COLOR GERMAN
Dictionary Plus

Oxford
COLOR GERMAN
Dictionary Plus

Third edition

GERMAN–ENGLISH
ENGLISH–GERMAN

DEUTSCH–ENGLISCH
ENGLISCH–DEUTSCH

OXFORD
UNIVERSITY PRESS
Great Clarendon Street, Oxford OX2 6DP

Oxford University Press is a department of the University of Oxford.
It furthers the University's objective of excellence in research, scholarship, and education by publishing worldwide in

Oxford New York

Auckland Cape Town Dar es Salaam Hong Kong Karachi
Kuala Lumpur Madrid Melbourne Mexico City Nairobi
New Delhi Shanghai Taipei Toronto

With offices in

Argentina Austria Brazil Chile Czech Republic France Greece
Guatemala Hungary Italy Japan Poland Portugal Singapore
South Korea Switzerland Thailand Turkey Ukraine Vietnam

Oxford is a registered trade mark of Oxford University Press
in the UK and in certain other countries

Published in the United States
by Oxford University Press Inc., New York

First published as the Oxford German Minidictionary 2005
Supplementary material first published by OUP in 2004, 2005, and 2006
This edition published 2007

British Library Cataloguing in Publication Data

Data available

Library of Congress Cataloging in Publication Data

Data available

Typeset by Interactive Sciences Ltd
Printed in Italy
by Legoprint S.p.A.

ISBN 978–0–19–921471–6
ISBN 978–0–19–921893–6 (US edition)

10 9 8 7 6 5 4 3 2 1

Contents

Preface

This is a dictionary designed primarily for students of German. Its clear presentation and use of color make it easily accessible. This edition contains new material on texting. In addition, the notes on German life and culture have been expanded. It also contains a list of the German words you must know, making it even more useful for students who wish to improve their vocabulary.

Contributors

Third Edition

Editors:
Nicholas Rollin
Roswitha Morris
Eva Vennebusch

Supplementary Material:
Robin Sawers
Neil and Roswitha Morris
Valerie Grundy
Eva Vennebusch

Second Edition Revised

Editor:
Gundhild Prowe

Second Edition

Editors:
Roswitha Morris
Robin Sawers

First Edition

Editors:
Gundhild Prowe
Jill Schneider

Proprietary terms

This dictionary includes some words which are, or are asserted to be, proprietary names or trademarks. Their inclusion does not imply that they have acquired for legal purposes a non-proprietary or general significance, nor is any other judgement implied concerning their legal status. In cases where the editor has some evidence that a word is used as a proprietary name or trademark this is indicated by the symbol ®, but no judgement concerning the legal status of such words is made or implied thereby.

Introduction

The text of this dictionary reflects recent changes to the spelling of German ratified in July 1996. The symbol * has been introduced to refer from the old spelling to the new, preferred one:

Äs* *nt* **-ses, -se = Ass**
dasein* *vi sep (sein)* = **da sein**, *s.* **da**
Schiffahrt* f = **Schifffahrt**

Where both the old and new forms are valid, an equals sign = is used to refer to the preferred form:

aufwändig adj = **aufwendig**

When such forms follow each other alphabetically, they are given with commas, with the preferred form in first place:

Panter, Panther m **-s**, - panther

In phrases, *od* (oder) is used:

...deine(r,s) *poss pron* yours;
die D~en *od* **d~en** *pl* your family *sg*

On the English–German side, only the preferred German form is given.

- A swung dash ~ represents the headword or that part of the headword preceding a vertical bar |. The initial letter of a German headword is given to show whether or not it is a capital.
- The vertical bar | follows the part of the headword which is not repeated in compounds or derivatives.
- Square brackets [ ] are used for optional material.
- Words in round brackets give you either grammatical information or help in choosing the correct translation. Some of these words are abbreviated; for full form see p. xviii.
- A bullet • indicates a new part of speech within an entry.
- *od* (oder) and *or* denote that words or portions of a phrase are synonymous. An oblique stroke / is used where there is a difference in usage or meaning.

- ≈ is used where no exact equivalent exists in the other language.
- A dagger † indicates that a German verb is irregular and that the parts can be found in the verb table on pp.615–620. Compound verbs are not listed there as they follow the pattern of the basic verb.
- The stressed vowel is marked in a German headword by _ (long) or . (short). A phonetic transcription is only given for words which do not follow the normal rules of pronunciation. These rules can be found on pp.x–xi.
- German headword nouns are followed by the gender and, with the exception of compound nouns, by the genitive and plural. These are only given at compound nouns if they present some difficulty. Otherwise the user should refer to the final element.
- Nouns that decline like adjectives are entered as follows: **-e(r)** m/f, **-e(s)** nt.
- Adjectives which have no undeclined form are entered in the feminine form with the masculine and neuter in brackets **-e(r,s)**.
- The reflexive pronoun **sich** is accusative unless marked (*dat*).

Verbs

- (sein) indicates that an intransitive verb is conjugated with the auxillary verb 'sein' in the perfect tense.
- (haben) indicates that an intransitive verb is conjugated with the auxillary verb 'haben' in the perfect tense.
- If neither 'sein' or 'haben' is shown, the verb is completely regular.

A new feature for this edition is the list of German words you must know, which can be found in the centre section of the dictionary. A [C] symbol next to a headword means that there is more information on this subject in the A–Z of German life and culture found in the centre section. An exclamation mark [!] indicates colloquial language, and a cross [✖] indicates slang.

Phonetic symbols used for German words

a	**Hand**	hant
a:	**Bahn**	ba:n
ɐ	**Ober**	'o:bɐ
ɐ̯	**Uhr**	u:ɐ̯
ã	**Conférencier**	kõferã'si̯e:
ã:	**Abonnement**	abɔnə'mã:
a͜i	**weit**	va͜it
a͜u	**Haut**	ha͜ut
b	**Ball**	bal
ç	**ich**	ɪç
d	**dann**	dan
d͜ʒ	**Gin**	d͜ʒɪn
e	**Metall**	me'tal
e:	**Beet**	be:t
ɛ	**mästen**	'mɛstən
ɛ:	**wählen**	'vɛ:lən
ɛ̃	**Cousin**	ku'zɛ̃:
ə	**Nase**	'na:zə
f	**Faß**	fas
g	**Gast**	gast
h	**haben**	'ha:bən
i	**Rivale**	ri'va:lə
i:	**viel**	fi:l
i̯	**Aktion**	ak't͜si̯o:n
ɪ	**Birke**	'bɪrkə
j	**ja**	ja:
k	**kalt**	kalt
l	**Last**	last
m	**Mast**	mast
n	**Naht**	na:t
ŋ	**lang**	laŋ
o	**Moral**	mo'ra:l
o:	**Boot**	bo:t
o̯	**loyal**	lo̯a'ja:l
õ	**Konkurs**	kõ'kʊrs
õ:	**Ballon**	ba'lõ:
ɔ	**Post**	pɔst
ø	**Ökonom**	øko'no:m
ø:	**Öl**	ø:l
œ	**göttlich**	'gœtliç
ɔ͜y	**heute**	'hɔ͜ytə
p	**Pakt**	pakt
r	**Rast**	rast
s	**Hast**	hast
ʃ	**Schal**	ʃa:l
t	**Tal**	ta:l
t͜s	**Zahl**	t͜sa:l
tʃ	**Couch**	ka͜utʃ
u	**Kupon**	ku'põ:
u:	**Hut**	hu:t
u̯	**aktuell**	ak'tu̯ɛl
ʊ	**Pult**	pʊlt
v	**was**	vas
x	**Bach**	bax
y	**Physik**	fy'zi:k
y:	**Rübe**	'ry:bə
y̆	**Nuance**	'ny̆ã:sə
ʏ	**Fülle**	'fʏlə
z	**Nase**	'na:zə
ʒ	**Regime**	re'ʒi:m

? Glottal stop, e.g. **Koordination** / ko?ɔrdina't͜sio:n /.

: length sign after a vowel, e.g. **Chrom** / kro:m /.

' Stress mark before stressed syllable, e.g. **Balkon** / bal'kõ:/.

Guide to German pronunciation

Consonants

Produced as in English with the following exceptions:

b	as	*p*	at the end of a word or syllable
d	as	*t*	at the end of a word or syllable
g	as	*k*	at the end of a word or syllable
ch	as in Scottish *loch*		after **a**, **o**, **u**, **au**
	like an exaggerated *h* as in *huge*		after **i**, **e**, **ä**, **ö**, **ü**, **eu**, **ei**
-chs	as	*x*	(as in *box*)
-ig	as	-ich/ɪç /	when **a** suffix
j	as	*y*	(as in *yes*)
ps			the **p** is pronounced
pn			the **p** is pronounced
qu	as	*k + v*	
s	as	*z*	(as in *zero*) at the beginning of a word
	as	*s*	(as in *bus*) at the end of a word or syllable, before a consonant, or when doubled
sch	as	*sh*	
sp	as	*shp*	at the beginning of a word
st	as	*sht*	at the beginning of a word
v	as	*f*	(as in *for*)
	as	*v*	(as in *very*) within a word

w	as	*v*	(as in *very*)
z	as	*ts*	

Vowels

Approximately as follows:

a	short	as	*u*	(as in *but*)
	long	as	*a*	(as in *car*)
e	short	as	*e*	(as in *pen*)
	long	as	*a*	(as in *paper*)
i	short	as	*i*	(as in *bit*)
	long	as	*ee*	(as in queen)
o	short	as	*o*	(as in *hot*)
	long	as	o	(as in *pope*)
u	short	as	*oo*	(as in *foot*)
	long	as	*oo*	(as in *boot*)

Vowels are always short before a double consonant, and long when followed by an **h** or when double

ie	is pronounced	*ee*	(as in *keep*)

Diphthongs

au	as	*ow*	(as in *how*)
ei **ai**	as	*y*	(as in *my*)
eu **äu**	as	*oy*	(as in *boy*)

Pronunciation of the alphabet

English/Englisch		*German/Deutsch*
eɪ	**a**	a:
bi:	**b**	be:
si:	**c**	t͜se:
di:	**d**	de:
i:	**e**	e:
ef	**f**	ɛf
dʒi:	**g**	ge:
eɪtʃ	**h**	ha:
aɪ	**i**	i:
dʒeɪ	**j**	jɔt
keɪ	**k**	ka:
el	**l**	ɛl
em	**m**	ɛm
en	**n**	ɛn
əʊ	**o**	o:
pi:	**p**	pe:
kju:	**q**	ku:
a:(r)	**r**	ɛr
es	**s**	ɛs
ti:	**t**	te:
ju:	**u**	u:
vi:	**v**	fau
'dʌblju:	**w**	ve:
eks	**x**	ɪks
waɪ	**y**	'ʏpsilɔn
zed	**z**	tsɛt
eɪ umlaut	**ä**	ɛ:
əʊ umlaut	**ö**	ø:
ju: umlaut	**ü**	y:
es'zed	**ß**	ɛs'tsɛt

Glossary of grammatical terms

Abbreviation
A shortened form of a word or phrase: **etc.** = **usw.**

Accusative
The case of a direct object; some German prepositions take the accusative

Active
In the active form the subject of the verb performs the action: **he asked** = **er hat gefragt**

Adjective
A word describing a noun: **a *red* pencil** = **ein *roter* Stift**

Adverb
A word that describes or changes the meaning of a verb, an adjective, or another adverb: **she sings *beautifully*** = **sie singt *schön***

Article
The definite article, **the** = **der/die/das**, and indefinite article, **a/an** = **ein/eine/ein**, used in front of a noun

Attributive
An adjective or noun is attributive when it is used directly before a noun: **the *black* dog** = **der *schwarze* Hund**; ***farewell* speech** = **Abschiedsrede**

Auxiliary verb
One of the verbs – as German **haben, sein, werden** – used to form the perfect or future tense: **I *will* help** = **ich *werde* helfen**

Cardinal number
A whole number representing a quantity: **one/two/three** = **eins/zwei/drei**

Case
The form of a noun, pronoun, adjective, or article that shows the part it plays in a sentence; there are four cases in German – nominative, accusative, genitive, and dative

Clause
A self-contained section of a sentence that contains a subject and a verb

Collective noun
A noun that is singular in form but refers to a group of individual persons or things, e.g. **royalty**, **grain**

Collocate
A word that regularly occurs with another; in German, **Buch** is a typical collocate of the verb **lesen**

Comparative
The form of an adjective or adverb that makes it "more": **smaller** = **kleiner**, **more clearly** = **klarer**

Compound adjective
An adjective formed from two or more separate words: **selbstbewusst (selbst + bewusst)** = **self-confident**

Compound noun
A noun formed from two or more separate words: **der Flughafen (Flug+Hafen)** = **airport**

Compound verb
A verb formed by adding a prefix to a simple verb; in German, some compound verbs are separable **(an|fangen)**, and some are inseparable **(verlassen)**

Conditional tense
A tense of a verb that expresses what would happen if something else occurred: **he would go** = **er würde gehen**

Conjugation
Variation of the form of a verb to show tense, person, mood, etc.

Conjunction
A word used to join clauses together: **and** = **und**, **because** = **weil**

Dative
The case of an indirect object; many German prepositions take the dative

Declension
The form of a noun, pronoun, or adjective that corresponds to a particular case, number, or gender; some German nouns decline like adjectives, e.g. **Beamte, Taube**

Definite article:
the = **der/die/das**

Demonstrative pronoun
A pronoun indicating the person or thing referred to; ***this*** **is my bicycle** = ***das*** **ist mein Fahrrad**

Direct object
The noun or pronoun directly affected by the verb: **he caught *the ball*** = **er fing *den Ball***

Direct speech
A speaker's actual words or the use of these in writing

Ending
Letters added to the stem of verbs, as well as to nouns and adjectives, according to tense, case, etc.

Feminine
One of the three noun genders in German: **die Frau** = **the woman**

Future tense
The tense of a verb that refers to something that will happen in the future: **I will go** = **ich werde gehen**

Gender
One of the three groups of nouns in German: masculine, feminine, or neuter

Genitive
The case that shows possession; some prepositions in German take the genitive

Imperative
A form of a verb that expresses a command: **go away!** = **geh weg!**

Imperfect tense
The tense of a verb that refers to an uncompleted or a habitual action in the past: **I went there every Friday** = **ich ging jeden Freitag dorthin**

Impersonal verb
A verb in English used only with **'it'**, and in German only with **'es'**: **it is raining** = **es regnet**

Indeclinable adjective
An adjective that has no inflected forms, as German **klasse, Moskauer**

Indefinite article:
a/an = **ein/eine/ein**

Indefinite pronoun
A pronoun that does not identify a specific person or object: **one** = **man**, **something** = **etwas**

Indicative form
The form of a verb used when making a statement of fact or asking questions of fact: **he is just coming** = **er kommt**

gleich

Indirect object
The noun or pronoun indirectly affected by the verb, at which the direct object is aimed: **I gave *him* the book** = **ich gab *ihm* das Buch**

Indirect speech
A report of what someone has said which does not reproduce the exact words

Infinitive
The basic part of a verb: **to play** = **spielen**

Inflect
To change the ending or form of a word to show its tense or its grammatical relation to other words: **gehe** and **gehst** are inflected forms of the verb **gehen**

Inseparable verb
A verb with a prefix that can never be separated from it: **verstehen, ich verstehe**

Interjection
A sound, word, or remark expressing a strong feeling such as anger, fear, or joy: **oh!** = **ach!**

Interrogative pronoun
A pronoun that asks a question: **who?** = **wer?**

Intransitive verb
A verb that does not have a direct object: **he died suddenly** = **er ist plötzlich gestorben**

Irregular verb
A verb that does not follow one of the set patterns and has its own individual forms

Masculine
One of the three noun genders in German: **der Mann** = **the man**, **der Stuhl** = **the chair**

Modal verb
A verb that is used with another verb (not a modal) to express permission, obligation, possibility, etc., as German **können, sollen**, English **might, should**

Negative
expressing refusal or denial; **there aren't any** = **es gibt keine**

Neuter
One of the three noun genders in German: **das Buch** = **the book**, **das Kind** = **the child**

Nominative
The case of the subject of a sentence; in sentences with **sein** and **werden** the noun after the verb is in the nominative: **that is my car** = **das ist mein Auto**

Noun
A word that names a person or a thing

Number
The state of being either singular or plural

Object
The word or words naming the person or thing acted upon by a verb or preposition, as **'Buch'** in **er las das Buch** or **'ihm'** in **ich traue ihm**

Ordinal number
A number that shows a person's or thing's position in a series: **the *twenty-first* century** = **das *einundzwanzigste* Jahrhundert**, **the *second* door on the left** = **die *zweite* Tür links**

Part of speech
A grammatical term for the function of a word; noun, verb, adjective, etc., are parts of speech.

Passive
In the passive form the subject of the

verb experiences the action rather than performs it: **he was asked** = **er wurde gefragt**

Past participle
The part of a verb used to form past tenses: **she had *gone***, **er hat *gelogen***

Perfect tense
The tense of a verb that refers to a completed action in the past or an action that started in the past and is still going on: **I have already eaten** = **ich habe schon gegessen**; **I have been reading all day** = **ich habe den ganzen Tag gelesen**

Person
Any of the three groups of personal pronouns and forms taken by verbs; the **first person** (e.g. **I**/**ich**) refers to the person(s) speaking, the **second person** (e.g. **you**/**du**) refers to the person(s) spoken to; the **third person** (e.g. **he**/**er**) refers to the persons spoken about

Personal pronoun
A pronoun that refers to a person or thing: **he/she/it** = **er/sie/es**

Phrasal verb
A verb in English combined with a preposition or an adverb to have a particular meaning: **run away** = **weglaufen**

Phrase
A self-contained section of a sentence that does not contain a full verb

Pluperfect tense
The tense of a verb that refers to something that happened before a particular point in the past: **als ich ankam, *war* er schon *losgefahren*** = **when I arrived, he *had* already *left***

Plural
Of nouns etc., referring to more than one: **the trees** = **die Bäume**

Possessive adjective
An adjective that shows possession, belonging to someone or something; **my** = **mein/meine/mein**

Possessive pronoun
A pronoun that shows possession, belonging to someone or something: **mine** = **meiner/meine/meins**

Predicate
The part of a sentence that says something about the **subject**, e.g. **went home** in **John went home**

Predicative
An adjective is predicative when it comes after a verb such as **be** or **become** in English, or after **sein** or **werden** in German: **she is beautiful** = **sie ist schön**

Prefix
A letter or group of letters added to the beginning of a word to change its meaning; in German, the prefix can move from separable verbs (**an|fangen**), but stays fixed to inseparable verbs (**verlassen**)

Preposition
A word that stands in front of a noun or pronoun, relating it to the rest of the sentence; in German prepositions are always followed by a particular case, usually either the accusative or dative, but occasionally the genitive: **with** = **mit (+ dative)**, **for** = für **(+ accusative)**, **because of** = **wegen (+ genitive)**

Present participle
The part of a verb that in English ends in **–ing**, and in German adds **–d** to the infinitive: **asking** = **fragend**

Present tense
The tense of a verb that refers to

something happening now: **I make** = **ich mache**

Pronoun
A word that stands instead of a noun: **he** = **er**, **she** = **sie**, **mine** = **meiner/meine/meins**

Proper noun
A name of a person, place, institution, etc., in English written with a capital letter at the start; **Germany**, the **Atlantic**, **Karl**, **Europa** are all proper nouns

Reflexive pronoun
A pronoun that goes with a reflexive verb: in German **mich, dich, sich, uns, euch, sich**

Reflexive verb
A verb whose object is the same as its subject; in German, it is used with a reflexive pronoun: **du sollst dich waschen** = **you should wash yourself**

Regular verb
A verb that follows a set pattern in its different forms

Relative pronoun
A pronoun that introduces a subordinate clause, relating to a person or thing mentioned in the main clause: **the man *who* visited us** = **der Mann, *der* uns besucht hat**

Reported Speech
Another name for **Indirect speech**

Sentence
A sequence of words, with a subject and a verb, that can stand on their own to make a statement, ask a question, or give a command

Separable verb
A verb with a prefix that can be separated from it in some tenses: **anfangen, anzufangen, angefangen,** but **ich fange an, du fingst an**

Singular
Of nouns etc., referring to just one: **the tree** = **der Baum**

Stem
The part of a verb to which endings are added; **fahr-** is the stem of **fahren**

Subject
In a clause or sentence, the noun or pronoun that causes the action of the verb: ***he* caught the ball** = ***er* fing den Ball**

Subjunctive
A verb form that is used to express doubt or unlikelihood: **if I were to tell you that ...** = **wenn ich dir sagen würde, dass ...**

Subordinate clause
A clause which adds information to the main clause of a sentence but cannot be used as a sentence by itself

Suffix
A letter or group of letters joined to the end of a word to make another word, as **–heit in Schönheit**

Superlative
The form of an adjective or adverb that makes it "most": **the *smallest* house** = **das *kleinste* Haus**, **most clearly** = **am klarsten**

Tense
The form of a verb that tells when the action takes place: present, future, imperfect, perfect, pluperfect

Transitive verb
A verb that is used with a direct object: **she read the book** = **sie las das Buch**

Verb
A word or group of words that describes an action: **the children *are playing*** = **die Kinder *spielen***

Abbreviations/Abkürzungen

adjective	*adj*	Adjektiv
abbreviation	*abbr*	Abkürzung
accusative	*acc*	Akkusativ
Administration	*Admin*	Administration
adverb	*adv*	Adverb
American	*Amer*	amerikanisch
Anatomy	*Anat*	Anatomie
attributive	*attrib*	attributiv
Austrian	*Aust*	österreichisch
Motor vehicles	*Auto*	Automobil
Aviation	*Aviat*	Luftfahrt
Botany	*Bot*	Botanik
collective	*coll*	Kollektivum
Commerce	*Comm*	Handel
conjunction	*conj*	Konjunktion
Cookery	*Culin*	Kochkunst
dative	*dat*	Dativ
definite article	*def art*	bestimmter Artikel
demonstrative	*dem*	Demonstrativ-
Electricity	*Electr*	Elektrizität
something	*etw*	etwas
feminine	*f*	Femininum
figurative	*fig*	figurativ
genitive	*gen*	Genitiv
Geography	*Geog*	Geographie
Grammar	*Gram*	Grammatik
impersonal	*impers*	unpersönlich
inseparable	*insep*	untrennbar
interjection	*int*	Interjektion
invariable	*inv*	unveränderlich
someone	*jd*	jemand
someone (dat)	*jdm*	jemandem
someone (acc)	*jdn*	jemanden
someone's	*jds*	jemandes
Law	*Jur*	Jura
Language	*Lang*	Sprache

Abbreviations/Abkürzungen

masculine	*m*	Maskulinum
Mathematics	*Math*	Mathematik
Medicine	*Med*	Medizin
Military	*Mil*	Militär
Music	*Mus*	Musik
noun	*n*	Substantiv
Nautical	*Naut*	nautisch
nominative	*nom*	Nominativ
neuter	*nt*	Neutrum
or	*od*	oder
pejorative	*pej*	abwertend
Photography	*Phot*	Fotografie
Physics	*Phys*	Physik
plural	*pl*	Plural
Politics	*Pol*	Politik
possessive	*poss*	Possessiv-
past participle	*pp*	zweites Partizip
predicative	*pred*	prädikativ
prefix	*pref*	Präfix, Vorsilbe
preposition	*prep*	Präposition
present	*pres*	Präsens
present participle	*pres p*	erstes Partizip
pronoun	*pron*	Pronomen
past tense	*pt*	Präteritum
Railway	*Rail*	Eisenbahn
regular	*reg*	regelmäßig
relative	*rel*	Relativ-
Religion	*Relig*	Religion
see	*s.*	siehe
School	*Sch*	Schule
separable	*sep*	trennbar
singular	*sg*	Singular
someone	*s.o.*	jemand
Technical	*Techn*	Technik
Telephone	*Teleph*	Telefon
Theatre	*Theat*	Theater
University	*Univ*	Universität
intransitive verb	*vi*	intransitives Verb
reflexive verb	*vr*	reflexives Verb
transitive verb	*vt*	transitives Verb
Zoology	*Zool*	Zoologie

Abbreviations/Abkürzungen

familiar	[!]	familiär
slang	[✖]	Slang
old spelling	*	alte Schreibung
proprietary term	®	Markenzeichen
see A–Z of German life and culture	[C]	
short stress	.	
long stress	_	
no exact equivalent	≈	
irregular verb	†	
phrasal verb	■	

German – English

Aa

Aal m **-[e]s,-e** eel

Aas nt **-es** carrion; ✖ swine

ab prep (+ dat) from • adv off; (weg) away; (auf Fahrplan) departs; **ab und zu** now and then; **auf und ab** up and down

abändern vt sep alter; (abwandeln) modify

Abbau m dismantling; (Kohlen-) mining. **a~en** vt sep dismantle; mine (Kohle)

abbeißen† vt sep bite off

abbeizen vt sep strip

abberufen† vt sep recall

abbestellen vt sep cancel; **jdn a~** put s.o. off

abbiegen† vi sep (sein) turn off; **[nach] links a~** turn left

Abbildung f **-,-en** illustration

abblättern vi sep (sein) flake off

abblend|en vt/i sep (haben) **[die Scheinwerfer] a~en** dip one's headlights. **A~licht** nt dipped headlights pl

abbrechen† v sep • vt break off; (abreißen) demolish; (Computer) cancel • vi (sein/haben) break off

abbrennen† v sep • vt burn off; (niederbrennen) burn down • vi (sein) burn down

abbringen† vt sep dissuade (**von** from)

Abbruch m demolition; (Beenden) breaking off

abbuchen vt sep debit

abbürsten vt sep brush down; (entfernen) brush off

abdanken vi sep (haben) resign; (Herrscher:) abdicate

abdecken vt sep uncover; (abnehmen) take off; (zudecken) cover; **den Tisch a~** clear the table

abdichten vt sep seal

abdrehen vt sep turn off

Abdruck m (pl **⸚e**) impression. **a~en** vt sep print

abdrücken vt/i sep (haben) fire; **sich a~** leave an impression

Abend m **-s,-e** evening; **am A~** in the evening; **heute A~** this evening, tonight; **gestern A~** yesterday evening, last night. 🅲**A~brot** nt supper. **A~essen** nt dinner; (einfacher) supper. **A~mahl** nt (Relig) [Holy] Communion. **a~s** adv in the evening

Abenteuer nt **-s,-** adventure; (Liebes-) affair. **a~lich** adj fantastic

aber conj but; **oder a~** or else • adv (wirklich) really

Aber|glaube m superstition. **a~gläubisch** adj superstitious

abfahr|en† v sep • vi (sein) leave; (Auto:) drive off • vt take away; (entlangfahren) drive along; use (Fahrkarte); **abgefahrene Reifen** worn tyres. **A~t** f departure; (Talfahrt) descent; (Piste) run; (Ausfahrt) exit

Abfall m refuse, rubbish; (auf der Straße) litter; (Industrie-) waste

abfallen† vi sep (sein) drop, fall; (übrig bleiben) be left (**für** for); (sich neigen) slope away. **a~d** adj sloping

Abfallhaufen m rubbish-dump

abfällig adj disparaging

abfangen† vt sep intercept

abfärben vi sep (haben) (Farbe:) run; (Stoff:) not be colour-fast

abfassen vt sep draft

abfertigen vt sep attend to; (zollamtlich) clear; **jdn kurz a~** ! give s.o. short shrift

abfeuern vt sep fire

🅲 *see A-Z of German life and culture*

a

abfind|en† vt sep pay off; (entschädigen) compensate; **sich a~en mit** come to terms with. **A~ung** f **-,-en** compensation

abfliegen† vi sep (sein) fly off; (Aviat) take off

abfließen† vi sep (sein) drain or run away

Abflug m (Aviat) departure

Abfluss m drainage; (Öffnung) drain. **A~rohr** nt drain-pipe

abfragen vt sep **jdn** od **jdm Vokabeln a~** test s.o. on vocabulary

Abfuhr f - removal; (fig) rebuff

abführ|en vt sep take or lead away. **A~mittel** nt laxative

abfüllen vt sep **auf** od **in Flaschen a~** bottle

Abgase ntpl exhaust fumes

abgeben† vt sep hand in; (abliefern) deliver; (verkaufen) sell; (zur Aufbewahrung) leave; (Fußball) pass; (ausströmen) give off; (abfeuern) fire; (verlauten lassen) give; cast (Stimme); **jdm etw a~** give s.o. a share of sth

abgehen† v sep •vi (sein) leave; (Theat) exit; (sich lösen) come off; (abgezogen werden) be deducted •vt walk along

abgehetzt adj harassed. **abgelegen** adj remote. **abgeneigt** adj **etw** (dat) **nicht abgeneigt sein** not be averse to sth. **abgenutzt** adj worn. **Abgeordnete(r)** m/f deputy; (Pol) Member of Parliament. **abgepackt** adj pre-packed

abgeschieden adj secluded

abgeschlossen adj (fig) complete; (Wohnung) self-contained. **abgesehen** prep apart (from **von**). **abgespannt** adj exhausted. **abgestanden** adj stale. **abgestorben** adj dead; (Glied) numb. **abgetragen** adj worn. **abgewetzt** adj threadbare

abgewinnen† vt sep win (**jdm** from s.o.); **etw** (dat) **Geschmack a~** get a taste for sth

abgewöhnen vt sep **jdm/sich das Rauchen a~** cure s.o. of/give up smoking

abgießen† vt sep pour off; drain (Gemüse)

Abgott m idol

abgöttisch adv **a~ lieben** idolize

abgrenz|en vt sep divide off; (fig) define. **A~ung** f - demarcation

Abgrund m abyss; (fig) depths pl

abgucken vt sep [!] copy

Abguss m cast

abhacken vt sep chop off

abhaken vt sep tick off

abhalten† vt sep keep off; (hindern) keep, prevent (**von** from); (veranstalten) hold

abhanden adv **a~ kommen** get lost

Abhandlung f treatise

Abhang m slope

abhängen[1] vt sep (reg) take down; (abkuppeln) uncouple

abhäng|en[2]† vi sep (haben) depend (**von** on). **a~ig** adj dependent (**von** on). **A~igkeit** f - dependence

abhärten vt sep toughen up

abheben† v sep •vt take off; (vom Konto) withdraw; **sich a~** stand out (**gegen** against) •vi (haben) (Cards) cut [the cards]; (Aviat) take off; (Rakete:) lift off

abheften vt sep file

Abhilfe f remedy

abholen vt sep collect

abhör|en vt sep listen to; (überwachen) tap; **jdn** od **jdm Vokabeln a~en** test s.o. on vocabulary. **A~gerät** nt bugging device

▣ **Abitur** nt **-s** ≈ A levels pl

abkaufen vt sep buy (dat from)

abklingen† vi sep (sein) die away; (nachlassen) subside

▣ *see* A-Z of German life and culture

abkochen vt sep boil

abkommen† vi sep (sein) **a~ von** stray from; (aufgeben) give up. **A~** nt **-s,-** agreement

Abkömmling m **-s,-e** descendant

abkratzen vt sep scrape off

abkühlen vt/i sep (sein) cool; **sich a~** cool [down]

Abkunft f - origin

abkuppeln vt sep uncouple

abkürz|en vt sep shorten; abbreviate (Wort). **A~ung** f short cut; (Wort) abbreviation

abladen† vt sep unload

Ablage f shelf; (für Akten) tray

ablager|n vt sep deposit. **A~ung** f **-,-en** deposit

ablassen† vt sep drain [off]; let off (Dampf)

Ablauf m drain; (Verlauf) course; (Ende) end; (einer Frist) expiry. **a~en†** v sep •vi (sein) run or drain off; (verlaufen) go off; (enden) expire; (Zeit:) run out; (Uhrwerk:) run down •vt walk along; (absuchen) scour (**nach** for)

ableg|en v sep •vt put down; discard (Karte); (abheften) file; (ausziehen) take off; sit, take (Prüfung); **abgelegte Kleidung** cast-offs pl •vi (haben) take off one's coat; (Naut) cast off. **A~er** m **-s,-** (Bot) cutting; (Schössling) shoot

ablehn|en vt sep refuse; (missbilligen) reject. **A~ung** f **-,-en** refusal; rejection

ableit|en vt sep divert; **sich a~en** be derived (**von**/**aus** from). **A~ung** f derivation; (Wort) derivative

ablenk|en vt sep deflect; divert (Aufmerksamkeit). **A~ung** f **-,-en** distraction

ablesen† vt sep read

ablicht|en vt sep photocopy. **A~ung** f photocopy

abliefern vt sep deliver

ablös|en vt sep detach; (abwechseln) relieve; **sich a~en** come off; (sich abwechseln) take turns. **A~ung** f relief

abmach|en vt sep remove; (ausmachen) arrange; (vereinbaren) agree. **A~ung** f **-,-en** agreement

abmager|n vi sep (sein) lose weight. **A~ungskur** f slimming diet

abmelden vt sep cancel; **sich a~** (im Hotel) check out; (Computer) log off

abmessen† vt sep measure

abmühen (sich) vr sep struggle

Abnäher m **-s,-** dart

abnehm|en† v sep •vt take off, remove; pick up (Hörer); **jdm etw a~en** take/(kaufen) buy sth from s.o. •vi (haben) decrease; (nachlassen) decline; (Person:) lose weight; (Mond:) wane. **A~er** m **-s,-** buyer

Abneigung f dislike (**gegen** of)

abnorm adj abnormal

abnutz|en vt sep wear out. **A~ung** f - wear [and tear]

Abon|nement /abɔnəˈmã:/ nt **-s,-s** subscription. **A~nent** m **-en, -en** subscriber. **a~nieren** vt take out a subscription to

Abordnung f **-,-en** deputation

abpassen vt sep wait for; **gut a~** time well

abraten† vi sep (haben) **jdm von etw a~** advise s.o. against sth

abräumen vt/i (haben) clear away

abrechn|en v sep •vt deduct •vi (haben) settle up. **A~ung** f settlement; (Rechnung) account

Abreise f departure. **a~n** vi sep (sein) leave

abreißen† v sep •vt tear off; (demolieren) pull down •vi (sein) come off

abrichten vt sep train

Abriss m demolition; (Übersicht) summary

abrufen† vt sep call away; (Computer) retrieve

abrunden vt sep round off

a

abrüst|en vi sep (haben) disarm. **A~ung** f disarmament

abrutschen vi sep (sein) slip

Absage f **-,-n** cancellation; (Ablehnung) refusal. **a~n** v sep •vt cancel •vi (haben) **[jdm] a~n** cancel an appointment [with s.o.]; (auf Einladung) refuse [s.o.'s invitation]

Absatz m heel; (Abschnitt) paragraph; (Verkauf) sale

abschaff|en vt sep abolish; get rid of (Auto, Hund)

abschalten vt/i sep (haben) switch off

Abscheu m - revulsion

abscheulich adj revolting

abschicken vt sep send off

Abschied m **-[e]s,-e** farewell; (Trennung) parting; **A~ nehmen** say goodbye (**von** to)

abschießen† vt sep shoot down; (abfeuern) fire; launch (Rakete)

abschirmen vt sep shield

abschlagen† vt sep knock off; (verweigern) refuse

Abschlepp|dienst m breakdown service. **a~en** vt sep tow away. **A~seil** nt tow-rope

abschließen† v sep •vt lock; (beenden, abmachen) conclude; make (Wette); balance (Bücher) •vi (haben) lock up; (enden) end. **a~d** adv in conclusion

Abschluss m conclusion. **A~zeugnis** nt diploma

abschmecken vt sep season

abschmieren vt sep lubricate

abschneiden† v sep •vt cut off •vi (haben) **gut/schlecht a~** do well/badly

Abschnitt m section; (Stadium) stage; (Absatz) paragraph

abschöpfen vt sep skim off

abschrauben vt sep unscrew

abschreck|en vt sep deter; (Culin) put in cold water (Ei). **a~end** adj repulsive. **A~ungsmittel** nt deterrent

abschreib|en† v sep •vt copy; (Comm & fig) write off •vi (haben) copy. **A~ung** f (Comm) depreciation

Abschrift f copy

Abschuss m shooting down; (Abfeuern) firing; (Raketen-) launch

abschüssig adj sloping; (steil) steep

abschwellen† vi sep (sein) go down

abseh|bar adj **in a~barer Zeit** in the foreseeable future. **a~en**† vt/i sep (haben) copy; (voraussehen) foresee; **a~en von** disregard; (aufgeben) refrain from

abseits adv apart; (Sport) offside •prep (+ gen) away from. **A~** nt - (Sport) offside

absend|en† vt sep send off. **A~er** m sender

absetzen v sep •vt put or set down; (ablagern) deposit; (abnehmen) take off; (abbrechen) stop; (entlassen) dismiss; (verkaufen) sell; (abziehen) deduct •vi (haben) pause

Absicht f **-,-en** intention; **mit A~** intentionally, on purpose

absichtlich adj intentional

absitzen† v sep •vi (sein) dismount •vt 🅸 serve (Strafe)

absolut adj absolute

absolvieren vt complete; (bestehen) pass

absonder|n vt sep separate; (ausscheiden) secrete. **A~ung** f **-,-en** secretion

absorbieren vt absorb

abspeisen vt sep fob off (**mit** with)

absperr|en vt sep cordon off; (abstellen) turn off; (SGer) lock. **A~ung** f **-,-en** barrier

abspielen vt sep play; (Fußball) pass; **sich a~** take place

Absprache f agreement

absprechen† vt sep arrange; **sich a~** agree

abspringen† vi sep (sein) jump off; (mit Fallschirm) parachute; (abgehen) come off

Absprung m jump

abspülen vt sep rinse

abstamm|en vi sep (haben) be descended (**von** from). **A~ung** f - descent

Abstand m distance; (zeitlich) interval; **A~ halten** keep one's distance

abstatten vt sep **jdm einen Besuch a~** pay s.o. a visit

Abstecher m **-s,-** detour

abstehen† vi sep (haben) stick out

absteigen† vi sep (sein) dismount; (niedersteigen) descend; (Fußball) be relegated

abstell|en vt sep put down; (lagern) store; (parken) park; (abschalten) turn off. **A~gleis** nt siding. **A~raum** m box-room

absterben† vi sep (sein) die; (gefühllos werden) go numb

Abstieg m **-[e]s,-e** descent; (Fußball) relegation

abstimm|en v sep • vi (haben) vote (**über** + acc on) • vt coordinate (**auf** + acc with). **A~ung** f vote

Abstinenzler m **-s, -** teetotaller

abstoßen† vt sep knock off; (verkaufen) sell; (fig: ekeln) repel. **a~d** adj repulsive

abstreiten† vt sep deny

Abstrich m (Med) smear

abstufen vt sep grade

Absturz m fall; (Aviat) crash

abstürzen vi sep (sein) fall; (Aviat) crash

absuchen vt sep search

absurd adj absurd

Abszess m **-es,-e** abscess

Abt m **-[e]s,¨-e** abbot

abtasten vt sep feel; (Techn) scan

abtauen vt/i sep (sein) thaw; (entfrosten) defrost

Abtei f **-,-en** abbey

Abteil nt compartment

Abteilung f **-,-en** section; (Admin, Comm) department

abtragen† vt sep clear; (einebnen) level; (abnutzen) wear out

abträglich adj detrimental (dat to)

abtreib|en† vt sep (Naut) drive off course; **ein Kind a~en lassen** have an abortion. **A~ung** f **-,-en** abortion

abtrennen vt sep detach; (abteilen) divide off

Abtreter m **-s,-** doormat

abtrocknen vt/i sep (haben) dry; **sich a~** dry oneself

abtropfen vi sep (sein) drain

abtun† vt sep (fig) dismiss

abwägen† vt sep (fig) weigh

abwandeln vt sep modify

abwarten v sep • vt wait for • vi (haben) wait [and see]

abwärts adv down[wards]

Abwasch m **-[e]s** washing-up; (Geschirr) dirty dishes pl. **a~en**† v sep • vt wash; wash up (Geschirr); (entfernen) wash off • vi (haben) wash up. **A~lappen** m dishcloth

Abwasser nt **-s,¨** sewage. **A~kanal** m sewer

abwechseln vi/r sep (haben) **[sich] a~** alternate; (Personen:) take turns. **a~d** adj alternate

Abwechslung f **-,-en** change; **zur A~** for a change

abwegig adj absurd

Abwehr f **-** defence; (Widerstand) resistance; (Pol) counter-espionage. **a~en** vt sep ward off. **A~system** nt immune system

abweich|en† vi sep (sein) deviate/ (von Regel) depart (**von** from); (sich unterscheiden) differ (**von** from). **a~end** adj divergent; (verschieden) different. **A~ung** f **-,-en** deviation

abweis|en† vt sep turn down; turn away (Person). **a~end** adj unfriendly. **A~ung** f rejection

abwenden† vt sep turn away; (verhindern) avert

abwerfen† vt sep throw off; throw (Reiter); (Aviat) drop; (Kartenspiel)

a

discard; shed (Haut, Blätter); yield (Gewinn)

abwert|en vt sep devalue. **A~ung** f -,-en devaluation

Abwesenheit f - absence; absent-mindedness

abwickeln vt sep unwind; (erledigen) settle

abwischen vt sep wipe

abzahlen vt sep pay off

abzählen vt sep count

Abzahlung f instalment

Abzeichen nt badge

abzeichnen vt sep copy

Abzieh|bild nt transfer. **a~en**† v sep •vt pull off; take off (Laken); strip (Bett); (häuten) skin; (Phot) print; run off (Kopien); (zurückziehen) withdraw; (abrechnen) deduct •vi (sein) go away, (Rauch:) escape

Abzug m withdrawal; (Abrechnung) deduction; (Phot) print (Korrektur-) proof; (am Gewehr) trigger; (A~söffnung) vent; **A~̈e** pl deductions

abzüglich prep (+ gen) less

Abzugshaube f [cooker] hood

abzweig|en v sep •vi (sein) branch off •vt divert. **A~ung** f -,-en junction; (Gabelung) fork

ach int oh; **a~ je!** oh dear! **a~ so** I see

Achse f -,-n axis; (Rad-) axle

Achsel f -,-n shoulder. **A~höhle** f armpit. **A~zucken** nt -s shrug

acht inv adj, **A~**[1] f -,-en eight

Acht[2] f **A~ geben** be careful; **A~ geben auf** (+ acc) look after; **außer A~ lassen** disregard; **sich in A~ nehmen** be careful

acht|e(r,s) adj eighth. **a~eckig** adj octagonal. **A~el** nt -s,- eighth

achten vt respect •vi (haben) **a~ auf** (+ acc) pay attention to; (aufpassen) look after

Achterbahn f roller-coaster

achtlos adj careless

achtsam adj careful

Achtung f - respect (**vor** + dat for); **A~!** look out!

acht|zehn inv adj eighteen. **a~zehnte(r,s)** adj eighteenth. **a~zig** a inv eighty. **a~zigste(r,s)** adj eightieth

Acker m -s,̈ field. **A~bau** m agriculture. **A~land** nt arable land

addieren vt/i (haben) add

Addition /-'tsi̯o:n/ f -,-en addition

ade int goodbye

Adel m -s nobility

Ader f -,-n vein

Adjektiv nt -s,-e adjective

Adler m -s,- eagle

adlig adj noble. **A~e(r)** m nobleman

Administration /-'tsi̯o:n/ f - administration

Admiral m -s,̈e admiral

adop|tieren vt adopt. **A~tion** f -,-en adoption. **A~tiveltern** pl adoptive parents. **A~tivkind** nt adopted child

Adrenalin nt -s adrenalin

Adres|se f -,-n address. **a~sieren** vt address

Adria f - Adriatic

Adverb nt -s,-ien adverb

Affäre f -,-n affair

Affe m -n,-n monkey; (Menschen-) ape

affektiert adj affected

affig adj affected; (eitel) vain

Afrika nt -s Africa

Afrikan|er(in) m -s,- (f -,-nen) African. **a~isch** adj African

After m -s,- anus

Agen|t(in) m -en,-en (f -,-nen) agent. **A~tur** f -,-en agency

Aggres|sion f -,-en aggression. **a~siv** adj aggressive

Agnostiker m -s,- agnostic

Ägypt|en /ɛ'gʏptən/ nt -s Egypt. **A~er(in)** m -s,- (f -,-nen)

Egyptian. **ä~isch** adj Egyptian

ähneln vi (haben) (+ dat) resemble; **sich ä~** be alike

ahnen vt have a presentiment of; (vermuten) suspect

Ahnen mpl ancestors. **A~forschung** f genealogy

ähnlich adj similar; **jdm ä~ sehen** resemble s.o. **Ä~keit** f -,-en similarity; resemblance

Ahnung f -,-en premonition; (Vermutung) idea, hunch

Ahorn m **-s,-e** maple

Ähre f **-,-n** ear [of corn]

Aids /e:ts/ nt - Aids

Airbag /'ɛ:ɐ̯bɛk/ m **-s, -s** (Auto) air bag

Akademie f **-,-n** academy

Akadem|iker(in) m **-s,-** (f **-,-nen**) university graduate. **a~isch** adj academic

akklimatisieren (sich) vr become acclimatized

Akkord m **-[e]s,-e** (Mus) chord. **A~arbeit** f piecework

Akkordeon nt **-s,-s** accordion

Akkumulator m **-s,-en** (Electr) accumulator

Akkusativ m **-s,-e** accusative. **A~objekt** nt direct object

Akrobat|(in) m **-en,-en** (f **-,-nen**) acrobat. **a~isch** adj acrobatic

Akt m **-[e]s,-e** act; (Kunst) nude

Akte f **-,-n** file; **A~n** documents. **A~ntasche** f briefcase

Aktie /'aktsi̯ə/ f **-,-n** (Comm) share. **A~ngesellschaft** f joint-stock company

Aktion /ak'tsi̯o:n/ f **-,-en** action. **A~är** m **-s,-e** shareholder

aktiv adj active

aktuell adj topical; (gegenwärtig) current

Akupunktur f - acupuncture

Akustik f - acoustics pl.

akut adj acute

Akzent m **-[e]s,-e** accent

akzept|abel adj acceptable. **a~ieren** vt accept

Alarm m **-s** alarm; (Mil) alert. **a~ieren** vt alert; (beunruhigen) alarm

Albdruck m nightmare

albern adj silly • vi (haben) play the fool

Albtraum m nightmare

Al|bum nt **-s,-ben** album

Algebra f - algebra

Algen fpl algae

Algerien /-i̯ən/ nt **-s** Algeria

Alibi nt **-s,-s** alibi

Alimente pl maintenance sg

Alkohol m **-s** alcohol. **a~frei** adj non-alcoholic

Alkohol|iker(in) m **-s,-** (f **-,-nen**) alcoholic. **a~isch** adj alcoholic

Alkopop nt **-(s), -s** alcopop

all inv pron **all das/mein Geld** all the/my money; **all dies** all this

All nt **-s** universe

alle pred adj finished

all|e(r,s) pron all; (jeder) every; **a~es** everything, all; (alle Leute) everyone; **a~e** pl all; **a~es Geld** all the money; **a~e beide** both [of them/us]; **a~e Tage** every day; **a~e drei Jahre** every three years; **ohne a~en Grund** without any reason; **vor a~em** above all; **a~es in a~em** all in all; **a~es aussteigen!** all change!

Allee f **-,-n** avenue

allein adv alone; (nur) only; **a~ stehend** single; **a~ der Gedanke** the mere thought; **von a~[e]** of its/(Person) one's own accord; (automatisch) automatically • conj but. **A~erziehende(r)** m/f single parent. **a~ig** adj sole. **A~stehende** pl single people

allemal adv every time; (gewiss) certainly

allenfalls adv at most; (eventuell) possibly

a

aller|beste(r,s) adj very best; **am a~besten** best of all. **a~dings** adv indeed; (zwar) admittedly. **a~erste(r,s)** adj very first

Allergie f -,-n allergy

allergisch adj allergic (**gegen** to)

Aller|heiligen nt -s All Saints Day. **a~höchstens** adv at the very most. **a~lei** inv adj all sorts of • pron all sorts of things. **a~letzte(r,s)** adj very last. **a~liebste(r,s)** adj favourite • adv **am a~liebsten** for preference; **am a~liebsten haben** like best of all. **a~meiste(r,s)** adj most • adv **am a~meisten** most of all. **A~seelen** nt -s All Souls Day. **a~wenigste(r,s)** adj very least • adv **am a~wenigsten** least of all

allgemein adj general; **im A~en (a~en)** in general. **A~heit** f - community; (Öffentlichkeit) general public

Allianz f -,-en alliance

Alligator m -s,-en alligator

alliiert adj allied; **die A~en** pl the Allies

all|jährlich adj annual. **a~mählich** adj gradual

Alltag m working day; **der A~** (fig) everyday life

alltäglich adj daily; (gewöhnlich) everyday; (Mensch) ordinary

alltags adv on weekdays

allzu adv [far] too; **a~ oft** all too often; **a~ vorsichtig** over-cautious

Alm f -,-en alpine pasture

Almosen ntpl alms

Alpdruck* m = **Albdruck**

Alpen pl Alps

Alphabet nt -[e]s,-e alphabet. **a~isch** adj alphabetical

Alptraum* m = **Albtraum**

als conj as; (zeitlich) when; (mit Komparativ) than; **nichts als** nothing but; **als ob** as if or though

also adv & conj so; **a~ gut** all right then; **na a~!** there you are!

alt adj old; (gebraucht) second-hand; (ehemalig) former; **alt werden** grow old

Alt m -s, -e (Mus) contralto

Altar m -s,⸚e altar

Alt|e(r) m/f old man/woman; **die A~en** old people. **A~eisen** nt scrap iron. **A~enheim** nt old people's home

Alter nt -s,- age; (Bejahrtheit) old age; **im A~ von** at the age of

älter adj older; **mein ä~er Bruder** my elder brother

altern vi (sein) age

Alternative f -,-n alternative

Alters|grenze f age limit. **A~heim** nt old people's home. **A~rente** f old-age pension. **a~schwach** adj old and infirm. **A~vorsorge** f provision for old age

Alter|tum nt -s,⸚er antiquity. **a~tümlich** adj old; (altmodisch) old-fashioned

altklug adj precocious

alt|modisch adj old-fashioned. **A~papier** nt waste paper. **A~warenhändler** m second-hand dealer

Alufolie f [aluminium] foil

Aluminium nt -s aluminium, (Amer) aluminum

am prep = **an dem; am Montag** on Monday; **am Morgen** in the morning; **am besten** [the] best

Amateur /-'tøːɐ̯/ m -s,-e amateur

Ambition /-'tsi̯oːn/ f -,-en ambition

Amboss m -es,-e anvil

ambulan|t adj out-patient • adv **a~t behandeln** treat as an out-patient. **A~z** f -,-en out-patients' department

Ameise f -,-n ant

amen int, **A~** nt -s amen

Amerika nt -s America

Amerikan|er(in) m -s,- (f -,-nen) American. **a~isch** adj American

Ammoniak nt -s ammonia

Amnestie f -,-n amnesty

amoralisch adj amoral

Ampel f **-,-n** traffic lights pl

Amphitheater nt amphitheatre

Amput|ation /-'tsi̯o:n/ f **-,-en** amputation. **a~ieren** vt amputate

Amsel f **-,-n** blackbird

Amt nt **-[e]s,¨er** office; (Aufgabe) task; (Teleph) exchange. **a~lich** adj official. **A~szeichen** nt dialling tone

Amulett nt **-[e]s,-e** [lucky] charm

amüs|ant adj amusing. **a~ieren** vt amuse; **sich a~ieren** be amused (**über** + acc at); (sich vergnügen) enjoy oneself

an

• preposition (+ dative)

! Note that **an** plus **dem** can become **am**

····➤ (räumlich) on; (Gebäude, Ort) at. **an der Wand** on the wall. **Frankfurt an der Oder** Frankfurt on [the] Oder. **an der Ecke** at the corner. **am Bahnhof** at the station. **an vorbei** past. **am 24. Mai** on May 24th

····➤ (zeitlich) on. **am Montag** on Monday. **an jedem Sonntag** every Sunday

····➤ (sonstige Verwendungen) **arm/reich an Vitaminen** low/rich in vitamins. **jdn an etw erkennen** recognize s.o. by sth. **an etw leiden** suffer from sth. **an einer Krankheit sterben** die of a disease. **an [und für] sich** actually

• preposition (+ accusative)

! Note that **an** plus **das** can become **ans**

····➤ to. **schicke es an deinen Bruder** send it to your brother. **er ging ans Fenster** he went to the window

····➤ (auf, gegen) on. **etw an die Wand hängen** to hang sth on the wall. **lehne es an den Baum** lean it on or against the tree

····➤ (sonstige Verwendungen) **an etw/jdn glauben** believe in sth/s.o. **an etw denken** think of sth. **sich an etw erinnern** remember sth

• adverb

····➤ (auf Fahrplan) **Köln an: 9.15** arriving Cologne 09.15

····➤ (angeschaltet) on. **die Waschmaschine/der Fernseher/das Licht/das Gas ist an** the washing machine/television/light/gas is on

····➤ (ungefähr) around; about. **an [die] €20000** around or about €20,000

····➤ (in die Zukunft) **von heute an** from today (onwards)

analog adj analogous; (Computer) analog. **A~ie** f **-,-n** analogy

Analphabet m **-en,-en** illiterate person. **A~entum** nt **-s** illiteracy

Analy|se f **-,-n** analysis. **a~sieren** vt analyse. **A~tiker** m **-s,-** analyst. **a~tisch** adj analytical

Anämie f **-** anaemia

Ananas f **-,-[se]** pineapple

Anatomie f **-** anatomy

Anbau m cultivation; (Gebäude) extension. **a~en** vt sep build on; (anpflanzen) cultivate, grow

anbei adv enclosed

anbeißen† v sep • vt take a bite of • vi (haben) (Fisch:) bite

anbeten vt sep worship

Anbetracht m **in A~** (+ gen) in view of

anbieten† vt sep offer; **sich a~** offer (**zu** to)

anbinden† vt sep tie up

Anblick m sight. **a~en** vt sep look at

anbrechen† v sep • vt start on; break into (Vorräte) • vi (sein) begin; (Tag:) break; (Nacht:) fall

anbrennen† v sep • vt light • vi (sein) burn

anbringen† vt sep bring [along]; (befestigen) fix

Anbruch m (fig) dawn; **bei A~ des**

a

Tages/der Nacht at daybreak/ nightfall

Andacht f **-,-en** reverence; (Gottesdienst) prayers pl

andächtig adj reverent; (fig) rapt

andauern vi sep (haben) last; (anhalten) continue. **a∼d** adj persistent; (ständig) constant

Andenken nt **-s,-** memory; (Souvenir) souvenir

ander|e(r,s) adj other; (verschieden) different; (nächste) next; **ein a∼er, eine a∼e** another • pron **der a∼e/die a∼en** the other/others; **ein a∼er** another [one]; (Person) someone else; **kein a∼er** no one else; **einer nach dem a∼en** one after the other; **alles a∼e/nichts a∼es** everything/nothing else; **unter a∼em** among other things. **a∼enfalls** adv otherwise. **a∼erseits** adv on the other hand. **a∼mal** adv **ein a∼mal** another time

ändern vt alter; (wechseln) change; **sich ä∼** change

anders pred adj different; **a∼ werden** change • adv differently; (riechen, schmecken) different; (sonst) else; **jemand a∼** someone else

andersherum adv the other way round

anderthalb inv adj one and a half; **a∼ Stunden** an hour and a half

Änderung f **-,-en** alteration; (Wechsel) change

andeut|en vt sep indicate; (anspielen) hint at. **A∼ung** f **-,-en** indication; hint

Andrang m rush (**nach** for); (Gedränge) crush

androhen vt sep **jdm etw a∼** threaten s.o. with sth

aneignen vt sep **sich** (dat) **a∼** appropriate; (lernen) learn

aneinander adv & prefix together; (denken) of one another; **a∼ vorbei** past one another; **a∼ geraten** quarrel

Anekdote f **-,-n** anecdote

anerkannt adj acknowledged

anerkenn|en† vt sep acknowledge, recognize; (würdigen) appreciate. **a∼end** adj approving. **A∼ung** f - acknowledgement, recognition; appreciation

anfahren† v sep • vt deliver; (streifen) hit • vi (sein) start

Anfall m fit, attack. **a∼en**† v sep • vt attack • vi (sein) arise; (Zinsen:) accrue

anfällig adj susceptible (**für** to); (zart) delicate

Anfang m **-s,¨e** beginning, start; **zu** od **am A∼** at the beginning; (anfangs) at first. **a∼en**† vt/i sep (haben) begin, start; (tun) do

Anfänger(in) m **-s,-** (f **-,-nen**) beginner

anfangs adv at first. **A∼buchstabe** m initial letter. **A∼gehalt** nt starting salary

anfassen vt sep touch; (behandeln) treat; tackle (Arbeit); **sich a∼** hold hands

anfechten† vt sep contest

anfertigen vt sep make

anfeuchten vt sep moisten

anflehen vt sep implore, beg

Anflug m (Avia) approach

anforder|n vt sep demand; (Comm) order. **A∼ung** f demand

Anfrage f enquiry. **a∼n** vi sep (haben) enquire, ask

anfreunden (sich) vr sep make friends (**mit** with)

anfügen vt sep add

anfühlen vt sep feel; **sich weich a∼** feel soft

anführ|en vt sep lead; (zitieren) quote; (angeben) give. **A∼er** m leader. **A∼ungszeichen** ntpl quotation marks

Angabe f statement; (Anweisung) instruction; (Tennis) service; **nähere A∼n** particulars

angeb|en† v sep • vt state; give (Namen, Grund); (anzeigen) indicate; set (Tempo) • vi (haben) (Tennis) serve; (!: protzen) show off. **A∼er(in)** m

-s,- (f -,-nen) [!] show-off. **A~erei** f - [!] showing-off

angeblich adj alleged

angeboren adj innate; (Med) congenital

Angebot nt offer; (Auswahl) range; **A~ und Nachfrage** supply and demand

angebracht adj appropriate

angeheiratet adj (Onkel, Tante) by marriage

angeheitert adj [!] tipsy

angehen† v sep • vi (sein) begin, start; (Licht, Radio:) come on; (anwachsen) take root; **a~ gegen** fight • vt attack; tackle (Arbeit); (bitten) ask (**um** for); (betreffen) concern

angehör|en vi sep (haben) (+ dat) belong to. **A~ige(r)** m/f relative

Angeklagte(r) m/f accused

Angel f -,-n fishing-rod; (Tür-) hinge

Angelegenheit f matter

Angel|haken m fish-hook. **a~n** vi (haben) fish (**nach** for); **a~n gehen** go fishing • vt (fangen) catch. **A~rute** f fishing-rod

angelsächsisch adj Anglo-Saxon

angemessen adj commensurate (dat with); (passend) appropriate

angenehm adj pleasant; (bei Vorstellung) **a~!** delighted to meet you!

angeregt adj animated

angesehen adj respected; (Firma) reputable

angesichts prep (+ gen) in view of

angespannt adj intent; (Lage) tense

Angestellte(r) m/f employee

angewandt adj applied

angewiesen adj dependent (**auf** + acc on); **auf sich selbst a~** on one's own

angewöhnen vt sep **jdm etw a~** get s.o. used to sth; **sich** (dat) **etw a~** get into the habit of doing sth

Angewohnheit f habit

Angina f - tonsillitis

angleichen† vt sep adjust (dat to)

anglikanisch adj Anglican

Anglistik f - English [language and literature]

Angorakatze f Persian cat

angreif|en† vt sep attack; tackle (Arbeit); (schädigen) damage. **A~er** m -s,- attacker; (Pol) aggressor

angrenzen vi sep (haben) adjoin (**an etw** acc sth). **a~d** adj adjoining

Angriff m attack; **in A~ nehmen** tackle. **a~slustig** adj aggressive

Angst f -,¨e fear; (Psychology) anxiety; (Sorge) worry (**um** about); **A~ haben** be afraid (**vor** + dat of); (sich sorgen) be worried (**um** about); **jdm A~ machen** frighten s.o.

ängstigen vt frighten; (Sorge machen) worry; **sich ä~** be frightened; be worried (**um** about)

ängstlich adj nervous; (scheu) timid; (verängstigt) frightened, scared; (besorgt) anxious

angucken vt sep [!] look at

angurten (sich) vr sep fasten one's seat belt

anhaben† vt sep have on; **er/es kann mir nichts a~** (fig) he/it cannot hurt me

anhalt|en† v sep • vt stop; hold (Atem); **jdn zur Arbeit a~en** urge s.o. to work • vi (haben) stop; (andauern) continue. **a~end** adj persistent. **A~er(in)** m -s,- (f -,-nen) hitchhiker; **per A~er fahren** hitchhike. **A~spunkt** m clue

anhand prep (+ gen) with the aid of

Anhang m appendix

anhängen[1] vt sep (reg) hang up; (befestigen) attach

anhäng|en[2]† vi (haben) be a follower of. **A~er** m -s,- follower; (Auto) trailer; (Schild) [tie-on] label; (Schmuck) pendant. **A~erin** f -,-nen follower. **a~lich** adj affectionate

anhäufen vt sep pile up

a

Anhieb m **auf A~** straight away

Anhöhe f hill

anhören vt sep listen to; **sich gut a~** sound good

animieren vt encourage (**zu** to)

Anis m **-es** aniseed

Anker m **-s,-** anchor; **vor A~ gehen** drop anchor. **a~n** vi (haben) anchor; (liegen) be anchored

anketten vt sep chain up

Anklage f accusation; (Jur) charge; (Ankläger) prosecution. **A~bank** f dock. **a~n** vt sep accuse (gen of); (Jur) charge (gen with)

Ankläger m accuser; (Jur) prosecutor

anklammern vt sep clip on; **sich a~** cling (**an** + acc to)

ankleben v sep •vt stick on •vi (sein) stick (**an** + dat to)

anklicken vt sep click on

anklopfen vi sep (haben) knock

anknipsen vt sep [!] switch on

ankommen† vi sep (sein) arrive; (sich nähern) approach; **gut a~** arrive safely; (fig) go down well (**bei** with); **nicht a~ gegen** (fig) be no match for; **a~ auf** (+ acc) depend on; **das kommt darauf an** it [all] depends

ankreuzen vt sep mark with a cross

ankündig|en vt sep announce. **A~ung** f announcement

Ankunft f - arrival

ankurbeln vt sep (fig) boost

anlächeln vt sep smile at

anlachen vt sep smile at

Anlage f **-,-n** installation; (Industrie-) plant; (Komplex) complex; (Geld-) investment; (Plan) layout; (Beilage) enclosure; (Veranlagung) aptitude; (Neigung) predisposition; **[öffentliche] A~n** [public] gardens; **als A~** enclosed

Anlass m **-es,¨-e** reason; (Gelegenheit) occasion; **A~ geben zu** give cause for

anlass|en† vt sep (Auto) start; [!] leave on (Licht); keep on (Mantel). **A~er** m **-s,-** starter

anlässlich prep (+ gen) on the occasion of

Anlauf m (Sport) run-up; (fig) attempt. **a~en**† v sep •vi (sein) start; (beschlagen) mist up; (Metall:) tarnish; **rot a~en** blush •vt (Naut) call at

anlegen v sep •vt put (**an** + acc against); put on (Kleidung, Verband); lay back (Ohren); aim (Gewehr); (investieren) invest; (ausgeben) spend (**für** on); draw up (Liste); **es darauf a~** (fig) aim (**zu** to) •vi (haben) (Schiff:) moor; **a~ auf** (+ acc) aim at

anlehnen vt sep lean (**an** + acc against); **sich a~** lean (**an** + acc on)

Anleihe f **-,-n** loan

anleit|en vt sep instruct. **A~ung** f instructions pl

anlernen vt sep train

Anliegen nt **-s,-** request; (Wunsch) desire

anlieg|en† vi sep (haben) **[eng] a~en** fit closely; **[eng] a~end** close-fitting. **A~er** mpl residents; **'A~er frei'** 'access for residents only'

anlügen† vt sep lie to

anmachen vt sep [!] fix; (anschalten) turn on; dress (Salat)

anmalen vt sep paint

Anmarsch m (Mil) approach

anmeld|en vt sep announce; (Admin) register; **sich a~en** say that one is coming; (Admin) register; (Sch) enrol; (im Hotel) check in; (beim Arzt) make an appointment; (Computer) log on. **A~ung** f announcement; (Admin) registration; (Sch) enrolment; (Termin) appointment

anmerk|en vt sep mark; **sich** (dat) **etw a~en lassen** show sth. **A~ung** f **-,-en** note

Anmut f - grace; (Charme) charm

anmutig adj graceful

annähen vt sep sew on

annäher|nd adj approximate. **A~ungsversuche** mpl advances

Annahme f -,-n acceptance; (Adoption) adoption; (Vermutung) assumption

annehm|bar adj acceptable. **a~en†** vt sep accept; (adoptieren) adopt; acquire (Gewohnheit); (sich zulegen, vermuten) assume; **angenommen, dass** assuming that. **A~lichkeiten** fpl comforts

Anno adv **A~ 1920** in the year 1920

Annon|ce /a'nõ:sə/ f -,-n advertisement. **a~cieren** vt/i (haben) advertise

annullieren vt annul; cancel

Anomalie f -,-n anomaly

anonym adj anonymous

Anorak m -s,-s anorak

anordn|en vt sep arrange; (befehlen) order. **A~ung** f arrangement; order

anorganisch adj inorganic

anormal adj abnormal

anpass|en vt sep try on; (angleichen) adapt (dat to); **sich a~** adapt (dat to). **A~ung** f - adaptation. **a~ungsfähig** adj adaptable. **A~ungsfähigkeit** f adaptability

Anpfiff m (Sport) kick-off

Anprall m -[e]s impact. **a~en** vi sep (sein) strike (**an etw** acc sth)

anpreisen† vt sep commend

Anprob|e f fitting. **a~ieren** vt sep try on

anrechnen vt sep count (**als** as); (berechnen) charge for; (verrechnen) allow (Summe)

Anrecht nt right (**auf** + acc to)

Anrede f [form of] address. **a~n** vt sep address; speak to

anreg|en vt sep stimulate; (ermuntern) encourage (**zu** to); (vorschlagen) suggest. **a~end** adj stimulating. **A~ung** f stimulation; (Vorschlag) suggestion

Anreise f journey; (Ankunft) arrival. **a~n** vi sep (sein) arrive

Anreiz m incentive

Anrichte f -,-n sideboard. **a~n** vt sep (Culin) prepare; (garnieren) garnish (**mit** with); (verursachen) cause

anrüchig adj disreputable

Anruf m call. **A~beantworter** m -s,- answering machine. **a~en†** v sep •vt call to; (bitten) call on (**um** for); (Teleph) ring •vi (haben) ring (**bei jdm** s.o.)

anrühren vt sep touch; (verrühren) mix

ans prep = **an das**

Ansage f announcement. **a~n** vt sep announce

ansamm|eln vt sep collect; (anhäufen) accumulate; **sich a~eln** collect; (sich häufen) accumulate; (Leute:) gather. **A~lung** f collection; (Menschen-) crowd

ansässig adj resident

Ansatz m beginning; (Versuch) attempt

anschaffen vt sep [**sich** dat] **etw a~en** acquire/(kaufen) buy sth

anschalten vt sep switch on

anschau|en vt sep look at. **a~lich** adj vivid. **A~ung** f -,-en (fig) view

Anschein m appearance. **a~end** adv apparently

anschirren vt sep harness

Anschlag m notice; (Vor-) estimate; (Überfall) attack (**auf** + acc on); (Mus) touch; (Techn) stop. **a~en†** v sep •vt put up (Aushang); strike (Note, Taste); cast on (Masche); (beschädigen) chip •vi (haben) strike/(stoßen) knock (**an** + acc against); (wirken) be effective •vi (sein) knock (**an** + acc against)

anschließen† v sep •vt connect (**an** + acc to); (zufügen) add; **sich a~ an** (+ acc) (anstoßen) adjoin; (folgen) follow; (sich anfreunden) become friendly with; **sich jdm a~** join s.o. •vi (haben) **a~ an** (+ acc) adjoin; (folgen) follow. **a~d** adj adjoining; (zeitlich) following •adv afterwards

a

Anschluss m connection; (Kontakt) contact; **A~ finden** make friends; **im A~ an** (+ acc) after

anschmiegsam adj affectionate

anschmieren vt sep smear

anschnallen vt sep strap on; **sich a~** fasten one's seat-belt

anschneiden† vt sep cut into; broach (Thema)

anschreiben† vt sep write (**an** + acc on); (Comm) put on s.o.'s account; (sich wenden) write to

Anschrift f address

anschuldig|en vt sep accuse. **A~ung** f **-,-en** accusation

anschwellen† vi sep (sein) swell

ansehen† vt sep look at; (einschätzen) regard (**als** as); [**sich** dat] **etw a~** look at sth; (TV) watch sth. **A~** nt **-s** respect; (Ruf) reputation

ansehnlich adj considerable

ansetzen v sep • vt join (**an** + acc to); (veranschlagen) estimate • vi (haben) (anbrennen) burn; **zum Sprung a~** get ready to jump

Ansicht f view; **meiner A~ nach** in my view; **zur A~** (Comm) on approval. **A~s[post]karte** f picture postcard. **A~ssache** f matter of opinion

ansiedeln (sich) vr sep settle

ansonsten adv apart from that

anspannen vt sep hitch up; (anstrengen) strain; tense (Muskel)

Anspielung f **-,-en** allusion; hint

Anspitzer m **-s,-** pencil-sharpener

Ansprache f address

ansprechen† v sep • vt speak to; (fig) appeal to • vi (haben) respond (**auf** + acc to)

anspringen† v sep • vt jump at • vi (sein) (Auto) start

Anspruch m claim/(Recht) right (**auf** + acc to); **A~ haben** be entitled (**auf** + acc to); **in A~ nehmen** make use of; (erfordern) demand; take up (Zeit); occupy (Person); **hohe A~̈e stellen** be very demanding. **a~slos** adj undemanding. **a~svoll** adj demanding; (kritisch) discriminating; (vornehm) up-market

anstacheln vt sep (fig) spur on

Anstalt f **-,-en** institution

Anstand m decency; (Benehmen) [good] manners pl

anständig adj decent; (ehrbar) respectable; (richtig) proper

anstandslos adv without any trouble

anstarren vt sep stare at

anstatt conj & prep (+ gen) instead of

ansteck|en v sep • vt pin (**an** + acc to/on); put on (Ring); (anzünden) light; (in Brand stecken) set fire to; (Med) infect; **sich a~en** catch an infection (**bei** from) • vi (haben) be infectious. **a~end** adj infectious. **A~ung** f **-,-en** infection

anstehen† vi sep (haben) queue

anstelle prep (+ gen) instead of

anstell|en vt sep put, stand (**an** + acc against); (einstellen) employ; (anschalten) turn on; (tun) do; **sich a~en** queue [up]. **A~ung** f employment; (Stelle) job

Anstieg m **-[e]s,-e** climb; (fig) rise

anstifte|n vt sep cause; (anzetteln) instigate

Anstoß m (Anregung) impetus; (Stoß) knock; (Fußball) kick-off; **A~ erregen** give offence. **a~en†** v sep • vt knock; (mit dem Ellbogen) nudge • vi (sein) knock (**an** + acc against) • vi (haben) adjoin (**an etw** acc sth); **a~en auf** (+ acc) drink to; **mit der Zunge a~en** lisp

anstößig adj offensive

anstrahlen vt sep floodlight

anstreichen† vt sep paint; (anmerken) mark

anstreng|en vt sep strain; (ermüden) tire; **sich a~en** exert oneself; (sich bemühen) make an effort (**zu** to). **a~end** adj strenuous; (ermüdend) tiring. **A~ung** f **-,-en** strain; (Mühe) effort

Anstrich m coat [of paint]

Ansturm m rush; (Mil) assault

Ansuchen nt **-s,-** request

Antarktis f - Antarctic

Anteil m share; **A~ nehmen** take an interest (**an** + dat in). **A~nahme** f - interest (**an** + dat in); (Mitgefühl) sympathy

Antenne f **-,-n** aerial

Anthologie f **-,-n** anthology

Anthrax m - anthrax

Anthropologie f - anthropology

Anti|alkoholiker m teetotaller. **A~biotikum** nt **-s,-ka** antibiotic

antik adj antique. **A~e** f - [classical] antiquity

Antikörper m antibody

Antilope f **-,-n** antelope

Antipathie f - antipathy

Antiquariat nt **-[e]s,-e** antiquarian bookshop

Antiquitäten fpl antiques. **A~händler** m antique dealer

Antrag m **-[e]s,¨-e** proposal; (Pol) motion; (Gesuch) application. **A~steller** m **-s,-** applicant

antreffen† vt sep find

antreten† v sep •vt start; take up (Amt) •vi (sein) line up

Antrieb m urge; (Techn) drive; **aus eigenem A~** of one's own accord

Antritt m start; **bei A~ eines Amtes** when taking office

antun† vt sep **jdm etw a~** do sth to s.o.; **sich** (dat) **etwas a~** take one's own life

Antwort f **-,-en** answer, reply (**auf** + acc to). **a~en** vt/i (haben) answer (**jdm** s.o.)

anvertrauen vt sep entrust/ (mitteilen) confide (**jdm** to s.o.)

Anwalt m **-[e]s,¨-e, Anwältin** f **-,-nen** lawyer; (vor Gericht) counsel

Anwandlung f **-,-en** fit (**von** of)

Anwärter(in) m(f) candidate

anweis|en† vt sep assign (dat to); (beauftragen) instruct. **A~ung** f instruction; (Geld-) money order

anwend|en vt sep apply (**auf** + acc to); (gebrauchen) use. **A~ung** f application; use

anwerben† vt sep recruit

Anwesen nt **-s,-** property

anwesen|d adj present (**bei** at); **die A~den** those present. **A~heit** f - presence

anwidern vt sep disgust

Anwohner mpl residents

Anzahl f number

anzahl|en vt sep pay a deposit on. **A~ung** f deposit

anzapfen vt sep tap

Anzeichen nt sign

Anzeige f **-,-n** announcement; (Inserat) advertisement; **A~ erstatten gegen jdn** report s.o. to the police. **a~n** vt sep announce; (inserieren) advertise; (melden) report [to the police]; (angeben) indicate

anzieh|en† vt sep •vt attract; (festziehen) tighten; put on (Kleider, Bremse); (ankleiden) dress; **sich a~en** get dressed. **a~end** adj attractive. **A~ungskraft** f attraction; (Phys) gravity

Anzug m suit

anzüglich adj suggestive

anzünden vt sep light; (in Brand stecken) set fire to

anzweifeln vt sep question

apart adj striking

Apathie f - apathy

apathisch adj apathetic

Aperitif m **-s,-s** aperitif

Apfel m **-s,¨** apple

Apfelsine f **-,-n** orange

Apostel m **-s,-** apostle

Apostroph m **-s,-e** apostrophe

Apothek|e f **-,-n** pharmacy. **A~er(in)** m **-s,-** (f **-,-nen**) pharmacist, [dispensing] chemist

Apparat m **-[e]s,-e** device; (Phot) camera; (Radio, TV) set; (Teleph)

telephone; **am A~!** speaking!

Appell m **-s,-e** appeal; (Mil) roll-call. **a~ieren** vi (haben) appeal (**an** + acc to)

Appetit m **-s** appetite; **guten A~!** enjoy your meal! **a~lich** adj appetizing

Applaus m **-es** applause

Aprikose f **-,-n** apricot

April m **-[s]** April

Aquarell nt **-s,-e** water-colour

Aquarium nt **-s,-ien** aquarium

Äquator m **-s** equator

Ära f - era

Araber(in) m **-s,-** (f **-,-nen**) Arab

arabisch adj Arab; (Geog) Arabian; (Ziffer) Arabic

Arbeit f **-,-en** work; (Anstellung) employment, job; (Aufgabe) task; (Sch) [written] test; (Abhandlung) treatise; (Qualität) workmanship; **sich an die A~ machen** set to work; **sich** (dat) **viel A~ machen** go to a lot of trouble. **a~en** v sep • vi (haben) work (**an** + dat on) • vt make. **A~er(in)** m **-s,-** (f **-,-nen**) worker; (Land-, Hilfs-) labourer. **A~erklasse** f working class

Arbeit|geber m **-s,-** employer. **A~nehmer** m **-s,-** employee

C **Arbeits|amt** nt employment exchange. **A~erlaubnis, A~genehmigung** f work permit. **A~kraft** f worker. **a~los** adj unemployed; **~los sein** be out of work. **A~lose(r)** m/f unemployed person; **die A~losen** the unemployed pl. **A~losenunterstützung** f unemployment benefit. **A~losigkeit** f - unemployment

arbeitsparend adj labour-saving

Arbeitsplatz m job

Archäo|loge m **-n,-n** archaeologist. **A~logie** f - archaeology

C *see A-Z of German life and culture*

Arche f - **die A~ Noah** Noah's Ark

Architek|t(in) m **-en,-en** (f **-,-nen**) architect. **a~tonisch** adj architectural. **A~tur** f - architecture

Archiv nt **-s,-e** archives pl

Arena f **-,-nen** arena

arg adj bad; (groß) terrible

Argentin|ien /-i̯ən/ nt **-s** Argentina. **a~isch** adj Argentinian

Ärger m **-s** annoyance; (Unannehmlichkeit) trouble. **ä~lich** adj annoyed; (leidig) annoying; **ä~lich sein** be annoyed. **ä~n** vt annoy; (necken) tease; **sich ä~n** get annoyed (**über jdn/etw** with s.o./about sth). **Ä~nis** nt **-ses, -se** annoyance; **öffentliches Ä~nis** public nuisance

Arglist f - malice

arglos adj unsuspecting

Argument nt **-[e]s,-e** argument. **a~ieren** vi (haben) argue (**dass** that)

Arie /ˈaːri̯ə/ f **-,-n** aria

Aristo|krat m **-en,-en** aristocrat. **A~kratie** f - aristocracy. **a~kratisch** adj aristocratic

Arkt|is f - Arctic. **a~isch** adj Arctic

arm adj poor

Arm m **-[e]s,-e** arm; **jdn auf den Arm nehmen** Ⓕ pull s.o.'s leg

Armaturenbrett nt instrument panel; (Auto) dashboard

Armband nt (pl **-bänder**) bracelet; (Uhr-) watch-strap. **A~uhr** f wrist-watch

Arm|e(r) m/f poor man/woman; **die A~en** the poor pl

Armee f **-,-n** army

Ärmel m **-s,-** sleeve. **Ä~kanal** m [English] Channel. **ä~los** adj sleeveless

Arm|lehne f arm. **A~leuchter** m candelabra

ärmlich adj poor; (elend) miserable

armselig adj miserable

Armut f - poverty

Arran|gement /arãʒəˈmã:/ nt **-s,-s** arrangement. **a~gieren** vt arrange

arrogant adj arrogant

Arsch m **-[e]s,¨e** (vulgar) arse

Arsen nt **-s** arsenic

Art f **-,-en** manner; (Weise) way; (Natur) nature; (Sorte) kind; (Biology) species; **auf diese Art** in this way

Arterie /-iə/ f **-,-n** artery

Arthritis f - arthritis

artig adj well-behaved

Artikel m **-s,-** article

Artillerie f - artillery

Artischocke f **-,-n** artichoke

Arznei f **-,-en** medicine

Arzt m **-[e]s,¨e** doctor

Ärzt|in f **-,-nen** [woman] doctor. **ä~lich** adj medical

As* nt **-ses,-se** = **Ass**

Asbest m **-[e]s** asbestos

Asche f - ash. **A~nbecher** m ashtray. **A~rmittwoch** m Ash Wednesday

Asiat|(in) m **-en,-en** (f **-,-nen**) Asian. **a~isch** adj Asian

Asien /ˈa:ziən/ nt **-s** Asia

asozial adj antisocial

Aspekt m **-[e]s,-e** aspect

Asphalt m **-[e]s** asphalt. **a~ieren** vt asphalt

Ass nt **-es,-e** ace

Assistent(in) m **-en,-en** (f **-,-nen**) assistant

Ast m **-[e]s,¨e** branch

ästhetisch adj aesthetic

Asth|ma nt **-s** asthma. **a~matisch** adj asthmatic

Astro|loge m **-n,-n** astrologer. **A~logie** f - astrology. **A~naut** m **-en,-en** astronaut. **A~nomie** f - astronomy

Asyl nt **-s,-e** home; (Pol) asylum. **A~bewerber(in)** m **-e, -** (f **-en, -en**) asylum seeker

Atelier /-ˈlie:/ nt **-s,-s** studio

Atem m **-s** breath. **a~los** adj breathless. **A~zug** m breath

Atheist m **-en,-en** atheist

Äther m **-s** ether

Äthiopien /-iən/ nt **-s** Ethiopia

Athlet|(in) m **-en,-en** (f **-,-nen**) athlete. **a~isch** adj athletic

Atlant|ik m **-s** Atlantic. **a~isch** adj Atlantic; **der A~ische Ozean** the Atlantic Ocean

Atlas m **-lasses,-lanten** atlas

atmen vt/i (haben) breathe

Atmosphäre f **-,-n** atmosphere

Atmung f - breathing

Atom nt **-s,-e** atom. **A~bombe** f atom bomb. **A~krieg** m nuclear war

Atten|tat nt **-[e]s,-e** assassination attempt. **A~täter** m assassin

Attest nt **-[e]s,-e** certificate

Attrak|tion /-ˈtsio:n/ f **-,-en** attraction. **a~tiv** adj attractive

Attribut nt **-[e]s,-e** attribute

ätzen vt corrode; (Med) cauterize; (Kunst) etch. **ä~d** adj corrosive; (Spott) caustic

au int ouch; **au fein!** oh good!

Aubergine /obɛrˈʒi:nə/ f **-,-n** aubergine

auch adv & conj also, too; (außerdem) what's more; (selbst) even; **a~ wenn** even if; **sie weiß es a~ nicht** she doesn't know either; **wer/wie/was a~ immer** whoever/however/whatever

Audienz f **-,-en** audience

audiovisuell adj audio-visual

Auditorium nt **-s,-ien** (Univ) lecture hall

a

auf

- preposition (+ dative)

····➤ (nicht unter) on. **auf dem Tisch** on the table. **auf Deck** on deck. **auf der Erde** on earth. **auf der Welt** in the world. **auf der Straße** in the street

····➤ (bei Institution, Veranstaltung usw.) at; (bei Gebäude, Zimmer) in. **auf der Schule/Uni** at school/university. **auf einer Party/Hochzeit** at a party/wedding. **Geld auf der Bank haben** have money in the bank. **sie ist auf ihrem Zimmer** she's in her room. **auf einem Lehrgang** on a course. **auf Urlaub** on holiday

- preposition (+ accusative)

····➤ (nicht unter) on[to]. **er legte das Buch auf den Tisch** he laid the book on the table. **auf eine Mauer steigen** climb onto a wall. **auf die Straße gehen** go [out] into the street

····➤ (bei Institution, Veranstaltung usw.) to. **auf eine Party/die Toilette gehen** go to a party/the toilet. **auf die Schule/Uni gehen** go to school/university. **auf einen Lehrgang/auf Urlaub gehen** go on a course/on holiday

····➤ (bei Entfernung) **auf 10 km [Entfernung] zu sehen/hören** visible/audible for [a distance of] 10 km

····➤ (zeitlich) (wie lange) for; (bis) until; (wann) on. **auf Jahre [hinaus]** for years [to come]. **auf ein paar Tage** for a few days. **etw auf nächsten Mittwoch verschieben** postpone sth until next Wednesday. **das fällt auf einen Montag** it falls on a Monday

····➤ (Art und Weise) in. **auf diese [Art und] Weise** in this way. **auf Deutsch/Englisch** in German/English

····➤ (aufgrund) **auf Wunsch** on request. **auf meine Bitte** on or at my request. **auf Befehl** on command

····➤ (Proportion) to. **ein Teelöffel auf einen Liter Wasser** one teaspoon to one litre of water. **auf die Sekunde/den Millimeter [genau]** [precise] to the nearest second/millimetre

····➤ (Toast) to. **auf deine Gesundheit!** your health!

- adverb

····➤ (aufgerichtet, aufgestanden) up. **auf!** (steh auf!) up you get! **auf und ab** (hin und her) up and down

····➤ (aufsetzen) **Helm/Hut/Brille auf!** helmet/hat/glasses on!

····➤ (geöffnet, offen) open. **Fenster/Mund auf!** open the window/your mouth!

aufatmen vi sep (haben) heave a sigh of relief

aufbahren vt sep lay out

Aufbau m construction; (Struktur) structure. **a~en** v sep •vt construct, build; (errichten) erect; (schaffen) build up; (arrangieren) arrange; **sich a~en** (fig) be based (**auf** + dat on) •vi (haben) be based (**auf** + dat on)

aufbauschen vt sep puff out; (fig) exaggerate

aufbekommen† vt sep get open; (Sch) be given [as homework]

aufbessern vt sep improve; (erhöhen) increase

aufbewahr|en vt sep keep; (lagern) store. **A~ung** f - safe keeping; storage; (Gepäck-) left-luggage office

aufblas|bar adj inflatable. **a~en**† vt sep inflate

aufbleiben† vi sep (sein) stay open; (Person:) stay up

aufblenden vt/i sep (haben) (Auto) switch to full beam

aufblühen vi sep (sein) flower

aufbocken vt sep jack up

aufbrauchen vt sep use up

aufbrechen† v sep •vt break open •vi (sein) (Knospe:) open; (sich aufmachen) set out, start

aufbringen† vt sep raise (Geld); find (Kraft)

Aufbruch m start, departure

aufbrühen vt sep make (Tee)

aufbürden vt sep **jdm etw a~** (fig) burden s.o. with sth

aufdecken vt sep (auflegen) put on; (abdecken) uncover; (fig) expose

aufdrehen vt sep turn on

aufdringlich adj persistent

aufeinander adv one on top of the other; (schießen) at each other; (warten) for each other; **a~ folgend** successive; (Tage) consecutive.

Aufenthalt m stay; **10 Minuten A~ haben** (Zug:) stop for 10 minutes. **A~serlaubnis, A~sgenehmigung** f residence permit. **A~sraum** m recreation room; (im Hotel) lounge

Auferstehung f - resurrection

aufessen† vt sep eat up

auffahr|en† vi sep (sein) drive up; (aufprallen) crash, run (**auf** + acc into). **A~t** f drive; (Autobahn-) access road, slip road; (Bergfahrt) ascent

auffallen† vi sep (sein) be conspicuous; **unangenehm a~** make a bad impression

auffällig adj conspicuous

auffangen† vt sep catch; pick up

auffass|en vt sep understand; (deuten) take. **A~ung** f understanding; (Ansicht) view

aufforder|n vt sep ask; (einladen) invite. **A~ung** f request; invitation

auffrischen v sep •vt freshen up; revive (Erinnerung); **seine Englischkenntnisse a~** brush up one's English

aufführ|en vt sep perform; (angeben) list; **sich a~en** behave. **A~ung** f performance

auffüllen vt sep fill up

Aufgabe f task; (Rechen-) problem; (Verzicht) giving up; **A~n** (Sch) homework sg

Aufgang m way up; (Treppe) stairs pl; (der Sonne) rise

aufgeben† v sep •vt give up; post (Brief); send (Telegramm); place (Bestellung); register (Gepäck); put in the paper (Annonce); **jdm eine Aufgabe a~** set s.o. a task; **jdm Suppe a~** serve s.o. with soup •vi (haben) give up

Aufgebot nt contingent (**an** + dat of); (Relig) banns pl

aufgedunsen adj bloated

aufgehen† vi sep (sein) open; (sich lösen) come undone; (Teig, Sonne:) rise; (Saat:) come up; (Math) come out exactly; **in Flammen a~** go up in flames

aufgelegt adj **gut/schlecht a~ sein** be in a good/bad mood

aufgeregt adj excited; (erregt) agitated

aufgeschlossen adj (fig) openminded

aufgeweckt adj (fig) bright

aufgießen† vt sep pour on; (aufbrühen) make (Tee)

aufgreifen† vt sep pick up; take up (Vorschlag, Thema)

aufgrund prep (+ gen) on the strength of

Aufguss m infusion

aufhaben† v sep •vt have on; **den Mund a~** have one's mouth open; **viel a~** (Sch) have a lot of homework •vi (haben) be open

aufhalten† vt sep hold up; (anhalten) stop; (abhalten) keep; (offenhalten) hold open; hold out (Hand); **sich a~** stay; (sich befassen) spend one's time (**mit** on)

aufhäng|en vt/i sep (haben) hang up; (henken) hang; **sich a~en** hang oneself. **A~er** m **-s,-** loop

aufheben† vt sep pick up; (hochheben) raise; (aufbewahren) keep; (beenden) end; (rückgängig machen) lift; (abschaffen) abolish; (Jur) quash (Urteil); repeal (Gesetz); (ausgleichen) cancel out; **gut aufgehoben sein** be well looked after

aufheitern vt sep cheer up; **sich a~** (Wetter:) brighten up

a

aufhellen vt sep lighten; **sich a~** (Himmel:) brighten

aufhetzen vt sep incite

aufholen v sep • vt make up • vi (haben) catch up; (zeitlich) make up time

aufhören vi sep (haben) stop

aufklappen vt/i sep (sein) open

aufklär|en vt sep solve; **jdn a~en** enlighten s.o.; **sich a~en** be solved; (Wetter:) clear up. **A~ung** f solution; enlightenment; (Mil) reconnaissance; **sexuelle A~ung** sex education

aufkleb|en vt sep stick on. **A~er** m **-s,-** sticker

aufknöpfen vt sep unbutton

aufkochen v sep • vt bring to the boil • vi (sein) come to the boil

aufkommen† vi sep (sein) start; (Wind:) spring up; (Mode:) come in

aufkrempeln vt sep roll up

aufladen† vt sep load; (Electr) charge

Auflage f impression; (Ausgabe) edition; (Zeitungs-) circulation

auflassen† vt sep leave open; leave on (Hut)

Auflauf m crowd; (Culin) ≈ soufflé

auflegen v sep • vt apply (**auf** + acc to); put down (Hörer); **neu a~** reprint • vi (haben) ring off

auflehn|en (sich) vr sep (fig) rebel. **A~ung** f - rebellion

auflesen† vt sep pick up

aufleuchten vi sep (haben) light up

auflös|en vt sep dissolve; close (Konto); **sich a~en** dissolve; (Nebel:) clear. **A~ung** f dissolution; (Lösung) solution

aufmach|en v sep • vt open; (lösen) undo; **sich a~en** set out (**nach** for) • vi (haben) open; **jdm a~en** open the door to s.o. **A~ung** f **-,-en** get-up

aufmerksam adj attentive; **a~ werden auf** (+ acc) notice; **jdn a~ machen auf** (+ acc) draw s.o.'s attention to. **A~keit** f **-,-en** attention; (Höflichkeit) courtesy

aufmuntern vt sep cheer up

Aufnahme f **-,-n** acceptance; (Empfang) reception; (in Klub, Krankenhaus) admission; (Einbeziehung) inclusion; (Beginn) start; (Foto) photograph; (Film-) shot; (Mus) recording; (Band-) tape recording. **a~fähig** adj receptive. **A~prüfung** f entrance examination

aufnehmen† vt sep pick up; (absorbieren) absorb; take (Nahrung, Foto); (fassen) hold; (annehmen) accept; (leihen) borrow; (empfangen) receive; (in Klub, Krankenhaus) admit; (beherbergen, geistig erfassen) take in; (einbeziehen) include; (beginnen) take up; (niederschreiben) take down; (filmen) film, shoot; (Mus) record; **auf Band a~** tape[-record]

aufopfer|n vt sep sacrifice; **sich a~n** sacrifice oneself. **A~ung** f self-sacrifice

aufpassen vi sep (haben) pay attention; (sich vorsehen) take care; **a~ auf** (+ acc) look after

Aufprall m **-[e]s** impact. **a~en** vi sep (sein) **a~en auf** (+ acc) hit

aufpumpen vt sep pump up, inflate

aufputsch|en vt sep incite. **A~mittel** nt stimulant

aufquellen† vi sep (sein) swell

aufraffen vt sep pick up; **sich a~** pick oneself up; (fig) pull oneself together

aufragen vi sep (sein) rise [up]

aufräumen vt/i sep (haben) tidy up; (wegräumen) put away

aufrecht adj & adv upright. **a~erhalten†** vt sep (fig) maintain

aufreg|en vt excite; (beunruhigen) upset; (ärgern) annoy; **sich a~en** get excited; (sich erregen) get worked up. **a~end** adj exciting. **A~ung** f excitement

aufreiben† vt sep chafe; (fig) wear down. **a~d** adj trying

aufreißen† v sep • vt tear open; dig up (Straße); open wide (Augen, Mund)

•vi (sein) split open

aufrichtig adj sincere. **A~keit** f - sincerity

aufrollen vt sep roll up; (entrollen) unroll

aufrücken vi sep (sein) move up; (fig) be promoted

Aufruf m appeal (**an** + dat to); **a~en**† vt sep call out (Namen); **jdn a~en** call s.o.'s name

Aufruhr m **-s,-e** turmoil; (Empörung) revolt

aufrühr|en vt sep stir up. **A~er** m **-s,-** rebel. **a~erisch** adj inflammatory; (rebellisch) rebellious

aufrunden vt sep round up

aufrüsten vi sep (haben) arm

aufsagen vt sep recite

aufsässig adj rebellious

Aufsatz m top; (Sch) essay

aufsaugen† vt sep soak up

aufschauen vi sep (haben) look up (**zu** at/(fig) to)

aufschichten vt sep stack up

aufschieben† vt sep slide open; (verschieben) put off, postpone

Aufschlag m impact; (Tennis) service; (Hosen-) turn-up; (Ärmel-) upturned cuff; (Revers) lapel; (Comm) surcharge. **a~en**† v sep •vt open; crack (Ei); (hochschlagen) turn up; (errichten) put up; (erhöhen) increase; cast on (Masche); **sich** (dat) **das Knie a~en** cut [open] one's knee •vi (haben) hit (**auf etw** acc/dat sth); (Tennis) serve; (teurer werden) go up

aufschließen† v sep •vt unlock •vi (haben) unlock the door

aufschlussreich adj revealing; (lehrreich) informative

aufschneiden† v sep •vt cut open; (in Scheiben) slice •vi (haben) [!] exaggerate

Aufschnitt m sliced sausage, cold meat [and cheese]

aufschrauben vt sep screw on; (abschrauben) unscrew

Aufschrei m [sudden] cry

aufschreiben† vt sep write down; **jdn a~** (Polizist:) book s.o.

Aufschrift f inscription; (Etikett) label

Aufschub m delay; (Frist) grace

aufschürfen vt sep **sich** (dat) **das Knie a~** graze one's knee

aufschwingen† **(sich)** vr sep find the energy (**zu** for)

Aufschwung m (fig) upturn

aufsehen† vi sep (haben) look up (**zu** at/(fig) to). **A~** nt **-s A~ erregen** cause a sensation; **A~ erregend** sensational

Aufseher(in) m **-s,-** (f **-,-nen**) supervisor; (Gefängnis-) warder

aufsetzen vt sep put on; (verfassen) draw up; (entwerfen) draft; **sich a~** sit up

Aufsicht f supervision; (Person) supervisor. **A~srat** m board of directors

aufsperren vt sep open wide

aufspielen v sep •vi (haben) play •vr **sich a~** show off

aufspießen vt sep spear

aufspringen† vi sep (sein) jump up; (aufprallen) bounce; (sich öffnen) burst open

aufspüren vt sep track down

aufstacheln vt sep incite

Aufstand m uprising, rebellion

aufständisch adj rebellious

aufstehen† vi sep (sein) get up; (offen sein) be open; (fig) rise up

aufsteigen† vi sep (sein) get on; (Reiter:) mount; (Bergsteiger:) climb up; (hochsteigen) rise [up]; (fig: befördert werden) rise (**zu** to); (Sport) be promoted

aufstell|en vt sep put up; (Culin) put on; (postieren) post; (in einer Reihe) line up; (nominieren) nominate; (Sport) select (Mannschaft); make out (Liste); lay down (Regel); make (Behauptung); set up (Rekord). **A~ung** f nomination; (Liste) list

Aufstieg m **-[e]s, -e** ascent; (fig) rise; (Sport) promotion

a

Aufstoßen nt **-s** burping
aufstrebend adj (fig) ambitious
Aufstrich m [sandwich] spread
aufstützen vt sep rest (**auf** + acc on); **sich a∼** lean (**auf** + acc on)
Auftakt m (fig) start
auftauchen vi sep (sein) emerge; (fig) turn up; (Frage:) crop up
auftauen vt/i sep (sein) thaw
aufteil|en vt sep divide [up]. **A∼ung** f division
auftischen vt sep serve [up]
Auftrag m **-[e]s,¨e** task; (Kunst) commission; (Comm) order; **im A∼** (+ gen) on behalf of. **a∼en**† vt sep apply; (servieren) serve; (abtragen) wear out; **jdm a∼en** instruct s.o. (**zu** to). **A∼geber** m **-s,-** client
auftrennen vt sep unpick, undo
auftreten† vi sep (sein) tread; (sich benehmen) behave, act; (Theat) appear; (die Bühne betreten) enter; (vorkommen) occur
Auftrieb m buoyancy; (fig) boost
Auftritt m (Theat) appearance; (auf die Bühne) entrance; (Szene) scene
aufwachen vi sep (sein) wake up
aufwachsen† vi sep (sein) grow up
Aufwand m **-[e]s** expenditure; (Luxus) extravagance; (Mühe) trouble; **A∼ treiben** be extravagant
aufwändig adj = **aufwendig**
aufwärmen vt sep heat up; (fig) rake up; **sich a∼** warm oneself; (Sport) warm up
Aufwartefrau f cleaner
aufwärts adv upwards; (bergauf) uphill; **es geht a∼ mit jdm/etw** someone/something is improving
Aufwartung f **-** cleaner
aufwecken vt sep wake up
aufweichen v sep •vt soften •vi (sein) become soft
aufweisen† vt sep have, show
aufwend|en† vt sep spend; **Mühe a∼en** take pains. **a∼ig** adj lavish; (teuer) expensive
aufwert|en vt sep revalue. **A∼ung** f revaluation
aufwickeln vt sep roll up; (auswickeln) unwrap
Aufwiegler m **-s,-** agitator
aufwisch|en vt sep wipe up; wash (Fußboden). **A∼lappen** m floorcloth
aufwühlen vt sep churn up
aufzähl|en vt sep enumerate, list. **A∼ung** f list
aufzeichn|en vt sep record; (zeichnen) draw. **A∼ung** f recording; **A∼ungen** notes
aufziehen† v sep •vt pull up; hoist (Segel); (öffnen) open; draw (Vorhang); (großziehen) bring up; rear (Tier); mount (Bild); thread (Perlen); wind up (Uhr); (🄸: necken) tease •vi (sein) approach
Aufzug m hoist; (Fahrstuhl) lift, (Amer) elevator; (Prozession) procession; (Theat) act
Augapfel m eyeball
Auge nt **-s,-n** eye; (Punkt) spot; **vier A∼n werfen** throw a four; **gute A∼n** good eyesight; **unter vier A∼n** in private; **im A∼ behalten** keep in sight; (fig) bear in mind
Augenblick m moment; **A∼!** just a moment! **a∼lich** adj immediate; (derzeitig) present •adv immediately; (derzeit) at present
Augen|braue f eyebrow. **A∼höhle** f eye socket. **A∼licht** nt sight. **A∼lid** nt eyelid
August m **-[s]** August
Auktion /ˈtsi̯oːn/ f **-,-en** auction
Aula f **-,-len** (Sch) [assembly] hall
Au-pair-Mädchen /oˈpɛːr-/ nt aupair
aus prep (+ dat) out of; (von) from; (bestehend) [made] of; **aus Angst** from or out of fear; **aus Spaß** for fun •adv out; (Licht, Radio) off; **aus sein auf** (+ acc) be after; **aus und ein** in and out; **von sich aus** of one's own accord; **von mir aus** as far as I'm concerned
ausarbeiten vt sep work out

ausarten vi sep (sein) degenerate (**in** + acc into)

ausatmen vt/i sep (haben) breathe out

ausbauen vt sep remove; (vergrößern) extend; (fig) expand

ausbedingen† vt sep **sich** (dat) **a~** insist on; (zur Bedingung machen) stipulate

ausbesser|n vt sep mend, repair. **A~ung** f repair

ausbeulen vt sep remove the dents from; (dehnen) make baggy

ausbild|en vt sep train; (formen) form; (entwickeln) develop; **sich a~en** train (**als/zu** as); (entstehen) develop. **A~ung** f training; (Sch) education

ausbitten† vt sep **sich** (dat) **a~** ask for; (verlangen) insist on

ausblasen† vt sep blow out

ausbleiben† vi sep (sein) fail to appear/ (Erfolg:) materialize; (nicht heimkommen) stay out

Ausblick m view

ausbrech|en† vi sep (sein) break out; (Vulkan:) erupt; (fliehen) escape; **in Tränen a~en** burst into tears. **A~er** m runaway

ausbreit|en vt sep spread [out]. **A~ung** f spread

Ausbruch m outbreak; (Vulkan-) eruption; (Wut-) outburst; (Flucht) escape, break-out

ausbrüten vt sep hatch

Ausdauer f perseverance; (körperlich) stamina. **a~nd** adj persevering; (unermüdlich) untiring

ausdehnen vt sep stretch; (fig) extend; **sich a~** stretch; (Phys & fig) expand; (dauern) last

ausdenken† vt sep **sich** (dat) **a~** think up; (sich vorstellen) imagine

Ausdruck m expression; (Fach-) term; (Computer) printout. **a~en** vt sep print

ausdrücken vt sep squeeze out; squeeze (Zitrone); stub out (Zigarette); (äußern) express

ausdrucks|los adj expressionless. **a~voll** adj expressive

auseinander adv apart; (entzwei) in pieces; **a~ falten** unfold; **a~ gehen** part; (Linien, Meinungen:) diverge; (Ehe:) break up; **a~ halten** tell apart; **a~ nehmen** take apart or to pieces; **a~ setzen** explain (**jdm** to s.o.); **sich a~ setzen** sit apart; (sich aussprechen) have it out (**mit jdm** with s.o.); come to grips (**mit einem Problem** with a problem). **A~setzung** f **-,-en** discussion; (Streit) argument

auserlesen adj select, choice

Ausfahrt f drive; (Autobahn-, Garagen-) exit

Ausfall m failure; (Absage) cancellation; (Comm) loss. **a~en**† vi sep (sein) fall out; (versagen) fail; (abgesagt werden) be cancelled; **gut/ schlecht a~en** turn out to be good/poor

ausfallend, **ausfällig** adj abusive

ausfertig|en vt sep make out. **A~ung** f **-,-en in doppelter A~ung** in duplicate

ausfindig adj **a~ machen** find

Ausflug m excursion, outing

Ausflügler m **-s,-** [day-]tripper

Ausfluss m outlet; (Abfluss) drain; (Med) discharge

ausfragen vt sep question

Ausfuhr f **-,-en** (Comm) export

ausführ|en vt sep take out; (Comm) export; (erklären) explain. **a~lich** adj detailed • adv in detail. **A~ung** f execution; (Comm) version; (äußere) finish; (Qualität) workmanship; (Erklärung) explanation

Ausgabe f issue; (Buch-) edition; (Comm) version

Ausgang m way out, exit; (Flugsteig) gate; (Ende) end; (Ergebnis) outcome. **A~spunkt** m starting point. **A~ssperre** f curfew

ausgeben† vt sep hand out; issue (Fahrkarten); spend (Geld); **sich a~ als** pretend to be

ausgebildet adj trained

a

a

ausgebucht adj fully booked; (Vorstellung) sold out

ausgefallen adj unusual

ausgefranst adj frayed

ausgeglichen adj [well-]balanced

ausgeh|en† vi sep (sein) go out; (Haare:) fall out; (Vorräte, Geld:) run out; (verblassen) fade; **gut/schlecht a~en** end well/badly; **davon a~en, dass** assume that. **A~verbot** nt curfew

ausgelassen adj high-spirited

ausgemacht adj agreed

ausgenommen conj except; **a~ wenn** unless

ausgeprägt adj marked

ausgeschlossen pred adj out of the question

ausgeschnitten adj low-cut

ausgesprochen adj marked •adv decidedly

ausgestorben adj extinct; **[wie] a~** (Straße:) deserted

Ausgestoßene(r) m/f outcast

ausgezeichnet adj excellent

ausgiebig adj extensive; (ausgedehnt) long; **a~ Gebrauch machen von** make full use of

ausgießen† vt sep pour out

Ausgleich m **-[e]s** balance; (Entschädigung) compensation. **a~en**† v sep •vt balance; even out (Höhe); (wettmachen) compensate for; **sich a~en** balance out •vi (haben) (Sport) equalize. **A~streffer** m equalizer

ausgrab|en† vt sep dig up; (Archaeology) excavate. **A~ung** f **-,-en** excavation

Ausguss m [kitchen] sink

aushaben† vt sep have finished (Buch)

aushalten† vt sep bear, stand; hold (Note); (Unterhalt zahlen für) keep; **nicht auszuhalten, nicht zum A~** unbearable

aushändigen vt sep hand over

aushängen[1] vt sep (reg) display; take off its hinges (Tür)

aushäng|en[2]† vi sep (haben) be displayed. **A~eschild** nt sign

ausheben† vt sep excavate

aushecken vt sep (fig) hatch

aushelfen† vi sep (haben) help out (**jdm** s.o.)

Aushilf|e f [temporary] assistant; **zur A~e** to help out. **A~skraft** f temporary worker. **a~sweise** adv temporarily

aushöhlen vt sep hollow out

auskennen† **(sich)** vr sep know one's way around; **sich mit/in etw** (dat) **a~** know all about sth

auskommen† vi sep (sein) manage (**mit/ohne** with/without); (sich vertragen) get on (**gut** well)

auskugeln vt sep **sich** (dat) **den Arm a~** dislocate one's shoulder

auskühlen vt/i sep (sein) cool

auskundschaften vt sep spy out

Auskunft f **-,⸚e** information; (A~sstelle) information desk/ (Büro) bureau; (Teleph) enquiries pl; **eine A~** a piece of information

auslachen vt sep laugh at

Auslage f [window] display; **A~n** expenses

Ausland nt **im/ins A~** abroad

Ausländ|er(in) m **-s,-** (f **-,-nen**) foreigner. **a~isch** adj foreign

Auslandsgespräch nt international call

auslass|en† vt sep let out; let down (Saum); (weglassen) leave out; (versäumen) miss; (Culin) melt; (fig) vent (Ärger) (**an** + dat on). **A~ungszeichen** nt apostrophe

Auslauf m run. **a~en**† vi sep (sein) run out; (Farbe:) run; (Naut) put to sea; (Modell:) be discontinued

ausleeren vt sep empty [out]

ausleg|en vt sep lay out; display (Waren); (auskleiden) line (**mit** with); (bezahlen) pay; (deuten) interpret. **A~ung** f **-,-en** interpretation

ausleihen† vt sep lend; **sich** (dat) **a~** borrow

Auslese f - selection; (fig) pick; (Elite) elite

auslieferǀn vt sep hand over; (Jur) extradite. **A~ung** f handing over; (Jur) extradition; (Comm) distribution

ausloggen vi sep log off or out

auslosen vt sep draw lots for

auslösǀen vt sep set off, trigger; (fig) cause; arouse (Begeisterung); (einlösen) redeem; pay a ransom for (Gefangene). **A~er** m **-s,-** trigger; (Phot) shutter release

Auslosung f draw

auslüften vt/i sep (haben) air

ausmachen vt sep put out; (abschalten) turn off; (abmachen) arrange; (erkennen) make out; (betragen) amount to; (wichtig sein) matter

Ausmaß nt extent; **A~e** dimensions

Ausnahmǀe f **-,-n** exception. **A~ezustand** m state of emergency. **a~slos** adv without exception. **a~sweise** adv as an exception

ausnehmen† vt sep take out; gut (Fisch); **sich gut a~** look good. **a~d** adv exceptionally

ausnutzǀen, **ausnützǀen** vt sep exploit. **A~ung** f exploitation

auspacken vt sep unpack; (auswickeln) unwrap

ausplaudern vt sep let out, blab

ausprobieren vt sep try out

Auspuff m **-s** exhaust [system]. **A~gase** ntpl exhaust fumes. **A~rohr** nt exhaust pipe

auspusten vt sep blow out

ausradieren vt sep rub out

ausrauben vt sep rob

ausräuchern vt sep smoke out; fumigate (Zimmer)

ausräumen vt sep clear out

ausrechnen vt sep work out

Ausrede f excuse. **a~n** v sep •vi (haben) finish speaking •vt **jdm etw a~n** talk s.o. out of sth

ausreichen vi sep (haben) be enough. **a~d** adj adequate

Ausreise f departure. **a~n** vi sep (sein) leave the country. **A~visum** nt exit visa

ausreißen† v sep •vt pull or tear out •vi (sein) [!] run away

ausrenken vt sep dislocate

ausrichten vt sep align; (bestellen) deliver; (erreichen) achieve; **jdm a~** tell s.o. (**dass** that); **ich soll Ihnen Grüße von X a~** X sends [you] his regards

ausrotten vt sep exterminate; (fig) eradicate

Ausruf m exclamation. **a~en**† vt sep exclaim; call out (Namen); (verkünden) proclaim; **jdn a~en lassen** put out a call for s.o. **A~ezeichen** nt exclamation mark

ausruhen vt/i sep (haben) rest; **sich a~** have a rest

ausrüstǀen vt sep equip. **A~ung** f equipment; (Mil) kit

ausrutschen vi sep (sein) slip

Aussage f **-,-n** statement; (Jur) testimony, evidence; (Gram) predicate. **a~n** vt/i sep (haben) state; (Jur) give evidence, testify

ausschalten vt sep switch off

Ausschank m sale of alcoholic drinks; (Bar) bar

Ausschau f - **A~ halten nach** look out for

ausscheiden† vi sep (sein) leave; (Sport) drop out; (nicht in Frage kommen) be excluded

ausschenken vt sep pour out

ausscheren vi sep (sein) (Auto) pull out

ausschildern vt sep signpost

ausschimpfen vt sep tell off

ausschlafen† vi/r sep (haben) **[sich] a~** get enough sleep; (morgens) sleep late

Ausschlag m (Med) rash; **den A~ geben** (fig) tip the balance. **a~gebend** adj decisive

a

ausschließ|en† vt sep lock out; (fig) exclude; (entfernen) expel. **a~lich** adj exclusive

ausschlüpfen vi sep (sein) hatch

Ausschluss m exclusion; expulsion; **unter A~ der Öffentlichkeit** in camera

ausschneiden† vt sep cut out

Ausschnitt m excerpt, extract; (Zeitungs-) cutting; (Hals-) neckline

ausschöpfen vt sep ladle out; (Naut) bail out; exhaust (Möglichkeiten)

ausschreiben† vt sep write out; (ausstellen) make out; (bekanntgeben) announce; put out to tender (Auftrag)

Ausschreitungen fpl riots; (Exzesse) excesses

Ausschuss m committee; (Comm) rejects pl

ausschütten vt sep tip out; (verschütten) spill; (leeren) empty

aussehen† vi sep (haben) look; **wie sieht er/es aus?** what does he/it look like? **A~** nt **-s** appearance

außen adv [on the] outside; **nach a~** outwards. **A~bordmotor** m outboard motor. **A~handel** m foreign trade. **A~minister** m Foreign Minister. **A~politik** f foreign policy. **A~seite** f outside. **A~seiter** m **-s,-** outsider; (fig) misfit. **A~stände** mpl outstanding debts

außer prep (+ dat) except [for], apart from; (außerhalb) out of; **a~ sich** (fig) beside oneself •conj except; **a~ wenn** unless. **a~dem** adv in addition, as well •conj moreover

äußer|e(r,s) adj external; (Teil, Schicht) outer. **Ä~e(s)** nt exterior; (Aussehen) appearance

außer|ehelich adj extramarital. **a~gewöhnlich** adj exceptional. **a~halb** prep (+ gen) outside •adv **a~halb wohnen** live outside town

äußer|lich adj external; (fig) outward. **ä~n** vt express; **sich ä~n** comment; (sich zeigen) manifest itself

außerordentlich adj extraordinary

äußerst adv extremely

äußerste|(r,s) adj outermost; (weiteste) furthest; (höchste) utmost, extreme; (letzte) last; (schlimmste) worst. **Ä~(s)** nt **das Ä~** the limit; (Schlimmste) the worst; **sein Ä~s tun** do one's utmost; **aufs Ä~** extremely

Äußerung f **-,-en** comment; (Bemerkung) remark

aussetzen v sep •vt expose (dat to); abandon (Kind); launch (Boot); offer (Belohnung); **etwas auszusetzen haben an** (+ dat) find fault with •vi (haben) stop; (Motor:) cut out

Aussicht f **-,-en** view/(fig) prospect (**auf** + acc of); **weitere A~en** (Meteorology) further outlook sg. **a~slos** adj hopeless

ausspannen v sep •vt spread out; unhitch (Pferd) •vi (haben) rest

aussperren vt sep lock out

ausspielen v sep •vt play (Karte); (fig) play off (**gegen** against) •vi (haben) (Kartenspiel) lead

Aussprache f pronunciation; (Gespräch) talk

aussprechen† vt sep pronounce; (äußern) express; **sich a~** talk; come out (**für/gegen** in favour of/ against)

Ausspruch m saying

ausspucken v sep •vt spit out •vi (haben) spit

ausspülen vt sep rinse out

ausstatt|en vt sep equip. **A~ung** f **-,-en** equipment; (Innen-) furnishings pl; (Theat) scenery and costumes pl

ausstehen† v sep •vt suffer; **Angst a~** be frightened; **ich kann sie nicht a~** I can't stand her •vi (haben) be outstanding

aussteigen† vi sep (sein) get out; (aus Bus, Zug) get off; **alles a~!** all change!

ausstell|en vt sep exhibit; (Comm) display; (ausfertigen) make out;

issue (Pass). **A~ung** f exhibition; (Comm) display

aussterben† vi sep (sein) die out; (Biology) become extinct

Aussteuer f trousseau

Ausstieg m **-[e]s,-e** exit

ausstopfen vt sep stuff

ausstoßen† vt sep emit; utter (Fluch); heave (Seufzer); (ausschließen) expel

ausstrahl|en vt/i sep (sein) radiate, emit; (Radio, TV) broadcast. **A~ung** f radiation

ausstrecken vt sep stretch out; put out (Hand)

ausstreichen† vt sep cross out

ausströmen v sep •vi (sein) pour out; (entweichen) escape •vt emit; (ausstrahlen) radiate

aussuchen vt sep pick, choose

Austausch m exchange. **a~bar** adj interchangeable. **a~en** vt sep exchange; (auswechseln) replace

austeilen vt sep distribute

Auster f **-,-n** oyster

austragen† vt sep deliver; hold (Wettkampf); play (Spiel)

Austral|ien /-i̯ən/ nt **-s** Australia. **A~ier(in)** m **-s,-** (f **-,-nen**) Australian. **a~isch** adj Australian

austreiben† vt sep drive out; (Relig) exorcize

austreten† v sep •vt stamp out; (abnutzen) wear down •vi (sein) come out; (ausscheiden) leave (**aus etw** sth); **[mal] a~** ⊡ go to the loo

austrinken† vt/i sep (haben) drink up; (leeren) drain

Austritt m resignation

austrocknen vt/i sep (sein) dry out

ausüben vt sep practise; carry on (Handwerk); exercise (Recht); exert (Druck, Einfluss)

Ausverkauf m [clearance] sale. **a~t** adj sold out

Auswahl f choice, selection; (Comm) range; (Sport) team

auswählen vt sep choose, select

Auswander|er m emigrant. **a~n** vi sep (sein) emigrate. **A~ung** f emigration

auswärt|ig adj non-local; (ausländisch) foreign. **a~s** adv outwards; (Sport) away. **A~sspiel** nt away game

auswaschen† vt sep wash out

auswechseln vt sep change; (ersetzen) replace; (Sport) substitute

Ausweg m (fig) way out

ausweichen† vi sep (sein) get out of the way; **jdm/etw a~en** avoid/ (sich entziehen) evade someone/ something

Ausweis m **-es,-e** pass; (Mitglieds-, Studenten-) card. **a~en**† vt sep deport; **sich a~en** prove one's identity. **A~papiere** ntpl identification papers. **A~ung** f deportation

auswendig adv by heart

auswerten vt sep evaluate

auswickeln vt sep unwrap

auswirk|en (sich) vr sep have an effect (**auf** + acc on). **A~ung** f effect; (Folge) consequence

auswringen vt sep wring out

auszahlen vt sep pay out; (entlohnen) pay off; (abfinden) buy out; **sich a~** (fig) pay off

auszählen vt sep count; (Boxen) count out

Auszahlung f payment

auszeichn|en vt sep (Comm) price; (ehren) honour; (mit einem Preis) award a prize to; (Mil) decorate; **sich a~en** distinguish oneself. **A~ung** f honour; (Preis) award; (Mil) decoration; (Sch) distinction

ausziehen† v sep •vt pull out; (auskleiden) undress; take off (Mantel, Schuhe) •vi (sein) move out; (sich aufmachen) set out

Auszug m departure; (Umzug) move; (Ausschnitt) extract; (Bank-) statement

Auto nt **-s,-s** car; **A~ fahren** drive;

(mitfahren) go in the car. ◘**A~bahn** f motorway

Autobiographie f autobiography

Auto|bus m bus. **A~fahrer(in)** m(f) driver, motorist. **A~fahrt** f drive

Autogramm nt **-s,-e** autograph

Automat m **-en,-en** automatic device; (Münz-) slot-machine; (Verkaufs-) vending-machine; (Fahrkarten-) machine; (Techn) robot. **A~ik** f **-** automatic mechanism; (Auto) automatic transmission

automatisch adj automatic

Autonummer f registration number

Autopsie f **-,-n** autopsy

Autor m **-s,-en** author

Auto|reisezug m Motorail. **A~rennen** nt motor race

Autorin f **-,-nen** author[ess]

Autori|sation /-'tsi̯o:n/ f **-** authorization. **A~tät** f **-,-en** authority

Auto|schlosser m motor mechanic. **A~skooter** m **-s,-** dodgem. **A~stopp** m **-s per A~stopp fahren** hitch-hike. **A~verleih** m car hire [firm]. **A~waschanlage** f car wash

autsch int ouch

Axt f **-,⸚e** axe

Bb

B, b /be:/ nt **-** (Mus) B flat

Baby /'be:bi/ nt **-s,-s** baby. **B~ausstattung** f layette. **B~sitter** m **-s,-** babysitter

Bach m **-[e]s,⸚e** stream

Backbord nt **-[e]s** port [side]

Backe f **-,-n** cheek

backen vt/i† (haben) bake; (braten) fry

Backenzahn m molar

Bäcker m **-s,-** baker. **B~ei** f **-,-en, B~laden** m baker's shop

Back|obst nt dried fruit. **B~ofen** m oven. **B~pfeife** f ! slap in the face. **B~pflaume** f prune. **B~pulver** nt baking-powder. **B~stein** m brick

Bad nt **-[e]s,⸚er** bath; (Zimmer) bathroom; (Schwimm-) pool; (Ort) spa

Bade|anstalt f swimming baths pl. **B~anzug** m swim-suit. **B~hose** f swimming trunks pl. **B~kappe** f bathing-cap. **B~mantel** m bathrobe. **b~n** vi (haben) have a bath; (im Meer) bathe •vt bath; (waschen) bathe. **B~ort** m seaside resort. **B~wanne** f bath. **B~zimmer** nt bathroom

Bagger m **-s,-** excavator; (Nass-) dredger. **B~see** m flooded gravel-pit

Bahn f **-,-en** path; (Astronomy) orbit; (Sport) track; (einzelne) lane; (Rodel-) run; (Stoff-) width; (Eisen-) railway; (Zug) train; (Straßen-) tram. **b~brechend** adj (fig) pioneering. **B~hof** m [railway] station. **B~steig** m **-[e]s,-e** platform. **B~übergang** m level crossing

Bahre f **-,-n** stretcher

Baiser /bɛ'ze:/ nt **-s,-s** meringue

Bake f **-,-n** (Naut, Aviat) beacon

Bakterien /-i̯ən/ fpl bacteria

Balanc|e /ba'lã:sə/ f **-** balance. **b~ieren** vt/i (haben/sein) balance

bald adv soon; (fast) almost

Baldachin /-xi:n/ m **-s,-e** canopy

bald|ig adj early; (Besserung) speedy.

◘ *see* A-Z of German life and culture

b~möglichst adv as soon as possible

Balg nt & m **-[e]s,¨er** [!] brat

Balkan m **-s** Balkans pl

Balken m **-s,-** beam

Balkon /bal'kõ:/ m **-s,-s** balcony; (Theat) circle

Ball[1] m **-[e]s,¨e** ball

Ball[2] m **-[e]s,¨e** (Tanz) ball

Ballade f **-,-n** ballad

Ballast m **-[e]s** ballast. **B~stoffe** mpl roughage sg

Ballen m **-s,-** bale; (Anat) ball of the hand/(Fuß-) foot; (Med) bunion

Ballerina f **-,-nen** ballerina

Ballett nt **-s,-e** ballet

Ballon /ba'lõ:/ m **-s,-s** balloon

Balsam m **-s** balm

Balt|ikum nt **-s** Baltic States pl. **b~isch** adj Baltic

Bambus m **-ses,-se** bamboo

banal adj banal

Banane f **-,-n** banana

Banause m **-n,-n** philistine

Band[1] nt **-[e]s,¨er** ribbon; (Naht-, Ton-, Ziel-) tape; **am laufenden B~** [!] non-stop

Band[2] m **-[e]s,¨e** volume

Band[3] nt **-[e]s,-e** (fig) bond

Band[4] /bɛnt/ f **-,-s** [jazz] band

Bandag|e /ban'da:ʒə/ f **-,-n** bandage. **b~ieren** vt bandage

Bande f **-,-n** gang

bändigen vt control, restrain; (zähmen) tame

Bandit m **-en,-en** bandit

Band|maß nt tape-measure. **B~scheibe** f (Anat) disc. **B~wurm** m tapeworm

Bang|e f **B~e haben** be afraid; **jdm B~e machen** frighten s.o. **b~en** vi (haben) fear (**um** for)

Banjo nt **-s,-s** banjo

Bank[1] f **-,¨e** bench

Bank[2] f **-,-en** (Comm) bank. **B~einzug** m direct debit

Bankett nt **-s,-e** banquet

Bankier /baŋ'ki̯e:/ m **-s,-s** banker

Bankkonto nt bank account

Bankrott m **-s,-s** bankruptcy. **b~** adj bankrupt

Bankwesen nt banking

Bann m **-[e]s,-e** (fig) spell. **b~en** vt exorcize; (abwenden) avert; **[wie] gebannt** spellbound

Banner nt **-s,-** banner

bar adj (rein) sheer; (Gold) pure; **b~es Geld** cash; **[in] bar bezahlen** pay cash

Bar f **-,-s** bar

Bär m **-en,-en** bear

Baracke f **-,-n** (Mil) hut

Barb|ar m **-en,-en** barbarian. **b~arisch** adj barbaric

bar|fuß adv barefoot. **B~geld** nt cash

barmherzig adj merciful

barock adj baroque. **B~** nt & m **-[s]** baroque

Barometer nt **-s,-** barometer

Baron m **-s,-e** baron. **B~in** f **-,-nen** baroness

Barren m **-s,-** (Gold-) bar, ingot; (Sport) parallel bars pl. **B~gold** nt gold bullion

Barriere f **-,-n** barrier

Barrikade f **-,-n** barricade

barsch adj gruff

Barsch m **-[e]s,-e** (Zool) perch

Bart m **-[e]s,¨e** beard; (der Katze) whiskers pl

bärtig adj bearded

Barzahlung f cash payment

Basar m **-s,-e** bazaar

Base[1] f **-,-n** [female] cousin

Base[2] f **-,-n** (Chemistry) alkali, base

Basel nt **-s** Basle

basieren vi (haben) be based (**auf** + dat on)

Basilikum nt **-s** basil

b

Basis f **-,Basen** base; (fig) basis

basisch adj (Chemistry) alkaline

Bask|enmütze f beret. **b~isch** adj Basque

Bass m **-es,¨-e** bass

Bassin /ba'sɛ̃ː/ nt **-s,-s** pond; (Brunnen-) basin; (Schwimm-) pool

Bassist m **-en,-en** bass player; (Sänger) bass

Bast m **-[e]s** raffia

basteln vt make • vi (haben) do handicrafts

Batterie f **-,-n** battery

Bau[1] m **-[e]s,-e** burrow; (Fuchs-) earth

Bau[2] m **-[e]s,-ten** construction; (Gebäude) building; (Auf-) structure; (Körper-) build; (B~stelle) building site. **B~arbeiten** fpl building work sg; (Straßen-) roadworks

Bauch m **-[e]s, Bäuche** abdomen, belly; (Magen) stomach; (Bauchung) bulge. **b~ig** adj bulbous. **B~nabel** m navel. **B~redner** m ventriloquist. **B~schmerzen** mpl stomach-ache sg. **B~speicheldrüse** f pancreas

bauen vt build; (konstruieren) construct • vi (haben) build (**an etw** dat sth); **b~ auf** (+ acc) (fig) rely on

Bauer[1] m **-n,-n** farmer; (Schach) pawn

Bauer[2] nt **-s,-** [bird]cage

bäuerlich adj rustic

Bauern|haus nt farmhouse. **B~hof** m farm

bau|fällig adj dilapidated. **B~genehmigung** f planning permission. **B~gerüst** nt scaffolding. **B~jahr** nt year of construction. **B~kunst** f architecture. **b~lich** adj structural

Baum m **-[e]s, Bäume** tree

baumeln vi (haben) dangle

bäumen (sich) vr rear [up]

Baum|schule f [tree] nursery. **B~wolle** f cotton

Bausch m **-[e]s, Bäusche** wad; **in B~ und Bogen** (fig) wholesale. **b~en** vt puff out

Bau|sparkasse f building society. **B~stein** m building brick. **B~stelle** f building site; (Straßen-) roadworks pl. **B~unternehmer** m building contractor

Bayer|(in) m **-n,-n** (f **-,-nen**) Bavarian. ◼**B~n** nt **-s** Bavaria

bay[e]risch adj Bavarian

Bazillus m **-,-len** bacillus

beabsichtig|en vt intend. **b~t** adj intended; intentional

beacht|en vt take notice of; (einhalten) observe; (folgen) follow; **nicht b~en** ignore. **b~lich** adj considerable. **B~ung** f **-** observance; **etw** (dat) **keine B~ung schenken** take no notice of sth

◼**Beamte(r)** m, **Beamtin** f **-,-nen** official; (Staats-) civil servant; (Schalter-) clerk

beanspruchen vt claim; (erfordern) demand

beanstand|en vt find fault with; (Comm) make a complaint about. **B~ung** f **-,-en** complaint

beantragen vt apply for

beantworten vt answer

bearbeiten vt work; (weiter-) process; (behandeln) treat (**mit** with); (Admin) deal with; (redigieren) edit; (Theat) adapt; (Mus) arrange

Beatmungsgerät nt ventilator

beaufsichtig|en vt supervise. **B~ung** f **-** supervision

beauftragen vt instruct; commission (Künstler)

bebauen vt build on; (bestellen) cultivate

beben vi (haben) tremble

Becher m **-s,-** beaker; (Henkel-) mug; (Joghurt-, Sahne-) carton

Becken nt **-s,-** basin; pool; (Mus) cymbals pl; (Anat) pelvis

bedacht adj careful; **darauf b~** anxious (**zu** to)

◼ *see A-Z of German life and culture*

bedächtig adj careful; slow

bedanken (sich) vr thank (**bei jdm** s.o.)

Bedarf m **-s** need/(Comm) demand (**an** + dat for); **bei B~** if required. **B~shaltestelle** f request stop

bedauer|lich adj regrettable. **b~licherweise** adv unfortunately. **b~n** vt regret; (bemitleiden) feel sorry for; **bedaure**! sorry! **b~nswert** adj pitiful; (bedauerlich) regrettable

bedeckt adj covered; (Himmel) overcast

bedenken† vt consider; (überlegen) think over. **B~** pl misgivings; **ohne B~** without hesitation

bedenklich adj doubtful; (verdächtig) dubious; (ernst) serious

bedeut|en vi (haben) mean. **b~end** adj important; (beträchtlich) considerable. **B~ung** f **-,-en** meaning; (Wichtigkeit) importance. **b~ungslos** adj meaningless; (unwichtig) unimportant. **b~ungsvoll** adj significant; (vielsagend) meaningful

bedien|en vt serve; (betätigen) operate; **sich [selbst] b~en** help oneself. **B~ung** f **-,-en** service; (Betätigung) operation; (Kellner) waiter; (Kellnerin) f waitress. **B~ungsgeld** nt service charge

Bedingung f **-,-en** condition; **B~en** conditions; (Comm) terms. **b~slos** adj unconditional

bedroh|en vt threaten. **b~lich** adj threatening. **B~ung** f threat

bedrücken vt depress

bedruckt adj printed

bedürf|en† vi (haben) (+ gen) need. **B~nis** nt **-ses,-se** need

Beefsteak /ˈbi:fste:k/ nt **-s,-s** steak; **deutsches B~** hamburger

beeilen (sich) vr hurry; hasten (**zu** to)

beeindrucken vt impress

beeinflussen vt influence

beeinträchtigen vt mar; (schädigen) impair

beengen vt restrict

beerdig|en vt bury. **B~ung** f **-,-en** funeral

Beere f **-,-n** berry

Beet nt **-[e]s,-e** (Horticulture) bed

Beete f **-,-n Rote B~** beetroot

befähig|en vt enable; (qualifizieren) qualify. **B~ung** f - qualification; (Fähigkeit) ability

befahrbar adj passable

befallen† vt attack; (Angst:) seize

befangen adj shy; (gehemmt) self-conscious; (Jur) biased. **B~heit** f - shyness; self-consciousness; bias

befassen (sich) vr concern oneself/(behandeln) deal (**mit** with)

Befehl m **-[e]s,-e** order; (Leitung) command (**über** + acc of). **b~en** † vt **jdm etw b~en** order s.o. to do sth • vi (haben) give the orders. **B~sform** f (Gram) imperative. **B~shaber** m **-s,-** commander

befestigen vt fasten (**an** + dat to); (Mil) fortify

befeuchten vt moisten

befinden† **(sich)** vr be. **B~** nt **-s** [state of] health

beflecken vt stain

befolgen vt follow

beförder|n vt transport; (im Rang) promote. **B~ung** f **-,-en** transport; promotion

befragen vt question

befrei|en vt free; (räumen) clear (**von** of); (freistellen) exempt (**von** from); **sich b~en** free oneself. **B~er** m **-s,-** liberator. **B~ung** f - liberation; exemption

befreunden (sich) vr make friends; **befreundet sein** be friends

befriedig|en vt satisfy. **b~end** adj satisfying; (zufrieden stellend) satisfactory. **B~ung** f - satisfaction

befrucht|en vt fertilize. **B~ung** f - fertilization; **künstliche B~ung** artificial insemination

Befugnis f **-,-se** authority

b

Befund m result

befürcht|en vt fear. **B~ung** f -,-en fear

befürworten vt support

begab|t adj gifted. **B~ung** f -,-en gift, talent

begeben† (**sich**) vr go; **sich in Gefahr b~** expose oneself to danger

begegn|en vi (sein) **jdm/etw b~en** meet someone/something. **B~ung** f -,-en meeting

begehr|en vt desire. **b~t** adj sought-after

begeister|n vt **jdn b~n** arouse someone's enthusiasm. **b~t** adj enthusiastic; (eifrig) keen. **B~ung** f - enthusiasm

Begierde f -,-n desire

Beginn m -s beginning. **b~en†** vt/i (haben) start, begin

beglaubigen vt authenticate

begleichen† vt settle

begleit|en vt accompany. **B~er** m -s,- companion; (Mus) accompanist. **B~ung** f -,-en company; (Mus) accompaniment

beglück|en vt make happy. **b~wünschen** vt congratulate (**zu** on)

begnadig|en vt (Jur) pardon. **B~ung** f -,-en (Jur) pardon

begraben† vt bury

Begräbnis n -ses,-se burial; (Feier) funeral

begreif|en† vt understand; **nicht zu b~en** incomprehensible. **b~lich** adj understandable

begrenz|en vt form the boundary of; (beschränken) restrict. **b~t** adj limited. **B~ung** f -,-en restriction; (Grenze) boundary

Begriff m -[e]s,-e concept; (Ausdruck) term; (Vorstellung) idea

begründ|en vt give one's reason for. **b~et** adj justified. **B~ung** f -,-en reason

begrüß|en vt greet; (billigen) welcome. **b~enswert** adj welcome. **B~ung** f - greeting; welcome

begünstigen vt favour

begütert adj wealthy

behaart adj hairy

behäbig adj portly

behag|en vi (haben) please (**jdm** s.o.). **B~en** nt -s contentment; (Genuss) enjoyment. **b~lich** adj comfortable. **B~lichkeit** f - comfort

behalten† vt keep; (sich merken) remember

Behälter m -s,- container

behand|eln vt treat; (sich befassen) deal with. **B~lung** f treatment

beharr|en vi (haben) persist (**auf** + dat in). **b~lich** adj persistent

behaupt|en vt maintain; (vorgeben) claim; (sagen) say; (bewahren) retain; **sich b~en** hold one's own. **B~ung** f -,-en assertion; claim; (Äußerung) statement

beheben† vt remedy

behelf|en† (**sich**) vr make do (**mit** with). **b~smäßig** adj makeshift • adv provisionally

beherbergen vt put up

beherrsch|en vt rule over; (dominieren) dominate; (meistern, zügeln) control; (können) know. **b~t** adj self-controlled. **B~ung** f - control

beherzigen vt heed

behilflich adj **jdm b~ sein** help s.o.

behinder|n vt hinder; (blockieren) obstruct. **b~t** adj handicapped; (schwer) disabled. **B~te(r)** m/f handicapped/disabled person. **B~ung** f -,-en obstruction; (Med) handicap; disability

Behörde f -,-n [public] authority

behüte|n vt protect. **b~t** adj sheltered

behutsam adj careful; (zart) gentle

bei

• preposition (+ dative)

> **!** Note that **bei** plus **dem** can become **beim**

····➤ (nahe) near; (dicht an, neben) by; (als Begleitung) with. **wer steht da bei ihm?** who is standing there next to or with him? **etw bei sich haben** have sth with or on one. **bleiben Sie beim Gepäck/bei den Kindern** stay with the luggage/the children. **war heute ein Brief für mich bei der Post?** was there a letter for me in the post today?

····➤ (an) by. **jdn bei der Hand nehmen** take s.o. by the hand

····➤ (in der Wohnung von) at ... 's home or house/flat. **bei mir [zu Hause]** at my home or [!] place. **bei seinen Eltern leben** live with one's parents. **wir sind bei Ulrike eingeladen** we have been invited to Ulrike's. **bei Schmidt** at the Schmidts'; (Geschäft) at Schmidts'; (auf Briefen) c/o Schmidt. **bei jdm/ einer Firma arbeiten** work for s.o./a firm. **bei uns tut man das nicht** we don't do that where I come from.

····➤ (gegenwärtig) at; (verwickelt) in. **bei einer Hochzeit/einem Empfang** at a wedding/reception. **bei einem Unfall** in an accident

····➤ (im Falle von) in the case of, with; (bei Wetter) in. **wie bei den Römern** as with the Romans. **bei Nebel** in fog, if there is fog. **bei dieser Hitze** in this heat

····➤ (angesichts) with; (trotz) in spite of. **bei deinen guten Augen** with your good eyesight. **bei all seinen Bemühungen** in spite of or despite all his efforts

····➤ (Zeitpunkt) at, on. **bei diesen Worten errötete er** he blushed at this or on hearing this. **bei seiner Ankunft** on his arrival. **bei Tag/ Nacht** by day/night.

····➤ (Gleichzeitigkeit, mit Verbalsubstantiv) **beim ... en** while or when ... ing. **beim Spazierengehen im Walde** while walking in the woods. **beim Überqueren der Straße** when crossing the road. **sie war beim Lesen** she was reading. **wir waren beim Frühstück** we were having breakfast

beibehalten† vt sep keep

beibringen† vt sep **jdm etw b~** teach s.o. sth; (mitteilen) break sth to s.o.; (zufügen) inflict sth on s.o.

Beicht|e f -,-n confession. **b~en** vt/i (haben) confess. **B~stuhl** m confessional

beide adj & pron both; **b~s** both; **dreißig b~** (Tennis) thirty all. **b~rseitig** adj mutual. **b~rseits** adv & prep (+ gen) on both sides (of)

beieinander adv together

Beifahrer(in) m(f) [front-seat] passenger; (Motorrad) pillion passenger

Beifall m **-[e]s** applause; (Billigung) approval; **B~ klatschen** applaud

beifügen vt sep add; (beilegen) enclose

beige /bɛːʒ/ inv adj beige

beigeben† vt sep add

Beihilfe f financial aid; (Studien-) grant; (Jur) aiding and abetting

Beil nt **-[e]s,-e** hatchet, axe

Beilage f supplement; (Gemüse) vegetable

beiläufig adj casual

beilegen vt sep enclose; (schlichten) settle

Beileid nt condolences pl. **B~sbrief** m letter of condolence

beiliegend adj enclosed

beim prep = **bei dem; b~ Militär** in the army; **b~ Frühstück** at breakfast

beimessen† vt sep (fig) attach (dat to)

Bein nt **-[e]s,-e** leg; **jdm ein B~ stellen** trip s.o. up

beinah[e] adv nearly, almost

Beiname m epithet

b

beipflichten vi sep (haben) agree (dat with)

Beirat m advisory committee

beisammen adv together; **b~ sein** be together

Beisein nt presence

beiseite adv aside; (abseits) apart; **b~ legen** put aside; (sparen) put by

beisetz|en vt sep bury. **B~ung** f **-,-en** funeral

Beispiel nt example; **zum B~** for example. **b~sweise** adv for example

beißen† vt/i (haben) bite; (brennen) sting; **sich b~** (Farben:) clash

Bei|stand m **-[e]s** help. **b~stehen**† vi sep (haben) **jdm b~stehen** help s.o.

beistimmen vi sep (haben) agree

Beistrich m comma

Beitrag m **-[e]s,¨e** contribution; (Mitglieds-) subscription; (Versicherungs-) premium; (Zeitungs-) article. **b~en**† vt/i sep (haben) contribute

bei|treten† vi sep (sein) (+ dat) join. **B~tritt** m joining

Beize f **-,-n** (Holz-) stain

beizeiten adv in good time

beizen vt stain (Holz)

bejahen vt answer in the affirmative; (billigen) approve of

bejahrt adj aged, old

bekämpf|en vt fight. **B~ung** f fight (gen against)

bekannt adj well-known; (vertraut) familiar; **jdn b~ machen** introduce s.o.; **etw b~ machen** od **geben** announce sth; **b~ werden** become known. **B~e(r)** m/f acquaintance; (Freund) friend. **B~gabe** f announcement. **b~lich** adv as is well known. **B~machung** f **-,-en** announcement; (Anschlag) notice. **B~schaft** f **-** acquaintance; (Leute) acquaintances pl; (Freunde) friends pl

bekehr|en vt convert. **B~ung** f **-,-en** conversion

bekenn|en† vt confess, profess (Glauben); **sich [für] schuldig b~en** admit one's guilt. **B~tnis** nt **-ses,-se** confession; (Konfession) denomination

beklag|en vt lament; (bedauern) deplore; **sich b~en** complain. **b~enswert** adj unfortunate. **B~te(r)** m/f (Jur) defendant

bekleid|en vt hold (Amt). **B~ung** f clothing

Beklemmung f **-,-en** feeling of oppression

bekommen† vt get; have (Baby); catch (Erkältung) • vi (sein) **jdm gut b~** do s.o. good; (Essen:) agree with s.o.

beköstig|en vt feed. **B~ung** f **-** board; (Essen) food

bekräftigen vt reaffirm

bekreuzigen (sich) vr cross oneself

bekümmert adj troubled; (besorgt) worried

bekunden vt show

Belag m **-[e]s,¨e** coating; (Fußboden-) covering; (Brot-) topping; (Zahn-) tartar; (Brems-) lining

belager|n vt besiege. **B~ung** f **-,-en** siege

Belang m **von B~** of importance; **B~e** pl interests. **b~los** adj irrelevant; (unwichtig) trivial

belassen† vt leave; **es dabei b~** leave it at that

belasten vt load; (fig) burden; (beanspruchen) put a strain on; (Comm) debit; (Jur) incriminate

belästigen vt bother; (bedrängen) pester; (unsittlich) molest

Belastung f **-,-en** load; (fig) strain; (Comm) debit. **B~smaterial** nt incriminating evidence. **B~szeuge** m prosecution witness

belaufen† **(sich)** vr amount (**auf** + acc to)

belauschen vt eavesdrop on

beleb|en vt (fig) revive; (lebhaft machen) enliven. **b~t** adj lively; (Straße) busy

Beleg m **-[e]s,-e** evidence; (Beispiel) instance (**für** of); (Quittung) receipt. **b~en** vt cover/(garnieren) garnish (**mit** with); (besetzen) reserve; (Univ) enrol for; (nachweisen) provide evidence for; **den ersten Platz b~en** (Sport) take first place. **B~schaft** f **-,-en** workforce. **b~t** adj occupied; (Zunge) coated; (Stimme) husky; **b~te Brote** open sandwiches

belehren vt instruct

beleidig|en vt offend; (absichtlich) insult. **B~ung** f **-,-en** insult

belesen adj well-read

beleucht|en vt light; (anleuchten) illuminate. **B~ung** f **-,-en** illumination

Belg|ien /-i̯ən/ nt **-s** Belgium. **B~ier(in)** m **-s,-** (f **-,-nen**) Belgian. **b~isch** adj Belgian

belicht|en vt (Phot) expose. **B~ung** f **-** exposure

Belieb|en nt **-s nach B~en** [just] as one likes. **b~ig** adj **eine b~ige Zahl** any number you like • adv **b~ig oft** as often as one likes. **b~t** adj popular

bellen vi (haben) bark

belohn|en vt reward. **B~ung** f **-,-en** reward

belustig|en vt amuse. **B~ung** f **-,-en** amusement

bemalen vt paint

bemängeln vt criticize

bemannt adj manned

bemerk|bar adj **sich b~bar machen** attract attention. **b~en** vt notice; (äußern) remark. **b~enswert** adj remarkable. **B~ung** f **-,-en** remark

bemitleiden vt pity

bemüh|en vt trouble; **sich b~en** try (**zu** to; **um etw** to get sth); (sich kümmern) attend (**um** to); **b~t sein** endeavour (**zu** to). **B~ung** f **-,-en** effort

benachbart adj neighbouring

benachrichtig|en vt inform; (amtlich) notify. **B~ung** f **-,-en** notification

benachteiligen vt discriminate against; (ungerecht sein) treat unfairly

benehmen† **(sich)** vr behave. **B~** nt **-s** behaviour

beneiden vt envy (**um etw** sth)

Bengel m **-s,-** boy; (Rüpel) lout

benötigen vt need

benutz|en, (SGer) **benütz|en** vt use; take (Bahn) **B~ung** f use

Benzin nt **-s** petrol

beobacht|en vt observe. **B~er** m **-s,-** observer. **B~ung** f **-,-en** observation

bequem adj comfortable; (mühelos) easy; (faul) lazy. **b~en (sich)** vr deign (**zu** to). **B~lichkeit** f **-,-en** comfort; (Faulheit) laziness

berat|en† vt advise; (überlegen) discuss; **sich b~en** confer • vi (haben) discuss (**über etw** acc sth); (beratschlagen) confer. **B~er(in)** m **-s,-**, (f **-,-nen**) adviser. **B~ung** f **-,-en** guidance; (Rat) advice; (Besprechung) discussion; (Med, Jur) consultation

berechn|en vt calculate; (anrechnen) charge for; (abfordern) charge. **B~ung** f calculation

berechtig|en vt entitle; (befugen) authorize; (fig) justify. **b~t** adj justified, justifiable. **B~ung** f **-,-en** authorization; (Recht) right; (Rechtmäßigkeit) justification

bered|en vt talk about; **sich b~en** talk. **B~samkeit** f **-** eloquence

beredt adj eloquent

Bereich m **-[e]s,-e** area; (fig) realm; (Fach-) field

bereichern vi enrich

bereit adj ready. **b~en** vt prepare; (verursachen) cause; give (Überraschung). **b~halten**† vt sep have/(ständig) keep ready. **b~legen** vt sep put out [ready]. **b~machen** vt sep get ready. **b~s** adv already

Bereitschaft f **-,-en** readiness;

b

b

(Einheit) squad. **B~sdienst** m **B~sdienst haben** (Mil) be on stand-by; (Arzt:) be on call. **B~spolizei** f riot police

bereit|stehen† vi sep (haben) be ready. **b~stellen** vt sep put out ready; (verfügbar machen) make available. **B~ung** f - preparation. **b~willig** adj willing

bereuen vt regret

Berg m -[e]s,-e mountain; (Anhöhe) hill; **in den B~en** in the mountains. **b~ab** adv downhill. **B~arbeiter** m miner. **b~auf** adv uphill. **B~bau** m -[e]s mining

bergen† vt recover; (Naut) salvage; (retten) rescue

Berg|führer m mountain guide. **b~ig** adj mountainous. **B~kette** f mountain range. **B~mann** m (pl -leute) miner. **B~steiger(in)** m -s,- (f -,-nen) mountaineer, climber

Bergung f - recovery; (Naut) salvage; (Rettung) rescue

Berg|wacht f mountain rescue service. **B~werk** nt mine

Bericht m -[e]s,-e report; (Reise-) account. **b~en** vt/i (haben) report; (erzählen) tell (**von** of). **B~erstatter(in)** m -s,- (f -,-nen) reporter

berichtigen vt correct

beriesel|n vt irrigate. **B~ungsanlage** f sprinkler system

Berlin nt -s Berlin. **B~er** m -s,- Berliner

Bernhardiner m -s,- St Bernard

Bernstein m amber

berüchtigt adj notorious

berücksichtig|en vt take into consideration. **B~ung** f - consideration

Beruf m profession; (Tätigkeit) occupation; (Handwerk) trade. **b~en**† vt appoint; **sich b~en** refer (**auf** + acc to); (vorgeben) plead (**auf etw** acc sth); • adj competent; **b~en sein** be destined (**zu** to). **b~lich** adj professional; (Ausbildung) vocational • adv professionally; **b~lich tätig sein** work, have a job. **B~sberatung** f vocational guidance. **B~sausbildung** f professional training. **b~smäßig** adv professionally. **B~sschule** f vocational school. **B~ssoldat** m regular soldier. **b~stätig** adj working; **b~stätig sein** work, have a job. **B~stätige(r)** m/f working man/woman. **B~ung** f -,-en appointment; (Bestimmung) vocation; (Jur) appeal; **B~ung einlegen** appeal. **B~ungsgericht** nt appeal court

beruhen vi (haben) be based (**auf** + dat on)

beruhig|en vt calm [down]; (zuversichtlich machen) reassure. **b~end** adj calming; (tröstend) reassuring; (Med) sedative. **B~ung** f - calming; reassurance; (Med) sedation. **B~ungsmittel** nt sedative; (bei Psychosen) tranquillizer

berühmt adj famous. **B~heit** f -,-en fame; (Person) celebrity

berühr|en vt touch; (erwähnen) touch on. **B~ung** f -,-en touch; (Kontakt) contact

besänftigen vt soothe

Besatz m -es,⸚e trimming

Besatzung f -,-en crew; (Mil) occupying force

beschädig|en vt damage. **B~ung** f -,-en damage

beschaffen vt obtain, get • adj **so b~ sein, dass** be such that. **B~heit** f - consistency

beschäftig|en vt occupy; (Arbeitgeber:) employ; **sich b~en** occupy oneself. **b~t** adj busy; (angestellt) employed (**bei** at). **B~ung** f -,-en occupation; (Anstellung) employment

beschämt adj ashamed; (verlegen) embarrassed

beschatten vt shade; (überwachen) shadow

Bescheid m -[e]s information; **jdm B~ sagen** od **geben** let s.o. know; **B~ wissen** know

see A-Z of German life and culture

bescheiden adj modest. **B~heit** f - modesty

bescheinen† vt shine on; **von der Sonne beschienen** sunlit

bescheinig|en vt certify. **B~ung** f -,-en [written] confirmation; (Schein) certificate

beschenken vt give a present/presents to

Bescherung f -,-en distribution of Christmas presents

beschildern vt signpost

beschimpf|en vt abuse, swear at. **B~ung** f -,-en abuse

beschirmen vt protect

Beschlag m **in B~ nehmen** monopolize. **b~en**† vt shoe • vi (sein) steam or mist up • adj steamed or misted up. **B~nahme** f -,-n confiscation; (Jur) seizure. **b~nahmen** vt confiscate; (Jur) seize

beschleunig|en vt hasten; (schneller machen) speed up (Schritt) • vi (haben) accelerate. **B~ung** f - acceleration

beschließen† vt decide; (beenden) end • vi (haben) decide (**über** + acc about)

Beschluss m decision

beschmutzen vt make dirty

beschneid|en† vt trim; (Horticulture) prune; (Relig) circumcise. **B~ung** f - circumcision

beschnüffeln vt sniff at

beschönigen vt (fig) gloss over

beschränken vt limit, restrict; **sich b~ auf** (+ acc) confine oneself to

beschrankt adj (Bahnübergang) with barrier[s]

beschränk|t adj limited; (geistig) dull-witted. **B~ung** f -,-en limitation, restriction

beschreib|en† vt describe. **B~ung** f -,-en description

beschuldig|en vt accuse. **B~ung** f -,-en accusation

beschummeln vt [!] cheat

Beschuss m (Mil) fire; (Artillerie-) shelling

beschütz|en vt protect. **B~er** m -s,- protector

Beschwer|de f -,-n complaint; **B~den** (Med) trouble sg. **b~en** vt weight down; **sich b~en** complain. **b~lich** adj difficult

beschwindeln vt cheat (**um** out of); (belügen) lie to

beschwipst adj [!] tipsy

beseitig|en vt remove. **B~ung** f - removal

Besen m **-s,-** broom

besessen adj obsessed (**von** by)

besetz|en vt occupy; fill (Posten); (Theat) cast (Rolle); (verzieren) trim (**mit** with). **b~t** adj occupied; (Toilette, Leitung) engaged; (Zug, Bus) full up; **der Platz ist b~t** this seat is taken. **B~tzeichen** nt engaged tone. **B~ung** f -,-en occupation; (Theat) cast

besichtig|en vt look round (Stadt); (prüfen) inspect; (besuchen) visit. **B~ung** f -,-en visit; (Prüfung) inspection; (Stadt-) sightseeing

besiedelt adj **dünn/dicht b~** sparsely/densely populated

besiegen vt defeat

besinn|en† **(sich)** vr think, reflect; (sich erinnern) remember (**auf jdn/etw** someone/something). **B~ung** f - reflection; (Bewusstsein) consciousness; **bei/ohne B~ung** conscious/unconscious. **b~ungslos** adj unconscious

Besitz m possession; (Eigentum, Land-) property; (Gut) estate. **b~en**† vt own, possess; (haben) have. **B~er(in)** m **-s,-** (f **-,-nen**) owner; (Comm) proprietor

besoffen adj [x] drunken; **b~ sein** be drunk

besonder|e(r,s) adj special; (bestimmt) particular; (gesondert) separate. **b~s** adv [e]specially, particularly; (gesondert) separately

besonnen adj calm

besorg|en vt get; (kaufen) buy;

b

(erledigen) attend to; (versorgen) look after. **b~t** adj worried/(bedacht) concerned (**um** about). **B~ung** f -,-en errand; **B~ungen machen** do shopping

bespitzeln vt spy on

besprech|en† vt discuss; (rezensieren) review. **B~ung** f -,-en discussion; review; (Konferenz) meeting

besser adj & adv better. **b~n** vt improve; **sich b~n** get better. **B~ung** f - improvement; **gute B~ung!** get well soon!

Bestand m **-[e]s,¨e** existence; (Vorrat) stock (**an** + dat of)

beständig adj constant; (Wetter) settled; **b~ gegen** resistant to

Bestand|saufnahme f stocktaking. **B~teil** m part

bestätig|en vt confirm; acknowledge (Empfang); **sich b~en** prove to be true. **B~ung** f **-,-en** confirmation

bestatt|en vt bury. **B~ung** f **-,-en** funeral

Bestäubung f - pollination

bestaunen vt gaze at in amazement; (bewundern) admire

best|e(r,s) adj best; **b~en Dank!** many thanks! **B~e(r,s)** m/f/nt best; **sein B~es tun** do one's best

bestech|en† vt bribe; (bezaubern) captivate. **b~end** adj captivating. **b~lich** adj corruptible. **B~ung** f - bribery. **B~ungsgeld** nt bribe

Besteck nt **-[e]s,-e** [set of] knife, fork and spoon; (coll) cutlery

bestehen† vi (haben) exist; (fortdauern) last; (bei Prüfung) pass; **~ aus** consist/(gemacht sein) be made of; **~ auf** (+ dat) insist on •vt pass (Prüfung)

besteig|en† vt climb; (aufsteigen) mount; ascend (Thron). **B~ung** f ascent

bestell|en vt order; (vor-) book; (ernennen) appoint; (bebauen) cultivate; (ausrichten) tell; **zu sich b~en** send for; **b~t sein** have an appointment; **kann ich etwas b~en?** can I take a message? **B~schein** m order form. **B~ung** f order; (Botschaft) message; (Bebauung) cultivation

besteuer|n vt tax. **B~ung** f - taxation

Bestie /ˈbɛsti̯ə/ f **-,-n** beast

bestimm|en vt fix; (entscheiden) decide; (vorsehen) intend; (ernennen) appoint; (ermitteln) determine; (definieren) define; (Gram) qualify •vi (haben) be in charge (**über** + acc of). **~t** adj definite; (gewiss) certain; (fest) firm. **B~ung** f fixing; (Vorschrift) regulation; (Ermittlung) determination; (Definition) definition; (Zweck) purpose; (Schicksal) destiny. **B~ungsort** m destination

Bestleistung f (Sport) record

bestraf|en vt punish. **B~ung** f **-,-en** punishment

Bestrahlung f radiotherapy

Bestreb|en nt **-s** endeavour; (Absicht) aim. **B~ung** f **-,-en** effort

bestreiten† vt dispute; (leugnen) deny; (bezahlen) pay for

bestürz|t adj dismayed; (erschüttert) stunned. **B~ung** f - dismay, consternation

Bestzeit f (Sport) record [time]

Besuch m **-[e]s,-e** visit; (kurz) call; (Schul-) attendance; (Gast) visitor; (Gäste) visitors pl; **B~ haben** have a visitor/visitors; **bei jdm zu** od **auf B~ sein** be staying with s.o. **~en** vt visit; (kurz) call on; (teilnehmen) attend; go to (Schule, Ausstellung). **B~er(in)** m **-s,-** (f **-,-nen**) visitor; caller. **B~szeit** f visiting hours pl

betagt adj aged, old

betätig|en vt operate; **sich b~en** work (**als** as). **B~ung** f **-,-en** operation; (Tätigkeit) activity

betäub|en vt stun; (Lärm:) deafen; (Med) anaesthetize; (lindern) ease; deaden (Schmerz); **wie b~t** dazed. **B~ung** f - daze; (Med) anaesthesia. **B~ungsmittel** nt anaesthetic

Bete f **-,-n Rote B~** beetroot

beteilig|en vt give a share to; **sich b~en** take part (**an** + dat in); (beitragen) contribute (**an** + dat to). **b~t** adj **b~t sein** take part/(an Unfall) be involved/(Comm) have a share (**an** + dat in); **alle B~ten** all those involved. **B~ung** f **-,-en** participation; involvement; (Anteil) share

beten vi (haben) pray

Beton /be'tɔŋ/ m **-s** concrete

betonen vt stressed, emphasize

beton|t adj stressed; (fig) pointed. **B~ung** f **-,-en** stress

Betracht m **in B~ ziehen** consider; **außer B~ lassen** disregard; **nicht in B~ kommen** be out of the question. **b~en** vt look at; (fig) regard (**als** as)

beträchtlich adj considerable

Betrachtung f **-,-en** contemplation; (Überlegung) reflection

Betrag m **-[e]s,¨e** amount. **b~en**† vt amount to; **sich b~en** behave. **B~en** nt **-s** behaviour; (Sch) conduct

betreff|en† vt affect; (angehen) concern. **b~end** adj relevant. **b~s** prep (+ gen) concerning

betreiben† vt (leiten) run; (ausüben) carry on

betreten† vt step on; (eintreten) enter; '**B~ verboten**' 'no entry'; (bei Rasen) 'keep off [the grass]'

betreu|en vt look after. **B~er(in)** m **-s,-** (f **-,-nen**) helper; (Kranken-) nurse. **B~ung** f **-** care

Betrieb m business; (Firma) firm; (Treiben) activity; (Verkehr) traffic; **außer B~** not in use; (defekt) out of order

Betriebs|anleitung, **B~anweisung** f operating instructions pl. **B~ferien** pl firm's holiday. **B~leitung** f management. **B~rat** m works committee. **B~störung** f breakdown

betrinken† **(sich)** vr get drunk

betroffen adj disconcerted; **b~ sein** be affected (**von** by)

betrüb|en vt sadden. **b~t** adj sad

Betrug m **-[e]s** deception; (Jur) fraud

betrüg|en† vt cheat, swindle; (Jur) defraud; (in der Ehe) be unfaithful to. **B~er(in)** m **-s,-** (f **-,-nen**) swindler. **B~erei** f **-,-en** fraud

betrunken adj drunken; **b~ sein** be drunk. **B~e(r)** m drunk

Bett nt **-[e]s,-en** bed. **B~couch** f sofa-bed. **B~decke** f blanket; (Tages-) bedspread

Bettel|ei f **-** begging. **b~n** vi (haben) beg

Bettler(in) m **-s,-** (f **-,-nen**) beggar

Bettpfanne f bedpan

Betttuch (**Bettuch**) nt sheet

Bett|wäsche f bed linen. **B~zeug** nt bedding

betupfen vt dab (**mit** with)

beug|en vt bend; (Gram) decline; conjugate (Verb); **sich b~en** bend; (lehnen) lean; (sich fügen) submit (dat to). **B~ung** f **-,-en** (Gram) declension; conjugation

Beule f **-,-n** bump; (Delle) dent

beunruhig|en vt worry; **sich b~en** worry. **B~ung** f **-** worry

beurlauben vt give leave to

beurteil|en vt judge. **B~ung** f **-,-en** judgement; (Ansicht) opinion

Beute f **-** booty, haul; (Jagd-) bag; (eines Raubtiers) prey

Beutel m **-s,-** bag; (Tabak- & Zool) pouch. **B~tier** nt marsupial

Bevölkerung f **-,-en** population

bevollmächtigen vt authorize

bevor conj before; **b~ nicht** until

bevormunden vt treat like a child

bevorstehen† vi sep (haben) approach; (unmittelbar) be imminent. **b~d** adj approaching, forthcoming; **unmittelbar b~d** imminent

bevorzug|en vt prefer; (begünstigen)

b

favour. **b~t** adj privileged; (Behandlung) preferential

bewachen vt guard

Bewachung f - guard; **unter B~** under guard

bewaffn|en vt arm. **b~et** adj armed. **B~ung** f - armament; (Waffen) arms pl

bewahren vt protect (**vor** + dat from); (behalten) keep; **die Ruhe b~** keep calm

bewähren (sich) vr prove one's/(Ding:) its worth; (erfolgreich sein) prove a success

bewähr|t adj reliable; (erprobt) proven. **B~ung** f - (Jur) probation. **B~ungsfrist** f [period of] probation. **B~ungsprobe** f (fig) test

bewältigen vt cope with; (überwinden) overcome

bewässer|n vt irrigate. **B~ung** f - irrigation

bewegen[1] vt (reg) move; **sich b~** move; (körperlich) take exercise

bewegen[2]† vt **jdn dazu b~, etw zu tun** induce s.o. to do sth

Beweg|grund m motive. **b~lich** adj movable, mobile; (wendig) agile. **B~lichkeit** f - mobility; agility. **B~ung** f -,-en movement; (Phys) motion; (Rührung) emotion; (Gruppe) movement; **körperliche B~ung** physical exercise. **b~ungslos** adj motionless

Beweis m **-es,-e** proof; (Zeichen) token; **B~e** evidence sg. **b~en**† vt prove; (zeigen) show; **sich b~en** prove oneself/(Ding:) itself. **B~material** nt evidence

bewerb|en† **(sich)** vr apply (**um** for; **bei** to). **B~er(in)** m **-s,-** (f **-,-nen**) applicant. **B~ung** f **-,-en** application

bewerten vt value; (einschätzen) rate; (Sch) mark, grade

bewilligen vt grant

bewirken vt cause; (herbeiführen) bring about

bewirt|en vt entertain. **B~ung** f - hospitality

bewohn|bar adj habitable. **b~en** vt inhabit, live in. **B~er(in)** m **-s,-** (f **-,-nen**) resident, occupant; (Einwohner) inhabitant

bewölk|en (sich) vr cloud over; **b~t** cloudy. **B~ung** f - clouds pl

bewunder|n vt admire. **b~nswert** adj admirable. **B~ung** f - admiration

bewusst adj conscious (gen of); (absichtlich) deliberate. **b~los** adj unconscious. **B~losigkeit** f - unconsciousness; **B~sein** nt **-s** consciousness; (Gewissheit) awareness; **bei B~sein** conscious

bezahl|en vt/i (haben) pay; pay for (Ware, Essen). **B~ung** f - payment; (Lohn) pay. **B~fernsehen** nt pay television; pay TV

bezaubern vt enchant

bezeichn|en vt mark; (bedeuten) denote; (beschreiben, nennen) describe (**als** as). **b~end** adj typical. **B~ung** f marking; (Beschreibung) description (**als** as); (Ausdruck) term; (Name) name

bezeugen vt testify to

bezichtigen vt accuse (gen of)

bezieh|en† vt cover; (einziehen) move into; (beschaffen) obtain; (erhalten) get; (in Verbindung bringen) relate (**auf** + acc to); **sich b~en** (bewölken) cloud over; **sich b~en auf** (+ acc) refer to; **das Bett frisch b~en** put clean sheets on the bed. **B~ung** f **-,-en** relation; (Verhältnis) relationship; (Bezug) respect; **B~ungen haben** have connections. **b~ungsweise** adv respectively; (vielmehr) or rather

Bezirk m **-[e]s,-e** district

Bezug m cover; (Kissen-) case; (Beschaffung) obtaining; (Kauf) purchase; (Zusammenhang) reference; **B̈~e** pl earnings; **B~ nehmen** refer (**auf** + acc to); **in B~ auf** (+ acc) regarding

bezüglich prep (+ gen) regarding • adj relating (**auf** + acc to)

bezwecken vt (fig) aim at

bezweifeln vt doubt

BH /beːˈhaː/ m **-[s],-[s]** bra

Bibel f **-,-n** Bible

Biber m **-s,-** beaver

Biblio|thek f **-,-en** library. **B~thekar(in)** m **-s,-** (f **-,-nen**) librarian

biblisch adj biblical

bieg|en† vt bend; **sich b~en** bend •vi (sein) curve (**nach** to); **um die Ecke b~en** turn the corner. **b~sam** adj flexible, supple. **B~ung** f **-,-en** bend

Biene f **-,-n** bee. **B~nstock** m beehive. **B~nwabe** f honey-comb

Bier nt **-s,-e** beer. **B~deckel** m beer-mat. **B~krug** m beer-mug

bieten† vt offer; (bei Auktion) bid

Bifokalbrille f bifocals pl

Bigamie f **-** bigamy

bigott adj over-pious

Bikini m **-s,-s** bikini

Bilanz f **-,-en** balance sheet; (fig) result; **die B~ ziehen** (fig) draw conclusions (**aus** from)

Bild nt **-[e]s,-er** picture; (Theat) scene

bilden vt form; (sein) be; (erziehen) educate

Bild|erbuch nt picture-book. **B~fläche** f screen. **B~hauer** m **-s,-** sculptor. **b~lich** adj pictorial; (figurativ) figurative. **B~nis** nt **-ses,-se** portrait. **B~punkt** m pixel. **B~schirm** m (TV) screen. **B~schirmgerät** nt visual display unit, VDU. **b~schön** adj very beautiful

Bildung f **-** formation; (Erziehung) education; (Kultur) culture

Billard /ˈbɪljart/ nt **-s** billiards sg. **B~tisch** m billiard table

Billett /bɪlˈjɛt/ nt **-[e]s,-e** & **-s** ticket

Billiarde f **-,-n** thousand million million

billig adj cheap; (dürftig) poor; **recht und b~** right and proper. **b~en** vt approve. **B~flieger** m low-cost airline. **B~ung** f **-** approval

Billion /bɪlˈjoːn/ f **-,-en** million million, billion

Bimsstein m pumice stone

Binde f **-,-n** band; (Verband) bandage; (Damen-) sanitary towel. **B~hautentzündung** f conjunctivitis. **b~n**† vt tie (**an** + acc to); make (Strauß); bind (Buch); (fesseln) tie up; (Culin) thicken; **sich b~n** commit oneself. **B~strich** m hyphen. **B~wort** nt (pl **-wörter**) (Gram) conjunction

Bind|faden m string. **B~ung** f **-,-en** (fig) tie; (Beziehung) relationship; (Verpflichtung) commitment; (Ski-) binding; (Textiles) weave

binnen prep (+ dat) within. **B~handel** m home trade

Bio- prefix organic

Bio|chemie f biochemistry. **b~dynamisch** m organic. **B~graphie**, **B~grafie** f **-,-n** biography

Bio|hof m organic farm. **B~laden** m health-food store

Biolog|e m **-n,-n** biologist. **B~ie** f **-** biology. **b~isch** adj biological; **b~ischer Anbau** organic farming; **b~isch angebaut** organically grown

Bioterrorismus m bioterrorism

Birke f **-,-n** birch [tree]

Birm|a nt **-s** Burma. **b~anisch** adj Burmese

Birn|baum m pear-tree. **B~e** f **-,-n** pear; (Electr) bulb

bis prep (+ acc) as far as, [up] to; (zeitlich) until, till; (spätestens) by; **bis zu** up to; **bis auf** (+ acc) (einschließlich) [down] to; (ausgenommen) except [for]; **drei bis vier Minuten** three to four minutes; **bis morgen!** see you tomorrow! •conj until

Bischof m **-s,¨e** bishop

bisher adv so far, up to now

Biskuit|rolle /bɪsˈkviːt-/ f Swiss roll. **B~teig** m sponge mixture

Biss m **-es,-e** bite

bisschen inv pron **ein b~** a bit, a

see A-Z of German life and culture

b

little; **kein b∼** not a bit

Biss|en m **-s,-** bite, mouthful. **b∼ig** adj vicious; (fig) caustic

bisweilen adv from time to time

bitt|e adv please; (nach Klopfen) come in; (als Antwort auf 'danke') don't mention it, you're welcome; **wie b∼e?** pardon? **B∼e** f **-,-n** request/(dringend) plea (**um** for). **b∼en**† vt/i (haben) ask/(dringend) beg (**um** for); (einladen) invite, ask. **b∼end** adj pleading

bitter adj bitter. **B∼keit** f **-** bitterness. **b∼lich** adv bitterly

Bittschrift f petition

bizarr adj bizarre

bläh|en vt swell; (Vorhang, Segel:) billow • vi (haben) cause flatulence. **B∼ungen** fpl flatulence sg, [!] wind sg

Blamage /bla'ma:ʒə/ f **-,-n** humiliation; (Schande) disgrace

blamieren vt disgrace; **sich b∼** disgrace oneself; (sich lächerlich machen) make a fool of oneself

blanchieren /blã'ʃi:rən/ vt (Culin) blanch

blank adj shiny. **B∼oscheck** m blank cheque

Blase f **-,-n** bubble; (Med) blister; (Anat) bladder. **b∼n**† vt/i (haben) blow; play (Flöte). **B∼nentzündung** f cystitis

Blas|instrument nt wind instrument. **B∼kapelle** f brass band

blass adj pale; (schwach) faint

Blässe f **-** pallor

Blatt nt **-[e]s,⸚er** (Bot) leaf; (Papier) sheet; (Zeitung) paper

Blattlaus f greenfly

blau adj, **B∼** nt **-s,-** blue; **b∼er Fleck** bruise; **b∼es Auge** black eye; **b∼ sein** [!] be tight; **Fahrt ins B∼e** mystery tour. **B∼beere** f bilberry. **B∼licht** nt blue flashing light

Blech nt **-[e]s,-e** sheet metal; (Weiß-) tin; (Platte) metal sheet; (Back-) baking sheet; (Mus) brass; ([!]: Unsinn) rubbish. **B∼schaden** m (Auto) damage to the bodywork

Blei nt **-[e]s** lead

Bleibe f **-** place to stay. **b∼n**† vi (sein) remain, stay; (übrig-) be left; **ruhig b∼n** keep calm; **bei etw b∼n** (fig) stick to sth; **b∼n Sie am Apparat** hold the line; **etw b∼n lassen** not do sth. **b∼nd** adj permanent; (anhaltend) lasting

bleich adj pale. **b∼en**† vi (sein) bleach; (ver-) fade • vt (reg) bleach. **B∼mittel** nt bleach

blei|ern adj leaden. **∼frei** adj unleaded. **B∼stift** m pencil. **B∼stiftabsatz** m stiletto heel. **B∼stiftspitzer** m **-s,-** pencil sharpener

Blende f **-,-n** shade, shield; (Sonnen-) [sun] visor; (Phot) diaphragm; (Öffnung) aperture; (an Kleid) facing. **b∼n** vt dazzle, blind

Blick m **-[e]s,-e** look; (kurz) glance; (Aussicht) view; **auf den ersten B∼** at first sight. **b∼en** vi (haben) look/(kurz) glance (**auf** + acc at). **B∼punkt** m (fig) point of view

blind adj blind; (trübe) dull; **b∼er Alarm** false alarm; **b∼er Passagier** stowaway. **B∼darm** m appendix. **B∼darmentzündung** f appendicitis. **B∼e(r)** m/f blind man/woman; **die B∼en** the blind pl. **B∼enhund** m guidedog. **B∼enschrift** f braille. **B∼gänger** m **-s,-** (Mil) dud. **B∼heit** f **-** blindness

blink|en vi (haben) flash; (funkeln) gleam; (Auto) indicate. **B∼er** m **-s,-** (Auto) indicator. **B∼licht** nt flashing light

blinzeln vi (haben) blink

Blitz m **-es,-e** [flash of] lightning; (Phot) flash. **B∼ableiter** m lightning-conductor. **b∼artig** adj lightning • adv like lightning. **b∼en** vi (haben) flash; (funkeln) sparkle; **es hat geblitzt** there was a flash of lightning. **B∼eis** nt sheet ice. **B∼licht** nt (Phot) flash. **b∼sauber** adj spick and span. **b∼schnell** adj lightning • adv like lightning

Block m **-[e]s,¨e** block • **-[e]s,-s** & **¨e** pad; (Häuser-) block

Blockade f **-,-n** blockade

Blockflöte f recorder

blockieren vt block; (Mil) blockade

Blockschrift f block letters pl

blöd[e] adj feeble-minded; (dumm) stupid

Blödsinn m **-[e]s** idiocy; (Unsinn) nonsense

blöken vi (haben) bleat

blond adj fair-haired; (Haar) fair

bloß adj bare; (alleinig) mere • adv only, just

bloß|legen vt sep uncover. **b~stellen** vt sep compromise

Bluff m **-s,-s** bluff. **b~en** vt/i (haben) bluff

blühen vi (haben) flower; (fig) flourish. **b~d** adj flowering; (fig) flourishing, thriving

Blume f **-,-n** flower; (vom Wein) bouquet. **B~nbeet** nt flower-bed. **B~ngeschäft** nt flower-shop, florist's. **B~nkohl** m cauliflower. **B~nmuster** nt floral design. **B~nstrauß** m bunch of flowers. **B~ntopf** m flowerpot; (Pflanze) pot plant. **B~nzwiebel** f bulb

blumig adj (fig) flowery

Bluse f **-,-n** blouse

Blut nt **-[e]s** blood. **b~arm** adj anaemic. **B~bahn** f blood-stream. **B~bild** nt blood count. **B~druck** m blood pressure. **b~dürstig** adj bloodthirsty

Blüte f **-,-n** flower, bloom; (vom Baum) blossom; (B~zeit) flowering period; (Baum-) blossom time; (Höhepunkt) peak, prime

Blut|egel m **-s,-** leech. **b~en** vi (haben) bleed

Blüten|blatt nt petal. **B~staub** m pollen

Blut|er m **-s,-** haemophiliac. **B~erguss** m bruise. **B~gefäß** nt blood-vessel. **B~gruppe** f blood group. **b~ig** adj bloody. **B~körperchen** nt **-s,-** corpuscle. **B~probe** f blood test. **b~rünstig** adj (fig) bloody, gory. **B~schande** f incest. **B~spender** m blood donor. **B~sturz** m haemorrhage. **B~transfusion, B~übertragung** f blood transfusion. **B~ung** f **-,-en** bleeding; (Med) haemorrhage; (Regel-) period. **b~unterlaufen** adj bruised; (Auge) bloodshot. **B~vergiftung** f blood-poisoning. **B~wurst** f black pudding

Bö f **-,-en** gust; (Regen-) squall

Bob m **-s,-s** bob[-sleigh]

Bock m **-[e]s,¨e** buck; (Ziege) billy goat; (Schaf) ram; (Gestell) support. **b~ig** adj ! stubborn. **B~springen** nt leap-frog

Boden m **-s,¨** ground; (Erde) soil; (Fuß-) floor; (Grundfläche) bottom; (Dach-) loft, attic. **B~satz** m sediment. **B~schätze** mpl mineral deposits. **B~see (der)** Lake Constance

Bogen m **-s,-** & **¨** curve; (Geometry) arc; (beim Skilauf) turn; (Architecture) arch; (Waffe, Geigen-) bow; (Papier) sheet; **einen großen B~ um jdn/etw machen** ! give s.o./sth a wide berth. **B~schießen** nt archery

Bohle f **-,-n** [thick] plank

Böhm|en nt **-s** Bohemia. **b~isch** adj Bohemian

Bohne f **-,-n** bean; **grüne B~n** French beans

bohner|n vt polish. **B~wachs** nt floor-polish

bohr|en vt/i (haben) drill (**nach** for); drive (Tunnel); sink (Brunnen); (Insekt:) bore. **B~er** m **-s,-** drill. **B~insel** f [offshore] drilling rig. **B~turm** m derrick

Boje f **-,-n** buoy

Böllerschuss m gun salute

Bolzen m **-s,-** bolt; (Stift) pin

bombardieren vt bomb; (fig) bombard (**mit** with)

Bombe f **-,-n** bomb. **B~nangriff** m bombing raid. **B~nerfolg** m huge success

see A-Z of German life and culture

b

Bon /bɔŋ/ m **-s,-s** voucher; (Kassen-) receipt

Bonbon /bɔŋ'bɔŋ/ m & nt **-s,-s** sweet

Bonus m **-[ses],-[se]** bonus

Boot nt **-[e]s,-e** boat. **B~ssteg** m landing-stage

Bord[1] nt **-[e]s,-e** shelf

Bord[2] m (Naut) **an B~** aboard, on board; **über B~** overboard. **B~buch** nt log[-book]

Bordell nt **-s,-e** brothel

Bordkarte f boarding-pass

borgen vt borrow; **jdm etw b~** lend s.o. sth

Borke f **-,-n** bark

Börse f **-,-n** purse; (Comm) stock exchange. **B~nmakler** m stockbroker

Borst|e f **-,-n** bristle. **b~ig** adj bristly

Borte f **-,-n** braid

Böschung f **-,-en** embankment

böse adj wicked, evil; (unartig) naughty; (schlimm) bad; (zornig) cross; **jdm** od **auf jdn b~ sein** be cross with s.o.

bos|haft adj malicious, spiteful. **B~heit** f **-,-en** malice; spite; (Handlung) spiteful act/(Bemerkung) remark

böswillig adj malicious

Botani|k f **-** botany. **B~ker(in)** m **-s,-** (f **-,-nen**) botanist

Bot|e m **-n,-n** messenger. **B~engang** m errand. **B~schaft** f **-,-en** message; (Pol) embassy. **B~schafter** m **-s,-** ambassador

Bouillon /bʊl'jɔŋ/ f **-,-s** clear soup. **B~würfel** m stock cube

Bowle /'bo:lə/ f **-,-n** punch

Box f **-,-en** box; (Pferde-) loose box; (Lautsprecher-) speaker; (Autorennen) pit

box|en vi (haben) box •vt punch. **B~en** nt **-s** boxing. **B~enluder** nt pit babe. **B~er** m **-s,-** boxer. **B~stopp** m pit stop

brachliegen† vi sep (haben) lie fallow

Branche /'brã:ʃə/ f **-,-n** [line of] business. **B~nverzeichnis** nt (Teleph) classified directory

Brand m **-[e]s,⸚e** fire; (Med) gangrene; (Bot) blight; **in B~ geraten** catch fire; **in B~ setzen** od **stecken** set on fire. **B~bombe** f incendiary bomb

Brand|stifter m arsonist. **B~stiftung** f arson

Brandung f **-** surf

Brand|wunde f burn. **B~zeichen** nt brand

Branntwein m spirit; (coll) spirits pl. **B~brennerei** f distillery

bras|ilianisch adj Brazilian. **B~ilien** nt **-s** Brazil

Brat|apfel m baked apple. **b~en**† vt/i (haben) roast; (in der Pfanne) fry. **B~en** m **-s,-** roast; (B~stück) joint. **b~fertig** adj oven-ready. **B~hähnchen** nt roasting chicken. **B~kartoffeln** fpl fried potatoes. **B~pfanne** f frying-pan

Bratsche f **-,-n** (Mus) viola

Bratspieß m spit

Brauch m **-[e]s,Bräuche** custom. **b~bar** adj usable; (nützlich) useful. **b~en** vt need; (ge-, verbrauchen) use; take (Zeit); **er b~t es nur zu sagen** he only has to say

Braue f **-,-n** eyebrow

brau|en vt brew. **B~er** m **-s,-** brewer. **B~erei** f **-,-en** brewery

braun adj, **B~** nt **-s,-** brown; **b~ werden** (Person:) get a tan; **b~ [gebrannt] sein** be [sun-]tanned

Bräune f **-** [sun-]tan. **b~n** vt/i (haben) brown; (in der Sonne) tan

Braunschweig nt **-s** Brunswick

Brause f **-,-n** (Dusche) shower; (an Gießkanne) rose; (B~limonade) fizzy drink

Braut f **-,⸚e** bride; (Verlobte) fiancée

Bräutigam m **-s,-e** bridegroom; (Verlobter) fiancé

Brautkleid nt wedding dress

Brautpaar nt bridal couple; (Verlobte) engaged couple

brav adj good; (redlich) honest • adv dutifully; (redlich) honestly

bravo int bravo!

BRD abbr (**Bundesrepublik Deutschland**) FRG

Brech|eisen nt jemmy; (B~stange) crowbar. **b~en**† vt break; (Phys) refract (Licht); (erbrechen) vomit; **sich b~en** (Wellen:) break; (Licht:) be refracted; **sich** (dat) **den Arm b~en** break one's arm • vi (sein) break • vi (haben) vomit, be sick. **B~reiz** m nausea. **B~stange** f crowbar

Brei m **-[e]s,-e** paste; (Culin) purée; (Hafer-) porridge

breit adj wide; (Schultern, Grinsen) broad. **B~band** nt broadband. **B~e** f **-,-n** width; breadth; (Geog) latitude. **b~en** vt spread (**über** + acc over). **B~engrad** m [degree of] latitude. **B~enkreis** m parallel

Bremse[1] f **-,-n** horsefly

Bremse[2] f **-,-n** brake. **b~n** vt slow down; (fig) restrain • vi (haben) brake

Bremslicht nt brake-light

brenn|bar adj combustible; **leicht b~bar** highly [in]flammable. **b~en**† vi (haben) burn; (Licht:) be on; (Zigarette:) be alight; (weh tun) smart, sting • vt burn; (rösten) roast; (im Brennofen) fire; (destillieren) distil. **b~end** adj burning; (angezündet) lighted; (fig) fervent. **B~er** m **-s, -** burner. **B~erei** f **-,-en** distillery

Brennessel* f = **Brennnessel**

Brenn|holz nt firewood. **B~ofen** m kiln. **B~nessel** f stinging nettle. **B~punkt** m (Phys) focus. **B~spiritus** m methylated spirits. **B~stoff** m fuel. **B~stoffzelle** f fuel cell

Bretagne /bre'tanjə/ **(die) -** Brittany

Brett nt **-[e]s,-er** board; (im Regal) shelf; **schwarzes B~** notice board. **B~spiel** nt board game

Brezel f **-,-n** pretzel

Bridge /brɪtʃ/ nt **-** (Spiel) bridge

Brief m **-[e]s,-e** letter. **B~beschwerer** m **-s,-** paperweight. **B~freund(in)** m(f) pen-friend. **B~kasten** m letter-box. **B~kopf** m letter-head. **b~lich** adj & adv by letter. **B~marke** f [postage] stamp. **B~öffner** m paper-knife. **B~papier** nt notepaper. **B~tasche** f wallet. **B~träger** m postman. **B~umschlag** m envelope. **B~wahl** f postal vote. **B~wechsel** m correspondence

Brikett nt **-s,-s** briquette

Brillant m **-en,-en** [cut] diamond

Brille f **-,-n** glasses pl, spectacles pl; (Schutz-) goggles pl; (Klosett-) toilet seat

bringen† vt bring; (fort-) take; (ein-) yield; (veröffentlichen) publish; (im Radio) broadcast; show (Film); **ins Bett b~** put to bed; **jdn nach Hause b~** take/(begleiten) see s.o. home; **um etw b~** deprive of sth; **jdn dazu b~, etw zu tun** get s.o. to do sth; **es weit b~** (fig) go far

Brise f **-,-n** breeze

Brit|e m **-n,-n, B~in** f **-,-nen** Briton. **b~isch** adj British

Bröck|chen nt **-s,-** (Culin) crouton. **b~elig** adj crumbly; (Gestein) friable. **b~eln** vt/i (haben/sein) crumble

Brocken m **-s,-** chunk; (Erde, Kohle) lump

Brokat m **-[e]s,-e** brocade

Brokkoli pl broccoli sg

Brombeere f blackberry

Bronchitis f **-** bronchitis

Bronze /'brõ:sə/ f **-,-n** bronze

Brosch|e f **-,-n** brooch. **b~iert** adj paperback. **B~üre** f **-,-n** brochure; (Heft) booklet

Brösel mpl (Culin) breadcrumbs

Brot nt **-[e]s,-e** bread; **ein B~** a loaf [of bread]; (Scheibe) a slice of bread

Brötchen nt **-s,-** [bread] roll

b

Brotkrümel m breadcrumb

Bruch m **-[e]s,⸚e** break; (Brechen) breaking; (Rohr-) burst; (Med) fracture; (Eingeweide-) rupture, hernia; (Math) fraction; (fig) breach; (in Beziehung) break-up

brüchig adj brittle

Bruch|landung f crash-landing. **B~rechnung** f fractions pl. **B~stück** nt fragment. **B~teil** m fraction

Brücke f **-,-n** bridge; (Teppich) rug

Bruder m **-s,⸚** brother

brüderlich adj brotherly, fraternal

Brügge nt **-s** Bruges

Brüh|e f **-,-n** broth, stock. **B~würfel** m stock cube

brüllen vt/i (haben) roar

brumm|eln vt/i (haben) mumble. **b~en** vi (haben) (Insekt:) buzz; (Bär:) growl; (Motor:) hum; (murren) grumble. **B~er** m **-s,-** [!] bluebottle. **b~ig** adj [!] grumpy

brünett adj dark-haired

Brunnen m **-s,-** well; (Spring-) fountain; (Heil-) spa water

brüsk adj brusque

Brüssel nt **-s** Brussels

Brust f **-,⸚e** chest; (weibliche, Culin: B~stück) breast. **B~bein** nt breastbone

brüsten (sich) vr boast

Brust|fellentzündung f pleurisy. **B~schwimmen** nt breaststroke

Brüstung f **-,-en** parapet

Brustwarze f nipple

Brut f **-,-en** incubation

brutal adj brutal

brüten vi (haben) sit (on eggs); (fig) ponder (**über** + dat over)

Brutkasten m (Med) incubator

brutto adv, **B~-** prefix gross

BSE f **-** BSE

Bub m **-en,-en** (SGer) boy. **B~e** m **-n,-n** (Karte) jack, knave

Buch nt **-[e]s,⸚er** book; **B~ führen** keep a record (**über** + acc of); **die B⸚er führen** keep the accounts

Buche f **-,-n** beech

buchen vt book; (Comm) enter

Bücher|ei f **-,-en** library. **B~regal** nt bookcase, bookshelves pl. **B~schrank** m bookcase

Buchfink m chaffinch

Buch|führung f bookkeeping. **B~halter(in)** m **-s,-** (f **-,-nen**) bookkeeper, accountant. **B~haltung** f bookkeeping, accountancy; (Abteilung) accounts department. **B~handlung** f bookshop

Büchse f **-,-n** box; (Konserven-) tin, can

Buch|stabe m **-n,-n** letter. **b~stabieren** vt spell [out]. **b~stäblich** adv literally

Bucht f **-,-en** (Geog) bay

Buchung f **-,-en** booking, reservation; (Comm) entry

Buckel m **-s,-** hump; (Beule) bump; (Hügel) hillock

bücken (sich) vr bend down

bucklig adj hunchbacked

Bückling m **-s,-e** smoked herring

Buddhis|mus m **-** Buddhism. **B~t(in)** m **-en,-en** (f **-,-nen**) Buddhist. **b~tisch** adj Buddhist

Bude f **-,-n** hut; (Kiosk) kiosk; (Markt-) stall; ([!]: Zimmer) room

Budget /bʏ'dʒe:/ nt **-s,-s** budget

Büfett nt **-[e]s,-e** sideboard; (Theke) bar; **kaltes B~** cold buffet

Büffel m **-s,-** buffalo

Bügel m **-s,-** frame; (Kleider-) coathanger; (Steig-) stirrup; (Brillen-) sidepiece. **B~brett** nt ironing-board. **B~eisen** nt iron. **B~falte** f crease. **b~frei** adj non-iron. **b~n** vt/i (haben) iron

Bühne f -,-n stage. **B~nbild** nt set. **B~neingang** m stage door

Buhrufe mpl boos

Bukett nt -[e]s,-e bouquet

Bulgarien /-i̯ən/ nt -s Bulgaria

Bull|auge nt (Naut) porthole. **B~dogge** f bulldog. **B~dozer** m -s,- bulldozer. **B~e** m -n,-n bull; (sl: Polizist) cop

Bumme|l m -s,- [!] stroll. **B~lei** f - [!] dawdling

bummel|ig adj [!] slow; (nachlässig) careless. **b~n** vi (sein) [!] stroll • vi (haben) [!] dawdle. **B~streik** m go-slow. **B~zug** m [!] slow train

Bums m -es,-e [!] bump, thump

Bund[1] nt -[e]s,-e bunch

Bund[2] m -[e]s,⸚e association; (Bündnis) alliance; (Pol) federation; (Rock-, Hosen-) waistband; **der B~** the Federal Government

Bündel nt -s,- bundle. **b~n** vt bundle [up]

Bundes|- prefix Federal. **B~genosse** m ally. **B~kanzler** m Federal Chancellor. **B~land** nt [federal] state; (Aust) province. **B~liga** f German national league. **B~rat** m Upper House of Parliament. **B~regierung** f Federal Government. **B~republik** f **die B~republik Deutschland** the Federal Republic of Germany. **B~tag** m Lower House of Parliament. **B~wehr** f [Federal German] Army

bünd|ig adj & adv **kurz und b~ig** short and to the point. **B~nis** nt -ses,-se alliance

Bunker m -s,- bunker; (Luftschutz-) shelter

bunt adj coloured; (farbenfroh) colourful; (grell) gaudy; (gemischt) varied; (wirr) confused; **b~e Platte** assorted cold meats. **B~stift** m crayon

Bürde f -,-n (fig) burden

Burg f -,-en castle

Bürge m -n,-n guarantor. **b~n** vi (haben) **b~n für** vouch for; (fig) guarantee

Bürger|(in) m -s,- (f -,-nen) citizen. **B~krieg** m civil war. **b~lich** adj civil; (Pflicht) civic; (mittelständisch) middle-class. **B~liche(r)** m/f commoner. **B~meister** m mayor. **B~rechte** npl civil rights. **B~steig** m -[e]s,-e pavement

Bürgschaft f -,-en surety

Burgunder m -s,- (Wein) Burgundy

Büro nt -s,-s office. **B~angestellte(r)** m/f office worker. **B~klammer** f paper clip. **B~kratie** f -,-n bureaucracy. **b~kratisch** adj bureaucratic

Bursche m -n,-n lad, youth

Bürste f -,-n brush. **b~n** vt brush. **B~nschnitt** m crew cut

Bus m -ses,-se bus; (Reise-) coach

Busch m -[e]s,⸚e bush

Büschel nt -s,- tuft

buschig adj bushy

Busen m -s,- bosom

Bussard m -s,-e buzzard

Buße f -,-n penance; (Jur) fine

Bußgeld nt (Jur) fine

Büste f -,-n bust; (Schneider-) dummy. **B~nhalter** m -s,- bra

Butter f - butter. **B~blume** f buttercup. **B~brot** nt slice of bread and butter. **B~milch** f buttermilk. **b~n** vt butter

b.w. abbr (**bitte wenden**) P.T.O.

see A-Z of German life and culture

Cc

ca. abbr (**circa**) about

Café /ka'fe:/ nt **-s,-s** café

Camcorder /'kamkɔrdɐ/ m **-s, -** camcorder

camp|en /'kɛmpən/ vi (haben) go camping. **C~ing** nt **-s** camping. **C~ingplatz** m campsite

Caravan /'ka[:]ravan/ m **-s,-s** (Auto) caravan; (Kombi) estate car

CD /tse:'de:/ f **-,-s** compact disc, CD. **CD-ROM** f **-,-(s)** CD-ROM

Cell|ist(in) /tʃɛ'lɪst(ɪn)/ m **-en,-en** (f **-,-nen**) cellist. **C~o** nt **-,-los** & **-li** cello

Celsius /'tsɛlziʊs/ inv Celsius, centigrade

Cent /tsɛnt/ m **-[s], -[s]** cent

Champagner /ʃam'panjɐ/ m **-s** champagne

Champignon /'ʃampɪnjɔŋ/ m **-s,-s** [field] mushroom

Chance /'ʃã:s[ə]/ f **-,-n** chance

Chaos /'ka:ɔs/ nt **-** chaos

Charakter /ka'raktɐ/ m **-s,-e** character. **c~isieren** vt characterize. **c~istisch** adj characteristic (**für** of)

charm|ant /ʃar'mant/ adj charming. **C~e** m **-s** charm

Charter|flug /'tʃ-, 'ʃartɐ-/ m charter flight. **c~n** vt charter

Chassis /ʃa'si:/ nt **-,-** chassis

Chauffeur /ʃɔ'fø:ɐ̯/ m **-s,-e** chauffeur; (Taxi-) driver

Chauvinist /ʃovi'nɪst/ m **-en,-en** chauvinist

Chef /ʃɛf/ m **-s,-s** head; 🅘 boss

Chemie /çe'mi:/ f **-** chemistry

Chem|iker(in) /'çe:-/ m **-s,-** (f **-,-nen**) chemist. **c~isch** adj chemical; **c~ische Reinigung** dry-cleaning; (Geschäft) dry-cleaner's

Chicorée /'ʃɪkore:/ m **-s** chicory

Chiffre /'ʃɪfɐ, 'ʃɪfrə/ f **-,-n** cipher

Chile /'çi:le/ nt **-s** Chile

Chin|a /'çi:na/ nt **-s** China. **C~ese** m **-n,-n**, **C~esin** f **-,-nen** Chinese. **c~esisch** adj Chinese. **C~esisch** nt **-[s]** (Lang) Chinese

Chip /tʃɪp/ m **-s,-s** [micro]chip. **C~s** pl crisps

Chirurg /çi'rʊrk/ m **-en,-en** surgeon. **C~ie** f **-** surgery

Chlor /klo:ɐ̯/ nt **-s** chlorine

Choke /tʃo:k/ m **-s,-s** (Auto) choke

Cholera /'ko:lera/ f **-** cholera

cholerisch /ko'le:rɪʃ/ adj irascible

Cholesterin /ço-, kolɛste'ri:n/ nt **-s** cholesterol

Chor /ko:ɐ̯/ m **-[e]s,¨e** choir

Choreographie, **Choreografie** /koreogra'fi:/ f **-,-n** choreography

Christ /krɪst/ m **-en,-en** Christian. **C~baum** m Christmas tree. **C~entum** nt **-s** Christianity **c~lich** adj Christian

Christus /'krɪstʊs/ m **-ti** Christ

Chrom /kro:m/ nt **-s** chromium

Chromosom /kromo'zo:m/ nt **-s,-en** chromosome

Chronik /'kro:nɪk/ f **-,-en** chronicle

chronisch /'kro:nɪʃ/ adj chronic

Chrysantheme /krʏzan'te:mə/ f **-,-n** chrysanthemum

circa /'tsɪrka/ adv about

Clique /'klɪkə/ f **-,-n** clique

Clou /klu:/ m **-s,-s** highlight, 🅘 high spot

Clown /klaun/ m **-s,-s** clown

Club /klʊp/ m **-s,-s** club

Cocktail /'kɔkteːl/ m **-s,-s** cocktail

Code /'koːt/ m **-s,-s** code

Comic-Heft /'kɔmɪk-/ nt comic

Computer /kɔm'pjuːtɐ/ m **-s,-** computer. **c∼isieren** vt computerize. **C∼spiel** nt computer game

Conférencier /kõ'ferã'sieː/ m **-s,-** compère

Cord /kɔrt/ m **-s, C∼samt** m corduroy

Couch /kautʃ/ f **-,-s** settee

Cousin /ku'zɛ̃ː/ m **-s,-s** [male] cousin. **C∼e** f **-,-n** [female] cousin

Creme /kreːm/ f **-s,-s** cream; (Speise) cream dessert

Curry /'kari, 'kœri/ nt & m **-s** curry powder • nt **-s,-s** (Gericht) curry

Cursor /'køːɐ̯sɐ/ m **-s, -** cursor

Cyberspace /'saibɐspeːs/ m **-** cyberspace

da adv there; (hier) here; (zeitlich) then; (in dem Fall) in that case; **von da an** from then on; **da sein** be there/(hier) here; (existieren) exist; **wieder da sein** be back • conj as, since

dabei (emphatic: **dabei**) adv nearby; (daran) with it; (eingeschlossen) included; (hinsichtlich) about it; (währenddem) during this; (gleichzeitig) at the same time; (doch) and yet; **dicht d∼** close by; **d∼ sein** be present; (mitmachen) be involved; **d∼ sein, etw zu tun** be just doing sth

Dach nt **-[e]s,¨er** roof. **D∼boden** m loft. **D∼luke** f skylight. **D∼rinne** f gutter

Dachs m **-es,-e** badger

Dachsparren m **-s,-** rafter

Dackel m **-s,-** dachshund

dadurch (emphatic: **dadurch**) adv through it/them; (Ursache) by it; (deshalb) because of that; **d∼, dass** because

dafür (emphatic: **dafür**) adv for it/them; (anstatt) instead; (als Ausgleich) but [on the other hand]; **d∼, dass** considering that; **ich kann nichts dafür** it's not my fault

dagegen (emphatic: **dagegen**) adv against it/them; (Mittel, Tausch) for it; (verglichen damit) by comparison; (jedoch) however; **hast du was d∼?** do you mind?

daheim adv at home

daher (emphatic: **daher**) adv from there; (deshalb) for that reason; **das kommt d∼, weil** that's because • conj that is why

dahin (emphatic: **dahin**) adv there; **bis d∼** up to there; (bis dann) until/(Zukunft) by then; **jdn d∼ bringen, dass er etw tut** get s.o. to do sth

dahinten adv back there

dahinter (emphatic: **dahinter**) adv behind it/them; **d∼ kommen** (fig) get to the bottom of it

Dahlie /-iə/ f **-,-n** dahlia

dalassen† vt sep leave there

daliegen† vi sep (haben) lie there

damalig adj at that time; **der d∼e Minister** the then minister

damals adv at that time

Damast m **-es,-e** damask

Dame f **-,-n** lady; (Karte, Schach) queen; (D∼spiel) draughts sg. **d∼nhaft** adj ladylike

damit (emphatic: **damit**) adv with it/them; (dadurch) by it; **hör auf d∼!** stop it! • conj so that

Damm m **-[e]s,¨e** dam

dämmer|ig adj dim. **D~licht** nt twilight. **d~n** vi (haben) (Morgen:) dawn; **es d~t** it is getting light/ (abends) dark. **D~ung** f dawn; (Abend-) dusk

Dämon m **-s,-en** demon

d

Dampf m **-es,¨e** steam; (Chemistry) vapour. **d~en** vi (haben) steam

dämpfen vt (Culin) steam; (fig) muffle (Ton); lower (Stimme)

Dampf|er m **-s,-** steamer. **D~kochtopf** m pressure-cooker. **D~maschine** f steam engine. **D~walze** f steamroller

danach (emphatic: **danach**) adv after it/them; (suchen) for it/them; (riechen) of it; (später) afterwards; (entsprechend) accordingly; **es sieht d~ aus** it looks like it

Däne m **-n,-n** Dane

daneben (emphatic: **daneben**) adv beside it/them; (außerdem) in addition; (verglichen damit) by comparison

Dän|emark nt **-s** Denmark. **D~in** f **-,-nen** Dane. **d~isch** adj Danish

Dank m **-es** thanks pl; **vielen D~!** thank you very much! **d~** prep (+ dat or gen) thanks to. **d~bar** adj grateful; (erleichtert) thankful; (lohnend) rewarding. **D~barkeit** f - gratitude. **d~e** adv **d~e [schön** od **sehr]!** thank you [very much]! **d~en** vi (haben) thank (**jdm** s.o.); (ablehnen) decline; **nichts zu d~en!** don't mention it!

dann adv then; **selbst d~, wenn** even if

daran (emphatic: **daran**) adv on it/ them; at it/them; (denken) of it; **nahe d~** on the point (**etw zu tun** of doing sth). **d~setzen** vt sep **alles d~setzen** do one's utmost (**zu** to)

darauf (emphatic: **darauf**) adv on it/ them; (warten) for it; (antworten) to it; (danach) after that; (d~hin) as a result. **d~hin** adv as a result

daraus (emphatic: **daraus**) adv out of or from it/them; **er macht sich nichts d~** he doesn't care for it

darlegen vt sep expound; (erklären) explain

Darlehen nt **-s,-** loan

Darm m **-[e]s,¨e** intestine

darstell|en vt sep represent; (bildlich) portray; (Theat) interpret; (spielen) play; (schildern) describe. **D~er** m **-s,-** actor. **D~erin** f **-,-nen** actress. **D~ung** f representation; interpretation; description

darüber (emphatic: **darüber**) adv over it/them; (höher) above it/ them; (sprechen, lachen, sich freuen) about it; (mehr) more; **d~ hinaus** beyond [it]; (dazu) on top of that

darum (emphatic: **darum**) adv round it/them; (bitten, kämpfen) for it; (deshalb) that is why; **d~, weil** because

darunter (emphatic: **darunter**) adv under it/them; (tiefer) below it/ them; (weniger) less; (dazwischen) among them

das def art & pron s. **der**

dasein* vi sep (sein) = **da sein**, s. **da**. **D~** nt **-s** existence

dass conj that

dasselbe pron s. **derselbe**

Daten|sichtgerät nt visual display unit, VDU. **D~verarbeitung** f data processing

datieren vt/i (haben) date

Dativ m **-s,-e** dative. **D~objekt** nt indirect object

Dattel f **-,-n** date

Datum nt **-s,-ten** date; **Daten** dates; (Angaben) data

Dauer f - duration, length; (Jur) term; **auf die D~** in the long run. **D~auftrag** m standing order. **d~haft** adj lasting, enduring; (fest) durable. **D~karte** f season ticket. **d~n** vi (haben) last; **lange d~n** take a long time. **d~nd** adj lasting; (ständig) constant. **D~welle** f perm

Daumen m **-s,-** thumb; **jdm den D~ drücken** od **halten** keep one's fingers crossed for s.o.

Daunen fpl down sg. **D~decke** f [down-filled] duvet

davon (emphatic: **davon**) adv from it/them; (dadurch) by it; (damit) with it/them; (darüber) about it; (Menge) of it/them; **das kommt d~!** it serves you right! **d~kommen**† vi sep (sein) escape (**mit dem Leben** with one's life). **d~laufen**† vi sep (sein) run away. **d~machen (sich)** vr sep [!] make off. **d~tragen**† vt sep carry off; (erleiden) suffer; (gewinnen) win

davor (emphatic: **davor**) adv in front of it/them; (sich fürchten) of it; (zeitlich) before it/them

dazu (emphatic: **dazu**) adv to it/them; (damit) with it/them; (dafür) for it; **noch d~** in addition to that; **jdn d~ bringen, etw zu tun** get s.o. to do sth; **ich kam nicht d~** I didn't get round to [doing] it. **d~kommen**† vi sep (sein) arrive [on the scene]; (hinzukommen) be added. **d~rechnen** vt sep add to it/them

dazwischen (emphatic: **dazwischen**) adv between them; in between; (darunter) among them. **d~kommen**† vi sep (sein) (fig) crop up; **wenn nichts d~kommt** if all goes well

Debat|te f -,-n debate; **zur D~te stehen** be at issue. **d~tieren** vt/i (haben) debate

Debüt /de'by:/ nt **-s,-s** début

Deck nt **-[e]s,-s** (Naut) deck; **an D~** on deck. **D~bett** nt duvet

Decke f **-,-n** cover; (Tisch-) tablecloth; (Bett-) blanket; (Reise-) rug; (Zimmer-) ceiling; **unter einer D~ stecken** [!] be in league

Deckel m **-s,-** lid; (Flaschen-) top; (Buch-) cover

decken vt cover; tile (Dach); lay (Tisch); (schützen) shield; (Sport) mark; meet (Bedarf); **jdn d~** (fig) cover up for s.o.; **sich d~** (fig) cover oneself (**gegen** against); (übereinstimmen) coincide

Deckname m pseudonym

Deckung f **-** (Mil) cover; (Sport) defence; (Mann-) marking; (Boxen) guard; (Sicherheit) security; **in D~ gehen** take cover

defin|ieren vt define. **D~ition** f **-,-en** definition

Defizit nt **-s,-e** deficit

deformiert adj deformed

deftig adj [!] (Mahlzeit) hearty; (Witz) coarse

Degen m **-s,-** sword; (Fecht-) épée

degeneriert adj (fig) degenerate

degradieren vt (Mil) demote; (fig) degrade

dehn|bar adj elastic. **d~en** vt stretch; lengthen (Vokal); **sich d~en** stretch

Deich m **-[e]s,-e** dike

dein poss pron your. **d~e(r,s)** poss pron yours; **die D~en** od **d~en** pl your family sg. **d~erseits** adv for your part. **d~etwegen** adv for your sake; (wegen dir) because of you, on your account. **d~etwillen** adv **um d~etwillen** for your sake. **d~ige** poss pron **der/die/das d~ige** yours. **d~s** poss pron yours

Dekan m **-s,-e** dean

Deklin|ation /-'tsi̯o:n/ f **-,-en** declension. **d~ieren** vt decline

Dekolleté, **Dekolletee** /dekɔl'te:/ nt **-s,-s** low neckline

Dekor m & nt **-s** decoration. **D~ateur** m **-s,-e** interior decorator; (Schaufenster-) window-dresser. **D~ation** f **-,-en** decoration; (Schaufenster-) window-dressing; (Auslage) display. **d~ativ** adj decorative. **d~ieren** vt decorate; dress (Schaufenster)

Deleg|ation /-'tsi̯o:n/ f **-,-en** delegation. **D~ierte(r)** m/f delegate

delikat adj delicate; (lecker) delicious; (taktvoll) tactful. **D~essengeschäft** nt delicatessen

Delikt nt **-[e]s,-e** offence

Delinquent m **-en,-en** offender

Delle f **-,-n** dent

Delphin m **-s,-e** dolphin

d

d

Delta nt **-s,-s** delta

dem def art & pron s. **der**

dementieren vt deny

dem|entsprechend adj corresponding; (passend) appropriate • adv accordingly; (passend) appropriately. **d~nächst** adv soon; (in Kürze) shortly

Demokrat m **-en,-en** democrat. **D~ie** f **-,-n** democracy. **d~isch** adj democratic

demolieren vt wreck

Demonstr|ant m **-en,-en** demonstrator. **D~ation** f **-,-en** demonstration. **d~ieren** vt/i (haben) demonstrate

demontieren vt dismantle

Demoskopie f **-** opinion research

Demut f **-** humility

den def art & pron s. **der. d~en** pron s. **der**

denk|bar adj conceivable. **d~en†** vt/i (haben) think (**an** + acc of); (sich erinnern) remember (**an etw** acc sth); **das kann ich mir d~en** I can imagine [that]; **ich d~e nicht daran** I have no intention of doing it. **D~mal** nt memorial; (Monument) monument. **d~würdig** adj memorable

denn conj for; **besser/mehr d~ je** better/more than ever • adv **wie/wo d~?** but how/where? **warum d~ nicht?** why ever not? **es sei d~ [, dass]** unless

dennoch adv nevertheless

Denunz|iant m **-en,-en** informer. **d~ieren** vt denounce

Deodorant nt **-s,-s** deodorant

deplaciert, deplatziert /-'tsi:ɐt/ adj (fig) out of place

Deponie f **-,-n** dump. **d~ren** vt deposit

deportieren vt deport

Depot /de'po:/ nt **-s,-s** depot; (Lager) warehouse; (Bank-) safe deposit

Depression f **-,-en** depression

deprimieren vt depress

der, die, das, pl **die**

• definite article

acc **den, die, das**, pl **die**; gen **des, der, des**, pl **der**; dat **dem, der, dem**, pl **den**

····➤ the. **der Mensch** the person; (als abstrakter Begriff) man. **die Natur** nature. **das Leben** life. **das Lesen/Tanzen** reading/dancing. **sich** (dat) **das Gesicht/die Hände waschen** wash one's face/hands. **3 Euro das Pfund** 3 euros a pound

• pronoun

acc **den, die, das**, pl **die**; gen **dessen, deren, dessen**, pl **deren**; dat **dem, der, dem**, pl **denen**

• demonstrative pronoun

····➤ that; (pl) those

····➤ (attributiv) **der Mann war es** it was 'that man

····➤ (substantivisch) he, she, it; (pl) they. **der war es** it was 'him. **die da** (person) that woman/girl; (thing) that one

• relative pronoun

····➤ (Person) who. **der Mann, der/dessen Sohn hier arbeitet** the man who/whose son works here. **die Frau, mit der ich Tennis spiele** the woman with whom I play tennis, the woman I play tennis with. **das Mädchen, das ich gestern sah** the girl I saw yesterday

····➤ (Ding) which, that. **ich sah ein Buch, das mich interessierte** I saw a book that interested me. **die CD, die ich mir anhöre** the CD I am listening to. **das Auto, mit dem wir nach Deutschland fahren** the car we are going to Germany in or in which we are going to Germany

derb adj tough; (kräftig) strong; (grob) coarse; (unsanft) rough

deren pron s. **der**

dergleichen inv adj such • pron such a thing/such things

der-/die-/dasselbe, pl **dieselben**

pron the same; **ein- und dasselbe** one and the same thing

derzeit adv at present

des def art s. **der**

Desert|eur /-'tøːɐ̯/ m **-s,-e** deserter. **d~ieren** vi (sein/haben) desert

desgleichen adv likewise •pron the like

deshalb adv for this reason; (also) therefore

Design nt **-s, -s** design

Designer(in) /di'zainɐ, -nərɪn/ m **-s,-** (f **-,-nen**) designer

Desin|fektion /dɛsʔɪnfɛk'tsi̯oːn/ f disinfecting. **D~fektionsmittel** nt disinfectant. **d~fizieren** vt disinfect

dessen pron s. **der**

Destill|ation /-'tsi̯oːn/ f - distillation. **d~ieren** vt distil

desto adv **je mehr d~besser** the more the better

deswegen adv = **deshalb**

Detektiv m **-s,-e** detective

Deton|ation /-'tsi̯oːn/ f **-,-en** explosion. **d~ieren** vi (sein) explode

deut|en vt interpret; predict (Zukunft) •vi (haben) point (**auf** + acc at/(fig) to). **d~lich** adj clear; (eindeutig) plain

deutsch adj German. **D~** nt **-[s]** (Lang) German; **auf D~** in German. **D~e(r)** m/f German. **D~land** nt **-s** Germany

Deutung f **-,-en** interpretation

Devise f **-,-n** motto. **D~n** pl foreign currency or exchange sg

Dezember m **-s,-** December

dezent adj unobtrusive; (diskret) discreet

Dezernat nt **-[e]s,-e** department

Dezimalzahl f decimal

d.h. abbr (das heißt) i.e.

Dia nt **-s,-s** (Phot) slide

Diabet|es m - diabetes. **D~iker** m **-s,-** diabetic

Diadem nt **-s,-e** tiara

Diagnose f **-,-n** diagnosis

diagonal adj diagonal. **D~e** f **-,-n** diagonal

Diagramm nt **-s,-e** diagram; (Kurven-) graph

Diakon m **-s,-e** deacon

Dialekt m **-[e]s,-e** dialect

Dialog m **-[e]s,-e** dialogue

Diamant m **-en,-en** diamond

Diapositiv nt **-s,-e** (Phot) slide

Diaprojektor m slide projector

Diät f **-,-en** (Med) diet; **D~ leben** be on a diet

dich pron (acc of **du**) you; (reflexive) yourself

dicht adj dense; (dick) thick; (undurchlässig) airtight; (wasser-) watertight •adv densely; (nahe) close (**bei** to). **D~e** f density. **d~en**[1] vt make watertight

dicht|en[2] vi (haben) write poetry. •vt write. **D~er(in)** m **-s,-** (f **-,-nen**) poet. **d~erisch** adj poetic. **D~ung**[1] f **-,-en** poetry; (Gedicht) poem

Dichtung[2] f **-,-en** seal; (Ring) washer; (Auto) gasket

dick adj thick; (beleibt) fat; (geschwollen) swollen; (fam: eng) close; **d~ machen** be fattening. **d~flüssig** adj thick; (Phys) viscous. **D~kopf** m ! stubborn person; **einen D~kopf haben** be stubborn

die def art & pron s. **der**

Dieb|(in) m **-[e]s,-e** (f **-,-nen**) thief. **d~isch** adj thieving; (Freude) malicious. **D~stahl** m **-[e]s,¨-e** theft

Diele f **-,-n** floorboard; (Flur) hall

dien|en vi (haben) serve. **D~er** m **-s,-** servant; (Verbeugung) bow. **D~erin** f **-,-nen** maid, servant

Dienst m **-[e]s,-e** service; (Arbeit) work; (Amtsausübung) duty; **außer D~** off duty; (pensioniert) retired; **D~ haben** work; (Soldat, Arzt:) be on duty

d

d

Dienstag m Tuesday. **d~s** adv on Tuesdays

Dienst|bote m servant. **d~frei** adj **d~freier Tag** day off; **d~frei haben** have time off; (Soldat, Arzt:) be off duty. **D~grad** m rank. **D~leistung** f service. **d~lich** adj official • adv **d~lich verreist** away on business. **D~mädchen** nt maid. **D~reise** f business trip. **D~stelle** f office. **D~stunden** fpl office hours

dies inv pron this. **d~bezüglich** adj relevant • adv regarding this matter. **d~e(r,s)** pron this; (pl) these; (substantivisch) this [one]; (pl) these; **d~e Nacht** tonight; (letzte) last night

dieselbe pron s. **derselbe**

Dieselkraftstoff m diesel [oil]

diesmal adv this time

Dietrich m **-s,-e** skeleton key

Diffamation /-'tsi̯o:n/ f - defamation

Differential* /-'tsi̯a:l/ nt **-s,-e** = **Differenzial**

Differenz f **-,-en** difference. **D~ial** nt **-s,-e** differential. **d~ieren** vt/i (haben) differentiate (**zwischen** + dat between)

digital adj digital

Digital- prefix digital. **D~kamera** f digital camera. **D~uhr** f digital clock/watch

digitalisieren vt digitize

Dikt|at nt **-[e]s,-e** dictation. **D~ator** m **-s,-en** dictator. **D~atur** f **-,-en** dictatorship. **d~ieren** vt/i (haben) dictate

Dill m **-s** dill

Dimension f **-,-en** dimension

Ding nt **-[e]s,-e** & [!] **-er** thing; **guter D~e sein** be cheerful; **vor allen D~en** above all

Dinosaurier /-i̯ɐ/ m **-s,-** dinosaur

Diözese f **-,-n** diocese

Diphtherie f - diphtheria

Diplom nt **-s,-e** diploma; (Univ) degree

Diplomat m **-en,-en** diplomat

dir pron (dat of **du**) [to] you; (reflexive) yourself; **ein Freund von dir** a friend of yours

direkt adj direct • adv directly; (wirklich) really. **D~ion** f - management; (Vorstand) board of directors. **D~or** m **-s,-en**, **D~orin** f **-,-nen** director; (Bank-, Theater-) manager; (Sch) head; (Gefängnis) governor. **D~übertragung** f live transmission

Dirig|ent m **-en,-en** (Mus) conductor. **d~ieren** vt direct; (Mus) conduct

Dirndl nt **-s,-** dirndl [dress]

Discounter m **-s, -** discount supermarket

Diskette f **-,-n** floppy disc

Disko f **-,-s** [!] disco. **D~thek** f **-,-en** discothèque

diskret adj discreet

Diskus m **-,-se** & **Disken** discus

Disku|ssion f **-,-en** discussion. **d~tieren** vt/i (haben) discuss

disponieren vi (haben) make arrangements; **d~ [können] über** (+ acc) have at one's disposal

Disqualifi|kation /-'tsi̯o:n/ f disqualification. **d~zieren** vt disqualify

Dissertation /-'tsi̯o:n/ f **-,-en** dissertation

Dissident m **-en,-en** dissident

Distanz f **-,-en** distance. **d~ieren** **(sich)** vr dissociate oneself (**von** from). **d~iert** adj aloof

Distel f **-,-n** thistle

Disziplin f **-,-en** discipline. **d~arisch** adj disciplinary. **d~iert** adj disciplined

dito adv ditto

diverse attrib a pl various

Divid|ende f **-,-en** dividend. **d~ieren** vt divide (**durch** by)

Division f **-,-en** division

DJH abbr (**Deutsche Jugendherberge**) [German] youth hostel

DM abbr (**Deutsche Mark**) DM

doch conj & adv but; (dennoch) yet; (trotzdem) after all; **wenn d~ ...** ! if only ... ! **nicht d~!** don't!

Docht m **-[e]s,-e** wick

Dock nt **-s,-s** dock. **d~en** vt/i (haben) dock

Dogge f **-,-n** Great Dane

Dogm|a nt **-s,-men** dogma. **d~atisch** adj dogmatic

Dohle f **-,-n** jackdaw

Doktor m **-s,-en** doctor. **D~arbeit** f [doctoral] thesis

Dokument nt **-[e]s,-e** document. **D~arbericht** m documentary. **D~arfilm** m documentary film

Dolch m **-[e]s,-e** dagger

Dollar m **-s,-** dollar

dolmetsch|en vt/i (haben) interpret. **D~er(in)** m **-s,-** (f **-,-nen**) interpreter

Dom m **-[e]s,-e** cathedral

Domino nt **-s,-s** dominoes sg. **D~stein** m domino

Dompfaff m **-en,-en** bullfinch

Donau f **-** Danube

Donner m **-s** thunder. **d~n** vi (haben) thunder

Donnerstag m Thursday. **d~s** adv on Thursdays

doof adj [!] stupid

Doppel nt **-s,-** duplicate; (Tennis) doubles pl. **D~bett** nt double bed. **D~decker** m **-s,-** doubledecker [bus]. **d~deutig** adj ambiguous. **D~gänger** m **-s,-** double. **D~kinn** nt double chin. **d~klicken** vi (haben) double-click (**auf** + acc on). **D~name** m double-barrelled name. **D~punkt** m (Gram) colon. **D~stecker** m two-way adaptor. **d~t** adj double; (Boden) false; **in d~ter Ausfertigung** in duplicate; **die d~te Menge** twice the amount • adv doubly; (zweimal) twice; **d~t so viel** twice as much. **D~zimmer** nt double room

Dorf nt **-[e]s,¨-er** village. **D~bewohner** m villager

dörflich adj rural

Dorn m **-[e]s,-en** thorn. **d~ig** adj thorny

Dorsch m **-[e]s,-e** cod

dort adv there. **d~ig** adj local

Dose f **-,-n** tin, can

dösen vi (haben) doze

Dosen|milch f evaporated milk. **D~öffner** m tin or can opener. **D~pfand** nt deposit (on beer cans etc)

dosieren vt measure out

Dosis f **-, Dosen** dose

Dotter m & nt **-s,-** [egg] yolk

Dozent(in) m **-en,-en** (f **-,-nen**) (Univ) lecturer

Dr. abbr (**Doktor**) Dr

Drache m **-n,-n** dragon. **D~n** m **-s,-** kite. **D~nfliegen** nt hang-gliding

Draht m **-[e]s,¨-e** wire; **auf D~** [!] on the ball. **D~seilbahn** f cable railway

Dram|a nt **-s,-men** drama. **D~atik** f **-** drama. **D~atiker** m **-s,-** dramatist. **d~atisch** adj dramatic

dran adv [!] = **daran; gut/schlecht d~ sein** be well off/in a bad way; **ich bin d~** it's my turn

Drang m **-[e]s** urge; (Druck) pressure

dräng|eln vt/i (haben) push; (bedrängen) pester. **d~en** vt push; (bedrängen) urge; **sich d~en** crowd (**um** round) • vi (haben) push; (eilen) be urgent; **d~en auf** (+ acc) press for

dran|halten† **(sich)** vr sep hurry. **d~kommen**† vi sep (sein) have one's turn

drauf adv [!] = **darauf; d~ und dran sein** be on the point (**etw zu tun** of doing sth). **D~gänger** m **-s,-** daredevil

draußen adv outside; (im Freien) out of doors

drechseln vt (Techn) turn

Dreck m **-s** dirt; (Morast) mud

Dreh m **-s** [!] knack; **den D~ heraushaben** have got the hang of

d

it. **D~bank** f lathe. **D~bleistift** m propelling pencil. **D~buch** nt screenplay, script. **d~en** vt turn; (im Kreis) rotate; (verschlingen) twist; roll (Zigarette); shoot (Film); **lauter/leiser d~en** turn up/down; **sich d~en** turn; (im Kreis) rotate; (schnell) spin; (Wind:) change; **sich d~en um** revolve around; (sich handeln) be about • vi (haben) turn; (Wind:) change; **an etw** (dat) **d~en** turn sth. **D~stuhl** m swivel chair. **D~tür** f revolving door. **D~ung** f -,-en turn; (im Kreis) rotation. **D~zahl** f number of revolutions

drei inv adj, **D~** f -,-en three; (Sch) ≈ pass. **D~eck** nt -[e]s,-e triangle. **d~eckig** adj triangular. **d~erlei** inv adj three kinds of • pron three things. **d~fach** adj triple. **d~mal** adv three times. **D~rad** nt tricycle

dreißig inv adj thirty. **d~ste(r,s)** adj thirtieth

dreiviertel* inv adj = **drei viertel**, s. **viertel**. **D~stunde** f three-quarters of an hour

dreizehn inv adj thirteen. **d~te(r,s)** adj thirteenth

dreschen† vt thresh

dress|ieren vt train. **D~ur** f - training

dribbeln vi (haben) dribble

Drill m -[e]s (Mil) drill. **d~en** vt drill

Drillinge mpl triplets

dringlich adj urgent

Drink m -[s],-s [alcoholic] drink

drinnen adv inside

dritt adv **zu d~** in threes; **wir waren zu d~** there were three of us. **d~e(r,s)** adj third; **ein D~er** a third person. **d~el** inv adj third. **D~el** nt -s,- third. **d~ens** adv thirdly. **d~rangig** adj third-rate

Drog|e f -,-n drug. **D~enabhängige(r)** m/f drug addict. **D~erie** f -,-n chemist's shop. **D~ist** m -en,-en chemist

drohen vi (haben) threaten (**jdm** s.o.)

dröhnen vi (haben) resound; (tönen) boom

Drohung f -,-en threat

drollig adj funny; (seltsam) odd

Drops m -,- [fruit] drop

Drossel f -,-n thrush

drosseln vt (Techn) throttle; (fig) cut back

drüben adv over there

Druck[1] m -[e]s,⸚e pressure; **unter D~ setzen** (fig) pressurize

Druck[2] m -[e]s,-e printing; (Schrift, Reproduktion) print. **D~buchstabe** m block letter

drucken vt print

drücken vt/i (haben) press; (aus-) squeeze; (Schuh:) pinch; (umarmen) hug; **Preise d~** force down prices; (an Tür) **d~** push; **sich d~** [!] make oneself scarce; **sich d~ vor** (+ dat) [!] shirk. **d~d** adj heavy; (schwül) oppressive

Drucker m -s,- printer

Druckerei f -,-en printing works

Druck|fehler m misprint. **D~knopf** m press-stud. **D~luft** f compressed air. **D~sache** f printed matter. **D~schrift** f type; (Veröffentlichung) publication; **in D~schrift** in block letters pl

Druckstelle f bruise

Drüse f -,-n (Anat) gland

Dschungel m -s,- jungle

du pron (familiar address) you; **auf Du und Du** on familiar terms

Dübel m -s,- plug

Dudelsack m bagpipes pl

Duell nt -s,-e duel

Duett nt -s,-e [vocal] duet

Duft m -[e]s,⸚e fragrance, scent; (Aroma) aroma. **d~en** vi (haben) smell (**nach** of)

dulden vt tolerate; (erleiden) suffer • vi (haben) suffer

dumm adj stupid; (unklug) foolish; ([!]: lästig) awkward; **wie d~!** how annoying! **d~erweise** adv stupidly; (leider) unfortunately. **D~heit** f -,-en stupidity; (Torheit) foolishness; (Handlung) folly.

D~kopf m [!] fool.

dumpf adj dull

Düne f -,-n dune

Dung m -s manure

Düng|emittel nt fertilizer. **d~en** vt fertilize. **D~er** m -s,- fertilizer

dunk|el adj dark; (vage) vague; (fragwürdig) shady; **d~les Bier** brown ale; **im D~eln** in the dark

Dunkel|heit f - darkness. **D~kammer** f dark-room. **d~n** vi (haben) get dark

dünn adj thin; (Buch) slim; (spärlich) sparse; (schwach) weak

Dunst m **-es,¨e** mist, haze; (Dampf) vapour

dünsten vt steam

dunstig adj misty, hazy

Duo nt **-s,-s** [instrumental] duet

Duplikat nt **-[e]s,-e** duplicate

Dur nt - (Mus) major [key]

durch prep (+ acc) through; (mittels) by; **[geteilt] d~** (Math) divided by •adv **die Nacht d~** throughout the night; **d~ und d~ nass** wet through

durchaus adv absolutely; **d~ nicht** by no means

durchblättern vt sep leaf through

durchblicken vi sep (haben) look through; **d~ lassen** (fig) hint at

Durchblutung f circulation

durchbohren vt insep pierce

durchbrechen[1]† vt/i sep (haben) break [in two]

durchbrechen[2]† vt insep break through; break (Schallmauer)

durchbrennen† vi sep (sein) burn through; (Sicherung:) blow

Durchbruch m breakthrough

durchdrehen v sep •vt mince •vi (haben/sein) [!] go crazy

durchdringen† vi sep (sein) penetrate; (sich durchsetzen) get one's way. **d~d** adj penetrating; (Schrei) piercing

durcheinander adv in a muddle; (Person) confused; **d~ bringen** muddle [up]; confuse (Person); **d~ geraten** get mixed up; **d~ reden** all talk at once. **D~** nt **-s** muddle

durchfahren vi sep (sein) drive through; (Zug:) go through

Durchfahrt f journey/drive through; **auf der D~** passing through; **'D~ verboten'** 'no thoroughfare'

Durchfall m diarrhoea. **d~en**† vi sep (sein) fall through; ([!]: versagen) flop; (bei Prüfung) fail

Durchfuhr f - (Comm) transit

durchführ|bar adj feasible. **d~en** vt sep carry out

Durchgang m passage; (Sport) round; **'D~ verboten'** 'no entry'. **D~sverkehr** m through traffic

durchgeben† vt sep pass through; (übermitteln) transmit; (Radio, TV) broadcast

durchgebraten adj **gut d~** well done

durchgehen† vi sep (sein) go through; (davonlaufen) run away; (Pferd:) bolt; **jdm etw d~ lassen** let s.o. get away with sth. **d~d** adj continuous; **d~d geöffnet** open all day; **d~der Zug** through train

durchgreifen† vi sep (haben) reach through; (vorgehen) take drastic action. **d~d** adj drastic

durchhalte|n† v sep (fig) •vi (haben) hold out •vt keep up. **D~vermögen** nt stamina

durchkommen† vi sep (sein) come through; (gelangen, am Telefon) get through

durchlassen† vt sep let through

durchlässig adj permeable; (undicht) leaky

Durchlauferhitzer m **-s,-** geyser

durchlesen† vt sep read through

durchleuchten vt insep X-ray

durchlöchert adj riddled with holes

durchmachen vt sep go through; (erleiden) undergo

Durchmesser m **-s,-** diameter

durchnässt adj wet through

durchnehmen† vt sep (Sch) do

durchnummeriert adj numbered consecutively

d

durchpausen vt sep trace

durchqueren vt insep cross

Durchreiche f **-,-n** hatch

Durchreise f journey through; **auf der D~** passing through. **d~n** vi sep (sein) pass through

durchreißen† vt/i sep (sein) tear

Durchsage f **-,-n** announcement. **d~n** vt sep announce

Durchschlag m carbon copy; (Culin) colander. **d~en**† v sep • vt (Culin) rub through a sieve; **sich d~en** (fig) struggle through • vi (sein) (Sicherung:) blow

durchschlagend adj (fig) effective; (Erfolg) resounding

durchschneiden† vt sep cut

Durchschnitt m average; **im D~** on average. **d~lich** adj average • adv on average. **D~s-** prefix average

Durchschrift f carbon copy

durchsehen† v sep • vi (haben) see through • vt look through

durchseihen vt sep strain

durchsetzen vt sep force through; **sich d~** assert oneself; (Mode:) catch on

Durchsicht f check

durchsichtig adj transparent

durchsickern vi sep (sein) seep through; (Neuigkeit:) leak out

durchstehen† vt sep (fig) come through

durchstreichen† vt sep cross out

durchsuch|en vt insep search. **D~ung** f **-,-en** search

durchwachsen adj (Speck) streaky; (!: gemischt) mixed

durchwählen vi sep (haben) (Teleph) dial direct

durchweg adv without exception

durchwühlen vt insep rummage through; ransack (Haus)

Durchzug m through draught

dürfen†

• transitive & auxiliary verb

····➤ (Erlaubnis haben zu) be allowed; may, can. **etw [tun] dürfen** be allowed to do sth. **darf ich das tun?** may or can I do that? **nein, das darfst du nicht** no you may not or cannot [do that]. **er sagte mir, ich dürfte sofort gehen** he told me I could go at once. **hier darf man nicht rauchen** smoking is prohibited here. **sie darf/durfte es nicht sehen** she must not/was not allowed to see it.

····➤ (in Höflichkeitsformeln) may. **darf ich rauchen?** may I smoke? **darf/dürfte ich um diesen Tanz bitten?** may/might I have the pleasure of this dance?

····➤ **dürfte** (sollte) should, ought. **jetzt dürften sie dort angekommen sein** they should or ought to be there by now. **das dürfte nicht allzu schwer sein** that should not be too difficult. **ich hätte es nicht tun/sagen dürfen** I ought not to have done/said it

• intransitive verb

····➤ (irgendwohin gehen dürfen) be allowed to go; may go; can go. **darf ich nach Hause?** may or can I go home? **sie durfte nicht ins Theater** she was not allowed to go the theatre

dürftig adj poor; (Mahlzeit) scanty

dürr adj dry; (Boden) arid; (mager) skinny. **D~e** f **-,-n** drought

Durst m **-[e]s** thirst; **D~ haben** be thirsty. **d~ig** adj thirsty

Dusche f **-,-n** shower. **d~n** vi/r (haben) **[sich] d~n** have a shower

Düse f **-,-n** nozzle. **D~nflugzeug** nt jet

Dutzend nt **-s,-e** dozen. **d~weise** adv by the dozen

duzen vt **jdn d~** call s.o. 'du'

DVD f **-, -s** DVD

Dynam|ik f **-** dynamics sg; (fig) dynamism. **d~isch** adj dynamic; (Rente) index-linked

Dynamit nt **-es** dynamite

Dynamo m **-s,-s** dynamo

Dynastie f **-,-n** dynasty

D-Zug /'de:-/ m express [train]

Ee

Ebbe f **-,-n** low tide

eben adj level; (glatt) smooth; **zu e~er Erde** on the ground floor • adv just; (genau) exactly; **e~ noch** only just; (gerade vorhin) just now; **das ist es e~!** that's just it! **E~bild** nt image

Ebene f **-,-n** (Geog) plain; (Geometry) plane; (fig: Niveau) level

eben|falls adv also; **danke, e~falls** thank you, [the] same to you. **E~holz** nt ebony. **e~so** adv just the same; (ebenso sehr) just as much; **e~so gut** just as good; adv just as well; **e~so sehr** just as much; **e~so viel** just as much/many; **e~so wenig** just as little/few; (noch) no more

Eber m **-s,-** boar

ebnen vt level; (fig) smooth

Echo nt **-s,-s** echo

echt adj genuine, real; authentic • adv [!] really; typically. **E~heit** f **-** authenticity

Eck|ball m (Sport) corner. **E~e** f **-,-n** corner; **um die E~e bringen** [!] bump off. **e~ig** adj angular; (Klammern) square; (unbeholfen) awkward. **E~zahn** m canine tooth

Ecu, ECU /e'ky:/ m **-[s],-[s]** ecu

edel adj noble; (wertvoll) precious; (fein) fine. **e~mütig** adj magnanimous. **E~stahl** m stainless steel. **E~stein** m precious stone

Efeu m **-s** ivy

Effekt m **-[e]s,-e** effect. **E~en** pl securities. **e~iv** adj actual; (wirksam) effective

EG f **-** abbr (**Europäische Gemeinschaft**) EC

egal adj **das ist mir e~** [!] it's all the same to me • adv **e~ wie/wo** no matter how/where

Egge f **-,-n** harrow

Ego|ismus m **-** selfishness. **E~ist(in)** m **-en,-en** (f **-,-nen**) egoist. **e~istisch** adj selfish

eh adv (Aust, [!]) anyway

ehe conj before; **ehe nicht** until

Ehe f **-,-n** marriage. **E~bett** nt double bed. **E~bruch** m adultery. **E~frau** f wife. **e~lich** adj marital; (Recht) conjugal; (Kind) legitimate

ehemalig adj former. **e~s** adv formerly

Ehe|mann m (pl **-männer**) husband. **E~paar** nt married couple

eher adv earlier, sooner; (lieber, vielmehr) rather; (mehr) more

Ehering m wedding ring

Ehr|e f **-,-n** honour. **e~en** vt honour. **e~enamtlich** adj honorary • adv in an honorary capacity. **E~engast** m guest of honour. **e~enhaft** adj honourable. **E~ensache** f point of honour. **E~enwort** nt word of honour. **e~erbietig** adj deferential. **E~furcht** f reverence; (Scheu) awe. **e~fürchtig** adj reverent.

E~gefühl nt sense of honour. **E~geiz** m ambition. **e~geizig** adj ambitious. **e~lich** adj honest; **e~lich gesagt** to be honest. **E~lichkeit** f - honesty. **e~los** adj dishonourable. **e~würdig** adj venerable; (als Anrede) Reverend

Ei nt **-[e]s,-er** egg

Eibe f **-,-n** yew

Eiche f **-,-n** oak. **E~l** f **-,-n** acorn

eichen vt standardize

Eichhörnchen nt **-s,-** squirrel

Eid m **-[e]s,-e** oath

Eidechse f **-,-n** lizard

eidlich adj sworn • adv on oath

Eidotter m & nt egg yolk

Eier|becher m egg-cup. **E~kuchen** m pancake; (Omelett) omelette. **E~schale** f eggshell. **E~schnee** m beaten egg-white. **E~stock** m ovary

Eifer m **-s** eagerness. **E~sucht** f jealousy. **e~süchtig** adj jealous

eifrig adj eager

Eigelb nt **-[e]s,-e** [egg] yolk

eigen adj own; (typisch) characteristic (dat of); (seltsam) odd; (genau) particular. **E~art** f peculiarity. **e~artig** adj peculiar. **e~händig** adj personal; (Unterschrift) own. **E~heit** f **-,-en** peculiarity. **E~name** m proper name. **e~nützig** adj selfish. **e~s** adv specially. **E~schaft** f **-,-en** quality; (Phys) property; (Merkmal) characteristic; (Funktion) capacity. **E~schaftswort** nt (pl **-wörter**) adjective. **E~sinn** m obstinacy. **e~sinnig** adj obstinate

eigentlich adj actual, real; (wahr) true • adv actually, really; (streng genommen) strictly speaking

Eigen|tor nt own goal. **E~tum** nt **-s** property. **E~tümer(in)** m **-s,-** (f **-,-nen**) owner. **E~tumswohnung** f freehold flat. **e~willig** adj self-willed; (Stil) highly individual

eignen (sich) vr be suitable

Eil|brief m express letter. **E~e** f - hurry; **E~e haben** be in a hurry; (Sache:) be urgent. **e~en** vi (sein) hurry • (haben) (drängen) be urgent. **e~ig** adj hurried; (dringend) urgent; **es e~ig haben** be in a hurry. **E~zug** m semi-fast train

Eimer m **-s,-** bucket; (Abfall-) bin

ein

• indefinite article

····➤ a, (vor Vokal) an. **ein Kleid/Apfel/Hotel/Mensch** a dress/an apple/a[n] hotel/a human being. **so ein** such a. **was für ein ...** (Frage) what kind of a ... ? (Ausruf) what a ... !

• adjective

····➤ (Ziffer) one. **eine Minute** one minute. **wir haben nur eine Stunde** we only have an/(betont) one hour. **eines Tages/Abends** one day/evening

····➤ (derselbe) the same. **einer Meinung sein** be of the same opinion. **mit jdm in einem Zimmer schlafen** sleep in the same room as s.o.

einander pron one another

Einäscherung f **-,-en** cremation

einatmen vt/i sep (haben) inhale, breathe in

Einbahnstraße f one-way street

einbalsamieren vt sep embalm

Einband m binding

Einbau m installation; (Montage) fitting. **e~en** vt sep install; (montieren) fit. **E~küche** f fitted kitchen

einbegriffen pred adj included

Einberufung f call-up

Einbettzimmer nt single room

einbeulen vt sep dent

einbeziehen† vt sep **[mit] e~** include; (berücksichtigen) take into account

einbiegen† vi sep (sein) turn

einbild|en vt sep **sich** (dat) **etw e~en** imagine sth; **sich** (dat) **viel e~en** be conceited. **E~ung** f imagination; (Dünkel) conceit. **E~ungskraft** f imagination

einblenden vt sep fade in

Einblick m insight

einbrech|en† vi sep (haben/sein) break in; **bei uns ist eingebrochen worden** we have been burgled. **E~er** m burglar

einbringen† vt sep get in; bring in (Geld)

Einbruch m burglary; **bei E~ der Nacht** at nightfall

einbürger|n vt sep naturalize. **E~ung** f - naturalization

einchecken /-tʃɛkən/ vt/i sep (haben) check in

eindecken (sich) vr sep stock up

eindeutig adj unambiguous; (deutlich) clear

eindicken vt sep (Culin) thicken

eindringen† vi sep (sein) **e~en in** (+ acc) penetrate into; (mit Gewalt) force one's/(Wasser:) its way into; (Mil) invade

Eindruck m impression

eindrücken vt sep crush

eindrucksvoll adj impressive

ein|e(r,s) pron one; (jemand) someone; (man) one, you

einebnen vt sep level

eineiig adj (Zwillinge) identical

eineinhalb inv adj one and a half; **e~ Stunden** an hour and a half

Einelternfamilie f one-parent family

einengen vt sep restrict

Einer m **-s,-** (Math) unit. **e~** pron s. **eine(r,s). e~lei** inv adj • attrib adj one kind of; (eintönig, einheitlich) the same • pred adj ⓘ immaterial; **es ist mir e~lei** it's all the same to me. **e~seits** adv on the one hand

einfach adj simple; (Essen) plain; (Faden, Fahrt) single; **e~er Soldat** private. **E~heit** f - simplicity

einfädeln vt sep thread; (fig; arrangieren) arrange

einfahr|en† v sep • vi (sein) arrive; (Zug:) pull in • vt (Auto) run in. **E~t** f arrival; (Eingang) entrance, way in; (Auffahrt) drive; (Autobahn-) access road; **keine E~t** no entry

Einfall m idea; (Mil) invasion. **e~en**† vi sep (sein) collapse; (eindringen) invade; **jdm e~en** occur to s.o.; **was fällt ihm ein!** what does he think he is doing!

Einfalt f - naïvety

einfarbig adj of one colour; (Stoff, Kleid) plain

einfass|en vt sep edge; set (Edelstein). **E~ung** f border, edging

einfetten vt sep grease

Einfluss m influence. **e~reich** adj influential

einförmig adj monotonous. **E~keit** f - monotony

einfrieren† vt/i sep (sein) freeze

einfügen vt sep insert; (einschieben) interpolate; **sich e~** fit in

einfühlsam adj sensitive

Einfuhr f **-,-en** import

einführ|en vt sep introduce; (einstecken) insert; (einweisen) initiate; (Comm) import. **e~end** adj introductory. **E~ung** f introduction; (Einweisung) initiation

Eingabe f petition; (Computer) input

Eingang m entrance, way in; (Ankunft) arrival

eingebaut adj built-in; (Schrank) fitted

eingeben† vt sep hand in; (Computer) feed in

eingebildet adj imaginary; (überheblich) conceited

Eingeborene(r) m/f native

eingehen† v sep • vi (sein) come in; (ankommen) arrive; (einlaufen) shrink; (sterben) die; (Zeitung, Firma:) fold; **auf etw** (acc) **e~** go into sth; (annehmen) agree to sth • vt enter into; contract (Ehe); make (Wette); take (Risiko)

eingemacht adj (Culin) bottled

eingenommen pred adj (fig) taken (**von** with); prejudiced (**gegen** against)

eingeschneit adj snowbound

e

eingeschrieben adj registered

Einge|ständnis nt admission. **e~stehen**† vt sep admit

eingetragen adj registered

Eingeweide pl bowels, entrails

eingewöhnen (sich) vr sep settle in

e

eingießen† vt sep pour in; (einschenken) pour

eingleisig adj single-track

eingliederIn vt sep integrate. **E~ung** f integration

eingravieren vt sep engrave

eingreifen† vi sep (haben) intervene. **E~** nt **-s** intervention

Eingriff m intervention; (Med) operation

einhaken vt/r sep **jdn e~** od **sich bei jdm e~** take someone's arm

einhalten† v sep •vt keep; (befolgen) observe •vi (haben) stop

einhändigen vt sep hand in

einhängen vt sep hang; put down (Hörer)

einheimisch adj local; (eines Landes) native; (Comm) homeproduced. **E~e(r)** m/f local, native

Einheit f **-,-en** unity; (Maß-, Mil) unit. **e~lich** adj uniform. **E~spreis** m standard price; (Fahrpreis) flat fare

einholen vt sep catch up with; (aufholen) make up for; (erbitten) seek; (einkaufen) buy

einhüllen vt sep wrap

einhundert inv adj one hundred

einig adj united; [**sich** (dat)] **e~ sein** be in agreement

einig|e(r,s) pron some; (ziemlich viel) quite a lot of; (substantivisch) **e~e** pl some; (mehrere) several; (ziemlich viele) quite a lot; **e~es** sg some things; **vor e~er Zeit** some time ago

einigen vt unite; unify (Land); **sich e~** come to an agreement

einigermaßen adv to some extent; (ziemlich) fairly; (ziemlich gut) fairly well

Einigkeit f **-** unity; (Übereinstimmung) agreement

einjährig adj one-year-old; **e~e Pflanze** annual

einkalkulieren vt sep take into account

einkassieren vt sep collect

Einkauf m purchase; (Einkaufen) shopping; **Einkäufe machen** do some shopping. **e~en** vt sep buy; **e~en gehen** go shopping. **E~swagen** m shopping trolley

einklammern vt sep bracket

Einklang m harmony; **in E~ stehen** be in accord (**mit** with)

einkleben vt sep stick in

einkleiden vt sep fit out

einklemmen vt sep clamp

einkochen v sep •vi (sein) boil down •vt preserve, bottle

Einkommen nt **-s** income. **E~[s]steuer** f income tax

Einkünfte pl income sg; (Einnahmen) revenue sg

einlad|en† vt sep load; (auffordern) invite; (bezahlen für) treat. **E~ung** f invitation

Einlage f enclosure; (Schuh-) arch support; (Programm-) interlude; (Comm) investment; (Bank-) deposit; **Suppe mit E~** soup with noodles/ dumplings

Ein|lass m **-es** admittance. **e~lassen**† vt sep let in; run (Bad, Wasser); **sich auf etw** (acc) **e~lassen** get involved in sth

einleben (sich) vr sep settle in

Einlege|arbeit f inlaid work. **e~n** vt sep put in; lay in (Vorrat); lodge (Protest); (einfügen) insert; (Auto) engage (Gang); (Culin) pickle; (marinieren) marinade; **eine Pause e~n** have a break. **E~sohle** f insole

einleit|en vt sep initiate; (eröffnen) begin. **E~ung** f introduction

einleuchten vi sep (haben) be clear (dat to). **e~d** adj convincing

einliefer|n vt sep take (**ins**

Krankenhaus to hospital). **E~ung** f admission

einlösen vt sep cash (Scheck); redeem (Pfand); (fig) keep

einmachen vt sep preserve

einmal adv once; (eines Tages) one or some day; **noch/schon e~** again/ before; **noch e~ so teuer** twice as expensive; **auf e~** at the same time; (plötzlich) suddenly; **nicht e~** not even. **E~eins** nt - [multiplication] tables pl. **e~ig** adj (einzigartig) unique; ([!]: großartig) fantastic

einmarschieren vi sep (sein) march in

einmisch|en (sich) vr sep interfere. **E~ung** f interference

Einnahme f **-,-n** taking; (Mil) capture; **E~n** pl income sg; (Einkünfte) revenue sg; (Comm) receipts; (eines Ladens) takings

einnehmen† vt sep take; have (Mahlzeit); (Mil) capture; take up (Platz)

einordnen vt sep put in its proper place; (klassifizieren) classify; **sich e~** fit in; (Auto) get in lane

einpacken vt sep pack

einparken vt sep park

einpflanzen vt sep plant; implant (Organ)

einplanen vt sep allow for

einprägen vt sep impress (**jdm** [up]on s.o.); **sich** (dat) **etw e~en** memorize sth

einrahmen vt sep frame

einrasten vi sep (sein) engage

einräumen vt sep put away; (zugeben) admit; (zugestehen) grant

einrechnen vt sep include

einreden v sep •vt **jdm/sich** (dat) **etw e~** persuade s.o./oneself of sth

einreiben† vt sep rub (**mit** with)

einreichen vt sep submit; **die Scheidung e~** file for divorce

Einreih|er m **-s,-** single-breasted suit. **e~ig** adj single-breasted

Einreise f entry. **e~n** vi sep (sein) enter (**nach Irland** Ireland)

einrenken vt sep (Med) set

einricht|en vt sep fit out; (möblieren) furnish; (anordnen) arrange; (Med) set (Bruch); (eröffnen) set up; **sich e~en** furnish one's home; (sich einschränken) economize; (sich vorbereiten) prepare (**auf** + acc for). **E~ung** f furnishing; (Möbel) furnishings pl; (Techn) equipment; (Vorrichtung) device; (Eröffnung) setting up; (Institution) institution; (Gewohnheit) practice

einrosten vi sep (sein) rust; (fig) get rusty

eins inv adj & pron one; **noch e~** one other thing; **mir ist alles e~** [!] it's all the same to me. **E~** f **-,-en** one; (Sch) ≈ A

einsam adj lonely; (allein) solitary; (abgelegen) isolated. **E~keit** f - loneliness; solitude; isolation

einsammeln vt sep collect

Einsatz m use; (Mil) mission; (Wett-) stake; (E~teil) insert; **im E~** in action

einschalt|en vt sep switch on; (einschieben) interpolate; (fig: beteiligen) call in; **sich e~en** (fig) intervene. **E~quote** f (TV) viewing figures pl; ≈ ratings pl

einschätzen vt sep assess; (bewerten) rate

einschenken vt sep pour

einscheren vi sep (sein) pull in

einschicken vt sep send in

einschieben† vt sep push in; (einfügen) insert

einschiff|en (sich) vr sep embark. **E~ung** f - embarkation

einschlafen† vi sep (sein) go to sleep; (aufhören) peter out

einschläfern vt sep lull to sleep; (betäuben) put out; (töten) put to sleep. **e~d** adj soporific

Einschlag m impact. **e~en**† v sep •vt knock in; (zerschlagen) smash; (drehen) turn; take (Weg); take up (Laufbahn) •vi (haben) hit/(Blitz:)

e

strike (**in etw** acc sth); (Erfolg haben) be a hit

einschleusen vt sep infiltrate

einschließ|en† vt sep lock in; (umgeben) enclose; (einkreisen) surround; (einbeziehen) include; **sich e~en** lock oneself in; **Bedienung eingeschlossen** service included. **e~lich** adv inclusive • prep (+ gen) including

e

einschneiden† vt/i sep (haben) **[in] etw** (acc) **e~** cut into sth. **e~d** adj (fig) drastic

Einschnitt m cut; (Med) incision; (Lücke) gap; (fig) decisive event

einschränk|en vt sep restrict; (reduzieren) cut back; **sich e~en** economize. **E~ung** f **-,-en** restriction; (Reduzierung) reduction; (Vorbehalt) reservation

Einschreib|[e]brief m registered letter. **e~en†** vt sep enter; register (Brief); **sich e~en** put one's name down; (sich anmelden) enrol. **E~en** nt registered letter/packet; **als** od **per E~en** by registered post

einschüchtern vt sep intimidate

Einsegnung f **-,-en** confirmation

einsehen† vt sep inspect; (lesen) consult; (begreifen) see

einseitig adj one-sided; (Pol) unilateral • adv on one side; (fig) one-sidedly; (Pol) unilaterally

einsenden† vt sep send in

einsetzen v sep • vt put in; (einfügen) insert; (verwenden) use; put on (Zug); call out (Truppen); (Mil) deploy; (ernennen) appoint; (wetten) stake; (riskieren) risk • vi (haben) start; (Winter, Regen:) set in

Einsicht f insight; (Verständnis) understanding; (Vernunft) reason. **e~ig** adj understanding

Einsiedler m hermit

einsinken† vi sep (sein) sink in

einspannen vt sep harness; **jdn e~** [!] rope s.o. in

einsparen vt sep save

einsperren vt sep shut/(im Gefängnis) lock up

einsprachig adj monolingual

einspritzen vt sep inject

Einspruch m objection; **E~ erheben** object; (Jur) appeal

einspurig adj single-track; (Auto) single-lane

einst adv once; (Zukunft) one day

Einstand m (Tennis) deuce

einstecken vt sep put in; post (Brief); (Electr) plug in; ([!]: behalten) pocket; ([!]: hinnehmen) take; suffer (Niederlage); **etw e~** put sth in one's pocket

einsteigen† vi sep (sein) get in; (in Bus/Zug) get on

einstell|en vt sep put in; (anstellen) employ; (aufhören) stop; (regulieren) adjust, set; (Optik) focus; tune (Motor, Zündung); tune to (Sender); **sich e~en** turn up; (Schwierigkeiten:) arise; **sich e~en auf** (+ acc) adjust to; (sich vorbereiten) prepare for. **E~ung** f employment; (Regulierung) adjustment; (TV, Auto) tuning; (Haltung) attitude

einstig adj former

einstimmig adj unanimous. **E~keit** f - unanimity

einstöckig adj single-storey

einstudieren vt sep rehearse

einstufen vt sep classify

Ein|sturz m collapse. **e~stürzen** vi sep (sein) collapse

einstweilen adv for the time being; (inzwischen) meanwhile

eintasten vt sep key in

eintauchen vt/i sep (sein) dip in

eintauschen vt sep exchange

eintausend inv adj one thousand

einteil|en vt sep divide (**in** + acc into); (Biology) classify; **sich** (dat) **seine Zeit gut e~en** organize one's time well. **e~ig** adj one-piece. **E~ung** f division

eintönig adj monotonous. **E~keit** f - monotony

Eintopf m, **E~gericht** nt stew

Eintracht f - harmony

Eintrag m **-[e]s,⸚e** entry. **e∼en**† vt sep enter; (Admin) register; **sich e∼en** put one's name down

einträglich adj profitable

Eintragung f **-,-en** registration

eintreffen† vi sep (sein) arrive; (fig) come true

eintreiben† vt sep drive in; (einziehen) collect

eintreten† v sep • vi (sein) enter; (geschehen) occur; **in einen Klub e∼** join a club; **e∼ für** (fig) stand up for • vt kick in

Eintritt m entrance; (zu Veranstaltung) admission; (Beitritt) joining; (Beginn) beginning. **E∼skarte** f [admission] ticket

einüben vt sep practise

einundachtzig inv adj eighty-one

Einvernehmen nt **-s** understanding; (Übereinstimmung) agreement

einverstanden adj **e∼ sein** agree

Einverständnis nt agreement; (Zustimmung) consent

Einwand m **-[e]s,⸚e** objection

Einwander|er m immigrant. **e∼n** vi sep (sein) immigrate. **E∼ung** f immigration

einwandfrei adj perfect

einwärts adv inwards

einwechseln vt sep change

einwecken vt sep preserve, bottle

Einweg- prefix non-returnable

einweichen vt sep soak

einweih|en vt sep inaugurate; (Relig) consecrate; (einführen) initiate; **in ein Geheimnis e∼en** let into a secret. **E∼ung** f **-,-en** inauguration; consecration; initiation

einweisen† vt sep direct; (einführen) initiate; **ins Krankenhaus e∼** send to hospital

einwerfen† vt sep insert; post (Brief); (Sport) throw in

einwickeln vt sep wrap [up]

einwillig|en vi sep (haben) consent, agree (**in** + acc to). **E∼ung** f **-** consent

Einwohner|(in) m **-s,-** (f **-,-nen**) inhabitant. **E∼zahl** f population

Einwurf m interjection; (Einwand) objection; (Sport) throw-in; (Münz-) slot

Einzahl f (Gram) singular

einzahl|en vt sep pay in. **E∼ung** f payment; (Einlage) deposit

einzäunen vt sep fence in

Einzel nt **-s,-** (Tennis) singles pl. **E∼bett** nt single bed. **E∼gänger** m **-s,-** loner. **E∼haft** f solitary confinement. **E∼handel** m retail trade. **E∼händler** m retailer. **E∼haus** nt detached house. **E∼heit** f **-,-en** detail. **E∼karte** f single ticket. **E∼kind** nt only child

einzeln adj single; (individuell) individual; (gesondert) separate; odd (Handschuh, Socken); **e∼e Fälle** some cases. **E∼e(r,s)** pron **der/die E∼e** the individual; **E∼e** pl some; **im E∼en** in detail

Einzel|teil nt [component] part. **E∼zimmer** nt single room

einziehen† v sep • vt pull in; draw in (Atem, Krallen); (Zool, Techn) retract; indent (Zeile); (aus dem Verkehr ziehen) withdraw; (beschlagnahmen) confiscate; (eintreiben) collect; make (Erkundigungen); (Mil) call up • vi (sein) enter; (umziehen) move in; (eindringen) penetrate

einzig adj only; (einmalig) unique; **eine e∼e Frage** a a single question • adv only; **e∼ und allein** solely. **E∼e(r,s)** pron **der/die/das E∼e** the only one; **ein/kein E∼er** a/not a single one; **das E∼e, was mich stört** the only thing that bothers me

Eis nt **-es** ice; (Speise-) ice-cream; **Eis am Stiel** ice lolly; **Eis laufen** skate. **E∼bahn** f ice rink. **E∼bär** m polar bear. **E∼becher** m ice-cream sundae. **E∼berg** m iceberg. **E∼diele** f ice-cream parlour

Eisen nt **-s,-** iron. **E∼bahn** f railway

eisern adj iron; (fest) resolute; **e∼er**

e

Vorhang (Theat) safety curtain; (Pol) Iron Curtain

Eis|fach nt freezer compartment. **e~gekühlt** adj chilled. **e~ig** adj icy. **E~kaffee** m iced coffee. **E~lauf** m skating. **E~läufer(in)** m(f) skater. **E~pickel** m ice-axe. **E~scholle** f ice-floe. **E~vogel** m kingfisher. **E~würfel** m icecube. **E~zapfen** m icicle. **E~zeit** f ice age

eitel adj vain; (rein) pure. **E~keit** f - vanity

Eiter m **-s** pus. **e~n** vi (haben) discharge pus

Eiweiß nt **-es,-e** egg-white

Ekel m **-s** disgust; (Widerwille) revulsion. **e~haft** adj nauseating; (widerlich) repulsive. **e~n** vt/i (haben) **mich** od **mir e~t [es] davor** it makes me feel sick •vr **sich e~n vor** (+ dat) find repulsive

eklig adj disgusting, repulsive

Ekzem nt **-s,-e** eczema

elastisch adj elastic; (federnd) springy; (fig) flexible

Elch m **-[e]s,-e** elk

Elefant m **-en,-en** elephant

elegan|t adj elegant. **E~z** f - elegance

Elektri|ker m **-s,-** electrician. **e~sch** adj electric

Elektrizität f - electricity. **E~swerk** nt power station

Elektr|oartikel mpl electrical appliances. **E~ode** f **-,-n** electrode. **E~onik** f - electronics sg. **e~onisch** adj electronic

Elend nt **-s** misery; (Armut) poverty. **e~** adj miserable; (krank) poorly; (gemein) contemptible. **E~sviertel** nt slum

elf inv adj, **E~** f **-,-en** eleven

Elfe f **-,-n** fairy

Elfenbein nt ivory

Elfmeter m (Fußball) penalty

elfte(r,s) adj eleventh

Ell[en]bogen m elbow

Ellip|se f **-,-n** ellipse. **e~tisch** adj elliptical

Elsass nt - Alsace

elsässisch adj Alsatian

Elster f **-,-n** magpie

elter|lich adj parental. **E~n** pl parents. **e~nlos** adj orphaned. **E~nteil** m parent

Email /e'mai/ nt **-s,-s**, **E~le** f **-,-n** enamel

E-Mail /'i:me:l/ f **-,-s** e-mail; e-mail message

Emanzi|pation /-'tsi̯o:n/ f - emancipation. **e~piert** adj emancipated

Embargo nt **-s,-s** embargo

Embryo m **-s,-s** embryo

Emigr|ant(in) m **-en,-en** (f **-,-nen**) emigrant. **E~ation** f - emigration. **e~ieren** vi (sein) emigrate

Empfang m **-[e]s,¨-e** reception; (Erhalt) receipt; **in E~ nehmen** receive; (annehmen) accept. **e~en**† vt receive; (Biology) conceive

Empfäng|er m **-s,-** recipient; (Post-) addressee; (Zahlungs-) payee; (Radio, TV) receiver. **E~nis** f - (Biology) conception

Empfängnisverhütung f contraception. **E~smittel** nt contraceptive

Empfangs|bestätigung f receipt. **E~dame** f receptionist. **E~halle** f [hotel] foyer

empfehl|en† vt recommend. **E~ung** f **-,-en** recommendation; (Gruß) regards pl

empfind|en† vt feel. **e~lich** adj sensitive (**gegen** to); (zart) delicate. **E~lichkeit** f - sensitivity; delicacy; tenderness; touchiness. **E~ung** f **-,-en** sensation; (Regung) feeling

empor adv (literarisch) up[wards]

empören vt incense; **sich e~** be indignant; (sich auflehnen) rebel

Emporkömmling m **-s,-e** upstart

empör|t adj indignant. **E~ung** f - indignation; (Auflehnung) rebellion

Ende nt **-s,-n** end; (eines Films, Romans) ending; (!: Stück) bit; **zu E~ sein** be finished; **etw zu E~ schreiben** finish writing sth; **am E~** at the end; (schließlich) in the end; (!: vielleicht) perhaps; (!: erschöpft) at the end of one's tether

end|en vi (haben) end. **e~gültig** adj final; (bestimmt) definite

Endivie /-i̯ə/ f **-,-n** endive

end|lich adv at last, finally; (schließlich) in the end. **e~los** adj endless. **E~station** f terminus. **E~ung** f **-,-en** (Gram) ending

Energie f **-** energy

energisch adj resolute; (nachdrücklich) vigorous

eng adj narrow; (beengt) cramped; (anliegend) tight; (nah) close; **e~ anliegend** tight-fitting

Engagement /ãgaʒə'mã:/ nt **-s,-s** (Theat) engagement; (fig) commitment

Engel m **-s,-** angel

England nt **-s** England

Engländer m **-s,-** Englishman; (Techn) monkey-wrench; **die E~** the English pl. **E~in** f **-,-nen** Englishwoman

englisch adj English. **E~** nt **-[s]** (Lang) English; **auf E~** in English

Engpass m (fig) bottleneck

en gros /ã'gro:/ adv wholesale

Enkel m **-s,-** grandson; **E~** pl grandchildren. **E~in** f **-,-nen** granddaughter. **E~kind** nt grandchild. **E~sohn** m grandson. **E~tochter** f granddaughter

Ensemble /ã'sã:bəl/ nt **-s,-s** ensemble; (Theat) company

entart|en vi (sein) degenerate. **e~et** adj degenerate

entbehren vt do without; (vermissen) miss

entbind|en† vt release (**von** from); (Med) deliver (**von** of) • vi (haben) give birth. **E~ung** f delivery. **E~ungsstation** f maternity ward

entdeck|en vt discover. **E~er** m **-s,-** discoverer; (Forscher) explorer. **E~ung** f **-,-en** discovery

Ente f **-,-n** duck

entehren vt dishonour

enteignen vt dispossess; expropriate (Eigentum)

enterben vt disinherit

Enterich m **-s,-e** drake

entfallen† vi (sein) not apply; **auf jdn e~** be s.o.'s share

entfern|en vt remove; **sich e~en** leave. **e~t** adj distant; (schwach) vague; **zwei Kilometer e~t** two kilometres away; **e~t verwandt** distantly related. **E~ung** f **-,-en** removal; (Abstand) distance; (Reichweite) range

entfliehen† vi (sein) escape

entfremden vt alienate

entfrosten vt defrost

entführ|en vt abduct, kidnap; hijack (Flugzeug). **E~er** m abductor, kidnapper; hijacker. **E~ung** f abduction, kidnapping; hijacking

entgegen adv towards • prep (+ dat) contrary to. **e~gehen**† vi sep (sein) (+ dat) go to meet; (fig) be heading for. **e~gesetzt** adj opposite; (gegensätzlich) opposing. **e~kommen**† vi sep (sein) (+ dat) come to meet; (zukommen auf) come towards; (fig) oblige. **E~kommen** nt **-s** helpfulness; (Zugeständnis) concession. **e~kommend** adj approaching; (Verkehr) oncoming; (fig) obliging. **e~nehmen**† vt sep accept. **e~wirken** vi sep (haben) (+ dat) counteract; (fig) oppose

entgegn|en vt reply (**auf** + acc to). **E~ung** f **-,-en** reply

entgehen† vi sep (sein) (+ dat) escape; **jdm e~** (unbemerkt bleiben) escape s.o.'s notice; **sich** (dat) **etw e~ lassen** miss sth

Entgelt nt **-[e]s** payment; **gegen E~** for money

entgleis|en vi (sein) be derailed; (fig) make a gaffe. **E~ung** f **-,-en** derailment; (fig) gaffe

entgräten vt fillet, bone

Enthaarungsmittel nt depilatory

enthalt|en† vt contain; **in etw** (dat) **e~en sein** be contained/(eingeschlossen) included in sth; **sich der Stimme e~en** (Pol) abstain. **e~sam** adj abstemious. **E~ung** f (Pol) abstention

enthaupten vt behead

e

entheben† vt **jdn seines Amtes e~** relieve s.o. of his post

Enthüllung f **-,-en** revelation

Enthusias|mus m - enthusiasm. **E~t** m **-en,-en** enthusiast

entkernen vt stone; core (Apfel)

entkleiden vt undress; **sich e~en** undress

entkommen† vi (sein) escape

entkorken vt uncork

entladen† vt unload; (Electr) discharge; **sich e~** discharge; (Gewitter:) break; (Zorn:) explode

entlang adv & prep (+ preceding acc or following dat) along; **die Straße e~** along the road; **an etw** (dat) **e~** along sth. **e~fahren**† vi sep (sein) drive along. **e~gehen**† vi sep (sein) walk along

entlarven vt unmask

entlass|en† vt dismiss; (aus Krankenhaus) discharge; (aus der Haft) release. **E~ung** f **-,-en** dismissal; discharge; release

entlast|en vt relieve the strain on; ease (Gewissen, Verkehr); relieve (**von** of); (Jur) exonerate. **E~ung** f - relief; exoneration

entlaufen† vi (sein) run away

entleeren vt empty

entlegen adj remote

entlohnen vt pay

entlüft|en vt ventilate. **E~er** m **-s,-** extractor fan. **E~ung** f ventilation

entmündigen vt declare incapable of managing his own affairs

entmutigen vt discourage

entnehmen† vt take (dat from); (schließen) gather (dat from)

entpuppen (sich) vr (fig) turn out (**als etw** to be sth)

entrahmt adj skimmed

entrichten vt pay

entrinnen† vi (sein) escape

entrüst|en vt fill with indignation; **sich e~en** be indignant (**über** + acc at). **e~et** adj indignant. **E~ung** f - indignation

entsaft|en vt extract the juice from. **E~er** m **-s,-** juice extractor

entsagen vi (haben) (+ dat) renounce

entschädig|en vt compensate. **E~ung** f **-,-en** compensation

entschärfen vt defuse

entscheid|en† vt/i (haben) decide; **sich e~en** decide; (Sache:) be decided. **e~end** adj decisive; (kritisch) crucial. **E~ung** f decision

entschließen† **(sich)** vr decide, make up one's mind; **sich anders e~** change one's mind

entschlossen adj determined; (energisch) resolute; **kurz e~** without hesitation. **E~heit** f - determination

Entschluss m decision

entschlüsseln vt decode

entschuld|bar adj excusable. **e~igen** vt excuse; **sich e~igen** apologize (**bei** to); **e~igen Sie [bitte]!** sorry! (bei Frage) excuse me. **E~igung** f **-,-en** apology; (Ausrede) excuse; **um E~igung bitten** apologize

entsetz|en vt horrify. **E~en** nt **-s** horror. **e~lich** adj horrible; (schrecklich) terrible

Entsorgung f - waste disposal

entspann|en vt relax; **sich e~en** relax; (Lage:) ease. **E~ung** f - relaxation; easing; (Pol) détente

entsprech|en† vi (haben) (+ dat) correspond to; (übereinstimmen) agree with. **e~end** adj corresponding; (angemessen) appropriate; (zuständig) relevant • adv correspondingly; appropriately; (demgemäß) accordingly • prep (+ dat) in accordance with

entspringen† vi (sein) (Fluss:) rise; (fig) arise, spring (dat from)

entstammen vi (sein) come/ (abstammen) be descended (dat from)

entsteh|en† vi (sein) come into being; (sich bilden) form; (sich entwickeln) develop; (Brand:) start; (stammen) originate. **E~ung** f - origin; formation; development

entstell|en vt disfigure; (verzerren) distort. **E~ung** f disfigurement; distortion

entstört adj (Electr) suppressed

enttäusch|en vt disappoint. **E~ung** f disappointment

entwaffnen vt disarm

entwässer|n vt drain. **E~ung** f - drainage

entweder conj & adv either

entwerfen† vt design; (aufsetzen) draft; (skizzieren) sketch

entwert|en vt devalue; (ungültig machen) cancel. **E~er** m **-s,-** ticket-cancelling machine. **E~ung** f devaluation; cancelling

entwick|eln vt develop; **sich e~eln** develop. **E~lung** f **-,-en** development; (Biology) evolution. **E~lungsland** nt developing country

entwöhnen vt wean (gen from); cure (Süchtige)

entwürdigend adj degrading

Entwurf m design; (Konzept) draft; (Skizze) sketch

entwurzeln vt uproot

entzie|hen† vt take away (dat from); **jdm den Führerschein e~hen** disqualify s.o. from driving; **sich e~hen** (+ dat) withdraw from. **E~hungskur** f treatment for drug/alcohol addiction

entziffern vt decipher

Entzug m withdrawal; (Vorenthaltung) deprivation

entzünd|en vt ignite; (anstecken) light; (fig: erregen) inflame; **sich e~en** ignite; (Med) become inflamed. **e~et** adj (Med) inflamed. **e~lich** adj inflammable. **E~ung** f (Med) inflammation

entzwei adj broken

Enzian m **-s,-e** gentian

Enzyklo|pädie f **-,-en** encyclopaedia. **e~pädisch** adj encyclopaedic

Enzym nt **-s,-e** enzyme

Epidemie f **-,-n** epidemic

Epi|lepsie f - epilepsy. **E~leptiker(in)** m **-s,-** (f **-,-nen**) epileptic. **e~leptisch** adj epileptic

Epilog m **-s,-e** epilogue

Episode f **-,-n** episode

Epoche f **-,-n** epoch

Epos nt -, **Epen** epic

er pron he; (Ding, Tier) it

erachten vt consider (**für nötig** necessary). **E~** nt **-s meines E~s** in my opinion

erbarmen (sich) vr have pity/ (Gott:) mercy (gen on). **E~** nt **-s** pity; mercy

erbärmlich adj wretched

erbauen vt build; (fig) edify; **nicht erbaut von** [!] not pleased about

Erbe[1] m **-n,-n** heir

Erbe[2] nt **-s** inheritance; (fig) heritage. **e~n** vt inherit

erbeuten vt get; (Mil) capture

Erbfolge f (Jur) succession

erbieten† **(sich)** vr offer (**zu** to)

Erbin f **-,-nen** heiress

erbitten† vt ask for

erbittert adj bitter; (heftig) fierce

erblassen vi (sein) turn pale

erblich adj hereditary

erblicken vt catch sight of

erblinden vi (sein) go blind

erbrechen† vt vomit • vi/r **[sich] e~**

[C] *see* A-Z of German life and culture

vomit. **E~** nt **-s** vomiting

Erbschaft f -,**-en** inheritance

Erbse f -,**-n** pea

Erb|stück nt heirloom. **E~teil** nt inheritance

Erd|apfel m (Aust) potato. **E~beben** nt **-s,-** earthquake. **E~beere** f strawberry

e

Erde f -,**-n** earth; (Erdboden) ground; (Fußboden) floor. **e~n** vt (Electr) earth

erdenklich adj imaginable

Erd|gas nt natural gas. **E~geschoss** nt ground floor. **E~kugel** f globe. **E~kunde** f geography. **E~nuss** f peanut. **E~öl** nt [mineral] oil

erdrosseln vt strangle

erdrücken vt crush to death

Erd|rutsch m landslide. **E~teil** m continent

erdulden vt endure

ereignen (sich) vr happen

Ereignis nt **-ses,-se** event. **e~los** adj uneventful. **e~reich** adj eventful

Eremit m **-en,-en** hermit

erfahr|en† vt learn, hear; (erleben) experience • adj experienced. **E~ung** f -,**-en** experience; **in E~ung bringen** find out

erfassen vt seize; (begreifen) grasp; (einbeziehen) include; (aufzeichnen) record

erfind|en† vt invent. **E~er** m **-s,-** inventor. **e~erisch** adj inventive. **E~ung** f -,**-en** invention

Erfolg m **-[e]s,-e** success; (Folge) result; **E~ haben** be successful. **e~en** vi (sein) take place; (geschehen) happen. **e~los** adj unsuccessful. **e~reich** adj successful

erforder|lich adj required, necessary. **e~n** vt require, demand

erforsch|en vt explore; (untersuchen) investigate. **E~ung** f exploration; investigation

erfreu|en vt please. **e~lich** adj pleasing. **e~licherweise** adv happily. **e~t** adj pleased

erfrier|en† vi (sein) freeze to death; (Glied:) become frostbitten; (Pflanze:) be killed by the frost. **E~ung** f -,**-en** frostbite

erfrisch|en vt refresh. **E~ung** f -,**-en** refreshment

erfüll|en vt fill; (nachkommen) fulfil; serve (Zweck); discharge (Pflicht:) **sich e~en** come true. **E~ung** f fulfilment

erfunden invented

ergänz|en vt complement; (hinzufügen) add. **E~ung** f complement; supplement; (Zusatz) addition

ergeben† vt produce; (zeigen) show, establish; **sich e~en** result; (Schwierigkeit:) arise; (kapitulieren) surrender; (sich fügen) submit • adj devoted; (resigniert) resigned

Ergebnis nt **-ses,-se** result. **e~los** adj fruitless

ergiebig adj productive; (fig) rich

ergreifen† vt seize; take (Maßnahme, Gelegenheit); take up (Beruf); (rühren) move; **die Flucht e~** flee. **e~d** adj moving

ergriffen adj deeply moved. **E~heit** f - emotion

ergründen vt (fig) get to the bottom of

erhaben adj raised; (fig) sublime

Erhalt m **-[e]s** receipt. **e~en**† vt receive, get; (gewinnen) obtain; (bewahren) preserve, keep; (instand halten) maintain; (unterhalten) support; **am Leben e~en** keep alive • adj **gut/schlecht e~en** in good/bad condition; **e~en bleiben** survive

erhältlich adj obtainable

Erhaltung f - preservation; maintenance

erhängen (sich) vr hang oneself

erheb|en† vt raise; levy (Steuer); charge (Gebühr); **Anspruch e~en** lay claim (**auf** + acc to); **Protest e~en** protest; **sich e~en** rise;

(Frage:) arise. **e~lich** adj considerable. **E~ung** f **-,-en** elevation; (Anhöhe) rise; (Aufstand) uprising; (Ermittlung) survey

erheiter|n vt amuse. **E~ung** f - amusement

erhitzen vt heat

erhöh|en vt raise; (fig) increase; **sich e~en** rise, increase. **E~ung** f **-,-en** increase

erhol|en (sich) vr recover (**von** from); (nach Krankheit) convalesce; (sich ausruhen) have a rest. **e~sam** adj restful. **E~ung** f - recovery; (Ruhe) rest

erinner|n vt remind (**an** + acc of); **sich e~n** remember (**an jdn/etw** s.o./sth). **E~ung** f **-,-en** memory; (Andenken) souvenir

erkält|en (sich) vr catch a cold; **e~et sein** have a cold. **E~ung** f **-,-en** cold

erkenn|bar adj recognizable; (sichtbar) visible. **e~en†** vt recognize; (wahrnehmen) distinguish. **E~tnis** f **-,-se** recognition; realization; (Wissen) knowledge; **die neuesten E~tnisse** the latest findings

Erker m **-s,-** bay

erklär|en vt declare; (erläutern) explain; **sich bereit e~en** agree (**zu** to). **e~end** adj explanatory. **e~lich** adj explicable; (verständlich) understandable. **e~licherweise** adv understandably. **E~ung** f **-,-en** declaration; explanation; **öffentliche E~ung** public statement

erkrank|en vi (sein) fall ill; be taken ill (**an** + dat with). **E~ung** f **-,-en** illness

erkundig|en (sich) vr enquire (**nach jdm/etw** after s.o./about sth). **E~ung** f **-,-en** enquiry

erlangen vt attain, get

Erlass m **-es,¨-e** (Admin) decree; (Befreiung) exemption; (Straf-) remission

erlassen† vt (Admin) issue; **jdm etw e~** exempt s.o. from sth; let s.o. off (Strafe)

erlauben vt allow, permit; **ich kann es mir nicht e~** I can't afford it

Erlaubnis f - permission. **E~schein** m permit

erläutern vt explain

Erle f **-,-n** alder

erleb|en vt experience; (mit-) see; have (Überraschung). **E~nis** nt **-ses,-se** experience

erledigen vt do; (sich befassen mit) deal with; (beenden) finish; (entscheiden) settle; (töten) kill

erleichter|n vt lighten; (vereinfachen) make easier; (befreien) relieve; (lindern) ease. **e~t** adj relieved. **E~ung** f - relief

erleiden† vt suffer

erleuchten vt illuminate; **hell erleuchtet** brightly lit

erlogen adj untrue, false

Erlös m **-es** proceeds pl

erlöschen† vi (sein) go out; (vergehen) die; (aussterben) die out; (ungültig werden) expire; **erloschener Vulkan** extinct volcano

erlös|en vt save; (befreien) release (**von** from); (Relig) redeem. **e~t** adj relieved. **E~ung** f release; (Erleichterung) relief; (Relig) redemption

ermächtig|en vt authorize. **E~ung** f **-,-en** authorization

Ermahnung f exhortation; admonition

ermäßig|en vt reduce. **E~ung** f **-,-en** reduction

ermessen† vt judge; (begreifen) appreciate. **E~** nt **-s** discretion; (Urteil) judgement; **nach eigenem E~** at one's own discretion

ermitt|eln vt establish; (herausfinden) find out •vi (haben) investigate (**gegen jdn** s.o.). **E~lungen** fpl investigations. **E~lungsverfahren** nt (Jur) preliminary inquiry

ermöglichen vt make possible

ermord|en vt murder. **E~ung** f **-,-en** murder

ermüd|en vt tire •vi (sein) get tired. **E~ung** f - tiredness

ermutigen vt encourage. **e~d** adj encouraging

ernähr|en vt feed; (unterhalten) support, keep; **sich e~en von** live/ (Tier:) feed on. **E~er** m **-s,-** breadwinner. **E~ung** f - nourishment; nutrition; (Kost) diet

e

ernenn|en† vt appoint. **E~ung** f **-,-en** appointment

erneu|ern vt renew; (auswechseln) replace; change (Verband); (renovieren) renovate. **E~erung** f renewal; replacement; renovation. **e~t** adj renewed; (neu) new •adv again

ernst adj serious; **e~ nehmen** take seriously. **E~** m **-es** seriousness; **im E~** seriously; **mit einer Drohung E~ machen** carry out a threat; **ist das dein E~?** are you serious? **e~haft** adj serious. **e~lich** adj serious

Ernte f **-,-n** harvest; (Ertrag) crop. **E~dankfest** nt harvest festival. **e~n** vt harvest; (fig) reap, win

ernüchter|n vt sober up; (fig) bring down to earth. **e~nd** adj (fig) sobering

Erober|er m **-s,-** conqueror. **e~n** vt conquer. **E~ung** f **-,-en** conquest

eröffn|en vt open; **jdm etw e~en** announce sth to s.o. **E~ung** f opening; (Mitteilung) announcement

erörter|n vt discuss. **E~ung** f **-,-en** discussion

Erot|ik f - eroticism. **e~isch** adj erotic

Erpel m **-s,-** drake

erpicht adj **e~ auf** (+ acc) keen on

erpress|en vt extort; blackmail (Person). **E~er** m **-s,-** blackmailer. **E~ung** f - extortion; blackmail

erprob|en vt test. **e~t** adj proven

erraten† vt guess

erreg|bar adj excitable. **e~en** vt excite; (hervorrufen) arouse; **sich e~en** get worked up. **e~end** adj exciting. **E~er** m **-s,-** (Med) germ. **e~t** adj agitated; (hitzig) heated. **E~ung** f - excitement

erreich|bar adj within reach; (Ziel) attainable; (Person) available. **e~en** vt reach; catch (Zug); live to (Alter); (durchsetzen) achieve

errichten vt erect

erringen† vt gain, win

erröten vi (sein) blush

Errungenschaft f **-,-en** achievement; (!: Anschaffung) acquisition

Ersatz m **-es** replacement, substitute; (Entschädigung) compensation. **E~reifen** m spare tyre. **E~teil** nt spare part

erschaffen† vt create

erschein|en† vi (sein) appear; (Buch:) be published. **E~ung** f **-,-en** appearance; (Person) figure; (Phänomen) phenomenon; (Symptom) symptom; (Geist) apparition

erschieß|en† vt shoot [dead]. **E~ungskommando** nt firing squad

erschlaffen vi (sein) go limp

erschlagen† vt beat to death; (tödlich treffen) strike dead; **vom Blitz e~ werden** be killed by lightning

erschließen† vt develop

erschöpf|en vt exhaust. **e~t** adj exhausted. **E~ung** f - exhaustion

erschrecken† vi (sein) get a fright •vt (reg) startle; (beunruhigen) alarm; **du hast mich e~t** you gave me a fright

erschrocken adj frightened; (erschreckt) startled

erschütter|n vt shake; (ergreifen) upset deeply. **E~ung** f **-,-en** shock

erschwinglich adj affordable

ersehen† vt (fig) see (**aus** from)

ersetzen vt replace; make good (Schaden); refund (Kosten); **jdm etw**

e~ compensate s.o. for sth

ersichtlich adj obvious, apparent

erspar|en vt save. **E~nis** f **-,-se** saving; **E~nisse** savings

erst adv (zuerst) first; (noch nicht mehr als) only; (nicht vor) not until; **e~ dann** only then; **eben e~** [only] just

erstarren vi (sein) solidify; (gefrieren) freeze; (steif werden) go stiff; (vor Schreck) be paralysed

erstatten vt (zurück-) refund; **Bericht e~** report (**jdm** to s.o.)

Erstaufführung f first performance, première

erstaun|en vt amaze, astonish. **E~en** nt amazement, astonishment. **e~lich** adj amazing

Erst|ausgabe f first edition. **e~e(r,s)** adj first; (beste) best; **e~e Hilfe** first aid. **E~e(r)** m/f first; (Beste) best; **fürs E~e** for the time being; **als E~es** first of all; **er kam als E~er** he arrived first

erstechen† vt stab to death

ersteigern vt buy at an auction

erst|ens adv firstly, in the first place. **e~ere(r,s)** adj the former; **der/die/das E~ere** the former

ersticken vt suffocate; smother (Flammen) •vi (sein) suffocate. **E~** nt **-s** suffocation; **zum E~** stifling

erstklassig adj first-class

ersuchen vt ask, request. **E~** nt **-s** request

ertappen vt [!] catch

erteilen vt give (**jdm** s.o.)

ertönen vi (sein) sound; (erschallen) ring out

Ertrag m **-[e]s,¨e** yield. **e~en†** vt bear

erträglich adj bearable; (leidlich) tolerable

ertränken vt drown

ertrinken† vi (sein) drown

erübrigen (sich) vr be unnecessary

erwachsen adj grown-up. **E~e(r)** m/f adult, grown-up

erwäg|en† vt consider. **E~ung** f **-,-en** consideration; **in E~ung ziehen** consider

erwähn|en vt mention. **E~ung** f **-,-en** mention

erwärmen vt warm; **sich e~** warm up; (fig) warm (**für** to)

erwart|en vt expect; (warten auf) wait for. **E~ung** f **-,-en** expectation

erweisen† vt prove; (bezeigen) do (Gefallen, Dienst, Ehre); **sich e~ als** prove to be

erweitern vt widen; dilate (Pupille); (fig) extend, expand

Erwerb m **-[e]s** acquisition; (Kauf) purchase; (Brot-) livelihood; (Verdienst) earnings pl. **e~en†** vt acquire; (kaufen) purchase. **e~slos** adj unemployed. **e~stätig** adj employed

erwider|n vt reply; return (Besuch, Gruß). **E~ung** f **-,-en** reply

erwirken vt obtain

erwürgen vt strangle

Erz nt **-es,-e** ore

erzähl|en vt tell (**jdm** s.o.) •vi (haben) talk (**von** about). **E~er** m **-s,-** narrator. **E~ung** f **-,-en** story, tale

Erzbischof m archbishop

erzeug|en vt produce; (Electr) generate. **E~er** m **-s,-** producer. **E~nis** nt **-ses,-se** product; **landwirtschaftliche E~nisse** farm produce sg.

erzieh|en† vt bring up; (Sch) educate. **E~er** m **-s,-** [private] tutor. **E~erin** f **-,-nen** governess. **E~ung** f **-** upbringing; education

erzielen vt achieve; score (Tor)

erzogen adj **gut/schlecht e~** well/ badly brought up

es
• pronoun
····➤ (Sache) it; (weibliche Person) she/her; (männliche Person) he/him. **ich bin es** it's me. **wir sind traurig, ihr seid es auch** we are sad, and so are you. **er ist es, der ...** he is the one who ... **es sind Studenten** they are students
····➤ (impers) it. **es hat geklopft** there was a knock. **es klingelt** someone is ringing. **es wird schöner** the weather is improving. **es geht ihm gut/schlecht** he is well/unwell. **es lässt sich aushalten** it is bearable. **es gibt** there is or (pl) are
····➤ (als formales Objekt) **er hat es gut** he has it made; he's well off. **er meinte es gut** he meant well. **ich hoffe/glaube es** I hope/think so

e

Esche f -,-n ash

Esel m -s,- donkey; (!: Person) ass

Eskimo m -[s],-[s] Eskimo

Eskort|e f -,-n (Mil) escort. **e~ieren** vt escort

essbar adj edible

essen† vt/i (haben) eat; **zu Mittag/Abend e~** have lunch/supper; **e~ gehen** eat out. **E~** nt -s,- food; (Mahl) meal; (festlich) dinner

Esser(in) m -s,- (f -,-nen) eater

Essig m -s vinegar. **E~gurke** f [pickled] gherkin

Esslöffel m ≈ dessertspoon. **Essstäbchen** ntpl chopsticks. **Esstisch** m dining-table. **Esswaren** fpl food sg; (Vorräte) provisions. **Esszimmer** nt dining-room

Estland nt -s Estonia

Estragon m -s tarragon

etablieren (sich) vr establish oneself/(Geschäft:) itself

Etage /e'ta:ʒə/ f -,-n storey. **E~nbett** nt bunk-beds pl. **E~nwohnung** f flat

Etappe f -,-n stage

Etat /e'ta:/ m -s,-s budget

Eth|ik f - ethic; (Sittenlehre) ethics sg. **e~isch** adj ethical

ethnisch adj ethnic; **e~e Säuberung** ethnic cleansing

Etikett nt -[e]s,-e[n] label; (Preis-) tag. **e~ieren** vt label

Etui /e'tvi:/ nt -s,-s case

etwa adv (ungefähr) about; (zum Beispiel) for instance; (womöglich) perhaps; **nicht e~, dass ...** not that ... ; **denkt nicht e~ ...** don't imagine ...

etwas pron something; (fragend/verneint) anything; (ein bisschen) some, a little; **sonst noch e~?** anything else? **so e~ Ärgerliches!** what a nuisance! • adv a bit

Etymologie f - etymology

euch pron (acc of **ihr** pl) you; (dat) [to] you; (reflexive) yourselves; (einander) each other

euer poss pron pl your. **e~e, e~t-** s. **eure, euret-**

Eule f -,-n owl

Euphorie f - euphoria

eur|e poss pron pl your. **e~e(r,s)** poss pron yours. **e~etwegen** adv for your sake; (wegen euch) because of you, on your account. **e~etwillen** adv **um e~etwillen** for your sake. **e~ige** poss pron **der/die/das e~ige** yours

Euro m -[s],[-s] euro. **E~-** prefix Euro-

Europa nt -s Europe. **E~-** prefix European

Europä|er(in) m -s,- (f -,-nen) European. **e~isch** adj European

Euter nt -s,- udder

evakuier|en vt evacuate. **E~ung** f - evacuation

evan|gelisch adj Protestant. **E~gelium** nt -s,-ien gospel

eventuell adj possible • adv possibly; (vielleicht) perhaps

Evolution /-'tsi̯o:n/ f - evolution

ewig adj eternal; (endlos) never-ending; **e~ dauern** ! take ages. **E~keit** f - eternity

Examen nt -s,- & -mina (Sch) examination

Exemplar nt **-s,-e** specimen; (Buch) copy. **e~isch** adj exemplary

exerzieren vt/i (haben) (Mil) drill; (üben) practise

exhumieren vt exhume

Exil nt **-s** exile

Existenz f **-,-en** existence; (Lebensgrundlage) livelihood

existieren vi (haben) exist

exklusiv adj exclusive. **e~e** prep (+ gen) excluding

exkommunizieren vt excommunicate

Exkremente npl excrement sg

Expedition /-'tsi̯o:n/ f **-,-en** expedition

Experiment nt **-[e]s,-e** experiment. **e~ieren** vi (haben) experiment

Experte m **-n,-n** expert

explo|dieren vi (sein) explode. **E~sion** f **-,-en** explosion

Expor|t m **-[e]s,-e** export. **E~teur** m **-s,-e** exporter. **e~tieren** vt export

extra adv separately; (zusätzlich) extra; (eigens) specially; (!: absichtlich) on purpose

extravagan|t adj flamboyant; (übertrieben) extravagant

extravertiert adj extrovert

extrem adj extreme. **E~ist** m **-en,-en** extremist

Exzellenz f - (title) Excellency

Exzentr|iker m **-s,-** eccentric. **e~isch** adj eccentric

Ff

Fabel f **-,-n** fable. **f~haft** adj ! fantastic

Fabrik f **-,-en** factory. **F~ant** m **-en,-en** manufacturer. **F~at** nt **-[e]s,-e** product; (Marke) make. **F~ation** f - manufacture

Fach nt **-[e]s,¨er** compartment; (Schub-) drawer; (Gebiet) field; (Sch) subject. **F~arbeiter** m skilled worker. **F~arzt** m, **F~ärztin** f specialist. **F~ausdruck** m technical term

Fächer m **-s,-** fan

Fach|gebiet nt field. **f~kundig** adj expert. **f~lich** adj technical; (beruflich) professional. **F~mann** m (pl **-leute**) expert. **f~männisch** adj expert. **F~schule** f technical college. **F~werkhaus** nt half-timbered house. **F~wort** nt (pl **-wörter**) technical term

Fackel f **-,-n** torch

fade adj insipid; (langweilig) dull

Faden m **-s,¨** thread; (Bohnen-) string; (Naut) fathom

Fagott nt **-[e]s,-e** bassoon

fähig adj capable (**zu**/gen of); (tüchtig) able, competent. **F~keit** f **-,-en** ability; competence

fahl adj pale

fahnd|en vi (haben) search (**nach** for). **F~ung** f **-,-en** search

Fahne f **-,-n** flag; (Druck-) galley [proof]; **eine F~ haben** ! reek of alcohol. **F~nflucht** f desertion

Fahr|ausweis m ticket. **F~bahn** f carriageway; (Straße) road. **f~bar** adj mobile

Fähre f **-,-n** ferry

fahr|en† vi (sein) go, travel; (Fahrer:) drive; (Radfahrer:) ride; (verkehren) run, (ab-) leave; (Schiff:) sail; **mit dem Auto/Zug f~en** go by car/train; **was ist in ihn gefahren?** ! what has got into him? • vt drive; ride (Fahrrad); take (Kurve). **f~end**

adj moving; (f~bar) mobile; (nicht sesshaft) travelling. **F~er** m **-s,-** driver. **F~erflucht** f failure to stop after an accident. **F~erhaus** nt driver's cab. **F~erin** f **-,-nen** woman driver. **F~gast** m passenger. **F~geld** nt fare. **F~gestell** nt chassis; (Aviat) undercarriage. **F~karte** f ticket. **F~kartenschalter** m ticket office. **f~lässig** adj negligent. **F~lässigkeit** f - negligence. **F~lehrer** m driving instructor. **F~plan** m timetable. **f~planmäßig** adj scheduled • adv according to/(pünktlich) on schedule. **F~preis** m fare. **F~prüfung** f driving test. **F~rad** nt bicycle. **F~schein** m ticket. **F~schule** f driving school. **F~schüler(in)** m(f) learner driver. **F~stuhl** m lift

f

Fahrt f **-,-en** journey; (Auto) drive; (Ausflug) trip; (Tempo) speed

Fährte f **-,-n** track; (Witterung) scent

Fahr|tkosten pl travelling expenses. **F~werk** nt undercarriage. **F~zeug** nt **-[e]s,-e** vehicle; (Wasser-) craft, vessel

fair /fɛːɐ̯/ adj fair

Fakultät f **-,-en** faculty

Falke m **-n,-n** falcon

Fall m **-[e]s,⸚e** fall; (Jur, Med, Gram) case; **im F~[e]** in case (gen of); **auf jeden F~** in any case; (bestimmt) definitely; **für alle F~e** just in case; **auf keinen F~** on no account

Falle f **-,-n** trap

fallen† vi (sein) fall; (sinken) go down; **[im Krieg] f~** be killed in the war; **f~ lassen** drop (etw, fig: Plan, jdn); make (Bemerkung)

fällen vt fell; (fig) pass (Urteil)

fällig adj due; (Wechsel) mature; **längst f~** long overdue. **F~keit** f - (Comm) maturity

falls conj in case; (wenn) if

Fallschirm m parachute. **F~jäger** m paratrooper. **F~springer** m parachutist

Falltür f trapdoor

falsch adj wrong; (nicht echt, unaufrichtig) false; (gefälscht) forged; (Geld) counterfeit; (Schmuck) fake • adv wrongly; falsely; (singen) out of tune; **f~ gehen** (Uhr:) be wrong

fälschen vt forge, fake

Falschgeld nt counterfeit money

fälschlich adj wrong; (irrtümlich) mistaken

Falsch|meldung f false report; (absichtlich) hoax report. **F~münzer** m **-s,-** counterfeiter

Fälschung f **-,-en** forgery, fake

Falte f **-,-n** fold; (Rock-) pleat; (Knitter-) crease; (im Gesicht) line; wrinkle

falten vt fold

Falter m **-s,-** butterfly; moth

faltig adj creased; (Gesicht) lined; wrinkled

familiär adj family ; (vertraut, zudringlich) familiar; (zwanglos) informal

Familie /-i̯ə/ f **-,-n** family. **F~nforschung** f genealogy. **F~nname** m surname. **F~nplanung** f family planning. **F~nstand** m marital status

Fan /fɛn/ m **-s,-s** fan

Fana|tiker m **-s,-** fanatic. **f~tisch** adj fanatical

Fanfare f **-,-n** trumpet; (Signal) fanfare

Fang m **-[e]s,⸚e** capture; (Beute) catch; **F~e** (Krallen) talons; (Zähne) fangs. **F~arm** m tentacle. **f~en**† vt catch; (ein-) capture; **gefangen nehmen** take prisoner. **F~en** nt **-s** **F~en spielen** play tag. **F~frage** f catch question

Fantasie f **-,-n** = **Phantasie**

Farb|aufnahme f colour photograph. **F~band** nt (pl **-bänder**) typewriter ribbon. **F~e** f **-,-n** colour; (Maler-) paint; (zum Färben) dye; (Karten) suit. **f~echt** adj colour-fast

färben vt colour; dye (Textilien, Haare)

see A-Z of German life and culture

•vi (haben) not be colour-fast

farb|enblind adj colour-blind. **f~enfroh** adj colourful. **F~film** m colour film. **f~ig** adj coloured •adv in colour. **F~ige(r)** m/f coloured man/woman. **F~kasten** m box of paints. **f~los** adj colourless. **F~stift** m crayon. **F~stoff** m dye; (Lebensmittel-) colouring. **F~ton** m shade

Färbung f **-,-en** colouring

Farn m **-[e]s,-e** fern

Färse f **-,-n** heifer

Fasan m **-[e]s,-e[n]** pheasant

Faschierte(s) nt (Aust) mince

Fasching m **-s** (SGer) carnival

Faschis|mus m **-** fascism. **F~t** m **-en,-en** fascist. **f~tisch** adj fascist

Faser f **-,-n** fibre

Fass nt **-es,⸚er** barrel, cask; **Bier vom F~** draught beer

Fassade f **-,-n** façade

fassbar adj comprehensible; (greifbar) tangible

fassen vt take [hold of], grasp; (ergreifen) seize; (fangen) catch; (ein-) set; (enthalten) hold; (fig: begreifen) take in, grasp; conceive (Plan); make (Entschluss); **sich f~** compose oneself; **sich kurz f~** be brief; **nicht zu f~** (fig) unbelievable •vi (haben) **f~ an** (+ acc) touch

Fassung f **-,-en** mount; (Edelstein-) setting; (Electr) socket; (Version) version; (Beherrschung) composure; **aus der F~ bringen** disconcert. **f~slos** adj shaken; (erstaunt) flabbergasted. **F~svermögen** nt capacity

fast adv almost, nearly; **f~ nie** hardly ever

fast|en vi (haben) fast. **F~enzeit** f Lent. **F~nacht** f Shrovetide; (Karneval) carnival. **F~nachtsdienstag** m Shrove Tuesday

fatal adj fatal; (peinlich) embarrassing

Fata Morgana f **- -,- -nen** mirage

fauchen vi (haben) spit, hiss •vt snarl

faul adj lazy; (verdorben) rotten, bad; (Ausrede) lame

faul|en vi (sein) rot; (Zahn:) decay; (verwesen) putrefy. **f~enzen** vi (haben) be lazy. **F~enzer** m **-s,-** lazy-bones sg. **F~heit** f **-** laziness

Fäulnis f **-** decay

Fauna f **-** fauna

Faust f **-,Fäuste** fist; **auf eigene F~** (fig) off one's own bat. **F~handschuh** m mitten. **F~schlag** m punch

Fauxpas /fo'pa/ m **-,-** gaffe

Favorit(in) /favo'ri:t(ɪn)/ m **-en,-en** (f **-,-nen**) (Sport) favourite

Fax nt **-,-[e]** fax. **f~en** vt fax

Faxen fpl [!] antics; **F~ machen** fool about

Faxgerät nt fax machine

Februar m **-s,-e** February

fecht|en† vi (haben) fence. **F~er** m **-s,-** fencer

Feder f **-,-n** feather; (Schreib-) pen; (Spitze) nib; (Techn) spring. **F~ball** m shuttlecock; (Spiel) badminton. **F~busch** m plume. **f~leicht** adj as light as a feather. **f~n** vi (haben) be springy; (nachgeben) give; (hoch-) bounce. **f~nd** adj springy; (elastisch) elastic. **F~ung** f **-** (Techn) springs pl; (Auto) suspension

Fee f **-,-n** fairy

Fegefeuer nt purgatory

fegen vt sweep

Fehde f **-,-n** feud

fehl adj **f~ am Platze** out of place. **F~betrag** m deficit. **f~en** vi (haben) be missing/(Sch) absent; (mangeln) be lacking; **mir f~t die Zeit** I haven't got the time; **was f~t ihm?** what's the matter with him? **das hat uns noch gefehlt!** that's all we need! **f~end** adj missing; (Sch) absent

Fehler m **-s,-** mistake, error; (Sport & fig) fault; (Makel) flaw. **f~frei** adj

see A-Z of German life and culture

f

faultless. **f~haft** adj faulty. **f~los** adj flawless

Fehl|geburt f miscarriage. **F~griff** m mistake. **F~kalkulation** f miscalculation. **F~schlag** m failure. **f~schlagen†** vi sep (sein) fail. **F~start** m (Sport) false start. **F~zündung** f (Auto) misfire

Feier f -,-n celebration; (Zeremonie) ceremony; (Party) party. **F~abend** m end of the working day; **F~abend machen** stop work. **f~lich** adj solemn; (fömlich) formal. **f~n** vt celebrate; hold (Fest) • vi (haben) celebrate. **F~tag** m [public] holiday; (kirchlicher) feast-day; **erster/zweiter F~tag** Christmas Day / Boxing Day. **f~tags** adv on public holidays

f

feige adj cowardly; **f~ sein** be a coward • adv in a cowardly way

Feige f -,-n fig

Feig|heit f - cowardice. **F~ling** m -s,-e coward

Feile f -,-n file. **f~n** vt/i (haben) file

feilschen vi (haben) haggle

fein adj fine; (zart) delicate; (Strümpfe) sheer; (Unterschied) subtle; (scharf) keen; (vornehm) refined; (prima) great; **sich f~ machen** dress up. **F~arbeit** f precision work

Feind(in) m -es,-e (f -,-nen) enemy. **f~lich** adj enemy; (f~selig) hostile. **F~schaft** f -,-en enmity

fein|fühlig adj sensitive. **F~gefühl** nt sensitivity; (Takt) delicacy. **F~heit** f -,-en fineness; delicacy; subtlety; refinement; **F~heiten** subtleties. **F~kostgeschäft** nt delicatessen [shop]

feist adj fat

Feld nt -[e]s,-er field; (Fläche) ground; (Sport) pitch; (Schach-) square; (auf Formular) box. **F~bett** nt camp-bed. **F~forschung** f fieldwork. **F~herr** m commander. **F~stecher** m -s,- field-glasses pl. **F~webel** m -s,- (Mil) sergeant. **F~zug** m campaign

Felge f -,-n [wheel] rim

Fell nt -[e]s,-e (Zool) coat; (Pelz) fur; (abgezogen) skin, pelt

Fels m -en,-en rock. **F~block** m boulder. **F~en** m -s,- rock

Femininum nt -s,-na (Gram) feminine

Feminist|(in) m -en,-en (f -,-nen) feminist. **f~isch** adj feminist

Fenchel m -s fennel

Fenster nt -s,- window. **F~brett** nt window sill. **F~scheibe** f [window-]pane

Ferien /'fe:ri̯ən/ pl holidays; (Univ) vacation sg; **F~ haben** be on holiday. **F~ort** m holiday resort

Ferkel nt -s,- piglet

fern adj distant; **der F~e Osten** the Far East; **sich f~ halten** keep away • adv far away; **von f~** from a distance • prep (+ dat) far [away] from. **F~bedienung** f remote control. **F~e** f - distance; **in weiter F~e** far away; (zeitlich) in the distant future. **f~er** adj further • adv (außerdem) furthermore; (in Zukunft) in future. **f~gelenkt** adj remote-controlled; (Rakete) guided. **F~gespräch** nt long-distance call. **F~glas** nt binoculars pl. **F~kurs[us]** m correspondence course. **F~licht** nt (Auto) full beam. **F~meldewesen** nt telecommunications pl. **F~rohr** nt telescope. **F~schreiben** nt telex

Fernseh|apparat m television set. **f~en†** vi sep (haben) watch television. **F~en** nt -s television. **F~er** m -s,- [television] viewer; (Gerät) television set

Fernsprech|amt nt telephone exchange. **F~er** m telephone

Fern|steuerung f remote control. **F~studium** nt distance learning

Ferse f -,-n heel

fertig adj finished; (bereit) ready; (Comm) ready-made; (Gericht) ready-to-serve; **f~ werden mit** finish; (bewältigen) cope with; **f~ sein** have finished; (fig) be through (**mit jdm** with s.o.); (!: erschöpft) be all in/ (seelisch) shattered; **etw f~**

bringen manage to do sth; (beenden) finish sth; **etw/jdn f~ machen** finish sth; (bereitmachen) get sth/s.o. ready; (!: erschöpfen) wear s.o. out; (seelisch) shatter s.o.; **sich f~ machen** get ready; **etw f~ stellen** complete sth • adv **f~ essen/lesen** finish eating/reading. **F~bau** m (pl **-bauten**) prefabricated building. **f~en** vt make. **F~gericht** nt ready-to-serve meal. **F~haus** nt prefabricated house. **F~keit** f **-,-en** skill. **F~stellung** f completion. **F~ung** f - manufacture

fesch adj ! attractive

Fessel f **-,-n** ankle

fesseln vt tie up; tie (**an** + acc to); (fig) fascinate

fest adj firm; (nicht flüssig) solid; (erstarrt) set; (haltbar) strong; (nicht locker) tight; (feststehend) fixed; (ständig) steady; (Anstellung) permanent; (Schlaf) sound; (Blick, Stimme) steady; **f~ werden** harden; (Gelee:) set; **f~e Nahrung** solids pl • adv firmly; tightly; steadily; soundly; (kräftig, tüchtig) hard; **f~ schlafen** be fast asleep; **f~ angestellt** permanent

Fest nt **-[e]s,-e** celebration; (Party) party; (Relig) festival; **frohes F~!** happy Christmas!

fest|binden† vt sep tie (**an** + dat to). **f~bleiben**† vi sep (sein) (fig) remain firm. **f~halten**† v sep • vt hold on to; (aufzeichnen) record; **sich f~halten** hold on • vi (haben) **f~halten an** (+ dat) (fig) stick to; cling to (Tradition). **f~igen** vt strengthen. **F~iger** m **-s,-** styling lotion/(Schaum-) mousse. **F~igkeit** f - (s. **fest**) firmness; solidity; strength; steadiness. **F~land** nt mainland; (Kontinent) continent. **f~legen** vt sep (fig) fix, settle; lay down (Regeln); tie up (Geld); **sich f~legen** commit oneself

festlich adj festive. **F~keiten** fpl festivities

fest|liegen† vi sep (haben) be fixed, settled. **f~machen** v sep • vt fasten/(binden) tie (**an** + dat to); (f~legen) fix, settle • vi (haben) (Naut) moor. **F~mahl** nt feast. **F~nahme** f **-,-n** arrest. **f~nehmen**† vt sep arrest. **F~netz** nt landline network. **F~platte** f hard disk. **f~setzen** vt sep fix, settle; (inhaftieren) gaol; **sich f~setzen** collect. **f~sitzen**† vi sep (haben) be firm/(Schraube:) tight; (haften) stick; (nicht weiterkommen) be stuck. **F~spiele** npl festival sg. **f~stehen**† vi sep (haben) be certain. **f~stellen** vt sep fix; (ermitteln) establish; (bemerken) notice; (sagen) state. **F~tag** m special day

Festung f **-,-en** fortress

Festzug m [grand] procession

Fete /'fe:tə, 'fɛ:tə/ f **-,-n** party

fett adj fat; fatty; (fettig) greasy; (üppig) rich; (Druck) bold. **F~** nt **-[e]s,-e** fat; (flüssig) grease. **f~arm** adj low-fat. **f~en** vt grease • vi (haben) be greasy. **F~fleck** m grease mark. **f~ig** adj greasy

Fetzen m **-s,-** scrap; (Stoff) rag

feucht adj damp, moist; (Luft) humid. **F~igkeit** f - dampness; (Nässe) moisture; (Luft-) humidity. **F~igkeitscreme** f moisturizer

Feuer nt **-s,-** fire; (für Zigarette) light; (Begeisterung) passion; **F~ machen** light a fire. **F~alarm** m fire alarm. **f~gefährlich** adj [in]flammable. **F~leiter** f fire escape. **F~löscher** m **-s,-** fire extinguisher. **F~melder** m **-s,-** fire alarm. **f~n** vi (haben) fire (**auf** + acc on). **F~probe** f (fig) test. **f~rot** adj crimson. **F~stein** m flint. **F~stelle** f hearth. **F~treppe** f fire escape. **F~wache** f fire station. **F~waffe** f firearm. **F~wehr** f **-,-en** fire brigade. **F~wehrauto** nt fire engine. **F~wehrmann** m (pl **-männer** & **-leute**) fireman. **F~werk** nt firework display, fireworks pl. **F~zeug** nt lighter

feurig adj fiery; (fig) passionate

Fiaker m **-s,-** (Aust) horse-drawn cab

Fichte f **-,-n** spruce

Fieber nt **-s** [raised] temperature; **F~ haben** have a temperature. **f~n** vi (haben) be feverish. **F~thermometer** nt thermometer

fiebrig adj feverish

Figur f -,-en figure; (Roman-, Film-) character; (Schach-) piece

Filet /fi'le:/ nt -s,-s fillet

Filiale f -,-n (Comm) branch

Filigran nt -s filigree

Film m -[e]s,-e film; (Kino-) film; (Schicht) coating. **f~en** vt/i (haben) film. **F~kamera** f cine/(für Kinofilm) film camera

f

Filt|er m & (Techn) nt -s,- filter; (Zigaretten-) filter-tip. **f~ern** vt filter. **F~erzigarette** f filter-tipped cigarette. **f~rieren** vt filter

Filz m -es felt. **F~stift** m felt-tipped pen

Fimmel m -s,- [!] obsession

Finale nt -s,- (Mus) finale; (Sport) final

Finanz f -,-en finance. **F~amt** nt tax office. **f~iell** adj financial. **f~ieren** vt finance. **F~minister** m minister of finance

find|en† vt find; (meinen) think; **den Tod f~en** meet one's death; **wie f~est du das?** what do you think of that? **es wird sich f~en** it'll turn up; (fig) it'll be all right •vi (haben) find one's way. **F~er** m -s,- finder. **F~erlohn** m reward. **f~ig** adj resourceful

Finesse f -,-n (Kniff) trick; **F~n** (Techn) refinements

Finger m -s,- finger; **die F~ lassen von** [!] leave alone. **F~abdruck** m finger mark; (Admin) fingerprint. **F~hut** m thimble. **F~nagel** m fingernail. **F~spitze** f fingertip. **F~zeig** m -[e]s,-e hint

Fink m -en,-en finch

Finn|e m -n,-n, **F~in** f -,-nen Finn. **f~isch** adj Finnish. **F~land** nt -s Finland

finster adj dark; (düster) gloomy; (unheildrohend) sinister. **F~nis** f - darkness; (Astronomy) eclipse

Firm|a f -,-men firm, company

Firmen|wagen m company car. **F~zeichen** nt trade mark, logo

Firmung f -,-en (Relig) confirmation

Firnis m -ses,-se varnish. **f~sen** vt varnish

First m -[e]s,-e [roof] ridge

Fisch m -[e]s,-e fish; **F~e** (Astrology) Pisces. **F~dampfer** m trawler. **f~en** vt/i (haben) fish. **F~er** m -s,- fisherman. **F~erei** f - fishing. **F~händler** m fishmonger. **F~reiher** m heron

Fiskus m - **der F~** the Treasury

fit adj fit. **Fitness** f - fitness

fix adj [!] quick; (geistig) bright; **f~e Idee** obsession; **fix und fertig** all finished; (bereit) all ready; ([!]: erschöpft) shattered. **F~er** m -s,- [x] junkie

fixieren vt stare at; (Phot) fix

Fjord m -[e]s,-e fiord

flach adj flat; (eben) level; (niedrig) low; (nicht tief) shallow

Flachbildschirm m flat screen

Fläche f -,-n area; (Ober-) surface; (Seite) face. **F~nmaß** nt square measure

Flachs m -es flax. **f~blond** adj flaxen-haired; (Haar) flaxen

flackern vi (haben) flicker

Flagge f -,-n flag

Flair /flɛ:ɐ̯/ nt -s air, aura

Flak f -,-[s] anti-aircraft artillery/ (Geschütz) gun

flämisch adj Flemish

Flamme f -,-n flame; (Koch-) burner

Flanell m -s (Textiles) flannel

Flank|e f -,-n flank. **f~ieren** vt flank

Flasche f -,-n bottle. **F~nbier** nt bottled beer. **F~nöffner** m bottle-opener. **F~npfand** nt deposit (on bottle)

flatter|haft adj fickle. **f~n** vi (sein/ haben) flutter; (Segel:) flap

flau adj (schwach) faint; (Comm) slack

Flaum m -[e]s down. **f~ig** adj downy; **f~ig rühren** (Aust Culin) cream

flauschig adj fleecy; (Spielzeug) fluffy

Flausen fpl ⊡ silly ideas

Flaute f **-,-n** (Naut) calm; (Comm) slack period; (Schwäche) low

fläzen (sich) vr ⊡ sprawl

Flechte f **-,-n** (Med) eczema; (Bot) lichen; (Zopf) plait. **f~n†** vt plait; weave (Korb)

Fleck m **-[e]s,-e[n]** spot; (größer) patch; (Schmutz-) stain, mark; **blauer F~** bruise. **f~en** vi (haben) stain. **f~enlos** adj spotless. **F~entferner** m **-s,-** stain remover. **f~ig** adj stained

Fledermaus f bat

Flegel m **-s,-** lout. **f~haft** adj loutish

flehen vi (haben) beg (**um** for)

Fleisch nt **-[e]s** flesh; (Culin) meat; (Frucht-) pulp; **F~ fressend** carnivorous. **F~er** m **-s,-** butcher. **F~fresser** m **-s,-** carnivore. **f~ig** adj fleshy. **f~lich** adj carnal. **F~wolf** m mincer

Fleiß m **-es** diligence; **mit F~** diligently; (absichtlich) on purpose. **f~ig** adj diligent; (arbeitsam) industrious

fletschen vt **die Zähne f~** (Tier:) bare its teeth

flex|ibel adj flexible; (Einband) limp. **F~ibilität** f **-** flexibility

flicken vt mend; (mit Flicken) patch. **F~** m **-s,-** patch

Flieder m **-s** lilac

Fliege f **-,-n** fly; (Schleife) bow-tie. **f~n†** vi (sein) fly; (geworfen werden) be thrown; (⊡: fallen) fall; (⊡: entlassen werden) be fired/(von der Schule) expelled; **in die Luft f~n** blow up •vt fly. **f~nd** adj flying. **F~r** m **-s,-** airman; (Pilot); pilot; (⊡: Flugzeug) plane. **F~rangriff** m air raid

flieh|en† vi (sein) flee (**vor** + dat from); (entweichen) escape •vt shun. **f~end** adj fleeing; (Kinn, Stirn) receding

Fliese f **-,-n** tile

Fließ|band nt assembly line. **f~en†** vi (sein) flow; (aus Wasserhahn) run. **f~end** adj flowing; (Wasser) running; (Verkehr) moving; (geläufig) fluent

flimmern vi (haben) shimmer; (TV) flicker

flink adj nimble; (schnell) quick

Flinte f **-,-n** shotgun

Flirt /flœɐ̯t/ m **-s,-s** flirtation. **f~en** vi (haben) flirt

Flitter m **-s** sequins pl. **F~wochen** fpl honeymoon sg

flitzen vi (sein) ⊡ dash

Flock|e f **-,-n** flake; (Wolle) tuft. **f~ig** adj fluffy

Floh m **-[e]s,⸚e** flea. **F~spiel** nt tiddly-winks sg

Flora f **-** flora

Florett nt **-[e]s,-e** foil

florieren vi (haben) flourish

Floskel f **-,-n** [empty] phrase

Floß nt **-es,⸚e** raft

Flosse f **-,-n** fin; (Seehund-, Gummi-) flipper; (sl: Hand) paw

Flöt|e f **-,-n** flute; (Block-) recorder. **f~en** vi (haben) play the flute/recorder; (⊡: pfeifen) whistle •vt play on the flute/recorder. **F~ist(in)** m **-en,-en** (f **-,-nen**) flautist

flott adj quick; (lebhaft) lively; (schick) smart

Flotte f **-,-n** fleet

flottmachen vt sep **wieder f~** (Naut) refloat; get going again (Auto); put back on its feet (Unternehmen)

Flöz nt **-es,-e** [coal] seam

Fluch m **-[e]s,⸚e** curse. **f~en** vi (haben) curse, swear

Flucht f **-** flight; (Entweichen) escape; **die F~ ergreifen** take flight. **f~artig** adj hasty

flücht|en vi (sein) flee (**vor** + dat from); (entweichen) escape •vr **sich f~en** take refuge. **f~ig** adj fugitive; (kurz) brief; (Blick)

f

fleeting; (Bekanntschaft) passing; (oberflächlich) cursory; (nicht sorgfältig) careless. **f~ig kennen** know slightly. **F~igkeitsfehler** m slip. **F~ling** m **-s,-e** fugitive; (Pol) refugee

Fluchwort nt (pl **-wörter**) swear word

Flug m **-[e]s,¨e** flight. **F~abwehr** f anti-aircraft defence

f

Flügel m **-s,-** wing; (Fenster-) casement; (Mus) grand piano

Fluggast m [air] passenger

flügge adj fully-fledged

Flug|gesellschaft f airline. **F~hafen** m airport. **F~lotse** m air-traffic controller. **F~platz** m airport; (klein) airfield. **F~preis** m air fare. **F~schein** m air ticket. **F~schneise** f flight path. **F~schreiber** m **-s,-** flight recorder. **F~schrift** f pamphlet. **F~steig** m **-[e]s,-e** gate. **F~zeug** nt **-[e]s,-e** aircraft, plane

Flunder f **-,-n** flounder

flunkern vi (haben) [!] tell fibs

Flur m **-[e]s,-e** [entrance] hall; (Gang) corridor

Fluss m **-es,¨e** river; (Fließen) flow; **im F~** (fig) in a state of flux. **f~abwärts** adv downstream. **f~aufwärts** adv upstream

flüssig adj liquid; (Lava) molten; (fließend) fluent; (Verkehr) freely moving. **F~keit** f **-,-en** liquid; (Anat) fluid

Flusspferd nt hippopotamus

flüstern vt/i (haben) whisper

Flut f **-,-en** high tide; (fig) flood

Föderation /-'tsi̯o:n/ f **-,-en** federation

Fohlen nt **-s,-** foal

Föhn m **-s** föhn [wind]; (Haartrockner) hairdrier. **f~en** vt [blow-]dry

Folg|e f **-,-n** consequence; (Reihe) succession; (Fortsetzung) instalment; (Teil) part. **f~en** vi (sein) follow (**jdm/etw** s.o./sth); (zuhören) listen (dat to); **wie f~t** as follows •(haben) (gehorchen) obey (**jdm** s.o.). **f~end** adj following; **F~endes** the following

folger|n vt conclude (**aus** from). **F~ung** f **-,-en** conclusion

folg|lich adv consequently. **f~sam** adj obedient

Folie /'fo:li̯ə/ f **-,-n** foil; (Plastik-) film

Folklore f **-** folklore

Folter f **-,-n** torture. **f~n** vt torture

Fön ® m **-s,-e** hairdrier

Fonds /fõ:/ m **-,-** fund

fönen* vt = **föhnen**

Förder|band nt (pl **-bänder**) conveyor belt. **f~lich** adj beneficial

fordern vt demand; (beanspruchen) claim; (zum Kampf) challenge

fördern vt promote; (unterstützen) encourage; (finanziell) sponsor; (gewinnen) extract

Forderung f **-,-en** demand; (Anspruch) claim

Förderung f **-** promotion; encouragement; (Techn) production

Forelle f **-,-n** trout

Form f **-,-en** form; (Gestalt) shape; (Culin, Techn) mould; (Back-) tin; **[gut] in F~** in good form

Formalität f **-,-en** formality

Format nt **-[e]s,-e** format; (Größe) size; (fig: Bedeutung) stature

formatieren vt format

Formel f **-,-n** formula

formen vt shape, mould; (bilden) form; **sich f~** take shape

förmlich adj formal

form|los adj shapeless; (zwanglos) informal. **F~sache** f formality

Formular nt **-s,-e** [printed] form

formulier|en vt formulate, word. **F~ung** f **-,-en** wording

forsch|en vi (haben) search (**nach** for). **f~end** adj searching. **F~er** m **-s,-** research scientist; (Reisender) explorer. **F~ung** f **-,-en** research

Forst m **-[e]s,-e** forest

Förster m **-s,-** forester

Forstwirtschaft f forestry

Fort nt **-s,-s** (Mil) fort

fort adv away; **f~ sein** be away; (gegangen/verschwunden) have gone; **und so f~** and so on; **in einem f~** continuously. **F~bewegung** f locomotion. **F~bildung** f further education/training. **f~bleiben**† vi sep (sein) stay away. **f~bringen**† vt sep take away. **f~fahren**† vi sep (sein) go away • (haben/sein) continue (**zu** to). **f~fallen**† vi sep (sein) be dropped/(ausgelassen) omitted; (entfallen) no longer apply; (aufhören) cease. **f~führen** vt sep continue. **f~gehen**† vi sep (sein) leave, go away; (ausgehen) go out; (andauern) go on. **f~geschritten** adj advanced; (spät) late. **F~geschrittene(r)** m/f advanced student. **f~lassen**† vt sep let go; (auslassen) omit. **f~laufen**† vi sep (sein) run away; (sich f~setzen) continue. **f~laufend** adj consecutive. **f~pflanzen (sich)** vr sep reproduce; (Ton, Licht:) travel. **F~pflanzung** f - reproduction. **F~pflanzungsorgan** nt reproductive organ. **f~schicken** vt sep send away; (abschicken) send off. **f~schreiten**† vi sep (sein) continue; (Fortschritte machen) progress, advance. **f~schreitend** adj progressive; (Alter) advancing. **F~schritt** m progress; **F~schritte machen** make progress. **f~schrittlich** adj progressive. **f~setzen** vt sep continue; **sich f~setzen** continue. **F~setzung** f -,-en continuation; (Folge) instalment; **F~setzung folgt** to be continued. **F~setzungsroman** m serialized novel, serial. **f~während** adj constant. **f~ziehen**† v sep • vt pull away • vi (sein) move away

Fossil nt **-s,-ien** fossil

Foto nt **-s,-s** photo. **F~apparat** m camera. **f~gen** adj photogenic

Fotograf|(in) m **-en,-en** (f **-,-nen**) photographer. **F~ie** f **-,-n** photography; (Bild) photograph. **f~ieren** vt take a photo[graph] of • vi (haben) take photographs. **f~isch** adj photographic

Fotohandy nt camera phone

Fotokopie f photocopy. **f~ren** vt photocopy. **F~rgerät** nt photocopier

Föt|us m **-,-ten** foetus

Foul /faul/ nt **-s,-s** (Sport) foul. **f~en** vt foul

Fracht f **-,-en** freight. **F~er** m **-s,-** freighter. **F~gut** nt freight. **F~schiff** nt cargo boat

Frack m **-[e]s,⸚e** & **-s** tailcoat

Frage f **-,-n** question; **nicht in F~ kommen** s. **infrage**. **F~bogen** m questionnaire. **f~n** vt (haben) ask; **sich f~n** wonder (**ob** whether). **f~nd** adj questioning. **F~zeichen** nt question mark

frag|lich adj doubtful; (Person, Sache) in question. **f~los** adv undoubtedly

Fragment nt **-[e]s,-e** fragment

fragwürdig adj questionable; (verdächtig) dubious

Fraktion /-ˈtsi̯oːn/ f **-,-en** parliamentary party

Franken[1] m **-s,-** (Swiss) franc

Franken[2] nt **-s** Franconia

frankieren vt stamp, frank

Frankreich nt **-s** France

Fransen fpl fringe sg

Franz|ose m **-n,-n** Frenchman; **die F~osen** the French pl. **F~ösin** f **-,-nen** Frenchwoman. **f~ösisch** adj French. **F~ösisch** nt **-[s]** (Lang) French

Fraß m **-es** feed; (pej: Essen) muck

Fratze f **-,-n** grotesque face; (Grimasse) grimace

Frau f **-,-en** woman; (Ehe-) wife; **F~ Thomas** Mrs Thomas; **Unsere Liebe F~** (Relig) Our Lady

Frauen|arzt m, **F~ärztin** f gynaecologist. **F~rechtlerin** f **-,-nen** feminist

Fräulein nt **-s,-** single woman; (jung) young lady; (Anrede) Miss

f

f

frech adj cheeky; (unverschämt) impudent. **F~heit** f -,-en cheekiness; impudence; (Äußerung) impertinence

frei adj free; (freischaffend) freelance; (Künstler) independent; (nicht besetzt) vacant; (offen) open; (bloß) bare; **f~er Tag** day off; **sich** (dat) **f~ nehmen** take time off; **f~ machen** (räumen) clear; vacate (Platz); (befreien) liberate; **f~ lassen** leave free; **ist dieser Platz f~?** is this seat taken? '**Zimmer f~**' 'vacancies' • adv freely; (ohne Notizen) without notes; (umsonst) free

Frei|bad nt open-air swimming pool. **f~beruflich** adj & adv freelance. **F~e** nt **im F~en** in the open air, out of doors. **F~gabe** f release. **f~geben**† v sep • vt release; (eröffnen) open; **jdm einen Tag f~geben** give s.o. a day off • vi (haben) **jdm f~geben** give s.o. time off. **f~gebig** adj generous. **F~gebigkeit** f - generosity. **f~haben**† v sep • vt **eine Stunde f~haben** have an hour off; (Sch) have a free period • vi (haben) be off work/(Sch) school; (beurlaubt sein) have time off. **f~händig** adv without holding on

Freiheit f -,-en freedom, liberty. **F~sstrafe** f prison sentence

Frei|herr m baron. **F~körperkultur** f naturism. **F~lassung** f - release. **F~lauf** m free-wheel. **f~legen** vt sep expose. **f~lich** adv admittedly; (natürlich) of course. **F~lichttheater** nt open-air theatre. **f~machen** vt sep (frankieren) frank; (entkleiden) bare; **einen Tag f~machen** take a day off. **F~maurer** m Freemason. **f~schaffend** adj freelance. **f~schwimmen**† **(sich)** v sep pass one's swimming test. **f~sprechen**† vt sep acquit. **F~spruch** m acquittal. **f~stehen**† vi sep (haben) stand empty; **es steht ihm f~** (fig) he is free (**zu** to). **f~stellen** vt sep exempt (**von** from); **jdm etw f~stellen** leave sth up to s.o. **F~stil** m freestyle. **F~stoß** m free kick

Freitag m Friday. **f~s** adv on Fridays

Frei|tod m suicide. **F~umschlag** m stamped envelope. **f~weg** adv freely; (offen) openly. **f~willig** adj voluntary. **F~willige(r)** m/f volunteer. **F~zeichen** nt ringing tone; (Rufzeichen) dialling tone. **F~zeit** f free or spare time; (Muße) leisure. **F~zeit-** prefix leisure; **F~zeitbekleidung** f casual wear. **f~zügig** adj unrestricted; (großzügig) liberal

fremd adj foreign; (unbekannt) strange; (nicht das eigene) other people's; **ein f~er Mann** a stranger; **f~e Leute** strangers; **unter f~em Namen** under an assumed name; **ich bin hier f~** I'm a stranger here. **F~e** f - **in der F~e** away from home; (im Ausland) in a foreign country. **F~e(r)** m/f stranger; (Ausländer) foreigner; (Tourist) tourist. **F~enführer** m [tourist] guide. **F~enverkehr** m tourism. **F~enzimmer** nt room [to let]; (Gäste-) guest room. **f~gehen**† vi sep (sein) [!] be unfaithful. **F~sprache** f foreign language. **F~wort** nt (pl **-wörter**) foreign word

Freske f -,-n, **Fresko** nt **-s,-ken** fresco

Fresse f -,-n [✱] (Mund) gob; (Gesicht) mug. **f~n**† vt/i (haben) eat. **F~n** nt **-s** feed; (sl: Essen) grub

Fressnapf m feeding bowl

Freud|e f -,-n pleasure; (innere) joy; **mit F~en** with pleasure; **jdm eine F~e machen** please s.o. **f~ig** adj joyful

freuen vt please; **sich f~** be pleased (**über** + acc about); **sich f~ auf** (+ acc) look forward to; **es freut mich** I'm glad (**dass** that)

Freund m **-es,-e** friend; (Verehrer) boyfriend. **F~in** f -,**-nen** friend; (Liebste) girlfriend. **f~lich** adj kind; (umgänglich) friendly; (angenehm) pleasant. **f~licherweise** adv kindly. **F~lichkeit** f -,**-en** kindness; friendliness; pleasantness

Freundschaft f -,-en friendship; **F~ schließen** become friends. **f~lich** adj friendly

Frieden m -s peace; **F~ schließen** make peace; **im F~** in peacetime; **lass mich in F~!** leave me alone! **F~svertrag** m peace treaty

Fried|hof m cemetery. **f~lich** adj peaceful

frieren† vi (haben) (Person:) be cold; impers **es friert/hat gefroren** it is freezing/there has been a frost; **frierst du?** are you cold? • (sein) (gefrieren) freeze

Fries m -es,-e frieze

frisch adj fresh; (sauber) clean; (leuchtend) bright; (munter) lively; (rüstig) fit; **sich f~ machen** freshen up • adv freshly, newly; **ein Bett f~ beziehen** put clean sheets on a bed; **f~ gestrichen!** wet paint! **F~e** f - freshness; brightness; liveliness; fitness. **F~haltepackung** f vacuum pack

Fri|seur /fri'zø:ɐ̯/ m -s,-e hairdresser; (Herren-) barber. **F~seursalon** m hairdressing salon. **F~seuse** f -,-n hairdresser

frisier|en vt **jdn/sich f~en** do someone's/one's hair; **die Bilanz/einen Motor f~en** ⊡ fiddle the accounts/soup up an engine

Frisör m -s,-e = **Friseur**

Frist f -,-en period; (Termin) deadline; (Aufschub) time; **drei Tage F~** three days' grace. **f~los** adj instant

Frisur f -,-en hairstyle

frittieren vt deep-fry

frivol /fri'vo:l/ adj frivolous

froh adj happy; (freudig) joyful; (erleichtert) glad

fröhlich adj cheerful; (vergnügt) merry. **F~keit** f - cheerfulness; merriment

fromm adj devout; (gutartig) docile

Frömmigkeit f - devoutness

Fronleichnam m Corpus Christi

Front f -,-en front. **f~al** adj frontal; (Zusammenstoß) head-on • adv from the front; (zusammenstoßen) head-on. **F~alzusammenstoß** m head-on collision

Frosch m -[e]s,¨e frog. **F~laich** m frog-spawn. **F~mann** m (pl -männer) frogman

Frost m -[e]s,¨e frost. **F~beule** f chilblain

frösteln vi (haben) shiver

frost|ig adj frosty. **F~schutzmittel** nt antifreeze

Frottee nt & m -s towelling; **F~[hand]tuch** nt terry towel

frottieren vt rub down

Frucht f -,¨e fruit; **F~ tragen** bear fruit. **f~bar** adj fertile; (fig) fruitful. **F~barkeit** f - fertility

früh adj early • adv early; (morgens) in the morning; **heute f~** this morning; **von f~ an** od **auf** from an early age. **F~aufsteher** m -s,- early riser. **F~e** f - **in aller F~e** bright and early; **in der F~e** (SGer) in the morning. **f~er** adv earlier; (eher) sooner; (ehemals) formerly; (vor langer Zeit) in the old days; **f~er oder später** sooner or later; **ich wohnte f~er in X** I used to live in X. **f~ere(r,s)** adj earlier; (ehemalig) former; (vorige) previous; **in f~eren Zeiten** in former times. **f~estens** adv at the earliest. **F~geburt** f premature birth/(Kind) baby. **F~jahr** nt spring. **F~ling** m -s,-e spring. **f~morgens** adv early in the morning. **f~reif** adj precocious

Frühstück nt breakfast. **f~en** vi (haben) have breakfast

frühzeitig adj & adv early; (vorzeitig) premature

Frustr|ation /-'tsi̯o:n/ f -,-en frustration. **f~ieren** vt frustrate

Fuchs m -es,¨e fox; (Pferd) chestnut. **f~en** vt ⊡ annoy

Füchsin f -,-nen vixen

Fuge[1] f -,-n joint

Fuge[2] f -,-n (Mus) fugue

füg|en vt fit (**in** + acc into); (an-)

see A-Z of German life and culture

join (**an** + acc on to); (dazu-) add (**zu** to); **sich f~en** fit (**in** + acc into); adjoin/(folgen) follow (**an etw** acc sth); (fig: gehorchen) submit (dat to). **f~sam** adj obedient. **F~ung** f **-,-en eine F~ung des Schicksals** a stroke of fate

fühl|bar adj noticeable. **f~en** vt/i (haben) feel; **sich f~en** feel (**krank/einsam** ill/lonely); (!: stolz sein) fancy oneself. **F~er** m **-s,-** feeler. **F~ung** f - contact

f

Fuhre f **-,-n** load

führ|en vt lead; guide (Tourist); (geleiten) take; (leiten) run; (befehligen) command; (verkaufen) stock; bear (Namen); keep (Liste, Bücher); **bei** od **mit sich f~en** carry •vi (haben) lead; (verlaufen) go, run; **zu etw f~en** lead to sth. **f~end** adj leading. **F~er** m **-s,-** leader; (Fremden-) guide; (Buch) guide[book]. **F~erhaus** nt driver's cab. **F~erschein** m driving licence; **den F~erschein machen** take one's driving test. **F~erscheinentzug** m disqualification from driving. **F~ung** f **-,-en** leadership; (Leitung) management; (Mil) command; (Betragen) conduct; (Besichtigung) guided tour; (Vorsprung) lead; **in F~ung gehen** go into the lead

Fuhr|unternehmer m haulage contractor. **F~werk** nt cart

Fülle f **-,-n** abundance, wealth (**an** + dat of); (Körper-) plumpness. **f~n** vt fill; (Culin) stuff

Füllen nt **-s,-** foal

Füll|er m **-s,-** !, **F~federhalter** m fountain pen. **F~ung** f **-,-en** filling; (Braten-) stuffing

fummeln vi (haben) fumble (**an** + dat with)

Fund m **-[e]s,-e** find

Fundament nt **-[e]s,-e** foundations pl. **f~al** adj fundamental

Fundbüro nt lost-property office

fünf inv adj, **F~** f **-,-en** five; (Sch) ≈ fail mark. **F~linge** mpl quintuplets. **f~te(r,s)** adj fifth. **f~zehn** inv adj fifteen. **f~zehnte(r,s)** adj fifteenth. **f~zig** inv adj fifty. **f~zigste(r,s)** adj fiftieth

fungieren vi (haben) act (**als** as)

Funk m **-s** radio. **F~e** m **-n,-n** spark. **f~eln** vi (haben) sparkle; (Stern:) twinkle. **F~en** m **-s,-** spark. **f~en** vt radio. **F~sprechgerät** nt walkie-talkie. **F~spruch** m radio message. **F~streife** f [police] radio patrol

Funktion /-ˈtsi̯oːn/ f **-,-en** function; (Stellung) position; (Funktionieren) working; **außer F~** out of action. **F~är** m **-s,-e** official. **f~ieren** vi (haben) work

für prep (+ acc) for; **Schritt für Schritt** step by step; **was für [ein]** what [a]! (fragend) what sort of [a]? **Für** nt **das Für und Wider** the pros and cons pl

Furche f **-,-n** furrow

Furcht f - fear (**vor** + dat of); **F~ erregend** terrifying. **f~bar** adj terrible

fürcht|en vt/i (haben) fear; **sich f~en** be afraid (**vor** + dat of). **f~erlich** adj dreadful

füreinander adv for each other

Furnier nt **-s,-e** veneer. **f~t** adj veneered

Fürsorg|e f care; (Admin) welfare; (!: Geld) ≈ social security. **F~er(in)** m **-s,-** (f **-,-nen**) social worker. **f~lich** adj solicitous

Fürst m **-en,-en** prince. **F~entum** nt **-s,¨er** principality. **F~in** f **-,-nen** princess

Furt f **-,-en** ford

Furunkel m **-s,-** (Med) boil

Fürwort nt (pl **-wörter**) pronoun

Furz m **-es,-e** (vulgar) fart

Fusion f **-,-en** fusion; (Comm) merger

Fuß m **-es,¨e** foot; (Aust: Bein) leg; (Lampen-) base; (von Weinglas) stem; **zu Fuß** on foot; **zu Fuß gehen** walk; **auf freiem Fuß** free. **F~abdruck** m footprint. **F~abtreter** m **-s,-** doormat.

F~ball m football. **F~ballspieler** m footballer. **F~balltoto** nt football pools pl. **F~bank** f footstool. **F~boden** m floor

Fussel f -,-n & m -s,-[n] piece of fluff; **F~n** fluff sg. **f~n** vi (haben) shed fluff

fußen vi (haben) be based (**auf** + dat on)

Fußgänger|(in) m -s,- (f -,-nen) pedestrian. **F~brücke** f footbridge. **F~zone** f pedestrian precinct

Fuß|geher m -s,- (Aust) = **F~gänger. F~gelenk** nt ankle. **F~hebel** m pedal. **F~nagel** m toenail. **F~note** f footnote. **F~pflege** f chiropody. **F~rücken** m instep. **F~sohle** f sole of the foot. **F~tritt** m kick. **F~weg** m footpath; **eine Stunde F~weg** an hour's walk

futsch pred adj 🅸 gone

Futter[1] nt **-s** feed; (Trocken-) fodder

Futter[2] nt **-s,-** (Kleider-) lining

Futteral nt **-s,-e** case

füttern[1] vt feed

füttern[2] vt line

Futur nt **-s** (Gram) future

Gg

Gabe f -,-n gift; (Dosis) dose

Gabel f -,-n fork. **g~n (sich)** vr fork. **G~stapler** m -s,- fork-lift truck. **G~ung** f -,-en fork

gackern vi (haben) cackle

gaffen vi (haben) gape, stare

Gage /ˈgaːʒə/ f -,-n (Theat) fee

gähnen vi (haben) yawn

Gala f - ceremonial dress

Galavorstellung f gala performance

Galerie f -,-n gallery

Galgen m -s,- gallows sg. **G~frist** f 🅸 reprieve

Galionsfigur f figurehead

Galle f - bile; (G~nblase) gall-bladder. **G~nblase** f gall-bladder. **G~nstein** m gallstone

Galopp m **-s** gallop; **im G~** at a gallop. **g~ieren** vi (sein) gallop

gamm|eln vi (haben) 🅸 loaf around. **G~ler(in)** m -s,- (f -,-nen) drop-out

Gams f -,-en (Aust) chamois

Gämse f -,-n chamois

Gang m -[e]s,⸚e walk; (G~art) gait; (Boten-) errand; (Funktionieren) running; (Verlauf, Culin) course; (Durch-) passage; (Korridor) corridor; (zwischen Sitzreihen) aisle, gangway; (Anat) duct; (Auto) gear; **in G~ bringen** get going; **im G~e sein** be in progress; **Essen mit vier G⸚en** four-course meal

gängig adj common; (Comm) popular

Gangschaltung f gear change

Gangster /ˈgɛŋstɐ/ m **-s,-** gangster

Ganove m **-n,-n** 🅸 crook

Gans f -,⸚e goose

Gänse|blümchen nt **-s,-** daisy. **G~füßchen** ntpl inverted commas. **G~haut** f goose-pimples pl. **G~rich** m **-s,-e** gander

ganz adj whole, entire; (vollständig) complete; (🅸: heil) undamaged, intact; **die g~e Zeit** all the time, the whole time; **eine g~e Weile/ Menge** quite a while/lot; inv **g~ Deutschland** the whole of Germany; **wieder g~ machen** 🅸 mend; **im Großen und G~en** on the whole • adv quite; (völlig) completely, entirely; (sehr) very; **nicht g~** not quite; **g~ allein** all on one's own; **g~ und gar** completely, totally; **g~ und gar nicht** not at all. **G~e(s)** nt whole. **g~jährig** adv all the year round. **g~tägig** adj & adv full-time; (geöffnet) all day. **g~tags** adv all day; (arbeiten) full-time

gar[1] adj done, cooked

gar[2] adv **gar nicht/nichts/niemand** not/nothing/no one at all

Garage /ga'ra:ʒə/ f **-,-n** garage

Garantie f **-,-n** guarantee. **g~ren** vt/i (haben) **[für] etw g~ren** guarantee sth. **G~schein** m guarantee

Garderobe f **-,-n** (Kleider) wardrobe; (Ablage) cloakroom; (Künstler-) dressing-room. **G~nfrau** f cloakroom attendant

Gardine f **-,-n** curtain

garen vt/i (haben) cook

gären† vi (haben) ferment; (fig) seethe

Garn nt **-[e]s,-e** yarn; (Näh-) cotton

Garnele f **-,-n** shrimp; prawn

garnieren vt decorate; (Culin) garnish

Garnison f **-,-en** garrison

Garnitur f **-,-en** set; (Möbel-) suite

Garten m **-s,⸚** garden. **G~arbeit** f gardening. **G~bau** m horticulture. **G~haus** nt, **G~laube** f summerhouse. **G~schere** f secateurs pl

Gärtner|(in) m **-s,-** (f **-,-nen**) gardener. **G~ei** f **-,-en** nursery

Gärung f **-** fermentation

Gas nt **-es,-e** gas; **Gas geben** [!] accelerate. **G~maske** f gas mask. **G~pedal** nt (Auto) accelerator

Gasse f **-,-n** alley; (Aust) street

Gast m **-[e]s,⸚e** guest; (Hotel-) visitor; (im Lokal) patron; **zum Mittag G⸚e haben** have people to lunch; **bei jdm zu G~ sein** be staying with s.o. **G~arbeiter** m foreign worker. **G~bett** nt spare bed

see A-Z of German life and culture

Gäste|bett nt spare bed. **G~buch** nt visitors' book. **G~zimmer** nt [hotel] room; (privat) spare room

gast|freundlich adj hospitable. **G~freundschaft** f hospitality. **G~geber** m **-s,-** host. **G~geberin** f **-,-nen** hostess. **G~haus** nt, **G~hof** m inn, hotel

gastlich adj hospitable

Gastronomie f **-** gastronomy

Gast|spiel nt guest performance. **G~spielreise** f (Theat) tour. **G~stätte** f restaurant. **G~wirt** m landlord. **G~wirtin** f landlady. **G~wirtschaft** f restaurant

Gas|werk nt gasworks sg. **G~zähler** m gas meter

Gatte m **-n,-n** husband

Gattin f **-,-nen** wife

Gattung f **-,-en** kind; (Biology) genus; (Kunst) genre

Gaudi f **-** (Aust, [!]) fun

Gaumen m **-s,-** palate

Gauner m **-s,-** crook, swindler. **G~ei** f **-,-en** swindle

Gaze /'ga:zə/ f **-** gauze

Gazelle f **-,-n** gazelle

Gebäck nt **-s** [cakes and] pastries pl; (Kekse) biscuits pl

Gebälk nt **-s** timbers pl

geballt adj (Faust) clenched

Gebärde f **-,-n** gesture

gebär|en† vt give birth to, bear; **geboren werden** be born. **G~mutter** f womb, uterus

Gebäude nt **-s,-** building

Gebeine ntpl [mortal] remains

Gebell nt **-s** barking

geben† vt give; (tun, bringen) put; (Karten) deal; (aufführen) perform; (unterrichten) teach; **etw verloren g~** give sth up as lost; **viel/wenig g~ auf** (+ acc) set great/little store by; **sich g~** (nachlassen) wear off; (besser werden) get better; (sich verhalten) behave • impers **es gibt** there is/are; **was gibt es Neues/zum Mittag/im Kino?** what's the news/for lunch/on at the cinema? **es wird Regen g∼** it's going to rain •vi (haben) (Karten) deal

Gebet nt **-[e]s,-e** prayer

Gebiet nt **-[e]s,-e** area; (Hoheits-) territory; (Sach-) field

gebieten† vt command; (erfordern) demand •vi (haben) rule

Gebilde nt **-s,-** structure

gebildet adj educated; (kultiviert) cultured

Gebirg|e nt **-s,-** mountains pl. **g∼ig** adj mountainous

Gebiss nt **-es,-e** teeth pl; (künstliches) false teeth pl; dentures pl, (des Zaumes) bit

geblümt adj floral, flowered

gebogen adj curved

geboren adj born; **g∼er Deutscher** German by birth; **Frau X, g∼e Y** Mrs X, née Y

Gebot nt **-[e]s,-e** rule

gebraten adj fried

Gebrauch m use; (Sprach-) usage; **Gebräuche** customs; **in G∼** in use; **G∼ machen von** make use of. **g∼en** vt use; **zu nichts zu g∼en** useless

gebräuchlich adj common; (Wort) in common use

Gebrauch|sanleitung, G∼sanweisung f directions pl for use. **g∼t** adj used; (Comm) secondhand. **G∼twagen** m used car

gebrechlich adj frail, infirm

gebrochen adj broken •adv **g∼Englisch sprechen** speak broken English

Gebrüll nt **-s** roaring

Gebühr f **-,-en** charge, fee; **über G∼** excessively. **g∼end** adj due; (geziemend) proper. **g∼enfrei** adj free •adv free of charge. **g∼enpflichtig** adj & adv subject to a charge; **g∼enpflichtige Straße** toll road

Geburt f **-,-en** birth; **von G∼** by birth. **G∼enkontrolle, G∼enregelung** f birth control. **G∼enziffer** f birth rate

gebürtig adj native (**aus** of); **g∼er Deutscher** German by birth

Geburts|datum nt date of birth. **G∼helfer** m obstetrician. **G∼hilfe** f obstetrics sg. **G∼ort** m place of birth. **G∼tag** m birthday. **G∼urkunde** f birth certificate

Gebüsch nt **-[e]s,-e** bushes pl

Gedächtnis nt **-ses** memory; **aus dem G∼** from memory

Gedanke m **-ns,-n** thought (**an** + acc of); (Idee) idea; **sich** (dat) **G∼n machen** worry (**über** + acc about). **g∼nlos** adj thoughtless; (zerstreut) absent-minded. **G∼nstrich** m dash

Gedärme ntpl intestines; (Tier-) entrails

Gedeck nt **-[e]s,-e** place setting; (auf Speisekarte) set meal

gedeihen† vi (sein) thrive, flourish

gedenken† vi (haben) propose (**etw zu tun** to do sth); **jds g∼** remember s.o. **G∼** nt **-s** memory

Gedenk|feier f commemoration. **G∼gottesdienst** m memorial service

Gedicht nt **-[e]s,-e** poem

Gedräng|e nt **-s** crush, crowd. **g∼t** adj (knapp) concise •adv **g∼t voll** packed

Geduld f **-** patience; **G∼ haben** be patient. **g∼en (sich)** vr be patient. **g∼ig** adj patient. **G∼[s]spiel** nt puzzle

gedunsen adj bloated

geehrt adj honoured; **Sehr g∼er Herr X** Dear Mr X

geeignet adj suitable; **im g∼en Moment** at the right moment

Gefahr f **-,-en** danger; **in G∼** in danger; **auf eigene G∼** at one's own risk; **G∼ laufen** run the risk (**etw zu tun** of doing sth)

gefähr|den vt endanger; (fig) jeopardize. **g∼lich** adj dangerous

gefahrlos adj safe

Gefährt nt **-[e]s,-e** vehicle

g

Gefährte m **-n,-n, Gefährtin** f **-,-nen** companion

gefahrvoll adj dangerous, perilous

Gefälle nt **-s,-** slope; (Straßen-) gradient

gefallen† vi (haben) **jdm g~** please s.o.; **er/es gefällt mir** I like him/it; **sich** (dat) **etw g~ lassen** put up with sth

Gefallen¹ m **-s,-** favour

Gefallen² nt **-s** pleasure (**an** + dat in); **dir zu G~** to please you

Gefallene(r) m soldier killed in the war

gefällig adj pleasing; (hübsch) attractive; (hilfsbereit) obliging; **noch etwas g~?** will there be anything else? **G~keit** f **-,-en** favour; (Freundlichkeit) kindness

Gefangen|e(r) m/f prisoner. **G~nahme** f **-** capture. **g~nehmen*** vt sep = **g~ nehmen**, s. **fangen**. **G~schaft** f **-** captivity

Gefängnis nt **-ses,-se** prison; (Strafe) imprisonment. **G~strafe** f imprisonment; (Urteil) prison sentence. **G~wärter** m [prison] warder

Gefäß nt **-es,-e** container; (Blut-) vessel

gefasst adj composed; (ruhig) calm; **g~ sein auf** (+ acc) be prepared for

gefedert adj sprung

gefeiert adj celebrated

Gefieder nt **-s** plumage

gefleckt adj spotted

Geflügel nt **-s** poultry. **G~klein** nt **-s** giblets pl. **g~t** adj winged

Geflüster nt **-s** whispering

Gefolge nt **-s** retinue, entourage

gefragt adj popular

Gefreite(r) m lance corporal

gefrier|en† vi (sein) freeze. **G~fach** nt freezer compartment. **G~punkt** m freezing point. **G~schrank** m upright freezer. **G~truhe** f chest freezer

gefroren adj frozen

gefügig adj compliant; (gehorsam) obedient

Gefühl nt **-[e]s,-e** feeling; (Empfindung) sensation; (G~sregung) emotion; **im G~ haben** know instinctively. **g~los** adj insensitive; (herzlos) unfeeling; (taub) numb. **g~smäßig** adj emotional; (instinktiv) instinctive. **G~sregung** f emotion. **g~voll** adj sensitive; (sentimental) sentimental

gefüllt adj filled; (voll) full

gefürchtet adj feared, dreaded

gefüttert adj lined

gegeben adj given; (bestehend) present; (passend) appropriate. **g~enfalls** adv if need be

gegen prep (+ acc) against; (Sport) versus; (g~über) to[-wards]; (Vergleich) compared with; (Richtung, Zeit) towards; (ungefähr) around; **ein Mittel g~** a remedy for • adv **g~ 100 Leute** about 100 people. **G~angriff** m counter-attack

Gegend f **-,-en** area, region; (Umgebung) neighbourhood

gegeneinander adv against/ (gegenüber) towards one another

Gegen|fahrbahn f opposite carriageway. **G~gift** nt antidote. **G~maßnahme** f countermeasure. **G~satz** m contrast; (Widerspruch) contradiction; (G~teil) opposite; **im G~satz zu** unlike. **g~seitig** adj mutual; **sich g~seitig hassen** hate one another. **G~stand** m object; (Gram, Gesprächs-) subject. **G~stück** nt counterpart; (G~teil) opposite. **G~teil** nt opposite, contrary; **im G~teil** on the contrary. **g~teilig** adj opposite

gegenüber prep (+ dat) opposite; (Vergleich) compared with; **jdm g~ höflich sein** be polite to s.o. • adv opposite. **G~** nt **-s** person opposite. **g~liegend** adj opposite. **g~stehen†** vi sep (haben) (+ dat) face; **feindlich g~stehen** (+ dat) be hostile to. **g~stellen** vt sep confront; (vergleichen) compare

Gegen|verkehr m oncoming traffic. **G~vorschlag** m counter-proposal. **G~wart** f **-** present;

(Anwesenheit) presence. **g~wärtig** adj present •adv at present. **G~wehr** f - resistance. **G~wert** m equivalent. **G~wind** m head wind. **g~zeichnen** vt sep countersign

geglückt adj successful

Gegner|(in) m **-s,-** (f **-,-nen**) opponent. **g~isch** adj opposing

Gehabe nt **-s** affected behaviour

Gehackte(s) nt mince

Gehalt nt **-[e]s,¨-er** salary. **G~serhöhung** f rise

gehässig adj spiteful

gehäuft adj heaped

Gehäuse nt **-s,-** case; (TV, Radio) cabinet; (Schnecken-) shell

Gehege nt **-s,-** enclosure

geheim adj secret; **g~ halten** keep secret; **im g~en** secretly. **G~dienst** m Secret Service. **G~nis** nt **-ses,-se** secret. **g~nisvoll** adj mysterious

gehemmt adj (fig) inhibited

gehen†

• intransitive verb (sein)

····➤ (sich irgendwohin begeben) go; (zu Fuß) walk. **tanzen/schwimmen/einkaufen gehen** go dancing/swimming/shopping. **schlafen gehen** go to bed. **zum Arzt gehen** go to the doctor's. **in die Schule gehen** go to school. **auf und ab gehen** walk up and down. **über die Straße gehen** cross the street

····➤ (weggehen; fam: abfahren) go; leave. **ich muss bald gehen** I must go soon. **Sie können gehen** you may go. **der Zug geht um zehn Uhr** [!] the train leaves or goes at ten o'clock

····➤ (funktionieren) work. **der Computer geht wieder/nicht mehr** the computer is working again/has stopped working. **meine Uhr geht falsch/richtig** my watch is wrong/right

····➤ (möglich sein) be possible. **ja, das geht** yes, I or we can manage that. **das geht nicht** that can't be done; ([!]: ist nicht akzeptabel) it's not good enough, it's not on [!]. **es geht einfach nicht, dass du so spät nach Hause kommst** it simply won't do for you to come home so late

····➤ ([!]: gerade noch angehen) **es geht [so]** it is all right. **Wie war die Party? — Es ging so** How was the party? — Not bad or So-so

····➤ (sich entwickeln) do; go. **der Laden geht gut** the shop is doing well. **es geht alles nach Wunsch** everything is going to plan

····➤ (impers) **wie geht es Ihnen?** how are you? **jdm geht es gut/schlecht** (gesundheitlich) s.o. is doing well/badly

····➤ (impers; sich um etw handeln) **es geht um** it concerns. **worum geht es hier?** what is this all about? **es geht ihr nur ums Geld** she is only interested in money

Geheul nt **-s** howling

Gehilfe m **-n,-n, Gehilfin** f **-,-nen** trainee; (Helfer) assistant

Gehirn nt **-s** brain; (Verstand) brains pl **G~erschütterung** f concussion. **G~hautentzündung** f meningitis. **G~wäsche** f brainwashing

gehoben adj (fig) superior

Gehöft nt **-[e]s,-e** farm

Gehör nt **-s** hearing

gehorchen vi (haben) (+ dat) obey

gehören vi (haben) belong (dat to); **dazu gehört Mut** that takes courage; **es gehört sich nicht** it isn't done

gehörlos adj deaf

Gehörn nt **-s,-e** horns pl; (Geweih) antlers pl

gehorsam adj obedient. **G~** m **-s** obedience

Geh|steig m **-[e]s,-e** pavement. **G~weg** m = **Gehsteig;** (Fußweg) footpath

Geier m **-s,-** vulture

g

g

Geig|e f -,-n violin. **g~en** vi (haben) play the violin •vt play on the violin. **G~er(in)** m -s,- (f -,-nen) violinist

geil adj lecherous; randy; (!: toll) great

Geisel f -,-n hostage

Geiß f -,-en (SGer) [nanny-]goat. **G~blatt** nt honeysuckle

Geist m -[e]s,-er mind; (Witz) wit; (Gesinnung) spirit; (Gespenst) ghost; **der Heilige G~** the Holy Ghost or Spirit

geistes|abwesend adj absent-minded. **G~blitz** m brainwave. **g~gegenwärtig** adv with great presence of mind. **g~gestört** adj [mentally] deranged. **g~krank** adj mentally ill. **G~krankheit** f mental illness. **G~wissenschaften** fpl arts. **G~zustand** m mental state

geist|ig adj mental; (intellektuell) intellectual. **g~lich** adj spiritual; (religiös) religious; (Musik) sacred; (Tracht) clerical. **G~liche(r)** m clergyman. **G~lichkeit** f - clergy. **g~reich** adj clever; (witzig) witty

Geiz m -es meanness. **g~en** vi (haben) be mean (**mit** with). **G~hals** m ! miser. **g~ig** adj mean, miserly. **G~kragen** m ! miser

Gekicher nt -s giggling

geknickt adj ! dejected

gekonnt adj accomplished •adv expertly

gekränkt adj offended, hurt

Gekritzel nt -s scribble

Gelächter nt -s laughter

geladen adj loaded

gelähmt adj paralysed

Geländer nt -s,- railings pl; (Treppen-) banisters

gelangen vi (sein) reach/(fig) attain (**zu etw/an etw** acc sth)

gelassen adj composed; (ruhig) calm. **G~heit** f - equanimity; (Fassung) composure

Gelatine /ʒela-/ f - gelatine

geläufig adj common, current; (fließend) fluent; **jdm g~ sein** be familiar to s.o.

gelaunt adj **gut/schlecht g~ sein** be in a good/bad mood

gelb adj yellow; (bei Ampel) amber; **das G~e vom Ei** the yolk of the egg. **G~** nt -s,- yellow. **g~lich** adj yellowish. **G~sucht** f jaundice

Geld nt -es,-er money; **öffentliche G~er** public funds. **G~automat** m cashpoint machine. **G~beutel** m, **G~börse** f purse. **G~geber** m -s,- backer. **g~lich** adj financial. **G~mittel** ntpl funds. **G~schein** m banknote. **G~schrank** m safe. **G~strafe** f fine. **G~stück** nt coin

Gelee /ʒe'le:/ nt -s,-s jelly

gelegen adj situated; (passend) convenient

Gelegenheit f -,-en opportunity, chance; (Anlass) occasion; (Comm) bargain; **bei G~** some time. **G~sarbeit** f casual work. **G~skauf** m bargain

gelegentlich adj occasional •adv occasionally; (bei Gelegenheit) some time

Gelehrte(r) m/f scholar

Geleit nt -[e]s escort; **freies G~** safe conduct. **g~en** vt escort

Gelenk nt -[e]s,-e joint. **g~ig** adj supple; (Techn) flexible

gelernt adj skilled

Geliebte(r) m/f lover

gelingen† vi (sein) succeed, be successful. **G~** nt -s success

gellend adj shrill

geloben vt promise [solemnly]; **das Gelobte Land** the Promised Land

Gelöbnis nt -ses,-se vow

gelöst adj (fig) relaxed

gelten† vi (haben) be valid; (Regel:) apply; **g~ als** be regarded as; **etw nicht g~ lassen** not accept sth; **wenig/viel g~** be worth/(fig) count for little/a lot; **jdm g~** be meant for s.o.; **das gilt nicht** that doesn't count. **g~d** adj valid; (Preise) current; (Meinung) prevailing; **g~d machen** assert (Recht, Forderung); bring to bear (Einfluss)

Geltung f - validity; (Ansehen) prestige; **zur G~ bringen** set off

Gelübde nt **-s,-** vow

gelungen adj successful

Gelüst nt **-[e]s,-e** desire

gemächlich adj leisurely • adv in a leisurely manner

Gemahl m **-s,-e** husband. **G~in** f **-,-nen** wife

Gemälde nt **-s,-** painting. **G~galerie** f picture gallery

gemäß prep (+ dat) in accordance with

gemäßigt adj moderate; (Klima) temperate

gemein adj common; (unanständig) vulgar; (niederträchtig) mean; **g~er Soldat** private

Gemeinde f **-,-n** [local] community; (Admin) borough; (Pfarr-) parish; (bei Gottesdienst) congregation. **G~rat** m local council/(Person) councillor. **G~wahlen** fpl local elections

gemein|gefährlich adj dangerous. **G~heit** f **-,-en** commonness; vulgarity; meanness; (Bemerkung, Handlung) mean thing [to say/do]; **so eine G~heit!** how mean! **G~kosten** pl overheads. **g~nützig** adj charitable. **g~sam** adj common • adv together

Gemeinschaft f **-,-en** community. **g~lich** adj joint; (Besitz) communal • adv jointly; (zusammen) together. **G~sarbeit** f team work

Gemenge nt **-s,-** mixture

Gemisch nt **-[e]s,-e** mixture. **g~t** adj mixed

Gemme f **-,-n** engraved gem

Gemse* f **-,-n** = **Gämse**

Gemurmel nt **-s** murmuring

Gemüse nt **-s,-** vegetable; (coll) vegetables pl. **G~händler** m greengrocer

gemustert adj patterned

Gemüt nt **-[e]s,-er** nature, disposition; (Gefühl) feelings pl

gemütlich adj cosy; (gemächlich) leisurely; (zwanglos) informal; (Person) genial; **es sich** (dat) **g~ machen** make oneself comfortable. **G~keit** f - cosiness

Gen nt **-s,-e** gene

genau adj exact, precise; (Waage, Messung) accurate; (sorgfältig) meticulous; (ausführlich) detailed; **nichts G~es wissen** not know any details; **g~ genommen** strictly speaking; **g~!** exactly! **G~igkeit** f - exactitude; precision; accuracy; meticulousness

genauso adv just the same; (g~ sehr) just as much; **g~ teuer** just as expensive; **g~ gut** just as good; adv just as well; **g~ sehr** just as much; **g~ viel** just as much/many; **g~ wenig** just as little/few; (noch) no more

Gendarm /ʒãˈdarm/ m **-en,-en** (Aust) policeman

Genealogie f - genealogy

genehmig|en vt grant; approve (Plan). **G~ung** f **-,-en** permission; (Schein) permit

geneigt adj sloping, inclined; (fig) well-disposed (dat towards)

General m **-s,⸚e** general. **G~direktor** m managing director. **G~probe** f dress rehearsal. **G~streik** m general strike

Generation /-ˈtsi̯oːn/ f **-,-en** generation

Generator m **-s,-en** generator

generell adj general

genes|en† vi (sein) recover. **G~ung** f - recovery; (Erholung) convalescence

Genetik f - genetics sg

genetisch adj genetic

Genf nt **-s** Geneva. **G~er** adj Geneva; **G~er See** Lake Geneva

g

see A-Z of German life and culture

genial adj brilliant. **G~ität** f genius

Genick nt **-s,-e** [back of the] neck; **sich** (dat) **das G~ brechen** break one's neck

Genie /ʒe'ni:/ nt **-s,-s** genius

genieren /ʒe'ni:rən/ vt embarrass; **sich g~** feel or be embarrassed

genieß|bar adj fit to eat/drink. **g~en†** vt enjoy; (verzehren) eat/drink

g

Genitiv m **-s,-e** genitive

genmanipuliert adj genetically modified

Genom nt **-s, -e** genome

Genosse m **-n,-n** (Pol) comrade. **G~nschaft** f **-,-en** cooperative

Gentechnologie f genetic engineering

genug inv adj & adv enough

Genüge f **zur G~** sufficiently. **g~n** vi (haben) be enough. **g~nd** inv adj sufficient, enough; (Sch) fair • adv sufficiently, enough

Genuss m **-es,⸚e** enjoyment; (Vergnügen) pleasure; (Verzehr) consumption

geöffnet adj open

Geo|graphie, G~grafie f - geography. **g~graphisch, g~grafisch** adj geographical. **G~logie** f - geology. **g~logisch** adj geological. **G~meter** m **-s,-** surveyor. **G~metrie** f - geometry. **g~metrisch** adj geometric[al]

geordnet adj well-ordered; (stabil) stable; **alphabetisch g~** in alphabetical order

Gepäck nt **-s** luggage, baggage. **G~ablage** f luggage-rack. **G~aufbewahrung** f left-luggage office. **G~schein** m left-luggage ticket; (Aviat) baggage check. **G~träger** m porter; (Fahrrad-) luggage carrier; (Dach-) roof-rack

Gepard m **-s,-e** cheetah

gepflegt adj well-kept; (Person) well-groomed; (Hotel) first-class

gepunktet adj spotted

gerade adj straight; (direkt) direct; (aufrecht) upright; (aufrichtig) straightforward; (Zahl) even • adv straight; directly; (eben) just; (genau) exactly; (besonders) especially; **g~ sitzen/stehen** sit/stand [up] straight; **g~ erst** only just. **G~** f **-,-n** straight line. **g~aus** adv straight ahead/on. **g~heraus** adv (fig) straight out. **g~so** adv just the same; **g~so gut** just as good; adv just as well. **g~stehen†** vi sep (haben) (fig) accept responsibility (**für** for). **g~zu** adv virtually; (wirklich) absolutely

Geranie /-i̯ə/ f **-,-n** geranium

Gerät nt **-[e]s,-e** tool; (Acker-) implement; (Küchen-) utensil; (Elektro-) appliance; (Radio-, Fernseh-) set; (Turn-) piece of apparatus; (coll) equipment

geraten† vi (sein) get; **in Brand g~** catch fire; **in Wut g~** get angry; **gut g~** turn out well

Geratewohl nt **aufs G~** at random

geräuchert adj smoked

geräumig adj spacious, roomy

Geräusch nt **-[e]s,-e** noise. **g~los** adj noiseless

gerben vt tan

gerecht adj just; (fair) fair. **g~fertigt** adj justified. **G~igkeit** f - justice; fairness

Gerede nt **-s** talk

geregelt adj regular

gereizt adj irritable

Geriatrie f - geriatrics sg

Gericht[1] nt **-[e]s,-e** (Culin) dish

Gericht[2] nt **-[e]s,-e** court [of law]; **vor G~** in court; **das Jüngste G~** the Last Judgement. **g~lich** adj judicial; (Verfahren) legal • adv **g~lich vorgehen** take legal action. **G~shof** m court of justice. **G~smedizin** f forensic medicine. **G~ssaal** m court room. **G~svollzieher** m **-s,-** bailiff

gerieben adj grated; (!: schlau) crafty

gering adj small; (niedrig) low;

(g~fügig) slight. **g~fügig** adj slight. **g~schätzig** adj contemptuous; (Bemerkung) disparaging. **g~ste(r,s)** adj least; **nicht im G~sten** not in the least

gerinnen† vi (sein) curdle; (Blut:) clot

Gerippe nt **-s,-** skeleton; (fig) framework

gerissen adj [!] crafty

Germ m **-[e]s** & (Aust) f **-** yeast

German|e m **-n,-n** [ancient] German. **g~isch** adj Germanic. **G~istik** f **-** German [language and literature]

gern[e] adv gladly; **g~ haben** like; (lieben) be fond of; **ich tanze g~** I like dancing; **willst du mit?—g~!** do you want to come?—I'd love to!

Gerste f **-** barley. **G~nkorn** nt (Med) stye

Geruch m **-[e]s,¨e** smell (**von/nach** of). **g~los** adj odourless. **G~ssinn** m sense of smell

Gerücht nt **-[e]s,-e** rumour

gerührt adj (fig) moved, touched

Gerümpel nt **-s** lumber, junk

Gerüst nt **-[e]s,-e** scaffolding; (fig) framework

gesammelt adj collected; (gefasst) composed

gesamt adj entire, whole. **G~ausgabe** f complete edition. **G~eindruck** m overall impression. **G~heit** f **-** whole. **G~schule** f comprehensive school. **G~summe** f total

Gesandte(r) m/f envoy

Gesang m **-[e]s,¨e** singing; (Lied) song; (Kirchen-) hymn. **G~verein** m choral society

Gesäß nt **-es** buttocks pl

Geschäft nt **-[e]s,-e** business; (Laden) shop, store; (Transaktion) deal; **schmutzige G~e** shady dealings; **ein gutes G~ machen** do very well (**mit** out of). **g~ig** adj busy; (Treiben) bustling. **G~igkeit** f **-** activity. **g~lich** adj business ● adv on business

Geschäfts|brief m business letter. **G~führer** m manager; (Vereins-) secretary. **G~mann** m (pl **-leute**) businessman. **G~stelle** f office; (Zweigstelle) branch. **g~tüchtig** adj **g~tüchtig sein** be a good businessman/-woman. **G~zeiten** fpl hours of business

geschehen† vi (sein) happen (dat to); **das geschieht dir recht!** it serves you right! **gern g~!** you're welcome! **G~** nt **-s** events pl

gescheit adj clever

Geschenk nt **-[e]s,-e** present, gift

Geschicht|e f **-,-n** history; (Erzählung) story; ([!]: Sache) business. **g~lich** adj historical

Geschick nt **-[e]s** fate; (Talent) skill. **G~lichkeit** f **-** skilfulness, skill. **g~t** adj skilful; (klug) clever

geschieden adj divorced

Geschirr nt **-s,-e** (coll) crockery; (Porzellan) china; (Service) service; (Pferde-) harness; **schmutziges G~** dirty dishes pl. **G~spülmaschine** f dishwasher. **G~tuch** nt tea towel

Geschlecht nt **-[e]s,-er** sex; (Gram) gender; (Generation) generation. **g~lich** adj sexual. **G~skrankheit** f venereal disease. **G~steile** ntpl genitals. **G~sverkehr** m sexual intercourse. **G~swort** nt (pl **-wörter**) article

geschliffen adj (fig) polished

Geschmack m **-[e]s,¨e** taste; (Aroma) flavour; (G~ssinn) sense of taste; **einen guten G~ haben** (fig) have good taste. **g~los** adj tasteless; **g~los sein** (fig) be in bad taste. **g~voll** adj (fig) tasteful

Geschoss nt **-es,-e** missile; (Stockwerk) storey, floor

Geschrei nt **-s** screaming; (fig) fuss

Geschütz nt **-es,-e** gun, cannon

geschützt adj protected; (Stelle) sheltered

Geschwader nt **-s,-** squadron

see A-Z of German life and culture

Geschwätz nt **-es** talk

geschweige conj **g~ denn** let alone

Geschwindigkeit f **-,-en** speed; (Phys) velocity. **G~sbegrenzung, G~sbeschränkung** f speed limit

Geschwister pl brother[s] and sister[s]; siblings

geschwollen adj swollen; (fig) pompous

Geschworene|(r) m/f juror; **die G~n** the jury sg

g

Geschwulst f **-,¨e** swelling; (Tumor) tumour

geschwungen adj curved

Geschwür nt **-s,-e** ulcer

gesellig adj sociable; (Zool) gregarious; (unterhaltsam) convivial; **g~er Abend** social evening

Gesellschaft f **-,-en** company; (Veranstaltung) party; **die G~** society; **jdm G~ leisten** keep s.o. company. **g~lich** adj social. **G~sspiel** nt party game

Gesetz nt **-es,-e** law. **G~entwurf** m bill. **g~gebend** adj legislative. **G~gebung** f **-** legislation. **g~lich** adj legal. **g~mäßig** adj lawful; (gesetzlich) legal. **g~widrig** adj illegal

gesichert adj secure

Gesicht nt **-[e]s,-er** face; (Aussehen) appearance. **G~sfarbe** f complexion. **G~spunkt** m point of view. **G~szüge** mpl features

Gesindel nt **-s** riff-raff

Gesinnung f **-,-en** mind; (Einstellung) attitude

gesondert adj separate

Gespann nt **-[e]s,-e** team; (Wagen) horse and cart/carriage

gespannt adj taut; (fig) tense; (Beziehungen) strained; (neugierig) eager; (erwartungsvoll) expectant; **g~ sein, ob** wonder whether; **auf etw g~ sein** look forward eagerly to sth

Gespenst nt **-[e]s,-er** ghost. **g~isch** adj ghostly; (unheimlich) eerie

Gespött nt **-[e]s** mockery; **zum G~ werden** become a laughing stock

Gespräch nt **-[e]s-e** conversation; (Telefon-) call; **ins G~ kommen** get talking; **im G~ sein** be under discussion. **g~ig** adj talkative. **G~sthema** nt topic of conversation

Gestalt f **-,-en** figure; (Form) shape, form; **G~ annehmen** (fig) take shape. **g~en** vt shape; (organisieren) arrange; (schaffen) create; (entwerfen) design; **sich g~en** turn out

Geständnis nt **-ses,-se** confession

Gestank m **-s** stench, [bad] smell

gestatten vt allow, permit; **nicht gestattet** prohibited; **g~ Sie?** may I?

Geste /ˈgɛ-, ˈgeːstə/ f **-,-n** gesture

Gesteck nt **-[e]s,-e** flower arrangement

gestehen† vt/i (haben) confess; confess to (Verbrechen)

Gestein nt **-[e]s,-e** rock

Gestell nt **-[e]s,-e** stand; (Flaschen-) rack; (Rahmen) frame

gesteppt adj quilted

gestern adv yesterday; **g~ Nacht** last night

gestrandet adj stranded

gestreift adj striped

gestrichelt adj (Linie) dotted

gestrichen adj **g~er Teelöffel** level teaspoon[ful]

gestrig /ˈgɛstrɪç/ adj yesterday's; **am g~en Tag** yesterday

Gestrüpp nt **-s,-e** undergrowth

Gestüt nt **-[e]s,-e** stud [farm]

Gesuch nt **-[e]s,-e** request; (Admin) application. **g~t** adj sought-after

gesund adj healthy; **g~ sein** be in good health; (Sport, Getränk:) be good for one; **wieder g~ werden** get well again

Gesundheit f **-** health; **G~!** (bei Niesen) bless you! **g~lich** adj health; **g~licher Zustand** state of health • adv **es geht ihm g~lich**

gut/schlecht he is in good/poor health. **g~sschädlich** adj harmful

getäfelt adj panelled

Getöse nt **-s** racket, din

Getränk nt **-[e]s,-e** drink. **G~ekarte** f wine-list

getrauen vt **sich** (dat) **etw g~** dare [to] do sth; **sich g~** dare

Getreide nt **-s** (coll) grain

getrennt adj separate; **g~ leben** live apart; **g~ schreiben** write as two words

getreu adj faithful • prep (+ dat) true to. **g~lich** adv faithfully

Getriebe nt **-s,-** bustle; (Techn) gear; (Auto) transmission; (Gehäuse) gearbox

getrost adv with confidence

Getto nt **-s,-s** ghetto

Getue nt **-s** [!] fuss

Getümmel nt **-s** tumult

geübt adj skilled

Gewächs nt **-es,-e** plant

gewachsen adj **jdm g~ sein** be a match for s.o.

Gewächshaus nt greenhouse

gewagt adj daring

gewählt adj refined

gewahr adj **g~ werden** become aware (acc/gen of)

Gewähr f **-** guarantee

gewähr|en vt grant; (geben) offer. **g~leisten** vt guarantee

Gewahrsam m **-s** safekeeping; (Haft) custody

Gewalt f **-,-en** power; (Kraft) force; (Brutalität) violence; **mit G~** by force. **G~herrschaft** f tyranny. **g~ig** adj powerful; ([!]: groß) enormous; (stark) tremendous. **g~sam** adj forcible; (Tod) violent. **g~tätig** adj violent. **G~tätigkeit** f **-,-en** violence; (Handlung) act of violence

Gewand nt **-[e]s,¨er** robe

gewandt adj skilful. **G~heit** f **-** skill

Gewebe nt **-s,-** fabric; (Anat) tissue

Gewehr nt **-s,-e** rifle, gun

Geweih nt **-[e]s,-e** antlers pl

Gewerb|e nt **-s,-** trade. **g~lich** adj commercial. **g~smäßig** adj professional

Gewerkschaft f **-,-en** trade union. **G~ler(in)** m **-s,-** (f **-,-nen**) trade unionist

Gewicht nt **-[e]s,-e** weight; (Bedeutung) importance. **G~heben** nt **-s** weight lifting

Gewinde nt **-s,-** [screw] thread

Gewinn m **-[e]s,-e** profit; (fig) gain, benefit; (beim Spiel) winnings pl; (Preis) prize; (Los) winning ticket. **G~beteiligung** f profit-sharing. **g~en†** vt win; (erlangen) gain; (fördern) extract • vi (haben) win; **g~en an** (+ dat) gain in. **g~end** adj engaging. **G~er(in)** m **-s,-** (f **-,-nen**) winner

Gewirr nt **-s,-e** tangle; (Straßen-) maze

gewiss adj certain

Gewissen nt **-s,-** conscience. **g~haft** adj conscientious. **g~los** adj unscrupulous. **G~sbisse** mpl pangs of conscience

gewissermaßen adv to a certain extent; (sozusagen) as it were

Gewissheit f **-** certainty

Gewitt|er nt **-s,-** thunderstorm. **g~rig** adj thundery

gewogen adj (fig) well-disposed (dat towards)

gewöhnen vt **jdn/sich g~ an** (+ acc) get s.o. used to/get used to; **[an] jdn/etw gewöhnt sein** be used to s.o./sth

Gewohnheit f **-,-en** habit. **G~srecht** nt common law

gewöhnlich adj ordinary; (üblich) usual; (ordinär) common

gewohnt adj customary; (vertraut) familiar; (üblich) usual; **etw** (acc) **g~ sein** be used to sth

Gewölbe nt **-s,-** vault

Gewühl nt **-[e]s** crush

gewunden adj winding

Gewürz nt **-es,-e** spice. **G~nelke** f clove

gezackt adj serrated

gezähnt adj serrated; (Säge) toothed

Gezeiten fpl tides

gezielt adj specific; (Frage) pointed

geziert adj affected

gezwungen adj forced. **g~ermaßen** adv of necessity

g

Gicht f - gout

Giebel m **-s,-** gable

Gier f - greed (**nach** for). **g~ig** adj greedy

gieß|en† vt pour; water (Blumen, Garten); (Techn) cast • v impers **es g~t** it is pouring [with rain]. **G~kanne** f watering can

Gift nt **-[e]s,-e** poison; (Schlangen-) venom; (Med) toxin. **g~ig** adj poisonous; (Schlange) venomous; (Med, Chemistry) toxic; (fig) spiteful. **G~müll** m toxic waste. **G~pilz** m toadstool

Gilde f **-,-n** guild

Gin /dʒɪn/ m **-s** gin

Ginster m **-s** (Bot) broom

Gipfel m **-s,-** summit, top; (fig) peak. **G~konferenz** f summit conference. **g~n** vi (haben) culminate (**in** + dat in)

Gips m **-es** plaster. **G~verband** m (Med) plaster cast

Giraffe f **-,-n** giraffe

Girlande f **-,-n** garland

Girokonto /'ʒiːro-/ nt current account

Gischt m **-[e]s** & f **-** spray

Gitar|re f **-,-n** guitar. **G~rist(in)** m **-en,-en** (f **-,-nen**) guitarist

Gitter nt **-s,-** bars pl; (Rost) grating, grid; (Geländer, Zaun) railings pl; (Fenster-) grille; (Draht-) wire screen

Glanz m **-es** shine; (von Farbe, Papier) gloss; (Seiden-) sheen; (Politur) polish; (fig) brilliance; (Pracht) splendour

glänzen vi (haben) shine. **g~d** adj shining, bright; (Papier) glossy; (fig) brilliant

glanz|los adj dull. **G~stück** nt masterpiece

Glas nt **-es,¨-er** glass; (Brillen-) lens; (Fern-) binoculars pl; (Marmeladen-) [glass] jar. **G~er** m **-s,-** glazier

glasieren vt glaze; ice (Kuchen)

glas|ig adj glassy; (durchsichtig) transparent. **G~scheibe** f pane

Glasur f **-,-en** glaze; (Culin) icing

glatt adj smooth; (eben) even; (Haar) straight; (rutschig) slippery; (einfach) straightforward; (Absage) flat; **g~ streichen** smooth out; **g~ rasiert** clean-shaven; **g~ gehen** go off smoothly; **das ist g~ gelogen** it's a downright lie

Glätte f - smoothness; (Rutschigkeit) slipperiness

Glatt|eis nt [black] ice. **g~weg** adv [!] outright

Glatz|e f **-,-n** bald patch; (Voll-) bald head; **eine G~e bekommen** go bald. **g~köpfig** adj bald

Glaube m **-ns** belief (**an** + acc in); (Relig) faith; **G~n schenken** (+ dat) believe. **g~n** vt/i (haben) believe (**an** + acc in); (vermuten) think; **jdm g~n** believe s.o.; **nicht zu g~n** unbelievable, incredible. **G~nsbekenntnis** nt creed

gläubig adj religious; (vertrauend) trusting. **G~e(r)** m/f (Relig) believer; **die G~en** the faithful. **G~er** m **-s,-** (Comm) creditor

glaub|lich adj **kaum g~lich** scarcely believable. **g~würdig** adj credible; (Person) reliable

gleich adj same; (identisch) identical; (g~wertig) equal; **g~ bleibend** constant; **2 mal 5 [ist] g~ 10** two times 5 equals 10; **das ist mir g~** it's all the same to me; **ganz g~, wo/wer** no matter where/who • adv equally; (übereinstimmend) identically, the same; (sofort) immediately; (in Kürze) in a minute; (fast) nearly; (direkt) right. **g~altrig** adj [of] the same age. **g~bedeutend** adj synonymous.

g~berechtigt adj equal. **G~berechtigung** f equality

gleichen† vi (haben) **jdm/etw g~** be like or resemble s.o./something

gleich|ermaßen adv equally. **g~falls** adv also, likewise; **danke g~falls** thank you, the same to you. **G~gewicht** nt balance; (Phys & fig) equilibrium. **g~gültig** adj indifferent; (unwichtig) unimportant. **G~gültigkeit** f indifference. **g~machen** vt sep make equal; **dem Erdboden g~machen** raze to the ground. **g~mäßig** adj even, regular; (beständig) constant. **G~mäßigkeit** f - regularity

Gleichnis nt **-ses,-se** parable

Gleich|schritt m **im G~schritt** in step. **g~setzen** vt sep equate/ (g~stellen) place on a par (dat/**mit** with). **g~stellen** vt sep place on a par (dat with). **G~strom** m direct current

Gleichung f **-,-en** equation

gleichwertig adv adj of equal value. **g~zeitig** adj simultaneous

Gleis nt **-es,-e** track; (Bahnsteig) platform; **G~ 5** platform 5

gleiten† vi (sein) glide; (rutschen) slide. **g~d** adj sliding; **g~de Arbeitszeit** flexitime

Gleitzeit f flexitime

Gletscher m **-s,-** glacier

Glied nt **-[e]s,-er** limb; (Teil) part; (Ketten-) link; (Mitglied) member; (Mil) rank. **g~ern** vt arrange; (einteilen) divide. **G~maßen** fpl limbs

glitschig adj slippery

glitzern vi (haben) glitter

global adj global

globalisier|en vt globalize. **G~ung** f **-,-en** globalization

Globus m **-** & **-busses,-ben** & **-busse** globe

Glocke f **-,-n** bell. **G~nturm** m bell tower, belfry

glorreich adj glorious

Glossar nt **-s,-e** glossary

Glosse f **-,-n** comment

glotzen vi (haben) stare

Glück nt **-[e]s** [good] luck; (Zufriedenheit) happiness; **G~ bringend** lucky; **G~/kein G~ haben** be lucky/unlucky; **zum G~** luckily, fortunately; **auf gut G~** on the off chance; (wahllos) at random. **g~en** vi (sein) succeed

glücklich adj lucky, fortunate; (zufrieden) happy; (sicher) safe • adv happily; safely. **g~erweise** adv luckily, fortunately

Glücksspiel nt game of chance; (Spielen) gambling

Glückwunsch m good wishes pl; (Gratulation) congratulations pl; **herzlichen G~!** congratulations! (zum Geburtstag) happy birthday! **G~karte** f greetings card

Glüh|birne f light bulb. **g~en** vi (haben) glow. **g~end** adj glowing; (rot-) red-hot; (Hitze) scorching; (leidenschaftlich) fervent. **G~faden** m filament. **G~wein** m mulled wine. **G~würmchen** nt **-s,-** glow-worm

Glukose f - glucose

Glut f - embers pl; (Röte) glow; (Hitze) heat; (fig) ardour

Glyzinie /-i̯ə/ f **-,-n** wisteria

GmbH abbr (**Gesellschaft mit beschränkter Haftung**) ≈ plc

Gnade f - mercy; (Gunst) favour; (Relig) grace. **G~nfrist** f reprieve

gnädig adj gracious; (mild) lenient; **g~e Frau** Madam

Gnom m **-en,-en** gnome

Gobelin /gobəˈlɛ̃ː/ m **-s,-s** tapestry

Gold nt **-[e]s** gold. **g~en** adj gold; (g~farben) golden. **G~fisch** m goldfish. **g~ig** adj sweet, lovely. **G~lack** m wallflower. **G~regen** m laburnum. **G~schmied** m goldsmith

Golf[1] m **-[e]s,-e** (Geog) gulf

Golf[2] nt **-s** golf. **G~platz** m golf course. **G~schläger** m golf club. **G~spieler(in)** m(f) golfer

Gondel f **-,-n** gondola; (Kabine) cabin

g

gönnen vt **jdm etw g~** not begrudge s.o. sth; **jdm etw nicht g~** begrudge s.o. sth

googeln vt/i ® google

Gör nt **-s,-en, Göre** f **-,-n** [!] kid

Gorilla m **-s,-s** gorilla

Gosse f **-,-n** gutter

Got|ik f - Gothic. **g~isch** adj Gothic

Gott m **-[e]s,⸚er** God; (Myth) god

Götterspeise f jelly

g

Gottes|dienst m service. **G~lästerung** f blasphemy

Gottheit f **-,-en** deity

Göttin f **-,-nen** goddess

göttlich adj divine

gottlos adj ungodly; (atheistisch) godless

Grab nt **-[e]s,⸚er** grave

graben† vi (haben) dig

Graben m **-s,⸚** ditch; (Mil) trench

Grab|mal nt tomb. **G~stein** m gravestone, tombstone

Grad m **-[e]s,-e** degree

Graf m **-en,-en** count

Grafik f **-,-en** graphics sg; (Kunst) graphic arts pl; (Druck) print

Gräfin f **-,-nen** countess

grafisch adj graphic; **g~e Darstellung** diagram

Grafschaft f **-,-en** county

Gram m **-s** grief

grämen (sich) vr grieve

Gramm nt **-s,-e** gram

Gram|matik f **-,-en** grammar. **g~matikalisch** adj grammatical

Granat m **-[e]s,-e** garnet. **G~e** f **-,-n** shell; (Hand-) grenade

Granit m **-s,-e** granite

Gras nt **-es,⸚er** grass. **g~en** vi (haben) graze. **G~hüpfer** m **-s,-** grasshopper

grässlich adj dreadful

Grat m **-[e]s,-e** [mountain] ridge

Gräte f **-,-n** fishbone

Gratifikation /-'tsi̯o:n/ f **-,-en** bonus

gratis adv free [of charge]. **G~probe** f free sample

Gratu|lant(in) m **-en,-en** (f **-,-nen**) well-wisher. **G~lation** f **-,-en** congratulations pl; (Glückwünsche) best wishes pl. **g~lieren** vi (haben) **jdm g~lieren** congratulate s.o. (**zu** on); (zum Geburtstag) wish s.o. happy birthday

grau adj, **G~** nt **-s,-** grey

Gräuel m **-s,-** horror

grauen v impers **mir graut [es] davor** I dread it. **G~** nt **-s** dread. **g~haft** adj gruesome; (grässlich) horrible

gräulich adj horrible

grausam adj cruel. **G~keit** f **-,-en** cruelty

graus|en v impers **mir graust davor** I dread it. **G~en** nt **-s** horror, dread. **g~ig** adj gruesome

gravieren vt engrave. **g~d** adj (fig) serious

graziös adj graceful

greifen† vt take hold of; (fangen) catch • vi (haben) reach (**nach** for); **um sich g~** (fig) spread

Greis m **-es,-e** old man. **G~in** f **-,-nen** old woman

grell adj glaring; (Farbe) garish; (schrill) shrill

Gremium nt **-s,-ien** committee

Grenz|e f **-,-n** border; (Staats-) frontier; (Grundstücks-) boundary; (fig) limit. **g~en** vi (haben) border (**an** + acc on). **g~enlos** adj boundless; (maßlos) infinite

Griech|e m **-n,-n** Greek. **G~enland** nt **-s** Greece. **G~in** f **-,-nen** Greek woman. **g~isch** adj Greek. **G~isch** nt **-[s]** (Lang) Greek

Grieß m **-es** semolina

Griff m **-[e]s,-e** grasp, hold; (Hand-) movement of the hand; (Tür-, Messer-) handle; (Schwert-) hilt.

g~bereit adj handy

Grill m **-s,-s** grill; (Garten-) barbecue

Grille f **-,-n** (Zool) cricket

grill|en vt grill; (im Freien) barbecue •vi (haben) have a barbecue. **G~fest** nt barbecue

Grimasse f **-,-n** grimace; **G~n schneiden** pull faces

grimmig adj furious; (Kälte) bitter

grinsen vi (haben) grin

Grippe f **-,-n** influenza, [!] flu

grob adj coarse; (unsanft, ungefähr) rough; (unhöflich) rude; (schwer) gross; (Fehler) bad; **g~ geschätzt** roughly. **G~ian** m **-s,-e** brute

Groll m **-[e]s** resentment. **g~en** vi (haben) be angry (dat with); (Donner:) rumble

Grönland nt **-s** Greenland

Gros nt **-es,-** (Maß) gross

Groschen m **-s,-** (Aust) groschen; [!] ten-pfennig piece

groß adj big; (Anzahl, Summe) large; (bedeutend, stark) great; (g~artig) grand; (Buchstabe) capital; **g~e Ferien** summer holidays; **der größte Teil** the majority or bulk; **g~ werden** (Person:) grow up; **g~ in etw** (dat) **sein** be good at sth; **G~ und Klein** young and old; **im G~en und Ganzen** on the whole •adv (feiern) in style; ([!]: viel) much

groß|artig adj magnificent. **G~aufnahme** f close-up. **G~britannien** nt **-s** Great Britain. **G~buchstabe** m capital letter. **G~e(r)** m/f **unser G~er** our eldest; **die G~en** the grown-ups; (fig) the great pl

Größe f **-,-n** size; (Ausmaß) extent; (Körper-) height; (Bedeutsamkeit) greatness; (Math) quantity; (Person) great figure

Großeltern pl grandparents

Groß|handel m wholesale trade. **G~händler** m wholesaler. **G~macht** f superpower. **g~mütig** adj magnanimous. **G~mutter** f grandmother. **G~schreibung** f capitalization. **g~spurig** adj pompous; (überheblich) arrogant. **G~stadt** f [large] city. **g~städtisch** adj city; **G~teil** m large proportion; (Hauptteil) bulk

größtenteils adv for the most part

groß|tun† **(sich)** vr sep brag. **G~vater** m grandfather. **g~ziehen**† vt sep bring up; rear (Tier). **g~zügig** adj generous. **G~zügigkeit** f - generosity

Grotte f **-,-n** grotto

Grübchen nt **-s,-** dimple

Grube f **-,-n** pit

grübeln vi (haben) brood

Gruft f **-,¨-e** [burial] vault

grün adj green; **im G~en** out in the country; **die G~en** the Greens

Grund m **-[e]s,¨-e** ground; (Boden) bottom; (Hinter-) background; (Ursache) reason; **aus diesem G~e** for this reason; **im G~e [genommen]** basically; **auf G~ laufen** (Naut) run aground; **zu G~e richten/gehen** s. **zugrunde**. **G~begriffe** mpl basics. **G~besitzer** m landowner

gründ|en vt found, set up; start (Familie); (fig) base (**auf** + acc on); **sich g~en** be based (**auf** + acc on). **G~er(in)** m **-s,-** (f **-,-nen**) founder

Grund|farbe f primary colour. **G~form** f (Gram) infinitive. [A-Z] **G~gesetz** nt (Pol) constitution. **G~lage** f basis, foundation

gründlich adj thorough. **G~keit** f - thoroughness

Gründonnerstag m Maundy Thursday

Grund|regel f basic rule. **G~riss** m ground plan; (fig) outline. **G~satz** m principle. **g~sätzlich** adj fundamental; (im Allgemeinen) in principle; (prinzipiell) on principle. [A-Z] **G~schule** f primary school.

[A-Z] see A-Z of German life and culture

G~stück nt plot [of land]

Gründung f **-,-en** foundation

Grün|span m verdigris. **G~streifen** m grass verge; (Mittel-) central reservation

grunzen vi (haben) grunt

Gruppe f **-,-n** group; (Reise-) party

gruppieren vt group

Grusel|geschichte f horror story. **g~ig** adj creepy

g

Gruß m **-es,⸚e** greeting; (Mil) salute; **einen schönen G~ an X** give my regards to X; **viele/herzliche G~e** regards; **Mit freundlichen G~en** Yours sincerely/faithfully

grüßen vt/i (haben) say hallo (**jdn** to s.o.); (Mil) salute; **g~ Sie X von mir** give my regards to X; **grüß Gott!** (SGer, Aust) good morning/afternoon/evening!

gucken vi (haben) [!] look

Guerilla /ge'rɪlja/ f **-** guerrilla warfare. **G~kämpfer** m guerrilla

Gulasch nt & m **-[e]s** goulash

gültig adj valid

Gummi m & nt **-s,-[s]** rubber; (Harz) gum. **G~band** nt (pl **-bänder**) elastic or rubber band

gummiert adj gummed

Gummi|knüppel m truncheon. **G~stiefel** m gumboot, wellington. **G~zug** m elastic

Gunst f **-** favour

günstig adj favourable; (passend) convenient

Gurgel f **-,-n** throat. **g~n** vi (haben) gargle

Gurke f **-,-n** cucumber; (Essig-) gherkin

Gurt m **-[e]s,-e** strap; (Gürtel) belt; (Auto) safety belt. **G~band** nt (pl **-bänder**) waistband

Gürtel m **-s,-** belt. **G~linie** f waistline. **G~rose** f shingles sg

Guss m **-es,⸚e** (Techn) casting; (Strom) stream; (Regen-) downpour; (Torten-) icing. **G~eisen** nt cast iron

gut adj good; (Gewissen) clear; (gütig) kind (**zu** to); **jdm gut sein** be fond of s.o.; **im G~en** amicably; **schon gut** that's all right • adv well; (schmecken, riechen) good; (leicht) easily; **gut zu sehen** clearly visible; **gut drei Stunden** a good three hours

Gut nt **-[e]s,⸚er** possession, property; (Land-) estate; **Gut und Böse** good and evil; **Güter** (Comm) goods

Gutacht|en nt **-s,-** expert's report. **G~er** m **-s,-** expert

gutartig adj good-natured; (Med) benign

Gute|(s) nt **etwas/nichts G~s** something/nothing good; **G~s tun** do good; **alles G~!** all the best!

Güte f **-,-n** goodness, kindness; (Qualität) quality

Güterzug m goods train

gut|gehen* vi sep (sein) = **gut gehen**, s. **gehen. g~gehend*** adj = **gut gehend**, s. **gehen. g~gläubig** adj trusting. **g~haben†** vt sep **fünfzig Euro g~haben** have fifty euros credit (**bei** with). **G~haben** nt **-s,-** [credit] balance; (Kredit) credit

gut|machen vt sep make up for; make good (Schaden). **g~mütig** adj good-natured. **G~mütigkeit** f **-** good nature. **G~schein** m credit note; (Bon) voucher; (Geschenk-) gift token. **g~schreiben†** vt sep credit. **G~schrift** f credit

Guts|haus nt manor house

gut|tun* vi sep (haben) = **gut tun**, s. **tun. g~willig** adj willing

[C] **Gymnasium** nt **-s,-ien** ≈ grammar school

Gymnastik f **-** [keep-fit] exercises pl; (Turnen) gymnastics sg

Gynäko|loge m **-n,-n** gynaecologist. **G~logie** f **-** gynaecology

[C] see A-Z of German life and culture

Hh

H, h /haː/ nt -,- (Mus) B, b

Haar nt **-[e]s,-e** hair; **sich** (dat) **die Haare** od **das H~ waschen** wash one's hair; **um ein H~** [!] very nearly. **H~bürste** f hairbrush. **h~en** vi (haben) shed hairs; (Tier:) moult • vr **sich h~en** moult. **h~ig** adj hairy; [!] tricky. **H~klemme** f hair grip. **H~nadelkurve** f hairpin bend. **H~schnitt** m haircut. **H~spange** f slide. **H~waschmittel** nt shampoo

Habe f - possessions pl

haben†

• transitive verb

····> have; (im Präsens) have got [!]. **er hat kein Geld** he has no money or [!] he hasn't got any money. **ich habe/hatte die Grippe** I've got flu/had flu. **was haben Sie da?** what have you got there? **wenn ich die Zeit hätte** if I had the time

····> (empfinden) **Angst/Hunger/Durst haben** be frightened/hungry/thirsty. **was hat er?** what's wrong with him?

····> (+ Adj., es) **es gut/schlecht haben** be well/badly off. **es schwer haben** be having a difficult time

····> (+ zu) (müssen) **du hast zu gehorchen** you must obey

• auxiliary verb

····> have. **ich habe/hatte ihn eben gesehen** I have or I've/I had or I'd just seen him. **er hat es gewusst** he knew it. **er hätte ihr geholfen** he would have helped her

• reflexive verb

····> ([!]: sich aufregen) make a fuss. **hab dich nicht so!** don't make such a fuss!

Habgier f greed. **h~ig** adj greedy

Habicht m **-[e]s,-e** hawk

Hachse f **-,-n** (Culin) knuckle

Hackbraten m meat loaf

Hacke[1] f **-,-n** hoe; (Spitz-) pick

Hacke[2] f **-,-n**, **Hacken** m **-s,-** heel

hack|en vt hoe; (schlagen, zerkleinern) chop; (Vogel:) peck. **H~fleisch** nt mince

Hafen m **-s,¨** harbour; (See-) port. **H~arbeiter** m docker. **H~stadt** f port

Hafer m **-s** oats pl. **H~flocken** fpl [rolled] oats

Haft f - (Jur) custody; (H~strafe) imprisonment. **h~bar** adj (Jur) liable. **H~befehl** m warrant

haften vi (haben) cling; (kleben) stick; (bürgen) vouch/(Jur) be liable **(für** for)

Häftling m **-s,-e** detainee

Haftpflicht f (Jur) liability. **H~versicherung** f (Auto) third-party insurance

Haftung f - (Jur) liability

Hagebutte f **-,-n** rose hip

Hagel m **-s** hail. **h~n** vi (haben) hail

hager adj gaunt

Hahn m **-[e]s,¨e** cock; (Techn) tap

Hähnchen nt **-s,-** (Culin) chicken

Hai[fisch] m **-[e]s,-e** shark

Häkchen nt **-s,-** tick

häkel|n vt/i (haben) crochet. **H~nadel** f crochet hook

Haken m **-s,-** hook; (Häkchen) tick; ([!]: Schwierigkeit) snag. **h~** vt hook **(an** + acc to). **H~kreuz** nt swastika

halb adj half; **auf h~em Weg** halfway • adv half; **h~ drei** half past two; **fünf [Minuten] vor/nach h~ vier** twenty-five [minutes] past

h

three/to four. **H~e(r,s)** f/m/nt half [a litre]

halber prep (+ gen) for the sake of; **Geschäfte h~** on business

Halbfinale nt semifinal

halbieren vt halve, divide in half; (Geometry) bisect

Halb|insel f peninsula. **H~kreis** m semicircle. **H~kugel** f hemisphere. **h~laut** adj low • adv in an undertone. **h~mast** adv at half-mast. **H~mond** m half moon. **H~pension** f half board. **h~rund** adj semicircular. **H~schuh** m [flat] shoe. **h~tags** adv [for] half a day; **h~tags arbeiten** ≈ work part-time. **H~ton** m semitone. **h~wegs** adv half-way; (ziemlich) more or less. **h~wüchsig** adj adolescent. **H~zeit** f (Sport) half-time; (Spielzeit) half

Halde f **-,-n** dump, tip

Hälfte f **-,-n** half; **zur H~** half

Halfter f **-,-n** & nt **-s,-** holster

Halle f **-,-n** hall; (Hotel-) lobby; (Bahnhofs-) station concourse

hallen vi (haben) resound; (wider-) echo

Hallen- prefix indoor

hallo int hallo

Halluzination /-ˈtsi̯oːn/ f **-,-en** hallucination

Halm m **-[e]s,-e** stalk; (Gras-) blade

Hals m **-es,⸚e** neck; (Kehle) throat; **aus vollem H~e** at the top of one's voice; (lachen) out loud. **H~band** nt (pl **-bänder**) collar. **H~schmerzen** mpl sore throat sg

halt int stop! (Mil) halt!; [!] wait a minute!

Halt m **-[e]s,-e** hold; (Stütze) support; (innerer) stability; (Anhalten) stop; **H~ machen** stop. **h~bar** adj durable; (Textiles) hard-wearing; (fig) tenable; **h~bar bis** (Comm) use by

halten† vt hold; make (Rede); give (Vortrag); (einhalten, bewahren) keep; [**sich** (dat)] **etw h~** keep (Hund); take (Zeitung); **h~ für** regard as; **viel h~ von** think highly of; **sich links h~** keep left; **sich h~ an** (+ acc) (fig) keep to • vi (haben) hold; (haltbar sein, bestehen bleiben) keep; (Freundschaft, Blumen:) last; (Halt machen) stop; **auf sich** (acc) **h~** take pride in oneself; **zu jdm h~** be loyal to s.o.

Halte|stelle f stop. **H~verbot** nt waiting restriction; **'H~verbot'** 'no waiting'

Haltung f **-,-en** (Körper-) posture; (Verhalten) manner; (Einstellung) attitude; (Fassung) composure; (Halten) keeping

Hammel m **-s,-** ram; (Culin) mutton. **H~fleisch** nt mutton

Hammer m **-s,⸚** hammer

hämmern vt/i (haben) hammer

Hamster m **-s,-** hamster. **h~n** vt/i [!] hoard

Hand f **-,⸚e** hand; **jdm die H~ geben** shake hands with s.o.; **rechter/linker H~** on the right/left; **zweiter H~** second-hand; **unter der H~** unofficially; (geheim) secretly; **H~ und Fuß haben** (fig) be sound. **H~arbeit** f manual work; (handwerklich) handicraft; (Nadelarbeit) needlework; (Gegenstand) hand-made article. **H~ball** m [German] handball. **H~bewegung** f gesture. **H~bremse** f handbrake. **H~buch** nt handbook, manual

Händedruck m handshake

Handel m **-s** trade, commerce; (Unternehmen) business; (Geschäft) deal; **H~ treiben** trade. **h~n** vi (haben) act; (Handel treiben) trade (**mit** in); **von etw** od **über etw** (acc) **h~n** deal with sth; **sich h~n um** be about, concern. **H~smarine** f merchant navy. **H~sschiff** nt merchant vessel. **H~sschule** f commercial college. **H~sware** f merchandise

Hand|feger m **-s,-** brush. **H~fläche** f palm. **H~gelenk** nt wrist. **H~gemenge** nt **-s,-** scuffle. **H~gepäck** nt hand luggage. **h~geschrieben** adj hand-written. **h~greiflich** adj tangible;

h~greiflich werden become violent. **H~griff** m handle

handhaben vt insep (reg) handle

Handikap /'hɛndikɛp/ nt **-s,-s** handicap

Handkuss m kiss on the hand

Händler m **-s,-** dealer, trader

handlich adj handy

Handlung f **-,-en** act; (Handeln) action; (Roman-) plot; (Geschäft) shop. **H~sweise** f conduct

Hand|schellen fpl handcuffs. **H~schlag** m handshake. **H~schrift** f handwriting; (Text) manuscript. **H~schuh** m glove. **H~stand** m handstand. **H~tasche** f handbag. **H~tuch** nt towel

Handwerk nt craft, trade. **H~er** m **-s,-** craftsman; (Arbeiter) workman

Handy /'hɛndi/ nt **-s,-s** mobile phone, cell phone Amer

Hanf m **-[e]s** hemp

Hang m **-[e]s,¨e** slope; (fig) inclination

Hänge|brücke f suspension bridge. **H~matte** f hammock

hängen[1] vt (reg) hang

hängen[2]† vi (haben) hang; **h~ an** (+ dat) (fig) be attached to; **h~ lassen** leave

Hannover nt **-s** Hanover

hänseln vt tease

hantieren vi (haben) busy oneself

Happen m **-s,-** mouthful; **einen H~ essen** have a bite to eat

Harfe f **-,-n** harp

Harke f **-,-n** rake. **h~n** vt/i (haben) rake

harmlos adj harmless; (arglos) innocent

Harmonie f **-,-n** harmony

Harmonika f **-,-s** accordion; (Mund-) mouth organ

harmonisch adj harmonious

Harn m **-[e]s** urine. **H~blase** f bladder

Harpune f **-,-n** harpoon

hart adj hard; (heftig) violent; (streng) harsh

Härte f **-,-n** hardness; (Strenge) harshness; (Not) hardship. **h~n** vt harden

Hart|faserplatte f hardboard. **h~näckig** adj stubborn; (ausdauernd) persistent. **H~näckigkeit** f **-** stubbornness; persistence

Harz nt **-es,-e** resin

Haschee nt **-s,-s** (Culin) hash

Haschisch nt & m **-[s]** hashish

Hase m **-n,-n** hare

Hasel f **-,-n** hazel. **H~maus** f dormouse. **H~nuss** f hazel nut

Hass m **-es** hatred

hassen vt hate

hässlich adj ugly; (unfreundlich) nasty. **H~keit** f **-** ugliness; nastiness

Hast f **-** haste. **h~ig** adj hasty, adv -ily, hurried

hast, hat, hatte, hätte s. **haben**

Haube f **-,-n** cap; (Trocken-) drier; (Kühler-) bonnet

Hauch m **-[e]s** breath; (Luft-) breeze; (Duft) whiff; (Spur) tinge. **h~dünn** adj very thin

Haue f **-,-n** pick; (!: Prügel) beating. **h~n**† vt beat; (hämmern) knock; (meißeln) hew; **sich h~n** fight; **übers Ohr h~n** ! cheat • vi (haben) bang (**auf** + acc on); **jdm ins Gesicht h~n** hit s.o. in the face

Haufen m **-s,-** heap, pile; (Leute) crowd

häufen vt heap or pile [up]; **sich h~** pile up; (zunehmen) increase

häufig adj frequent

Haupt nt **-[e]s, Häupter** head. **H~bahnhof** m main station. **H~fach** nt main subject. **H~gericht** nt main course

Häuptling m **-s,-e** chief

Haupt|mahlzeit f main meal. **H~mann** m (pl **-leute**) captain. **H~post** f main post office. **H~quartier** nt headquarters pl.

H~rolle f lead; (fig) leading role. **H~sache** f main thing; **in der H~sache** in the main. **h~sächlich** adj main. **H~satz** m main clause. **H~stadt** f capital. **H~verkehrsstraße** f main road. **H~verkehrszeit** f rush hour. **H~wort** nt (pl **-wörter**) noun

Haus nt **-es, Häuser** house; (Gebäude) building; (Schnecken-) shell; **zu H~e** at home; **nach H~e** home. **H~arbeit** f housework; (Sch) homework. **H~arzt** m family doctor. **H~aufgaben** fpl homework sg. **H~besetzer** m **-s,-** squatter

h

hausen vi (haben) live; (wüten) wreak havoc

Haus|frau f housewife. **h~gemacht** adj home-made. **H~halt** m **-[e]s,-e** household; (Pol) budget. **h~halten**† vi sep (haben) **h~halten mit** manage carefully; conserve (Kraft). **H~hälterin** f **-,-nen** housekeeper. **H~haltsgeld** nt housekeeping [money]. **H~haltsplan** m budget. **H~herr** m head of the household; (Gastgeber) host

Hausierer m **-s,-** hawker

Hauslehrer m [private] tutor. **H~in** f governess

häuslich adj domestic, (Person) domesticated

Haus|meister m caretaker. **H~ordnung** f house rules pl. **H~putz** m cleaning. **H~rat** m **-[e]s** household effects pl. **H~schlüssel** m front-door key. **H~schuh** m slipper. **H~suchung** f [police] search. **H~suchungsbefehl** m search warrant. **H~tier** nt domestic animal; (Hund, Katze) pet. **H~tür** f front door. **H~wirt** m landlord. **H~wirtin** f landlady

Haut f **-,Häute** skin; (Tier-) hide. **H~arzt** m dermatologist

häuten vt skin; **sich h~** moult

haut|eng adj skin-tight. **H~farbe** f colour; (Teint) complexion

Hebamme f **-,-n** midwife

Hebel m **-s,-** lever

heben† vt lift; (hoch-, steigern) raise; **sich h~** rise; (Nebel:) lift; (sich verbessern) improve

hebräisch adj Hebrew

hecheln vi (haben) pant

Hecht m **-[e]s,-e** pike

Heck nt **-s,-s** (Naut) stern; (Aviat) tail; (Auto) rear

Hecke f **-,-n** hedge

Heck|fenster nt rear window. **H~tür** f hatchback

Heer nt **-[e]s,-e** army

Hefe f **-** yeast

Heft nt **-[e]s,-e** booklet; (Sch) exercise book; (Zeitschrift) issue. **h~en** vt (nähen) tack; (stecken) pin/ (klammern) clip/(mit Heftmaschine) staple (**an** + acc to). **H~er** m **-s,-** file

heftig adj fierce, violent; (Regen) heavy; (Schmerz, Gefühl) intense

Heft|klammer f staple; (Büro-) paper clip. **H~maschine** f stapler. **H~zwecke** f **-,-n** drawing pin

Heide[1] m **-n,-n** heathen

Heide[2] f **-,-n** heath; (Bot) heather. **H~kraut** nt heather

Heidelbeere f bilberry

Heidin f **-,-nen** heathen

heikel adj difficult, tricky

heil adj undamaged, intact; (Person) unhurt; **mit h~er Haut** [!] unscathed

Heil nt **-s** salvation

Heiland m **-s** (Relig) Saviour

Heil|anstalt f sanatorium; (Nerven-) mental hospital. **H~bad** nt spa. **h~bar** adj curable

Heilbutt m **-[e]s,-e** halibut

heilen vt cure; heal (Wunde) •vi (sein) heal

Heilgymnastik f physiotherapy

heilig adj holy; (geweiht) sacred; **der H~e Abend** Christmas Eve; **die h~e Anna** Saint Anne; (Feiertag); **h~ sprechen** canonize. **H~abend** m Christmas Eve. **H~e(r)** m/f saint.

H~enschein m halo. **H~keit** f - sanctity, holiness. **H~tum** nt **-s,¨-er** shrine

heil|kräftig adj medicinal. **H~kräuter** ntpl medicinal herbs. **H~mittel** nt remedy. **H~praktiker** m **-s,-** practitioner of alternative medicine. **H~sarmee** f Salvation Army. **H~ung** f - cure

Heim nt **-[e]s,-e** home; (Studenten-) hostel. **h~** adv home

Heimat f **-,-en** home; (Land) native land. **H~stadt** f home town

heim|begleiten vt sep see home. **H~computer** m home computer. **h~fahren†** v sep •vi (sein) go/drive home •vt take/drive home. **H~fahrt** f way home. **h~gehen†** vi sep (sein) go home

heimisch adj native, indigenous; (Pol) domestic

Heim|kehr f - return [home]. **h~kehren** vi sep (sein) return home. **h~kommen†** vi sep (sein) come home

heimlich adj secret; **etw h~ tun** do sth secretly. **H~keit** f **-,-en** secrecy; **H~keiten** secrets

Heim|reise f journey home. **H~spiel** nt home game. **h~suchen** vt sep afflict. **h~tückisch** adj treacherous; (Krankheit) insidious. **h~wärts** adv home. **H~weg** m way home. **H~weh** nt **-s** homesickness; **H~weh haben** be homesick. **H~werker** m **-s,-** [home] handyman. **h~zahlen** vt sep **jdm etw h~zahlen** (fig) pay s.o. back for sth

Heirat f **-,-en** marriage. **h~en** vt/i (haben) marry. **H~santrag** m proposal; **jdm einen H~santrag machen** propose to s.o.

heiser adj hoarse. **H~keit** f - hoarseness

heiß adj hot; (hitzig) heated; (leidenschaftlich) fervent

heißen† vi (haben) be called; (bedeuten) mean; **ich heiße ...** my name is ...; **wie h~Sie?** what is your name? **wie heißt ... auf Englisch?** what's the English for ...? •vt call; **jdn etw tun h~** tell s.o. to do sth

heiter adj cheerful; (Wetter) bright; (amüsant) amusing; **aus h~em Himmel** (fig) out of the blue

Heiz|anlage f heating; (Auto) heater. **H~decke** f electric blanket. **h~en** vt heat; light (Ofen) •vi (haben) put the heating on; (Ofen:) give out heat. **H~gerät** nt heater. **H~kessel** m boiler. **H~körper** m radiator. **H~lüfter** m **-s,-** fan heater. **H~material** nt fuel. **H~ung** f **-,-en** heating; (Heizkörper) radiator

Hektar nt & m **-s,-** hectare

Held m **-en,-en** hero. **h~enhaft** adj heroic. **H~entum** nt **-s** heroism. **H~in** f **-,-nen** heroine

helf|en† vi (haben) help (**jdm** s.o.); (nützen) be effective; **sich** (dat) **nicht zu h~en wissen** not know what to do; **es hilft nichts** it's no use. **H~er(in)** m **-s,-** (f **-,-nen**) helper, assistant

hell adj light; (Licht ausstrahlend, klug) bright; (Stimme) clear; (!: völlig) utter; **h~es Bier** ≈ lager •adv brightly

Hell|igkeit f - brightness. **H~seher(in)** m **-s,-** (f **-,-nen**) clairvoyant

Helm m **-[e]s,-e** helmet

Hemd nt **-[e]s,-en** vest; (Ober-) shirt

Hemisphäre f **-,-n** hemisphere

hemm|en vt check; (verzögern) impede; (fig) inhibit. **H~ung** f **-,-en** (fig) inhibition; (Skrupel) scruple; **H~ungen haben** be inhibited. **h~ungslos** adj unrestrained

Hendl nt **-s,-[n]** (Aust) chicken

Hengst m **-[e]s,-e** stallion

Henkel m **-s,-** handle

Henne f **-,-n** hen

her adv here; (zeitlich) ago; **her mit ... !** give me ... ! **von Norden/weit her** from the north/far away; **vom Thema her** as far as the subject is concerned; **her sein** come (**von** from); **es ist schon lange her** it was a long time ago

herab adv down [here]; **von oben h~** from above; (fig) condescending

herablassen† vt sep let down; **sich h~** condescend (**zu** to)

herab|sehen† vi sep (haben) look down (**auf** + acc on). **h~setzen** vt sep reduce, cut; (fig) belittle

Heraldik f - heraldry

heran adv near; **[bis] h~ an** (+ acc) up to. **h~kommen**† vi sep (sein) approach; **h~kommen an** (+ acc) come up to; (erreichen) get at; (fig) measure up to. **h~machen (sich)** vr sep **sich h~machen an** (+ acc) approach; get down to (Arbeit). **h~wachsen**† vi sep (sein) grow up. **h~ziehen**† v sep •vt pull up (**an** + acc to); (züchten) raise; (h~bilden) train; (hinzuziehen) call in •vi (sein) approach

herauf adv up [here]; **die Treppe h~** up the stairs. **h~setzen** vt sep raise, increase

heraus adv out (**aus** of); **h~ damit** od **mit der Sprache!** out with it! **h~bekommen**† vt sep get out; (ausfindig machen) find out; (lösen) solve; **Geld h~bekommen** get change. **h~finden**† v sep •vt find out •vi (haben) find one's way out. **h~fordern** vt sep provoke; challenge (Person). **H~forderung** f provocation; challenge. **H~gabe** f handing over; (Admin) issue; (Veröffentlichung) publication. **h~geben**† vt sep hand over; (Admin) issue; (veröffentlichen) publish; edit (Zeitschrift); **jdm Geld h~geben** give s.o. change •vi (haben) give change (**auf** + acc for). **H~geber** m **-s,-** publisher; editor. **h~halten**† **(sich)** vr sep (fig) keep out (**aus** of). **h~kommen**† vi sep (sein) come out; (aus Schwierigkeit, Takt) get out; **auf eins** od **dasselbe h~kommen** [!] come to the same thing. **h~lassen**† vt sep let out. **h~nehmen**† vt sep take out; **sich zu viel h~nehmen** (fig) take liberties. **h~reden (sich)** vr sep make excuses. **h~rücken** v sep •vt move out; (hergeben) hand over •vi (sein) **h~rücken mit** hand over; (fig: sagen) come out with. **h~schlagen**† vt sep knock out; (fig) gain. **h~stellen** vt sep put out; **sich h~stellen** turn out (**als** to be; **dass** that). **h~ziehen**† vt sep pull out

herb adj sharp; (Wein) dry; (fig) harsh

herbei adv here. **h~führen** vt sep (fig) bring about. **h~schaffen** vt sep get. **h~sehnen** vt sep long for

Herberg|e f **-,-n** [youth] hostel; (Unterkunft) lodging. **H~svater** m warden

herbestellen vt sep summon

herbitten† vt sep ask to come

herbringen† vt sep bring [here]

Herbst m **-[e]s,-e** autumn. **h~lich** adj autumnal

Herd m **-[e]s,-e** stove, cooker

Herde f **-,-n** herd; (Schaf-) flock

herein adv in [here]; **h~!** come in! **h~bitten**† vt sep ask in. **h~fallen**† vi sep (sein) [!] be taken in (**auf** + acc by). **h~kommen**† vi sep (sein) come in. **h~lassen**† vt sep let in. **h~legen** vt sep [!] take for a ride

Herfahrt f journey/drive here

herfallen† vi sep (sein) **~ über** (+ acc) attack; fall upon (Essen)

hergeben† vt sep hand over; (fig) give up

hergehen† vi sep (sein) **h~ vor** (+ dat) walk along in front of; **es ging lustig her** [!] there was a lot of merriment

herholen vt sep fetch; **weit hergeholt** (fig) far-fetched

Hering m **-s,-e** herring; (Zeltpflock) tent peg

her|kommen† vi sep (sein) come here; **wo kommt das her?** where does it come from? **h~kömmlich** adj traditional. **H~kunft** f - origin

herleiten vt sep derive

hermachen vt sep **viel/wenig h~** be impressive/unimpressive; (wichtig nehmen) make a lot of/little fuss (**von** of); **sich h~ über** (+ acc) fall upon; tackle (Arbeit)

Hermelin[1] nt **-s,-e** (Zool) stoat

Hermelin[2] m **-s,-e** (Pelz) ermine

Hernie /ˈhɛrni̯ə/ f **-,-n** hernia

Heroin nt **-s** heroin

heroisch adj heroic

Herr m **-n,-en** gentleman; (Gebieter) master (**über** + acc of); **[Gott,] der H~** the Lord [God]; **H~ Meier** Mr Meier; **Sehr geehrte H~en** Dear Sirs. **H~enhaus** nt manor [house]. **h~enlos** adj ownerless; (Tier) stray

Herrgott m **der H~** the Lord

herrichten vt sep prepare; **wieder h~** renovate

Herrin f **-,-nen** mistress

herrlich adj marvellous; (großartig) magnificent

Herrschaft f **-,-en** rule; (Macht) power; (Kontrolle) control; **meine H~en!** ladies and gentlemen!

herrsch|en vi (haben) rule; (verbreitet sein) prevail; **es h~te Stille** there was silence. **H~er(in)** m **-s,-** (f **-,-nen**) ruler

herrühren vi sep (haben) stem (**von** from)

herstammen vi sep (haben) come (**aus/von** from)

herstell|en vt sep establish; (Comm) manufacture, make. **H~er** m **-s,-** manufacturer, maker. **H~ung** f - establishment; manufacture

herüber adv over [here]

herum adv **im Kreis h~** [round] in a circle; **falsch h~** the wrong way round; **um ... h~** round ... ; (ungefähr) [round] about ... ; **h~ sein** be over. **h~drehen** vt sep turn round/(wenden) over; turn (Schlüssel). **h~gehen**† vi sep (sein) walk around; (Zeit:) pass; **h~gehen um** go round. **h~kommen**† vi sep (sein) get about; **h~kommen um** get round; come round (Ecke); **um etw [nicht] h~kommen** (fig) [not] get out of sth. **h~sitzen**† vi sep (haben) sit around; **h~sitzen um** sit round. **h~sprechen**† **(sich)** vr sep (Gerücht:) get about. **h~treiben**† **(sich)** vr sep hang around. **h~ziehen**† vi sep (sein) move around; (ziellos) wander about

herunter adv down [here]; **die Treppe h~** down the stairs. **h~fallen**† vi fall off. **h~gekommen** adj (fig) run-down; (Gebäude) dilapidated; (Person) down-at-heel. **h~kommen**† vi sep (sein) come down; (fig) go to rack and ruin; (Firma, Person:) go downhill; (gesundheitlich) get run down. **h~laden** sep vt † download. **h~lassen**† vt sep let down, lower. **h~machen** vt sep [!] reprimand; (herabsetzen) run down. **h~spielen** vt sep (fig) play down

hervor adv out (**aus** of). **h~bringen**† vt sep produce; utter (Wort). **h~gehen**† vi sep (sein) come/(sich ergeben) emerge/(folgen) follow (**aus** from). **h~heben**† vt sep (fig) stress, emphasize. **h~ragen** vi sep (haben) jut out; (fig) stand out. **h~ragend** adj (fig) outstanding. **h~rufen**† vt sep (fig) cause. **h~stehen**† vi sep (haben) protrude. **h~treten**† vi sep (sein) protrude, bulge; (fig) stand out. **h~tun**† **(sich)** vr sep (fig) distinguish oneself; (angeben) show off

Herweg m way here

Herz nt **-ens,-en** heart; (Kartenspiel) hearts pl; **sich** (dat) **ein H~ fassen** pluck up courage. **H~anfall** m heart attack

herzhaft adj hearty; (würzig) savoury

herziehen† v sep •vt **hinter sich** (dat) **h~** pull along [behind one] •vi (sein) **hinter jdm h~** follow along behind s.o.; **über jdn h~** [!] run s.o. down

herz|ig adj sweet, adorable. **H~infarkt** m heart attack. **H~klopfen** nt **-s** palpitations pl

herzlich adj cordial; (warm) warm; (aufrichtig) sincere; **h~en Dank!** many thanks! **h~e Grüße** kind regards

herzlos adj heartless

Herzog m **-s,¨-e** duke. **H~in** f **-,-nen** duchess. **H~tum** nt **-s,¨-er** duchy

Herzschlag m heartbeat; (Med) heart failure

Hessen nt **-s** Hesse

heterosexuell adj heterosexual

Hetze f **-** rush; (Kampagne) virulent campaign (**gegen** against). **h∼n** vt chase; **sich h∼n** hurry

Heu nt **-s** hay

Heuchelei f **-** hypocrisy

heuch|eln vt feign • vi (haben) pretend. **H∼ler(in)** m **-s,-** (f **-,-nen**) hypocrite. **h∼lerisch** adj hypocritical

h

heuer adv (Aust) this year

heulen vi (haben) howl; (!: weinen) cry

Heu|schnupfen m hay fever. **H∼schober** m **-s,-** haystack. **H∼schrecke** f **-,-n** grasshopper

heut|e adv today; (heutzutage) nowadays; **h∼e früh** od **Morgen** this morning; **von h∼e auf morgen** from one day to the next. **h∼ig** adj today's; (gegenwärtig) present; **der h∼ige Tag** today. **h∼zutage** adv nowadays

Hexe f **-,-n** witch. **h∼n** vi (haben) work magic. **H∼nschuss** m lumbago

Hieb m **-[e]s,-e** blow; (Peitschen-) lash; **H∼e** hiding sg

hier adv here; **h∼ sein/bleiben/lassen/behalten** be/stay/leave/keep here; **h∼ und da** here and there; (zeitlich) now and again

hier|auf adv on this/these; (antworten) to this; (zeitlich) after this. **h∼aus** adv out of or from this/these. **h∼durch** adv through this/these; (Ursache) as a result of this. **h∼her** adv here. **h∼hin** adv here. **h∼in** adv in this/these. **h∼mit** adv with this/these; (Comm) herewith; (Admin) hereby. **h∼nach** adv after this/these; (demgemäß) according to this/these. **h∼über** adv over/(höher) above this/these; (sprechen, streiten) about this/these. **h∼von** adv from this/these; (h∼über) about this/these; (Menge) of this/these. **h∼zu** adv to this/these; (h∼für) for this/these.

h∼zulande adv here

hiesig adj local. **H∼e(r)** m/f local

Hilf|e f **-,-n** help, aid; **um H∼e rufen** call for help. **h∼los** adj helpless. **H∼losigkeit** f **-** helplessness. **h∼reich** adj helpful

Hilfs|arbeiter m unskilled labourer. **h∼bedürftig** adj needy; **h∼bedürftig sein** be in need of help. **h∼bereit** adj helpful. **H∼kraft** f helper. **H∼mittel** nt aid. **H∼verb** nt auxiliary verb

Himbeere f raspberry

Himmel m **-s,-** sky; (Relig & fig) heaven; (Bett-) canopy; **unter freiem H∼** in the open air. **H∼bett** nt four-poster [bed]. **H∼fahrt** f Ascension

himmlisch adj heavenly

hin adv there; **hin und her** to and fro; **hin und zurück** there and back; (Rail) return; **hin und wieder** now and again; **an** (+ dat) ... **hin** along; **auf** (+ acc) ... **hin** in reply to (Brief, Anzeige); on (jds Rat); **zu** od **nach** ... **hin** towards; **hin sein** ! be gone; **es ist noch lange hin** it's a long time yet

hinauf adv up [there]. **h∼gehen**† vi sep (sein) go up. **h∼setzen** vt sep raise

hinaus adv out [there]; (nach draußen) outside; **zur Tür h∼** out of the door; **auf Jahre h∼** for years to come; **über etw** (acc) **h∼** beyond sth; (Menge) [over and] above sth; **über etw** (acc) **h∼ sein** (fig) be past sth. **h∼gehen**† vi sep (sein) go out; (Zimmer:) face (**nach Norden** north); **h∼gehen über** (+ acc) go beyond, exceed. **h∼laufen**† vi sep (sein) run out; **h∼laufen auf** (+ acc) (fig) amount to. **h∼lehnen (sich)** vr sep lean out. **h∼schieben**† vt sep push out; (fig) put off. **h∼werfen**† vt sep throw out; (!: entlassen) fire. **h∼wollen**† vi sep (haben) want to go out; **h∼wollen auf** (+ acc) (fig) aim at. **h∼ziehen**† v sep • vt pull out; (in die Länge ziehen) drag out; (verzögern) delay; **sich h∼ziehen** drag on; be delayed • vi (sein) move out. **h∼zögern** vt delay; **sich h~zögern** be delayed

Hinblick m **im H~ auf** (+ acc) in view of; (hinsichtlich) regarding

hinder|lich adj awkward; **jdm h~lich sein** hamper s.o. **h~n** vt hamper; (verhindern) prevent. **H~nis** nt **-ses,-se** obstacle. **H~nisrennen** nt steeplechase

Hindu m **-s,-s** Hindu.

hindurch adv through it/them

hinein adv in [there]; (nach drinnen) inside; **h~ in** (+ acc) into. **h~fallen**† vi sep (sein) fall in. **h~gehen**† vi sep (sein) go in; **h~gehen in** (+ acc) go into. **h~reden** vi sep (haben) **jdm h~reden** interrupt s.o.; (sich einmischen) interfere in s.o.'s affairs. **h~versetzen (sich)** vr sep **sich in jds Lage h~versetzen** put oneself in s.o.'s position. **h~ziehen**† vt sep pull in; **h~ziehen in** (+ acc) pull into; **in etw** (acc) **h~gezogen werden** (fig) become involved in sth

hin|fahren† v sep •vi (sein) go/drive there •vt take/drive there. **H~fahrt** f journey/drive there; (Rail) outward journey. **h~fallen**† vi sep (sein) fall. **h~fliegen**† v sep •vi (sein) fly there; [!] fall •vt fly there. **H~flug** m flight there; (Aviat) outward flight

Hingeb|ung f **-** devotion. **h~ungsvoll** adj devoted

hingehen† vi sep (sein) go/(zu Fuß) walk there; (vergehen) pass; **h~ zu** go up to; **wo gehst du hin**? where are you going?

hingerissen adj rapt; **h~ sein** be carried away (**von** by)

hinhalten† vt sep hold out; (warten lassen) keep waiting

hinken vi (haben/sein) limp

hin|knien (sich) vr sep kneel down. **h~kommen**† vi sep (sein) get there; (h~gehören) belong, go; ([!]: auskommen) manage (**mit** with); ([!]: stimmen) be right. **h~laufen**† vi sep (sein) run/(gehen) walk there. **h~legen** vt sep lay or put down; **sich h~legen** lie down.

h~nehmen† vt sep (fig) accept

hinreichen v sep •vt hand (dat to) •vi (haben) extend (**bis** to); (ausreichen) be adequate. **h~d** adj adequate

Hinreise f journey there; (Rail) outward journey

hinreißen† vt sep (fig) carry away; **sich h~ lassen** get carried away. **h~d** adj ravishing

hinricht|en vt sep execute. **H~ung** f execution

hinschreiben† vt sep write there; (aufschreiben) write down

hinsehen† vi sep (haben) look

hinsetzen vt sep put down; **sich h~** sit down

Hinsicht f **- in dieser H~** in this respect; **in finanzieller H~** financially. **h~lich** prep (+ gen) regarding

hinstellen vt sep put or set down; park (Auto)

hinstrecken vt sep hold out; **sich h~** extend

hinten adv at the back; **dort h~** back there; **nach/von h~** to the back/from behind. **h~herum** adv round the back; [!] by devious means

hinter prep (+ dat/acc) behind; (nach) after; **h~ jdm/etw herlaufen** run after s.o./something; **h~ etw** (dat) **stecken** (fig) be behind sth; **h~ etw** (acc) **kommen** (fig) get to the bottom of sth; **etw h~ sich** (acc) **bringen** get sth over [and done] with

Hinterbliebene pl (Admin) surviving dependants; **die H~n** the bereaved family sg

hintere|(r,s) adj back, rear; **h~s Ende** far end

hintereinander adv one behind/ (zeitlich) after the other; **dreimal h~** three times in succession

Hintergedanke m ulterior motive

hintergehen† vt deceive

Hinter|grund m background.

h

H~halt m **-[e]s,-e** ambush. **h~hältig** adj underhand

hinterher adv behind, after; (zeitlich) afterwards

Hinter|hof m back yard. **H~kopf** m back of the head

hinterlassen† vt leave [behind]; (Jur) leave, bequeath (dat to). **H~schaft** f **-,-en** (Jur) estate

hinterlegen vt deposit

Hinter|leib m (Zool) abdomen. **H~list** f deceit. **h~listig** adj deceitful. **H~n** m **-s,-** [!] bottom, backside. **H~rad** nt rear or back wheel. **h~rücks** adv from behind. **h~ste(r,s)** adj last; **h~ste Reihe** back row. **H~teil** nt [!] behind. **H~treppe** f back stairs pl

hinterziehen† vt (Admin) evade

hinüber adv over or across [there]; **h~ sein** ([!]: unbrauchbar, tot) have had it. **h~gehen**† vi sep (sein) go over or across; **h~gehen über** (+ acc) cross

hinunter adv down [there]. **h~gehen**† vi sep (sein) go down. **h~schlucken** vt sep swallow

Hinweg m way there

hinweg adv away, off; **h~ über** (+ acc) over; **über eine Zeit h~** over a period. **h~kommen**† vt sep (sein) **h~kommen über** (+ acc) (fig) get over. **h~sehen**† vi sep (haben) **h~sehen über** (+ acc) see over; (fig) overlook. **h~setzen (sich)** vr sep **sich h~setzen über** (+ acc) ignore

Hinweis m **-es,-e** reference; (Andeutung) hint; (Anzeichen) indication; **unter H~ auf** (+ acc) with reference to. **h~en**† v sep •vi (haben) point (**auf** + acc to) •vt **jdn auf etw** (acc) **h~en** point sth out to s.o.

hinwieder adv on the other hand

hin|zeigen vi sep (haben) point (**auf** + acc to). **h~ziehen**† vt sep pull; (fig: in die Länge ziehen) drag out; (verzögern) delay; **sich h~ziehen** drag on

hinzu adv in addition. **h~fügen** vt sep add. **h~kommen**† vt sep (sein) be added; (ankommen) arrive [on the scene]; join (**zu jdm** s.o.). **h~ziehen**† vt sep call in

Hiobsbotschaft f bad news sg

Hirn nt **-s** brain; (Culin) brains pl. **H~hautentzündung** f meningitis

Hirsch m **-[e]s,-e** deer; (männlich) stag; (Culin) venison

Hirse f **-** millet

Hirt m **-en,-en**, **Hirte** m **-n,-n** shepherd

hissen vt hoist

Histor|iker m **-s,-** historian. **h~isch** adj historical; (bedeutend) historic

Hitz|e f **-** heat. **h~ig** adj (fig) heated; (Person) hot-headed; (jähzornig) hot-tempered. **H~schlag** m heat-stroke

H-Milch /'ha:-/ f long-life milk

Hobby nt **-s,-s** hobby

Hobel m **-s,-** (Techn) plane; (Culin) slicer. **h~n** vt/i (haben) plane. **H~späne** mpl shavings

hoch adj (attrib **hohe(r,s)**) high; (Baum, Mast) tall; (Offizier) high-ranking; (Alter) great; (Summe) large; (Strafe) heavy; **hohe Schuhe** ankle boots •adv high; (sehr) highly; **h~ gewachsen** tall; **h~ begabt** highly gifted; **h~ gestellte Persönlichkeit** important person; **die Treppe h~** up the stairs; **sechs Mann h~** six of us/them. **H~** nt **-s,-s** cheer; (Meteorology) high

Hoch|achtung f high esteem. **H~achtungsvoll** adv Yours faithfully. **H~betrieb** m great activity; **in den Geschäften herrscht H~betrieb** the shops are terribly busy. [C] **H~deutsch** nt High German. **H~druck** m high pressure. **H~ebene** f plateau. **h~fahren**† vi sep (sein) go up; (auffahren) start up; (aufbrausen) flare up. **h~gehen**† vi sep (sein) go up; (explodieren) blow up; (aufbrausen) flare up. **h~gestellt** attrib adj (Zahl) superior; (fig) ***h~ gestellt**, s. **hoch**. **H~glanz** m high gloss.

[C] see A-Z of German life and culture

h~gradig adj extreme. **h~hackig** adj high-heeled. **h~halten†** vt sep hold up; (fig) uphold. **H~haus** nt high-rise building. **h~heben†** vt sep lift up; raise (Hand). **h~kant** adv on end. **h~kommen†** vi sep (sein) come up; (aufstehen) get up; (fig) get on [in the world]. **H~konjunktur** f boom. **h~krempeln** vt sep roll up. **h~leben** vi sep (haben) **h~leben lassen** give three cheers for; **H~mut** m pride, arrogance. **h~näsig** adj ! snooty. **H~ofen** m blast-furnace. **h~ragen** vi sep rise [up]; (Turm:) soar. **H~ruf** m cheer. **H~saison** f high season. **h~schlagen†** vt sep turn up (Kragen). **H~schule** f university; (Musik-, Kunst-) academy. **H~sommer** m midsummer. **H~spannung** f high/(fig) great tension. **h~spielen** vt sep (fig) magnify. **H~sprung** m high jump

höchst adv extremely, most

Hochstapler m **-s,-** confidence trickster

höchst|e(r,s) adj highest; (Baum, Turm) tallest; (oberste, größte) top; **es ist h~e Zeit** it is high time. **h~ens** adv at most; (es sei denn) except perhaps. **H~geschwindigkeit** f top or maximum speed. **H~maß** nt maximum. **h~persönlich** adv in person. **H~preis** m top price. **H~temperatur** f maximum temperature

Hoch|verrat m high treason. **H~wasser** nt high tide; (Überschwemmung) floods pl. **H~würden** m **-s** Reverend; (Anrede) Father

Hochzeit f **-,-en** wedding. **H~skleid** nt wedding dress. **H~sreise** f honeymoon [trip]. **H~stag** m wedding day/(Jahrestag) anniversary

Hocke f **- in der H~ sitzen** squat. **h~n** vi (haben) squat •vr **sich h~n** squat down

Hocker m **-s,-** stool

Höcker m **-s,-** bump; (Kamel-) hump

Hockey /hɔki/ nt **-s** hockey

Hode f **-,-n**, **Hoden** m **-s,-** testicle

Hof m **-[e]s,¨-e** [court]yard; (Bauern-) farm; (Königs-) court; (Schul-) playground; (Astronomy) halo

hoffen vt/i (haben) hope (**auf** + acc for). **h~tlich** adv I hope so, hopefully

Hoffnung f **-,-en** hope. **h~slos** adj hopeless. **h~svoll** adj hopeful

höflich adj polite. **H~keit** f **-,-en** politeness, courtesy

hohe(r,s) adj s. **hoch**

Höhe f **-,-n** height; (Aviat, Geog) altitude; (Niveau) level; (einer Summe) size; (An-) hill

Hoheit f **-,-en** (Staats-) sovereignty; (Titel) Highness. **H~sgebiet** nt [sovereign] territory. **H~szeichen** nt national emblem

Höhe|nlinie f contour line. **H~nsonne** f sun lamp. **H~punkt** m (fig) climax, peak. **h~r** adj & adv higher; **h~re Schule** secondary school

hohl adj hollow; (leer) empty

Höhle f **-,-n** cave; (Tier-) den; (Hohlraum) cavity; (Augen-) socket

Hohl|maß nt measure of capacity. **H~raum** m cavity

Hohn m **-s** scorn, derision

höhnen vt deride

holen vt fetch, get; (kaufen) buy; (nehmen) take (**aus** from)

Holland nt **-s** Holland

Holländ|er m **-s,-** Dutchman; **die H~er** the Dutch pl. **H~erin** f **-,-nen** Dutchwoman. **h~isch** adj Dutch

Höll|e f **-** hell. **h~isch** adj infernal; (schrecklich) terrible

Holunder m **-s** (Bot) elder

Holz nt **-es,¨-er** wood; (Nutz-) timber. **H~blasinstrument** nt woodwind instrument

hölzern adj wooden

Holz|hammer m mallet. **h~ig** adj

see A-Z of German life and culture

woody. **H~kohle** f charcoal. **H~schnitt** m woodcut. **H~wolle** f wood shavings pl

Homöopathie f - homoeopathy

homöopathisch adj homoeopathic

homosexuell adj homosexual. **H~e(r)** m/f homosexual

Honig m **-s** honey. **H~wabe** f honeycomb

Hono|rar nt **-s,-e** fee. **h~rieren** vt remunerate; (fig) reward

Hopfen m **-s** hops pl; (Bot) hop

hopsen vi (sein) jump

horchen vi (haben) listen (**auf** + acc to); (heimlich) eavesdrop

hören vt hear; (an-) listen to •vi (haben) hear; (horchen) listen; (gehorchen) obey; **h~ auf** (+ acc) listen to

Hör|er m **-s,-** listener; (Teleph) receiver. **H~funk** m radio. **H~gerät** nt hearing aid

Horizon|t m **-[e]s** horizon. **h~tal** adj horizontal

Hormon nt **-s,-e** hormone

Horn nt **-s,¨-er** horn. **H~haut** f hard skin; (Augen-) cornea

Hornisse f **-,-n** hornet

Horoskop nt **-[e]s,-e** horoscope

Horrorfilm m horror film

Hör|saal m (Univ) lecture hall. **H~spiel** nt radio play

Hort m **-[e]s,-e** (Schatz) hoard; (fig) refuge. **h~en** vt hoard

Hortensie /-i̯ə/ f **-,-n** hydrangea

Hose f **-,-n**, **Hosen** pl trousers pl. **H~nrock** m culottes pl. **H~nschlitz** m fly, flies pl. **H~nträger** mpl braces

Hostess f **-,-tessen** hostess; (Aviat) air hostess

Hostie /ˈhɔsti̯ə/ f **-,-n** (Relig) host

Hotel nt **-s,-s** hotel

hübsch adj pretty; (nett) nice

Hubschrauber m **-s,-** helicopter

Huf m **-[e]s,-e** hoof. **H~eisen** nt horseshoe

Hüft|e f **-,-n** hip. **H~gürtel** m **-s,-** girdle

Hügel m **-s,-** hill. **h~ig** adj hilly

Huhn nt **-s,¨-er** chicken; (Henne) hen

Hühn|chen nt **-s,-** chicken. **H~erauge** nt corn. **H~erstall** m henhouse

Hülle f **-,-n** cover; (Verpackung) wrapping; (Platten-) sleeve. **h~n** vt wrap

Hülse f **-,-n** (Bot) pod; (Etui) case. **H~nfrüchte** fpl pulses

human adj humane. **H~ität** f - humanity

Hummel f **-,-n** bumble bee

Hummer m **-s,-** lobster

Hum|or m **-s** humour; **H~or haben** have a sense of humour. **h~orvoll** adj humorous

humpeln vi (sein/haben) hobble

Humpen m **-s,-** tankard

Hund m **-[e]s,-e** dog; (Jagd-) hound. **H~ehütte** f kennel

hundert inv adj one/a hundred. **H~** nt **-s,-e** hundred; **H~e** od **h~e von** hundreds of. **H~jahrfeier** f centenary. **h~prozentig** adj & adv one hundred per cent. **h~ste(r,s)** adj hundredth. **H~stel** nt **-s,-** hundredth

Hündin f **-,-nen** bitch

Hüne m **-n,-n** giant

Hunger m **-s** hunger; **H~ haben** be hungry. **h~n** vi (haben) starve. **H~snot** f famine

hungrig adj hungry

Hupe f **-,-n** (Auto) horn. **h~n** vi (haben) sound one's horn

hüpfen vi (sein) skip; (Frosch:) hop; (Grashüpfer:) jump

Hürde f **-,-n** (Sport & fig) hurdle; (Schaf-) pen, fold

Hure f **-,-n** whore

hurra int hurray

husten vi (haben) cough. **H~** m **-s** cough. **H~saft** m cough mixture

Hut[1] m **-[e]s,¨-e** hat; (Pilz-) cap

Hut[2] f - **auf der H~ sein** be on

one's guard (**vor** + dat against)

hüten vt watch over; tend (Tiere); (aufpassen) look after; **das Bett h∼ müssen** be confined to bed; **sich h∼** be on one's guard (**vor** + dat against); **sich h∼, etw zu tun** take care not to do sth

Hütte f -,-n hut; (Hunde-) kennel; (Techn) iron and steel works. **H∼nkäse** m cottage cheese. **H∼nkunde** f metallurgy

Hyäne f -,-n hyena

hydraulisch adj hydraulic

Hygien|e /hy'gi̯e:nə/ f - hygiene. **h∼isch** adj hygienic

Hypno|se f - hypnosis. **h∼tisch** adj hypnotic. **H∼tiseur** m -s,-e hypnotist. **h∼tisieren** vt hypnotize

Hypochonder /hypo'xɔndɐ/ m -s,- hypochondriac

Hypothek f -,-en mortgage

Hypothese f -,-n hypothesis

Hys|terie f - hysteria. **h∼terisch** adj hysterical

Ii

ich pron I; **ich bins** it's me. **Ich** nt -[s],-[s] self; (Psychology) ego

IC-Zug /i'tse:-/ m inter-city train

ideal adj ideal. **I∼** nt -s,-e ideal. **I∼ismus** m - idealism. **I∼ist(in)** m -en,-en (f -,-nen) idealist. **i∼istisch** adj idealistic

Idee f -,-n idea; **fixe I∼** obsession

identifizieren vt identify

identisch adj identical

Identität f -, -en identity

Ideo|logie f -,-n ideology. **i∼logisch** adj ideological

idiomatisch adj idiomatic

Idiot m -en,-en idiot. **i∼isch** adj idiotic

idyllisch /i'dʏlɪʃ/ adj idyllic

Igel m -s,- hedgehog

ihm pron (dat of **er, es**) [to] him; (Ding, Tier) [to] it

ihn pron (acc of **er**) him; (Ding, Tier) it. **i∼en** pron (dat of **sie** pl) [to] them. **I∼en** pron (dat of **Sie**) [to] you

ihr pron (2nd pers pl) you • (dat of **sie** sg) [to] her; (Ding, Tier) [to] it • poss pron her; (Ding, Tier) its; (pl) their. **Ihr** poss pron your. **i∼e(r,s)** poss pron hers; (pl) theirs. **I∼e(r,s)** poss pron yours. **i∼erseits** adv for her/(pl) their part. **I∼erseits** adv on your part. **i∼etwegen** adv for her/(Ding, Tier) its/(pl) their sake; (wegen) because of her/it/them, on her/its/their account. **I∼etwegen** adv for your sake; (wegen) because of you, on your account. **i∼ige** poss pron **der/die/das i∼ige** hers; (pl) theirs. **I∼ige** poss pron **der/die/das I∼ige** yours. **i∼s** poss pron hers; (pl) theirs. **I∼s** poss pron yours

Ikone f -,-n icon

illegal adj illegal

Illus|ion f -,-en illusion. **i∼orisch** adj illusory

Illustr|ation /-'tsi̯o:n/ f -,-en illustration. **i∼ieren** vt illustrate. **I∼ierte** f -n,-[n] [illustrated] magazine

Iltis m -ses,-se polecat

im prep = **in dem**

Imbiss m snack. **I∼stube** f snack bar

Imit|ation /-'tsi̯o:n/ f -,-en imitation. **i∼ieren** vt imitate

Imker m -s,- bee-keeper

Immatrikul|ation /-'tsi̯o:n/ f - (Univ) enrolment. **i∼ieren** vt (Univ) enrol; **sich i∼ieren** enrol

immer adv always; **für i~** for ever; (endgültig) for good; **i~ noch** still; **i~ mehr** more and more; **was i~** whatever. **i~hin** adv (wenigstens) at least; (trotzdem) all the same; (schließlich) after all. **i~zu** adv all the time

Immobilien /-i̯ən/ pl real estate sg. **I~makler** m estate agent

immun adj immune (**gegen** to)

Imperialismus m - imperialism

impf|en vt vaccinate, inoculate. **I~stoff** m vaccine. **I~ung** f -,-en vaccination, inoculation

imponieren vi (haben) impress (**jdm** s.o.)

Impor|t m **-[e]s,-e** import. **I~teur** m **-s,-e** importer. **i~tieren** vt import

impoten|t adj (Med) impotent. **I~z** f - (Med) impotence

imprägnieren vt waterproof

Impressionismus m - impressionism

improvisieren vt/i (haben) improvise

imstande pred adj able (**zu** to); capable (**etw zu tun** of doing sth)

in prep (+ dat) in; (+ acc) into, in; (bei Bus, Zug) on; **in der Schule** at school; **in die Schule** to school • adj **in sein** be in

Inbegriff m embodiment

indem conj (während) while; (dadurch) by (+ -ing)

Inder(in) m **-s,-** (f **-,-nen**) Indian

indessen conj while • adv (unterdessen) meanwhile

Indian|er(in) m **-s,-** (f **-,-nen**) (American) Indian. **i~isch** adj Indian

Indien /ˈɪndi̯ən/ nt **-s** India

indirekt adj indirect

indisch adj Indian

indiskret adj indiscreet

indiskutabel adj out of the question

Individu|alist m **-en,-en** individualist. **I~alität** f - individuality. **i~ell** adj individual

Indizienbeweis /ɪnˈdiːtsi̯ən-/ m circumstantial evidence

industr|ialisiert adj industrialized. **I~ie** f -,-n industry. **i~iell** adj industrial

ineinander adv in/into one another

Infanterie f - infantry

Infektion /-ˈtsi̯oːn/ f **-,-en** infection. **I~skrankheit** f infectious disease

infizieren vt infect; **sich i~** become/ (Person:) be infected

Inflation /-ˈtsi̯oːn/ f - inflation. **i~är** adj inflationary

infolge prep (+ gen) as a result of. **i~dessen** adv consequently

Inform|atik f - information science. **I~ation** f **-,-en** information; **I~ationen** information sg. **i~ieren** vt inform; **sich i~ieren** find out (**über** + acc about)

infrage adv **etw i~ stellen** question sth; (ungewiss machen) make sth doubtful; **nicht i~ kommen** be out of the question

infrarot adj infra-red

Ingenieur /ɪnʒeˈni̯øːɐ̯/ m **-s,-e** engineer

Ingwer m **-s** ginger

Inhaber(in) m **-s,-** (f **-,-nen**) holder; (Besitzer) proprietor; (Scheck-) bearer

inhaftieren vt take into custody

inhalieren vt/i (haben) inhale

Inhalt m **-[e]s,-e** contents pl; (Bedeutung, Gehalt) content; (Geschichte) story. **I~sangabe** f summary. **I~sverzeichnis** nt list/ (in Buch) table of contents

Initiative /initsi̯aˈtiːvə/ f **-,-n** initiative

inklusive prep (+ gen) including • adv inclusive

inkonsequent adj inconsistent

inkorrekt adj incorrect

Inkubationszeit /-'tsi̯o:ns-/ f (Med) incubation period

Inland nt **-[e]s** home country; (Binnenland) interior. **I~sgespräch** nt inland call

inmitten prep (+ gen) in the middle of; (unter) amongst

innen adv inside; **nach i~** inwards. **I~architekt(in)** m(f) interior designer. **I~minister** m Minister of the Interior; (in UK) Home Secretary. **I~politik** f domestic policy. **I~stadt** f town centre

inner|e(r,s) adj inner; (Med, Pol) internal. **I~e(s)** nt interior; (Mitte) centre; (fig: Seele) inner being. **I~eien** fpl (Culin) offal sg. **i~halb** prep (+ gen) inside; (zeitlich & fig) within; (während) during • adv **i~halb von** within. **i~lich** adj internal

innig adj sincere

innovativ adj innovative

Innung f **-,-en** guild

ins prep = **in das**

Insasse m **-n,-n** inmate; (im Auto) occupant; (Passagier) passenger

insbesondere adv especially

Inschrift f inscription

Insekt nt **-[e]s,-en** insect. **I~envertilgungsmittel** nt insecticide

Insel f **-,-n** island

Inser|at nt **-[e]s,-e** [newspaper] advertisement. **i~ieren** vt/i (haben) advertise

insge|heim adv secretly. **i~samt** adv [all] in all

insofern, insoweit adv in this respect; **i~ als** in as much as

Insp|ektion /ɪnspɛk'tsi̯o:n/ f **-,-en** inspection. **I~ektor** m **-en,-en** inspector

Install|ateur /ɪnstala'tø:ɐ̯/ m **-s,-e** fitter; (Klempner) plumber. **i~ieren** vt install

instand adv **i~ halten** maintain; (pflegen) look after. **I~haltung** f - maintenance, upkeep

Instandsetzung f - repair

Instanz /-st-/ f **-,-en** authority

Instinkt /-st-/ m **-[e]s,-e** instinct. **i~iv** adj instinctive

Institut /-st-/ nt **-[e]s,-e** institute

Instrument /-st-/ nt **-[e]s,-e** instrument. **I~almusik** f instrumental music

Insulin nt **-s** insulin

inszenier|en vt (Theat) produce. **I~ung** f **-,-en** production

Integr|ation /-'tsi̯o:n/ f - integration. **i~ieren** vt integrate; **sich i~ieren** integrate

Intellekt m **-[e]s** intellect. **i~uell** adj intellectual

intelligen|t adj intelligent. **I~z** f - intelligence

Intendant m **-en,-en** director

Intensivstation f intensive-care unit

interaktiv adj interactive

inter|essant adj interesting. **I~esse** nt **-s,-n** interest; **I~esse haben** be interested (**an** + dat in). **I~essengruppe** f pressure group. **I~essent** m **-en,-en** interested party; (Käufer) prospective buyer. **i~essieren** vt interest; **sich i~essieren** be interested (**für** in)

Inter|nat nt **-[e]s,-e** boarding school. **i~national** adj international. **I~nist** m **-en,-en** specialist in internal diseases. **I~pretation** /-'ts:iʃo:n/ f **-,-en** interpretation. **i~pretieren** vt interpret. **I~vall** nt **-s,-e** interval. **I~vention** /-'ts:iʃo:n/ f **-,-en** intervention

🄲 **Internet** nt **-s,-s** Internet; **im I~** on the Internet

Interview /'ɪntɐvju:/ nt **-s,-s** interview. **i~en** vt interview

intim adj intimate

intoleran|t adj intolerant. **I~z** f - intolerance

intravenös adj intravenous

Intrige f **-,-n** intrigue

🄲 *see* A-Z of German life and culture

introvertiert adj introverted

Invalidenrente f disability pension

Invasion f **-,-en** invasion

Inven|tar nt **-s,-e** furnishings and fittings pl; (Techn) equipment; (Bestand) stock; (Liste) inventory. **I~tur** f **-,-en** stock-taking

investieren vt invest

inwie|fern adv in what way. **i~weit** adv how far, to what extent

Inzest m **-[e]s** incest

inzwischen adv in the meantime

Irak (der) -[s] Iraq. **i~isch** adj Iraqi

Iran (der) -[s] Iran. **i~isch** adj Iranian

irdisch adj earthly

Ire m **-n,-n** Irishman; **die I~n** the Irish pl

irgend adv **wenn i~ möglich** if at all possible. **i~ein** indefinite article some/any; **i~ein anderer** someone/anyone else. **i~eine(r,s)** pron any one; (jemand) someone/anyone. **i~etwas** pron something; anything. **i~jemand** pron someone; anyone. **i~wann** pron at some time [or other]/at any time. **i~was** pron [!] something [or other]/anything. **i~welche(r,s)** pron any. **i~wer** pron someone/anyone. **i~wie** adv somehow [or other]. **i~wo** adv somewhere

Irin f **-,-nen** Irishwoman

irisch adj Irish

Irland nt **-s** Ireland

Ironie f **-** irony

ironisch adj ironic

irre adj mad, crazy; ([!]: gewaltig) incredible. **I~(r)** m/f lunatic. **i~führen** vt sep (fig) mislead

irre|machen vt sep confuse. **i~n** vi/r (haben) **[sich] i~n** be mistaken • vi (sein) wander. **I~nanstalt** f, **I~nhaus** nt lunatic asylum. **i~werden**† vi sep (sein) get confused

Irrgarten m maze

irritieren vt irritate

Irr|sinn m madness, lunacy. **i~sinnig** adj mad; ([!]: gewaltig) incredible. **I~tum** m **-s,⸚er** mistake

Ischias m & nt **-** sciatica

Islam (der) -[s] Islam. **islamisch** adj Islamic

Island nt **-s** Iceland

Isolier|band nt insulating tape. **i~en** vt isolate; (Phys, Electr) insulate; (gegen Schall) soundproof. **I~ung** f **-** isolation; insulation; soundproofing

Isra|el /'ɪsraeːl/ nt **-s** Israel. **I~eli** m **-[s],-s** & f **-,-[s]** Israeli. **i~elisch** adj Israeli

ist s. **sein; er ist** he is

Ital|ien /-i̯ən/ nt **-s** Italy. **I~iener(in)** m **-s,-** (f **-,-nen**) Italian. **i~ienisch** adj Italian. **I~ienisch** nt **-[s]** (Lang) Italian

Jj

ja adv, **Ja** nt **-[s]** yes; **ich glaube ja** I think so; **ja nicht!** not on any account! **da seid ihr ja!** there you are!

Jacht f **-,-en** yacht

Jacke f **-,-n** jacket; (Strick-) cardigan

Jackett /ʒa'kɛt/ nt **-s,-s** jacket

Jade m **-[s]** & f **-** jade

Jagd f **-,-en** hunt; (Schießen) shoot; (Jagen) hunting; shooting; (fig) pursuit (**nach** of); **auf die J~ gehen** go hunting/shooting.

J~gewehr nt sporting gun. **J~hund** m gun-dog: (Hetzhund) hound

jagen vt hunt; (schießen) shoot; (verfolgen, wegjagen) chase; (treiben) drive; **sich j~** chase each other; **in die Luft j~** blow up • vi (haben) hunt, go hunting/shooting; (fig) chase (**nach** after) • vi (sein) race, dash

Jäger m **-s,-** hunter

Jahr nt **-[e]s,-e** year. **j~elang** adv for years. **J~eszahl** f year. **J~eszeit** f season. **J~gang** m year; (Wein) vintage. **J~hundert** nt century

jährlich adj annual, yearly

Jahr|markt m fair. **J~tausend** nt millennium. **J~zehnt** nt **-[e]s,-e** decade

Jähzorn m violent temper. **j~ig** adj hot-tempered

Jalousie /ʒalu'zi:/ f **-,-n** venetian blind

Jammer m **-s** misery

jämmerlich adj miserable; (Mitleid erregend) pitiful

jammern vi (haben) lament • vt **jdn j~** arouse s.o.'s pity

Jänner m **-s,-** (Aust) January

Januar m **-s,-e** January

Jap|an nt **-s** Japan. **J~aner(in)** m **-s,-** (f **-,-nen**) Japanese. **j~anisch** adj Japanese. **J~anisch** nt **-[s]** (Lang) Japanese

jäten vt/i (haben) weed

jaulen vi (haben) yelp

Jause f **-,-n** (Aust) snack

jawohl adv yes

Jazz /jats, dʒɛs/ m **-** jazz

je adv (jemals) ever; (jeweils) each; (pro) per; **je nach** according to; **seit eh und je** always • conj **je mehr, desto besser** the more the better • prep (+ acc) per

Jeans /dʒi:ns/ pl jeans

jed|e(r,s) pron every; (j~er Einzelne) each; (j~er Beliebige) any; (substantivisch) everyone; each one; anyone; **ohne j~en Grund** without any reason. **j~enfalls** adv in any case; (wenigstens) at least. **j~ermann** pron everyone. **j~erzeit** adv at any time. **j~esmal** adv every time

jedoch adv & conj however

jemals adv ever

jemand pron someone, somebody; (fragend, verneint) anyone, anybody

jen|e(r,s) pron that; (pl) those; (substantivisch) that one; (pl) those. **j~seits** prep (+ gen) [on] the other side of

jetzt adv now

jiddisch adj, **J~** nt **-[s]** Yiddish

Job /dʒɔp/ m **-s,-s** job. **j~ben** vi (haben) 🄵 work

Joch nt **-[e]s,-e** yoke

Jockei, **Jockey** /'dʒɔki/ m **-s,-s** jockey

Jod nt **-[e]s** iodine

jodeln vi (haben) yodel

Joga m & nt **-[s]** yoga

joggen /'dʒɔgən/ vi (haben/sein) jog

Joghurt, **Jogurt** m & nt **-[s]** yoghurt

Johannisbeere f redcurrant

Joker m **-s,-** (Karte) joker

Jolle f **-,-n** dinghy

Jongleur /ʒõ'glø:ɐ̯/ m **-s,-e** juggler

Jordanien /-i̯ən/ nt **-s** Jordan

Journalis|mus /ʒʊrna'lɪsmʊs/ m **-** journalism. **J~t(in)** m **-en,-en** (f **-,-nen**) journalist

Jubel m **-s** rejoicing, jubilation. **j~n** vi (haben) rejoice

Jubiläum nt **-s,-äen** jubilee; (Jahrestag) anniversary

jucken vi (haben) itch; **sich j~en** scratch; **es j~t mich** I have an itch

Jude m **-n,-n** Jew. **J~ntum** nt **-s** Judaism; (Juden) Jewry

Jüd|in f **-,-nen** Jewess. **j~isch** adj Jewish

Judo nt **-[s]** judo

Jugend f **-** youth; (junge Leute)

young people pl. **J~herberge** f youth hostel. **J~kriminalität** f juvenile delinquency. **j~lich** adj youthful. **J~liche(r)** m/f young man/woman. **J~liche** pl young people. **J~stil** m art nouveau

Jugoslawien /-ɪ̯ən/ nt **-s** Yugoslavia. **j~isch** adj Yugoslav

Juli m **-[s],-s** July

jung adj young; (Wein) new • pron **J~ und Alt** young and old. **J~e** m **-n,-n** boy. **J~e(s)** nt young animal/ bird; (Katzen-) kitten; (Bären-) cub; (Hunde-) pup; **die J~en** the young pl

Jünger m **-s,-** disciple

Jungfrau f virgin; (Astrology) Virgo. **J~geselle** m bachelor

Jüngling m **-s,-e** youth

jüngst|e(r,s) adj youngest; (neueste) latest; **in j~er Zeit** recently

Juni m **-[s],-s** June

Jura pl law sg

Jurist|(in) m **-en,-en** (f **-,-nen**) lawyer. **j~isch** adj legal

Jury /ʒy'ri:/ f **-,-s** jury; (Sport) judges pl

Justiz f **-** **die J~** justice

Juwel nt **-s,-en** & (fig) **-e** jewel. **J~ier** m **-s,-e** jeweller

Jux m **-es,-e** 🄸 joke; **aus Jux** for fun

Kk

Kabarett nt **-s,-s** & **-e** cabaret

Kabel nt **-s,-** cable. **K~fernsehen** nt cable television

Kabeljau m **-s,-e** & **-s** cod

Kabine f **-,-n** cabin; (Umkleide-) cubicle; (Telefon-) booth; (einer K~nbahn) car. **K~nbahn** f cable-car

Kabinett nt **-s,-e** (Pol) Cabinet

Kabriolett nt **-s,-s** convertible

Kachel f **-,-n** tile. **k~n** vt tile

Kadenz f **-,-en** (Mus) cadence

Käfer m **-s,-** beetle

🄲 **Kaffee** /'kafe:, ka'fe:/ m **-s,-s** coffee. **K~kanne** f coffee pot. **K~maschine** f coffee maker. **K~mühle** f coffee grinder

Käfig m **-s,-e** cage

kahl adj bare; (haarlos) bald; **k~ geschoren** shaven

Kahn m **-s,¨-e** boat; (Last-) barge

Kai m **-s,-s** quay

Kaiser m **-s,-** emperor. **K~in** f **-,-nen** empress. **k~lich** adj imperial. **K~reich** nt empire. **K~schnitt** m Caesarean [section]

Kajüte f **-,-n** (Naut) cabin

Kakao /ka'kau̯/ m **-s** cocoa

Kakerlak m **-s** & **-en,-en** cockroach

Kaktus m **-,-teen** cactus

Kalb nt **-[e]s,¨-er** calf. **K~fleisch** nt veal

Kalender m **-s,-** calendar; (Termin-) diary

Kaliber nt **-s,-** calibre; (Gewehr-) bore

Kalium nt **-s** potassium

Kalk m **-[e]s,-e** lime; (Kalzium) calcium. **k~en** vt whitewash. **K~stein** m limestone

Kalkul|ation /-'tsi̯o:n/ f **-,-en** calculation. **k~ieren** vt/i (haben) calculate

Kalorie f **-,-n** calorie

kalt adj cold; **mir ist k~** I am cold

Kälte f **-** cold; (Gefühls-) coldness; **10 Grad K~** 10 degrees below zero

🄲 *see* A-Z of German life and culture

Kalzium nt **-s** calcium

Kamel nt **-s,-e** camel

Kamera f **-,-s** camera

Kamerad(in) m **-en,-en** (f **-,-nen**) companion; (Freund) mate; (Mil, Pol) comrade

Kameramann m (pl **-männer** & **-leute**) cameraman

Kamille f **-** chamomile

Kamin m **-s,-e** fireplace; (SGer: Schornstein) chimney

Kamm m **-[e]s,¨e** comb; (Berg-) ridge; (Zool, Wellen-) crest

kämmen vt comb; **jdn/sich k~** comb someone's/one's hair

Kammer f **-,-n** small room; (Techn, Biology, Pol) chamber. **K~musik** f chamber music

Kammgarn nt (Textiles) worsted

Kampagne /kam'panjə/ f **-,-n** (Pol, Comm) campaign

Kampf m **-es,¨e** fight; (Schlacht) battle; (Wett-) contest; (fig) struggle

kämpf|en vi (haben) fight; **sich k~en durch** fight one's way through. **K~er(in)** m **-s,-** (f **-,-nen**) fighter

Kampfrichter m (Sport) judge

Kanada nt **-s** Canada

Kanad|ier(in) /-i̯ɐ, -i̯ərɪn/ m **-s,-** (f **-,-nen**) Canadian. **k~isch** adj Canadian

Kanal m **-s,¨e** canal; (Abfluss-) drain, sewer; (Radio, TV) channel; **der K~** the [English] Channel

Kanalisation /-'tsi̯o:n/ f **-** sewerage system, drains pl

Kanarienvogel /-i̯ən-/ m canary

Kanarisch adj **K~e Inseln** Canaries

Kandidat(in) m **-en,-en** (f **-,-nen**) candidate

kandiert adj candied

Känguru nt **-s,-s** kangaroo

Kaninchen nt **-s,-** rabbit

Kanister m **-s,-** canister; (Benzin-) can

Kännchen nt **-s,-** [small] jug; (Kaffee-) pot

Kanne f **-,-n** jug; (Tee-) pot; (Öl-) can; (große Milch-) churn

Kannibal|e m **-n,-n** cannibal. **K~ismus** m **-** cannibalism

Kanon m **-s,-s** canon; (Lied) round

Kanone f **-,-n** cannon, gun

kanonisieren vt canonize

Kantate f **-,-n** cantata

Kante f **-,-n** edge

Kanten m **-s,-** crust [of bread]

Kanter m **-s,-** canter

kantig adj angular

Kantine f **-,-n** canteen

🅒 **Kanton** m **-s,-e** (Swiss) canton

Kanu nt **-s,-s** canoe

Kanzel f **-,-n** pulpit; (Aviat) cockpit

Kanzler m **-s,-** chancellor

Kap nt **-s,-s** (Geog) cape

Kapazität f **-,-en** capacity

Kapelle f **-,-n** chapel; (Mus) band

kapern vt (Naut) seize

kapieren vt [!] understand

Kapital nt **-s** capital. **K~ismus** m **-** capitalism. **K~ist** m **-en,-en** capitalist. **k~istisch** adj capitalist

Kapitän m **-s,-e** captain

Kapitel nt **-s,-** chapter

Kaplan m **-s,¨e** curate

Kappe f **-,-n** cap

Kapsel f **-,-n** capsule; (Flaschen-) top

kaputt adj [!] broken; (zerrissen) torn; (defekt) out of order; (ruiniert) ruined; (erschöpft) worn out. **k~gehen**† vi sep (sein) [!] break; (zerreißen) tear; (defekt werden) pack up; (Ehe, Freundschaft:) break up. **k~lachen (sich)** vr sep [!] be in stitches. **k~machen** vt sep [!] break; (zerreißen) tear; (defekt machen) put out of order; (erschöpfen) wear out; **sich k~machen** wear oneself out

---

🅒 *see* A-Z of German life and culture

k

Kapuze f -,-n hood

Kapuzinerkresse f nasturtium

Karaffe f -,-n carafe; (mit Stöpsel) decanter

Karamell m -s caramel. **K~bonbon** m & nt ≈ toffee

Karat nt -[e]s,-e carat

Karawane f -,-n caravan

Kardinal m -s,¨e cardinal. **K~zahl** f cardinal number

Karfreitag m Good Friday

karg adj meagre; (frugal) frugal; (spärlich) sparse; (unfruchtbar) barren; (gering) scant

Karibik f - Caribbean

kariert adj check[ed]; (Papier) squared; **schottisch k~** tartan

Karik|atur f -,-en caricature; (Journalism) cartoon. **k~ieren** vt caricature

k

Karneval m -s,-e & -s carnival

Kärnten nt -s Carinthia

Karo nt -s,-s (Raute) diamond; (Viereck) square; (Muster) check (Kartenspiel) diamonds pl

Karosserie f -,-n bodywork

Karotte f -,-n carrot

Karpfen m -s,- carp

Karren m -s,- cart; (Hand-) barrow. **k~** vt cart

Karriere /ka'ri̯eːrə/ f -,-n career; **K~ machen** get to the top

Karte f -,-n card; (Eintritts-, Fahr-) ticket; (Speise-) menu; (Land-) map

Kartei f -,-en card index

Karten|spiel nt card game; (Spielkarten) pack of cards. **K~vorverkauf** m advance booking

Kartoffel f -,-n potato. **K~brei** m mashed potatoes

Karton /kar'tɔŋ/ m -s,-s cardboard; (Schachtel) carton

Karussell nt -s,-s & -e roundabout

Käse m -s,- cheese

Kaserne f -,-n barracks pl

Kasino nt -s,-s casino

Kasperle nt & m -s,- Punch. **K~theater** nt Punch and Judy show

Kasse f -,-n till; (Registrier-) cash register; (Zahlstelle) cash desk; (im Supermarkt) check out; (Theater-) box office; (Geld) pool [of money], ⓘ kitty; (Kranken-) health insurance scheme; **knapp bei K~ sein** ⓘ be short of cash. **K~nwart** m -[e]s,-e treasurer. **K~nzettel** m receipt

Kasserolle f -,-n saucepan

Kassette f -,-n cassette; (Film-, Farbband-) cartridge. **K~nrekorder** m -s,- cassette recorder

kassier|en vi (haben) collect the money/(im Bus) the fares •vt collect. **K~er(in)** m -s,- (f -,-nen) cashier

Kastanie /kas'taːni̯ə/ f -,-n [horse] chestnut, ⓘ conker

Kasten m -s,¨ box; (Brot-) bin; (Flaschen-) crate; (Brief-) letter box; (Aust: Schrank) cupboard

kastrieren vt castrate; neuter

Katalog m -[e]s,-e catalogue

Katalysator m -s,-en catalyst; (Auto) catalytic converter

Katapult nt -[e]s,-e catapult

Katarrh, Katarr m -s,-e catarrh

Katastrophe f -,-n catastrophe

Katechismus m - catechism

Kategorie f -,-n category

Kater m -s,- tom cat; (ⓘ: Katzenjammer) hangover

Kathedrale f -,-n cathedral

Kath|olik(in) m -en,-en (f -,-nen) Catholic. **k~olisch** adj Catholic. **K~olizismus** m - Catholicism

Kätzchen nt -s,- kitten; (Bot) catkin

Katze f -,-n cat. **K~njammer** m ⓘ hangover. **K~nsprung** m **ein K~nsprung** ⓘ a stone's throw

Kauderwelsch nt -[s] gibberish

kauen vt/i (haben) chew; bite (Nägel)

Kauf m -[e]s, **Käufe** purchase; **guter K~** bargain; **in K~ nehmen** (fig) put up with. **k~en** vt/i (haben) buy; **k~en bei** shop at

Käufer(in) m **-s,-** (f **-,-nen**) buyer; (im Geschäft) shopper

Kauf|haus nt department store. **K~laden** m shop

käuflich adj saleable; (bestechlich) corruptible; **k~ erwerben** buy

Kauf|mann m (pl **-leute**) businessman; (Händler) dealer; (Dialekt) grocer. **K~preis** m purchase price

Kaugummi m chewing gum

Kaulquappe f **-,-n** tadpole

kaum adv hardly

Kaution /-'tsi̯o:n/ f **-,-en** surety; (Jur) bail; (Miet-) deposit

Kautschuk m **-s** rubber

Kauz m **-es, Käuze** owl

Kavalier m **-s,-e** gentleman

Kavallerie f **-** cavalry

Kaviar m **-s** caviare

keck adj bold; cheeky

Kegel m **-s,-** skittle; (Geometry) cone. **K~bahn** f skittle-alley. **k~n** vi (haben) play skittles

Kehl|e f **-,-n** throat; **aus voller K~e** at the top of one's voice. **K~kopf** m larynx. **K~kopfentzündung** f laryngitis

Kehr|e f **-,-n** [hairpin] bend. **k~en** vi (haben) (fegen) sweep •vt sweep; (wenden) turn; **sich nicht k~en an** (+ acc) not care about. **K~icht** m **-[e]s** sweepings pl. **K~reim** m refrain. **K~seite** f (fig) drawback. **k~tmachen** vi sep (haben) turn back; (sich umdrehen) turn round

Keil m **-[e]s,-e** wedge

Keilriemen m fan belt

Keim m **-[e]s,-e** (Bot) sprout; (Med) germ. **k~en** vi (haben) germinate; (austreiben) sprout. **k~frei** adj sterile

kein pron no; not a; **k~e fünf Minuten** less than five minutes. **k~e(r,s)** pron no one, nobody; (Ding) none, not one. **k~esfalls** adv on no account. **k~eswegs** adv by no means. **k~mal** adv not once. **k~s** pron none, not one

Keks m **-[es],-[e]** biscuit

Kelch m **-[e]s,-e** goblet, cup; (Relig) chalice; (Bot) calyx

Kelle f **-,-n** ladle; (Maurer) trowel

Keller m **-s,-** cellar. **K~ei** f **-,-en** winery. **K~wohnung** f basement flat

Kellner m **-s,-** waiter. **K~in** f **-,-nen** waitress

keltern vt press

keltisch adj Celtic

Kenia nt **-s** Kenya

kenn|en† vt know; **k~en lernen** get to know; (treffen) meet; **sich k~en lernen** meet; (näher) get to know one another. **K~er** m **-s,-**, **K~erin** f **-,-nen** connoisseur; (Experte) expert. **k~tlich** adj recognizable; **k~tlich machen** mark. **K~tnis** f **-,-se** knowledge; **zur K~tnis nehmen** take note of; **in K~tnis setzen** inform (**von** of). **K~wort** nt (pl **-wörter**) reference; (geheimes) password. **K~zeichen** nt distinguishing mark or feature; (Merkmal) characteristic, (Markierung) marking; (Auto) registration. **k~zeichnen** vt distinguish; (markieren) mark

kentern vi (sein) capsize

Keramik f **-,-en** pottery

Kerbe f **-,-n** notch

Kerker m **-s,-** dungeon; (Gefängnis) prison

Kerl m **-s,-e** & **-s** [!] fellow, bloke

Kern m **-s,-e** pip; (Kirsch-) stone; (Nuss-) kernel; (Techn) core; (Atom-, Zell- & fig) nucleus; (Stadt-) centre; (einer Sache) heart. **K~energie** f nuclear energy. **K~gehäuse** nt core. **k~los** adj seedless. **K~physik** f nuclear physics sg

Kerze f **-,-n** candle. **K~nhalter** m **-s,-** candlestick

kess adj pert

Kessel m **-s,-** kettle

Kette f **-,-n** chain; (Hals-) necklace.

k

k~n vt chain (**an** + acc to). **K~nladen** m chain store

Ketze|r(in) m **-s,-** (f **-,-nen**) heretic. **K~rei** f - heresy

keuch|en vi (haben) pant. **K~husten** m whooping cough

Keule f **-,-n** club; (Culin) leg; (Hühner-) drumstick

keusch adj chaste

Khaki nt - khaki

kichern vi (haben) giggle

Kiefer¹ f **-,-n** pine[-tree]

Kiefer² m **-s,-** jaw

Kiel m **-s,-e** (Naut) keel

Kiemen fpl gills

Kies m **-es** gravel. **K~el** m **-s,-**, **K~elstein** m pebble

Kilo nt **-s,-[s]** kilo. **K~gramm** nt kilogram. **K~hertz** nt kilohertz. **K~meter** m kilometre. **K~meterstand** m ≈ mileage. **K~watt** nt kilowatt

Kind nt **-es,-er** child; **von K~ auf** from childhood

Kinder|arzt m, **K~ärztin** f paediatrician. **K~bett** nt child's cot. ◘**K~garten** m nursery school. **K~geld** nt child benefit. **K~lähmung** f polio. **k~leicht** adj very easy. **k~los** adj childless. **K~mädchen** nt nanny. **K~reim** m nursery rhyme. **K~spiel** nt children's game. ◘**K~tagesstätte** f day nursery. **K~teller** m children's menu. **K~wagen** m pram. **K~zimmer** nt child's/children's room; (für Baby) nursery

Kind|heit f - childhood. **k~isch** adj childish. **k~lich** adj childlike

kinetisch adj kinetic

Kinn nt **-[e]s,-e** chin. **K~lade** f jaw

Kino nt **-s,-s** cinema

Kiosk m **-[e]s,-e** kiosk

Kippe f **-,-n** (Müll-) dump; (**!**: Zigaretten-) fag end. **k~n** vt tilt; (schütten) tip (**in** + acc into) • vi (sein) topple

◘ *see* A-Z of German life and culture

Kirch|e f **-,-n** church. **K~enbank** f pew. **K~endiener** m verger. **K~enlied** nt hymn. **K~enschiff** nt nave. **K~hof** m churchyard. **k~lich** adj church • adv **k~lich getraut werden** be married in church. **K~turm** m church tower, steeple. **K~weih** f **-,-en** [village] fair

Kirmes f **-,-sen** = **Kirchweih**

Kirsche f **-,-n** cherry

Kissen nt **-s,-** cushion; (Kopf-) pillow

Kiste f **-,-n** crate; (Zigarren-) box

Kitsch m **-es** sentimental rubbish; (Kunst) kitsch

Kitt m **-s** [adhesive] cement; (Fenster-) putty

Kittel m **-s,-** overall, smock

Kitz nt **-es,-e** (Zool) kid

Kitz|el m **-s,-** tickle; (Nerven-) thrill. **k~eln** vt/i (haben) tickle. **k~lig** adj ticklish

kläffen vi (haben) yap

Klage f **-,-n** lament; (Beschwerde) complaint; (Jur) action. **k~n** vi (haben) lament; (sich beklagen) complaint; (Jur) sue

Kläger(in) m **-s,-** (f **-,-nen**) (Jur) plaintiff

klamm adj cold and damp; (steif) stiff. **K~** f **-,-en** (Geog) gorge

Klammer f **-,-n** (Wäsche-) peg; (Büro-) paper clip; (Heft-) staple; (Haar-) grip; (für Zähne) brace; (Techn) clamp; (Typography) bracket. **k~n (sich)** vr cling (**an** + acc to)

Klang m **-[e]s,⸚e** sound; (K~farbe) tone

Klapp|e f **-,-n** flap; (**!**: Mund) trap. **k~en** vt fold; (hoch-) tip up • vi (haben) **!** work out. **K~handy** nt folding mobile phone

Klapper f **-,-n** rattle. **k~n** vi (haben) rattle. **K~schlange** f rattlesnake

klapp|rig adj rickety; (schwach) decrepit. **K~stuhl** m folding chair

Klaps m **-es,-e** pat, smack

klar adj clear; **sich** (dat) **k~ werden** make up one's mind; (erkennen) realize (**dass** that); **sich** (dat) **k~** od **im K~en sein** realize (**dass** that) • adv clearly; ([!]: natürlich) of course

klären vt clarify; **sich k~** clear; (fig: sich lösen) resolve itself

Klarheit f -,- clarity

Klarinette f -,-n clarinet

klar|machen vt sep make clear (dat to); **sich** (dat) **etw k~machen** understand sth. **k~stellen** vt sep clarify

Klärung f - clarification

Klasse f -,-n class; (Sch) class, form; (Zimmer) classroom. **k~** inv adj [!] super. **K~narbeit** f [written] test. **K~nzimmer** nt classroom

Klass|ik f - classicism; (Epoche) classical period. **K~iker** m **-s,-** classical author/(Mus) composer. **k~isch** adj classical; (typisch) classic

Klatsch m **-[e]s** gossip. **K~base** f [!] gossip. **k~en** vt slap; **Beifall k~en** applaud • vi (haben) make a slapping sound; (im Wasser) splash; (tratschen) gossip; (applaudieren) clap. **k~nass** adj [!] soaking wet

klauen vt/i (haben) [!] steal

Klausel f -,-n clause

Klaustrophobie f - claustrophobia

Klausur f -,-en (Univ) paper

Klavier nt **-s,-e** piano. **K~spieler(in)** m(f) pianist

kleb|en vt stick/(mit Klebstoff) glue (**an** + acc to) • vi (haben) stick (**an** + dat to). **k~rig** adj sticky. **K~stoff** m adhesive, glue. **K~streifen** m adhesive tape

Klecks m **-es,-e** stain; (Tinten-) blot; (kleine Menge) dab. **k~en** vi (haben) make a mess

Klee m **-s** clover

Kleid nt **-[e]s,-er** dress; **K~er** dresses; (Kleidung) clothes. **k~en** vt dress; (gut stehen) suit. **K~erbügel** m coat hanger. **K~erbürste** f clothes brush. **K~erhaken** m coat-hook. **K~erschrank** m wardrobe. **k~sam** adj becoming. **K~ung** f - clothes pl, clothing. **K~ungsstück** nt garment

Kleie f - bran

klein adj small, little; (von kleinem Wuchs) short; **k~ schneiden** cut up small. **von k~ auf** from childhood. **K~arbeit** f painstaking work. **K~e(r,s)** m/f/nt little one. **K~geld** nt [small] change. **K~handel** m retail trade. **K~heit** f - smallness; (Wuchs) short stature. **K~holz** nt firewood. **K~igkeit** f -,-en trifle; (Mahl) snack. **K~kind** nt infant. **k~laut** adj subdued. **k~lich** adj petty

klein|schreiben† vt sep write with a small [initial] letter. **K~stadt** f small town. **k~städtisch** adj provincial

Kleister m **-s** paste. **k~n** vt paste

Klemme f -,-n [hair-]grip. **k~n** vt jam; **sich** (dat) **den Finger k~n** get one's finger caught • vi (haben) jam, stick

Klempner m **-s,-** plumber

Klerus (der) - the clergy

Klette f -,-n burr

kletter|n vi (sein) climb. **K~pflanze** f climber

Klettverschluss m Velcro ® fastening

klicken vi (haben) click

Klient(in) /kli'ɛnt(ɪn)/ m **-en,-en** (f **-,-nen**) (Jur) client

Kliff nt **-[e]s,-e** cliff

Klima nt **-s** climate. **K~anlage** f air conditioning

klimat|isch adj climatic. **k~isiert** adj air-conditioned

klimpern vi (haben) jingle; **k~ auf** (+ dat) tinkle on (Klavier); strum (Gitarre)

Klinge f -,-n blade

Klingel f -,-n bell. **k~n** vi (haben) ring; **es k~t** there's a ring at the door

klingen† vi (haben) sound

Klinik f -,-en clinic

Klinke f -,-n [door] handle

Klippe f -,-n [submerged] rock

Klips m **-es,-e** clip; (Ohr-) clip-on ear ring

klirren vi (haben) rattle; (Glas:) chink

Klo nt **-s,-s** ⓘ loo

Klon m **-s, -e** clone. **k∼en** vt clone

klopfen vi (haben) knock; (leicht) tap; (Herz:) pound; **es k∼te** there was a knock at the door

Klops m **-es,-e** meatball

Klosett nt **-s,-s** lavatory

Kloß m **-es,¨-e** dumpling

Kloster nt **-s,¨** monastery; (Nonnen-) convent

klösterlich adj monastic

Klotz m **-es,¨-e** block

Klub m **-s,-s** club

Kluft f **-,¨-e** cleft; (fig: Gegensatz) gulf

klug adj intelligent; (schlau) clever. **K∼heit** f **-** cleverness

Klump|en m **-s,-** lump

knabbern vt/i (haben) nibble

Knabe m **-n,-n** boy. **k∼nhaft** adj boyish

Knäckebrot nt crispbread

knack|en vt/i (haben) crack. **K∼s** m **-es,-e** crack

Knall m **-[e]s,-e** bang. **K∼bonbon** m cracker. **k∼en** vi (haben) go bang; (Peitsche:) crack • vt (ⓘ: werfen) chuck; **jdm eine k∼en** ⓘ clout s.o. **k∼ig** adj ⓘ gaudy

knapp adj (gering) scant; (kurz) short; (mangelnd) scarce; (gerade ausreichend) bare; (eng) tight. **K∼heit** f **-** scarcity

knarren vi (haben) creak

Knast m **-[e]s** ⓘ prison

knattern vi (haben) crackle; (Gewehr:) stutter

Knäuel m & nt **-s,-** ball

Knauf m **-[e]s, Knäufe** knob

knauserig adj ⓘ stingy

knautschen vt ⓘ crumple • vi (haben) crease

Knebel m **-s,-** gag. **k∼n** vt gag

Knecht m **-[e]s,-e** farm-hand; (fig) slave

kneif|en† vt pinch • vi (haben) pinch; (ⓘ: sich drücken) chicken out. **K∼zange** f pincers pl

Kneipe f **-,-n** ⓘ pub

knet|en vt knead; (formen) mould. **K∼masse** f Plasticine®

Knick m **-[e]s,-e** bend; (Kniff) crease. **k∼en** vt bend; (kniffen) fold; **geknickt sein** ⓘ be dejected

Knicks m **-es,-e** curtsy. **k∼en** vi (haben) curtsy

Knie nt **-s,-** knee

knien /ˈkniːən/ vi (haben) kneel • vr **sich k∼** kneel [down]

Kniescheibe f kneecap

Kniff m **-[e]s,-e** pinch; (Falte) crease; (ⓘ: Trick) trick. **k∼en** vt fold

knipsen vt (lochen) punch; (Phot) photograph • vi (haben) take a photograph/photographs

Knirps m **-es,-e** ⓘ little chap; ® (Schirm) telescopic umbrella

knirschen vi (haben) grate; (Schnee, Kies:) crunch

knistern vi (haben) crackle; (Papier:) rustle

Knitter|falte f crease. **k∼frei** adj crease-resistant. **k∼n** vi (haben) crease

knobeln vi (haben) toss (**um** for)

Knoblauch m **-s** garlic

Knöchel m **-s,-** ankle; (Finger-) knuckle

Knochen m **-s,-** bone. **K∼mark** nt bone marrow

knochig adj bony

Knödel m **-s,-** (SGer) dumpling

Knoll|e f **-,-n** tuber

Knopf m **-[e]s,¨-e** button; (Griff) knob

knöpfen vt button

Knopfloch nt buttonhole

Knorpel m **-s** gristle; (Anat) cartilage

Knospe f bud

Knoten m **-s,-** knot; (Med) lump;

(Haar-) bun, chignon. **k~** vt knot. **K~punkt** m junction

knüll|en vt crumple • vi (haben) crease. **K~er** m -s,- [!] sensation

knüpfen vt knot; (verbinden) attach (**an** + acc to)

Knüppel m -s,- club; (Gummi-) truncheon

knurren vi (haben) growl; (Magen:) rumble

knusprig adj crunchy, crisp

knutschen vi (haben) [!] smooch

k.o. /ka'ʔo:/ adj **k.o. schlagen** knock out; **k.o. sein** [!] be worn out

Koalition /koali'tsio:n/ f -,-en coalition

Kobold m -[e]s,-e goblin, imp

Koch m -[e]s,⸚e cook; (im Restaurant) chef. **K~buch** nt cookery book. **k~en** vt cook; (sieden) boil; make (Kaffee, Tee); **hart gekochtes Ei** hard-boiled egg • vi (haben) cook; (sieden) boil; [!] seethe (**vor** + dat with). **K~en** nt -s cooking; (Sieden) boiling. **k~end** adj boiling. **K~herd** m cooker, stove

Köchin f -,-nen [woman] cook

Koch|löffel m wooden spoon. **K~nische** f kitchenette. **K~platte** f hotplate. **K~topf** m saucepan

Köder m -s,- bait

Koffein /kɔfe'i:n/ nt -s caffeine. **k~frei** adj decaffeinated

Koffer m -s,- suitcase. **K~kuli** m luggage trolley. **K~raum** m (Auto) boot

Kognak /'kɔnjak/ m -s,-s brandy

Kohl m -[e]s cabbage

Kohle f -,-n coal. **K~[n]hydrat** nt -[e]s,-e carbohydrate. **K~nbergwerk** nt coal mine, colliery. **K~ndioxid** nt carbon dioxide. **K~nsäure** f carbon dioxide. **K~nstoff** m carbon

Koje f -,-n (Naut) bunk

Kokain /koka'i:n/ nt -s cocaine

kokett adj flirtatious. **k~ieren** vi (haben) flirt

Kokon /ko'kõ:/ m -s,-s cocoon

Kokosnuss f coconut

Koks m -es coke

Kolben m -s,- (Gewehr-) butt; (Mais-) cob; (Techn) piston; (Chemistry) flask

Kolibri m -s,-s humming bird

Kolik f -,-en colic

Kollaborateur /-'tø:ɐ̯/ m -s,-e collaborator

Kolleg nt -s,-s & -ien (Univ) course of lectures

Kolleg|e m -n,-n, **K~in** f -,-nen colleague. **K~ium** nt -s,-ien staff

Kollek|te f -,-n (Relig) collection. **K~tion** /-'tsi̯o:n/ f -,-en collection

Köln nt -s Cologne. **K~ischwasser, K~isch Wasser** nt eau-de-Cologne

Kolonie f -,-n colony

Kolonne f -,-n column; (Mil) convoy

Koloss m -es,-e giant

Koma nt -s,-s coma

Kombi m -s,-s = **K~wagen**. **K~nation** /-'tsi̯o:n/ f -,-en combination; (Folgerung) deduction; (Kleidung) co-ordinating outfit. **k~nieren** vt combine; (fig) reason; (folgern) deduce. **K~wagen** m estate car

Kombüse f -,-n (Naut) galley

Komet m -en,-en comet

Komfort /kɔm'fo:ɐ̯/ m -s comfort; (Luxus) luxury

Komik f - humour. **K~er** m -s,- comic, comedian

komisch adj funny; (Oper) comic; (sonderbar) odd, funny. **k~erweise** adv funnily enough

Komitee nt -s,-s committee

Komma nt -s,-s & -ta comma; (Dezimal-) decimal point; **drei K~ fünf** three point five

Kommando nt -s,-s order; (Befehlsgewalt) command; (Einheit) detachment. **K~brücke** f bridge

kommen† vi (sein) come; (eintreffen)

k

arrive; (gelangen) get (**nach** to); **k~ lassen** send for; **auf/hinter etw** (acc) **k~** think of/find out about sth; **um/zu etw k~** lose/acquire sth; **wieder zu sich k~** come round; **wie kommt das?** why is that? **k~d** adj coming; **k~den Montag** next Monday

Kommen|tar m **-s,-e** commentary; (Bemerkung) comment. **k~tieren** vt comment on

kommerziell adj commercial

Kommissar m **-s,-e** commissioner; (Polizei-) superintendent

Kommission f **-,-en** commission; (Gremium) committee

Kommode f **-,-n** chest of drawers

Kommunalwahlen fpl local elections

k

Kommunion f **-,-en** [Holy] Communion

Kommun|ismus m **-** Communism. **K~ist(in)** m **-en,-en** (f **-,-nen**) Communist. **k~istisch** adj Communist

kommunizieren vi (haben) receive [Holy] Communion

Komödie /ko'mø:di̯ə/ f **-,-n** comedy

Kompagnon /'kɔmpanjõ:/ m **-s,-s** (Comm) partner

Kompanie f **-,-n** (Mil) company

Komparse m **-n,-n** (Theat) extra

Kompass m **-es,-e** compass

komplett adj complete

Komplex m **-es,-e** complex

Komplikation /-'tsi̯o:n/ f **-,-en** complication

Kompliment nt **-[e]s,-e** compliment

Komplize m **-n,-n** accomplice

komplizier|en vt complicate. **k~t** adj complicated

Komplott nt **-[e]s,-e** plot

kompo|nieren vt/i (haben) compose. **K~nist** m **-en,-en** composer

Kompost m **-[e]s** compost

Kompott nt **-[e]s,-e** stewed fruit

Kompromiss m **-es,-e** compromise; **einen K~ schließen** compromise. **k~los** adj uncompromising

Konden|sation /-'tsi̯o:n/ f **-** condensation. **k~sieren** vt condense

Kondensmilch f evaporated/ (gesüßt) condensed milk

Kondition /-'tsi̯o:n/ f **-** (Sport) fitness; **in K~** in form

Konditor m **-s,-en** confectioner. **K~ei** f **-,-en** patisserie

Kondo|lenzbrief m letter of condolence. **k~lieren** vi (haben) express one's condolences

Kondom nt & m **-s,-e** condom

Konfekt nt **-[e]s** confectionery; (Pralinen) chocolates pl

Konfektion /-'tsi̯o:n/ f **-** ready-to-wear clothes pl

Konferenz f **-,-en** conference; (Besprechung) meeting

Konfession f **-,-en** [religious] denomination. **k~ell** adj denominational

Konfetti nt **-s** confetti

Konfirm|and(in) m **-en,-en** (f **-,-nen**) candidate for confirmation. **K~ation** f **-,-en** (Relig) confirmation. **k~ieren** vt (Relig) confirm

Konfitüre f **-,-n** jam

Konflikt m **-[e]s,-e** conflict

Konföderation /-'tsi̯o:n/ f confederation

konfus adj confused

Kongress m **-es,-e** congress

König m **-s,-e** king. **K~in** f **-,-nen** queen. **k~lich** adj royal; (hoheitsvoll) regal; (großzügig) handsome. **K~reich** nt kingdom

Konjunktiv m **-s,-e** subjunctive

Konjunktur f **-** economic situation; (Hoch-) boom

konkret adj concrete

Konkurren|t(in) m **-en,-en** (f **-,-nen**) competitor, rival. **K~z** f **-**

competition; **jdm K∼z machen** compete with s.o. **K∼zkampf** m competition, rivalry

konkurrieren vi (haben) compete

Konkurs m **-es,-e** bankruptcy

können†

• auxiliary verb

····➤ (vermögen) be able to; (Präsens) can; (Vergangenheit, Konditional) could. **ich kann nicht schlafen** I cannot or can't sleep. **kann ich Ihnen helfen?** can I help you? **kann/könnte das explodieren?** can/could it explode? **es kann sein, dass er kommt** he may come

! Distinguish **konnte** and **könnte** (both can be 'could'): **er konnte sie nicht retten** he couldn't or was unable to rescue them. **er konnte sie noch retten** he was able to rescue them. **er könnte sie noch retten, wenn** ... he could still rescue them if ...

····➤ (dürfen) can, may. **kann ich gehen?** can or may I go? **können wir mit[kommen]?** can or may we come too?

• transitive verb

····➤ (beherrschen) know (language); be able to play (game). **können Sie Deutsch?** do you know any German? **sie kann das [gut]** she can do that [well]. **ich kann nichts dafür** I can't help that, I'm not to blame

• intransitive verb

····➤ (fähig sein) **ich kann [heute] nicht** I can't [today]. **er kann nicht anders** there's nothing else he can do; (es ist seine Art) he can't help it. **er kann nicht mehr** [F] he can't go on; (nicht mehr essen) he can't eat any more

····➤ (irgendwohin gehen können) be able to go; can go. **ich kann nicht ins Kino** I can't go to the cinema. **er konnte endlich nach Florenz** at last he was able to go to Florence

konsequen|t adj consistent; (logisch) logical. **K∼z** f **-,-en** consequence

konservativ adj conservative

Konserv|en fpl tinned or canned food sg. **K∼endose** f tin, can. **K∼ierungsmittel** nt preservative

Konsonant m **-en,-en** consonant

Konstitution /-'tsi̯o:n/ f **-,-en** constitution. **k∼ell** adj constitutional

konstruieren vt construct; (entwerfen) design

Konstruk|tion /-'tsi̯o:n/ f **-,-en** construction; (Entwurf) design. **k∼tiv** adj constructive

Konsul m **-s,-n** consul. **K∼at** nt **-[e]s,-e** consulate

Konsum m **-s** consumption. **K∼güter** npl consumer goods

Kontakt m **-[e]s,-e** contact. **K∼linsen** fpl contact lenses. **K∼person** f contact

kontern vt/i (haben) counter

Kontinent /'kɔn-, kɔnti'nɛnt/ m **-[e]s,-e** continent

Konto nt **-s,-s** account. **K∼auszug** m [bank] statement. **K∼nummer** f account number. **K∼stand** m [bank] balance

Kontrabass m double bass

Kontroll|abschnitt m counterfoil. **K∼e** f **-,-n** control; (Prüfung) check. **K∼eur** m **-s,-e** [ticket] inspector. **k∼ieren** vt check; inspect (Fahrkarten); (beherrschen) control

Kontroverse f **-,-n** controversy

Kontur f **-,-en** contour

konventionell adj conventional

Konversationslexikon nt encyclopaedia

konvert|ieren vi (haben) (Relig) convert. **K∼it** m **-en,-en** convert

Konzentration /-'tsi̯o:n/ f **-,-en** concentration. **K∼slager** nt concentration camp

konzentrieren vt concentrate; **sich k∼** concentrate (**auf** + acc on)

Konzept nt **-[e]s,-e** [rough] draft;

jdn aus dem K~bringen put s.o. off his stroke

Konzern m **-s,-e** (Comm) group [of companies]

Konzert nt **-[e]s,-e** concert; (Klavier-) concerto

Konzession f **-,-en** licence; (Zugeständnis) concession

Konzil nt **-s,-e** (Relig) council

Kooperation /koʔɔpera'tsi̯o:n/ f co-operation

Koordin|ation /koʔɔrdina'tsi̯o:n/ f **-** co-ordination. **k~ieren** vt co-ordinate

Kopf m **-[e]s,¨-e** head; **ein K~ Kohl/Salat** a cabbage/lettuce; **aus dem K~** from memory; (auswendig) by heart; **auf dem K~** (verkehrt) upside down; **K~ stehen** stand on one's head; **sich** (dat) **den K~ waschen** wash one's hair; **sich** (dat) **den K~ zerbrechen** rack one's brains. **K~ball** m header

köpfen vt behead; (Fußball) head

Kopf|ende nt head. **K~haut** f scalp. **K~hörer** m headphones pl. **K~kissen** nt pillow. **k~los** adj panic-stricken. **K~rechnen** nt mental arithmetic. **K~salat** m lettuce. **K~schmerzen** mpl headache sg. **K~sprung** m header, dive. **K~stand** m headstand. **K~steinpflaster** nt cobblestones pl. **K~tuch** nt headscarf. **k~über** adv head first; (fig) headlong. **K~wäsche** f shampoo. **K~weh** nt headache

Kopie f **-,-n** copy. **k~ren** vt copy. **K~rschutz** m copy protection

Koppel[1] f **-,-n** enclosure; (Pferde-) paddock

Koppel[2] nt **-s,-** (Mil) belt. **k~n** vt couple

Koralle f **-,-n** coral

Korb m **-[e]s,¨-e** basket; **jdm einen K~ geben** (fig) turn s.o. down. **K~ball** m [kind of] netball

Kord m **-s** (Textiles) corduroy

Kordel f **-,-n** cord

Korinthe f **-,-n** currant

Kork m **-s,-e** cork. **K~en** m **-s,-** cork. **K~enzieher** m **-s,-** corkscrew

Korn nt **-[e]s,¨-er** grain, (Samen-) seed; (am Visier) front sight

Körn|chen nt **-s,-** granule. **k~ig** adj granular

Körper m **-s,-** body; (Geometry) solid. **K~bau** m build, physique. **k~behindert** adj physically disabled. **k~lich** adj physical; (Strafe) corporal. **K~pflege** f personal hygiene. **K~schaft** f **-,-en** corporation, body

korrekt adj correct. **K~or** m **-s,-en** proof reader. **K~ur** f **-,-en** correction. **K~urabzug** m proof

Korrespon|dent(in) m **-en,-en** (f **-,-nen**) correspondent. **K~denz** f **-,-en** correspondence

Korridor m **-s,-e** corridor

korrigieren vt correct

Korrosion f **-** corrosion

korrup|t adj corrupt. **K~tion** f **-** corruption

Korsett nt **-[e]s,-e** corset

koscher adj kosher

Kosename m pet name

Kosmet|ik f **-** beauty culture. **K~ika** ntpl cosmetics. **K~ikerin** f **-,-nen** beautician. **k~isch** adj cosmetic; (Chirurgie) plastic

kosm|isch adj cosmic. **K~onaut(in)** m **-en,-en** (f **-,-nen**) cosmonaut

Kosmos m **-** cosmos

Kost f **-** food; (Ernährung) diet; (Verpflegung) board

kostbar adj precious. **K~keit** f **-,-en** treasure

kosten[1] vt/i (haben) **[von] etw k~** taste sth

kosten[2] vt cost; (brauchen) take; **wie viel kostet es?** how much is it? **K~** pl expense sg, cost sg; (Jur) costs; **auf meine K~** at my expense. **K~[vor]anschlag** m estimate. **k~los** adj free • adv free [of charge]

köstlich adj delicious; (entzückend) delightful

Kostprobe f taste; (fig) sample

Kostüm nt **-s,-e** (Theat) costume; (Verkleidung) fancy dress; (Schneider-) suit. **k~iert** adj **k~iert sein** be in fancy dress

Kot m **-[e]s** excrement

Kotelett /kɔt'lɛt/ nt **-s,-s** chop, cutlet. **K~en** pl sideburns

Köter m **-s,-** (pej) dog

Kotflügel m (Auto) wing

kotzen vi (haben) ✖ throw up

Krabbe f **-,-n** crab, shrimp

krabbeln vi (sein) crawl

Krach m **-[e]s,⸚e** din, racket; (Knall) crash; (!: Streit) row; (!: Ruin) crash. **k~en** vi (haben) crash; **es hat gekracht** there was a bang/(!: Unfall) a crash •(sein) break, crack; (auftreffen) crash (**gegen** into)

krächzen vi (haben) croak

Kraft f **-,⸚e** strength; (Gewalt) force; (Arbeits-) worker; **in/außer K~** in/no longer in force. **K~fahrer** m driver. **K~fahrzeug** nt motor vehicle. **K~fahrzeugbrief** m [vehicle] registration document

kräftig adj strong; (gut entwickelt) sturdy; (nahrhaft) nutritious; (heftig) hard

kraft|los adj weak. **K~probe** f trial of strength. **K~stoff** m (Auto) fuel. **K~wagen** m motor car. **K~werk** nt power station

Kragen m **-s,-** collar

Krähe f **-,-n** crow

krähen vi (haben) crow

Kralle f **-,-n** claw

Kram m **-s** ! things pl, ! stuff; (Angelegenheiten) business. **k~en** vi (haben) rummage about (**in** + dat in; **nach** for)

Krampf m **-[e]s,⸚e** cramp. **K~adern** fpl varicose veins. **k~haft** adj convulsive; (verbissen) desperate

Kran m **-[e]s,⸚e** (Techn) crane

Kranich m **-s,-e** (Zool) crane

krank adj sick; (Knie, Herz) bad; **k~ sein/werden** be/fall ill. **K~e(r)** m/f sick man/woman, invalid; **die K~en** the sick pl

kränken vt offend, hurt

Kranken|bett nt sick bed. **K~geld** nt sickness benefit. **K~gymnast(in)** m **-en,-en** (f **-,-nen**) physiotherapist. **K~gymnastik** f physiotherapy. **K~haus** nt hospital. ◘**K~kasse** f health insurance scheme/(Amt) office. **K~pflege** f nursing. **K~saal** m [hospital] ward. **K~schein** m certificate of entitlement to medical treatment. **K~schwester** f nurse. **K~versicherung** f health insurance. **K~wagen** m ambulance

Krankheit f **-,-en** illness, disease

kränklich adj sickly

krankmelden vt sep **jdn k~** report s.o. sick; **sich k~** report sick

Kranz m **-es,⸚e** wreath

Krapfen m **-s,-** doughnut

Krater m **-s,-** crater

kratzen vt/i (haben) scratch. **K~er** m **-s,-** scratch

Kraul nt **-s** (Sport) crawl. **k~en**[1] vi (haben/sein) (Sport) do the crawl

kraulen[2] vt tickle; **sich am Kopf k~** scratch one's head

kraus adj wrinkled; (Haar) frizzy; (verworren) muddled. **K~e** f **-,-n** frill

kräuseln vt wrinkle; frizz (Haar-); gather (Stoff); **sich k~** wrinkle; (sich kringeln) curl; (Haar:) go frizzy

Kraut nt **-[e]s, Kräuter** herb; (SGer) cabbage; (Sauer-) sauerkraut

Krawall m **-s,-e** riot; (Lärm) row

Krawatte f **-,-n** [neck]tie

krea|tiv /krea'ti:f/ adj creative. **K~tur** f **-,-en** creature

Krebs m **-es,-e** crayfish; (Med) cancer; (Astrology) Cancer

Kredit m **-s,-e** credit; (Darlehen) loan;

◘ *see* A-Z of German life and culture

auf K~ on credit. K~karte f credit card

Kreid|e f - chalk. k~ig adj chalky

kreieren /kre'i:rən/ vt create

Kreis m -es,-e circle; (Admin) district

kreischen vt/i (haben) screech; (schreien) shriek

Kreisel m -s,- [spinning] top

kreis|en vi (haben) circle; revolve (**um** around). **k~förmig** adj circular. **K~lauf** m cycle; (Med) circulation. **K~säge** f circular saw. **K~verkehr** m [traffic] roundabout

Krem f -,-s & m -s,-e cream

Krematorium nt -s,-ien crematorium

Krempe f -,-n [hat] brim

k

krempeln vt turn (**nach oben** up)

Krepp m -s,-s & -e crêpe

Krepppapier nt crêpe paper

Kresse f -,-n cress; (Kapuziner-) nasturtium

Kreta nt -s Crete

Kreuz nt -es,-e cross; (Kreuzung) intersection; (Mus) sharp; (Kartenspiel) clubs pl; (Anat) small of the back; **über K~** crosswise; **das K~ schlagen** cross oneself. **k~en** vt cross; **sich k~en** cross; (Straßen:) intersect; (Meinungen:) clash •vi (haben/sein) cruise. **K~fahrt** f (Naut) cruise. **K~gang** m cloister

kreuzig|en vt crucify. **K~ung** f -,-en crucifixion

Kreuz|otter f adder, common viper. **K~ung** f -,-en intersection; (Straßen-) crossroads sg. **K~verhör** nt cross-examination. **k~weise** adv crosswise. **K~worträtsel** nt crossword [puzzle]. **K~zug** m crusade

kribbel|ig adj 🅸 edgy. **k~n** vi (haben) tingle; (kitzeln) tickle

kriech|en† vi (sein) crawl; (fig) grovel (**vor** + dat to). **K~spur** f (Auto) crawler lane. **K~tier** nt reptile

Krieg m -[e]s,-e war

kriegen vt 🅸 get; **ein Kind k~** have a baby

kriegs|beschädigt adj war-disabled. **K~dienstverweigerer** m -s,- conscientious objector. **K~gefangene(r)** m prisoner of war. **K~gefangenschaft** f captivity. **K~gericht** nt court martial. **K~list** f stratagem. **K~rat** m council of war. **K~recht** nt martial law

Krimi m -s,-s 🅸 crime story/film. **K~nalität** f - crime; (Vorkommen) crime rate. **K~nalpolizei** f criminal investigation department. **K~nalroman** m crime novel. **k~nell** adj criminal

Krippe f -,-n manger; (Weihnachts-) crib; (Kinder-) crèche. **K~nspiel** nt Nativity play

Krise f -,-n crisis

Kristall nt -s crystal; (geschliffen) cut glass

Kritik f -,-en criticism; (Rezension) review; **unter aller K~** 🅸 abysmal

Kriti|ker m -s,- critic; (Rezensent) reviewer. **k~sch** adj critical. **k~sieren** vt criticize; review

kritzeln vt/i (haben) scribble

Krokodil nt -s,-e crocodile

Krokus m -,-[se] crocus

Krone f -,-n crown; (Baum-) top

krönen vt crown

Kronleuchter m chandelier

Krönung f -,-en coronation; (fig: Höhepunkt) crowning event

Kropf m -[e]s,⸚e (Zool) crop; (Med) goitre

Kröte f -,-n toad

Krücke f -,-n crutch

Krug m -[e]s,⸚e jug; (Bier-) tankard

Krümel m -s,- crumb. **k~ig** adj crumbly. **k~n** vt crumble •vi (haben) be crumbly

krumm adj crooked; (gebogen) curved; (verbogen) bent

krümmen vt bend; crook (Finger); **sich k~** bend; (sich winden) writhe; (vor Lachen) double up

Krümmung f -,-en bend, curve

Krüppel m -s,- cripple

Kruste f -,-n crust; (Schorf) scab

Kruzifix nt -es,-e crucifix

Kub|a nt -s Cuba. **k~anisch** adj Cuban

Kübel m -s,- tub; (Eimer) bucket; (Techn) skip

Küche f -,-n kitchen; (Kochkunst) cooking; **kalte/warme K~** cold/ hot food

Kuchen m -s,- cake

Küchen|herd m cooker, stove. **K~maschine** f food processor, mixer. **K~schabe** f -,-n cockroach

Kuckuck m -s,-e cuckoo

Kufe f -,-n [sledge] runner

Kugel f -,-n ball; (Geometry) sphere; (Gewehr-) bullet; (Sport) shot. **k~förmig** adj spherical. **K~lager** nt ball-bearing. **k~n** vt/i (haben) roll; **sich k~n** (vor Lachen) fall about. **K~schreiber** m -s,- ballpoint [pen]. **k~sicher** adj bulletproof. **K~stoßen** nt -s shot-putting

Kuh f -,⸚e cow

kühl adj cool; (kalt) chilly. **K~box** f -,-en cool box. **K~e** f - coolness; chilliness. **k~en** vt cool; refrigerate (Lebensmittel); chill (Wein). **K~er** m -s,- (Auto) radiator. **K~erhaube** f bonnet. **K~fach** nt frozen-food compartment. **K~raum** m cold store. **K~schrank** m refrigerator. **K~truhe** f freezer. **K~wasser** nt [radiator] water

kühn adj bold

Kuhstall m cowshed

Küken nt -s,- chick; (Enten-) duckling

Kulissen fpl (Theat) scenery sg; (seitlich) wings; **hinter den K~** (fig) behind the scenes

Kult m -[e]s,-e cult

kultivier|en vt cultivate. **k~t** adj cultured

Kultur f -,-en culture. **K~beutel** m toilet bag. **k~ell** adj cultural. **K~film** m documentary film. **K~tourismus** m cultural tourism

Kultusminister m Minister of Education and Arts

Kümmel m -s caraway; (Getränk) kümmel

Kummer m -s sorrow, grief; (Sorge) worry; (Ärger) trouble

kümmer|lich adj puny; (dürftig) meagre; (armselig) wretched. **k~n** vt concern; **sich k~n um** look after; (sich befassen) concern oneself with; (beachten) take notice of

kummervoll adj sorrowful

Kumpel m -s,- [!] mate

Kunde m -n,-n customer. **K~ndienst** m [after-sales] service

Kundgebung f -,-en (Pol) rally

kündig|en vt cancel (Vertrag); give notice of withdrawal for (Geld); give notice to quit (Wohnung); **seine Stellung k~en** give [in one's] notice •vi (haben) give [in one's] notice; **jdm k~en** give s.o. notice. **K~ung** f -,-en cancellation; notice [of withdrawal/dismissal/to quit]; (Entlassung) dismissal. **K~ungsfrist** f period of notice

Kund|in f -,-nen [woman] customer. **K~schaft** f - clientele, customers pl

künftig adj future •adv in future

Kunst f -,⸚e art; (Können) skill. **K~faser** f synthetic fibre. **K~galerie** f art gallery. **K~geschichte** f history of art. **K~gewerbe** nt arts and crafts pl. **K~griff** m trick

Künstler m -s,- artist; (Könner) master. **K~in** f -,-nen [woman] artist. **k~isch** adj artistic

künstlich adj artificial

Kunst|stoff m plastic. **K~stück** nt trick; (große Leistung) feat. **k~voll** adj artistic; (geschickt) skilful

kunterbunt adj multicoloured; (gemischt) mixed

Kupfer nt -s copper

Kupon /ku'põ:/ m -s,-s voucher; (Zins-) coupon; (Stoff-) length

Kuppe f -,-n [rounded] top

k

Kuppel f -,-n dome

kupp|eln vt couple (**an** + acc to) • vi (haben) (Auto) operate the clutch. **K~lung** f -,-en coupling; (Auto) clutch

Kur f -,-en course of treatment, cure

Kür f -,-en (Sport) free exercise; (Eislauf) free programme

Kurbel f -,-n crank. **K~welle** f crankshaft

Kürbis m -ses,-se pumpkin

Kurier m -s,-e courier

kurieren vt cure

kurios adj curious, odd. **K~ität** f -,-en oddness; (Objekt) curiosity

Kurort m health resort; (Badeort) spa

Kurs m -es,-e course; (Aktien-) price. **K~buch** nt timetable

kursieren vi (haben) circulate

kursiv adj italic • adv in italics. **K~schrift** f italics pl

Kursus m -,Kurse course

Kurswagen m through carriage

Kurtaxe f visitors' tax

Kurve f -,-n curve; (Straßen-) bend

kurz adj short; (knapp) brief; (rasch) quick; (schroff) curt; **k~e Hosen** shorts; **vor k~em** a short time ago; **seit k~em** lately; **den Kürzeren ziehen** get the worst of it; **k~ vor** shortly before; **sich k~ fassen** be brief; **k~ und gut** in short; **zu k~ kommen** get less than one's fair share. **k~ärmelig** adj short-sleeved. **k~atmig** adj **k~atmig sein** be short of breath

Kürze f - shortness; (Knappheit) brevity; **in K~** shortly. **k~n** vt shorten; (verringern) cut

kurzfristig adj short-term • adv at short notice

kürzlich adv recently

Kurz|meldung f newsflash. **K~schluss** m short circuit. **K~schrift** f shorthand. **k~sichtig** adj short-sighted. **K~sichtigkeit** f - short-sightedness. **K~streckenrakete** f short-range missile

Kürzung f -,-en shortening; (Verringerung) cut (gen in)

Kurz|waren fpl haberdashery sg. **K~welle** f short wave

kuscheln (sich) vr snuggle (**an** + acc up to)

Kusine f -,-n [female] cousin

Kuss m -es,⸚e kiss

küssen vt/i (haben) kiss; **sich k~** kiss

Küste f -,-n coast

Küster m -s,- verger

Kutsch|e f -,-n [horse-drawn] carriage/(geschlossen) coach. **K~er** m -s,- coachman, driver

Kutte f -,-n (Relig) habit

Kutter m -s,- (Naut) cutter

Kuvert /ku'veːɐ̯/ nt -s,-s envelope

Ll

Labor nt -s,-s & -e laboratory. **L~ant(in)** m -en,-en (f -,-nen) laboratory assistant

Labyrinth nt -[e]s,-e maze, labyrinth

Lache f -,-n puddle; (Blut-) pool

lächeln vi (haben) smile. **L~** nt -s smile. **l~d** adj smiling

lachen vi (haben) laugh. **L~** nt -s laugh; (Gelächter) laughter

lächerlich adj ridiculous; **sich l~ machen** make a fool of oneself. **L~keit** f -,-en ridiculousness; (Kleinigkeit) triviality

see A-Z of German life and culture

Lachs m **-es,-e** salmon

Lack m **-[e]s,-e** varnish; (Japan-) lacquer; (Auto) paint. **l~en** vt varnish. **l~ieren** vt varnish; (spritzen) spray. **L~schuhe** mpl patent-leather shoes

laden† vt load; (Electr) charge; (Jur: vor-) summon

Laden m **-s,¨** shop; (Fenster-) shutter. **L~dieb** m shoplifter. **L~schluss** m [shop] closing time. **L~tisch** m counter

Laderaum m (Naut) hold

lädieren vt damage

Ladung f **-,-en** load; (Naut, Aviat) cargo; (elektrische) charge

Lage f **-,-n** position, situation; (Schicht) layer; **nicht in der L~ sein** not be in a position (**zu** to)

Lager nt **-s,-** camp; (L~haus) warehouse; (Vorrat) stock; (Techn) bearing; (Erz-, Ruhe-) bed; (eines Tieres) lair; **[nicht] auf L~** [not] in stock. **L~haus** nt warehouse. **l~n** vt store; (legen) lay; **sich l~n** settle. **L~raum** m store-room. **L~ung** f - storage

Lagune f **-,-n** lagoon

lahm adj lame. **l~en** vi (haben) be lame

lähmen vt paralyse

Lähmung f **-,-en** paralysis

Laib m **-[e]s,-e** loaf

Laich m **-[e]s** (Zool) spawn

Laie m **-n,-n** layman; (Theat) amateur. **l~nhaft** adj amateurish

Laken nt **-s,-** sheet

Lakritze f - liquorice

lallen vt/i (haben) mumble; (Baby:) babble

Lametta nt **-s** tinsel

Lamm nt **-[e]s,¨er** lamb

Lampe f **-,-n** lamp; (Decken-, Wand-) light; (Glüh-) bulb. **L~nfieber** nt stage fright

Lampion /lam'pi̯ɔŋ/ m **-s,-s** Chinese lantern

▣**Land** nt **-[e]s,¨er** country; (Fest-) land; (Bundes-) state, Land; (Aust) province; **auf dem L~e** in the country; **an L~ gehen** (Naut) go ashore. **L~arbeiter** m agricultural worker. **L~ebahn** f runway. **l~en** vt/i (sein) land; (▣: gelangen) end up

Ländereien pl estates

Länderspiel nt international

Landesverrat m treason

Landkarte f map

ländlich adj rural

Land|schaft f **-,-en** scenery; (Geog, Kunst) landscape; (Gegend) country[side]. **l~schaftlich** adj scenic; (regional) regional. **L~streicher** m **-s,-** tramp. ▣**L~tag** m state/(Aust) provincial parliament

Landung f **-,-en** landing

Land|vermesser m **-s,-** surveyor. **L~weg** m country lane; **auf dem L~weg** overland. **L~wirt** m farmer. **L~wirtschaft** f agriculture; (Hof) farm. **l~wirtschaftlich** adj agricultural

lang[1] adv & prep (+ preceding acc or preceding **an** + dat) along; **den** od **am Fluss l~** along the river

lang[2] adj long; (groß) tall; **seit l~em** for a long time • adv **eine Stunde l~** for an hour; **mein Leben l~** all my life. **l~ärmelig** adj long-sleeved. **l~atmig** adj long-winded. **l~e** adv a long time; (schlafen) late; **schon l~e** [for] a long time; (zurückliegend) a long time ago; **l~e nicht** not for a long time; (bei weitem nicht) nowhere near

Länge f **-,-n** length; (Geog) longitude; **der L~ nach** lengthways

Läng|engrad m degree of longitude. **l~er** adj & adv longer; (längere Zeit) [for] some time

Langeweile f - boredom; **L~ haben** be bored

lang|fristig adj long-term; (Vorhersage) long-range. **l~jährig** adj long-standing; (Erfahrung) long

▣ *see* A-Z of German life and culture

länglich adj oblong; **l~ rund** oval

längs adv & prep (+ gen/dat) along; (der Länge nach) lengthways

lang|sam adj slow. **L~samkeit** f - slowness

längst adv **[schon] l~** for a long time; (zurückliegend) a long time ago; **l~ nicht** nowhere near

Lang|strecken- prefix long-distance; (Mil, Aviat) long-range. **l~weilen** vt bore; **sich l~weilen** be bored. **l~weilig** adj boring

Lanze f -,-n lance

Lappalie /la'pa:li̯ə/ f -,-n trifle

Lappen m -s,- cloth; (Anat) lobe

Laptop m -s,-s laptop

Lärche f -,-n larch

Lärm m -s noise. **l~end** adj noisy

Larve /'larfə/ f -,-n larva; (Maske) mask

l

lasch adj listless; (schlaff) limp

Lasche f -,-n tab, flap

Laser /'le:-, 'la:zɐ/ m -s,- laser

lassen†

• transitive verb

····➤ (+ infinitive; veranlassen) **etw tun lassen** have or get sth done. **jdn etw tun lassen** make s.o. do sth; get s.o. to do sth **sich** dat **die Haare schneiden lassen** have or get one's hair cut. **jdn warten lassen** make or let s.o. wait; keep s.o. waiting. **jdn grüßen lassen** send one's regards to s.o. **jdn kommen/rufen lassen** send for s.o.

····➤ (+ infinitive; erlauben) let; allow; (hineinlassen/herauslassen) let or allow (**in** + acc into, **aus** + dat out of). **jdn etw tun lassen** let s.o. do sth; allow s.o. to do sth. **er ließ mich nicht ausreden** he didn't let me finish [what I was saying]

····➤ (belassen, bleiben lassen) leave. **jdn in Frieden lassen** leave s.o. in peace. **etw ungesagt lassen** leave sth unsaid

····➤ (unterlassen) stop. **das Rauchen lassen** stop smoking. **er kann es nicht lassen, sie zu quälen** he can't stop or he is forever tormenting her

····➤ (überlassen) **jdm etw lassen** let s.o. have sth

····➤ (als Aufforderung) **lass/lasst uns gehen/fahren!** let's go!

• reflexive verb

····➤ **das lässt sich machen** that can be done. **das lässt sich nicht beweisen** it can't be proved. **die Tür lässt sich leicht öffnen** the door opens easily

• intransitive verb

····➤ [!] **Lass mal. Ich mache das schon** Leave it. I'll do it

lässig adj casual. **L~keit** f - casualness

Lasso nt -s,-s lasso

Last f -,-en load; (Gewicht) weight; (fig) burden; **L~en** charges; (Steuern) taxes. **L~auto** nt lorry. **l~en** vi (haben) weigh heavily/ (liegen) rest (**auf** + dat on)

Laster¹ m -s,- [!] lorry

Laster² nt -s,- vice

läster|n vt blaspheme • vi (haben) make disparaging remarks (**über** + acc about). **L~ung** f -,-en blasphemy

lästig adj troublesome; **l~ sein/werden** be/become a nuisance

Last|kahn m barge. **L~[kraft]wagen** m lorry

Latein nt -[s] Latin. **L~amerika** nt Latin America. **l~isch** adj Latin

Laterne f -,-n lantern; (Straßen-) street lamp. **L~npfahl** m lamp-post

latschen vi (sein) [!] traipse

Latte f -,-n slat; (Tor-, Hochsprung-) bar

Latz m -es,⸚e bib

Lätzchen nt -s,- [baby's] bib

Latzhose f dungarees pl

Laub nt -[e]s leaves pl; (L~werk) foliage. **L~baum** m deciduous tree

Laube f -,-n summer-house

Laub|säge f fretsaw. **L~wald** m deciduous forest

Lauch m **-[e]s** leeks pl

Lauer f **auf der L~ liegen** lie in wait. **l~n** vi (haben) lurk; **l~n auf** (+ acc) lie in wait for

Lauf m **-[e]s, Läufe** run; (Laufen) running; (Verlauf) course; (Wett-) race; (Sport: Durchgang) heat; (Gewehr-) barrel; **im L~[e]** (+ gen) in the course of. **L~bahn** f career. **l~en**† vi (sein) run; (zu Fuß gehen) walk; (gelten) be valid; **Ski/Schlittschuh l~en** ski/skate. **l~end** adj running; (gegenwärtig) current; (regelmäßig) regular; **auf dem L~enden sein** be up to date •adv continually

Läufer m **-s,-** (Person, Teppich) runner; (Schach) bishop

Lauf|gitter nt play-pen. **L~masche** f ladder. **L~text** m marquee text. **L~zettel** m circular

Lauge f **-,-n** soapy water

Laun|e f **-,-n** mood; (Einfall) whim; **guter L~e sein, gute L~e haben** be in a good mood. **l~isch** adj moody

Laus f **-,Läuse** louse; (Blatt-) greenfly

lauschen vi (haben) listen

laut adj loud; (geräuschvoll) noisy; **l~ lesen** read aloud; **l~er stellen** turn up •prep (+ gen/dat) according to. **L~** m **-es,-e** sound

Laute f **-,-n** (Mus) lute

lauten vi (haben) (Text:) run, read

läuten vt/i (haben) ring

lauter adj pure; (ehrlich) honest; (Wahrheit) plain •adj inv sheer; (nichts als) nothing but

laut|hals adv at the top of one's voice, (lachen) out loud. **l~los** adj silent, (Stille) hushed. **L~schrift** f phonetics pl. **L~sprecher** m loudspeaker. **L~stärke** f volume

lauwarm adj lukewarm

Lava f **-,-ven** lava

Lavendel m **-s** lavender

lavieren vi (haben) manœuvre

Lawine f **-,-n** avalanche

Lazarett nt **-[e]s,-e** military hospital

leasen /ˈliːsən/ vt rent

Lebehoch nt cheer

leben vt/i (haben) live (**von** on); **leb wohl!** farewell! **L~** nt **-s,-** life, (Treiben) bustle; **am L~** alive. **l~d** adj living

lebendig adj live; (lebhaft) lively; (anschaulich) vivid; **l~ sein** be alive. **L~keit** f - liveliness; vividness

Lebens|abend m old age. **L~alter** nt age. **l~fähig** adj viable. **L~gefahr** f mortal danger; **in L~gefahr** in mortal danger; (Patient) critically ill. **l~gefährlich** adj extremely dangerous; (Verletzung) critical. **L~haltungskosten** pl cost of living sg. **l~länglich** adj life-long •adv for life. **L~lauf** m curriculum vitae. **L~mittel** ntpl food sg. **L~mittelgeschäft** nt food shop. **L~mittelhändler** m grocer. **L~retter** m rescuer; (beim Schwimmen) life-guard. **L~unterhalt** m livelihood; **seinen L~unterhalt verdienen** earn one's living. **L~versicherung** f life assurance. **L~wandel** m conduct. **l~wichtig** adj vital. **L~zeit** f **auf L~zeit** for life

Leber f **-,-n** liver. **L~fleck** m mole

Lebe|wesen nt living being. **L~wohl** nt **-s,-s** & **-e** farewell

leb|haft adj lively; (Farbe) vivid. **L~kuchen** m gingerbread. **l~los** adj lifeless. **L~zeiten** fpl **zu jds L~zeiten** in s.o.'s lifetime

leck adj leaking. **L~** nt **-s,-s** leak. **l~en**[1] vi (haben) leak

lecken[2] vi (haben) lick

lecker adj tasty. **L~bissen** m delicacy

Leder nt **-s,-** leather

ledig adj single, unmarried

leer adj empty; (unbesetzt) vacant; **l~ laufen** (Auto) idle. **l~en** vt empty; **sich l~en** empty. **L~lauf** m (Auto) neutral. **L~ung** f **-,-en** (Post) collection

l

legal adj legal. **l~isieren** vt legalize. **L~ität** f - legality

Legas|thenie f - dyslexia **L~theniker** m -s,- dyslexic

legen vt put; (hin-, ver-) lay; set (Haare); **sich l~** lie down; (nachlassen) subside

Legende f -,-n legend

leger /le'ʒeːɐ̯/ adj casual

Legierung f -,-en alloy

Legion f -,-en legion

Legislative f - legislature

legitim adj legitimate. **L~ität** f - legitimacy

Lehm m -s clay

Lehn|e f -,-n (Rücken-) back; (Arm-) arm. **l~en** vt lean (**an** + acc against); **sich l~en** lean (**an** + acc against) ● vi (haben) be leaning (**an** + acc against)

Lehr|buch nt textbook. ▣**L~e** f -,-n apprenticeship; (Anschauung) doctrine; (Theorie) theory; (Wissenschaft) science; (Erfahrung) lesson. **l~en** vt/i (haben) teach. **L~er** m -s,- teacher; (Fahr-) instructor. **L~erin** f -,-nen teacher. **L~erzimmer** nt staff-room. **L~fach** nt (Sch) subject. **L~gang** m course. **L~kraft** f teacher. **L~ling** m -s,-e apprentice; (Auszubildender) trainee. **L~plan** m syllabus. **l~reich** adj instructive. **L~stelle** f apprenticeship. **L~stuhl** m (Univ) chair. **L~zeit** f apprenticeship

Leib m -es,-er body; (Bauch) belly. **L~eserziehung** f (Sch) physical education. **L~gericht** nt favourite dish. **l~lich** adj physical; (blutsverwandt) real, natural. **L~wächter** m bodyguard

Leiche f -,-n [dead] body; corpse. **L~nbestatter** m -s,- undertaker. **L~nhalle** f mortuary. **L~nwagen** m hearse. **L~nzug** m funeral procession, cortège

Leichnam m -s,-e [dead] body

leicht adj light; (Stoff) lightweight; (gering) slight; (mühelos) easy; **jdm l~ fallen** be easy for s.o.; **etw l~ machen** make sth easy (**dat** for); **es sich** (dat) **l~ machen** take the easy way out; **etw l~ nehmen** (fig) take sth lightly. **L~athletik** f [track and field] athletics sg. **L~gewicht** nt (Boxen) lightweight. **l~gläubig** adj gullible. **l~hin** adv casually. **L~igkeit** f - lightness; (Mühelosigkeit) ease; (L~sein) easiness; **mit L~igkeit** with ease. **L~sinn** m carelessness; recklessness; (Frivolität) frivolity. **l~sinnig** adj careless; (unvorsichtig) reckless

Leid nt -[e]s sorrow, grief; (Böses) harm; **es tut mir L~** I am sorry; **er tut mir L~** I feel sorry for him. **l~** adj **jdn/etw l~ sein/werden** be/get tired of s.o./something

Leide|form f passive. **l~n**† vt/i (haben) suffer (**an** + dat from); **jdn/etw nicht l~n können** dislike s.o./something. **L~n** nt -s,- suffering; (Med) complaint; (Krankheit) disease. **l~nd** adj suffering. **L~nschaft** f -,-en passion. **l~nschaftlich** adj passionate

leider adv unfortunately; **l~ ja/nicht** I'm afraid so/not

Leier|kasten m barrel-organ. **l~n** vt/i (haben) wind; (herunter-) drone out

Leih|e f -,-n loan. **l~en**† vt lend; **sich** (dat) **etw l~en** borrow sth. **L~gabe** f loan. **L~gebühr** f rental; lending charge. **L~haus** nt pawnshop. **L~wagen** m hire-car. **l~weise** adv on loan

Leim m -s glue. **l~en** vt glue

Leine f -,-n rope; (Wäsche-) line; (Hunde-) lead, leash

Lein|en nt -s linen. **L~wand** f linen; (Kunst) canvas; (Film-) screen

leise adj quiet; (Stimme, Berührung) soft; (schwach) faint; (leicht) light; **l~r stellen** turn down

Leiste f -,-n strip; (Holz-) batten; (Anat) groin

leist|en vt achieve, accomplish; **sich** (dat) **etw l~en** treat oneself to sth; (▣: anstellen) get up to sth; **ich kann es mir nicht l~en** I can't afford it. **L∼ung** f -,-en achievement; (Sport, Techn) performance; (Produktion) output; (Zahlung) payment

Leit|artikel m leader, editorial. **l∼en** vt run, manage; (an-/hinführen) lead; (Mus, Techn, Phys) conduct; (lenken, schicken) direct. **l∼end** adj leading; (Posten) executive

Leiter[1] f -,-n ladder

Leit|er[2] m -s,- director; (Comm) manager; (Führer) leader; (Mus, Phys) conductor. **L∼erin** f -,-nen director; manageress; leader. **L∼planke** f crash barrier. **L∼spruch** m motto. **L∼ung** f -,-en (Führung) direction; (Comm) management; (Aufsicht) control; (Electr: Schnur) lead, flex; (Kabel) cable; (Telefon-) line; (Rohr-) pipe; (Haupt-) main. **L∼ungswasser** nt tap water

Lektion /-ˈtsi̯oːn/ f -,-en lesson

Lekt|or m -s,-en, **L∼orin** f -,-nen (Univ) assistant lecturer; (Verlags-) editor. **L∼üre** f -,-n reading matter

Lende f -,-n loin

lenk|en vt guide; (steuern) steer; (regeln) control; **jds Aufmerksamkeit auf sich** (acc) **l∼en** attract s.o.'s attention. **L∼rad** nt steering-wheel. **L∼stange** f handlebars pl. **L∼ung** f - steering

Leopard m -en,-en leopard

Lepra f - leprosy

Lerche f -,-n lark

lernen vt/i (haben) learn; (für die Schule) study

Lernkurve f learning curve

Lesb|ierin /ˈlɛsbi̯ərɪn/ f -,-nen lesbian. **l∼isch** adj lesbian

les|en† vt/i (haben) read; (Univ) lecture •vt pick, gather. **L∼en** nt -s reading. **L∼er(in)** m -s,- (f -,-nen) reader. **l∼erlich** adj legible. **L∼ezeichen** nt bookmark

lethargisch adj lethargic

Lettland nt -s Latvia

letzt|e(r,s) adj last; (neueste) latest; **in l∼er Zeit** recently; **l∼en Endes** in the end. **l∼ens** adv recently; (zuletzt) lastly. **l∼ere(r,s)** adj the latter; **der/die/das L∼ere (l∼ere)** the latter

Leucht|e f -,-n light. **l∼en** vi (haben) shine. **l∼end** adj shining. **L∼er** m -s,- candlestick. **L∼feuer** nt beacon. **L∼rakete** f flare. **L∼reklame** f neon sign. **L∼röhre** f fluorescent tube. **L∼turm** m lighthouse

leugnen vt deny

Leukämie f - leukaemia

Leumund m -s reputation

Leute pl people; (Mil) men; (Arbeiter) workers

Leutnant m -s,-s second lieutenant

Lexikon nt -s,-ka encyclopaedia; (Wörterbuch) dictionary

Libanon (der) -s Lebanon

Libelle f -,-n dragonfly

liberal adj (Pol) liberal

Libyen nt -s Libya

Licht nt -[e]s,-er light; (Kerze) candle; **L∼ machen** turn on the light. **l∼** adj bright; (Med) lucid; (spärlich) sparse. **L∼bild** nt [passport] photograph; (Dia) slide. **L∼blick** m (fig) ray of hope. **l∼en** vt thin out; **den Anker l∼en** (Naut) weigh anchor; **sich l∼en** become less dense; thin. **L∼hupe** f headlight flasher; **die L∼hupe betätigen** flash one's headlights. **L∼maschine** f dynamo. **L∼ung** f -,-en clearing

Lid nt -[e]s,-er [eye]lid. **L∼schatten** m eye-shadow

lieb adj dear; (nett) nice; (artig) good; **jdn l∼ haben** be fond of s.o.; (lieben) love s.o.; **es wäre mir l∼er** I should prefer it (**wenn** if)

Liebe f -,-n love. **l∼n** vt love; (mögen) like; **sich l∼n** love each other; (körperlich) make love. **l∼nd** adj loving. **l∼nswert** a lovable. **l∼nswürdig** adj kind. **l∼nswürdigerweise** adv very kindly

lieber adv rather; (besser) better; **l∼**

mögen like better; **ich trinke l~ Tee** I prefer tea

Liebes|brief m love letter. **L~dienst** m favour. **L~kummer** m heartache. **L~paar** nt [pair of] lovers pl

lieb|evoll adj loving, affectionate. **L~haber** m -s,- lover; (Sammler) collector. **L~haberei** f -,-en hobby. **L~kosung** f -,-en caress. **l~lich** adj lovely; (sanft) gentle; (süß) sweet. **L~ling** m -s,-e darling; (Bevorzugte) favourite. **L~lings-** prefix favourite. **l~los** adj loveless; (Eltern) uncaring; (unfreundlich) unkind. **L~schaft** f -,-en [love] affair. **l~ste(r,s)** adj dearest; (bevorzugt) favourite • adv **am l~sten** best [of all]; **jdn/etw am l~sten mögen** like s.o./something best [of all]. **L~ste(r)** m/f beloved; (Schatz) sweetheart

Lied nt -[e]s,-er song

liederlich adj slovenly; (unordentlich) untidy. **L~keit** f - slovenliness; untidiness

Lieferant m -en,-en supplier

liefer|bar adj (Comm) available. **l~n** vt supply; (zustellen) deliver; (hervorbringen) yield. **L~ung** f -,-en delivery; (Sendung) consignment

Liege f -,-n couch. **l~n**† vi (haben) lie; (gelegen sein) be situated; **l~n bleiben** remain lying [there]; (im Bett) stay in bed; (Ding:) be left; (Schnee:) settle; (Arbeit:) remain undone; (zurückgelassen werden) be left behind; **l~n lassen** leave; (zurücklassen) leave behind; (nicht fortführen) leave undone; **l~n an** (+ dat) (fig) be due to; (abhängen) depend on; **jdm [nicht] l~n** [not] suit s.o.; **mir liegt viel daran** it is very important to me. **L~stuhl** m deck-chair. **L~stütz** m -es,-e press-up, (Amer) push-up. **L~wagen** m couchette car

Lift m -[e]s,-e & -s lift

Liga f -,-gen league

Likör m -s,-e liqueur

lila inv adj mauve; (dunkel) purple

Lilie /ˈli:li̯ə/ f -,-n lily

Liliputaner(in) m -s,- (f -,-nen) dwarf

Limo f -,-[s] (!), **L~nade** f -,-n fizzy drink; lemonade

Limousine /limuˈzi:nə/ f -,-n saloon

lind adj mild

Linde f -,-n lime tree

linder|n vt relieve, ease. **L~ung** f - relief

Lineal nt -s,-e ruler

Linie /-i̯ə/ f -,-n line; (Zweig) branch; (Bus-) route; **L~ 4** number 4 [bus/tram]; **in erster L~** primarily. **L~nflug** m scheduled flight. **L~nrichter** m linesman

lin[i]iert adj lined, ruled

Link|e f -n,-n left side; (Hand) left hand; (Boxen) left; **die L~e** (Pol) the left. **l~e(r,s)** adj left; (Pol) leftwing; **l~e Masche** purl

links adv on the left; (bei Stoff) on the wrong side; (verkehrt) inside out; **l~ stricken** purl. **L~händer(in)** m -s,- (f -,-nen) lefthander. **l~händig** adj & adv lefthanded

Linoleum /-leʊm/ nt -s lino, linoleum

Linse f -,-n lens; (Bot) lentil

Lippe f -,-n lip. **L~nstift** m lipstick

Liquid|ation /-ˈtsi̯o:n/ f -,-en liquidation. **l~ieren** vt liquidate

lispeln vt/i (haben) lisp

List f -,-en trick, ruse

Liste f -,-n list

listig adj cunning, crafty

Litanei f -,-en litany

Litauen nt -s Lithuania

Liter m & nt -s,- litre

Literatur f - literature

Liturgie f -,-n liturgy

Litze f -,-n braid

Lizenz f -,-en licence

Lob nt -[e]s praise

Lobby /ˈlɔbi/ f - (Pol) lobby

loben vt praise

löblich adj praiseworthy

Lobrede f eulogy

Loch nt **-[e]s,⸚er** hole. **l~en** vt punch a hole/holes in; punch (Fahrkarte). **L~er** m **-s,-** punch

löcherig adj full of holes

Locke f **-,-n** curl. **l~n**[1] vt curl; **sich l~n** curl

locken[2] vt lure, entice; (reizen) tempt. **l~d** adj tempting

Lockenwickler m **-s,-** curler; (Rolle) roller

locker adj loose; (Seil) slack; (Erde) light; (zwanglos) casual; (zu frei) lax. **l~n** vt loosen; slacken (Seil); break up (Boden); relax (Griff); **sich l~n** become loose; (Seil:) slacken; (sich entspannen) relax

lockig adj curly

Lockmittel nt bait

Loden m **-s** (Textiles) loden

Löffel m **-s,-** spoon; (L~ voll) spoonful. **l~n** vt spoon up

Logarithmus m **-,-men** logarithm

Logbuch nt (Naut) log-book

Loge /ˈlo:ʒə/ f **-,-n** lodge; (Theat) box

Log|ik f - logic. **l~isch** adj logical

Logo nt **-s,-s** logo

Lohn m **-[e]s,⸚e** wages pl, pay; (fig) reward. **L~empfänger** m wage-earner. **l~en** vi|r (haben) **[sich] l~en** be worth it or worth while •vt be worth. **l~end** adj worthwhile; (befriedigend) rewarding. **L~erhöhung** f [pay] rise. **L~steuer** f income tax

Lok f **-,-s** 🄵 = **Lokomotive**

Lokal nt **-s,-e** restaurant; (Trink-) bar

Lokomotiv|e f **-,-n** engine, locomotive. **L~führer** m engine driver

London nt **-s** London. **L~er** adj London •m **-s,-** Londoner

Lorbeer m **-s,-en** laurel. **L~blatt** nt (Culin) bay-leaf

Lore f **-,-n** (Rail) truck

Los nt **-es,-e** lot; (Lotterie-) ticket; (Schicksal) fate

los pred adj **los sein** be loose; **jdn/etw los sein** be rid of s.o./something; **was ist [mit ihm] los?** what's the matter [with him]? •adv **los!** go on! **Achtung, fertig, los!** ready, steady, go!

lösbar adj soluble

losbinden† vt sep untie

Lösch|blatt nt sheet of blotting-paper. **l~en** vt put out, extinguish; quench (Durst); blot (Tinte); (tilgen) cancel; (streichen) delete

Löschfahrzeug nt fire-engine

lose adj loose

Lösegeld nt ransom

losen vt (haben) draw lots (**um** for)

lösen vt undo; (lockern) loosen; (entfernen) detach; (klären) solve; (auflösen) dissolve; cancel (Vertrag); break off (Beziehung); (kaufen) buy; **sich l~** come off; (sich trennen) detach oneself/itself; (lose werden) come undone; (sich klären) resolve itself; (sich auflösen) dissolve

los|fahren† vi sep (sein) start; (Auto:) drive off; **l~fahren nach** (+ dat) head for. **l~gehen**† vi sep (sein) set off; (🄵: anfangen) start; (Bombe:) go off; **l~gehen nach** (+ dat) head for; (fig: angreifen) go for. **l~kommen**† vi sep (sein) get away (**von** from). **l~lassen**† vt sep let go of; (freilassen) release

löslich adj soluble

los|lösen vt sep detach; **sich l~lösen** become detached; (fig) break away (**von** from). **l~machen** vt sep detach; untie. **l~reißen**† vt sep tear off; **sich l~reißen** break free; (fig) tear oneself away. **l~schicken** vt sep send off. **l~sprechen**† vt sep absolve (**von** from)

Losung f **-,-en** (Pol) slogan; (Mil) password

Lösung f **-,-en** solution. **L~smittel** nt solvent

loswerden† vt sep get rid of

Lot nt **-[e]s,-e** perpendicular; (Blei-) plumb[-bob]. **l~en** vt plumb

löt|en vt solder. **L~lampe** f blow-lamp

lotrecht adj perpendicular

Lotse m **-n,-n** (Naut) pilot. **l~n** vt (Naut) pilot; (fig) guide

Lotterie f **-,-n** lottery

Lotto nt **-s,-s** lotto; (Lotterie) lottery

Löw|e m **-n,-n** lion; (Astrology) Leo. **L~enzahn** m (Bot) dandelion. **L~in** f **-,-nen** lioness

loyal /lo̦aˈjaːl/ adj loyal. **L~ität** f **-** loyalty

Luchs m **-es,-e** lynx

Lücke f **-,-n** gap. **l~nhaft** adj incomplete; (Wissen) patchy. **l~nlos** adj complete; (Folge) unbroken

Luder nt **-s,-** ☒ (Frau) bitch

Luft f **-,¨e** air; **tief L~ holen** take a deep breath; **in die L~ gehen** explode. **L~angriff** m air raid. **L~aufnahme** f aerial photograph. **L~ballon** m balloon. **L~blase** f air bubble. **L~druck** m atmospheric pressure

lüften vt air; raise (Hut); reveal (Geheimnis)

Luft|fahrt f aviation. **L~fahrtgesellschaft** f airline. **L~gewehr** nt airgun. **l~ig** adj airy; (Kleid) light. **L~kissenfahrzeug** nt hovercraft. **L~krieg** m aerial warfare. **l~leer** adj **l~leerer Raum** vacuum. **L~linie** f **100 km L~linie** 100 km as the crow flies. **L~matratze** f air-bed, inflatable mattress. **L~pirat** m hijacker. **L~post** f airmail. **L~röhre** f windpipe. **L~schiff** nt airship. **L~schlange** f [paper] streamer. **L~schutzbunker** m air-raid shelter

Lüftung f **-** ventilation

Luft|veränderung f change of air. **L~waffe** f air force. **L~zug** m draught

Lüg|e f **-,-n** lie. **l~en**† vt/i (haben) lie. **L~ner(in)** m **-s,-** (f **-,-nen**) liar. **l~nerisch** adj untrue; (Person) untruthful

Luke f **-,-n** hatch; (Dach-) skylight

Lümmel m **-s,-** lout

Lump m **-en,-en** scoundrel. **L~en** m **-s,-** rag; **in L~en** in rags. **L~enpack** nt riff-raff. **L~ensammler** m rag-and-bone man. **l~ig** adj mean, shabby

Lunge f **-,-n** lungs pl; (L~nflügel) lung. **L~nentzündung** f pneumonia

Lupe f **-,-n** magnifying glass

Lurch m **-[e]s,-e** amphibian

Lust f **-,¨e** pleasure; (Verlangen) desire; (sinnliche Begierde) lust; **L~ haben** feel like (**auf etw** acc sth); **ich habe keine L~** I don't feel like it; (will nicht) I don't want to

lustig adj jolly; (komisch) funny; **sich l~ machen über** (+ acc) make fun of

Lüstling m **-s,-e** lecher

lust|los adj listless. **L~mörder** m sex killer. **L~spiel** nt comedy

lutsch|en vt/i (haben) suck. **L~er** m **-s,-** lollipop

Lüttich nt **-s** Liège

Luv f & nt **- nach Luv** (Naut) to windward

luxuriös adj luxurious

Luxus m **-** luxury

Lymph|drüse /ˈlʏmf-/ f, **L~knoten** m lymph gland

lynchen /ˈlʏnçən/ vt lynch

Lyr|ik f **-** lyric poetry. **L~iker** m **-s,-** lyric poet. **l~isch** adj lyrical

Mm

Machart f style

machen

• transitive verb

····➤ (herstellen, zubereiten) make (money, beds, music, exception, etc). **aus Plastik/Holz gemacht** made of plastic/wood. **sich** (dat) **etw machen lassen** have sth made. **etw aus jdm machen** make s.o. into sth. **jdn zum Präsidenten machen** make s.o. president. **er machte sich** (dat) **viele Freunde/Feinde** he made a lot of friends/enemies. **jdm/sich** (dat) **[einen] Kaffee machen** make [some] coffee for s.o./oneself. **ein Foto machen** take a photo

····➤ (verursachen) make, cause (difficulties); cause (pain, anxiety). **jdm Arbeit machen** make [extra] work for s.o., cause s.o. extra work. **jdm Mut/Hoffnung machen** give s.o. courage/hope. **das macht Hunger/Durst** this makes you hungry/thirsty. **das macht das Wetter** that's [because of] the weather

····➤ (ausführen, ordnen) do (job, repair, fam: room, washing, etc.).; take (walk, trip, exam, course). **sie machte mir die Haare** [!] she did my hair for me. **einen Besuch [bei jdm] machen** pay [s.o.] a visit

····➤ (tun) do (nothing, everything). **was machst du [da]?** what are you doing? **so etwas macht man nicht** that [just] isn't done

····➤ **was macht ... ?** (wie ist es um bestellt?) how is ...? **was macht die Gesundheit/Arbeit?** how are you keeping/how is the job [getting on]?

····➤ (Math: ergeben) be. **zwei mal zwei macht vier** two times two is four. **das macht 6 Euro [zusammen]** that's or that comes to six euros [altogether]

····➤ (schaden) **was macht das schon?** what does it matter? **[das] macht nichts!** [!] it doesn't matter

····➤ **mach's gut!** [!] look after yourself!; (auf Wiedersehen) so long!

• reflexive verb

····➤ **sich machen** [!] do well

····➤ **sich an etw** (acc) **machen** get down to sth. **sie machte sich an die Arbeit** she got down to work

• intransitive verb

····➤ **das macht hungrig/durstig** it makes you hungry/thirsty. **das macht dick** it's fattening

Macht f -,¨e power. **M~haber** m -s,- ruler

mächtig adj powerful • adv [!] terribly

machtlos adj powerless

Mädchen nt -s,- girl; (Dienst-) maid. **m~haft** adj girlish. **M~name** m girl's name; (vor der Ehe) maiden name

Made f -,-n maggot

madig adj maggoty

Madonna f -,-nen madonna

Magazin nt -s,-e magazine; (Lager) warehouse; store-room

Magd f -,¨e maid

Magen m -s,¨ stomach. **M~verstimmung** f stomach upset

mager adj thin; (Fleisch) lean; (Boden) poor; (dürftig) meagre. **M~keit** f - thinness; leanness. **M~sucht** f anorexia

Magie f - magic

Mag|ier /ˈmaːgi̯ɐ/ m -s,- magician. **m~isch** adj magic

Magistrat m -s,-e city council

Magnet m -en & -[e]s,-e magnet.

m~isch adj magnetic

Mahagoni nt **-s** mahogany

Mäh|drescher m **-s,-** combine harvester. **m~en** vt/i (haben) mow

Mahl nt **-[e]s,¨er** & **-e** meal

mahlen† vt grind

Mahlzeit f meal; **M~!** enjoy your meal!

Mähne f **-,-n** mane

mahn|en vt/i (haben) remind (**wegen** about); (ermahnen) admonish; (auffordern) urge (**zu** to). **M~ung** f **-,-en** reminder; admonition

Mai m **-[e]s,-e** May; **der Erste Mai** May Day. **M~glöckchen** nt **-s,-** lily of the valley

Mailand nt **-s** Milan

Mais m **-es** maize; (Culin) sweet corn

Majestät f **-,-en** majesty. **m~isch** adj majestic

Major m **-s,-e** major

m

Majoran m **-s** marjoram

makaber adj macabre

Makel m **-s,-** blemish; (Defekt) flaw

Makkaroni pl macaroni sg

Makler m **-s,-** (Comm) broker

Makrele f **-,-n** mackerel

Makrone f **-,-n** macaroon

mal adv (Math) times; (bei Maßen) by; ([!]: einmal) once; (eines Tages) one day; **nicht mal** not even

Mal nt **-[e]s,-e** time; **zum ersten/letzten Mal** for the first/last time; **ein für alle Mal** once and for all; **jedes Mal** every time; **jedes Mal, wenn** whenever

Mal|buch nt colouring book. **m~en** vt/i (haben) paint. **M~er** m **-s,-** painter. **M~erei** f **-,-en** painting. **M~erin** f **-,-nen** painter. **m~erisch** adj picturesque

Mallorca /ma'lɔrka, -'jɔrka/ nt **-s** Majorca

malnehmen† vt sep multiply (**mit** by)

Malz nt **-es** malt

Mama /'mama, ma'ma:/ f **-s** mummy

Mammut nt **-s,-e** & **-s** mammoth

mampfen vt [!] munch

man pron one, you; (die Leute) people, they; **man sagt** they say, it is said

manch|e(r,s) pron many a; **[so] m~es Mal** many a time; **m~e Leute** some people •(substantivisch) **m~er/m~e** many a man/woman; **m~e** pl some; (Leute) some people; (viele) many [people]; **m~es** some things; (vieles) many things. **m~erlei** inv adj various •pron various things

manchmal adv sometimes

Mandant(in) m **-en,-en** (f **-,-nen**) (Jur) client

Mandarine f **-,-n** mandarin

Mandat nt **-[e]s,-e** mandate; (Jur) brief; (Pol) seat

Mandel f **-,-n** almond; (Anat) tonsil. **M~entzündung** f tonsillitis

Manege /ma'ne:ʒə/ f **-,-n** ring; (Reit-) arena

Mangel[1] m **-s,¨** lack; (Knappheit) shortage; (Med) deficiency; (Fehler) defect

Mangel[2] f **-,-n** mangle

mangel|haft adj faulty, defective; (Sch) unsatisfactory. **m~n**[1] vi (haben) **es m~t an** (+ dat) there is a lack/(Knappheit) shortage of

mangeln[2] vt put through the mangle

Manie f **-,-n** mania

Manier f **-,-en** manner; **M~en** manners. **m~lich** adj well-mannered •adv properly

Manifest nt **-[e]s,-e** manifesto

Maniküre f **-,-n** manicure; (Person) manicurist. **m~n** vt manicure

Manko nt **-s,-s** disadvantage; (Fehlbetrag) deficit

Mann m **-[e]s,¨er** man; (Ehe-) husband

Männchen nt **-s,-** little man; (Zool) male

Mannequin /'manəkɛ̃/ nt **-s,-s** model

männlich adj male; (Gram & fig) masculine; (mannhaft) manly; (Frau) mannish. **M~keit** f - masculinity; (fig) manhood

Mannschaft f -,-**en** team; (Naut) crew

Manöv|er nt **-s,-** manœuvre; (Winkelzug) trick. **m~rieren** vt/i (haben) manœuvre

Mansarde f -,-**n** attic room; (Wohnung) attic flat

Manschette f -,-**n** cuff. **M~knopf** m cuff-link

Mantel m **-s,**¨ coat; overcoat

Manuskript nt **-[e]s,-e** manuscript

Mappe f -,-**n** folder; (Akten-) briefcase; (Schul-) bag

Märchen nt **-s,-** fairy-tales

Margarine f - margarine

Marienkäfer /ma'ri:ən-/ m lady-bird

Marihuana nt **-s** marijuana

Marine f marine; (Kriegs-) navy. **m~blau** adj navy [blue]

marinieren vt marinade

Marionette f -,-**n** puppet, marionette

Mark[1] f -,- (alte Währung) mark; **drei M~** three marks

Mark[2] nt **-[e]s** (Knochen-) marrow (Bot)pith; (Frucht-) pulp

markant adj striking

Marke f -,-**n** token; (rund) disc; (Erkennungs-) tag; (Brief-) stamp; (Lebensmittel-) coupon; (Spiel-) counter; (Markierung) mark; (Fabrikat) make; (Tabak-) brand. **M~nartikel** m branded article

markieren vt mark; (!: vortäuschen) fake

Markise f -,-**n** awning

Markstück nt one-mark piece

Markt m **-[e]s,**¨**e** market; (M~platz) market-place. **M~forschung** f market research

Marmelade f -,-**n** jam; (Orangen-) marmalade

Marmor m **-s** marble

Marokko nt **-s** Morocco

Marone f -,-**n** [sweet] chestnut

Marsch m **-[e]s,**¨**e** march. **m~** int (Mil) march!

Marschall m **-s,**¨**e** marshal

marschieren vi (sein) march

Marter f -,-**n** torture. **m~n** vt torture

Märtyrer(in) m **-s,-** (f -,-**nen**) martyr

Marxismus m - Marxism

März m -,-**e** March

Marzipan nt **-s** marzipan

Masche f -,-**n** stitch; (im Netz) mesh; (!: Trick) dodge. **M~ndraht** m wire netting

Maschin|e f -,-**n** machine; (Flugzeug) plane; (Schreib-) typewriter; **M~e schreiben** type. **m~egeschrieben** adj typewritten, typed. **m~ell** adj machine • adv by machine. **M~enbau** m mechanical engineering. **M~engewehr** nt machine-gun. **M~ist** m **-en,-en** machinist; (Naut) engineer

Masern pl measles sg

Maserung f -,-**en** [wood] grain

Maske f -,-**n** mask; (Theat) make-up

maskieren vt mask; **sich m~** dress up (**als** as)

maskulin adj masculine

Masochist m **-en,-en** masochist

Maß[1] nt **-es,-e** measure; (Abmessung) measurement; (Grad) degree; (Mäßigung) moderation; **in hohem Maße** to a high degree

Maß[2] f -,- (SGer) litre [of beer]

Massage /ma'sa:ʒə/ f -,-**n** massage

Massaker nt **-s,-** massacre

Maßband nt (pl **-bänder**) tape-measure

Masse f -,-**n** mass; (Culin) mixture;

see A-Z of German life and culture

m

(Menschen-) crowd; **eine M~ Arbeit** [!] masses of work. **m~nhaft** adv in huge quantities. **M~nproduktion** f mass production. **M~nvernichtungswaffen** fpl weapons of mass destruction. **m~nweise** adv in huge numbers

Masseu|r /ma'søːɐ̯/ m **-s,-e** masseur. **M~se** f **-,-n** masseuse

maß|gebend adj authoritative; (einflussreich) influential. **m~geblich** adj decisive. **m~geschneidert** adj made-to-measure

massieren vt massage

massig adj massive

mäßig adj moderate; (mittelmäßig) indifferent. **m~en** vt moderate; **sich m~en** moderate; (sich beherrschen) restrain oneself. **M~ung** f - moderation

massiv adj solid; (stark) heavy

m

Maß|krug m beer mug. **m~los** adj excessive; (grenzenlos) boundless; (äußerst) extreme. **M~nahme** f **-,-n** measure

Maßstab m scale; (Norm & fig) standard. **m~sgerecht, m~sgetreu** adj scale • adv to scale

Mast[1] m **-[e]s,-en** pole; (Überland-) pylon; (Naut) mast

Mast[2] f - fattening

mästen vt fatten

masturbieren vi (haben) masturbate

Material nt **-s,-ien** material; (coll) materials pl. **M~ismus** m - materialism. **m~istisch** adj materialistic

Mathe f - [!] maths sg

Mathe|matik f - mathematics sg. **M~matiker** m **-s,-** mathematician. **m~matisch** adj mathematical

Matinee f **-,-n** (Theat) morning performance

Matratze f **-,-n** mattress

Matrose m **-n,-n** sailor

Matsch m **-[e]s** mud; (Schnee-) slush

matt adj weak; (gedämpft) dim; (glanzlos) dull; (Politur, Farbe) matt. **M~** nt **-s** (Schach) mate

Matte f **-,-n** mat

Mattglas nt frosted glass

[C] **Matura** f - (Aust) ≈ A levels pl

Mauer f **-,-n** wall. **M~werk** nt masonry

Maul nt **-[e]s, Mäuler** (Zool) mouth; **halts M~!** [!] shut up! **M~- und Klauenseuche** f foot-and-mouth disease. **M~korb** m muzzle. **M~tier** nt mule. **M~wurf** m mole

Maurer m **-s,-** bricklayer

Maus f **-,Mäuse** mouse

Maut f **-,-en** (Aust) toll. **M~straße** f toll road

maximal adj maximum

Maximum nt **-s,-ma** maximum

Mayonnaise /majɔ'nɛːzə/ f **-,-n** mayonnaise

Mechan|ik /me'çaːnɪk/ f - mechanics sg; (Mechanismus) mechanism. **M~iker** m **-s,-** mechanic. **m~isch** adj mechanical. **m~isieren** vt mechanize. **M~ismus** m **-,-men** mechanism

meckern vi (haben) bleat; ([!]: nörgeln) grumble

Medaill|e /me'daljə/ f **-,-n** medal. **M~on** nt **-s,-s** medallion (Schmuck) locket

Medikament nt **-[e]s,-e** medicine

Medit|ation /-'tsi̯oːn/ f **-,-en** meditation. **m~ieren** vi (haben) meditate

Medium nt **-s,-ien** medium; **die Medien** the media

Medizin f **-,-en** medicine. **M~er** m **-s,-** doctor; (Student) medical student. **m~isch** adj medical; (heilkräftig) medicinal

Meer nt **-[e]s,-e** sea. **M~busen** m gulf. **M~enge** f strait. **M~esspiegel** m sea-level. **M~jungfrau** f mermaid. **M~rettich** m horseradish.

[C] *see* A-Z of German life and culture

M∼schweinchen nt **-s,-** guinea-pig

Mehl nt **-[e]s** flour. **M∼schwitze** f (Culin) roux

mehr pron & adv more; **nicht m∼** no more; (zeitlich) no longer; **nichts m∼** no more; (nichtsweiter) nothing else; **nie m∼** never again. **m∼eres** pron several things pl. **m∼fach** adj multiple; (mehrmalig) repeated • adv several times. **M∼fahrtenkarte** f book of tickets. **M∼heit** f **-,-en** majority. **m∼malig** adj repeated. **m∼mals** adv several times. **m∼sprachig** adj multilingual. **M∼wertsteuer** f value-added tax, VAT. **M∼zahl** f majority; (Gram) plural. **M∼zweck-** prefix multi-purpose

meiden† vt avoid, shun

Meile f **-,-n** mile. **m∼nweit** adv [for] miles

mein poss pron my. **m∼e(r,s)** poss pron mine; **die M∼en** od **m∼en** pl my family sg

Meineid m perjury

meinen vt mean; (glauben) think; (sagen) say

mein|erseits adv for my part. **m∼etwegen** adv for my sake; (wegen mir) because of me; (!: von mir aus) as far as I'm concerned

Meinung f **-,-en** opinion; **jdm die M∼ sagen** give s.o. a piece of one's mind. **M∼sumfrage** f opinion poll

Meise f **-,-n** (Zool) tit

Meißel m **-s,-** chisel. **m∼n** vt/i (haben) chisel

meist adv mostly; (gewöhnlich) usually. **m∼e** adj **der/die/das m∼e** most; **die m∼en Leute** most people; **am m∼en** [the] most • pron **das m∼e** most [of it]; **die m∼en** most. **m∼ens** adv mostly; (gewöhnlich) usually

Meister m **-s,-** master craftsman; (Könner) master; (Sport) champion. **m∼n** vt master. **M∼schaft** f **-,-en** mastery; (Sport) championship

meld|en vt report; (anmelden) register; (ankündigen) announce; **sich m∼en** report (**bei** to); (zum Militär) enlist; (freiwillig) volunteer; (Teleph) answer; (Sch) put up one's hand; (von sich hören lassen) get in touch (**bei** with). **M∼ung** f **-,-en** report; (Anmeldung) registration

melken† vt milk

Melodie f **-,-n** tune, melody

melodisch adj melodic; melodious

Melone f **-,-n** melon

Memoiren /meˈmo̯aːrən/ pl memoirs

Menge f **-,-n** amount, quantity; (Menschen-) crowd; (Math) set; **eine M∼ Geld** a lot of money. **m∼n** vt mix

Mensa f **-,-sen** (Univ) refectory

Mensch m **-en,-en** human being; **der M∼** man; **die M∼en** people; **jeder/kein M∼** everybody/nobody. **M∼enaffe** m ape. **m∼enfeindlich** adj antisocial. **M∼enfresser** m **-s,-** cannibal; (Zool) man-eater. **m∼enfreundlich** adj philanthropic. **M∼enleben** nt human life; (Lebenszeit) lifetime. **m∼enleer** adj deserted. **M∼enmenge** f crowd. **M∼enraub** m kidnapping. **M∼enrechte** ntpl human rights. **m∼enscheu** adj unsociable. **m∼enwürdig** adj humane. **M∼heit** f **- die M∼heit** mankind, humanity. **m∼lich** adj human; (human) humane. **M∼lichkeit** f **-** humanity

Menstru|ation /-ˈtsi̯oːn/ f **-** menstruation. **m∼ieren** vi (haben) menstruate

Mentalität f **-,-en** mentality

Menü nt **-s,-s** menu; (festes M∼) set meal

Meridian m **-s,-e** meridian

merk|bar adj noticeable. **M∼blatt** nt [explanatory] leaflet. **m∼en** vt notice; **sich** (dat) **etw m∼en** remember sth. **M∼mal** nt feature

merkwürdig adj odd, strange

m

see A-Z of German life and culture

Messe[1] f -,-n (Relig) mass; (Comm) [trade] fair

Messe[2] f -,-n (Mil) mess

messen† vt/i (haben) measure; (ansehen) look at; **[bei jdm] Fieber m~** take s.o.'s temperature; **sich mit jdm m~ können** be a match for s.o.

Messer nt -s,- knife

Messias m - Messiah

Messing nt -s brass

Messung f -,-en measurement

Metabolismus m - metabolism

Metall nt -s,-e metal. **m~isch** adj metallic

Metamorphose f -,-n metamorphosis

metaphorisch adj metaphorical

Meteor m -s,-e meteor. **M~ologie** f - meteorology

Meter m & nt -s,- metre. **M~maß** nt tape-measure

m

Method|e f -,-n method. **m~isch** adj methodical

Metropole f -,-n metropolis

Metzger m -s,- butcher. **M~ei** f -,-en butcher's shop

Meuterei f -,-en mutiny

meutern vi (haben) mutiny; ([!]: schimpfen) grumble

Mexikan|er(in) m -s,- (f -,-nen) Mexican. **m~isch** adj Mexican

Mexiko nt -s Mexico

miauen vi (haben) mew, miaow

mich pron (acc of **ich**) me; (reflexive) myself

Mieder nt -s,- bodice

Miene f -,-n expression

mies adj [!] lousy

Miet|e f -,-n rent; (Mietgebühr) hire charge; **zur M~e wohnen** live in rented accommodation. **m~en** vt rent (Haus, Zimmer); hire (Auto, Boot). **M~er(in)** m -s,- (f -,-nen) tenant. **m~frei** adj & adv rent-free. **M~shaus** nt block of rented flats. **M~vertrag** m lease. **M~wagen** m hire-car. **M~wohnung** f rented flat; (zu vermieten) flat to let

Migräne f -,-n migraine

Mikro|chip m microchip. **M~computer** m microcomputer. **M~film** m microfilm

Mikro|fon, **M~phon** nt -s,-e microphone. **M~skop** nt -s,-e microscope. **m~skopisch** adj microscopic

Mikrowelle f microwave. **M~nherd** m microwave oven

Milbe f -,-n mite

Milch f - milk. **M~glas** nt opal glass. **m~ig** adj milky. **M~mann** m (pl -**männer**) milkman. **M~straße** f Milky Way

mild adj mild; (nachsichtig) lenient. **M~e** f - mildness; leniency. **m~ern** vt make milder; (mäßigen) moderate; (lindern) ease; **sich m~ern** become milder; (sich mäßigen) moderate; (Schmerz:) ease; **m~ernde Umstände** mitigating circumstances

Milieu /mi'li̯ø:/ nt -s,-s [social] environment

Militär nt -s army; (Soldaten) troops pl; **beim M~** in the army. **m~isch** adj military

Miliz f -,-en militia

Milliarde /mɪ'li̯ardə/ f -,-n thousand million, billion

Milli|gramm nt milligram. **M~meter** m & nt millimetre. **M~meterpapier** nt graph paper

Million /mɪ'li̯o:n/ f -,-en million. **M~är** m -s,-e millionaire

Milz f - (Anat) spleen. **~brand** m anthrax

mimen vt ([!]: vortäuschen) act

Mimose f -,-n mimosa

Minderheit f -,-en minority

minderjährig adj (Jur) under-age. **M~e(r)** m/f (Jur) minor

mindern vt diminish; decrease

minderwertig adj inferior. **M~keit** f - inferiority. **M~keitskomplex** m inferiority complex

Mindest- prefix minimum. **m~e** adj & pron **der/die/das M~e** od **m~e** the least; **nicht im M~en** not in the least. **m~ens** adv at least. **M~lohn** m minimum wage. **M~maß** nt minimum

Mine f -,-n mine; (Bleistift-) lead; (Kugelschreiber-) refill. **M~nräumboot** nt minesweeper

Mineral nt **-s,-e** & **-ien** mineral. **m~isch** adj mineral. **M~wasser** nt mineral water

Miniatur f **-,-en** miniature

Minigolf nt miniature golf

minimal adj minimal

Minimum nt **-s,-ma** minimum

Mini|ster m, **-s,-** minister. **m~steriell** adj ministerial. **M~sterium** nt **-s,-ien** ministry

minus conj, adv & prep (+ gen) minus. **M~** nt **-** deficit; (Nachteil) disadvantage. **M~zeichen** nt minus [sign]

Minute f **-,-n** minute

mir pron (dat of **ich**) [to] me; (reflexive) myself

Misch|ehe f mixed marriage. **m~en** vt mix; blend (Tee, Kaffee); toss (Salat); shuffle (Karten); **sich m~en** mix; (Person;) mingle (**unter** + acc with); **sich m~en in** (+ acc) join in (Gespräch); meddle in (Angelegenheit) •vi (haben) shuffle the cards. **M~ling** m **-s,-e** half-caste. **M~ung** f **-,-en** mixture; blend

miserabel adj abominable

missachten vt disregard

Miss|achtung f disregard. **M~bildung** f deformity

missbilligen vt disapprove of

Miss|billigung f disapproval. **M~brauch** m abuse

missbrauchen vt abuse; (vergewaltigen) rape

Misserfolg m failure

Misse|tat f misdeed. **M~täter** m ! culprit

missfallen† vi (haben) displease (**jdm** s.o.)

Miss|fallen nt **-s** displeasure; (Missbilligung) disapproval. **M~geburt** f freak; (fig) monstrosity. **M~geschick** nt mishap; (Unglück) misfortune

miss|glücken vi (sein) fail. **m~gönnen** vt begrudge

misshandeln vt ill-treat

Misshandlung f ill-treatment

Mission f **-,-en** mission

Missionar(in) m **-s,-e** (f **-,-nen**) missionary

Missklang m discord

misslingen† vi (sein) fail; **es misslang ihr** she failed. **M~** nt **-s** failure

Missmut m ill humour. **m~ig** adj morose

missraten† vi (sein) turn out badly

Miss|stand m abuse; (Zustand) undesirable state of affairs. **M~stimmung** f discord; (Laune) bad mood

m

misstrauen vi (haben) **jdm/etw m~** mistrust s.o./sth; (Argwohn hegen) distrust s.o./sth

Misstrau|en nt **-s** mistrust; (Argwohn) distrust. **M~ensvotum** nt vote of no confidence. **m~isch** adj distrustful; (argwöhnisch) suspicious

Miss|verständnis nt misunderstanding. **m~verstehen**† vt misunderstand. **M~wirtschaft** f mismanagement

Mist m **-[e]s** manure; ! rubbish

Mistel f **-,-n** mistletoe

Misthaufen m dungheap

mit prep (+ dat) with; (sprechen) to; (mittels) by; (inklusive) including; (bei) at; **mit Bleistift** in pencil; **mit lauter Stimme** in a loud voice; **mit drei Jahren** at the age of three •adv (auch) as well; **mit anfassen** (fig) lend a hand

Mitarbeit f collaboration. **m~en** vi sep collaborate (**an** + dat on). **M~er(in)** m(f) collaborator; (Kollege) colleague; employee

Mitbestimmung f co-determination

mitbringen† vt sep bring [along]

miteinander adv with each other

Mitesser m (Med) blackhead

mitfahren† vi sep (sein) go/come along; **mit jdm m~** go with s.o.; (mitgenommen werden) be given a lift by s.o.

mitfühlen vi sep (haben) sympathize

mitgeben† vt sep **jdm etw m~** give s.o. sth to take with him

Mitgefühl nt sympathy

mitgehen† vi sep (sein) **mit jdm m~** go with s.o.

Mitgift f **-,-en** dowry

Mitglied nt member. **M~schaft** f **-** membership

mithilfe prep (+ gen) with the aid of

Mithilfe f assistance

m

mitkommen† vi sep (sein) come [along] too; (fig: folgen können) keep up; (verstehen) follow

Mitlaut m consonant

Mitleid nt pity, compassion; **M~ erregend** pitiful. **m~ig** adj pitying; (mitfühlend) compassionate. **m~slos** adj pitiless

mitmachen v sep •vt take part in; (erleben) go through •vi (haben) join in

Mitmensch m fellow man

mitnehmen† vt sep take along; (mitfahren lassen) give a lift to; (fig: schädigen) affect badly; (erschöpfen) exhaust; **'zum M~'** 'to take away'

mitreden vi sep (haben) join in [the conversation]; (mit entscheiden) have a say (**bei** in)

mitreißen† vt sep sweep along; (fig: begeistern) carry away; **m~d** rousing

mitsamt prep (+ dat) together with

mitschreiben† vt sep (haben) take down

Mitschuld f partial blame. **m~ig** adj **m~ig sein** be partly to blame

Mitschüler(in) m(f) fellow pupil

mitspielen vi sep (haben) join in; (Theat) be in the cast; (beitragen) play a part

Mittag m midday, noon; (Mahlzeit) lunch; (Pause) lunch-break; **heute/gestern M~** at lunch-time today/yesterday; **[zu] M~ essen** have lunch. **M~essen** nt lunch. **m~s** adv at noon; (als Mahlzeit) for lunch; **um 12 Uhr m~s** at noon. **M~spause** f lunch-hour; (Pause) lunch-break. **M~sschlaf** m after-lunch nap

Mittäter|(in) m(f) accomplice. **M~schaft** f **-** complicity

Mitte f **-,-n** middle; (Zentrum) centre; **die goldene M~** the golden mean; **M~ Mai** in mid-May; **in unserer M~** in our midst

mitteil|en vt sep **jdm etw m~en** tell s.o. sth; (amtlich) inform s.o. of sth. **M~ung** f **-,-en** communication; (Nachricht) piece of news

Mittel nt **-s,-** means sg; (Heil-) remedy; (Medikament) medicine; (M~wert) mean; (Durchschnitt) average; **M~** pl (Geld-) funds, resources. **m~** pred adj medium; (m~mäßig) middling. **M~alter** nt Middle Ages pl. **m~alterlich** adj medieval. **M~ding** nt (fig) cross. **m~europäisch** adj Central European. **M~finger** m middle finger. **m~los** adj destitute. **m~mäßig** adj middling; [**nur**] **m~mäßig** mediocre. **M~meer** nt Mediterranean. **M~punkt** m centre; (fig) centre of attention

mittels prep (+ gen) by means of

Mittel|schule f = **Realschule**. **M~smann** m (pl **-männer**) intermediary, go-between. **M~stand** m middle class. **m~ste(r,s)** adj middle. **M~streifen** m (Auto) central reservation. **M~stürmer** m centre-forward. **M~welle** f medium wave. **M~wort** nt (pl **-wörter**) participle

see A-Z of German life and culture

mitten adv **m~ in/auf** (dat/acc) in the middle of. **m~durch** adv [right] through the middle

Mitternacht f midnight

mittler|e(r,s) adj middle; (Größe, Qualität) medium; (durchschnittlich) mean, average. **m~weile** adv meanwhile; (seitdem) by now

Mittwoch m **-s,-e** Wednesday. **m~s** adv on Wednesdays

mitunter adv now and again

mitwirk|en vi sep (haben) take part; (helfen) contribute. **M~ung** f participation

mix|en vt mix. **M~er** m **-s,-** (Culin) liquidizer, blender

mobb|en vt bully, harass. **M~ing** nt **-s** bullying, harassment

Möbel pl furniture sg. **M~stück** nt piece of furniture. **M~wagen** m removal van

Mobiliar nt **-s** furniture

mobilisier|en vt mobilize. **M~ung** f **-** mobilization

Mobil|machung f **-** mobilization. **M~telefon** nt mobile phone

möblier|en vt furnish; **m~tes Zimmer** furnished room

mochte, möchte s. **mögen**

Mode f **-,-n** fashion; **M~ sein** be fashionable

Modell nt **-s,-e** model. **m~ieren** vt model

Modenschau f fashion show

Modera|tor m **-s,-en, M~torin** f **-,-nen** (TV) presenter

modern adj modern; (modisch) fashionable. **m~isieren** vt modernize

Mode|schmuck m costume jewellery. **M~schöpfer** m fashion designer

modisch adj fashionable

Modistin f **-,-nen** milliner

modrig adj musty

modulieren vt modulate

Mofa nt **-s,-s** moped

mogeln vi (haben) ⓘ cheat

mögen†

- transitive verb
  - ····➤ like. **sie mag ihn sehr [gern]** she likes him very much. **möchten Sie ein Glas Wein?** would you like a glass of wine? **lieber mögen** prefer. **ich möchte lieber Tee** I would prefer tea
- auxiliary verb
  - ····➤ (wollen) want to. **sie mochte nicht länger bleiben** she didn't want to stay any longer. **ich möchte ihn [gerne] sprechen** I'd like to speak to him. **möchtest du nach Hause?** do you want to go home? or would you like to go home?
  - ····➤ (Vermutung, Möglichkeit) may. **ich mag mich irren** I may be wrong. **wer/was mag das sein?** whoever/whatever can it be? **[das] mag sein** that may well be. **mag kommen, was da will** come what may

möglich adj possible; **alle m~en** all sorts of; **über alles M~e sprechen** talk about all sorts of things. **m~erweise** adv possibly. **M~keit** f **-,-en** possibility. **M~keitsform** f subjunctive. **m~st** adv if possible; **m~st viel** as much as possible

Mohn m **-s** poppy

Möhre, Mohrrübe f **-,-n** carrot

Mokka m **-s** mocha; (Geschmack) coffee

Molch m **-[e]s,-e** newt

Mole f **-,-n** (Naut) mole

Molekül nt **-s,-e** molecule

Molkerei f **-,-en** dairy

Moll nt **-** (Mus) minor

mollig adj cosy; (warm) warm; (rundlich) plump

Moment m **-s,-e** moment; **M~[mal]!** just a moment! **m~an** adj momentary; (gegenwärtig) at the moment

Monarch m **-en,-en** monarch. **M~ie** f **-,-n** monarchy

Monat m **-s,-e** month. **m~elang** adv for months. **m~lich** adj & adv monthly

Mönch m **-[e]s,-e** monk

Mond m **-[e]s,-e** moon

mondän adj fashionable

Mond|finsternis f lunar eclipse. **m~hell** adj moonlit. **M~sichel** f crescent moon. **M~schein** m moonlight

monieren vt criticize

Monitor m **-s,-en** (Techn) monitor

Monogramm nt **-s,-e** monogram

Mono|log m **-s,-e** monologue. **M~pol** nt **-s,-e** monopoly. **m~ton** adj monotonous

Monster nt **-s,-** monster

Monstrum nt **-s,-stren** monster

Monsun m **-s,-e** monsoon

Montag m Monday

Montage /mɔn'ta:ʒə/ f **-,-n** fitting; (Zusammenbau) assembly; (Film-) editing; (Kunst) montage

montags adv on Mondays

Montanindustrie f coal and steel industry

Monteur /mɔn'tø:ɐ̯/ m **-s,-e** fitter. **M~anzug** m overalls pl

montieren vt fit; (zusammenbauen) assemble

Monument nt **-[e]s,-e** monument. **m~al** a monumental

Moor nt **-[e]s,-e** bog; (Heide-) moor

Moos nt **es,-e** moss. **m~ig** adj mossy

Moped nt **-s,-s** moped

Mopp m **-s,-s** mop

Moral f **-** morals pl, (Selbstvertrauen) morale; (Lehre) moral. **m~isch** adj moral

Mord m **-[e]s,-e** murder, (Pol) assassination. **M~anschlag** m murder/assassination attempt. **m~en** vt/i (haben) murder, kill

Mörder m **-s,-** murderer, (Pol) assassin. **M~in** f **-,-nen** murderess. **m~isch** adj murderous; (!: schlimm) dreadful

morgen adv tomorrow; **m~ Abend** tomorrow evening

Morgen m **-s,-** morning; (Maß) ≈ acre; **am M~** in the morning; **heute/Montag M~** this/Monday morning. **M~dämmerung** f dawn. **M~rock** m dressing-gown. **M~rot** nt red sky in the morning. **m~s** adj in the morning

morgig adj tomorrow's; **der m~e Tag** tomorrow

Morphium nt **-s** morphine

morsch adj rotten

Morsealphabet nt Morse code

Mörtel m **-s** mortar

Mosaik /moza'i:k/ nt **-s,-e[n]** mosaic

Moschee f **-,-n** mosque

Mosel f **-** Moselle

Moskau nt **-s** Moscow

Moskito m **-s,-s** mosquito

Moslem m **-s,-s** Muslim

Motiv nt **-s,-e** motive; (Kunst) motif

Motor /'mo:tɔr, mo'to:ɐ̯/ m **-s,-en** engine; (Elektro-) motor. **M~boot** nt motor boat

motorisieren vt motorize

Motor|rad nt motor cycle. **M~roller** m motor scooter

Motte f **-,-n** moth. **M~nkugel** f mothball

Motto nt **-s,-s** motto

Möwe f **-,-n** gull

Mücke f **-,-n** gnat; (kleine) midge; (Stech-) mosquito

müd|e adj tired; **es m~e sein** be tired (**etw zu tun** of doing sth). **M~igkeit** f **-** tiredness

muffig adj musty; (!: mürrisch) grumpy

Mühe f **-,-n** effort; (Aufwand) trouble; **sich** (dat) **M~ geben** make an effort; (sich bemühen) try; nicht der **M~ wert** not worth while; mit **M~ und** Not with great difficulty; (gerade noch) only just. **m~los** adj effortless

muhen vi (haben) moo

Mühl|e f -,-n mill; (Kaffee-) grinder. **M~stein** m millstone

Müh|sal f -,-e (literarisch) toil; (Mühe) trouble. **m~sam** adj laborious; (beschwerlich) difficult

Mulde f -,-n hollow

Müll m -s refuse. **M~abfuhr** f refuse collection

Mullbinde f gauze bandage

Mülleimer m waste bin; (Mülltonne) dustbin

Müller m -s,- miller

Müll|halde f [rubbish] dump. **M~schlucker** m refuse chute. **M~tonne** f dustbin

multi|national adj multinational. **M~plikation** f -,-en multiplication. **m~plizieren** vt multiply

Mumie /ˈmuːmi̯ə/ f -,-n mummy

Mumm m -s [!] energy

Mumps m - mumps

Mund m -[e]s,⸚er mouth; **ein M~ voll Suppe** a mouthful of soup; **halt den M~!** [x] shut up! **M~art** f dialect. **m~artlich** adj dialect

Mündel nt & m -s,- (Jur) ward. **m~sicher** adj gilt-edged

münden vi (sein) flow/(Straße:) lead (**in** + acc into)

Mundharmonika f mouth-organ

mündig adj **m~ sein/werden** (Jur) be/come of age. **M~keit** f - (Jur) majority

mündlich adj verbal; **m~e Prüfung** oral

Mündung f -,-en (Fluss-) mouth; (Gewehr-) muzzle

Mundwinkel m corner of the mouth

Munition /-ˈtsi̯oːn/ f - ammunition

munkeln vt/i (haben) talk (**von** of); **es wird gemunkelt** rumour has it (**dass** that)

Münster nt -s,- cathedral

munter adj lively; (heiter) merry; **m~ sein** (wach) be wide awake; **gesund und m~** fit and well

Münz|e f -,-n coin; (M~stätte) mint. **M~fernsprecher** m payphone

mürbe adj crumbly; (Obst) mellow; (Fleisch) tender. **M~teig** m short pastry

Murmel f -,-n marble

murmeln vt/i (haben) murmur; (undeutlich) mumble

Murmeltier nt marmot

murren vt/i (haben) grumble

mürrisch adj surly

Mus nt -es purée

Muschel f -,-n mussel; [sea] shell

Museum /muˈzeːʊm/ nt -s,-seen museum

Musik f - music. **m~alisch** adj musical

Musiker(in) m -s,- (f -,-nen) musician

Musik|instrument nt musical instrument. **M~kapelle** f band. **M~pavillon** m bandstand

musisch adj artistic

musizieren vi (haben) make music

Muskat m -[e]s nutmeg

Muskel m -s,-n muscle. **M~kater** m stiff and aching muscles pl

muskulös adj muscular

Muslim|(in) m -s,-e (f -,-nen) Muslim. **m~isch** adj Muslim

muss s. **müssen**

Muße f - leisure

müssen†

- auxiliary verb

····➤ (gezwungen/verpflichtet/notwendig sein) have to; must. **er muss es tun** he must or has to do it; [!] he's got to do it. **ich musste schnell fahren** I had to drive fast. **das muss 1968 gewesen sein** it must have been in 1968. **er muss gleich hier sein** he must be here

m

at any moment

····➤ (in negativen Sätzen; ungezwungen) **sie muss es nicht tun** she does not have to *or* [!] she hasn't got to do it. **es musste nicht so sein** it didn't have to be like that

····➤ **es müsste** (sollte) **doch möglich sein** it ought to *or* should be possible. **du müsstest es mal versuchen** you ought to *or* should try it

• intransitive verb

····➤ (irgendwohin gehen müssen) have to *or* must go. **ich muss nach Hause/zum Arzt** I have to *or* must go home/to the doctor. **ich musste mal [aufs Klo]** I had to go [to the loo]

müßig adj idle

musste, müsste s. **müssen**

Muster nt **-s,-** pattern; (Probe) sample; (Vorbild) model. **M~beispiel** nt typical example; (Vorbild) perfect example. **m~gültig, m~haft** adj exemplary. **m~n** vt eye; (inspizieren) inspect. **M~ung** f **-,-en** inspection; (Mil) medical; (Muster) pattern

Mut m **-[e]s** courage; **jdm Mut machen** encourage s.o.; **zu M~e sein** feel like it; s. **zumute**

mut|ig adj courageous. **m~los** adj despondent

mutmaßen vt presume; (Vermutungen anstellen) speculate

Mutprobe f test of courage

Mutter[1] f **-,⸚** mother

Mutter[2] f **-,-n** (Techn) nut

Muttergottes f **-** madonna

Mutterland nt motherland

mütterlich adj maternal; (fürsorglich) motherly. **m~erseits** adv on one's/the mother's side

Mutter|mal nt birthmark; (dunkel) mole. **M~schaft** f **-** motherhood. **m~seelenallein** adj & adv all alone. **M~sprache** f mother tongue. **M~tag** m Mother's Day

Mütze f **-,-n** cap; **wollene M~** woolly hat

MwSt. abbr (**Mehrwertsteuer**) VAT

mysteriös adj mysterious

Mystik /ˈmʏstɪk/ f **-** mysticism

myth|isch adj mythical. **M~ologie** f **-** mythology

Nn

na int well; **na gut** all right then

Nabel m **-s,-** navel. **N~schnur** f umbilical cord

nach

• preposition (+ dative)

····➤ (räumlich) to. **nach London fahren** go to London. **der Zug nach München** the train to Munich; (noch nicht abgefahren) the train for Munich; the Munich train. **nach Hause gehen** go home. **nach Osten [zu]** eastwards; towards the east

····➤ (zeitlich) after; (Uhrzeit) past. **nach fünf Minuten/dem Frühstück** after five minutes/breakfast. **zehn [Minuten] nach zwei** ten [minutes] past two

····➤ ([räumliche und zeitliche] Reihenfolge) after. **nach Ihnen/dir!** after you!

····➤ (mit bestimmten Verben) for. **greifen/streben/schicken nach** grasp/strive/send for

····➤ (gemäß) according to. **nach der neuesten Mode gekleidet** dressed in [accordance with] the latest fashion. **dem Gesetz nach** in accordance with the law; by law.

nach meiner Ansicht od **Meinung, meiner Ansicht** od **Meinung nach** in my view or opinion. **nach etwas schmecken/riechen** taste/smell of sth
- adverb
····> (zeitlich) **nach und nach** little by little; gradually. **nach wie vor** still

nachahm|en vt sep imitate. **N~ung** f -,-en imitation

Nachbar|(in) m -n,-n (f -,-nen) neighbour. **N~haus** nt house next door. **n~lich** adj neighbourly; (Nachbar-) neighbouring. **N~schaft** f - neighbourhood

nachbestell|en vt sep reorder. **N~ung** f repeat order

nachbild|en vt sep copy, reproduce. **N~ung** f copy, reproduction

nachdatieren vt sep backdate

nachdem conj after; **je n~** it depends

nachdenk|en† vi sep (haben) think (**über** + acc about). **n~lich** adj thoughtful

nachdrücklich adj emphatic

nacheinander adv one after the other

Nachfahre m **-n,-n** descendant

Nachfolg|e f succession. **N~er(in)** m **-s,-** (f **-,-nen**) successor

nachforsch|en vi sep (haben) make enquiries. **N~ung** f enquiry

Nachfrage f (Comm) demand. **n~n** vi sep (haben) enquire

nachfüllen vt sep refill

nachgeben† v sep ●vi (haben) give way: (sich fügen) give in, yield ●vt **jdm Suppe n~** give s.o. more soup

Nachgebühr f surcharge

nachgehen† vi sep (sein) (Uhr:) be slow; **jdm/etw n~** follow s.o./something; follow up (Spur, Angelegenheit); pursue (Angelegenheit)

Nachgeschmack m after-taste

nachgiebig adj indulgent; (gefällig) compliant. **N~keit** f - indulgence; compliance

nachgrübeln vi sep (haben) ponder (**über** + acc on)

nachhaltig adj lasting

nachhelfen† vi sep (haben) help

nachher adv later; (danach) afterwards; **bis n~!** see you later!

Nachhilfeunterricht m coaching

Nachhinein adv **im N~** afterwards

nachhinken vi sep (sein) (fig) lag behind

nachholen vt sep (später holen) fetch later; (mehr holen) get more; (später machen) do later; (aufholen) catch up on

Nachkomme m **-n,-n** descendant. **n~n**† vi sep (sein) follow [later], come later; **etw** (dat) **n~n** (fig) comply with (Bitte); carry out (Pflicht). **N~nschaft** f - descendants pl, progeny

Nachkriegszeit f post-war period

Nachlass m **-es,¨e** discount; (Jur) [deceased's] estate

nachlassen† v sep ●vi (haben) decrease; (Regen, Hitze:) let up; (Schmerz:) ease; (Sturm:) abate; (Augen, Leistungen:) deteriorate ●vt **etw vom Preis n~** take sth off the price

nachlässig adj careless; (leger) casual; (unordentlich) sloppy. **N~keit** f - carelessness; sloppiness

nachlesen† vt sep look up

nachlöse|n vi sep (haben) pay one's fare on the train/on arrival. **N~schalter** m excess-fare office

nachmachen vt sep (später machen) do later; (imitieren) imitate, copy; (fälschen) forge

Nachmittag m afternoon; **heute/gestern N~** this/yesterday afternoon. **n~s** adv in the afternoon

Nachnahme f **etw per N~ schicken** send sth cash on delivery or COD

Nachname m surname

n

Nachporto nt excess postage

nachprüfen vt sep check, verify

Nachricht f -,-en [piece of] news sg; **N~en** news sg; **eine N~ hinterlassen** leave a message; **jdm N~ geben** inform s.o. **N~endienst** m (Mil) intelligence service

nachrücken vi sep (sein) move up

Nachruf m obituary

nachsagen vt sep repeat (**jdm** after s.o.); **jdm Schlechtes/Gutes n~** speak ill/well of s.o.

Nachsaison f late season

nachschicken vt sep (später schicken) send later; (hinterher-) send after (**jdm** s.o.); send on (Post) (**jdm** to s.o.)

nachschlagen† v sep •vt look up •vi (haben) **in einem Wörterbuch n~en** consult a dictionary; **jdm n~en** take after s.o.

Nachschrift f transcript; (Nachsatz) postscript

Nachschub m (Mil) supplies pl

n

nachsehen† v sep •vt (prüfen) check; (nachschlagen) look up; (hinwegsehen über) overlook •vi (haben) have a look; (prüfen) check; **im Wörterbuch n~** consult a dictionary

nachsenden† vt sep forward (Post) (**jdm** to s.o.); '**bitte n~**' 'please forward'

nachsichtig adj forbearing; lenient; indulgent

Nachsilbe f suffix

nachsitzen† vi sep (haben) **n~ müssen** be kept in [after school]; **jdn n~ lassen** give s.o. detention. **N~** nt **-s** (Sch) detention

Nachspeise f dessert, sweet

nachsprechen† vt sep repeat (**jdm** after s.o.)

nachspülen vt sep rinse

nächst /-çst/ prep (+ dat) next to. **n~beste(r,s)** adj first [available]; (zweitbeste) next best. **n~e(r,s)** adj next; (nächstgelegene) nearest; (Verwandte) closest; **in n~er Nähe** close by; **am n~en sein** be nearest or closest •pron **der/die/das N~e (n~e)** the next; **der N~e (n~e) bitte** next please; **als N~es (n~es)** next; **fürs N~e (n~e)** for the time being. **N~e(r)** m fellow man

nachstehend adj following •adv below

Nächst|enliebe f charity. **n~ens** adv shortly. **n~gelegen** adj nearest

nachsuchen vi sep (haben) search; **n~ um** request

Nacht f -,¨e night; **über/bei N~** overnight/at night; **morgen N~** tomorrow night; **heute N~** tonight; (letzte Nacht) last night; **gestern N~** last night; (vorletzte Nacht) the night before last. **N~dienst** m night duty

Nachteil m disadvantage; **zum N~** to the detriment (gen of)

Nacht|falter m moth. **N~hemd** nt night-dress; (Männer-) night-shirt

Nachtigall f -,-en nightingale

Nachtisch m dessert

Nachtklub m night-club

nächtlich adj nocturnal, night

Nacht|lokal nt night-club. **N~mahl** nt (Aust) supper

Nachtrag m postscript; (Ergänzung) supplement. **n~en**† vt sep add; **jdm etw n~en** (fig) bear a grudge against s.o. for sth. **n~end** adj vindictive; **n~end sein** bear grudges

nachträglich adj subsequent, later; (verspätet) belated •adv later; (nachher) afterwards; (verspätet) belatedly

Nacht|ruhe f night's rest; **angenehme N~ruhe!** sleep well! **n~s** adv at night; **2 Uhr n~s** 2 o'clock in the morning. **N~schicht** f night-shift. **N~tisch** m bedside table. **N~tischlampe** f bedside lamp. **N~topf** m chamber-pot. **N~wächter** m night-watchman. **N~zeit** f night-time

Nachuntersuchung f check-up

Nachwahl f by-election

Nachweis m **-es,-e** proof. **n~bar** adj demonstrable. **n~en†** vt sep prove; (aufzeigen) show; (vermitteln) give details of; **jdm nichts n~en können** have no proof against s.o.

Nachwelt f posterity

Nachwirkung f after-effect

Nachwuchs m new generation; (!: Kinder) offspring. **N~spieler** m young player

nachzahlen vt/i sep (haben) pay extra; (später zahlen) pay later; **Steuern n~** pay tax arrears

nachzählen vt/i sep (haben) count again; (prüfen) check

Nachzahlung f extra/later payment; (Gehalts-) back-payment

nachzeichnen vt sep copy

Nachzügler m **-s,-** late-comer; (Zurückgebliebener) straggler

Nacken m **-s,-** nape or back of the neck

nackt adj naked; (bloß, kahl) bare; (Wahrheit) plain. **N~heit** f **-** nakedness, nudity. **N~kultur** f nudism. **N~schnecke** f slug

Nadel f **-,-n** needle; (Häkel-) hook; (Schmuck-, Hut-) pin. **N~arbeit** f needlework. **N~baum** m conifer. **N~stich** m stitch; (fig) pinprick. **N~wald** m coniferous forest

Nagel m **-s,¨** nail. **N~haut** f cuticle. **N~lack** m nail varnish. **n~n** vt nail. **n~neu** adj brand-new

nagen vt/i (haben) gnaw (**an** + dat at); **n~d** (fig) nagging

Nagetier nt rodent

nah adj, adv & prep = **nahe**

Näharbeit f sewing

Nahaufnahme f close-up

nahe adj nearby; (zeitlich) imminent; (eng) close; **der N~ Osten** the Middle East; **in n~r Zukunft** in the near future; **von n~m** [from] close to; **n~ sein** be close (dat to) •adv near, close; (verwandt) closely; **n~ an** (+ acc/dat) near [to], close to; **n~ daran sein, etw zu tun** nearly do sth; **n~ liegen** be close; (fig) be highly likely; **n~ legen** (fig) recommend (**dat** to); **jdm n~ legen, etw zu tun** urge s.o. to do sth; **jdm n~ gehen** (fig) affect s.o. deeply; **jdm zu n~ treten** (fig) offend s.o. •prep (+ dat) near [to], close to

Nähe f **-** nearness, proximity; **aus der N~** [from] close to; **in der N~** near or close by

nahe|gehen* vi sep (sein) = **n~ gehen**, s. **nahe**. **n~legen*** vt sep = **n~ legen**, s. **nahe**. **n~liegen*** vi sep (haben) = **n~ liegen**, s. **nahe**

nähen vt/i (haben) sew; (anfertigen) make; (Med) stitch [up]

näher adj closer; (Weg) shorter; (Einzelheiten) further •adv closer; (genauer) more closely; **n~ kommen** come closer; (fig) get closer (**dat** to); **sich n~ erkundigen** make further enquiries; **n~ an** (+ acc/dat) nearer [to], closer to •prep (+ dat) nearer [to], closer to. **N~e[s]** nt [further] details pl. **n~n (sich)** vr approach

nahezu adv almost

Nähgarn nt [sewing] cotton

Nahkampf m close combat

Näh|maschine f sewing machine. **N~nadel** f sewing-needle

nähren vt feed; (fig) nurture

nahrhaft adj nutritious

Nährstoff m nutrient

Nahrung f **-** food, nourishment. **N~smittel** nt food

Nährwert m nutritional value

Naht f **-,¨e** seam; (Med) suture. **n~los** adj seamless

Nahverkehr m local service

Nähzeug nt sewing; (Zubehör) sewing kit

naiv /na'i:f/ adj naïve. **N~ität** f **-** naïvety

Name m **-ns,-n** name; **im N~n** (+ gen) in the name of; (handeln) on behalf of. **n~nlos** adj nameless; (unbekannt) unknown, anonymous.

n

N~nstag m name-day. **N~nsvetter** m namesake. **N~nszug** m signature. **n~ntlich** adv by name; (besonders) especially

namhaft adj noted; (ansehnlich) considerable; **n~ machen** name

nämlich adv (und zwar) namely; (denn) because

Nanotechnologie f nanotechnology

nanu int hallo

Napf m **-[e]s,⸚e** bowl

Narbe f **-,-n** scar

Narkose f **-,-n** general anaesthetic. **N~arzt** m anaesthetist. **N~mittel** nt anaesthetic

Narr m **-en,-en** fool; **zum N~en halten** make a fool of. **n~en** vt fool

Närr|in f **-,-nen** fool. **n~isch** adj foolish; (!: verrückt) crazy (**auf** + acc about)

Narzisse f **-,-n** narcissus

naschen vt/i (haben) nibble (**an** + dat at)

n

Nase f **-,-n** nose

näseln vi (haben) speak through one's nose; **n~d** nasal

Nasen|bluten nt **-s** nosebleed. **N~loch** nt nostril

Nashorn nt rhinoceros

nass adj wet

Nässe f **-** wet; wetness. **n~n** vt wet

Nation /na'tsi̯o:n/ f **-,-en** nation. **n~al** adj national. **N~alhymne** f national anthem. **N~alismus** m **-** nationalism. **N~alität** f **-,-en** nationality. **N~alspieler** m international

Natrium nt **-s** sodium

Natron nt **-s doppeltkohlensaures N~** bicarbonate of soda

Natter f **-,-n** snake; (Gift-) viper

Natur f **-,-en** nature; **von N~ aus** by nature. **n~alisieren** vt naturalize. **N~alisierung** f **-,-en** naturalization

see A-Z of German life and culture

Naturell nt **-s,-e** disposition

Natur|erscheinung f natural phenomenon. **N~forscher** m naturalist. **N~heilkunde** f natural medicine. **N~kunde** f natural history

natürlich adj natural • adv naturally; (selbstverständlich) of course. **N~keit** f **-** naturalness

natur|rein adj pure. **N~schutz** m nature conservation; **unter N~schutz stehen** be protected. **N~schutzgebiet** nt nature reserve. **N~wissenschaft** f [natural] science. **N~wissenschaftler** m scientist

nautisch adj nautical

Navigation /-'tsi̯o:n/ f **-** navigation

Nazi m **-s,-s** Nazi

n.Chr. abbr (**nach Christus**) AD

Nebel m **-s,-** fog; (leicht) mist

neben prep (+ dat/acc) next to, beside; (+ dat) (außer) apart from. **n~an** adv next door

Neben|anschluss m (Teleph) extension. **N~ausgaben** fpl incidental expenses

nebenbei adv in addition; (beiläufig) casually

Neben|bemerkung f passing remark. **N~beruf** m second job

nebeneinander adv next to each other, side by side

Neben|eingang m side entrance. **N~fach** nt (Univ) subsidiary subject. **N~fluss** m tributary

nebenher adv in addition

nebenhin adv casually

Neben|höhle f sinus. **N~kosten** pl additional costs. **N~produkt** nt by-product. **N~rolle** f supporting role; (Kleine) minor role. **N~sache** f unimportant matter. **n~sächlich** adj unimportant. **N~satz** m subordinate clause. **N~straße** f minor road; (Seiten-) side street. **N~wirkung** f side-effect. **N~zimmer** nt room next door

neblig adj foggy; (leicht) misty

neck|en vt tease. **N~erei** f -

teasing. **n∼isch** adj teasing

Neffe m **-n,-n** nephew

negativ adj negative. **N∼** nt **-s,-e** (Phot) negative

Neger m **-s,-** Negro

nehmen† vt take (dat from); **sich** (dat) **etw n∼** take sth; help oneself to (Essen)

Neid m **-[e]s** envy, jealousy. **n∼isch** adj envious, jealous (**auf** + acc of); **auf jdn n∼isch sein** envy s.o.

neig|en vt incline; (zur Seite) tilt; (beugen) bend; **sich n∼en** incline; (Boden:) slope; (Person:) bend (**über** + acc over) • vi (haben) **n∼en zu** (fig) have a tendency towards; be prone to (Krankheit); incline towards (Ansicht); **dazu n∼en, etw zu tun** tend to do sth. **N∼ung** f **-,-en** inclination; (Gefälle) slope; (fig) tendency

nein adv, **N∼** nt **-s** no

Nektar m **-s** nectar

Nelke f **-,-n** carnation; (Culin) clove

nenn|en† vt call; (taufen) name; (angeben) give; (erwähnen) mention; **sich n∼en** call oneself. **n∼enswert** adj significant

Neon nt **-s** neon. **N∼beleuchtung** f fluorescent lighting

Nerv m **-s,-en** nerve; **die N∼en verlieren** lose control of oneself. **n∼en** vt **jdn n∼en** ☒ get on s.o.'s nerves. **N∼enarzt** m neurologist. **n∼enaufreibend** adj nerve-racking. **N∼enkitzel** m ⓘ thrill. **N∼ensystem** nt nervous system. **N∼enzusammenbruch** m nervous breakdown

nervös adj nervy, edgy; (Med) nervous; **n∼ sein** be on edge

Nervosität f **-** nerviness, edginess

Nerz m **-es,-e** mink

Nessel f **-,-n** nettle

Nest nt **-[e]s,-er** nest; (ⓘ: Ort) small place

nett adj nice; (freundlich) kind

netto adv net

Netz nt **-es,-e** net; (Einkaufs-) string bag; (Spinnen-) web; (auf Landkarte) grid; (System) network; (Electr) mains pl. **N∼haut** f retina. **N∼karte** f area season ticket. **N∼werk** nt network

neu adj new; (modern) modern; **wie neu** as good as new; **das ist mir neu** it's news to me; **von n∼em** all over again • adv newly; (gerade erst) only just; (erneut) again; **etw neu schreiben** rewrite sth; **neu vermähltes Paar** newly-weds pl. **N∼auflage** f new edition; (unverändert) reprint. **N∼bau** m (pl **-ten**) new house/building

Neu|e(r) m/f new person, newcomer; (Schüler) new boy/girl. **N∼e(s)** nt **das N∼e** the new; **etwas N∼es** something new; (Neuigkeit) a piece of news; **was gibt's N∼es?** what's the news?

neuerdings adv [just] recently

neuest|e(r,s) adj newest; (letzte) latest; **seit n∼em** just recently. **N∼e** nt **das N∼e** the latest thing: (Neuigkeit) the latest news sg

neugeboren adj newborn

Neugier, **Neugierde** f **-** curiosity; (Wissbegierde) inquisitiveness

neugierig adj curious (**auf** + acc about); (wissbegierig) inquisitive

Neuheit f **-,-en** novelty; newness

Neuigkeit f **-,-en** piece of news; **N∼en** news sg

Neujahr nt New Year's Day; **über N∼** over the New Year

neulich adv the other day

Neumond m new moon

neun inv adj, **N∼** f **-,-en** nine. **n∼te(r,s)** adj ninth. **n∼zehn** inv adj nineteen. **n∼zehnte(r,s)** adj nineteenth. **n∼zig** inv adj ninety. **n∼zigste(r,s)** adj ninetieth

Neuralgie f **-,-n** neuralgia

neureich adj nouveau riche

Neurologe m **-n,-n** neurologist

Neurose f **-,-n** neurosis

Neuschnee m fresh snow

Neuseeland nt **-s** New Zealand

neuste(r,s) adj = **neueste(r,s)**

neutral adj neutral. **N~ität** f - neutrality

Neutrum nt **-s,-tra** neuter noun

neu|vermählt* adj **n~ vermählt**, s. **neu. N~zeit** f modern times pl

nicht adv not; **ich kann n~** I cannot or can't; **er ist n~ gekommen** he hasn't come; **bitte n~!** please don't! **n~ berühren!** do not touch! **du kennst ihn doch, n~?** you do know him, don't you?

Nichte f **-,-n** niece

Nichtraucher m non-smoker

nichts pron & a nothing; **n~ mehr** no more; **n~ ahnend** unsuspecting; **n~ sagend** meaningless; (uninteressant) nondescript. **N~** nt - nothingness; (fig: Leere) void

Nichtschwimmer m non-swimmer

nichts|nutzig adj good-for-nothing; (!: unartig) naughty. **n~sagend*** adj **n~ sagend**, s. **nichts. N~tun** nt **-s** idleness

n

Nickel nt **-s** nickel

nicken vi (haben) nod

Nickerchen nt **-s,-**, ! nap

nie adv never

nieder adj low • adv down. **n~brennen**† vt/i sep (sein) burn down. **N~deutsch** nt Low German. **N~gang** m (fig) decline. **n~gedrückt** adj (fig) depressed. **n~geschlagen** adj dejected, despondent. **N~kunft** f **-,¨e** confinement. **N~lage** f defeat

Niederlande (die) pl the Netherlands

Niederländ|er m **-s,-** Dutchman; **die N~er** the Dutch pl. **N~erin** f **-,-nen** Dutchwoman. **n~isch** adj Dutch

nieder|lassen† vt sep let down; **sich n~lassen** settle; (sich setzen) sit down. **N~lassung** f **-,-en** settlement; (Zweigstelle) branch. **n~legen** vt sep put or lay down; resign (Amt); **die Arbeit n~legen** go on strike. **n~metzeln** vt sep massacre. **N~sachsen** nt Lower Saxony. **N~schlag** m precipitation; (Regen) rainfall; (radioaktiver) fallout. **n~schlagen**† vt sep knock down; lower (Augen); (unterdrücken) crush. **n~schmettern** vt sep (fig) shatter. **n~setzen** vt sep put or set down; **sich n~setzen** sit down. **n~strecken** vt sep fell; (durch Schuss) gun down. **n~trächtig** adj base, vile. **n~walzen** vt sep flatten

niedlich adj pretty; sweet

niedrig adj low; (fig: gemein) base • adv low

niemals adv never

niemand pron nobody, no one

Niere f **-,-n** kidney; **künstliche N~** kidney machine

niesel|n vi (haben) drizzle. **N~regen** m drizzle

niesen vi (haben) sneeze. **N~** nt **-s** sneezing; (Nieser) sneeze

Niete[1] f **-,-n** rivet; (an Jeans) stud

Niete[2] f **-,-n** blank; ! failure

nieten vt rivet

Nikotin nt **-s** nicotine

Nil m **-[s]** Nile. **N~pferd** nt hippopotamus

nimmer adv (SGer) not any more; **nie und n~** never

nirgend|s, n~wo adv nowhere

Nische f **-,-n** recess, niche

nisten vi (haben) nest

Nitrat nt **-[e]s,-e** nitrate

Niveau /ni'vo:/ nt **-s,-s** level; (geistig, künstlerisch) standard

nix adv ! nothing

Nixe f **-,-n** mermaid

nobel adj noble; (!: luxuriös) luxurious; (!: großzügig) generous

noch adv still; (zusätzlich) as well; (mit Komparativ) even; **n~ nicht** not yet; **gerade n~** only just; **n~ immer** od **immer n~** still; **n~ letzte Woche** only last week; **wer n~?** who else? **n~ etwas** something else;

(Frage) anything else? **n~ einmal** again; **n~ ein Bier** another beer; **n~ größer** even bigger; **n~ so sehr** however much •conj **weder n~** ... neither nor ...

nochmals adv again

Nomad|e m **-n,-n** nomad. **n~isch** adj nomadic

nominier|en vt nominate. **N~ung** f **-,-en** nomination

Nonne f **-,-n** nun. **N~nkloster** nt convent

Nonstopflug m direct flight

Nord m **-[e]s** north. **N~amerika** nt North America

Norden m **-s** north

nordisch adj Nordic

nördlich adj northern; (Richtung) northerly •adv & prep (+ gen) **n~ [von] der Stadt** [to the] north of the town

Nordosten m north-east

Nord|pol m North Pole. **N~see** f **-** North Sea. **N~westen** m north-west

Nörgelei f **-,-en** grumbling

nörgeln vi (haben) grumble

Norm f **-,-en** norm; (Techn) standard; (Soll) quota

normal adj normal. **n~erweise** adv normally

normen vt standardize

Norwe|gen nt **-s** Norway. **N~ger(in)** m **-s,-** (f **-,-nen**) Norwegian. **n~gisch** adj Norwegian

Nost|algie f **-** nostalgia. **n~algisch** adj nostalgic

Not f **-,¨e** need; (Notwendigkeit) necessity; (Entbehrung) hardship; (seelisch) trouble; **Not leiden** be in need, suffer hardship; **Not leidende Menschen** needy people; **zur Not** if need be; (äußerstenfalls) at a pinch

Notar m **-s,-e** notary public

Not|arzt m emergency doctor. **N~ausgang** m emergency exit. **N~behelf** m **-[e]s,-e** makeshift. **N~bremse** f emergency brake. **N~dienst** m **N~dienst haben** be on call

Note f **-,-n** note; (Zensur) mark; **ganze/halbe N~** (Mus) semi-breve/minim; **N~n lesen** read music; **persönliche N~** personal touch. **N~nblatt** nt sheet of music. **N~nschlüssel** m clef

Notfall m emergency; **für den N~** just in case. **n~s** adv if need be

notieren vt note down; (Comm) quote; **sich** (dat) **etw n~** make a note of sth

nötig adj necessary; **n~ haben** need; **das N~ste** the essentials pl •adv urgently. **n~enfalls** adv if need be. **N~ung** f **-** coercion

Notiz f **-,-en** note; (Zeitungs-) item; **[keine] N~ nehmen von** take [no] notice of. **N~buch** nt notebook. **N~kalender** m diary

Not|lage f plight. **n~landen** vi (sein) make a forced landing. **N~landung** f forced landing. **n~leidend*** adj = **Not leidend**, s. **Not. N~lösung** f stopgap

Not|ruf m emergency call; (Naut, Aviat) distress call; (Nummer) emergency services number. **N~signal** nt distress signal. **N~stand** m state of emergency. **N~unterkunft** f emergency accommodation. **N~wehr** f **-** (Jur) self-defence

notwendig adj necessary; essential •adv urgently. **N~keit** f **-,-en** necessity

Notzucht f **-** (Jur) rape

Nougat /'nu:gat/ m & nt **-s** nougat

Novelle f **-,-n** novella; (Pol) amendment

November m **-s,-** November

Novize m **-n,-n, Novizin** f **-,-nen** (Relig) novice

Nu m **im Nu** [!] in a flash

nüchtern adj sober; (sachlich) matter-of-fact; (schmucklos) bare; (ohne Würze) bland; **auf n~en Magen** on an empty stomach

Nudel f **-,-n** piece of pasta; **N~n**

n

pasta sg; (Band-) noodles. **N~holz** nt rolling-pin

Nudist m **-en,-en** nudist

nuklear adj nuclear

null inv adj zero, nought; (Teleph) O; (Sport) nil; (Tennis) love; **n~ Fehler** no mistakes; **n~ und nichtig** (Jur) null and void. **N~** f **-,-en** nought, zero; (fig: Person) nonentity. **N~punkt** m zero

numerieren* vt = **nummerieren**

Nummer f **-,-n** number; (Ausgabe) issue; (Darbietung) item; (Zirkus-) act; (Größe) size. **n~ieren** vt number. **N~nschild** nt number-plate

nun adv now; (na) well; (halt) just; **nun gut!** very well then!

nur adv only, just; **wo kann sie nur sein?** wherever can she be? **er soll es nur versuchen!** just let him try!

Nürnberg nt **-s** Nuremberg

nuscheln vt/i (haben) mumble

Nuss f **-,⸚e** nut. **N~knacker** m **-s,-** nutcrackers pl

Nüstern fpl nostrils

Nut f **-,-en**, **Nute** f **-,-n** groove

Nutte f **-,-n** ☒ tart ☒

nutz|bar adj usable; **n~bar machen** utilize; cultivate (Boden). **n~bringend** adj profitable

nutzen vt use, utilize; (aus-) take advantage of • vi (haben) = **nützen. N~** m **-s** benefit; (Comm) profit; **N~ ziehen aus** benefit from; **von N~ sein** be useful

nützen vi (haben) be useful or of use (dat to); (Mittel:) be effective; **nichts n~** be useless or no use; **was nützt mir das?** what good is that to me? • vt = **nutzen**

nützlich adj useful. **N~keit** f - usefulness

nutz|los adj useless; (vergeblich) vain. **N~losigkeit** f - uselessness. **N~ung** f - use, utilization

Nylon /ˈnailɔn/ nt **-s** nylon

Nymphe /ˈnʏmfə/ f **-,-n** nymph

Oo

o int **o ja/nein!** oh yes/no!

Oase f **-,-n** oasis

ob conj whether; **ob reich, ob arm** rich or poor; **und ob**! ⊡ you bet!

Obacht f **O~ geben** pay attention; **O~**! look out!

Obdach nt **-[e]s** shelter. **o~los** adj homeless. **O~lose(r)** m/f homeless person; **die O~losen** the homeless pl

Obduktion /-ˈtsi̯oːn/ f **-,-en** post-mortem

O-Beine ntpl ⊡ bow-legs, bandy legs

oben adv at the top; (auf der Oberseite) on top; (eine Treppe hoch) upstairs; (im Text) above; **da o~** up there; **o~ im Norden** up in the north; **siehe o~** see above; **o~ auf** (+ acc/dat) on top of; **nach o~** up[wards]; (die Treppe hinauf) upstairs; **von o~** from above/upstairs; **von o~ bis unten** from top to bottom/(Person) to toe; **jdn von o~ bis unten mustern** look s.o. up and down; **o~ erwähnt** od **genannt** above-mentioned. **o~drein** adv on top of that

Ober m **-s,-** waiter

Ober|arm m upper arm. **O~arzt** m ≈ senior registrar. **O~deck** nt upper deck. **o~e(r,s)** adj upper; (höhere) higher. **O~fläche** f surface. **o~flächlich** adj superficial. **O~geschoss** nt upper storey. **o~halb** adv & prep (+ gen) above. **O~haupt** nt (fig) head.

O~haus nt (Pol) upper house; (in UK) House of Lords. **O~hemd** nt [man's] shirt. **o~irdisch** adj surface • adv above ground. **O~kiefer** m upper jaw. **O~körper** m upper part of the body. **O~leutnant** m lieutenant. **O~lippe** f upper lip

Obers nt - (Aust) cream

Ober|schenkel m thigh. **O~schule** f grammar school. **O~seite** f upper/(rechte Seite) right side

Oberst m **-en** & **-s,-en** colonel

oberste(r,s) adj top; (höchste) highest; (Befehlshaber, Gerichtshof) supreme; (wichtigste) first

Ober|stimme f treble. **O~teil** nt top. **O~weite** f chest/(der Frau) bust size

obgleich conj although

Obhut f - care

obig adj above

Objekt nt **-[e]s,-e** object; (Haus, Grundstück) property

Objektiv nt **-s,-e** lens. **o~** adj objective. **O~ität** f - objectivity

Oblate f **-,-n** (Relig) wafer

Obmann m (pl **-männer**) [jury] foreman; (Sport) referee

Oboe /o'bo:ə/ f **-,-n** oboe

Obrigkeit f - authorities pl

obschon conj although

Observatorium nt **-s,-ien** observatory

obskur adj obscure; dubious

Obst nt **-es** (coll) fruit. **O~baum** m fruit-tree. **O~garten** m orchard. **O~händler** m fruiterer

obszön adj obscene

O-Bus m trolley bus

obwohl conj although

Ochse m **-n,-n** ox

öde adj desolate; (unfruchtbar) barren; (langweilig) dull. **Öde** f - desolation; barrenness; dullness

oder conj or; **du kennst ihn doch, o~?** you know him, don't you?

Ofen m **-s,⸚** stove; (Heiz-) heater; (Back-) oven; (Techn) furnace

offen adj open; (Haar) loose; (Flamme) naked; (o~herzig) frank; (o~ gezeigt) overt; (unentschieden) unsettled; **o~e Stelle** vacancy; **Wein o~ verkaufen** sell wine by the glass; **o~ bleiben** remain open; **o~ halten** hold open (Tür); keep open (Mund, Augen); **o~ lassen** leave open; leave vacant (Stelle); **o~ stehen** be open; (Rechnung:) be outstanding; **jdm o~ stehen** (fig) be open to s.o.; adv **o~ gesagt** od **gestanden** to be honest. **o~bar** adj obvious • adv apparently. **o~baren** vt reveal. **O~barung** f **-,-en** revelation. **O~heit** f - frankness, openness. **o~sichtlich** adj obvious

offenstehen* vi sep (haben) = **offen stehen**, s. **offen**

öffentlich adj public. **Ö~keit** f - public; **in aller Ö~keit** in public, publicly

Offerte f **-,-n** (Comm) offer

offiziell adj official

Offizier m **-s,-e** (Mil) officer

öffn|en vt/i (haben) open; **sich ö~en** open. **Ö~er** m **-s,-** opener. **Ö~ung** f **-,-en** opening. **Ö~ungszeiten** fpl opening hours

oft adv often

öfter adv quite often. **ö~e(r,s)** adj frequent; **des Ö~en (ö~en)** frequently. **ö~s** adv [!] quite often

oh int oh!

ohne prep (+ acc) without; **o~ mich!** count me out! **oben o~** topless • conj **o~ zu überlegen** without thinking; **o~ dass ich es merkte** without my noticing it. **o~dies** adv anyway. **o~gleichen** pred adj unparalleled. **o~hin** adv anyway

Ohn|macht f **-,-en** faint; (fig) powerlessness; **in O~macht fallen** faint. **o~mächtig** adj unconscious; (fig) powerless; **o~mächtig werden** faint

Ohr nt **-[e]s,-en** ear

Öhr nt **-[e]s,-e** eye (of needle)

Ohrenschmalz nt ear-wax. **O~schmerzen** mpl earache sg

Ohrfeige f slap in the face. **o~n** vt **jdn o~n** slap s.o.'s face

Ohr|läppchen nt **-s,-** ear-lobe. **O~ring** m ear-ring. **O~wurm** m earwig

oje int oh dear!

okay /o'ke:/ adj & adv [!] OK

Öko|logie f **-** ecology. **ö~logisch** adj ecological. **Ö~nomie** f **-** economy; (Wissenschaft) economics sg. **ö~nomisch** adj economic; (sparsam) economical

Oktave f **-,-n** octave

Oktober m **-s,-** October

ökumenisch adj ecumenical

Öl nt **-[e]s,-e** oil; **in Öl malen** paint in oils. **Ölbaum** m olivetree. **ölen** vt oil. **Ölfarbe** f oil-paint. **Ölfeld** nt oilfield. **Ölgemälde** nt oil-painting. **ölig** adj oily

Oliv|e f **-,-n** olive. **O~enöl** nt olive oil

Ölmessstab m dip-stick. **Ölsardinen** fpl sardines in oil. **Ölstand** m oil-level. **Öltanker** m oil-tanker. **Ölteppich** m oil-slick

Olympiade f **-,-n** Olympic Games pl, Olympics pl

Olymp|iasieger(in) /o'lympi̯a-/ m(f) Olympic champion. **o~isch** adj Olympic; **O~ische Spiele** Olympic Games

Ölzeug nt oilskins pl

Oma f **-,-s** [!] granny

Omnibus m bus; (Reise-) coach

onanieren vi (haben) masturbate

Onkel m **-s,-** uncle

Opa m **-s,-s** [!] grandad

Opal m **-s,-e** opal

Oper f **-,-n** opera

Operation /-'tsi̯o:n/ f **-,-en** operation. **O~ssaal** m operating theatre

Operette f **-,-n** operetta

operieren vt operate on (Patient, Herz); **sich o~ lassen** have an operation •vi (haben) operate

Opernglas nt opera-glasses pl

Opfer nt **-s,-** sacrifice; (eines Unglücks) victim; **ein O~ bringen** make a sacrifice; **jdm/etw zum O~ fallen** fall victim to s.o./something. **o~n** vt sacrifice

Opium nt **-s** opium

Opposition /-'tsi̯o:n/ f **-** opposition. **O~spartei** f opposition party

Optik f **-** optics sg, ([!]: Objektiv) lens. **O~er** m **-s,-** optician

optimal adj optimum

Optimis|mus m **-** optimism. **O~t** m **-en,-en** optimist. **o~tisch** adj optimistic

optisch adj optical; (Eindruck) visual

Orakel nt **-s,-** oracle

Orange /o'rã:ʒə/ f **-,-n** orange. **o~** inv adj orange. **O~ade** f **-,-n** orangeade. **O~nmarmelade** f [orange] marmalade

Oratorium nt **-s,-ien** oratorio

Orchester /ɔr'kɛstɐ/ nt **-s,-** orchestra

Orchidee /ɔrçi'de:ə/ f **-,-n** orchid

Orden m **-s,-** (Ritter-, Kloster-) order; (Auszeichnung) medal, decoration

ordentlich adj neat, tidy; (anständig) respectable; (ordnungsgemäß, fam: richtig) proper; (Mitglied, Versammlung) ordinary; ([!]: gut) decent; ([!]: gehörig) good

Order f **-,-s & -n** order

ordinär adj common

Ordination /-'tsi̯o:n/ f **-,-en** (Relig) ordination; (Aust) surgery

ordn|en vt put in order; tidy; (an-) arrange. **O~er** m **-s,-** steward; (Akten-) file

Ordnung f **-** order; **O~ machen** tidy up; **in O~ bringen** put in order; (aufräumen) tidy; (reparieren) mend; (fig) put right; **in O~ sein**

be in order; (ordentlich sein) be tidy; (fig) be all right; **[geht] in O~!** OK! **o~sgemäß** adj proper. **O~sstrafe** f (Jur) fine. **o~swidrig** adj improper

Ordonnanz, **Ordonanz** f -,-en (Mil) orderly

Organ nt **-s,-e** organ; voice

Organisation /-'tsio:n/ f **-,-en** organization

organisch adj organic

organisieren vt organize; ((!): beschaffen) get [hold of]

Organismus m **-,-men** organism; (System) system

Organspenderkarte f donor card

Orgasmus m **-,-men** orgasm

Orgel f **-,-n** (Mus) organ. **O~pfeife** f organ-pipe

Orgie /'ɔrgiə/ f **-,-n** orgy

Orien|t /'o:riɛnt/ m **-s** Orient. **o~talisch** adj Oriental

orientier|en /oriɛn'ti:rən/ vt inform (**über** + acc about); **sich o~en** get one's bearings, orientate oneself; (unterrichten) inform oneself (**über** + acc about). **O~ung** f - orientation; **die O~ung verlieren** lose one's bearings

original adj original. **O~** nt **-s,-e** original. **O~übertragung** f live transmission

originell adj original; (eigenartig) unusual

Orkan m **-s,-e** hurricane

Ornament nt **-[e]s,-e** ornament

Ort m **-[e]s,-e** place; (Ortschaft) [small] town; **am Ort** locally; **am Ort des Verbrechens** at the scene of the crime

ortho|dox adj orthodox. **O~graphie**, **O~grafie** f - spelling. **O~päde** m **-n,-n** orthopaedic specialist

örtlich adj local

Ortschaft f **-,-en** [small] town; (Dorf) village; **geschlossene O~** (Auto) built-up area

Orts|gespräch nt (Teleph) local call. **O~verkehr** m local traffic. **O~zeit** f local time

Öse f **-,-n** eyelet; (Schlinge) loop; **Haken und Öse** hook and eye

Ost m **-[e]s** east

Osten m **-s** east; **nach O~** east

ostentativ adj pointed

Osteopath m **-en,-en** osteopath

Oster|ei /'o:stɐ?ai/ nt Easter egg. **O~fest** nt Easter. **O~glocke** f daffodil. **O~n** nt **-,-** Easter; **frohe O~n!** happy Easter!

Österreich nt **-s** Austria. **Ö~er** m, **-s,-**, **Ö~erin** f **-,-nen** Austrian. **ö~isch** adj Austrian

östlich adj eastern; (Richtung) easterly • adv & prep (+ gen) **ö~ [von] der Stadt** [to the] east of the town

Ostsee f Baltic [Sea]

Otter[1] m **-s,-** otter

Otter[2] f **-,-n** adder

Ouverture /uvɛr'ty:rə/ f **-,-n** overture

oval adj oval. **O~** nt **-s,-e** oval

Oxid, **Oxyd** nt **-[e]s,-e** oxide

Ozean m **-s,-e** ocean

Ozon nt **-s** ozone. **O~loch** nt hole in the ozone layer. **O~schicht** f ozone layer

Pp

paar pron inv **ein p~** a few; **ein p~ Mal** a few times; **alle p~ Tage** every few days. **P~** nt **-[e]s,-e** pair; (Ehe-, Liebes-) couple. **p~en** vt mate; (verbinden) combine; **sich p~en** mate. **P~ung** f **-,-en** mating. **p~weise** adv in pairs, in twos

Pacht f **-,-en** lease; (P~summe) rent. **p~en** vt lease

Pächter m **-s,-** lessee; (eines Hofes) tenant

Pachtvertrag m lease

Päckchen nt **-s,-** package, small packet

pack|en vt/i (haben) pack; (ergreifen) seize; (fig: fesseln) grip. **P~en** m **-s,-** bundle. **p~end** adj (fig) gripping. **P~papier** nt [strong] wrapping paper. **P~ung** f **-,-en** packet; (Med) pack

Pädagog|e m **-n,-n** educationalist; (Lehrer) teacher. **P~ik** f **-** educational science

Paddel nt **-s,-** paddle. **P~boot** nt canoe. **p~n** vt/i (haben/sein) paddle. **P~sport** m canoeing

Page /'pa:ʒə/ m **-n,-n** page

Paillette /pai'jɛtə/ f **-,-n** sequin

Paket nt **-[e]s,-e** packet; (Post-) parcel

Pakist|an nt **-s** Pakistan. **P~aner(in)** m **-s,-** (f **-,-nen**) Pakistani. **p~anisch** adj Pakistani

Palast m **-[e]s,¨e** palace

Paläst|ina nt **-s** Palestine. **P~inenser(in)** m **-s,-** (f **-,-nen**) Palestinian. **p~inensisch** adj Palestinian

Palette f **-,-n** palette

Palme f **-,-n** palm[-tree]

Pampelmuse f **-,-n** grapefruit

Panier|mehl nt (Culin) breadcrumbs pl. **p~t** adj (Culin) breaded

Panik f **-** panic

Panne f **-,-n** breakdown; (Reifen-) flat tyre; (Missgeschick) mishap

Panter, **Panther** m **-s,-** panther

Pantine f **-,-n** [wooden] clog

Pantoffel m **-s,-n** slipper; mule

Pantomime[1] f **-,-n** mime

Pantomime[2] m **-n,-n** mime artist

Panzer m **-s,-** armour; (Mil) tank; (Zool) shell. **p~n** vt armourplate. **P~schrank** m safe

Papa /'papa, pa'pa:/ m **-s,-s** daddy

Papagei m **-s & -en,-en** parrot

Papier nt **-[e]s,-e** paper. **P~korb** m waste-paper basket. **P~schlange** f streamer. **P~waren** fpl stationery sg

Pappe f **-** cardboard

Pappel f **-,-n** poplar

pappig adj [!] sticky

Papp|karton m, **P~schachtel** f cardboard box

Paprika m **-s,-[s]** [sweet] pepper; (Gewürz) paprika

Papst m **-[e]s,¨e** pope

päpstlich adj papal

Parade f **-,-n** parade

Paradies nt **-es,-e** paradise

Paraffin nt **-s** paraffin

Paragraf, **Paragraph** m **-en,-en** section

parallel adj & adv parallel. **P~e** f **-,-n** parallel

Paranuss f Brazil nut

Parasit m **-en,-en** parasite

parat adj ready

Parcours /par'ku:ɐ̯/ m -,- /-[s],-s/ (Sport) course

Pardon /par'dõ:/ int sorry!

Parfüm nt -s,-e & -s perfume, scent. **p~iert** adj perfumed, scented

parieren vi (haben) ! obey

Park m -s,-s park. **p~en** vt/i (haben) park. **P~en** nt -s parking; **'P~en verboten'** 'no parking'

Parkett nt -[e]s, -e parquet floor; (Theat) stalls pl

Park|haus nt multi-storey car park. **P~kralle** f wheel clamp. **P~lücke** f parking space. **P~platz** m car park; parking space. **P~scheibe** f parking-disc. **P~schein** m car-park ticket. **P~uhr** f parking-meter. **P~verbot** nt parking ban; **'P~verbot'** 'no parking'

Parlament nt -[e]s,-e parliament. **p~arisch** adj parliamentary

Parodie f -,-n parody

Parole f -,-n slogan; (Mil) password

Partei f -,-en (Pol, Jur) party; (Miet-) tenant; **für jdn P~ ergreifen** take s.o.'s part. **p~isch** adj biased

Parterre /par'tɛr/ nt -s,-s ground floor; (Theat) rear stalls pl

Partie f -,-n part; (Tennis, Schach) game; (Golf) round; (Comm) batch; **eine gute P~ machen** marry well

Partikel nt -s,- particle

Partitur f -,-en (Mus) full score

Partizip nt -s,-ien participle

Partner|(in) m -s,- (f -,-nen) partner. **P~schaft** f -,-en partnership. **P~stadt** f twin town

Party /'pa:ɐ̯ti/ f -,-s party

Parzelle f -,-n plot [of ground]

Pass m -es,¨e passport; (Geog, Sport) pass

Passage /pa'sa:ʒə/ f -,-n passage; (Einkaufs-) shopping arcade

Passagier /pasa'ʒi:ɐ̯/ m -s,-e passenger

Passant(in) m -en,-en (f -,-nen) passer-by

Passe f -,-n yoke

passen vi (haben) fit; (geeignet sein) be right (**für** for); (Sport) pass the ball; (aufgeben) pass; **p~ zu go** [well] with; (übereinstimmen) match; **jdm p~** fit s.o.; (gelegen sein) suit s.o.; **[ich] passe** pass. **p~d** adj suitable; (angemessen) appropriate; (günstig) convenient; (übereinstimmend) matching

passier|en vt pass; cross (Grenze); (Culin) rub through a sieve • vi (sein) happen (**jdm** to s.o.); **es ist ein Unglück p~t** there has been an accident. **P~schein** m pass

Passiv nt -s,-e (Gram) passive

Passstraße f pass

Paste f -,-n paste

Pastell nt -[e]s,-e pastel

Pastete f -,-n pie; (Gänseleber-) pâté

pasteurisieren /pastøri'zi:rən/ vt pasteurize

Pastor m -s,-en pastor

Pate m -n,-n godfather; (fig) sponsor; **P~n** godparents. **P~nkind** nt godchild

Patent nt -[e]s,-e patent; (Offiziers-) commission. **p~** adj ! clever; (Person) resourceful. **p~ieren** vt patent

Pater m -s,- (Relig) Father

Patholog|e m -n,-n pathologist. **p~isch** adj pathological

Patience /pa'si̯ã:s/ f -,-n patience

Patient(in) /pa'tsi̯ɛnt(ɪn)/ m -en,-en (f -,-nen) patient

Patin f -,-nen godmother

Patriot|(in) m -en,-en (f -,-nen) patriot. **p~isch** adj patriotic. **P~ismus** m - patriotism

Patrone f -,-n cartridge

Patrouille /pa'trʊljə/ f -,-n patrol

Patsch|e f **in der P~e sitzen** ! be in a jam. **p~nass** adj ! soaking wet

Patt nt -s stalemate

Patz|er m -s,- ! slip. **p~ig** adj ! insolent

P

Pauk|e f -,-n kettledrum; **auf die P~e hauen** [!] have a good time; (prahlen) boast. **p~en** vt/i (haben) [!] swot

pauschal adj all-inclusive; (einheitlich) flat-rate; (fig) sweeping (Urteil); **p~e Summe** lump sum. **P~e** f -,-n lump sum. **P~reise** f package tour. **P~summe** f lump sum

Pause[1] f -,-n break; (beim Sprechen) pause; (Theat) interval; (im Kino) intermission; (Mus) rest; **P~ machen** have a break

Pause[2] f -,-n tracing. **p~n** vt trace

pausenlos adj incessant

pausieren vi (haben) have a break; (ausruhen) rest

Pauspapier nt tracing-paper

Pavian m -s,-e baboon

Pavillon /'pavɪljõ/ m -s,-s pavilion

Pazifi|k m -s Pacific [Ocean]. **p~sch** adj Pacific

Pazifist m -en,-en pacifist

Pech nt -s pitch; (Unglück) bad luck; **P~ haben** be unlucky

Pedal nt -s,-e pedal

Pedant m -en,-en pedant

Pediküre f -,-n pedicure

Pegel m -s,- level; (Gerät) water-level indicator. **P~stand** m [water] level

peilen vt take a bearing on

peinigen vt torment

peinlich adj embarrassing, awkward; (genau) scrupulous; **es war mir sehr p~** I was very embarrassed

Peitsche f -,-n whip. **p~n** vt whip; (fig) lash • vi (sein) lash (**an** + acc against). **P~nhieb** m lash

Pelikan m -s,-e pelican

Pell|e f -,-n skin. **p~en** vt peel; shell (Ei); **sich p~en** peel

Pelz m -es,-e fur

Pendel nt -s,- pendulum. **p~n** vi (haben) swing • vi (sein) commute. **P~verkehr** m shuttle-service; (für Pendler) commuter traffic

Pendler m -s,- commuter

penetrant adj penetrating; (fig) obtrusive

Penis m -,-se penis

Penne f -,-n [!] school

Pension /pã'zi̯o:n/ f -,-en pension; (Hotel) guest-house; **bei voller/ halber P~** with full/half board. **P~är(in)** m -s,-e (f -,-nen) pensioner. **P~at** nt -[e]s,-e boarding-school. **p~ieren** vt retire. **P~ierung** f - retirement

Pensum nt -s [allotted] work

Peperoni f -,- chilli

per prep (+ acc) by

Perfekt nt -s (Gram) perfect

Perfektion /-'tsi̯o:n/ f - perfection

perforiert adj perforated

Pergament nt -[e]s,-e parchment. **P~papier** nt grease-proof paper

Period|e f -,-n period. **p~isch** adj periodic

Perl|e f -,-n pearl; (Glas-, Holz-) bead; (Sekt-) bubble. **P~mutt** nt -s mother-of-pearl

Pers|ien /-i̯ən/ nt -s Persia. **p~isch** adj Persian

Person f -,-en person; (Theat) character; **für vier P~en** for four people

Personal nt -s personnel, staff. **P~ausweis** m identity card. **P~chef** m personnel manager. **P~ien** pl personal particulars. **P~mangel** m staff shortage

persönlich adj personal • adv personally, in person. **P~keit** f -,-en personality

Perücke f -,-n wig

pervers adj [sexually] perverted. **P~ion** f -,-en perversion

Pessimis|mus m - pessimism. **P~t** m -en,-en pessimist. **p~tisch** adj pessimistic

Pest f - plague

Petersilie /-i̯ə/ f - parsley

Petroleum /-leum/ nt -s paraffin

Petze f **-,-n** [!] sneak. **p~n** vi (haben) [!] sneak

Pfad m **-[e]s,-e** path. **P~finder** m **-s,-** [Boy] Scout. **P~finderin** f **-,-nen** [Girl] Guide

Pfahl m **-[e]s,¨-e** stake, post

Pfalz (die) - the Palatinate

Pfand nt **-[e]s,¨-er** pledge; (beim Spiel) forfeit; (Flaschen-) deposit

pfänd|en vt (Jur) seize. **P~erspiel** nt game of forfeits

Pfandleiher m **-s,-** pawnbroker

Pfändung f **-,-en** (Jur) seizure

Pfann|e f **-,-n** [frying-]pan. **P~kuchen** m pancake

Pfarr|er m **-s,-** vicar, parson; (katholischer) priest. **P~haus** nt vicarage

Pfau m **-s,-en** peacock

Pfeffer m **-s** pepper. **P~kuchen** m gingerbread. **P~minze** f - (Bot) peppermint. **p~n** vt pepper; ([!]: schmeißen) chuck. **P~streuer** m **-s,-** pepperpot

Pfeif|e f **-,-n** whistle; (Tabak-, Orgel-) pipe. **p~en**† vt/i (haben) whistle; (als Signal) blow the whistle

Pfeil m **-[e]s,-e** arrow

Pfeiler m **-s,-** pillar; (Brücken-) pier

Pfennig m **-s,-e** pfennig

Pferch m **-[e]s,-e** [sheep] pen

Pferd nt **-es,-e** horse; **zu P~e** on horseback. **P~erennen** nt horse-race; (als Sport) [horse-]racing. **P~eschwanz** m horse's tail; (Frisur) pony-tail. **P~estall** m stable. **P~estärke** f horsepower

Pfiff m **-[e]s,-e** whistle

Pfifferling m **-s,-e** chanterelle

pfiffig adj [!] smart

Pfingst|en nt **-s** Whitsun. **P~rose** f peony

Pfirsich m **-s,-e** peach

Pflanz|e f **-,-n** plant. **p~en** vt plant. **P~enfett** nt vegetable fat. **p~lich** adj vegetable

Pflaster nt **-s,-** pavement; (Heft-) plaster. **p~n** vt pave

Pflaume f **-,-n** plum

Pflege f - care; (Kranken-) nursing; **in P~ nehmen** look after; (Admin) foster (Kind). **p~bedürftig** adj in need of care. **P~eltern** pl foster-parents. **P~kind** nt foster-child. **p~leicht** adj easy-care. **p~n** vt look after, care for; nurse (Kranke); cultivate (Künste, Freundschaft). **P~r(in)** m **-s,-** (f **-,-nen**) nurse; (Tier-) keeper

Pflicht f **-,-en** duty; (Sport) compulsory exercise/routine. **p~bewusst** adj conscientious. **P~gefühl** nt sense of duty

pflücken vt pick

Pflug m **-[e]s,¨-e** plough

pflügen vt/i (haben) plough

Pforte f **-,-n** gate

Pförtner m **-s,-** porter

Pfosten m **-s,-** post

Pfote f **-,-n** paw

Pfropfen m **-s,-** stopper; (Korken) cork. **p~** vt graft (**auf** + acc on [to]); ([!]: pressen) cram (**in** + acc into)

pfui int ugh

Pfund nt **-[e]s,-e** & - pound

Pfusch|arbeit f [!] shoddy work. **p~en** vi (haben) [!] botch one's work. **P~erei** f **-,-en** [!] botch-up

Pfütze f **-,-n** puddle

Phantasie f **-,-n** imagination; **P~n** fantasies; (Fieber-) hallucinations. **p~los** adj unimaginative. **p~ren** vi (haben) fantasize; (im Fieber) be delirious. **p~voll** adj imaginative

phantastisch adj fantastic

pharma|zeutisch adj pharmaceutical. **P~zie** f - pharmacy

Phase f **-,-n** phase

Philologie f - [study of] language and literature

Philosoph m **-en,-en** philosopher. **P~ie** f **-,-n** philosophy

philosophisch adj philosophical

P

Phobie f -,-n phobia
Phonet|ik f - phonetics sg. **p~isch** adj phonetic
Phosphor m -s phosphorus
Photo nt, Photo- = **Foto, Foto-**
Phrase f -,-n empty phrase
Physik f - physics sg. **p~alisch** adj physical
Physiker(in) m -s,- (f -,-nen) physicist
Physiologie f - physiology
physisch adj physical
Pianist(in) m -en,-en (f -,-nen) pianist
Pickel m -s,- pimple, spot; (Spitzhacke) pick. **p~ig** adj spotty
Picknick nt -s,-s picnic
piep[s]|en vi (haben) (Vogel:) cheep; (Maus:) squeak; (Techn) bleep. **P~er** m -s,- bleeper
Pier m -s,-e [harbour] pier
Pietät /pie'tɛ:t/ f - reverence. **p~los** adj irreverent
Pigment nt -[e]s,-e pigment. **P~ierung** f - pigmentation
Pik nt -s,-s (Karten) spades pl
pikant adj piquant; (gewagt) racy
piken vt [!] prick
pikiert adj offended, hurt
Pilger|(in) m -s,- (f -,-nen) pilgrim. **P~fahrt** f pilgrimage. **p~n** vi (sein) make a pilgrimage
Pille f -,-n pill
Pilot m -en,-en pilot
Pilz m -es,-e fungus; (essbarer) mushroom
pingelig adj [!] fussy
Pinguin m -s,-e penguin
Pinie /-iə/ f -,-n stone-pine
pinkeln vi (haben) [!] pee
Pinsel m -s,- [paint]brush
Pinzette f -,-n tweezers pl
Pionier m -s,-e (Mil) sapper; (fig) pioneer
Pirat m -en,-en pirate
Piste f -,-n (Ski-) run, piste; (Renn-) track; (Aviat) runway
Pistole f -,-n pistol
pitschnass adj [!] soaking wet
pittoresk adj picturesque
Pizza f -,-s pizza
Pkw /'pe:kave:/ m -s,-s car
plädieren vi (haben) plead (**für** for); **auf Freispruch p~** (Jur) ask for an acquittal
Plädoyer /plɛdoa'je:/ nt -s,-s (Jur) closing speech; (fig) plea
Plage f -,-n [hard] labour; (Mühe) trouble; (Belästigung) nuisance. **p~n** vt torment, plague; (bedrängen) pester; **sich p~n** struggle
Plakat nt -[e]s,-e poster
Plakette f -,-n badge
Plan m -[e]s,⸚e plan
Plane f -,-n tarpaulin; (Boden-) groundsheet
planen vt/i (haben) plan
Planet m -en,-en planet
planier|en vt level. **P~raupe** f bulldozer
Planke f -,-n plank
plan|los adj unsystematic. **p~mäßig** adj systematic; (Ankunft) scheduled
Plansch|becken nt paddling pool. **p~en** vi (haben) splash about
Plantage /plan'ta:ʒə/ f -,-n plantation
Planung f - planning
plappern vi (haben) chatter •vt talk (Unsinn)
plärren vi (haben) bawl
Plasma nt -s plasma
Plastik[1] f -,-en sculpture
Plast|ik[2] nt -s plastic. **p~isch** adj three-dimensional; (formbar) plastic; (anschaulich) graphic
Plateau /pla'to:/ nt -s,-s plateau
Platin nt -s platinum
platonisch adj platonic
plätschern vi (haben) splash; (Bach:)

P

babble • vi (sein) (Bach:) babble along

platt adj & adv flat. **P~** nt **-[s]** (Lang) Low German

Plättbrett nt ironing-board

Platte f **-,-n** slab; (Druck-) plate; (Metall-, Glas-) sheet; (Fliese) tile; (Koch-) hotplate; (Tisch-) top; (Schall-) record, disc; (zum Servieren) [flat] dish, platter; **kalte P~** assorted cold meats and cheeses pl

Plätt|eisen nt iron. **p~en** vt/i (haben) iron

Plattenspieler m record-player

Platt|form f **-,-en** platform. **P~füße** mpl flat feet

Platz m **-es,¨e** place; (von Häusern umgeben) square; (Sitz-) seat; (Sport-) ground; (Fußball-) pitch; (Tennis-) court; (Golf-) course; (freier Raum) room, space; **P~ nehmen** take a seat; **P~ machen** make room; **vom P~ stellen** (Sport) send off. **P~anweiserin** f **-,-nen** usherette

Plätzchen nt **-s,-** spot; (Culin) biscuit

platzen vi (sein) burst; (auf-) split; (!: scheitern) fall through; (Verlobung:) be off

Platz|karte f seat reservation ticket. **P~mangel** m lack of space. **P~patrone** f blank. **P~verweis** m (Sport) sending off. **P~wunde** f laceration

Plauderei f **-,-en** chat

plaudern vi (haben) chat

plausibel adj plausible

pleite adj ! **p~ sein** be broke: (Firma:) be bankrupt. **P~** f **-,-n** ! bankruptcy; (Misserfolg) flop; **P~ gehen** od **machen** go bankrupt

plissiert adj [finely] pleated

Plomb|e f **-,-n** seal; (Zahn-) filling. **p~ieren** vt seal; fill (Zahn)

plötzlich adj sudden

plump adj plump; clumsy

plumpsen vi (sein) ! fall

plündern vt/i (haben) loot

Plunderstück nt Danish pastry

Plural m **-s,-e** plural

plus adv, conj & prep (+ dat) plus. **P~** nt **-** surplus; (Gewinn) profit (Vorteil) advantage, plus. **P~punkt** m (Sport) point; (fig) plus

Po m **-s,-s** ! bottom

Pöbel m **-s** mob, rabble. **p~haft** adj loutish

pochen vi (haben) knock, (Herz:) pound; **p~ auf** (+ acc) (fig) insist on

pochieren /pɔ'ʃi:rən/ vt poach

Pocken pl smallpox sg

Podest nt **-[e]s,-e** rostrum

Podium nt **-s,-ien** platform; (Podest) rostrum

Poesie /poe'zi:/ f **-** poetry

poetisch adj poetic

Pointe /'po̯ɛ̃:tə/ f **-,-n** punchline (of a joke)

Pokal m **-s,-e** goblet; (Sport) cup

pökeln vt (Culin) salt

Poker nt **-s** poker

Pol m **-s,-e** pole. **p~ar** adj polar

Polarstern m pole-star

Pole m, **-n,-n** Pole. **P~n** nt **-s** Poland

Police /po'li:sə/ f **-,-n** policy

Polier m **-s,-e** foreman

polieren vt polish

Polin f **-,-nen** Pole

Politesse f **-,-n** [woman] traffic warden

Politik f **-** politics sg; (Vorgehen, Maßnahme) policy

Polit|iker(in) m **-s,-** (f, **-,-nen**) politician. **p~isch** adj political

Politur f **-,-en** polish

Polizei f **-** police pl. **p~lich** adj police • adv by the police; (sich anmelden) with the police. **P~streife** f police patrol. **P~stunde** f closing time. **P~wache** f police station

Polizist m **-en,-en** policeman. **P~in** f **-,-nen** policewoman

Pollen m **-s** pollen

polnisch adj Polish

Polster nt **-s,-** pad; (Kissen) cushion; (Möbel-) upholstery. **p~n** vt pad; upholster (Möbel). **P~ung** f - padding; upholstery

Polter|abend m eve-of-wedding party. **p~n** vi (haben) thump, bang

Polyäthylen nt **-s** polythene

Polyester m **-s** polyester

Polyp m **-en,-en** polyp. **P~en** pl adenoids pl

Pommes frites /pɔm'fri:t/ pl chips; (dünner) French fries

Pomp m **-s** pomp

Pompon /põ'põ:/ m **-s,-s** pompon

pompös adj ostentatious

Pony[1] nt **-s,-s** pony

Pony[2] m **-s,-s** fringe

Pop m **-[s]** pop

Popo m **-s,-s** [!] bottom

populär adj popular

Pore f **-,-n** pore

Porno|grafie, **Pornographie** f - pornography. **p~grafisch**, **p~graphisch** adj pornographic

Porree m **-s** leeks pl

Portal nt **-s,-e** portal

Portemonnaie /pɔrtmɔ'ne:/ nt **-s,-s** purse

Portier /pɔr'tie:/ m **-s,-s** doorman, porter

Portion /-'tsio:n/ f **-,-en** helping, portion

Portmonee nt **-s,-s** = **Portemonnaie**

Porto nt **-s** postage. **p~frei** adv post free, post paid

Porträ|t /pɔr'trɛ:/ nt **-s,-s** portrait. **p~tieren** vt paint a portrait of

Portugal nt **-s** Portugal

Portugies|e m **-n,-n, P~in** f **-,-nen** Portuguese. **p~isch** adj Portuguese

Portwein m port

[C] see A-Z of German life and culture

Porzellan nt **-s** china, porcelain

Posaune f **-,-n** trombone

Position /-'tsio:n/ f **-,-en** position

positiv adj positive. **P~** nt **-s,-e** (Phot) positive

Post f - post office; (Briefe) mail, post; **mit der P~** by post

postalisch adj postal

Post|amt nt post office. **P~anweisung** f postal money order. **P~bote** m postman

Posten m **-s,-** post; (Wache) sentry; (Waren-) batch; (Rechnungs-) item, entry

Poster nt & m **-s,-** poster

Postfach nt post-office or PO box

Post|karte f postcard. **p~lagernd** adv poste restante. **P~leitzahl** f postcode. **P~scheckkonto** nt ≈ National Girobank account. **P~stempel** m postmark

postum adj posthumous

post|wendend adv by return of post. **P~wertzeichen** nt [postage] stamp

Potenz f **-,-en** potency; (Math & fig) power

Pracht f - magnificence, splendour

prächtig adj magnificent; splendid

prachtvoll adj magnificent

Prädikat nt **-[e]s,-e** rating; (Comm) grade; (Gram) predicate

prägen vt stamp (**auf** + acc on); emboss (Leder); mint (Münze); coin (Wort); (fig) shape

prägnant adj succinct

prähistorisch adj prehistoric

prahl|en vi (haben) boast, brag (**mit** about)

Prakti|k f **-,-en** practice. **P~kant(in)** m **-en,-en** (f **-,-nen**) trainee

Prakti|kum nt **-s,-ka** practical training. **p~sch** adj practical; (nützlich) handy; (tatsächlich) virtual; **p~scher Arzt** general practitioner • adv practically; virtually; (in der Praxis) in practice. **p~zieren** vt/i (haben) practise; (anwenden) put into practice; (🅘: bekommen) get

Praline f -,-n chocolate

prall adj bulging; (dick) plump; (Sonne) blazing • adv **p~ gefüllt** full to bursting. **p~en** vi (sein) **p~ auf** (+ acc)/**gegen** collide with, hit; (Sonne:) blaze down on

Prämie /-i̯ə/ f -,-n premium; (Preis) award

präm[i]ieren vt award a prize to

Pranger m -s,- pillory

Pranke f -,-n paw

Präparat nt -[e]s,-e preparation

Präsens nt - (Gram) present

präsentieren vt present

Präsenz f - presence

Präservativ nt -s,-e condom

Präsident|(in) m -en,-en (f -,-nen) president. **P~schaft** f - presidency

Präsidium nt -s presidency; (Gremium) executive committee; (Polizei-) headquarters pl

prasseln vi (haben) (Regen:) beat down; (Feuer:) crackle

Präteritum nt -s imperfect

Praxis f -,-xen practice; (Erfahrung) practical experience; (Arzt-) surgery; **in der P~** in practice

Präzedenzfall m precedent

präzis[e] adj precise

predig|en vt/i (haben) preach. **P~t** f -,-en sermon

Preis m -es,-e price; (Belohnung) prize. **P~ausschreiben** nt competition

Preiselbeere f (Bot) cowberry; (Culin) ≈ cranberry

preisen† vt praise

preisgeben† vt sep abandon (dat to); reveal (Geheimnis)

preis|gekrönt adj award-winning. **p~günstig** adj reasonably priced • adv at a reasonable price. **P~lage** f price range. **p~lich** adj price • adv in price. **P~richter** m judge. **P~schild** nt price-tag. **P~träger(in)** m(f) prize-winner. **p~wert** adj reasonable

Prell|bock m buffers pl. **p~en** vt bounce; (verletzen) bruise; (🅘: betrügen) cheat. **P~ung** f -,-en bruise

🅒**Premiere** /prəˈmi̯eːrə/ f -,-n première

Premierminister(in) /prəˈmi̯eː-/ m(f) Prime Minister

Presse f -,-n press. **p~n** vt press

Pressluftbohrer m pneumatic drill

Preuß|en nt -s Prussia. **p~isch** adj Prussian

prickeln vi (haben) tingle

Priester m -s,- priest

prima inv adj 🅘 first-class, first-rate; (toll) fantastic

primär adj primary

Primel f -,-n primula

primitiv adj primitive

Prinz m -en,-en prince. **P~essin** f -,-nen princess

Prinzip nt -s,-ien principle. **p~iell** adj (Frage) of principle • adv on principle

Prise f -,-n **P~ Salz** pinch of salt

Prisma nt -s,-men prism

privat adj private, personal. **P~adresse** f home address. **p~isieren** vt privatize

Privileg nt -[e]s,-ien privilege. **p~iert** adj privileged

pro prep (+ dat) per. **Pro** nt - **das Pro und Kontra** the pros and cons pl

Probe f -,-n test, trial; (Menge, Muster) sample; (Theat) rehearsal; **auf die P~ stellen** put to the test; **ein Auto P~ fahren** test-drive a car. **p~n** vt/i (haben) (Theat) rehearse. **p~weise** adv on a trial basis. **P~zeit** f probationary period

probieren vt/i (haben) try; (kosten) taste; (proben) rehearse

Problem nt -s,-e problem.

🅒 *see A-Z of German life and culture*

P

p~atisch adj problematic

problemlos adj problem-free • adv without any problems

Produkt nt **-[e]s,-e** product

Produk|tion /-ˈtsi̯oːn/ f **-,-en** production. **p~tiv** adj productive

Produ|zent m **-en,-en** producer. **p~zieren** vt produce

Professor m **-s,-en** professor

Profi m **-s,-s** (Sport) professional

Profil nt **-s,-e** profile; (Reifen-) tread; (fig) image

Profit m **-[e]s,-e** profit. **p~ieren** vi (haben) profit (**von** from)

Prognose f **-,-n** forecast; (Med) prognosis

Programm nt **-s,-e** programme; (Computer-) program; (TV) channel; (Comm: Sortiment) range. **p~ieren** vt/i (haben) (Computer) program. **P~ierer(in)** m **-s,-** (f **-,-nen**) [computer] programmer

Projekt nt **-[e]s,-e** project

Projektor m **-s,-en** projector

Prolet m **-en,-en** boor. **P~ariat** nt **-[e]s** proletariat

Prolog m **-s,-e** prologue

P

Promenade f **-,-n** promenade

Promille pl ! alcohol level sg in the blood; **zu viel P~ haben** ! be over the limit

Prominenz f **-** prominent figures pl

Promiskuität f **-** promiscuity

promovieren vi (haben) obtain one's doctorate

prompt adj prompt

Pronomen nt **-s,-** pronoun

Propaganda f **-** propaganda; (Reklame) publicity

Propeller m **-s,-** propeller

Prophet m **-en,-en** prophet

prophezei|en vt prophesy. **P~ung** f **-,-en** prophecy

Proportion /-ˈtsi̯oːn/ f **-,-en** proportion

Prosa f **-** prose

prosit int cheers!

Prospekt m **-[e]s,-e** brochure; (Comm) prospectus

prost int cheers!

Prostitu|ierte f **-n,-n** prostitute. **P~tion** f **-** prostitution

Protest m **-[e]s,-e** protest

Protestant|(in) m **-en,-en** (f **-,-nen**) (Relig) Protestant. **p~isch** adj (Relig) Protestant

protestieren vi (haben) protest

Prothese f **-,-n** artificial limb; (Zahn-) denture

Protokoll nt **-s,-e** record; (Sitzungs-) minutes pl; (diplomatisches) protocol

protz|en vi (haben) show off (**mit etw** sth). **p~ig** adj ostentatious

Proviant m **-s** provisions pl

Provinz f **-,-en** province

Provision f **-,-en** (Comm) commission

provisorisch adj provisional, temporary

Provokation /-ˈtsi̯oːn/ f **-,-en** provocation

provozieren vt provoke

Prozedur f **-,-en** [lengthy] business

Prozent nt **-[e]s,-e** & **-** per cent; 5 **P~** 5 per cent. **P~satz** m percentage. **p~ual** adj percentage

Prozess m **-es,-e** process; (Jur) lawsuit; (Kriminal-) trial

Prozession f **-,-en** procession

Prozessor m **-s,-en** processor

prüde adj prudish

prüf|en vt test/(über-) check (**auf** + acc for); audit (Bücher); (Sch) examine; **p~ender Blick** searching look. **P~er** m **-s,-** inspector; (Buch-) auditor; (Sch) examiner. **P~ling** m **-s,-e** examination candidate. **P~ung** f **-,-en** examination; (Test) test; (Bücher-) audit; (fig) trial

Prügel m **-s,-** cudgel; **P~** pl hiding sg, beating sg. **P~ei** f -,-en brawl, fight. **p~n** vt beat, thrash

Prunk m **-[e]s** magnificence, splendour

Psalm m **-s,-en** psalm

Pseudonym nt **-s,-e** pseudonym

pst int shush!

Psychi|ater m **-s,-** psychiatrist. **P~atrie** f - psychiatry. **p~atrisch** adj psychiatric

psychisch adj psychological

Psycho|analyse f psychoanalysis. **P~loge** m **-n,-n** psychologist. **P~logie** f - psychology. **p~logisch** adj psychological

Pubertät f - puberty

Publi|kum nt **-s** public; (Zuhörer) audience; (Zuschauer) spectators pl. **p~zieren** vt publish

Pudding m **-s,-s** blancmange; (im Wasserbad gekocht) pudding

Pudel m **-s,-** poodle

Puder m & ⊡ nt **-s,-** powder. **P~dose** f [powder] compact. **p~n** vt powder. **P~zucker** m icing sugar

Puff m & nt **-s,-s** ⊠ brothel

Puffer m **-s,-** (Rail) buffer; (Culin) pancake. **P~zone** f buffer zone

Pull|i m **-s,-s** jumper. **P~over** m **-s,-** jumper; (Herren-) pullover

Puls m **-es** pulse. **P~ader** f artery

Pult nt **-[e]s,-e** desk

Pulver nt **-s,-** powder. **p~ig** adj powdery

Pulverkaffee m instant coffee

pummelig adj ⊡ chubby

Pumpe f **-,-n** pump. **p~n** vt/i (haben) pump; (⊡: leihen) lend; [**sich** (dat)] **etw p~n** (⊡: borgen) borrow sth

Pumps /pœmps/ pl court shoes

Punkt m **-[e]s,-e** dot; (Textiles) spot; (Geometry, Sport & fig) point; (Gram) full stop, period; **P~ sechs Uhr** at six o'clock sharp

pünktlich adj punctual. **P~keit** f - punctuality

Pupille f **-,-n** (Anat) pupil

Puppe f **-,-n** doll; (Marionette) puppet; (Schaufenster-, Schneider-) dummy; (Zool) chrysalis

pur adj pure; (⊡: bloß) sheer

Püree nt **-s,-s** purée; (Kartoffel-) mashed potatoes pl

purpurrot adj crimson

Purzel|baum m ⊡ somersault. **p~n** vi (sein) ⊡ tumble

Puste f - ⊡ breath. **p~n** vt/i (haben) ⊡ blow

Pute f **-,-n** turkey

Putsch m **-[e]s,-e** coup

Putz m **-es** plaster; (Staat) finery. **p~en** vt clean; (Aust) dry-clean; (zieren) adorn; **sich p~en** dress up; **sich** (dat) **die Zähne/Nase p~en** clean one's teeth/blow one's nose. **P~frau** f cleaner, charwoman. **p~ig** adj ⊡ amusing, cute; (seltsam) odd

Puzzlespiel /'pazl-/ nt jigsaw

Pyramide f **-,-n** pyramid

Qq

Quacksalber m **-s,-** quack

Quadrat nt **-[e]s,-e** square. **q~isch** adj square

quaken vi (haben) quack; (Frosch:) croak

Quäker(in) m **-s,-** (f **-,-nen**) Quaker

Qual f **-,-en** torment; (Schmerz) agony

quälen vt torment; (foltern) torture; (bedrängen) pester; **sich q~** torment oneself; (leiden) suffer; (sich mühen) struggle

Quälerei f -,-en torture

Qualifi|kation /-'tsi̯o:n/ f -,-en qualification. **q~zieren** vt qualify. **q~ziert** adj qualified; (fähig) competent; (Arbeit) skilled

Qualität f -,-en quality

Qualle f -,-n jellyfish

Qualm m -s [thick] smoke

qualvoll adj agonizing

Quantum nt -s,-ten quantity; (Anteil) share, quota

Quarantäne f - quarantine

Quark m -s quark, ≈ curd cheese

Quartal nt -s,-e quarter

Quartett nt -[e]s,-e quartet

Quartier nt -s,-e accommodation; (Mil) quarters pl

Quarz m -es quartz

quasseln vi (haben) 🄸 jabber

Quaste f -,-n tassel

Quatsch m -[e]s 🄸 nonsense, rubbish; **Q~ machen** (Unfug machen) fool around; (etw falsch machen) do a silly thing. **q~en** 🄸 vi (haben) talk; (Wasser, Schlamm:) squelch • vt talk

Quecksilber nt mercury

Quelle f -,-n spring; (Fluss- & fig) source

quengeln vi 🄸 whine

quer adv across, crosswise; (schräg) diagonally; **q~ gestreift** horizontally striped

Quere f - **der Q~ nach** across, crosswise; **jdm in die Q~ kommen** get in s.o.'s way

Quer|latte f crossbar. **Q~schiff** nt transept. **Q~schnitt** m cross-section. **q~schnittsgelähmt** adj paraplegic. **Q~straße** f side-street. **Q~verweis** m cross-reference

quetschen vt squash; (drücken) squeeze; (zerdrücken) crush; (Culin) mash; **sich q~ in** (+ acc) squeeze into

Queue /kø:/ nt -s,-s cue

quieken vi (haben) squeal; (Maus:) squeak

quietschen vi (haben) squeal; (Tür, Dielen:) creak

Quintett nt -[e]s,-e quintet

quirlen vt mix

Quitte f -,-n quince

quittieren vt receipt (Rechnung); sign for (Geldsumme, Sendung); **den Dienst q~** resign

Quittung f -,-en receipt

Quiz /kvɪs/ nt -,- quiz

Quote f -,-n proportion

Rr

Rabatt m -[e]s,-e discount

Rabatte f -,-n (Horticulture) border

Rabattmarke f trading stamp

Rabbiner m -s,- rabbi

Rabe m -n,-n raven

Rache f - revenge, vengeance

Rachen m -s,- pharynx

rächen vt avenge; **sich r~** take revenge (**an** + dat on); (Fehler:) cost s.o. dear

Rad nt -[e]s,⸚er wheel; (Fahr-) bicycle, 🄸 bike; **Rad fahren** cycle

Radar m & nt -s radar

Radau m -s 🄸 din, racket

radeln vi (sein) 🄸 cycle

Rädelsführer m ringleader

radfahr|en* vi sep (sein) **Rad**

fahren, s. **Rad. R~er(in)** m(f) **-s,-** (f **-,-nen**) cyclist

radier|en vt/i (haben) rub out; (Kunst) etch. **R~gummi** m eraser, rubber. **R~ung** f **-,-en** etching

Radieschen /-'di:sçən/ nt **-s,-** radish

radikal adj radical, drastic

Radio nt **-s,-s** radio

radioaktiv adj radioactive. **R~ität** f **-** radioactivity

Radius m **-,-ien** radius

Rad|kappe f hub-cap. **R~ler** m **-s,-** cyclist; (Getränk) shandy

raffen vt grab; (kräuseln) gather; (kürzen) condense

Raffin|ade f **-** refined sugar. **R~erie** f **-,-n** refinery. **R~esse** f **-,-n** refinement; (Schlauheit) cunning. **r~iert** adj ingenious; (durchtrieben) crafty

ragen vi (haben) rise [up]

Rahm m **-s** (SGer) cream

rahmen vt frame. **R~** m **-s,-** frame; (fig) framework; (Grenze) limits pl; (einer Feier) setting

Rakete f **-,-n** rocket; (Mil) missile

Rallye /'rɛli/ nt **-s,-s** rally

rammen vt ram

Rampe f **-,-n** ramp; (Theat) front of the stage

Ramsch m **-[e]s** junk

ran adv = **heran**

Rand m **-[e]s,¨er** edge; (Teller-, Gläser-, Brillen-) rim; (Zier-) border, edging; (Brief-) margin; (Stadt-) outskirts pl; (Ring) ring

randalieren vi (haben) rampage

Randstreifen m (Auto) hard shoulder

Rang m **-[e]s,¨e** rank; (Theat) tier; **erster/zweiter R~** (Theat) dress/ upper circle; **ersten R~es** first-class

rangieren /raŋ'ʒi:rən/ vt shunt • vi (haben) rank (**vor** + dat before)

Rangordnung f order of importance; (Hierarchie) hierarchy

Ranke f **-,-n** tendril; (Trieb) shoot

ranken (sich) vr (Bot) trail; (in die Höhe) climb

Ranzen m **-s,-** (Sch) satchel

ranzig adj rancid

Rappe m **-n,-n** black horse

Raps m **-es** (Bot) rape

rar adj rare; **er macht sich rar** [!] we don't see much of him. **R~ität** f **-,-en** rarity

rasant adj fast; (schnittig, schick) stylish

rasch adj quick

rascheln vi (haben) rustle

Rasen m **-s,-** lawn

rasen vi (sein) tear [along]; (Puls:) race; (Zeit:) fly; **gegen eine Mauer r~** career into a wall • vi (haben) rave; (Sturm:) rage. **r~d** adj furious; (tobend) raving; (Sturm, Durst) raging; (Schmerz) excruciating; (Beifall) tumultuous

Rasenmäher m lawn-mower

Rasier|apparat m razor. **r~en** vt shave; **sich r~en** shave. **R~klinge** f razor blade. **R~wasser** nt aftershave [lotion]

Raspel f **-,-n** rasp; (Culin) grater. **r~n** vt grate

Rasse f **-,-n** race. **R~hund** m pedigree dog

Rassel f **-,-n** rattle. **r~n** vi (haben) rattle; (Schlüssel:) jangle; (Kette:) clank

Rassendiskriminierung f racial discrimination

Rassepferd nt thoroughbred.

rassisch adj racial

Rassis|mus m **-** racism. **r~tisch** adj racist

Rast f **-,-en** rest. **R~platz** m picnic area. **R~stätte** f motorway restaurant [and services]

Rasur f **-,-en** shave

Rat m **-[e]s** [piece of] advice; **sich** (dat) **keinen Rat wissen** not know what to do; **zu Rat[e] ziehen** = **zurate ziehen**, s. **zurate**

Rate f **-,-n** instalment

raten† vt guess; (empfehlen) advise •vi (haben) guess; **jdm r~** advise s.o.

Ratenzahlung f payment by instalments

Rat|geber m **-s,-** adviser; (Buch) guide. **R~haus** nt town hall

ratifizier|en vt ratify. **R~ung** f **-,-en** ratification

Ration /ra'tsi̯o:n/ f **-,-en** ration. **r~ell** adj efficient. **r~ieren** vt ration

rat|los adj helpless; **r~los sein** not know what to do. **r~sam** pred adj advisable; prudent. **R~schlag** m piece of advice; **R~schläge** advice sg

Rätsel nt **-s,-** riddle; (Kreuzwort-) puzzle; (Geheimnis) mystery. **r~haft** adj puzzling, mysterious. **r~n** vi (haben) puzzle

Ratte f **-,-n** rat

rau adj rough; (unfreundlich) gruff; (Klima) harsh, raw; (heiser) husky; (Hals) sore

Raub m **-[e]s** robbery; (Menschen-) abduction; (Beute) loot, booty. **r~en** vt steal; abduct (Menschen)

Räuber m **-s,-** robber

Raub|mord m robbery with murder. **R~tier** nt predator. **R~vogel** m bird of prey

Rauch m **-[e]s** smoke. **r~en** vt/i (haben) smoke. **R~en** nt **-s** smoking; '**R~en verboten**' 'no smoking'. **R~er** m **-s**,-smoker

Räucher|lachs m smoked salmon. **r~n** vt (Culin) smoke

rauf adv = **herauf, hinauf**

rauf|en vt pull •vr/i (haben) **[sich] r~en** fight. **R~erei** f **-,-en** fight

rauh* adj = **rau**

Raum m **-[e]s, Räume** room; (Gebiet) area; (Welt-) space

räumen vt clear; vacate (Wohnung); evacuate (Gebäude, Gebiet, (Mil) Stellung); (bringen) put (**in/auf** + acc into/on); (holen) get (**aus** out of)

Raum|fahrer m astronaut. **R~fahrt** f space travel. **R~inhalt** m volume

räumlich adj spatial

Raum|pflegerin f cleaner. **R~schiff** nt spaceship

Räumung f - clearing; vacating; evacuation. **R~sverkauf** m clearance/closing-down sale

Raupe f **-,-n** caterpillar

raus adv = **heraus, hinaus**

Rausch m **-[e]s, Räusche** intoxication; (fig) exhilaration; **einen R~ haben** be drunk

rauschen vi (haben) (Wasser, Wind:) rush; (Bäume Blätter:) rustle •vi [!] (sein) rush [along]

Rauschgift nt [narcotic] drug; (coll) drugs pl. **R~süchtige(r)** m/f drug addict

räuspern (sich) vr clear one's throat

rausschmeißen† vt sep [!] throw out; (entlassen) sack

Raute f **-,-n** diamond

Razzia f **-,-ien** [police] raid

Reagenzglas nt test-tube

reagieren vi (haben) react (**auf** + acc to)

Reaktion /-'tsi̯o:n/ f **-,-en** reaction. **r~är** adj reactionary

Reaktor m **-s,-en** reactor

realisieren vt realize

Realis|mus m - realism. **R~t** m **-en,-en** realist. **r~tisch** adj realistic

Realität f **-,-en** reality

[C] **Realschule** f ≈ secondary modern school

Rebe f **-,-n** vine

Rebell m **-en,-en** rebel. **r~ieren** vi (haben) rebel. **R~ion** f **-,-en** rebellion

rebellisch adj rebellious

[C] see A-Z of German life and culture

r

Rebhuhn nt partridge

Rebstock m vine

Rechen m **-s,-** rake

Rechen|aufgabe f arithmetical problem; (Sch) sum. **R~maschine** f calculator

recherchieren /reʃɛr'ʃi:rən/ vt/i (haben) investigate; (Journalism) research

rechnen vi (haben) do arithmetic; (schätzen) reckon; (zählen) count (**zu** among; **auf** + acc on); **r~ mit** reckon with; (erwarten) expect ● vt calculate, work out; (fig) count (**zu** among). **R~** nt **-s** arithmetic

Rechner m **-s,-** calculator; (Computer) computer

Rechnung f **-,-en** bill; (Comm) invoice; (Berechnung) calculation; **R~ führen über** (+ acc) keep account of. **R~sjahr** nt financial year. **R~sprüfer** m auditor

Recht nt **-[e]s,-e** law; (Berechtigung) right (**auf** + acc to); **im R~ sein** be in the right; **R~ haben/behalten** be right; **R~ bekommen** be proved right; **jdm R~ geben** agree with s.o.; **mit** od **zu R~** rightly

recht adj right; (wirklich) real; **ich habe keine r~e Lust** I don't really feel like it; **es jdm r~ machen** please s.o.; **jdm r~ sein** be all right with s.o. **r~ vielen Dank** many thanks

Recht|e f **-n,-[n]** right side; (Hand) right hand; (Boxen) right; **die R~e** (Pol) the right; **zu meiner R~en** on my right. **r~e(r,s)** adj right; (Pol) right-wing; **r~e Masche** plain stitch. **R~e(r)** m/f **der/die R~e** the right man/woman; **R~e(s)** nt **das R~e** the right thing; **etwas R~es lernen** learn something useful; **nach dem R~en sehen** see that everything is all right

Rechteck nt **-[e]s,-e** rectangle. **r~ig** adj rectangular

rechtfertigen vt justify; **sich r~en** justify oneself

recht|haberisch adj opinionated. **r~lich** adj legal. **r~mäßig** adj legitimate

rechts adv on the right; (bei Stoff) on the right side; **von/nach r~** from/ to the right; **zwei r~, zwei links stricken** knit two, purl two. **R~anwalt** m, **R~anwältin** f lawyer

Rechtschreib|programm nt spell checker. **R~ung** f - spelling

Rechts|händer(in) m **-s,-** (f **-,-nen**) right-hander. **r~händig** adj & adv right-handed. **r~kräftig** adj legal. **R~streit** m law suit. **R~verkehr** m driving on the right. **r~widrig** adj illegal. **R~wissenschaft** f jurisprudence

rechtzeitig adj & adv in time

Reck nt **-[e]s,-e** horizontal bar

recken vt stretch

Redakteur /redak'tø:ɐ̯/ m **-s,-e** editor; (Radio, TV) producer

Redaktion /-'tsi̯o:n/ f **-,-en** editing; (Radio, TV) production; (Abteilung) editorial/production department

Rede f **-,-n** speech; **zur R~stellen** demand an explanation from; **nicht der R~ wert** not worth mentioning

reden vi (haben) talk (**von** about; **mit** to); (eine Rede halten) speak ● vt talk; speak (Wahrheit). **R~sart** f saying

Redewendung f idiom

redigieren vt edit

Redner m **-s,-** speaker

reduzieren vt reduce

Reeder m **-s,-** shipowner. **R~ei** f **-,-en** shipping company

Refer|at nt **-[e]s,-e** report; (Abhandlung) paper; (Abteilung) section. **R~ent(in)** m **-en,-en** (f **-,-nen**) speaker; (Sachbearbeiter) expert. **R~enz** f **-,-en** reference

Reflex m **-es,-e** reflex; (Widerschein) reflection. **R~ion** f **-,-en** reflection. **r~iv** adj reflexive

Reform f **-,-en** reform. **R~ation** f - (Relig) Reformation

Reform|haus nt health-food shop. **r~ieren** vt reform

Refrain /rə'frɛ̃:/ m **-s,-s** refrain

Regal nt **-s,-e** [set of] shelves pl

Regatta f **-,-ten** regatta

rege adj active; (lebhaft) lively; (geistig) alert; (Handel) brisk

Regel f **-,-n** rule; (Monats-) period. **r∼mäßig** adj regular. **r∼n** vt regulate; direct (Verkehr); (erledigen) settle. **r∼recht** adj real, proper • adv really. **R∼ung** f **-,-en** regulation; settlement

regen vt move; **sich r∼** move; (wach werden) stir

Regen m **-s,-** rain. **R∼bogen** m rainbow. **R∼bogenhaut** f iris

Regener|ation /-'tsi̯o:n/ f **-** regeneration. **r∼ieren** vt regenerate

Regen|mantel m raincoat. **R∼schirm** m umbrella. **R∼tag** m rainy day. **R∼wetter** nt wet weather. **R∼wurm** m earthworm

Regie /re'ʒi:/ f **-** direction; **R∼ führen** direct

regier|en vt/i (haben) govern, rule; (Monarch:) reign [over]; (Gram) take. **R∼ung** f **-,-en** government; (Herrschaft) rule; (eines Monarchen) reign

Regiment nt **-[e]s,-er** regiment

Region f **-,-en** region. **r∼al** adj regional

Regisseur /reʒɪ'sø:ɐ̯/ m **-s,-e** director

Register nt **-s,-** register; (Inhaltsverzeichnis) index; (Orgel-) stop

Regler m **-s,-** regulator

reglos adj & adv motionless

regn|en vi (haben) rain; **es r∼et** it is raining. **r∼erisch** adj rainy

regul|är adj normal; (rechtmäßig) legitimate. **r∼ieren** vt regulate

Regung f **-,-en** movement; (Gefühls-) emotion. **r∼slos** adj & adv motionless

Reh nt **-[e]s,-e** roe-deer; (Culin) venison

Rehbock m roebuck

reib|en† vt rub; (Culin) grate • vi (haben) rub. **R∼ung** f **-** friction. **r∼ungslos** adj (fig) smooth

reich adj rich (**an** + dat in)

Reich nt **-[e]s,-e** empire; (König-) kingdom; (Bereich) realm

Reiche(r) m/f rich man/woman; **die R∼en** the rich pl

reichen vt hand; (anbieten) offer • vi (haben) be enough; (in der Länge) be long enough; **r∼ bis zu** reach [up to]; (sich erstrecken) extend to; **mit dem Geld r∼** have enough money

reich|haltig adj extensive, large (Mahlzeit) substantial. **r∼lich** adj ample: (Vorrat) abundant. **R∼tum** m **-s,-tümer** wealth (**an** + dat of); **R∼tümer** riches. **R∼weite** f reach; (Techn, Mil) range

Reif m **-[e]s** [hoar-]frost

reif adj ripe; (fig) mature; **r∼ für** ready for. **r∼en** vi (sein) ripen; (Wein, Käse & fig) mature

Reifen m **-s,-** hoop; (Arm-) bangle; (Auto-) tyre. **R∼druck** m tyre pressure. **R∼panne** f puncture, flat tyre

reiflich adj careful

Reihe f **-,-n** row; (Anzahl & Math) series; **der R∼ nach** in turn; **wer ist an der R∼?** whose turn is it? **r∼n (sich)** vr **sich r∼n an** (+ acc) follow. **R∼nfolge** f order. **R∼nhaus** nt terraced house

Reiher m **-s,-** heron

Reim m **-[e]s,-e** rhyme. **r∼en** vt rhyme; **sich r∼en** rhyme

rein[1] adj pure; (sauber) clean; (Unsinn, Dummheit) sheer; **ins R∼e (r∼e) schreiben** make a fair copy of

rein[2] adv = **herein, hinein**

Reineclaude /rɛ:nə'klo:də/ f **-,-n** greengage

Reinfall m [!] let-down; (Misserfolg) flop

Rein|gewinn m net profit. **R∼heit** f **-** purity

reinig|en vt clean; (chemisch) dry-clean. **R∼ung** f **-,-en** cleaning; (chemische) dry-cleaning; (Geschäft) dry cleaner's

reinlegen vt sep put in; [!] dupe;

r

(betrügen) take for a ride

reinlich adj clean. **R~keit** f - cleanliness

Reis m **-es** rice

Reise f **-,-n** journey; (See-) voyage; (Urlaubs-, Geschäfts-) trip. **R~andenken** nt souvenir. **R~büro** nt travel agency. **R~bus** m coach. **R~führer** m tourist guide; (Buch) guide. **R~gesellschaft** f tourist group. **R~leiter(in)** m(f) courier. **r~n** vi (sein) travel. **R~nde(r)** m/f traveller. **R~pass** m passport. **R~scheck** m traveller's cheque. **R~veranstalter** m **-s,-** tour operator. **R~ziel** nt destination

Reisig nt **-s** brushwood

Reißaus m **R~ nehmen** [!] run away

Reißbrett nt drawing-board

reißen† vt tear; (weg-) snatch; (töten) kill; **Witze r~** crack jokes; **an sich** (acc) **r~**snatch; seize (Macht); **sich r~ um** [!] fight for •vi (sein) tear; (Seil, Faden:) break •vi (haben) **r~ an** (+ dat) pull at

Reißer m **-s,-** [!] thriller; (Erfolg) big hit

Reiß|nagel m = **R~zwecke. R~verschluss** m zip [fastener]. **R~wolf** m shredder. **R~zwecke** f **-,-n** drawing-pin

reit|en† vt/i (sein) ride. **R~er(in)** m **-s,-** (f **-,-nen**) rider. **R~hose** f riding breeches pl. **R~pferd** nt saddle-horse. **R~weg** m bridle-path

Reiz m **-es,-e** stimulus; (Anziehungskraft) attraction, appeal; (Charme) charm. **r~bar** adj irritable. **R~barkeit** f - irratability. **r~en** vt provoke; (Med) irritate; (interessieren, locken) appeal to, attract; arouse (Neugier); (beim Kartenspiel) bid. **R~ung** f **-,-en** (Med) irritation. **r~voll** adj attractive

rekeln (sich) vr [!] stretch

Reklamation /-'tsi̯o:n/ f **-,-en** (Comm) complaint

Reklam|e f **-,-n** advertising, publicity; (Anzeige) advertisement; (TV, Radio) commercial; **R~e machen** advertise (**für etw** sth). **r~ieren** vt complain about; (fordern) claim •vi (haben) complain

Rekord m **-[e]s,-e** record

Rekrut m **-en,-en** recruit

Rek|tor m **-s,-en** (Sch) head[master]; (Univ) vice-chancellor. **R~torin** f **-,-nen** head, headmistress; vice-chancellor

Relais /rə'lɛ:/ nt **-,-** /-s,-s/ (Electr) relay

relativ adj relative

Religi|on f **-,-en** religion; (Sch) religious education. **r~ös** adj religious

Reling f **-,-s** (Naut) rail

Reliquie /re'li:kvi̯ə/ f **-,-n** relic

rempeln vt jostle; (stoßen) push

Reneklode f **-,-n** greengage

Rennbahn f race-track; (Pferde-) racecourse. **R~boot** nt speed-boat. **r~en**† vi (sein) run; **um die Wette r~en** have a race. **R~en** nt **-s,-** race. **R~pferd** nt racehorse. **R~sport** m racing. **R~wagen** m racing car

renommiert adj renowned; (Hotel, Firma) of repute

renovier|en vt renovate; redecorate (Zimmer). **R~ung** f - renovation; redecoration

rentabel adj profitable

Rente f **-,-n** pension; **in R~ gehen** [!] retire. **R~nversicherung** f pension scheme

Rentier nt reindeer

rentieren (sich) vr be profitable; (sich lohnen) be worth while

Rentner(in) m **-s,-** (f **-,-nen**) [old-age] pensioner

Reparatur f **-,-en** repair. **R~werkstatt** f repair workshop; (Auto) garage

reparieren vt repair, mend

Reportage /-'ta:ʒə/ f **-,-n** report

Reporter(in) m **-s,-** (f **-,-nen**) reporter

r

repräsentativ adj representative (**für** of); (eindrucksvoll) imposing

Reprodu|ktion /-'tsi̯o:n/ f -,-en reproduction. **r~zieren** vt reproduce

Reptil nt **-s,-ien** reptile

Republik f -,-en republic. **r~anisch** adj republican

Requisiten pl (Theat) properties, [!] props

Reservat nt **-[e]s,-e** reservation

Reserve f -,-n reserve; (Mil, Sport) reserves pl. **R~rad** nt spare wheel

reservier|en vt reserve; **r~en lassen** book. **r~t** adj reserved. **R~ung** f -,-en reservation

Reservoir /rezɛr'vo̯a:ɐ̯/ nt **-s,-s** reservoir

Residenz f -,-en residence

Resign|ation /-'tsi̯o:n/ f - resignation. **r~ieren** vi (haben) (fig) give up. **r~iert** adj resigned

resolut adj resolute

Resonanz f -,-en resonanance

Respekt /-sp-, -ʃp-/ m **-[e]s** respect (**vor** + dat for). **r~ieren** vt respect

respektlos adj disrespectful

Ressort /rɛ'so:ɐ̯/ nt **-s,-s** department

Rest m **-[e]s,-e** remainder, rest; **R~e** remains; (Essens-) leftovers

Restaurant /rɛsto'rã:/ nt **-s,-s** restaurant

Restaur|ation /rɛstau̯ra'tsi̯o:n/ f - restoration. **r~ieren** vt restore

Rest|betrag m balance. **r~lich** adj remaining

Resultat nt **-[e]s,-e** result

rett|en vt save (**vor** + dat from); (aus Gefahr befreien) rescue; **sich r~en** save oneself; (flüchten) escape. **R~er** m **-s,-** rescuer; (fig) saviour

Rettich m **-s,-e** white radish

Rettung f -,-en rescue; (fig) salvation; **jds letzte R~** s.o.'s last hope. **R~sboot** nt lifeboat. **R~sdienst** m rescue service. **R~sgürtel** m lifebelt. **r~slos** adv hopelessly. **R~sring** m lifebelt. **R~ssanitäter(in)** m(f) paramedic. **R~swagen** m ambulance

retuschieren vt (Phot) retouch

Reue f - remorse; (Relig) repentance

Revanch|e /re'vã:ʃə/ f -,-n revenge; **R~e fordern** (Sport) ask for a return match. **r~ieren (sich)** vr take revenge; (sich erkenntlich zeigen) reciprocate (**mit** with)

Revers /re've:ɐ̯/ nt -,- /-[s],-s/ lapel

Revier nt **-s,-e** district; (Zool & fig) territory; (Polizei-) [police] station

Revision f -,-en revision; (Prüfung) check; (Jur) appeal

Revolution /-'tsi̯o:n/ f -,-en revolution. **r~är** adj revolutionary. **r~ieren** vt revolutionize

Revolver m **-s,-** revolver

rezen|sieren vt review. **R~sion** f -,-en review

Rezept nt **-[e]s,-e** prescription; (Culin) recipe

Rezession f -,-en recession

R-Gespräch nt reverse-charge call

Rhabarber m **-s** rhubarb

Rhein m **-s** Rhine. **R~land** nt **-s** Rhineland. **R~wein** m hock

Rhetorik f - rhetoric

Rheum|a nt **-s** rheumatism. **r~atisch** adj rheumatic. **R~atismus** m - rheumatism

Rhinozeros nt **-[ses],-se** rhinoceros

rhyth|misch /'rʏt-/ adj rhythmic[al]. **R~mus** m -,-men rhythm

richten vt direct (**auf** + acc at); address (Frage) (**an** + acc to); aim (Waffe) (**auf** + acc at); (einstellen) set; (vorbereiten) prepare; (reparieren) mend; **in die Höhe r~** raise [up]; **sich r~** be directed (**auf** + acc at; **gegen** against); (Blick:) turn (**auf** + acc on); **sich r~nach** comply with (Vorschrift); fit in with (jds Plänen); (abhängen) depend on •vi (haben) **r~ über** (+ acc) judge

Richter m **-s,-** judge

richtig adj right, correct; (wirklich,

echt) real; **das R~e** the right thing • adv correctly; really; **r~ stellen** put right (Uhr); (fig) correct (Irrtum); **die Uhr geht r~** the clock is right

Richtlinien fpl guidelines

Richtung f **-,-en** direction

riechen† vt/i (haben) smell (**nach** of; **an etw** dat sth)

Riegel m **-s,-** bolt; (Seife) bar

Riemen m **-s,-** strap; (Ruder) oar

Riese m **-n,-n** giant

rieseln vi (sein) trickle; (Schnee:) fall lightly

riesengroß adj huge, enormous

riesig adj huge; (gewaltig) enormous • adv [!] terribly

Riff nt **-[e]s,-e** reef

Rille f **-,-n** groove

Rind nt **-es,-er** ox; (Kuh) cow; (Stier) bull; (R~fleisch) beef; **R~er** cattle pl

Rinde f **-,-n** bark; (Käse-) rind; (Brot-) crust

Rinder|braten m roast beef. **R~wahnsinn** m [!] mad cow disease

Rindfleisch nt beef

Ring m **-[e]s,-e** ring

ringeln (sich) vr curl

ring|en† vi (haben) wrestle; (fig) struggle (**um/nach** for) • vt wring (Hände). **R~er** m **-s,-** wrestler. **R~kampf** m wrestling match; (als Sport) wrestling

rings|herum, **r~um** adv all around

Rinn|e f **-,-n** channel; (Dach-) gutter. **r~en**† vi (sein) run; (Sand:) trickle. **R~stein** m gutter

Rippe f **-,-n** rib. **R~nfellentzündung** f pleurisy

Risiko nt **-s,-s** & **-ken** risk

risk|ant adj risky. **r~ieren** vt risk

Riss m **-es,-e** tear; (Mauer-) crack; (fig) rift

rissig adj cracked; (Haut) chapped

Rist m **-[e]s,-e** instep

Ritt m **-[e]s,-e** ride

Ritter m **-s,-** knight

Ritual nt **-s,-e** ritual

Ritz m **-es,-e** scratch. **R~e** f **-,-n** crack; (Fels-) cleft; (zwischen Betten, Vorhängen) gap. **r~en** vt scratch

Rival|e m **-n,-n**, **R~in** f **-,-nen** rival. **R~ität** f **-,-en** rivalry

Robbe f **-,-n** seal

Robe f **-,-n** gown; (Talar) robe

Roboter m **-s,-** robot

robust adj robust

röcheln vi (haben) breathe noisily

Rochen m **-s,-** (Zool) ray

Rock[1] m **-[e]s,⸚e** skirt; (Jacke) jacket

Rock[2] m **-[s]** (Mus) rock

rodel|n vi (sein/haben) toboggan. **R~schlitten** m toboggan

roden vt clear (Land); grub up (Stumpf)

Rogen m **-s,-** [hard] roe

Roggen m **-s** rye

roh adj rough; (ungekocht) raw; (Holz) bare; (brutal) brutal. **R~bau** m **-[e]s,-ten** shell. **R~kost** f raw [vegetarian] food. **R~ling** m **-s,-e** brute. **R~öl** nt crude oil

Rohr nt **-[e]s,-e** pipe; (Geschütz-) barrel; (Bot) reed; (Zucker-, Bambus-) cane

Röhre f **-,-n** tube; (Radio-) valve; (Back-) oven

Rohstoff m raw material

Rokoko nt **-s** rococo

Roll|bahn f taxiway; (Start-/Landebahn) runway. **R~balken** m scroll bar

Rolle f **-,-n** roll; (Garn-) reel; (Draht-) coil; (Techn) roller; (Seil-) pulley; (Lauf-) castor; (Theat) part, role; **das spielt keine R~** (fig) that doesn't matter. **r~n** vt roll; (auf-) roll up; (Computer) scroll; **sich r~n** roll • vi (sein) roll; (Flugzeug:) taxi. **R~r** m **-s,-** scooter. **R~rblades®** /-ble:ds/ mpl Rollerblades®

Roll|feld nt airfield. **R~kragen** m

r

polo-neck. **R~mops** m rollmop[s] sg

Rollo nt **-s,-s** [roller] blind

Roll|schuh m roller-skate; **R~schuh laufen** roller-skate. **R~stuhl** m wheelchair. **R~treppe** f escalator

Rom nt **-s** Rome

Roman m **-s,-e** novel. **r~isch** adj Romanesque; (Sprache) Romance

Romant|ik f - romanticism. **r~isch** adj romantic

Röm|er(in) m **-s,-** (f **-,-nen**) Roman. **r~isch** adj Roman

Rommé, **Rommee** /'rɔme:/ nt **-s** rummy

röntgen vt X-ray. **R~aufnahme** f, **R~bild** nt X-ray. **R~strahlen** mpl X-rays

rosa inv adj, **R~** nt **-[s],-** pink

Rose f **-,-n** rose. **R~nkohl** m [Brussels] sprouts pl. **R~nkranz** m (Relig) rosary

Rosine f **-,-n** raisin

Rosmarin m **-s** rosemary

Ross nt **-es,⸚er** horse

Rost[1] m **-[e]s,-e** grating; (Kamin-) grate; (Brat-) grill

Rost[2] m **-[e]s** rust. **r~en** vi (haben) rust

rösten vt roast; toast (Brot)

rostfrei adj stainless

rostig adj rusty

rot adj, **Rot** nt **-s,-** red; **rot werden** turn red; (erröten) go red, blush

Röte f - redness; (Scham-) blush

Röteln pl German measles sg

röten vt redden; **sich r~** turn red

rothaarig adj red-haired

rotieren vi (haben) rotate

Rot|kehlchen nt **-s,-** robin. **R~kohl** m red cabbage

rötlich adj reddish

Rotwein m red wine

Rou|lade /ru'la:də/ f **-,-n** beef olive. **R~leau** nt **-s,-s** [roller] blind

Routin|e /ru'ti:nə/ f **-,-n** routine; (Erfahrung) experience. **r~emäßig** adj routine • adv routinely. **r~iert** adj experienced

Rowdy /'raudi/ m **-s,-s** hooligan

Rübe f **-,-n** beet; **rote R~** beetroot

Rubin m **-s,-e** ruby

Rubrik f **-,-en** column

Ruck m **-[e]s,-e** jerk

ruckartig adj jerky

rück|bezüglich adj (Gram) reflexive. **R~blende** f flashback. **R~blick** m (fig) review (**auf** + acc of). **r~blickend** adv in retrospect. **r~datieren** vt (infinitive & pp only) backdate

Rücken m **-s,-** back; (Buch-) spine; (Berg-) ridge. **R~lehne** f back. **R~mark** nt spinal cord. **R~schwimmen** nt backstroke. **R~wind** m following wind; (Aviat) tail wind

rückerstatten vt (infinitive & pp only) refund

Rückfahr|karte f return ticket. **R~t** f return journey

Rück|fall m relapse. **R~flug** m return flight. **R~frage** f [further] query. **r~fragen** vi (haben) (infinitive & pp only) check (**bei** with). **R~gabe** f return. **r~gängig** adj **r~gängig machen** cancel; break off (Verlobung). **R~grat** nt **-[e]s,-e** spine, backbone. **R~hand** f backhand. **R~kehr** f return. **R~lagen** fpl reserves. **R~licht** nt rear-light. **R~reise** f return journey

Rucksack m rucksack

Rück|schau f review. **R~schlag** m (Sport) return; (fig) set-back. **r~schrittlich** adj retrograde. **R~seite** f back; (einer Münze) reverse

Rücksicht f **-,-en** consideration. **R~nahme** f - consideration. **r~slos** adj inconsiderate; (schonungslos) ruthless. **r~svoll** adj considerate

Rück|sitz m back seat; (Sozius) pillion. **R~spiegel** m rear-view mirror. **R∼spiel** nt return match. **R∼stand** m (Chemistry) residue; (Arbeits-) backlog; **im R∼stand sein** be behind. **r∼ständig** adj (fig) backward. **R∼stau** m (Auto) tailback. **R∼strahler** m **-s,-** reflector. **R∼tritt** m resignation; (Fahrrad) back pedalling

rückwärt|ig adj back, rear. **r∼s** adv backwards. **R∼sgang** m reverse [gear]

Rückweg m way back

rück|wirkend adj retrospective. **R∼wirkung** f retrospective force; **mit R∼wirkung vom** backdated to. **R∼zahlung** f repayment

Rüde m **-n,-n** [male] dog

Rudel nt **-s,-** herd; (Wolfs-) pack; (Löwen-) pride

Ruder nt **-s,-** oar; (Steuer-) rudder; **am R∼** (Naut & fig) at the helm. **R∼boot** nt rowing boat. **r∼n** vt/i (haben/sein) row

Ruf m **-[e]s,-e** call; (laut) shout; (Telefon) telephone number; (Ansehen) reputation. **r∼en**† vt/i (haben) call (**nach** for); **r∼en lassen** send for

Ruf|name m forename by which one is known. **R∼nummer** f telephone number. **R∼zeichen** nt dialling tone

Rüge f **-,-n** reprimand. **r∼n** vt reprimand; (kritisieren) criticize

Ruhe f **-** rest; (Stille) quiet; (Frieden) peace; (innere) calm; (Gelassenheit) composure; **R∼ [da]!** quiet! **r∼los** adj restless. **r∼n** vi (haben) rest (**auf** + dat on); (Arbeit, Verkehr:) have stopped. **R∼pause** f rest, break. **R∼stand** m retirement; **im R∼stand** retired. **R∼störung** f disturbance of the peace. **R∼tag** m day of rest; **'Montag R∼tag'** 'closed on Mondays'

ruhig adj quiet; (erholsam) restful; (friedlich) peaceful; (unbewegt, gelassen) calm; **man kann r∼ darüber sprechen** there's no harm in talking about it

Ruhm m **-[e]s** fame; (Ehre) glory

rühmen vt praise

ruhmreich adj glorious

Ruhr f **-** (Med) dysentery

Rühr|ei nt scrambled eggs pl. **r∼en** vt move; (Culin) stir; **sich r∼en** move •vi (haben) stir; **r∼en an** (+ acc) touch; (fig) touch on. **r∼end** adj touching

Rührung f **-** emotion

Ruin m **-s** ruin. **R∼e** f **-,-n** ruin; ruins pl (gen of). **r∼ieren** vt ruin

rülpsen vi (haben) [!] belch

Rum m **-s** rum

Rumän|ien /-i̯ən/ nt **-s** Romania. **r∼isch** adj Romanian

Rummel m **-s** [!] hustle and bustle; (Jahrmarkt) funfair

Rumpelkammer f junk-room

Rumpf m **-[e]s,⸚e** body, trunk; (Schiffs-) hull; (Aviat) fuselage

rund adj round •adv approximately; **r∼ um** [a]round. **R∼blick** m panoramic view. **R∼brief** m circular [letter]

Runde f **-,-n** round; (Kreis) circle; (eines Polizisten) beat; (beim Rennen) lap; **eine R∼ Bier** a round of beer

Rund|fahrt f tour. **R∼frage** f poll

Rundfunk m radio; **im R∼** on the radio. **R∼gerät** nt radio [set]

Rund|gang m round; (Spaziergang) walk (**durch** round). **r∼heraus** adv straight out. **r∼herum** adv all around. **r∼lich** adj rounded; (mollig) plump. **R∼reise** f [circular] tour. **R∼schreiben** nt circular. **r∼um** adv all round. **R∼ung** f **-,-en** curve

Runzel f **-,-n** wrinkle

runzlig adj wrinkled

Rüpel m **-s,-** [!] lout

rupfen vt pull out; pluck (Geflügel)

Rüsche f **-,-n** frill

Ruß m **-es** soot

Russe m **-n,-n** Russian

Rüssel m **-s,-** (Zool) trunk

Russ|in f **-,-nen** Russian. **r~isch** adj Russian. **R~isch** nt **-[s]** (Lang) Russian

Russland nt **-s** Russia

rüsten vi (haben) prepare (**zu/für** for) •vr **sich r~** get ready

rüstig adj sprightly

rustikal adj rustic

Rüstung f **-,-en** armament; (Harnisch) armour. **R~skontrolle** f arms control

Rute f **-,-n** twig; (Angel-, Wünschel-) rod; (zur Züchtigung) birch; (Schwanz) tail

Rutsch m **-[e]s,-e** slide. **R~bahn** f slide. **R~e** f **-,-n** chute. **r~en** vt slide; (rücken) move •vi (sein) slide; (aus-, ab-) slip; (Auto) skid. **r~ig** adj slippery

rütteln vt shake •vi (haben) **r~ an** (+ dat) rattle

Ss

Saal m **-[e]s,Säle** hall; (Theat) auditorium; (Kranken-) ward

Saat f **-,-en** seed; (Säen) sowing; (Gesätes) crop

sabbern vi (haben) [!] slobber; (Baby:) dribble; (reden) jabber

Säbel m **-s,-** sabre

Sabo|tage /zabo'ta:ʒə/ f **-** sabotage. **S~teur** m **-s,-e** saboteur. **s~tieren** vt sabotage

Sach|bearbeiter m expert. **S~buch** nt non-fiction book

Sache f **-,-n** matter, business; (Ding) thing; (fig) cause

Sach|gebiet nt (fig) area, field. **s~kundig** adj expert. **s~lich** adj factual; (nüchtern) matter-of-fact

sächlich adj (Gram) neuter

Sachse m **-n,-n** Saxon. **S~n** nt **-s** Saxony

sächsisch adj Saxon

Sach|verhalt m **-[e]s** facts pl. **S~verständige(r)** m/f expert

Sack m **-[e]s,⸚e** sack

Sack|gasse f cul-de-sac; (fig) impasse. **S~leinen** nt sacking

Sadis|mus m **-** sadism. **S~t** m **-en,-en** sadist

säen vt/i (haben) sow

Safe /ze:f/ m **-s,-s** safe

Saft m **-[e]s,⸚e** juice; (Bot) sap. **s~ig** adj juicy

Sage f **-,-n** legend

Säge f **-,-n** saw. **S~mehl** nt sawdust

sagen vt say; (mitteilen) tell; (bedeuten) mean

sägen vt/i (haben) saw

sagenhaft adj legendary

Säge|späne mpl wood shavings. **S~werk** nt sawmill

Sahn|e f **-** cream. **S~ebonbon** m & nt ≈ toffee. **s~ig** adj creamy

Saison /zɛ'zõ:/ f **-,-s** season

Saite f **-,-n** (Mus, Sport) string. **S~ninstrument** nt stringed instrument

Sakko m & nt **-s,-s** sports jacket

Sakrament nt **-[e]s,-e** sacrament

Sakristei f **-,-en** vestry

Salat m **-[e]s,-e** salad. **S~soße** f salad-dressing

Salbe f **-,-n** ointment

Salbei m **-s** & f **-** sage

salben vt anoint

Saldo m **-s,-dos** & **-den** balance

Salon /za'lõ:/ m **-s,-s** salon

salopp adj casual; (Benehmen) informal

Salto m **-s,-s** somersault

Salut m **-[e]s,-e** salute. **s~ieren** vi (haben) salute

Salve f **-,-n** volley; (Geschütz-) salvo, (von Gelächter) burst

Salz nt **-es,-e** salt. **s~en**† vt salt. **S~fass** nt salt-cellar. **s~ig** adj salty. **S~kartoffeln** fpl boiled potatoes. **S~säure** f hydrochloric acid

Samen m **-s,-** seed; (Anat) semen, sperm

Sammel|becken nt reservoir. **s~n** vt/i (haben) collect; (suchen, versammeln) gather; **sich s~n** collect; (sich versammeln) gather; (sich fassen) collect oneself. **S~name** m collective noun

Samm|ler(in) m **-s,-** (f **-,-nen**) collector. **S~lung** f **-,-en** collection; (innere) composure

Samstag m **-s** Saturday. **s~s** adv on Saturdays

samt prep (+ dat) together with

Samt m **-[e]s** velvet

sämtlich indefinite pronoun inv all. **s~e(r,s)** indefinite pronoun all the; **s~e Werke** complete works

Sanatorium nt **-s,-ien** sanatorium

Sand m **-[e]s** sand

Sandale f **-,-n** sandal

Sand|bank f sandbank. **S~kasten** m sand-pit. **S~papier** nt sandpaper

sanft adj gentle

Sänger(in) m **-s,-**(f **-,-nen**) singer

sanieren vt clean up; redevelop (Gebiet); (modernisieren) modernize; make profitable (Industrie, Firma); **sich s~** become profitable

sanitär adj sanitary

Sanität|er m **-s,-** first-aid man; (Fahrer) ambulance man; (Mil) medical orderly. **S~swagen** m ambulance

Sanktion /zaŋk'tsi̯o:n/ f **-,-en** sanction. **s~ieren** vt sanction

Saphir m **-s,-e** sapphire

Sardelle f **-,-n** anchovy

Sardine f **-,-n** sardine

Sarg m **-[e]s,¨-e** coffin

Sarkasmus m **-** sarcasm

Satan m **-s** Satan; (!: Teufel) devil

Satellit m **-en,-en** satellite. **S~enfernsehen** nt satellite television. **S~enschüssel** f satellite dish. **S~entelefon** nt satphone

Satin /za'tɛŋ/ m **-s** satin

Satire f **-,-n** satire

satt adj full; (Farbe) rich; **s~ sein** have had enough [to eat]; **etw s~ haben** ! be fed up with sth

Sattel m **-s,¨-** saddle. **s~n** vt saddle. **S~zug** m articulated lorry

sättigen vt satisfy; (Chemistry & fig) saturate • vi (haben) be filling

Satz m **-es,¨-e** sentence; (Teil-) clause; (These) proposition; (Math) theorem; (Mus) movement; (Tennis, Zusammengehöriges) set; (Boden-) sediment; (Kaffee-) grounds pl; (Steuer-, Zins-) rate; (Druck-) setting; (Schrift-) type; (Sprung) leap, bound. **S~aussage** f predicate. **S~gegenstand** m subject. **S~zeichen** nt punctuation mark

Sau f **-,Säue** sow

sauber adj clean; (ordentlich) neat; (anständig) decent; **s~ machen** clean. **S~keit** f **-** cleanliness; neatness

säuberlich adj neat

Sauce /'zo:sə/ f **-,-n** sauce; (Braten-) gravy

Saudi-Arabien /-i̯ən/ nt **-s** Saudi Arabia

sauer adj sour; (Chemistry) acid; (eingelegt) pickled; (schwer) hard; **saurer Regen** acid rain

Sauerkraut nt sauerkraut

säuerlich adj slightly sour

Sauerstoff m oxygen

saufen† vt/i (haben) drink; ✖ booze

Säufer m **-s,-** ✖ boozer

saugen† vt/i (haben) suck; (staub-)

S

vacuum, hoover; **sich voll Wasser s~** soak up water

säugen vt suckle

Säugetier nt mammal

saugfähig adj absorbent

Säugling m **-s,-e** infant

Säule f **-,-n** column

Saum m **-[e]s,Säume** hem; (Rand) edge

säumen vt hem; (fig) line

Sauna f **-,-nas** & **-nen** sauna

Säure f **-,-n** acidity; (Chemistry) acid

sausen vi (haben) rush; (Ohren:) buzz •vi (sein) rush [along]

Saxophon, **Saxofon** nt **-s,-e** saxophone

S-Bahn f city and suburban railway

Scanner m **-s,-** scanner

sch int shush! (fort) shoo!

Schabe f **-,-n** cockroach

schaben vt/i (haben) scrape

schäbig adj shabby

Schablone f **-,-n** stencil; (Muster) pattern; (fig) stereotype

Schach nt **-s** chess; **S~!** check! **S~brett** nt chessboard

Schachfigur f chess-man

schachmatt adj **s~ setzen** checkmate; **s~!** checkmate!

Schachspiel nt game of chess

Schacht m **-[e]s,¨e** shaft

Schachtel f **-,-n** box; (Zigaretten-) packet

Schachzug m move

schade adj **s~ sein** be a pity or shame: **zu s~ für** too good for

Schädel m **-s**, skull. **S~bruch** m fractured skull

schaden vi (haben) (+ dat) damage; (nachteilig sein) hurt. **S~** m **-s,¨** damage; (Defekt) defect; (Nachteil) disadvantage. **S~ersatz** m damages pl. **S~freude** f malicious glee. **s~froh** adj gloating

schädig|en vt damage, harm. **S~ung** f **-,-en** damage

schädlich adj harmful

Schädling m **-s,-e** pest. **S~sbekämpfungsmittel** nt pesticide

Schaf nt **-[e]s,-e** sheep. **S~bock** m ram

Schäfer m **-s,-** shepherd. **S~hund** m sheepdog; **Deutscher S~hund** alsatian

schaffen[1]† vt create; (herstellen) establish; make (Platz)

schaffen[2] v (reg) •vt manage [to do]; pass (Prüfung); catch (Zug); (bringen) take

Schaffner m **-s,-** conductor; (Zug-) ticket-inspector

Schaffung f **-** creation

Schaft m **-[e]s,¨e** shaft; (Gewehr-) stock; (Stiefel-) leg

Schal m **-s,-s** scarf

Schale f **-,-n** skin; (abgeschält) peel; (Eier-, Nuss-, Muschel-) shell; (Schüssel) dish

schälen vt peel; **sich s~** peel

Schall m **-[e]s** sound. **S~dämpfer** m silencer. **s~dicht** adj soundproof. **s~en** vi (haben) ring out: (nachhallen) resound. **S~mauer** f sound barrier. **S~platte** f record, disc

schalt|en vt switch •vi (haben) switch/(Ampel:) turn (**auf** + acc **to**); (Auto) change gear; ([!]: begreifen) catch on. **S~er** m **-s,-** switch; (Post-, Bank-) counter; (Fahrkarten-) ticket window. **S~hebel** m switch; (Auto) gear lever. **S~jahr** nt leap year. **S~ung** f **-,-en** circuit: (Auto) gear change

Scham f **-** shame; (Anat) private parts pl

schämen (sich) vr be ashamed

scham|haft adj modest. **s~los** adj shameless

Schampon nt **-s** shampoo. **s~ieren** vt shampoo

Schande f **-** disgrace, shame

schändlich adj disgraceful

Schanktisch m bar

Schanze f, -,-n [ski-]jump

Schar f -,-en crowd; (Vogel-) flock

Scharade f -,-n charade

scharen vt **um sich s~** gather round one; **sich s~ um** flock round. **s~weise** adv in droves

scharf adj sharp; (stark) strong; (stark gewürzt) hot; (Geruch) pungent; (Wind, Augen, Verstand) keen; (streng) harsh; (Galopp) hard; (Munition) live; (Hund) fierce; **s~ einstellen** (Phot) focus; **s~ sein** (Phot) be in focus; **s~ sein auf** (+ acc) ▣ be keen on

Schärfe f sharpness; strength; hotness; pungency; keenness; harshness. **s~n** vt sharpen

Scharf|richter m executioner. **S~schütze** m marksman. **S~sinn** m astuteness

Scharlach m -s scarlet fever

Scharlatan m -s,-e charlatan

Scharnier nt -s,-e hinge

Schärpe f -,-n sash

scharren vi (haben) scrape; (Huhn) scratch • vt scrape

Schaschlik m & nt -s,-s kebab

Schatten m -s,- shadow; (schattige Stelle) shade. **S~riss** m silhouette. **S~seite** f shady side; (fig) disadvantage

schattier|en vt shade. **S~ung** f -,-en shading

schattig adj shady

Schatz m -es,⸚e treasure; (Freund, Freundin) sweetheart

schätzen vt estimate; (taxieren) value; (achten) esteem; (würdigen) appreciate

Schätzung f -,-en estimate; (Taxierung) valuation

Schau f -,-en show. **S~ bild** nt diagram

Schauder m -s shiver; (vor Abscheu) shudder. **s~haft** adj dreadful. **s~n** vi (haben) shiver; (vor Abscheu) shudder

schauen vi (haben) (SGer, Aust) look; **s~, dass** make sure that

Schauer m -s,- shower; (Schauder) shiver. **S~geschichte** f horror story. **s~lich** adj ghastly

Schaufel f -,-n shovel; (Kehr-) dustpan. **s~n** vt shovel; (graben) dig

Schaufenster nt shop-window. **S~puppe** f dummy

Schaukel f -,-n swing. **s~n** vt rock • vi (haben) rock; (auf einer Schaukel) swing; (schwanken) sway. **S~pferd** nt rocking-horse. **S~stuhl** m rocking-chair

Schaum m -[e]s foam; (Seifen-) lather; (auf Bier) froth; (als Frisier-, Rasiermittel) mousse

schäumen vi (haben) foam, froth; (Seife:) lather

Schaum|gummi m foam rubber. **s~ig** adj frothy; **s~ig rühren** (Culin) cream. **S~stoff** m [synthetic] foam. **S~wein** m sparkling wine

Schauplatz m scene

schaurig adj dreadful; (unheimlich) eerie

Schauspiel nt play; (Anblick) spectacle. **S~er** m actor. **S~erin** f actress

Scheck m -s,-s cheque. **S~buch, S~heft** nt cheque-book. **S~karte** f cheque card

Scheibe f -,-n disc; (Schieß-) target; (Glas-) pane; (Brot-, Wurst-) slice. **S~nwischer** m -s,- windscreen-wiper

Scheich m -s,-e & -s sheikh

Scheide f -,-n sheath; (Anat) vagina

scheid|en† vt separate; (unterscheiden) distinguish; dissolve (Ehe); **sich s~en lassen** get divorced • vi (sein) leave; (voneinander) part. **S~ung** f -,-en divorce

Schein m -[e]s,-e light; (Anschein) appearance; (Bescheinigung) certificate; (Geld-) note. **s~bar** adj apparent. **s~en**† vi (haben) shine; (den Anschein haben) seem, appear

scheinheilig adj hypocritical

S

Scheinwerfer m **-s,-** floodlight; (Such-) searchlight; (Auto) headlight; (Theat) spotlight

Scheiße f **-** (vulgar) shit. **s~n**† vi (haben) (vulgar) shit

Scheit nt **-[e]s,-e** log

Scheitel m **-s,-** parting

scheitern vi (sein) fail

Schelle f **-,-n** bell. **s~n** vi (haben) ring

Schellfisch m haddock

Schelm m **-s,-e** rogue

Schelte f **-** scolding

Schema nt **-s,-mata** model, pattern; (Skizze) diagram

Schemel m **-s,-** stool

Schenke f **-,-n** tavern

Schenkel m **-s,-** thigh

schenken vt give [as a present]; **jdm Vertrauen s~** trust s.o.

Scherbe f **-,-n** [broken] piece

Schere f **-,-n** scissors pl; (Techn) shears pl; (Hummer-) claw. **s~n**[1]† vt shear; crop (Haar)

scheren[2] vt (reg) [!] bother; **sich nicht s~ um** not care about

Scherenschnitt m silhouette

Scherereien fpl [!] trouble sg

Scherz m **-es,-e** joke; **im/zum S~** as a joke. **s~en** vi (haben) joke

scheu adj shy; (Tier) timid; **s~ werden** (Pferd:) shy

scheuchen vt shoo

scheuen vt be afraid of; (meiden) shun; **keine Mühe/Kosten s~** spare no effort/expense; **sich s~** be afraid (**vor** + dat of); shrink (**etw zu tun** from doing sth)

scheuern vt scrub; (reiben) rub; **[wund] s~n** chafe • vi (haben) rub, chafe

Scheuklappen fpl blinkers

Scheune f **-,-n** barn

Scheusal nt **-s,-e** monster

scheußlich adj horrible

Schi m **-s,-er** ski; **S~ fahren** od **laufen** ski

Schicht f **-,-en** layer; (Geology) stratum; (Gesellschafts-) class; (Arbeits-) shift. **S~arbeit** f shift work. **s~en** vt stack [up]

schick adj stylish; (Frau) chic. **S~** m **-[e]s** style

schicken vt/i (haben) send; **s~ nach** send for

Schicksal nt **-s,-e** fate. **S~sschlag** m misfortune

Schieb|edach nt (Auto) sun-roof. **s~en**† vt push; (gleitend) slide; ([!]: handeln mit) traffic in; **etw s~en auf** (+ acc) (fig) put sth down to; shift (Schuld) on to • vi (haben) push. **S~etür** f sliding door. **S~ung** f **-,-en** [!] illicit deal; (Betrug) rigging, fixing

Schieds|gericht nt panel of judges; (Jur) arbitration tribunal. **S~richter** m referee; (Tennis) umpire; (Jur) arbitrator

schief adj crooked; (unsymmetrisch) lopsided; (geneigt) slanting, sloping; (nicht senkrecht) leaning; (Winkel) oblique; (fig) false; suspicious • adv not straight; **s~ gehen** [!] go wrong

Schiefer m **-s** slate

schielen vi (haben) squint

Schienbein nt shin

Schiene f **-,-n** rail; (Gleit-) runner; (Med) splint. **s~n** vt (Med) put in a splint

Schieß|bude f shooting-gallery. **s~en**† vt shoot; fire (Kugel); score (Tor) • vi (haben) shoot, fire (**auf** + acc at). **S~scheibe** f target. **S~stand** m shooting-range

Schifahr|en nt skiing. **S~er(in)** m(f) skier

Schiff nt **-[e]s,-e** ship; (Kirchen-) nave; (Seiten-) aisle

Schiffahrt* f = **Schifffahrt**

schiff|bar adj navigable. **S~bruch** m shipwreck. **s~brüchig** adj shipwrecked. **S~fahrt** f shipping

Schikan|e f **-,-n** harassment; **mit allen S~en** [!] with every refinement. **s~ieren** vt harass

Schi|laufen nt **-s** skiing.

S~läufer(in) m(f) **-s,-** (f **-,-nen**) skier

Schild[1] m **-[e]s,-e** shield

Schild[2] nt **-[e]s,-er** sign; (Nummern-) plate; (Mützen-) badge; (Etikett) label

Schilddrüse f thyroid [gland]

schilder|n vt describe. **S~ung** f **-,-en** description

Schild|kröte f tortoise; (See-) turtle. **S~patt** nt **-[e]s** tortoiseshell

Schilf nt **-[e]s** reeds pl

schillern vi (haben) shimmer

Schimmel m **-s,-** mould; (Pferd) white horse. **s~n** vi (haben/sein) go mouldy

schimmern vi (haben) gleam

Schimpanse m **-n,-n** chimpanzee

schimpf|en vi (haben) grumble (**mit** at; **über** + acc about); scold (**mit jdm** s.o.) •vt call. **S~wort** nt (pl **-wörter**) swear-word

Schinken m **-s,-** ham. **S~speck** m bacon

Schippe f **-,-n** shovel. **s~n** vt shovel

Schirm m **-[e]s,-e** umbrella; (Sonnen-) sunshade; (Lampen-) shade; (Augen-) visor; (Mützen-) peak; (Ofen-, Bild-) screen; (fig: Schutz) shield. **S~herrschaft** f patronage. **S~mütze** f peaked cap

schizophren adj schizophrenic. **S~ie** f - schizophrenia

Schlacht f **-,-en** battle

schlachten vt slaughter, kill

Schlacht|feld nt battlefield. **S~hof** m abattoir

Schlacke f **-,-n** slag

Schlaf m **-[e]s** sleep; **im S~** in one's sleep. **S~anzug** m pyjamas pl

Schläfe f **-,-n** (Anat) temple

schlafen† vi (haben) sleep; **s~ gehen** go to bed; **er schläft noch** he is still asleep

schlaff adj limp; (Seil) slack; (Muskel) flabby

Schlaf|lied nt lullaby. **s~los** adj sleepless. **S~losigkeit** f - insomnia. **S~mittel** nt sleeping drug

schläfrig adj sleepy

Schlaf|saal m dormitory. **S~sack** m sleeping-bag. **S~tablette** f sleeping-pill. **S~wagen** m sleeping-car, sleeper. **s~wandeln** vi (haben/sein) sleep-walk. **S~zimmer** nt bedroom

Schlag m **-[e]s,¨e** blow; (Faust-) punch; (Herz-, Puls-, Trommel-) beat; (einer Uhr) chime; (Glocken-, Gong- & Med) stroke; (elektrischer) shock; (Art) type; **S¨~e bekommen** get a beating; **S~ auf S~** in rapid succession. **S~ader** f artery. **S~anfall** m stroke. **S~baum** m barrier

schlagen† vt hit, strike; (fällen) fell; knock (Loch, Nagel) (**in** + acc into); (prügeln, besiegen) beat; (Culin) whisk (Eiweiß); whip (Sahne); (legen) throw; (wickeln) wrap; **sich s~** fight •vi (haben) beat; (Tür:) bang; (Uhr:) strike; (melodisch) chime; **mit den Flügeln s~** flap its wings •vi (sein) **in etw** (acc) **s~** (Blitz, Kugel:) strike sth; **nach jdm s~** (fig) take after s.o.

Schlager m **-s,-** popular song; (Erfolg) hit

Schläger m **-s,-** racket; (Tischtennis-) bat; (Golf-) club; (Hockey-) stick. **S~ei** f **-,-en** fight, brawl

schlag|fertig adj quick-witted. **S~loch** nt pot-hole. **S~sahne** f whipped cream; (ungeschlagen) whipping cream. **S~seite** f (Naut) list. **S~stock** m truncheon. **S~wort** nt (pl **-worte**) slogan. **S~zeile** f headline. **S~zeug** nt (Mus) percussion. **S~zeuger** m **-s,-** percussionist; (in Band) drummer

Schlamm m **-[e]s** mud. **s~ig** adj muddy

Schlamp|e f **-,-n** ! slut. **s~en** vi (haben) ! be sloppy (**bei** in). **s~ig** adj slovenly; (Arbeit) sloppy

Schlange f **-,-n** snake; (Menschen-, Auto-) queue; **S~ stehen** queue

schlängeln (sich) vr wind; (Person:) weave (**durch** through)

S

schlank adj slim. **S~heitskur** f slimming diet

schlapp adj tired; (schlaff) limp

schlau adj clever; (gerissen) crafty; **ich werde nicht s~ daraus** I can't make head or tail of it

Schlauch m **-[e]s,Schläuche** tube; (Wasser-) hose[pipe]. **S~boot** nt rubber dinghy

Schlaufe f **-,-n** loop

schlecht adj bad; (böse) wicked; (unzulänglich) poor; **s~ werden** go bad; (Wetter:) turn bad; **mir ist s~** I feel sick; **s~ machen** ! run down. **s~gehen*** vi sep (sein) = **s~ gehen**, s. **gehen**

schlecken vt/i (haben) lick (**an etw** dat sth); (auf-) lap up

Schlegel m **-s,-** (SGer: Keule) leg; (Hühner-) drumstick

schleichen† vi (sein) creep; (langsam gehen/fahren) crawl • vr **sich s~** creep. **s~d** adj creeping

Schleier m **-s,-** veil; (fig) haze

Schleife f **-,-n** bow; (Fliege) bowtie; (Biegung) loop

schleifen[1] v (reg) • vt drag • vi (haben) trail, drag

schleifen[2]† vt grind; (schärfen) sharpen; cut (Edelstein, Glas)

Schleim m **-[e]s** slime; (Anat) mucus; (Med) phlegm. **s~ig** adj slimy

schlendern vi (sein) stroll

schlenkern vt/i (haben) swing; **s~ mit** swing; dangle (Beine)

Schlepp|dampfer m tug. **S~e** f **-,-n** train. **s~en** vt drag; (tragen) carry; (ziehen) tow; **sich s~en** drag oneself; (sich hinziehen) drag on; **sich s~en mit** carry. **S~er** m **-s,-** tug; (Traktor) tractor. **S~kahn** m barge. **S~lift** m T-bar lift. **S~tau** nt towrope; **ins S~tau nehmen** take in tow

Schleuder f **-,-n** catapult; (Wäsche-) spin-drier. **s~n** vt hurl; spin (Wäsche) • vi (sein) skid; **ins S~n geraten** skid. **S~sitz** m ejector seat

Schleuse f **-,-n** lock; (Sperre) sluice[-gate]. **s~n** vt steer

Schliche pl tricks

schlicht adj plain; simple

Schlichtung f **-** settlement; (Jur) arbitration

Schließe f **-,-n** clasp; buckle

schließen† vt close (ab-) lock; fasten (Kleid, Verschluss); (stilllegen) close down; (beenden, folgern) conclude; enter into (Vertrag); **sich s~** close; **etw s~ an** (+ acc) connect sth to; **sich s~ an** (+ acc) follow • vi (haben) close, (den Betrieb einstellen) close down; (den Schlüssel drehen) turn the key; (enden, folgern) conclude

Schließ|fach nt locker. **s~lich** adv finally, in the end; (immerhin) after all. **S~ung** f **-,-en** closure

Schliff m **-[e]s** cut; (Schleifen) cutting; (fig) polish

schlimm adj bad

Schlinge f **-,-n** loop; (Henkers-) noose; (Med) sling; (Falle) snare

Schlingel m **-s,-** ! rascal

schlingen† vt wind, wrap; tie (Knoten) • vt/i (haben) bolt one's food

Schlips m **-es,-e** tie

Schlitten m **-s,-** sledge; (Rodel-) toboggan; (Pferde-) sleigh; **S~ fahren** toboggan

schlittern vi (haben/ sein) slide

Schlittschuh m skate; **S~ laufen** skate. **S~läufer(in)** m(f) **-s,-** (f **-,-nen**) skater

Schlitz m **-es,-e** slit; (für Münze) slot; (Jacken-) vent; (Hosen-) flies pl. **s~en** vt slit

Schloss nt **-es,⸚er** lock; (Vorhänge-) padlock; (Verschluss) clasp; (Gebäude) castle; palace

Schlosser m **-s,-** locksmith; (Auto-) mechanic

Schlucht f **-,-en** ravine, gorge

schluchzen vi (haben) sob

Schluck m **-[e]s,-e** mouthful; (klein) sip

Schluckauf m **-s** hiccups pl

schlucken vt/i (haben) swallow

Schlummer m **-s** slumber

Schlund m **-[e]s** [back of the] throat; (fig) mouth

schlüpf|en vi (sein) slip; [**aus dem Ei**] **s~en** hatch. **S~er** m **-s,-** knickers pl. **s~rig** adj slippery

schlürfen vt/i (haben) slurp

Schluss m **-es,¨e** end; (S~folgerung) conclusion; **zum S~** finally; **S~ machen** stop (**mit etw** sth); finish (**mit jdm** with s.o.)

Schlüssel m **-s,-** key; (Schrauben-) spanner; (Geheim-) code; (Mus) clef. **S~bein** nt collar-bone. **S~bund** m & nt bunch of keys. **S~loch** nt keyhole

Schlussfolgerung f conclusion

schlüssig adj conclusive

Schluss|licht nt rear-light. **S~verkauf** m sale

schmächtig adj slight

schmackhaft adj tasty

schmal adj narrow; (dünn) thin; (schlank) slender; (karg) meagre

schmälern vt diminish; (herabsetzen) belittle

Schmalz[1] nt **-es** lard; (Ohren-) wax

Schmalz[2] m **-es** [!] schmaltz

Schmarotzer m **-s,-** parasite; (Person) sponger

schmatzen vi (haben) eat noisily

schmausen vi (haben) feast

schmecken vi (haben) taste (**nach** of); [**gut**] **s~** taste good • vt taste

Schmeichelei f **-,-en** flattery; (Kompliment) compliment

schmeichel|haft adj complimentary, flattering. **s~n** vi (haben) (+ dat) flatter

schmeißen† vt/i (haben) **s~** [**mit**] [!] chuck

Schmeißfliege f bluebottle

schmelz|en† vt/i (sein) melt; smelt (Erze). **S~wasser** nt melted snow and ice

Schmerbauch m [!] paunch

Schmerz m **-es,-en** pain; (Kummer) grief; **S~en haben** be in pain. **s~en** vt hurt; (fig) grieve • vi (haben) hurt, be painful. **S~ensgeld** nt compensation for pain and suffering. **s~haft** adj painful. **s~los** adj painless **s~stillend** adj pain-killing; **s~stillendes Mittel** analgesic, pain-killer. **S~tablette** f pain-killer

Schmetterball m (Tennis) smash

Schmetterling m **-s,-e** butterfly

schmettern vt hurl; (Tennis) smash; (singen) sing • vi (haben) sound

Schmied m **-[e]s,-e** blacksmith

Schmiede f **-,-n** forge. **S~eisen** nt wrought iron. **s~n** vt forge

Schmier|e f **-,-n** grease; (Schmutz) mess. **s~en** vt lubricate; (streichen) spread; (schlecht schreiben) scrawl • vi (haben) smudge; (schreiben) scrawl. **S~geld** nt [!] bribe. **s~ig** adj greasy; (schmutzig) grubby. **S~mittel** nt lubricant

Schminke f **-,-n** make-up. **s~n** vt make up; **sich s~n** put on make-up; **sich** (dat) **die Lippen s~n** put on lipstick

schmirgel|n vt sand down. **S~papier** nt emery-paper

schmollen vi (haben) sulk

schmor|en vt/i (haben) braise. **S~topf** m casserole

Schmuck m **-[e]s** jewellery; (Verzierung) ornament, decoration

schmücken vt decorate, adorn

schmuck|los adj plain. **S~stück** nt piece of jewellery

Schmuggel m **-s** smuggling. **s~n** vt smuggle. **S~ware** f contraband

Schmuggler m **-s,-** smuggler

schmunzeln vi (haben) smile

schmusen vi (haben) cuddle

Schmutz m **-es** dirt. **s~en** vi (haben) get dirty. **s~ig** adj dirty

Schnabel m **-s,¨** beak, bill; (eines Kruges) lip; (Tülle) spout

Schnalle f **-,-n** buckle. **s~n** vt

strap; (zu-) buckle

schnalzen vi (haben) **mit der Zunge s~** click one's tongue

schnapp|en vi (haben) **s~en nach** snap at; gasp for (Luft) • vt snatch, grab; ([!]: festnehmen) nab. **S~schloss** nt spring lock. **S~schuss** m snapshot

Schnaps m **-es,⸚e** schnapps

schnarchen vi (haben) snore

schnaufen vi (haben) puff, pant

Schnauze f **-,-n** muzzle; (eines Kruges) lip; (Tülle) spout

schnäuzen (sich) vr blow one's nose

Schnecke f **-,-n** snail; (Nackt-) slug; (Spirale) scroll. **S~nhaus** nt snail-shell

Schnee m **-s** snow; (Eier-) beaten egg-white. **S~besen** m whisk. **S~brille** f snow-goggles pl. **S~fall** m snow-fall. **S~flocke** f snowflake. **S~glöckchen** nt **-s,-** snowdrop. **S~kette** f snow chain. **S~mann** m (pl **-männer**) snowman. **S~pflug** m snowplough. **S~schläger** m whisk. **S~sturm** m snowstorm, blizzard. **S~wehe** f **-,-n** snowdrift

Schneide f **-,-n** [cutting] edge; (Klinge) blade

schneiden† vt cut; (in Scheiben) slice; (kreuzen) cross; (nicht beachten) cut dead; **Gesichter s~** pull faces; **sich s~** cut oneself; (über-) intersect

Schneider m **-s,-** tailor. **S~in** f **-,-nen** dressmaker. **s~n** vt make (Anzug, Kostüm)

Schneidezahn m incisor

schneien vi (haben) snow; **es schneit** it is snowing

Schneise f **-,-n** path

schnell adj quick; (Auto, Tempo) fast • adv quickly; (in s~em Tempo) fast; (bald) soon; **mach s~!** hurry up! **S~igkeit** f **-** rapidity; (Tempo) speed. **S~kochtopf** m pressure-cooker. **s~stens** adv as quickly as possible. **S~zug** m express [train]

schnetzeln vt cut into thin strips

Schnipsel m & nt **-s,-** scrap

Schnitt m **-[e]s,-e** cut; (Film-) cutting; (S~muster) [paper] pattern; **im S~** (durchschnittlich) on average

Schnitte f **-,-n** slice [of bread]

schnittig adj stylish; (stromlinienförmig) streamlined

Schnitt|lauch m chives pl. **S~muster** nt [paper] pattern. **S~punkt** m [point of] intersection. **S~stelle** f interface. **S~wunde** f cut

Schnitzel nt **-s,-** scrap; (Culin) escalope. **s~n** vt shred

schnitzen vt/i (haben) carve

schnodderig adj [!] brash

Schnorchel m **-s,-** snorkel

Schnörkel m **-s,-** flourish; (Kunst) scroll. **s~ig** adj ornate

schnüffeln vi (haben) sniff **(an etw** dat sth); ([!]: spionieren) snoop [around]

Schnuller m **-s,-** [baby's] dummy

Schnupf|en m **-s,-** [head] cold. **S~tabak** m snuff

schnuppern vt/i (haben) sniff **(an etw** dat sth)

Schnur f **-,⸚e** string; (Kordel) cord; (Electr) flex

schnüren vt tie; lace [up] (Schuhe)

Schnurr|bart m moustache. **s~en** vi (haben) hum; (Katze:) purr

Schnürsenkel m [shoe-]lace

Schock m **-[e]s,-s** shock. **s~en** vt [!] shock. **s~ieren** vt shock

Schöffe m **-n,-n** lay judge

Schokolade f **-** chocolate

Scholle f **-,-n** clod [of earth]; (Eis-) [ice-]floe; (Fisch) plaice

schon adv already; (allein) just; (sogar) even; (ohnehin) anyway; **s~ einmal** before; (jemals) ever; **s~ immer/oft/wieder** always/often/again; **s~ deshalb** for that reason alone; **das ist s~ möglich** that's quite possible; **ja s~, aber** well yes, but

schön adj beautiful; (Wetter) fine;

(angenehm, nett) nice; (gut) good; (!: beträchtlich) pretty; **s~en Dank!** thank you very much!

schonen vt spare; (gut behandeln) look after. **s~d** adj gentle

Schönheit f -,-en beauty. **S~sfehler** m blemish. **S~skonkurrenz** f beauty contest

Schonung f -,-en gentle care; (nach Krankheit) rest; (Baum-) plantation. **s~slos** adj ruthless

Schonzeit f close season

schöpf|en vt scoop [up]; ladle (Suppe); **Mut s~en** take heart. **s~erisch** adj creative. **S~kelle** f. **S~löffel** m ladle. **S~ung** f -,-en creation

Schoppen m -s,- (SGer) ≈ pint

Schorf m -[e]s scab

Schornstein m chimney. **S~feger** m -s,- chimney sweep

Schoß m -es,⸚e lap; (Frack-) tail

Schössling m -s,-e (Bot) shoot

Schote f -,-n pod; (Erbse) pea

Schotte m -n,-n Scot, Scotsman

Schottin f -nen Scot, Scotswoman

Schotter m -s gravel

schott|isch adj Scottish, Scots. **S~land** nt -s Scotland

schraffieren vt hatch

schräg adj diagonal; (geneigt) sloping; **s~ halten** tilt. **S~strich** m oblique stroke

Schramme f -,-n scratch

Schrank m -[e]s,⸚e cupboard; (Kleider-) wardrobe; (Akten-, Glas-) cabinet

Schranke f -,-n barrier

Schraube f -,-n screw; (Schiffs-) propeller. **s~n** vt screw; (ab-) unscrew; (drehen) turn. **S~nschlüssel** m spanner. **S~nzieher** m -s,- screwdriver

Schraubstock m vice

Schreck m -[e]s,-e fright. **S~en** m -s,- fright; (Entsetzen) horror

Schreck|gespenst nt spectre. **s~haft** adj easily frightened; (nervös) jumpy. **s~lich** adj terrible.

Schrei m -[e]s,-e cry, shout; (gellend) scream; **der letzte S~** ! the latest thing

schreib|en† vt/i (haben) write; (auf der Maschine) type; **richtig/falsch s~en** spell right/wrong; **sich s~en** (Wort:) be spelt; (korrespondieren) correspond. **S~en** nt -s,- writing; (Brief) letter. **S~fehler** m spelling mistake. **S~heft** nt exercise book. **S~kraft** f clerical assistant; (für Maschineschreiben) typist. **S~maschine** f typewriter. **S~tisch** m desk. **S~ung** f -,-en spelling. **S~waren** fpl stationery sg.

schreien† vt/i (haben) cry; (gellend) scream; (rufen, laut sprechen) shout

Schreiner m -s,- joiner

schreiten† vi (sein) walk

Schrift f -,-en writing; (Druck-) type; (Abhandlung) paper; **die Heilige S~** the Scriptures pl. **S~führer** m secretary. **s~lich** adj written • adv in writing. **S~sprache** f written language. **S~steller(in)** m -s,- (f -,-nen) writer. **S~stück** nt document. **S~zeichen** nt character

schrill adj shrill

Schritt m -[e]s,-e step; (Entfernung) pace; (Gangart) walk; (der Hose) crotch. **S~macher** m -s,- pace-maker. **s~weise** adv step by step

schroff adj precipitous; (abweisend) brusque; (unvermittelt) abrupt; (Gegensatz) stark

Schrot m & nt -[e]s coarse meal; (Blei-) small shot. **S~flinte** f shotgun

Schrott m -[e]s scrap[-metal]; **zu S~ fahren** ! write off. **S~platz** m scrap-yard

schrubben vt/i (haben) scrub

Schrull|e f -,-n whim; **alte S~e** ! old crone. **s~ig** adj cranky

schrumpfen vi (sein) shrink

schrump[e]lig adj wrinkled

Schub m -[e]s,⸚e (Phys) thrust;

(S~fach) drawer; (Menge) batch. **S~fach** nt drawer. **S~karre** f, **S~karren** m wheelbarrow. **S~lade** f drawer

Schubs m **-es,-e** push, shove. **s~en** vt push, shove

schüchtern adj shy. **S~heit** f - shyness

Schuft m **-[e]s,-e** (pej) swine

Schuh m **-[e]s,-e** shoe. **S~anzieher** m **-s,-** shoehorn. **S~band** nt (pl **-bänder**) shoe-lace. **S~creme** f shoe-polish. **S~löffel** m shoehorn. **S~macher** m **-s,-** shoemaker

Schul|abgänger m **-s,-** schoolleaver. **S~arbeiten, S~aufgaben** fpl homework sg.

Schuld f **-,-en** guilt; (Verantwortung) blame; (Geld-) debt; **S~en machen** get into debt; **S~ haben** be to blame (**an** + dat for); **jdm S~ geben** blame s.o. • **s~ sein** be to blame (**an** + dat for). **s~en** vt owe

schuldig adj guilty (gen of); (gebührend) due; **jdm etw s~sein** owe s.o. sth. **S~keit** f - duty

schuld|los adj innocent. **S~ner** m **-s,-** debtor. **S~spruch** m guilty verdict

🅒**Schule** f **-,-n** school; **in der/die S~** at/to school. **s~n** vt train

Schüler(in) m **-s,-** (f **-,-nen**) pupil

schul|frei adj **s~freier Tag** day without school; **wir haben morgen s~frei** there's no school tomorrow. **S~hof** m [school] playground. **S~jahr** nt school year; (Klasse) form. **S~kind** nt schoolchild. **S~stunde** f lesson

Schulter f **-,-n** shoulder. **S~blatt** nt shoulder-blade

Schulung f - training

schummeln vi (haben) 🅘 cheat

Schund m **-[e]s** trash

Schuppe f **-,-n** scale; **S~n** pl dandruff sg. **s~n (sich)** vr flake [off]

Schuppen m **-s,-** shed

🅒 *see* A-Z of German life and culture

schürf|en vt mine; **sich** (dat) **das Knie s~en** graze one's knee • vi (haben) **s~en nach** prospect for. **S~wunde** f abrasion, graze

Schürhaken m poker

Schurke m **-n,-n** villain

Schürze f **-,-n** apron

Schuss m **-es,⸚e** shot; (kleine Menge) dash

Schüssel f **-,-n** bowl; (TV) dish

Schuss|fahrt f (Ski) schuss. **S~waffe** f firearm

Schuster m **-s,-** = **Schuhmacher**

Schutt m **-[e]s** rubble. **S~abladeplatz** m rubbish dump

Schüttel|frost m shivering fit. **s~n** vt shake; **sich s~n** shake oneself/itself; (vor Ekel) shudder; **jdm die Hand s~n** shake s.o.'s hand

schütten vt pour; (kippen) tip; (ver-) spill • vi (haben) **es schüttet** it is pouring [with rain]

Schutz m **-es** protection; (Zuflucht) shelter; (Techn) guard; **S~ suchen** take refuge. **S~anzug** m protective suit. **S~blech** nt mudguard. **S~brille** f goggles pl

Schütze m **-n,-n** marksman; (Tor-) scorer; (Astrology) Sagittarius

schützen vt protect; (Zuflucht gewähren) shelter (**vor** + dat from) • vi (haben) give protection/shelter (**vor** + dat from)

Schutz|engel m guardian angel. **S~heilige(r)** m/f patron saint

Schützling m **-s,-e** charge

schutz|los adj defenceless, helpless. **S~mann** m (pl **-männer** & **-leute**) policeman. **S~umschlag** m dust-jacket

Schwaben nt **-s** Swabia

schwäbisch adj Swabian

schwach adj weak; (nicht gut; gering) poor; (leicht) faint

Schwäche f **-,-n** weakness. **s~n** vt weaken

schwäch|lich adj delicate. **S~ling** m **-s,-e** weakling

Schwachsinn m mental deficiency. **s~ig** adj mentally deficient; [!] idiotic

Schwager m **-s,¨** brother-in-law

Schwägerin f **-,-nen** sister-in-law

Schwalbe f **-,-n** swallow

Schwall m **-[e]s** torrent

Schwamm m **-[e]s,¨e** sponge; (SGer: Pilz) fungus; (essbar) mushroom. **s~ig** adj spongy

Schwan m **-[e]s,¨e** swan

schwanger adj pregnant

Schwangerschaft f **-,-en** pregnancy

Schwank m **-[e]s,¨e** (Theat) farce

schwank|en vi (haben) sway; (Boot:) rock; (sich ändern) fluctuate; (unentschieden sein) be undecided •(sein) stagger. **S~ung** f **-,-en** fluctuation

Schwanz m **-es,¨e** tail

schwänzen vt [!] skip; **die Schule s~** play truant

Schwarm m **-[e]s,¨e** swarm; (Fisch-) shoal; ([!]: Liebe) idol

schwärmen vi (haben) swarm; **s~ für** [!] adore; (verliebt sein) have a crush on

Schwarte f **-,-n** (Speck-) rind

schwarz adj black; ([!]: illegal) illegal; **s~er Markt** black market; **s~ gekleidet** dressed in black; **s~ auf weiß** in black and white; **s~ sehen** (fig) be pessimistic; **ins S~e treffen** score a bull's-eye. **S~** nt **-[e]s,-** black. **S~arbeit** f moonlighting. **s~arbeiten** vi sep (haben) moonlight. **S~e(r)** m/f black

Schwärze f **-** blackness. **s~n** vt blacken

Schwarz|fahrer m fare-dodger. **S~handel** m black market (**mit** in). **S~händler** m black marketeer. **S~markt** m black market. [C] **S~wald** m Black Forest. **s~weiß** adj black and white

schwatzen, (SGer) **schwätzen** vi (haben) chat; (klatschen) gossip; (Sch) talk [in class] •vt talk

Schwebe f **-** **in der S~** (fig) undecided. **S~bahn** f cable railway. **s~n** vi (haben) float; (fig) be undecided; (Verfahren:) be pending; **in Gefahr s~n** be in danger •(sein) float

Schwed|e m **-n,-n** Swede. **S~en** nt **-s** Sweden. **S~in** f **-,-nen** Swede. **s~isch** adj Swedish

Schwefel m **-s** sulphur

schweigen† vi (haben) be silent; **ganz zu s~ von** let alone. **S~** nt **-s** silence; **zum S~ bringen** silence

schweigsam adj silent; (wortkarg) taciturn

Schwein nt **-[e]s,-e** pig; (Culin) pork; [x] Schuft) swine; **S~ haben** [!] be lucky. **S~ebraten** m roast pork. **S~efleisch** nt pork. **S~erei** f **-,-en** [x] [dirty] mess; (Gemeinheit) dirty trick. **S~estall** m pigsty. **S~sleder** nt pigskin

Schweiß m **-es** sweat

schweißen vt weld

Schweiz (die) **-** Switzerland. **S~er** adj & m **-s,-**, **S~erin** f **-,-nen** Swiss. **s~erisch** adj Swiss

Schwelle f **-,-n** threshold; (Eisenbahn-) sleeper

schwell|en† vi (sein) swell. **S~ung** f **-,-en** swelling

schwer adj heavy; (schwierig) difficult; (mühsam) hard; (ernst) serious; (schlimm) bad; **3 Pfund s~ sein** weigh 3 pounds •adv heavily; with difficulty; (mühsam) hard; (schlimm, sehr) badly, seriously; **s~ krank/verletzt** seriously ill/ injured; **s~ hören** be hard of hearing; **etw s~ nehmen** take sth seriously; **jdm s~ fallen** be hard for s.o.; **es jdm s~ machen** make it or things difficult for s.o.; **sich s~ tun** have difficulty (**mit** with); **s~ zu sagen** difficult or hard to say

Schwere f **-** heaviness; (Gewicht) weight; (Schwierigkeit) difficulty;

[C] *see* A-Z of German life and culture

(Ernst) gravity. **S~losigkeit** f - weightlessness

schwer|fällig adj ponderous, clumsy. **S~gewicht** nt heavyweight. **s~hörig** adj **s~hörig sein** be hard of hearing. **S~kraft** f (Phys) gravity. **s~mütig** adj melancholic. **S~punkt** m centre of gravity; (fig) emphasis

Schwert nt **-[e]s,-er** sword. **S~lilie** f iris

Schwer|verbrecher m serious offender. **s~wiegend** adj weighty

Schwester f **-,-n** sister; (Kranken-) nurse. **s~lich** adj sisterly

Schwieger|eltern pl parents-in-law. **S~mutter** f mother-in-law. **S~sohn** m son-in-law. **S~tochter** f daughter-in-law. **S~vater** m father-in-law

schwierig adj difficult. **S~keit** f **-,-en** difficulty

Schwimm|bad nt swimming-baths pl. **S~becken** nt swimming-pool. **s~en†** vt/i (sein/haben) swim; (auf dem Wasser treiben) float. **S~weste** f life-jacket

Schwindel m **-s** dizziness, vertigo; (!: Betrug) fraud; (Lüge) lie. **S~anfall** m dizzy spell. **s~frei** adj **s~frei sein** have a good head for heights. **s~n** vi (haben) lie

Schwindl|er m **-s,-** liar; (Betrüger) fraud, con-man. **s~ig** adj dizzy; **mir ist** od **wird s~ig** I feel dizzy

schwing|en† vi (haben) swing; (Phys) oscillate; (vibrieren) vibrate •vt swing; wave (Fahne); (drohend) brandish. **S~ung** f **-,-en** oscillation; vibration

Schwips m **-es,-e einen S~ haben** ! be tipsy

schwitzen vi (haben) sweat; **ich s~e** I am hot

schwören† vt/i (haben) swear (**auf** + acc by)

schwul adj (!: homosexuell) gay

schwül adj close. **S~e** f - closeness

Schwung m **-[e]s,⸚e** swing; (Bogen) sweep; (Schnelligkeit) momentum; (Kraft) vigour. **s~los** adj dull. **s~voll** adj vigorous; (Bogen, Linie) sweeping; (mitreißend) spirited

Schwur m **-[e]s,⸚e** vow; (Eid) oath. **S~gericht** nt jury [court]

sechs inv adj, **S~** f **-,-en** six; (Sch) ≈ fail mark. **s~eckig** adj hexagonal. **s~te(r,s)** adj sixth

sech|zehn inv adj sixteen. **s~zehnte(r,s)** adj sixteenth. **s~zig** inv adj sixty. **s~zigste(r,s)** adj sixtieth

See[1] m **-s,-n** lake

See[2] f - sea; **an die/der See** to/at the seaside; **auf See** at sea. **S~fahrt** f [sea] voyage; (Schifffahrt) navigation. **S~gang** m **schwerer S~gang** rough sea. **S~hund** m seal. **s~krank** adj seasick

Seele f **-,-n** soul

seelisch adj psychological; (geistig) mental

See|macht f maritime power. **S~mann** m (pl **-leute**) seaman, sailor. **S~not** f **in S~not** in distress. **S~räuber** m pirate. **S~reise** f [sea] voyage. **S~rose** f water-lily. **S~sack** m kitbag. **S~stern** m starfish. **S~tang** m seaweed. **s~tüchtig** adj seaworthy. **S~zunge** f sole

Segel nt **-s,-** sail. **S~boot** nt sailing-boat. **S~flugzeug** nt glider. **s~n** vt/i (sein/haben) sail. **S~schiff** nt sailing-ship. **S~sport** m sailing. **S~tuch** nt canvas

Segen m **-s** blessing

Segler m **-s,-** yachtsman

segnen vt bless

sehen† vt see; watch (Fernsehsendung); **jdn/etw wieder s~** see s.o./sth again; **sich s~ lassen** show oneself •vi (haben) see; (blicken) look (**auf** + acc at); (ragen) show (**aus** above); **gut/schlecht s~** have good/bad eyesight; **vom S~ kennen** know by sight; **s~ nach** keep an eye on; (betreuen) look after; (suchen) look for. **s~swert, s~swürdig** adj worth seeing. **S~swürdigkeit** f **-,-en** sight

Sehne f **-,-n** tendon; (eines Bogens) string

S

sehnen (sich) vr long (**nach** for)

Sehn|sucht f - longing (**nach** for). **s~süchtig** adj longing; (Wunsch) dearest

sehr adv very; (mit Verb) very much; **so s~, dass** so much that

seicht adj shallow

seid s. **sein**[1]

Seide f -,-n silk

Seidel nt -s,- beer-mug

seiden adj silk **S~papier** nt tissue paper. **S~raupe** f silk-worm

seidig adj silky

Seife f -,-n soap. **S~npulver** nt soap powder. **S~nschaum** m lather

Seil nt -[e]s,-e rope; (Draht-) cable. **S~bahn** f cable railway. **s~springen**† vi (sein) (infinitive & pp only) skip. **S~tänzer(in)** m(f) tightrope walker

sein†[1]
- intransitive verb (sein)
- ····➤ be. **ich bin glücklich** I am happy. **er ist Lehrer/Schwede** he is a teacher/Swedish. **bist du es?** is that you? **sei still!** be quiet! **sie waren in Paris** they were in Paris. **morgen bin ich zu Hause** I shall be at home tomorrow. **er ist aus Berlin** he is or comes from Berlin
- ····➤ (impers + dat) **mir ist kalt/besser** I am cold/better. **ihr ist schlecht** she feels sick
- ····➤ (existieren) be. **es ist/sind ...** there is/are .... **es ist keine Hoffnung mehr** there is no more hope. **es sind vier davon** there are four of them. **es war einmal ein Prinz** once upon a time there was a prince
- auxiliary verb
- ····➤ (zur Perfektumschreibung) have. **er ist gestorben** he has died. **sie sind angekommen** they have arrived. **sie war dort gewesen** she had been there. **ich wäre gefallen** I would have fallen
- ····➤ (zur Bildung des Passivs) be. **wir sind gerettet worden/wir waren gerettet** we were saved
- ····➤ (+ zu + Infinitiv) be to be. **es war niemand zu sehen** there was no one to be seen. **das war zu erwarten** that was to be expected. **er ist zu bemitleiden** he is to be pitied. **die Richtlinien sind strengstens zu beachten** the guidelines are to be strictly followed

sein[2] poss pron his; (Ding, Tier) its; (nach man) one's; **sein Glück versuchen** try one's luck. **s~e(r,s)** poss pron his; (nach man) one's own; **das S~e tun** do one's share. **s~erseits** adv for his part. **s~erzeit** adv in those days. **s~etwegen** adv for his sake; (wegen ihm) because of him, on his account. **s~ige** poss pron **der/die/das s~ige** his

seins poss pron his; (nach man) one's own

seit conj & prep (+ dat) since; **s~ einiger** Zeit for some time [past]; **ich wohne s~ zehn Jahren hier** I've lived here for ten years. **s~dem** conj since • adv since then

Seite f -,-n side; (Buch-) page; **zur S~ treten** step aside; **auf der einen/anderen S~** (fig) on the one/other hand

seitens prep (+ gen) on the part of

Seiten|schiff nt [side] aisle. **S~sprung** m infidelity. **S~stechen** nt -s (Med) stitch. **S~straße** f side-street. **S~streifen** m verge; (Autobahn-) hard shoulder

seither adv since then

seit|lich adj side • adv at/on the side; **s~lich von** to one side of • prep (+ gen) to one side of. **s~wärts** adv on/to one side; (zur Seite) sideways

Sekret|är m -s,-e secretary; (Schrank) bureau. **S~ariat** nt -[e]s,-e secretary's office. **S~ärin** f -,-nen secretary

Sekt m -[e]s [German] sparkling wine

S

Sekte f **-,-n** sect

Sektor m **-s,-en** sector

Sekunde f **-,-n** second

Sekundenschlaf m microsleep

selber pron [!] = **selbst**

selbst pron oneself; **ich/du/er/sie s~** I myself /you yourself/ he himself/she herself; **wir/ihr/sie s~** we ourselves/you yourselves/ they themselves; **ich schneide mein Haar s~** I cut my own hair; **von s~** of one's own accord; (automatisch) automatically; **s~ gemacht** home-made •adv even

selbständig adj = **selbstständig. S~keit** f - = **Selbstständigkeit**

Selbst|bedienung f self-service. **S~befriedigung** f masturbation. **s~bewusst** adj self-confident. **S~bewusstsein** nt self-confidence. **S~bildnis** nt self-portrait. **S~erhaltung** f self-preservation. **s~gemacht*** adj = **s~ gemacht**, s. **selbst. s~haftend** adj self-adhesive. **S~hilfe** f self-help. **s~klebend** adj self-adhesive. **S~kostenpreis** m cost price. **S~laut** m vowel. **s~los** adj selfless. **S~mord** m suicide. **S~mordattentat** nt suicide attack. **S~mörder(in)** m(f) suicide. **s~mörderisch** adj suicidal. **S~porträt** nt self-portrait. **s~sicher** adj self-assured. **s~ständig** adj independent; self-employed (Handwerker); **sich s~ständig machen** set up on one's own. **S~ständigkeit** f - independence. **s~süchtig** adj selfish. **S~tanken** nt self-service (for petrol). **s~tätig** adj automatic. **S~versorgung** f self-catering. **s~verständlich** adj natural; **etw für s~verständlich halten** take sth for granted; **das ist s~verständlich** that goes without saying; **s~verständlich!** of course! **S~verteidigung** f self-defence. **S~vertrauen** nt self-confidence. **S~verwaltung** f self-government

selig adj blissfully happy; (Relig) blessed; (verstorben) late. **S~keit** f - bliss

Sellerie m **-s,-s** & f **-,-** celeriac; (Stangen-) celery

selten adj rare •adv rarely, seldom; (besonders) exceptionally. **S~heit** f **-,-en** rarity

seltsam adj odd, strange. **s~erweise** adv oddly

Semester nt **-s,-** (Univ) semester

Semikolon nt **-s,-s** semicolon

Seminar nt **-s,-e** seminar; (Institut) department; (Priester-) seminary

Semmel f **-,-n** (Aust, SGer) [bread] roll. **S~brösel** pl breadcrumbs

Senat m **-[e]s,-e** senate. **S~or** m **-s,-en** senator

senden[1]† vt send

sende|n[2] vt (reg) broadcast; (über Funk) transmit, send. **S~r** m **-s,-** [broadcasting] station; (Anlage) transmitter. **S~reihe** f series

Sendung f **-,-en** consignment, shipment; (TV) programme

Senf m **-s** mustard

senil adj senile. **S~ität** f - senility

Senior m **-s,-en** senior; **S~en** senior citizens. **S~enheim** nt old people's home

senken vt lower; bring down (Fieber, Preise); bow (Kopf); **sich s~** come down, fall; (absinken) subside

senkrecht adj vertical. **S~e** f **-n,-n** perpendicular

Sensation /-'tsio:n/ f **-,-en** sensation. **s~ell** adj sensational

Sense f **-,-n** scythe

sensibel adj sensitive

sentimental adj sentimental

September m **-s,-** September

Serie /'ze:riə/ f **-,-n** series; (Briefmarken) set; (Comm) range. **S~nnummer** f serial number

seriös adj respectable; (zuverlässig) reliable

Serpentine f **-,-n** winding road; (Kehre) hairpin bend

Serum nt **-s,Sera** serum

Server m **-s,-** server

Service[1] /zɛr'viːs/ nt **-[s],-** service, set

Service[2] /'zøːɐ̯vɪs/ m & nt **-s** (Comm, Tennis) service

servieren vt/i (haben) serve. **S~erin** f **-,-nen** waitress

Serviette f **-,-n** napkin, serviette

Servus int (Aust) cheerio; (Begrüßung) hallo

Sessel m **-s,-** armchair. **S~bahn** f, **S~lift** m chairlift

sesshaft adj settled

Set /zɛt/ nt & m **-[s],-s** set; (Deckchen) place-mat

setz|en vt put; (abstellen) set down; (hin-) sit down (Kind); move (Spielstein); (pflanzen) plant; (schreiben, wetten) put; **sich s~en** sit down; (sinken) settle •vi (sein) leap •vi (haben) **s~en auf** (+ acc) back

Seuche f **-,-n** epidemic

seufz|en vi (haben) sigh. **S~er** m **-s,-** sigh

Sex /zɛks/ m **-[es]** sex

Sexu|alität f **-** sexuality. **s~ell** adj sexual

sezieren vt dissect

Shampoo /ʃam'puː/, **Shampoon** /ʃam'poːn/ nt **-s** shampoo

siamesisch adj Siamese

sich reflexive pron oneself; (mit er/sie/es) himself/herself/itself; (mit sie pl) themselves; (mit Sie) yourself; (pl) yourselves; (einander) each other; **s~ kennen** know oneself/(einander) each other; **s~ waschen** have a wash; **s~** (dat) **die Haare kämmen** comb one's hair; **s~ wundern** be surprised; **s~ gut verkaufen** sell well; **von s~ aus** of one's own accord

Sichel f **-,-n** sickle

sicher adj safe; (gesichert) secure; (gewiss) certain; (zuverlässig) reliable; sure (Urteil); steady (Hand); (selbstbewusst) self-confident; **bist du s~?** are you sure? •adv safely; securely; certainly; reliably; self-confidently; (wahrscheinlich) most probably; **s~!** certainly!

s~gehen† vi sep (sein) (fig) be sure

Sicherheit f **-** safety; (Pol, Psych, Comm) security; (Gewissheit) certainty; (Zuverlässigkeit) reliability; (des Urteils) surety; (Selbstbewusstsein) self-confidence. **S~sgurt** m safety belt; (Auto) seat belt. **S~snadel** f safety pin

sicherlich adv certainly; (wahrscheinlich) most probably

sicher|n vt secure; (garantieren) safeguard; (schützen) protect; put the safety catch on (Pistole). **S~ung** f **-,-en** safeguard, protection; (Gewehr-) safety catch; (Electr) fuse

Sicht f **-** view; (S~weite) visibility; **auf lange S~** in the long term. **s~bar** adj visible. **S~vermerk** m visa. **S~weite** f visibility; **außer S~weite** out of sight

sie pron (nom) (sg) she; (Ding, Tier) it; (pl) they; (acc) (sg) her; (Ding, Tier) it; (pl) them

Sie pron you; **gehen/warten Sie!** go/wait!

Sieb nt **-[e]s,-e** sieve; (Tee-) strainer. **s~en**[1] vt sieve, sift

sieben[2] inv adj, **S~** f **-,-en** seven. **S~sachen** fpl [!] belongings. **s~te(r,s)** adj seventh

sieb|te(r,s) adj seventh. **s~zehn** inv adj seventeen. **s~zehnte(r,s)** adj seventeenth. **s~zig** inv adj seventy. **s~zigste(r,s)** adj seventieth

siede|n† vt/i (haben) boil. **S~punkt** m boiling point

Siedlung f **-,-en** [housing] estate; (Niederlassung) settlement

Sieg m **-[e]s,-e** victory

Siegel nt **-s,-** seal. **S~ring** m signet-ring

sieg|en vi (haben) win. **S~er(in)** m **-s,-** (f **-,-nen**) winner. **s~reich** adj victorious

siezen vt **jdn s~** call s.o. 'Sie'

Signal nt **-s,-e** signal

Silbe f **-,-n** syllable

Silber nt **-s** silver. **s~n** adj silver

Silhouette /zɪ'lu̯ɛtə/ f **-,-n** silhouette

Silizium nt **-s** silicon

Silo m & nt **-s,-s** silo

Silvester nt **-s** New Year's Eve

Sims m & nt **-es,-e** ledge

simsen vt/i text, send a text message

simultan adj simultaneous

sind s. **sein**[1]

Sinfonie f **-,-n** symphony

singen† vt/i (haben) sing

Singvogel m songbird

sinken† vi (sein) sink; (nieder-) drop; (niedriger werden) go down, fall; **den Mut s~ lassen** lose courage

Sinn m **-[e]s,-e** sense; (Denken) mind; (Zweck) point; **in gewissem S~e** in a sense; **es hat keinen S~** it is pointless. **S~bild** nt symbol

sinnlich adj sensory; (sexuell) sensual; (Genüsse) sensuous. **S~keit** f **-** sensuality; sensuousness

sinn|los adj senseless; (zwecklos) pointless. **s~voll** adj meaningful; (vernünftig) sensible

Sintflut f flood

Siphon /'zi:fõ/ m **-s,-s** siphon

Sippe f **-,-n** clan

Sirene f **-,-n** siren

Sirup m **-s,-e** syrup; treacle

Sitte f **-,-n** custom; **S~n** manners

sittlich adj moral. **S~keit** f **-** morality. **S~keitsverbrecher** m sex offender

sittsam adj well-behaved; (züchtig) demure

Situ|ation /-'tsi̯o:n/ f **-,-en** situation. **s~iert** adj **gut/schlecht s~iert** well/badly off

Sitz m **-es,-e** seat; (Passform) fit

sitzen† vi (haben) sit; (sich befinden) be; (passen) fit; ([!]: treffen) hit home; **[im Gefängnis] s~** [!] be in jail; [C] **s~ bleiben** remain seated; [!] (Sch) stay or be kept down; (nicht heiraten) be left on the shelf; **s~ bleiben auf** (+ dat) be left with

Sitz|gelegenheit f seat. **S~platz** m seat. **S~ung** f **-,-en** session

Sizilien /-i̯ən/ nt **-s** Sicily

Skala f **-,-len** scale; (Reihe) range

Skalpell nt **-s,-e** scalpel

skalpieren vt scalp

Skandal m **-s,-e** scandal. **s~ös** adj scandalous

Skandinav|ien /-i̯ən/ nt **-s** Scandinavia. **s~isch** adj Scandinavian

[C] **Skat** m **-s** skat

Skateboard /'ske:tbo:ɐ̯t/ nt **-s, -s** skateboard

Skelett nt **-[e]s,-e** skeleton

Skep|sis f **-** scepticism. **s~tisch** adj sceptical

Ski /ʃi:/ m **-s,-er** ski; **Ski fahren** od **laufen** ski. **S~fahrer(in), S~läufer(in)** m(f) **-s,-** (f **-,-nen**) skier. **S~sport** m skiing

Skizz|e f **-,-n** sketch. **s~ieren** vt sketch

Sklav|e m **-n,-n** slave. **S~erei** f **-** slavery. **S~in** f **-,-nen** slave

Skorpion m **-s,-e** scorpion; (Astrology) Scorpio

Skrupel m **-s,-** scruple. **s~los** adj unscrupulous

Skulptur f **-,-en** sculpture

Slalom m **-s,-s** slalom

Slaw|e m **-n,-n, S~in** f **-,-nen** Slav. **s~isch** adj Slav; (Lang) Slavonic

Slip m **-s,-s** briefs pl

Smaragd m **-[e]s,-e** emerald

Smoking m **-s,-s** dinner jacket

SMS-Nachricht f text message

Snob m **-s,-s** snob. **S~ismus** m **-** snobbery **s~istisch** adj snobbish

so adv so; (so sehr) so much; (auf diese Weise) like this/that; (solch) such; ([!]: sowieso) anyway; ([!]: umsonst) free; ([!]: ungefähr) about; **so viel** so

[C] *see* A-Z of German life and culture

much; **so gut/bald wie** as good/soon as; **so ein Zufall!** what a coincidence! **mir ist so, als ob** I feel as if; **so oder so** in any case; **so um zehn Euro** [!] about ten euros; **so?** really? •conj (also) so; (dann) then; **so dass** = **sodass**

sobald conj as soon as

Söckchen nt **-s,-** [ankle] sock

Socke f **-,-n** sock

Sockel m **-s,-** plinth, pedestal

Socken m **-s,-** sock

sodass conj so that

Sodawasser nt soda water

Sodbrennen nt **-s** heartburn

soeben adv just [now]

Sofa nt **-s,-s** settee, sofa

sofern adv provided [that]

sofort adv at once, immediately; (auf der Stelle) instantly

Software /'zɔftvɛːɐ̯/ f **-** software

sogar adv even

sogenannt adj so-called

sogleich adv at once

Sohle f **-,-n** sole; (Tal-) bottom

Sohn m **-[e]s,¨e** son

Sojabohne f soya bean

solange conj as long as

solch inv pron such; **s~ ein(e)** such a; **s~ einer/eine/eins** one/(Person) someone like that. **s~e(r,s)** pron such •(substantivisch) **ein s~er/eine s~e/ein s~es** one/(Person) someone like that; **s~e** pl those; (Leute) people like that

Soldat m **-en,-en** soldier

Söldner m **-s,-** mercenary

Solidarität f **-** solidarity

solide adj solid; (haltbar) sturdy; (sicher) sound; (anständig) respectable

Solist(in) m **-en,-en** (f **-,-nen**) soloist

Soll nt **-s** (Comm) debit; (Produktions-) quota

sollen†

• auxiliary verb

····➤ (Verpflichtung) be [supposed or meant] to. **er soll morgen zum Arzt gehen** he is [supposed] to go to the doctor tomorrow. **die beiden Flächen sollen fluchten** the two surfaces are meant to be or should be in alignment. **du solltest ihn anrufen** you were meant to phone him or should have phoned him

····➤ (Befehl) **du sollst sofort damit aufhören** you're to stop that at once. **er soll hereinkommen** he is to come in; (sagen Sie es ihm) tell him to come in

····➤ **sollte** (subjunctive) should; ought to. **wir sollten früher aufstehen** we ought to or should get up earlier. **das hätte er nicht tun/sagen sollen** he shouldn't have done/said that

····➤ (Zukunft, Geplantes) be to. **ich soll die Abteilung übernehmen** I am to take over the department. **du sollst dein Geld zurückbekommen** you are to or shall get your money back. **es soll nicht wieder vorkommen** it won't happen again. **sie sollten ihr Reiseziel nie erreichen** they were never to reach their destination

····➤ (Ratlosigkeit) be to; shall. **was soll man nur machen?** what is one to do?; what shall I/we do? **ich weiß nicht, was ich machen soll** I don't know what I should do or what to do

····➤ (nach Bericht) be supposed to. **er soll sehr reich sein** he is supposed or is said to be very rich. **sie soll geheiratet haben** they say or I gather she has got married

····➤ (Absicht) be meant or supposed to. **was soll dieses Bild darstellen?** what is this picture supposed to represent? **das sollte ein Witz sein** that was meant or supposed to be a joke

····➤ (in Bedingungssätzen) should. **sollte er anrufen, falls** od **wenn er anrufen sollte** should he or if he should telephone

• intransitive verb
····➤ (irgendwohin gehen sollen) be [supposed] to go. **er soll morgen zum Arzt/nach Berlin** he is [supposed] to go to the doctor/to Berlin tomorrow. **ich sollte ins Theater** I was supposed to go to the theatre
····➤ (sonstige Wendungen) **soll er doch!** let him! **was soll das?** what's that in aid of? [!]

Solo nt **-s,-los** & **-li** solo

somit adv therefore, so

Sommer m **-s,-** summer. **s~lich** adj summery; (Sommer-) summer • adv **s~lich warm** as warm as summer. **S~sprossen** fpl freckles

Sonate f **-,-n** sonata

Sonde f **-,-n** probe

Sonder|angebot nt special offer. **s~bar** adj odd. **S~fahrt** f special excursion. **S~fall** m special case. **s~gleichen** adv **eine Gemeinheit s~gleichen** unparalleled meanness. **S~ling** m **-s,-e** crank. **S~marke** f special stamp

sondern conj but; **nicht nur ... s~ auch** not only ... but also

Sonder|preis m special price. **S~schule** f special school

Sonett nt **-[e]s,-e** sonnet

Sonnabend m **-s,-e** Saturday. **s~s** adv on Saturdays

Sonne f **-,-n** sun. **s~n (sich)** vr sun oneself

Sonnen|aufgang m sunrise. **s~baden** vi (haben) sunbathe. **S~bank** f sun-bed. **S~blume** f sunflower. **S~brand** m sunburn. **S~brille** f sunglasses pl. **S~energie** f solar energy. **S~finsternis** f solar eclipse. **S~milch** f sun-tan lotion. **S~öl** nt sun-tan oil. **S~schein** m sunshine. **S~schirm** m sunshade. **S~stich** m sunstroke. **S~uhr** f sundial. **S~untergang** m sunset. **S~wende** f solstice

sonnig adj sunny

Sonntag m **-s,-e** Sunday. **s~s** adv on Sundays

sonst adv (gewöhnlich) usually; (im Übrigen) apart from that; (andernfalls) otherwise, or [else]; **wer/was/wie/wo s~?** who/what/how/where else? **s~ niemand** no one else; **s~ noch etwas?** anything else? **s~ noch Fragen?** any more questions? **s~ jemand** od **wer** someone/(fragend, verneint) anyone else; (irgendjemand) [just] anyone; **s~ wo** somewhere/(fragend, verneint) anywhere else; (irgendwo) [just] anywhere. **s~ig** adj other

sooft conj whenever

Sopran m **-s,-e** soprano

Sorge f **-,-n** worry (**um** about); (Fürsorge) care; **sich** (dat) **S~n machen** worry. **s~n** vi (haben) **s~n für** look after, care for; (vorsorgen) provide for; (sich kümmern) see to; **dafür s~n, dass** see or make sure that • vr **sich s~n** worry. **s~nfrei** adj carefree. **s~nvoll** adj worried. **S~recht** nt (Jur) custody

Sorg|falt f **-** care. **s~fältig** adj careful

Sorte f **-,-n** kind, sort; (Comm) brand

sort|ieren vt sort [out]; (Comm) grade. **S~iment** nt **-[e]s,-e** range

sosehr conj however much

Soße f **-,-n** sauce; (Braten-) gravy; (Salat-) dressing

Souvenir /zuvəˈniːɐ̯/ nt **-s,-s** souvenir

souverän /zuvəˈrɛːn/ adj sovereign

soviel conj however much; **s~ ich weiß** as far as I know • adv ***so viel**, s. **viel**

soweit conj as far as; (insoweit) [in] so far as • adv* **so weit**, s. **weit**

sowenig conj however little • adv ***so wenig**, s. **wenig**

sowie conj as well as; (sobald) as soon as

sowieso adv anyway, in any case

sowjet|isch adj Soviet. **S~union** f **-** Soviet Union

sowohl adv **s~ ... als** od **wie auch** as well as ...

sozial adj social; (Einstellung, Beruf) caring. **S~arbeit** f social work. **S~demokrat** m social democrat. **S~hilfe** f social security

Sozialis|mus m - socialism. **S~t** m **-en,-en** socialist

Sozial|versicherung f National Insurance. **S~wohnung** f ≈ council flat

Soziologie f - sociology

Sozius m **-,-se** (Comm) partner; (Beifahrersitz) pillion

Spachtel m **-s,-** & f **-,-n** spatula

Spagat m **-[e]s,-e** (Aust) string; **S~ machen** do the splits pl

Spaghetti, **Spagetti** pl spaghetti sg

Spalier nt **-s,-e** trellis

Spalt|e f **-,-n** crack; (Gletscher-) crevasse; (Druck-) column; (Orangen-) segment. **s~en**† vt split. **S~ung** f **-,-en** splitting; (Kluft) split; (Phys) fission

Span m **-[e]s,¨e** [wood] chip

Spange f **-,-n** clasp; (Haar-) slide; (Zahn-) brace

Span|ien /-i̯ən/ nt **-s** Spain. **S~ier** m **-s,-**, **S~ierin** f **-,-nen** Spaniard. **s~isch** adj Spanish. **S~isch** nt **-[s]** (Lang) Spanish

Spann m **-[e]s** instep

Spanne f **-,-n** span; (Zeit-) space; (Comm) margin

spann|en vt stretch; put up (Leine); (straffen) tighten; (an-) harness (**an** + acc to); **sich s~en** tighten •vi (haben) be too tight. **s~end** adj exciting. **S~ung** f **-,-en** tension; (Erwartung) suspense; (Electr) voltage

Spar|buch nt savings book. **S~büchse** f money-box. **s~en** vt/i (haben) save; (sparsam sein) economize (**mit**/**an** + dat on). **S~er** m **-s,-** saver

Spargel m **-s,-** asparagus

Spar|kasse f savings bank. **S~konto** nt deposit account

sparsam adj economical; (Person) thrifty. **S~keit** f - economy; thrift

Sparschwein nt piggy bank

Sparte f **-,-n** branch; (Zeitungs-) section; (Rubrik) column

Spaß m **-es,¨e** fun; (Scherz) joke; **im/aus/zum S~** for fun; **S~ machen** be fun; (Person:) be joking; **viel S~!** have a good time! **s~en** vi (haben) joke. **S~vogel** m joker

Spastiker m **-s,-** spastic

spät adj & adv late; **wie s~ ist es?** what time is it? **zu s~ kommen** be late

Spaten m **-s,-** spade

später adj later; (zukünftig) future •adv later

spätestens adv at the latest

Spatz m **-en,-en** sparrow

Spätzle pl (Culin) noodles

spazieren vi (sein) stroll; **s~ gehen** go for a walk

Spazier|gang m walk; **einen S~gang machen** go for a walk. **S~gänger(in)** m **-s,-** (f **-,-nen**) walker. **S~stock** m walking-stick

Specht m **-[e]s,-e** woodpecker

Speck m **-s** bacon. **s~ig** adj greasy

Spedi|teur /ʃpediˈtøːɐ̯/ m **-s,-e** haulage/(für Umzüge) removals contractor. **S~tion** f **-,-en** carriage, haulage; (Firma) haulage/(für Umzüge) removals firm

Speer m **-[e]s,-e** spear; (Sport) javelin

Speiche f **-,-n** spoke

Speichel m **-s** saliva

Speicher m **-s,-** warehouse; (Dialekt: Dachboden) attic; (Computer) memory. **s~n** vt store

Speise f **-,-n** food; (Gericht) dish; (Pudding) blancmange. **S~eis** nt ice-cream. **S~kammer** f larder. **S~karte** f menu. **s~n** vi (haben) eat •vt feed. **S~röhre** f oesophagus. **S~saal** m dining room. **S~wagen** m dining car

Spektrum nt **-s,-tra** spectrum

Spekul|ant m **-en,-en** speculator. **s~ieren** vi (haben) speculate; **s~ieren auf** (+ acc) [!] hope to get

S

Spelze f -,-n husk

spendabel adj generous

Spende f -,-n donation. **s~n** vt donate; give (Blut, Schatten); **Beifall s~n** applaud. **S~r** m -s,- donor; (Behälter) dispenser

spendieren vt pay for

Sperling m -s,-e sparrow

Sperre f -,-n barrier; (Verbot) ban; (Comm) embargo. **s~n** vt close; (ver-) block; (verbieten) ban; cut off (Strom, Telefon); stop (Scheck, Kredit); **s~n in** (+ acc) put in (Gefängnis, Käfig)

Sperr|holz nt plywood. **S~müll** m bulky refuse. **S~stunde** f closing time

Spesen pl expenses

spezial|isieren (sich) vr specialize (**auf** + acc in). **S~ist** m -en,-en specialist. **S~ität** f -,-en speciality

spicken vt (Culin) lard; **gespickt mit** (fig) full of •vi (haben) [!] crib (**bei** from)

[C] **Spiegel** m -s,- mirror; (Wasser-, Alkohol-) level. **S~bild** nt reflection. **S~ei** nt fried egg. **s~n** vt reflect; **sich s~n** be reflected •vi (haben) reflect [the light]; (glänzen) gleam. **S~ung** f -,-en reflection

Spiel nt -[e]s,-e game; (Spielen) playing; (Glücks-) gambling; (Schau-) play; (Satz) set; **auf dem S~ stehen** be at stake; **aufs S~ setzen** risk. **S~automat** m fruit machine. **S~bank** f casino. **S~dose** f musical box. **s~en** vt/i (haben) play; (im Glücksspiel) gamble; (vortäuschen) act; (Roman:) be set (**in** + dat in); **s~en mit** (fig) toy with

Spieler(in) m -s,- (f -,-nen) player; (Glücks-) gambler

Spiel|feld nt field, pitch. **S~marke** f chip. **S~plan** m programme. **S~platz** m playground. **S~raum** m (fig) scope; (Techn) clearance. **S~regeln** fpl rules [of the game]. **S~sachen** fpl toys. **S~verderber** m -s,- spoilsport. **S~waren** fpl toys. **S~warengeschäft** nt toyshop. **S~zeug** nt toy; (S~sachen) toys pl

Spieß m -es,-e spear; (Brat-) spit; skewer; (Fleisch-) kebab. **S~er** m -s,- [petit] bourgeois. **s~ig** adj bourgeois

Spike[s]reifen /'ʃpaik[s]-/ m studded tyre

Spinat m -s spinach

Spindel f -,-n spindle

Spinne f -,-n spider

spinn|en† vt/i (haben) spin; **er spinnt** [!] he's crazy. **S~[en]gewebe** nt, **S~webe** f -,-n cobweb

Spion m -s,-e spy

Spionage /ʃpio'naːʒə/ f - espionage, spying. **S~abwehr** f counter-espionage

spionieren vi (haben) spy

Spionin f -,-nen [woman] spy

Spiral|e f -,-n spiral. **s~ig** adj spiral

Spirituosen pl spirits

Spiritus m - alcohol; (Brenn-) methylated spirits pl. **S~kocher** m spirit stove

spitz adj pointed; (scharf) sharp; (schrill) shrill; (Winkel) acute. **S~bube** m scoundrel

Spitze f -,-n point; (oberer Teil) top; (vorderer Teil) front; (Pfeil-, Finger-, Nasen-) tip; (Schuh-, Strumpf-) toe; (Zigarren-, Zigaretten-) holder; (Höchstleistung) maximum; (Textiles) lace; ([!]: Anspielung) dig; **an der S~ liegen** be in the lead

Spitzel m -s,- informer

spitzen vt sharpen; purse (Lippen); prick up (Ohren). **S~geschwindigkeit** f top speed

Spitzname m nickname

Spleen /ʃpliːn/ m -s,-e obsession

Splitter m -s,- splinter. **s~n** vi (sein) shatter

sponsern vt sponsor

Spore f -,-n (Biology) spore

Sporn m -[e]s, **Sporen** spur

Sport m -[e]s sport; (Hobby) hobby.

[C] *see A-Z of German life and culture*

S

S~art f sport. **S~ler** m **-s,-** sportsman. **S~lerin** f **-,-nen** sportswoman. **s~lich** adj sports; (fair) sporting; (schlank) sporty. **S~platz** m sports ground. **S~verein** m sports club. **S~wagen** m sports car; (Kinder-) push-chair, (Amer) stroller

Spott m **-[e]s** mockery

spotten vi (haben) mock; **s~ über** (+ acc) make fun of; (höhnend) ridicule

spöttisch adj mocking

Sprach|e f **-,-n** language; (Sprechfähigkeit) speech; **zur S~e bringen** bring up. **S~fehler** m speech defect. **S~labor** nt language laboratory. **s~lich** adj linguistic. **s~los** adj speechless

Spray /ʃpreː/ nt & m **-s,-s** spray. **S~dose** f aerosol [can]

Sprechanlage f intercom

sprechen† vi (haben) speak/(sich unterhalten) talk (**über** + acc/**von** about/of); **Deutsch s~** speak German • vt speak; (sagen) say; pronounce (Urteil); **schuldig s~** find guilty; **Herr X ist nicht zu s~** Mr X is not available

Sprecher(in) m **-s,-** (f **-,-nen**) speaker; (Radio, TV) announcer; (Wortführer) spokesman, f spokeswoman

Sprechstunde f consulting hours pl; (Med) surgery. **S~nhilfe** f (Med) receptionist

Sprechzimmer nt consulting room

spreizen vt spread

spreng|en vt blow up; blast (Felsen); (fig) burst; (begießen) water; (mit Sprenger) sprinkle; dampen (Wäsche). **S~er** m **-s,-** sprinkler. **S~kopf** m warhead. **S~körper** m explosive device. **S~stoff** m explosive

Spreu f **-** chaff

Sprich|wort nt (pl **-wörter**) proverb. **s~wörtlich** adj proverbial

Springbrunnen m fountain

spring|en† vi (sein) jump; (Schwimmsport) dive; (Ball:) bounce; (spritzen) spurt; (zer-) break; (rissig werden) crack; (SGer: laufen) run. **S~er** m **-s,-** jumper; (Kunst-) diver; (Schach) knight. **S~reiten** nt show-jumping

Sprint m **-s,-s** sprint

Spritz|e f **-,-n** syringe; (Injektion) injection; (Feuer-) hose. **s~en** vt spray; (be-, ver-) splash; (Culin) pipe; (Med) inject • vi (haben) splash; (Fett:) spit • vi (sein) splash; (hervor-) spurt. **S~er** m **-s,-** splash; (Schuss) dash

spröde adj brittle; (trocken) dry

Sprosse f **-,-n** rung

Sprotte f **-,-n** sprat

Spruch m **-[e]s,⸚e** saying; (Denk-) motto; (Zitat) quotation. **S~band** nt (pl **-bänder**) banner

Sprudel m **-s,-** sparkling mineral water. **s~n** vi (haben/sein) bubble

Sprüh|dose f aerosol [can]. **s~en** vt spray • vi (sein) (Funken:) fly; (fig) sparkle

Sprung m **-[e]s,⸚e** jump, leap; (Schwimmsport) dive; (!: Katzen-) stone's throw; (Riss) crack. **S~brett** nt springboard. **S~schanze** f skijump. **S~seil** nt skipping rope

Spucke f **-** spit. **s~n** vt/i (haben) spit; (sich übergeben) be sick

Spuk m **-[e]s,-e** [ghostly] apparition. **s~en** vi (haben) (Geist:) walk; **in diesem Haus s~t es** this house is haunted

Spülbecken nt sink

Spule f **-,-n** spool

Spüle f **-,-n** sink

spulen vt spool

spül|en vt rinse; (schwemmen) wash; **Geschirr s~en** wash up • vi (haben) flush [the toilet]. **S~kasten** m cistern. **S~mittel** nt washing-up liquid

Spur f **-,-en** track; (Fahr-) lane; (Fährte) trail; (Anzeichen) trace; (Hinweis) lead

spürbar adj noticeable

spür|en vt feel; (seelisch) sense. **S~hund** m tracker dog

spurlos adv without trace

spurten vi (sein) put on a spurt

sputen (sich) vr hurry

Staat m **-[e]s,-en** state; (Land) country; (Putz) finery. **s~lich** adj state • adv by the state

Staatsangehörig|e(r) m/f national. **S~keit** f **-** nationality

Staats|anwalt m state prosecutor. **S~beamte(r)** m civil servant. **S~besuch** m state visit. **S~bürger(in)** m(f) national. **S~mann** m (pl **-männer**) statesman. **S~streich** m coup

Stab m **-[e]s,¨e** rod; (Gitter-) bar (Sport) baton; (Mil) staff

Stäbchen ntpl chopsticks

Stabhochsprung m pole-vault

stabil adj stable; (gesund) robust; (solide) sturdy

Stachel m **-s,-** spine; (Gift-) sting; (Spitze) spike. **S~beere** f gooseberry. **S~draht** m barbed wire. **S~schwein** nt porcupine

Stadion nt **-s,-ien** stadium

Stadium nt **-s,-ien** stage

Stadt f **-,¨e** town; (Groß-) city

städtisch adj urban; (kommunal) municipal

Stadt|mitte f town centre. **S~plan** m street map. **S~teil** m district

Staffel f **-,-n** team; (S~lauf) relay; (Mil) squadron

Staffelei f **-,-en** easel

Staffel|lauf m relay race. **s~n** vt stagger; (abstufen) grade

Stahl m **-s** steel. **S~beton** m reinforced concrete

Stall m **-[e]s,¨e** stable; (Kuh-) shed; (Schweine-) sty; (Hühner-) coop; (Kaninchen-) hutch

Stamm m **-[e]s¨e** trunk; (Sippe) tribe; (Wort-) stem. **S~baum** m family tree; (eines Tieres) pedigree

stammeln vt/i (haben) stammer

stammen vi (haben) come/(zeitlich) date (**von/aus** from)

stämmig adj sturdy

Stamm|kundschaft f regulars pl. **S~lokal** nt favourite pub

stampfen vi (haben) stamp; (Maschine:) pound • vi (sein) tramp • vt pound; mash (Kartoffeln)

Stand m **-[e]s,¨e** standing position; (Zustand) state; (Spiel-) score; (Höhe) level; (gesellschaftlich) class; (Verkaufs-) stall; (Messe-) stand; (Taxi-) rank; **auf den neuesten S~ bringen** up-date

Standard m **-s,-s** standard

Standbild nt statue

Ständer m **-s,-** stand; (Geschirr-) rack; (Kerzen-) holder

Standes|amt nt registry office. **S~beamte(r)** m registrar

standhaft adj steadfast

ständig adj constant; (fest) permanent

Stand|licht nt sidelights pl. **S~ort** m position; (Firmen-) location; (Mil) garrison. **S~punkt** m point of view. **S~uhr** f grandfather clock

Stange f **-,-n** bar; (Holz-) pole; (Gardinen-) rail; (Hühner-) perch; (Zimt-) stick; **von der S~** [!] off the peg

Stängel m **-s,-** stalk, stem

Stangenbohne f runner bean

Stanniol nt **-s** tin foil. **S~papier** nt silver paper

stanzen vt stamp; punch (Loch)

Stapel m **-s,-** stack, pile. **S~lauf** m launch[ing]. **s~n** vt stack or pile up

Star[1] m **-[e]s,-e** starling

Star[2] m **-[e]s** (Med) **[grauer] S~** cataract; **grüner S~** glaucoma

Star[3] m **-s,-s** (Theat, Sport) star

stark adj strong; (Motor) powerful; (Verkehr, Regen) heavy; (Hitze, Kälte) severe; (groß) big; (schlimm) bad; (dick) thick; (korpulent) stout • adv (sehr) very much

Stärk|e f **-,-n** strength; power; thickness; stoutness; (Größe) size; (Mais-, Wäsche-) starch. **S~emehl** nt cornflour. **s~en** vt strengthen; starch (Wäsche); **sich s~en** fortify oneself. **S~ung** f **-,-en** strengthening; (Erfrischung) refreshment

starr adj rigid; (steif) stiff

starren vi (haben) stare

Starr|sinn m obstinacy. **s~sinnig** adj obstinate

Start m **-s,-s** start; (Aviat) take-off. **S~bahn** f runway. **s~en** vi (sein) start; (Aviat) take off • vt start; (fig) launch

Station /-'tsi̯o:n/ f **-,-en** station; (Haltestelle) stop; (Abschnitt) stage; (Med) ward; **S~ machen** break one's journey. **s~är** adv as an inpatient. **s~ieren** vt station

statisch adj static

Statist(in) m **-en,-en** (f **-,-nen**) (Theat) extra

Statisti|k f **-,-en** statistics sg; (Aufstellung) statistics pl. **s~sch** adj statistical

Stativ nt **-s,-e** (Phot) tripod

statt prep (+ gen) instead of; **an seiner s~** in his place; **an Kindes s~ annehmen** adopt • conj **s~ etw zu tun** instead of doing sth. **s~dessen** adv instead

statt|finden† vi sep (haben) take place. **s~haft** adj permitted

Statue /'ʃta:tu̯ə/ f **-,-n** statue

Statur f **-** build, stature

Status m **-** status. **S~symbol** nt status symbol

Statut nt **-[e]s,-en** statute

Stau m **-[e]s,-s** congestion; (Auto) [traffic] jam; (Rück-) tailback

Staub m **-[e]s** dust; **S~ wischen** dust; **S~ saugen** vacuum, hoover

Staubecken nt reservoir

staub|ig adj dusty. **s~saugen** vt/i (haben) vacuum, hoover. **S~sauger** m vacuum cleaner, Hoover®

Staudamm m dam

stauen vt dam up; **sich s~** accumulate; (Autos:) form a tailback

staunen vi (haben) be amazed or astonished

Stau|see m reservoir. **S~ung** f **-,-en** congestion; (Auto) [traffic] jam

Steak /ʃte:k, ste:k/ nt **-s,-s** steak

stechen† vt stick (**in** + acc in); (verletzen) prick; (mit Messer) stab; (Insekt:) sting; (Mücke:) bite • vi (haben) prick; (Insekt:) sting; (Mücke:) bite; (mit Stechuhr) clock in/out; **in See s~** put to sea

Stech|ginster m gorse. **S~kahn** m punt. **S~palme** f holly. **S~uhr** f time clock

Steck|brief m 'wanted' poster. **S~dose** f socket. **s~en** vt put; (mit Nadel, Reißzwecke) pin; (pflanzen) plant • vi (haben) be; (fest-) be stuck; **s~ bleiben** get stuck; **den Schlüssel s~ lassen** leave the key in the lock

Steckenpferd nt hobby-horse

Steck|er m **-s,-** (Electr) plug. **S~nadel** f pin

Steg m **-[e]s,-e** foot-bridge; (Boots-) landing-stage; (Brillen-) bridge

stehen† vi (haben) stand; (sich befinden) be; (still-) be stationary; (Maschine, Uhr:) have stopped; **s~ bleiben** remain standing; (gebäude:) be left standing; (anhalten) stop; (Motor:) stall; (Zeit:) stand still; **vor dem Ruin s~** face ruin; **zu jdm/etw s~** (fig) stand by s.o./sth **jdm [gut] s~** suit s.o.; **sich gut s~** be on good terms; **es steht 3 zu 1** the score is 3–1. **s~d** adj standing; (sich nicht bewegend) stationary; (Gewässer) stagnant

Stehlampe f standard lamp

stehlen† vt/i (haben) steal; **sich s~** steal, creep

Steh|platz m standing place. **S~vermögen** nt stamina, staying-power

steif adj stiff

Steig|bügel m stirrup. **S~eisen** nt crampon

steigen† vi (sein) climb; (hochgehen) rise, go up; (Schulden, Spannung:) mount; **s~ auf** (+ acc) climb on [to] (Stuhl); climb (Berg, Leiter); get on (Pferd, Fahrrad); **s~ in** (+ acc) climb into; get in (Auto); get on (Bus, Zug); **s~ aus** climb out of; get out of (Bett, Auto); get off (Bus, Zug); **s~de Preise** rising prices

steiger|n vt increase; **sich s~n** increase; (sich verbessern) improve. **S~ung** f -,-en increase; improvement; (Gram) comparison

steil adj steep. **S~küste** f cliffs pl

Stein m **-[e]s,-e** stone; (Ziegel-) brick; (Spiel-) piece. **S~bock** m ibex; (Astrology) Capricorn. **S~bruch** m quarry. **S~garten** m rockery. **S~gut** nt earthenware. **s~ig** adj stony. **s~igen** vt stone. **S~kohle** f [hard] coal. **S~schlag** m rock fall

Stelle f **-,-n** place; (Fleck) spot; (Abschnitt) passage; (Stellung) job, post; (Behörde) authority; **auf der S~** immediately

stellen vt put; (aufrecht) stand; set (Wecker, Aufgabe); ask (Frage); make (Antrag, Forderung, Diagnose); **zur Verfügung s~** provide; **lauter/leiser s~** turn up/down; **kalt/warm s~** chill/keep hot; **sich s~** [go and] stand; give oneself up (**der Polizei** to the police); **sich tot s~** pretend to be dead; **gut gestellt sein** be well off

S

Stellen|anzeige f job advertisement. **S~vermittlung** f employment agency. **s~weise** adv in places

Stellung f **-,-en** position; (Arbeit) job; **S~nehmen** make a statement (**zu** on). **S~suche** f job-hunting

Stellvertreter m deputy

Stelzen fpl stilts. **s~** vi (sein) stalk

stemmen vt press; lift (Gewicht)

Stempel m **-s,-** stamp; (Post-) postmark; (Präge-) die; (Feingehalts-) hallmark. **s~n** vt stamp; hallmark (Silber); cancel (Marke)

Stengel* m **-s,-** = **Stängel**

Steno f - [!] shorthand

Steno|gramm nt **-[e]s,-e** shorthand text. **S~grafie** f - shorthand. **s~grafieren** vt take down in shorthand • vi (haben) do shorthand

Steppdecke f quilt

Steppe f **-,-n** steppe

Stepptanz m tap-dance

sterben† vi (sein) die (**an** + dat of); **im S~ liegen** be dying

sterblich adj mortal. **S~keit** f - mortality

stereo adv in stereo. **S~anlage** f stereo [system]

steril adj sterile. **s~isieren** vt sterilize. **S~ität** f - sterility

Stern m **-[e]s,-e** star. **S~bild** nt constellation. **S~chen** nt **-s,-** asterisk. **S~kunde** f astronomy. **S~schnuppe** f **-,-n** shooting star. **S~warte** f **-,-n** observatory

stets adv always

Steuer[1] nt **-s,-** steering-wheel; (Naut) helm; **am S~** at the wheel

Steuer[2] f **-,-n** tax

Steuer|bord nt **-[e]s** starboard [side]. **S~erklärung** f tax return. **s~frei** adj & adv tax-free. **S~mann** m (pl **-leute**) helmsman; (beim Rudern) cox. **s~n** vt steer; (Aviat) pilot; (Techn) control • vi (haben) be at the wheel/(Naut) helm. **s~pflichtig** adj taxable. **S~rad** nt steering-wheel. **S~ruder** nt helm. **S~ung** f - steering; (Techn) controls pl. **S~zahler** m **-s,-** taxpayer

Stewardess /'stjuːɐdɛs/ f **-,-en** air hostess, stewardess

Stich m **-[e]s,-e** prick; (Messer-) stab; (S~wunde) stab wound; (Bienen-) sting; (Mücken-) bite; (Schmerz) stabbing pain; (Näh-) stitch; (Kupfer-) engraving; (Kartenspiel) trick

stick|en vt/i (haben) embroider. **S~erei** f - embroidery

Stickstoff m nitrogen

Stiefel m **-s,-** boot

Stief|kind nt stepchild. **S~mutter**

f stepmother. **S~mütterchen** nt **-s,-** pansy. **S~sohn** m stepson. **S~tochter** f stepdaughter. **S~vater** m stepfather

Stiege f **-,-n** stairs pl

Stiel m **-[e]s,-e** handle; (Blumen-, Gläser-) stem; (Blatt-) stalk

Stier m **-[e]s,-e** bull; (Astrology) Taurus

Stierkampf m bullfight

Stift[1] m **-[e]s,-e** pin; (Nagel) tack; (Blei-) pencil; (Farb-) crayon

Stift[2] nt **-[e]s,-e** [endowed] foundation. **s~en** vt endow; (spenden) donate; create (Unheil, Verwirrung); bring about (Frieden). **S~ung** f **-,-en** foundation; (Spende) donation

Stil m **-[e]s,-e** style

still adj quiet; (reglos, ohne Kohlensäure) still; (heimlich) secret; **der S~e Ozean** the Pacific; **im S~en** secretly. **S~e** f **-** quiet; (Schweigen) silence

Stilleben* nt = **Stillleben**

stillen vt satisfy; quench (Durst); stop (Schmerzen, Blutung); breast-feed (Kind)

still|halten† vi sep (haben) keep still. **S~leben** nt still life. **s~legen** vt sep close down. **S~schweigen** nt silence. **S~stand** m standstill; **zum S~stand bringen/kommen** stop. **s~stehen**† vi sep (haben) stand still; (anhalten) stop; (Verkehr:) be at a standstill

Stimm|bänder ntpl vocal cords. **s~berechtigt** adj entitled to vote. **S~bruch** m **er ist im S~bruch** his voice is breaking

Stimme f **-,-n** voice; (Wahl-) vote

stimmen vi (haben) be right; (wählen) vote • vt tune

Stimmung f **-,-en** mood; (Atmosphäre) atmosphere

Stimmzettel m ballot-paper

stink|en† vi (haben) smell/(stark) stink (**nach** of). **S~tier** nt skunk

Stipendium nt **-s,-ien** scholarship; (Beihilfe) grant

Stirn f **-,-en** forehead

stochern vi (haben) **s~ in** (+ dat) poke (Feuer); pick at (Essen)

Stock[1] m **-[e]s,¨e** stick; (Ski-) pole; (Bienen-) hive; (Rosen-) bush; (Reb-) vine

Stock[2] m **-[e]s,-** storey, floor. **S~bett** nt bunk-beds pl.

stock|en vi (haben) stop; (Verkehr:) come to a standstill; (Person:) falter. **S~ung** f **-,-en** hold-up

Stockwerk nt storey, floor

Stoff m **-[e]s,-e** substance; (Textiles) fabric, material; (Thema) subject [matter]; (Gesprächs-) topic. **S~wechsel** m metabolism

stöhnen vi (haben) groan, moan

Stola f **-,-len** stole

Stollen m **-s,-** gallery; (Kuchen) stollen

stolpern vi (sein) stumble; **s~ über** (+ acc) trip over

stolz adj proud (**auf** + acc of). **S~** m **-es** pride

stopfen vt stuff; (stecken) put; (ausbessern) darn • vi (haben) be constipating

Stopp m **-s,-s** stop. **s~** int stop!

stoppelig adj stubbly

stopp|en vt stop; (Sport) time • vi (haben) stop. **S~uhr** f stop-watch

Stöpsel m **-s,-** plug; (Flaschen-) stopper

Storch m **-[e]s,¨e** stork

Store /ʃtoːɐ̯/ m **-s,-s** net curtain

stören vt disturb; disrupt (Rede); jam (Sender); (missfallen) bother • vi (haben) be a nuisance

stornieren vt cancel

störrisch adj stubborn

Störung f **-,-en** disturbance; disruption; (Med) trouble; (Radio) interference; **technische S~** technical fault

Stoß m **-es,¨e** push, knock; (mit

Ellbogen) dig; (Hörner-) butt; (mit Waffe) thrust; (Schwimm-) stroke; (Ruck) jolt; (Erd-) shock; (Stapel) stack, pile. **S~dämpfer** m **-s,-** shock absorber

stoßen† vt push, knock; (mit Füßen) kick; (mit Kopf) butt; (an-) poke, nudge; (treiben) thrust; **sich s~** knock oneself; **sich** (dat) **den Kopf s~** hit one's head • vi (haben) push; **s~ an** (+ acc) knock against; (angrenzen) adjoin • vi (sein) **s~ gegen** knock against; bump into (Tür); **s~ auf** (+ acc) bump into; (entdecken) come across; strike (Öl)

Stoß|stange f bumper. **S~verkehr** m rush-hour traffic. **S~zahn** m tusk. **S~zeit** f rush-hour

stottern vt/i (haben) stutter, stammer

Str. abbr (**Straße**) St

Strafanstalt f prison

Strafe f **-,-n** punishment; (Jur & fig) penalty; (Geld-) fine; (Freiheits-) sentence. **s~n** vt punish

straff adj tight, taut. **s~en** vt tighten

Strafgesetz nt criminal law

sträf|lich adj criminal. **S~ling** m **-s,-e** prisoner

Straf|mandat nt (Auto) [parking/speeding] ticket. **S~porto** nt excess postage. **S~raum** m penalty area. **S~stoß** m penalty. **S~tat** f crime

Strahl m **-[e]s,-en** ray; (einer Taschenlampe) beam; (Wasser-) jet. **s~en** vi (haben) shine; (funkeln) sparkle; (lächeln) beam. **S~enbehandlung** f radiotherapy. **S~ung** f - radiation

Strähne f **-,-n** strand

stramm adj tight

Strampel|höschen /-sç-/ nt **-s,-** rompers pl. **s~n** vi (haben) (Baby:) kick

Strand m **-[e]s,⸚e** beach. **s~en** vi (sein) run aground

Strang m **-[e]s,⸚e** rope

Strapaz|e f **-,-n** strain. **s~ieren** vt be hard on; tax (Nerven)

Strass m **- & -es** paste

Straße f **-,-n** road; (in der Stadt auch) street; (Meeres-) strait. **S~nbahn** f tram. **S~nkarte** f road-map. **S~nsperre** f road-block

Strat|egie f **-,-n** strategy. **s~egisch** adj strategic

Strauch m **-[e]s, Sträucher** bush

Strauß[1] m **-es, Sträuße** bunch [of flowers]; (Bukett) bouquet

Strauß[2] m **-es,-e** ostrich

streben vi (haben) strive (**nach** for) • vi (sein) head (**nach/zu** for)

Streber m **-s,-** pushy person

Strecke f **-,-n** stretch, section; (Entfernung) distance; (Rail) line; (Route) route

strecken vt stretch; (aus-) stretch out; (gerade machen) straighten; (Culin) thin down; **den Kopf aus dem Fenster s~** put one's head out of the window

Streich m **-[e]s,-e** prank, trick

streicheln vt stroke

streichen† vt spread; (weg-) smooth; (an-) paint; (aus-) delete; (kürzen) cut • vi (haben) **s~ über** (+ acc) stroke

Streichholz nt match

Streich|instrument nt stringed instrument. **S~käse** m cheese spread. **S~orchester** nt string orchestra. **S~ung** f **-,-en** deletion; (Kürzung) cut

Streife f **-,-n** patrol

streifen vt brush against; (berühren) touch; (verletzen) graze; (fig) touch on (Thema)

Streifen m **-s,-** stripe; (Licht-) streak; (auf der Fahrbahn) line; (schmales Stück) strip

Streifenwagen m patrol car

Streik m **-s,-s** strike; **in den S~ treten** go on strike. **S~brecher** m strike-breaker, (pej) scab. **s~en** vi (haben) strike; [!] refuse; (versagen) pack up

Streit m **-[e]s,-e** quarrel;

(Auseinandersetzung) dispute. **s~en†** vr/i (haben) **[sich] s~en** quarrel. **S~igkeiten** fpl quarrels. **S~kräfte** fpl armed forces

streng adj strict; (Blick, Ton) stern; (rau, nüchtern) severe; (Geschmack) sharp; **s~ genommen** strictly speaking. **S~e** f - strictness; sternness; severity

Stress m **-es,-e** stress

stressig adj stressful

streuen vt spread; (ver-) scatter; sprinkle (Zucker, Salz); **die Straßen s~** grit the roads

streunen vi (sein) roam

Strich m **-[e]s,-e** line; (Feder-, Pinsel-) stroke; (Morse-, Gedanken-) dash. **S~kode** m bar code. **S~punkt** m semicolon

Strick m **-[e]s,-e** cord; (Seil) rope

strick|en vt/i (haben) knit. **S~jacke** f cardigan. **S~leiter** f rope ladder. **S~nadel** f knitting-needle. **S~waren** fpl knitwear sg. **S~zeug** nt knitting

striegeln vt groom

strittig adj contentious

Stroh nt **-[e]s** straw. **S~blumen** fpl everlasting flowers. **S~dach** nt thatched roof. **S~halm** m straw

Strolch m **-[e]s,-e** ⊡ rascal

Strom m **-[e]s,⸚e** river; (Menschen-, Auto-, Blut-) stream; (Tränen-) flood; (Schwall) torrent; (Electr) current, power; **gegen den S~** (fig) against the tide. **s~abwärts** adv downstream. **s~aufwärts** adv upstream

strömen vi (sein) flow; (Menschen, Blut:) stream, pour

Strom|kreis m circuit. **s~linienförmig** adj streamlined. **S~sperre** f power cut

Strömung f **-,-en** current

Strophe f **-,-n** verse

Strudel m **-s,-** whirlpool; (SGer Culin) strudel

Strumpf m **-[e]s,⸚e** stocking; (Knie-) sock. **S~band** nt (pl **-bänder**) suspender. **S~hose** f tights pl

Strunk m **-[e]s,⸚e** stalk

struppig adj shaggy

Stube f **-,-n** room. **s~nrein** adj house-trained

Stuck m **-s** stucco

Stück nt **-[e]s,-e** piece; (Zucker-) lump; (Seife) tablet; (Theater-) play; (Gegenstand) item; (Exemplar) specimen; **ein S~** (Entfernung) some way. **S~chen** nt **-s,-** [little] bit. **s~weise** adv bit by bit; (einzeln) singly

Student|(in) m **-en,-en** (f **-,-nen**) student. **s~isch** adj student

Studie /-i̯ə/ f **-,-n** study

studieren vt/i (haben) study

Studio nt **-s,-s** studio

Studium nt **-s,-ien** studies pl

Stufe f **-,-n** step; (Treppen-) stair; (Raketen-) stage; (Niveau) level. **s~n** vt terrace; (staffeln) grade

Stuhl m **-[e]s,⸚e** chair; (Med) stools pl. **S~gang** m bowel movement

stülpen vt put (**über** + acc over)

stumm adj dumb; (schweigsam) silent

Stummel m **-s,-** stump; (Zigaretten-) butt; (Bleistift-) stub

Stümper m **-s,-** bungler

stumpf adj blunt; (Winkel) obtuse; (glanzlos) dull; (fig) apathetic. **S~** m **-[e]s,⸚e** stump

Stumpfsinn m apathy; tedium

Stunde f **-,-n** hour; (Sch) lesson

stunden vt **jdm eine Schuld s~** give s.o. time to pay a debt

Stunden|kilometer mpl kilometres per hour. **s~lang** adv for hours. **S~lohn** m hourly rate. **S~plan** m timetable. **s~weise** adv by the hour

stündlich adj & adv hourly

stur adj pigheaded

Sturm m **-[e]s,⸚e** gale; storm; (Mil) assault

stürm|en vi (haben) (Wind:) blow hard •vi (sein) rush •vt storm;

(bedrängen) besiege. **S~er** m **-s,-** forward. **s~isch** adj stormy; (Überfahrt) rough

Sturz m **-es,¨e** [heavy] fall; (Preis-) sharp drop; (Pol) overthrow

stürzen vi (sein) fall [heavily]; (in die Tiefe) plunge; (Preise:) drop sharply; (Regierung:) fall; (eilen) rush •vt throw; (umkippen) turn upside down; turn out (Speise, Kuchen); (Pol) overthrow, topple; **sich s~** throw oneself (**aus/in** + acc out of/into)

Sturzhelm m crash-helmet

Stute f **-,-n** mare

Stütze f **-,-n** support

stützen vt support; (auf-) rest; **sich s~ auf** (+ acc) lean on

stutzig adj puzzled; (misstrauisch) suspicious

Stützpunkt m (Mil) base

Substantiv nt **-s,-e** noun

Substanz f **-,-en** substance

Subvention /-'tsi̯o:n/ f **-,-en** subsidy. **s~ieren** vt subsidize

Such|e f - search; **auf der S~e nach** looking for. **s~en** vt look for; (intensiv) search for; seek (Hilfe, Rat); **'Zimmer gesucht'** 'room wanted' •vi (haben) look, search (**nach** for). **S~er** m **-s,-** (Phot) viewfinder. **S~maschine** f search engine

Sucht f **-,¨e** addiction; (fig) mania

süchtig adj addicted. **S~e(r)** m/f addict

Süd m **-[e]s** south. **S~afrika** nt South Africa. **S~amerika** nt South America. **s~deutsch** adj South German

Süden m **-s** south; **nach S~** south

Süd|frucht f tropical fruit. **s~lich** adj southern; (Richtung) southerly •adv & prep (+ gen) **s~lich der Stadt** south of the town. **S~pol** m South Pole. **s~wärts** adv southwards

Sühne f **-,-n** atonement; (Strafe) penalty. **s~n** vt atone for

Sultanine f **-,-n** sultana

Sülze f **-,-n** [meat] jelly

Summe f **-,-n** sum

summen vi (haben) hum; (Biene:) buzz •vt hum

summieren (sich) vr add up

Sumpf m **-[e]s,¨e** marsh, swamp

Sünd|e f **-,-n** sin. **S~enbock** m scapegoat. **S~er(in)** m **-s,-** (f **-,-nen**) sinner. **s~igen** vi (haben) sin

super inv adj [!] great. **S~markt** m supermarket

Suppe f **-,-n** soup. **S~nlöffel** m soup-spoon. **S~nteller** m soup plate. **S~nwürfel** m stock cube

Surf|brett /'sø:ɐ̯f-/ nt surfboard. **s~en** vi (haben) surf. **S~en** nt **-s** surfing

surren vi (haben) whirr

süß adj sweet. **S~e** f - sweetness. **s~en** vt sweeten. **S~igkeit** f **-,-en** sweet. **s~lich** adj sweetish; (fig) sugary. **S~speise** f sweet. **S~stoff** m sweetener. **S~waren** fpl confectionery sg, sweets pl. **S~wasser-** prefix freshwater

Sylvester nt **-s** = **Silvester**

Symbol nt **-s,-e** symbol. **S~ik** f - symbolism. **s~isch** adj symbolic

Sym|metrie f - symmetry. **s~metrisch** adj symmetrical

Sympathie f **-,-n** sympathy

sympathisch adj agreeable; (Person) likeable

Symptom nt **-s,-e** symptom. **s~atisch** adj symptomatic

Synagoge f **-,-n** synagogue

synchronisieren /zynkroni'zi:rən/ vt synchronize; dub (Film)

Syndikat nt **-[e]s,-e** syndicate

Syndrom nt **-s,-e** syndrome

synonym adj synonymous

Synthese f **-,-n** synthesis

Syrien /-i̯ən/ nt **-s** Syria

System nt **-s,-e** system. **s~atisch** adj systematic

Szene f **-,-n** scene

Tt

Tabak m **-s,-e** tobacco

Tabelle f **-,-n** table; (Sport) league table

Tablett nt **-[e]s,-s** tray

Tablette f **-,-n** tablet

tabu adj taboo. **T~** nt **-s,-s** taboo

Tacho m **-s,-s**, **Tachometer** m & nt speedometer

Tadel m **-s,-** reprimand; (Kritik) censure; (Sch) black mark. **t~los** adj impeccable. **t~n** vt reprimand; censure

Tafel f **-,-n** (Tisch, Tabelle) table; (Platte) slab; (Anschlag-, Hinweis-) board; (Gedenk-) plaque; (Schiefer-) slate; (Wand-) blackboard; (Bild-) plate; (Schokolade) bar

Täfelung f **-** panelling

Tag m **-[e]s,-e** day; **unter T~e** underground; **es wird Tag** it is getting light; **guten Tag!** good morning/afternoon!

Tage|buch nt diary. **t~lang** adv for days

Tages|anbruch m daybreak. **T~ausflug** m day trip. **T~decke** f bedspread. **T~karte** f day ticket; (Speise-) menu of the day. **T~licht** nt daylight. **T~mutter** f child-minder. **T~ordnung** f agenda. **T~rückfahrkarte** f day return [ticket]. **T~zeit** f time of the day. **T~zeitung** f daily [news]paper

täglich adj & adv daily; **zweimal t~** twice a day

tags adv by day; **t~ zuvor/darauf** the day before/after

tagsüber adv during the day

tag|täglich adj daily • adv every single day. **T~ung** f **-,-en** meeting; conference

Taill|e /'taljə/ f **-,-n** waist. **t~iert** adj fitted

Takt m **-[e]s,-e** tact; (Mus) bar; (Tempo) time; (Rhythmus) rhythm; **im T~** in time

Taktik f **-** tactics pl.

takt|los adj tactless. **T~losigkeit** f **-** tactlessness. **T~stock** m baton. **t~voll** adj tactful

Tal nt **-[e]s,¨er** valley

Talar m **-s,-e** robe; (Univ) gown

Talent nt **-[e]s,-e** talent. **t~iert** adj talented

Talg m **-s** tallow; (Culin) suet

Talsperre f dam

Tampon /tam'põ:/ m **-s,-s** tampon

Tank m **-s,-s** tank. **t~en** vt fill up with (Benzin) • vi (haben) fill up with petrol; (Aviat) refuel. **T~er** m **-s,-** tanker. **T~stelle** f petrol station. **T~wart** m **-[e]s,-e** petrol-pump attendant

Tanne f **-,-n** fir [tree]. **T~nbaum** m fir tree; (Weihnachtsbaum) Christmas tree. **T~nzapfen** m fir cone

Tante f **-,-n** aunt

Tantiemen /tan'ti̯e:mən/ pl royalties

Tanz m **-es,¨e** dance. **t~en** vt/i (haben) dance

Tänzer(in) m **-s,-** (f **-,-nen**) dancer

Tapete f **-,-n** wallpaper

tapezieren vt paper

tapfer adj brave. **T~keit** f **-** bravery

Tarif m **-s,-e** rate; (Verzeichnis) tariff

tarn|en vt disguise; (Mil) camouflage. **T~ung** f **-** disguise; camouflage

Tasche f **-,-n** bag; (Hosen-, Mantel-) pocket. **T~nbuch** nt paperback. **T~ndieb** m pickpocket. **T~ngeld** nt pocket-money. **T~nlampe** f torch. **T~nmesser** nt penknife.

T~ntuch nt handkerchief

Tasse f -,-n cup

Tastatur f -,-en keyboard

Tast|e f -,-n key; (Druck-) push button. **t~en** vi (haben) feel, grope (**nach** for) •vt key in (Daten); **sich t~en** feel one's way (zu to)

Tat f -,-en action; (Helden-) deed; (Straf-) crime; **auf frischer Tat ertappt** caught in the act

Täter(in) m -s,- (f -,-nen) culprit; (Jur) offender

tätig adj active; **t~ sein** work. **T~keit** f -,-en activity; (Arbeit) work, job

Tatkraft f energy

Tatort m scene of the crime

tätowier|en vt tattoo. **T~ung** f -,-en tattooing; (Bild) tattoo

Tatsache f fact. **T~nbericht** m documentary

tatsächlich adj actual

Tatze f -,-n paw

Tau[1] m -[e]s dew

Tau[2] nt -[e]s,-e rope

taub adj deaf; (gefühllos) numb

Taube f -,-n pigeon; dove. **T~nschlag** m pigeon loft

Taub|heit f - deafness. **t~stumm** adj deaf and dumb

tauch|en vt dip, plunge; (unter-) duck •vi (haben/sein) dive/(ein-) plunge (**in** + acc into); (auf-) appear (**aus** out of). **T~er** m -s,- diver. **T~eranzug** m diving-suit

tauen vi (sein) melt, thaw •impers **es taut** it is thawing

Tauf|becken nt font. **T~e** f -,-n christening, baptism. **t~en** vt christen, baptize. **T~pate** m godfather

taugen vi (haben) **etwas/nichts t~n be good**/no good

tauglich adj suitable; (Mil) fit

Tausch m -[e]s,-e exchange, ⓘ swap. **t~en** vt exchange/(handeln) barter (gegen for) •vi (haben) swap (**mit etw** sth; **mit jdm** with s.o.)

täuschen vt deceive, fool; betray (Vertrauen); **sich t~** delude oneself; (sich irren) be mistaken •vi (haben) be deceptive. **t~d** adj deceptive; (Ähnlichkeit) striking

Täuschung f -,-en deception; (Irrtum) mistake; (Illusion) delusion

tausend inv adj one/a thousand. **T~** nt -s,-e thousand. **T~füßler** m -s,- centipede. **t~ste(r, s)** adj thousandth. **T~stel** nt -s,- thousandth

Tau|tropfen m dewdrop. **T~wetter** nt thaw

Taxe f -,-n charge; (Kur-) tax; (Taxi) taxi

Taxi nt -s,-s taxi, cab

Taxi|fahrer m taxi driver. **T~stand** m taxi rank

Teakholz /'ti:k-/ nt teak

Team /ti:m/ nt -s,-s team

Techni|k f -,-en technology; (Methode) technique. **T~ker** m -s,- technician. **t~sch** adj technical; (technologisch) technological; **T~sche Hochschule** Technical University

Techno|logie f -,-n technology. **t~logisch** adj technological

Teddybär m teddy bear

Tee m -s,-s tea. **T~beutel** m tea-bag. **T~kanne** f teapot. **T~löffel** m teaspoon

Teer m -s tar. **t~en** vt tar

Tee|sieb nt tea strainer. **T~wagen** m [tea] trolley

Teich m -[e]s,-e pond

Teig m -[e]s,-e pastry; (Knet-) dough; (Rühr-) mixture; (Pfannkuchen-) batter. **T~rolle** f rolling-pin. **T~waren** fpl pasta sg

Teil m -[e]s,-e part; (Bestand-) component; (Jur) party; **zum T~** partly; **zum großen/größten T~** for the most part •m & nt -[e]s (Anteil) share; **ich für mein[en] T~** for my part •nt -[e]s,-e part; (Ersatz-) spare part; (Anbau-) unit

teil|bar adj divisible. **T~chen** nt -s,- particle. **t~en** vt divide; (auf-) share out; (gemeinsam haben) share;

(Pol) partition (Land); **sich** (dat) **etw t~en** share sth; **sich t~en** divide; (sich gabeln) fork; (Meinungen:) differ •vi (haben) share

Teilhaber m **-s,-** (Comm) partner

Teilnahme f **-** participation; (innere) interest; (Mitgefühl) sympathy

teilnehm|en† vi sep (haben) **t~en an** (+ dat) take part in; (mitfühlen) share [in]. **T~er(in)** m **-s,-** (f **-,-nen**) participant; (an Wettbewerb) competitor

teil|s adv partly. **T~ung** f **-,-en** division; (Pol) partition. **t~weise** adj partial •adv partially, partly. **T~zahlung** f part payment; (Rate) instalment. **T~zeitbeschäftigung** f part-time job

Teint /tɛ̃:/ m **-s,-s** complexion

Telearbeit f teleworking

Telefax nt fax

Telefon nt **-s,-e** [tele]phone. **T~anruf** m, **T~at** nt **-[e]s,-e** [tele]phone call. **T~buch** nt [tele]phone book. **t~ieren** vi (haben) [tele]phone

telefon|isch adj [tele]phone •adv by [tele]phone. **T~ist(in)** m **-en,-en** (f **-,-nen**) telephonist. **T~karte** f phone card. **T~nummer** f [tele]phone number. **T~zelle** f [tele]phone box

Telegraf m **-en,-en** telegraph. **T~enmast** m telegraph pole. **t~ieren** vi (haben) send a telegram. **t~isch** adj telegraphic •adv by telegram

Telegramm nt **-s,-e** telegram

Teleobjektiv nt telephoto lens

Telepathie f **-** telepathy

Teleskop nt **-s,-e** telescope

Telex nt **-,-[e]** telex. **t~en** vt telex

Teller m **-s,-** plate

Tempel m **-s,-** temple

Temperament nt **-s,-e** temperament; (Lebhaftigkeit) vivacity

Temperatur f **-,-en** temperature

Tempo nt **-s,-s** speed; **T~ [T~]!** hurry up!

Tendenz f **-,-en** trend; (Neigung) tendency

Tennis nt **-** tennis. **T~platz** m tennis-court. **T~schläger** m tennis-racket

Teppich m **-s,-e** carpet. **T~boden** m fitted carpet

Termin m **-s,-e** date; (Arzt-) appointment. **T~kalender** m [appointments] diary

Terpentin nt **-s** turpentine

Terrasse f **-,-n** terrace

Terrier /ˈtɛri̯ɐ/ m **-s,-** terrier

Terrine f **-,-n** tureen

Territorium nt **-s,-ien** territory

Terror m **-s** terror. **t~isieren** vt terrorize. **T~ismus** m **-** terrorism. **T~ist** m **-en,-en** terrorist

Tesafilm® m ≈ Sellotape®

Test m **-[e]s,-s** & **-e** test

Testament nt **-[e]s,-e** will; **Altes/Neues T~** Old/New Testament. **T~svollstrecker** m **-s,-** executor

testen vt test

Tetanus m **-** tetanus

teuer adj expensive; (lieb) dear; **wie t~?** how much?

Teufel m **-s,-** devil. **T~skreis** m vicious circle

teuflisch adj fiendish

Text m **-[e]s,-e** text; (Passage) passage; (Bild-) caption; (Lied-) lyrics pl. **T~er** m **-s,-** copywriter; (Schlager-) lyricist

Textilien /-i̯ən/ pl textiles; (Textilwaren) textile goods

Text|nachricht f text message. **T~verarbeitungssystem** nt word processor

Theater nt **-s,-** theatre; (!: Getue) fuss. **T~kasse** f box-office. **T~stück** nt play

Theke f **-,-n** bar; (Ladentisch) counter

Thema nt **-s,-men** subject

Themse f **-** Thames

Theolo|ge m **-n,-n** theologian. **T~gie** f - theology

theor|etisch adj theoretical. **T~ie** f -,-n theory

Therapeut(in) m **-en,-en** (f **-,-nen**) therapist

Therapie f **-,-n** therapy

Thermalbad nt thermal bath

Thermometer nt **-s,-** thermometer

Thermosflasche® f Thermos flask®

Thermostat m **-[e]s,-e** thermostat

These f **-,-n** thesis

Thrombose f **-,-n** thrombosis

Thron m **-[e]s,-e** throne. **t~en** vi (haben) sit [in state]. **T~folge** f succession. **T~folger** m **-s,-** heir to the throne

Thunfisch m tuna

Thymian m **-s** thyme

ticken vi (haben) tick

tief adj deep; (t~ liegend, niedrig) low; (t~gründig) profound; **t~er Teller** soup-plate •adv deep; low; (sehr) deeply, profoundly; (schlafen) soundly. **T~** nt **-s,-s** (Meteorology) depression. **T~bau** m civil engineering. **T~e** f **-,-n** depth. **T~garage** f underground car park. **t~gekühlt** adj [deep-]frozen

Tiefkühl|fach nt freezer compartment. **T~kost** f frozen food. **T~truhe** f deep-freeze

Tiefsttemperatur f minimum temperature

t

Tier nt **-[e]s,-e** animal. **T~arzt** m, **T~ärztin** f vet, veterinary surgeon. **T~garten** m zoo. **T~kreis** m zodiac. **T~kunde** f zoology. **T~quälerei** f cruelty to animals

Tiger m **-s,-** tiger

tilgen vt pay off (Schuld); (streichen) delete; (fig: auslöschen) wipe out

Tinte f **-,-n** ink. **T~nfisch** m squid

Tipp (Tip) m **-s,-s** [!] tip

tipp|en vt [!] type •vi (haben) (berühren) touch (**auf/an etw** acc sth); ([!]: Maschine schreiben) type; **t~en auf** (+ acc) ([!]: wetten) bet on. **T~schein** m pools/lottery coupon

tipptopp adj [!] immaculate

Tirol nt **-s** [the] Tyrol

Tisch m **-[e]s,-e** table; (Schreib-) desk; **nach T~** after the meal. **T~decke** f table-cloth. **T~gebet** nt grace. **T~ler** m **-s,-** joiner; (Möbel-) cabinet-maker. **T~rede** f after-dinner speech. **T~tennis** nt table tennis

Titel m **-s,-** title

Toast /to:st/ m **-[e]s,-e** toast; (Scheibe) piece of toast. **T~er** m **-s,-** toaster

toben vi (haben) rave; (Sturm:) rage; (Kinder:) play boisterously

Tochter f **-,⸚** daughter. **T~gesellschaft** f subsidiary

Tod m **-es** death

Todes|angst f mortal fear. **T~anzeige** f death announcement; (Zeitungs-) obituary. **T~fall** m death. **T~opfer** nt fatality, casualty. **T~strafe** f death penalty. **T~urteil** nt death sentence

todkrank adj dangerously ill

tödlich adj fatal; (Gefahr) mortal

Toilette /toa'lɛtə/ f **-,-n** toilet. **T~npapier** nt toilet paper

toler|ant adj tolerant. **T~anz** f - tolerance. **t~ieren** vt tolerate

toll adj crazy, mad; ([!]: prima) fantastic; (schlimm) awful •adv (sehr) very; (schlimm) badly. **t~kühn** adj foolhardy. **T~wut** f rabies. **t~wütig** adj rabid

Tölpel m **-s,-** fool

Tomate f **-,-n** tomato. **T~nmark** nt tomato purée

Tombola f **-,-s** raffle

Ton[1] m **-[e]s** clay

Ton[2] m **-[e]s,⸚e** tone; (Klang) sound; (Note) note; (Betonung) stress; (Farb-) shade; **der gute Ton** (fig) good form. **T~abnehmer** m **-s,-** pick-up. **t~angebend** adj (fig) leading.

T~art f tone [of voice]; (Mus) key. **T~band** nt (pl **-bänder**) tape. **T~bandgerät** nt tape recorder

tönen vi (haben) sound •vt tint

Tonleiter f scale

Tonne f -,-n barrel, cask: (Müll-) bin; (Maß) tonne, metric ton

Topf m **-[e]s,¨-e** pot; (Koch-) pan

Topfen m **-s** (Aust) ≈ curd cheese

Töpferei f **-,-en** pottery

Topf|lappen m oven-cloth. **T~pflanze** f potted plant

Tor nt **-[e]s,-e** gate; (Einfahrt) gateway; (Sport) goal

Torf m **-s** peat

torkeln vi (sein/habe) stagger

Tornister m **-s,-** knapsack; (Sch) satchel

Torpedo m **-s,-s** torpedo

Torpfosten m goal-post

Torte f **-,-n** gateau; (Obst-) flan

Tortur f **-,-en** torture

Torwart m **-s,-e** goalkeeper

tot adj dead; **tot geboren** stillborn; **sich tot stellen** pretend to be dead

total adj total. **T~schaden** m ≈ write-off

Tote|(r) m/f dead man/woman; (Todesopfer) fatality; **die T~n** the dead pl

töten vt kill

Toten|gräber m **-s,-** grave-digger. **T~kopf** m skull. **T~schein** m death certificate

totfahren† vt sep run over and kill

Toto nt & m **-s** football pools pl. **T~schein** m pools coupon

tot|schießen† vt sep shoot dead. **T~schlag** m (Jur) manslaughter. **t~schlagen†** vt sep kill

Tötung f **-,-en** killing; **fahrlässige T~** (Jur) manslaughter

Toup|et /tu'pe:/ nt **-s,-s** toupee. **t~ieren** vt back-comb

Tour /tu:ɐ̯/ f **-,-en** tour; (Ausflug) trip; (Auto-) drive; (Rad-) ride; (Strecke) distance; (Techn) revolution; (!: Weise) way

Touris|mus /tu'rɪsmʊs/ m - tourism. **T~t** m **-en,-en** tourist

Tournee /tʊr'ne:/ f **-,-n** tour

Trab m **-[e]s** trot

Trabant m **-en,-en** satellite

traben vi (haben/sein) trot

Tracht f **-,-en** [national] costume

Tradition /-'ts̮i̯o:n/ f **-,-en** tradition. **t~ell** adj traditional

Trag|bahre f stretcher. **t~bar** adj portable; (Kleidung) wearable

tragen† vt carry; (an-/ aufhaben) wear; (fig) bear •vi (haben) carry; **gut t~** (Baum:) produce a good crop

Träger m **-s,-** porter; (Inhaber) bearer; (eines Ordens) holder; (Bau-) beam; (Stahl-) girder; (Achsel-) [shoulder] strap. **T~kleid** nt pinafore dress

Trag|etasche f carrier bag. **T~flächenboot**, **T~flügelboot** nt hydrofoil

Trägheit f - sluggishness; (Faulheit) laziness; (Phys) inertia

Trag|ik f - tragedy. **t~isch** adj tragic

Tragödie /-i̯ə/ f **-,-n** tragedy

Train|er /'trɛ:nɐ/ m **-s,-** trainer; (Tennis-) coach. **t~ieren** vt/i (haben) train

Training /'trɛ:nɪŋ/ nt **-s** training. **T~sanzug** m tracksuit. **T~sschuhe** mpl trainers

Traktor m **-s,-en** tractor

trampeln vi (haben) stamp one's feet •vi (sein) trample (**auf** + acc on) •vt trample

trampen /'trɛmpən/ vi (sein) ! hitch-hike

Tranchiermesser /trã'ʃi:ɐ̯-/ nt carving knife

Träne f **-,-n** tear. **t~n** vi (haben) water. **T~ngas** nt tear-gas

Tränke f **-,-n** watering place; (Trog) drinking trough. **t~n** vt water

t

(Pferd); (nässen) soak (mit with)

Trans|formator m **-s,-en** transformer. **T~fusion** f **-,-en** [blood] transfusion

Transit /tran'zi:t/ m **-s** transit

Transparent nt **-[e]s,-e** banner; (Bild) transparency

transpirieren vi (haben) perspire

Transport m **-[e]s,-e** transport; (Güter-) consignment. **t~ieren** vt transport

Trapez nt **-es,-e** trapeze

Tratte f **-,-n** (Comm) draft

Traube f **-,-n** bunch of grapes; (Beere) grape; (fig) cluster. **T~nzucker** m glucose

trauen vi (haben) (+ dat) trust •vt marry; **sich t~** dare (**etw zu tun** [to] do sth); venture (**in** + acc/**aus** into/out of)

Trauer f **-** mourning; (Schmerz) grief (**um** for); **T~ tragen** be [dressed] in mourning. **T~fall** m bereavement. **T~feier** f funeral service. **t~n** vi (haben) grieve; **t~n um** mourn [for]. **T~spiel** nt tragedy. **T~weide** f weeping willow

Traum m **-[e]s, Träume** dream

Trauma nt **-s,-men** trauma

träumen vt/i (haben) dream

traumhaft adj dreamlike; (schön) fabulous

traurig adj sad; (erbärmlich) sorry. **T~keit** f **-** sadness

Trau|ring m wedding-ring. **T~schein** m marriage certificate. **T~ung** f **-,-en** wedding [ceremony]

Treff nt **-s,-s** (Karten) spades pl

treff|en† vt hit; (Blitz:) strike; (fig: verletzen) hurt; (zusammenkommen mit) meet; take (Maßnahme); **sich t~en** meet (**mit jdm** s.o.); **sich gut t~en** be convenient; **es gut/schlecht t~en** be lucky/unlucky •vi (haben) hit the target; **t~en auf** (+ acc) meet; (fig) meet with. **T~en** nt **-s,-** meeting. **T~er** m **-s,-** hit; (Los) winner. **T~punkt** m meeting-place

treiben† vt drive; (sich befassen mit) do; carry on (Gewerbe); indulge in (Luxus); get up to (Unfug); **Handel t~** trade •vi (sein) drift; (schwimmen) float •vi (haben) (Bot) sprout. **T~** nt **-s** activity

Treib|haus nt hothouse. **T~hauseffekt** m greenhouse effect. **T~holz** nt driftwood. **T~riemen** m transmission belt. **T~sand** m quicksand. **T~stoff** m fuel

trenn|bar adj separable. **t~en** vt separate/(abmachen) detach (**von** from); divide, split (Wort); **sich t~en** separate; (auseinander gehen) part; **sich t~en von** leave; (fortgeben) part with. **T~ung** f **-,-en** separation; (Silben-) division. **T~ungsstrich** m hyphen. **T~wand** f partition

trepp|ab adv downstairs. **t~auf** adv upstairs

Treppe f **-,-n** stairs pl; (Außen-) steps pl. **T~ngeländer** nt banisters pl

Tresor m **-s,-e** safe

Tresse f **-,-n** braid

Treteimer m pedal bin

treten† vi (sein/haben) step; (versehentlich) tread; (ausschlagen) kick (**nach** at); **in Verbindung t~** get in touch •vt tread; (mit Füßen) kick

treu adj faithful; (fest) loyal. **T~e** f **-** faithfulness; loyalty; (eheliche) fidelity. **T~ekarte** f loyalty card. **T~händer** m **-s,-** trustee. **t~los** adj disloyal; (untreu) unfaithful

Tribüne f **-,-n** platform; (Zuschauer-) stand

Trichter m **-s,-** funnel; (Bomben-) crater

Trick m **-s,-s** trick. **T~film** m cartoon. **t~reich** adj clever

Trieb m **-[e]s,-e** drive, urge; (Instinkt) instinct; (Bot) shoot. **T~verbrecher** m sex offender. **T~werk** nt (Aviat) engine; (Uhr-) mechanism

triefen† vi (haben) drip; (nass sein) be dripping (**von/vor** + dat with)

Trigonometrie f **-** trigonometry

Trikot[1] /tri'ko:/ m **-s** (Textiles) jersey

Trikot² nt **-s,-s** (Sport) jersey; (Fußball-) shirt

Trimester nt **-s,-** term

Trimm-dich nt **-s** keep-fit

trimmen vt trim; tune (Motor); **sich t~** keep fit

trink|en† vt/i (haben) drink. **T~er(in)** m **-s,-** (f **-,-nen**) alcoholic. **T~geld** nt tip. **T~spruch** m toast

trist adj dreary

Tritt m **-[e]s,-e** step; (Fuß-) kick. **T~brett** nt step

Triumph m **-s,-e** triumph. **t~ieren** vi (haben) rejoice

trocken adj dry. **T~haube** f drier. **T~heit** f **-,-en** dryness; (Dürre) drought. **t~legen** vt sep change (Baby); drain (Sumpf). **T~milch** f powdered milk

trockn|en vt/i (sein) dry. **T~er** m **-s,-** drier

Trödel m **-s** [!] junk. **t~n** vi (haben) dawdle

Trödler m **-s,-** [!] slowcoach; (Händler) junk-dealer

Trog m **-[e]s,⸚e** trough

Trommel f **-,-n** drum. **T~fell** nt ear-drum. **t~n** vi (haben) drum

Trommler m **-s,-** drummer

Trompete f **-,-n** trumpet. **T~r** m **-s,-** trumpeter

Tropen pl tropics

Tropf m **-[e]s,-e** (Med) drip

tröpfeln vt/i (sein/haben) drip

tropfen vt/i (sein/haben) drip. **T~** m **-s,-** drop; (fallend) drip. **t~weise** adv drop by drop

Trophäe /tro'fɛ:ə/ f **-,-n** trophy

tropisch adj tropical

Trost m **-[e]s** consolation, comfort

tröst|en vt console, comfort; **sich t~en** console oneself. **t~lich** adj comforting

trost|los adj desolate; (elend) wretched; (reizlos) dreary. **T~preis** m consolation prize

Trott m **-s** amble; (fig) routine

Trottel m **-s,-** [!] idiot

Trottoir /trɔ'to̯a:ɐ̯/ nt **-s,-s** pavement

trotz prep (+ gen) despite, in spite of. **T~** m **-es** defiance. **t~dem** adv nevertheless. **t~ig** adj defiant; stubborn

trübe adj dull; (Licht) dim; (Flüssigkeit) cloudy; (fig) gloomy

Trubel m **-s** bustle

trüben vt dull; make cloudy (Flüssigkeit); (fig) spoil; strain (Verhältnis) **sich t~** (Flüssigkeit:) become cloudy; (Himmel:) cloud over; (Augen:) dim

Trüb|sal f **-** misery. **T~sinn** m melancholy. **t~sinnig** adj melancholy

trügen† vt deceive • vi (haben) be deceptive

Trugschluss m fallacy

Truhe f **-,-n** chest

Trümmer pl rubble sg; (T~teile) wreckage sg, (fig) ruins

Trumpf m **-[e]s,⸚e** trump [card]. **t~en** vi (haben) play trumps

Trunk m **-[e]s** drink. **T~enheit** f **-** drunkenness; **T~enheit am Steuer** drink-driving

Trupp m **-s,-s** group; (Mil) squad. **T~e** f **-,-n** (Mil) unit; (Theat) troupe; **T~en** troops

Truthahn m turkey

Tschech|e m **-n,-n**, **T~in** f **-,-nen** Czech. **t~isch** adj Czech. **T~oslowakei (die) -** Czechoslovakia

tschüs, **tschüss** int bye, cheerio

Tuba f **-,-ben** (Mus) tuba

Tube f **-,-n** tube

Tuberkulose f **-** tuberculosis

Tuch nt **-[e]s,⸚er** cloth; (Hals-, Kopf-) scarf; (Schulter-) shawl

tüchtig adj competent; (reichlich, beträchtlich) good; (groß) big • adv competently; (ausreichend) well

Tück|e f **-,-n** malice. **t~isch** adj malicious; (gefährlich) treacherous

Tugend f -,en virtue. **t~haft** adj virtuous

Tülle f -,-n spout

Tulpe f -,-n tulip

Tümmler m -s,- porpoise

Tumor m -s,-en tumour

Tümpel m -[e]s,- pond

Tumult m -[e]s,-e commotion; (Aufruhr) riot

tun† vt do; take (Schritt, Blick); work (Wunder); (bringen) put (**in** + acc into); **sich tun** happen; **jdm etwas tun** hurt s.o.; **das tut nichts** it doesn't matter •vi (haben) act (**als ob** as if); **er tut nur so** he's just pretending; **jdm/etw gut tun** do s.o./sth good; **zu tun haben** have things/work to do; **[es] zu tun haben mit** have to deal with. **Tun** nt -s actions pl

Tünche f -,-n whitewash; (fig) veneer. **t~n** vt whitewash

Tunesien /-i̯ən/ nt -s Tunisia

Tunfisch m = **Thunfisch**

Tunnel m -s,- tunnel

tupf|en vt dab •vi (haben) **t~en an/auf** (+ acc) touch. **T~en** m -s,- spot. **T~er** m -s,- spot; (Med) swab

Tür f -,-en door

Turban m -s,-e turban

Turbine f -,-n turbine

Türk|e m -n,-n Turk. **T~ei (die)** - Turkey. **T~in** f -,-nen Turk

türkis inv adj turquoise

türkisch adj Turkish

Turm m -[e]s,¨-e tower; (Schach) rook, castle

Türm|chen nt -s,- turret. **t~en** vt pile [up]; **sich t~en** pile up

Turmspitze f spire

turn|en vi (haben) do gymnastics. **T~en** nt -s gymnastics sg; (Sch) physical education, [!] gym. **T~er(in)** m -s,- (f -,-nen) gymnast. **T~halle** f gymnasium

Turnier nt -s,-e tournament; (Reit-) show

Turnschuhe mpl gym shoes; trainers

Türschwelle f doorstep, threshold

Tusche f -,-n [drawing] ink

tuscheln vt/i (haben) whisper

Tüte f -,-n bag; (Comm) packet; (Eis-) cornet; **in die T~ blasen** [!] be breathalysed

TÜV m - ≈ MOT [test]

Typ m -s,-en type; ([!]: Kerl) bloke. **T~e** f -,-n type

Typhus m - typhoid

typisch adj typical (**für** of)

Typus m -, **Typen** type

Tyrann m -en,-en tyrant. **T~ei** f - tyranny. **t~isch** adj tyrannical. **t~isieren** vt tyrannize

Uu

U-Bahn f underground

übel adj bad; (hässlich) nasty; **mir ist ü~** I feel sick; **jdm etw ü~ nehmen** hold sth against s.o. **Ü~keit** f - nausea

üben vt/i (haben) practise

über prep (+ dat/acc) over; (höher als) above; (betreffend) about; (Buch, Vortrag) on; (Scheck, Rechnung) for; (quer ü~) across; **ü~ Köln fahren** go via Cologne; **ü~ Ostern** over Easter; **die Woche ü~** during the week; **Fehler ü~ Fehler** mistake after mistake •adv **ü~ und ü~** all over; **jdm ü~ sein** be better/ (stärker) stronger than s.o. •adj [!] **ü~ sein** be left over; **etw ü~ sein**

be fed up with sth

überall adv everywhere

überanstrengen vt insep overtax; strain (Augen)

überarbeiten vt insep revise; **sich ü~en** overwork

überbieten† vt insep outbid; (übertreffen) surpass

Überblick m overall view; (Abriss) summary

überblicken vt insep overlook; (abschätzen) assess

überbringen† vt insep deliver

überbrücken vt insep (fig) bridge

überbuchen vt insep overbook

überdies adv moreover

überdimensional adj oversized

Überdosis f overdose

überdrüssig adj **ü~ sein/werden** be/grow tired (gen of)

übereignen vt insep transfer

übereilt adj over-hasty

übereinander adv one on top of/ above the other; (sprechen) about each other

überein|kommen† vi sep (sein) agree. **Ü~kunft** f - agreement. **ü~stimmen** vi sep (haben) agree; (Zahlen:) tally; (Ansichten:) coincide; (Farben:) match. **Ü~stimmung** f agreement

überfahren† vt insep run over

Überfahrt f crossing

Überfall m attack; (Bank-) raid

überfallen† vt insep attack; raid (Bank); (bestürmen) bombard (**mit** with)

Überfluss m abundance; (Wohlstand) affluence

überflüssig adj superfluous

überfordern vt insep overtax

überführ|en vt insep transfer; (Jur) convict (gen of). **Ü~ung** f transfer; (Straße) flyover; (Fußgänger-) foot-bridge

überfüllt adj overcrowded

Übergabe f handing over; transfer

Übergang m crossing; (Wechsel) transition

übergeben† vt insep hand over; (übereignen) transfer; **sich ü~** be sick

übergehen† vt insep (fig) pass over; (nicht beachten) ignore; (auslassen) leave out

Übergewicht nt excess weight; (fig) predominance; **Ü~ haben** be overweight

über|greifen† vi sep (haben) spread (**auf** + acc to). **Ü~griff** m infringement

über|groß adj outsize; (übertrieben) exaggerated. **Ü~größe** f outsize

überhand adv **ü~ nehmen** increase alarmingly

überhäufen vt insep inundate (**mit** with)

überhaupt adv (im Allgemeinen) altogether; (eigentlich) anyway; (überdies) besides; **ü~ nicht/nichts** not/nothing at all

überheblich adj arrogant. **Ü~keit** f - arrogance

überhol|en vt insep overtake; (reparieren) overhaul. **ü~t** adj outdated. **Ü~ung** f **-,-en** overhaul. **Ü~verbot** nt 'Ü~verbot' 'no overtaking'

überhören vt insep fail to hear; (nicht beachten) ignore

überirdisch adj supernatural

überkochen vi sep (sein) boil over

überlassen† vt insep **jdm etw ü~** leave sth to s.o.; (geben) let s.o. have sth; **sich** (dat) **selbst ü~ sein** be left to one's own devices

Überlauf m overflow

überlaufen† vi sep (sein) overflow; (Mil, Pol) defect

Überläufer m defector

überleben vt/i insep (haben) survive. **Ü~de(r)** m/f survivor

überlegen[1] vt sep put over

überlegen[2] v insep ● vt [**sich** dat] **ü~** think over, consider; **es sich** (dat)

anders ü~ change one's mind •vi (haben) think, reflect

überlegen³ adj superior. **Ü~heit** f - superiority

Überlegung f -,-en reflection

überliefer|n vt insep hand down. **Ü~ung** f tradition

überlisten vt insep outwit

Übermacht f superiority

übermäßig adj excessive

Übermensch m superman. **ü~lich** adj superhuman

übermitteln vt insep convey; (senden) transmit

übermorgen adv the day after tomorrow

übermüdet adj overtired

Über|mut m high spirits pl. **ü~mütig** adj high-spirited

übernächst|e(r,s) adj next but one; **ü~es Jahr** the year after next

übernacht|en vi insep (haben) stay overnight. **Ü~ung** f -,-en overnight stay; **Ü~ung und Frühstück** bed and breakfast

Übernahme f - taking over; (Comm) take-over

übernatürlich adj supernatural

übernehmen† vt insep take over; (annehmen) take on; **sich ü~** overdo things; (finanziell) over-reach oneself

überqueren vt insep cross

überrasch|en vt insep surprise. **ü~end** adj surprising; (unerwartet) unexpected. **Ü~ung** f -,-en surprise

U

überreden vt insep persuade

Überreste mpl remains

Überschall- prefix supersonic

überschätzen vt insep overestimate

Überschlag m rough estimate; (Sport) somersault

überschlagen¹† vt sep cross (Beine)

überschlagen²† vt insep estimate roughly; (auslassen) skip; **sich ü~** somersault; (Ereignisse:) happen fast •adj tepid

überschneiden† **(sich)** vr insep intersect, cross; (zusammenfallen) overlap

überschreiten† vt insep cross; (fig) exceed

Überschrift f heading; (Zeitungs-) headline

Über|schuss m surplus. **ü~schüssig** adj surplus

überschwemm|en vt insep flood; (fig) inundate. **Ü~ung** f -,-en flood

Übersee in/nach Ü~ overseas; **aus/von Ü~** from overseas. **Ü~dampfer** m ocean liner. **ü~isch** adj overseas

übersehen† vt insep look out over; (abschätzen) assess; (nicht sehen) overlook, miss; (ignorieren) ignore

übersenden† vt insep send

übersetzen¹ vi sep (haben/sein) cross [over]

übersetz|en² vt insep translate. **Ü~er(in)** m -s,- (f -,-nen) translator. **Ü~ung** f -,-en translation

Übersicht f overall view; (Abriss) summary; (Tabelle) table. **ü~lich** adj clear

Übersiedlung f move

überspielen vt insep (fig) cover up; **auf Band ü~** tape

überstehen† vt insep come through; get over (Krankheit); (überleben) survive

übersteigen† vt insep climb [over]; (fig) exceed

überstimmen vt insep outvote

Überstunden fpl overtime sg; **Ü~ machen** work overtime

überstürz|en vt insep rush; **sich ü~en** (Ereignisse:) happen fast. **ü~t** adj hasty

übertrag|bar adj transferable; (Med) infectious. **ü~en**† vt insep transfer; (übergeben) assign (dat to); (Techn, Med) transmit; (Radio, TV) broadcast; (übersetzen) translate;

(anwenden) apply (**auf** + acc to) • adj transferred, figurative. **Ü~ung** f **-,-en** transfer; transmission; broadcast; translation, application

übertreffen† vt insep surpass; (übersteigen) exceed; **sich selbst ü~** excel oneself

übertreib|en† vt insep exaggerate; (zu weit treiben) overdo. **Ü~ung** f **-,-en** exaggeration

übertreten[1]† vi sep (sein) step over the line; (Pol) go over/(Relig) convert (**zu** to)

übertret|en[2]† vt insep infringe; break (Gesetz). **Ü~ung** f **-,-en** infringement; breach

übertrieben adj exaggerated

übervölkert adj overpopulated

überwachen vt insep supervise; (kontrollieren) monitor; (bespitzeln) keep under surveillance

überwältigen vt insep overpower; (fig) overwhelm

überweis|en† vt insep transfer; refer (Patienten). **Ü~ung** f transfer; (ärztliche) referral

überwiegen† v insep • vi (haben) predominate, • vt outweigh

überwind|en† vt insep overcome; **sich ü~en** force oneself. **Ü~ung** f effort

Über|zahl f majority. **ü~zählig** adj spare

überzeug|en vt insep convince; **sich [selbst] ü~en** satisfy oneself. **ü~end** adj convincing. **Ü~ung** f **-,-en** conviction

überziehen[1]† vt sep put on

überziehen[2]† vt insep cover; overdraw (Konto)

Überzug m cover; (Schicht) coating

üblich adj usual; (gebräuchlich) customary

U-Boot nt submarine

übrig adj remaining; (andere) other; **alles Ü~e** [all] the rest; **im Ü~en** besides; (ansonsten) apart from that; **ü~ sein** od **bleiben** be left [over]; **etw ü~ lassen** leave sth [over]; **uns blieb nichts anderes ü~** we had no choice

Übung f **-,-en** exercise; (Üben) practice; **außer** od **aus der Ü~** out of practice

Ufer nt **-s,-** shore; (Fluss-) bank

Uhr f **-,-en** clock; (Armband-) watch; (Zähler) meter; **um ein U~** at one o'clock; **wie viel U~ ist es?** what's the time? **U~macher** m **-s,-** watch and clockmaker. **U~werk** nt clock/watch mechanism. **U~zeiger** m [clock-/watch-]hand. **U~zeit** f time

Uhu m **-s,-s** eagle owl

UKW abbr (Ultrakurzwelle) VHF

ulkig adj funny; (seltsam) odd

Ulme f **-,-n** elm

Ultimatum nt **-s,-ten** ultimatum

Ultra|kurzwelle f very high frequency. **U~leichtflugzeug** nt microlight [aircraft]

Ultraschall m ultrasound

ultraviolett adj ultraviolet

um prep (+ acc) [a]round; (Uhrzeit) at; (bitten) for; (streiten) over; (sich sorgen) about; (betrügen) out of; (bei Angabe einer Differenz) by; **um [... herum]** around, [round] about; **Tag um Tag** day after day; **um seinetwillen** for his sake • adv (ungefähr) around, about; **um sein** ! be over; (Zeit) be up • conj **um zu** to; (Absicht) [in order] to; **zu müde, um zu ...** too tired to ...

umarm|en vt insep embrace, hug. **U~ung** f **-,-en** embrace, hug

Umbau m rebuilding; conversion (**zu** into). **u~en** vt sep rebuild; convert (**zu** into)

Umbildung f reorganization; (Pol) reshuffle

umbinden† vt sep put on

umblättern v sep • vt turn [over] • vi (haben) turn the page

umbringen† vt sep kill; **sich u~** kill oneself

umbuchen v sep • vt change; (Comm) transfer • vi (haben) change one's booking

umdrehen v sep •vt turn round/ (wenden) over; turn (Schlüssel); (umkrempeln) turn inside out; **sich u~** turn round; (im Liegen) turn over •vi (haben/sein) turn back

Umdrehung f turn; (Motor-) revolution

umeinander adv around each other; **sich u~ sorgen** worry about each other

umfahren[1]† vt sep run over

umfahren[2]† vt insep go round; bypass (Ort)

umfallen† vi sep (sein) fall over; (Person:) fall down

Umfang m girth; (Geometry) circumference; (Größe) size

umfangreich adj extensive; (dick) big

umfassen vt insep consist of, comprise; (umgeben) surround. **u~d** adj comprehensive

Umfrage f survey, poll

umfüllen vt sep transfer

umfunktionieren vt sep convert

Umgang m [social] contact; (Umgehen) dealing (**mit** with)

Umgangssprache f colloquial language

umgeb|en† vt/i insep (haben) surround •adj **u~en von** surrounded by. **U~ung** f **-,-en** surroundings pl

umgehen† vt insep avoid; (nicht beachten) evade; (Straße:) bypass

umgehend adj immediate

Umgehungsstraße f bypass

umgekehrt adj inverse; (Reihenfolge) reverse; **es war u~** it was the other way round

umgraben† vt sep dig [over]

Umhang m cloak

umhauen† vt sep knock down; (fällen) chop down

umhören (sich) vr sep ask around

Umkehr f **-** turning back. **u~en** v sep •vi (sein) turn back •vt turn round; turn inside out (Tasche); (fig) reverse

umkippen v sep •vt tip over; (versehentlich) knock over •vi (sein) fall over; (Boot:) capsize

Umkleide|kabine f changing-cubicle. **u~n (sich)** vr sep change. **U~raum** m changing-room

umknicken v sep •vt bend; (falten) fold •vi (sein) bend; (mit dem Fuß) go over on one's ankle

umkommen† vi sep (sein) perish

Umkreis m surroundings pl; **im U~ von** within a radius of

umkreisen vt insep circle; (Astronomy) revolve around; (Satellit:) orbit

umkrempeln vt sep turn up; (von innen nach außen) turn inside out; (ändern) change radically

Umlauf m circulation; (Astronomy) revolution. **U~bahn** f orbit

Umlaut m umlaut

umlegen vt sep lay or put down; flatten (Getreide); turn down (Kragen); put on (Schal); throw (Hebel); (verlegen) transfer; (!: töten) kill

umleit|en vt sep divert. **U~ung** f diversion

umliegend adj surrounding

umpflanzen vt sep transplant

umranden vt insep edge

umräumen vt sep rearrange

umrechn|en vt sep convert. **U~ung** f conversion

umreißen† vt insep outline

Umriss m outline

umrühren vt/i sep (haben) stir

ums pron = **um das**

Umsatz m (Comm) turnover

umschalten vt/i sep (haben) switch over; **auf Rot u~** (Ampel:) change to red

Umschau f **U~ halten nach** look out for

Umschlag m cover; (Schutz-) jacket; (Brief-) envelope; (Med) compress; (Hosen-) turn-up. **u~en**† v sep •vt turn up; turn over (Seite); (fällen)

chop down •vi (sein) topple over; (Wetter:) change; (Wind:) veer

umschließen† vt insep enclose

umschreib|en vt insep define; (anders ausdrücken) paraphrase

umschulen vt sep retrain; (Sch) transfer to another school

Umschwung m (fig) change; (Pol) U-turn

umsehen† **(sich)** vr sep look round; (zurück) look back; **sich u~ nach** look for

umsein* vi sep (sein) **um sein**, s. **um**

umseitig adj & adv overleaf

umsetzen vt sep move; (umpflanzen) transplant; (Comm) sell

umsied|eln v sep •vt resettle •vi (sein) move. **U~lung** f resettlement

umso conj **~ besser/mehr** all the better/more; **je mehr, ~ besser** the more the better

umsonst adv in vain; (grundlos) without reason; (gratis) free

Umstand m circumstance; (Tatsache) fact; (Aufwand) fuss; (Mühe) trouble; **unter U~en** possibly; **jdm U~e machen** put s.o. to trouble; **in andern U~en** pregnant

umständlich adj laborious; (kompliziert) involved

Umstands|kleid nt maternity dress. **U~wort** nt (pl **-wörter**) adverb

Umstehende pl bystanders

umsteigen† vi sep (sein) change

umstellen[1] vt insep surround

umstell|en[2] vt sep rearrange; transpose (Wörter); (anders einstellen) reset; (Techn) convert; (ändern) change; **sich u~en** adjust. **U~ung** f rearrangement; transposition; resetting; conversion; change; adjustment

umstritten adj controversial; (ungeklärt) disputed

umstülpen vt sep turn upside down; (von innen nach außen) turn inside out

Um|sturz m coup. **u~stürzen** v sep •vt overturn; (Pol) overthrow •vi (sein) fall over

umtaufen vt sep rename

Umtausch m exchange. **u~en** vt sep change; exchange (**gegen** for)

umwechseln vt sep change

Umweg m detour; **auf U~en** (fig) in a roundabout way

Umwelt f environment. **u~freundlich** adj environmentally friendly. **U~schutz** m protection of the environment

umwerfen† vt sep knock over; (fig) upset (Plan)

umziehen† v sep •vi (sein) move •vt change; **sich u~** change

umzingeln vt insep surround

Umzug m move; (Prozession) procession

unabänderlich adj irrevocable; (Tatsache) unalterable

unabhängig adj independent; **u~ davon, ob** irrespective of whether. **U~keit** f - independence

unablässig adj incessant

unabsehbar adj incalculable

unabsichtlich adj unintentional

unachtsam adj careless

unangebracht adj inappropriate

unangenehm adj unpleasant; (peinlich) embarrassing

Unannehmlichkeiten fpl trouble sg

unansehnlich adj shabby

unanständig adj indecent

unappetitlich adj unappetizing

Unart f -,-en bad habit. **u~ig** adj naughty

unauffällig adj inconspicuous; unobtrusive

unaufgefordert adv without being asked

unauf|haltsam adj inexorable. **u~hörlich** adj incessant

unaufmerksam adj inattentive

unaufrichtig adj insincere
unausbleiblich adj inevitable
unausstehlich adj insufferable
unbarmherzig adj merciless
unbeabsichtigt adj unintentional
unbedenklich adj harmless • adv without hesitation
unbedeutend adj insignificant; (geringfügig) slight
unbedingt adj absolute; **nicht u~** not necessarily
unbefriedig|end adj unsatisfactory. **u~t** adj dissatisfied
unbefugt adj unauthorized • adv without authorization
unbegreiflich adj incomprehensible
unbegrenzt adj unlimited • adv indefinitely
unbegründet adj unfounded
Unbehagen nt unease; (körperlich) discomfort
unbekannt adj unknown; (nicht vertraut) unfamiliar. **U~e(r)** m/f stranger
unbekümmert adj unconcerned; (unbeschwert) carefree
unbeliebt adj unpopular. **U~heit** f unpopularity
unbemannt adj unmanned
unbemerkt adj & adv unnoticed
unbenutzt adj unused
unbequem adj uncomfortable; (lästig) awkward
unberechenbar adj unpredictable
unberechtigt adj unjustified; (unbefugt) unauthorized
unberührt adj untouched; (fig) virgin; (Landschaft) unspoilt
unbescheiden adj presumptuous
unbeschrankt adj unguarded
unbeschränkt adj unlimited • adv without limit
unbeschwert adj carefree
unbesiegt adj undefeated
unbespielt adj blank
unbeständig adj inconsistent; (Wetter) unsettled
unbestechlich adj incorruptible
unbestimmt adj indefinite: (Alter) indeterminate; (ungewiss) uncertain; (unklar) vague
unbestritten adj undisputed • adv indisputably
unbeteiligt adj indifferent; **u~ an** (+ dat) not involved in
unbetont adj unstressed
unbewacht adj unguarded
unbewaffnet adj unarmed
unbeweglich adj & adv motionless, still
unbewohnt adj uninhabited
unbewusst adj unconscious
unbezahlbar adj priceless
unbrauchbar adj useless
und conj and; **und so weiter** and so on; **nach und nach** bit by bit
Undank m ingratitude. **u~bar** adj ungrateful; (nicht lohnend) thankless. **U~barkeit** f ingratitude
undeutlich adj indistinct; vague
undicht adj leaking; **u~e Stelle** leak
Unding nt absurdity
undiplomatisch adj undiplomatic
unduldsam adj intolerant
undurch|dringlich adj impenetrable; (Miene) inscrutable. **u~führbar** adj impracticable
undurch|lässig adj impermeable. **u~sichtig** adj opaque; (fig) doubtful
uneben adj uneven. **U~heit** f **-,-en** unevenness; (Buckel) bump
unecht adj false; **u~er Schmuck** imitation jewellery
unehelich adj illegitimate
uneinig adj (fig) divided; [**sich** (dat)] **u~ sein** disagree
uneins adj **~ sein** be at odds
unempfindlich adj insensitive

u

(**gegen** to); (widerstandsfähig) tough; (Med) immune

unendlich adj infinite; (endlos) endless. **U~keit** f - infinity

unentbehrlich adj indispensable

unentgeltlich adj free, (Arbeit) unpaid • adv free of charge

unentschieden adj undecided; (Sport) drawn; **u~ spielen** draw. **U~** nt **-s,-** draw

unentschlossen adj indecisive; (unentschieden) undecided

unentwegt adj persistent; (unaufhörlich) incessant

unerfahren adj inexperienced. **U~heit** f - inexperience

unerfreulich adj unpleasant

unerhört adj enormous; (empörend) outrageous

unerklärlich adj inexplicable

unerlässlich adj essential

unerlaubt adj unauthorized • adv without permission

unerschwinglich adj prohibitive

unersetzlich adj irreplaceable; (Verlust) irreparable

unerträglich adj unbearable

unerwartet adj unexpected

unerwünscht adj unwanted; (Besuch) unwelcome

unfähig adj incompetent; **u~, etw zu tun** incapable of doing sth; (nicht in der Lage) unable to do sth. **U~keit** f incompetence; inability (**zu** to)

unfair adj unfair

Unfall m accident. **U~flucht** f failure to stop after an accident. **U~station** f casualty department

unfassbar adj incomprehensible

Unfehlbarkeit f - infallibility

unfolgsam adj disobedient

unförmig adj shapeless

unfreiwillig adj involuntary; (unbeabsichtigt) unintentional

unfreundlich adj unfriendly; (unangenehm) unpleasant. **U~keit** f unfriendliness; unpleasantness

Unfriede[n] m discord

unfruchtbar adj infertile; (fig) unproductive. **U~keit** f infertility

Unfug m **-s** mischief; (Unsinn) nonsense

Ungar|(in) m **-n,-n** (f **-,-nen**) Hungarian. **u~isch** adj Hungarian. **U~n** nt **-s** Hungary

ungeachtet prep (+ gen) in spite of; **dessen u~** notwithstanding [this]. **ungebraucht** adj unused. **ungedeckt** adj uncovered; (Sport) unmarked; (Tisch) unlaid

Ungeduld f impatience. **u~ig** adj impatient

ungeeignet adj unsuitable

ungefähr adj approximate, rough

ungefährlich adj harmless

ungeheuer adj enormous. **U~** nt **-s,-** monster

ungehorsam adj disobedient. **U~** m disobedience

ungeklärt adj unsolved; (Frage) unsettled; (Ursache) unknown

ungelegen adj inconvenient

ungelernt adj unskilled

ungemütlich adj uncomfortable; (unangenehm) unpleasant

ungenau adj inaccurate; vague. **U~igkeit** f **-,-en** inaccuracy

ungeniert /ˈʊnʒeniːɐ̯t/ adj uninhibited • adv openly

ungenießbar adj inedible; (Getränk) undrinkable. **ungenügend** adj inadequate; (Sch) unsatisfactory. **ungepflegt** adj neglected; (Person) unkempt. **ungerade** adj (Zahl) odd

ungerecht adj unjust. **U~igkeit** f **-,-en** injustice

ungern adv reluctantly

ungesalzen adj unsalted

Ungeschick|lichkeit f clumsiness. **u~t** adj clumsy

ungeschminkt adj without make-up; (Wahrheit) unvarnished.

ungesetzlich adj illegal. **ungestört** adj undisturbed. **ungesund** adj unhealthy. **ungesüßt** adj unsweetened. **ungetrübt** adj perfect

Ungetüm nt **-s,-e** monster

ungewiss adj uncertain; **im Ungewissen sein/lassen** be/leave in the dark. **U~heit** f uncertainty

ungewöhnlich adj unusual. **ungewohnt** adj unaccustomed; (nicht vertraut) unfamiliar

Ungeziefer nt **-s** vermin

ungezogen adj naughty

ungezwungen adj informal; (natürlich) natural

ungläubig adj incredulous

unglaublich adj incredible, unbelievable

ungleich adj unequal; (verschieden) different. **U~heit** f - inequality. **u~mäßig** adj uneven

Unglück nt **-s,-e** misfortune; (Pech) bad luck; (Missgeschick) mishap; (Unfall) accident. **u~lich** adj unhappy; (ungünstig) unfortunate. **u~licherweise** adv unfortunately

ungültig adj invalid; (Jur) void

ungünstig adj unfavourable; (unpassend) inconvenient

Unheil nt **-s** disaster; **U~ anrichten** cause havoc

unheilbar adj incurable

unheimlich adj eerie; (gruselig) creepy; (!: groß) terrific • adv eerily; (!: sehr) terribly

unhöflich adj rude. **U~keit** f rudeness

unhygienisch adj unhygienic

Uni f **-,-s** ! university

uni /y'ni:/ inv adj plain

Uniform f **-,-en** uniform

uninteressant adj uninteresting

Union f **-,-en** union

universell adj universal

Universität f **-,-en** university

Universum nt **-s** universe

unkenntlich adj unrecognizable

unklar adj unclear; (ungewiss) uncertain; (vage) vague; **im U~en (u~en) sein** be in the dark

unkompliziert adj uncomplicated

Unkosten pl expenses

Unkraut nt weed; (coll) weeds pl; **U~ jäten** weed. **U~vertilgungsmittel** nt weed-killer

unlängst adv recently

unlauter adj dishonest; (unfair) unfair

unleserlich adj illegible

unleugbar adj undeniable

unlogisch adj illogical

Unmenge f enormous amount/ (Anzahl) number

Unmensch m ! brute. **u~lich** adj inhuman

unmerklich adj imperceptible

unmittelbar adj immediate; (direkt) direct

unmöbliert adj unfurnished

unmodern adj old-fashioned

unmöglich adj impossible. **U~keit** f - impossibility

Unmoral f immorality. **u~isch** adj immoral

unmündig adj under-age

Unmut m displeasure

unnatürlich adj unnatural

unnormal adj abnormal

unnötig adj unnecessary

unord|entlich adj untidy; (nachlässig) sloppy. **U~nung** f disorder; (Durcheinander) muddle

unorthodox adj unorthodox • adv in an unorthodox manner

unparteiisch adj impartial

unpassend adj inappropriate; (Moment) inopportune

unpersönlich adj impersonal

unpraktisch adj impractical

unpünktlich adj unpunctual • adv late

unrealistisch adj unrealistic

unrecht adj wrong •n **jdm u~ tun** do s.o. an injustice. **U~** nt wrong; **zu U~** wrongly; **U~ haben** be wrong; **jdm U~ geben** disagree with s.o. **u~mäßig** adj unlawful

unregelmäßig adj irregular

unreif adj unripe; (fig) immature

unrein adj impure; (Luft) polluted; (Haut) bad; **ins U~e schreiben** make a rough draft of

unrentabel adj unprofitable

Unruh|e f **-,-n** restlessness; (Erregung) agitation; (Besorgnis) anxiety; **U~en** (Pol) unrest sg. **u~ig** adj restless; (laut) noisy; (besorgt) anxious

uns pron (acc/dat of **wir**) us; (reflexive) ourselves; (einander) each other

unsauber adj dirty; (nachlässig) sloppy

unschädlich adj harmless

unscharf adj blurred

unschätzbar adj inestimable

unscheinbar adj inconspicuous

unschlagbar adj unbeatable

unschlüssig adj undecided

Unschuld f **-** innocence; (Jungfräulichkeit) virginity. **u~ig** adj innocent

unselbstständig, **unselbständig** adj dependent •adv **u~ denken** not think for oneself

unser poss pron our. **u~e(r,s)** poss pron ours. **u~erseits** adv for our part. **u~twegen** adv for our sake; (wegen uns) because of us, on our account

unsicher adj unsafe; (ungewiss) uncertain; (nicht zuverlässig) unreliable; (Schritte, Hand) unsteady; (Person) insecure •adv unsteadily. **U~heit** f uncertainty; unreliability; insecurity

unsichtbar adj invisible

Unsinn m nonsense. **u~ig** adj nonsensical, absurd

Unsitt|e f bad habit. **u~lich** adj indecent

unsportlich adj not sporty; (unfair) unsporting

uns|re(r,s) poss pron = **unsere(r,s)**. **u~rige** poss pron **der/die/das u~rige** ours

unsterblich adj immortal. **U~keit** f immortality

Unsumme f vast sum

unsympathisch adj unpleasant; **er ist mir u~** I don't like him

untätig adj idle

untauglich adj unsuitable; (Mil) unfit

unten adv at the bottom; (auf der Unterseite) underneath; (eine Treppe tiefer) downstairs; (im Text) below; **hier/da u~** down here/there; **nach u~** down[wards]; (die Treppe hinunter) downstairs; **siehe u~** see below

unter prep (+ dat/acc) under; (niedriger als) below; (inmitten, zwischen) among; **u~ anderem** among other things; **u~ der Woche** during the week; **u~ sich** by themselves

Unter|arm m forearm. **U~bewusstsein** nt subconscious

unterbieten† vt insep undercut; beat (Rekord)

unterbinden† vt insep stop

unterbrech|en† vt insep interrupt; break (Reise). **U~ung** f **-,-en** interruption, break

unterbringen† vt sep put; (beherbergen) put up

unterdessen adv in the meantime

Unterdrückung f **-** suppression; oppression

untere(r,s) adj lower

untereinander adv one below the other; (miteinander) among ourselves/yourselves/themselves

unterernähr|t adj undernourished. **U~ung** f malnutrition

Unterführung f underpass; (Fußgänger-) subway

Untergang m (der Sonne) setting; (Naut) sinking; (Zugrundegehen) disappearance; (der Welt) end

Untergebene(r) m/f subordinate

untergehen† vi sep (sein) (Astronomy) set; (versinken) go under; (Schiff:) go down, sink; (zugrunde gehen) disappear; (Welt:) come to an end

Untergeschoss nt basement

Untergrund m foundation; (Hintergrund) background. **U~bahn** f underground [railway]

unterhaken vt sep **jdn u~** take s.o.'s arm; **untergehakt** arm in arm

unterhalb adv & prep (+ gen) below

Unterhalt m maintenance

unterhalt|en† vt insep maintain; (ernähren) support; (betreiben) run; (erheitern) entertain; **sich u~en** talk; (sich vergnügen) enjoy oneself. **U~ung** f **-,-en** maintenance; (Gespräch) conversation; (Zeitvertreib) entertainment

Unter|haus nt (Pol) lower house; (in UK) House of Commons. **U~hemd** nt vest. **U~hose** f underpants pl. **u~irdisch** adj & adv underground

Unterkiefer m lower jaw

unterkommen† vi sep (sein) find accommodation; (eine Stellung finden) get a job

Unterkunft f **-,-künfte** accommodation

Unterlage f pad; **U~n** papers

Unterlass m **ohne U~** incessantly

Unterlassung f **-,-en** omission

unterlegen adj inferior; (Sport) losing; **zahlenmäßig u~** outnumbered (dat by). **U~e(r)** m/f loser

Unterleib m abdomen

unterliegen† vi insep (sein) lose (dat to); (unterworfen sein) be subject (dat to)

Unterlippe f lower lip

Untermiete f **zur U~ wohnen** be a lodger. **U~r(in)** m(f) lodger

unternehm|en† vt insep undertake; take (Schritte); **etw/nichts u~en** do sth/nothing. **U~en** nt **-s,-** undertaking, enterprise (Betrieb) concern. **U~er** m **-s,-** employer; (Bau-) contractor; (Industrieller) industrialist. **u~ungslustig** adj enterprising

Unteroffizier m non-commissioned officer

unterordnen vt sep subordinate

Unterredung f **-,-en** talk

Unterricht m **-[e]s** teaching; (Privat-) tuition; (U~sstunden) lessons pl

unterrichten vt/i insep (haben) teach; (informieren) inform; **sich u~** inform oneself

Unterrock m slip

untersagen vt insep forbid

Untersatz m mat; (mit Füßen) stand; (Gläser-) coaster

unterscheid|en† vt/i insep (haben) distinguish; (auseinander halten) tell apart; **sich u~en** differ. **U~ung** f **-,-en** distinction

Unterschied m **-[e]s,-e** difference; (Unterscheidung) distinction; **im U~ zu ihm** unlike him. **u~lich** adj different; (wechselnd) varying

unterschlag|en† vt insep embezzle; (verheimlichen) suppress. **U~ung** f **-,-en** embezzlement; suppression

Unterschlupf m **-[e]s** shelter; (Versteck) hiding-place

unterschreiben† vt/i insep (haben) sign

Unter|schrift f signature; (Bild-) caption. **U~seeboot** nt submarine

Unterstand m shelter

unterste(r,s) adj lowest, bottom

unterstehen† v insep ●vi (haben) be answerable (dat to); (unterliegen) be subject (dat to)

unterstellen[1] vt sep put

underneath; (abstellen) store; **sich u~** shelter

unterstellen[2] vt insep place under the control (dat of); (annehmen) assume; (fälschlich zuschreiben) impute (dat to)

unterstreichen† vt insep underline

unterstütz|en vt insep support; (helfen) aid. **U~ung** f **-,-en** support; (finanziell) aid; (regelmäßiger Betrag) allowance; (Arbeitslosen-) benefit

untersuch|en vt insep examine; (Jur) investigate; (prüfen) test; (überprüfen) check; (durchsuchen) search. **U~ung** f **-,-en** examination; investigation; test; check; search. **U~ungshaft** f detention on remand

Untertan m **-s** & **-en,-en** subject

Untertasse f saucer

Unterteil nt bottom (part)

Untertitel m subtitle

untervermieten vt/i insep (haben) sublet

Unterwäsche f underwear

unterwegs adv on the way; (außer Haus) out; (verreist) away

Unterwelt f underworld

unterzeichnen vt insep sign

unterziehen† vt insep **etw einer Untersuchung/Überprüfung u~** examine/ check sth; **sich einer Operation/Prüfung u~** have an operation/take a test

Untier nt monster

untragbar adj intolerable

untrennbar adj inseparable

untreu adj disloyal; (in der Ehe) unfaithful. **U~e** f disloyalty; infidelity

untröstlich adj inconsolable

unübersehbar adj obvious; (groß) immense

ununterbrochen adj incessant

unveränderlich adj invariable; (gleichbleibend) unchanging

unverändert adj unchanged

unverantwortlich adj irresponsible

unverbesserlich adj incorrigible

unverbindlich adj non-committal; (Comm) not binding •adv without obligation

unverdaulich adj indigestible

unver|gesslich adj unforgettable. **u~gleichlich** adj incomparable. **u~heiratet** adj unmarried. **u~käuflich** adj not for sale; (Muster) free

unverkennbar adj unmistakable

unverletzt adj unhurt

unvermeidlich adj inevitable

unver|mindert adj & adv undiminished. **u~mutet** adj unexpected

Unver|nunft f folly. **u~nünftig** adj foolish

unverschämt adj insolent; ([!]: ungeheuer) outrageous. **U~heit** f **-,-en** insolence

unver|sehens adv suddenly. **u~sehrt** adj unhurt; (unbeschädigt) intact

unverständlich adj incomprehensible; (undeutlich) indistinct

unverträglich adj incompatible; (Person) quarrelsome; (unbekömmlich) indigestible

unver|wundbar adj invulnerable. **u~wüstlich** adj indestructible; (Person, Humor) irrepressible; (Gesundheit) robust. **u~zeihlich** adj unforgivable

unverzüglich adj immediate

unvollendet adj unfinished

unvollkommen adj imperfect; (unvollständig) incomplete

unvollständig adj incomplete

unvor|bereitet adj unprepared. **u~hergesehen** adj unforeseen

unvorsichtig adj careless

unvorstellbar adj unimaginable
unvorteilhaft adj unfavourable; (nicht hübsch) unattractive
unwahr adj untrue. **U~heit** f -,-en untruth. **u~scheinlich** adj unlikely; (unglaublich) improbable; ([!]: groß) incredible
unweit adv & prep (+ gen) not far
unwesentlich adj unimportant
Unwetter nt -s,- storm
unwichtig adj unimportant
unwider|legbar adj irrefutable. **u~stehlich** adj irresistible
Unwill|e m displeasure. **u~ig** adj angry; (widerwillig) reluctant
unwirklich adj unreal
unwirksam adj ineffective
unwirtschaftlich adj uneconomic
unwissen|d adj ignorant. **U~heit** f - ignorance
unwohl adj unwell; (unbehaglich) uneasy
unwürdig adj unworthy (gen of)
Unzahl f vast number. **unzählig** adj innumerable, countless
unzerbrechlich adj unbreakable
unzerstörbar adj indestructible
unzertrennlich adj inseparable
Unzucht f sexual offence; **gewerbsmäßige U~** prostitution
unzüchtig adj indecent; (Schriften) obscene
unzufrieden adj dissatisfied; (innerlich) discontented. **U~heit** f dissatisfaction
unzulässig adj inadmissible
unzurechnungsfähig adj insane. **U~keit** f insanity
unzusammenhängend adj incoherent
unzutreffend adj inapplicable; (falsch) incorrect
unzuverlässig adj unreliable
unzweifelhaft adj undoubted
üppig adj luxuriant; (überreichlich) lavish
uralt adj ancient
Uran nt -s uranium
Uraufführung f first performance
Urenkel m great-grandson; (pl) great-grandchildren
Urgroß|mutter f great-grandmother. **U~vater** m great-grandfather
Urheber m -s,- originator; (Verfasser) author. **U~recht** nt copyright
Urin m -s,-e urine
Urkunde f -,-n certificate; (Dokument) document
Urlaub m -s holiday; (Mil, Admin) leave; **auf U~** on holiday/leave; **U~ haben** be on holiday/leave. **U~er(in)** m -s,- (f -,-nen) holiday-maker. **U~sort** m holiday resort
Urne f -,-n urn; (Wahl-) ballot-box
Ursache f cause; (Grund) reason; **keine U~!** don't mention it!
Ursprung m origin
ursprünglich adj original; (anfänglich) initial; (natürlich) natural
Urteil nt -s,-e judgement; (Meinung) opinion; (U~sspruch) verdict; (Strafe) sentence. **u~en** vi (haben) judge
Urwald m primeval forest; (tropischer) jungle
Urzeit f primeval times pl
USA pl USA sg
usw. abbr (**und so weiter**) etc.
utopisch adj Utopian

Vv

Vakuum /'va:kuʊm/ nt **-s** vacuum. **v~verpackt** adj vacuum-packed

Vanille /va'nɪljə/ f - vanilla

variieren vt/i (haben) vary

Vase /'va:zə/ f **-,-n** vase

Vater m **-s,¨** father. **V~land** nt fatherland

väterlich adj paternal; (fürsorglich) fatherly. **v~erseits** adv on one's/the father's side

Vater|schaft f - fatherhood; (Jur) paternity. **V~unser** nt **-s,-** Lord's Prayer

v. Chr. abbr (**vor Christus**) BC

Vegetar|ier(in) /vege'ta:ri̯ɐ, -i̯ərɪn/ m(f) **-s,-** (f **-,-nen**) vegetarian. **v~isch** adj vegetarian

Veilchen nt **-s,-n** violet

Vene /'ve:nə/ f **-,-n** vein

Venedig /ve'ne:dɪç/ nt **-s** Venice

Ventil /vɛn'ti:l/ nt **-s,-e** valve. **V~ator** m **-s,-en** fan

verabred|en vt arrange; **sich [mit jdm] v~en** arrange to meet [s.o.]. **V~ung** f **-,-en** arrangement; (Treffen) appointment

verabschieden vt say goodbye to; (aus dem Dienst) retire; pass (Gesetz); **sich v~** say goodbye

verachten vt despise

Verachtung f - contempt

verallgemeinern vt/i (haben) generalize

veränder|lich adj changeable; (Math) variable. **v~n** vt change; **sich v~n** change; (beruflich) change one's job. **V~ung** f change

verängstigt adj frightened, scared

verankern vt anchor

veranlag|t adj **künstlerisch/musikalisch v~t sein** have an artistic/a musical bent; **praktisch v~t** practically minded. **V~ung** f **-,-en** disposition; (Neigung) tendency; (künstlerisch) bent

veranlassen vt (reg) arrange for; (einleiten) institute; **jdn v~** prompt s.o. (**zu** to)

veranschlagen vt (reg) estimate

veranstalt|en vt organize; hold, give (Party); make (Lärm). **V~er** m **-s,-** organizer. **V~ung** f **-,-en** event

verantwort|lich adj responsible; **v~lich machen** hold responsible. **V~ung** f - responsibility. **v~ungsbewusst** adj responsible. **v~ungslos** adj irresponsible. **v~ungsvoll** adj responsible

verarbeiten vt use; (Techn) process; (verdauen & fig) digest

verärgern vt annoy

verausgaben (sich) vr spend all one's money (or) strength

veräußern vt sell

Verb /vɛrp/ nt **-s,-en** verb

Verband m **-[e]s,¨e** association; (Mil) unit; (Med) bandage; (Wund-) dressing. **V~szeug** nt first-aid kit

verbann|en vt exile; (fig) banish. **V~ung** f - exile

verbergen† vt hide; **sich v~** hide

verbesser|n vt improve; (berichtigen) correct. **V~ung** f **-,-en** improvement; correction

verbeug|en (sich) vr bow. **V~ung** f bow

verbeulen vt dent

verbiegen† vt bend

verbieten† vt forbid; (Admin) prohibit, ban

verbillig|en vt reduce [in price]. **v~t** adj reduced

verbinden† vt connect (**mit** to);

(zusammenfügen) join; (verknüpfen) combine; (in Verbindung bringen) associate; (Med) bandage; dress (Wunde); **jdm verbunden sein** (fig) be obliged to s.o.

verbindlich adj friendly; (bindend) binding

Verbindung f connection; (Verknüpfung) combination; (Kontakt) contact; (Vereinigung) association; **chemiche V~** chemical compound; **in V~ stehen/sich in V~ setzen** be/get in touch

verbissen adj grim

verbitter|n vt make bitter. **v~t** adj bitter. **V~ung** f - bitterness

verblassen vi (sein) fade

Verbleib m **-s** whereabouts pl

verbleit adj (Benzin) leaded

verblüff|en vt amaze, astound. **V~ung** f - amazement

verblühen vi (sein) wither, fade

verbluten vi (sein) bleed to death

verborgen vt lend

Verbot nt **-[e]s,-e** ban. **v~en** adj forbidden; (Admin) prohibited

Verbrauch m **-[e]s** consumption. **v~en** vt use; consume (Lebensmittel); (erschöpfen) use up. **V~er** m **-s,-** consumer

Verbrechen† nt **-s,-** crime

Verbrecher m **-s,-** criminal

verbreit|en vt spread. **v~et** adj widespread. **V~ung** f - spread; (Verbreiten) spreading

verbrenn|en† vt/i (sein) burn; cremate (Leiche). **V~ung** f **-,-en** burning; cremation; (Wunde) burn

verbringen† vt spend

V

verbrühen vt scald

verbuchen vt enter

verbünd|en (sich) vr form an alliance. **V~ete(r)** m/f ally

verbürgen vt guarantee; **sich v~ für** vouch for

Verdacht m **-[e]s** suspicion; **in** or **im V~ haben** suspect

verdächtig adj suspicious. **v~en** vt suspect (gen of). **V~te(r)** m/f suspect

verdamm|en vt condemn; (Relig) damn. **v~t** adj & adv ☒ damned; **v~t!** damn!

verdampfen vt/i (sein) evaporate

verdanken vt owe (dat to)

verdau|en vt digest. **v~lich** adj digestible. **V~ung** f - digestion

Verdeck nt **-[e]s,-e** hood; (Oberdeck) top deck

verderb|en† vi (sein) spoil; (Lebensmittel:) go bad • vt spoil; **ich habe mir den Magen verdorben** I have an upset stomach. **V~en** nt **-s** ruin. **v~lich** adj perishable; (schädlich) pernicious

verdien|en vt/i (haben) earn; (fig) deserve. **V~er** m **-s,-** wage-earner

Verdienst[1] m **-[e]s** earnings pl

Verdienst[2] nt **-[e]s,-e** merit

verdient adj well-deserved

verdoppeln vt double

verdorben adj spoilt, ruined; (Magen) upset; (moralisch) corrupt; (verkommen) depraved

verdreh|en vt twist; roll (Augen); (fig) distort. **v~t** adj ! crazy

verdreifachen vt treble, triple

verdrücken vt crumple; (!: essen) polish off; **sich v~** ! slip away

Verdruss m **-es** annoyance

verdünnen vt dilute; **sich v~** taper off

verdunst|en vi (sein) evaporate. **V~ung** f - evaporation

verdursten vi (sein) die of thirst

veredeln vt refine; (Horticulture) graft

verehr|en vt revere; (Relig) worship; (bewundern) admire; (schenken) give. **V~er(in)** m **-s,-** (f **-,-nen**) admirer. **V~ung** f - veneration; worship; admiration

vereidigen vt swear in

Verein m **-s,-e** society; (Sport-) club

vereinbar adj compatible. **v~en** vt

arrange. **V~ung** f -,-en agreement

vereinfachen vt simplify

vereinheitlichen vt standardize

vereinig|en vt unite; merge (Firmen); **wieder v~en** reunite; reunify (Land); **sich v~en** unite; **V~te Staaten [von Amerika]** United States sg [of America]. **V~ung** f -,-en union; (Organisation) organization

vereinzelt adj isolated • adv occasionally

vereist adj frozen; (Straße) icy

vereitert adj septic

verenden vi (sein) die

verengen vt restrict; **sich v~** narrow; (Pupille:) contract

vererb|en vt leave (dat to); (Biology & fig) pass on (dat to). **V~ung** f - heredity

verfahren† vi (sein) proceed; **v~ mit** deal with • vr **sich v~** lose one's way • adj muddled. **V~** nt -s,- procedure; (Techn) process; (Jur) proceedings pl

Verfall m decay; (eines Gebäudes) dilapidation; (körperlich & fig) decline; (Ablauf) expiry. **v~en†** vi (sein) decay; (Person, Sitten:) decline; (ablaufen) expire; **v~en in** (+ acc) lapse into; **v~en auf** (+ acc) hit on (Idee)

verfärben (sich) vr change colour; (Stoff:) discolour

verfass|en vt write; (Jur) draw up; (entwerfen) draft. **V~er** m -s,- author. **V~ung** f (Pol) constitution; (Zustand) state

verfaulen vi (sein) rot, decay

verfechten† vt advocate

verfehlen vt miss

verfeinde|n (sich) vr become enemies; **v~t sein** be enemies

verfeinern vt refine; (verbessern) improve

verfilmen vt film

verfluch|en vt curse. **v~t** adj & adv [!] damned; **v~t!** damn!

verfolg|en vt pursue; (folgen) follow; (bedrängen) pester; (Pol) persecute; **strafrechtlich v~en** prosecute. **V~er** m -s,- pursuer. **V~ung** f - pursuit; persecution

verfrüht adj premature

verfügbar adj available

verfüg|en vt order; (Jur) decree • vi (haben) **v~en über** (+ acc) have at one's disposal. **V~ung** f -,-en order; (Jur) decree; **jdm zur V~ung stehen** be at s.o.'s disposal

verführ|en vt seduce; tempt. **V~ung** f seduction; temptation

vergangen adj past; (letzte) last. **V~heit** f - past; (Gram) past tense

vergänglich adj transitory

vergas|en vt gas. **V~er** m -s,- carburettor

vergeb|en† vt award (**an** + dat to); (weggeben) give away; (verzeihen) forgive. **v~lich** adj futile, vain • adv in vain. **V~ung** f - forgiveness

vergehen† vi (sein) pass; **sich v~** violate (**gegen etw** sth). **V~** nt -s,- offence

vergelt|en† vt repay. **V~ung** f - retaliation; (Rache) revenge

vergessen† vt forget; (liegen lassen) leave behind

vergesslich adj forgetful. **V~keit** f - forgetfulness

vergeuden vt waste, squander

vergewaltig|en vt rape. **V~ung** f -,-en rape

vergießen† vt spill; shed (Tränen, Blut)

vergift|en vt poison. **V~ung** f -,-en poisoning

Vergissmeinnicht nt -[e]s,-[e] forget-me-not

vergittert adj barred

verglasen vt glaze

Vergleich m -[e]s,-e comparison; (Jur) settlement. **v~bar** adj comparable. **v~en†** vt compare (**mit** with/to)

vergnüg|en (sich) vr enjoy oneself. **V~en** nt -s,- pleasure;

(Spaß) fun; **viel V∼en!** have a good time! **v∼t** adj cheerful; (zufrieden) happy. **V∼ungen** fpl entertainments

vergolden vt gild; (plattieren) gold-plate

vergraben† vt bury

vergriffen adj out of print

vergrößer|n vt enlarge; (Linse:) magnify; (vermehren) increase; (erweitern) extend; expand (Geschäft); **sich v∼n** grow bigger; (Firma:) expand; (zunehmen) increase. **V∼ung** f -,-en magnification; increase; expansion; (Phot) enlargement. **V∼ungsglas** nt magnifying glass

vergüt|en vt pay for; **jdm etw v∼en** reimburse s.o. for sth. **V∼ung** f -,-en remuneration; (Erstattung) reimbursement

verhaft|en vt arrest. **V∼ung** f -,-en arrest

verhalten† (sich) vr behave; (handeln) act; (beschaffen sein) be. **V∼** nt -s behaviour, conduct

Verhältnis nt -ses,-se relationship; (Liebes-) affair; (Math) ratio; **V∼se** circumstances; conditions. **v∼mäßig** adv comparatively, relatively

verhand|eln vt discuss; (Jur) try • vi (haben) negotiate. **V∼lung** f (Jur) trial; **V∼lungen** negotiations

Verhängnis nt -ses fate, doom

verhärten vt/i (sein) harden

verhasst adj hated

verhätscheln vt spoil

verhauen† vt [!] beat; make a mess of (Prüfung)

verheilen vi (sein) heal

verheimlichen vt keep secret

verheirat|en (sich) vr get married (**mit** to); **sich wieder v∼en** remarry. **v∼et** adj married

verhelfen† vi (haben) **jdm zu etw v∼** help s.o. get sth

verherrlichen vt glorify

verhexen vt bewitch

verhindern vt prevent; **v∼t sein** be unable to come

Verhör nt -s,-e interrogation; **ins V∼ nehmen** interrogate. **v∼en** vt interrogate; **sich v∼en** mishear

verhungern vi (sein) starve

verhüt|en vt prevent. **V∼ung** f - prevention. **V∼ungsmittel** nt contraceptive

verirren (sich) vr get lost

verjagen vt chase away

verjüngen vt rejuvenate

verkalkt adj [!] senile

verkalkulieren (sich) vr miscalculate

Verkauf m sale; **zum V∼** for sale. **v∼en** vt sell; **zu v∼en** for sale

Verkäufer(in) m(f) seller; (im Geschäft) shop assistant

Verkehr m -s traffic; (Kontakt) contact; (Geschlechts-) intercourse; **aus dem V∼ ziehen** take out of circulation. **v∼en** vi (haben) operate; (Bus, Zug:) run; (Umgang haben) associate, mix (**mit** with); (Gast sein) visit (**bei jdm** s.o.)

Verkehrs|ampel f traffic lights pl. **V∼unfall** m road accident. **V∼verein** m tourist office. **V∼zeichen** nt traffic sign

verkehrt adj wrong; **v∼ herum** adv the wrong way round; (links) inside out

verklagen vt sue (**auf** + acc for)

verkleid|en vt disguise; (Techn) line; **sich v∼en** disguise oneself; (für Kostümfest) dress up. **V∼ung** f -,-en disguise; (Kostüm) fancy dress; (Techn) lining

verkleiner|n vt reduce [in size]. **V∼ung** f - reduction

verknittern vt/i (sein) crumple

verknüpfen vt knot together

verkommen† vi (sein) be neglected; (sittlich) go to the bad; (verfallen) decay; (Haus:) fall into disrepair; (Gegend:) become run-down; (Lebensmittel:) go bad • adj neglected; (sittlich) depraved; (Haus)

V

dilapidated; (Gegend) run-down

verkörpern vt embody, personify

verkraften vt cope with

verkrampft adj (fig) tense

verkriechen† **(sich)** vr hide

verkrümmt adj crooked, bent

verkrüppelt adj crippled; (Glied) deformed

verkühl|en (sich) vr catch a chill. **V~ung** f **-,-en** chill

verkümmern vi (sein) waste/ (Pflanze:) wither away

verkünden vt announce; pronounce (Urteil)

verkürzen vt shorten; (verringern) reduce; (abbrechen) cut short; while away (Zeit)

Verlag m **-[e]s,-e** publishing firm

verlangen vt ask for; (fordern) demand; (berechnen) charge. **V~** nt **-s** desire; (Bitte) request

verlänger|n vt extend; lengthen (Kleid); (zeitlich) prolong; renew (Pass, Vertrag); (Culin) thin down. **V~ung** f **-,-en** extension; renewal. **V~ungsschnur** f extension cable

verlassen† vt leave; (im Stich lassen) desert; **sich v~ auf** (+ acc) rely or depend on •adj deserted. **V~heit** f - desolation

verlässlich adj reliable

Verlauf m course; **im V~** (+ gen) in the course of. **v~en**† vi (sein) run; (ablaufen) go; **gut v~en** go [off] well •vr **sich v~en** lose one's way

verlegen vt move; (verschieben) postpone; (vor-) bring forward; (verlieren) mislay; (versperren) block; (legen) lay (Teppich, Rohre); (veröffentlichen) publish; **sich v~ auf** (+ acc) take up (Beruf); resort to (Bitten) •adj embarrassed. **V~heit** f - embarrassment

Verleger m **-s,-** publisher

verleihen† vt lend; (gegen Gebühr) hire out; (überreichen) award, confer; (fig) give

verlernen vt forget

verletz|en vt injure; (kränken) hurt; (verstoßen gegen) infringe; violate (Grenze). **v~end** adj hurtful, wounding. **V~te(r)** m/f injured person; (bei Unfall) casualty. **V~ung** f **-,-en** (Verstoß) infringement; violation

verleugnen vt deny; disown (Freund)

verleumd|en vt slander; (schriftlich) libel. **v~erisch** adj slanderous; libellous. **V~ung** f **-,-en** slander; (schriftlich) libel

verlieben (sich) vr fall in love (**in** + acc with); **verliebt sein** be in love (**in** + acc with)

verlier|en† vt lose; shed (Laub) •vi (haben) lose (**an etw** dat sth). **V~er** m **-s,-** loser

verlob|en (sich) vr get engaged (**mit** to); **v~t sein** be engaged. **V~te** f fiancée. **V~te(r)** m fiancé. **V~ung** f **-,-en** engagement

verlock|en vt tempt. **V~ung** f **-,-en** temptation

verloren adj lost; **v~ gehen** get lost

verlos|en vt raffle. **V~ung** f **-,-en** raffle; (Ziehung) draw

Verlust m **-[e]s,-e** loss

vermachen vt leave, bequeath

Vermächtnis nt **-ses,-se** legacy

vermähl|en (sich) vr marry. **V~ung** f **-,-en** marriage

vermehren vt increase; propagate (Pflanzen); **sich v~** increase; (sich fortpflanzen) breed

vermeiden† vt avoid

Vermerk m **-[e]s,-e** note. **v~en** vt note [down]

vermessen† vt measure; survey (Gelände) •adj presumptuous

vermiet|en vt let, rent [out]; hire out (Boot, Auto); **zu v~en** to let; (Boot:) for hire. **V~er** m landlord. **V~erin** f landlady

vermindern vt reduce

vermischen vt mix

vermissen vt miss

vermisst adj missing

vermitteln vi (haben) mediate • vt arrange; (beschaffen) find; place (Arbeitskräfte)

Vermittl|er m **-s,-** agent; (Schlichter) mediator. **V~ung** f **-,-en** arrangement; (Agentur) agency; (Teleph) exchange; (Schlichtung) mediation

Vermögen nt **-s,-** fortune. **v~d** adj wealthy

vermut|en vt suspect; (glauben) presume. **v~lich** adj probable • adv presumably. **V~ung** f **-,-en** supposition; (Verdacht) suspicion

vernachlässigen vt neglect

vernehm|en† vt hear; (verhören) question; (Jur) examine. **V~ung** f **-,-en** questioning

verneigen (sich) vr bow

verneln|en vt answer in the negative; (ablehnen) reject. **v~end** adj negative. **V~ung** f **-,-en** negative answer

vernicht|en vt destroy; (ausrotten) exterminate. **V~ung** f **-** destruction; extermination

Vernunft f **-** reason

vernünftig adj reasonable, sensible

veröffentlich|en vt publish. **V~ung** f **-,-en** publication

verordn|en vt prescribe (dat for). **V~ung** f **-,-en** prescription; (Verfügung) decree

verpachten vt lease [out]

verpack|en vt pack; (einwickeln) wrap. **V~ung** f packaging; wrapping

verpassen vt miss; (!: geben) give

verpfänden vt pawn

verpflanzen vt transplant

verpfleg|en vt feed: **sich selbst v~en** cater for oneself. **V~ung** f **-** board; (Essen) food; **Unterkunft und V~ung** board and lodging

verpflicht|en vt oblige; (einstellen) engage; (Sport) sign; **sich v~en** undertake/(versprechen) promise (**zu** to); (vertraglich) sign a contract. **V~ung** f **-,-en** obligation, commitment

verprügeln vt beat up, thrash

Verputz m **-es** plaster. **v~en** vt plaster

Verrat m **-[e]s** betrayal, treachery. **v~en**† vt betray; give away (Geheimnis)

Verräter m **-s,-** traitor

verrech|nen vt settle; clear (Scheck); **sich v~nen** make a mistake; (fig) miscalculate. **V~nungsscheck** m crossed cheque

verreisen vi (sein) go away; **verreist sein** be away

verrenken vt dislocate

verrichten vt perform, do

verriegeln vt bolt

verringer|n vt reduce; **sich v~n** decrease. **V~ung** f **-** reduction; decrease

verrost|en vi (sein) rust. **v~et** adj rusty

verrückt adj crazy, mad. **V~e(r)** m/f lunatic, **V~heit** f **-,-en** madness; (Torheit) folly

verrühren vt mix

verrunzelt adj wrinkled

verrutschen vt (sein) slip

Vers /fɛrs/ m **-es,-e** verse

versag|en vi (haben) fail • vt **sich etw v~en** deny oneself sth. **V~en** nt **-s,-** failure. **V~er** m **-s,-** failure

versalzen† vt put too much salt in/on; (fig) spoil

versamm|eln vt assemble. **V~lung** f assembly, meeting

Versand m **-[e]s** dispatch. **V~haus** nt mail-order firm

versäumen vt miss; lose (Zeit); (unterlassen) neglect; **[es] v~en, etw zu tun** fail to do sth

verschärfen vt intensify; tighten (Kontrolle); increase (Tempo); aggravate (Lage); **sich v~** intensify; increase; (Lage:) worsen

V

verschätzen (sich) vr **sich v~ in** (+ dat) misjudge

verschenken vt give away

verscheuchen vt shoo/(jagen) chase away

verschicken vt send; (Comm) dispatch

verschieb|en† vt move; (aufschieben) put off, postpone; **sich v~en** move, shift; (verrutschen) slip; (zeitlich) be postponed. **V~ung** f shift; postponement

verschieden adj different; **v~e** pl different; (mehrere) various; **V~es** some things; (dieses und jenes) various things; **das ist v~** it varies • adv differently; **v~ groß** of different sizes. **v~artig** adj diverse

verschimmel|n vi (sein) go mouldy. **v~t** adj mouldy

verschlafen† vi (haben) oversleep • vt sleep through (Tag); **sich v~** oversleep • adj sleepy

verschlagen† vt lose (Seite); **jdm die Sprache/den Atem v~** leave s.o. speechless/take s.o.'s breath away • adj sly

verschlechter|n vt make worse; **sich v~n** get worse, deteriorate. **V~ung** f **-,-en** deterioration

Verschleiß m **-es** wear and tear

verschleppen vt carry off; (entführen) abduct; spread (Seuche); neglect (Krankheit); (hinausziehen) delay

verschleudern vt sell at a loss

verschließen† vt close; (abschließen) lock; (einschließen) lock up

verschlimmer|n vt make worse; aggravate (Lage); **sich v~n** get worse, deteriorate. **V~ung** f **-,-en** deterioration

verschlossen adj reserved. **V~heit** f - reserve

verschlucken vt swallow; **sich v~** choke (**an** + dat on)

Verschluss m **-es,¨-e** fastener, clasp; (Koffer-) catch; (Flaschen-) top; (luftdicht) seal; (Phot) shutter

verschlüsselt adj coded

verschmelzen† vt/i (sein) fuse

verschmerzen vt get over

verschmutz|en vt soil; pollute (Luft) • vi (sein) get dirty. **V~ung** f - pollution

verschneit adj snow-covered

verschnörkelt adj ornate

verschnüren vt tie up

verschollen adj missing

verschonen vt spare

verschossen adj faded

verschränken vt cross

verschreiben† vt prescribe; **sich v~** make a slip of the pen

verschulden vt be to blame for. **V~** nt **-s** fault

verschuldet adj **v~ sein** be in debt

verschütten vt spill; (begraben) bury

verschweigen† vt conceal, hide

verschwend|en vt waste. **V~ung** f - extravagance; (Vergeudung) waste

verschwiegen adj discreet

verschwinden† vi (sein) disappear; **[mal] v~** [!] spend a penny

verschwommen adj blurred

verschwör|en† **(sich)** vr conspire. **V~ung** f **-,-en** conspiracy

versehen† vt perform; hold (Posten); keep (Haushalt); **v~ mit** provide with; **sich v~** make a mistake. **V~** nt **-s,-** oversight; (Fehler) slip; **aus V~** by mistake. **v~tlich** adv by mistake

Versehrte(r) m disabled person

versengen vt singe; (stärker) scorch

versenken vt sink

versessen adj keen (**auf** + acc on)

versetz|en vt move; transfer (Person); (Sch) move up; (verpfänden) pawn; (verkaufen) sell; (vermischen) blend; **jdn v~en** ([!]: warten lassen) stand s.o. up; **jdm in Angst/**

Erstaunen v~en frighten/astonish s.o.; **sich in jds Lage v~en** put oneself in s.o.'s place. **V~ung** f -,-en move; transfer; (Sch) move to a higher class

verseuchen vt contaminate

versicher|n vt insure; (bekräftigen) affirm; **jdm v~n** assure s.o. (**dass** that). **V~ung** f -,-en insurance; assurance

versiegeln vt seal

versiert /vɛr'ʒiːɐ̯t/ adj experienced

versilbert adj silver-plated

Versmaß /'fɛrs-/ nt metre

versöhn|en vt reconcile; **sich v~en** become reconciled. **V~ung** f -,-en reconciliation

versorg|en vt provide, supply (**mit** with); provide for (Familie); (betreuen) look after. **V~ung** f - provision, supply; (Betreuung) care

verspät|en (sich) vr be late. **v~et** adj late; (Zug) delayed; (Dank) belated. **V~ung** f - lateness; **V~ung haben** be late

versperren vt block; bar (Weg)

verspiel|en vt gamble away. **v~t** adj playful

verspotten vt mock, ridicule

versprech|en† vt promise; **sich v~en** make a slip of the tongue; **sich** (dat) **viel v~en von** have high hopes of; **ein viel v~ender Anfang** a promising start. **V~en** nt -s,- promise. **V~ungen** fpl promises

verstaatlich|en vt nationalize. **V~ung** f - nationalization

Verstand m -[e]s mind; (Vernunft) reason; **den V~ verlieren** go out of one's mind

verständig adj sensible; (klug) intelligent. **v~en** vt notify, inform; **sich v~en** communicate; (sich verständlich machen) make oneself understood. **V~ung** f - notification; communication; (Einigung) agreement

verständlich adj comprehensible; (deutlich) clear; (begreiflich) understandable; **sich v~ machen** make oneself understood. **v~erweise** adv understandably

Verständnis nt -ses understanding

verstärk|en vt strengthen, reinforce; (steigern) intensify, increase; amplify (Ton). **V~er** m -s,- amplifier. **V~ung** f reinforcement; increase; amplification; (Truppen) reinforcements pl

verstaubt adj dusty

verstauchen vt sprain

Versteck nt -[e]s,-e hiding-place; **V~ spielen** play hide-and-seek. **v~en** vt hide; **sich v~en** hide

verstehen† vt understand; (können) know; **falsch v~** misunderstand; **sich v~** understand one another; (auskommen) get on

versteiger|n vt auction. **V~ung** f auction

versteinert adj fossilized

verstell|en vt adjust; (versperren) block; (verändern) disguise; **sich v~en** pretend. **V~ung** f - pretence

versteuern vt pay tax on

verstimm|t adj disgruntled; (Magen) upset; (Mus) out of tune. **V~ung** f - ill humour; (Magen-) upset

verstockt adj stubborn

verstopf|en vt plug; (versperren) block; **v~t** blocked; (Person) constipated. **V~ung** f -,-en blockage; (Med) constipation

verstorben adj late, deceased. **V~e(r)** m/f deceased

verstört adj bewildered

Verstoß m infringement. **v~en**† vt disown •vi (haben) **v~en gegen** contravene, infringe

verstreuen vt scatter

verstümmeln vt mutilate; garble (Text)

Versuch m -[e]s,-e attempt; (Experiment) experiment. **v~en** vt (haben) try; **v~t sein** be tempted (**zu** to). **V~ung** f -,-en temptation

vertagen vt adjourn; (aufschieben) postpone; **sich v~** adjourn

vertauschen vt exchange; (verwechseln) mix up

verteidig|en vt defend. **V~er** m -s,- defender; (Jur) defence counsel. **V~ung** f -,-en defence

verteil|en vt distribute; (zuteilen) allocate; (ausgeben) hand out; (verstreichen) spread. **V~ung** f - distribution; allocation

vertief|en vt deepen; **v~t sein in** (+ acc) be engrossed in. **V~ung** f -,-en hollow, depression

vertikal /vɛrti'ka:l/ adj vertical

vertilgen vt exterminate; kill [off] (Unkraut)

vertippen (sich) vr make a typing mistake

vertonen vt set to music

Vertrag m -[e]s,⸚e contract; (Pol) treaty

vertragen† vt tolerate, stand; take (Kritik, Spaß); **sich v~** get on

vertraglich adj contractual

verträglich adj good-natured; (bekömmlich) digestible

vertrauen vi (haben) trust (**jdm/etw** s.o./sth; **auf** + acc in). **V~** nt -s trust, confidence (**zu** in); **im V~** in confidence. **v~swürdig** adj trustworthy

vertraulich adj confidential; (intim) familiar

vertraut adj intimate; (bekannt) familiar. **V~heit** f - intimacy; familiarity

vertreib|en† vt drive away; drive out (Feind); (Comm) sell; **sich** (dat) **die Zeit v~en** pass the time. **V~ung** f -,-en expulsion

vertret|en† vt represent; (einspringen für) stand in or deputize for; (verfechten) support; hold (Meinung); **sich** (dat) **den Fuß v~en** twist one's ankle. **V~er** m -s,- representative; deputy; (Arzt-) locum; (Verfechter) supporter. **V~ung** f -,-en representation; (Person) deputy; (eines Arztes) locum; (Handels-) agency

Vertrieb m -[e]s (Comm) sale

vertrocknen vi (sein) dry up

verüben vt commit

verunglücken vi (sein) be involved in an accident; (❗: missglücken) go wrong; **tödlich v~** be killed in an accident

verunreinigen vt pollute; (verseuchen) contaminate

verursachen vt cause

verurteil|en vt condemn; (Jur) convict (**wegen** of); sentence (**zum Tode** to death). **V~ung** f - condemnation; (Jur) conviction

vervielfachen vt multiply

vervielfältigen vt duplicate

vervollständigen vt complete

verwählen (sich) vr misdial

verwahren vt keep; (verstauen) put away

verwahrlost adj neglected; (Haus) dilapidated

Verwahrung f - keeping; **in V~ nehmen** take into safe keeping

verwaist adj orphaned

verwalt|en vt administer; (leiten) manage; govern (Land). **V~er** m -s,- administrator; manager. **V~ung** f -,-en administration; management; government

verwand|eln vt transform, change (**in** + acc into) **sich v~eln** change, turn (**in** + acc into). **V~lung** f transformation

verwandt adj related (**mit** to). **V~e(r)** m/f relative. **V~schaft** f - relationship; (Menschen) relatives pl

verwarn|en vt warn, caution. **V~ung** f warning, caution

verwechs|eln vt mix up, confuse; (halten für) mistake (**mit** for). **V~lung** f -,-en mix-up

verweiger|n vt/i (haben) refuse (**jdm etw** s.o. sth). **V~ung** f refusal

Verweis m -es,-e reference (**auf** +

acc to); (Tadel) reprimand; **v~en**† vt refer (**auf/an** + acc to); (tadeln) reprimand; **von der Schule v~en** expel

verwelken vi (sein) wilt

verwend|en† vt use; spend (Zeit, Mühe). **V~ung** f use

verwerten vt utilize, use

verwesen vi (sein) decompose

verwick|eln vt involve (**in** + acc in); **sich v~eln** get tangled up. **v~elt** adj complicated

verwildert adj wild; (Garten) overgrown; (Aussehen) unkempt

verwinden† vt (fig) get over

verwirklichen vt realize

verwirr|en vt tangle up; (fig) confuse; **sich v~en** get tangled; (fig) become confused. **v~t** adj confused. **V~ung** f - confusion

verwischen vt smudge

verwittert adj weathered

verwitwet adj widowed

verwöhn|en vt spoil. **v~t** adj spoilt

verworren adj confused

verwund|bar adj vulnerable. **v~en** vt wound

verwunder|lich adj surprising. **v~n** vt surprise; **sich v~n** be surprised. **V~ung** f - surprise

Verwund|ete(r) m wounded soldier; **die V~eten** the wounded pl. **V~ung** f -,-en wound

verwüst|en vt devastate, ravage. **V~ung** f -,-en devastation

verzählen (sich) vr miscount

verzaubern vt bewitch; (fig) enchant; **v~ in** (+ acc) turn into

Verzehr m **-s** consumption. **v~en** vt eat

verzeih|en† vt forgive; **v~en Sie!** excuse me! **V~ung** f - forgiveness; **um V~ung bitten** apologize; **V~ung!** sorry! (bei Frage) excuse me!

Verzicht m **-[e]s** renunciation (**auf** + acc of). **v~en** vi (haben) do without; **v~en auf** (+ acc) give up; renounce (Recht, Erbe)

verziehen† vt pull out of shape; (verwöhnen) spoil; **sich v~** lose shape; (Holz:) warp; (Gesicht:) twist; (verschwinden) disappear; (Nebel:) disperse; (Gewitter:) pass • vi (sein) move [away]

verzier|en vt decorate. **V~ung** f **-,-en** decoration

verzinsen vt pay interest on

verzöger|n vt delay; (verlangsamen) slow down. **V~ung** f **-,-en** delay

verzollen vt pay duty on; **haben Sie etwas zu v~?** have you anything to declare?

verzweif|eln vi (sein) despair. **v~elt** adj desperate. **V~lung** f - despair; (Ratlosigkeit) desperation

verzweigen (sich) vr branch [out]

Veto /'ve:to/ nt **-s,-s** veto

Vetter m **-s,-n** cousin

vgl. abbr (**vergleiche**) cf.

Viadukt /vi̯a'dʊkt/ nt **-[e]s,-e** viaduct

Video /'vi:deo/ nt **-s,-s** video. **V~handy** nt vision phone. **V~kassette** f video cassette. **V~recorder** m **-s,-** video recorder

Vieh nt **-[e]s** livestock; (Rinder) cattle pl; (🅸: Tier) creature

viel pron a great deal/🅸 a lot of; (pl) many, 🅸 a lot of; (substantivisch) **v~[es]** much, 🅸 a lot; **nicht/so/wie/zu v~** not/so/how/too much/ (pl) many; **v~e** pl many; **das v~e Geld** all that money • adv much, 🅸 a lot; **v~ mehr/weniger** much more/less; **v~zu groß/klein** much or far too big/small; **so v~ wie möglich** as much as possible; **so/zu v~ arbeiten** work so/too much

viel|deutig adj ambiguous. **v~fach** adj multiple • adv many times; (🅸: oft) frequently. **V~falt** f - diversity, [great] variety

vielleicht adv perhaps, maybe; (🅸: wirklich) really

vielmals adv very much

vielmehr adv rather; (im Gegenteil) on the contrary

vielseitig adj varied; (Person) versatile. **V~keit** f - versatility

vielversprechend* adj = **viel versprechend**, s. **versprechen**

vier inv adj, **V~** f -,-en four; (Sch) ≈ fair. **V~eck** nt -[e]s,-e oblong, rectangle; (Quadrat) square. **v~eckig** adj oblong, rectangular; square. **V~linge** mpl quadruplets

viertel /'fɪrtəl/ inv adj quarter; **um v~ neun** at [a] quarter past eight; **um drei v~ neun** at [a] quarter to nine. **V~** nt -s,- quarter; (Wein) quarter litre; **V~ vor/nach sechs** [a] quarter to/past six. **V~finale** nt quarter-final. **V~jahr** nt three months pl; (Comm) quarter. **v~jährlich** adj & adv quarterly. **V~stunde** f quarter of an hour

vier|zehn /'fɪr-/ inv adj fourteen. **v~zehnte(r,s)** adj fourteenth. **v~zig** inv adj forty. **v~zigste(r,s)** adj fortieth

Villa /'vɪla/ f -,-len villa

violett /vi̯o'lɛt/ adj violet

Vio|line /vi̯o'li:nə/ f -,-n violin. **V~linschlüssel** m treble clef

Virus /'vi:rʊs/ nt -,-ren virus

Visier /vi'zi:ɐ̯/ nt -s,-e visor

Visite /vi'zi:tə/ f -,-n round; **V~ machen** do one's round

Visum /'vi:zʊm/ nt -s,-sa visa

Vitamin /vita'mi:n/ nt -s,-e vitamin

Vitrine /vi'tri:nə/ f -,-n display cabinet/(im Museum) case

Vizepräsident /'fi:tsə-/ m vice president

Vogel m -s,¨ bird; **einen V~ haben** [!] have a screw loose. **V~scheuche** f -,-n scarecrow

Vokabeln /vo'ka:bəln/ fpl vocabulary sg

Vokal /vo'ka:l/ m -s,-e vowel

Volant /vo'lã:/ m -s,-s flounce

Volk nt -[e]s,¨er people sg; (Bevölkerung) people pl

Völker|kunde f ethnology. **V~mord** m genocide. **V~recht** nt international law

Volks|abstimmung f plebiscite. **V~fest** nt public festival. [C] **V~hochschule** f adult education classes pl/(Gebäude) centre. **V~lied** nt folk-song. **V~tanz** m folk-dance. **v~tümlich** adj popular. **V~wirt** m economist. **V~wirtschaft** f economics sg. **V~zählung** f [national] census

voll adj full (**von** od **mit** of); (Haar) thick; (Erfolg, Ernst) complete; (Wahrheit) whole; **v~ machen** fill up; **v~ tanken** fill up with petrol • adv (ganz) completely; (arbeiten) full-time; (auszahlen) in full; **v~ und ganz** completely

Vollblut nt thoroughbred

vollende|n vt insep complete. **v~t** adj perfect

Vollendung f completion; (Vollkommenheit) perfection

voller inv adj full of

Volleyball /'vɔli-/ m volleyball

vollführen vt insep perform

vollfüllen vt sep fill up

Vollgas nt **V~ geben** put one's foot down; **mit V~** flat out

völlig adj complete

volljährig adj **v~ sein** (Jur) be of age. **V~keit** f - (Jur) majority

Vollkaskoversicherung f fully comprehensive insurance

vollkommen adj perfect; (völlig) complete

Voll|kornbrot nt wholemeal bread. **V~macht** f -,-en authority; (Jur) power of attorney. **V~mond** m full moon. **V~pension** f full board

vollständig adj complete

vollstrecken vt insep execute; carry out (Urteil)

volltanken* vi sep (haben) = **voll tanken**, s. **voll**

Volltreffer m direct hit

vollzählig adj complete

[C] *see* A-Z of German life and culture

V

vollziehen† vt insep carry out; perform (Handlung); consummate (Ehe); **sich v~** take place

Volt /vɔlt/ nt **-[s],-** volt

Volumen /voˈluːmən/ nt **-s,-** volume

vom prep = **von dem**

von

• preposition (+ dative)

> ! Note that **von dem** can become **vom**

····➤ (räumlich) from; (nach Richtungen) of. **von hier an** from here on[ward]. **von Wien aus** [starting] from Vienna. **nördlich/südlich von Mannheim** [to the] north/ south of Mannheim. **rechts/links von mir** to the right/left of me; on my right/left

····➤ (zeitlich) from. **von jetzt an** from now on. **von heute/morgen an** [as] from today/tomorrow; starting today/tomorrow

····➤ (zur Angabe des Urhebers, der Ursache; nach Passiv) by. **der Roman ist von Fontane** the novel is by Fontane. **sie hat ein Kind von ihm**. she has a child by him. **er ist vom Blitz erschlagen worden** he was killed by lightning

····➤ (anstelle eines Genitivs; Hingehören, Beschaffenheit, Menge etc.) of. **ein Stück von dem Kuchen** a piece of the cake. **einer von euch** one of you. **eine Fahrt von drei Stunden** a drive of three hours; a three-hour drive. **das Brot von gestern** yesterday's bread. **ein Tal von erstaunlicher Schönheit** a valley of extraordinary beauty

····➤ (beftreffend) about. **handeln/ wissen/erzählen** od **reden von ...** be/know/talk about .... **eine Geschichte von zwei Elefanten** a story about or of two elephants

V

voneinander adv from each other; (abhängig) on each other

vonseiten prep (+ gen) on the part of

vonstatten adv **v~ gehen** take place

vor prep (+ dat/acc) in front of; (zeitlich, Reihenfolge) before; (+ dat) (bei Uhrzeit) to; (warnen, sich fürchten) of; (schützen, davonlaufen) from; (Respekt haben) for; **vor Angst zittern** tremble with fear; **vor drei Tagen** three days ago; **vor allen Dingen** above all •adv forward; **vor und zurück** backwards and forwards

Vorabend m eve

voran adv at the front; (voraus) ahead; (vorwärts) forward. **v~gehen**† vi sep (sein) lead the way; (Fortschritte machen) make progress. **v~kommen**† vi sep (sein) make progress; (fig) get on

Vor|anschlag m estimate. **V~anzeige** f advance notice. **V~arbeiter** m foreman

voraus adv ahead (dat of); (vorn) at the front; (vorwärts) forward **•im Voraus** in advance. **v~bezahlen** vt sep pay in advance. **v~gehen**† vi sep (sein) go on ahead; **jdm/etw v~gehen** precede s.o./sth. **V~sage** f **-,-n** prediction. **v~sagen** vt sep predict

voraussetz|en vt sep take for granted; (erfordern) require; **vorausgesetzt, dass** provided that. **V~ung** f **-,-en** assumption; (Erfordernis) prerequisite

voraussichtlich adj anticipated, expected •adv probably

Vorbehalt m **-[e]s,-e** reservation

vorbei adv past (**an jdm/etw** s.o./ sth); (zu Ende) over. **v~fahren**† vi sep (sein) drive/go past. **v~gehen**† vi sep (sein) go past; (verfehlen) miss; (vergehen) pass; (!: besuchen) drop in (**bei** on)

vorbereit|en vt sep prepare; prepare for (Reise); **sich v~en** prepare [oneself] (**auf** + acc for). **V~ung** f **-,-en** preparation

vorbestellen vt sep order/(im Theater, Hotel) book in advance

vorbestraft adj **v~ sein** have a [criminal] record

Vorbeugung f **-** prevention

Vorbild nt model. **v~lich** adj

exemplary, model • adv in an exemplary manner

vorbringen† vt sep put forward; offer (Entschuldigung)

vordatieren vt sep post-date

Vorder|bein nt foreleg. **v~e(r,s)** adj front. **V~grund** m foreground. **V~rad** nt front wheel. **V~seite** f front; (einer Münze) obverse. **v~ste(r,s)** adj front, first. **V~teil** nt front

vor|drängeln (sich) vr sep ! jump the queue. **v~drängen (sich)** vr sep push forward. **v~dringen**† vi sep (sein) advance

voreilig adj rash

voreingenommen adj biased, prejudiced. **V~heit** f - bias

vorenthalten† vt sep withhold

vorerst adv for the time being

Vorfahr m **-en,-en** ancestor

Vorfahrt f right of way; **'V~ beachten'** 'give way'. **V~sstraße** f ≈ major road

Vorfall m incident. **v~en**† vi sep (sein) happen

vorfinden† vt sep find

Vorfreude f [happy] anticipation

vorführ|en vt sep present, show; (demonstrieren) demonstrate; (aufführen) perform. **V~ung** f presentation; demonstration; performance

Vor|gabe f (Sport) handicap. **V~gang** m occurrence; (Techn) process. **V~gänger(in)** m **-s,-** (f **-,-nen**) predecessor

vorgehen† vi sep (sein) go forward; (voraus-) go on ahead; (Uhr:) be fast; (wichtig sein) take precedence; (verfahren) act, proceed; (geschehen) happen, go on. **V~** nt **-s** action

vor|geschichtlich adj prehistoric. **V~geschmack** m foretaste. **V~gesetzte(r)** m/f superior. **v~gestern** adv the day before yesterday; **v~gestern Abend** the evening before last

vorhaben† vt sep propose, intend (**zu** to); **etw v~** have sth planned. **V~** nt **-s,-** plan

Vorhand f (Sport) forehand

vorhanden adj existing; **v~ sein** exist; be available

Vorhang m curtain

Vorhängeschloss nt padlock

vorher adv before[hand]

vorhergehend adj previous

vorherrschend adj predominant

Vorher|sage f **-,-n** prediction: (Wetter-) forecast. **v~sagen** vt sep predict; forecast (Wetter). **v~sehen**† vt sep foresee

vorhin adv just now

vorige(r,s) adj last, previous

Vor|kehrungen fpl precautions. **V~kenntnisse** fpl previous knowledge sg

vorkommen† vi sep (sein) happen; (vorhanden sein) occur; (nach vorn kommen) come forward; (hervorkommen) come out; (zu sehen sein) show; **jdm bekannt v~** seem familiar to s.o.

Vorkriegszeit f pre-war period

vorlad|en† vt sep (Jur) summons. **V~ung** f summons

Vorlage f model; (Muster) pattern; (Gesetzes-) bill

vorlassen† vt sep admit; **jdn v~** ! let s.o. pass; (den Vortritt lassen) let s.o. go first

Vor|lauf m (Sport) heat. **V~läufer** m forerunner. **v~läufig** adj provisional; (zunächst) for the time being. **v~laut** adj forward. **V~leben** nt past

vorleg|en vt sep put on (Kette); (unterbreiten) present; (vorzeigen) show. **V~er** m **-s,-** mat; (Bett-) rug

vorles|en† vt sep read [out]; **jdm v~en** read to s.o. **V~ung** f lecture

vorletzt|e(r,s) adj last ... but one; **v~es Jahr** the year before last

Vorliebe f preference

vorliegen† vt sep (haben) be present/(verfügbar) available;

(bestehen) exist, be

vorlügen† vt sep lie (dat to)

vormachen vt sep put up; put on (Kette); push (Riegel); (zeigen) demonstrate; **jdm etwas v~** (!: täuschen) kid s.o.

Vormacht f supremacy

vormals adv formerly

vormerken vt sep make a note of; (reservieren) reserve

Vormittag m morning; **gestern/ heute V~** yesterday/this morning. **v~s** adv in the morning

Vormund m **-[e]s,-munde** & **-münder** guardian

vorn adv at the front; **nach v~** to the front; **von v~** from the front/ (vom Anfang) beginning; **von v~ anfangen** start afresh

Vorname m first name

vorne adv = **vorn**

vornehm adj distinguished; smart

vornehmen† vt sep carry out; **sich** (dat) **v~, etw zu tun** plan to do sth

vornherein adv **von v~herein** from the start

Vor|ort m suburb. **V~rang** m priority, precedence (**vor** + dat over). **V~rat** m **-[e]s,-e** supply, stock (**an** + dat of). **v~rätig** adj available; **v~rätig haben** have in stock. **V~ratskammer** f larder. **V~recht** nt privilege. **V~richtung** f device

Vorrunde f qualifying round

vorsagen vt/i sep (haben) recite; **jdm v~** tell s.o. the answer

Vor|satz m resolution. **v~sätzlich** adj deliberate; (Jur) premeditated

Vorschau f preview; (Film-) trailer

Vorschein m **zum V~kommen** appear

Vorschlag m suggestion, proposal. **v~en†** vt sep suggest, propose

vorschnell adj rash

vorschreiben† vt sep lay down; dictate (dat to); **vorgeschriebene Dosis** prescribed dose

Vorschrift f regulation; (Anweisung) instruction; **jdm V~en machen** tell s.o. what to do. **v~smäßig** adj correct

Vorschule f nursery school

Vorschuss m advance

vorseh|en† v sep • vt intend (**für/ als** for/as); (planen) plan; **sich v~en** be careful (**vor** + dat of) • vi (haben) peep out. **V~ung** f **-** providence

Vorsicht f **-** care; (bei Gefahr) caution; **V~!** careful! (auf Schild) 'caution'. **v~ig** adj careful; cautious. **V~smaßnahme** f precaution

Vorsilbe f prefix

Vorsitz m chairmanship; **den V~ führen** be in the chair. **V~ende(r)** m/f chairman

Vorsorge f **V~ treffen** take precautions; make provisions (**für** for). **v~n** vi sep (haben) provide (**für** for)

Vorspeise f starter

Vorspiel nt prelude. **v~en** v sep • vt perform/ (Mus) play (dat for) • vi (haben) audition

vorsprechen† v sep • vt recite; (zum Nachsagen) say (dat to) • vi (haben) (Theat) audition; **bei jdm v~** call on s.o.

Vor|sprung m projection; (Fels-) ledge; (Vorteil) lead (**vor** + dat over). **V~stadt** f suburb. **V~stand** m board [of directors]; (Vereins-) committee; (Partei-) executive

vorsteh|en† vi sep (haben) project, protrude; **einer Abteilung v~en** be in charge of a department. **V~er** m **-s,-** head

vorstell|en vt sep put forward (Bein, Uhr); (darstellen) represent; (bekanntmachen) introduce; **sich v~en** introduce oneself; (als Bewerber) go for an interview; **sich** (dat) **etw v~en** imagine sth. **V~ung** f introduction; (bei Bewerbung) interview; (Aufführung) performance; (Idee) idea; (Phantasie) imagination. **V~ungsgespräch** nt interview

V

Vorstoß m advance

Vorstrafe f previous conviction

Vortag m day before

vortäuschen vt sep feign, fake

Vorteil m advantage. **v~haft** adj advantageous; flattering

Vortrag m **-[e]s,⸚e** talk; (wissenschaftlich) lecture. **v~en**† vt sep perform; (aufsagen) recite; (singen) sing; (darlegen) present (dat to)

vortrefflich adj excellent

Vortritt m precedence; **jdm den V~ lassen** let s.o. go first

vorüber adv **v~ sein** be over; **an etw** (dat) **v~** past sth. **v~gehend** adj temporary

Vor|urteil nt prejudice. **V~verkauf** m advance booking

vorverlegen vt sep bring forward

Vor|wahl[nummer] f dialling code. **V~wand** m **-[e]s,⸚e** pretext; (Ausrede) excuse

vorwärts adv forward[s]; **v~ kommen** make progress; (fig) get on or ahead

vorwegnehmen† vt sep anticipate

vorweisen† vt sep show

vorwiegend adv predominantly

Vorwort nt (pl **-worte**) preface

Vorwurf m reproach; **jdm Vorwürfe machen** reproach s.o. **v~svoll** adj reproachful

Vorzeichen nt sign; (fig) omen

vorzeigen vt sep show

vorzeitig adj premature

vorziehen† vt sep pull forward; draw (Vorhang); (lieber mögen) prefer; favour

Vor|zimmer nt anteroom; (Büro) outer office. **V~zug** m preference; (gute Eigenschaft) merit, virtue; (Vorteil) advantage

vorzüglich adj excellent

vulgär /vʊl'gɛːɐ̯/ adj vulgar • adv in a vulgar way

Vulkan /vʊl'kaːn/ m **-s,-e** volcano

Ww

Waage f **-,-n** scales pl; (Astrology) Libra. **w~recht** adj horizontal

Wabe f **-,-n** honeycomb

wach adj awake; (aufgeweckt) alert; **w~ werden** wake up

Wach|e f **-,-n** guard; (Posten) sentry; (Dienst) guard duty; (Naut) watch; (Polizei-) station; **W~e halten** keep watch. **W~hund** m guard-dog

Wacholder m **-s** juniper

Wachposten m sentry

Wachs nt **-es** wax

wach|sam adj vigilant. **W~keit** f - vigilance

wachsen†[1] vi (sein) grow

wachs|en[2] vt (reg) wax. **W~figur** f waxwork

Wachstum nt **-s** growth

Wächter m **-s,-** guard; (Park-) keeper; (Parkplatz-) attendant

Wacht|meister m [police] constable. **W~posten** m sentry

wackel|ig adj wobbly; (Stuhl) rickety; (Person) shaky. **W~kontakt** m loose connection. **w~n** vi (haben) wobble; (zittern) shake

Wade f **-,-n** (Anat) calf

Waffe f **-,-n** weapon; **W~n** arms

Waffel f **-,-n** waffle; (Eis-) wafer

Waffen|ruhe f cease-fire.

W~schein m firearms licence. **W~stillstand** m armistice

Wagemut m daring

wagen vt risk; **es w~, etw zu tun** dare [to] do sth; **sich w~** (gehen) venture

Wagen m **-s,-** cart; (Eisenbahn-) carriage, coach; (Güter-) wagon; (Kinder-) pram; (Auto) car. **W~heber** m **-s,-** jack

Waggon /va'gõ:/ m **-s,-s** wagon

Wahl f **-,-en** choice; (Pol, Admin) election; (geheime) ballot; **zweite W~** (Comm) seconds pl

wähl|en vt/i (haben) choose; (Pol, Admin) elect; (stimmen) vote; (Teleph) dial. **W~er(in)** m **-s,-** (f **-,-nen**) voter. **w~erisch** adj choosy, fussy

Wahl|fach nt optional subject. **w~frei** adj optional. **W~kampf** m election campaign. **W~kreis** m constituency. **W~lokal** nt polling-station. **w~los** adj indiscriminate

Wahl|spruch m motto. **W~urne** f ballot-box

Wahn m **-[e]s** delusion; (Manie) mania

Wahnsinn m madness. **w~ig** adj mad, insane; ([!]: unsinnig) crazy; ([!]: groß) terrible; **w~ig werden** go mad • adv [!] terribly. **W~ige(r)** m/f maniac

wahr adj true; (echt) real; **du kommst doch, nicht w~?** you are coming, aren't you?

während prep (+ gen) during • conj while; (wohingegen) whereas

Wahrheit f **-,-en** truth. **w~sgemäß** adj truthful

wahrnehm|en† vt sep notice; (nutzen) take advantage of; exploit (Vorteil); look after (Interessen). **W~ung** f **-,-en** perception

Wahrsagerin f **-,-nen** fortune teller

wahrscheinlich adj probable. **W~keit** f **-** probability

Währung f **-,-en** currency

Wahrzeichen nt symbol

Waise f **-,-n** orphan. **W~nhaus** nt orphanage. **W~nkind** nt orphan

Wal m **-[e]s,-e** whale

Wald m **-[e]s,¨er** wood; (groß) forest. **w~ig** adj wooded

Waliser m **-s,-** Welshman

Waliserin f **-,-nen** Welshwoman

walisisch adj Welsh

Wall m **-[e]s,¨e** mound

Wallfahr|er(in) m(f) pilgrim. **W~t** f pilgrimage

Walnuss f walnut

Walze f **-,-n** roller. **w~n** vt roll

Walzer m **-s,-** waltz

Wand f **-,¨e** wall; (Trenn-) partition; (Seite) side; (Fels-) face

Wandel m **-s** change

Wander|er m **-s,-**, **W~in** f **-,-nen** hiker, rambler. **w~n** vi (sein) hike, ramble; (ziehen) travel; (gemächlich gehen) wander; (ziellos) roam. **W~schaft** f **-** travels pl. **W~ung** f **-,-en** hike, ramble. **W~weg** m footpath

Wandlung f **-,-en** change, transformation

Wand|malerei f mural. **W~tafel** f blackboard. **W~teppich** m tapestry

Wange f **-,-n** cheek

wann adv when

Wanne f **-,-n** tub

Wanze f **-,-n** bug

[C] **Wappen** nt **-s,-** coat of arms. **W~kunde** f heraldry

war, **wäre** s. **sein**[1]

Ware f **-,-n** article; (Comm) commodity; (coll) merchandise; **W~n** goods. **W~nhaus** nt department store. **W~nprobe** f sample. **W~nzeichen** nt trademark

warm adj warm; (Mahlzeit) hot; **w~ machen** heat • adv warmly; **w~ essen** have a hot meal

Wärm|e f **-** warmth; (Phys) heat; **10**

[C] *see* A-Z of German life and culture

Grad W~e 10 degrees above zero. **w~en** vt warm; heat (Essen, Wasser). **W~flasche** f hot-water bottle

Warn|blinkanlage f hazard [warning] lights pl. **w~en** vt/i (haben) warn (**vor** + dat of). **W~ung** f **-,-en** warning

Warteliste f waiting list

warten vi (haben) wait (**auf** + acc for) • vt service

Wärter(in) m **-s,-** (f **-,-nen**) keeper; (Museums-) attendant; (Gefängnis-) warder; (Kranken-) orderly

Warte|raum, W~saal m waiting-room. **W~zimmer** nt (Med) waiting-room

Wartung f **-** (Techn) service

warum adv why

Warze f **-,-n** wart

was pron what • rel pron that; **alles, was ich brauche** all [that] I need • indefinite pronoun ([!]: etwas) something; (fragend, verneint) anything; **so was Ärgerliches!** what a nuisance! • adv [!] (warum) why; (wie) how

wasch|bar adj washable. **W~becken** nt wash-basin

Wäsche f **-** washing; (Unter-) underwear

waschecht adj colour-fast

Wäscheklammer f clothes-peg

waschen† vt wash; **sich w~** have a wash; **W~ und Legen** shampoo and set • vi (haben) do the washing

Wäscherei f **-,-en** laundry

Wäsche|schleuder f spin-drier. **W~trockner** m tumble-drier

Wasch|küche f laundry-room. **W~lappen** m face-flannel. **W~maschine** f washing machine. **W~mittel** nt detergent. **W~pulver** nt washing-powder. **W~salon** m launderette. **W~zettel** m blurb

Wasser nt **-s** water. **W~ball** m beach-ball; (Spiel) water polo. **w~dicht** adj watertight; (Kleidung) waterproof. **W~fall** m waterfall. **W~farbe** f water-colour. **W~hahn** m tap. **W~kraft** f water-power. **W~kraftwerk** nt hydroelectric power-station. **W~leitung** f water-main; **aus der W~leitung** from the tap. **W~mann** m (Astrology) Aquarius

wässern vt soak; (begießen) water • vi (haben) water

Wasser|ski nt **-s** water-skiing. **W~stoff** m hydrogen. **W~straße** f waterway. **W~waage** f spirit-level

wässrig adj watery

watscheln vi (sein) waddle

Watt nt **-s,-** (Phys) watt

Watt|e f **-** cotton wool. **w~iert** adj padded; (gesteppt) quilted

WC /ve'tse:/ nt **-s,-s** WC

Web|cam f **-,-s** web camera. **W~design** nt web design

web|en vt/i (haben) weave. **W~er** m **-s,-** weaver

Web|seite /'vep-/ f web page. **W~site** f **-, -s** website

Wechsel m **-s,-** change; (Tausch) exchange; (Comm) bill of exchange. **W~geld** nt change. **w~haft** adj changeable. **W~jahre** npl menopause sg. **W~kurs** m exchange rate. **w~n** vt change; (tauschen) exchange • vi (haben) change; vary. **w~nd** adj changing; varying. **W~strom** m alternating current. **W~stube** f bureau de change

weck|en vt wake [up]; (fig) awaken • vi (haben) (Wecker:) go off. **W~er** m **-s,-** alarm [clock]

wedeln vi (haben) wave; **mit dem Schwanz w~** wag its tail

weder conj **w~ ... noch** neither ... nor

Weg m **-[e]s,-e** way; (Fuß-) path; (Fahr-) track; (Gang) errand; **sich auf den Weg machen** set off

weg adv away, off; (verschwunden) gone; **weg sein** be away; (gegangen/verschwunden) have gone; **Hände weg!** hands off!

wegen prep (+ gen) because of; (um

W

... willen) for the sake of; (bezüglich) about

weg|fahren† vi sep (sein) go away; (abfahren) leave. **W~fahrsperre** f immobilizer. **w~fallen**† vi sep (sein) be dropped/(ausgelassen) omitted; (entfallen) no longer apply. **w~geben**† vt sep give away. **w~gehen**† vi sep (sein) leave, go away; (ausgehen) go out. **w~kommen**† vi sep (sein) get away; (verloren gehen) disappear; **schlecht w~kommen** [!] get a raw deal. **w~lassen**† vt sep let go; (auslassen) omit. **w~laufen**† vi sep (sein) run away. **w~räumen** vt sep put away; (entfernen) clear away. **w~schicken** vt sep send away; (abschicken) send off. **w~tun**† vt sep put away; (wegwerfen) throw away

Wegweiser m **-s,-** signpost

weg|werfen† vt sep throw away. **w~ziehen**† v sep •vt pull away •vi (sein) move away

weh adj sore; **weh tun** hurt; (Kopf, Rücken:) ache; **jdm weh tun** hurt s.o.

wehe int alas; **w~ [dir/euch]!** (drohend) don't you dare!

wehen vi (haben) blow; (flattern) flutter •vt blow

Wehen fpl contractions

Wehr[1] nt **-[e]s,-e** weir

Wehr[2] f **sich zur W~ setzen** resist. [C] **W~dienst** m military service. **W~dienstverweigerer** m **-s,-** conscientious objector

wehren (sich) vr resist; (gegen Anschuldigung) protest; (sich sträuben) refuse

wehr|los adj defenceless. **W~macht** f armed forces pl. **W~pflicht** f conscription

Weib nt **-[e]s,-er** woman; (Ehe-) wife. **W~chen** nt **-s,-** (Zool) female. **w~lich** adj feminine; (Biology) female

weich adj soft; (gar) done

Weiche f **-,-n** (Rail) points pl

Weich|heit f **-** softness. **w~lich** adj soft; (Charakter) weak. **W~spüler** m **-s,-** (Textiles) conditioner. **W~tier** nt mollusc

Weide[1] f **-,-n** (Bot) willow

Weide[2] f **-,-n** pasture. **w~n** vt/i (haben) graze

weiger|n (sich) vr refuse. **W~ung** f **-,-en** refusal

Weihe f **-,-n** consecration; (Priester-) ordination. **w~n** vt consecrate; (zum Priester) ordain

Weiher m **-s,-** pond

Weihnacht|en nt **-s** & pl Christmas. **w~lich** adj Christmassy. **W~sbaum** m Christmas tree. **W~slied** nt Christmas carol. **W~smann** m (pl **-männer**) Father Christmas. **W~stag** m **erster/zweiter W~stag** Christmas Day/Boxing Day

Weih|rauch m incense. **W~wasser** nt holy water

weil conj because; (da) since

Weile f **-** while

Wein m **-[e]s,-e** wine; (Bot) vines pl; (Trauben) grapes pl. **W~bau** m winegrowing. **W~berg** m vineyard. **W~brand** m **-[e]s** brandy

weinen vt/i (haben) cry, weep

Wein|glas nt wine glass. **W~karte** f wine list. **W~lese** f grape harvest. **W~liste** f wine list. **W~probe** f wine tasting. **W~rebe** f, **W~stock** m vine. [C] **W~stube** f wine bar. **W~traube** f bunch of grapes; (W~beere) grape

weise adj wise

Weise f **-,-n** way; (Melodie) tune

Weisheit f **-,-en** wisdom. **W~szahn** m wisdom tooth

weiß adj, **W~** nt **-,-** white

weissag|en vt/i insep (haben) prophesy. **W~ung** f **-,-en** prophecy

Weiß|brot nt white bread. **W~e(r)** m/f white man/woman. **w~en** vt whitewash. **W~wein** m white wine

[C] *see* A-Z of German life and culture

Weisung f -,-en instruction; (Befehl) order

weit adj wide; (ausgedehnt) extensive; (lang) long • adv widely; (offen, öffnen) wide; (lang) far; **von w~em** from a distance; **bei w~em** by far; **w~ und breit** far and wide; **ist es noch w~?** is it much further? **so w~ wie möglich** as far as possible; **ich bin so w~** I'm ready; **w~ verbreitet** widespread; **w~ reichende Folgen** far-reaching consequences

Weite f -,-n expanse; (Entfernung) distance; (Größe) width. **w~n** vt widen; stretch (Schuhe)

weiter adj further • adv further; (außerdem) in addition; (anschließend) then; **etw w~ tun** go on doing sth; **w~ nichts/niemand** nothing/no one else; **und so w~** and so on

weiter|e(r,s) adj further; **ohne w~es** just like that; (leicht) easily

weiter|erzählen vt sep go on with; (w~sagen) repeat. **w~fahren†** vi sep (sein) go on. **w~geben†** vt sep pass on. **w~hin** adv (immer noch) still; (in Zukunft) in future; (außerdem) furthermore; **etw w~hin tun** go on doing sth. **w~machen** vi sep (haben) carry on

weit|gehend adj extensive • adv to a large extent. **w~sichtig** adj long-sighted; (fig) far-sighted. **W~sprung** m long jump. **w~verbreitet** adj = **w~ verbreitet**, s. **weit**

Weizen m -s wheat

welch inv pron what; **w~ ein(e)** what a. **w~e(r,s)** pron which; **um w~e Zeit?** at what time? • rel pron which; (Person) who • indefinite pronoun some; (fragend) any; **was für w~e?** what sort of?

Wellblech nt corrugated iron

Well|e f -,-n wave; (Techn) shaft. **W~enlänge** f wavelength. **W~enlinie** f wavy line. **W~enreiten** nt surfing. **W~ensittich** m -s,-e budgerigar. **w~ig** adj wavy.

Wellness f - mental and physical wellbeing

🅒 **Welt** f -,-en world; **auf der W~** in the world; **auf die** od **zur W~ kommen** be born. **W~all** nt universe. **w~berühmt** adj world-famous. **w~fremd** adj unworldly. **W~kugel** f globe. **w~lich** adj worldly; (nicht geistlich) secular

Weltmeister|(in) m(f) world champion. **W~schaft** f world championship

Weltraum m space. **W~fahrer** m astronaut

Weltrekord m world record

wem pron (dat of **wer**) to whom

wen pron (acc of **wer**) whom

🅒 **Wende** f -,-n change. **W~kreis** m (Geog) tropic

Wendeltreppe f spiral staircase

wenden[1] vt (reg) turn • vi (haben) turn [round]

wenden[2]† (& reg) vt turn; **sich w~** turn; **sich an jdn w~** turn/(schriftlich) write to s.o.

Wend|epunkt m (fig) turning-point. **W~ung** f -,-en turn; (Biegung) bend; (Veränderung) change

wenig pron little; (pl) few; **so/zu w~** so/too little/(pl) few; **w~e** pl few • adv little; (kaum) not much; **so w~ wie möglich** as little as possible. **w~er** pron less; (pl) fewer; **immer w~er** less and less • adv & conj less. **w~ste(r,s)** least; **am w~sten** least [of all]. **w~stens** adv at least

wenn conj if; (sobald) when; **immer w~** whenever; **w~ nicht** od **außer w~** unless; **w~ auch** even though

wer pron who; (!: jemand) someone; (fragend) anyone

Werbe|agentur f advertising agency. **w~n†** vt recruit; attract (Kunden, Besucher) • vi (haben) **w~n für** advertise; canvass for (Partei). **W~spot** m -s,-s commercial

Werbung f - advertising

🅒 *see A-Z of German life and culture*

W

werden†
- intransitive verb (sein)
  - ····➤ (+ adjective) become; get; (allmählich) grow. **müde/alt/länger werden** become or get/grow tired/old/longer. **taub/blind/wahnsinnig werden** go deaf/blind/mad. **blass werden** become or turn pale. **krank werden** become or fall ill. **es wird warm/dunkel** it is getting warm/dark. **mir wurde schlecht/schwindlig** I began to feel sick/dizzy
  - ····➤ (+ noun) become. **Arzt/Lehrer/Mutter werden** become a doctor/teacher/mother. **er will Lehrer werden** he wants to be a teacher. **was ist aus ihm geworden?** what has become of him?
  - ····➤ **werden zu** become; turn into. **das Erlebnis wurde zu einem Albtraum** the experience became or turned into a nightmare. **zu Eis werden** turn into ice
- auxiliary verb
  - ····➤ (Zukunft) will; shall. **er wird bald hier sein** he will or he'll soon be here. **wir werden sehen** we shall see. **es wird bald regnen** it's going to rain soon
  - ····➤ (Konjunktiv) **würde(n)** would. **ich würde es kaufen, wenn ...** I would buy it if .... **würden Sie so nett sein?** would you be so kind?
  - ····➤ (beim Passiv; pp **worden**) be. **geliebt/geboren werden** be loved/born. **du wirst gerufen** you are being called. **er wurde gebeten** he was asked. **es wurde gemunkelt** it was rumoured. **mir wurde gesagt, dass** ... I was told that .... **das Haus ist soeben/1995 renoviert worden** the house has just been renovated/was renovated in 1995

werfen† vt throw; cast (Blick, Schatten); **sich w∼** (Holz:) warp

Werft f -,-en shipyard

Werk nt -[e]s,-e work; (Fabrik) works sg, factory; (Trieb-) mechanism. **W∼en** nt -s (Sch) handicraft. **W∼statt** f -,¨en workshop; (Auto-) garage. **W∼tag** m weekday. **w∼tags** adv on weekdays. **w∼tätig** adj working

Werkzeug nt tool; (coll) tools pl. **W∼leiste** f toolbar

Wermut m -s vermouth

wert adj **viel w∼** worth a lot; **nichts w∼ sein** be worthless; **jds w∼ sein** be worthy of s.o. **W∼** m -[e]s,-e value; (Nenn-) denomination; **im W∼ von** worth. **w∼en** vt rate

Wert|gegenstand m object of value. **w∼los** adj worthless. **W∼minderung** f depreciation. **W∼papier** nt (Comm) security. **W∼sachen** fpl valuables. **w∼voll** adj valuable

Wesen nt -s,- nature; (Lebe-) being; (Mensch) creature

wesentlich adj essential; (grundlegend) fundamental • adv considerably, much

weshalb adv why

Wespe f -,-n wasp

wessen pron (gen of **wer**) whose

westdeutsch adj West German

Weste f -,-n waistcoat

Westen m -s west

Western m -[s],- western

Westfalen nt -s Westphalia

Westindien nt West Indies pl

west|lich adj western; (Richtung) westerly • adv & prep (+ gen) **w∼lich [von] der Stadt** [to the] west of the town. **w∼wärts** adv westwards

weswegen adv why

Wettbewerb m -s,-e competition

Wette f -,-n bet; **um die W∼ laufen** race (**mit jdm** s.o.)

wetten vt/i (haben) bet (**auf** + acc on); **mit jdm w∼** have a bet with s.o.

Wetter nt -s,- weather; (Un-) storm. **W∼bericht** m weather report. **W∼vorhersage** f weather forecast. **W∼warte** f -,-n meteorological station

Wett|kampf m contest.

W~kämpfer(in) m(f) competitor. **W~lauf** m race. **W~rennen** nt race. **W~streit** m contest

Whisky m **-s** whisky

wichtig adj important; **w~ nehmen** take seriously. **W~keit** f - importance

Wicke f **-,-n** sweet pea

Wickel m **-s,-** compress

wickeln vt wind; (ein-) wrap; (bandagieren) bandage; **ein Kind frisch w~** change a baby

Widder m **-s,-** ram; (Astrology) Aries

wider prep (+ acc) against; (entgegen) contrary to; **w~ Willen** against one's will

widerlegen vt insep refute

wider|lich adj repulsive. **W~rede** f contradiction; **keine W~rede!** don't argue!

widerrufen† vt/i insep (haben) retract; revoke (Befehl)

Widersacher m **-s,-** adversary

widersetzen (sich) vr insep resist (**jdm/etw** s.o./sth)

widerspiegeln vt sep reflect

widersprechen† vi insep (haben) contradict (**jdm/etw** s.o./something)

Wider|spruch m contradiction; (Protest) protest. **w~sprüchlich** adj contradictory. **w~spruchslos** adv without protest

Widerstand m resistance; **W~ leisten** resist. **w~sfähig** adj resistant; (Bot) hardy

widerstehen† vi insep (haben) resist (**jdm/etw** s.o./sth); (anwidern) be repugnant (**jdm** to s.o.)

Widerstreben nt **-s** reluctance

widerwärtig adj disagreeable

Widerwill|e m aversion, repugnance. **w~ig** adj reluctant

widm|en vt dedicate (dat to); (verwenden) devote (dat to); **sich w~en** (+ dat) devote oneself to. **W~ung** f **-,-en** dedication

wie adv how; **wie viel** how much/ (pl) many; **um wie viel Uhr?** at what time? **wie viele?** how many? **wie ist Ihr Name?** what is your name? **wie ist das Wetter?** what is the weather like? •conj as; (gleich wie) like; (sowie) as well as; (als) when, as; **so gut wie** as good as; **nichts wie** nothing but

wieder adv again; **jdn/etw w~ erkennen** recognize s.o./something; **etw w~ verwenden/verwerten** reuse/recycle sth; **etw w~ gutmachen** make up for (Schaden); redress (Unrecht); (bezahlen) pay for sth

Wiederaufbau m reconstruction

wieder|bekommen† vt sep get back. **W~belebung** f - resuscitation. **w~bringen†** vt sep bring back. **w~erkennen*†** vt sep = **w~ erkennen**, s. **wieder**. **w~geben†** vt sep give back, return; (darstellen) portray; (ausdrücken, übersetzen) render; (zitieren) quote. **W~geburt** f reincarnation

Wiedergutmachung f - reparation; (Entschädigung) compensation

wiederherstellen vt sep reestablish; restore (Gebäude); restore to health (Kranke)

wiederhol|en vt insep repeat; (Sch) revise; **sich w~en** recur; (Person:) repeat oneself. **w~t** adj repeated. **W~ung** f **-,-en** repetition; (Sch) revision

Wieder|hören nt **auf W~hören!** goodbye! **W~käuer** m **-s,-** ruminant. **W~kehr** f - return; (W~holung) recurrence. **w~kommen†** vi sep (sein) come back

wiedersehen* vt sep = **wieder sehen**, s. **sehen**. **W~** nt **-s,-** reunion; **auf W~!** goodbye!

wiedervereinig|en* vt sep = **wieder vereinigen**, s. **vereinigen**. ▣**W~ung** f reunification

wieder|verwenden*† vt sep = **w~ verwenden**, s. **wieder**.

▣ *see A-Z of German life and culture*

W

w∼verwerten* vt sep = **w∼ verwerten**, s. **wieder**

Wiege f **-,-n** cradle

wiegen[1]† vt/i (haben) weigh

wiegen[2] vt (reg) rock. **W∼lied** nt lullaby

wiehern vi (haben) neigh

Wien nt **-s** Vienna. **W∼er** adj Viennese • m **-s,-** Viennese • f **-,-** ≈ frankfurter. **w∼erisch** adj Viennese

Wiese f **-,-n** meadow

Wiesel nt **-s,-** weasel

wieso adv why

wieviel* pron = **wie viel**, s. **wie**. **w∼te(r,s)** adj which; **der W∼te ist heute?** what is the date today?

wieweit adv how far

wild adj wild; (Stamm) savage; **w∼er Streik** wildcat strike; **w∼ wachsen** grow wild. **W∼** nt **-[e]s** game; (Rot-) deer; (Culin) venison. **W∼e(r)** m/f savage

Wilder|er m **-s,-** poacher. **w∼n** vt/i (haben) poach

Wild|heger, **W∼hüter** m **-s,-** gamekeeper. **W∼leder** nt suede. **W∼nis** f **-** wilderness. **W∼schwein** nt wild boar. **W∼westfilm** m western

Wille m **-ns** will

Willenskraft f will-power

willig adj willing

willkommen adj welcome; **w∼ heißen** welcome. **W∼** nt **-s** welcome

wimmeln vi (haben) swarm

wimmern vi (haben) whimper

Wimpel m **-s,-** pennant

Wimper f **-,-n** [eye]lash; **W∼ntusche** f mascara

Wind m **-[e]s,-e** wind

Winde f **-,-n** (Techn) winch

Windel f **-,-n** nappy

winden† vt wind; make (Kranz); **in die Höhe w∼** winch up; **sich w∼** wind (**um** round); (sich krümmen) writhe

Wind|hund m greyhound. **w∼ig** adj windy. **W∼mühle** f windmill. **W∼park** m wind farm. **W∼pocken** fpl chickenpox sg. **W∼schutzscheibe** f windscreen. **W∼stille** f calm. **W∼stoß** m gust of wind. **W∼surfen** nt windsurfing

Windung f **-,-en** bend; (Spirale) spiral

Winkel m **-s,-** angle; (Ecke) corner. **W∼messer** m **-s,-** protractor

winken vi (haben) wave

Winter m **-s,-** winter. **w∼lich** adj wintry; (Winter-) winter **W∼schlaf** m hibernation; **W∼sport** m winter sports pl

Winzer m **-s,-** winegrower

winzig adj tiny, minute

Wipfel m **-s,-** [tree-]top

Wippe f **-,-n** see-saw

wir pron we; **wir sind es** it's us

Wirbel m **-s,-** eddy; (Drehung) whirl; (Trommel-) roll; (Anat) vertebra; (Haar-) crown; (Aufsehen) fuss. **w∼n** vt/i (sein/haben) whirl. **W∼säule** f spine. **W∼sturm** m cyclone. **W∼tier** nt vertebrate. **W∼wind** m whirlwind

wird s. **werden**

wirken vi (haben) have an effect (**auf** + acc on); (zur Geltung kommen) be effective; (tätig sein) work; (scheinen) seem • vt (Textiles) knit

wirklich adj real. **W∼keit** f **-,-en** reality

wirksam adj effective

Wirkung f **-,-en** effect. **w∼slos** adj ineffective. **w∼svoll** adj effective

wirr adj tangled; (Haar) tousled; (verwirrt, verworren) confused

Wirt m **-[e]s,-e** landlord. **W∼in** f **-,-nen** landlady

Wirtschaft f **-,-en** economy; (Gast-) restaurant; (Kneipe) pub. **w∼en** vi (haben) manage one's finances. **w∼lich** adj economic; (sparsam) economical. **W∼sflüchtling** m economic refugee. **W∼sgeld** nt housekeeping [money].

W∼sprüfer m auditor

Wirtshaus nt inn; (Kneipe) pub

wischen vt/i (haben) wipe; wash (Fußboden)

wissen† vt/i (haben) know; **weißt du noch?** do you remember? **nichts w∼ wollen von** not want anything to do with. **W∼** nt **-s** knowledge; **meines W∼s** to my knowledge

Wissenschaft f **-,-en** science. **W∼ler** m **-s,-** academic; (Natur-) scientist. **w∼lich** adj academic; scientific

wissenswert adj worth knowing

witter|n vt scent; (ahnen) sense. **W∼ung** f **-** scent; (Wetter) weather

Witwe f **-,-n** widow. **W∼r** m **-s,-** widower

Witz m **-es,-e** joke; (Geist) wit. **W∼bold** m **-[e]s,-e** joker. **w∼ig** adj funny; witty

wo adv where; (als) when; (irgendwo) somewhere; **wo immer** wherever • conj seeing that; (obwohl) although; (wenn) if

woanders adv somewhere else

wobei adv how; (relativ) during the course of which

Woche f **-,-n** week. **W∼nende** nt weekend. **W∼nkarte** f weekly ticket. **w∼nlang** adv for weeks. **W∼ntag** m day of the week; (Werktag) weekday. **w∼tags** adv on weekdays

wöchentlich adj & adv weekly

Wodka m **-s** vodka

wofür adv what ... for; (relativ) for which

Woge f **-,-n** wave

woher adv where from; **woher weißt du das?** how do you know that? **wohin** adv where [to]; **wohin gehst du?** where are you going?

wohl adv well; (vermutlich) probably; (etwa) about; (zwar) perhaps; **w∼ kaum** hardly; **sich w∼ fühlen** feel well/(behaglich) comfortable; **jdm w∼ tun** do s.o. good. **W∼** nt **-[e]s** welfare, well-being; **zum W∼** (+ gen) for the good of; **zum W∼!** cheers!

Wohl|befinden nt well-being. **W∼behagen** nt feeling of well-being. **W∼ergehen** nt **-s** welfare. **w∼erzogen** adj well brought-up

Wohlfahrt f **-** welfare. **W∼sstaat** m Welfare State

wohl|habend adj prosperous, well-to-do. **w∼ig** adj comfortable. **w∼schmeckend** adj tasty

Wohlstand m prosperity. **W∼sgesellschaft** f affluent society

Wohltat f [act of] kindness; (Annehmlichkeit) treat; (Genuss) bliss

Wohltät|er m benefactor. **w∼ig** adj charitable

wohl|tuend adj agreeable. **w∼tun*** vi sep (haben) = **w∼ tun**, s. **wohl**

Wohlwollen nt **-s** goodwill; (Gunst) favour. **w∼d** adj benevolent

Wohn|block m block of flats. **w∼en** vi (haben) live; (vorübergehend) stay. **W∼gegend** f residential area. **w∼haft** adj resident. **W∼haus** nt house. **W∼heim** nt hostel; (Alten-) home. **w∼lich** adj comfortable. **W∼mobil** nt **-s,-e** camper. **W∼ort** m place of residence. **W∼sitz** m place of residence

Wohnung f **-,-en** flat; (Unterkunft) accommodation. **W∼snot** f housing shortage

Wohn|wagen m caravan. **W∼zimmer** nt living-room

wölb|en vt curve; arch (Rücken). **W∼ung** f **-,-en** curve; (Architecture) vault

Wolf m **-[e]s,⸚e** wolf; (Fleisch-) mincer; (Reiß-) shredder

Wolk|e f **-,-n** cloud. **W∼enbruch** m cloudburst. **W∼enkratzer** m skyscraper. **w∼enlos** adj cloudless. **w∼ig** adj cloudy

Woll|decke f blanket. **W∼e** f **-,-n** wool

wollen† [1]
- auxiliary verb
  - (den Wunsch haben) want to. **ich will nach Hause gehen** I want to go home. **ich wollte Sie fragen, ob ...** I wanted to ask you if ...
  - (im Begriff sein) be about to. **wir wollten gerade gehen** we were just about to go
  - (sich in der gewünschten Weise verhalten) **will nicht** refuses to. **der Motor will nicht anspringen** the engine won't start
- intransitive verb
  - want to. **ob du willst oder nicht** whether you want to or not. **ganz wie du willst** just as you like
  - (!: irgendwohin zu gehen wünschen) **ich will nach Hause** I want to go home. **zu wem wollen Sie?** who[m] do you want to see?
  - (!: funktionieren) **will nicht** won't go. **meine Beine wollen nicht mehr** my legs are giving up !
- transitive verb
  - want; (beabsichtigen) intend. **er will nicht, dass du ihm hilfst** he does not want you to help him. **das habe ich nicht gewollt** I never intended or meant that to happen

Wollsachen fpl woollens

womit adv what ... with; (relativ) with which. **wonach** adv what ... after/(suchen) for/(riechen) of; (relativ) after/for/of which

woran adv what ... on/(denken, sterben) of; (relativ) on/of which; **woran hast du ihn erkannt?** how did you recognize him? **worauf** adv what on .../(warten) for; (relativ) on/for which; (woraufhin) whereupon. **woraus** adv what ... from; (relativ) from which

W

Wort nt -[e]s,⸚er & -e word; **jdm ins W~ fallen** interrupt s.o.

Wörterbuch nt dictionary

Wort|führer m spokesman. **w~getreu** adj & adv word-for-word. **w~karg** adj taciturn. **W~laut** m wording

wörtlich adj literal; (wortgetreu) word-for-word

wort|los adj silent • adv without a word. **W~schatz** m vocabulary. **W~spiel** nt pun, play on words

worüber adv what ... over/(lachen, sprechen) about; (relativ) over/about which. **worum** adv what ... round/(bitten, kämpfen) for; (relativ) round/for which; **worum geht es?** what is it about? **wovon** adv what ... from/(sprechen) about; (relativ) from/about which. **wovor** adv what ... in front of; (sich fürchten) what of; (relativ) in front of which; of which. **wozu** adv what ... to/(brauchen, benutzen) for; (relativ) to/for which; **wozu?** what for?

Wrack nt **-s,-s** wreck

wringen† vt wring

Wucher|preis m extortionate price. **W~ung** f **-,-en** growth

Wuchs m **-es** growth; (Gestalt) stature

Wucht f - force

wühlen vi (haben) rummage; (in der Erde) burrow • vt dig

Wulst m **-[e]s,⸚e** bulge; (Fett-) roll

wund adj sore; **w~ reiben** chafe; **sich w~ liegen** get bedsores. **W~brand** m gangrene

Wunde f **-,-n** wound

Wunder nt **-s,-** wonder, marvel; (übernatürliches) miracle; **kein W~!** no wonder! **w~bar** adj miraculous; (herrlich) wonderful. **W~kind** nt infant prodigy. **w~n** vt surprise; **sich w~n** be surprised (**über** + acc at). **w~schön** adj beautiful

Wundstarrkrampf m tetanus

Wunsch m **-[e]s,⸚e** wish; (Verlangen) desire; (Bitte) request

wünschen vt want; **sich** (dat) **etw w~** want sth; (bitten um) ask for sth; **jdm Glück/gute Nacht w~** wish s.o. luck/good night; **Sie w~?** can I help you? **w~swert** adj desirable

Wunschkonzert nt musical request programme

wurde, **würde** s. **werden**

Würde f **-,-n** dignity; (Ehrenrang) honour. **w~los** adj undignified. **W~nträger** m dignitary. **w~voll** adj dignified •adv with dignity

würdig adj dignified; (wert) worthy

Wurf m **-[e]s,⸚e** throw; (Junge) litter

Würfel m **-s,-** cube; (Spiel-) dice; (Zucker-) lump. **w~n** vi (haben) throw the dice; **w~n um** play dice for •vt throw; (in Würfel schneiden) dice. **W~zucker** m cube sugar

würgen vt choke •vi (haben) retch; choke (**an** + dat on)

Wurm m **-[e]s,⸚er** worm; (Made) maggot. **w~en** vi (haben) **jdn w~en** [!] rankle [with s.o.]

Wurst f **-,⸚e** sausage; **das ist mir W~** [!] I couldn't care less

Würze f **-,-n** spice; (Aroma) aroma

Wurzel f **-,-n** root; **W~n schlagen** take root. **w~n** vi (haben) root

würz|en vt season. **w~ig** adj tasty; (aromatisch) aromatic; (pikant) spicy

wüst adj chaotic; (wirr) tangled; (öde) desolate; (wild) wild; (schlimm) terrible

Wüste f **-,-n** desert

Wut f **-** rage, fury. **W~anfall** m fit of rage

wüten vi (haben) rage. **w~d** adj furious; **w~d machen** infuriate

Xx

x /ɪks/ inv adj (Math) x; [!] umpteen. **X-Beine** ntpl knock-knees. **x-beinig**, **X-beinig** adj knock-kneed. **x-beliebig** adj [!] any. **x-mal** adv [!] umpteen times

Yy

Yoga /ˈjoːga/ m & nt **-[s]** yoga

Zz

Zack|e f -,-n point; (Berg-) peak; (Gabel-) prong. **z~ig** adj jagged; (gezackt) serrated

zaghaft adj timid; (zögernd) tentative

zäh adj tough; (hartnäckig) tenacious. **z~flüssig** adj viscous; (Verkehr) slow-moving. **Z~igkeit** f - toughness; tenacity

Zahl f -,-en number; (Ziffer, Betrag) figure

zahlen vt/i (haben) pay; (bezahlen) pay for; **bitte z~!** the bill please!

zählen vi (haben) count; **z~ zu** (fig) be one/(pl) some of •vt count; **z~ zu** add to; (fig) count among

zahlenmäßig adj numerical

Zähler m -s,- meter

Zahl|grenze f fare-stage. **Z~karte** f paying-in slip. **z~los** adj countless. **z~reich** adj numerous; (Anzahl, Gruppe) large •adv in large numbers. **Z~ung** f -,-en payment; **in Z~ung nehmen** take in part-exchange

Zählung f -,-en count

Zahlwort nt (pl **-wörter**) numeral

zahm adj tame

zähmen vt tame; (fig) restrain

Zahn m -[e]s,⸚e tooth; (am Zahnrad) cog. **Z~arzt** m, **Z~ärztin** f dentist. **Z~belag** m plaque. **Z~bürste** f toothbrush. **Z~fleisch** nt gums pl. **z~los** adj toothless. **Z~pasta** f -,-en toothpaste. **Z~rad** nt cog-wheel. **Z~schmelz** m enamel. **Z~schmerzen** mpl toothache sg. **Z~spange** f brace. **Z~stein** m tartar. **Z~stocher** m -s,- toothpick

Zange f -,-n pliers pl; (Kneif-) pincers pl; (Kohlen-, Zucker-) tongs pl; (Geburts-) forceps pl

Zank m -[e]s squabble. **z~en** vr **sich z~en** squabble

Zäpfchen nt -s,- (Anat) uvula; (Med) suppository

zapfen vt tap, draw. **Z~streich** m (Mil) tattoo

Zapf|hahn m tap. **Z~säule** f petrol-pump

zappeln vi (haben) wriggle; (Kind:) fidget

zart adj delicate; (weich, zärtlich) tender; (sanft) gentle. **Z~gefühl** nt tact

zärtlich adj tender; (liebevoll) loving. **Z~keit** f -,-en tenderness; (Liebkosung) caress

Zauber m -s magic; (Bann) spell. **Z~er** m -s,- magician. **z~haft** adj enchanting. **Z~künstler** m conjuror. **z~n** vi (haben) do magic; (Zaubertricks ausführen) do conjuring tricks •vt produce as if by magic. **Z~stab** m magic wand. **Z~trick** m conjuring trick

Zaum m -[e]s,Zäume bridle

Zaun m -[e]s,Zäune fence

z.B. abbr (**zum Beispiel**) e.g.

Zebra nt -s,-s zebra. **Z~streifen** m zebra crossing

Zeche f -,-n bill; (Bergwerk) pit

zechen vi (haben) [!] drink

Zeder f -,-n cedar

Zeh m -[e]s,-en toe. **Z~e** f -,-n toe; (Knoblauch-) clove

zehn inv adj, **Z~** f -,-en ten. **z~te(r,s)** adj tenth. **Z~tel** nt -s,- tenth

Zeichen nt -s,- sign; (Signal) signal. **Z~setzung** f - punctuation. **Z~trickfilm** m cartoon

zeichn|en vt/i (haben) draw; (kenn-)

mark; (unter-) sign. **Z~ung** f **-,-en** drawing

Zeige|finger m index finger. **z~n** vt show; **sich z~n** appear; (sich herausstellen) become clear ● vi (haben) point (**auf** + acc to). **Z~r** m **-s,-** pointer; (Uhr-) hand

Zeile f **-,-n** line; (Reihe) row

Zeit f **-,-en** time; **sich** (dat) **Z~ lassen** take one's time; **es hat Z~** theres's no hurry; **mit der Z~** in time; **in nächster Z~** in the near future; **zur Z~** (rechtzeitig) in time; *(derzeit) s. **zurzeit**; **eine Z~ lang** for a time or while

Zeit|alter nt age, era. **z~gemäß** adj modern, up-to-date. **Z~genosse** m, **Z~genossin** f contemporary. **z~genössisch** adj contemporary. **z~ig** adj & adv early

zeitlich adj (Dauer) in time; (Folge) chronological. ● adv **z~ begrenzt** for a limited time

zeit|los adj timeless. **Z~lupe** f slow motion. **Z~punkt** m time. **z~raubend** adj time-consuming. **Z~raum** m period. **Z~schrift** f magazine, periodical

Zeitung f **-,-en** newspaper. **Z~spapier** nt newspaper

Zeit|verschwendung f waste of time. **Z~vertreib** m pastime. **z~weise** adv at times. **Z~wort** nt (pl **-wörter**) verb. **Z~zünder** m time fuse

Zelle f **-,-n** cell; (Telefon-) box

Zelt nt **-[e]s,-e** tent; (Fest-) marquee. **z~en** vi (haben) camp. **Z~en** nt **-s** camping. **Z~plane** f tarpaulin. **Z~platz** m campsite

Zement m **-[e]s** cement

zen|sieren vt (Sch) mark; censor (Presse, Film). **Z~sur** f **-,-en** (Sch) mark; (Presse-) censorship

Zentimeter m & nt centimetre. **Z~maß** nt tape-measure

Zentner m **-s,-** [metric] hundredweight (50 kg)

zentral adj central. **Z~e** f **-,-n** central office; (Partei-) headquarters pl; (Teleph) exchange. **Z~heizung** f central heating

Zentrum nt **-s,-tren** centre

zerbrech|en† vt/i (sein) break. **z~lich** adj fragile

zerdrücken vt crush

Zeremonie f **-,-n** ceremony

Zerfall m disintegration; (Verfall) decay. **z~en**† vi (sein) disintegrate; (verfallen) decay

zergehen† vi (sein) melt; (sich auflösen) dissolve

zerkleinern vt chop/(schneiden) cut up; (mahlen) grind

zerknüllen vt crumple [up]

zerkratzen vt scratch

zerlassen† vt melt

zerlegen vt take to pieces, dismantle; (zerschneiden) cut up; (tranchieren) carve

zerlumpt adj ragged

zermalmen vt crush

zermürben vt (fig) wear down

zerplatzen vi (sein) burst

zerquetschen vt squash; crush

Zerrbild nt caricature

zerreißen† vt tear; (in Stücke) tear up; break (Faden, Seil) ● vi (sein) tear; break

zerren vt drag; pull (Muskel) ● vi (haben) pull (**an** + dat at)

zerrissen adj torn

zerrütten vt ruin, wreck; shatter (Nerven)

zerschlagen† vt smash; smash up (Möbel); **sich z~** (fig) fall through; (Hoffnung:) be dashed

zerschmettern vt/i (sein) smash

zerschneiden† vt cut; (in Stücke) cut up

zersplittern vi (sein) splinter; (Glas:) shatter ● vt shatter

zerspringen† vi (sein) shatter; (bersten) burst

Zerstäuber m **-s,-** atomizer

see A-Z of German life and culture

zerstör|en vt destroy; (zunichte machen) wreck. **Z~er** m **-s,-** destroyer. **Z~ung** f destruction

zerstreu|en vt scatter; disperse (Menge); dispel (Zweifel); **sich z~en** disperse; (sich unterhalten) amuse oneself. **z~t** adj absent-minded

Zertifikat nt **-[e]s,-e** certificate

zertrümmern vt smash [up]; wreck (Gebäude, Stadt)

Zettel m **-s,-** piece of paper; (Notiz) note; (Bekanntmachung) notice

Zeug nt **-s** [!] stuff; (Sachen) things pl; (Ausrüstung) gear; **dummes Z~** nonsense

Zeuge m **-n,-n** witness. **z~n** vi (haben) testify; **z~n von** (fig) show •vt father. **Z~naussage** f testimony. **Z~nstand** m witness box

Zeugin f **-,-nen** witness

Zeugnis nt **-ses,-se** certificate; (Sch) report; (Referenz) reference; (fig: Beweis) evidence

Zickzack m **-[e]s,-e** zigzag

Ziege f **-,-n** goat

Ziegel m **-s,-** brick; (Dach-) tile. **Z~stein** m brick

ziehen† vt pull; (sanfter; zücken; zeichnen) draw; (heraus-) pull out; extract (Zahn); raise (Hut); put on (Bremse); move (Schachfigur); (dehnen) stretch; make (Grimasse, Scheitel); (züchten) breed; grow (Rosen); **nach sich z~** (fig) entail •vr **sich z~** (sich erstrecken) run; (sich verziehen) warp •vi (haben) pull (**an** + dat on/at); (Tee, Ofen:) draw; (Culin) simmer; **es zieht** there is a draught; **solche Filme z~ nicht mehr** films like that are no longer popular •vi (sein) (um-) move (**nach** to); (Menge:) march; (Vögel:) migrate; (Wolken, Nebel:) drift

Ziehharmonika f accordion

Ziehung f **-,-en** draw

Ziel nt **-[e]s,-e** destination; (Sport) finish; (Z~scheibe & Mil) target; (Zweck) aim, goal. **z~bewusst** adj purposeful. **z~en** vi (haben) aim (**auf** + acc at). **z~los** adj aimless. **Z~scheibe** f target

ziemlich adj [!] fair •adv rather, fairly

Zier|de f **-,-n** ornament. **z~en** vt adorn

zierlich adj dainty

Ziffer f **-,-n** figure, digit; (Zahlzeichen) numeral. **Z~blatt** nt dial

Zigarette f **-,-n** cigarette

Zigarre f **-,-n** cigar

Zigeuner(in) m **-s,-** (f **-,-nen**) gypsy

Zimmer nt **-s,-** room. **Z~mädchen** nt chambermaid. **Z~mann** m (pl **-leute**) carpenter. **Z~nachweis** m accommodation bureau. **Z~pflanze** f house plant

Zimt m **-[e]s** cinnamon

Zink nt **-s** zinc

Zinn m **-s** tin; (Gefäße) pewter

Zins|en mpl interest sg; **Z~en tragen** earn interest. **Z~eszins** m **-es,-en** compound interest. **Z~fuß, Z~satz** m interest rate

Zipfel m **-s,-** corner; (Spitze) point

zirka adv about

Zirkel m **-s,-** [pair of] compasses pl; (Gruppe) circle

Zirkul|ation /-'tsio:n/ f - circulation. **z~ieren** vi (sein) circulate

Zirkus m **-,-se** circus

zirpen vi (haben) chirp

zischen vi (haben) hiss; (Fett:) sizzle •vt hiss

Zit|at nt **-[e]s,-e** quotation. **z~ieren** vt/i (haben) quote

Zitr|onat nt **-[e]s** candied lemon-peel. **Z~one** f **-,-n** lemon

zittern vi (haben) tremble; (vor Kälte) shiver; (beben) shake

zittrig adj shaky

Zitze f **-,-n** teat

zivil adj civilian; (Ehe, Recht) civil. **Z~** nt **-s** civilian clothes pl. [C] **Z~dienst** m community service

Zivili|sation /-'tsi̯o:n/ f -,-en civilization. **z~sieren** vt civilize. **z~siert** adj civilized • adv in a civilized manner

Zivilist m **-en,-en** civilian

zögern vi (haben) hesitate. **Z~** nt **-s** hesitation. **z~d** adj hesitant

Zoll[1] m **-[e]s,-** inch

Zoll[2] m **-[e]s,¨-e** [customs] duty; (Behörde) customs pl. **Z~abfertigung** f customs clearance. **Z~beamte(r)** m customs officer. **z~frei** adj & adv duty-free. **Z~kontrolle** f customs check

Zone f **-,-n** zone

Zoo m **-s,-s** zoo

zoologisch adj zoological

Zopf m **-[e]s,¨-e** plait

Zorn m **-[e]s** anger. **z~ig** adj angry

zu

• preposition (+ dative)

> ! Note that **zu dem** can become **zum** and **zu der**, **zur**

....> (Richtung) to; (bei Beruf) into. **wir gehen zur Schule** we are going to school. **ich muss zum Arzt** I must go to the doctor's. **zu ... hin** towards. **er geht zum Theater/Militär** he is going into the theatre/army

....> (zusammen mit) with. **zu dem Käse gab es Wein** there was wine with the cheese. **zu etw passen** go with sth

....> (räumlich; zeitlich) at. **zu Hause** at home. **zu ihren Füßen** at her feet. **zu Ostern** at Easter. **zur Zeit** (+ gen) at the time of

....> (preislich) at; for. **zum halben Preis** at half price. **das Stück zu zwei Euro** at or for two euros each. **eine Marke zu 60 Cent** a 60-cent stamp

....> (Zweck, Anlass) for. **zu diesem Zweck** for this purpose. **zum Spaß** for fun. **zum Lesen** for reading. **zum Geburtstag bekam ich** ... for my birthday I got ... .

zum ersten Mal for the first time

....> (Art und Weise) **zu meinem Erstaunen/Entsetzen** to my surprise/horror. **zu Fuß/Pferde** on foot/horseback. **zu Dutzenden** by the dozen. **wir waren zu dritt/viert** there were three/four of us

....> (Zahlenverhältnis) to. **es steht 5 zu 3** the score is 5–3

....> (Ziel, Ergebnis) into. **zu etw werden** turn into sth

....> (gegenüber) to; towards. **freundlich/hässlich zu jdm sein** be friendly/nasty to s.o.

....> (über) on; about. **sich zu etw äußern** to comment on sth

• adverb

....> (allzu) too. **zu groß/viel/weit** too big/much/far

....> (Richtung) towards. **nach dem Fluss zu** towards the river

....> (geschlossen) closed; (an Schalter, Hahn) off. **Augen zu!** close your eyes! **Tür zu!** shut the door!

• conjunction

....> to. **etwas zu essen** something to eat. **nicht zu glauben** unbelievable. **zu erörternde Probleme** problems to be discussed

zualler|erst adv first of all. **z~letzt** adv last of all

Zubehör nt **-s** accessories pl

zubereit|en vt sep prepare. **Z~ung** f - preparation; (in Rezept) method

zubinden† vt sep tie [up]

zubring|en† vt sep spend. **Z~er** m **-s,-** access road; (Bus) shuttle

Zucchini /tsu'ki:ni/ pl courgettes

Zucht f **-,-en** breeding; (Pflanzen-) cultivation; (Art, Rasse) breed; (von Pflanzen) strain; (Z~farm) farm; (Pferde-) stud

zücht|en vt breed; cultivate, grow (Rosen). **Z~er** m **-s,-** breeder; grower

Zuchthaus nt prison

Züchtung f **-,-en** breeding; (Pflanzen-) cultivation; (Art, Rasse) breed; (von Pflanzen) strain

zucken vi (haben) twitch; (sich z~d

bewegen) jerk; (Blitz:) flash; (Flamme:) flicker • vt **die Achseln z~** shrug one's shoulders

Zucker m **-s** sugar. **Z~dose** f sugar basin. **Z~guss** m icing. **z~krank** adj diabetic. **Z~krankheit** f diabetes. **z~n** vt sugar. **Z~rohr** nt sugar cane. **Z~rübe** f sugar beet. **Z~watte** f candyfloss

zudecken vt sep cover up; (im Bett) tuck up; cover (Topf)

zudem adv moreover

zudrehen vt sep turn off

zueinander adv to one another; **z~ passen** go together; **z~ halten** (fig) stick together

zuerkennen† vt sep award (dat to)

zuerst adv first; (anfangs) at first

zufahr|en† vi sep (sein) **z~en auf** (+ acc) drive towards. **Z~t** f access; (Einfahrt) drive

Zufall m chance; (Zusammentreffen) coincidence; **durch Z~** by chance/ coincidence. **z~en**† vi sep (sein) close, shut; **jdm z~en** (Aufgabe:) fall/(Erbe:) go to s.o.

zufällig adj chance, accidental • adv by chance

Zuflucht f refuge; (Schutz) shelter

zufolge prep (+ dat) according to

zufrieden adj contented; (befriedigt) satisfied; **sich z~ geben** be satisfied; **jdn z~ lassen** leave s.o. in peace; **jdn z~ stellen** satisfy s.o.; **z~ stellend** satisfactory. **Z~heit** f **-** contentment; satisfaction

zufrieren† vi sep (sein) freeze over

zufügen vt sep inflict (dat on); do (Unrecht) (dat to)

Zufuhr f **-** supply

Zug m **-[e]s,⸚e** train; (Kolonne) column; (Um-) procession; (Mil) platoon; (Vogelschar) flock; (Ziehen, Zugkraft) pull; (Wandern, Ziehen) migration; (Schluck, Luft-) draught; (Atem-) breath; (beim Rauchen) puff; (Schach-) move; (beim Schwimmen, Rudern) stroke; (Gesichts-) feature; (Wesens-) trait

Zugabe f (Geschenk) [free] gift; (Mus) encore

Zugang m access

zugänglich adj accessible; (Mensch:) approachable

Zugbrücke f drawbridge

zugeben† vt sep add; (gestehen) admit; (erlauben) allow

zugehen† vi sep (sein) close; **jdm z~** be sent to s.o.; **z~ auf** (+ acc) go towards; **dem Ende z~** draw to a close; (Vorräte:) run low; **auf der Party ging es lebhaft zu** the party was pretty lively

Zugehörigkeit f **-** membership

Zügel m **-s,-** rein

zugelassen adj registered

zügel|los adj unrestrained. **z~n** vt rein in; (fig) curb

Zuge|ständnis nt concession. **z~stehen**† vt sep grant

zügig adj quick

Zugkraft f pull; (fig) attraction

zugleich adv at the same time

Zugluft f draught

zugreifen† vi sep (haben) grab it/ them; (bei Tisch) help oneself; (bei Angebot) jump at it; (helfen) lend a hand

zugrunde adv **z~ richten** destroy; **z~ gehen** be destroyed; (sterben) die; **z~ liegen** form the basis (dat of)

zugunsten prep (+ gen) in favour of; (Sammlung) in aid of

zugute adv **jdm/etw z~ kommen** benefit s.o./something

Zugvogel m migratory bird

zuhalten† v sep • vt keep closed; (bedecken) cover; **sich** (dat) **die Nase z~** hold one's nose

Zuhälter m **-s,-** pimp

zuhause adv = **zu Hause**, s. **Haus**. **Z~** nt **-s,-** home

zuhör|en vi sep (haben) listen (dat to). **Z~er(in)** m(f) listener

zujubeln vi sep (haben) **jdm z~** cheer s.o.

zukleben vt sep seal

zuknöpfen vt sep button up

zukommen† vi sep (sein) **z~ auf** (+ acc) come towards; (sich nähern) approach; **z~ lassen** send (**jdm** s.o.); devote (Pflege) (dat to); **jdm z~** be s.o.'s right

Zukunft f - future. **zukünftig** adj future • adv in future

zulächeln vi sep (haben) smile (dat at)

zulangen vi sep (haben) help oneself

zulassen† vt sep allow, permit; (teilnehmen lassen) admit; (Admin) license, register; (geschlossen lassen) leave closed; leave unopened (Brief)

zulässig adj permissible

Zulassung f **-,-en** admission; registration; (Lizenz) licence

zuleide adv **jdm etwas z~ tun** hurt s.o.

zuletzt adv last; (schließlich) in the end

zuliebe adv **jdm/etw z~** for the sake of someone/something

zum prep = **zu dem; zum Spaß** for fun; **etw zum Lesen** sth to read

zumachen v sep • vt close, shut; do up (Jacke); seal (Umschlag); turn off (Hahn); (stilllegen) close down • vi (haben) close, shut; (stillgelegt werden) close down

zumal adv especially • conj especially since

zumindest adv at least

zumutbar adj reasonable

zumute adv **mir ist nicht danach z~** I don't feel like it

zumut|en vt sep **jdm etw z~en** ask or expect sth of s.o.; **sich** (dat) **zu viel z~en** overdo things. **Z~ung** f - imposition

zunächst adv first [of all]; (anfangs) at first; (vorläufig) for the moment • prep (+ dat) nearest to

Zunahme f **-,-n** increase

Zuname m surname

zünd|en vt/i (haben) ignite. **Z~er** m **-s,-** detonator, fuse. **Z~holz** nt match. **Z~kerze** f sparking-plug. **Z~schlüssel** m ignition key. **Z~schnur** f fuse. **Z~ung** f **-,-en** ignition

zunehmen† vi sep (haben) increase (**an** + dat in); (Mond:) wax; (an Gewicht) put on weight. **z~d** adj increasing

Zuneigung f - affection

Zunft f **-,¨e** guild

Zunge f **-,-n** tongue. **Z~nbrecher** m tongue-twister

zunutze adj **sich** (dat) **etw z~ machen** make use of sth; (ausnutzen) take advantage of sth

zuoberst adv right at the top

zuordnen vt sep assign (dat to)

zupfen vt/i (haben) pluck (**an** + dat at); pull out (Unkraut)

zur prep = **zu der; zur Schule** to school; **zur Zeit** at present

zurate adv **z~ ziehen** consult

zurechnungsfähig adj of sound mind

zurecht|finden† **(sich)** vr sep find one's way. **z~kommen**† vi sep (sein) cope (**mit** with); (rechtzeitig kommen) be in time. **z~legen** vt sep put out ready; **sich** (dat) **eine Ausrede z~legen** have an excuse all ready. **z~machen** vt sep get ready. **Z~weisung** f reprimand

zureden vi sep (haben) **jdm z~** try to persuade s.o.

zurichten vt sep prepare; (beschädigen) damage; (verletzen) injure

zuriegeln vt sep bolt

zurück adv back; **Berlin, hin und z~** return to Berlin. **z~bekommen**† vt sep get back. **z~bleiben**† vi sep (sein) stay behind; (nicht mithalten) lag behind. **z~bringen**† vt sep bring back; (wieder hinbringen) take back. **z~erstatten** vt sep refund. **z~fahren**† v sep • vt drive back • vi (sein) return, go back; (im Auto) drive back; (z~weichen) recoil. **z~finden**† vi sep (haben) find one's way back. **z~führen** v sep • vt take back; (fig) attribute (**auf** + acc to) • vi (haben) lead back. **z~geben**† vt sep give back, return. **z~geblieben** adj retarded. **z~gehen**† vi sep (sein) go back, return; (abnehmen) go down; **z~gehen auf** (+ acc) (fig) go back to

zurückgezogen adj secluded. **Z~heit** f - seclusion

zurückhalt|en† vt sep hold back; (abhalten) stop; **sich z~en** restrain oneself. **z~end** adj reserved. **Z~ung** f - reserve

zurück|kehren vi sep (sein) return. **z~kommen**† vi sep (sein) come back, return; (ankommen) get back. **z~lassen**† vt sep leave behind; (z~kehren lassen) allow back. **z~legen** vt sep put back; (reservieren) keep; (sparen) put by; cover (Strecke). **z~liegen**† vi sep (haben) be in the past; (Sport) be behind; **das liegt lange zurück** that was long ago. **z~melden (sich)** vr sep report back. **z~schicken** vt sep send back. **z~schlagen**† v sep • vi (haben) hit back • vt hit back; (umschlagen) turn back. **z~schrecken**† vi sep (sein) shrink back, recoil; (fig) shrink (**vor** + dat from). **z~stellen** vt sep put back; (reservieren) keep; (fig) put aside; (aufschieben) postpone. **z~stoßen**† v sep • vt push back • vi (sein) reverse, back. **z~treten**† vi sep (sein) step back; (vom Amt) resign; (verzichten) withdraw. **z~weisen**† vt sep turn away; (fig) reject. **z~zahlen** vt sep pay back. **z~ziehen**† vt sep draw back; (fig) withdraw; **sich z~ziehen** withdraw; (vom Beruf) retire

Zuruf m shout. **z~en**† vt sep shout (dat to)

zurzeit adv at present

Zusage f -,-n acceptance; (Versprechen) promise. **z~n** v sep • vt promise • vi (haben) accept

zusammen adv together; (insgesamt) altogether; **z~ sein** be together. **Z~arbeit** f co-operation. **z~arbeiten** vi sep (haben) co-operate. **z~bauen** vt sep assemble. **z~bleiben**† vi sep (sein) stay together. **z~brechen**† vi sep (sein) collapse. **Z~bruch** m collapse; (Nerven- & fig) breakdown. **z~fallen**† vi sep (sein) collapse; (zeitlich) coincide. **z~fassen** vt sep summarize, sum up. **Z~fassung** f summary. **z~fügen** vt sep fit together. **z~gehören** vi sep (haben) belong together; (z~passen) go together. **z~gesetzt** adj (Gram) compound. **z~halten**† v sep • vt hold together; (beisammenhalten) keep together • vi (haben) (fig) stick together. **Z~hang** m connection; (Kontext) context. **z~hanglos** adj incoherent. **z~klappen** v sep • vt fold up • vi (sein) collapse. **z~kommen**† vi sep (sein) meet; (sich sammeln) accumulate. **Z~kunft** f -,¨e meeting. **z~laufen**† vi sep (sein) gather; (Flüssigkeit:) collect; (Linien:) converge. **z~leben** vi sep (haben) live together. **z~legen** v sep • vt put together; (z~falten) fold up; (vereinigen) amalgamate; pool (Geld) • vi (haben) club together. **z~nehmen**† vt sep gather up; summon up (Mut); collect (Gedanken); **sich z~nehmen** pull oneself together. **z~passen** vi sep (haben) go together, match. **Z~prall** m collision. **z~rechnen** vt sep add up. **z~schlagen**† vt sep smash up; (prügeln) beat up. **z~schließen**† **(sich)** vr sep join together; (Firmen:) merge. **Z~schluss** m union; (Comm) merger

Zusammensein nt -s get-together

zusammensetz|en vt sep put together; (Techn) assemble; **sich z~en** sit [down] together; (bestehen) be made up (**aus** from). **Z~ung** f -,-en composition; (Techn) assembly; (Wort) compound

zusammen|stellen vt sep put together; (gestalten) compile. **Z~stoß** m collision; (fig) clash. **z~treffen**† vi sep (sein) meet; (zeitlich) coincide. **z~zählen** vt sep add up. **z~ziehen**† v sep • vt draw together; (addieren) add up; (konzentrieren) mass; **sich z~ziehen**

contract; (Gewitter:) gather • vi (sein) move in together; move in (**mit** with)

Zusatz m addition; (Jur) rider; (Lebensmittel-) additive. **zusätzlich** adj additional • adv in addition

zuschau|en vi sep (haben) watch. **Z~er(in)** m **-s,-** (f **-,-nen**) spectator; (TV) viewer

Zuschlag m surcharge; (Zug) supplement. **z~pflichtig** adj (Zug) for which a supplement is payable

zuschließen† v sep • vt lock • vi (haben) lock up

zuschneiden† vt sep cut out; cut to size (Holz)

zuschreiben† vt sep attribute (dat to); **jdm die Schuld z~** blame s.o.

Zuschrift f letter; (auf Annonce) reply

zuschulden adv **sich** (dat) **etwas z~ kommen lassen** do wrong

Zuschuss m contribution; (staatlich) subsidy

zusehends adv visibly

zusein* vi sep (sein) = **zu sein**, s. **zu**

zusenden† vt sep send (dat to)

zusetzen v sep • vt add; (einbüßen) lose

zusicher|n vt sep promise. **Z~ung** f promise.

zuspielen vt sep (Sport) pass

zuspitzen (sich) vr sep (fig) become critical

Zustand m condition, state

zustande adv **z~ bringen/kommen** bring/come about

zuständig adj competent; (verantwortlich) responsible

zustehen† vi sep (haben) **jdm z~** be s.o.'s right; (Urlaub:) be due to s.o.

zusteigen† vi sep (sein) get on; **noch jemand zugestiegen?** ≈ tickets please; (im Bus) ≈ any more fares please?

zustell|en vt sep block; (bringen) deliver. **Z~ung** f delivery

zusteuern v sep • vi (sein) head (**auf** + acc for) • vt contribute

zustimm|en vi sep (haben) agree; (billigen) approve (dat of). **Z~ung** f consent; approval

zustoßen† vi sep (sein) happen (dat to)

Zustrom m influx

Zutat f (Culin) ingredient

zuteil|en vt sep allocate; assign (Aufgabe). **Z~ung** f allocation

zutiefst adv deeply

zutragen† vt sep carry/(fig) report (dat to); **sich z~** happen

zutrau|en vt sep **jdm etw z~** believe s.o. capable of sth. **Z~en** nt **-s** confidence

zutreffen† vi sep (haben) be correct; **z~ auf** (+ acc) apply to

Zutritt m admittance

zuunterst adv right at the bottom

zuverlässig adj reliable. **Z~keit** f - reliability

Zuversicht f - confidence. **z~lich** adj confident

zuviel* pron & adv = **zu viel**, s. **viel**

zuvor adv before; (erst) first

zuvorkommen† vi sep (sein) (+ dat) anticipate. **z~d** adj obliging

Zuwachs m **-es** increase

Zuwanderung f immigration

zuwege adv **z~ bringen** achieve

zuweilen adv now and then

zuweisen† vt sep assign

Zuwendung f donation; (Fürsorge) care

zuwenig* pron & adv = **zu wenig**, s. **wenig**

zuwerfen† vt sep slam (Tür); **jdm etw z~** throw s.o. sth

zuwider adv **jdm z~ sein** be repugnant to s.o. • prep (+ dat) contrary to

zuzahlen vt sep pay extra

zuziehen† v sep • vt pull tight; draw (Vorhänge); (hinzu-) call in; **sich** (dat) **etw z~** contract (Krankheit);

sustain (Verletzung); incur (Zorn) • vi (sein) move into the area

zuzüglich prep (+ gen) plus

Zwang m -[e]s,⁻e compulsion; (Gewalt) force; (Verpflichtung) obligation

zwängen vt squeeze

zwanglos adj informal. **Z~igkeit** f - informality

Zwangsjacke f straitjacket

zwanzig inv adj twenty. **z~ste(r,s)** adj twentieth

zwar adv admittedly

Zweck m -[e]s,-e purpose; (Sinn) point. **z~los** adj pointless. **z~mäßig** adj suitable; (praktisch) functional

zwei inv adj, **Z~** f -,-en two; (Sch) ≈ B. **Z~bettzimmer** nt twin-bedded room

zweideutig adj ambiguous

zwei|erlei inv adj two kinds of • pron two things. **z~fach** adj double

Zweifel m -s,- doubt. **z~haft** adj doubtful; (fragwürdig) dubious. **z~los** adv undoubtedly. **z~n** vi (haben) doubt (**an etw** dat sth)

Zweig m -[e]s,-e branch. **Z~stelle** f branch [office]

Zwei|kampf m duel. **z~mal** adv twice. **z~reihig** adj (Anzug) double-breasted. **z~sprachig** adj bilingual

zweit adv **zu z~** in twos; **wir waren zu z~** there were two of us. **z~beste(r,s)** adj second-best. **z~e(r,s)** adj second

zweitens adv secondly

Zwerchfell nt diaphragm

Zwerg m -[e]s,-e dwarf

Zwickel m -s,- gusset

zwicken vt/i (haben) pinch

Zwieback m -[e]s,⁻e rusk

Zwiebel f -,-n onion; (Blumen-)bulb

Zwielicht nt half-light; (Dämmerlicht) twilight. **z~ig** adj shady

Zwiespalt m conflict

Zwilling m -s,-e twin; **Z~e** (Astrology) Gemini

zwingen† vt force; **sich z~** force oneself. **z~d** adj compelling

Zwinger m -s,- run; (Zucht-) kennels pl

zwinkern vi (haben) blink; (als Zeichen) wink

Zwirn m -[e]s button thread

zwischen prep (+ dat/acc) between; (unter) among[st]. **Z~bemerkung** f interjection. **z~durch** adv in between; (in der Z~zeit) in the meantime. **Z~fall** m incident. **Z~landung** f stopover. **Z~raum** m gap, space. **Z~wand** f partition. **Z~zeit** f **in der Z~zeit** in the meantime

Zwist m -[e]s,-e discord; (Streit) feud

zwitschern vi (haben) chirp

zwo inv adj two

zwölf inv adj twelve. **z~te(r,s)** adj twelfth

Zylind|er m -s,- cylinder; (Hut) top hat. **z~risch** adj cylindrical

Zyn|iker m -s,- cynic. **z~isch** adj cynical. **Z~ismus** m - cynicism

Zypern nt -s Cyprus

Zypresse f -,-n cypress

Zyste /ˈtsʏstə/ f -,-n cyst

Games, Culture, Letter-Writing

Test yourself with word games

This section contains a number of word games which will help you to use your dictionary more effectively and to build up your knowledge of German vocabulary and usage an entertaining way. You will find answers to all puzzles and games at the end of the section.

1 Join Up the Nouns

These German nouns are all made up of two separate words, but they have split apart. Draw a line between two pieces of paper that make up a noun. Watch out: one of the first words goes with two of the second words!

When you've made all the German words, do the same for the English translations and match them up with the German.

Flug
Wetter
Auto
Stadt
Post
Blumen

karte
bericht
mitte
topf
hafen
bahn
plan

street
town
motor
post
weather
flower
air

pot
card
centre
way
map
report
port

2 Wordsearch

Fifteen German words are hidden among the letters in the grid. Can you find them all? Watch out: six of the words read downwards, while all the others read across.

To help you, here are the English meanings of the German words. You can tick them off as you find the German.

ace
almost
also
better
daughter
opera
powder
quay
rough
save
speak
ten
under
village
wide

M	W	N	B	U	N	T	E	R	V
Z	E	H	N	C	X	Z	L	K	J
H	I	G	F	P	U	L	V	E	R
D	T	O	C	H	T	E	R	S	A
D	S	P	R	E	C	H	E	N	P
O	B	E	S	S	E	R	A	O	I
R	U	R	K	U	F	A	S	T	A
F	Y	T	A	R	E	W	S	Q	U
Z	X	C	I	V	B	R	A	U	C
N	R	E	T	T	E	N	M	L	H

3 Odd Meaning Out

One word can have several different meanings. In the following exercise, only two of the three English translations given for each German word are correct. Use the dictionary to spot the odd one out, and then look up the right German translation for it:

fordern	demand challenge convince
Schnee	snow icing beaten egg-white
patent	obvious resourceful clever
Haken	tick hake hook
Brause	bruise fizzy drink shower
neben	next to apart from foggy
Pilz	mushroom fungus beer
schwer	swift difficult heavy
gerade	straight grand even
drehen	turn shoot catch
Strom	power storm stream
Blase	blanket blister bladder

4 Troubleshooting

Our computer has developed some annoying little problems. Can you help put them right?

First, when we type any three-letter word beginning with d, the computer shows three d's on the screen! The problem words are all highlighted in our "Recipe of the Week". Can you correct them in the box above each word?

Ddd Rezept ddd Woche

Für ddd Kuchenteig ddd Butter in Stückchen schneiden und mit ddd Mehl vermischen. Ddd Gemisch mit ddd Honig und ddd Milch zu einem festen Teig verarbeiten. Ddd Äpfel waschen, halbieren und in ddd Pfanne mit ddd Butter, ddd Zimt und ddd Zitronensaft aufkochen lassen. Ddd Teig in ddd Form geben und mit ddd Obst belegen. Ddd Kuchen in ddd Backofen schieben und 35 Minuten backen.

5 Crossword

If you need to, you can use the dictionary to solve this crossword. Just translate the clues into German, and write the translations in capital letters.

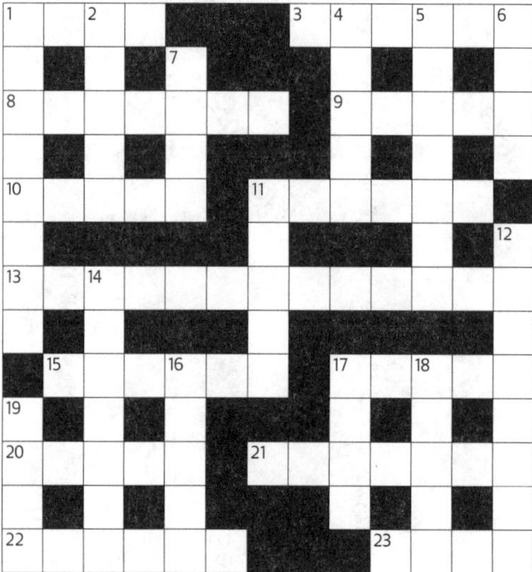

Across

1 mature (4)
3 journeys (6)
8 advertisement, small ad (7)
9 pale (adjective) (5)
10 to hurry (5)
11 few (6)
13 a (male) industrialist (13)
15 to catch (6)
17 (male) Russian (5)
20 price or prize (5)
21 bags or pockets (7)
22 saddle (noun) (6)
23 stove (4)

Down

1 (female) rider (8)
2 island (5)
4 heiress (5)
5 asparagus (7)
6 nest (4)
7 crane (machine) (4)
11 goods, or (they) were (5)
12 to appoint (8)
14 dialect (7)
16 alley (5)
17 pink (4)
18 sheep (5)
19 epic (noun) (4)

6 Curly Words

One word is missing in each of the curly lists. Which day, month, capital city, and number are missing?

Can you write out the four lists in the right order?

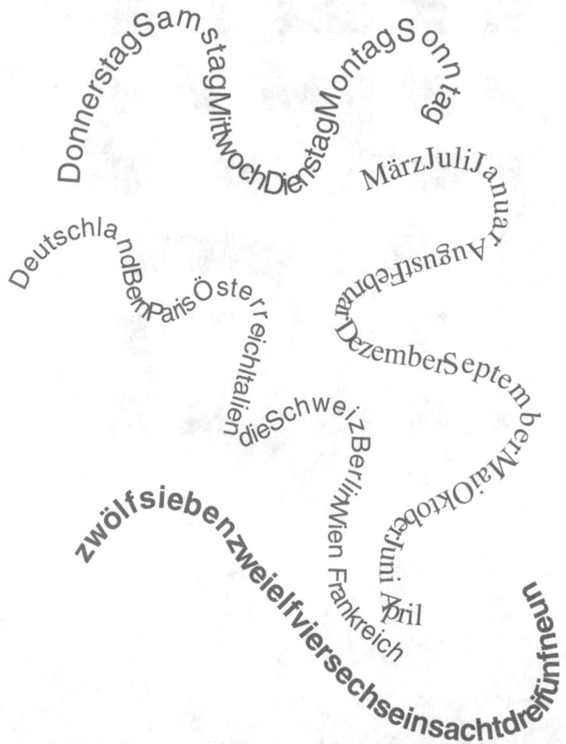

7 Sporting Links

Can you match each piece of sporting equipment to the right sport? Can you translate the sports into German?

das Seil	**archery**
die Zielscheibe	**tennis**
der Schlittschuh	**skittles**
der Tennisschläger	**surfing**
der Kegel	**mountaineering**
der Ski	**football**
der Federball	**swimming**
das Segel	**golf**
die Kugel	**skating**
der Fußball	**riding**
die Flosse	**cycling**
der Zügel	**gymnastics**
das Sprungbrett	**skiing**
das Fahrrad	**fencing**
der Golfschläger	**diving**
die Turnschuhe	**shot-put**
das Florett	**sailing**
das Surfbrett	**badminton**

Answers

1

Flughafen	airport
Wetterbericht	weather report
Autobahn	motorway
Stadtmitte	town centre
Stadtplan	street map
Postkarte	postcard
Blumentopf	flowerpot

2

Ass	ace	rau	rough
fast	almost	retten	save
auch	also	sprechen	speak
besser	better	zehn	ten
Tochter	daughter	unter	under
Oper	opera	Dorf	village
Pulver	powder	weit	wide
Kai	quay		

3

convince	überzeugen
icing	Zuckerguss
obvious	offensichtlich
hake	Seehecht
bruise	blauer Fleck
foggy	neblig
beer	Bier
swift	schnell
grand	großartig
catch	fangen
storm	Sturm
blanket	Decke

4

Das Rezept **der** Woche

Für **den** Kuchenteig **die** Butter in Stückchen schneiden und mit **dem** Mehl vermischen. **Das** Gemisch mit **dem** Honig und **der** Milch zu einem festen Teig verarbeiten. **Die** Äpfel waschen, halbieren und in **der** Pfanne mit **der** Butter, **dem** Zimt und **dem** Zitronensaft aufkochen lassen. **Den** Teig in **die** Form geben und mit **dem** Obst belegen. **Den** Kuchen in **den** Backofen schieben und 35 Minuten backen.

5

6

Freitag; Sonntag, Montag, Dienstag, Mittwoch, Donnerstag, Freitag, Samstag;
November; Januar, Februar, März, April, Mai, Juni, Juli, August, September, **Oktober**, November, Dezember;
Rom; Deutschland/Berlin, Österreich/Wien, die Schweiz/Bern, Frankreich/Paris, Italien/Rom;
zehn; eins, zwei, drei, vier, fünf, sechs, sieben, acht, neun, zehn, elf, zwölf.

7

das Fahrrad	bicycle	cycling	das Radfahren
der Federball	shuttlecock	badminton	der Federball
das Florett	foil	fencing	das Fechten
die Flosse	flipper	swimming	das Schwimmen
der Fußball	football	football	der Fußball
der Golfschläger	golf-club	golf	das Golf
der Kegel	skittle	skittles	das Kegeln
die Kugel	shot	shot-put	das Kugelstoßen
der Schlittschuh	ice-skate	skating	das Eislaufen
das Segel	sail	sailing	der Segelsport
das Seil	rope	mountaineering	das Bergsteigen
der Ski	ski	skiing	das Skilaufen
das Sprungbrett	springboard	diving	das Kunstspringen
das Surfbrett	surfboard	surfing	das Surfen
der Tennisschläger	tennis-racket	tennis	das Tennis
die Turnschuhe	gym shoes	gymnastics	das Turnen
die Zielscheibe	target	archery	das Bogenschießen
der Zügel	rein	riding	das Reiten

Calendar of traditions, festivals, and holidays in German-speaking countries

January

1 8 15 22 29
2 9 16 23 30
3 10 17 24 31
4 11 18 25
5 12 19 26
6 13 20 27
7 14 21 28

February

1 8 15 22
2 9 16 23
3 10 17 24
4 11 18 25
5 12 19 26
6 13 20 27
7 **14** 21 28

March

1 8 15 22 29
2 9 16 23 30
3 10 17 24 31
4 11 18 25
5 12 19 26
6 13 20 27
7 14 21 28

April

1 8 15 22 29
2 9 16 23 30
3 10 17 24 31
4 11 18 25
5 12 19 26
6 13 20 27
7 **14** 21 28

May

1 8 15 22 29
2 9 16 23 30
3 10 17 24 31
4 11 18 25
5 12 19 26
6 13 20 27
7 14 21 28

June

1 8 15 22 29
2 9 16 23 30
3 10 17 24
4 11 18 25
5 12 19 26
6 13 20 27
7 14 21 28

July

1 8 15 22 29
2 9 16 23 30
3 10 17 24 31
4 11 18 25
5 12 19 26
6 13 20 27
7 14 21 28

August

1 8 15 22 29
2 9 16 23 30
3 10 17 24 31
4 11 18 25
5 12 19 26
6 13 20 27
7 14 21 28

September

1 8 15 22 29
2 9 16 23 30
3 10 17 24
4 11 18 25
5 12 19 26
6 13 20 27
7 14 21 28

October

1 8 15 22 29
2 9 16 23 30
3 10 17 24 **31**
4 11 18 25
5 12 19 **26**
6 13 20 27
7 14 21 28

November

1 8 15 22 29
2 9 16 23 30
3 10 17 24
4 **11** 18 25
5 12 19 26
6 13 20 27
7 14 21 28

December

1 8 15 22 29
2 9 16 23 30
3 10 17 **24** **31**
4 11 18 **25**
5 12 19 **26**
6 13 20 27
7 14 21 28

1 January

Neujahr New Year's Day is always a public holiday and tends to be a quiet day when people are recovering from the *Silvester* celebrations.

6 January

Heilige Drei Könige Epiphany or Twelfth Night is a public holiday in Austria and some parts of southern Germany. In some areas, children dressed up as the Three Kings go from house to house to bless the homes for the coming year and collect money for charity. This is also traditionally the day when the Christmas tree is taken down.

2 February

Mariä Lichtmess Candlemas is celebrated in the Catholic church but is not a public holiday.

1 April

Erster April April Fool's Day is the time to make an April fool of your family and friends (*jdn. in den April schicken*) or to play an April fool trick (*Aprilscherz*).

1 May

Erster Mai May Day is a public holiday in Germany, Austria, and Switzerland. It is celebrated by trade unions as *Labour Day*, often with rallies and demonstrations. Many people simply use the day for a family outing or picnic, and in rural areas maypoles are put up in the villages.

3 October

Tag der deutschen Einheit Germany's national holiday, the *Day of German Unity* commemorates German reunification on 3 October 1990.

26 October

Nationalfeiertag Austria's national holiday.

31 October

Reformationstag Reformation Day is a public holiday in some mainly Protestant parts of Germany and commemorates the Reformation.

1 November

Allerheiligen All Saints' Day is a public holiday in Catholic parts of Germany and Austria.

2 November

Allerseelen All Souls' Day is the day when Catholics remember their dead by visiting the cemeteries to pray and place wreaths, flowers, and lighted candles on the graves. This is often done on 1 November as *Allerseelen* is not a public holiday.

11 November

Martinstag St Martin's day is not a public holiday, but in Catholic areas the charitable Saint is commemorated with processions where children carry lanterns and sing songs. Traditional food includes the *Martinsgans* (roast goose) and *Martinsbrezel* (a kind of soft pretzel).

6 December

Nikolaustag On the eve of St Nicholas' Day, children put out their boots in the hope of finding presents and fruit, nuts, and sweets in the morning. The

Saint may also turn up in person, looking much like Santa Claus or Father Christmas.

24 December

Heiligabend Christmas Eve is not a public holiday but many firms and shops close early for the Christmas period. This is the day when traditionally the Christmas tree is put up and decorated. Christmas presents are given in the evening, and many people attend midnight mass.

25 December

Erster Weihnachtstag Christmas Day is a public holiday in Germany, Austria, and Switzerland. It tends to be a quiet day for family get-togethers, often with a traditional lunch of goose or carp.

26 December

Zweiter Weihnachtstag Boxing Day is a public holiday in Germany, Austria, and Switzerland. In Austria and Switzerland it is called *Stephanstag* (St Stephen's day).

31 December

Silvester New Year's Eve is not a bank holiday, but firms and shops tend to close early. A party, or at least a meal with friends, is a must for *Silvester* evening. At midnight, the new year is toasted in Sekt (German sparkling wine), and everybody goes outside to admire the fireworks.

Movable feasts

Rosenmontag The day before Shrove Tuesday is not an official public holiday but many people, especially in the Rhineland, get the day off work or school to take part in the *Karneval* celebrations, which involve masked balls, fancy-dress parties, and parades. The street parades in Düsseldorf, Cologne, Mainz, and other cities are attended by thousands of revellers and shown live on television.

Faschingsdienstag Shrove Tuesday is the final day of *Fasching* (Carnival) in Southern Germany, with processions and fancy dress parties similar to Rosenmontag in the Northwest. In the far south, ancient customs to drive out the winter with bells and drums survive. The pre-Lent carnival in and around the Rhineland is called Karneval. Almost every town has its own carnival prince and princess, and organizes a street parade with decorated floats, which is watched by thousands of revellers in fancy dress.

Aschermittwoch Ash Wednesday marks the end of the carnival season and the beginning of Lent. This day is celebrated in the Catholic Church but is not a public holiday.

Karfreitag Good Friday is a public holiday and generally a very quiet day.

Catholics traditionally eat fish on this day.

Ostern Easter traditions include hiding Easter eggs (often dyed hardboiled eggs, or the chocolate variety) in the garden for the children. The *Osterhase* (Easter bunny) is supposed to have brought them. Ostermontag (Easter Monday) is also a public holiday.

Weißer Sonntag (Sunday after Easter) In the Catholic Church, first communion is traditionally taken on this Sunday.

Muttertag (second Sunday in May) On Mothers' Day, children of all ages give their mothers small gifts, cards, or flowers.

Christi Himmelfahrt (40 days after Easter) Ascension day is a public holiday in Germany, Austria, and Switzerland. This day is also Fathers' day when fathers traditionally go out on daytrips or pub crawls.

Pfingsten (seventh Sunday after Easter) As *Pfingstmontag* (Whit Monday) is also a public holiday in Germany, Austria, and Switzerland, Whitsun is a popular time to have a long weekend away.

Fronleichnam (second Thursday after Whitsun) Corpus Christi is a public holiday in Austria and in parts of Germany and Switzerland. In Catholic areas, processions and open-air masses are held.

Buß- und Bettag (third Wednesday in November, 11 days before the first Advent Sunday) This 'day of repentance and prayer' is a public holiday only in some parts of Germany.

Volkstrauertag (second Sunday before the beginning of Advent) In Germany, this is a national day of mourning to commemorate the dead of both world wars, and the victims of the Nazis.

Totensonntag (last Sunday before the beginning of Advent) Protestants remember their dead on this day.

Advent The four weeks leading up to Christmas, beginning with the **1. Adventssonntag** (first Sunday in Advent) in late November or early December, still have a special significance in Germany, even for non-religious people. An Advent wreath with four candles is present in almost every German household during this time, and on each Sunday of Advent one more candle is lit.

A–Z of German life and culture

Abendbrot, Abendessen

For most Germans, MITTAGESSEN is still the main meal of the day. *Abendbrot* or *Abendessen* normally consists of bread, cheese, meats, perhaps a salad, and a hot drink. It is eaten by the whole family at about 6 or 7 p.m. *Abendessen* can also refer to a cooked meal, especially for people who are out at work all day.

Abitur

This is the final exam taken by pupils at a GYMNASIUM, usually when they are about 19. The result is based on continuous assessment during the last two years before the *Abitur*, plus examinations in four subjects. The *Abitur* is the obligatory qualification for university entrance.

Ampel-Koalition

A term describing any coalition between the SPD (the party colour is red), the FDP (yellow), and the Green Party. This type of coalition has become increasingly common in local government over the last ten years, with some LÄNDER ruled in this way.

AOK - Allgemeine Ortskrankenkasse

The largest health insurance organization in Germany. Foreign visitors to Germany who need medical assistance can get the necessary forms at the local *AOK* office.

Arbeitsamt

The local employment office to be found in every German town. It provides career guidance, helps the unemployed find new jobs, and processes all claims for ARBEITSLOSENGELD and related benefits. Unemployed people have to report to the *Arbeitsamt* once every three months to prove they are still looking for work.

Arbeitslosengeld

This is the benefit paid to all unemployed people who are looking for a new job and have already made a minimum contribution to the ARBEITSLOSENVERSICHERUNG. The benefit is a proportion of the person's previous pay, and is higher for people supporting children. After one year, it is reduced and called *Arbeitslosenhilfe*.

Arbeitslosenversicherung

This is the compulsory state-run insurance against unemployment. All *Arbeiter* and *Angestellte* have to pay into this scheme and in return are entitled to ARBEITSLOSENGELD and related benefits. This area has been subject to wide-ranging reforms in recent years.

ARD

An umbrella organization for the regional broadcasting stations of the various German LÄNDER, financed by licence fees plus a certain amount of advertising. The *ARD* broadcasts DAS ERSTE.

Autobahn
Germany's motorway network is very extensive and not subject to a general speed limit, other than a recommended limit of about 80 mph. Many motorways have only two lanes. To ease congestion, lorries are not allowed to use the *Autobahn* on Sundays.

BAföG - Bundesausbildungsförderungsgesetz
The grant which about a quarter of German students receive from the state. Whether they are entitled to *BAföG*, and how much they get, depends on the students' and their parents' financial circumstances. Half of the money is given in the form of a loan which has to be repaid later.

Bayern
Bayern (Bavaria), Germany's largest and southernmost land, is known for its beautiful scenery (the Alps and their foothills, as well as forests, rivers, and lakes, picturesque towns and villages), its excellent beer and food, and its lively cosmopolitan capital München (Munich). The Bavarians are said to be warm and hospitable, but also fiercely independent and very conservative.

Bayreuth
The Bavarian city of Bayeuth is a magnet for opera fans. The German composer Richard Wagner (1813–83) lived there, and since 1876 the Richard Wagner Festival has been staged annually. The Bayeuth festival theatre was built by Ludwig II, King of Bavaria, who was Wagner's greatest admirer.

Beamte
This term covers civil servants and other officials, but also occupations like teachers and lecturers. *Beamte* are legally obliged to support the democratic system in Germany and are not allowed to go on strike. In return, they enjoy many privileges, such as total job security, private health insurance, and exemption from social security contributions.

Berlin
After WIEDERVEREINIGUNG, Berlin took over from Bonn as the capital of Germany, but the German government did not start moving there until 1998. This vibrant city in the heart of Europe lies on the river Spree. It has about 3.5 million inhabitants and is a major cultural and industrial centre.

Berufsausbildung
▶ LEHRE.

Berufsschule
A college for young people who are doing a LEHRE. They attend *Berufsschule* 2 days a week (or sometimes in blocks of several weeks) to continue their general education and receive formal training in their chosen type of job.

Besenwirtschaft
An inn set up by a local wine-grower for a few weeks after the new wine has been made. An inflated pig's bladder is hung up outside the door to show that the new vintage may be sampled there. This is mainly found in Southern Germany.

Bier

Germany and Austria rank among the world's top beer consumers. Germans brew more than 5000 varieties, and each beer tastes different. German beer is brewed according to the *Reinheitsgebot* (brewing regulations) of 1516, which stipulate that no ingredients other than hops, malted barley, yeast and water may be used. The standard pale ale or lager is a Helles, a dark beer is a *Dunkles*, and a wheat beer is a *Weißbier* (south), *Weizenbier* (north-west) and *Weiße* (Berlin). A *Biergarten* is a rustic open-air pub, or beer garden, which is traditional in Bavaria and Austria.

Biergarten

A rustic open-air pub which is traditional in Bavaria but can now be found throughout Germany. It is usually set up for the summer in the yard of a pub or restaurant. A *Biergarten* is the best place to enjoy a beer and a simple meal on a summer's day.

Bild Zeitung

Germany's largest-selling daily newspaper, *Bild* is a typical tabloid with huge headlines, lots of photos, scandal stories, gossip, and nude models. It is known for its right-wing views. *Bild* sells about 4.5 million copies every day, almost eight times more than any other newspaper in Germany. Its Sunday edition is called *Bild am Sonntag*.

Bodensee

This is the German name for Lake Constance, Germany's biggest lake, bordered by Germany, Switzerland, and Austria. The river Rhine flows through it. This popular recreation area enjoys a particularly mild climate, especially on the three islands Lindau, Mainau, and Reichenau.

Bonn

Bonn was the capital of the Federal Republic of Germany from 1949 until **BERLIN** was made the capital of a reunified Germany and it remains home to a number of government institutions. This relatively small, quiet city of about 300,000 inhabitants enjoys a picturesque location on the river Rhine.

Bund

This term refers to the federal state as the top level of government, as opposed to the individual **LÄNDER** which make up the Federal Republic. *Bund* and *Länder* have different responsibilities, with the *Bund* in charge of foreign policy, defence, transport, health, employment, etc.

Bundesbank

Properly called the *Deutsche Bundesbank*, Germany's central bank is located in Frankfurt/Main. With the introduction of the Euro in 1999, some of its functions have passed to the European Central Bank (also in Frankfurt).

Bundeskanzler

The Chancellor is the head of government in Germany and Austria. The German chancellor is normally elected for 4 years by the MPs in the BUNDESTAG after being proposed by the BUNDESPRÄSIDENT. He chooses the ministers and decides on government policies.

Bundesland

▶ LAND.

Bundespräsident

The President is the head of state in Germany and Austria. The German president is elected for 5 years by the MPs and delegates from the LÄNDER. He (so far there have not been any women) acts mainly as a figurehead, representing Germany abroad, and does not get involved in party politics, although he often takes a moral lead in major issues like the reform of the education system.

Bundesrat

This is the upper house of the German parliamentary system, where the LÄNDER are represented. The *Bundesrat* members are appointed by the Länder governments. It has to approve laws affecting the *Länder*, and also any changes to the GRUNDGESETZ. Sometimes the opposition parties actually hold a majority in the *Bundesrat*, which allows them to influence German legislation.

Bundestag

The lower house of the German parliament, which is elected every four years by the German people. The *Bundestag* is responsible for federal legislation, the federal budget, and electing the BUNDESKANZLER. Half of the MPs are elected directly and half by proportional representation, in a complicated voting system where each voter has two votes.

Bundeswappen

▶ WAPPEN

Bundeswehr

This is the name for the German armed forces, which come under the control of the defence minister. The *Bundeswehr* consists of professional soldiers and conscripts serving their WEHRDIENST. Until 1994, the GRUNDGESETZ did not allow German forces to be deployed abroad, but they now take part in certain operations, notably UN peacekeeping missions.

Bündnis 90/Die Grünen

This party came into being in 1993 as the result of a merger of the West German Green party and civil rights movements of the former GDR. It is the third largest force in the German parliament, committed to environmental and social issues.

CDU - Christlich-Demokratische Union

One of the main German political parties. It was founded in 1945 and is committed to Christian and conservative values. The *CDU* is not active in Bavaria.

▶ CSU.

Christkind

Traditionally, it is *Das Christkind* (the Christ Child) who brings Christmas presents to children on Christmas Eve. The concept of *der Weihnachtsmann* (Father Christmas) is relatively new in Germany.

CSU - Christlich-Soziale Union

The Bavarian sister party of the CDU. It was founded in 1946 and has enjoyed an absolute majority in Bavaria for over 30 years. Politically, it stands to the right of the *CDU*.

Das Erste

Also called **ERSTES PROGRAMM**, this is the first German public TV channel, broadcast by ARD. Programming includes news, information, films, and entertainment. There is a limited amount of advertising, which is concentrated in 'blocks' at certain times of day and not after 8 p.m.

Der Spiegel

One of Germany's best-selling weekly news and current affairs magazines, *Der Spiegel* was founded in 1947 and is published in Hamburg. It has a liberal to left-wing outlook and has become synonymous with investigative journalism in Germany, as it has brought to light a number of major scandals in German business and politics over the years.

Deutsche Post

The previously state-run German postal system has undergone wide-ranging reforms in recent years which effectively removed the *Deutsche Post* monopoly in 2002. The number of post offices has been reduced, but small post office agencies can now be found in shops, newsagents, and petrol stations. German letter boxes are yellow. Postal charges are relatively high, but the service is very reliable.

Deutsche Telekom

The previously state-run German telecommunications service has undergone extensive reforms and gradual privatization and is now a public limited company. Since 1998 when the market was opened up to competition, *Deutsche Telekom* has ceased to have a monopoly.

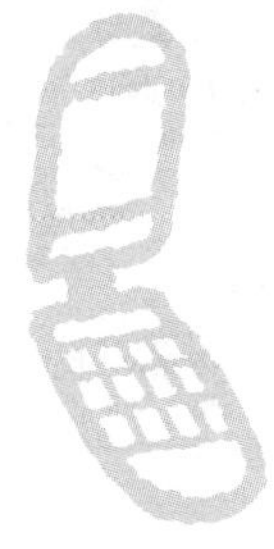

Deutsche Welle

The German equivalent of the BBC World Service, this radio station is financed and controlled by the German government and broadcasts programmes on German politics, business, arts, and culture, aimed at listeners abroad.

Die Republikaner

This ultra right-wing party was founded in 1983 and quickly became notorious for its xenophobic and nationalistic aims. After some success in the early 90s it now has very little support and is not represented in the **BUNDESTAG**.

Die Welt
A national daily newspaper which was founded in 1946 and is published in Hamburg. It has a large business section and is considered to be right-wing in its views.

Die Zeit
Germany's 'heaviest' weekly newspaper is published in Hamburg and is considered essential reading for academics and intellectuals. Former BUNDESKANZLER Helmut Schmidt is a joint editor. The paper offers in-depth analysis of current issues in politics, society, culture, and the arts.

Documenta
This international contemporary arts exhibition takes place in Kassel every four to five years. It includes drama, music and film events. *Documenta* 12 will take place in 2007. The events are subsidized by state and private sponsors.

Drittes Programm
One of the eight regional television channels run by the ard and focussing on regional affairs and educational programmes.

Duales System
This is a waste disposal and recycling system which was introduced in Germany in 1993 and is operated by the private company *DSD*. All packaging materials marked with the GRÜNER PUNKT symbol are collected separately, and sorted into plastics, glass, paper, and metal for recycling. Non-recyclable and compostable waste is still collected by the local refuse collection service.

Eigenheim
The level of home ownership in Germany is rising but still far lower than in Britain. Many people happily live in rented flats or houses, but most dream of buying or building their *Eigenheim* (own home) one day and save up towards it through the system of BAUSPAREN. German houses tend to be large and solidly built, usually with cellars, and are therefore relatively expensive. First-time buyers are usually middle-aged and expect to stay in their home for the rest of their lives.

Einwohnermeldeamt
Anybody who moves to Germany or relocates within Germany is legally obliged to register their address with the *Einwohnermeldeamt* within a week.

Entwerter
When travelling on buses and trams in Germany it is important to remember that you have to cancel (*entwerten*) your ticket in one of the *Entwerter* machines located inside the bus or tram. Your ticket, even if you have just bought it from the driver, is not valid without the stamp from the *Entwerter*.

Erste, Das
▶ DAS ERSTE.

Eurocheque
The Eurocheque is the standard cheque issued by banks in Germany. It is backed up by the *Eurochequekarte* which can also be used at cash machines and for payments in shops. Although plastic cards have become more popular in Germany, many people (and shops and restaurants) still prefer cash.

Fachhochschule
This type of university provides shorter, more vocational and practically-based courses than those available at a HOCHSCHULE.

Fahrschule
Learner drivers in Germany have to take lessons from a qualified driving instructor at a *Fahrschule* (driving school) in a specially adapted car with dual controls. It is quite common to have 20 or 30 driving lessons before sitting the driving test, as there is no other way of getting driving practice on the road.

Fasching, Fastnachtszeit
The carnival season begins at Epiphany and ends on *Aschermittwoch* (Ash Wednesday) for Lent. Depending on the region, it is also called *Karneval* or *Fasnet*, and is celebrated in Germany, Austria and Switzerland. Celebrations reach a climax on *Faschingsdienstag*, or *Rosenmontag* in the Rhineland, when there are street processions.

FDP - Freie Demokratische Partei
The German Liberal party, which was founded in 1948. This relatively small party tends to gain only 5 to 10% of the vote at general elections, but it has held the balance of power in various coalition governments both with the SPD and the CDU/CSU. It supports a free-market economy and the freedom of the individual.

Focus
A relatively new weekly news and current affairs magazine published in Munich. It was set up in 1993 and is aimed at a centre-right readership, especially businesspeople and professionals. *Focus* has become a serious competitor of DER SPIEGEL, with shorter, easier-to-read articles and a more modern presentation.

Frankfurter Allgemeine Zeitung (FAZ)
One of Germany's most serious and widely respected daily newspapers. It was founded in 1945 and is published in Frankfurt/Main. It tends to have a centre-left to liberal outlook.

Frühstück
Breakfast in Germany typically consists of strong coffee, slices of bread or fresh rolls with butter, jam, honey, sliced cheese and meat, and maybe a boiled egg. For working people and schoolchildren, who have little time for breakfast first thing in the morning, a *zweites Frühstück* is common at around 10 a.m.

Gastarbeiter
The term used for foreign workers from southern European countries, mainly Turkey, former Yugoslavia, and Italy, many of whom came to Germany in the 60s and 70s. Despite the time that they have lived in Germany and the fact that their children have grown up there, integration is still a widely discussed issue.

Gemeinde
The lowest level of local government, run by a local council chaired by the *Bürgermeister* (mayor). *Gemeinden* have their own budget, with income from local taxes. They pass local legislation and administer local affairs.

Gesamthochschule

A type of university established in some LÄNDER following reforms in the 60s and combining HOCHSCHULE and FACHHOCHSCHULE under one roof, thereby offering greater flexibility and a wider choice of subjects to the student.

Gesamtschule

A comprehensive secondary school introduced in the 70s and designed to replace the traditional division into GYMNASIUM, REALSCHULE, and HAUPTSCHULE. Pupils are taught different subjects at their own level and may take any of the school-leaving exams, including the ABITUR.

Goethe-Institut

An organization for promoting German language and culture abroad. It is based in Munich and runs about 140 institutes in over 70 countries, offering German language classes, cultural events such as exhibitions, films and seminars, and a library of German books and magazines and other documentation, which is open to the public.

Grundgesetz

The written German constitution which came into force in May 1949. It lays down the basic rights of German citizens, the relationship between BUND and LÄNDER, and the legal framework of the German state.

Grundschule

The primary school which all German children attend for four years from the age of 6 (some children do not start until they are 7). Lessons are intense but pupils only attend school for about 4 hours a day. At the end of the *Grundschule*, teachers and parents decide together which type of secondary school the child should attend.

Grüner Punkt

A symbol used to mark packaging materials which can be recycled. Any packaging carrying this logo is collected separately under the DUALES SYSTEM recycling scheme. Manufacturers have to buy a licence from the recycling company *DSD* to entitle them to use this symbol.

Gymnasium

The secondary school which prepares pupils for the abitur. The *Gymnasium* is attended after the GRUNDSCHULE by the most academically-inclined pupils. They spend nine years at this school, and during the last three years, they have some choice as to which subjects they study.

▶ SCHULE.

Hauptschule

The secondary school which prepares pupils for the HAUPTSCHULABSCHLUSS (school-leaving certificate). The *Hauptschule* aims to give the least academically-inclined children a sound educational grounding. Pupils stay at the *Hauptschule* for 5 or 6 years after the GRUNDSCHULE.

▶ SCHULE, LEHRE.

Heurige

This is an Austrian term for both a new wine and an inn with new wine on tap, especially an inn with its own vineyard in the Vienna region. A garland of pine twigs outside the gates of the *Heurige* shows that the new barrel has been tapped.

Hochschule

German *Hochschulen* (universities) do not charge fees, and anybody who has passed the **ABITUR** is entitled to go to university (except for some subjects which have a **NUMERUS CLAUSUS**). They tend to be very large and impersonal institutions. Students may receive a **BAFÖG** grant and often take more than the minimum 8 semesters (4 years) to complete their course.

Hochdeutsch

There are many regional dialects in Germany, Austria and Switzerland. *Hochdeutsch* (High German) is the standard language that can be understood by all German speakers. Newspapers and books are generally printed in *Hochdeutsch*.

ICE - Intercityexpresszug

This high-speed train runs at two-hour intervals on a number of main routes in Germany, offering shorter journey times and better facilities than ordinary trains. A futuristic new *ICE* station has been built at Frankfurt airport.

Internet

A wealth of useful information on German politics, culture, and so on can be obtained on the Internet, which is very popular in Germany. All the main German newspapers have web sites (e.g. http://www.focus.de), as do the television channels (e.g. http://www.ard.de) and organizations like the GOETHE-INSTITUT (http://goethe.de). In addition, many German towns and cities have web sites (e.g. http://www.berlin.de).

Kaffee

This refers not only to coffee as a drink but also to the small meal taken at about 4 in the afternoon, consisting of coffee and cakes or biscuits. It is often a social occasion as it is common to invite family or friends for *Kaffee* und *Kuchen* (rather than for lunch or dinner), especially on birthdays and other family occasions.

Kanton

The name for the individual autonomous states that make up Switzerland. There are 26 *Kantone*, with the largest having just over 1 million inhabitants. Each *Kanton* has its own government and its own constitution.

Kindergarten

Every German pre-school child has the right to attend *Kindergarten* (nursery or play school) between the ages of 3 and 6. Kindergarten concentrates on play, crafts, singing etc., and aims to foster the child's social and emotional development. There is no formal teaching at all, this being reserved for the **GRUNDSCHULE**.

Kindertagesstätte

Often called *Kita* for short, this is a day nursery intended for the children of working parents. The age range is usually from babies to 6, although some *Kitas* also offer after-school care for older children.

Krankenkasse

There are many different health insurance organizations in Germany with the AOK being the largest. Contributions are high, due to the high standard (and cost) of health care in Germany. The *Krankenkassen* issue their members with plastic cards which entitle them to treatment by the doctor of their choice.

Kur
A health cure in a spa town may last up to 6 weeks and usually involves a special diet, exercise programmes, physiotherapy and massage. The cure is intended for people with minor complaints or who are recovering from illness, and it plays an important role in preventative medicine in Germany.

Ladenschlusszeit
The strict regulations governing shop closing times in Germany were relaxed in 1996. Shops are allowed to stay open until 8 p.m. on weekdays and 4 p.m. on Saturdays, and bakeries may open for 3 hours on Sundays. However, the actual opening times vary, depending on the location and size of the shop.

Land
Germany is a federal republic consisting of 16 member states called *Länder* or *Bundesländer*. Five so-called neue *Bundesländer* were added after reunification in 1990. The Land has a degree of autonomy and is responsible for all educational and cultural affairs, the police, the environment, and local government. Austria is a federal state consisting of 9 *Länder*, and the Swiss equivalent is a **KANTON**.

Landtag
The parliament of a **LAND**, which is elected every 4 to 5 years using a similar mixed system of voting as for the **BUNDESTAG** elections.

Lehre
This type of apprenticeship is still the normal way to learn a trade or train for a practical career in Germany. A *Hauptschulabschluss* is the minimum requirement, although many young people with a *Realschulabschluss* or even Lehre opt to train in this way. A Lehre takes about 2 to 3 years and involves practial training by a **MEISTER(IN)** backed up by lessons at a **BERUFSSCHULE**, with an exam at the end.

Love Parade
A festival of techno music and dance which takes place in Berlin every summer, with about 1 million mainly young people attending. Originally a celebration of youth culture, it has become a major tourist attraction.

Markt
Weekly markets are still held in most German cities and towns, usually laid out very attractively in the picturesque market squares. Fresh fruit and vegetables, flowers, eggs, cheese and other dairy products, bread, meat and fish are available directly from the producer. Many Germans still buy most of their provisions *auf dem Markt*.

Matura
▶ **ABITUR**

Meister(in)

A master craftsman or craftswoman who has completed rigorous training in his/her trade or vocation and has passed a final exam after several years' experience in a job. A *Meister(in)* is allowed to set up in business and train young people who are doing their **LEHRE**.

Mittagessen

This is a cooked meal eaten in the middle of the day and is the main meal of the day for most Germans. Schoolchildren come home from school in time for *Mittagessen* and most large companies have canteens where hot meals are served at lunchtime. On a Sunday, *Mittagessen* might consist of a starter like a clear broth, followed by a roast with gravy, boiled potatoes and vegetables, and a dessert.

Namenstag

This day is celebrated by many Germans, especially Catholics, in the same way as a birthday. It is the day dedicated to the saint whose name the person carries so, for example, someone called Martin would celebrate their *Namenstag* on *Martinstag* (November 11).

Nationalrat

In Austria the *Nationalrat* is the Federal Assembly's lower house, whose 183 members are elected for four years under a system of proportional representation. In Switzerland, the *Nationalrat* is made up of 200 representatives.

Numerus clausus

The *Numerus clausus* system is used to limit the number of students studying certain oversubscribed subjects such as medicine at German universities. It means that only those students who have achieved a minimum average mark in their **ABITUR** are admitted.

Oktoberfest

Germany's biggest beer festival and funfair, which takes places every year in Munich. Over 16 days more than 5 million litres of beer are drunk in marquees erected by the major breweries. The festival goes back to 1810, when a horse race was held to celebrate the wedding of Ludwig, Crown Prince of Bavaria.

Orientierungsstufe

The name given to the first two years at a **HAUPTSCHULE**, a **REALSCHULE**, or a **GYMNASIUM**. During this time pupils can find out if they are suited to the type of school they are attending, and at the end of the two years they may transfer to a different school.

Ossi

A colloquial and sometimes derogatory term for someone from East Germany, as opposed to a **WESSI** (someone from West Germany).

Polterabend

This is Germany's answer to stag and hen nights. The *Polterabend* usually takes place a few days before the wedding and takes the form of a large party for the family and friends of both bride and groom. Traditionally, the guests smash some crockery, as this is supposed to bring luck to the couple.

Post

▶ **DEUTSCHE POST**.

Prater
Vienna's largest amusement park was a private game reserve for the Austrian royal family until 1766. The *Prater* is famous for its old-fashioned carousels. A *Riesenrad*, big wheel or Ferris wheel, with a diameter of 67 metres was built there for the World Exhibition of 1897.

Premiere
Germany's main Pay-TV channel was introduced in 1991 and can be received via satellite or cable. *Premiere* subscribers can watch the latest feature films, sports events, cultural programmes, and documentaries uninterrupted by advertising.

Realschule
The secondary school which prepares pupils for the *Realschulabschluss* (school-leaving certificate). This type of school is in between HAUPTSCHULE and GYMNASIUM, catering for less academic children who will probably train for a practical career. Pupils stay at the *Realschule* for 6 years after the GRUNDSCHULE. ▶ SCHULE, LEHRE.

Rechtschreibreform
After much controversy, a reform aiming to simplify the strict rules governing German spelling and punctuation was finally implemented in 1998. The old spelling is still acceptable for a transitional period until 2005, but most newspapers and some new books already use the new spelling.

Reichstag
This historic building in the centre of Berlin became the seat of the BUNDESTAG in 1999. The refurbishment of the *Reichstag* included the addition of a glass cupola, with a walkway open to visitors, which provides a spectacular viewing platform and addition to the Berlin skyline.

Republikaner
▶ DIE REPUBLIKANER.

RTL
Germany's largest privately-owned television channel is the market leader in commercial television. It broadcasts films, sport, news, and entertainment and regularly achieves the highest viewing figures.

Salzburger Festspiele
The Austrian city of Salzburg, the home of Wolfgang Amadeus Mozart (1756-91), hosts this annual festival as a tribute to the great composer. Every summer since 1920, Mozart-lovers have enjoyed his music at the Salzburg Festival.

SAT 1
Germany's second largest privately-owned television channel broadcasts films, news, sport, and entertainment. It was the first commercial channel in the country.

3SAT
This satellite TV channel is run jointly by ARD, ZDF, and Swiss and Austrian TV.

Schule
German children do not start school until they are 6, and they are not allowed to leave school until they are at least 15. All children attend the GRUNDSCHULE for four years (six in Berlin) and either a HAUPTSCHULE, REALSCHULE, GYMNASIUM, or GESAMTSCHULE, depending on their ability. Some students stay at school

until they are over 20 due to the system of "SITZEN BLEIBEN".

Schultag - 1. Schultag

The first day at school is a big event for a German child, involving a ceremony at school and sometimes at church. The child is given a *Schultüte*, a large cardboard cone containing pens, small gifts, and sweets, to mark this special occasion.

Schützenfest

An annual festival celebrated in most towns, involving a shooting competition, parade, and fair. The winners of the shooting competition are crowned *Schützenkönig* and *Schützenkönigin* for the year.

Schwarzwald

This is the German name for the Black Forest, a mountainous area in south-western Germany and a popular holiday destination for Germans and foreign tourists alike. The name refers to the large coniferous forests in the area.

Schweizerische Eidgenossenschaft

The Swiss Confederation is the official name for Switzerland. The confederation was established in 1291 when the cantons of Uri, Schwyz and Unterwalden swore to defend their traditional rights against the Habsburg Empire. The unified federal state as it is known today was formed in 1848.

sitzen bleiben

If German pupils fail more than one subject in their end-of-year school report, they have to repeat the year. This is colloquially referred to as *sitzen bleiben*, and it means that some pupils do not manage to sit their ABITUR until they are 20.

Skat

A popular card game for three players playing with 32 German cards. Keen players meet regularly for a game or even join a *Skat* club.

Sozialabgaben

This term refers to the contributions every German taxpayer has to make towards the four main state insurance schemes: pension, health, nursing care, and unemployment. Altogether this amounts to over 40% of gross income, with employee and employer paying half each.

SPD - Sozialdemokratische Partei Deutschlands

One of the main German political parties and the party with the biggest membership. Re-formed after the war in 1945, it is a workers' party supporting social democratic values.

Spiegel

▶ DER SPIEGEL.

Stammtisch

A large table reserved for regulars in most German pubs. The word is also used to refer to the group of people who meet around this table for a drink and lively discussion.

Stasi - Staatssicherheitsdienst
The secret service in the former GDR. With the help of an extensive network of informers, the *Stasi* built up personal files on over 6 million people, that is one third of the population. It was disbanded a year before re-unification.

Süddeutsche Zeitung
This respected daily national newspaper was founded in 1945 and is published in Munich. It has a liberal outlook and is read mainly in southern Germany.

Volkshochschule (VHS)
A local adult education centre that can be found in every German town. The *VHS* offers low-cost daytime and evening classes in a wide range of subjects, including crafts, languages, music, and exercise.

Waldorfschule
An increasingly popular type of private school originally founded by the Austrian anthroposophist Rudolf Steiner in the 1920s. The main aim of these schools is to develop pupils' creative and cognitive abilities through music, art, and crafts.

Wappen
BUNDESWAPPEN: The federal coat of arms features a heraldic eagle, which was originally the emblem of Roman emperors. It was incorporated into the coat of arms of the German Empire when it was founded in 1871. In 1950 it was revived as the official coat of arms of the Federal Republic of Germany.

Wehrdienst
Compulsory military service for young men in Germany (10 months), Switzerland (3 months), and Austria (6 months). Young Germans are generally called up when they are 19, although there are certain exemptions. Conscientious objectors may apply to do **ZIVILDIENST** instead.

Weihnachtsmarkt
During the weeks of Advent, these Christmas markets take place in most German towns, selling Christmas decorations, handmade toys and crib figures, traditional Christmas biscuits, and mulled wine to sustain the shoppers.

Weinstube
A cosy wine bar which offers a wide choice of wines and usually also serves a few dishes which are considered to go well with wine. A *Weinstube* tends to be more upmarket than an ordinary pub, or else fairly rustic, especially in wine-growing areas.

Welt
▶ **DIE WELT**.

Wende
This word can refer to any major political or social change or turning point, but it is used especially to refer to the collapse of Communism in 1989, which was symbolized by the fall of the Berlin wall and eventually led to the WIEDERVEREINIGUNG in 1990.

Wessi
A colloquial and sometimes derogatory term for someone from West Germany, as opposed to an OSSI. The expression *Besserwessi*, a pun on *Besserwisser* ('know-all') is used by East Germans to describe a *Wessi* who thinks he knows it all.

Westdeutsche Allgemeine Zeitung (WAZ)
Germany's highest-circulation serious national paper. It was founded in 1948 and is published in Essen, catering mainly for the densely populated Ruhr area.

Wiedervereinigung
This is the German word for the reunification of Germany which officially took place on 3 October 1990, when the former GDR was incorporated into the Federal Republic. The huge financial and social costs of reunification are still being felt throughout Germany.

ZDF - Zweites Deutsches Fernsehen
The second German public TV channel which was founded in 1961 and broadcasts the *Zweites Programm* with entertainment, news, information, and a limited amount of advertising.

Zeit
▶ DIE ZEIT.

Zivildienst
Community service which recognized conscientious objectors in Germany and Austria can choose to carry out instead of WEHRDIENST. It lasts 3 months longer than *Wehrdienst* (2 months longer in Austria) and usually involves caring for children, the elderly, the disabled, or the sick.

Zürcher Festspiele
The Zurich festival in Switzerland is an annual celebration of classical music, opera, dance and art, with special performances held throughout the city. The festival conclues with a brilliant Midsummer Night's Ball in central Zurich.

Letter-writing

Holiday postcard

- Beginnings (informal): '*Lieber*' here because it's a man; if it's a woman, use *Liebe* e.g. *Liebe Elke*.
  To two people, repeat '*Liebe(r)*': *Lieber Hans, liebe Elke*.
  To a family: *Liebe Schmidts, Liebe Familie Schmidt*, or just *Liebe Leute*.

- Address: Note that the title (*Herrn, Frau, Fräulein*) stands on the line above the name. *Herr* always has an n on the end in addresses.
  The house number comes after the street name.
  The postcode comes before the place, and if you're writing from outside the country put a D- for Germany, A- for Austria or CH- for Switzerland in front of it.

Heidelberg, den 6.8. 2007

Lieber Hans!

Einen schönen Gruß aus Alt-Heidelberg! Wir sind erst zwei Tage hier, aber schon sehr angetan von der Stadt und Umgebung, trotz der vielen Touristen. Wir waren gestern abend in einem Konzert im Schlosshof, eine wunderbare Stimmung! Morgen machen wir eine Bootsfahrt, dann geht's am Donnerstag wieder nach Hause. Hoffentlich ist deine Mutter inzwischen wieder gesund.

Bis bald

Max und Sophie

Herrn

Hans Matthäus

Brucknerstr. 26

91052 Erlangen

- Endings (informal): *Herzlich* or *Herzlichst, Herzliche Grüße*; more affectionately: *Alles Liebe*; *Bis bald* = See you soon .

Christmas and New Year wishes

On a card:

Frohe Weihnachten und viel Glück im neuen Jahr

A bit more formal: Ein gesegnetes Weihnachtsfest und die besten Wünsche zum neuen Jahr

A bit less formal: Fröhliche Weihnachten und einen guten Rutsch ins neue Jahr

In a letter:

- On most personal letters German speakers don't put their address at the top, but just the name of the place and the date

Würzburg, den 20.12.2007

Liebe Karin, lieber Ferdinand,

euch und euren Kindern wünschen wir von Herzen frohe Weihnachten und ein glückliches neues Jahr. Wir hoffen, es geht euch allen gut, und dass wir uns bald mal wieder sehen werden. Es kommt uns so vor, als hätten wir uns eine Ewigkeit nicht gesehen.

Das vergangene Jahr war für uns sehr ereignisreich. Thomas hatte im Sommer einen Unfall mit dem Fahrrad, und brach sich den Arm und das Schlüsselbein. Sabine hat das Abitur gerade noch bestanden und ist jetzt an der Uni in Erlangen, studiert Sport. Der arme Michael ist im Oktober arbeitslos geworden und sucht immer noch nach einer Stelle.

Ihr müsst unbedingt vorbeikommen, wenn ihr das nächste Mal in der Gegend seid. Ruft doch einfach ein paar Tage vorher an, damit wir etwas ausmachen können.

Mit herzlichen Grüßen

Eure Gabi und Michael

Invitation (informal)

Hamm, den 22.4.2007

Liebe Jennie,

wäre es möglich, dass du **1** in den Sommerferien zu uns kommst? Katrin und Gottfried würden sich riesig freuen (ich und mein Mann natürlich auch). Wir planen eine Reise zum Bodensee Ende Juli/Anfang August, du **1** könntest gerne mitfahren. Es ist wirklich sehr schön dort unten. Wir werden wahrscheinlich zelten – hoffentlich hast du **1** nichts dagegen!

Schreib bald, ob das für dich in Frage kommt.

Herzliche Grüße

Monika Pfortner

■ Beginning: if you put a comma after the name on the first line (which is usual), the letter proper should start with a small letter.

1 *du*, *dich*, *dein* etc.: although many people still write these with a capital in letters, this is not necessary. But the formal *Sie*, *Ihnen*, *Ihr* must always have a capital.

Invitation (formal)

Invitations to parties are usually by word of mouth, while for weddings, announcements rather than invitations are usually sent out:

Irene Brinkmann — Stefan Hopf

Wir heiraten am Samstag, den 20. April 2007, um 14 Uhr in der Pfarrkirche Landsberg.

Goethestraße 12	Ulrichsweg 4
Landsberg	Altötting

Accepting an invitation

Edinburgh, den 2.5.2007

Liebe Frau Pfortner,

recht herzlichen Dank für Ihre liebe Einladung. Da ich noch keine festen Pläne für die Sommerferien habe, möchte ich sie sehr gerne annehmen. Allerdings darf ich nicht mehr als vier bis fünf Tage weg sein, da es meiner Mutter nicht sehr gut geht. Sie **1** *müssen mir sagen, was ich mitbringen soll (außer Edinburgh Rock!). Ist es sehr warm am Bodensee? Kann man im See schwimmen?*

Natürlich habe ich nichts gegen Zelten. Auch hier in Schottland bei Wind und Regen macht es mir Spaß!

Ich freue mich auf ein baldiges Wiedersehen.

Herzliche Grüße

Jennie Stewart

1 Since this is a letter from a younger person writing to the mother of a friend, she uses the formal *Sie* form and possessive *Ihr* (always with capitals), and writes to her as *"Frau Pfortner"*. On the other hand it was quite natural for Frau Pfortner to use the *du* form to her.

Enquiry to a tourist office

■ The subject of the letter is centred.

■ A simple business-style letter. The recipient's address is on the left and the sender's on the right, with the date below.

Verkehrsverein Heidelberg e.V.
Friedrich-Ebert-Anlage 2
69117 Heidelberg

Silvia Sommer
Tannenweg 23
48149 Münster

24. April 2007

Hotels und Pensionen in Heidelberg

Sehr geehrte Damen und Herren,

würden Sie mir bitte freundlicherweise eine Liste der Hotels und Pensionen (der mittleren Kategorie) am Ort zusenden?

Ich möchte bitte auch Informationen über Busfahrten zu den Sehenswürdigkeiten der Umgebung in der zweiten Augusthälfte haben.

Mit freundlichen Grüßen

Silvia Sommer

■ This is the standard formula for starting a business letter addressed to a firm or organization, and not to a particular person.

■ *"Mit freundlichen Grüßen"* is the standard ending for a formal or business letter; another possibility is *"Mit besten Grüßen"*.

Booking a hotel room

Hotel Goldener Pflug
Ortsstraße 7
69235 Steinbach

Tobias Schwarz
Gartenstr. 19
76530 Baden-Baden

16. Juli 2007

Sehr geehrte Damen und Herren,

Ich wurde durch die Broschüre "Hotels und Pensionen im Naturpark Odenwald (Ausgabe 2000)" auf ihr Hotel aufmerksam.

Ich möchte für mich und meine Frau für die Zeit vom 2. bis 11. August (neun Nächte) ein ruhiges Doppelzimmer mit Dusche reservieren, sowie ein Einzelzimmer für unseren Sohn.

Falls Sie für diese Zeit etwas Passendes haben, informieren Sie mich doch bitte über den Preis und darüber, ob Sie eine Anzahlung wünschen.

Mit freundlichen Grüßen

Tobias Schwarz

Booking a campsite

For a business letter to a particular person, use *"Sehr geehrte(r)"* and the name. (If this letter were to a man, it would start *"Sehr geehrter Herr Sattler"*).

Camilla Stumpf
Saalgasse 10
60311 Frankfurt

Camping am See
Frau Bettina Sattler
Auweg 6-10
87654 Waldenkirchen

Frankfurt, den 16.04.2007

Sehr geehrte Frau Sattler,

Ihr Campingplatz wurde mir von Herrn Stephan Seidel empfohlen, der schon mehrmals bei Ihnen war. **1** Ich würde nun gerne vom 18. bis 25. Juli mit zwei Freunden eine Woche bei Ihnen verbringen. Könnten Sie uns bitte einen Zeltplatz **2** möglichst in unmittelbarer Nähe des Sees **3** reservieren?

Würden Sie mir freundlicherweise mitteilen, ob Sie meine Reservierung annehmen können und ob Sie eine Anzahlung wünschen?

Außerdem wäre ich Ihnen dankbar für eine kurze Wegbeschreibung von der Autobahn.

Mit vielem Dank im Voraus und freundlichen Grüßen

Camilla Stumpf

1 Or if you have found the campsite in a guide, say e.g.: *"Ich habe Ihre Anschrift dem ADAC-Campingführer 2000 entnommen"*.

2 Or if you have a caravan: *"einen Stellplatz für einen Wohnwagen"*.

3 Alternatives: *"in schattiger/geschützter Lage"*.

Cancelling a reservation

Herrn
Hans Knauer
Gasthaus Sonnenblick
Hauptstr. 6
D-94066 Bad Füssing
Germany

Aberdeen, den 2.6.2007

Sehr geehrter Herr Knauer,

leider muss ich meine Reservierung für die Woche vom 7. bis 13. August **1** rückgängig machen. Wegen unvorhergesehener Umstände **2** muss ich auf meinen Urlaub verzichten.

Es tut mir aufrichtig Leid, dass ich so spät abbestellen muss, und hoffe, dass Sie deswegen keine Unannehmlichkeiten haben.

Mit freundlichen Grüßen

Robert McDonald

1 Or: "*für die Zeit vom 7. bis 20. August*" etc.

2 Or more precisely: "*Durch den überraschenden Tod meines Vaters/die Krankheit meines Mannes*" etc.

Sending an e-mail

The illustration shows a typical interface for sending e-mail.

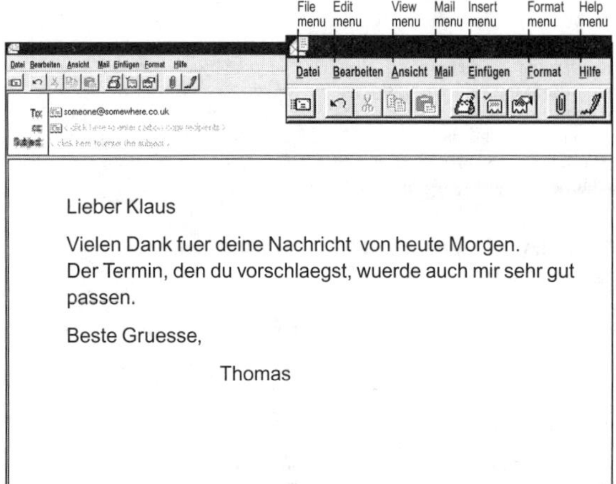

Texting

The basic principles governing German SMS abbreviations are similar to those governing English SMS. Certain words or syllables are represented by letters or numbers that sound the same. Most punctuation is usually omitted, umlauts are rarely used, and there are no strict rules about upper and lower case. For example 'viele Grüße' can be 'vlg'. Sentences are shortened by leaving out certain letters – 'bist du noch wach?' might read 'bidunowa'. Often just the initial letter of a word is used, as in 'ff' for 'Fortsetzung folgt'. Many English abbreviations have made it into German text messages.
For example '4u' (for you) is often used for 'für dich'.

Glossary of German SMS abbreviations

Abbreviation	Meaning
8ung	Achtung
ads	alles deine Schuld
akla?	alles klar?
aws	auf Wiedersehen
bb	bis bald
bda	bis dann
bidunowa?	bist du noch wach?
braduhi?	brauchst du Hilfe?
bs	bis später
dad	denke an dich
d	der
div	danke im Voraus
dubido	du bist doof
ff	Fortsetzung folgt
g	grinsen
g&k	Gruß und Kuss
gn8	gute Nacht
gngn	geht nicht, gibts nicht
hahu	habe Hunger
hdl	habe dich lieb
hdos	halt die Ohren steif
hegl	herzlichen Glückwunsch
ild	ich liebe dich
jon	jetzt oder nie
katze?	kannst du tanzen?
ko5mispä	komme 5 Minuten später
l8er	later = später
lg	liebe Grüße
lidumino	liebst du mich noch?
mamima	mail mir mal
mumidire	muss mit dir reden
n8	Nacht
nfd	nur für dich
pg	Pech gehabt
rumian	ruf mich an
sfh	Schluss für heute
siw	soweit ich weiß
sms	schreib mir schnell
sz	schreib zurück
tabu	tausend Bussis
vegimini	vergiss mich nicht
vlg	viele Grüße
vv	viel Vergnügen
wamaduheu?	was machst du heute?
waudi	warte auf dich
we	Wochenende
zdom?	zu dir oder zu mir?

Emoticons	
:-)	lächeln, glücklich
:-))	sehr glücklich
:-|	Stirnrunzeln
:-e	enttäuscht
:-(	unglücklich, traurig
:-((	sehr unglücklich
:->	sarkastisch
%-)	verwirrt
:~(or :'-(	weinen
;-)	zwinkern
|-o	müde
:-\	skeptisch
:-D	lachen
:-<>	erstaunt
:-p	rausgestreckte Zunge
:-O	schreien
O:-)	Engel
:-* or :-x	Kuss
:-o	Schock
@}-,-'–	Rose

The German words you must know

A

Abend der
aber
Abfahrt die
Achtung
Adresse die
all
allein
alles
als
also
alt
Amerikaner der
Ampel die
an
anbieten
Anfang der
Angebot das
angenehm
Ankunft die
annehmen
anrufen
Antwort die
Apfel der
Apotheke die
April
Arbeit die
arm
Arm der
Arzt der
auch
auf
aufstehen
Auge das
August
aus
Ausgang der
Auskunft die
aussehen
außen
Austausch der
Ausweis der
Autobahn die

B

Bäckerei die
Badezimmer das
Bahnhof der
bald
Bank die
bauen
Bauer der
Baum der
beginnen
bei
Bein das
bekommen
benützen
Berg der
berühmt
besetzt
besonders
bestellen
Besuch der
Bett das
bezahlen
Bier das
Bild das
billig
bis
bitte
blau
bleiben
Blick der
brauchen
braun
brechen
breit
Brief der
Brille die
Brot das
Brötchen das
Bruder der
Buch das
Burg die

C

Campingplatz der
Chef der
Computer der

D

da
danken
dann
das
dass
decken
deutsch
Deutsch
Deutsche der
Deutschland
Dezember
dick
Dienstag
dieser
doch
Donnerstag
Dorf das
dort
drehen
dritte
Drogerie die
drücken
dünn
durch
dürfen
durstig
Dusche die

E

Ei das
eigen
ein/eine/ein
einfach
Einfahrt die
einige
einsteigen
Eintritt der
einverstanden
Einwohner der
Eis das
Ende das
eng
Engländer der
englisch
entlang
Entschuldigung die
Erbse die
Erdbeere die
Erfolg der
erlauben
erst
essen
etwas
Euro der

F

Fabrik die
fahren
Fahrer der
Fahrkarte die
Fahrrad das
Fahrt die
fallen
falsch
Familie die
Familienname der
Farbe die
fast
Februar
fehlen
Fehler der
Feld das
Fenster das
Ferien die
fest
finden

Finger der
Fisch der
flach
Flasche die
Fleisch das
Flughafen der
Flugzeug das
Fluss der
Frage die
Frau die
Fräulein das
frei
Freitag
freitags
Fremde der
Freund der
froh
früh
Frühling der
Frühstück das
für
furchtbar
Fuß der

G

ganz
Gang der
Garten der
Gast der
geben
geboren
gefallen
gefährlich
gegen
gegenüber
gehen
gelb
Geld das
genau
genug
gerade
gern
Geschäft das
geschehen
Geschenk das
geschieden
geschlossen
gestern
Gesundheit die
gewinnen
Gewitter das
gewöhnlich
Glas das
glauben
gleich
Gleis das
glücklich
Grad der
grau
groß
Größe die
grün
Gruppe die
gut

H

Haar das
haben
halb
Hallo
Haltestelle die
halten
Hand die
Handy das
hart
Haus das
Heft das
heiß
heißen
Hemd das
Herbst der
Herr der
heute
hier
Hilfe die
hinter
hinunter
hoch
Hof der
hoffen
holen
hören
Hotel das
hübsch
Hund der
hungrig

I

Idee die
immer
in
Industrie die
Informatik die
innen

J

ja
Jahr das
Januar
jeder
jemand
jener
jetzt
Juli
jung
Junge der
Juni

K

Kaffee der
kalt
Kamera die
Karte die
Käse der
Kasse die
Katze die
kaufen
Kaufhaus das
kein
Kellner der
kennen
Kind das
Kino das
Kirche die
Klasse die
Kleid das
klein
Knie das
Kohl der
komisch
kommen
Konditorei die
können
Kopf der
kostenlos
krank
Krankheit die
Kreis der
kriegen
Kuchen der
Küche die
kühl
Kunst die
kurz

L

lachen
Laden der
Land das
lang
langsam
lassen
laufen
laut
Lebensmittel die
leer
Lehrer der
leicht
Leid tun
leider
lernen
lesen
Leute die
Liebe die
liegen
Linie die
links
Liste die
Lohn der
los
Luft die
Lust haben

M

machen
Mädchen das
Mahlzeit die
Mai
Mal das
man
Mann der
Mappe die
Markt der

Meer das
mehr
Menge die
Mensch der
Menü das
Messer das
Metzgerei die
mieten
Milch die
Minute die
mit
Mittag der
Mittagessen das
Mittwoch
Möbel das
mögen
möglich
Monat der
Montag
morgen
Morgen der
müde
Musik die
müssen
Mutter die

N

nach
Nachmittag der
Nachrichten die
nächst
Nacht die
Name der
Nase die
nass
natürlich
neben
nehmen
nein
neu
nicht
nichts
nie
niemand
noch
Norden der
nötig
November
null
nur
nützlich

O

Obst das
oder
offen
öffnen
ohne
Ohr das
Oktober
Onkel der
Osten der
Österreich
Österreicher der

P

Papier das
Park der
Parkplatz der
Partner der
passieren
Pause die
Person die
Pferd das
Pflanze die
Plan der
Platz der
plötzlich
Polizei die
Polizist der
Post die
Postkarte die
Preis der
prima
probieren
Prüfung die
putzen

Q

Quadrat das

R

Rad das
rauchen
Rechnung die
rechts
Regel die
regnen
reich
reichen
Reise die
Reisende der
reisen
reiten
reservieren
Rettung die
richtig
Richtung die
Rock der
rot
Rücken der
ruhig

S

Saft der
sagen
Salz das
Samstag
satt
sauber
S-Bahn die
Schachtel die
schaden
Schaf das
Scheibe die
Schein der
schicken
schieben
Schinken der
schlafen
schlecht
schließen
schlimm
Schloss das
schmecken
Schmerzen die
schmutzig
Schnee der
schnell
Schokolade die
schon
schön
schrecklich
schreiben
Schuh der
Schule die
schwach
schwarz
Schweinefleisch das
Schweiz die
schweizerisch
schwer
Schwester die
schwierig
Schwimmbad das
See der
See die
sehen
sehr
sein
seit
Selbstbedienung die
selten
Serie die
Sessel der
sich setzen
sicher
singen
Sitz der
Ski fahren
so
Socke die
sofort
Sohn der
sollen
Sommer der
Sonne die
Sonntag
Spaß
spät
Speisekarte die
Spiel das
sportlich
Sprache die
sprechen
Stadt die
Stadtplan der
stark
stehen
steigen

Stelle die
sterben
Stimme die
Strand der
Straße die
Straßenbahn die
streng
Stück das
Student der
Stuhl der
Stunde die
Sturm der
suchen
Süden der
Suppe die
süß

T

Tafel die
Tag der
täglich
Tankstelle die
Tanz der
Tasche die
Tasse die
Tee der
Telefon das
Teller der
teuer
Tier das
Tisch der
Tochter die
toll
Torte die
Tourist der
tragen
treffen
Treppe die
trinken
trocken
tun
Tür die
Tüte die

U

U-Bahn die
über
Uhr die
um
umsteigen
und
ungefähr
unmöglich
unter
Unterkunft die
Unterschied der
Urlaub der

V

Vater der
sich verabschieden
verboten
verbringen
verdienen
Verein der
vergessen
vergleichen
verkaufen
Verkehr der
verlassen
verlieren
verschieden
verstehen
Verzeihung die
viel
vielleicht
Vogel der
voll
von
vor
Vormittag der
Vorname der
Vorsicht
vorziehen

W

Wagen der
wählen
während
wahrscheinlich
Wand die
wandern
wann
warm
warum
was
Wasser das
wechseln
Wecker der
wegen
weil
Wein der
weiß
weit
welcher
Welt die
wenig
wenn
wer
werden
wert
Westen der
Wetter das
wichtig
wie
wieder
willkommen
Winter der
wirklich
wissen
wo
Woche die
wohnen
Wohnung die
wollen
Wort das
wunderbar
Wurst die

Z

zahlen
Zahn der
zeigen
Zeit die
Zeitung die
Zentrum das
ziehen
Zigarette die
Zimmer das
zu
Zucker der
Zug der
zurückgehen
zurückkommen
zweite
zwischen

English – German

Aa

a /ə/, betont /eɪ/

vor einem Vokal **an**

• indefinite article

····➤ ein (m), eine (f), ein (nt). **a problem** ein Problem. **an apple** ein Apfel. **a cat** eine Katze. **have you got a pencil?** hast du einen Bleistift? **I gave it to a beggar** ich gab es einem Bettler

! There are some cases where **a** is not translated, such as when talking about people's professions or nationalities: **she is a lawyer** sie ist Rechtsanwältin. **he's an Italian** er ist Italiener

····➤ (with 'not') kein (m), keine (f), kein (nt), keine (pl). **that's not a problem/not a good idea** das ist kein Problem/keine gute Idee. **there was not a chance that ...** es bestand keine Möglichkeit, dass .... **she did not say a word** sie sagte kein Wort. **I didn't tell a soul** ich habe es keinem Menschen gesagt

····➤ (per; each) pro. **£300 a week** 300 Pfund pro Woche. **30 miles an hour** 30 Meilen pro Stunde. (in prices) **it costs 90p a pound** es kostet 90 Pence das Pfund.

aback /ə'bæk/ adv **be taken ~** verblüfft sein

abandon /ə'bændən/ vt verlassen; (give up) aufgeben

abate /ə'beɪt/ vi nachlassen

abattoir /'æbətwɑ:(r)/ n Schlachthof m

abb|ey /'æbɪ/ n Abtei f. **~ot** n Abt m

abbreviat|e /ə'bri:vɪeɪt/ vt abkürzen. **~ion** n Abkürzung f

abdicat|e /'æbdɪkeɪt/ vi abdanken. **~ion** n Abdankung f

abdom|en /'æbdəmən/ n Unterleib m. **~inal** adj Unterleibs-

abduct /əb'dʌkt/ vt entführen. **~ion** n Entführung f

aberration /æbə'reɪʃn/ n Abweichung f; (mental) Verwirrung f

abeyance /ə'beɪəns/ n **in ~** [zeitweilig] außer Kraft

abhor /əb'hɔ:(r)/ vt (pt/pp **abhorred**) verabscheuen. **~rent** adj abscheulich

abide /ə'baɪd/ vt (pt/pp **abided**) (tolerate) aushalten; ausstehen (person)

ability /ə'bɪlətɪ/ n Fähigkeit f; (talent) Begabung f

abject /'æbdʒekt/ adj erbärmlich; (humble) demütig

ablaze /ə'bleɪz/ adj in Flammen

able /'eɪbl/ adj (**-r,-st**) fähig; **be ~ to do sth** etw tun können. **~-'bodied** adj körperlich gesund

ably /'eɪblɪ/ adv gekonnt

abnormal /æb'nɔ:ml/ adj anormal; (Med) abnorm. **~ity** n Abnormität f. **~ly** adv ungewöhnlich

aboard /ə'bɔ:d/ adv & prep an Bord (+ gen)

abol|ish /ə'bɒlɪʃ/ vt abschaffen. **~ition** n Abschaffung f

abominable /ə'bɒmɪnəbl/ adj, **-bly** adv abscheulich

aborigines /æbə'rɪdʒəni:z/ npl Ureinwohner pl

abort /ə'bɔ:t/ vt abtreiben. **~ion** n Abtreibung f. **~ive** adj (attempt) vergeblich

about /ə'baʊt/ adv umher, herum; (approximately) ungefähr; **be ~** (in circulation) umgehen; (in existence) vorhanden sein; **be ~ to do sth** im Begriff sein, etw zu tun; **there was no one ~** es war kein Mensch da; **run/play ~**

herumlaufen/-spielen •prep um (+ acc) [... herum]; (concerning) über (+ acc); **what is it ~?** worum geht es? (book:) wovon handelt es? **I know nothing ~ it** ich weiß nichts davon; **talk/know ~** reden/ wissen von

about: ~-'face n, **-'turn** n Kehrtwendung f

above /ə'bʌv/ adv oben •prep über (+ dat/acc); **~ all** vor allem

above: ~-'board adj legal. **~-mentioned** adj oben erwähnt

abrasive /ə'breɪsɪv/ adj Scheuer-; (remark) verletzend •n Scheuermittel nt; (Techn) Schleifmittel nt

abreast /ə'brest/ adv nebeneinander; **keep ~ of** Schritt halten mit

abridge /ə'brɪdʒ/ vt kürzen

abroad /ə'brɔːd/ adv im Ausland; **go ~** ins Ausland fahren

abrupt /ə'brʌpt/ adj abrupt; (sudden) plötzlich; (curt) schroff

abscess /'æbsɪs/ n Abszess m

absence /'æbsəns/ n Abwesenheit f

absent /'æbsənt/ adj abwesend; **be ~** fehlen

absentee /æbsən'tiː/ n Abwesende(r) m/f

absent-minded /æbsənt'maɪndɪd/ adj geistesabwesend; (forgetful) zerstreut

absolute /'æbsəluːt/ adj absolut

absorb /əb'sɔːb/ vt absorbieren, aufsaugen; **~ed in** vertieft in (+ acc). **~ent** adj saugfähig

absorption /əb'sɔːpʃn/ n Absorption f

abstain /əb'steɪn/ vi sich enthalten (**from** gen)

abstemious /əb'stiːmɪəs/ adj enthaltsam

abstention /əb'stenʃn/ n (Pol) [Stimm]enthaltung f

abstract /'æbstrækt/ adj abstrakt •n (summary) Abriss m

absurd /əb'sɜːd/ adj absurd. **~ity** n Absurdität f

abundan|ce /ə'bʌndəns/ n Fülle f (**of** an + dat). **~t** adj reichlich

abuse[1] /ə'bjuːz/ vt missbrauchen; (insult) beschimpfen

abus|e[2] /ə'bjuːs/ n Missbrauch m; (insults) Beschimpfungen pl. **~ive** ausfallend

abysmal /ə'bɪʒml/ adj [!] katastrophal

abyss /ə'bɪs/ n Abgrund m

academic /ækə'demɪk/ adj, **-ally** adv akademisch

academy /ə'kædəmɪ/ n Akademie f

accelerat|e /ək'seləreɪt/ vt/i beschleunigen. **~ion** n Beschleunigung f. **~or** n (Auto) Gaspedal nt

accent /'æksənt/ n Akzent m

accept /ək'sept/ vt annehmen; (fig) akzeptieren •vi zusagen. **~able** adj annehmbar. **~ance** n Annahme f; (of invitation) Zusage f

access /'ækses/ n Zugang m. **~ible** adj zugänglich

accessor|y /ək'sesərɪ/ n (Jur) Mitschuldige(r) m/f; **~ies** pl (fashion) Accessoires pl; (Techn) Zubehör nt

accident /'æksɪdənt/ n Unfall m; (chance) Zufall m; **by ~** zufällig; (unintentionally) versehentlich. **~al** adj zufällig; (unintentional) versehentlich

acclaim /ə'kleɪm/ vt feiern (**as** als)

acclimatize /ə'klaɪmətaɪz/ vt **become ~d** sich akklimatisieren

accommodat|e /ə'kɒmədeɪt/ vt unterbringen. **~ing** adj entgegenkommend. **~ion** n (rooms) Unterkunft f

accompan|iment /ə'kʌmpənɪmənt/ n Begleitung f. **~ist** n (Mus) Begleiter(in) m(f)

accompany /ə'kʌmpənɪ/ vt (pt/pp **-ied**) begleiten

accomplice /ə'kʌmplɪʃ/ n Komplize/-zin m/f

accomplish /ə'kʌmplɪʃ/ vt erfüllen (task); (achieve) erreichen. **~ed** adj fähig. **~ment** n Fertigkeit f; (achievement) Leistung f

accord /ə'kɔ:d/ n **of one's own ~** aus eigenem Antrieb. **~ance** n **in ~ance with** entsprechend (+ dat)

according /ə'kɔ:dɪŋ/ adv **~ to** nach (+ dat). **~ly** adv entsprechend

accordion /ə'kɔ:dɪən/ n Akkordeon nt

account /ə'kaʊnt/ n Konto nt; (bill) Rechnung f; (description) Darstellung f; (report) Bericht m; **~s** pl (Comm) Bücher pl; **on ~ of** wegen (+ gen); **on no ~** auf keinen Fall; **take into ~** in Betracht ziehen, berücksichtigen • vi **~ for** Rechenschaft ablegen für; (explain) erklären

accountant /ə'kaʊntənt/ n Buchhalter(in) m(f); (chartered) Wirtschaftsprüfer m

accumulat|e /ə'kju:mjʊleɪt/ vt ansammeln, anhäufen • vi sich ansammeln, sich anhäufen. **~ion** n Ansammlung f, Anhäufung f

accura|cy /'ækʊrəsɪ/ n Genauigkeit f. **~te** adj genau

accusation /ækju:'zeɪʃn/ n Anklage f

accusative /ə'kju:zətɪv/ adj & n **~ [case]** (Gram) Akkusativ m

accuse /ə'kju:z/ vt (Jur) anklagen (**of** gen); **~ s.o. of doing sth** jdn beschuldigen, etw getan zu haben

accustom /ə'kʌstəm/ vt gewöhnen (**to** an + dat); **grow** or **get ~ed to** sich gewöhnen an (+ acc). **~ed** adj gewohnt

ace /eɪs/ n (Cards, Sport) Ass nt

ache /eɪk/ n Schmerzen pl • vi weh tun, schmerzen

achieve /ə'tʃi:v/ vt leisten; (gain) erzielen; (reach) erreichen. **~ment** n (feat) Leistung f

acid /'æsɪd/ adj sauer; (fig) beißend • n Säure f. **~ity** n Säure f. **~'rain** n saurer Regen m

acknowledge /ək'nɒlɪdʒ/ vt anerkennen; (admit) zugeben; erwidern (greeting); **~ receipt of** den Empfang bestätigen (+ gen). **~ment** n Anerkennung f; (of letter) Empfangsbestätigung f

acne /'æknɪ/ n Akne f

acorn /'eɪkɔ:n/ n Eichel f

acoustic /ə'ku:stɪk/ adj, **-ally** adv akustisch. **~s** npl Akustik f

acquaint /ə'kweɪnt/ vt **be ~ed with** kennen; vertraut sein mit (fact). **~ance** n (person) Bekannte(r) m/f; **make s.o.'s ~ance** jdn kennen lernen

acquire /ə'kwaɪə(r)/ vt erwerben

acquisit|ion /ækwɪ'zɪʃn/ n Erwerb m; (thing) Erwerbung f. **~ive** adj habgierig

acquit /ə'kwɪt/ vt (pt/pp **acquitted**) freisprechen

acre /'eɪkə(r)/ n ≈ Morgen m

acrimon|ious /'ækrɪ'məʊnɪəs/ adj bitter

acrobat /'ækrəbæt/ n Akrobat(in) m(f). **~ic** adj akrobatisch

across /ə'krɒs/ adv hinüber/herüber; (wide) breit; (not lengthwise) quer; (in crossword) waagerecht; **come ~ sth** auf etw (acc) stoßen; **go ~** hinübergehen; **bring ~** herüberbringen • prep über (+ acc); (on the other side of) auf der anderen Seite (+ gen)

act /ækt/ n Tat f; (action) Handlung f; (law) Gesetz nt; (Theat) Akt m; (item) Nummer f • vi handeln; (behave) sich verhalten; (Theat) spielen; (pretend) sich verstellen; **~ as** fungieren als • vt spielen (role). **~ing** adj (deputy) stellvertretend • n (Theat) Schauspielerei f

action /'ækʃn/ n Handlung f; (deed) Tat f; (Mil) Einsatz m; (Jur) Klage f; (effect) Wirkung f; (Techn) Mechanismus m; **out of ~** (machine:) außer Betrieb; **take ~** handeln; **killed in ~** gefallen

activate /'æktɪveɪt/ vt betätigen

activ|e /'æktɪv/ adj aktiv; **on ~e service** im Einsatz. **~ity** n Aktivität f

act|or /'æktə(r)/ n Schauspieler m.

a

~**ress** n Schauspielerin f

actual /'æktʃʊəl/ adj eigentlich; (real) tatsächlich

acupuncture /'ækjʊ-/ n Akupunktur f

acute /ə'kju:t/ adj scharf; (angle) spitz; (illness) akut. ~**ly** adv sehr

ad /æd/ n [!] = **advertisement**

AD abbr (**Anno Domini**) n.Chr.

adamant /'ædəmənt/ adj **be ~ that** darauf bestehen, dass

adapt /ə'dæpt/ vt anpassen; bearbeiten (play) •vi sich anpassen. ~**able** adj anpassungsfähig

adaptation /ædæp'teɪʃn/ n (Theat) Bearbeitung f

add /æd/ vt hinzufügen; (Math) addieren •vi zusammenzählen, addieren; ~ **to** hinzufügen zu; (fig: increase) steigern; (compound) verschlimmern. ~ **up** vt zusammenzählen (figures) •vi zusammenzählen, addieren

adder /'ædə(r)/ n Kreuzotter f

addict /'ædɪkt/ n Süchtige(r) m/f

addict|ed /ə'dɪktɪd/ adj süchtig; ~**ed to drugs** drogensüchtig. ~**ion** n Sucht f

addition /ə'dɪʃn/ n Hinzufügung f; (Math) Addition f; (thing added) Ergänzung f; **in ~** zusätzlich. ~**al** adj zusätzlich

additive /'ædɪtɪv/ n Zusatz m

address /ə'dres/ n Adresse f, Anschrift f; (speech) Ansprache f •vt adressieren (**to** an + acc); (speak to) anreden (person); sprechen vor (+ dat) (meeting). ~**ee** n Empfänger m

adequate /'ædɪkwət/ adj ausreichend

adhere /əd'hɪə(r)/ vi kleben/(fig) festhalten (**to** an + dat)

adhesive /əd'hi:sɪv/ adj klebend •n Klebstoff m

adjacent /ə'dʒeɪsnt/ adj angrenzend

adjective /'ædʒɪktɪv/ n Adjektiv nt

adjoin /ə'dʒɔɪn/ vt angrenzen an (+ acc). ~**ing** adj angrenzend

adjourn /ə'dʒɜ:n/ vt vertagen (**until** auf + acc) •vi sich vertagen. ~**ment** n Vertagung f

adjudicate /ə'dʒu:dɪkeɪt/ vi (in competition) Preisrichter sein

adjust /ə'dʒʌst/ vt einstellen; (alter) verstellen •vi sich anpassen (**to** dat). ~**able** adj verstellbar. ~**ment** n Einstellung f; Anpassung f

ad lib /æd'lɪb/ adv aus dem Stegreif •vi (pt/pp **ad libbed**) [!] improvisieren

administer /əd'mɪnɪstə(r)/ vt verwalten; verabreichen (medicine)

administration /ədmɪnɪ'streɪʃn/ n Verwaltung f; (Pol) Regierung f

admirable /'ædmərəbl/ adj bewundernswert

admiral /'ædmərəl/ n Admiral m

admiration /ædmə'reɪʃn/ n Bewunderung f

admire /əd'maɪə(r)/ vt bewundern. ~**r** n Verehrer(in) m(f)

admission /əd'mɪʃn/ n Eingeständnis nt; (entry) Eintritt m

admit /əd'mɪt/ vt (pt/pp **admitted**) (let in) hereinlassen; (acknowledge) zugeben; ~ **to sth** etw zugeben. ~**tance** n Eintritt m. ~**tedly** adv zugegebenermaßen

admonish /əd'mɒnɪʃ/ vt ermahnen

adolescen|ce /ædə'lesns/ n Jugend f, Pubertät f. ~**t** adj Jugend-; (boy, girl) halbwüchsig •n Jugendliche(r) m/f

adopt /ə'dɒpt/ vt adoptieren; ergreifen (measure); (Pol) annehmen (candidate). ~**ion** n Adoption f

ador|able /ə'dɔ:rəbl/ adj bezaubernd. ~**ation** n Anbetung f

adore /ə'dɔ:(r)/ vt (worship) anbeten; ([!]: like) lieben

adorn /ə'dɔ:n/ vt schmücken. ~**ment** n Schmuck m

Adriatic /eɪdrɪ'ætɪk/ adj & n ~ **[Sea]** Adria f

adrift /ə'drɪft/ adj **be ~** treiben

adroit /ə'drɔɪt/ adj gewandt, geschickt

adulation /ædjʊ'leɪʃn/ n Schwärmerei f

adult /'ædʌlt/ n Erwachsene(r) m/f

adulterate /ə'dʌltəreɪt/ vt verfälschen; panschen (wine)

adultery /ə'dʌltərɪ/ n Ehebruch m

advance /əd'vɑːns/ n Fortschritt m; (Mil) Vorrücken nt; (payment) Vorschuss m; **in ~** im Voraus •vi vorankommen; (Mil) vorrücken; (make progress) Fortschritte machen •vt fördern (cause); vorbringen (idea); vorschießen (money). **~d** adj fortgeschritten; (progressive) fortschrittlich. **~ment** n Förderung f; (promotion) Beförderung f

advantage /əd'vɑːntɪdʒ/ n Vorteil m; **take ~ of** ausnutzen. **~ous** adj vorteilhaft

adventur|e /əd'ventʃə(r)/ n Abenteuer nt. **~er** n Abenteurer m. **~ous** adj abenteuerlich; (person) abenteuerlustig

adverb /'ædvɜːb/ n Adverb nt

adverse /'ædvɜːs/ adj ungünstig

advert /'ædvɜːt/ n [!] = **advertisement**

advertise /'ædvətaɪz/ vt Reklame machen für; (by small ad) inserieren •vi Reklame machen; inserieren

advertisement /əd'vɜːtɪsmənt/ n Anzeige f; (publicity) Reklame f; (small ad) Inserat nt

advertis|er /'ædvətaɪzə(r)/ n Inserent m. **~ing** n Werbung f

advice /əd'vaɪs/ n Rat m

advisable /əd'vaɪzəbl/ adj ratsam

advis|e /əd'vaɪz/ vt raten (**s.o.** jdm); (counsel) beraten; (inform) benachrichtigen; **~e s.o. against sth** jdm von etw abraten •vi raten. **~er** n Berater(in) m(f). **~ory** adj beratend

advocate¹ /'ædvəkət/ n (supporter) Befürworter m

advocate² /'ædvəkeɪt/ vt befürworten

aerial /'eərɪəl/ adj Luft- •n Antenne f

aerobics /eə'rəʊbɪks/ n Aerobic nt

aero|drome /'eərədrəʊm/ n Flugplatz m. **~plane** n Flugzeug nt

aerosol /'eərəsɒl/ n Spraydose f

aesthetic /iːs'θetɪk/ adj ästhetisch

affair /ə'feə(r)/ n Angelegenheit f, Sache f; (scandal) Affäre f; **[love-]~** [Liebes]verhältnis nt

affect /ə'fekt/ vt sich auswirken auf (+ acc); (concern) betreffen; (move) rühren; (pretend) vortäuschen. **~ation** n Affektiertheit f. **~ed** adj affektiert

affection /ə'fekʃn/ n Liebe f. **~ate** adj liebevoll

affirm /ə'fɜːm/ vt behaupten

affirmative /ə'fɜːmətɪv/ adj bejahend •n Bejahung f

afflict /ə'flɪkt/ vt **be ~ed with** behaftet sein mit. **~ion** n Leiden nt

affluen|ce /'æfluəns/ n Reichtum m. **~t** adj wohlhabend. **~t society** n Wohlstandsgesellschaft f

afford /ə'fɔːd/ vt **be able to ~ sth** sich (dat) etw leisten können. **~able** adj erschwinglich

affront /ə'frʌnt/ n Beleidigung f •vt beleidigen

afloat /ə'fləʊt/ adj **be ~** (ship:) flott sein; **keep ~** (person:) sich über Wasser halten

afraid /ə'freɪd/ adj **be ~** Angst haben (**of** vor + dat); **I'm ~ not** leider nicht; **I'm ~ so** [ja] leider

Africa /'æfrɪkə/ n Afrika nt. **~n** adj afrikanisch •n Afrikaner(in) m(f)

after /'ɑːftə(r)/ adv danach •prep nach (+ dat); **~ that** danach; **~ all** schließlich; **the day ~ tomorrow** übermorgen; **be ~** aus sein auf (+ acc) •conj nachdem

after: ~-effect n Nachwirkung f. **~math** /-mɑːθ/ n Auswirkungen pl. **~'noon** n Nachmittag m; **good ~noon!** guten Tag! **~-sales service** n Kundendienst m. **~shave** n Rasierwasser nt. **~thought** n nachträglicher Einfall m. **~wards** adv nachher

a

again /ə'gen/ adv wieder; (once more) noch einmal; ~ **and** ~ immer wieder

against /ə'genst/ prep gegen (+ acc)

age /eɪdʒ/ n Alter nt; (era) Zeitalter nt; **~s** [!] ewig; **under** ~ minderjährig; **of** ~ volljährig; **two years of** ~ zwei Jahre alt •v (pres p **ageing**) •vt älter machen •vi altern; (mature) reifen

aged[1] /eɪdʒd/ adj ~ **two** zwei Jahre alt

aged[2] /'eɪdʒɪd/ adj betagt •n **the** ~ pl die Alten

ageless /'eɪdʒlɪʃ/ adj ewig jung

agency /'eɪdʒənsɪ/ n Agentur f; (office) Büro nt

agenda /ə'dʒendə/ n Tagesordnung f

agent /'eɪdʒənt/ n Agent(in) m(f); (Comm) Vertreter(in) m(f); (substance) Mittel nt

aggravat|e /'ægrəveɪt/ vt verschlimmern; ([!]: annoy) ärgern. **~ion** n [!] Ärger m

aggregate /'ægrɪgət/ adj gesamt •n Gesamtzahl f; (sum) Gesamtsumme f

aggress|ion /ə'greʃn/ n Aggression f. **~ive** adj aggressiv. **~or** n Angreifer(in) m(f)

aggro /'ægrəʊ/ n [!] Ärger m

aghast /ə'gɑ:st/ adj entsetzt

agil|e /'ædʒaɪl/ adj flink, behände; (mind) wendig. **~ity** n Flinkheit f, Behändigkeit f

agitat|e /'ædʒɪteɪt/ vt bewegen; (shake) schütteln •vi (fig) ~ **for** agitieren für. **~ed** adj erregt. **~ion** n Erregung f; (Pol) Agitation f

ago /ə'gəʊ/ adv vor (+ dat); **a long time** ~ vor langer Zeit; **how long** ~ **is it?** wie lange ist es her?

agony /'ægənɪ/ n Qual f; **be in** ~ furchtbare Schmerzen haben

agree /ə'gri:/ vt vereinbaren; (admit) zugeben; ~ **to do sth** sich bereit erklären, etw zu tun •vi (people, figures:) übereinstimmen; (reach agreement) sich einigen; (get on) gut miteinander auskommen; (consent) einwilligen (**to** in + acc); ~ **with s.o.** jdm zustimmen; (food:) jdm bekommen; ~ **with sth** (approve of) mit etw einverstanden sein

agreeable /ə'gri:əbl/ adj angenehm

agreed /ə'gri:d/ adj vereinbart

agreement /ə'gri:mənt/ n Übereinstimmung f; (consent) Einwilligung f; (contract) Abkommen nt; **reach** ~ sich einigen

agricultur|al /ægrɪ'kʌltʃərəl/ adj landwirtschaftlich. **~e** n Landwirtschaft f

aground /ə'graʊnd/ adj gestrandet; **run** ~ (ship:) stranden

ahead /ə'hed/ adv **straight** ~ geradeaus; **be** ~ **of s.o./sth** vor jdm/etw sein; (fig) voraus sein; **go on** ~ vorgehen; **get** ~ vorankommen; **go** ~**!** [!] bitte! **look/plan** ~ vorausblicken/ -planen

aid /eɪd/ n Hilfe f; (financial) Unterstützung f; **in** ~ **of** zugunsten (+ gen) •vt helfen (+ dat)

Aids /eɪdz/ n Aids nt

aim /eɪm/ n Ziel nt; **take** ~ zielen •vt richten (**at** auf + acc); •vi zielen (**at** auf + acc); ~ **to do sth** beabsichtigen, etw zu tun. **~less** adj ziellos

air /eə(r)/ n Luft f; (expression) Miene f; (appearance) Anschein m; **be on the** ~ (programme:) gesendet werden; (person:) auf Sendung sein; **by** ~ auf dem Luftweg; (airmail) mit Luftpost •vt lüften; vorbringen (views)

air: ~ **bag** n (Auto) Airbag m. **~-conditioned** adj klimatisiert. **~-conditioning** n Klimaanlage f. **~craft** n Flugzeug nt. **~field** n Flugplatz m. ~ **force** n Luftwaffe f. ~ **freshener** n Raumspray nt. **~gun** n Luftgewehr nt.

~**hostess** n Stewardess f. ~ **letter** n Aerogramm nt. ~**line** n Fluggesellschaft f. ~**mail** n Luftpost f. ~**man** n Flieger m. ~**plane** n (Amer) Flugzeug nt. ~**port** n Flughafen m. ~**-raid** n Luftangriff m. ~**-raid shelter** n Luftschutzbunker m. ~**ship** n Luftschiff nt. ~ **ticket** n Flugschein m. ~**tight** adj luftdicht. ~**-traffic controller** n Fluglotse m

airy /'eərɪ/ adj luftig; (manner) nonchalant

aisle /aɪl/ n Gang m

ajar /ə'dʒɑ:(r)/ adj angelehnt

alarm /əlɑ:m/ n Alarm m; (device) Alarmanlage f; (clock) Wecker m; (fear) Unruhe f • vt erschrecken

alas /ə'læs/ int ach!

album /'ælbəm/ n Album nt

alcohol /'ælkəhɒl/ n Alkohol m. ~**ic** adj alkoholisch • n Alkoholiker(in) m(f). ~**ism** n Alkoholismus m

alert /ə'lɜ:t/ adj aufmerksam • n Alarm m

algebra /'ældʒɪbrə/ n Algebra f

Algeria /æl'dʒɪərɪə/ n Algerien nt

alias /'eɪlɪəs/ n Deckname m • adv alias

alibi /'ælɪbaɪ/ n Alibi nt

alien /'eɪlɪən/ adj fremd • n Ausländer(in) m(f)

alienate /'eɪlɪəneɪt/ vt entfremden

alight[1] /ə'laɪt/ vi aussteigen (**from** aus)

alight[2] adj **be** ~ brennen; **set** ~ anzünden

align /ə'laɪn/ vt ausrichten. ~**ment** n Ausrichtung f

alike /ə'laɪk/ adj & adv ähnlich; (same) gleich; **look** ~ sich (dat) ähnlich sehen

alive /ə'laɪv/ adj lebendig; **be** ~ leben; **be** ~ **with** wimmeln von

all /ɔ:l/

• adjective

····➤ (plural) alle. **all [the] children** alle Kinder. **all our children** alle unsere Kinder. **all the books** alle Bücher. **all the others** alle anderen

····➤ (singular = whole) ganz. **all the wine** der ganze Wein. **all the town** die ganze Stadt. **all my money** mein ganzes Geld; all mein Geld. **all day** den ganzen Tag. **all Germany** ganz Deutschland

• pronoun

····➤ (plural = all persons/things) alle. **all are welcome** alle sind willkommen. **they all came** sie sind alle gekommen. **are we all here?** sind wir alle da? **the best pupils of all** die besten Schüler (von allen). **the most beautiful of all** der/die/das schönste von allen

····➤ (singular = everything) alles. **that is all** das ist alles. **all that I possess** alles, was ich besitze

····➤ **all of** ganz; (with plural) alle. **all of the money** das ganze Geld. **all of the paintings** alle Gemälde. **all of you/them** Sie/sie alle

····➤ (in phrases) **all in all** alles in allem. **in all** insgesamt. **most of all** am meisten. **once and for all** ein für alle Mal. **not at all** gar nicht

• adverb

····➤ (completely) ganz. **she was all alone** sie war ganz allein. **I was all dirty** ich war ganz schmutzig

····➤ (in scores) **four all** vier zu vier

····➤ **all right** (things) in Ordnung. **is everything all right?** ist alles in Ordnung? **is that all right for you?** passt das Ihnen? **I'm all right** mir geht es gut. **did you get home all right?** sind Sie gut nach Hause gekommen? **is it all right to go in?** kann ich reingehen? **yes, all right** ja, gut. **work out all right** gut gehen; klappen [!]

····➤ (in phrases) **all but** (almost) fast. **all at once** auf einmal. **all the better** umso besser. **all the same** (nevertheless) trotzdem

a

allege /ə'ledʒ/ vt behaupten. **~d** adj angeblich

allegiance /ə'liːdʒəns/ n Treue f

allerg|ic /ə'lɜːdʒɪk/ adj allergisch (**to** gegen). **~y** n Allergie f

alleviate /ə'liːvɪeɪt/ vt lindern

alley /'ælɪ/ n Gasse f; (for bowling) Bahn f

alliance /ə'laɪəns/ n Verbindung f; (Pol) Bündnis nt

allied /'ælaɪd/ adj alliiert

alligator /'ælɪgeɪtə(r)/ n Alligator m

allocat|e /'æləkeɪt/ vt zuteilen; (share out) verteilen. **~ion** n Zuteilung f

allot /ə'lɒt/ vt (pt/pp **allotted**) zuteilen (**s.o.** jdm)

allow /ə'laʊ/ vt erlauben; (give) geben; (grant) gewähren; (reckon) rechnen; (agree, admit) zugeben; **~ for** berücksichtigen; **~ s.o. to do sth** jdm erlauben, etw zu tun; **be ~ed to do sth** etw tun dürfen

allowance /ə'laʊəns/ n [finanzielle] Unterstützung f; **make ~s for** berücksichtigen

alloy /'ælɔɪ/ n Legierung f

allude /ə'luːd/ vi anspielen (**to** auf + acc)

allusion /ə'luːʒn/ n Anspielung f

ally[1] /'ælaɪ/ n Verbündete(r) m/f; **the Allies** pl die Alliierten

ally[2] /ə'laɪ/ vt (pt/pp **-ied**) verbinden; **~ oneself with** sich verbünden mit

almighty /ɔːl'maɪtɪ/ adj allmächtig; (!: big) Riesen- •n **the A~** der Allmächtige

almond /'ɑːmənd/ n (Bot) Mandel f

almost /'ɔːlməʊst/ adv fast, beinahe

alone /ə'ləʊn/ adj & adv allein; **leave me ~** lass mich in Ruhe; **leave that ~!** lass die Finger davon! **let ~** ganz zu schweigen von

along /ə'lɒŋ/ prep entlang (+ acc); **~ the river** den Fluss entlang •adv **~ with** zusammen mit; **all ~** die ganze Zeit; **come ~** komm doch; **I'll bring it ~** ich bringe es mit

along'side adv daneben •prep neben (+ dat)

aloud /ə'laʊd/ adv laut

alphabet /'ælfəbet/ n Alphabet nt. **~ical** adj alphabetisch

alpine /'ælpaɪn/ adj alpin; **A~** Alpen-

Alps /ælps/ npl Alpen pl

already /ɔːl'redɪ/ adv schon

Alsace /æl'sæs/ n Elsass nt

Alsatian /æl'seɪʃn/ n (dog) [deutscher] Schäferhund m

also /'ɔːlsəʊ/ adv auch

altar /'ɔːltə(r)/ n Altar m

alter /'ɔːltə(r)/ vt ändern •vi sich verändern. **~ation** n Änderung f

alternate[1] /'ɔːltəneɪt/ vi [sich] abwechseln •vt abwechseln

alternate[2] /ɔːl'tɜːnət/ adj abwechselnd; **on ~ days** jeden zweiten Tag

alternative /ɔːl'tɜːnətɪv/ adj andere(r,s); **~ medicine** Alternativmedizin f •n Alternative f. **~ly** adv oder aber

although /ɔːl'ðəʊ/ conj obgleich, obwohl

altitude /'æltɪtjuːd/ n Höhe f

altogether /ɔːltə'geðə(r)/ adv insgesamt; (on the whole) alles in allem

aluminium /æljʊ'mɪnɪəm/ n, (Amer) **aluminum** n Aluminium nt

always /'ɔːlweɪz/ adv immer

am /æm/ see **be**

a.m. abbr (**ante meridiem**) vormittags

amass /ə'mæs/ vt anhäufen

amateur /'æmətə(r)/ n Amateur m •attrib Amateur-; (Theat) Laien-. **~ish** adj laienhaft

amaze /ə'meɪz/ vt erstaunen. **~d** adj erstaunt. **~ment** n Erstaunen nt

amazing /ə'meɪzɪŋ/ adj erstaunlich

ambassador /æm'bæsədə(r)/ n Botschafter m

amber /'æmbə(r)/ n Bernstein m • adj (colour) gelb

ambigu|ity /æmbɪ'gju:ətɪ/ n Zweideutigkeit f. **~ous** adj, **-ly** adv zweideutig

ambiti|on /æm'bɪʃn/ n Ehrgeiz m; (aim) Ambition f. **~ous** adj ehrgeizig

amble /'æmbl/ vi schlendern

ambulance /'æmbjʊləns/ n Krankenwagen m. **~ man** n Sanitäter m

ambush /'æmbʊʃ/ n Hinterhalt m • vt aus dem Hinterhalt überfallen

amen /ɑ:'men/ int amen

amend /ə'mend/ vt ändern. **~ment** n Änderung f

amenities /ə'mi:nətɪz/ npl Einrichtungen pl

America /ə'merɪkə/ n Amerika nt. **~n** adj amerikanisch • n Amerikaner(in) m(f). **~nism** n Amerikanismus m

amiable /'eɪmɪəbl/ adj nett

amicable /'æmɪkəbl/ adj, **-bly** adv freundschaftlich; (agreement) gütlich

amid[st] /ə'mɪd[st]/ prep inmitten (+ gen)

ammonia /ə'məʊnɪə/ n Ammoniak nt

ammunition /æmjʊ'nɪʃn/ n Munition f

amnesty /'æmnəstɪ/ n Amnestie f

among[st] /ə'mʌŋ[st]/ prep unter (+ dat/acc); **~ yourselves** untereinander

amoral /eɪ'mɒrəl/ adj amoralisch

amorous /'æmərəs/ adj zärtlich

amount /ə'maʊnt/ n Menge f; (sum of money) Betrag m; (total) Gesamtsumme f • vi **~ to** sich belaufen auf (+ acc); (fig) hinauslaufen auf (+ acc)

amphibi|an /æm'fɪbɪən/ n Amphibie f. **~ous** adj amphibisch

amphitheatre /'æmfɪ-/ n Amphitheater nt

ample /'æmpl/ adj (**-r,-st**) reichlich; (large) füllig

amplif|ier /'æmplɪfaɪə(r)/ n Verstärker m. **~y** vt (pt/pp **-ied**) weiter ausführen; verstärken (sound)

amputat|e /'æmpjʊteɪt/ vt amputieren. **~ion** n Amputation f

amuse /ə'mju:z/ vt amüsieren, belustigen; (entertain) unterhalten. **~ment** n Belustigung f; Unterhaltung f

amusing /ə'mju:zɪŋ/ adj amüsant

an /ən/, betont /æn/ see **a**

anaem|ia /ə'ni:mɪə/ n Blutarmut f, Anämie f. **~ic** adj blutarm

anaesthetic /ænəs'θetɪk/ n Narkosemittel nt, Betäubungsmittel nt; **under [an] ~** in Narkose

anaesthetist /ə'ni:sθətɪst/ n Narkosearzt m

analogy /ə'nælədʒɪ/ n Analogie f

analyse /'ænəlaɪz/ vt analysieren

analysis /ə'næləsɪs/ n Analyse f

analyst /'ænəlɪst/ n Chemiker(in) m(f); (psychologist) Analytiker m

analytical /ænə'lɪtɪkl/ adj analytisch

anarch|ist /'ænəkɪst/ n Anarchist m. **~y** n Anarchie f

anatom|ical /ænə'tɒmɪkl/ adj anatomisch. **~y** n Anatomie f

ancest|or /'ænsestə(r)/ n Vorfahr m. **~ry** n Abstammung f

anchor /'æŋkə(r)/ n Anker m • vi ankern • vt verankern

ancient /'eɪnʃənt/ adj alt

and /ənd/, betont /ænd/ conj und; **~ so on** und so weiter; **six hundred ~ two** sechshundertzwei; **more ~ more** immer mehr; **nice ~ warm** schön warm

anecdote /'ænɪkdəʊt/ n Anekdote f

angel /'eɪndʒl/ n Engel m. **~ic** adj engelhaft

anger /'æŋgə(r)/ n Zorn m • vt zornig machen

a

angle /ˈæŋgl/ n Winkel m; (fig) Standpunkt m; **at an ~** schräg

angler /ˈæŋglə(r)/ n Angler m

Anglican /ˈæŋglɪkən/ adj anglikanisch • n Anglikaner(in) m(f)

Anglo-Saxon /æŋgləʊˈsæksn/ adj angelsächsich • n (Lang) Angelsächsisch nt

angry /ˈæŋgrɪ/ adj, **-ily** adv zornig; **be ~ with** böse sein auf (+ acc)

anguish /ˈæŋgwɪʃ/ n Qual f

angular /ˈæŋgjʊlə(r)/ adj eckig; (features) kantig

animal /ˈænɪml/ n Tier nt • adj tierisch

animat|e /ˈænɪmeɪt/ vt beleben. **~ed** adj lebhaft

animosity /ænɪˈmɒsətɪ/ n Feindseligkeit f

ankle /ˈæŋkl/ n [Fuß]knöchel m

annex[e] /ˈæneks/ n Nebengebäude nt; (extension) Anbau m

annihilate /əˈnaɪəleɪt/ vt vernichten

anniversary /ænɪˈvɜːsərɪ/ n Jahrestag m

annotate /ˈænəteɪt/ vt kommentieren

announce /əˈnaʊns/ vt bekannt geben; (over loudspeaker) durchsagen; (at reception) ankündigen; (Radio, TV) ansagen; (in newspaper) anzeigen. **~ment** n Bekanntgabe f, Bekanntmachung f; Durchsage f; Ansage f; Anzeige f. **~r** n Ansager(in) m(f)

annoy /əˈnɔɪ/ vt ärgern; (pester) belästigen; **get ~ed** sich ärgern. **~ance** n Ärger m. **~ing** adj ärgerlich

annual /ˈænjʊəl/ adj jährlich • n (book) Jahresalbum nt

anonymous /əˈnɒnɪməs/ adj anonym

anorak /ˈænəræk/ n Anorak m

anorexi|a /ænəˈreksɪə/ n Magersucht f; **be ~c** an Magersucht leiden

another /əˈnʌðə(r)/ adj & pron ein anderer/eine andere/ein anderes; (additional) noch ein(e); **~ [one]** noch einer/eine/eins; **~ time** ein andermal; **one ~** einander

answer /ˈɑːnsə(r)/ n Antwort f; (solution) Lösung f • vt antworten (**s.o.** jdm); beantworten (question, letter); **~ the door/telephone** an die Tür/ans Telefon gehen • vi antworten; (Teleph) sich melden; **~ back** eine freche Antwort geben. **~ing machine** n (Teleph) Anrufbeantworter m

ant /ænt/ n Ameise f

antagonis|m /ænˈtægənɪzm/ n Antagonismus m. **~tic** adj feindselig

Antarctic /æntˈɑːktɪk/ n Antarktis f

antelope /ˈæntɪləʊp/ n Antilope f

antenatal /æntɪˈneɪtl/ adj **~ care** Schwangerschaftsfürsorge f

antenna /ænˈtenə/ n Fühler m; (Amer: aerial) Antenne f

anthem /ˈænθəm/ n Hymne f

anthology /ænˈθɒlədʒɪ/ n Anthologie f

anthrax /ˈænθræks/ n Milzbrand m, Anthrax m

anthropology /ænθrəˈpɒlədʒɪ/ n Anthropologie f

antibiotic /æntɪbaɪˈɒtɪk/ n Antibiotikum nt

anticipat|e /ænˈtɪsɪpeɪt/ vt vorhersehen; (forestall) zuvorkommen (+ dat); (expect) erwarten. **~ion** n Erwartung f

antiˈclimax n Enttäuschung f

antiˈclockwise adj & adv gegen den Uhrzeigersinn

antics /ˈæntɪks/ npl Mätzchen pl

antidote /ˈæntɪdəʊt/ n Gegengift nt

ˈantifreeze n Frostschutzmittel nt

antipathy /ænˈtɪpəθɪ/ n Abneigung f, Antipathie f

antiquated /ˈæntɪkweɪtɪd/ adj veraltet

antique /ænˈtiːk/ adj antik • n

Antiquität f. ~ **dealer** n Antiquitätenhändler m

antiquity /æn'tɪkwətɪ/ n Altertum nt

anti'septic adj antiseptisch •n Antiseptikum nt

anti'social adj asozial; [!] ungesellig

antlers /'æntləz/ npl Geweih nt

anus /'eɪnəs/ n After m

anvil /'ænvɪl/ n Amboss m

anxiety /æŋ'zaɪətɪ/ n Sorge f

anxious /'æŋkʃəs/ adj ängstlich; (worried) besorgt; **be ~ to do sth** etw gerne machen wollen

any /'enɪ/ adj irgendein(e); pl irgendwelche; (every) jede(r,s); pl alle; (after negative) kein(e); pl keine; **~ colour/number you like** eine beliebige Farbe/Zahl; **have you ~ wine/apples?** haben Sie Wein/Äpfel? •pron [irgend]einer/eine/eins; pl [irgend]welche; (some) welche(r,s); pl welche; (all) alle pl; (negative) keiner/keine/keins; pl keine; **I don't want ~ of it** ich will nichts davon; **there aren't ~** es gibt keine •adv noch; **~ quicker/slower** noch schneller/langsamer; **is it ~ better?** geht es etwas besser? **would you like ~ more?** möchten Sie noch [etwas]? **I can't eat ~ more** ich kann nichts mehr essen

'anybody pron [irgend]jemand; (after negative) niemand; **~ can do that** das kann jeder

'anyhow adv jedenfalls; (nevertheless) trotzdem; (badly) irgendwie

'anyone pron = **anybody**

'anything pron [irgend]etwas; (after negative) nichts; (everything) alles

'anyway adv jedenfalls; (in any case) sowieso

'anywhere adv irgendwo; (after negative) nirgendwo; (be, live) überall; (go) überallhin

apart /ə'pɑːt/ adv auseinander; **live ~** getrennt leben; **~ from** abgesehen von

apartment /ə'pɑːtmənt/ n Zimmer nt; (flat) Wohnung f

ape /eɪp/ n [Menschen]affe m •vt nachäffen

aperitif /ə'perətiːf/ n Aperitif m

apologetic /əpɒlə'dʒetɪk/ adj, **-ally** adv entschuldigend; **be ~** sich entschuldigen

apologize /ə'pɒlədʒaɪz/ vi sich entschuldigen (**to** bei)

apology /ə'pɒlədʒɪ/ n Entschuldigung f

apostle /ə'pɒsl/ n Apostel m

apostrophe /ə'pɒstrəfɪ/ n Apostroph m

appal /ə'pɔːl/ vt (pt/pp **appalled**) entsetzen. **~ling** adj entsetzlich

apparatus /æpə'reɪtəs/ n Apparatur f; (Sport) Geräte pl; (single piece) Gerät nt

apparent /ə'pærənt/ adj offenbar; (seeming) scheinbar. **~ly** adv offenbar, anscheinend

appeal /ə'piːl/ n Appell m, Aufruf m; (request) Bitte f; (attraction) Reiz m; (Jur) Berufung f •vi appellieren (**to** an + acc); (ask) bitten (**for** um); (be attractive) zusagen (**to** dat); (Jur) Berufung einlegen. **~ing** adj ansprechend

appear /ə'pɪə(r)/ vi erscheinen; (seem) scheinen; (Theat) auftreten. **~ance** n Erscheinen nt; (look) Aussehen nt; **to all ~ances** allem Anschein nach

appendicitis /əpendɪ'saɪtɪs/ n Blinddarmentzündung f

appendix /ə'pendɪks/ n (pl **-ices** /-ɪsiːz/) (of book) Anhang m •(pl **-es**) (Anat) Blinddarm m

appetite /'æpɪtaɪt/ n Appetit m

appetizing /'æpɪtaɪzɪŋ/ adj appetitlich

applau|d /ə'plɔːd/ vt/i Beifall klatschen (+ dat). **~se** n Beifall m

apple /'æpl/ n Apfel m

appliance /ə'plaɪəns/ n Gerät nt

applicable /'æplɪkəbl/ adj anwendbar (**to** auf + acc); (on form)

a

not ~ nicht zutreffend

applicant /'æplɪkənt/ n Bewerber(in) m(f)

application /æplɪ'keɪʃn/ n Anwendung f; (request) Antrag m; (for job) Bewerbung f; (diligence) Fleiß m

applied /ə'plaɪd/ adj angewandt

apply /ə'plaɪ/ vt (pt/pp **-ied**) auftragen (paint); anwenden (force, rule) •vi zutreffen (**to** auf + acc); **~ for** beantragen; sich bewerben um (job)

appoint /ə'pɔɪnt/ vt ernennen; (fix) festlegen. **~ment** n Ernennung f; (meeting) Verabredung f; (at doctor's, hairdresser's) Termin m; (job) Posten m; **make an ~ment** sich anmelden

appreciable /ə'pri:ʃəbl/ adj merklich; (considerable) beträchtlich

appreciat|e /ə'pri:ʃɪeɪt/ vt zu schätzen wissen; (be grateful for) dankbar sein für; (enjoy) schätzen; (understand) verstehen •vi (increase in value) im Wert steigen. **~ion** n (gratitude) Dankbarkeit f. **~ive** adj dankbar

apprehens|ion /æprɪ'henʃn/ n Festnahme f; (fear) Angst f. **~ive** adj ängstlich

apprentice /ə'prentɪs/ n Lehrling m. **~ship** n Lehre f

approach /ə'prəʊtʃ/ n Näherkommen nt; (of time) Nahen nt; (access) Zugang m; (road) Zufahrt f •vi sich nähern; (time:) nahen •vt sich nähern (+ dat); (with request) herantreten an (+ acc); (set about) sich heranmachen an (+ acc). **~able** adj zugänglich

appropriate /ə'prəʊprɪət/ adj angebracht, angemessen

approval /ə'pru:vl/ n Billigung f; **on ~** zur Ansicht

approv|e /ə'pru:v/ vt billigen •vi **~e of sth/s.o.** mit etw/jdm einverstanden sein. **~ing** adj anerkennend

approximate /ə'prɒksɪmət/ adj, **-ly** adv ungefähr

approximation /əprɒksɪ'meɪʃn/ n Schätzung f

apricot /'eɪprɪkɒt/ n Aprikose f

April /'eɪprəl/ n April m; **make an ~ fool of** in den April schicken

apron /'eɪprən/ n Schürze f

apt /æpt/ adj passend; **be ~ to do sth** dazu neigen, etw zu tun

aqualung /'ækwəlʌŋ/ n Tauchgerät nt

aquarium /ə'kweərɪəm/ n Aquarium nt

aquatic /ə'kwætɪk/ adj Wasser-

Arab /'ærəb/ adj arabisch •n Araber(in) m(f). **~ian** adj arabisch

Arabic /'ærəbɪk/ adj arabisch

arbitrary /'ɑ:bɪtrərɪ/ adj, **-ily** adv willkürlich

arbitrat|e /'ɑ:bɪtreɪt/ vi schlichten. **~ion** n Schlichtung f

arc /ɑ:k/ n Bogen m

arcade /ɑ:'keɪd/ n Laubengang m; (shops) Einkaufspassage f

arch /ɑ:tʃ/ n Bogen m; (of foot) Gewölbe nt •vt **~ its back** (cat:) einen Buckel machen

archaeological /ɑ:kɪə'lɒdʒɪkl/ adj archäologisch

archaeolog|ist /ɑ:kɪ'ɒlədʒɪst/ n Archäologe m/-login f. **~y** n Archäologie f

archaic /ɑ:'keɪɪk/ adj veraltet

arch'bishop /ɑ:tʃ-/ n Erzbischof m

archer /'ɑ:tʃə(r)/ n Bogenschütze m. **~y** n Bogenschießen nt

architect /'ɑ:kɪtekt/ n Architekt(in) m(f). **~ural** adj architektonisch

architecture /'ɑ:kɪtektʃə(r)/ n Architektur f

archives /'ɑ:kaɪvz/ npl Archiv nt

archway /'ɑ:tʃweɪ/ n Torbogen m

Arctic /'ɑ:ktɪk/ adj arktisch •n **the ~** die Arktis

ardent /'ɑ:dənt/ adj leidenschaftlich

ardour /'ɑ:də(r)/ n Leidenschaft f

arduous /'ɑːdjʊəs/ adj mühsam

are /ɑː(r)/ see **be**

area /'eərɪə/ n (surface) Fläche f; (Geometry) Flächeninhalt m; (region) Gegend f; (fig) Gebiet nt

arena /ə'riːnə/ n Arena f

Argentina /ɑːdʒən'tiːnə/ n Argentinien nt

Argentin|e /'ɑːdʒəntaɪn/, **~ian** /-'tɪnɪən/ adj argentinisch

argue /'ɑːgjuː/ vi streiten (**about** über + acc); (two people:) sich streiten; (debate) diskutieren; **don't ~!** keine Widerrede! • vt (debate) diskutieren; (reason) **~ that** argumentieren, dass

argument /'ɑːgjʊmənt/ n Streit m, Auseinandersetzung f; (reasoning) Argument nt; **have an ~** sich streiten. **~ative** adj streitlustig

aria /'ɑːrɪə/ n Arie f

arise /ə'raɪz/ vi (pt **arose**, pp **arisen**) sich ergeben (**from** aus)

aristocracy /ærɪ'stɒkrəsɪ/ n Aristokratie f

aristocrat /'ærɪstəkræt/ n Aristokrat(in) m(f). **~ic** adj aristokratisch

arithmetic /ə'rɪθmətɪk/ n Rechnen nt

arm /ɑːm/ n Arm m; (of chair) Armlehne f; **~s** pl (weapons) Waffen pl; (Heraldry) Wappen nt • vt bewaffnen

armament /'ɑːməmənt/ n Bewaffnung f; **~s** pl Waffen pl

'armchair n Sessel m

armed /ɑːmd/ adj bewaffnet; **~ forces** Streitkräfte pl

armour /'ɑːmə(r)/ n Rüstung f. **~ed** adj Panzer-

'armpit n Achselhöhle f

army /'ɑːmɪ/ n Heer nt; (specific) Armee f; **join the ~** zum Militär gehen

aroma /ə'rəʊmə/ n Aroma nt, Duft m. **~tic** adj aromatisch

arose /ə'rəʊz/ see **arise**

around /ə'raʊnd/ adv **[all] ~** rings herum; **he's not ~** er ist nicht da; **travel ~** herumreisen • prep um (+ acc) ... herum; (approximately, nearly) gegen

arouse /ə'raʊz/ vt aufwecken; (excite) erregen

arrange /ə'reɪndʒ/ vt arrangieren; anordnen (furniture, books); (settle) abmachen. **~ment** n Anordnung f; (agreement) Vereinbarung f; (of flowers) Gesteck nt; **make ~ments** Vorkehrungen treffen

arrest /ə'rest/ n Verhaftung f; **under ~** verhaftet • vt verhaften

arrival /ə'raɪvl/ n Ankunft f; **new ~s** pl Neuankömmlinge pl

arrive /ə'raɪv/ vi ankommen; **~ at** (fig) gelangen zu

arrogan|ce /'ærəgəns/ n Arroganz f. **~t** adj arrogant

arrow /'ærəʊ/ n Pfeil m

arse /ɑːs/ n (vulgar) Arsch m

arson /'ɑːsn/ n Brandstiftung f. **~ist** n Brandstifter m

art /ɑːt/ n Kunst f; **work of ~** Kunstwerk nt; **~s and crafts** pl Kunstgewerbe nt; **A~s** pl (Univ) Geisteswissenschaften pl

artery /'ɑːtərɪ/ n Schlagader f, Arterie f

'art gallery n Kunstgalerie f

arthritis /ɑː'θraɪtɪs/ n Arthritis f

artichoke /'ɑːtɪtʃəʊk/ n Artischocke f

article /'ɑːtɪkl/ n Artikel m; (object) Gegenstand m; **~ of clothing** Kleidungsstück nt

artificial /ɑːtɪ'fɪʃl/ adj künstlich

artillery /ɑː'tɪlərɪ/ n Artillerie f

artist /'ɑːtɪst/ n Künstler(in) m(f)

artiste /ɑː'tiːst/ n (Theat) Artist(in) m(f)

artistic /ɑː'tɪstɪk/ adj, **-ally** adv künstlerisch

as /æz/ conj (because) da; (when) als; (while) während • prep als; **as a child/foreigner** als Kind/Ausländer • adv **as well** auch; **as soon as** sobald; **as much as** so viel wie; **as quick as you** so schnell wie du; **as you know** wie Sie wissen; **as far as I'm concerned** was mich betrifft

asbestos /æz'bestɒs/ n Asbest m

ascend /ə'send/ vi [auf]steigen •vt besteigen (throne)

ascent /ə'sent/ n Aufstieg m

ascertain /æsə'teɪn/ vt ermitteln

ash[1] /æʃ/ n (tree) Esche f

ash[2] n Asche f

ashamed /ə'ʃeɪmd/ adj beschämt; **be ~** sich schämen (**of** über + acc)

ashore /ə'ʃɔ:(r)/ adv an Land

'**ashtray** n Aschenbecher m

Asia /'eɪʃə/ n Asien nt. **~n** adj asiatisch •n Asiat(in) m(f). **~tic** adj asiatisch

aside /ə'saɪd/ adv beiseite

ask /ɑ:sk/ vt/i **fragen**; stellen (question); (invite) einladen; **~ for** bitten um; verlangen (s.o.); **~ after** sich erkundigen nach; **~ s.o. in** jdn hereinbitten; **~ s.o. to do sth** jdn bitten, etw zu tun

asleep /ə'sli:p/ adj **be ~** schlafen; **fall ~** einschlafen

asparagus /ə'spærəgəs/ n Spargel m

aspect /'æspekt/ n Aspekt m

asphalt /'æsfælt/ n Asphalt m

aspire /ə'spaɪə(r)/ vi **~ to** streben nach

ass /æs/ n Esel m

assail /ə'seɪl/ vt bestürmen. **~ant** n Angreifer(in) m(f)

assassin /ə'sæsɪn/ n Mörder(in) m(f). **~ate** vt ermorden. **~ation** n [politischer] Mord m

assault /ə'sɔ:lt/ n (Mil) Angriff m; (Jur) Körperverletzung f •vt [tätlich] angreifen

assemble /ə'sembl/ vi sich versammeln •vt versammeln; (Techn) montieren

assembly /ə'semblɪ/ n Versammlung f; (Sch) Andacht f; (Techn) Montage f. **~ line** n Fließband nt

assent /ə'sent/ n Zustimmung f

assert /ə'sɜ:t/ vt behaupten; **~ oneself** sich durchsetzen. **~ion** n Behauptung f

assess /ə'ses/ vt bewerten; (fig & for tax purposes) einschätzen: schätzen (value). **~ment** n Einschätzung f; (of tax) Steuerbescheid m

asset /'æset/ n Vorteil m; **~s** pl (money) Vermögen nt; (Comm) Aktiva pl

assign /ə'saɪn/ vt zuweisen (**to** dat). **~ment** n (task) Aufgabe f

assist /ə'sɪst/ vt/i helfen (+ dat). **~ance** n Hilfe f. **~ant** adj Hilfs- •n Assistent(in) m(f); (in shop) Verkäufer(in) m(f)

associat|e[1] /ə'səʊʃɪeɪt/ vt verbinden; (Psychology) assoziieren •vi **~ with** verkehren mit. **~ion** n Verband m

associate[2] /ə'səʊʃɪət/ adj assoziiert •n Kollege m/-gin f

assort|ed /ə'sɔ:tɪd/ adj gemischt. **~ment** n Mischung f

assum|e /ə'sju:m/ vt annehmen; übernehmen (office); **~ing that** angenommen, dass

assumption /ə'sʌmpʃn/ n Annahme f; **on the ~** in der Annahme (**that** dass)

assurance /ə'ʃʊərəns/ n Versicherung f; (confidence) Selbstsicherheit f

assure /ə'ʃʊə(r)/ vt versichern (**s.o.** jdm); **I ~ you [of that]** das versichere ich Ihnen. **~d** adj sicher

asterisk /'æstərɪsk/ n Sternchen nt

asthma /'æsmə/ n Asthma nt

astonish /ə'stɒnɪʃ/ vt erstaunen. **~ing** adj erstaunlich. **~ment** n Erstaunen nt

astray /ə'streɪ/ adv **go ~** verloren gehen; (person:) sich verlaufen

astride /ə'straɪd/ adv rittlings •prep rittlings auf (+ dat/acc)

astrolog|er /ə'strɒlədʒə(r)/ n Astrologe m/-gin f. **~y** n Astrologie f

astronaut /'æstrənɔ:t/ n Astronaut(in) m(f)

astronom|er /ə'strɒnəmə(r)/ n Astronom m. **~ical** adj astronomisch. **~y** n Astronomie f

astute /ə'stju:t/ adj scharfsinnig

asylum /ə'saɪləm/ n Asyl nt; **[lunatic] ~** Irrenanstalt f. **~-seeker** n Asylbewerber(in) m(f)

at /æt/, unbetont /ət/
• preposition
····➤ (expressing place) an (+ dat). **at the station** am Bahnhof. **at the end** am Ende. **at the corner** an der Ecke. **at the same place** an der gleichen Stelle
····➤ (at s.o.'s house or shop) bei (+ dat). **at Lisa's** bei Lisa. **at my uncle's** bei meinem Onkel. **at the baker's/butcher's** beim Bäcker/Fleischer
····➤ (inside a building) in (+ dat). **at the theatre/supermarket** im Theater/Supermarkt. **we spent the night at a hotel** wir übernachteten in einem Hotel. **he is still at the office** er ist noch im Büro
····➤ (expressing time) (with clock time) um; (with main festivals) zu. **at six o'clock** um sechs Uhr. **at midnight** um Mitternacht. **at midday** um zwölf Uhr mittags. **at Christmas/Easter** zu Weihnachten/Ostern
····➤ (expressing age) mit. **at [the age of] forty** mit vierzig; im Alter von vierzig
····➤ (expressing price) zu. **at £2.50 [each]** zu od für [je] 2,50 Pfund
····➤ (expressing speed) mit. **at 30 m.p.h.** mit dreißig Meilen pro Stunde
····➤ (in phrases) **good/bad at languages** gut/schlecht in Sprachen. **two at a time** zwei auf einmal. **at that** (at that point) dabei; (at that provocation) daraufhin; (moreover) noch dazu

ate /et/ see **eat**

atheist /'eɪθɪɪst/ n Atheist(in) m(f)

athlet|e /'æθli:t/ n Athlet(in) m(f). **~ic** adj sportlich. **~ics** n Leichtathletik f

Atlantic /ət'læntɪk/ adj & n **the ~ [Ocean]** der Atlantik

atlas /'ætləs/ n Atlas m

atmosphere /'ætməsfɪə(r)/ n Atmosphäre f

atom /'ætəm/ n Atom nt. **~ bomb** n Atombombe f

atomic /ə'tɒmɪk/ adj Atom-

atrocious /ə'trəʊʃəs/ adj abscheulich

atrocity /ə'trɒsətɪ/ n Gräueltat f

attach /ə'tætʃ/ vt befestigen (**to** an + dat); beimessen (importance) (**to** dat); **be ~ed to** (fig) hängen an (+ dat)

attack /ə'tæk/ n Angriff m; (Med) Anfall m •vt/i angreifen. **~er** n Angreifer m

attain /ə'teɪn/ vt erreichen. **~able** adj erreichbar

attempt /ə'tempt/ n Versuch m •vt versuchen

attend /ə'tend/ vt anwesend sein bei; (go regularly to) besuchen; (take part in) teilnehmen an (+ dat); (accompany) begleiten; (doctor:) behandeln •vi anwesend sein; (pay attention) aufpassen; **~ to** sich kümmern um; (in shop) bedienen. **~ance** n Anwesenheit f; (number) Besucherzahl f. **~ant** n Wärter(in) m(f); (in car park) Wächter m

attention /ə'tenʃn/ n Aufmerksamkeit f; **~!** (Mil) stillgestanden! **pay ~** aufpassen; **pay ~ to** beachten, achten auf (+ acc)

attentive /ə'tentɪv/ adj aufmerksam

attic /'ætɪk/ n Dachboden m

attitude /'ætɪtju:d/ n Haltung f

attorney /ə'tɜ:nɪ/ n (Amer: lawyer) Rechtsanwalt m; **power of ~** Vollmacht f

attract /ə'trækt/ vt anziehen; erregen (attention); **~ s.o.'s attention** jds Aufmerksamkeit auf

a

sich (acc) lenken. ~**ion** n Anziehungskraft f; (charm) Reiz m; (thing) Attraktion f. ~**ive** adj, **-ly** adv attraktiv

attribute /ə'trɪbju:t/ vt zuschreiben (**to** dat)

aubergine /'əʊbəʒi:n/ n Aubergine f

auburn /'ɔ:bən/ adj kastanienbraun

auction /'ɔ:kʃn/ n Auktion f Versteigerung f •vt versteigern. ~**eer** n Auktionator m

audaci|ous /ɔ:'deɪʃəs/ adj verwegen. ~**ty** n Verwegenheit f; (impudence) Dreistigkeit f

audible /'ɔ:dəbl/ adj, **-bly** adv hörbar

audience /'ɔ:dɪəns/ n Publikum nt; (Theat, TV) Zuschauer pl; (Radio) Zuhörer pl; (meeting) Audienz f

audit /'ɔ:dɪt/ n Bücherrevision f •vt (Comm) prüfen

audition /ɔ:'dɪʃn/ n (Theat) Vorsprechen nt; (Mus) Vorspielen nt (for singer) Vorsingen nt •vi vorsprechen; vorspielen; vorsingen

auditor /'ɔ:dɪtə(r)/ n Buchprüfer m

auditorium /ɔ:dɪ'tɔ:rɪəm/ n Zuschauerraum m

August /'ɔ:gəst/ n August m

aunt /ɑ:nt/ n Tante f

au pair /əʊ'peə(r)/ n ~ **[girl]** Au-pair-Mädchen nt

aura /'ɔ:rə/ n Fluidum nt

auspicious /ɔ:'spɪʃəs/ adj günstig; (occasion) freudig

auster|e /ɒ'stɪə(r)/ adj streng; (simple) nüchtern. ~**ity** n Strenge f; (hardship) Entbehrung f

Australia /ɒ'streɪlɪə/ n Australien nt. ~**n** adj australisch •n Australier(in) m(f)

Austria /'ɒstrɪə/ n Österreich nt ~**n** adj österreichisch •n Österreicher(in) m(f)

authentic /ɔ:'θentɪk/ adj echt, authentisch. ~**ate** vt beglaubigen. ~**ity** n Echtheit f

author /'ɔ:θə(r)/ n Schriftsteller m, Autor m; (of document) Verfasser m

authoritarian /ɔ:θɒrɪ'teərɪən/ adj autoritär

authoritative /ɔ:'θɒrɪtətɪv/ adj maßgebend

authority /ɔ:'θɒrətɪ/ n Autorität f; (public) Behörde f; **in** ~ verantwortlich

authorization /ɔ:θəraɪ'zeɪʃn/ n Ermächtigung f

authorize /'ɔ:θəraɪz/ vt ermächtigen (s.o.); genehmigen (sth)

autobi'ography /ɔ:tə-/ n Autobiographie f

autograph /'ɔ:tə-/ n Autogramm nt

automatic /ɔ:tə'mætɪk/ adj, **-ally** adv automatisch

automation /ɔ:tə'meɪʃn/ n Automation f

automobile /'ɔ:təməbi:l/ n Auto nt

autonom|ous /ɔ:'tɒnəməs/ adj autonom. ~**y** n Autonomie f

autumn /'ɔ:təm/ n Herbst m. ~**al** adj herbstlich

auxiliary /ɔ:g'zɪlɪərɪ/ adj Hilfs- •n Helfer(in) m(f), Hilfskraft f

avail /ə'veɪl/ n **to no** ~ vergeblich

available /ə'veɪləbl/ adj verfügbar; (obtainable) erhältlich

avalanche /'ævəlɑ:nʃ/ n Lawine f

avenge /ə'vendʒ/ vt rächen

avenue /'ævənju:/ n Allee f

average /'ævərɪdʒ/ adj Durchschnitts-, durchschnittlich •n Durchschnitt m; **on** ~ im Durchschnitt, durchschnittlich •vt durchschnittlich schaffen

averse /ə'vɜ:s/ adj **not be** ~**e to sth** etw (dat) nicht abgeneigt sein

avert /ə'vɜ:t/ vt abwenden

aviary /'eɪvɪərɪ/ n Vogelhaus nt

aviation /eɪvɪ'eɪʃn/ n Luftfahrt f

avocado /ævə'kɑ:dəʊ/ n Avocado f

avoid /ə'vɔɪd/ vt vermeiden; ~ **s.o.** jdm aus dem Weg gehen. ~**able**

adj vermeidbar. **~ance** n Vermeidung f

await /ə'weɪt/ vt warten auf (+ acc)

awake /ə'weɪk/ adj wach; **wide ~** hellwach •vi (pt **awoke**, pp **awoken**) erwachen

awaken /ə'weɪkn/ vt wecken •vi erwachen. **~ing** n Erwachen nt

award /ə'wɔ:d/ n Auszeichnung f; (prize) Preis m •vt zuerkennen (**to s.o.** dat); verleihen (prize)

aware /ə'weə(r)/ adj **become ~** gewahr werden (**of** gen); **be ~ that** wissen, dass. **~ness** n Bewusstsein nt

away /ə'weɪ/ adv weg, fort; (absent) abwesend; **four kilometres ~** vier Kilometer entfernt; **play ~** (Sport) auswärts spielen. **~ game** n Auswärtsspiel nt

awful /'ɔ:fl/ adj furchtbar

awkward /'ɔ:kwəd/ adj schwierig; (clumsy) ungeschickt; (embarrassing) peinlich; (inconvenient) ungünstig. **~ly** adv ungeschickt; (embarrassedly) verlegen

awning /'ɔ:nɪŋ/ n Markise f

awoke(n) /ə'wəʊk(n)/ see **awake**

axe /æks/ n Axt f •vt (pres p **axing**) streichen

axle /'æksl/ n (Techn) Achse f

Bb

B /bi:/ n (Mus) H nt

baboon /bə'bu:n/ n Pavian m

baby /'beɪbɪ/ n Baby nt; (Amer, [!]) Schätzchen nt

baby: ~ish adj kindisch. **~-sit** vi babysitten. **~-sitter** n Babysitter m

bachelor /'bætʃələ(r)/ n Junggeselle m

back /bæk/ n Rücken m; (reverse) Rückseite f; (of chair) Rückenlehne f; (Sport) Verteidiger m; **at**/(Auto) **in the ~** hinten; **on the ~** auf der Rückseite; **~ to front** verkehrt •adj Hinter- •adv zurück; **~ here/there** hier/da hinten; **~ at home** zu Hause; **go/pay ~** zurückgehen/-zahlen •vt (support) unterstützen; (with money) finanzieren; (Auto) zurücksetzen; (Betting) [Geld] setzen auf (+ acc); (cover the back of) mit einer Verstärkung versehen •vi (Auto) zurücksetzen. **~ down** vi klein beigeben. **~ in** vi rückwärts hineinfahren. **~ out** vi rückwärts hinaus-/herausfahren; (fig) aussteigen (**of** aus). **~ up** vt unterstützen; (confirm) bestätigen •vi (Auto) zurücksetzen

back: ~ache n Rückenschmerzen pl. **~biting** n gehässiges Gerede nt. **~bone** n Rückgrat nt. **~date** vt rückdatieren; **~dated to** rückwirkend von. **~ 'door** n Hintertür f

backer /'bækə(r)/ n Geldgeber m

back: ~'fire vi (Auto) fehlzünden; (fig) fehlschlagen. **~ground** n Hintergrund m; **family ~ground** Familienverhältnisse pl. **~hand** n (Sport) Rückhand f. **~'handed** adj (compliment) zweifelhaft

backing /'bækɪŋ/ n (support) Unterstützung f; (material) Verstärkung f

back: ~lash n (fig) Gegenschlag m. **~log** n Rückstand m (**of** an + dat). **~pack** n Rucksack m. **~ 'seat** n Rücksitz m. **~side** n [!] Hintern m. **~stroke** n Rückenschwimmen nt. **~-up** n Unterstützung f; (Amer: traffic jam) Stau m

backward /'bækwəd/ adj zurückgeblieben; (country)

b

rückständig •adv rückwärts. **~s** rückwärts; **~s and forwards** hin und her

back'yard n Hinterhof m; **not in my ~yard** [!] nicht vor meiner Haustür

bacon /'beɪkn/ n [Schinken]speck m

bacteria /bæk'tɪərɪə/ npl Bakterien pl

bad /bæd/ adj (**worse, worst**) schlecht; (serious) schwer, schlimm; (naughty) unartig; **~ language** gemeine Ausdrucksweise f; **feel ~** sich schlecht fühlen; (feel guilty) ein schlechtes Gewissen haben

badge /bædʒ/ n Abzeichen nt

badger /'bædʒə(r)/ n Dachs m •vt plagen

badly /'bædlɪ/ adv schlecht; (seriously) schwer; **~ off** schlecht gestellt; **~ behaved** unerzogen; **want ~** sich (dat) sehnsüchtig wünschen; **need ~** dringend brauchen

bad-'mannered adj mit schlechten Manieren

badminton /'bædmɪntən/ n Federball m

bad-'tempered adj schlecht gelaunt

baffle /'bæfl/ vt verblüffen

bag /bæg/ n Tasche f; (of paper) Tüte f; (pouch) Beutel m; **~s of** [!] jede Menge •vt ([!]: reserve) in Beschlag nehmen

baggage /'bægɪdʒ/ n [Reise]gepäck nt

baggy /'bægɪ/ adj (clothes) ausgebeult

'bagpipes npl Dudelsack m

bail /beɪl/ n Kaution f; **on ~** gegen Kaution •vt **~ s.o. out** jdn gegen Kaution freibekommen; (fig) jdm aus der Patsche helfen

bait /beɪt/ n Köder m •vt mit einem Köder versehen; (fig: torment) reizen

bake /beɪk/ vt/i backen

baker /'beɪkə(r)/ n Bäcker m; **~'s [shop]** Bäckerei f. **~y** n Bäckerei f

baking /'beɪkɪŋ/ n Backen nt. **~-powder** n Backpulver nt

balance /'bæləns/ n (equilibrium) Gleichgewicht nt, Balance f; (scales) Waage f; (Comm) Saldo m; (outstanding sum) Restbetrag m; **[bank] ~** Kontostand m; **in the ~** (fig) in der Schwebe •vt balancieren; (equalize) ausgleichen; (Comm) abschließen (books) •vi balancieren; (fig & Comm) sich ausgleichen. **~d** adj ausgewogen

balcony /'bælkənɪ/ n Balkon m

bald /bɔːld/ adj (**-er, -est**) kahl; (person) kahlköpfig

bald|ly adv unverblümt. **~ness** n Kahlköpfigkeit f

ball¹ /bɔːl/ n Ball m; (Billiards, Croquet) Kugel f; (of yarn) Knäuel m & nt; **on the ~** [!] auf Draht

ball² n (dance) Ball m

ball-'bearing n Kugellager nt

ballerina /bælə'riːnə/ n Ballerina f

ballet /'bæleɪ/ m Ballett nt. **~ dancer** n Balletttänzer(in) m(f)

balloon /bə'luːn/ n Luftballon m; (Aviat) Ballon m

ballot /'bælət/ n [geheime] Wahl f; (on issue) [geheime] Abstimmung f. **~-box** n Wahlurne f. **~-paper** n Stimmzettel m

ball: ~point ['pen] n Kugelschreiber m. **~room** n Ballsaal m

balm /bɑːm/ n Balsam m

balmy /'bɑːmɪ/ adj sanft

Baltic /'bɔːltɪk/ adj & n **the ~ [Sea]** die Ostsee

bamboo /bæm'buː/ n Bambus m

ban /bæn/ n Verbot nt •vt (pt/pp **banned**) verbieten

banal /bə'nɑːl/ adj banal. **~ity** n Banalität f

banana /bə'nɑːnə/ n Banane f

band /bænd/ n Band nt; (stripe) Streifen m; (group) Schar f; (Mus) Kapelle f

bandage /'bændɪdʒ/ n Verband m; (for support) Bandage f •vt verbinden; bandagieren (limb)

b. & b. abbr **bed and breakfast**

bandit /'bændɪt/ n Bandit m

band: ~stand n Musikpavillon m. **~wagon** n **jump on the ~wagon** (fig) sich einer erfolgreichen Sache anschließen

bang /bæŋ/ n (noise) Knall m; (blow) Schlag m • adv **go ~** knallen • int bums! peng! • vt knallen; (shut noisily) zuknallen; (strike) schlagen auf (+ acc); **~ one's head** sich (dat) den Kopf stoßen (**on** an + acc) • vi schlagen; (door:) zuknallen

banger /'bæŋə(r)/ n (firework) Knallfrosch m; ([!]: sausage) Wurst f; **old ~** ([!]: car) Klapperkiste f

bangle /'bæŋgl/ n Armreifen m

banish /'bænɪʃ/ vt verbannen

banisters /'bænɪstəz/ npl [Treppen]geländer nt

banjo /'bændʒəʊ/ n Banjo nt

bank[1] /bæŋk/ n (of river) Ufer nt; (slope) Hang m • vi (Aviat) in die Kurve gehen

bank[2] n Bank f • **~ on** vt sich verlassen auf (+ acc)

'bank account n Bankkonto nt

banker /'bæŋkə(r)/ n Bankier m

bank: ~ 'holiday n gesetzlicher Feiertag m. **~ing** n Bankwesen nt. **~note** n Banknote f

bankrupt /'bæŋkrʌpt/ adj bankrott; **go ~** Bankrott machen • n Bankrotteur m • vt Bankrott machen. **~cy** n Bankrott m

banner /'bænə(r)/ n Banner nt; (carried by demonstrators) Transparent nt, Spruchband nt

banquet /'bæŋkwɪt/ n Bankett nt

baptism /'bæptɪzm/ n Taufe f

baptize /bæp'taɪz/ vt taufen

bar /bɑː(r)/ n Stange f; (of cage) [Gitter]stab m; (of gold) Barren m; (of chocolate) Tafel f; (of soap) Stück nt; (long) Riegel m; (café) Bar f; (counter) Theke f; (Mus) Takt m; (fig: obstacle) Hindernis nt; **parallel ~s** (Sport) Barren m; **behind ~s** [!] hinter Gittern • vt (pt/pp **barred**) versperren (way, door); ausschließen (person)

barbar|ic /bɑː'bærɪk/ adj barbarisch. **~ity** n Barbarei f. **~ous** adj barbarisch

barbecue /'bɑːbɪkjuː/ n Grill m; (party) Grillfest nt • vt [im Freien] grillen

barbed /'bɑːbd/ adj **~ wire** Stacheldraht m

barber /'bɑːbə(r)/ n [Herren]friseur m

'bar code n Strichkode m

bare /beə(r)/ adj (**-r, -st**) nackt, bloß; (tree) kahl; (empty) leer; (mere) bloß

bare: ~back adv ohne Sattel. **~faced** adj schamlos. **~foot** adv barfuß. **~'headed** adj mit unbedecktem Kopf

barely /'beəlɪ/ adv kaum

bargain /'bɑːgɪn/ n (agreement) Geschäft nt; (good buy) Gelegenheitskauf m; **into the ~** noch dazu; **make a ~** sich einigen • vi handeln; (haggle) feilschen; **~ for** (expect) rechnen mit

barge /bɑːdʒ/ n Lastkahn m; (towed) Schleppkahn m • vi **~ in** [!] hereinplatzen

baritone /'bærɪtəʊn/ n Bariton m

bark[1] /bɑːk/ n (of tree) Rinde f

bark[2] n Bellen nt • vi bellen

barley /'bɑːlɪ/ n Gerste f

bar: ~maid n Schankmädchen nt. **~man** Barmann m

barmy /'bɑːmɪ/ adj [!] verrückt

barn /bɑːn/ n Scheune f

barometer /bə'rɒmɪtə(r)/ n Barometer nt

baron /'bærn/ n Baron m. **~ess** n Baronin f

barracks /'bærəks/ npl Kaserne f

barrage /'bærɑːʒ/ n (in river) Wehr nt; (Mil) Sperrfeuer nt; (fig) Hagel m

barrel /'bærl/ n Fass nt; (of gun) Lauf m; (of cannon) Rohr nt. **~-organ** n Drehorgel f

b

barren /ˈbærn/ adj unfruchtbar; (landscape) öde

barricade /bærɪˈkeɪd/ n Barrikade f •vt verbarrikadieren

barrier /ˈbærɪə(r)/ n Barriere f; (across road) Schranke f; (Rail) Sperre f; (fig) Hindernis nt

barrow /ˈbærəʊ/ n Karre f, Karren m

base /beɪs/ n Fuß m; (fig) Basis f; (Mil) Stützpunkt m •vt stützen (**on** auf + acc); **be ~d on** basieren auf (+ dat)

base: ~ball n Baseball m. **~less** adj unbegründet. **~ment** n Kellergeschoss nt

bash /bæʃ/ n Schlag m; **have a ~!** [!] probier es mal! •vt hauen

basic /ˈbeɪsɪk/ adj Grund-; (fundamental) grundlegend; (essential) wesentlich; (unadorned) einfach; **the ~s** das Wesentliche. **~ally** adv grundsätzlich

basin /ˈbeɪsn/ n Becken nt; (for washing) Waschbecken nt; (for food) Schüssel f

basis /ˈbeɪsɪs/ n (pl **-ses** /-si:z/) Basis f

bask /bɑ:sk/ vi sich sonnen

basket /ˈbɑ:skɪt/ n Korb m. **~ball** n Basketball m

Basle /bɑ:l/ n Basel nt

bass /beɪs/ adj Bass-; **~ voice** Bassstimme f •n Bass m; (person) Bassist m

bassoon /bəˈsu:n/ n Fagott nt

bastard /ˈbɑ:stəd/ n [✖] Schuft m

bat[1] /bæt/ n Schläger m; **off one's own ~** [!] auf eigene Faust •vt (pt/pp **batted**) schlagen; **not ~ an eyelid** (fig) nicht mit der Wimper zucken

bat[2] n (Zool) Fledermaus f

batch /bætʃ/ n (of people) Gruppe f; (of papers) Stoß m; (of goods) Sendung f; (of bread) Schub m

bath /bɑ:θ/ n (pl **~s** /bɑ:ðz/) Bad nt; (tub) Badewanne f; **~s** pl Badeanstalt f; **have a ~** baden

bathe /beɪð/ n Bad nt •vt/i baden. **~r** n Badende(r) m/f

bathing /ˈbeɪðɪŋ/ n Baden nt. **~-cap** n Bademütze f. **~-costume** n Badeanzug m

bath: ~-mat n Badematte f. **~room** n Badezimmer nt. **~-towel** n Badetuch nt

battalion /bəˈtælɪən/ n Bataillon nt

batter /ˈbætə(r)/ n (Culin) flüssiger Teig m •vt schlagen. **~ed** adj (car) verbeult; (wife) misshandelt

battery /ˈbætərɪ/ n Batterie f

battle /ˈbætl/ n Schlacht f; (fig) Kampf m •vi (fig) kämpfen (**for** um)

battle: ~field n Schlachtfeld nt. **~ship** n Schlachtschiff nt

batty /ˈbætɪ/ adj [!] verrückt

Bavaria /bəˈveərɪə/ n Bayern nt. **~n** adj bayrisch •n Bayer(in) m(f)

bawl /bɔ:l/ vt/i brüllen

bay[1] /beɪ/ n (Geog) Bucht f; (in room) Erker m

bay[2] n (Bot) [echter] Lorbeer m. **~-leaf** n Lorbeerblatt nt

bayonet /ˈbeɪənet/ n Bajonett nt

bay ˈwindow n Erkerfenster nt

bazaar /bəˈzɑ:(r)/ n Basar m

BC abbr (**before Christ**) v.Chr.

be /bi:/

(pres **am, are, is**, pl **are**; pt **was**, pl **were**; pp **been**)

• intransitive verb

····> (expressing identity, nature, state, age etc.) sein. **he is a teacher** er ist Lehrer. **she is French** sie ist Französin. **he is very nice** er ist sehr nett. **I am tall** ich bin groß. **you are thirty** du bist dreißig. **it was very cold** es war sehr kalt

····> (expressing general position) sein; (lie) liegen; (stand) stehen. **where is the bank?** wo ist die Bank? **the book is on the table** das Buch liegt auf dem Tisch. **the vase is**

on the shelf die Vase steht auf dem Brett

····➤ (feel) **I am cold/hot** mir ist kalt/heiß. **I am ill** ich bin krank. **I am well** mir geht es gut. **how are you?** wie geht es Ihnen?

····➤ (date) **it is the 5th today** heute haben wir den Fünften

····➤ (go, come, stay) sein. **I have been to Vienna** ich bin in Wien gewesen. **have you ever been to London?** bist du schon einmal in London gewesen? **has the postman been?** war der Briefträger schon da? **I've been here for an hour** ich bin seit einer Stunde hier

····➤ (origin) **where are you from?** woher stammen od kommen Sie? **she is from Australia** sie stammt od ist aus Australien

····➤ (cost) kosten. **how much are the eggs?** was kosten die Eier?

····➤ (in calculations) **two threes are six** zweimal drei ist od sind sechs

····➤ (exist) **there is/are** es gibt (+ acc). **there's no fish left** es gibt keinen Fisch mehr

• auxiliary verb

····➤ (forming continuous tenses: not translated) **I'm working** ich arbeite. **I'm leaving tomorrow** ich reise morgen [ab]. **they were singing** sie sangen. **they will be coming on Tuesday** sie kommen am Dienstag

····➤ (forming passive) werden. **the child was found** das Kind wurde gefunden. **German is spoken here** hier wird Deutsch gesprochen; hier spricht man Deutsch

····➤ (expressing arrangement, obligation, destiny) sollen. **I am to go/inform you** ich soll gehen/Sie unterrichten. **they were to fly today** sie sollten heute fliegen. **you are to do that immediately** das sollst du sofort machen. **you are not to ...** (prohibition) du darfst nicht .... **they were never to meet again** (destiny) sie sollten sich nie wieder treffen

····➤ (in short answers) **Are you disappointed? — Yes I am** Bist du enttäuscht? — Ja. (negating previous statement) **Aren't you coming? — Yes I am!** Kommst du nicht? — Doch!

····➤ (in tag questions) **isn't it? wasn't she? aren't they?** etc. nicht wahr. **it's a beautiful house, isn't it?** das Haus ist sehr schön, nicht wahr?

beach /biːtʃ/ n Strand m

bead /biːd/ n Perle f

beak /biːk/ n Schnabel m

beam /biːm/ n Balken m; (of light) Strahl m • vi strahlen. **~ing** adj [freude]strahlend

bean /biːn/ n Bohne f

bear[1] /beə(r)/ n Bär m

bear[2] vt/i (pt **bore**, pp **borne**) tragen; (endure) ertragen; gebären (child); **~ right** sich rechts halten. **~able** adj erträglich

beard /bɪəd/ n Bart m. **~ed** adj bärtig

bearer /ˈbeərə(r)/ n Träger m; (of news, cheque) Überbringer m; (of passport) Inhaber(in) m(f)

bearing /ˈbeərɪŋ/ n Haltung f; (Techn) Lager nt; **get one's ~s** sich orientieren

beast /biːst/ n Tier nt; (!: person) Biest nt

beastly /ˈbiːstlɪ/ adj ! scheußlich; (person) gemein

beat /biːt/ n Schlag m; (of policeman) Runde f; (rhythm) Takt m • vt/i (pt **beat**, pp **beaten**) schlagen; (thrash) verprügeln; klopfen (carpet); (hammer) hämmern (**on** an + acc); **~ it!** ! hau ab! **it ~s me** ! das begreife ich nicht. **~ up** vt zusammenschlagen

beat|en /ˈbiːtn/ adj **off the ~en track** abseits. **~ing** n Prügel pl

beauti|ful /ˈbjuːtɪfl/ adj schön. **~fy** vt (pt/pp **-ied**) verschönern

beauty /ˈbjuːtɪ/ n Schönheit f. **~ parlour** n Kosmetiksalon m. **~ spot** n Schönheitsfleck m; (place) landschaftlich besonders reizvolles Fleckchen nt.

b

b

beaver /'bi:və(r)/ n Biber m

became /bɪ'keɪm/ see **become**

because /bɪ'kɒz/ conj weil • adv ~ **of** wegen (+ gen)

becom|e /bɪ'kʌm/ vt/i (pt **became**, pp **become**) werden. **~ing** adj (clothes) kleidsam

bed /bed/ n Bett nt; (layer) Schicht f; (of flowers) Beet nt; **in ~** im Bett; **go to ~** ins od zu Bett gehen; **~ and breakfast** Zimmer mit Frühstück. **~clothes** npl, **~ding** n Bettzeug nt. **~room** n Schlafzimmer nt

'bedside n **at his ~** an seinem Bett. **~ 'lamp** n Nachttischlampe f. **~ 'table** n Nachttisch m

bed: ~'sitter n, **~-'sitting-room** n Wohnschlafzimmer nt. **~spread** n Tagesdecke f. **~time** n **at ~time** vor dem Schlafengehen

bee /bi:/ n Biene f

beech /bi:tʃ/ n Buche f

beef /bi:f/ n Rindfleisch nt. **~burger** n Hamburger m

bee: ~hive n Bienenstock m. **~-line** n **make a ~-line for** 🄸 zusteuern auf (+ acc)

been /bi:n/ see **be**

beer /bɪə(r)/ n Bier nt

beet /bi:t/ n (Amer: beetroot) rote Bete f; **[sugar] ~** Zuckerrübe f

beetle /'bi:tl/ n Käfer m

'beetroot n rote Bete f

before /bɪ'fɔ:(r)/ prep vor (+ dat/acc); **the day ~ yesterday** vorgestern; **~ long** bald • adv vorher; (already) schon; **never ~** noch nie; **~ that** davor • conj (time) ehe, bevor. **~hand** adv vorher, im Voraus

beg /beg/ v (pt/pp **begged**) • vi betteln • vt (entreat) anflehen; (ask) bitten (**for** um)

began /bɪ'gæn/ see **begin**

beggar /'begə(r)/ n Bettler(in) m(f); 🄸 Kerl m

begin /bɪ'gɪn/ vt/i (pt **began**, pp **begun**, pres p **beginning**) anfangen, beginnen; **to ~ with** anfangs. **~ner** n Anfänger(in) m(f). **~ning** n Anfang m, Beginn m

begun /bɪ'gʌn/ see **begin**

behalf /bɪ'hɑ:f/ n **on ~ of** im Namen von; **on my ~** meinetwegen

behave /bɪ'heɪv/ vi sich verhalten; **~ oneself** sich benehmen

behaviour /bɪ'heɪvjə(r)/ n Verhalten nt; **good/bad ~** gutes/schlechtes Benehmen nt

behind /bɪ'haɪnd/ prep hinter (+ dat/acc); **be ~ sth** hinter etw (dat) stecken • adv hinten; (late) im Rückstand; **a long way ~** weit zurück • n 🄸 Hintern m. **~hand** adv im Rückstand

beige /beɪʒ/ adj beige

being /'bi:ɪŋ/ n Dasein nt; **living ~** Lebewesen nt; **come into ~** entstehen

belated /bɪ'leɪtɪd/ adj verspätet

belfry /'belfrɪ/ n Glockenstube f; (tower) Glockenturm m

Belgian /'beldʒən/ adj belgisch • n Belgier(in) m(f)

Belgium /'beldʒəm/ n Belgien nt

belief /bɪ'li:f/ n Glaube m

believable /bɪ'li:vəbl/ adj glaubhaft

believe /bɪ'li:v/ vt/i glauben (**s.o.** jdm; **in** an + acc). **~r** n (Relig) Gläubige(r) m/f

belittle /bɪ'lɪtl/ vt herabsetzen

bell /bel/ n Glocke f; (on door) Klingel f

bellow /'beləʊ/ vt/i brüllen

belly /'belɪ/ n Bauch m

belong /bɪ'lɒŋ/ vi gehören (**to** dat); (be member) angehören (**to** dat). **~ings** npl Sachen pl

beloved /bɪ'lʌvɪd/ adj geliebt • n Geliebte(r) m/f

below /bɪ'ləʊ/ prep unter (+ dat/acc) • adv unten; (Naut) unter Deck

belt /belt/ n Gürtel m; (area) Zone f; (Techn) [Treib]riemen m • vi (🄸: rush) rasen • vt (🄸: hit) hauen

bench /bentʃ/ n Bank f; (work-) Werkbank f

bend /bend/ n Biegung f; (in road) Kurve f; **round the ~** [!] verrückt • v (pt/pp **bent**) • vt biegen; beugen (arm, leg) • vi sich bücken; (thing:) sich biegen; (road:) eine Biegung machen. **~ down** vi sich bücken. **~ over** vi sich vornüberbeugen

beneath /bɪ'ni:θ/ prep unter (+ dat/ acc); **~ him** (fig) unter seiner Würde • adv darunter

benefactor /'benɪfæktə(r)/ n Wohltäter(in) m(f)

beneficial /benɪ'fɪʃl/ adj nützlich

benefit /'benɪfɪt/ n Vorteil m; (allowance) Unterstützung f; (insurance) Leistung f; **sickness ~** Krankengeld nt • v (pt/pp **-fited**, pres p **-fiting**) • vt nützen (+ dat) • vi profitieren (**from** von)

benevolen|ce /bɪ'nevələns/ n Wohlwollen nt. **~t** adj wohlwollend

bent /bent/ see **bend** • adj (person) gebeugt; (distorted) verbogen; ([!]: dishonest) korrupt; **be ~ on doing sth** darauf erpicht sein, etw zu tun • n Hang m, Neigung f (**for** zu); **artistic ~** künstlerische Ader f

bequeath /bɪ'kwi:ð/ vt vermachen (**to** dat)

bereave|d /bɪ'ri:vd/ n **the ~d** pl die Hinterbliebenen

beret /'bereɪ/ n Baskenmütze f

Berne /bɜ:n/ n Bern nt

berry /'berɪ/ n Beere f

berth /bɜ:θ/ n (on ship) [Schlaf]koje f; (ship's anchorage) Liegeplatz m; **give a wide ~ to** [!] einen großen Bogen machen um

beside /bɪ'saɪd/ prep neben (+ dat/ acc); **~ oneself** außer sich (dat)

besides /bɪ'saɪdz/ prep außer (+ dat) • adv außerdem

besiege /bɪ'si:dʒ/ vt belagern

best /best/ adj & n beste(r,s); **the ~** der/die/das Beste; **at ~** bestenfalls; **all the ~!** alles Gute! **do one's ~** sein Bestes tun; **the ~ part of a year** fast ein Jahr; **to the ~ of my knowledge** so viel ich weiß; **make the ~ of it** das Beste daraus machen • adv am besten; **as ~ I could** so gut ich konnte. **~ 'man** n ≈ Trauzeuge m. **~'seller** n Bestseller m

bet /bet/ n Wette f • v (pt/pp **bet** or **betted**) • vt **~ s.o. £5** mit jdm um £5 wetten • vi wetten; **~ on** [Geld] setzen auf (+ acc)

betray /bɪ'treɪ/ vt verraten. **~al** n Verrat m

better /'betə(r)/ adj besser; **get ~** sich bessern; (after illness) sich erholen • adv besser; **~ off** besser dran; **~ not** lieber nicht; **all the ~** umso besser; **the sooner the ~** je eher, desto besser; **think ~ of sth** sich eines Besseren besinnen; **you'd ~ stay** du bleibst am besten hier • vt verbessern; (do better than) übertreffen; **~ oneself** sich verbessern

between /bɪ'twi:n/ prep zwischen (+ dat/acc); **~ you and me** unter uns; **~ us** (together) zusammen • adv **[in] ~** dazwischen

beware /bɪ'weə(r)/ vi sich in Acht nehmen (**of** vor + dat); **~ of the dog!** Vorsicht, bissiger Hund!

bewilder /bɪ'wɪldə(r)/ vt verwirren. **~ment** n Verwirrung f

bewitch /bɪ'wɪtʃ/ vt verzaubern; (fig) bezaubern

beyond /bɪ'jɒnd/ prep über (+ acc) ... hinaus; (further) weiter als; **~ reach** außer Reichweite; **~ doubt** ohne jeden Zweifel; **it's ~ me** [!] das geht über meinen Horizont • adv darüber hinaus

bias /'baɪəs/ n Voreingenommenheit f; (preference) Vorliebe f; (Jur) Befangenheit f • vt (pt/pp **biased**) (influence) beeinflussen. **~ed** adj voreingenommen; (Jur) befangen

bib /bɪb/ n Lätzchen nt

Bible /'baɪbl/ n Bibel f

biblical /'bɪblɪkl/ adj biblisch

bibliography /bɪblɪ'ɒgrəfɪ/ n Bibliographie f

bicycle /ˈbaɪsɪkl/ n Fahrrad nt •vi mit dem Rad fahren

bid /bɪd/ n Gebot nt; (attempt) Versuch m •vt/i (pt/pp **bid**, pres p **bidding**) bieten (**for** auf + acc); (Cards) reizen

bidder /ˈbɪdə(r)/ n Bieter(in) m(f)

bide /baɪd/ vt ~ **one's time** den richtigen Moment abwarten

big /bɪg/ adj (**bigger, biggest**) groß •adv **talk** ~ [!] angeben

bigam|ist /ˈbɪgəmɪst/ n Bigamist m. ~**y** n Bigamie f

big-ˈheaded adj [!] eingebildet

bigot /ˈbɪgət/ n Eiferer m. ~**ed** adj engstirnig

ˈbigwig n [!] hohes Tier nt

bike /baɪk/ n [!] [Fahr]rad nt

bikini /bɪˈki:nɪ/ n Bikini m

bile /baɪl/ n Galle f

bilingual /baɪˈlɪŋgwəl/ adj zweisprachig

bilious /ˈbɪljəs/ adj (Med) ~ **attack** verdorbener Magen m

bill[1] /bɪl/ n Rechnung f; (poster) Plakat nt; (Pol) Gesetzentwurf m; (Amer: note) Banknote f; ~ **of exchange** Wechsel m •vt eine Rechnung schicken (+ dat)

bill[2] n (beak) Schnabel m

ˈbillfold n (Amer) Brieftasche f

billiards /ˈbɪljədz/ n Billard nt

billion /ˈbɪljən/ n (thousand million) Milliarde f; (million million) Billion f

bin /bɪn/ n Mülleimer m; (for bread) Kasten m

bind /baɪnd/ vt (pt/pp **bound**) binden (**to** an + acc); (bandage) verbinden; (Jur) verpflichten; (cover the edge of) einfassen. ~**ing** adj verbindlich •n Einband m; (braid) Borte f; (on ski) Bindung f

binge /bɪndʒ/ n [!] **go on the** ~ eine Sauftour machen

binoculars /bɪˈnɒkjʊləz/ npl **[pair of]** ~ Fernglas nt

bio|ˈchemistry /baɪəʊ-/ n Biochemie f. ~**degradable** adj biologisch abbaubar

biograph|er /baɪˈɒgrəfə(r)/ n Biograph(in) m(f). ~**y** n Biographie f

biological /baɪəˈlɒdʒɪkl/ adj biologisch

biolog|ist /baɪˈɒlədʒɪst/ n Biologe m. ~**y** n Biologie f

bioˈterrorism /baɪəʊ-/ n Bioterrorismus m

birch /bɜ:tʃ/ n Birke f; (whip) Rute f

bird /bɜ:d/ n Vogel m; ([!]: girl) Mädchen nt; **kill two** ~**s with one stone** zwei Fliegen mit einer Klappe schlagen

Biro ® /ˈbaɪrəʊ/ n Kugelschreiber m

birth /bɜ:θ/ n Geburt f

birth: ~ **certificate** n Geburtsurkunde f. ~**-control** n Geburtenregelung f. ~**day** n Geburtstag m. ~**-rate** n Geburtenziffer f

biscuit /ˈbɪskɪt/ n Keks m

bishop /ˈbɪʃəp/ n Bischof m

bit[1] /bɪt/ n Stückchen nt; (for horse) Gebiss nt; (Techn) Bohreinsatz m; **a** ~ ein bisschen; ~ **by** ~ nach und nach; **a** ~ **of bread** ein bisschen Brot; **do one's** ~ sein Teil tun

bit[2] see **bite**

bitch /bɪtʃ/ n Hündin f; [✖] Luder nt. ~**y** adj gehässig

bit|e /baɪt/ n Biss m; **[insect]** ~ Stich m; (mouthful) Bissen m •vt/i (pt **bit**, pp **bitten**) beißen; (insect:) stechen; kauen (one's nails). ~**ing** adj beißend

bitten /ˈbɪtn/ see **bite**

bitter /ˈbɪtə(r)/ adj bitter; ~**ly cold** bitterkalt •n bitteres Bier nt. ~**ness** n Bitterkeit f

bitty /ˈbɪtɪ/ adj zusammengestoppelt

bizarre /bɪˈzɑ:(r)/ adj bizarr

black /blæk/ adj (**-er, -est**) schwarz; **be** ~**and blue** grün und blau sein •n Schwarz nt; (person) Schwarze(r) m/f •vt schwärzen; boykottieren (goods)

black: ~berry n Brombeere f. **~bird** n Amsel f. **~board** n (Sch) [Wand]tafel f. **~'currant** n schwarze Johannisbeere f

blacken vt/i schwärzen

black: ~ 'eye n blaues Auge nt. **B~ 'Forest** n Schwarzwald m. **~ 'ice** n Glatteis nt. **~list** vt auf die schwarze Liste setzen. **~mail** n Erpressung f •vt erpressen. **~mailer** n Erpresser(in) m(f). **~ 'market** n schwarzer Markt m. **~-out** n **have a ~-out** (Med) das Bewusstsein verlieren. **~ 'pudding** n Blutwurst f

bladder /'blædə(r)/ n (Anat) Blase f

blade /bleɪd/ n Klinge f; (of grass) Halm m

blame /bleɪm/ n Schuld f •vt die Schuld geben (+ dat); **no one is to ~** keiner ist schuld daran. **~less** adj schuldlos

bland /blænd/ adj **(-er, -est)** mild

blank /blæŋk/ adj leer; (look) ausdruckslos •n Lücke f; (cartridge) Platzpatrone f. **~ 'cheque** n Blankoscheck m

blanket /'blæŋkɪt/ n Decke f; **wet ~** [!] Spielverderber(in) m(f)

blare /bleə(r)/ vt/i schmettern

blasé /'blɑːzeɪ/ adj blasiert

blast /blɑːst/ n (gust) Luftstoß m; (sound) Schmettern nt; (of horn) Tuten nt •vt sprengen •int [x] verdammt. **~ed** adj [x] verdammt

'blast-off n (of missile) Start m

blatant /'bleɪtənt/ adj offensichtlich

blaze /bleɪz/ n Feuer nt •vi brennen

blazer /'bleɪzə(r)/ n Blazer m

bleach /bliːtʃ/ n Bleichmittel nt •vt/i bleichen

bleak /bliːk/ adj **(-er, -est)** öde; (fig) trostlos

bleary-eyed /'blɪərɪ-/ adj mit trüben/(on waking up) verschlafenen Augen

bleat /bliːt/ vi blöken

bleed /bliːd/ v (pt/pp **bled**) •vi bluten •vt entlüften (radiator)

bleep /bliːp/ n Piepton m •vi piepsen •vt mit dem Piepser rufen. **~er** n Piepser m

blemish /'blemɪʃ/ n Makel m

blend /blend/ n Mischung f •vt mischen •vi sich vermischen

bless /bles/ vt segnen. **~ed** adj heilig; [x] verflixt. **~ing** n Segen m

blew /bluː/ see **blow**[2]

blight /blaɪt/ n (Bot) Brand m

blind /blaɪnd/ adj blind; (corner) unübersichtlich; **~ man/woman** Blinde(r) m/f •n **[roller] ~** Rouleau nt •vt blenden

blind: ~ 'alley n Sackgasse f. **~fold** adj & adv mit verbundenen Augen •n Augenbinde f •vt die Augen verbinden (+ dat). **~ly** adv blindlings. **~ness** n Blindheit f

blink /blɪŋk/ vi blinzeln; (light:) blinken

bliss /blɪs/ n Glückseligkeit f. **~ful** adj glücklich

blister /'blɪstə(r)/ n (Med) Blase f

blitz /blɪts/ n [!] Großaktion f

blizzard /'blɪzəd/ n Schneesturm m

bloated /'bləʊtɪd/ adj aufgedunsen

blob /blɒb/ n Klecks m

block /blɒk/ n Block m; (of wood) Klotz m; (of flats) [Wohn]block m •vt blockieren. **~ up** vt zustopfen

blockade /blɒ'keɪd/ n Blockade f •vt blockieren

blockage /'blɒkɪdʒ/ n Verstopfung f

block: ~head n [!] Dummkopf m. **~ 'letters** npl Blockschrift f

bloke /bləʊk/ n [!] Kerl m

blonde /blɒnd/ adj blond •n Blondine f

blood /blʌd/ n Blut nt

blood: ~-curdling adj markerschütternd. **~ donor** n Blutspender m. **~ group** n Blutgruppe f. **~hound** n Bluthund m. **~-poisoning** n Blutvergiftung f. **~ pressure** n

b

Blutdruck m. ~**shed** n Blutvergießen nt. ~**shot** adj blutunterlaufen. ~ **sports** npl Jagdsport m. ~**-stained** adj blutbefleckt. ~ **test** n Blutprobe f. ~**thirsty** adj blutdürstig. ~**-vessel** n Blutgefäß nt

bloody /'blʌdɪ/ adj blutig; ☒ verdammt. ~**-'minded** adj ☒ stur

bloom /blu:m/ n Blüte f • vi blühen

blossom /'blɒsəm/ n Blüte f • vi blühen

blot /blɒt/ n [Tinten]klecks m; (fig) Fleck m • ~ **out** vt (fig) auslöschen

blotch /blɒtʃ/ n Fleck m. ~**y** adj fleckig

'**blotting-paper** n Löschpapier nt

blouse /blaʊz/ n Bluse f

blow[1] /bləʊ/ n Schlag m

blow[2] v (pt **blew**, pp **blown**) • vt blasen; (fam; squander) verpulvern; ~ **one's nose** sich (dat) die Nase putzen • vi blasen; (fuse:) durchbrennen. ~ **away** vt wegblasen • vi wegfliegen. ~ **down** vt umwehen • vi umfallen. ~ **out** vt (extinguish) ausblasen. ~ **over** vi umfallen; (fig: die down) vorübergehen. ~ **up** vt (inflate) aufblasen; (enlarge) vergrößern; (shatter by explosion) sprengen • vi explodieren

'**blowlamp** n Lötlampe f

blown /bləʊn/ see **blow**[2]

'**blowtorch** n (Amer) Lötlampe f

blowy /'bləʊɪ/ adj windig

blue /blu:/ adj (**-r, -st**) blau; **feel** ~ deprimiert sein • n Blau nt; **have the** ~**s** deprimiert sein; **out of the** ~ aus heiterem Himmel

blue: ~**bell** n Sternhyazinthe f. ~**berry** n Heidelbeere f. ~**bottle** n Schmeißfliege f. ~ **film** n Pornofilm m. ~**print** n (fig) Entwurf m

bluff /blʌf/ n Bluff m • vi bluffen

blunder /'blʌndə(r)/ n Schnitzer m • vi einen Schnitzer machen

blunt /blʌnt/ adj stumpf; (person) geradeheraus. ~**ly** adv unverblümt, geradeheraus

blur /blɜ:(r)/ n **it's all a** ~ alles ist verschwommen • vt (pt/pp **blurred**) verschwommen machen; ~**red** verschwommen

blush /blʌʃ/ n Erröten nt • vi erröten

bluster /'blʌstə(r)/ n Großtuerei f. ~**y** adj windig

boar /bɔ:(r)/ n Eber m

board /bɔ:d/ n Brett nt; (for notices) schwarzes Brett nt; (committee) Ausschuss m; (of directors) Vorstand m; **on** ~ an Bord; **full** ~ Vollpension f; ~ **and lodging** Unterkunft und Verpflegung pl • vt einsteigen in (+ acc); (Naut, Aviat) besteigen • vi an Bord gehen. ~ **up** vt mit Brettern verschlagen

boarder /'bɔ:də(r)/ n Pensionsgast m; (Sch) Internatsschüler(in) m(f)

board: ~**-game** n Brettspiel nt. ~**ing-house** n Pension f. ~**ing-school** n Internat nt

boast /bəʊst/ vt sich rühmen (+ gen) • vi prahlen (**about** mit). ~**ful** adj prahlerisch

boat /bəʊt/ n Boot nt; (ship) Schiff nt

bob /bɒb/ vi (pt/pp **bobbed**) ~ **up and down** sich auf und ab bewegen

'**bob-sleigh** n Bob m

bodily /'bɒdɪlɪ/ adj körperlich • adv (forcibly) mit Gewalt

body /'bɒdɪ/ n Körper m; (corpse) Leiche f; (corporation) Körperschaft f. ~**guard** n Leibwächter m. ~ **part** n Leichenteil nt. ~**work** n (Auto) Karosserie f

bog /bɒg/ n Sumpf m

bogus /'bəʊgəs/ adj falsch

boil[1] /bɔɪl/ n Furunkel m

boil[2] n **bring/come to the** ~ zum Kochen bringen/kommen • vt/i kochen; ~**ed potatoes** Salzkartoffeln pl. ~ **down** vi (fig) hinauslaufen (**to** auf + acc). ~ **over** vi überkochen

boiler /'bɔɪlə(r)/ n Heizkessel m

'boiling point n Siedepunkt m

boisterous /'bɔɪstərəs/ adj übermütig

bold /bəʊld/ adj (**-er, -est**) kühn; (Printing) fett. **~ness** n Kühnheit f

bolster /'bəʊlstə(r)/ n Nackenrolle f •vt **~ up** Mut machen (+ dat)

bolt /bəʊlt/ n Riegel m; (Techn) Bolzen m •vt schrauben (**to** an + acc); verriegeln (door); hinunterschlingen (food) •vi abhauen; (horse:) durchgehen

bomb /bɒm/ n Bombe f •vt bombardieren

bombard /bɒm'bɑ:d/ vt beschießen; (fig) bombardieren

bombastic /bɒm'bæstɪk/ adj bombastisch

bomber /'bɒmə(r)/ n (Aviat) Bomber m; (person) Bombenleger(in) m(f)

bond /bɒnd/ n (fig) Band nt; (Comm) Obligation f

bone /bəʊn/ n Knochen m; (of fish) Gräte f •vt von den Knochen lösen (meat); entgräten (fish). **~-'dry** adj knochentrocken

bonfire /'bɒn-/ n Gartenfeuer nt; (celebratory) Freudenfeuer nt

bonus /'bəʊnəs/ n Prämie f; (gratuity) Gratifikation f; (fig) Plus nt

bony /'bəʊnɪ/ adj knochig; (fish) grätig

boo /bu:/ int buh! •vt ausbuhen •vi buhen

boob /bu:b/ n (🅸: mistake) Schnitzer m

book /bʊk/ n Buch nt; (of tickets) Heft nt; **keep the ~s** (Comm) die Bücher führen •vt/i buchen; (reserve) [vor]bestellen; (for offence) aufschreiben

book: ~case n Bücherregal nt. **~-ends** npl Buchstützen pl. **~ing-office** n Fahrkartenschalter m. **~keeping** n Buchführung f. **~let** n Broschüre f. **~maker** n Buchmacher m. **~mark** n Lesezeichen nt. **~seller** n Buchhändler(in) m(f). **~shop** n Buchhandlung f. **~stall** n Bücherstand m

boom /bu:m/ n (Comm) Hochkonjunktur f; (upturn) Aufschwung m •vi dröhnen; (fig) blühen

boon /bu:n/ n Segen m

boost /bu:st/ n Auftrieb m •vt Auftrieb geben (+ dat)

boot /bu:t/ n Stiefel m; (Auto) Kofferraum m

booth /bu:ð/ n Bude f; (cubicle) Kabine f

booty /'bu:tɪ/ n Beute f

booze /bu:z/ n 🅸 Alkohol m •vi 🅸 saufen

border /'bɔ:də(r)/ n Rand m; (frontier) Grenze f; (in garden) Rabatte f •vi **~ on** grenzen an (+ acc). **~line case** n Grenzfall m

bore[1] /bɔ:(r)/ see **bear**[2]

bor|e[2] n (of gun) Kaliber nt; (person) langweiliger Mensch m; (thing) langweilige Sache f •vt langweilen; **be ~ed** sich langweilen. **~edom** n Langeweile f. **~ing** adj langweilig

born /bɔ:n/ pp **be ~** geboren werden •adj geboren

borne /bɔ:n/ see **bear**[2]

borrow /'bɒrəʊ/ vt [sich (dat)] borgen od leihen (**from** von)

bosom /'bʊzm/ n Busen m

boss /bɒs/ n 🅸 Chef m •vt herumkommandieren. **~y** adj herrschsüchtig

botanical /bə'tænɪkl/ adj botanisch

botan|ist /'bɒtənɪst/ n Botaniker(in) m(f). **~y** n Botanik f

both /bəʊθ/ adj & pron beide; **~[of] the children** beide Kinder; **~ of them** beide [von ihnen] •adv **~ men and women** sowohl Männer als auch Frauen

bother /'bɒðə(r)/ n Mühe f; (minor trouble) Ärger m •int 🅸 verflixt! •vt belästigen; (disturb) stören •vi sich kümmern (**about** um)

b

bottle /ˈbɒtl/ n Flasche f •vt auf Flaschen abfüllen; (preserve) einmachen

bottle: ~-neck n (fig) Engpass m. **~-opener** n Flaschenöffner m

bottom /ˈbɒtəm/ adj unterste(r,s) •n (of container) Boden m; (of river) Grund m; (of page, hill) Fuß m; (buttocks) Hintern m; **at the ~** unten; **get to the ~ of sth** (fig) hinter etw (acc) kommen

bought /bɔːt/ see **buy**

bounce /baʊns/ vi [auf]springen; (cheque:) [!] nicht gedeckt sein •vt aufspringen lassen (ball)

bouncer /ˈbaʊnsə(r)/ n [!] Rausschmeißer m

bound[1] /baʊnd/ n Sprung m •vi springen

bound[2] see **bind** •adj **~ for** (ship) mit Kurs auf (+ acc); **be ~ to do sth** etw bestimmt machen; (obliged) verpflichtet sein, etw zu machen

boundary /ˈbaʊndərɪ/ n Grenze f

bounds /baʊndz/ npl (fig) Grenzen pl; **out of ~** verboten

bouquet /bʊˈkeɪ/ n [Blumen]strauß m; (of wine) Bukett nt

bourgeois /ˈbʊəʒwɑː/ adj (pej) spießbürgerlich

bout /baʊt/ n (Med) Anfall m; (Sport) Kampf m

bow[1] /bəʊ/ n (weapon & Mus) Bogen m; (knot) Schleife f

bow[2] /baʊ/ n Verbeugung f •vi sich verbeugen •vt neigen (head)

bow[3] /baʊ/ n (Naut) Bug m

bowel /ˈbaʊəl/ n Darm m. **~s** pl Eingeweide pl

bowl[1] /bəʊl/ n Schüssel f; (shallow) Schale f

bowl[2] n (ball) Kugel f •vt/i werfen. **~ over** vt umwerfen

bowler /ˈbəʊlə(r)/ n (Sport) Werfer m

bowling /ˈbəʊlɪŋ/ n Kegeln nt. **~-alley** n Kegelbahn f

bowls /bəʊlz/ n Bowlsspiel nt

bow-ˈtie /bəʊ-/ n Fliege f

box[1] /bɒks/ n Schachtel f; (wooden) Kiste f; (cardboard) Karton m; (Theat) Loge f

box[2] vt/i (Sport) boxen

box|er /ˈbɒksə(r)/ n Boxer m. **~ing** n Boxen nt. **B~ing Day** n zweiter Weihnachtstag m

box: ~-office n (Theat) Kasse f. **~-room** n Abstellraum m

boy /bɔɪ/ n Junge m. **~ band** n Jungenband f

boycott /ˈbɔɪkɒt/ n Boykott m •vt boykottieren

boy: ~friend n Freund m. **~ish** adj jungenhaft

bra /brɑː/ n BH m

brace /breɪs/ n Strebe f, Stütze f; (dental) Zahnspange f; **~s** npl Hosenträger mpl

bracelet /ˈbreɪslɪt/ n Armband nt

bracing /ˈbreɪsɪŋ/ adj stärkend

bracket /ˈbrækɪt/ n Konsole f; (group) Gruppe f; (Printing) **round/square ~s** runde/eckige Klammern •vt einklammern

brag /bræg/ vi (pt/pp **bragged**) prahlen (**about** mit)

braille /breɪl/ n Blindenschrift f

brain /breɪn/ n Gehirn nt; **~s** (fig) Intelligenz f

brain: ~less adj dumm. **~wash** vt einer Gehirnwäsche unterziehen. **~wave** n Geistesblitz m

brainy /ˈbreɪnɪ/ adj klug

brake /breɪk/ n Bremse f •vt/i bremsen. **~-light** n Bremslicht nt

bramble /ˈbræmbl/ n Brombeerstrauch m

branch /brɑːntʃ/ n Ast m; (fig) Zweig m; (Comm) Zweigstelle f; (shop) Filiale f •vi sich gabeln

brand /brænd/ n Marke f •vt (fig) brandmarken als

brandish /ˈbrændɪʃ/ vt schwingen

brand-ˈnew adj nagelneu

brandy /ˈbrændɪ/ n Weinbrand m

brash /bræʃ/ adj nassforsch

brass /brɑːs/ n Messing nt; (Mus) Blech nt; **top ~** [!] hohe Tiere pl. **~ band** n Blaskapelle f

brassy /'brɑːsɪ/ adj [!] ordinär

brat /bræt/ n (pej) Balg nt

bravado /brə'vɑːdəʊ/ n Forschheit f

brave /breɪv/ adj (**-r, -st**) tapfer • vt die Stirn bieten (+ dat). **~ry** n Tapferkeit f

bravo /brɑː'vəʊ/ int bravo!

brawl /brɔːl/ n Schlägerei f

brawn /brɔːn/ n (Culin) Sülze f

brawny /'brɔːnɪ/ adj muskulös

bray /breɪ/ vi iahen

brazen /'breɪzn/ adj unverschämt

Brazil /brə'zɪl/ n Brasilien nt. **~ian** adj brasilianisch. **~ nut** n Paranuss f

breach /briːtʃ/ n Bruch m; (Mil & fig) Bresche f; **~ of contract** Vertragsbruch m

bread /bred/ n Brot nt; **slice of ~ and butter** Butterbrot nt. **~crumbs** npl Brotkrümel pl; (Culin) Paniermehl nt

breadth /bredθ/ n Breite f

break /breɪk/ n Bruch m; (interval) Pause f; (interruption) Unterbrechung f; ([!]: chance) Chance f • v (pt **broke**, pp **broken**) • vt brechen; (smash) zerbrechen; (damage) kaputtmachen [!]; (interrupt) unterbrechen; **~ one's arm** sich (dat) den Arm brechen • vi brechen; (day:) anbrechen; (storm:) losbrechen; (thing:) kaputtgehen [!]; (rope, thread:) reißen; (news:) bekannt werden; **his voice is ~ing** er ist im Stimmbruch. **~ away** vi sich losreißen/(fig) sich absetzen (**from** von). **~ down** vi zusammenbrechen; (Techn) eine Panne haben; (negotiations:) scheitern • vt aufbrechen (door); aufgliedern (figures). **~ in** vi einbrechen. **~ off** vt/i abbrechen; lösen (engagement). **~ out** vi ausbrechen. **~ up** vt zerbrechen • vi (crowd:) sich zerstreuen; (marriage, couple:) auseinander gehen; (Sch) Ferien bekommen

break|able /'breɪkəbl/ adj zerbrechlich. **~age** n Bruch m. **~down** n (Techn) Panne f; (Med) Zusammenbruch m; (of figures) Aufgliederung f. **~er** n (wave) Brecher m

breakfast /'brekfəst/ n Frühstück nt

break: ~through n Durchbruch m. **~water** n Buhne f

breast /brest/ n Brust f. **~bone** n Brustbein nt. **~-feed** vt stillen. **~-stroke** n Brustschwimmen nt

breath /breθ/ n Atem m; **out of ~** außer Atem; **under one's ~** vor sich (acc) hin

breathe /briːð/ vt/i atmen. **~ in** vt/i einatmen. **~ out** vt/i ausatmen

breathing n Atmen nt

breath: /'breθ/: **~less** adj atemlos. **~-taking** adj atemberaubend

bred /bred/ see **breed**

breed /briːd/ n Rasse f • v (pt/pp **bred**) • vt züchten; (give rise to) erzeugen • vi sich vermehren. **~er** n Züchter m. **~ing** n Zucht f; (fig) [gute] Lebensart f

breez|e /briːz/ n Lüftchen nt; (Naut) Brise f. **~y** adj windig

brevity /'brevətɪ/ n Kürze f

brew /bruː/ n Gebräu nt • vt brauen; kochen (tea). **~er** n Brauer m. **~ery** n Brauerei f

bribe /braɪb/ n (money) Bestechungsgeld nt • vt bestechen. **~ry** n Bestechung f

brick /brɪk/ n Ziegelstein m, Backstein m

'bricklayer n Maurer m

bridal /'braɪdl/ adj Braut-

bride /braɪd/ n Braut f. **~groom** n Bräutigam m. **~smaid** n Brautjungfer f

bridge[1] /brɪdʒ/ n Brücke f; (of nose) Nasenrücken m; (of spectacles) Steg m

bridge[2] n (Cards) Bridge nt

bridle /'braɪdl/ n Zaum m

b

brief[1] /bri:f/ adj (**-er, -est**) kurz; **be ~** (person:) sich kurz fassen

brief[2] n Instruktionen pl; (Jur: case) Mandat nt. **~case** n Aktentasche f

brief|ing /'bri:fɪŋ/ n Informationsgespräch nt. **~ly** adv kurz. **~ness** n Kürze f

briefs /bri:fs/ npl Slip m

brigade /brɪ'geɪd/ n Brigade f

bright /braɪt/ adj (**-er, -est**) hell; (day) heiter; **~ red** hellrot

bright|en /'braɪtn/ v **~en [up]** •vt aufheitern •vi sich aufheitern. **~ness** n Helligkeit f

brilliance /'brɪljəns/ n Glanz m; (of person) Genialität f

brilliant /'brɪljənt/ adj glänzend; (person) genial

brim /brɪm/ n Rand m; (of hat) Krempe f

bring /brɪŋ/ vt (pt/pp **brought**) bringen; **~ them with you** bring sie mit; **I can't b~ myself to do it** ich bringe es nicht fertig. **~ about** vt verursachen. **~ along** vt mitbringen. **~ back** vt zurückbringen. **~ down** vt herunterbringen; senken (price). **~ off** vt vollbringen. **~ on** vt (cause) verursachen. **~ out** vt herausbringen. **~ round** vt vorbeibringen; (persuade) überreden; wieder zum Bewusstsein bringen (unconscious person). **~ up** vt heraufbringen; (vomit) erbrechen; aufziehen (children); erwähnen (question)

brink /brɪŋk/ n Rand m

brisk /brɪsk/ adj (**-er, -est**), **-ly** adv lebhaft; (quick) schnell

bristle /'brɪsl/ n Borste f

Brit|ain /'brɪtn/ n Großbritannien nt. **~ish** adj britisch; **the ~ish** die Briten pl. **~on** n Brite m/Britin f

Brittany /'brɪtənɪ/ n die Bretagne

brittle /'brɪtl/ adj brüchig, spröde

broad /brɔ:d/ adj (**-er, -est**) breit; (hint) deutlich; **in ~ daylight** am helllichten Tag. **~ beans** npl dicke Bohnen pl

broadband /'brɔ:dbænd/ n Breitband nt

'broadcast n Sendung f •vt/i (pt/pp **-cast**) senden. **~er** n Rundfunk- und Fernsehpersönlichkeit f. **~ing** n Funk und Fernsehen pl

broaden /'brɔ:dn/ vt verbreitern; (fig) erweitern •vi sich verbreitern

broadly /'brɔ:dlɪ/ adv breit; **~ speaking** allgemein gesagt

broad'minded adj tolerant

broccoli /'brɒkəlɪ/ n inv Brokkoli pl

brochure /'brəʊʃə(r)/ n Broschüre f

broke /brəʊk/ see **break** •adj [!] pleite

broken /'brəʊkn/ see **break** •adj zerbrochen, [!] kaputt. **~-hearted** adj untröstlich

broker /'brəʊkə(r)/ n Makler m

brolly /'brɒlɪ/ n [!] Schirm m

bronchitis /brɒŋ'kaɪtɪs/ n Bronchitis f

bronze /brɒnz/ n Bronze f

brooch /brəʊtʃ/ n Brosche f

brood /bru:d/ vi (fig) grübeln

broom /bru:m/ n Besen m; (Bot) Ginster m

broth /brɒθ/ n Brühe f

brothel /'brɒθl/ n Bordell nt

brother /'brʌðə(r)/ n Bruder m

brother: ~-in-law n (pl **-s-in-law**) Schwager m. **~ly** adj brüderlich

brought /brɔ:t/ see **bring**

brow /braʊ/ n Augenbraue f; (forehead) Stirn f; (of hill) [Berg]kuppe f

brown /braʊn/ adj (**-er, -est**) braun; **~ 'paper** Packpapier nt •n Braun nt •vt bräunen •vi braun werden

browse /braʊz/ vi (read) schmökern; (in shop) sich umsehen. **~r** n (Computing) Browser m

bruise /bru:z/ n blauer Fleck m •vt beschädigen (fruit); **~ one's arm** sich (dat) den Arm quetschen

brunette /bru:'net/ n Brünette f

brush /brʌʃ/ n Bürste f; (with handle)

Handfeger m; (for paint, pastry) Pinsel m; (bushes) Unterholz nt; (fig: conflict) Zusammenstoß m •vt bürsten; putzen (teeth); ~ **against** streifen [gegen]; ~ **aside** (fig) abtun. ~ **off** vt abbürsten. ~ **up** vt/i (fig) ~ **up [on]** auffrischen

brusque /brʊsk/ adj brüsk

Brussels /ˈbrʌslz/ n Brüssel nt. ~ **sprouts** npl Rosenkohl m

brutal /ˈbru:tl/ adj brutal. ~**ity** n Brutalität f

brute /bru:t/ n Unmensch m. ~ **force** n rohe Gewalt f

BSE abbr (**bovine spongiform encephalopathy**) BSE f

bubble /ˈbʌbl/ n [Luft]blase f •vi sprudeln

buck[1] /bʌk/ n (deer & Gym) Bock m; (rabbit) Rammler m •vi (horse:) bocken

buck[2] n (Amer [!]) Dollar m

buck[3] n **pass the ~** die Verantwortung abschieben

bucket /ˈbʌkɪt/ n Eimer m

buckle /ˈbʌkl/ n Schnalle f •vt zuschnallen •vi sich verbiegen

bud /bʌd/ n Knospe f

buddy /ˈbʌdɪ/ n [!] Freund m

budge /bʌdʒ/ vt bewegen •vi sich [von der Stelle] rühren

budget /ˈbʌdʒɪt/ n Budget nt; (Pol) Haushaltsplan m; (money available) Etat m •vi (pt/pp **budgeted**) ~ **for sth** etw einkalkulieren

buff /bʌf/ adj (colour) sandfarben •n Sandfarbe f; [!] Fan m •vt polieren

buffalo /ˈbʌfələʊ/ n (inv or pl **-es**) Büffel m

buffer /ˈbʌfə(r)/ n (Rail) Puffer m

buffet[1] /ˈbʊfeɪ/ n Büfett nt; (on station) Imbissstube f

buffet[2] /ˈbʌfɪt/ vt (pt/pp **buffeted**) hin und her werfen

bug /bʌg/ n Wanze f; ([!]: virus) Bazillus m; ([!]: device) Abhörgerät nt, [!] Wanze f •vt (pt/pp **bugged**) [!] verwanzen (room); abhören (telephone); (Amer: annoy) ärgern

bugle /ˈbju:gl/ n Signalhorn

build /bɪld/ n (of person) Körperbau m •vt/i (pt/pp **built**) bauen. ~ **on** vt anbauen (**to** an + acc). ~ **up** vt aufbauen •vi zunehmen

builder /ˈbɪldə(r)/ n Bauunternehmer m

building /ˈbɪldɪŋ/ n Gebäude nt. ~ **site** n Baustelle f. ~ **society** n Bausparkasse f

built /bɪlt/ see **build.** ~**-in** adj eingebaut. ~**-in ˈcupboard** n Einbauschrank m. ~**-up area** n bebautes Gebiet nt; (Auto) geschlossene Ortschaft f

bulb /bʌlb/ n [Blumen]zwiebel f; (Electr) [Glüh]birne f

bulbous /ˈbʌlbəs/ adj bauchig

Bulgaria /bʌlˈgeərɪə/ n Bulgarien nt

bulg|e /bʌldʒ/ n Ausbauchung f •vi sich ausbauchen. ~**ing** adj prall; (eyes) hervorquellend

bulk /bʌlk/ n Masse f; (greater part) Hauptteil m. ~**y** adj sperrig; (large) massig

bull /bʊl/ n Bulle m, Stier m

ˈbulldog n Bulldogge f

bulldozer /ˈbʊldəʊzə(r)/ n Planierraupe f

bullet /ˈbʊlɪt/ n Kugel f

bulletin /ˈbʊlɪtɪn/ n Bulletin nt

ˈbullet-proof adj kugelsicher

ˈbullfight n Stierkampf m. ~**er** n Stierkämpfer m

ˈbullfinch n Dompfaff m

bullock /ˈbʊlək/ n Ochse m

bull: ~ring n Stierkampfarena f. **~'s-eye** n **score a ~'s-eye** ins Schwarze treffen

bully /ˈbʊlɪ/ n Tyrann m •vt tyrannisieren

bum /bʌm/ n [✖] Hintern m

bumble-bee /ˈbʌmbl-/ n Hummel f

bump /bʌmp/ n Bums m; (swelling) Beule f; (in road) holperige Stelle f •vt stoßen; ~ **into** stoßen gegen; (meet) zufällig treffen. ~ **off** vt [!] um die Ecke bringen

b

bumper /ˈbʌmpə(r)/ adj Rekord- •n (Auto) Stoßstange f

bumpy /ˈbʌmpɪ/ adj holperig

bun /bʌn/ n Milchbrötchen nt; (hair) [Haar]knoten m

bunch /bʌntʃ/ n (of flowers) Strauß m; (of radishes, keys) Bund m; (of people) Gruppe f; ~ **of grapes** [ganze] Weintraube f

bundle /ˈbʌndl/ n Bündel nt •vt ~ **[up]** bündeln

bungalow /ˈbʌŋgələʊ/ n Bungalow m

bungle /ˈbʌŋgl/ vt verpfuschen

bunk /bʌŋk/ n [Schlaf]koje f. **~-beds** npl Etagenbett nt

bunker /ˈbʌŋkə(r)/ n Bunker m

bunny /ˈbʌnɪ/ n [!] Kaninchen nt

buoy /bɔɪ/ n Boje f

buoyan|cy /ˈbɔɪənsɪ/ n Auftrieb m. **~t** adj **be ~t** schwimmen

burden /ˈbɜ:dn/ n Last f

bureau /ˈbjʊərəʊ/ n (pl **-x** or **-s**) (desk) Sekretär m; (office) Büro nt

bureaucracy /bjʊəˈrɒkrəsɪ/ n Bürokratie f

bureaucratic /bjʊərəkrætɪk/ adj bürokratisch

burger /ˈbɜ:gə(r)/ n Hamburger m

burglar /ˈbɜ:glə(r)/ n Einbrecher m. **~ alarm** n Alarmanlage f

burglary n Einbruch m

burgle /ˈbɜ:gl/ vt einbrechen in (+ acc); **they have been ~d** bei ihnen ist eingebrochen worden

burial /ˈberɪəl/ n Begräbnis nt

burly /ˈbɜ:lɪ/ adj stämmig

Burm|a /ˈbɜ:mə/ n Birma nt. **~ese** adj birmanisch

burn /bɜ:n/ n Verbrennung f; (on skin) Brandwunde f; (on material) Brandstelle f •v (pt/pp **burnt** or **burned**) •vt verbrennen •vi brennen; (food:) anbrennen. **~ down** vt/i niederbrennen

burner /ˈbɜ:nə(r)/ n Brenner m

burnt /bɜ:nt/ see **burn**

burp /bɜ:p/ vi [!] aufstoßen

burrow /ˈbʌrəʊ/ n Bau m •vi wühlen

burst /bɜ:st/ n Bruch m; (surge) Ausbruch m •v (pt/pp **burst**) •vt platzen machen •vi platzen; (bud:) aufgehen; **~ into tears** in Tränen ausbrechen

bury /ˈberɪ/ vt (pt/pp **-ied**) begraben; (hide) vergraben

bus /bʌs/ n [Auto]bus m

bush /bʊʃ/ n Strauch m; (land) Busch m. **~y** adj buschig

busily /ˈbɪzɪlɪ/ adv eifrig

business /ˈbɪznɪs/ n Angelegenheit f; (Comm) Geschäft nt; **on ~** geschäftlich; **he has no ~** er hat kein Recht (**to** zu); **mind one's own ~** sich um seine eigenen Angelegenheiten kümmern; **that's none of your ~** das geht Sie nichts an. **~-like** adj geschäftsmäßig. **~man** n Geschäftsmann m

ˈbus-stop n Bushaltestelle f

bust[1] /bʌst/ n Büste f

bust[2] adj [!] kaputt; **go ~** Pleite gehen •v (pt/pp **busted** or **bust**) [!] •vt kaputtmachen •vi kaputtgehen

busy /ˈbɪzɪ/ adj beschäftigt; (day) voll; (street) belebt; (with traffic) stark befahren; (Amer Teleph) besetzt; **be ~** zu tun haben •vt **~ oneself** sich beschäftigen (**with** mit)

but /bʌt/, unbetont /bət/ conj aber; (after negative) sondern •prep außer (+ dat); **~ for** (without) ohne (+ acc); **the last ~ one** der/die/das vorletzte; **the next ~ one** der/die/das übernächste •adv nur

butcher /ˈbʊtʃə(r)/ n Fleischer m, Metzger m; **~'s [shop]** Fleischerei f, Metzgerei f •vt [ab]schlachten

butler /ˈbʌtlə(r)/ n Butler m

butt /bʌt/ n (of gun) [Gewehr]kolben

m; (fig: target) Zielscheibe f; (of cigarette) Stummel m; (for water) Regentonne f •vi ~ **in** unterbrechen

butter /'bʌtə(r)/ n Butter f •vt mit Butter bestreichen. ~ **up** vt [!] schmeicheln (+ dat)

butter: ~**cup** adj Butterblume f, Hahnenfuß m. ~**fly** n Schmetterling m

buttocks /'bʌtəks/ npl Gesäß nt

button /'bʌtn/ n Knopf m •vt ~ **[up]** zuknöpfen. ~**hole** n Knopfloch nt

buy /baɪ/ n Kauf m •vt (pt/pp **bought**) kaufen. ~**er** n Käufer(in) m(f)

buzz /bʌz/ n Summen nt •vi summen

buzzer /'bʌzə(r)/ n Summer m

by /baɪ/ prep (close to) bei (+ dat); (next to) neben (+ dat/acc); (past) an (+ dat) ... vorbei; (to the extent of) um (+ acc); (at the latest) bis; (by means of) durch; **by Mozart/Dickens** von Mozart/Dickens; ~ **oneself** allein; ~ **the sea** am Meer; ~ **car/bus** mit dem Auto/Bus; ~ **sea** mit dem Schiff; ~ **day/night** bei Tag/ Nacht; ~ **the hour** pro Stunde; ~ **the metre** meterweise; **six metres** ~ **four** sechs mal vier Meter; **win** ~ **a length** mit einer Länge Vorsprung gewinnen; **miss the train** ~ **a minute** den Zug um eine Minute verpassen •adv ~ **and large** im Großen und Ganzen; **put** ~ beiseite legen; **go/pass** ~ vorbeigehen

bye /baɪ/ int [!] tschüs

by: ~**-election** n Nachwahl f. ~**pass** n Umgehungsstraße f; (Med) Bypass m •vt umfahren. ~**-product** n Nebenprodukt m. ~**stander** n Zuschauer(in) m(f)

Cc

cab /kæb/ n Taxi nt; (of lorry, train) Führerhaus nt

cabaret /'kæbəreɪ/ n Kabarett nt

cabbage /'kæbɪdʒ/ n Kohl m

cabin /'kæbɪn/ n Kabine f; (hut) Hütte f

cabinet /'kæbɪnɪt/ n Schrank m; **[display]** ~ Vitrine f; **C**~ (Pol) Kabinett nt

cable /'keɪbl/ n Kabel nt; (rope) Tau nt. ~ **'railway** n Seilbahn f. ~ **'television** n Kabelfernsehen nt

cackle /'kækl/ vi gackern

cactus /'kæktəs/ n (pl **-ti** or **-tuses**) Kaktus m

cadet /kə'det/ n Kadett m

cadge /kædʒ/ vt/i [!] schnorren

Caesarean /sɪ'zeərɪən/ adj & n ~ **[section]** Kaiserschnitt m

café /'kæfeɪ/ n Café nt

cafeteria /kæfə'tɪərɪə/ n Selbstbedienungsrestaurant nt

cage /keɪdʒ/ n Käfig m

cagey /'keɪdʒɪ/ adj [!] **be** ~ mit der Sprache nicht herauswollen

cake /keɪk/ n Kuchen m; (of soap) Stück nt. ~**d** adj verkrustet (**with** mit)

calamity /kə'læmətɪ/ n Katastrophe f

calculat|e /'kælkjʊleɪt/ vt berechnen; (estimate) kalkulieren. ~**ing** adj (fig) berechnend. ~**ion** n Rechnung f, Kalkulation f. ~**or** n Rechner m

calendar /'kælɪndə(r)/ n Kalender m

calf[1] /kɑːf/ n (pl **calves**) Kalb nt

C

calf² n (pl **calves**) (Anat) Wade f

calibre /'kælɪbə(r)/ n Kaliber nt

call /kɔ:l/ n Ruf m; (Teleph) Anruf m; (visit) Besuch m •vt rufen; (Teleph) anrufen; (wake) wecken; ausrufen (strike) (name) nennen; **be ~ed** heißen •vi rufen; **~ [in** or **round]** vorbeikommen. **~ back** vt zurückrufen •vi noch einmal vorbeikommen. **~ for** vt rufen nach; (demand) verlangen; (fetch) abholen. **~ off** vt zurückrufen (dog); (cancel) absagen. **~ on** vt bitten (**for** um); (appeal to) appellieren an (+ acc); (visit) besuchen. **~ out** vt rufen; aufrufen (names) •vi rufen. **~ up** vt (Mil) einberufen; (Teleph) anrufen

call: ~-box n Telefonzelle f. **~ centre** n Callcenter nt. **~er** n Besucher m; (Teleph) Anrufer m. **~ing** n Berufung f. **~-up** n (Mil) Einberufung f

calm /kɑ:m/ adj (**-er, -est**) ruhig •n Ruhe f •vt **~ [down]** beruhigen •vi **~ down** sich beruhigen. **~ness** n Ruhe f; (of sea) Stille f

calorie /'kælərɪ/ n Kalorie f

calves /kɑ:vz/ npl see **calf**¹ & ²

camcorder /'kæmkɔ:də(r)/ n Camcorder m

came /keɪm/ see **come**

camel /'kæml/ n Kamel nt

camera /'kæmərə/ n Kamera f

camouflage /'kæməflɑ:ʒ/ n Tarnung f •vt tarnen

camp /kæmp/ n Lager nt •vi campen; (Mil) kampieren

campaign /kæm'peɪn/ n Feldzug m; (Comm, Pol) Kampagne f •vi (Pol) im Wahlkampf arbeiten

camp: ~-bed n Feldbett nt. **~er** n Camper m; (Auto) Wohnmobil nt. **~ing** n Camping nt. **~site** n Campingplatz m

can¹ /kæn/ n (for petrol) Kanister m; (tin) Dose f, Büchse f; **a ~ of beer** eine Dose Bier

can² /kæn/, unbetont /kən/

pres **can**, pt **could**

• modal verb

····➤ (be able to) können. **I can't** or **cannot go** ich kann nicht gehen. **she couldn't** or **could not go** (was unable to) sie konnte nicht gehen; (would not be able to) sie könnte nicht gehen. **he could go if he had time** er könnte gehen, wenn er Zeit hätte. **if I could go** wenn ich gehen könnte. **that cannot be true** das kann nicht stimmen

····➤ (know how to) können. **can you swim?** können Sie schwimmen? **she can drive** sie kann Auto fahren

····➤ (be allowed to) dürfen. **you can't smoke here** hier dürfen Sie nicht rauchen. **can I go?** kann ich gehen?

····➤ (in requests) können. **can I have a glass of water, please?** kann ich ein Glas Wasser haben, bitte? **could you ring me tomorrow?** könnten Sie mich morgen anrufen?

····➤ **could** (expressing possibility) könnte. **that could be so** das könnte od kann sein. **I could have killed him** ich hätte ihn umbringen können

Canad|a /'kænədə/ n Kanada nt. **~ian** adj kanadisch •n Kanadier(in) m(f)

canal /kə'næl/ n Kanal m

canary /kə'neərɪ/ n Kanarienvogel m

cancel /'kænsl/ vt/i (pt/pp **cancelled**) absagen; abbestellen (newspaper); (Computing) abbrechen; **be ~led** ausfallen. **~lation** n Absage f

cancer /'kænsə(r)/ n (also Astrology) **C~** Krebs m. **~ous** adj krebsig

candid /'kændɪd/ adj offen

candidate /'kændɪdət/ n Kandidat(in) m(f)

candle /'kændl/ n Kerze f. **~stick** n Kerzenständer m, Leuchter m

candy /'kændɪ/ n (Amer)

Süßigkeiten pl; **[piece of] ~** Bonbon m

cane /keɪn/ n Rohr nt; (stick) Stock m • vt mit dem Stock züchtigen

canine /'keɪnaɪn/ adj Hunde-. **~ tooth** n Eckzahn m

cannabis /'kænəbɪs/ n Haschisch nt

canned /kænd/ adj Dosen-, Büchsen-

cannibal /'kænɪbl/ n Kannibale m. **~ism** n Kannibalismus m

cannon /'kænən/ n inv Kanone f

cannot /'kænɒt/ see **can**[2]

canoe /kə'nu:/ n Paddelboot nt; (Sport) Kanu nt

'can-opener n Dosenöffner m

can't /kɑ:nt/ = **cannot.** See **can**[2]

canteen /kæn'ti:n/ n Kantine f; **~ of cutlery** Besteckkasten m

canter /'kæntə(r)/ n Kanter m • vi kantern

canvas /'kænvəs/ n Segeltuch nt; (Art) Leinwand f; (painting) Gemälde nt

canvass /'kænvəs/ vi um Stimmen werben

canyon /'kænjən/ n Cañon m

cap /kæp/ n Kappe f, Mütze f; (nurse's) Haube f; (top, lid) Verschluss m

capability /keɪpə'bɪlətɪ/ n Fähigkeit f

capable /'keɪpəbl/ adj, **-bly** adv fähig; **be ~ of doing sth** fähig sein, etw zu tun

capacity /kə'pæsətɪ/ n Fassungsvermögen nt; (ability) Fähigkeit f; **in my ~ as** in meiner Eigenschaft als

cape[1] /keɪp/ n (cloak) Cape nt

cape[2] n (Geog) Kap nt

capital /'kæpɪtl/ adj (letter) groß • n (town) Hauptstadt f; (money) Kapital nt; (letter) Großbuchstabe m

capital|ism /'kæpɪtəlɪzm/ n Kapitalismus m. **~ist** adj kapitalistisch • n Kapitalist m. **~ 'letter** n Großbuchstabe m. **~ 'punishment** n Todesstrafe f

capsize /kæp'saɪz/ vi kentern • vt zum Kentern bringen

captain /'kæptɪn/ n Kapitän m; (Mil) Hauptmann m • vt anführen (team)

caption /'kæpʃn/ n Überschrift f; (of illustration) Bildtext m

captivate /'kæptɪveɪt/ vt bezaubern

captiv|e /'kæptɪv/ adj **hold/take ~e** gefangen halten/nehmen • n Gefangene(r) m/f. **~ity** n Gefangenschaft f

capture /'kæptʃə(r)/ n Gefangennahme f • vt gefangen nehmen; [ein]fangen (animal); (Mil) einnehmen (town)

car /kɑ:(r)/ n Auto nt, Wagen m; **by ~** mit dem Auto od Wagen

caramel /'kærəmel/ n Karamell m

carat /'kærət/ n Karat nt

caravan /'kærəvæn/ n Wohnwagen m; (procession) Karawane f

carbon /'kɑ:bən/ n Kohlenstoff m; (paper) Kohlepapier nt; (copy) Durchschlag m

carbon: ~ copy n Durchschlag m. **~ paper** n Kohlepapier nt

carburettor /kɑ:bjʊ'retə(r)/ n Vergaser m

carcass /'kɑ:kəs/ n Kadaver m

card /kɑ:d/ n Karte f

'cardboard n Pappe f, Karton m. **~ 'box** n Pappschachtel f; (large) [Papp]karton m

'card-game n Kartenspiel nt

cardigan /'kɑ:dɪgən/ n Strickjacke f

cardinal /'kɑ:dɪnl/ adj Kardinal- • n (Relig) Kardinal m

card 'index n Kartei f

care /keə(r)/ n Sorgfalt f; (caution) Vorsicht f; (protection) Obhut f; (looking after) Pflege f; (worry) Sorge f; **~ of** (on letter abbr **c/o**) bei; **take ~** vorsichtig sein; **take into ~** in Pflege nehmen; **take ~ of** sich kümmern um • vi **~ for** (like) mögen; (look after) betreuen; **I don't ~** das ist mir gleich

C

career /kə'rɪə(r)/ n Laufbahn f; (profession) Beruf m •vi rasen

care: ~free adj sorglos. **~ful** adj sorgfältig; (cautious) vorsichtig. **~less** adj nachlässig. **~lessness** n Nachlässigkeit f. **~r** n Pflegende(r) m/f

'caretaker n Hausmeister m

'car ferry n Autofähre f

cargo /'kɑ:gəʊ/ n (pl **-es**) Ladung f

Caribbean /kærɪ'bi:ən/ n **the ~** die Karibik

caricature /'kærɪkətjʊə(r)/ n Karikatur f •vt karikieren

caring /'keərɪŋ/ adj (parent) liebevoll; (profession, attitude) sozial

carnation /kɑ:'neɪʃn/ n Nelke f

carnival /'kɑ:nɪvl/ n Karneval m

carol /'kærl/ n **[Christmas] ~** Weihnachtslied nt

carp[1] /kɑ:p/ n inv Karpfen m

carp[2] vi nörgeln

'car park n Parkplatz m; (multi-storey) Parkhaus nt; (underground) Tiefgarage f

carpent|er /'kɑ:pɪntə(r)/ n Zimmermann m; (joiner) Tischler m. **~ry** n Tischlerei f

carpet /'kɑ:pɪt/ n Teppich m

carriage /'kærɪdʒ/ n Kutsche f; (Rail) Wagen m; (of goods) Beförderung f; (cost) Frachtkosten pl; (bearing) Haltung f

carrier /'kærɪə(r)/ n Träger(in) m(f); (Comm) Spediteur m; **~[-bag]** Tragetasche f

carrot /'kærət/ n Möhre f, Karotte f

carry /'kærɪ/ vt/i (pt/pp **-ied**) tragen; **be carried away** [!] hingerissen sein. **~ off** vt wegtragen; gewinnen (prize). **~ on** vi weitermachen; **~ on with** [!] eine Affäre haben mit •vt führen; (continue) fortführen. **~ out** vt hinaus-/heraustragen; (perform) ausführen

cart /kɑ:t/ n Karren m; **put the ~ before the horse** das Pferd beim Schwanz aufzäumen •vt karren; ([!]: carry) schleppen

carton /'kɑ:tn/ n [Papp]karton m; (for drink) Tüte f; (of cream, yoghurt) Becher m

cartoon /kɑ:'tu:n/ n Karikatur f; (joke) Witzzeichnung f; (strip) Comic Strips pl; (film) Zeichentrickfilm m. **~ist** n Karikaturist m

cartridge /'kɑ:trɪdʒ/ n Patrone f; (for film) Kassette f

carve /kɑ:v/ vt schnitzen; (in stone) hauen; (Culin) aufschneiden

carving /'kɑ:vɪŋ/ n Schnitzerei f. **~-knife** n Tranchiermesser nt

'car wash n Autowäsche f; (place) Autowaschanlage f

case[1] /keɪs/ n Fall m; **in any ~** auf jeden Fall; **just in ~** für alle Fälle; **in ~ he comes** falls er kommt

case[2] n Kasten m; (crate) Kiste f; (for spectacles) Etui nt; (suitcase) Koffer m; (for display) Vitrine f

cash /kæʃ/ n Bargeld nt; **pay [in] ~** [in] bar bezahlen; **~ on delivery** per Nachnahme •vt einlösen (cheque). **~ desk** n Kasse f

cashier /kæ'ʃɪə(r)/ n Kassierer(in) m(f)

cash: ~point [machine] n Geldautomat m. **~ register** n Registrierkasse f

cassette /kə'set/ n Kassette f. **~ recorder** n Kassettenrecorder m

cast /kɑ:st/ n (mould) Form f; (model) Abguss m; (Theat) Besetzung f; **[plaster] ~** (Med) Gipsverband m •vt (pt/pp **cast**) (throw) werfen; (shed) abwerfen; abgeben (vote); gießen (metal); (Theat) besetzen (role). **~ off** vi (Naut) ablegen

castle /'kɑ:sl/ n Schloss nt; (fortified) Burg f; (Chess) Turm m

'cast-offs npl abgelegte Kleidung f

castor /'kɑ:stə(r)/ n (wheel) [Lauf]rolle f

'castor sugar n Streuzucker m

casual /'kæʒʊəl/ adj (chance) zufällig; (offhand) lässig; (informal) zwanglos; (not permanent)

Gelegenheits-; ~ **wear** Freizeitbekleidung f

casualty /'kæʒʊəltɪ/ n [Todes]opfer nt; (injured person) Verletzte(r) m/f; ~ **[department]** Unfallstation f

cat /kæt/ n Katze f

catalogue /'kætəlɒg/ n Katalog m •vt katalogisieren

catapult /'kætəpʌlt/ n Katapult nt •vt katapultieren

cataract /'kætərækt/ n (Med) grauer Star m

catarrh /kə'tɑ:(r)/ n Katarrh m

catastroph|e /kə'tæstrəfɪ/ n Katastrophe f. **~ic** adj katastrophal

catch /kætʃ/ n (of fish) Fang m; (fastener) Verschluss m; (on door) Klinke f; (!: snag) Haken m ! •v (pt/pp **caught**) •vt fangen; (be in time for) erreichen; (travel by) fahren mit; bekommen (illness); ~ **a cold** sich erkälten; ~ **sight of** erblicken; ~ **s.o. stealing** jdn beim Stehlen erwischen; ~ **one's finger in the door** sich (dat) den Finger in der Tür [ein]klemmen •vi (burn) anbrennen; (get stuck) klemmen. ~ **on** vi ! (understand) kapieren; (become popular) sich durchsetzen. ~ **up** vt einholen •vi aufholen; ~ **up with** einholen (s.o.); nachholen (work)

catching /'kætʃɪŋ/ adj ansteckend

catch: **~-phrase** n, **~word** n Schlagwort nt

catchy /'kætʃɪ/ adj einprägsam

categor|ical /kætɪ'gɒrɪkl/ adj kategorisch. **~y** n Kategorie f

cater /'keɪtə(r)/ vi ~ **for** beköstigen; (firm:) das Essen liefern für (party); (fig) eingestellt sein auf (+ acc). **~ing** n (trade) Gaststättengewerbe nt

caterpillar /'kætəpɪlə(r)/ n Raupe f

cathedral /kə'θi:drl/ n Dom m, Kathedrale f

Catholic /'kæθəlɪk/ adj katholisch •n Katholik(in) m(f). **C ~ism** n Katholizismus m

cattle /'kætl/ npl Vieh nt

catty /'kætɪ/ adj boshaft

caught /kɔ:t/ see **catch**

cauliflower /'kɒlɪ-/ n Blumenkohl m

cause /kɔ:z/ n Ursache f; (reason) Grund m; **good** ~ gute Sache f •vt verursachen; ~ **s.o. to do sth** jdn veranlassen, etw zu tun

caution /'kɔ:ʃn/ n Vorsicht f; (warning) Verwarnung f •vt (Jur) verwarnen

cautious /'kɔ:ʃəs/ adj vorsichtig

cavalry /'kævəlrɪ/ n Kavallerie f

cave /keɪv/ n Höhle f •vi ~ **in** einstürzen

cavern /'kævən/ n Höhle f

caviare /'kævɪɑ:(r)/ n Kaviar m

cavity /'kævətɪ/ n Hohlraum m; (in tooth) Loch nt

CCTV abbr (**closed-circuit television**) CCTV nt; (surveillance) Videoüberwachung f

CD abbr (**compact disc**) CD f; **~-ROM** CD-ROM f

cease /si:s/ vt/i aufhören. **~-fire** n Waffenruhe f. **~less** adj unaufhörlich

cedar /'si:də(r)/ n Zeder f

ceiling /'si:lɪŋ/ n [Zimmer]decke f; (fig) oberste Grenze f

celebrat|e /'selɪbreɪt/ vt/i feiern. **~ed** adj berühmt (**for** wegen). **~ion** n Feier f

celebrity /sɪ'lebrətɪ/ n Berühmtheit f

celery /'selərɪ/ n [Stangen]sellerie m & f

cell /sel/ n Zelle f

cellar /'selə(r)/ n Keller m

cellist /'tʃelɪst/ n Cellist(in) m(f)

cello /'tʃeləu/ n Cello nt

cellphone /'selfəʊn/ n Handy nt

Celsius /'selsɪəs/ adj Celsius

Celt /kelt/ n Kelte m/ Keltin f. **~ic** adj keltisch

cement /sɪ'ment/ n Zement m; (adhesive) Kitt m

C

cemetery /ˈsemətrɪ/ n Friedhof m

censor /ˈsensə(r)/ n Zensor m • vt zensieren. **~ship** n Zensur f

census /ˈsensəs/ n Volkszählung f

cent /sent/ n Cent m

centenary /senˈtiːnərɪ/ n, (Amer) **centennial** n Hundertjahrfeier f

center /ˈsentə(r)/ n (Amer) = **centre**

centi|grade /ˈsentɪ-/ adj Celsius. **~metre** n Zentimeter m & nt

central /ˈsentrəl/ adj zentral. **~ ˈheating** n Zentralheizung f. **~ize** vt zentralisieren

centre /ˈsentə(r)/ n Zentrum nt; (middle) Mitte f • v (pt/pp **centred**) • vt zentrieren. **~-ˈforward** n Mittelstürmer m

century /ˈsentʃərɪ/ n Jahrhundert nt

ceramic /sɪˈræmɪk/ adj Keramik-

cereal /ˈsɪərɪəl/ n Getreide nt; (breakfast food) Frühstücksflocken pl

ceremon|ial /serɪˈməʊnɪəl/ adj zeremoniell, feierlich • n Zeremoniell nt. **~ious** adj formell

ceremony /ˈserɪmənɪ/ n Zeremonie f, Feier f

certain /ˈsɜːtn/ adj sicher; (not named) gewiss; **for ~** mit Bestimmtheit; **make ~** (check) sich vergewissern (**that** dass); (ensure) dafür sorgen (**that** dass); **he is ~ to win** er wird ganz bestimmt siegen. **~ly** adv bestimmt, sicher; **~ly not!** auf keinen Fall! **~ty** n Sicherheit f, Gewissheit f; **it's a ~ty** es ist sicher

certificate /səˈtɪfɪkət/ n Bescheinigung f; (Jur) Urkunde f; (Sch) Zeugnis nt

certify /ˈsɜːtɪfaɪ/ vt (pt/pp **-ied**) bescheinigen; (declare insane) für geisteskrank erklären

cf. abbr (compare) vgl.

chafe /tʃeɪf/ vt wund reiben

chaffinch /ˈtʃæfɪntʃ/ n Buchfink m

chain /tʃeɪn/ n Kette f • vt ketten (**to** an + acc). **~ up** vt anketten

chain: ~ reˈaction n Kettenreaktion f. **~-smoker** n Kettenraucher m. **~ store** n Kettenladen m

chair /tʃeə(r)/ n Stuhl m; (Univ) Lehrstuhl m; (Adm) Vorsitzende(r) m/f. **~-lift** n Sessellift m. **~man** n Vorsitzende(r) m/f

chalet /ˈʃæleɪ/ n Chalet nt

chalk /tʃɔːk/ n Kreide f

challeng|e /ˈtʃælɪndʒ/ n Herausforderung f; (Mil) Anruf m • vt herausfordern; (Mil) anrufen; (fig) anfechten (statement). **~er** n Herausforderer m. **~ing** adj herausfordernd; (demanding) anspruchsvoll

chamber /ˈtʃeɪmbə(r)/ n Kammer f; **C~ of Commerce** Handelskammer f. **~ music** n Kammermusik f

chamois /ˈʃæmɪ/ n **~[-leather]** Ledertuch nt

champagne /ʃæmˈpeɪn/ n Champagner m

champion /ˈtʃæmpɪən/ n (Sport) Meister(in) m(f); (of cause) Verfechter m • vt sich einsetzen für. **~ship** n (Sport) Meisterschaft f

chance /tʃɑːns/ n Zufall m; (prospect) Chancen pl; (likelihood) Aussicht f; (opportunity) Gelegenheit f; **by ~** zufällig; **take a ~** ein Risiko eingehen; **give s.o. a ~** jdm eine Chance geben • attrib zufällig • vt **~ it** es riskieren

chancellor /ˈtʃɑːnsələ(r)/ n Kanzler m; (Univ) Rektor m

chancy /ˈtʃɑːnsɪ/ adj riskant

change /tʃeɪndʒ/ n Veränderung f; (alteration) Änderung f; (money) Wechselgeld nt; **for a ~** zur Abwechslung • vt wechseln; (alter) ändern; (exchange) umtauschen (**for** gegen); (transform) verwandeln; trocken legen (baby); **~ one's clothes** sich umziehen; **~ trains** umsteigen • vi sich verändern; (**~** clothes) sich umziehen; (**~** trains) umsteigen; **all ~!** alles aussteigen!

changeable /ˈtʃeɪndʒəbl/ adj wechselhaft

ˈchanging-room n Umkleideraum m

channel /ˈtʃænl/ n Rinne f; (Radio, TV) Kanal m; (fig) Weg m; **the [English] C~** der Ärmelkanal; **the C~ Islands** die Kanalinseln

chant /tʃɑːnt/ vt singen; (demonstrators:) skandieren

chao|s /ˈkeɪɒs/ n Chaos nt. **~tic** adj chaotisch

chap /tʃæpl/ n [!] Kerl m

chapel /ˈtʃæpl/ n Kapelle f

chaplain /ˈtʃæplɪn/ n Geistliche(r) m

chapped /tʃæpt/ adj (skin) aufgesprungen

chapter /ˈtʃæptə(r)/ n Kapitel nt

character /ˈkærɪktə(r)/ n Charakter m; (in novel, play) Gestalt f; (Printing) Schriftzeichen nt; **out of ~** uncharakteristisch; **quite a ~** [!] ein Original

characteristic /kærɪktəˈrɪstɪk/ adj, **-ally** adv charakteristisch (**of** für) • n Merkmal nt

characterize /ˈkærɪktəraɪz/ vt charakterisieren

charge /tʃɑːdʒ/ n (price) Gebühr f; (Electr) Ladung f; (attack) Angriff m; (Jur) Anklage f; **free of ~** kostenlos; **be in ~** verantwortlich sein (**of** für); **take ~** die Aufsicht übernehmen (**of** über + acc) • vt berechnen (fee); (Electr) laden; (attack) angreifen; (Jur) anklagen (**with** gen); **~ s.o. for sth** jdm etw berechnen

charitable /ˈtʃærɪtəbl/ adj wohltätig; (kind) wohlwollend

charity /ˈtʃærətɪ/ n Nächstenliebe f; (organization) wohltätige Einrichtung f; **for ~** für Wohltätigkeitszwecke

charm /tʃɑːm/ n Reiz m; (of person) Charme f; (object) Amulett nt • vt bezaubern. **~ing** adj reizend; (person, smile) charmant

chart /tʃɑːt/ n Karte f; (table) Tabelle f

charter /ˈtʃɑːtə(r)/ n **~ [flight]** Charterflug m • vt chartern; **~ed accountant** Wirtschaftsprüfer, Wirtschaftsprüferin m(f)

chase /tʃeɪs/ n Verfolgungsjagd f • vt jagen, verfolgen. **~ away** or **off** vt wegjagen

chassis /ˈʃæsɪ/ n (pl **chassis**) Chassis nt

chaste /tʃeɪst/ adj keusch

chat /tʃæt/ n Plauderei f; **have a ~ with** plaudern mit • vi (pt/pp **chatted**) plaudern. **~ show** n Talkshow f

chatter /ˈtʃætə(r)/ n Geschwätz nt • vi schwatzen; (child:) plappern; (teeth:) klappern. **~box** n [!] Plappermaul nt

chatty /ˈtʃætɪ/ adj geschwätzig

chauffeur /ˈʃəʊfə(r)/ n Chauffeur m

cheap /tʃiːp/ adj & adv (**-er, -est**) billig. **~en** vt entwürdigen

cheat /tʃiːt/ n Betrüger(in) m(f); (at games) Mogler m • vt betrügen • vi (at games) mogeln [!]

check[1] /tʃek/ adj (squared) kariert • n Karo nt

check[2] n Überprüfung f; (inspection) Kontrolle f; (Chess) Schach nt; (Amer: bill) Rechnung f; (Amer: cheque) Scheck m; (Amer: tick) Haken m; **keep a ~ on** kontrollieren • vt [über]prüfen; (inspect) kontrollieren; (restrain) hemmen; (stop) aufhalten • vi **[go and] ~** nachsehen. **~ in** vi sich anmelden; (Aviat) einchecken • vt abfertigen; einchecken. **~ out** vi sich abmelden. **~ up** vi prüfen, kontrollieren; **~ up on** überprüfen

checked /tʃekt/ adj kariert

check: ~-out n Kasse f. **~room** n (Amer) Garderobe f. **~-up** n (Med) [Kontroll]untersuchung f

cheek /tʃiːk/ n Backe f; (impudence) Frechheit f. **~y** adj, **-ily** adv frech

cheer /tʃɪə(r)/ n Beifallsruf m; **three ~s** ein dreifaches Hoch (**for** auf + acc); **~s!** prost! (goodbye) tschüs! • vt zujubeln (+ dat) • vi jubeln. **~ up** vt aufmuntern; aufheitern • vi munterer werden. **~ful** adj fröhlich. **~fulness** n Fröhlichkeit f

C

cheerio /tʃɪərɪ'əʊ/ int [!] tschüs!

cheese /tʃi:z/ n Käse m. **~cake** n Käsekuchen m

chef /ʃef/ n Koch m

chemical /'kemɪkl/ adj chemisch •n Chemikalie f

chemist /'kemɪst/ n (pharmacist) Apotheker(in) m(f); (scientist) Chemiker(in) m(f); **~'s [shop]** Drogerie f; (dispensing) Apotheke f. **~ry** n Chemie f

cheque /tʃek/ n Scheck m. **~-book** n Scheckbuch nt. **~ card** n Scheckkarte f

cherish /'tʃerɪʃ/ vt lieben; (fig) hegen

cherry /'tʃerɪ/ n Kirsche f •attrib Kirsch-

chess /tʃes/ n Schach nt

chess: ~board n Schachbrett nt. **~-man** n Schachfigur f

chest /tʃest/ n Brust f; (box) Truhe f

chestnut /'tʃesnʌt/ n Esskastanie f, Marone f; (horse-) [Ross]kastanie f

chest of 'drawers n Kommode f

chew /tʃu:/ vt kauen. **~ing-gum** n Kaugummi m

chick /tʃɪk/ n Küken nt

chicken /'tʃɪkɪn/ n Huhn nt •attrib Hühner- •adj [!] feige

chief /tʃi:f/ adj Haupt- •n Chef m; (of tribe) Häuptling m. **~ly** adv hauptsächlich

child /tʃaɪld/ n (pl **~ren**) Kind nt

child: ~birth n Geburt f. **~hood** n Kindheit f. **~ish** adj kindisch. **~less** adj kinderlos. **~like** adj kindlich. **~-minder** n Tagesmutter f

children /'tʃɪldrən/ npl see **child**

Chile /'tʃɪlɪ/ n Chile nt

chill /tʃɪl/ n Kälte f; (illness) Erkältung f •vt kühlen

chilly /'tʃɪlɪ/ adj kühl; **I felt ~** mich fröstelte [es]

chime /tʃaɪm/ vi läuten; (clock:) schlagen

chimney /'tʃɪmnɪ/ n Schornstein m. **~-pot** n Schornsteinaufsatz m. **~-sweep** n Schornsteinfeger m

chin /tʃɪn/ n Kinn nt

china /'tʃaɪnə/ n Porzellan nt

Chin|a n China nt. **~ese** adj chinesisch •n (Lang) Chinesisch nt; **the ~ese** pl die Chinesen

chink[1] /tʃɪŋk/ n (slit) Ritze f

chink[2] n Geklirr nt •vi klirren; (coins:) klimpern

chip /tʃɪp/ n (fragment) Span m; (in china, paintwork) angeschlagene Stelle f; (Computing, Gambling) Chip m; **~s** pl (Culin) Pommes frites pl; (Amer: crisps) Chips pl •vt (pt/pp **chipped**) (damage) anschlagen. **~ped** adj angeschlagen

chirp /tʃɜ:p/ vi zwitschern; (cricket:) zirpen. **~y** adj [!] munter

chit /tʃɪt/ n Zettel m

chocolate /'tʃɒkələt/ n Schokolade f; (sweet) Praline f

choice /tʃɔɪs/ n Wahl f; (variety) Auswahl f •adj auserlesen

choir /'kwaɪə(r)/ n Chor m. **~boy** n Chorknabe m

choke /tʃəʊk/ n (Auto) Choke m •vt würgen; (to death) erwürgen •vi sich verschlucken; **~ on** [fast] ersticken an (+ dat)

choose /tʃu:z/ vt/i (pt **chose**, pp **chosen**) wählen; (select) sich (dat) aussuchen; **~ to do/go** [freiwillig] tun/gehen; **as you ~** wie Sie wollen

choos[e]y /'tʃu:zɪ/ adj [!] wählerisch

chop /tʃɒp/ n (blow) Hieb m; (Culin) Kotelett nt •vt (pt/pp **chopped**) hacken. **~ down** vt abhacken; fällen (tree). **~ off** vt abhacken

chop|per /'tʃɒpə(r)/ n Beil nt; [!] Hubschrauber m. **~py** adj kabbelig

'chopsticks npl Essstäbchen pl

choral /'kɔ:rəl/ adj Chor-

chord /kɔ:d/ n (Mus) Akkord m

chore /tʃɔ:(r)/ n lästige Pflicht f; **[household] ~s** Hausarbeit f

chorus /ˈkɔːrəs/ n Chor m; (of song) Refrain m

chose, chosen see **choose**

Christ /kraɪst/ n Christus m

christen /ˈkrɪsn/ vt taufen

Christian /ˈkrɪstʃən/ adj christlich •n Christ(in) m(f). **~ity** n Christentum nt. **~ name** n Vorname m

Christmas /ˈkrɪsməs/ n Weihnachten nt. **~ card** n Weihnachtskarte f. **~ ˈDay** n erster Weihnachtstag m. **~ ˈEve** n Heiligabend m. **~ tree** n Weihnachtsbaum m

chrome /krəʊm/ n, **chromium** n Chrom nt

chronic /ˈkrɒnɪk/ adj chronisch

chronicle /ˈkrɒnɪkl/ n Chronik f

chrysanthemum /krɪˈsænθəməm/ n Chrysantheme f

chubby /ˈtʃʌbɪ/ adj mollig

chuck /tʃʌk/ vt [!] schmeißen. **~ out** vt [!] rausschmeißen

chuckle /ˈtʃʌkl/ vi in sich (acc) hineinlachen

chum /tʃʌm/ n Freund(in) m(f)

chunk /tʃʌŋk/ n Stück nt

church /tʃɜːtʃ/ n Kirche f. **~yard** n Friedhof m

churn /tʃɜːn/ vt **~ out** am laufenden Band produzieren

cider /ˈsaɪdə(r)/ n ≈ Apfelwein m

cigar /sɪˈgɑː(r)/ n Zigarre f

cigarette /sɪgəˈret/ n Zigarette f

cine-camera /ˈsɪnɪ-/ n Filmkamera f

cinema /ˈsɪnɪmə/ n Kino nt

cinnamon /ˈsɪnəmən/ n Zimt m

circle /ˈsɜːkl/ n Kreis m; (Theat) Rang m •vt umkreisen •vi kreisen

circuit /ˈsɜːkɪt/ n Runde f; (racetrack) Rennbahn f; (Electr) Stromkreis m. **~ous** adj **~ route** Umweg m

circular /ˈsɜːkjʊlə(r)/ adj kreisförmig •n Rundschreiben nt. **~ ˈsaw** n Kreissäge f. **~ ˈtour** n Rundfahrt f

circulat|e /ˈsɜːkjʊleɪt/ vt in Umlauf setzen •vi zirkulieren. **~ion** n Kreislauf m; (of newspaper) Auflage f

circumference /ʃəˈkʌmfərəns/ n Umfang m

circumstance /ˈsɜːkəmstəns/ n Umstand m; **~s** pl Umstände pl; (financial) Verhältnisse pl

circus /ˈsɜːkəs/ n Zirkus m

cistern /ˈsɪstən/ n (tank) Wasserbehälter m; (of WC) Spülkasten m

cite /saɪt/ vt zitieren

citizen /ˈsɪtɪzn/ n Bürger(in) m(f). **~ship** n Staatsangehörigkeit f

citrus /ˈsɪtrəs/ n **~ [fruit]** Zitrusfrucht f

city /ˈsɪtɪ/ n [Groß]stadt f

civic /ˈsɪvɪk/ adj Bürger-

civil /ˈʃɪvl/ adj bürgerlich; (aviation, defence) zivil; (polite) höflich. **~ engiˈneering** n Hoch- und Tiefbau m

civilian /sɪˈvɪljən/ adj Zivil-; **in ~ clothes** in Zivil •n Zivilist m

civiliz|ation /sɪvəlaɪˈzeɪʃn/ n Zivilisation f. **~e** vt zivilisieren

civil: ~ˈservant n Beamte(r) m/ Beamtin f. **C~ ˈService** n Staatsdienst m

claim /kleɪm/ n Anspruch m; (application) Antrag m; (demand) Forderung f; (assertion) Behauptung f •vt beanspruchen; (apply for) beantragen; (demand) fordern; (assert) behaupten; (collect) abholen

clam /klæm/ n Klaffmuschel f

clamber /ˈklæmbə(r)/ vi klettern

clammy /ˈklæmɪ/ adj feucht

clamour /ˈklæmə(r)/ n Geschrei nt •vi **~ for** schreien nach

clamp /klæmp/ n Klammer f; **[wheel] ~** Parkkralle f •vt [ein]spannen •vi [!] **~ down on** vorgehen gegen

clan /klæn/ n Clan m

clang /klæŋ/ n Schmettern nt. **~er** n [!] Schnitzer m

clank /klæŋk/ vi klirren

C

clap /klæp/ n **give s.o. a ~** jdm Beifall klatschen; **~ of thunder** Donnerschlag m • vt/i (pt/pp **clapped**) Beifall klatschen (+ dat); **~ one's hands** [in die Hände] klatschen

clari|fication /klærɪfɪ'keɪʃn/ n Klärung f. **~fy** vt/i (pt/pp **-ied**) klären

clarinet /klærɪ'net/ n Klarinette f

clarity /'klærətɪ/ n Klarheit f

clash /klæʃ/ n Geklirr nt; (fig) Konflikt m • vi klirren; (colours:) sich beißen; (events:) ungünstig zusammenfallen

clasp /klɑ:sp/ n Verschluss m • vt ergreifen; (hold) halten

class /klɑ:s/ n Klasse f; **travel first/second ~** erster/zweiter Klasse reisen • vt einordnen

classic /'klæsɪk/ adj klassisch • n Klassiker m. **~al** adj klassisch

classi|fication /klæsɪfɪ'keɪʃn/ n Klassifikation f. **~fy** vt (pt/pp **-ied**) klassifizieren

'classroom n Klassenzimmer nt

classy /'klɑ:sɪ/ adj ! schick

clatter /'klætə(r)/ n Geklapper nt • vi klappern

clause /klɔ:z/ n Klausel f; (Gram) Satzteil m

claw /klɔ:/ n Kralle f; (of bird of prey & Techn) Klaue f; (of crab, lobster) Schere f • vt kratzen

clay /kleɪ/ n Lehm m; (pottery) Ton m

clean /kli:n/ adj (**-er, -est**) sauber • adv glatt • vt sauber machen; putzen (shoes, windows); **~ one's teeth** sich (dat) die Zähne putzen; **have sth ~ed** etw reinigen lassen. **~ up** vt sauber machen

cleaner /'kli:nə(r)/ n Putzfrau f; (substance) Reinigungsmittel nt; **[dry] ~'s** chemische Reinigung f

cleanliness /'klenlɪnɪs/ n Sauberkeit f

cleanse /klenz/ vt reinigen

clear /klɪə(r)/ adj (**-er, -est**) klar; (obvious) eindeutig; (distinct) deutlich; (conscience) rein; (without obstacles) frei; **make sth ~** etw klarmachen (**to** dat) • adv **stand ~** zurücktreten; **keep ~ of** aus dem Wege gehen (+ dat) • vt räumen; abräumen (table); (acquit) freisprechen; (authorize) genehmigen; (jump over) überspringen; **~ one's throat** sich räuspern • vi (fog:) sich auflösen. **~ away** vt wegräumen. **~ off** vi ! abhauen. **~ out** vt ausräumen • vi ! abhauen. **~ up** vt (tidy) aufräumen; (solve) aufklären • vi (weather): sich aufklären

clearance /'klɪərəns/ n Räumung f; (authorization) Genehmigung f; (customs) [Zoll]abfertigung f; (Techn) Spielraum m. **~ sale** n Räumungsverkauf m

clench /klentʃ/ vt **~ one's fist** die Faust ballen; **~ one's teeth** die Zähne zusammenbeißen

clergy /'klɜ:dʒɪ/ npl Geistlichkeit f. **~man** n Geistliche(r) m

clerk /klɑ:k/, Amer: /klɜ:k/ n Büroangestellte(r) m/f; (Amer: shop assistant) Verkäufer(in) m(f)

clever /'klevə(r)/ adj (**-er, -est**), **-ly** adv klug; (skilful) geschickt

cliché /'kli:ʃeɪ/ n Klischee nt

click /klɪk/ vi klicken

client /'klaɪənt/ n Kunde m/ Kundin f; (Jur) Klient(in) m(f)

cliff /klɪf/ n Kliff nt

climat|e /'klaɪmət/ n Klima nt

climax /'klaɪmæks/ n Höhepunkt m

climb /klaɪm/ n Aufstieg m • vt besteigen (mountain); steigen auf (+ acc) (ladder, tree) • vi klettern; (rise) steigen; (road:) ansteigen. **~ down** vi hinunter-/herunterklettern; (from ladder, tree) heruntersteigen; ! nachgeben

climber /'klaɪmə(r)/ n Bergsteiger m; (plant) Kletterpflanze f

cling /klɪŋ/ vi (pt/pp **clung**) sich klammern (**to** an + acc); (stick) haften (**to** an + dat). **~ film** n Sichtfolie f mit Hafteffekt

clinic /ˈklɪnɪk/ n Klinik f. **~al** adj klinisch

clink /klɪŋk/ vi klirren

clip[1] /klɪp/ n Klammer f; (jewellery) Klipp m •vt (pt/pp **clipped**) anklammern (**to** an + acc)

clip[2] n (extract) Ausschnitt m •vt schneiden; knipsen (ticket). **~ping** n (extract) Ausschnitt m

cloak /kləʊk/ n Umhang m. **~room** n Garderobe f; (toilet) Toilette f

clobber /ˈklɒbə(r)/ n [!] Zeug nt •vt ([!]: hit, defeat) schlagen

clock /klɒk/ n Uhr f; ([!]: speedometer) Tacho m •vi **~ in/out** stechen

clock: ~wise adj & adv im Uhrzeigersinn. **~work** n Uhrwerk nt; (of toy) Aufziehmechanismus m; **like ~work** [!] wie am Schnürchen

clod /klɒd/ n Klumpen m

clog /klɒg/ vt/i (pt/pp **clogged**) **~ [up]** verstopfen

cloister /ˈklɔɪstə(r)/ n Kreuzgang m

clone /kləʊn/ n Klon m • vt klonen

close[1] /kləʊs/ adj (**-r, -st**) nah[e] (**to** dat); (friend) eng; (weather) schwül; **have a ~ shave** [!] mit knapper Not davonkommen •adv nahe •n (street) Sackgasse f

close[2] /kləʊz/ n Ende nt; **draw to a ~** sich dem Ende nähern •vt zumachen, schließen; (bring to an end) beenden; sperren (road) •vi sich schließen; (shop:) schließen, zumachen; (end) enden. **~ down** vt schließen; stilllegen (factory) •vi schließen; (factory:) stillgelegt werden

closely /ˈkləʊslɪ/ adv eng, nah[e]; (with attention) genau

closet /ˈklɒzɪt/ n (Amer) Schrank m

close-up /ˈkləʊs-/ n Nahaufnahme f

closure /ˈkləʊʒə(r)/ n Schließung f; (of factory) Stilllegung f; (of road) Sperrung f

clot /klɒt/ n [Blut]gerinnsel nt; ([!]: idiot) Trottel m

cloth /klɒθ/ n Tuch nt

clothe /kləʊð/ vt kleiden

clothes /kləʊðz/ npl Kleider pl. **~-line** n Wäscheleine f

clothing /ˈkləʊðɪŋ/ n Kleidung f

cloud /klaʊd/ n Wolke f •vi **~ over** sich bewölken

cloudy /ˈklaʊdɪ/ adj wolkig, bewölkt; (liquid) trübe

clout /klaʊt/ n [!] Schlag m; (influence) Einfluss m

clove /kləʊv/ n [Gewürz]nelke f; **~ of garlic** Knoblauchzehe f

clover /ˈkləʊvə(r)/ n Klee m. **~ leaf** n Kleeblatt nt

clown /klaʊn/ n Clown m •vi **~ [about]** herumalbern

club /klʌb/ n Klub m; (weapon) Keule f; (Sport) Schläger m; **~s** pl (Cards) Kreuz nt, Treff nt

clue /klu:/ n Anhaltspunkt m; (in crossword) Frage f; **I haven't a ~** [!] ich habe keine Ahnung

clump /klʌmp/ n Gruppe f

clumsiness /ˈklʌmzɪnɪs/ n Ungeschicklichkeit f

clumsy /ˈklʌmzɪ/ adj , **-ily** adv ungeschickt; (unwieldy) unförmig

clung /klʌŋ/ see **cling**

clutch /klʌtʃ/ n Griff m; (Auto) Kupplung f; **be in s.o.'s ~es** [!] in jds Klauen sein •vt festhalten; (grab) ergreifen •vi **~ at** greifen nach

clutter /ˈklʌtə(r)/ n Kram m •vt **~ [up]** vollstopfen

c/o abbr (**care of**) bei

coach /kəʊtʃ/ n [Reise]bus m; (Rail) Wagen m; (horse-drawn) Kutsche f; (Sport) Trainer m •vt Nachhilfestunden geben (+ dat); (Sport) trainieren

coal /kəʊl/ n Kohle f

coalition /kəʊəˈlɪʃn/ n Koalition f

ˈ**coal-mine** n Kohlenbergwerk nt

coarse /kɔ:s/ adj (**-r, -st**) grob

coast /kəʊst/ n Küste f •vi (freewheel) im Freilauf fahren; (Auto) im Leerlauf fahren. **~er** n (mat) Untersatz m

C

coast: ~guard n Küstenwache f. **~line** n Küste f

coat /kəʊt/ n Mantel m; (of animal) Fell nt; (of paint) Anstrich m; **~ of arms** Wappen nt •vt überziehen; (with paint) streichen. **~-hanger** n Kleiderbügel m. **~-hook** n Kleiderhaken m

coating /ˈkəʊtɪŋ/ n Überzug m, Schicht f; (of paint) Anstrich m

coax /kəʊks/ vt gut zureden (+ dat)

cobble¹ /ˈkɒbl/ n Kopfstein m; **~s** pl Kopfsteinpflaster nt

cobble² vt flicken. **~r** n Schuster m

cobweb /ˈkɒb-/ n Spinnengewebe nt

cock /kɒk/ n Hahn m; (any male bird) Männchen nt •vt (animal:) **~ its ears** die Ohren spitzen; **~ the gun** den Hahn spannen

cockerel /ˈkɒkərəl/ n [junger] Hahn m

cockney /ˈkɒknɪ/ n (dialect) Cockney nt; (person) Cockney m

cock: ~pit n (Aviat) Cockpit nt. **~roach** /-rəʊtʃ/ n Küchenschabe f. **~tail** n Cocktail m. **~-up** n ✖ **make a ~-up** Mist bauen (**of** bei)

cocky /ˈkɒkɪ/ adj ⓘ eingebildet

cocoa /ˈkəʊkəʊ/ n Kakao m

coconut /ˈkəʊkənʌt/ n Kokosnuss f

cod /kɒd/ n inv Kabeljau m

COD abbr (**cash on delivery**) per Nachnahme

coddle /ˈkɒdl/ vt verhätscheln

code /kəʊd/ n Kode m; (Computing) Code m; (set of rules) Kodex m. **~d** adj verschlüsselt

coerc|e /kəʊˈɜːs/ vt zwingen. **~ion** n Zwang m

coffee /ˈkɒfɪ/ n Kaffee m

coffee: ~-grinder n Kaffeemühle f. **~-pot** n Kaffeekanne f. **~-table** n Couchtisch m

coffin /ˈkɒfɪn/ n Sarg m

cogent /ˈkəʊdʒənt/ adj überzeugend

coherent /kəʊˈhɪərənt/ adj zusammenhängend; (comprehensible) verständlich

coil /kɔɪl/ n Rolle f; (Electr) Spule f; (one ring) Windung f •vt **~[up]** zusammenrollen

coin /kɔɪn/ n Münze f •vt prägen

coincide /kəʊɪnˈsaɪd/ vi zusammenfallen; (agree) übereinstimmen

coinciden|ce /kəʊˈɪnsɪdəns/ n Zufall m. **~tal** adj zufällig

coke /kəʊk/ n Koks m

Coke ® n (drink) Cola f

cold /kəʊld/ adj (**-er, -est**) kalt; **I am** or **feel ~** mir ist kalt •n Kälte f; (Med) Erkältung f

cold: ~-ˈblooded adj kaltblütig. **~-ˈhearted** adj kaltherzig. **~ly** adv (fig) kalt, kühl. **~ness** n Kälte f

collaborat|e /kəˈlæbəreɪt/ vi zusammenarbeiten (**with** mit); **~e on sth** mitarbeiten bei etw. **~ion** n Zusammenarbeit f, Mitarbeit f; (with enemy) Kollaboration f. **~or** n Mitarbeiter(in) m(f); Kollaborateur m

collaps|e /kəˈlæps/ n Zusammenbruch m; Einsturz m •vi zusammenbrechen; (roof, building) einstürzen. **~ible** adj zusammenklappbar

collar /ˈkɒlə(r)/ n Kragen m; (for animal) Halsband nt. **~-bone** n Schlüsselbein nt

colleague /ˈkɒliːg/ n Kollege m/ Kollegin f

collect /kəˈlekt/ vt sammeln; (fetch) abholen; einsammeln (tickets); einziehen (taxes) •vi sich [an]sammeln •adv **call ~** (Amer) ein R-Gespräch führen

collection /kəˈlekʃn/ n Sammlung f; (in church) Kollekte f; (of post) Leerung f; (designer's) Kollektion f

collector /kəˈlektə(r)/ n Sammler(in) m(f)

college /ˈkɒlɪdʒ/ n College nt

collide /kəˈlaɪd/ vi

zusammenstoßen

colliery /'kɒlɪərɪ/ n Kohlengrube f

collision /kə'lɪʒn/ n Zusammenstoß m

colloquial /kə'ləʊkwɪəl/ adj umgangssprachlich

Cologne /kə'ləʊn/ n Köln nt

colon /'kəʊlən/ n Doppelpunkt

colonel /'kɜ:nl/ n Oberst m

colonial /kə'ləʊnɪəl/ adj Kolonial-

colony /'kɒlənɪ/ n Kolonie f

colossal /kə'lɒsl/ adj riesig

colour /'kʌlə(r)/ n Farbe f; (complexion) Gesichtsfarbe f; (race) Hautfarbe f; **off ~** ▣ nicht ganz auf der Höhe •vt färben; **~ [in]** ausmalen

colour: ~-blind adj farbenblind. **~ed** adj farbig •n (person) Farbige(r) m/f. **~-fast** adj farbecht. **~ film** n Farbfilm m. **~ful** adj farbenfroh. **~less** adj farblos. **~ photo[graph]** n Farbaufnahme f. **~ television** n Farbfernsehen nt

column /'kɒləm/ n Säule f; (of soldiers, figures) Kolonne f; (Printing) Spalte f; (newspaper) Kolumne f

comb /kəʊm/ n Kamm m •vt kämmen; (search) absuchen; **~ one's hair** sich (dat) [die Haare] kämmen

combat /'kɒmbæt/ n Kampf m

combination /kɒmbɪ'neɪʃn/ n Kombination f

combine[1] /kəm'baɪn/ vt verbinden •vi sich verbinden; (people:) sich zusammenschließen

combine[2] /'kɒmbaɪn/ n (Comm) Konzern m

combustion /kəm'bʌstʃn/ n Verbrennung f

come /kʌm/ vi (pt **came**, pp **come**) kommen; (reach) reichen (**to** an + acc); **that ~ s to £10** das macht £10; **~ into money** zu Geld kommen; **~ true** wahr werden; **~ in two sizes** in zwei Größen erhältlich sein; **the years to ~** die kommenden Jahre; **how ~?** ▣ wie das? **~ about** vi geschehen. **~ across** vi herüberkommen; ▣ klar werden •vt stoßen auf (+ acc). **~ apart** vi sich auseinander nehmen lassen; (accidentally) auseinander gehen. **~ away** vi weggehen; (thing:) abgehen. **~ back** vi zurückkommen. **~ by** vi vorbeikommen •vt (obtain) bekommen. **~ in** vi hereinkommen. **~ off** vi abgehen; (take place) stattfinden; (succeed) klappen ▣. **~ out** vi herauskommen; (book:) erscheinen; (stain:) herausgehen. **~ round** vi vorbeikommen; (after fainting) [wieder] zu sich kommen; (change one's mind) sich umstimmen lassen. **~ to** vi [wieder] zu sich kommen. **~ up** vi heraufkommen; (plant:) aufgehen; (reach) reichen (**to** bis); **~ up with** sich (dat) einfallen lassen

'**come-back** n Comeback nt

comedian /kə'mi:dɪən/ n Komiker m

'**come-down** n Rückschritt m

comedy /'kɒmədɪ/ n Komödie f

comet /'kɒmɪt/ n Komet m

comfort /'kʌmfət/ n Bequemlichkeit f; (consolation) Trost m •vt trösten

comfortable /'kʌmfətəbl/ adj, **-bly** adv bequem

'**comfort station** n (Amer) öffentliche Toilette f

comfy /'kʌmfɪ/ adj ▣ bequem

comic /'kɒmɪk/ adj komisch •n Komiker m; (periodical) Comic-Heft nt

coming /'kʌmɪŋ/ adj kommend •n Kommen nt

comma /'kɒmə/ n Komma nt

command /kə'mɑ:nd/ n Befehl m; (Mil) Kommando nt; (mastery) Beherrschung f •vt befehlen (+ dat); kommandieren (army)

command|er /kə'mɑ:ndə(r)/ n Befehlshaber m. **~ing officer** n Befehlshaber m

C

commemorat|e /kə'meməreɪt/ vt gedenken (+ gen). **~ion** n Gedenken nt

commence /kə'mens/ vt/i anfangen, beginnen

commend /kə'mend/ vt loben; (recommend) empfehlen (**to** dat)

comment /'kɒment/ n Bemerkung f; **no ~!** kein Kommentar! •vi sich äußern (**on** zu); **~ on** (an event) kommentieren

commentary /'kɒməntrɪ/ n Kommentar m; **[running] ~** (Radio, TV) Reportage f

commentator /'kɒmənteɪtə(r)/ n Kommentator m; (Sport) Reporter m

commerce /'kɒmɜ:s/ n Handel m

commercial /kə'mɜ:ʃl/ adj kommerziell •n (Radio, TV) Werbespot m

commission /kə'mɪʃn/ n (order for work) Auftrag m; (body of people) Kommission f; (payment) Provision f; (Mil) [Offiziers]patent nt; **out of ~** außer Betrieb •vt beauftragen (s.o.); in Auftrag geben (thing); (Mil) zum Offizier ernennen

commit /kə'mɪt/ vt (pt/pp **committed**) begehen; (entrust) anvertrauen (**to** dat); (consign) einweisen (**to** in + acc); **~ oneself** sich festlegen; (involve oneself) sich engagieren. **~ment** n Verpflichtung f; (involvement) Engagement nt. **~ted** adj engagiert

committee /kə'mɪtɪ/ n Ausschuss m, Komitee nt

common /'kɒmən/ adj (**-er, -est**) gemeinsam; (frequent) häufig; (ordinary) gewöhnlich; (vulgar) ordinär •n Gemeindeland nt; **have in ~** gemeinsam haben; **House of C~s** Unterhaus nt

common: ~ly adv allgemein. **C~ 'Market** n Gemeinsamer Markt m. **~place** adj häufig. **~-room** n Aufenthaltsraum m. **~ 'sense** n gesunder Menschenverstand m

commotion /kə'məʊʃn/ n Tumult m

communal /'kɒmjʊnl/ adj gemeinschaftlich

communicate /kə'mju:nɪkeɪt/ vt mitteilen (**to** dat); übertragen (disease) •vi sich verständigen

communication /kəmju:nɪ'keɪʃn/ n Verständigung f; (contact) Verbindung f; (message) Mitteilung f; **~s** pl (technology) Nachrichtenwesen nt

communicative /kə'mju:nɪkətɪv/ adj mitteilsam

Communion /kə'mju:nɪən/ n **[Holy] ~** das [heilige] Abendmahl; (Roman Catholic) die [heilige] Kommunion

communis|m /'kɒmjʊnɪzm/ n Kommunismus m. **~t** adj kommunistisch •n Kommunist(in) m(f)

community /kə'mju:nətɪ/ n Gemeinschaft f; **local ~** Gemeinde f

commute /kə'mju:t/ vi pendeln. **~r** n Pendler(in) m(f)

compact /kəm'pækt/ adj kompakt

companion /kəm'pænjən/ n Begleiter(in) m(f). **~ship** n Gesellschaft f

company /'kʌmpənɪ/ n Gesellschaft f; (firm) Firma f; (Mil) Kompanie f; (!: guests) Besuch m. **~ car** n Firmenwagen m

comparable /'kɒmpərəbl/ adj vergleichbar

comparative /kəm'pærətɪv/ adj vergleichend; (relative) relativ •n (Gram) Komparativ m. **~ly** adv verhältnismäßig

compare /kəm'peə(r)/ vt vergleichen (**with/to** mit) •vi sich vergleichen lassen

comparison /kəm'pærɪsn/ n Vergleich m

compartment /kəm'pɑ:tmənt/ n Fach nt; (Rail) Abteil nt

compass /'kʌmpəs/ n Kompass m

compassion /kəm'pæʃn/ n Mitleid nt. **~ate** adj mitfühlend

compatible /kəm'pætəbl/ adj vereinbar; (drugs) verträglich; (Techn) kompatibel; **be ~** (people:)

[gut] zueinander passen

compatriot /kəm'pætrɪət/ n Landsmann m /-männin f

compel /kəm'pel/ vt (pt/pp **compelled**) zwingen

compensat|e /'kɑmpənseɪt/ vt entschädigen. **~ion** n Entschädigung f; (fig) Ausgleich m

compete /kəm'pi:t/ vi konkurrieren; (take part) teilnehmen (**in** an + dat)

competen|ce /'kɒmpɪtəns/ n Fähigkeit f. **~t** adj fähig

competition /kɒmpə'tɪʃn/ n Konkurrenz f; (contest) Wettbewerb m; (in newspaper) Preisausschreiben nt

competitive /kəm'petətɪv/ adj (Comm) konkurrenzfähig

competitor /kəm'petɪtə(r)/ n Teilnehmer m; (Comm) Konkurrent m

compile /kəm'paɪl/ vt zusammenstellen

complacen|cy /kəm'pleɪsənsɪ/ n Selbstzufriedenheit f. **~t** adj selbstzufrieden

complain /kəm'pleɪn/ vi klagen (**about/of** über + acc); (formally) sich beschweren. **~t** n Klage f; (formal) Beschwerde f; (Med) Leiden nt

complement[1] /'kɒmplɪmənt/ n Ergänzung f; **full ~** volle Anzahl f

complement[2] /'kɒmplɪment/ vt ergänzen

complete /kəm'pli:t/ adj vollständig; (finished) fertig; (utter) völlig •vt vervollständigen; (finish) abschließen; (fill in) ausfüllen. **~ly** adv völlig

completion /kəm'pli:ʃn/ n Vervollständigung f; (end) Abschluss m

complex /'kɒmpleks/ adj komplex •n Komplex m

complexion /kəm'plekʃn/ n Teint m; (colour) Gesichtsfarbe f

complexity /kəm'pleksətɪ/ n Komplexität f

complicat|e /'kɒmplɪkeɪt/ vt komplizieren. **~ed** adj kompliziert. **~ion** n Komplikation f

compliment /'kɒmplɪmənt/ n Kompliment nt; **~s** pl Grüße pl •vt ein Kompliment machen (+ dat). **~ary** adj schmeichelhaft; (given free) Frei-

comply /kəm'plaɪ/ vi (pt/pp **-ied**) **~ with** nachkommen (+ dat)

compose /kəm'pəʊz/ vt verfassen; (Mus) komponieren; **be ~d of** sich zusammensetzen aus. **~r** n Komponist m

composition /kɒmpə'zɪʃn/ n Komposition f; (essay) Aufsatz m

compost /'kɒmpɒst/ n Kompost m

composure /kəm'pəʊʒə(r)/ n Fassung f

compound /'kɒmpaʊnd/ adj zusammengesetzt; (fracture) kompliziert •n (Chemistry) Verbindung f; (Gram) Kompositum nt

comprehen|d /kɒmprɪ'hend/ vt begreifen, verstehen. **~sible** adj, **-bly** adv verständlich. **~sion** n Verständnis nt

comprehensive /kɒmprɪ'hensɪv/ adj & n umfassend; **~ [school]** Gesamtschule f. **~ insurance** n (Auto) Vollkaskoversicherung f

compress /kəm'pres/ vt zusammenpressen; **~ed air** Druckluft f

comprise /kəm'praɪz/ vt umfassen, bestehen aus

compromise /'kɒmprəmaɪz/ n Kompromiss m •vt kompromittieren (person) •vi einen Kompromiss schließen

compuls|ion /kəm'pʌlʃn/ n Zwang m. **~ive** adj zwanghaft. **~ory** adj obligatorisch

comput|e /kəm'pju:t/ vb berechnen. **~er** Computer m. **~er game** n Computerspiel. **~erize** vt computerisieren (data); auf Computer umstellen (firm). **~-'literate** adj mit Computern vertraut. **~ing** n Computertechnik f

comrade /'kɒmreɪd/ n Kamerad m; (Pol) Genosse m/Genossin f

con[1] /kɒn/ see **pro**

con[2] n [!] Schwindel m • vt (pt/pp **conned**) [!] beschwindeln

concave /'kɒŋkeɪv/ adj konkav

conceal /kən'si:l/ vt verstecken; (keep secret) verheimlichen

concede /kən'si:d/ vt zugeben; (give up) aufgeben

conceit /kən'si:t/ n Einbildung f. **~ed** adj eingebildet

conceivable /kən'si:vəbl/ adj denkbar

conceive /kən'si:v/ vt (child) empfangen; (fig) sich (dat) ausdenken • vi schwanger werden

concentrat|e /'kɒnsəntreɪt/ vt konzentrieren • vi sich konzentrieren. **~ion** n Konzentration f

concern /kən'sɜ:n/ n Angelegenheit f; (worry) Sorge f; (Comm) Unternehmen nt • vt (be about, affect) betreffen; (worry) kümmern; **be ~ed about** besorgt sein um; **~ oneself with** sich beschäftigen mit; **as far as I am ~ed** was mich angeht od betrifft. **~ing** prep bezüglich (+ gen)

concert /'kɒnsət/ n Konzert nt

concerto /kən'tʃeətəʊ/ n Konzert nt

concession /kən'seʃn/ n Zugeständnis nt; (Comm) Konzession f; (reduction) Ermäßigung f

concise /kən'saɪs/ adj kurz

conclude /kən'klu:d/ vt/i schließen

conclusion /kən'klu:ʒn/ n Schluss m; **in ~** abschließend, zum Schluss

conclusive /kən'klu:sɪv/ adj schlüssig

concoct /kən'kɒkt/ vt zusammenstellen; (fig) fabrizieren. **~ion** n Zusammenstellung f; (drink) Gebräu nt

concrete /'kɒnkri:t/ adj konkret • n Beton m • vt betonieren

concurrently /kən'kʌrəntlɪ/ adv gleichzeitig

concussion /kən'kʌʃn/ n Gehirnerschütterung f

condemn /kən'dem/ vt verurteilen; (declare unfit) für untauglich erklären. **~ation** n Verurteilung f

condensation /kɒnden'seɪʃn/ n Kondensation f

condense /kən'dens/ vt zusammenfassen

condescend /kɒndɪ'send/ vi sich herablassen (**to** zu). **~ing** adj herablassend

condition /kən'dɪʃn/ n Bedingung f; (state) Zustand m; **~s** pl Verhältnisse pl; **on ~ that** unter der Bedingung, dass • vt (mentally) konditionieren. **~al** adj bedingt • n (Gram) Konditional m. **~er** n Pflegespülung f; (for fabrics) Weichspüler m

condolences /kən'dəʊlənsɪz/ npl Beileid nt

condom /'kɒndəm/ n Kondom nt

condominium /kɒndə'mɪnɪəm/ n (Amer) ≈ Eigentumswohnung f

conduct[1] /'kɒndʌkt/ n Verhalten nt; (Sch) Betragen nt

conduct[2] /kən'dʌkt/ vt führen; (Phys) leiten; (Mus) dirigieren. **~or** n Dirigent m; (of bus) Schaffner m; (Phys) Leiter m

cone /kəʊn/ Kegel m; (Bot) Zapfen m; (for ice-cream) [Eis]tüte f; (Auto) Leitkegel m

confectioner /kən'fekʃənə(r)/ n Konditor m. **~y** n Süßwaren pl

conference /'kɒnfərəns/ n Konferenz f

confess /kən'fes/ vt/i gestehen; (Relig) beichten. **~ion** n Geständnis nt; (Relig) Beichte f

confetti /kən'fetɪ/ n Konfetti nt

confide /kən'faɪd/ vt anvertrauen • vi **~ in s.o.** sich jdm anvertrauen

confidence /'kɒnfɪdəns/ n (trust) Vertrauen nt; (self-assurance)

Selbstvertrauen nt; (secret) Geheimnis nt; **in ~** im Vertrauen. **~ trick** n Schwindel m

confident /'kɒnfɪdənt/ adj zuversichtlich; (self-assured) selbstsicher

confidential /kɒnfɪ'denʃl/ adj vertraulich

configuration /kənfɪgə'reɪʃn/ n Anordnung f, Konfiguration f

confine /kən'faɪn/ vt beschränken (**to** auf + acc). **~d** adj (narrow) eng

confirm /kən'fɜ:m/ vt bestätigen; (Relig) konfirmieren; (Roman Catholic) firmen. **~ation** n Bestätigung f; Konfirmation f; Firmung f

confiscat|e /'kɒnfɪskeɪt/ vt beschlagnahmen. **~ion** n Beschlagnahme f

conflict[1] /'kɒnflɪkt/ n Konflikt m

conflict[2] /kən'flɪkt/ vi im Widerspruch stehen (**with** zu). **~ing** adj widersprüchlich

conform /kən'fɔ:m/ vi (person:) sich anpassen; (thing:) entsprechen (**to** dat). **~ist** n Konformist m

confounded /kən'faʊndɪd/ adj [!] verflixt

confront /kən'frʌnt/ vt konfrontieren. **~ation** n Konfrontation f

confus|e /kən'fju:z/ vt verwirren; (mistake for) verwechseln (**with** mit). **~ing** adj verwirrend. **~ion** n Verwirrung f; (muddle) Durcheinander nt

congenial /kən'dʒi:nɪəl/ adj angenehm

congest|ed /kən'dʒestɪd/ adj verstopft; (with people) überfüllt. **~ion** n Verstopfung f; Überfüllung f

congratulat|e /kən'grætjʊleɪt/ vt gratulieren (+ dat) (**on** zu). **~ions** npl Glückwünsche pl; **~ions!** [ich] gratuliere!

congregation /kɒŋgrɪ'geɪʃn/ n (Relig) Gemeinde f

congress /'kɒŋgres/ n Kongress m. **~man** n Kongressabgeordnete(r) m

conical /'kɒnɪkl/ adj kegelförmig

conifer /'kɒnɪfə(r)/ n Nadelbaum m

conjecture /kən'dʒektʃə(r)/ n Mutmaßung f

conjunction /kən'dʒʌŋkʃn/ n Konjunktion f; **in ~ with** zusammen mit

conjur|e /'kʌndʒə(r)/ vi zaubern • vt **~e up** heraufbeschwören. **~or** n Zauberkünstler m

conk /kɒŋk/ vi **~ out** [!] (machine:) kaputtgehen

conker /'kɒŋkə(r)/ n [!] Kastanie f

'con-man n [!] Schwindler m

connect /kə'nekt/ vt verbinden (**to** mit); (Electr) anschließen (**to** an + acc) • vi verbunden sein; (train:) Anschluss haben (**with** an + acc); **be ~ed with** zu tun haben mit; (be related to) verwandt sein mit

connection /kə'nekʃn/ n Verbindung f; (Rail, Electr) Anschluss m; **in ~ with** in Zusammenhang mit. **~s** npl Beziehungen pl

connoisseur /kɒnə'sɜ:(r)/ n Kenner m

conquer /'kɒŋkə(r)/ vt erobern; (fig) besiegen. **~or** n Eroberer m

conquest /'kɒŋkwest/ n Eroberung f

conscience /'kɒnʃəns/ n Gewissen nt

conscientious /kɒnʃɪ'enʃəs/ adj gewissenhaft

conscious /'kɒnʃəs/ adj bewusst; **[fully] ~** bei [vollem] Bewusstsein; **be/become ~ of sth** sich (dat) etw (gen) bewusst sein/werden. **~ness** n Bewusstsein nt

conscript /'kɒnskrɪpt/ n Einberufene(r) m

consecrat|e /'kɒnsɪkreɪt/ vt weihen; einweihen (church). **~ion** n Weihe f; Einweihung f

consecutive /kən'sekjʊtɪv/ adj aufeinanderfolgend. **-ly** adv fortlaufend

C

consent /kən'sent/ n Einwilligung f, Zustimmung f •vi einwilligen (**to** in + acc), zustimmen (**to** dat)

consequen|ce /'kɒnsɪkwəns/ n Folge f. **~t** adj daraus folgend. **~tly** adv folglich

conservation /kɒnsə'veɪʃn/ n Erhaltung f, Bewahrung f. **~ist** n Umweltschützer m

conservative /kən'sɜːvətɪv/ adj konservativ; (estimate) vorsichtig. **C~** (Pol) adj konservativ •n Konservative(r) m/f

conservatory /kən'sɜːvətrɪ/ n Wintergarten m

conserve /kən'sɜːv/ vt erhalten, bewahren; sparen (energy)

consider /kən'sɪdə(r)/ vt erwägen; (think over) sich (dat) überlegen; (take into account) berücksichtigen; (regard as) betrachten als; **~ doing sth** erwägen, etw zu tun. **~able** adj, **-ably** adv erheblich

consider|ate /kən'sɪdərət/ adj rücksichtsvoll. **~ation** n Erwägung f; (thoughtfulness) Rücksicht f; (payment) Entgelt nt; **take into ~ation** berücksichtigen. **~ing** prep wenn man bedenkt (**that** dass)

consist /kən'sɪst/ vi **~ of** bestehen aus

consisten|cy /kən'sɪstənsɪ/ n Konsequenz f; (density) Konsistenz f. **~t** adj konsequent; (unchanging) gleichbleibend. **~tly** adv konsequent; (constantly) ständig

consolation /kɒnsə'leɪʃn/ n Trost m. **~ prize** n Trostpreis m

console /kən'səʊl/ vt trösten

consonant /'kɒnsənənt/ n Konsonant m

conspicuous /kən'spɪkjʊəs/ adj auffällig

conspiracy /kən'spɪrəsɪ/ n Verschwörung f

constable /'kʌnstəbl/ n Polizist m

constant /'kɒnstənt/ adj beständig; (continuous) ständig

constipat|ed /'kɒnstɪpeɪtɪd/ adj verstopft. **~ion** n Verstopfung f

constituency /kən'stɪtjʊənsɪ/ n Wahlkreis m

constitut|e /'kɒnstɪtjuːt/ vt bilden. **~ion** n (Pol) Verfassung f; (of person) Konstitution f

constraint /kən'streɪnt/ n Zwang m; (restriction) Beschränkung f; (strained manner) Gezwungenheit f

construct /kən'strʌkt/ vt bauen. **~ion** n Bau m; (Gram) Konstruktion f; (interpretation) Deutung f; **under ~ion** im Bau

consul /'kɒnsl/ n Konsul m. **~ate** n Konsulat nt

consult /kən'sʌlt/ vt [um Rat] fragen; konsultieren (doctor); nachschlagen in (+ dat) (book). **~ant** n Berater m; (Med) Chefarzt m. **~ation** n Beratung f; (Med) Konsultation f

consume /kən'sjuːm/ vt verzehren; (use) verbrauchen. **~r** n Verbraucher m

consumption /kən'sʌmpʃn/ n Konsum m; (use) Verbrauch m

contact /'kɒntækt/ n Kontakt m; (person) Kontaktperson f •vt sich in Verbindung setzen mit. **~ 'lenses** npl Kontaktlinsen pl

contagious /kən'teɪdʒəs/ adj direkt übertragbar

contain /kən'teɪn/ vt enthalten; (control) beherrschen. **~er** n Behälter m; (Comm) Container m

contaminat|e /kən'tæmɪneɪt/ vt verseuchen. **~ion** n Verseuchung f

contemplat|e /'kɒntəmpleɪt/ vt betrachten; (meditate) nachdenken über (+ acc). **~ion** n Betrachtung f; Nachdenken nt

contemporary /kən'tempərərɪ/ adj zeitgenössisch •n Zeitgenosse m/ -genossin f

contempt /kən'tempt/ n Verachtung f; **beneath ~** verabscheuungswürdig. **~ible** adj verachtenswert. **~uous** adj verächtlich

content[1] /'kɒntent/ n (also **contents**) pl Inhalt m

content[2] /kən'tent/ adj zufrieden •n **to one's heart's ~** nach Herzenslust •vt **~ oneself** sich begnügen (**with** mit). **~ed** adj zufrieden

contentment /kən'tentmənt/ n Zufriedenheit f

contest /'kɒntest/ n Kampf m; (competition) Wettbewerb m. **~ant** n Teilnehmer m

context /'kɒntekst/ n Zusammenhang m

continent /'kɒntɪnənt/ n Kontinent m

continental /kɒntɪ'nentl/ adj Kontinental-. **~ breakfast** n kleines Frühstück nt. **~ quilt** n Daunendecke f

continual /kən'tɪnjʊəl/ adj dauernd

continuation /kəntɪnjʊ'eɪʃn/ n Fortsetzung f

continue /kən'tɪnju:/ vt fortsetzen; **~ doing** or **to do sth** fortfahren, etw zu tun; **to be ~d** Fortsetzung folgt •vi weitergehen; (doing sth) weitermachen; (speaking) fortfahren; (weather:) anhalten

continuity /kɒntɪ'nju:ətɪ/ n Kontinuität f

continuous /kən'tɪnjʊəs/ adj anhaltend, ununterbrochen

contort /kən'tɔ:t/ vt verzerren. **~ion** n Verzerrung f

contour /'kɒntʊə(r)/ n Kontur f; (line) Höhenlinie f

contracep|tion /kɒntrə'sepʃn/ n Empfängnisverhütung f. **~tive** n Empfängnisverhütungsmittel nt

contract[1] /'kɒntrækt/ n Vertrag m

contract[2] /kən'trækt/ vi sich zusammenziehen. **~or** n Unternehmer m

contradict /kɒntrə'dɪkt/ vt widersprechen (+ dat). **~ion** n Widerspruch m. **~ory** adj widersprüchlich

contralto /kən'træltəʊ/ n Alt m; (singer) Altistin f

contraption /kən'træpʃn/ n [!] Apparat m

contrary /'kɒntrərɪ/ adj & adv entgegengesetzt; **~ to** entgegen (+ dat) •n Gegenteil nt; **on the ~** im Gegenteil

contrast[1] /'kɒntrɑ:st/ n Kontrast m

contrast[2] /kən'trɑ:st/ vt gegenüberstellen (**with** dat) •vi einen Kontrast bilden (**with** zu). **~ing** adj gegensätzlich; (colour) Kontrast-

contribut|e /kən'trɪbju:t/ vt/i beitragen; beisteuern (money); (donate) spenden. **~ion** n Beitrag m; (donation) Spende f. **~or** n Beitragende(r) m/f

contrivance /kən'traɪvəns/ n Vorrichtung f

control /kən'trəʊl/ n Kontrolle f; (mastery) Beherrschung f; (Techn) Regler m; **~s** pl (of car, plane) Steuerung f; **get out of ~** außer Kontrolle geraten •vt (pt/pp **controlled**) kontrollieren; (restrain) unter Kontrolle halten; **~ oneself** sich beherrschen

controvers|ial /kɒntrə'vɜ:ʃl/ adj umstritten. **~y** n Kontroverse f

convalesce /kɒnvə'les/ vi sich erholen. **~nce** n Erholung f

convalescent /kɒnvə'lesnt/ adj **~ home** n Erholungsheim nt

convenience /kən'vi:nɪəns/ n Bequemlichkeit f; **[public] ~** öffentliche Toilette f; **with all modern ~s** mit allem Komfort

convenient /kən'vi:nɪənt/ adj günstig; **be ~ for s.o.** jdm gelegen sein od jdm passen; **if it is ~ [for you]** wenn es Ihnen passt

convent /'kɒnvənt/ n [Nonnen-]kloster nt

convention /kən'venʃn/ n (custom) Brauch m, Sitte f. **~al** adj konventionell

converge /kən'vɜ:dʒ/ vi zusammenlaufen

conversation /kɒnvə'seɪʃn/ n Gespräch nt; (Sch) Konversation f

conversion /kən'vɜ:ʃn/ n Umbau m; (Relig) Bekehrung f; (calculation) Umrechnung f

C

convert¹ /ˈkɒnvɜːt/ n Bekehrte(r) m/f, Konvertit m

convert² /kənˈvɜːt/ vt bekehren (person); (change) umwandeln (**into** in + acc); umbauen (building); (calculate) umrechnen; (Techn) umstellen. **~ible** adj verwandelbar •n (Auto) Kabrio[lett] nt

convex /ˈkɒnveks/ adj konvex

convey /kənˈveɪ/ vt befördern; vermitteln (idea, message). **~or belt** n Förderband nt

convict¹ /ˈkɒnvɪkt/ n Sträfling m

convict² /kənˈvɪkt/ vt verurteilen (**of** wegen). **~ion** n Verurteilung f; (belief) Überzeugung f; **previous ~ion** Vorstrafe f

convinc|e /kənˈvɪns/ vt überzeugen. **~ing** adj überzeugend

convoy /ˈkɒnvɔɪ/ n Konvoi m

convulse /kənˈvʌls/ vt **be ~ed** sich krümmen (**with** vor + dat)

coo /kuː/ vi gurren

cook /kʊk/ n Koch m/ Köchin f •vt/i kochen; **is it ~ed?** ist es gar? **~ the books** [!] die Bilanz frisieren. **~book** n Kochbuch nt

cooker /ˈkʊkə(r)/ n [Koch]herd m; (apple) Kochapfel m. **~y** n Kochen nt. **~y book** n Kochbuch nt

cookie /ˈkʊkɪ/ n (Amer) Keks m

cool /kuːl/ adj (**-er, -est**) kühl •n Kühle f •vt kühlen •vi abkühlen. **~-box** n Kühlbox f. **~ness** n Kühle f

coop /kuːp/ vt **~ up** einsperren

co-operat|e /kəʊˈɒpəreɪt/ vi zusammenarbeiten. **~ion** n Kooperation f

co-operative /kəʊˈɒpərətɪv/ adj hilfsbereit •n Genossenschaft f

cop /kɒp/ n [!] Polizist m

cope /kəʊp/ vi [!] zurechtkommen; **~ with** fertig werden mit

copious /ˈkəʊpɪəs/ adj reichlich

copper¹ /ˈkɒpə(r)/ n Kupfer nt •adj kupfern

copper² n [!] Polizist m

copper ˈbeech n Blutbuche f

coppice /ˈkɒpɪs/ n, **copse** n Gehölz nt

copy /ˈkɒpɪ/ n Kopie f; (book) Exemplar nt •vt (pt/pp **-ied**) kopieren; (imitate) nachahmen; (Sch) abschreiben

copy: ~right n Copyright nt. **~-writer** n Texter m

coral /ˈkɒrl/ n Koralle f

cord /kɔːd/ n Schnur f; (fabric) Cordsamt m; **~s** pl Cordhose f

cordial /ˈkɔːdɪəl/ adj herzlich •n Fruchtsirup m

cordon /ˈkɔːdn/ n Kordon m •vt **~ off** absperren

corduroy /ˈkɔːdərɔɪ/ n Cordsamt m

core /kɔː(r)/ n Kern m; (of apple, pear) Kerngehäuse nt

cork /kɔːk/ n Kork m; (for bottle) Korken m. **~screw** n Korkenzieher m

corn¹ /kɔːn/ n Korn nt; (Amer: maize) Mais m

corn² n (Med) Hühnerauge nt

corned beef /kɔːndˈbiːf/ n Cornedbeef nt

corner /ˈkɔːnə(r)/ n Ecke f; (bend) Kurve f; (football) Eckball m •vt (fig) in die Enge treiben; (Comm) monopolisieren (market). **~stone** n Eckstein m

cornet /ˈkɔːnɪt/ n (Mus) Kornett nt; (for ice-cream) [Eis]tüte f

corn: ~flour n, (Amer) **~starch** n Stärkemehl nt

corny /ˈkɔːnɪ/ adj [!] abgedroschen

coronation /kɒrəˈneɪʃn/ n Krönung f

coroner /ˈkɒrənə(r)/ n Beamte(r) m, der verdächtige Todesfälle untersucht

corporal /ˈkɔːpərəl/ n (Mil) Stabsunteroffizier m

corps /kɔː(r)/ n (pl **corps** /kɔːz/) Korps nt

corpse /kɔːps/ n Leiche f

correct /kəˈrekt/ adj richtig; (proper)

korrekt •vt verbessern; (text, school work) korrigieren. **~ion** n Verbesserung f; (Typ) Korrektur f

correspond /kɒrɪ'spɒnd/ vi entsprechen (**to** dat); (two things:) sich entsprechen; (write) korrespondieren. **~ence** n Briefwechsel m; (Comm) Korrespondenz f. **~ent** n Korrespondent(in) m(f). **~ing** adj entsprechend

corridor /'kɒrɪdɔ:(r)/ n Gang m; (Pol, Aviat) Korridor m

corro|de /kə'rəʊd/ vt zerfressen •vi rosten. **~sion** n Korrosion f

corrugated /'kɒrəgeɪtɪd/ adj gewellt. **~ iron** n Wellblech nt

corrupt /kə'rʌpt/ adj korrupt •vt korrumpieren; (spoil) verderben. **~ion** n Korruption f

corset /'kɔ:sɪt/ n Korsett nt

Corsica /'kɔ:sɪkə/ n Korsika nt

cosh /kɒʃ/ n Totschläger m

cosmetic /kɒz'metɪk/ adj kosmetisch •n **~s** pl Kosmetika pl

cosset /'kɒsɪt/ vt verhätscheln

cost /kɒst/ n Kosten pl; **~s** pl (Jur) Kosten; **at all ~s** um jeden Preis •vt (pt/pp **cost**) kosten; **it ~ me £20** es hat mich £20 gekostet •vt (pt/pp **costed**) **~ [out]** die Kosten kalkulieren für

costly /'kɒstlɪ/ adj teuer

cost: ~ of 'living n Lebenshaltungskosten pl. **~ price** n Selbstkostenpreis m

costume /'kɒstju:m/ n Kostüm nt; (national) Tracht f. **~ jewellery** n Modeschmuck m

cosy /'kəʊzɪ/ adj gemütlich •n (tea-, egg-) Wärmer m

cot /kɒt/ n Kinderbett nt; (Amer: camp bed) Feldbett nt

cottage /'kɒtɪdʒ/ n Häuschen nt. **~ 'cheese** n Hüttenkäse m

cotton /'kɒtn/ n Baumwolle f; (thread) Nähgarn nt •adj baumwollen •vi **~ on** (!) kapieren

cotton 'wool n Watte f

couch /kaʊtʃ/ n Liege f

couchette /ku:'ʃet/ n (Rail) Liegeplatz m

cough /kɒf/ n Husten m •vi husten. **~ up** vt/i husten; ((!): pay) blechen

'cough mixture n Hustensaft m

could /kʊd/, unbetont /kəd/ see **can**[2]

council /'kaʊnsl/ n Rat m; (Admin) Stadtverwaltung f; (rural) Gemeindeverwaltung f. **~ house** n ≈ Sozialwohnung f

councillor /'kaʊnsələ(r)/ n Ratsmitglied nt

'council tax n Gemeindesteuer f

count[1] /kaʊnt/ n Graf m

count[2] n Zählung f; **keep ~** zählen •vt/i zählen. **~ on** vt rechnen auf (+ acc)

counter[1] /'kaʊntə(r)/ n (in shop) Ladentisch m; (in bank) Schalter m; (in café) Theke f; (Games) Spielmarke f

counter[2] adj Gegen- •vt/i kontern

counter'act vt entgegenwirken (+ dat)

'counterfeit /-fɪt/ adj gefälscht

'counterfoil n Kontrollabschnitt m

'counterpart n Gegenstück nt

counter-pro'ductive adj **be ~** das Gegenteil bewirken

'countersign vt gegenzeichnen

countess /'kaʊntɪs/ n Gräfin f

countless /'kaʊntlɪs/ adj unzählig

country /'kʌntrɪ/ n Land nt; (native land) Heimat f; (countryside) Landschaft f; **in the ~** auf dem Lande. **~man** n **[fellow] ~man** Landsmann m. **~side** n Landschaft f

county /'kaʊntɪ/ n Grafschaft f

coup /ku:/ n (Pol) Staatsstreich m

couple /'kʌpl/ n Paar nt; **a ~ of** (two) zwei •vt verbinden

coupon /'ku:pɒn/ n Kupon m; (voucher) Gutschein m; (entry form) Schein m

courage /'kʌrɪdʒ/ n Mut m. **~ous** adj mutig

courgettes /kʊəˈʒets/ npl Zucchini pl

courier /ˈkʊrɪə(r)/ n Bote m; (diplomatic) Kurier m; (for tourists) Reiseleiter(in) m(f)

course /kɔːs/ n (Naut, Sch) Kurs m; (Culin) Gang m; (for golf) Platz m; **~ of treatment** (Med) Kur f; **of ~** natürlich, selbstverständlich; **in the ~ of** im Lauf[e] (+ gen)

court /kɔːt/ n Hof m; (Sport) Platz m; (Jur) Gericht nt

courteous /ˈkɜːtɪəs/ adj höflich

courtesy /ˈkɜːtəsɪ/ n Höflichkeit f

court: ~ ˈmartial n (pl **~s martial**) Militärgericht nt. **~yard** n Hof m

cousin /ˈkʌzn/ n Vetter m, Cousin m; (female) Kusine f

cove /kəʊv/ n kleine Bucht f

cover /ˈkʌvə(r)/ n Decke f; (of cushion) Bezug m; (of umbrella) Hülle f; (of typewriter) Haube f; (of book, lid) Deckel m; (of magazine) Umschlag m; (protection) Deckung f, Schutz m; **take ~** Deckung nehmen; **under separate ~** mit getrennter Post •vt bedecken; beziehen (cushion); decken (costs, needs); zurücklegen (distance); berichten über (+ acc) event; (insure) versichern. **~ up** vt zudecken; (fig) vertuschen

coverage /ˈkʌvərɪdʒ/ n (Journalism) Berichterstattung f (**of** über + acc)

cover: ~ing n Decke f; (for floor) Belag m. **~-up** n Vertuschung f

cow /kaʊ/ n Kuh f

coward /ˈkaʊəd/ n Feigling m. **~ice** n Feigheit f. **~ly** adj feige

ˈcowboy n Cowboy m; [!] unsolider Handwerker m

cower /ˈkaʊə(r)/ vi sich [ängstlich] ducken

ˈcowshed n Kuhstall m

cox /kɒks/ n, **coxswain** n Steuermann m

coy /kɔɪ/ adj (**-er, -est**) gespielt schüchtern

crab /kræb/ n Krabbe f

crack /kræk/ n Riss m; (in china, glass) Sprung m; (noise) Knall m; ([!]: joke) Witz m; ([!]: attempt) Versuch m •adj [!] erstklassig •vt knacken (nut, code); einen Sprung machen in (+ acc) (china, glass); [!] reißen (joke); [!] lösen (problem) •vi (china, glass:) springen; (whip:) knallen. **~ down** vi [!] durchgreifen

cracked /krækt/ adj gesprungen; (rib) angebrochen; ([!]: crazy) verrückt

cracker /ˈkrækə(r)/ n (biscuit) Kräcker m; (firework) Knallkörper m; **[Christmas] ~** Knallbonbon m. **~s** adj **be ~s** [!] einen Knacks haben

crackle /ˈkrækl/ vi knistern

cradle /ˈkreɪdl/ n Wiege f

craft n Handwerk nt; (technique) Fertigkeit f. **~sman** n Handwerker m

crafty /ˈkrɑːftɪ/ adj , **-ily** adv gerissen

crag /kræg/ n Felszacken m

cram /kræm/ v (pt/pp **crammed**) •vt hineinstopfen (**into** in + acc); vollstopfen (**with** mit) •vi (for exams) pauken

cramp /kræmp/ n Krampf m. **~ed** adj eng

cranberry /ˈkrænbərɪ/ n (Culin) Preiselbeere f

crane /kreɪn/ n Kran m; (bird) Kranich m

crank /kræŋk/ n [!] Exzentriker m

ˈcrankshaft n Kurbelwelle f

crash /kræʃ/ n (noise) Krach m; (Auto) Zusammenstoß m; (Aviat) Absturz m •vi krachen (**into** gegen); (cars:) zusammenstoßen; (plane:) abstürzen •vt einen Unfall haben mit (car)

crash: ~-helmet n Sturzhelm m. **~-landing** n Bruchlandung f

crate /kreɪt/ n Kiste f

crater /ˈkreɪtə(r)/ n Krater m

crawl /krɔːl/ n (Swimming) Kraul nt; **do the ~** kraulen; **at a ~** im Kriechtempo •vi kriechen; (baby:) krabbeln; **~ with** wimmeln von

crayon /'kreɪən/ n Wachsstift m; (pencil) Buntstift m

craze /kreɪz/ n Mode f

crazy /'kreɪzɪ/ adj verrückt; **be ~ about** verrückt sein nach

creak /kri:k/ vi knarren

cream /kri:m/ n Sahne f; (Cosmetic, Med, Culin) Creme f •adj (colour) cremefarben •vt (Culin) cremig rühren. **~y** adj sahnig; (smooth) cremig

crease /kri:s/ n Falte f; (unwanted) Knitterfalte f •vt falten; (accidentally) zerknittern •vi knittern

creat|e /kri:'eɪt/ vt schaffen. **~ion** n Schöpfung f. **~ive** adj schöpferisch. **~or** n Schöpfer m

creature /'kri:tʃə(r)/ n Geschöpf nt

crèche /kreʃ/ n Kinderkrippe f

credibility /kredə'bɪlətɪ/ n Glaubwürdigkeit f

credible /'kredəbl/ adj glaubwürdig

credit /'kredɪt/ n Kredit m; (honour) Ehre f •vt glauben; **~ s.o. with sth** (Comm) jdm etw gutschreiben; (fig) jdm etw zuschreiben. **~able** adj lobenswert

credit: ~ card n Kreditkarte f. **~or** n Gläubiger m

creep /kri:p/ vi (pt/pp **crept**) schleichen •n [!] fieser Kerl m; **it gives me the ~s** es ist mir unheimlich. **~er** n Kletterpflanze f. **~y** adj gruselig

cremat|e /krɪ'meɪt/ vt einäschern. **~ion** n Einäscherung f

crêpe /kreɪp/ n Krepp m. **~ paper** n Krepppapier nt

crept /krept/ see **creep**

crescent /'kresənt/ n Halbmond m

cress /kres/ n Kresse f

crest /krest/ n Kamm m; (coat of arms) Wappen nt

crew /kru:/ n Besatzung f; (gang) Bande f. **~ cut** n Bürstenschnitt m

crib[1] /krɪb/ n Krippe f

crib[2] vt/i (pt/pp **cribbed**) [!] abschreiben

cricket /'krɪkɪt/ n Kricket nt. **~er** n Kricketspieler m

crime /kraɪm/ n Verbrechen nt; (rate) Kriminalität f

criminal /'krɪmɪnl/ adj kriminell, verbrecherisch; (law, court) Straf- •n Verbrecher m

crimson /'krɪmzn/ adj purpurrot

crinkle /'krɪŋkl/ vt/i knittern

cripple /'krɪpl/ n Krüppel m •vt zum Krüppel machen; (fig) lahmlegen. **~d** adj verkrüppelt

crisis /'kraɪsɪs/ n (pl **-ses** /-si:z/) Krise f

crisp /'krɪsp/ adj (**-er, -est**) knusprig. **~bread** n Knäckebrot nt. **~s** npl Chips pl

criss-cross /'krɪs-/ adj schräg gekreuzt

criterion /kraɪ'tɪərɪən/ n (pl **-ria** /-rɪə/) Kriterium nt

critic /'krɪtɪk/ n Kritiker m. **~al** adj kritisch. **~ally** adv kritisch; **~ally ill** schwer krank

criticism /'krɪtɪsɪzm/ n Kritik f

criticize /'krɪtɪsaɪz/ vt kritisieren

croak /krəʊk/ vi krächzen; (frog:) quaken

crockery /'krɒkərɪ/ n Geschirr nt

crocodile /'krɒkədaɪl/ n Krokodil nt

crocus /'krəʊkəs/ n (pl **-es**) Krokus m

crony /'krəʊnɪ/ n Kumpel m

crook /krʊk/ n (stick) Stab m; ([!]: criminal) Schwindler m, Gauner m

crooked /'krʊkɪd/ adj schief; (bent) krumm; ([!]: dishonest) unehrlich

crop /krɒp/ n Feldfrucht f; (harvest) Ernte f •v (pt/pp **cropped**) •vt stutzen •vi **~ up** [!] zur Sprache kommen; (occur) dazwischenkommen

croquet /'krəʊkeɪ/ n Krocket nt

cross /krɒs/ adj (annoyed) böse (**with** auf + acc); **talk at ~ purposes** aneinander vorbeireden •n Kreuz nt; (Bot, Zool) Kreuzung f •vt kreuzen (cheque, animals); überqueren (road); ~ **oneself** sich bekreuzigen; ~ **one's arms** die Arme verschränken; ~ **one's legs** die Beine übereinander schlagen; **keep one's fingers ~ed for s.o.** jdm die Daumen drücken; **it ~ed my mind** es fiel mir ein •vi (go across) hinübergehen/-fahren; (lines:) sich kreuzen. ~ **out** vt durchstreichen

cross: ~-'country n (Sport) Crosslauf m. **~-'eyed** adj schielend; **be ~-eyed** schielen. **~fire** n Kreuzfeuer nt. **~ing** n Übergang m; (sea journey) Überfahrt f. **~roads** n [Straßen]kreuzung f. **~-'section** n Querschnitt m. **~wise** adv quer. **~word** n **~word [puzzle]** Kreuzworträtsel nt

crotchety /'krɒtʃɪtɪ/ adj griesgrämig

crouch /kraʊtʃ/ vi kauern

crow /krəʊ/ n Krähe f; **as the ~ flies** Luftlinie

crowd /kraʊd/ n [Menschen]menge f •vi sich drängen. **~ed** adj [gedrängt] voll

crown /kraʊn/ n Krone f •vt krönen; überkronen (tooth)

crucial /'kru:ʃl/ adj höchst wichtig; (decisive) entscheidend (**to** für)

crude /'kru:d/ adj (**-r, -st**) primitiv; (raw) roh

cruel /'kru:əl/ adj (**crueller, cruellest**) grausam (**to** gegen). **~ty** n Grausamkeit f

cruis|e /kru:z/ n Kreuzfahrt f •vi kreuzen; (car:) fahren. **~er** n (Mil) Kreuzer m; (motor boat) Kajütboot nt

crumb /krʌm/ n Krümel m

crumb|le /'krʌmbl/ vt/i krümeln; (collapse) einstürzen

crumple /'krʌmpl/ vt zerknittern •vi knittern

crunch /krʌntʃ/ n [!] **when it comes to the ~** wenn es [wirklich] drauf ankommt •vt mampfen •vi knirschen

crusade /kru:'seɪd/ n Kreuzzug m; (fig) Kampagne f. **~r** n Kreuzfahrer m; (fig) Kämpfer m

crush /krʌʃ/ n (crowd) Gedränge nt •vt zerquetschen; zerknittern (clothes); (fig: subdue) niederschlagen

crust /krʌst/ n Kruste f

crutch /krʌtʃ/ n Krücke f

cry /kraɪ/ n Ruf m; (shout) Schrei m; **a far ~ from** (fig) weit entfernt von •vi (pt/pp **cried**) (weep) weinen; (baby:) schreien; (call) rufen

crypt /krɪpt/ n Krypta f. **~ic** adj rätselhaft

crystal /'krɪstl/ n Kristall m; (glass) Kristall nt

cub /kʌb/ n (Zool) Junge(s) nt

Cuba /'kju:bə/ n Kuba nt

cubby-hole /'kʌbɪ-/ n Fach nt

cub|e /kju:b/ n Würfel m. **~ic** adj Kubik-

cubicle /'kju:bɪkl/ n Kabine f

cuckoo /'kʊku:/ n Kuckuck m. **~ clock** n Kuckucksuhr f

cucumber /'kju:kʌmbə(r)/ n Gurke f

cuddl|e /'kʌdl/ vt herzen •vi **~e up to** sich kuscheln an (+ acc). **~y** adj kuschelig

cue[1] /kju:/ n Stichwort nt

cue[2] n (Billiards) Queue nt

cuff /kʌf/ n Manschette f; (Amer: turn-up) [Hosen]aufschlag m; (blow) Klaps m; **off the ~** [!] aus dem Stegreif. **~-link** n Manschettenknopf m

cul-de-sac /'kʌldəsæk/ n Sackgasse f

culinary /'kʌlɪnərɪ/ adj kulinarisch

culprit /'kʌlprɪt/ n Täter m

cult /kʌlt/ n Kult m

cultivate /'kʌltɪveɪt/ vt anbauen (crop); bebauen (land)

cultural /'kʌltʃərəl/ adj kulturell

culture /'kʌltʃə(r)/ n Kultur f. **~d** adj kultiviert

cumbersome /'kʌmbəsəm/ adj hinderlich; (unwieldy) unhandlich

cunning /'kʌnɪŋ/ adj listig •n List f

cup /kʌp/ n Tasse f; (prize) Pokal m

cupboard /'kʌbəd/ n Schrank m

Cup 'Final n Pokalendspiel nt

curable /'kjʊərəbl/ adj heilbar

curate /'kjʊərət/ n Vikar m; (Roman Catholic) Kaplan m

curb /kɜːb/ vt zügeln

curdle /'kɜːdl/ vi gerinnen

cure /kjʊə(r)/ n [Heil]mittel nt •vt heilen; (salt) pökeln; (smoke) räuchern; gerben (skin)

curiosity /kjʊərɪ'ɒsətɪ/ n Neugier f; (object) Kuriosität f

curious /'kjʊərɪəs/ adj neugierig; (strange) merkwürdig, seltsam

curl /kɜːl/ n Locke f •vt locken •vi sich locken

curly /'kɜːlɪ/ adj lockig

currant /'kʌrənt/ n (dried) Korinthe f

currency /'kʌrənsɪ/ n Geläufigkeit f; (money) Währung f; **foreign ~** Devisen pl

current /'kʌrənt/ adj augenblicklich, gegenwärtig; (in general use) geläufig, gebräuchlich •n Strömung f; (Electr) Strom m. **~ affairs** or **events** npl Aktuelle(s) nt. **~ly** adv zurzeit

curriculum /kə'rɪkjʊləm/ n Lehrplan m. **~ vitae** n Lebenslauf m

curry /'kʌrɪ/ n Curry nt & m; (meal) Currygericht nt

curse /kɜːs/ n Fluch m •vt verfluchen •vi fluchen

cursor /'kɜːsə(r)/ n Cursor m

cursory /'kɜːsərɪ/ adj flüchtig

curt /kɜːt/ adj barsch

curtain /'kɜːtn/ n Vorhang m

curtsy /'kɜːtsɪ/ n Knicks m •vi (pt/pp **-ied**) knicksen

curve /kɜːv/ n Kurve f •vi einen Bogen machen; **~ to the right/left** nach rechts/links biegen. **~d** adj gebogen

cushion /'kʊʃn/ n Kissen nt •vt dämpfen; (protect) beschützen

cushy /'kʊʃɪ/ adj [!] bequem

custard /'kʌstəd/ n Vanillesoße f

custom /'kʌstəm/ n Brauch m; (habit) Gewohnheit f; (Comm) Kundschaft f. **~ary** adj üblich; (habitual) gewohnt. **~er** n Kunde m/ Kundin f

customs /'kʌstəmz/ npl Zoll m. **~ officer** n Zollbeamte(r) m

cut /kʌt/ n Schnitt m; (Med) Schnittwunde f; (reduction) Kürzung f; (in price) Senkung f; **~ [of meat]** [Fleisch]stück nt •vt/i (pt/pp **cut**, pres p **cutting**) schneiden; (mow) mähen; abheben (cards); (reduce) kürzen; senken (price); **~ one's finger** sich in den Finger schneiden; **~ s.o.'s hair** jdm die Haare schneiden; **~ short** abkürzen. **~ back** vt zurückschneiden; (fig) einschränken, kürzen. **~ down** vt fällen; (fig) einschränken. **~ off** vt abschneiden; (disconnect) abstellen; **be ~ off** (Teleph) unterbrochen werden. **~ out** vt ausschneiden; (delete) streichen; **be ~ out for** [!] geeignet sein zu. **~ up** vt zerschneiden; (slice) aufschneiden

'cut-back n Kürzung f

cute /kjuːt/ adj **(-r, -st)** [!] niedlich

cut 'glass n Kristall nt

cutlery /'kʌtlərɪ/ n Besteck nt

cutlet /'kʌtlɪt/ n Kotelett nt

'cut-price adj verbilligt

cutting /'kʌtɪŋ/ adj (remark) bissig •n (from newspaper) Ausschnitt m; (of plant) Ableger m

CV abbr **curriculum vitae**

cyberspace /'saɪbəspeɪs/ n Cyberspace m

cycl|e /'saɪkl/ n Zyklus m; (bicycle) [Fahr]rad nt •vi mit dem Rad fahren. **~ing** n Radfahren nt. **~ist** n Radfahrer(in) m(f)

cylind|er /ˈsɪlɪndə(r)/ n Zylinder m. **~rical** adj zylindrisch

cynic /ˈsɪnɪk/ n Zyniker m. **~al** adj zynisch. **~ism** n Zynismus m

Cyprus /ˈsaɪprəs/ n Zypern nt

Czech /tʃek/ adj tschechisch; **~ Republic** Tschechische Republik f •n Tscheche m/ Tschechin f

c d

Dd

dab /dæb/ n Tupfer m; (of butter) Klecks m

dabble /ˈdæbl/ vi **~ in sth** (fig) sich nebenbei mit etw befassen

dachshund /ˈdækshʊnd/ n Dackel m

dad[dy] /ˈdæd[i]/ n ! Vati m

daddy-ˈlong-legs n [Kohl]schnake f; (Amer: spider) Weberknecht m

daffodil /ˈdæfədɪl/ n Osterglocke f, gelbe Narzisse f

daft /dɑːft/ adj (**-er, -est**) dumm

dagger /ˈdægə(r)/ n Dolch m

dahlia /ˈdeɪlɪə/ n Dahlie f

daily /ˈdeɪlɪ/ adj & adv täglich

dainty /ˈdeɪntɪ/ adj zierlich

dairy /ˈdeərɪ/ n Molkerei f; (shop) Milchgeschäft nt. **~ products** pl Milchprodukte pl

daisy /ˈdeɪzɪ/ n Gänseblümchen nt

dam /dæm/ n [Stau]damm m •vt (pt/pp **dammed**) eindämmen

damag|e /ˈdæmɪdʒ/ n Schaden m (**to** an + dat); **~es** pl (Jur) Schadenersatz m •vt beschädigen; (fig) beeinträchtigen

damn /dæm/ adj, int & adv ! verdammt •n **I don't care** or **give a ~** ! ich schere mich einen Dreck darum •vt verdammen. **~ation** n Verdammnis f

damp /dæmp/ adj (**-er, -est**) feucht •n Feuchtigkeit f

damp|en vt anfeuchten; (fig) dämpfen. **~ness** n Feuchtigkeit f

dance /dɑːns/ n Tanz m; (function) Tanzveranstaltung f •vt/i tanzen. **~ music** n Tanzmusik f

dancer /ˈdɑːnsə(r)/ n Tänzer(in) m(f)

dandelion /ˈdændɪlaɪən/ n Löwenzahn m

dandruff /ˈdændrʌf/ n Schuppen pl

Dane /deɪn/ n Däne m/Dänin f

danger /ˈdeɪndʒə(r)/ n Gefahr f; **in/out of ~** in/außer Gefahr. **~ous** adj gefährlich; **~ously ill** schwer erkrankt

dangle /ˈdæŋgl/ vi baumeln •vt baumeln lassen

Danish /ˈdeɪnɪʃ/ adj dänisch. **~ ˈpastry** n Hefeteilchen nt

Danube /ˈdænjuːb/ n Donau f

dare /deə(r)/ vt/i (challenge) herausfordern (**to** zu); **~ [to] do sth** [es] wagen, etw zu tun. **~devil** n Draufgänger m

daring /ˈdeərɪŋ/ adj verwegen •n Verwegenheit f

dark /dɑːk/ adj (**-er, -est**) dunkel; **~ blue/brown** dunkelblau/ -braun; **~ horse** (fig) stilles Wasser nt •n Dunkelheit f; **after ~** nach Einbruch der Dunkelheit; **in the ~** im Dunkeln

dark|en /ˈdɑːkn/ vt verdunkeln •vi dunkler werden. **~ness** n Dunkelheit f

ˈdark-room n Dunkelkammer f

darling /ˈdɑːlɪŋ/ adj allerliebst •n Liebling m

darn /dɑːn/ vt stopfen

dart /dɑːt/ n Pfeil m; **~s** sg (game)

[Wurf]pfeil m •vi flitzen

dash /dæʃ/ n (Printing) Gedankenstrich m; **a ~ of milk** ein Schuss Milch •vi rennen •vt schleudern. **~ off** vi losstürzen •vt (write quickly) hinwerfen

'dashboard n Armaturenbrett nt

data /'deɪtə/ npl & sg Daten pl. **~ processing** n Datenverarbeitung f

date[1] /deɪt/ n (fruit) Dattel f

date[2] n Datum nt; 🄸 Verabredung f; **to ~** bis heute; **out of ~** überholt; (expired) ungültig; **be up to ~** auf dem Laufenden sein •vt/i datieren; (Amer, fam: go out with) ausgehen mit

dated /'deɪtɪd/ adj altmodisch

dative /'deɪtɪv/ adj & n (Gram) **~ [case]** Dativ m

daub /dɔ:b/ vt beschmieren (**with** mit); schmieren (paint)

daughter /'dɔ:tə(r)/ n Tochter f. **~-in-law** n (pl **~s-in-law**) Schwiegertochter f

dawdle /'dɔ:dl/ vi trödeln

dawn /dɔ:n/ n Morgendämmerung f; **at ~** bei Tagesanbruch •vi anbrechen; **it ~ed on me** (fig) es ging mir auf

day /deɪ/ n Tag m; **~ by ~** Tag für Tag; **~ after ~** Tag um Tag; **these ~s** heutzutage; **in those ~s** zu der Zeit

day: ~-dream n Tagtraum m •vi [mit offenen Augen] träumen. **~light** n Tageslicht nt. **~time** n **in the ~time** am Tage

daze /deɪz/ n **in a ~** wie benommen. **~d** adj benommen

dazzle /'dæzl/ vt blenden

dead /ded/ adj tot; (flower) verwelkt; (numb) taub; **~ body** Leiche f; **~ centre** genau in der Mitte •adv **~ tired** todmüde; **~ slow** sehr langsam •n **the ~** pl die Toten; **in the ~ of night** mitten in der Nacht

deaden /'dedn/ vt dämpfen (sound); betäuben (pain)

dead: ~ 'end n Sackgasse f. **~ 'heat** n totes Rennen nt. **~line** n [letzter] Termin m

deadly /'dedlɪ/ adj tödlich; (🄸: dreary) sterbenslangweilig

deaf /def/ adj (**-er, -est**) taub; **~ and dumb** taubstumm

deaf|en /'defn/ vt betäuben; (permanently) taub machen. **~ening** adj ohrenbetäubend. **~ness** n Taubheit f

deal /di:l/ n (transaction) Geschäft nt; **whose ~?** (Cards) wer gibt? **a good** or **great ~** eine Menge; **get a raw ~** 🄸 schlecht wegkommen •v (pt/pp **dealt** /delt/) •vt (Cards) geben; **~ out** austeilen •vi **~ in** handeln mit; **~ with** zu tun haben mit; (handle) sich befassen mit; (cope with) fertig werden mit; (be about) handeln von; **that's been dealt with** das ist schon erledigt

deal|er /'di:lə(r)/ n Händler m

dean /di:n/ n Dekan m

dear /dɪə(r)/ adj (**-er, -est**) lieb; (expensive) teuer; (in letter) liebe(r,s)/ (formal) sehr geehrte(r,s) •n Liebe(r) m/f •int **oh ~!** oje! **~ly** adv (love) sehr; (pay) teuer

death /deθ/ n Tod m; **three ~s** drei Todesfälle. **~ certificate** n Sterbeurkunde f

deathly adj **~ silence** Totenstille f •adv **~ pale** totenblass

death: ~ penalty n Todesstrafe f. **~-trap** n Todesfalle f

debatable /dɪ'beɪtəbl/ adj strittig

debate /dɪ'beɪt/ n Debatte f •vt/i debattieren

debauchery /dɪ'bɔ:tʃərɪ/ n Ausschweifung f

debit /'debɪt/ n **~ [side]** Soll nt •vt (pt/pp **debited**) belasten; abbuchen (sum)

debris /'debri:/ n Trümmer pl

debt /det/ n Schuld f; **in ~** verschuldet. **~or** n Schuldner m

début /'deɪbu:/ n Debüt nt

decade /'dekeɪd/ n Jahrzehnt nt

decaden|ce /'dekədəns/ n

Dekadenz f. **~t** adj dekadent

decaffeinated /dɪ'kæfɪneɪtɪd/ adj koffeinfrei

decay /dɪ'keɪ/ n Verfall m; (rot) Verwesung f; (of tooth) Zahnfäule f •vi verfallen; (rot) verwesen; (tooth:) schlecht werden

deceased /dɪ'si:sd/ adj verstorben •n **the ~d** der/die Verstorbene

deceit /dɪ'si:t/ n Täuschung f. **~ful** adj unaufrichtig

deceive /dɪ'si:v/ vt täuschen; (be unfaithful to) betrügen

December /dɪ'sembə(r)/ n Dezember m

decency /'di:sənsɪ/ n Anstand m

decent /'di:sənt/ adj anständig

decept|ion /dɪ'sepʃn/ n Täuschung f; (fraud) Betrug m. **~ive** adj täuschend

decide /dɪ'saɪd/ vt entscheiden •vi sich entscheiden (**on** für)

decided /dɪ'saɪdɪd/ adj entschieden

decimal /'desɪml/ adj Dezimal- •n Dezimalzahl f. **~ 'point** n Komma nt

decipher /dɪ'saɪfə(r)/ vt entziffern

decision /dɪ'sɪʒn/ n Entscheidung f; (firmness) Entschlossenheit f

decisive /dɪ'saɪsɪv/ adj ausschlaggebend; (firm) entschlossen

deck[1] /dek/ vt schmücken

deck[2] n (Naut) Deck nt; **on ~** an Deck; **~ of cards** (Amer) [Karten]spiel nt. **~-chair** n Liegestuhl m

declaration /deklə'reɪʃn/ n Erklärung f

declare /dɪ'kleə(r)/ vt erklären; angeben (goods); **anything to ~?** etwas zu verzollen?

decline /dɪ'klaɪn/ n Rückgang m; (in health) Verfall m •vt ablehnen; (Gram) deklinieren •vi ablehnen; (fall) sinken; (decrease) nachlassen

decommission /di:kə'mɪʃn/ vt stilllegen; außer Dienst stellen (Schiff)

décor /'deɪkɔ:(r)/ n Ausstattung f

decorat|e /'dekəreɪt/ vt (adorn) schmücken; verzieren (cake); (paint) streichen; (wallpaper) tapezieren; (award medal to) einen Orden verleihen (+ dat). **~ion** n Verzierung f; (medal) Orden m; **~ions** pl Schmuck m. **~ive** adj dekorativ. **~or** n **painter and ~or** Maler und Tapezierer m

decoy /'di:kɔɪ/ n Lockvogel m

decrease[1] /'di:kri:s/ n Verringerung f; (in number) Rückgang m

decrease[2] /dɪ'kri:s/ vt verringern; herabsetzen (price) •vi sich verringern; (price:) sinken

decrepit /dɪ'krepɪt/ adj altersschwach

dedicat|e /'dedɪkeɪt/ vt widmen; (Relig) weihen. **~ed** adj hingebungsvoll; (person) aufopfernd. **~ion** n Hingabe f; (in book) Widmung f

deduce /dɪ'dju:s/ vt folgern (**from** aus)

deduct /dɪ'dʌkt/ vt abziehen

deduction /dɪ'dʌkʃn/ n Abzug m; (conclusion) Folgerung f

deed /di:d/ n Tat f; (Jur) Urkunde f

deep /di:p/ adj (**-er, -est**) tief; **go off the ~ end** [!] auf die Palme gehen •adv tief

deepen /'di:pn/ vt vertiefen

deep-'freeze n Gefriertruhe f; (upright) Gefrierschrank m

deer /dɪə(r)/ n inv Hirsch m; (roe) Reh nt

deface /dɪ'feɪs/ vt beschädigen

default /dɪ'fɔ:lt/ n **win by ~** (Sport) kampflos gewinnen

defeat /dɪ'fi:t/ n Niederlage f; (defeating) Besiegung f; (rejection) Ablehnung f •vt besiegen; ablehnen; (frustrate) vereiteln

defect /'di:fekt/ n Fehler m; (Techn) Defekt m. **~ive** adj fehlerhaft; (Techn) defekt

defence /dɪ'fens/ n Verteidigung f.

~**less** adj wehrlos

defend /dɪ'fend/ vt verteidigen; (justify) rechtfertigen. ~**ant** n (Jur) Beklagte(r) m/f; (in criminal court) Angeklagte(r) m/f

defensive /dɪ'fensɪv/ adj defensiv

defer /dɪ'fɜ:(r)/ vt (pt/pp **deferred**) (postpone) aufschieben

deferen|ce /'defərəns/ n Ehrerbietung f. ~**tial** adj ehrerbietig

defian|ce /dɪ'faɪəns/ n Trotz m; **in ~ce of** zum Trotz (+ dat). ~**t** adj aufsässig

deficien|cy /dɪ'fɪʃənsɪ/ n Mangel m. ~**t** adj mangelhaft

deficit /'defɪsɪt/ n Defizit nt

define /dɪ'faɪn/ vt bestimmen; definieren (word)

definite /'defɪnɪt/ adj bestimmt; (certain) sicher

definition /defɪ'nɪʃn/ n Definition f; (Phot, TV) Schärfe f

definitive /dɪ'fɪnətɪv/ adj endgültig; (authoritative) maßgeblich

deflat|e /dɪ'fleɪt/ vt die Luft auslassen aus. ~**ion** n (Comm) Deflation f

deflect /dɪ'flekt/ vt ablenken

deform|ed /dɪ'fɔ:md/ adj missgebildet. ~**ity** n Missbildung f

defraud /dɪ'frɔ:d/ vt betrügen (**of** um)

defray /dɪ'freɪ/ vt bestreiten

defrost /di:'frɒst/ vt entfrosten; abtauen (fridge); auftauen (food)

deft /deft/ adj (**-er, -est**) geschickt. ~**ness** n Geschicklichkeit f

defuse /di:'fju:z/ vt entschärfen

defy /dɪ'faɪ/ vt (pt/pp **-ied**) trotzen (+ dat); widerstehen (+ dat) (attempt)

degrading /dɪ'greɪdɪŋ/ adj entwürdigend

degree /dɪ'gri:/ n Grad m; (Univ) akademischer Grad m; **20 ~s** 20 Grad

de-ice /di:'aɪs/ vt enteisen

deity /'di:ɪtɪ/ n Gottheit f

dejected /dɪ'dʒektɪd/ adj niedergeschlagen

delay /dɪ'leɪ/ n Verzögerung f; (of train, aircraft) Verspätung f; **without ~** unverzüglich • vt aufhalten; (postpone) aufschieben • vi zögern

delegate[1] /'delɪgət/ n Delegierte(r) m/f

delegat|e[2] /'delɪgeɪt/ vt delegieren. ~**ion** n Delegation f

delet|e /dɪ'li:t/ vt streichen. ~**ion** n Streichung f

deliberate /dɪ'lɪbərət/ adj absichtlich; (slow) bedächtig

delicacy /'delɪkəsɪ/ n Feinheit f; Zartheit f; (food) Delikatesse f

delicate /'delɪkət/ adj fein; (fabric, health) zart; (situation) heikel; (mechanism) empfindlich

delicatessen /delɪkə'tesn/ n Delikatessengeschäft nt

delicious /dɪ'lɪʃəs/ adj köstlich

delight /dɪ'laɪt/ n Freude f • vt entzücken • vi **~ in** sich erfreuen an (+ dat). ~**ed** adj hocherfreut; **be ~ed** sich sehr freuen. ~**ful** adj reizend

delinquent /dɪ'lɪŋkwənt/ adj straffällig • n Straffällige(r) m/f

deli|rious /dɪ'lɪrɪəs/ adj **be ~rious** im Delirium sein. ~**rium** n Delirium nt

deliver /dɪ'lɪvə(r)/ vt liefern; zustellen (post, newspaper); halten (speech); überbringen (message); versetzen (blow); (set free) befreien; **~ a baby** ein Kind zur Welt bringen. ~**y** n Lieferung f; (of post) Zustellung f; (Med) Entbindung f; **cash on ~y** per Nachnahme

delta /'deltə/ n Delta nt

deluge /'delju:dʒ/ n Flut f; (heavy rain) schwerer Guss m

delusion /dɪ'lu:ʒn/ n Täuschung f

de luxe /də'lʌks/ adj Luxus-

demand /dɪ'mɑ:nd/ n Forderung f; (Comm) Nachfrage f; **in ~** gefragt;

d

on ~ auf Verlangen • vt verlangen, fordern (**of**/**from** von). **~ing** adj anspruchsvoll

demented /dɪˈmentɪd/ adj verrückt

demister /diːˈmɪstə(r)/ n (Auto) Defroster m

d

demo /ˈdeməʊ/ n (pl **~s**) [!] Demonstration f

democracy /dɪˈmɒkrəsɪ/ n Demokratie f

democrat /ˈdeməkræt/ n Demokrat m. **~ic** adj, **-ally** adv demokratisch

demo|lish /dɪˈmɒlɪʃ/ vt abbrechen; (destroy) zerstören. **~lition** n Abbruch m

demon /ˈdiːmən/ n Dämon m

demonstrat|e /ˈdemənstreɪt/ vt beweisen; vorführen (appliance) • vi (Pol) demonstrieren. **~ion** n Vorführung f; (Pol) Demonstration f

demonstrator /ˈdemənstreɪtə(r)/ n Vorführer m; (Pol) Demonstrant m

demoralize /dɪˈmɒrəlaɪz/ vt demoralisieren

demote /dɪˈməʊt/ vt degradieren

demure /dɪˈmjʊə(r)/ adj sittsam

den /den/ n Höhle f; (room) Bude f

denial /dɪˈnaɪəl/ n Leugnen nt; **official ~** Dementi nt

denim /ˈdenɪm/ n Jeansstoff m; **~s** pl Jeans pl

Denmark /ˈdenmɑːk/ n Dänemark nt

denounce /dɪˈnaʊns/ vt denunzieren; (condemn) verurteilen

dens|e /dens/ adj (**-r**, **-st**) dicht; ([!]: stupid) blöd[e]. **~ity** n Dichte f

dent /dent/ n Delle f, Beule f • vt einbeulen; **~ed** verbeult

dental /ˈdentl/ adj Zahn-; (treatment) zahnärztlich. **~ floss** n Zahnseide f. **~ surgeon** n Zahnarzt m

dentist /ˈdentɪst/ n Zahnarzt m/ -ärztin f. **~ry** n Zahnmedizin f

denture /ˈdentʃə(r)/ n Zahnprothese f; **~s** pl künstliches Gebiss nt

deny /dɪˈnaɪ/ vt (pt/pp **-ied**) leugnen; (officially) dementieren; **~ s.o. sth** jdm etw verweigern

deodorant /diːˈəʊdərənt/ n Deodorant nt

depart /dɪˈpɑːt/ vi abfahren; (Aviat) abfliegen; (go away) weggehen/ -fahren; (deviate) abweichen (**from** von)

department /dɪˈpɑːtmənt/ n Abteilung f; (Pol) Ministerium nt. **~ store** n Kaufhaus nt

departure /dɪˈpɑːtʃə(r)/ n Abfahrt f; (Aviat) Abflug m; (from rule) Abweichung f

depend /dɪˈpend/ vi abhängen (**on** von); (rely) sich verlassen (**on** auf + acc); **it all ~s** das kommt darauf an. **~able** adj zuverlässig. **~ant** n Abhängige(r) m/f. **~ence** n Abhängigkeit f. **~ent** adj abhängig (**on** von)

depict /dɪˈpɪkt/ vt darstellen

deplor|able /dɪˈplɔːrəbl/ adj bedauerlich. **~e** vt bedauern

deploy /dɪˈplɔɪ/ vt (Mil) einsetzen

depopulate /diːˈpɒpjʊleɪt/ vt entvölkern

deport /dɪˈpɔːt/ vt deportieren, ausweisen. **~ation** n Ausweisung f

depose /dɪˈpəʊz/ vt absetzen

deposit /dɪˈpɒzɪt/ n Anzahlung f; (against damage) Kaution f; (on bottle) Pfand nt; (sediment) Bodensatz m; (Geology) Ablagerung f • vt (pt/pp **deposited**) legen; (for safety) deponieren; (Geology) ablagern. **~ account** n Sparkonto nt

depot /ˈdepəʊ/ n Depot nt; (Amer: railway station) Bahnhof m

deprav|e /dɪˈpreɪv/ vt verderben. **~ed** adj verkommen

depreciat|e /dɪˈpriːʃɪeɪt/ vi an Wert verlieren. **~ion** n Wertminderung f; (Comm) Abschreibung f

depress /dɪˈpres/ vt deprimieren; (press down) herunterdrücken. **~ed** adj deprimiert. **~ing** adj deprimierend. **~ion** n Vertiefung f; (Med) Depression f; (weather) Tiefdruckgebiet nt

deprivation /deprɪˈveɪʃn/ n Entbehrung f

deprive /dɪˈpraɪv/ vt ~ **s.o. of sth** jdm etw entziehen. **~d** adj benachteiligt

depth /depθ/ n Tiefe f; **in ~** gründlich; **in the ~s of winter** im tiefsten Winter

deputize /ˈdepjʊtaɪz/ vi ~ **for** vertreten

deputy /ˈdepjʊtɪ/ n Stellvertreter m • attrib stellvertretend

derail /dɪˈreɪl/ vt **be ~ed** entgleisen. **~ment** n Entgleisung f

derelict /ˈderəlɪkt/ adj verfallen; (abandoned) verlassen

derisory /dɪˈraɪsərɪ/ adj höhnisch; (offer) lächerlich

derivation /derɪˈveɪʃn/ n Ableitung f

derivative /dɪˈrɪvətɪv/ adj abgeleitet • n Ableitung f

derive /dɪˈraɪv/ vt/i (obtain) gewinnen (**from** aus); **be ~d from** (word:) hergeleitet sein aus

derogatory /dɪˈrɒgətrɪ/ adj abfällig

derv /dɜːv/ n Diesel[kraftstoff] m

descend /dɪˈsend/ vt/i hinunter-/heruntergehen; (vehicle, lift:) hinunter-/herunterfahren; **be ~ed from** abstammen von. **~ant** n Nachkomme m

descent /dɪˈsent/ n Abstieg m; (lineage) Abstammung f

describe /dɪˈskraɪb/ vt beschreiben

descrip|tion /dɪˈskrɪpʃn/ n Beschreibung f; (sort) Art f. **~tive** adj beschreibend; (vivid) anschaulich

desecrate /ˈdesɪkreit/ vt entweihen

desert[1] /ˈdezət/ n Wüste f. **~ island** verlassene Insel f

desert[2] /dɪˈzɜːt/ vt verlassen • vt desertieren. **~ed** adj verlassen. **~er** n (Mil) Deserteur m. **~ion** n Fahnenflucht f

deserv|e /dɪˈzɜːv/ vt verdienen. **~edly** adv verdientermaßen. **~ing** adj verdienstvoll

design /dɪˈzaɪn/ n Entwurf m; (pattern) Muster nt; (construction) Konstruktion f; (aim) Absicht f • vt entwerfen; (construct) konstruieren; **be ~ed for** bestimmt sein für

designer /dɪˈzaɪnə(r)/ n Designer m; (Techn) Konstrukteur m; (Theat) Bühnenbildner m

desirable /dɪˈzaɪrəbl/ adj wünschenswert; (sexually) begehrenswert

desire /dɪˈzaɪə(r)/ n Wunsch m; (longing) Verlangen nt (**for** nach); (sexual) Begierde f • vt [sich (dat)] wünschen; (sexually) begehren

desk /desk/ n Schreibtisch m; (Sch) Pult nt

desolat|e /ˈdesələt/ adj trostlos. **~ion** n Trostlosigkeit f

despair /dɪˈspeə(r)/ n Verzweiflung f; **in ~** verzweifelt • vi verzweifeln

desperat|e /ˈdespərət/ adj verzweifelt; (urgent) dringend; **be ~e for** dringend brauchen. **~ion** n Verzweiflung f

despicable /dɪˈspɪkəbl/ adj verachtenswert

despise /dɪˈspaɪz/ vt verachten

despite /dɪˈspaɪt/ prep trotz (+ gen)

despondent /dɪˈspɒndənt/ adj niedergeschlagen

dessert /dɪˈzɜːt/ n Dessert nt, Nachtisch m. **~ spoon** n Dessertlöffel m

destination /destɪˈneɪʃn/ n [Reise]ziel nt; (of goods) Bestimmungsort m

destiny /ˈdestɪnɪ/ n Schicksal nt

destitute /ˈdestɪtjuːt/ adj völlig mittellos

destroy /dɪˈstrɔɪ/ vt zerstören; (totally) vernichten. **~er** n (Naut) Zerstörer m

destruc|tion /dɪˈstrʌkʃn/ n Zerstörung f; Vernichtung f. **~tive** adj zerstörerisch; (fig) destruktiv

detach /dɪˈtætʃ/ vt abnehmen; (tear

off) abtrennen. **~able** adj abnehmbar. **~ed** adj **~ed house** Einzelhaus nt

detail /'di:teɪl/ n Einzelheit f, Detail nt; **in ~** ausführlich • vt einzeln aufführen. **~ed** adj ausführlich

d

detain /dɪ'teɪn/ vt aufhalten; (police:) in Haft behalten; (take into custody) in Haft nehmen

detect /dɪ'tekt/ vt entdecken; (perceive) wahrnehmen. **~ion** n Entdeckung f

detective /dɪ'tektɪv/ n Detektiv m. **~ story** n Detektivroman m

detention /dɪ'tenʃn/ n Haft f; (Sch) Nachsitzen nt

deter /dɪ'tɜ:(r)/ vt (pt/pp **deterred**) abschrecken; (prevent) abhalten

detergent /dɪ'tɜ:dʒənt/ n Waschmittel nt

deteriorat|e /dɪ'tɪərɪəreɪt/ vi sich verschlechtern. **~ion** n Verschlechterung f

determination /dɪtɜ:mɪ'neɪʃn/ n Entschlossenheit f

determine /dɪ'tɜ:mɪn/ vt bestimmen. **~d** adj entschlossen

deterrent /dɪ'terənt/ n Abschreckungsmittel nt

detest /dɪ'test/ vt verabscheuen. **~able** adj abscheulich

detonate /'detəneɪt/ vt zünden

detour /'di:tʊə(r)/ n Umweg m

detract /dɪ'trækt/ vi **~ from** beeinträchtigen

detriment /'detrɪmənt/ n **to the ~ (of)** zum Schaden (+ gen). **~al** adj schädlich (**to** dat)

deuce /dju:s/ n (Tennis) Einstand m

devaluation /di:væljʊ'eɪʃn/ n Abwertung f

de'value vt abwerten (currency)

devastat|e /'devəsteɪt/ vt verwüsten. **~ing** adj verheerend. **~ion** n Verwüstung f

develop /dɪ'veləp/ vt entwickeln; bekommen (illness); erschließen (area) • vi sich entwickeln (**into** zu). **~er** n **[property] ~er** Bodenspekulant m

development /dɪ'veləpmənt/ n Entwicklung f

deviat|e /'di:vɪeɪt/ vi abweichen. **~ion** n Abweichung f

device /dɪ'vaɪs/ n Gerät nt; (fig) Mittel nt

devil /'devl/ n Teufel m. **~ish** adj teuflisch

devious /'di:vɪəs/ adj verschlagen

devise /dɪ'vaɪz/ vt sich (dat) ausdenken

devot|e /dɪ'vəʊt/ vt widmen (**to** dat). **~ed** adj ergeben; (care) liebevoll; **be ~ed to s.o.** sehr an jdm hängen

devotion /dɪ'vəʊʃn/ n Hingabe f

devour /dɪ'vaʊə(r)/ vt verschlingen

devout /dɪ'vaʊt/ adj fromm

dew /dju:/ n Tau m

dexterity /dek'sterətɪ/ n Geschicklichkeit f

diabet|es /daɪə'bi:ti:z/ n Zuckerkrankheit f. **~ic** n Diabetiker(in) m(f)

diabolical /daɪə'bɒlɪkl/ adj teuflisch

diagnose /daɪəg'nəʊz/ vt diagnostizieren

diagnosis /daɪəg'nəʊsɪs/ n (pl **-oses** /-si:z/) Diagnose f

diagonal /daɪ'ægənl/ adj diagonal • n Diagonale f

diagram /'daɪəgræm/ n Diagramm nt

dial /'daɪəl/ n (of clock) Zifferblatt nt; (Techn) Skala f; (Teleph) Wählscheibe f • vt/i (pt/pp **dialled**) (Teleph) wählen; **~ direct** durchwählen

dialect /'daɪəlekt/ n Dialekt m

dialling: ~ code n Vorwahlnummer f. **~ tone** n Amtszeichen nt

dialogue /'daɪəlɒg/ n Dialog m

diameter /daɪ'æmɪtə(r)/ n Durchmesser m

diamond /'daɪəmənd/ n Diamant

m; (cut) Brillant m; (shape) Raute f; **~s** pl (Cards) Karo nt

diaper /ˈdaɪəpə(r)/ n (Amer) Windel f

diarrhoea /daɪəˈriːə/ n Durchfall m

diary /ˈdaɪərɪ/ n Tagebuch nt; (for appointments) [Termin]kalender m

dice /daɪs/ n inv Würfel m

dictat|e /dɪkˈteɪt/ vt/i diktieren. **~ion** n Diktat nt

dictator /dɪkˈteɪtə(r)/ n Diktator m. **~ial** adj diktatorisch. **~ship** n Diktatur f

dictionary /ˈdɪkʃənrɪ/ n Wörterbuch nt

did /dɪd/ see **do**

didn't /ˈdɪdnt/ = **did not**

die[1] /daɪ/ n (Techn) Prägestempel m; (metal mould) Gussform f

die[2] vi (pres p **dying**) sterben (**of** an + dat); (plant, animal:) eingehen; (flower:) verwelken; **be dying to do sth** [!] darauf brennen, etw zu tun; **be dying for sth** [!] sich nach etw sehnen.
~ down vi nachlassen; (fire:) herunterbrennen. **~ out** vi aussterben

diesel /ˈdiːzl/ n Diesel m. **~ engine** n Dieselmotor m

diet /ˈdaɪət/ n Kost f; (restricted) Diät f; (for slimming) Schlankheitskur f; **be on a ~** Diät leben; eine Schlankheitskur machen •vi Diät leben; eine Schlankheitskur machen

differ /ˈdɪfə(r)/ vi sich unterscheiden; (disagree) verschiedener Meinung sein

differen|ce /ˈdɪfrəns/ n Unterschied m; (disagreement) Meinungsverschiedenheit f. **~t** adj andere(r,s); (various) verschiedene; **be ~t** anders sein (**from** als)

differential /dɪfəˈrenʃl/ adj Differenzial- •n Unterschied m; (Techn) Differenzial nt

differentiate /dɪfəˈrenʃɪeɪt/ vt/i unterscheiden (**between** zwischen + dat)

differently /ˈdɪfrəntlɪ/ adv anders

difficult /ˈdɪfɪkəlt/ adj schwierig, schwer. **~y** n Schwierigkeit f

diffiden|ce /ˈdɪfɪdəns/ n Zaghaftigkeit f. **~t** adj zaghaft

dig /dɪg/ n (poke) Stoß m; (remark) spitze Bemerkung f; (archaeological) Ausgrabung f •vt/i (pt/pp **dug**, pres p **digging**) graben; umgraben (garden). **~ out** vt ausgraben. **~ up** vt ausgraben; umgraben (garden); aufreißen (street)

digest /dɪˈdʒest/ vt verdauen. **~ible** adj verdaulich. **~ion** n Verdauung f

digit /ˈdɪdʒɪt/ n Ziffer f; (finger) Finger m; (toe) Zehe f. **~ize** vt digitalisieren

digital /ˈdɪdʒɪtl/ adj Digital-; **~ camera** Digitalkamera f; **~ television** Digitalfernsehen nt

dignified /ˈdɪgnɪfaɪd/ adj würdevoll

dignity /ˈdɪgnɪtɪ/ n Würde f

dilapidated /dɪˈlæpɪdeɪtɪd/ adj baufällig

dilatory /ˈdɪlətərɪ/ adj langsam

dilemma /dɪˈlemə/ n Dilemma nt

dilettante /dɪlɪˈtæntɪ/ n Dilettant(in) m(f)

diligen|ce /ˈdɪlɪdʒəns/ n Fleiß m. **~t** adj fleißig

dilute /daɪˈluːt/ vt verdünnen

dim /dɪm/ adj (**dimmer, dimmest**), **-ly** adv (weak) schwach; (dark) trüb[e]; (indistinct) undeutlich; ([!]: stupid) dumm, [!] doof •v (pt/pp **dimmed**) •vt dämpfen

dime /daɪm/ n (Amer) Zehncentstück nt

dimension /daɪˈmenʃn/ n Dimension f; **~s** pl Maße pl

diminutive /dɪˈmɪnjʊtɪv/ adj winzig •n Verkleinerungsform f

dimple /ˈdɪmpl/ n Grübchen nt

din /dɪn/ n Krach m, Getöse nt

dine /daɪn/ vi speisen. **~r** n Speisende(r) m/f; (Amer: restaurant) Esslokal nt

dinghy /ˈdɪŋgɪ/ n Dinghi nt;

d

d

(inflatable) Schlauchboot nt

dingy /'dɪndʒɪ/ adj trübe

dining /'daɪnɪŋ/: **~-car** n Speisewagen m. **~-room** n Esszimmer nt. **~-table** n Esstisch m

dinner /'dɪnə(r)/ n Abendessen nt; (at midday) Mittagessen nt; (formal) Essen nt. **~-jacket** n Smoking m

dinosaur /'daɪnəsɔ:(r)/ n Dinosaurier m

diocese /'daɪəsɪs/ n Diözese f

dip /dɪp/ n (in ground) Senke f; (Culin) Dip m •v (pt/pp **dipped**) vt [ein]tauchen; **~ one's headlights** (Auto) [die Scheinwerfer] abblenden •vi sich senken

diploma /dɪ'pləʊmə/ n Diplom nt

diplomacy /dɪ'pləʊməsɪ/ n Diplomatie f

diplomat /'dɪpləmæt/ n Diplomat m. **~ic** adj, **-ally** adv diplomatisch

'dip-stick n (Auto) Ölmessstab m

dire /'daɪə(r)/ adj (**-r, -st**) bitter; (consequences) furchtbar

direct /dɪ'rekt/ adj & adv direkt •vt (aim) richten (**at** auf / (fig) an + acc); (control) leiten; (order) anweisen; **~ a film/play** bei einem Film/Theaterstück Regie führen

direction /dɪ'rekʃn/ n Richtung f; (control) Leitung f; (of play, film) Regie f; **~s** pl Anweisungen pl; **~s for use** Gebrauchsanweisung f

directly /dɪ'rektlɪ/ adv direkt; (at once) sofort

director /dɪ'rektə(r)/ n (Comm) Direktor m; (of play, film) Regisseur m, Regisseurin f

directory /dɪ'rektərɪ/ n Verzeichnis nt; (Teleph) Telefonbuch nt

dirt /dɜ:t/ n Schmutz m; (soil) Erde f; **~ cheap** 🅸 spottbillig

dirty /'dɜ:tɪ/ adj schmutzig

dis|a'bility /dɪs-/ n Behinderung f. **~abled** adj [körper]behindert

disad'vantage n Nachteil m; **at a ~** im Nachteil. **~d** adj benachteiligt

disa'gree vi nicht übereinstimmen (**with** mit); **I ~** ich bin anderer Meinung; **oysters ~ with me** Austern bekommen mir nicht

disa'greeable adj unangenehm

disa'greement n Meinungsverschiedenheit f

disap'pear vi verschwinden. **~ance** n Verschwinden nt

disap'point vt enttäuschen. **~ment** n Enttäuschung f

disap'proval n Missbilligung f

disap'prove vi dagegen sein; **~ of** missbilligen

dis'arm vt entwaffnen •vi (Mil) abrüsten. **~ament** n Abrüstung f. **~ing** adj entwaffnend

disast|er /dɪ'zɑ:stə(r)/ n Katastrophe f; (accident) Unglück nt. **~rous** adj katastrophal

disbe'lief n Ungläubigkeit f; **in ~** ungläubig

disc /dɪsk/ n Scheibe f; (record) [Schall]platte f; (CD) CD f

discard /dɪ'skɑ:d/ vt ablegen; (throw away) wegwerfen

discerning /dɪ'sɜ:nɪŋ/ adj anspruchsvoll

'discharge[1] n Ausstoßen nt; (Naut, Electr) Entladung f; (dismissal) Entlassung f; (Jur) Freispruch m; (Med) Ausfluss m

dis'charge[2] vt ausstoßen; (Naut, Electr) entladen; (dismiss) entlassen; (Jur) freisprechen (accused)

disciplinary /'dɪsɪplɪnərɪ/ adj disziplinarisch

discipline /'dɪsɪplɪn/ n Disziplin f •vt Disziplin beibringen (+ dat); (punish) bestrafen

'disc jockey n Diskjockey m

dis'claim vt abstreiten. **~er** n Verzichterklärung f

dis'clos|e vt enthüllen. **~ure** n Enthüllung f

disco /'dɪskəʊ/ n 🅸 Disko f

dis'colour vt verfärben •vi sich verfärben

dis'comfort n Beschwerden pl;

(fig) Unbehagen nt

discon'nect vt trennen; (Electr) ausschalten; (cut supply) abstellen

discon'tent n Unzufriedenheit f. **~ed** adj unzufrieden

discon'tinue vt einstellen; (Comm) nicht mehr herstellen

'discord n Zwietracht f; (Mus & fig) Missklang m

discothèque /'dɪskətek/ n Diskothek f

'discount n Rabatt m

dis'courage vt entmutigen; (dissuade) abraten (+ dat)

dis'courteous adj unhöflich

discover /dɪ'skʌvə(r)/ vt entdecken. **~y** n Entdeckung f

discreet /dɪ'skri:t/ adj diskret

discretion /dɪ'skreʃn/ n Diskretion f; (judgement) Ermessen nt

discriminat|e /dɪ'skrɪmɪneɪt/ vi unterscheiden (**between** zwischen + dat); **~e against** diskriminieren. **~ing** adj anspruchsvoll. **~ion** n Diskriminierung f

discus /'dɪskəs/ n Diskus m

discuss /dɪ'skʌs/ vt besprechen; (examine critically) diskutieren. **~ion** n Besprechung f; Diskussion f

disdain /dɪs'deɪn/ n Verachtung f

disease /dɪ'zi:z/ n Krankheit f

disem'bark vi an Land gehen

disen'chant vt ernüchtern

disen'gage vt losmachen

disen'tangle vt entwirren

dis'figure vt entstellen

dis'grace n Schande f; **in ~** in Ungnade •vt Schande machen (+ dat). **~ful** adj schändlich

disgruntled /dɪs'grʌntld/ adj verstimmt

disguise /dɪs'gaɪz/ n Verkleidung f; **in ~** verkleidet •vt verkleiden; verstellen (voice)

disgust /dɪs'gʌst/ n Ekel m; **in ~** empört •vt anekeln; (appal) empören. **~ing** adj eklig; (appalling) abscheulich

dish /dɪʃ/ n Schüssel f; (shallow) Schale f; (small) Schälchen nt; (food) Gericht nt. **~ out** vt austeilen. **~ up** vt auftragen

'dishcloth n Spültuch nt

dis'hearten vt entmutigen

dis'honest adj, **-ly** adv unehrlich. **~y** n Unehrlichkeit f

dis'honour n Schande f. **~able** adj, **-bly** adv unehrenhaft

'dishwasher n Geschirrspülmaschine f

disil'lusion vt ernüchtern. **~ment** n Ernüchterung f

disin'fect vt desinfizieren. **~ant** n Desinfektionsmittel nt

disin'herit vt enterben

dis'integrate vi zerfallen

dis'jointed adj unzusammenhängend

disk /dɪsk/ n = **disc**

dis'like n Abneigung f •vt nicht mögen

dislocate /'dɪsləkeɪt/ vt ausrenken

dis'lodge vt entfernen

dis'loyal adj illoyal. **~ty** n Illoyalität f

dismal /'dɪzməl/ adj trüb[e]; (person) trübselig

dismantle /dɪs'mæntl/ vt auseinander nehmen; (take down) abbauen

dis'may n Bestürzung f. **~ed** adj bestürzt

dis'miss vt entlassen; (reject) zurückweisen. **~al** n Entlassung f; Zurückweisung f

diso'bedien|ce n Ungehorsam m. **~t** adj ungehorsam

diso'bey vt/i nicht gehorchen (+ dat); nicht befolgen (rule)

dis'order n Unordnung f; (Med) Störung f. **~ly** adj unordentlich

dis'organized adj unorganisiert

dis'own vt verleugnen

disparaging /dɪ'spærɪdʒɪŋ/ adj abschätzig

d

dispassionate /dɪ'spæʃənət/ adj gelassen; (impartial) unparteiisch

dispatch /dɪ'spætʃ/ n (Comm) Versand m; (Mil) Nachricht f; (report) Bericht m • vt [ab]senden; (kill) töten

dispel /dɪ'spel/ vt (pt/pp **dispelled**) vertreiben

dispensary /dɪ'spensərɪ/ n Apotheke f

dispense /dɪ'spens/ vt austeilen; ~ **with** verzichten auf (+ acc). ~**r** n (device) Automat m

disperse /dɪ'spɜːs/ vt zerstreuen • vi sich zerstreuen

dispirited /dɪ'spɪrɪtɪd/ adj entmutigt

display /dɪ'spleɪ/ n Ausstellung f; (Comm) Auslage f; (performance) Vorführung f • vt zeigen; ausstellen (goods)

dis'please vt missfallen (+ dat)

dis'pleasure n Missfallen nt

disposable /dɪ'spəʊzəbl/ adj Wegwerf-; (income) verfügbar

disposal /dɪ'spəʊzl/ n Beseitigung f; **be at s.o.'s** ~ jdm zur Verfügung stehen

dispose /dɪ'spəʊz/ vi ~ **of** beseitigen; (deal with) erledigen

disposition /dɪspə'zɪʃn/ n Veranlagung f; (nature) Wesensart f

disproportionate /dɪsprə'pɔːʃənət/ adj unverhältnismäßig

dis'prove vt widerlegen

dispute /dɪ'spjuːt/ n Disput m; (quarrel) Streit m • vt bestreiten

disqualifi'cation n Disqualifikation f

dis'qualify vt disqualifizieren; ~ **s.o. from driving** jdm den Führerschein entziehen

disre'gard vt nicht beachten

disre'pair n **fall into** ~ verfallen

dis'reputable adj verrufen

disre'pute n Verruf m

disre'spect n Respektlosigkeit f. ~**ful** adj respektlos

disrupt /dɪs'rʌpt/ vt stören. ~**ion** n Störung f

dissatis'faction n Unzufriedenheit f

dis'satisfied adj unzufrieden

dissect /dɪ'sekt/ vt zergliedern; (Med) sezieren. ~**ion** n Zergliederung f; (Med) Sektion f

dissent /dɪ'sent/ n Nichtübereinstimmung f • vi nicht übereinstimmen

dissident /'dɪsɪdənt/ n Dissident m

dis'similar adj unähnlich (**to** dat)

dissociate /dɪ'səʊʃɪeɪt/ vt ~ **oneself** sich distanzieren (**from** von)

dissolute /'dɪsəluːt/ adj zügellos; (life) ausschweifend

dissolve /dɪ'zɒlv/ vt auflösen • vi sich auflösen

dissuade /dɪ'sweɪd/ vt abbringen (**from** von)

distance /'dɪstəns/ n Entfernung f; **long/short** ~ lange/kurze Strecke f; **in the/from a** ~ in/aus der Ferne

distant /'dɪstənt/ adj fern; (aloof) kühl; (relative) entfernt

dis'tasteful adj unangenehm

distil /dɪ'stɪl/ vt (pt/pp **distilled**) brennen; (Chemistry) destillieren. ~**lery** n Brennerei f

distinct /dɪ'stɪŋkt/ adj deutlich; (different) verschieden. ~**ion** n Unterschied m; (Sch) Auszeichnung f. ~**ive** adj kennzeichnend; (unmistakable) unverwechselbar. ~**ly** adv deutlich

distinguish /dɪ'stɪŋgwɪʃ/ vt/i unterscheiden; (make out) erkennen; ~ **oneself** sich auszeichnen. ~**ed** adj angesehen; (appearance) distinguiert

distort /dɪ'stɔːt/ vt verzerren; (fig) verdrehen. ~**ion** n Verzerrung f; (fig) Verdrehung f

distract /dɪ'strækt/ vt ablenken. ~**ion** n Ablenkung f; (despair) Verzweiflung f

distraught /dɪ'strɔ:t/ adj [völlig] aufgelöst

distress /dɪ'stres/ n Kummer m; (pain) Schmerz m; (poverty, danger) Not f •vt Kummer/Schmerz bereiten (+ dat); (sadden) bekümmern; (shock) erschüttern. **~ing** adj schmerzlich; (shocking) erschütternd

distribut|e /dɪ'strɪbju:t/ vt verteilen; (Comm) vertreiben. **~ion** n Verteilung f; Vertrieb m. **~or** n Verteiler m

district /'dɪstrɪkt/ n Gegend f; (Admin) Bezirk m

dis'trust n Misstrauen nt •vt misstrauen (+ dat). **~ful** adj misstrauisch

disturb /dɪ'stɜ:b/ vt stören; (perturb) beunruhigen; (touch) anrühren. **~ance** n Unruhe f; (interruption) Störung f. **~ed** adj beunruhigt; **[mentally] ~ed** geistig gestört. **~ing** adj beunruhigend

dis'used adj stillgelegt; (empty) leer

ditch /dɪtʃ/ n Graben m •vt (!: abandon) fallen lassen (plan)

dither /'dɪðə(r)/ vi zaudern

ditto /'dɪtəʊ/ n dito; ! ebenfalls

dive /daɪv/ n [Kopf]sprung m; (Aviat) Sturzflug m; (!: place) Spelunke f •vi einen Kopfsprung machen; (when in water) tauchen; (Aviat) einen Sturzflug machen; (!: rush) stürzen

diver /'daɪvə(r)/ n Taucher m; (Sport) [Kunst]springer m

diverse /daɪ'vɜ:s/ adj verschieden

diversify /daɪ'vɜ:sɪfaɪ/ vt/i (pt/pp **-ied**) variieren; (Comm) diversifizieren

diversion /daɪ'vɜ:ʃn/ n Umleitung f; (distraction) Ablenkung f

diversity /daɪ'vɜ:sətɪ/ n Vielfalt f

divert /daɪ'vɜ:t/ vt umleiten; ablenken (attention); (entertain) unterhalten

divide /dɪ'vaɪd/ vt teilen; (separate) trennen; (Math) dividieren (**by** durch) •vi sich teilen

dividend /'dɪvɪdend/ n Dividende f

divine /dɪ'vaɪn/ adj göttlich

diving /'daɪvɪŋ/ n (Sport) Kunstspringen nt. **~-board** n Sprungbrett nt

divinity /dɪ'vɪnətɪ/ n Göttlichkeit f; (subject) Theologie f

division /dɪ'vɪʒn/ n Teilung f; (separation) Trennung f; (Math, Mil) Division f; (Parl) Hammelsprung m; (line) Trennlinie f; (group) Abteilung f

divorce /dɪ'vɔ:s/ n Scheidung f •vt sich scheiden lassen von. **~d** adj geschieden; **get ~d** sich scheiden lassen

DIY abbr **do-it-yourself**

dizziness /'dɪzɪnɪs/ n Schwindel m

dizzy /'dɪzɪ/ adj schwindlig; **I feel ~** mir ist schwindlig

do /du:/, unbetont /də/

3 sg pres tense **does**; pt **did**; pp **done**

• transitive verb

····➤ (perform) machen (homework, housework, exam, handstand etc); tun (duty, favour, something, nothing); vorführen (trick, dance); durchführen (test). **what are you doing?** was tust od machst du? **what can I do for you?** was kann ich für Sie tun? **do something!** tu doch etwas! **have you nothing better to do?** hast du nichts Besseres zu tun? **do the washing-up/cleaning** abwaschen/sauber machen

····➤ (as job) **what does your father do?** was macht dein Vater?; was ist dein Vater von Beruf?

····➤ (clean) putzen; (arrange) [zurecht]machen (hair)

····➤ (cook) kochen; (roast, fry) braten. **well done** (meat) durch[gebraten]. **the potatoes aren't done yet** die Kartoffeln sind noch nicht richtig durch

····➤ (solve) lösen (problem, riddle); machen (puzzle)

d

····➤ (!: swindle) reinlegen. **do s.o. out of sth** jdn um etw bringen

• intransitive verb

····➤ (with as or adverb) es tun; es machen. **do as they do** mach es wie sie. **he can do as he likes** er kann tun od machen, was er will. **you did well** du hast es gut gemacht

····➤ (get on) vorankommen; (in exams) abschneiden. **do well/badly at school** gut/schlecht in der Schule sein. **how are you doing?** wie geht's dir? **how do you do?** (formal) guten Tag!

····➤ **will do** (serve purpose) es tun; (suffice) [aus]reichen; (be suitable) gehen. **that won't do** das geht nicht. **that will do!** jetzt aber genug!

• auxiliary verb

····➤ (in questions) **do you know him?** kennst du ihn? **what does he want?** was will er?

····➤ (in negation) **I don't** or **do not wish to take part** ich will nicht teilnehmen. **don't be so noisy!** seid [doch] nicht so laut!

····➤ (as verb substitute) **you mustn't act as he does** du darfst nicht so wie er handeln. **come in, do!** komm doch herein!

····➤ (in tag questions) **don't you, doesn't he** etc. nicht wahr. **you went to Paris, didn't you?** du warst in Paris, nicht wahr?

····➤ (in short questions) **Does he live in London? — Yes, he does** Wohnt er in London? — Ja, stimmt

····➤ (for special emphasis) **I do love Greece** Griechenland gefällt mir wirklich gut

····➤ (for inversion) **little did he know that ...** er hatte keine Ahnung, dass ...

• noun

pl **do's** or **dos** /du:z/

····➤ (!: celebration) Feier f

• phrasal verbs

• **do away with** vt abschaffen. ▪ **do for** vt !: **do for s.o.** jdn fertig machen !; **be done for** erledigt sein. ▪ **do in** vt (sl: kill) kaltmachen ✖. ▪ **do up** vt (fasten) zumachen; binden (shoe-lace, bow-tie); (wrap) einpacken; (renovate) renovieren. ▪ **do with** vt: **I could do with ...** ich brauche .... ▪ **do without** vt: **do without sth** auf etw (acc) verzichten; vi darauf verzichten

docile /'dəʊsaɪl/ adj fügsam

dock¹ /dɒk/ n (Jur) Anklagebank f

dock² n Dock nt •vi anlegen. **~er** n Hafenarbeiter m. **~yard** n Werft f

doctor /'dɒktə(r)/ n Arzt m/ Ärztin f; (Univ) Doktor m •vt kastrieren; (spay) sterilisieren

doctrine /'dɒktrɪn/ n Lehre f

document /'dɒkjʊmənt/ n Dokument nt. **~ary** adj Dokumentar- •n Dokumentarbericht m; (film) Dokumentarfilm m

dodge /dɒdʒ/ n ! Trick m, Kniff m •vt/i ausweichen (+ dat)

dodgy /'dɒdʒɪ/ adj ! (awkward) knifflig; (dubious) zweifelhaft

doe /dəʊ/ n Ricke f; (rabbit) [Kaninchen]weibchen nt

does /dʌz/ see **do**

doesn't /'dʌznt/ = **does not**

dog /dɒg/ n Hund m

dog: ~-biscuit n Hundekuchen m. **~-collar** n Hundehalsband nt; (Relig, !) Kragen m eines Geistlichen. **~-eared** adj **be ~-eared** Eselsohren haben

dogged /'dɒgɪd/ adj beharrlich

dogma /'dɒgmə/ n Dogma nt. **~tic** adj dogmatisch

do-it-yourself /du:ɪtjə'self/ n Heimwerken nt. **~ shop** n Heimwerkerladen m

doldrums /'dɒldrəmz/ npl **be in the ~** niedergeschlagen sein; (business:) daniederliegen

dole /dəʊl/ n ! Stempelgeld nt; **be on the ~** arbeitslos sein •vt **~ out** austeilen

doll /dɒl/ n Puppe f •vt ! **~ oneself up** sich herausputzen

dollar /ˈdɒlə(r)/ n Dollar m

dolphin /ˈdɒlfɪn/ n Delphin m

domain /dəˈmeɪn/ n Gebiet nt

dome /dəʊm/ n Kuppel m

domestic /dəˈmestɪk/ adj häuslich; (Pol) Innen-; (Comm) Binnen-. ~ **animal** n Haustier nt. ~ **flight** n Inlandflug m

dominant /ˈdɒmɪnənt/ adj vorherrschend

dominat|e /ˈdɒmɪneɪt/ vt beherrschen •vi dominieren. ~**ion** n Vorherrschaft f

domineering /dɒmɪˈnɪə(r)ɪŋ/ adj herrschsüchtig

domino /ˈdɒmɪnəʊ/ n (pl **-es**) Dominostein m; ~**es** sg (game) Domino nt

donat|e /dəʊˈneɪt/ vt spenden. ~**ion** n Spende f

done /dʌn/ see **do**

donkey /ˈdɒŋkɪ/ n Esel m; ~**'s years** [!] eine Ewigkeit. ~**-work** n Routinearbeit f

donor /ˈdəʊnə(r)/ n Spender m, Spenderin f

don't /dəʊnt/ = **do not**

doom /du:m/ n Schicksal nt; (ruin) Verhängnis nt

door /dɔ:(r)/ n Tür f; **out of** ~**s** im Freien

door: ~**man** n Portier m. ~**mat** n [Fuß]abtreter m. ~**step** n Türschwelle f; **on the** ~**step** vor der Tür. ~**way** n Türöffnung f

dope /dəʊp/ n [!] Drogen pl; ([!]: information) Informationen pl; ([!]: idiot) Trottel m •vt betäuben; (Sport) dopen

dormant /ˈdɔ:mənt/ adj ruhend

dormitory /ˈdɔ:mɪtərɪ/ n Schlafsaal m

dormouse /ˈdɔ:-/ n Haselmaus f

dosage /ˈdəʊsɪdʒ/ n Dosierung f

dose /dəʊs/ n Dosis f

dot /dɒt/ n Punkt m; **on the** ~ pünktlich

dote /dəʊt/ vi ~ **on** vernarrt sein in (+ acc)

dotted /ˈdɒtɪd/ adj ~ **line** punktierte Linie f; **be** ~ **with** bestreut sein mit

dotty /ˈdɒtɪ/ adj [!] verdreht

double /ˈdʌbl/ adj & adv doppelt; (bed, chin) Doppel-; (flower) gefüllt •n das Doppelte; (person) Doppelgänger m; ~**s** pl (Tennis) Doppel nt; •vt verdoppeln; (fold) falten •vi sich verdoppeln. ~ **up** vi sich krümmen (**with** vor + dat)

double: ~**-ˈbass** n Kontrabass m. ~**-breasted** adj zweireihig. ~**-click** vt/i doppelklicken (**on** auf + acc). ~**-ˈcross** vt ein Doppelspiel treiben mit. ~**-ˈdecker** n Doppeldecker m. ~ **ˈglazing** n Doppelverglasung f. ~ **ˈroom** n Doppelzimmer nt

doubly /ˈdʌblɪ/ adv doppelt

doubt /daʊt/ n Zweifel m •vt bezweifeln. ~**ful** adj zweifelhaft; (disbelieving) skeptisch. ~**less** adv zweifellos

dough /dəʊ/ n [fester] Teig m; ([!]: money) Pinke f. ~**nut** n Berliner [Pfannkuchen] m

dove /dʌv/ n Taube f

dowdy /ˈdaʊdɪ/ adj unschick

down¹ /daʊn/ n (feathers) Daunen pl

down² adv unten; (with movement) nach unten; **go** ~ hinuntergehen; **come** ~ herunterkommen; ~ **there** da unten; **£50** ~ £50 Anzahlung; ~**!** (to dog) Platz! ~ **with ...!** nieder mit ...! •prep ~ **the road/stairs** die Straße/Treppe hinunter; ~ **the river** den Fluss abwärts •vt [!] (drink) runterkippen; ~ **tools** die Arbeit niederlegen

down: ~**cast** adj niedergeschlagen. ~**fall** n Sturz m; (ruin) Ruin m. ~**-ˈhearted** adj entmutigt. ~**ˈhill** adv bergab. ~**load** vt herunterladen. ~ **payment** n Anzahlung f. ~**pour** n Platzregen m. ~**right** adj & adv ausgesprochen. ~**size** vt verschlanken • vi abspecken.

~'**stairs** adv unten; (go) nach unten •adj im Erdgeschoss. ~'**stream** adv stromabwärts. ~-**to-'earth** adj sachlich. ~**town** adv (Amer) im Stadtzentrum. ~**ward** adj nach unten; (slope) abfallend •adv ~**[s]** abwärts, nach unten

doze /dəʊz/ n Nickerchen nt •vi dösen. ~ **off** vi einnicken

dozen /'dʌzn/ n Dutzend nt

Dr abbr **doctor**

draft[1] /drɑːft/ n Entwurf m; (Comm) Tratte f; (Amer Mil) Einberufung f •vt entwerfen; (Amer Mil) einberufen

draft[2] n (Amer) = **draught**

drag /dræg/ n **in** ~ [!] (man) als Frau gekleidet •vt (pt/pp **dragged**) schleppen; absuchen (river). ~ **on** vi sich in die Länge ziehen

dragon /'drægən/ n Drache m. ~-**fly** n Libelle f

drain /dreɪn/ n Abfluss m; (underground) Kanal m; **the** ~**s** die Kanalisation •vt entwässern (land); ablassen (liquid); das Wasser ablassen aus (tank); abgießen (vegetables); austrinken (glass) •vi ~ **[away]** ablaufen

drain|age /'dreɪnɪdʒ/ n Kanalisation f; (of land) Dränage f. ~**ing board** n Abtropfbrett nt. ~-**pipe** n Abflussrohr nt

drake /dreɪk/ n Enterich m

drama /'drɑːmə/ n Drama nt

dramatic /drə'mætɪk/ adj, **-ally** adv dramatisch

dramat|ist /'dræmətɪst/ n Dramatiker m. ~**ize** vt für die Bühne bearbeiten; (fig) dramatisieren

drank /dræŋk/ see **drink**

drape /dreɪp/ n (Amer) Vorhang m •vt drapieren

drastic /'dræstɪk/ adj, **-ally** adv drastisch

draught /drɑːft/ n [Luft]zug m; ~**s** sg (game) Damespiel nt; **there is a** ~ es zieht

draught beer n Bier nt vom Fass

draughty /'drɑːftɪ/ adj zugig

draw /drɔː/ n Attraktion f; (Sport) Unentschieden nt; (in lottery) Ziehung f •v (pt **drew**, pp **drawn**) •vt ziehen; (attract) anziehen; zeichnen (picture); abheben (money); ~ **the curtains** die Vorhänge zuziehen/ (back) aufziehen •vi (Sport) unentschieden spielen. ~ **back** vt zurückziehen •vi (recoil) zurückweichen. ~ **in** vt einziehen •vi einfahren. ~ **out** vt herausziehen; abheben (money) •vi ausfahren. ~ **up** vt aufsetzen (document); herrücken (chair) •vi [an]halten

draw: ~**back** n Nachteil m. ~**bridge** n Zugbrücke f

drawer /drɔː(r)/ n Schublade f

drawing /'drɔːɪŋ/ n Zeichnung f

drawing: ~-**board** n Reißbrett nt. ~-**pin** n Reißzwecke f. ~-**room** n Wohnzimmer nt

drawl /drɔːl/ n schleppende Aussprache f

drawn /drɔːn/ see **draw**

dread /dred/ n Furcht f (**of** vor + dat) •vt fürchten. ~**ful** adj, **-fully** adv fürchterlich

dream /driːm/ n Traum m •vt/i (pt/pp **dreamt** or **dreamed**) träumen (**about/of** von)

dreary /'drɪərɪ/ adj trüb[e]; (boring) langweilig

dregs /dregz/ npl Bodensatz m

drench /drentʃ/ vt durchnässen

dress /dres/ n Kleid nt; (clothing) Kleidung f •vt anziehen; (Med) verbinden; ~ **oneself, get** ~**ed** sich anziehen •vi sich anziehen. ~ **up** vi sich schön anziehen; (in disguise) sich verkleiden (**as** als)

dress: ~ **circle** n (Theat) erster Rang m. ~**er** n (furniture) Anrichte f; (Amer: dressing-table) Frisiertisch m

dressing n (Culin) Soße f; (Med) Verband m

dressing: ~-**gown** n Morgenmantel m. ~-**room** n

Ankleidezimmer nt; (Theat) [Künstler]garderobe f. **~-table** n Frisiertisch m

dress: ~maker n Schneiderin f. **~ rehearsal** n Generalprobe f

drew /druː/ see **draw**

dried /draɪd/ adj getrocknet; **~ fruit** Dörrobst nt

drier /ˈdraɪə(r)/ n Trockner m

drift /drɪft/ n Abtrift f; (of snow) Schneewehe f; (meaning) Sinn m •vi treiben; (off course) abtreiben; (snow:) Wehen bilden; (fig) (person:) sich treiben lassen

drill /drɪl/ n Bohrer m; (Mil) Drill m •vt/i bohren (**for** nach); (Mil) drillen

drily /ˈdraɪlɪ/ adv trocken

drink /drɪŋk/ n Getränk nt; (alcoholic) Drink m; (alcohol) Alkohol m •vt/i (pt **drank**, pp **drunk**) trinken. **~ up** vt/i austrinken

drink|able /ˈdrɪŋkəbl/ adj trinkbar. **~er** n Trinker m

ˈdrinking-water n Trinkwasser nt

drip /drɪp/ n Tropfen nt; (drop) Tropfen m; (Med) Tropf m; (🄸: person) Niete f •vi (pt/pp **dripped**) tropfen

drive /draɪv/ n [Auto]fahrt f; (entrance) Einfahrt f; (energy) Elan m; (Psychology) Trieb m; (Pol) Aktion f; (Sport) Treibschlag m; (Techn) Antrieb m •v (pt **drove**, pp **driven**) •vt treiben; fahren (car); (Sport: hit) schlagen; (Techn) antreiben; **~ s.o. mad** 🄸 jdn verrückt machen; **what are you driving at?** 🄸 worauf willst du hinaus? •vi fahren. **~ away** vt vertreiben •vi abfahren. **~ off** vt vertreiben •vi abfahren. **~ on** vi weiterfahren. **~ up** vi vorfahren

drivel /ˈdrɪvl/ n 🄸 Quatsch m

driven /ˈdrɪvn/ see **drive**

driver /ˈdraɪvə(r)/ n Fahrer(in) m(f); (of train) Lokführer m

driving: ~ lesson n Fahrstunde f. **~ licence** n Führerschein m. **~ school** n Fahrschule f. **~ test** Fahrprüfung f

drizzle /ˈdrɪzl/ n Nieselregen m •vi nieseln

drone /drəʊn/ n (sound) Brummen nt

droop /druːp/ vi herabhängen

drop /drɒp/ n Tropfen m; (fall) Fall m; (in price, temperature) Rückgang m •v (pt/pp **dropped**) •vt fallen lassen; abwerfen (bomb); (omit) auslassen; (give up) aufgeben •vi fallen; (fall lower) sinken; (wind:) nachlassen. **~ in** vi vorbeikommen. **~ off** vt absetzen (person) •vi abfallen; (fall asleep) einschlafen. **~ out** vi herausfallen; (give up) aufgeben

drought /draʊt/ n Dürre f

drove /drəʊv/ see **drive**

drown /draʊn/ vi ertrinken •vt ertränken; übertönen (noise); **be ~ed** ertrinken

drowsy /ˈdraʊzɪ/ adj schläfrig

drudgery /ˈdrʌdʒərɪ/ n Plackerei f

drug /drʌg/ n Droge f •vt (pt/pp **drugged**) betäuben

drug: ~ addict n Drogenabhängige(r) m/f. **~store** n (Amer) Drogerie f; (dispensing) Apotheke f

drum /drʌm/ n Trommel f; (for oil) Tonne f •v (pt/pp **drummed**) •vi trommeln •vt **~sth into s.o.** 🄸 jdm etw einbläuen. **~mer** n Trommler m; (in pop-group) Schlagzeuger m. **~stick** n Trommelschlegel m; (Culin) Keule f

drunk /drʌŋk/ see **drink** •adj betrunken; **get ~** sich betrinken •n Betrunkene(r) m

drunk|ard /ˈdrʌŋkəd/ n Trinker m. **~en** adj betrunken

dry /draɪ/ adj (**drier, driest**) trocken •vt/i trocknen. **~ up** vt/i austrocknen

dry: ~-ˈclean vt chemisch reinigen. **~-ˈcleaner's** n (shop) chemische Reinigung f. **~ness** n Trockenheit f

dual /ˈdjuːəl/ adj doppelt

d

dual 'carriageway n ≈ Schnellstraße f

dubious /'dju:brəs/ adj zweifelhaft

duchess /'dʌtʃɪs/ n Herzogin f

duck /dʌk/ n Ente f •vt (in water) untertauchen •vi sich ducken

duct /dʌkt/ n Rohr nt; (Anat) Gang m

dud /dʌd/ adj [!] nutzlos; (coin) falsch; (cheque) ungedeckt; (forged) gefälscht

due /dju:/ adj angemessen; **be ~** fällig sein; (baby:) erwartet werden; (train:) planmäßig ankommen; **~ to** (owing to) wegen (+ gen); **be ~ to** zurückzuführen sein auf (+ acc) •adv **~ west** genau westlich

duel /'dju:əl/ n Duell nt

duet /dju:'et/ n Duo nt; (vocal) Duett nt

dug /dʌg/ see **dig**

duke /dju:k/ n Herzog m

dull /dʌl/ adj (**-er, -est**) (overcast, not bright) trüb[e]; (not shiny) matt; (sound) dumpf; (boring) langweilig; (stupid) schwerfällig

duly /'dju:lɪ/ adv ordnungsgemäß

dumb /dʌm/ adj (**-er, -est**) stumm. **~ down** vt/i verflachen

dummy /'dʌmɪ/ n (tailor's) [Schneider]puppe f; (for baby) Schnuller m; (Comm) Attrappe f

dump /dʌmp/ n Abfallhaufen m; (for refuse) Müllhalde f, Deponie f; ([!]: town) Kaff nt; **be down in the ~s** [!] deprimiert sein •vt abladen

dumpling /'dʌmplɪŋ/ n Kloß m

dunce /dʌns/ n Dummkopf m

dune /dju:n/ n Düne f

dung /dʌŋ/ n Mist m

dungarees /dʌŋgə'ri:z/ npl Latzhose f

dungeon /'dʌndʒən/ n Verlies nt

dunk /dʌŋk/ vt eintunken

duo /'dju:əʊ/ n Paar nt; (Mus) Duo nt

dupe /dju:p/ n Betrogene(r) m/f •vt betrügen

duplicate[1] /'dju:plɪkət/ n Doppel nt; **in ~** in doppelter Ausfertigung f

duplicat|e[2] /'dju:plɪkeɪt/ vt kopieren; (do twice) zweimal machen

durable /'djʊərəbl/ adj haltbar

duration /djʊə'reɪʃn/ n Dauer f

during /'djʊərɪŋ/ prep während (+ gen)

dusk /dʌsk/ n [Abend]dämmerung f

dust /dʌst/ n Staub m •vt abstauben; (sprinkle) bestäuben (**with** mit) •vi Staub wischen

dust: ~bin n Mülltonne f. **~-cart** n Müllwagen m. **~er** n Staubtuch nt. **~-jacket** n Schutzumschlag m. **~man** n Müllmann m. **~pan** n Kehrschaufel f

dusty /'dʌstɪ/ adj staubig

Dutch /dʌtʃ/ adj holländisch •n (Lang) Holländisch nt; **the ~** pl die Holländer. **~man** n Holländer m

dutiful /'dju:tɪfl/ adj pflichtbewusst

duty /'dju:tɪ/ n Pflicht f; (task) Aufgabe f; (tax) Zoll m; **be on ~** Dienst haben. **~-free** adj zollfrei

duvet /'du:veɪ/ n Steppdecke f

DVD abbr (**digital versatile disc**) DVD f

dwarf /dwɔ:f/ n (pl **-s** or **dwarves**) Zwerg m

dwell /dwel/ vi (pt/pp **dwelt**); **~ on** (fig) verweilen bei. **~ing** n Wohnung f

dwindle /'dwɪndl/ vi abnehmen, schwinden

dye /daɪ/ n Farbstoff m •vt (pres p **dyeing**) färben

dying /'daɪɪŋ/ see **die**[2]

dynamic /daɪ'næmɪk/ adj dynamisch

dynamite /'daɪnəmaɪt/ n Dynamit nt

dyslex|ia /dɪs'leksɪə/ n Legasthenie f. **~ic** adj legasthenisch; **be ~ic** Legastheniker sein

Ee

each /iːtʃ/ adj & pron jede(r,s); (per) je; ~ **other** einander; **£1** ~ £1 pro Person; (for thing) pro Stück

eager /ˈiːgə(r)/ adj eifrig; **be** ~ **to do sth** etw gerne machen wollen. ~**ness** n Eifer m

eagle /ˈiːgl/ n Adler m

ear n Ohr nt. ~**ache** n Ohrenschmerzen pl. ~**-drum** n Trommelfell nt

earl /ɜːl/ n Graf m

early /ˈɜːlɪ/ adj & adv (**-ier, -iest**) früh; (reply) baldig; **be** ~ früh dran sein

earn /ɜːn/ vt verdienen

earnest /ˈɜːnɪst/ adj ernsthaft • n **in** ~ im Ernst

earnings /ˈɜːnɪŋz/ npl Verdienst m

ear: ~**phones** npl Kopfhörer pl. ~**-ring** n Ohrring m; (clip-on) Ohrklips m. ~**shot** n **within/out of** ~**shot** in/außer Hörweite

earth /ɜːθ/ n Erde f; (of fox) Bau m • vt (Electr) erden

earthenware /ˈɜːθn-/ n Tonwaren pl

earthly /ˈɜːθlɪ/ adj irdisch; **be no** ~ **use** [!] völlig nutzlos sein

ˈ**earthquake** n Erdbeben nt

earthy /ˈɜːθɪ/ adj erdig; (coarse) derb

ease /iːz/ n Leichtigkeit f • vt erleichtern; lindern (pain) • vi (pain:) nachlassen; (situation:) sich entspannen

easily /ˈiːzɪlɪ/ adv leicht, mit Leichtigkeit

east /iːst/ n Osten m; **to the** ~ **of** östlich von • adj Ost-, ost- • adv nach Osten

Easter /ˈiːstə(r)/ n Ostern nt • attrib Oster-. ~ **egg** n Osterei nt

east|erly /ˈiːstəlɪ/ adj östlich. ~**ern** adj östlich. ~**ward[s]** adv nach Osten

easy /ˈiːzɪ/ adj leicht; **take it** ~ [!] sich schonen; **go** ~ **with** [!] sparsam umgehen mit

easy: ~ **chair** n Sessel m. ~ˈ**going** adj gelassen

eat /iːt/ vt/i (pt **ate**, pp **eaten**) essen; (animal:) fressen. ~ **up** vt aufessen

eatable /ˈiːtəbl/ adj genießbar

eau-de-Cologne /əʊdəkəˈləʊn/ n Kölnisch Wasser nt

eaves /iːvz/ npl Dachüberhang m. ~**drop** vi (pt/pp ~ **dropped**) [heimlich] lauschen

ebb /eb/ n (tide) Ebbe f • vi zurückgehen; (fig) verebben

ebony /ˈebənɪ/ n Ebenholz nt

EC abbr (**European Community**) EG f

eccentric /ɪkˈsentrɪk/ adj exzentrisch • n Exzentriker m

ecclesiastical /ɪkliːzɪˈæstɪkl/ adj kirchlich

echo /ˈekəʊ/ n (pl **-es**) Echo nt, Widerhall m • v (pt/pp **echoed**, pres p **echoing**) • vi widerhallen (**with** von)

eclipse /ɪˈklɪps/ n (Astronomy) Finsternis f

ecolog|ical /iːkəˈlɒdʒɪkl/ adj ökologisch. ~**y** n Ökologie f

e-commerce /iːˈkɒmɜːs/ n E-Commerce m

economic /iːkəˈnɒmɪk/ adj wirtschaftlich. ~**al** adj sparsam. ~**ally** adv wirtschaftlich; (thriftily) sparsam. ~ **refugee** n Wirtschaftsflüchtling m. ~**s** n Volkswirtschaft f

economist /ɪˈkɒnəmɪst/ n Volkswirt m; (Univ) Wirtschaftswissenschaftler m

economize /ɪ'kɒnəmaɪz/ vi sparen (**on** an + dat)

economy /ɪ'kɒnəmɪ/ n Wirtschaft f; (thrift) Sparsamkeit f

ecstasy /'ekstəsɪ/ n Ekstase f

ecstatic /ɪk'stætɪk/ adj, **-ally** adv ekstatisch

eczema /'eksɪmə/ n Ekzem nt

eddy /'edɪ/ n Wirbel m

edge /edʒ/ n Rand m; (of table, lawn) Kante f; (of knife) Schneide f; **on ~** [!] nervös •vt einfassen. **~ forward** vi sich nach vorn schieben

edgy /'edʒɪ/ adj [!] nervös

edible /'edɪbl/ adj essbar

edifice /'edɪfɪs/ n [großes] Gebäude nt

edit /'edɪt/ vt (pt/pp **edited**) redigieren; herausgeben (anthology, dictionary); schneiden (film, tape)

edition /ɪ'dɪʃn/ n Ausgabe f; (impression) Auflage f

editor /'edɪtə(r)/ n Redakteur m; (of anthology, dictionary) Herausgeber m; (of newspaper) Chefredakteur m; (of film) Cutter(in) m(f)

editorial /edɪ'tɔːrɪəl/ adj redaktionell, Redaktions- •n (in newspaper) Leitartikel m

educate /'edjʊkeɪt/ vt erziehen. **~d** adj gebildet

education /edjʊ'keɪʃn/ n Erziehung f; (culture) Bildung f. **~al** adj pädagogisch; (visit) kulturell

eel /iːl/ n Aal m

eerie /'ɪərɪ/ adj unheimlich

effect /ɪ'fekt/ n Wirkung f, Effekt m; **take ~** in Kraft treten

effective /ɪ'fektɪv/ adj wirksam, effektiv; (striking) wirkungsvoll, effektvoll; (actual) tatsächlich. **~ness** n Wirksamkeit f

effeminate /ɪ'femɪnət/ adj unmännlich

effervescent /efə'vesnt/ adj sprudelnd

efficiency /ɪ'fɪʃənsɪ/ n Tüchtigkeit f; (of machine, organization) Leistungsfähigkeit f

efficient /ɪ'fɪʃənt/ adj tüchtig; (machine, organization) leistungsfähig; (method) rationell. **~ly** adv gut; (function) rationell

effort /'efət/ n Anstrengung f; **make an ~** sich (dat) Mühe geben. **~less** adj mühelos

e.g. abbr (**exempli gratia**) z.B.

egalitarian /ɪgælɪ'teərɪən/ adj egalitär

egg n Ei nt. **~-cup** n Eierbecher m. **~shell** n Eierschale f

ego /'iːgəʊ/ n Ich nt. **~ism** n Egoismus m. **~ist** n Egoist m. **~tism** n Ichbezogenheit f. **~tist** n ichbezogener Mensch m

Egypt /'iːdʒɪpt/ n Ägypten nt. **~ian** adj ägyptisch •n Ägypter(in) m(f)

eiderdown /'aɪdə-/ n (quilt) Daunendecke f

eigh|t /eɪt/ adj acht •n Acht f; (boat) Achter m. **~'teen** adj achtzehn. **~'teenth** adj achtzehnte(r,s)

eighth /eɪtθ/ adj achte(r,s) •n Achtel nt

eightieth /'eɪtɪɪθ/ adj achtzigste(r,s)

eighty /'eɪtɪ/ adj achtzig

either /'aɪðə(r)/ adj & pron **~ [of them]** einer von [den] beiden; (both) beide; **on ~ side** auf beiden Seiten •adv **I don't ~** ich auch nicht •conj **~ ... or** entweder ... oder

eject /ɪ'dʒekt/ vt hinauswerfen

elaborate /ɪ'læbərət/ adj kunstvoll; (fig) kompliziert

elapse /ɪ'læps/ vi vergehen

elastic /ɪ'læstɪk/ adj elastisch. **~ 'band** n Gummiband nt

elasticity /ɪlæs'tɪsətɪ/ n Elastizität f

elated /ɪ'leɪtɪd/ adj überglücklich

elbow /'elbəʊ/ n Ellbogen m

elder[1] /'eldə(r)/ n Holunder m

eld|er[2] adj ältere(r,s) •n **the ~er** der/die Ältere. **~erly** adj alt. **~est**

adj älteste(r,s) • n **the ~est** der/die Älteste

elect /ɪ'lekt/ vt wählen. **~ion** n Wahl f

elector /ɪ'lektə(r)/ n Wähler(in) m(f). **~ate** n Wählerschaft f

electric /ɪ'lektrɪk/ adj, **-ally** adv elektrisch

electrical /ɪ'lektrɪkl/ adj elektrisch; **~ engineering** Elektrotechnik f

electric: ~ 'blanket n Heizdecke f. **~ 'fire** n elektrischer Heizofen m

electrician /ɪlek'trɪʃn/ n Elektriker m

electricity /ɪlek'trɪsətɪ/ n Elektrizität f; (supply) Strom m

electrify /ɪ'lektrɪfaɪ/ vt (pt/pp **-ied**) elektrifizieren. **~ing** adj (fig) elektrisierend

electrocute /ɪ'lektrəkju:t/ vt durch einen elektrischen Schlag töten

electrode /ɪ'lektrəʊd/ n Elektrode f

electronic /ɪlek'trɒnɪk/ adj elektronisch. **~s** n Elektronik f

elegance /'elɪgəns/ n Eleganz f

elegant /'elɪgənt/ adj elegant

elegy /'elɪdʒɪ/ n Elegie f

element /'elɪmənt/ n Element nt. **~ary** adj elementar

elephant /'elɪfənt/ n Elefant m

elevat|e /'elɪveɪt/ vt heben; (fig) erheben. **~ion** n Erhebung f

elevator /'elɪveɪtə(r)/ n (Amer) Aufzug m, Fahrstuhl m

eleven /ɪ'levn/ adj elf • n Elf f. **~th** adj elfte(r,s); **at the ~th hour** [!] in letzter Minute

eligible /'elɪdʒəbl/ adj berechtigt

eliminate /ɪ'lɪmɪneɪt/ vt ausschalten

élite /eɪ'li:t/ n Elite f

elm /elm/ n Ulme f

elocution /elə'kju:ʃn/ n Sprecherziehung f

elope /ɪ'əʊp/ vi durchbrennen [!]

eloquen|ce /'eləkwəns/ n Beredsamkeit f. **~t** adj, **-ly** adv beredt

else /els/ adv sonst; **nothing ~** sonst nichts; **or ~** oder; (otherwise) sonst; **someone/somewhere ~** jemand/irgendwo anders; **anyone ~** jeder andere; (as question) sonst noch jemand? **anything ~** alles andere; (as question) sonst noch etwas? **~where** adv woanders

elucidate /ɪ'lu:sɪdeɪt/ vt erläutern

elusive /ɪ'lu:sɪv/ adj **be ~** schwer zu fassen sein

emaciated /ɪ'meɪsɪeɪtɪd/ adj abgezehrt

e-mail /'i:meɪl/ n E-Mail f • vt per E-Mail übermitteln (Ergebnisse, Datei usw.); **~ s.o.** jdm eine E-Mail schicken. **~ address** n E-Mail-Adresse f. **~ message** n E-Mail f

emancipat|ed /ɪ'mænsɪpeɪtɪd/ adj emanzipiert. **~ion** n Emanzipation f; (of slaves) Freilassung f

embankment /ɪm'bæŋkmənt/ n Böschung f; (of railway) Bahndamm m

embark /ɪm'bɑ:k/ vi sich einschiffen. **~ation** n Einschiffung f

embarrass /ɪm'bærəs/ vt in Verlegenheit bringen. **~ed** adj verlegen. **~ing** adj peinlich. **~ment** n Verlegenheit f

embassy /'embəsɪ/ n Botschaft f

embellish /ɪm'belɪʃ/ vt verzieren; (fig) ausschmücken

embezzle /ɪm'bezl/ vt unterschlagen. **~ment** n Unterschlagung f

emblem /'embləm/ n Emblem nt

embodiment /ɪm'bɒdɪmənt/ n Verkörperung f

embody /ɪm'bɒdɪ/ vt (pt/pp **-ied**) verkörpern; (include) enthalten

embrace /ɪm'breɪs/ n Umarmung f • vt umarmen; (fig) umfassen • vi sich umarmen

embroider /ɪm'brɔɪdə(r)/ vt besticken; sticken (design) • vi sticken. **~y** n Stickerei f

embryo /'embrɪəʊ/ n Embryo m

emerald /'emərəld/ n Smaragd m

emer|ge /ɪ'mɜːdʒ/ vi auftauchen (**from** aus); (become known) sich herausstellen; (come into being) entstehen. **~gence** n Auftauchen nt; Entstehung f

e

emergency /ɪ'mɜːdʒənsɪ/ n Notfall m. **~ exit** n Notausgang m

emigrant /'emɪgrənt/ n Auswanderer m

emigrat|e /'emɪgreɪt/ vi auswandern. **~ion** n Auswanderung f

eminent /'emɪnənt/ adj eminent

emission /ɪ'mɪʃn/ n Ausstrahlung f; (of pollutant) Emission f

emit /ɪ'mɪt/ vt (pt/pp **emitted**) ausstrahlen (light, heat); ausstoßen (smoke, fumes, cry)

emotion /ɪ'məʊʃn/ n Gefühl nt. **~al** adj emotional; **become ~al** sich erregen

empathy /'empəθɪ/ n Einfühlungsvermögen nt

emperor /'empərə(r)/ n Kaiser m

emphasis /'emfəsɪs/ n Betonung f

emphasize /'emfəsaɪz/ vt betonen

emphatic /ɪm'fætɪk/ adj, **-ally** adv nachdrücklich

empire /'empaɪə(r)/ n Reich nt

employ /ɪm'plɔɪ/ vt beschäftigen; (appoint) einstellen; (fig) anwenden. **~ee** n Beschäftigte(r) m/f; (in contrast to employer) Arbeitnehmer m. **~er** n Arbeitgeber m. **~ment** n Beschäftigung f; (work) Arbeit f. **~ment agency** n Stellenvermittlung f

empress /'emprɪs/ n Kaiserin f

emptiness /'emptɪnɪs/ n Leere f

empty /'emptɪ/ adj leer •vt leeren; ausleeren (container) •vi sich leeren

emulsion /ɪ'mʌlʃn/ n Emulsion f

enable /ɪ'neɪbl/ vt **~ s.o. to** es jdm möglich machen, zu

enact /ɪ'nækt/ vt (Theat) aufführen

enamel /ɪ'næml/ n Email nt; (on teeth) Zahnschmelz m; (paint) Lack m

enchant /ɪn'tʃɑːnt/ vt bezaubern. **~ing** adj bezaubernd. **~ment** n Zauber m

encircle /ɪn'sɜːkl/ vt einkreisen

enclos|e /ɪn'kləʊz/ vt einschließen; (in letter) beilegen (**with** dat). **~ure** n (at zoo) Gehege nt; (in letter) Anlage f

encore /'ɒŋkɔː(r)/ n Zugabe f •int bravo!

encounter /ɪn'kaʊntə(r)/ n Begegnung f •vt begegnen (+ dat); (fig) stoßen auf (+ acc)

encourag|e /ɪn'kʌrɪdʒ/ vt ermutigen; (promote) fördern. **~ement** n Ermutigung f. **~ing** adj ermutigend

encroach /ɪn'krəʊtʃ/ vi **~ on** eindringen in (+ acc) (land)

encyclopaed|ia /ɪnsaɪklə'piːdɪə/ n Enzyklopädie f, Lexikon nt. **~ic** adj enzyklopädisch

end /end/ n Ende nt; (purpose) Zweck m; **in the ~** schließlich; **at the ~ of May** Ende Mai; **on ~** hochkant; **for days on ~** tagelang; **make ~s meet** [!] [gerade] auskommen; **no ~ of** [!] unheimlich viel(e) •vt beenden •vi enden; **~ up in** ([!]: arrive at) landen in (+ dat)

endanger /ɪn'deɪndʒə(r)/ vt gefährden

endeavour /ɪn'devə(r)/ n Bemühung f •vi sich bemühen (**to** zu)

ending /'endɪŋ/ n Schluss m, Ende nt; (Gram) Endung f

endless /'endlɪs/ adj endlos

endorse /en'dɔːs/ vt (Comm) indossieren; (confirm) bestätigen. **~ment** n (Comm) Indossament nt; (fig) Bestätigung f; (on driving licence) Strafvermerk m

endow /ɪn'daʊ/ vt stiften; **be ~ed with** (fig) haben

endurance /ɪn'djʊərəns/ n Durchhaltevermögen nt; **beyond ~** unerträglich

endure /ɪn'djʊə(r)/ vt ertragen

enemy /'enəmɪ/ n Feind m •attrib feindlich

energetic /enə'dʒetɪk/ adj tatkräftig; **be ~** voller Energie sein

energy /'enədʒɪ/ n Energie f

enforce /ɪn'fɔːs/ vt durchsetzen. **~d** adj unfreiwillig

engage /ɪn'geɪdʒ/ vt einstellen (staff); (Theat) engagieren; (Auto) einlegen (gear) •vi sich beteiligen (**in** an + dat); (Techn) ineinandergreifen. **~d** adj besetzt; (person) beschäftigt; (to be married) verlobt; **get ~d** sich verloben (**to** mit). **~ment** n Verlobung f; (appointment) Verabredung f; (Mil) Gefecht nt

engaging /ɪn'geɪdʒɪŋ/ adj einnehmend

engine /'endʒɪn/ n Motor m; (Naut) Maschine f; (Rail) Lokomotive f; (of jet plane) Triebwerk nt. **~-driver** n Lokomotivführer m

engineer /endʒɪ'nɪə(r)/ n Ingenieur m; (service, installation) Techniker m; (Naut) Maschinist m; (Amer) Lokomotivführer m. **~ing** n **[mechanical] ~ing** Maschinenbau m

England /'ɪŋglənd/ n England nt

English /'ɪŋglɪʃ/ adj englisch; **the ~ Channel** der Ärmelkanal •n (Lang) Englisch nt; **in ~** auf Englisch; **into ~** ins Englische; **the ~** pl die Engländer. **~man** n Engländer m. **~woman** n Engländerin f

engrav|e /ɪn'greɪv/ vt eingravieren. **~ing** n Stich m

enhance /ɪn'hɑːns/ vt verschönern; (fig) steigern

enigma /ɪ'nɪgmə/ n Rätsel nt. **~tic** adj rätselhaft

enjoy /ɪn'dʒɔɪ/ vt genießen; **~ oneself** sich amüsieren; **~ cooking** gern kochen; **I ~ed it** es hat mir gut gefallen/ (food:) geschmeckt. **~able** adj angenehm, nett. **~ment** n Vergnügen nt

enlarge /ɪn'lɑːdʒ/ vt vergrößern. **~ment** n Vergrößerung f

enlist /ɪn'lɪst/ vt (Mil) einziehen; **~ s.o.'s help** jdn zur Hilfe heranziehen •vi (Mil) sich melden

enliven /ɪn'laɪvn/ vt beleben

enmity /'enmətɪ/ n Feindschaft f

enormity /ɪ'nɔːmətɪ/ n Ungeheuerlichkeit f

enormous /ɪ'nɔːməs/ adj riesig

enough /ɪ'nʌf/ a, adv & n genug; **be ~** reichen; **funnily ~** komischerweise

enquir|e /ɪn'kwaɪə(r)/ vi sich erkundigen (**about** nach). **~y** n Erkundigung f; (investigation) Untersuchung f

enrage /ɪn'reɪdʒ/ vt wütend machen

enrich /ɪn'rɪtʃ/ vt bereichern

enrol /ɪn'rəʊl/ v (pt/pp **-rolled**) •vt einschreiben •vi sich einschreiben

ensemble /ɒn'sɒmbl/ n (clothing & Mus) Ensemble nt

enslave /ɪn'sleɪv/ vt versklaven

ensue /ɪn'sjuː/ vi folgen; (result) sich ergeben (**from** aus)

ensure /ɪn'ʃʊə(r)/ vt sicherstellen; **~ that** dafür sorgen, dass

entail /ɪn'teɪl/ vt erforderlich machen; **what does it ~?** was ist damit verbunden?

entangle /ɪn'tæŋgl/ vt **get ~d** sich verfangen (**in** in + dat)

enter /'entə(r)/ vt eintreten/ (vehicle:) einfahren in (+ acc); einreisen in (+ acc) (country); (register) eintragen; sich anmelden zu (competition) •vi eintreten; (vehicle:) einfahren; (Theat) auftreten; (register as competitor) sich anmelden; (take part) sich beteiligen (**in** an + dat)

enterpris|e /'entəpraɪz/ n Unternehmen nt; (quality) Unternehmungsgeist m. **~ing** adj unternehmend

entertain /entə'teɪn/ vt unterhalten; (invite) einladen; (to meal) bewirten (guest) •vi unterhalten; (have guests) Gäste haben. **~er** n Unterhalter m. **~ment** n Unterhaltung f

enthral /ɪn'θrɔ:l/ vt (pt/pp **enthralled**) **be ~led** gefesselt sein (**by** von)

enthuse /ɪn'θju:z/ vi **~ over** schwärmen von

e

enthusias|m /ɪn'θju:zɪæzm/ n Begeisterung f. **~t** n Enthusiast m. **~tic** adj, **-ally** adv begeistert

entice /ɪn'taɪs/ vt locken. **~ment** n Anreiz m

entire /ɪn'taɪə(r)/ adj ganz. **~ly** adv ganz, völlig. **~ty** n **in its ~ty** in seiner Gesamtheit

entitle /ɪn'taɪtl/ vt berechtigen; **~d** ... mit dem Titel ...; **be ~d to sth** das Recht auf etw (acc) haben. **~ment** n Berechtigung f; (claim) Anspruch m (**to auf** + acc)

entrance /'entrəns/ n Eintritt m; (Theat) Auftritt m; (way in) Eingang m; (for vehicle) Einfahrt f. **~ fee** n Eintrittsgebühr f

entrant /'entrənt/ n Teilnehmer(in) m(f)

entreat /ɪn'tri:t/ vt anflehen (**for** um)

entrust /ɪn'trʌst/ vt **~ s.o. with sth, ~ sth to s.o.** jdm etw anvertrauen

entry /'entrɪ/ n Eintritt m; (into country) Einreise f; (on list) Eintrag m; **no ~** Zutritt/ (Auto) Einfahrt verboten

envelop /ɪn'veləp/ vt (pt/pp **enveloped**) einhüllen

envelope /'envələʊp/ n [Brief]umschlag m

enviable /'envɪəbl/ adj beneidenswert

envious /'envɪəs/ adj neidisch (**of** auf + acc)

environment /ɪn'vaɪərənmənt/ n Umwelt f

environmental /ɪnvaɪərən'mentl/ adj Umwelt-. **~ist** n Umweltschützer m. **~ly** adv **~ly friendly** umweltfreundlich

envisage /ɪn'vɪzɪdʒ/ vt sich (dat) vorstellen

envoy /'envɔɪ/ n Gesandte(r) m

envy /'envɪ/ n Neid m • vt (pt/pp **-ied**) **~ s.o. sth** jdn um etw beneiden

epic /'epɪk/ adj episch • n Epos nt

epidemic /epɪ'demɪk/ n Epidemie f

epilep|sy /'epɪlepsɪ/ n Epilepsie f. **~tic** adj epileptisch • n Epileptiker(in) m(f)

epilogue /'epɪlɒg/ n Epilog m

episode /'epɪsəʊd/ n Episode f; (instalment) Folge f

epitome /ɪ'pɪtəmɪ/ n Inbegriff m

epoch /'i:pɒk/ n Epoche f. **~-making** adj epochemachend

equal /'i:kwl/ adj gleich (**to** dat); **be ~ to a task** einer Aufgabe gewachsen sein • n Gleichgestellte(r) m/f • vt (pt/pp **equalled**) gleichen (+ dat); (fig) gleichkommen (+ dat). **~ity** n Gleichheit f

equalize /'i:kwəlaɪz/ vt/i ausgleichen

equally /'i:kwəlɪ/ adv gleich; (divide) gleichmäßig; (just as) genauso

equat|e /ɪ'kweɪt/ vt gleichsetzen (**with** mit). **~ion** n (Math) Gleichung f

equator /ɪ'kweɪtə(r)/ n Äquator m

equestrian /ɪ'kwestrɪən/ adj Reit-

equilibrium /i:kwɪ'lɪbrɪəm/ n Gleichgewicht nt

equinox /'i:kwɪnɒks/ n Tagundnachtgleiche f

equip /ɪ'kwɪp/ vt (pt/pp **equipped**) ausrüsten; (furnish) ausstatten. **~ment** n Ausrüstung f; Ausstattung f

equity /'ekwətɪ/ n Gerechtigkeit f

equivalent /ɪ'kwɪvələnt/ adj gleichwertig; (corresponding) entsprechend • n Äquivalent nt; (value) Gegenwert m; (counterpart) Gegenstück nt

era /'ɪərə/ n Ära f, Zeitalter nt

eradicate /ɪ'rædɪkeɪt/ vt ausrotten

erase /ɪ'reɪz/ vt ausradieren; (from tape) löschen

erect /ɪ'rekt/ adj aufrecht • vt errichten. **~ion** n Errichtung f; (building) Bau m; (Physiology) Erektion f

ero|de /ɪ'rəʊd/ vt (water:) auswaschen; (acid:) angreifen. **~sion** n Erosion f

erotic /ɪ'rɒtɪk/ adj erotisch

errand /'erənd/ n Botengang m

erratic /ɪ'rætɪk/ adj unregelmäßig; (person) unberechenbar

erroneous /ɪ'rəʊnɪəs/ adj falsch; (belief, assumption) irrig

error /'erə(r)/ n Irrtum m; (mistake) Fehler m; **in ~** irrtümlicherweise

erupt /ɪ'rʌpt/ vi ausbrechen. **~ion** n Ausbruch m

escalat|e /'eskəleɪt/ vt/i eskalieren. **~or** n Rolltreppe f

escape /ɪ'skeɪp/ n Flucht f; (from prison) Ausbruch m; **have a narrow ~** gerade noch davonkommen • vi flüchten; (prisoner:) ausbrechen; entkommen (**from** aus; **from s.o.** jdm); (gas:) entweichen • vt **the name ~s me** der Name entfällt mir

escapism /ɪ'skeɪpɪzm/ n Eskapismus m

escort[1] /'eskɔ:t/ n (of person) Begleiter m; (Mil) Eskorte f

escort[2] /ɪ'skɔ:t/ vt begleiten; (Mil) eskortieren

Eskimo /'eskɪməʊ/ n Eskimo m

esoteric /esə'terɪk/ adj esoterisch

especially /ɪ'speʃəlɪ/ adv besonders

espionage /'espɪənɑ:ʒ/ n Spionage f

essay /'eseɪ/ n Aufsatz m

essence /'esns/ n Wesen nt; (Chemistry, Culin) Essenz f

essential /ɪ'senʃl/ adj wesentlich; (indispensable) unentbehrlich • n **the ~s** das Wesentliche; (items) das Nötigste. **~ly** adv im Wesentlichen

establish /ɪ'stæblɪʃ/ vt gründen; (form) bilden; (prove) beweisen

estate /ɪ'steɪt/ n Gut nt; (possessions) Besitz m; (after death) Nachlass m; (housing) [Wohn]siedlung f. **~ agent** n Immobilienmakler m. **~ car** n Kombi[wagen] m

esteem /ɪ'sti:m/ n Achtung f • vt hochschätzen

estimate[1] /'estɪmət/ n Schätzung f; (Comm) [Kosten]voranschlag m; **at a rough ~** grob geschätzt

estimat|e[2] /'estɪmeɪt/ vt schätzen. **~ion** n Einschätzung f

estuary /'estjʊərɪ/ n Mündung f

etc. /et'setərə/ abbr (**et cetera**) und so weiter, usw.

eternal /ɪ't3:nl/ adj ewig

eternity /ɪ'θ3:nətɪ/ n Ewigkeit f

ethic|al /'eθɪkl/ adj ethisch; (morally correct) moralisch einwandfrei. **~s** n Ethik f

Ethiopia /i:θɪ'əʊpɪə/ n Äthiopien nt

ethnic /'eθnɪk/ adj ethnisch. **~ cleansing** n ethnische Säuberung

etiquette /'etɪket/ n Etikette f

EU abbr (**European Union**) EU f

eulogy /'ju:lədʒɪ/ n Lobrede f

euphemis|m /'ju:fəmɪzm/ n Euphemismus m. **~tic** adj, **-ally** adv verhüllend

euro /'jʊərəʊ/ n Euro m. **E~cheque** n Euroscheck m. **E~land** n Euroland nt

Europe /'jʊərəp/ n Europa nt

European /jʊərə'pi:ən/ adj europäisch; **~ Union** Europäische Union f • n Europäer(in) m(f)

eurosceptic /'jʊərəʊskeptɪk/ n Euroskeptiker(in) m(f)

evacuat|e /ɪ'vækjʊeɪt/ vt evakuieren; räumen (building, area). **~ion** n Evakuierung f; Räumung f

evade /ɪ'veɪd/ vt sich entziehen (+ dat); hinterziehen (taxes)

evaluat|e /ɪvæljʊ'eɪt/ vt einschätzen **~ion** n Beurteilung f, Einschätzung f

evange|lical /i:væn'dʒelɪkl/ adj

e

evangelisch. **~list** n Evangelist m

evaporat|e /ɪ'væpəreɪt/ vi verdunsten. **~ion** n Verdampfung f

evasion /ɪ'veɪʒn/ n Ausweichen nt; **tax ~** Steuerhinterziehung f

evasive /ɪ'veɪsɪv/ adj ausweichend; **be ~** ausweichen

even /'i:vn/ adj (level) eben; (same, equal) gleich; (regular) gleichmäßig; (number) gerade; **get ~ with** [!] es jdm heimzahlen •adv sogar, selbst; **~ so** trotzdem; **not ~** nicht einmal •vt **~ the score** ausgleichen

evening /'i:vnɪŋ/ n Abend m; **this ~** heute Abend; **in the ~** abends, am Abend. **~ class** n Abendkurs m

evenly /'i:vnlɪ/ adv gleichmäßig

event /ɪ'vent/ n Ereignis nt; (function) Veranstaltung f; (Sport) Wettbewerb m. **~ful** adj ereignisreich

eventual /ɪ'ventjʊəl/ adj **his ~ success** der Erfolg, der ihm schließlich zuteil wurde. **~ly** adv schließlich

ever /'evə(r)/ adv je[mals]; **not ~** nie; **for ~** für immer; **hardly ~** fast nie; **~ since** seitdem

'evergreen n immergrüner Strauch m/ (tree) Baum m

ever'lasting adj ewig

every /'evrɪ/ adj jede(r,s); **~ one** jede(r,s) Einzelne; **~ other day** jeden zweiten Tag

every: ~body pron jeder[mann]; alle pl. **~day** adj alltäglich. **~one** pron jeder[mann]; alle pl. **~thing** pron alles. **~where** adv überall

evict /ɪ'vɪkt/ vt [aus der Wohnung] hinausweisen. **~ion** n Ausweisung f

eviden|ce /'evɪdəns/ n Beweise pl; (Jur) Beweismaterial nt; (testimony) Aussage f; **give ~ce** aussagen. **~t** adj offensichtlich

evil /'i:vl/ adj böse •n Böse nt

evoke /ɪ'vəʊk/ vt heraufbeschwören

evolution /i:və'lu:ʃn/ n Evolution f

evolve /ɪ'vɒlv/ vt entwickeln •vi sich entwickeln

ewe /ju:/ n Schaf nt

exact /ɪg'zækt/ adj genau; **not ~ly** nicht gerade. **~ness** n Genauigkeit f

exaggerat|e /ɪg'zædʒəreɪt/ vt/i übertreiben. **~ion** n Übertreibung f

exam /ɪg'zæm/ n [!] Prüfung f

examination /ɪgzæmɪ'neɪʃn/ n Untersuchung f; (Sch) Prüfung f

examine /ɪg'zæmɪn/ vt untersuchen; (Sch) prüfen

example /ɪg'zɑ:mpl/ n Beispiel nt (**of** für); **for ~** zum Beispiel; **make an ~ of** ein Exempel statuieren an (+ dat)

exasperat|e /ɪg'zæspəreɪt/ vt zur Verzweiflung treiben. **~ion** n Verzweiflung f

excavat|e /'ekskəveɪt/ vt ausschachten; ausgraben (site). **~ion** n Ausgrabung f

exceed /ɪk'si:d/ vt übersteigen. **~ingly** adv äußerst

excel /ɪk'sel/ v (pt/pp **excelled**) vi sich auszeichnen •vt **~ oneself** sich selbst übertreffen

excellen|ce /'eksələns/ n Vorzüglichkeit f. **~t** adj ausgezeichnet, vorzüglich

except /ɪk'sept/ prep außer (+ dat); **~ for** abgesehen von •vt ausnehmen

exception /ɪk'sepʃn/ n Ausnahme f. **~al** adj außergewöhnlich

excerpt /'eksɜ:pt/ n Auszug m

excess /ɪk'ses/ n Übermaß nt (**of** an + dat); (surplus) Überschuss m; **~es** pl Exzesse pl

excessive /ɪk'sesɪv/ adj übermäßig

exchange /ɪks'tʃeɪndʒ/ n Austausch m; (Teleph) Fernsprechamt nt; (Comm) [Geld]wechsel m; **in ~** dafür •vt austauschen (**for** gegen); tauschen (places). ~ **rate** n Wechselkurs m

excitable /ɪk'saɪtəbl/ adj [leicht] erregbar

excit|e /ɪk'saɪt/ vt aufregen; (cause) erregen. **~ed** adj aufgeregt; **get ~ed** sich aufregen. **~ement** n Aufregung f; Erregung f. **~ing** adj aufregend; (story) spannend

exclaim /ɪk'skleɪm/ vt/i ausrufen

exclamation /eksklə'meɪʃn/ n Ausruf m. ~ **mark** n, (Amer) ~ **point** n Ausrufezeichen nt

exclu|de /ɪk'sklu:d/ vt ausschließen. **~ding** prep ausschließlich (+ gen). **~sion** n Ausschluss m

exclusive /ɪk'sklu:sɪv/ adj ausschließlich; (select) exklusiv

excrement /'ekskrɪmənt/ n Kot m

excrete /ɪk'skri:t/ vt ausscheiden

excruciating /ɪk'skru:ʃɪeɪtɪŋ/ adj grässlich

excursion /ɪk'skɜ:ʃn/ n Ausflug m

excusable /ɪk'skju:zəbl/ adj entschuldbar

excuse[1] /ɪk'skju:s/ n Entschuldigung f; (pretext) Ausrede f

excuse[2] /ɪk'skju:z/ vt entschuldigen; ~ **me!** Entschuldigung!

ex-di'rectory adj **be** ~ nicht im Telefonbuch stehen

execute /'eksɪkju:t/ vt ausführen; (put to death) hinrichten

execution /eksɪ'kju:ʃn/ n Ausführung f; Hinrichtung f

executive /ɪg'zekjʊtɪv/ adj leitend •n leitende(r) Angestellte(r) m/f; (Pol) Exekutive f

exemplary /ɪg'zemplərɪ/ adj beispielhaft

exemplify /ɪg'zemplɪfaɪ/ vt (pt/pp **-ied**) veranschaulichen

exempt /ɪg'zempt/ adj befreit •vt befreien (**from** von). **~ion** n Befreiung f

exercise /'eksəsaɪz/ n Übung f; **physical** ~ körperliche Bewegung f •vt (use) ausüben; bewegen (horse) •vi sich bewegen. ~ **book** n [Schul]heft nt

exert /ɪg'zɜ:t/ vt ausüben; ~ **oneself** sich anstrengen. **~ion** n Anstrengung f

exhale /eks'heɪl/ vt/i ausatmen

exhaust /ɪg'zɔ:st/ n (Auto) Auspuff m; (fumes) Abgase pl •vt erschöpfen. **~ed** adj erschöpft. **~ing** adj anstrengend. **~ion** n Erschöpfung f. **~ive** adj (fig) erschöpfend

exhibit /ɪg'zɪbɪt/ n Ausstellungsstück nt; (Jur) Beweisstück nt •vt ausstellen

exhibition /eksɪ'bɪʃn/ n Ausstellung f; (Univ) Stipendium nt. **~ist** n Exhibitionist(in) m(f)

exhibitor /ɪg'zɪbɪtə(r)/ n Aussteller m

exhilarat|ing /ɪg'zɪləreɪtɪŋ/ adj berauschend. **~ion** n Hochgefühl nt

exhume /ɪg'zju:m/ vt exhumieren

exile /'eksaɪl/ n Exil nt; (person) im Exil Lebende(r) m/f •vt ins Exil schicken

exist /ɪg'zɪst/ vi bestehen, existieren. **~ence** n Existenz f; **be in ~ence** existieren

exit /'eksɪt/ n Ausgang m; (Auto) Ausfahrt f; (Theat) Abgang m

exorbitant /ɪg'zɔ:bɪtənt/ adj übermäßig hoch

exotic /ɪg'zɒtɪk/ adj exotisch

expand /ɪk'spænd/ vt ausdehnen; (explain better) weiter ausführen •vi sich ausdehnen; (Comm) expandieren

expans|e /ɪk'spæns/ n Weite f. **~ion** n Ausdehnung f; (Techn, Pol, Comm) Expansion f

expect /ɪk'spekt/ vt erwarten; (suppose) annehmen; **I ~ so** wahrscheinlich

expectan|cy /ɪk'spektənsɪ/ n Erwartung f. **~t** adj erwartungsvoll; **~t mother** werdende Mutter f

e

expectation /ekspek'teɪʃn/ n Erwartung f

expedient /ɪk'spi:dɪənt/ adj zweckdienlich

expedite /'ekspɪdaɪt/ vt beschleunigen

expedition /ekspɪ'dɪʃn/ n Expedition f

expel /ɪk'spel/ vt (pt/pp **expelled**) ausweisen (**from** aus); (from school) von der Schule verweisen

expenditure /ɪk'spendɪtʃə(r)/ n Ausgaben pl

expense /ɪk'spens/ n Kosten pl; **business ~s** pl Spesen pl; **at my ~** auf meine Kosten

expensive /ɪk'spensɪv/ adj teuer

experience /ɪk'spɪərɪəns/ n Erfahrung f; (event) Erlebnis nt •vt erleben. **~d** adj erfahren

experiment /ɪk'sperɪmənt/ n Versuch m, Experiment nt •/-ment/ vi experimentieren. **~al** adj experimentell

expert /'ekspɜ:t/ adj fachmännisch •n Fachmann m, Experte m

expertise /ekspɜ:'ti:z/ n Sachkenntnis f

expire /ɪk'spaɪə(r)/ vi ablaufen

expiry /ɪk'spaɪərɪ/ n Ablauf m

explain /ɪk'spleɪn/ vt erklären

explana|tion /eksplə'neɪʃn/ n Erklärung f. **~tory** adj erklärend

explicit /ɪk'splɪsɪt/ adj deutlich

explode /ɪk'spləʊd/ vi explodieren •vt zur Explosion bringen

exploit[1] /'eksplɔɪt/ n [Helden]tat f

exploit[2] /ɪk'splɔɪt/ vt ausbeuten. **~ation** n Ausbeutung f

exploration /eksplə'reɪʃn/ n Erforschung f

explore /ɪk'splɔ:(r)/ vt erforschen. **~r** n Forschungsreisende(r) m

explos|ion /ɪk'spləʊʒn/ n Explosion f. **~ive** adj explosiv •n Sprengstoff m

export[1] /'ekspɔ:t/ n Export m, Ausfuhr f

export[2] /ɪk'spɔ:t/ vt exportieren, ausführen. **~er** n Exporteur m

expos|e /ɪk'spəʊz/ vt freilegen; (to danger) aussetzen (**to** dat); (reveal) aufdecken; (Phot) belichten. **~ure** n Aussetzung f; (Med) Unterkühlung f; (Phot) Belichtung f; **24 ~ures** 24 Aufnahmen

express /ɪk'spres/ adv (send) per Eilpost •n (train) Schnellzug m •vt ausdrücken; **~ oneself** sich ausdrücken. **~ion** n Ausdruck m. **~ive** adj ausdrucksvoll. **~ly** adv ausdrücklich

expulsion /ɪk'spʌlʃn/ n Ausweisung f; (Sch) Verweisung f von der Schule

exquisite /ek'skwɪzɪt/ adj erlesen

extend /ɪk'stend/ vt verlängern; (stretch out) ausstrecken; (enlarge) vergrößern •vi sich ausdehnen; (table:) sich ausziehen lassen

extension /ɪk'stenʃn/ n Verlängerung f; (to house) Anbau m; (Teleph) Nebenanschluss m

extensive /ɪk'stensɪv/ adj weit; (fig) umfassend. **~ly** adv viel

extent /ɪk'stent/ n Ausdehnung f; (scope) Ausmaß nt, Umfang m; **to a certain ~** in gewissem Maße

exterior /ɪk'stɪərɪə(r)/ adj äußere(r,s) •n **the ~** das Äußere

exterminat|e /ɪk'stɜ:mɪneɪt/ vt ausrotten. **~ion** n Ausrottung f

external /ɪk'stɜ:nl/ adj äußere(r,s); **for ~ use only** (Med) nur äußerlich. **~ly** adv äußerlich

extinct /ɪk'stɪŋkt/ adj ausgestorben; (volcano) erloschen. **~ion** n Aussterben nt

extinguish /ɪk'stɪŋgwɪʃ/ vt löschen. **~er** n Feuerlöscher m

extort /ɪk'stɔ:t/ vt erpressen. **~ion** n Erpressung f

extortionate /ɪk'stɔ:ʃənət/ adj übermäßig hoch

extra /'ekstrə/ adj zusätzlich •adv extra; (especially) besonders •n (Theat) Statist(in) m(f); **~s** pl Nebenkosten pl; (Auto) Extras pl

extract[1] /'ekstrækt/ n Auszug m

extract² /ɪk'strækt/ vt herausziehen; ziehen (tooth)

extraordinary /ɪk'strɔ:dɪnərɪ/ adj, **-ily** adv außerordentlich; (strange) seltsam

extravagan|ce /ɪk'strævəgəns/ n Verschwendung f; **an ~ce** ein Luxus m. **~t** adj verschwenderisch

extrem|e /ɪk'stri:m/ adj äußerste(r,s); (fig) extrem •n Extrem nt; **in the ~e** im höchsten Grade. **~ely** adv äußerst. **~ist** n Extremist m

extricate /'ekstrɪkeɪt/ vt befreien

extrovert /'ekstrəvɜ:t/ n extravertierter Mensch m

exuberant /ɪg'zju:bərənt/ adj überglücklich

exude /ɪg'zju:d/ vt absondern; (fig) ausstrahlen

exult /ɪg'zʌlt/ vi frohlocken

eye /aɪ/ n Auge nt; (of needle) Öhr nt; (for hook) Öse f; **keep an ~ on** aufpassen auf (+ acc) •vt (pt/pp **eyed**, pres p **ey[e]ing**) ansehen

eye: ~ brow n Augenbraue f. **~lash** n Wimper f. **~lid** n Augenlid nt. **~-shadow** n Lidschatten m. **~sight** n Sehkraft f. **~sore** n [!] Schandfleck m. **~witness** n Augenzeuge m

Ff

fable /'feɪbl/ n Fabel f

fabric /'fæbrɪk/ n Stoff m

fabrication /fæbrɪ'keɪʃn/ n Erfindung f

fabulous /'fæbjʊləs/ adj [!] phantastisch

façade /fə'sɑ:d/ n Fassade f

face /feɪs/ n Gesicht nt; (surface) Fläche f; (of clock) Zifferblatt nt; **pull ~s** Gesichter schneiden; **in the ~ of** angesichts (+ gen); **on the ~ of it** allem Anschein nach •vt/i gegenüberstehen (+ dat); **~ north** (house:) nach Norden liegen; **~ the fact that** sich damit abfinden, dass

face: ~-flannel n Waschlappen m. **~less** adj anonym. **~-lift** n Gesichtsstraffung f

facet /'fæsɪt/ n Facette f; (fig) Aspekt m

facetious /fə'si:ʃəs/ adj spöttisch

facial /'feɪʃl/ adj Gesichts-

facile /'fæsaɪl/ adj oberflächlich

facilitate /fə'sɪlɪteɪt/ vt erleichtern

facilit|y /fə'sɪlətɪ/ n Leichtigkeit f; (skill) Gewandtheit f; **~ies** pl Einrichtungen pl

facsimile /fæk'sɪməlɪ/ n Faksimile nt

fact /fækt/ n Tatsache f; **in ~** tatsächlich; (actually) eigentlich

faction /'fækʃn/ n Gruppe f

factor /'fæktə(r)/ n Faktor m

factory /'fæktərɪ/ n Fabrik f

factual /'fæktʃʊəl/ adj sachlich

faculty /'fækəltɪ/ n Fähigkeit f; (Univ) Fakultät f

fad /fæd/ n Fimmel m

fade /feɪd/ vi verblassen; (material:) verbleichen; (sound:) abklingen; (flower:) verwelken.

fag /fæg/ n (chore) Plage f; ([!]: cigarette) Zigarette f

fail /feɪl/ n **without ~** unbedingt •vi (attempt:) scheitern; (grow weak) nachlassen; (break down) versagen; (in exam) durchfallen; **~ to do sth** etw nicht tun •vt nicht bestehen (exam); durchfallen lassen (candidate); (disappoint) enttäuschen

failing /'feɪlɪŋ/ n Fehler m

failure /'feɪljə(r)/ n Misserfolg m; (breakdown) Versagen nt; (person) Versager m

faint /feɪnt/ adj (**-er, -est**) schwach; **I feel ~** mir ist schwach •n Ohnmacht f •vi ohnmächtig werden. **~ness** n Schwäche f

fair[1] /feə(r)/ n Jahrmarkt m; (Comm) Messe f

f

fair[2] adj (**-er, -est**) (hair) blond; (skin) hell; (weather) heiter; (just) gerecht, fair; (quite good) ziemlich gut; (Sch) genügend; **a ~ amount** ziemlich viel •adv **play ~** fair sein. **~ly** adv gerecht; (rather) ziemlich. **~ness** n Blondheit f; Helle f; Gerechtigkeit f; (Sport) Fairness f

fairy /'feərɪ/ n Elfe f; **good/wicked ~** gute/böse Fee f. **~ story, ~-tale** n Märchen nt

faith /feɪθ/ n Glaube m; (trust) Vertrauen nt (**in** zu)

faithful /'feɪθfl/ adj treu; (exact) genau; **Yours ~ly** Hochachtungsvoll. **~ness** n Treue f; Genauigkeit f

fake /feɪk/ adj falsch •n Fälschung f; (person) Schwindler m •vt fälschen; (pretend) vortäuschen

falcon /'fɔ:lkən/ n Falke m

fall /fɔ:l/ n Fall m; (heavy) Sturz m; (in prices) Fallen nt; (Amer: autumn) Herbst m; **have a ~** fallen •vi (pt **fell**, pp **fallen**) fallen; (heavily) stürzen; (night:) anbrechen; **~ in love** sich verlieben; **~ back on** zurückgreifen auf (+ acc); **~ for s.o.** [!] sich in jdn verlieben; **~ for sth** [!] auf etw (acc) hereinfallen. **~ about** vi (with laughter) sich [vor Lachen] kringeln. **~ down** vi umfallen; (thing:) herunterfallen; (building:) einstürzen. **~ in** vi hineinfallen; (collapse) einfallen; (Mil) antreten; **~ in with** sich anschließen (+ dat). **~ off** vi herunterfallen; (diminish) abnehmen. **~ out** vi herausfallen; (hair:) ausfallen; (quarrel) sich überwerfen. **~ over** vi hinfallen. **~ through** vi durchfallen; (plan:) ins Wasser fallen

fallacy /'fæləsɪ/ n Irrtum m

fallible /'fæləbl/ adj fehlbar

'fall-out n [radioaktiver] Niederschlag m

false /fɔ:ls/ adj falsch; (artificial) künstlich. **~hood** n Unwahrheit f. **~ly** adv falsch

false 'teeth npl [künstliches] Gebiss nt

falsify /'fɔ:lsɪfaɪ/ vt (pt/pp **-ied**) fälschen

falter /'fɔ:ltə(r)/ vi zögern

fame /feɪm/ n Ruhm m.

familiar /fə'mɪljə(r)/ adj vertraut; (known) bekannt; **too ~** familiär. **~ity** n Vertrautheit f. **~ize** vt vertraut machen (**with** mit)

family /'fæməlɪ/ n Familie f

family: ~ 'doctor n Hausarzt m. **~ 'life** n Familienleben nt. **~ 'planning** n Familienplanung f. **~ 'tree** n Stammbaum m

famine /'fæmɪn/ n Hungersnot f

famished /'fæmɪʃt/ adj sehr hungrig

famous /'feɪməs/ adj berühmt

fan[1] /fæn/ n Fächer m; (Techn) Ventilator m

fan[2] n (admirer) Fan m

fanatic /fə'nætɪk/ n Fanatiker m. **~al** adj fanatisch. **~ism** n Fanatismus m

fanciful /'fænsɪfl/ adj phantastisch; (imaginative) phantasiereich

fancy /'fænsɪ/ n Phantasie f; **I have taken a real ~ to him** er hat es mir angetan •adj ausgefallen •vt (believe) meinen; (imagine) sich (dat) einbilden; ([!]: want) Lust haben auf (+ acc); **~ that!** stell dir vor! (really) tatsächlich! **~ 'dress** n Kostüm nt

fanfare /'fænfeə(r)/ n Fanfare f

fang /fæŋ/ n Fangzahn m

'fan heater n Heizlüfter m

fantas|ize /'fæntəsaɪz/ vi phantasieren. **~tic** adj phantastisch. **~y** n Phantasie f

far /fɑ:(r)/ adv weit; (much) viel; **by**

~ bei weitem; ~ **away** weit weg; **as ~ as I know** soviel ich weiß; **as ~ as the church** bis zur Kirche •adj **at the ~ end** am anderen Ende; **the F~ East** der Ferne Osten

farc|e /fɑːs/ n Farce f. **~ical** adj lächerlich

fare /feə(r)/ n Fahrpreis m; (money) Fahrgeld nt; (food) Kost f; **air ~** Flugpreis m

farewell /feəˈwel/ int (literary) lebe wohl! •n Lebewohl nt

far-ˈfetched adj weit hergeholt

farm /fɑːm/ n Bauernhof m •vi Landwirtschaft betreiben •vt bewirtschaften (land). **~er** n Landwirt m

farm: ~house n Bauernhaus nt. **~ing** n Landwirtschaft f. **~yard** n Hof m

far: ~-ˈreaching adj weit reichend. **~-ˈsighted** adj (fig) umsichtig; (Amer: long-sighted) weitsichtig

farther /ˈfɑːðə(r)/ adv weiter; **~ off** weiter entfernt

fascinat|e /ˈfæsɪneɪt/ vt faszinieren. **~ing** adj faszinierend. **~ion** n Faszination f

fascis|m /ˈfæʃɪzm/ n Faschismus m. **~t** n Faschist m •adj faschistisch

fashion /ˈfæʃn/ n Mode f; (manner) Art f. **~able** adj, **-bly** adv modisch

fast /fɑːst/ adj & adv (**-er, -est**) schnell; (firm) fest; (colour) waschecht; **be ~** (clock:) vorgehen; **be ~ asleep** fest schlafen

fasten /ˈfɑːsn/ vt zumachen; (fix) befestigen (**to** an + dat). **~er** n, **~ing** n Verschluss m

fastidious /fəˈstɪdɪəs/ adj wählerisch; (particular) penibel

fat /fæt/ adj (**fatter, fattest**) dick; (meat) fett •n Fett nt

fatal /ˈfeɪtl/ adj tödlich; (error) verhängnisvoll. **~ity** n Todesopfer nt. **~ly** adv tödlich

fate /feɪt/ n Schicksal nt. **~ful** adj verhängnisvoll

ˈfat-head n [!] Dummkopf m

father /ˈfɒːðə(r)/ n Vater m; **F ~ Christmas** der Weihnachtsmann •vt zeugen

father: ~hood n Vaterschaft f. **~-in-law** n (pl **~s-in-law**) Schwiegervater m. **~ly** adj väterlich

fathom /ˈfæðəm/ n (Naut) Faden m •vt verstehen

fatigue /fəˈtiːg/ n Ermüdung f

fatten /ˈfætn/ vt mästen (animal)

fatty /ˈfætɪ/ adj fett; (foods) fetthaltig

fatuous /ˈfætjʊəs/ adj albern

fault /fɔːlt/ n Fehler m; (Techn) Defekt m; (Geology) Verwerfung f; **at ~** im Unrecht; **find ~ with** etwas auszusetzen haben an (+ dat); **it's your ~** du bist schuld. **~less** adj fehlerfrei

faulty /ˈfɔːltɪ/ adj fehlerhaft

favour /ˈfeɪvə(r)/ n Gunst f; **I am in ~** ich bin dafür; **do s.o. a ~** jdm einen Gefallen tun •vt begünstigen; (prefer) bevorzugen. **~able** adj, **-bly** adv günstig; (reply) positiv

favourit|e /ˈfeɪvərɪt/ adj Lieblings- •n Liebling m; (Sport) Favorit(in) m(f). **~ism** n Bevorzugung f

fawn /fɔːn/ adj rehbraun •n Hirschkalb nt

fax /fæks/ n Fax nt •vt faxen (**s.o.** jdm). **~ machine** n Faxgerät nt

fear /fɪə(r)/ n Furcht f, Angst f (**of** vor + dat) •vt/i fürchten

fear|ful /ˈfɪəfl/ adj besorgt; (awful) furchtbar. **~less** adj furchtlos

feas|ibility /fiːzəˈbɪlətɪ/ n Durchführbarkeit f. **~ible** adj durchführbar; (possible) möglich

feast /fiːst/ n Festmahl nt; (Relig) Fest nt •vi **~ [on]** schmausen

feat /fiːt/ n Leistung f

feather /ˈfeðə(r)/ n Feder f

feature /ˈfiːtʃə(r)/ n Gesichtszug m; (quality) Merkmal nt; (article) Feature nt •vt darstellen

February /ˈfebrʊərɪ/ n Februar m

fed /fed/ see **feed** •adj **be ~ up** [!] die Nase voll haben (**with** von)

federal /ˈfedərəl/ adj Bundes-

federation /fedəˈreɪʃn/ n Föderation f

fee /fiː/ n Gebühr f; (professional) Honorar nt

feeble /ˈfiːbl/ adj (**-r, -st**), **-bly** adv schwach

f

feed /fiːd/ n Futter nt; (for baby) Essen nt •v (pt/pp **fed**) •vt füttern; (support) ernähren; (into machine) eingeben; speisen (computer) •vi sich ernähren (**on** von)

ˈ**feedback** n Feedback nt

feel /fiːl/ v (pt/pp **felt**) •vt fühlen; (experience) empfinden; (think) meinen •vi sich fühlen; **~ soft/hard** sich weich/hart anfühlen; **I ~ hot/ill** mir ist heiß/schlecht; **~ing** n Gefühl nt; **no hard ~ings** nichts für ungut

feet /fiːt/ see **foot**

feline /ˈfiːlaɪn/ adj Katzen-; (catlike) katzenartig

fell[1] /fel/ vt fällen

fell[2] see **fall**

fellow /ˈfeləʊ/ n ([!]: man) Kerl m

fellow: ~-ˈcountryman n Landsmann m. **~ men** pl Mitmenschen pl

felt[1] /felt/ see **feel**

felt[2] n Filz m. **~[-tipped] ˈpen** n Filzstift m

female /ˈfiːmeɪl/ adj weiblich •nt Weibchen nt; (pej: woman) Weib nt

femin|ine /ˈfemɪnɪn/ adj weiblich •n (Gram) Femininum nt. **~inity** n Weiblichkeit f. **~ist** adj feministisch •n Feminist(in) m(f)

fenc|e /fens/ n Zaun m; ([!]: person) Hehler m •vi (Sport) fechten •vt **~e in** einzäunen. **~er** n Fechter m. **~ing** n Zaun m; (Sport) Fechten nt

fender /ˈfendə(r)/ n Kaminvorsetzer m; (Naut) Fender m; (Amer: wing) Kotflügel m

ferment /fəˈment/ vi gären •vt gären lassen

fern /fɜːn/ n Farn m

feroc|ious /fəˈrəʊʃəs/ adj wild. **~ity** n Wildheit f

ferry /ˈferɪ/ n Fähre f

fertil|e /ˈfɜːtaɪl/ adj fruchtbar. **~ity** n Fruchtbarkeit f

fertilize /ˈfɜːtəlaɪz/ vt befruchten; düngen (land). **~r** n Dünger m

fervent /ˈfɜːvənt/ adj leidenschaftlich

fervour /ˈfɜːvə(r)/ n Leidenschaft f

festival /ˈfestɪvl/ n Fest nt; (Mus, Theat) Festspiele pl

festiv|e /ˈfestɪv/ adj festlich. **~ities** npl Feierlichkeiten pl

festoon /feˈstuːn/ vt behängen (**with** mit)

fetch /fetʃ/ vt holen; (collect) abholen; (be sold for) einbringen

fetching /ˈfetʃɪŋ/ adj anziehend

fête /feɪt/ n Fest nt •vt feiern

feud /fjuːd/ n Fehde f

feudal /ˈfjuːdl/ adj Feudal-

fever /ˈfiːvə(r)/ n Fieber nt. **~ish** adj fiebrig; (fig) fieberhaft

few /fjuː/ adj (**-er, -est**) wenige; **every ~ days** alle paar Tage •n **a ~** ein paar; **quite a ~** ziemlich viele

fiancé /fɪˈɒnseɪ/ n Verlobte(r) m. **fiancée** n Verlobte f

fiasco /fɪˈæskəʊ/ n Fiasko nt

fib /fɪb/ n kleine Lüge

fibre /ˈfaɪbə(r)/ n Faser f

fiction /ˈfɪkʃn/ n Erfindung f; **[works of] ~** Erzählungsliteratur f. **~al** adj erfunden

fictitious /fɪkˈtɪʃəs/ adj [frei] erfunden

fiddle /ˈfɪdl/ n [!] Geige f; (cheating) Schwindel m •vi herumspielen (**with** mit) •vt [!] frisieren (accounts)

fiddly /ˈfɪdlɪ/ adj knifflig

fidelity /fɪˈdelətɪ/ n Treue f

fidget /ˈfɪdʒɪt/ vi zappeln. **~y** adj zappelig

field /fiːld/ n Feld nt; (meadow) Wiese f; (subject) Gebiet nt

field: ~ events npl Sprung- und Wurfdisziplinen pl. **F~ 'Marshal** n Feldmarschall m

fiendish /ˈfiːndɪʃ/ adj teuflisch

fierce /fɪəs/ adj (**-r, -st**) wild; (fig) heftig. **~ness** n Wildheit f; (fig) Heftigkeit f

fiery /ˈfaɪərɪ/ adj feurig

fifteen /fɪfˈtiːn/ adj fünfzehn •n Fünfzehn f. **~th** adj fünfzehnte(r,s)

fifth /fɪfθ/ adj fünfte(r,s)

fiftieth /ˈfɪftɪɪθ/ adj fünfzigste(r,s)

fifty /ˈfɪftɪ/ adj fünfzig

fig /fɪg/ n Feige f

fight /faɪt/ n Kampf m; (brawl) Schlägerei f; (between children, dogs) Rauferei f •v (pt/pp **fought**) •vt kämpfen gegen; (fig) bekämpfen •vi kämpfen; (brawl) sich schlagen; (children, dogs:) sich raufen. **~er** n Kämpfer m; (Aviat) Jagdflugzeug nt. **~ing** n Kampf m

figurative /ˈfɪgjərətɪv/ adj bildlich, übertragen

figure /ˈfɪgə(r)/ n (digit) Ziffer f; (number) Zahl f; (sum) Summe f; (carving, sculpture, woman's) Figur f; (form) Gestalt f; (illustration) Abbildung f; **good at ~s** gut im Rechnen •vi (appear) erscheinen •vt (Amer: think) glauben

filch /fɪltʃ/ vt [!] klauen

file[1] /faɪl/ n Akte f; (for documents) [Akten]ordner m •vt ablegen (documents); (Jur) einreichen

file[2] n (line) Reihe f; **in single ~** im Gänsemarsch

file[3] n (Techn) Feile f •vt feilen

fill /fɪl/ n **eat one's ~** sich satt essen •vt füllen; plombieren (tooth) •vi sich füllen. **~ in** vt auffüllen; ausfüllen (form). **~ out** vt ausfüllen (form). **~ up** vi sich füllen •vt vollfüllen; (Auto) volltanken; ausfüllen (questionnaire)

fillet /ˈfɪlɪt/ n Filet nt •vt (pt/pp **filleted**) entgräten

filling /ˈfɪlɪŋ/ n Füllung f; (of tooth) Plombe f. **~ station** n Tankstelle f

filly /ˈfɪlɪ/ n junge Stute f

film /fɪlm/ n Film m •vt/i filmen; verfilmen (book). **~ star** n Filmstar m

filter /ˈfɪltə(r)/ n Filter m •vt filtern

filth /fɪlθ/ n Dreck m. **~y** adj dreckig

fin /fɪn/ n Flosse f

final /ˈfaɪnl/ adj letzte(r,s); (conclusive) endgültig •n (Sport) Endspiel nt; **~s** pl (Univ) Abschlussprüfung f

finale /fɪˈnɑːlɪ/ n Finale nt

final|ist /ˈfaɪnəlɪst/ n Finalist(in) m(f)

final|ize /ˈfaɪnəlaɪz/ vt endgültig festlegen. **~ly** adv schließlich

finance /faɪˈnæns/ n Finanz f •vt finanzieren

financial /faɪˈnænʃl/ adj finanziell

find /faɪnd/ n Fund m •vt (pt/pp **found**) finden; (establish) feststellen; **go and ~** holen; **try to ~** suchen. **~ out** vt herausfinden; (learn) erfahren •vi (enquire) sich erkundigen

fine[1] /faɪn/ n Geldstrafe f •vt zu einer Geldstrafe verurteilen

fine[2] adj (**-r, -st**), **-ly** adv fein; (weather) schön; **he's ~** es geht ihm gut •adv gut; **cut it ~** [!] sich (dat) wenig Zeit lassen

finesse /fɪˈnes/ n Gewandtheit f

finger /ˈfɪŋgə(r)/ n Finger m •vt anfassen

finger: ~-nail n Fingernagel m. **~print** n Fingerabdruck m. **~tip** n Fingerspitze f

finicky /ˈfɪnɪkɪ/ adj knifflig; (choosy) wählerisch

finish /ˈfɪnɪʃ/ n Schluss m; (Sport) Finish nt; (line) Ziel nt; (of product) Ausführung f •vt beenden; (use up) aufbrauchen; **~ one's drink** austrinken; **~ reading** zu Ende lesen •vi fertig werden;

f

(performance:) zu Ende sein; (runner:) durchs Ziel gehen

Finland /'fɪnlənd/ n Finnland nt

Finn /fɪn/ n Finne m/ Finnin f. **~ish** adj finnisch

fir /fɜ:(r)/ n Tanne f

fire /'faɪə(r)/ n Feuer nt; (forest, house) Brand m; **be on ~** brennen; **catch ~** Feuer fangen; **set ~ to** anzünden; (arsonist:) in Brand stecken; **under ~** unter Beschuss • vt brennen (pottery); abfeuern (shot); schießen mit (gun); (!: dismiss) feuern • vi schießen (**at** auf + acc); (engine:) anspringen

fire: ~ alarm n Feuermelder m. **~ brigade** n Feuerwehr f. **~-engine** n Löschfahrzeug nt. **~ extinguisher** n Feuerlöscher m. **~man** n Feuerwehrmann m. **~place** n Kamin m. **~side** n **by** or **at the ~side** am Kamin. **~ station** n Feuerwache f. **~wood** n Brennholz nt. **~work** n Feuerwerkskörper m; **~works** pl (display) Feuerwerk nt

firm[1] /fɜ:m/ n Firma f

firm[2] adj (**-er, -est**) fest; (resolute) entschlossen; (strict) streng

first /fɜ:st/ adj & n erste(r,s); **at ~** zuerst; **at ~ sight** auf den ersten Blick; **from the ~** von Anfang an • adv zuerst; (firstly) erstens

first: ~ 'aid n erste Hilfe. **~-'aid kit** n Verbandkasten m. **~-class** adj erstklassig; (Rail) erster Klasse • /-'-/ adv (travel) erster Klasse. **~ 'floor** n erster Stock; (Amer: ground floor) Erdgeschoss nt. **~ly** adv erstens. **~name** n Vorname m. **~-rate** adj erstklassig

fish /fɪʃ/ n Fisch m • vt/i fischen; (with rod) angeln

fish: ~bone n Gräte f. **~erman** n Fischer m. **~ 'finger** n Fischstäbchen nt

fishing /'fɪʃɪŋ/ n Fischerei f. **~ boat** n Fischerboot nt. **~-rod** n Angel[rute] f

fish: ~monger /-mʌŋgə(r)/ n Fischhändler m. **~y** adj Fisch-; (!: suspicious) verdächtig

fission /'fɪʃn/ n (Phys) Spaltung f

fist /fɪst/ n Faust f

fit[1] /fɪt/ n (attack) Anfall m

fit[2] adj (**fitter, fittest**) (suitable) geeignet; (healthy) gesund; (Sport) fit; **~ to eat** essbar

fit[3] n (of clothes) Sitz m; **be a good ~** gut passen • v (pt/pp **fitted**) • vi (be the right size) passen • vt anbringen (**to** an + dat); (install) einbauen; **~ with** versehen mit. **~ in** vi hineinpassen; (adapt) sich einfügen (**with** in + acc) • vt (accommodate) unterbringen

fit|ness n Eignung f; **[physical] ~ness** Gesundheit f; (Sport) Fitness f. **~ted** adj eingebaut; (garment) tailliert

fitted: ~ 'carpet n Teppichboden m. **~ 'kitchen** n Einbauküche f. **~ 'sheet** n Spannlaken nt

fitting /'fɪtɪŋ/ adj passend • n (of clothes) Anprobe f; (of shoes) Weite f; (Techn) Zubehörteil nt; **~s** pl Zubehör nt

five /faɪv/ adj fünf • n Fünf f. **~r** n Fünfpfundschein m

fix /fɪks/ n (sl: drugs) Fix m; **be in a ~** ! in der Klemme sitzen • vt befestigen (**to** an + dat); (arrange) festlegen; (repair) reparieren; (Phot) fixieren; **~ a meal** Essen machen

fixed /'fɪkst/ adj fest

fixture /'fɪkstʃə(r)/ n (Sport) Veranstaltung f; **~s and fittings** zu einer Wohnung gehörende Einrichtungen pl

fizz /fɪz/ vi sprudeln

fizzle /'fɪzl/ vi **~ out** verpuffen

fizzy /'fɪzɪ/ adj sprudelnd. **~ drink** n Brause[limonade] f

flabbergasted /'flæbəgɑ:stɪd/ adj **be ~** platt sein !

flabby /'flæbɪ/ adj schlaff

flag /flæg/ n Fahne f; (Naut) Flagge f

'flag-pole n Fahnenstange f

flagrant /'fleɪgrənt/ adj flagrant

'flagstone n [Pflaster]platte f

flair /fleə(r)/ n Begabung f

flake /fleɪk/ n Flocke f •vi ~ **[off]** abblättern

flamboyant /flæm'bɔɪənt/ adj extravagant

flame /fleɪm/ n Flamme f

flan /flæn/ n **[fruit]** ~ Obsttorte f

flank /flæŋk/ n Flanke f

flannel /'flænl/ n Flanell m; (for washing) Waschlappen m

flap /flæp/ n Klappe f; **in a** ~ [!] aufgeregt •v (pt/pp **flapped**) vi flattern; [!] sich aufregen •vt ~ **its wings** mit den Flügeln schlagen

flare /fleə(r)/ n Leuchtsignal nt. •vi ~ **up** auflodern; ([!]: get angry) aufbrausen

flash /flæʃ/ n Blitz m; **in a** ~ [!] im Nu •vi blitzen; (repeatedly) blinken; ~ **past** vorbeirasen

flash: ~**back** n Rückblende f. ~**er** n (Auto) Blinker m. ~**light** n (Phot) Blitzlicht nt; (Amer: torch) Taschenlampe f. ~**y** adj auffällig

flask /flɑːsk/ n Flasche f

flat /flæt/ adj (**flatter, flattest**) flach; (surface) eben; (refusal) glatt; (beer) schal; (battery) verbraucht/ (Auto) leer; (tyre) platt; (Mus) **A** ~ As nt; **B** ~ B nt •n Wohnung f; ([!]: puncture) Reifenpanne f

flat: ~**ly** adv (refuse) glatt. ~ **rate** n Einheitspreis m

flatten /'flætn/ vt platt drücken

flatter /'flætə(r)/ vt schmeicheln (+ dat). ~**y** n Schmeichelei f

flat 'tyre n Reifenpanne f

flaunt /flɔːnt/ vt prunken mit

flautist /'flɔːtɪst/ n Flötist(in) m(f)

flavour /'fleɪvə(r)/ n Geschmack m •vt abschmecken. ~**ing** n Aroma nt

flaw /flɔː/ n Fehler m. ~**less** adj tadellos; (complexion) makellos

flea /fliː/ n Floh m

fleck /flek/ n Tupfen m

fled /fled/ see **flee**

flee /fliː/ v (pt/pp **fled**) •vi fliehen (**from** vor + dat) •vt flüchten aus

fleec|e /fliːs/ n Vlies nt •vt [!] schröpfen

fleet /fliːt/ n Flotte f; (of cars) Wagenpark m

fleeting /'fliːtɪŋ/ adj flüchtig

Flemish /'flemɪʃ/ adj flämisch

flesh /fleʃ/ n Fleisch nt

flew /fluː/ see **fly**[2]

flex[1] /fleks/ vt anspannen (muscle)

flex[2] n (Electr) Schnur f

flexib|ility /fleksə'bɪlətɪ/ n Biegsamkeit f; (fig) Flexibilität f. ~**le** adj biegsam; (fig) flexibel

flick /flɪk/ vt schnippen

flicker /'flɪkə(r)/ vi flackern

flier /'flaɪə(r)/ n = **flyer**

flight[1] /flaɪt/ n (fleeing) Flucht f

flight[2] n (flying) Flug m; ~ **of stairs** Treppe f

'flight recorder n Flugschreiber m

flimsy /'flɪmzɪ/ adj dünn; (excuse) fadenscheinig

flinch /flɪntʃ/ vi zurückzucken

fling /flɪŋ/ vt (pt/pp **flung**) schleudern

flint /flɪnt/ n Feuerstein m

flip /flɪp/ vt/i schnippen; ~ **through** durchblättern

flippant /'flɪpənt/ adj leichtfertig

flirt /flɜːt/ n kokette Frau f •vi flirten

flirtat|ion /flɜː'teɪʃn/ n Flirt m. ~**ious** adj kokett

flit /flɪt/ vi (pt/pp **flitted**) flattern

float /fləʊt/ n Schwimmer m; (in procession) Festwagen m; (money) Wechselgeld nt •vi (thing:) schwimmen; (person:) sich treiben lassen; (in air) schweben

flock /flɒk/ n Herde f; (of birds) Schwarm m •vi strömen

flog /flɒg/ vt (pt/pp **flogged**) auspeitschen; ([!]: sell) verkloppen

flood /flʌd/ n Überschwemmung f; (fig) Flut f •vt überschwemmen

'floodlight n Flutlicht nt •vt (pt/pp **floodlit**) anstrahlen

f

floor /flɔ:(r)/ n Fußboden m; (storey) Stock m

floor: ~ board n Dielenbrett nt. **~-polish** n Bohnerwachs nt. **~ show** n Kabarettvorstellung f

flop /flɒp/ n [!] (failure) Reinfall m; (Theat) Durchfall m •vi (pt/pp **flopped**) [!] (fail) durchfallen

floppy /'flɒpɪ/ adj schlapp. **~ 'disc** n Diskette f

floral /'flɔ:rl/ adj Blumen-

florid /'flɒrɪd/ adj (complexion) gerötet; (style) blumig

florist /'flɒrɪst/ n Blumenhändler(in) m(f)

flounder /'flaʊndə(r)/ vi zappeln

flour /'flaʊə(r)/ n Mehl nt

flourish /'flʌrɪʃ/ n große Geste f; (scroll) Schnörkel m •vi gedeihen; (fig) blühen •vt schwenken

flout /flaʊt/ vt missachten

flow /fləʊ/ n Fluss m; (of traffic, blood) Strom m •vi fließen

flower /'flaʊə(r)/ n Blume f •vi blühen

flower: ~-bed n Blumenbeet nt. **~pot** n Blumentopf m. **~y** adj blumig

flown /fləʊn/ see **fly**[2]

flu /flu:/ n [!] Grippe f

fluctuat|e /'flʌktjʊeɪt/ vi schwanken. **~ion** n Schwankung f

fluent /'flu:ənt/ adj fließend

fluff /flʌf/ n Fusseln pl; (down) Flaum m. **~y** adj flauschig

fluid /'flu:ɪd/ adj flüssig, (fig) veränderlich •n Flüssigkeit f

fluke /flu:k/ n [glücklicher] Zufall m

flung /flʌŋ/ see **fling**

fluorescent /flʊə'resnt/ adj fluoreszierend

fluoride /'flʊəraɪd/ n Fluor nt

flush /flʌʃ/ n (blush) Erröten nt •vi rot werden •vt spülen •adj in einer Ebene (**with** mit); ([!]: affluent) gut bei Kasse

flustered /'flʌstəd/ adj nervös

flute /flu:t/ n Flöte f

flutter /'flʌtə(r)/ n Flattern nt •vi flattern

fly[1] /flaɪ/ n (pl **flies**) Fliege f

fly[2] v (pt **flew**, pp **flown**) •vi fliegen; (flag:) wehen; (rush) sausen •vt fliegen; führen (flag)

fly[3] n, & **flies** pl (on trousers) Hosenschlitz m

flyer /'flaɪə(r)/ n Flieger(in) m(f); (leaflet) Flugblatt nt

foal /fəʊl/ n Fohlen nt

foam /fəʊm/ n Schaum m; (synthetic) Schaumstoff m •vi schäumen

fob /fɒb/ vt (pt/pp **fobbed**) **~ sth off** etw andrehen (**on s.o.** jdm); **~ s.o. off** jdn abspeisen (**with** mit)

focal /'fəʊkl/ n Brenn-

focus /'fəʊkəs/ n Brennpunkt m; **in ~** scharf eingestellt •v (pt/pp **focused** or **focussed**) •vt einstellen (**on** auf + acc) •vi (fig) sich konzentrieren (**on** auf + acc)

fog /fɒg/ n Nebel m

foggy /'fɒgɪ/ adj (**foggier, foggiest**) neblig

'fog-horn n Nebelhorn nt

foible /'fɔɪbl/ n Eigenart f

foil[1] /fɔɪl/ n Folie f; (Culin) Alufolie f

foil[2] vt (thwart) vereiteln

foil[3] n (Fencing) Florett nt

fold n Falte f; (in paper) Kniff m •vt falten; **~ one's arms** die Arme verschränken •vi sich falten lassen; (fail) eingehen. **~ up** vt zusammenfalten; zusammenklappen (chair) •vi sich zusammenfalten/-klappen lassen; [!] (business:) eingehen

fold|er /'fəʊldə(r)/ n Mappe f. **~ing** adj Klapp-

foliage /'fəʊlɪɪdʒ/ n Blätter pl; (of tree) Laub nt

folk /fəʊk/ npl Leute pl

folk: ~-dance n Volkstanz m. **~-song** n Volkslied nt

follow /'fɒləʊ/ vt/i folgen (+ dat); (pursue) verfolgen; (in vehicle) nachfahren (+ dat). **~ up** vt nachgehen (+ dat)

follow|er /ˈfɒləʊə(r)/ n Anhänger(in) m(f). **~ing** adj folgend • n Folgende(s) nt; (supporters) Anhängerschaft f • prep im Anschluss an (+ acc)

folly /ˈfɒlɪ/ n Torheit f

fond /fɒnd/ adj (**-er, -est**) liebevoll; **be ~ of** gern haben; gern essen (food)

fondle /ˈfɒndl/ vt liebkosen

fondness /ˈfɒndnɪs/ n Liebe f (**for** zu)

food /fu:d/ n Essen nt; (for animals) Futter nt; (groceries) Lebensmittel pl

food poisoning n Lebensmittelvergiftung f

fool[1] /fu:l/ n (Culin) Fruchtcreme f

fool[2] n Narr m; **make a ~ of oneself** sich lächerlich machen • vt hereinlegen • vi **~ around** herumalbern

ˈfool|hardy adj tollkühn. **~ish** adj dumm. **~ishness** n Dummheit f. **~proof** adj narrensicher

foot /fʊt/ n (pl **feet**) Fuß m; (measure) Fuß m (30,48 cm); (of bed) Fußende nt; **on ~** zu Fuß; **on one's feet** auf den Beinen; **put one's ~ in it** ! ins Fettnäpfchen treten

foot: ~-and-ˈmouth [disease] n Maul- und Klauenseuche f. **~ball** n Fußball m. **~baller** n Fußballspieler m. **~ball pools** npl Fußballtoto nt. **~-bridge** n Fußgängerbrücke f. **~hills** npl Vorgebirge nt. **~hold** n Halt m. **~ing** n Halt m. **~lights** npl Rampenlicht nt. **~note** n Fußnote f. **~path** n Fußweg m. **~print** n Fußabdruck m. **~step** n Schritt m; **follow in s.o.'s ~steps** (fig) in jds Fußstapfen treten. **~wear** n Schuhwerk nt

for /fɔ:(r)/, unstressed /fə(r)/

• preposition

····➤ (on behalf of; in place of; in favour of) für (+ acc). **I did it for you** ich habe es für dich gemacht. **I work for him/for a bank** ich arbeite für ihn/für eine Bank. **be for doing sth** dafür sein, etw zu tun. **cheque/bill for £5** Scheck/Rechnung über 5 Pfund. **for nothing** umsonst. **what have you got for a cold?** was haben Sie gegen Erkältungen?

····➤ (expressing reason) wegen (+ gen); (with emotion) aus. **famous for these wines** berühmt wegen dieser Weine od für diese Weine. **he was sentenced to death for murder** er wurde wegen Mordes zum Tode verurteilt. **were it not for you/your help** ohne dich/deine Hilfe. **for fear/love of** aus Angst vor (+ dat)/aus Liebe zu (+ dat)

····➤ (expressing purpose) (with action, meal) zu (+ dat); (with object) für (+ acc). **it's for washing the car** es ist zum Autowaschen. **we met for a discussion** wir trafen uns zu einer Besprechung. **for pleasure** zum Vergnügen. **meat for lunch** Fleisch zum Mittagessen. **what is that for?** wofür od wozu ist das? **a dish for nuts** eine Schale für Nüsse

····➤ (expressing direction) nach (+ dat); (less precise) in Richtung. **the train for Oxford** der Zug nach Oxford. **they were heading** or **making for London** sie fuhren in Richtung London

····➤ (expressing time) (completed process) ... lang; (continuing process) seit (+ dat). **I lived here for two years** ich habe zwei Jahre [lang] hier gewohnt. **I have been living here for two years** ich wohne hier seit zwei Jahren. **we are staying for a week** wir werden eine Woche bleiben

····➤ (expressing difficulty, impossibility, embarrassment etc.) + dat. **it's impossible/inconvenient for her** es ist ihr unmöglich/ungelegen. **it was embarrassing for our teacher** unserem Lehrer war es peinlich

• conjunction

····➤ denn. **he's not coming for he has no money** er kommt nicht mit, denn er hat kein Geld

forbade /fəˈbæd/ see **forbid**

f

forbid /fəˈbɪd/ vt (pt **forbade**, pp **forbidden**) verbieten (**s.o.** jdm). **~ding** adj bedrohlich; (stern) streng

force /fɔːs/ n Kraft f; (of blow) Wucht f; (violence) Gewalt f; **in ~** gültig; (in large numbers) in großer Zahl; **come into ~** in Kraft treten; **the ~s** pl die Streitkräfte pl •vt zwingen; (break open) aufbrechen

forced /fɔːst/ adj gezwungen; **~ landing** Notlandung f

force: ~-ˈfeed vt (pt/pp **-fed**) zwangsernähren. **~ful** adj energisch

forceps /ˈfɔːseps/ n inv Zange f

forcible /ˈfɔːsəbl/ adj gewaltsam

ford /fɔːd/ n Furt f •vt durchwaten; (in vehicle) durchfahren

fore /fɔː(r)/ adj vordere(r,s)

fore: ~arm n Unterarm m. **~cast** n Voraussage f; (for weather) Vorhersage f •vt (pt/pp **~cast**) voraussagen, vorhersagen. **~finger** n Zeigefinger m. **~gone** adj **be a ~gone conclusion** von vornherein feststehen. **~ground** n Vordergrund m. **~head** /ˈfɒrɪd/ n Stirn f. **~hand** n Vorhand f

foreign /ˈfɒrən/ adj ausländisch; (country) fremd; **he is ~** er ist Ausländer. **~ currency** n Devisen pl. **~er** n Ausländer(in) m(f). **~ language** n Fremdsprache f

Foreign: ~ Office n ≈ Außenministerium nt. **~ ˈSecretary** n ≈ Außenminister m

fore: ~leg n Vorderbein nt. **~man** n Vorarbeiter m. **~most** adj führend •adv **first and ~most** zuallererst. **~name** n Vorname m. **~runner** n Vorläufer m

foreˈsee vt (pt **-saw**, pp **-seen**) voraussehen, vorhersehen. **~able** adj **in the ~able future** in absehbarer Zeit

ˈforesight n Weitblick m

forest /ˈfɒrɪst/ n Wald m. **~er** n Förster m

forestry /ˈfɒrɪstrɪ/ n Forstwirtschaft f

ˈforetaste n Vorgeschmack m

forever /fəˈrevə(r)/ adv für immer

foreˈwarn vt vorher warnen

foreword /ˈfɔːwɜːd/ n Vorwort nt

forfeit /ˈfɔːfɪt/ n (in game) Pfand nt •vt verwirken

forgave /fəˈgeɪv/ see **forgive**

forge /fɔːdʒ/ n Schmiede f •vt schmieden; (counterfeit) fälschen. **~r** n Fälscher m. **~ry** n Fälschung f

forget /fəˈget/ vt/i (pt **-got**, pp **-gotten**) vergessen; verlernen (language, skill). **~ful** adj vergesslich. **~fulness** n Vergesslichkeit f. **~-me-not** n Vergissmeinnicht nt

forgive /fəˈgɪv/ vt (pt **-gave**, pp **-given**) **~ s.o. for sth** jdm etw vergeben od verzeihen

forgot(ten) /fəˈgɒt(n)/ see **forget**

fork /fɔːk/ n Gabel f; (in road) Gabelung f •vi (road:) sich gabeln; **~ right** rechts abzweigen

fork-lift ˈtruck n Gabelstapler m

forlorn /fəˈlɔːn/ adj verlassen; (hope) schwach

form /fɔːm/ n Form f; (document) Formular nt; (bench) Bank f; (Sch) Klasse f •vt formen (**into** zu); (create) bilden •vi sich bilden; (idea:) Gestalt annehmen

formal /ˈfɔːml/ adj formell, förmlich. **~ity** n Förmlichkeit f; (requirement) Formalität f

format /ˈfɔːmæt/ n Format nt • vt formatieren

formation /fɔːˈmeɪʃn/ n Formation f

former /ˈfɔmə(r)/ adj ehemalig; **the ~** der/die/das Erstere. **~ly** adv früher

formidable /ˈfɔmɪdəbl/ adj gewaltig

formula /ˈfɔːmjʊlə/ n (pl **-ae** or **-s**) Formel f

formulate /ˈfɔːmjʊleɪt/ vt formulieren

forsake /fəˈseɪk/ vt (pt **-sook** /-sʊk/,

pp **-saken**) verlassen

fort /fɔ:t/ n (Mil) Fort nt

forth /fɔ:θ/ adv **back and** ~ hin und her; **and so** ~ und so weiter

forth: ~'coming adj bevorstehend; ([!]: communicative) mitteilsam. **~right** adj direkt

fortieth /'fɔ:tɪɪθ/ adj vierzigste(r,s)

fortification /fɔ:tɪfɪ'keɪʃn/ n Befestigung f

fortify /'fɔ:tɪfaɪ/ vt (pt/pp **-ied**) befestigen; (fig) stärken

fortnight /'fɔ:t-/ n vierzehn Tage pl. **~ly** adj vierzehntäglich • adv alle vierzehn Tage

fortress /'fɔ:trɪs/ n Festung f

fortunate /'fɔ:tʃʊnət/ adj glücklich; **be** ~ Glück haben. **~ly** adv glüklicherweise

fortune /'fɔ:tʃu:n/ n Glück nt; (money) Vermögen nt. **~-teller** n Wahrsagerin f

forty /'fɔ:tɪ/ adj vierzig

forward /'fɔ:wəd/ adv vorwärts; (to the front) nach vorn • adj Vorwärts-; (presumptuous) anmaßend • n (Sport) Stürmer m • vt nachsenden (letter). **~s** adv vorwärts

fossil /'fɒsl/ n Fossil nt

foster /'fɒstə(r)/ vt fördern; in Pflege nehmen (child). **~-child** n Pflegekind nt. **~-mother** n Pflegemutter f

fought /fɔ:t/ see **fight**

foul /faʊl/ adj (**-er, -est**) widerlich; (language) unflätig; ~ **play** (Jur) Mord m • n (Sport) Foul nt • vt verschmutzen; (obstruct) blockieren; (Sport) foulen

found[1] /faʊnd/ see **find**

found[2] vt gründen

foundation /faʊn'deɪʃn/ n (basis) Gundlage f; (charitable) Stiftung f; **~s** pl Fundament nt

founder /'faʊndə(r)/ n Gründer(in) m(f)

foundry /'faʊndrɪ/ n Gießerei f

fountain /'faʊntɪn/ n Brunnen m

four /fɔ:(r)/ adj vier • n Vier f

four: ~'teen adj vierzehn • n Vierzehn f. **~'teenth** adj vierzehnte(r,s)

fourth /fɔ:θ/ adj vierte(r,s)

fowl /faʊl/ n Geflügel nt

fox /fɒks/ n Fuchs m • vt (puzzle) verblüffen

foyer /'fɔɪeɪ/ n Foyer nt; (in hotel) Empfangshalle f

fraction /'frækʃn/ n Bruchteil m; (Math) Bruch m

fracture /'fræktʃə(r)/ n Bruch m • vt/i brechen

fragile /'frædʒaɪl/ adj zerbrechlich

fragment /'frægmənt/ n Bruchstück nt, Fragment nt

fragran|ce /'freɪgrəns/ n Duft m. **~t** adj duftend

frail /freɪl/ adj (**-er, -est**) gebrechlich

frame /freɪm/ n Rahmen m; (of spectacles) Gestell nt; (Anat) Körperbau m • vt einrahmen; (fig) formulieren; [x] ein Verbrechen anhängen (+ dat). **~work** n Gerüst nt; (fig) Gerippe nt

franc /fræŋk/ n (French, Belgian) Franc m; (Swiss) Franken m

France /frɑ:ns/ n Frankreich nt

franchise /'fræntʃaɪz/ n (Pol) Wahlrecht nt; (Comm) Franchise nt

frank /fræŋk/ adj offen

frankfurter /'fræŋkfɜ:tə(r)/ n Frankfurter f

frantic /'fræntɪk/ adj, **-ally** adv verzweifelt; außer sich (dat) (**with** vor)

fraternal /frə'tɜ:nl/ adj brüderlich

fraud /frɔ:d/ n Betrug m; (person) Betrüger(in) m(f)

fray /freɪ/ vi ausfransen

freak /fri:k/ n Missbildung f; (person) Missgeburt f • adj anormal

freckle /'frekl/ n Sommersprosse f

free /fri:/ adj (**freer, freest**) frei; (ticket, copy, time) Frei-; (lavish) freigebig; ~ **[of charge]** kostenlos; **set** ~ freilassen; (rescue) befreien • vt (pt/pp **freed**) freilassen; (rescue) befreien; (disentangle) freibekommen

free: ~**dom** n Freiheit f. ~**hold** n [freier] Grundbesitz m. ~**lance** adj & adv freiberuflich. ~**ly** adv frei; (voluntarily) freiwillig; (generously) großzügig. **F**~**mason** n Freimaurer m. ~**-range** adj ~**-range eggs** Landeier pl. ~ **'sample** n Gratisprobe f. ~**style** n Freistil m. ~**way** n (Amer) Autobahn f

freez|e /fri:z/ vt (pt **froze**, pp **frozen**) einfrieren; stoppen (wages) • vi **it's** ~**ing** es friert

freez|er /'fri:zə(r)/ n Gefriertruhe f; (upright) Gefrierschrank m. ~**ing** adj eiskalt • n **five degrees below** ~**ing** fünf Grad unter Null

freight /freɪt/ n Fracht f. ~**er** n Frachter m. ~ **train** n Güterzug m

French /frentʃ/ adj französisch • n (Lang) Französisch nt; **the** ~ pl die Franzosen

French: ~ **'beans** npl grüne Bohnen pl. ~ **'bread** n Stangenbrot nt. ~**' fries** npl Pommes frites pl. ~**man** n Franzose m. ~ **'window** n Terrassentür f. ~**woman** n Französin f

frenzy /'frenzɪ/ n Raserei f

frequency /'fri:kwənsɪ/ n Häufigkeit f; (Phys) Frequenz f

frequent[1] /'fri:kwənt/ adj häufig

frequent[2] /frɪ'kwent/ vt regelmäßig besuchen

fresh /freʃ/ adj (**-er, -est**) frisch; (new) neu; (cheeky) frech

freshness /'freʃnɪs/ n Frische f

'freshwater adj Süßwasser-

fret /fret/ vi (pt/pp **fretted**) sich grämen. ~**ful** adj weinerlich

'fretsaw n Laubsäge f

friction /'frɪkʃn/ n Reibung f; (fig) Reibereien pl

Friday /'fraɪdeɪ/ n Freitag m

fridge /frɪdʒ/ n Kühlschrank m

fried /fraɪd/ see **fry**[2] • adj gebraten; ~ **egg** Spiegelei nt

friend /frend/ n Freund(in) m(f). ~**liness** n Freundlichkeit f. ~**ly** adj freundlich; ~**ly with** befreundet mit. ~**ship** n Freundschaft f

fright /fraɪt/ n Schreck m

frighten /'fraɪtn/ vt Angst machen (+ dat); (startle) erschrecken; **be** ~**ed** Angst haben (**of** vor + dat). ~**ing** adj Angst erregend

frightful /'fraɪtfl/ adj schrecklich

frigid /'frɪdʒɪd/ adj frostig; (sexually) frigide. ~**ity** n Frostigkeit f; Frigidität f

frill /frɪl/ n Rüsche f; (paper) Manschette f. ~**y** adj rüschenbesetzt

fringe /frɪndʒ/ n Fransen pl; (of hair) Pony m; (fig: edge) Rand m

frisk /frɪsk/ vi herumspringen • vt (search) durchsuchen

frisky /'frɪskɪ/ adj lebhaft

fritter /'frɪtə(r)/ vt ~ **[away]** verplempern [!]

frivol|ity /frɪ'vɒlətɪ/ n Frivolität f. ~**ous** adj frivol, leichtfertig

fro /frəʊ/ see **to**

frock /frɒk/ n Kleid nt

frog /frɒk/ n Frosch m. ~**man** n Froschmann m

frolic /'frɒlɪk/ vi (pt/pp **frolicked**) herumtollen

from /frɒm/ prep von (+ dat); (out of) aus (+ dat); (according to) nach (+ dat); ~ **Monday** ab Montag; ~ **that day** seit dem Tag

front /frʌnt/ n Vorderseite f; (fig) Fassade f; (of garment) Vorderteil nt; (sea~) Strandpromenade f; (Mil, Pol, Meteorol) Front f; **in** ~ **of** vor; **in** or **at the** ~ vorne; **to the** ~ nach vorne • adj vordere(r,s); (page, row) erste(r,s); (tooth, wheel) Vorder-

front: ~ **'door** n Haustür f. ~ **'garden** n Vorgarten m

frontier /'frʌntɪə(r)/ n Grenze f

frost /frɒst/ n Frost m; (hoar-~)

Raureif m; **ten degrees of ~** zehn Grad Kälte. **~bite** n Erfrierung f. **~bitten** adj erfroren

frost|ed /ˈfrɒstɪd/ adj **~ed glass** Mattglas nt. **~ing** n (Amer Culin) Zuckerguss m. **~y** adj, **-ily** adv frostig

froth /frɒθ/ n Schaum m • vi schäumen. **~y** adj schaumig

frown /fraʊn/ n Stirnrunzeln nt • vi die Stirn runzeln

froze /frəʊz/ see **freeze**

frozen /ˈfrəʊzn/ see **freeze** • adj gefroren; (Culin) tiefgekühlt; **I'm ~** [!] mir ist eiskalt. **~ food** n Tiefkühlkost f

frugal /ˈfru:gl/ adj sparsam; (meal) frugal

fruit /fru:t/ n Frucht f; (collectively) Obst nt. **~ cake** n englischer [Tee]kuchen m

fruitful adj fruchtbar

fruit: ~ juice n Obstsaft m. **~less** adj fruchtlos. **~ ˈsalad** n Obstsalat m

fruity /ˈfru:tɪ/ adj fruchtig

frustrat|e /frʌˈstreɪt/ vt vereiteln; (Psychology) frustrieren. **~ion** n Frustration f

fry /fraɪ/ vt/i (pt/pp **fried**) [in der Pfanne] braten. **~ing-pan** n Bratpfanne f

fuel /ˈfju:əl/ n Brennstoff m; (for car) Kraftstoff m; (for aircraft) Treibstoff m

fugitive /ˈfju:dʒətɪv/ n Flüchtling m

fulfil /fʊlˈfɪl/ vt (pt/pp **-filled**) erfüllen. **~ment** n Erfüllung f

full /fʊl/ adj & adv (**-er, -est**) voll; (detailed) ausführlich; (skirt) weit; **~ of** voll von (+ dat), voller (+ gen); **at ~ speed** in voller Fahrt • n **in ~** vollständig

full: ~ ˈmoon n Vollmond m. **~-scale** adj (model) in Originalgröße; (rescue, alert) großangelegt. **~ ˈstop** n Punkt m. **~-time** adj ganztägig • adv ganztags

fully /ˈfʊlɪ/ adv völlig; (in detail) ausführlich

fumble /ˈfʌmbl/ vi herumfummeln (**with** an + dat)

fume /fju:m/ vi vor Wut schäumen

fumes /fju:mz/ npl Dämpfe pl; (from car) Abgase pl

fun /fʌn/ n Spaß m; **for ~** aus od zum Spaß; **make ~ of** sich lustig machen über (+ acc); **have ~!** viel Spaß!

function /ˈfʌŋkʃn/ n Funktion f; (event) Veranstaltung f • vi funktionieren; (serve) dienen (**as** als). **~al** adj zweckmäßig

fund /fʌnd/ n Fonds m; (fig) Vorrat m; **~s** pl Geldmittel pl • vt finanzieren

fundamental /fʌndəˈmentl/ adj grundlegend; (essential) wesentlich

funeral /ˈfju:nərl/ n Beerdigung f; (cremation) Feuerbestattung f

funeral: ~ march n Trauermarsch m. **~ service** n Trauergottesdienst m

ˈfunfair n Jahrmarkt m

fungus /ˈfʌŋgəs/ n (pl **-gi** /-gaɪ/) Pilz m

funnel /ˈfʌnl/ n Trichter m; (on ship, train) Schornstein m

funnily /ˈfʌnɪlɪ/ adv komisch; **~ enough** komischerweise

funny /ˈfʌnɪ/ adj komisch

fur /fɜ:(r)/ n Fell nt; (for clothing) Pelz m; (in kettle) Kesselstein m. **~ ˈcoat** n Pelzmantel m

furious /ˈfjʊərɪəs/ adj wütend (**with** auf + acc)

furnace /ˈfɜ:nɪs/ n (Techn) Ofen m

furnish /ˈfɜ:nɪʃ/ vt einrichten; (supply) liefern. **~ed** adj **~ed room** möbliertes Zimmer nt. **~ings** npl Einrichtungsgegenstände pl

furniture /ˈfɜ:nɪtʃə(r)/ n Möbel pl

further /ˈfɜ:ðə(r)/ adj weitere(r,s); **at the ~ end** am anderen Ende; **until ~ notice** bis auf weiteres • adv weiter; **~ off** weiter entfernt • vt fördern

f

furthermore /fɜ:ðə'mɔ:(r)/ adv außerdem

furthest /'fɜ:ðɪst/ adj am weitesten entfernt •adv am weitesten

fury /'fjʊərɪ/ n Wut f

fuse[1] /fju:z/ n (of bomb) Zünder m; (cord) Zündschnur f

fuse[2] n (Electr) Sicherung f •vt/i verschmelzen; **the lights have ~d** die Sicherung [für das Licht] ist durchgebrannt. **~-box** n Sicherungskasten m

fuselage /'fju:zəlɑ:ʒ/ n (Aviat) Rumpf m

fuss /fʌs/ n Getue nt; **make a ~ of** verwöhnen; (caress) liebkosen •vi Umstände machen

fussy /'fʌsɪ/ adj wählerisch; (particular) penibel

futil|e /'fju:taɪl/ adj zwecklos. **~ity** n Zwecklosigkeit f

future /'fju:tʃə(r)/ adj zukünftig •n Zukunft f; (Gram) [erstes] Futur nt

futuristic /fju:tʃə'rɪstɪk/ adj futuristisch

fuzzy /'fʌzɪ/ adj (hair) kraus; (blurred) verschwommen

Gg

gabble /'gæbl/ vi schnell reden

gable /'geɪbl/ n Giebel m

gadget /'gædʒɪt/ n [kleines] Gerät nt

Gaelic /'geɪlɪk/ n Gälisch nt

gag /gæg/ n Knebel m; (joke) Witz m; (Theat) Gag m •vt (pt/pp **gagged**) knebeln

gaiety /'geɪətɪ/ n Fröhlichkeit f

gaily /'geɪlɪ/ adv fröhlich

gain /geɪn/ n Gewinn m; (increase) Zunahme f •vt gewinnen; (obtain) erlangen; **~ weight** zunehmen •vi (clock:) vorgehen

gait /geɪt/ n Gang m

gala /'gɑ:lə/ n Fest nt •attrib Gala-

galaxy /'gæləksɪ/ n Galaxie f; **the G~** die Milchstraße

gale /geɪl/ n Sturm m

gallant /'gælənt/ adj tapfer; (chivalrous) galant. **~ry** n Tapferkeit f

'gall-bladder n Gallenblase f

gallery /'gælərɪ/ n Galerie f

galley /'gælɪ/ n (ship's kitchen) Kombüse f; **~ [proof]** [Druck]fahne f

gallon /'gælən/ n Gallone f (= 4,5 l; Amer = 3,785 l)

gallop /'gæləp/ n Galopp m •vi galoppieren

gallows /'gæləʊz/ n Galgen m

galore /gə'lɔ(r)/ adv in Hülle und Fülle

gamble /'gæmbl/ n (risk) Risiko nt •vi [um Geld] spielen; **~ on** (rely) sich verlassen auf (+ acc). **~r** n Spieler(in) m(f)

game /geɪm/ n Spiel nt; (animals, birds) Wild nt; **~s** (Sch) Sport m •adj (brave) tapfer; (willing) bereit (**for** zu). **~keeper** n Wildhüter m

gammon /'gæmən/ n [geräucherter] Schinken m

gang /gæŋ/ n Bande f; (of workmen) Kolonne f

gangling /'gæŋglɪŋ/ adj schlaksig

gangmaster /'gæŋmɑ:stə(r)/ n Aufseher(in) m(f) von (meist illegalen) Gelegenheitsarbeitern

gangrene /'gæŋgri:n/ n Wundbrand m

gangster /'gæŋstə(r)/ n Gangster m

gangway /'gæŋweɪ/ n Gang m; (Naut, Aviat) Gangway f

gaol /dʒeɪl/ n Gefängnis nt •vt ins Gefängnis sperren. **~er** n Gefängniswärter m

gap /gæp/ n Lücke f; (interval) Pause f; (difference) Unterschied m

gap|e /geɪp/ vi gaffen; **~e at** anstarren. **~ing** adj klaffend

garage /ˈgærɑːʒ/ n Garage f; (for repairs) Werkstatt f; (for petrol) Tankstelle f

garbage /ˈgɑːbɪdʒ/ n Müll m. **~ can** n (Amer) Mülleimer m

garbled /ˈgɑːbld/ adj verworren

garden /ˈgɑːdn/ n Garten m; **[public] ~s** pl [öffentliche] Anlagen pl •vi im Garten arbeiten. **~er** n Gärtner(in) m(f). **~ing** n Gartenarbeit f

gargle /ˈgɑːgl/ n (liquid) Gurgelwasser nt •vi gurgeln

garish /ˈgeərɪʃ/ adj grell

garland /ˈgɑːlənd/ n Girlande f

garlic /ˈgɑːlɪk/ n Knoblauch m

garment /ˈgɑːmənt/ n Kleidungsstück nt

garnet /ˈgɑːnɪt/ n Granat m

garnish /ˈgɑːnɪʃ/ n Garnierung f •vt garnieren

garrison /ˈgærɪsn/ n Garnison f

garrulous /ˈgærʊləs/ adj geschwätzig

garter /ˈgɑːtə(r)/ n Strumpfband nt; (Amer: suspender) Strumpfhalter m

gas /gæs/ n Gas nt; (Amer, fam: petrol) Benzin nt •v (pt/pp **gassed**) •vt vergasen •vi [!] schwatzen. **~ cooker** n Gasherd m. **~ ˈfire** n Gasofen m

gash /gæʃ/ n Schnitt m; (wound) klaffende Wunde f

gasket /ˈgæskɪt/ n (Techn) Dichtung f

gas: ~ mask n Gasmaske f. **~-meter** n Gaszähler m

gasoline /ˈgæsəliːn/ n (Amer) Benzin nt

gasp /gɑːsp/ vi keuchen; (in surprise) hörbar die Luft einziehen

ˈgas station n (Amer) Tankstelle f

gastric /ˈgæstrɪk/ adj Magen-

gastronomy /gæˈstrɒnəmɪ/ n Gastronomie f

gate /geɪt/ n Tor nt; (to field) Gatter nt; (barrier) Schranke f; (at airport) Flugsteig m

gate: ~crasher n ungeladener Gast m. **~way** n Tor nt

gather /ˈgæðə(r)/ vt sammeln; (pick) pflücken; (conclude) folgern (**from** aus) •vi sich versammeln; (storm:) sich zusammenziehen. **~ing** n **family ~ing** Familientreffen nt

gaudy /ˈgɔːdɪ/ adj knallig

gauge /geɪdʒ/ n Stärke f; (Rail) Spurweite f; (device) Messinstrument nt

gaunt /gɔːnt/ adj hager

gauze /gɔːz/ n Gaze f

gave /geɪv/ see **give**

gawky /ˈgɔːkɪ/ adj schlaksig

gay /geɪ/ adj (**-er, -est**) fröhlich; (homosexual) homosexuell

gaze /geɪz/ n [langer] Blick m •vi sehen; **~ at** ansehen

GB abbr **Great Britain**

gear /gɪə(r)/ n Ausrüstung f; (Techn) Getriebe nt; (Auto) Gang m; **change ~** schalten

gear: ~box n (Auto) Getriebe nt. **~-lever** n, (Amer) **~-shift** n Schalthebel m

geese /giːs/ see **goose**

gel /dʒel/ n Gel nt

gelatine /ˈdʒelətɪn/ n Gelatine f

gem /dʒem/ n Juwel nt

gender /ˈdʒendə(r)/ n (Gram) Geschlecht nt

gene /dʒiːn/ n Gen nt

genealogy /dʒiːnɪˈælədʒɪ/ n Genealogie f

general /ˈdʒenrəl/ adj allgemein •n General m; **in ~** im Allgemeinen. **~ eˈlection** n allgemeine Wahlen pl

g

g

generaliz|ation /dʒenrəlaɪ'zeɪʃn/ n Verallgemeinerung f. **~e** vi verallgemeinern

generally /'dʒenrəlɪ/ adv im Allgemeinen

general prac'titioner n praktischer Arzt m

generate /'dʒenəreɪt/ vt erzeugen

generation /dʒenə'reɪʃn/ n Generation f

generator /'dʒenəreɪtə(r)/ n Generator m

generosity /dʒenə'rɒsɪtɪ/ n Großzügigkeit f

generous /'dʒenərəs/ adj großzügig

genetic /dʒə'netɪk/ adj, **-ally** adv genetisch. **~ally modified** gentechnisch verändert; genmanipuliert. **~ engineering** n Gentechnologie f

Geneva /dʒɪ'ni:və/ n Genf nt

genial /'dʒi:nɪəl/ adj freundlich

genitals /'dʒenɪtlz/ pl [äußere] Geschlechtsteile pl

genitive /'dʒenɪtɪv/ adj & n **~ [case]** Genitiv m

genius /'dʒi:nɪəs/ n (pl **-uses**) Genie nt; (quality) Genialität f

genome /'dʒi:nəʊm/ n Genom nt

genre /'ʒɑ̃rə/ n Gattung f, Genre nt

gent /dʒent/ n [!] Herr m; **the ~s** sg die Herrentoilette f

genteel /dʒen'ti:l/ adj vornehm

gentle /'dʒentl/ adj (**-r, -st**) sanft

gentleman /'dʒentlmən/ n Herr m; (well-mannered) Gentleman m

gent|leness /'dʒentlnɪs/ n Sanftheit f. **~ly** adv sanft

genuine /'dʒenjʊɪn/ adj echt; (sincere) aufrichtig. **~ly** adv (honestly) ehrlich

geograph|ical /dʒɪə'græfɪkl/ adj geographisch. **~y** n Geographie f, Erdkunde f

geological /dʒɪə'lɒdʒɪkl/ adj geologisch

geolog|ist /dʒɪ'ɒlədʒɪst/ n Geologe m/-gin f. **~y** n Geologie f

geometr|ic(al) /dʒɪə'metrɪk(l)/ adj geometrisch. **~y** n Geometrie f

geranium /dʒə'reɪnɪəm/ n Geranie f

geriatric /dʒerɪ'ætrɪk/ adj geriatrisch • n geriatrischer Patient m

germ /dʒɜ:m/ n Keim m; **~s** pl [!] Bazillen pl

German /'dʒɜ:mən/ adj deutsch • n (person) Deutsche(r) m/f; (Lang) Deutsch nt; **in ~** auf Deutsch; **into ~** ins Deutsche

Germanic /dʒə'mænɪk/ adj germanisch

Germany /'dʒɜ:mənɪ/ n Deutschland nt

germinate /'dʒɜ:mɪneɪt/ vi keimen

gesticulate /dʒe'stɪkjʊleɪt/ vi gestikulieren

gesture /'dʒestʃə(r)/ n Geste f

get /get/ v

pt **got**, pp **got** (Amer also **gotten**), pres p **getting**

• transitive verb

····➤ (obtain, receive) bekommen, [!] kriegen; (procure) besorgen; (buy) kaufen; (fetch) holen. **get a job/taxi for s.o.** jdm einen Job verschaffen/ein Taxi besorgen. **I must get some bread** ich muss Brot holen. **get permission** die Erlaubnis erhalten. **I couldn't get her on the phone** ich konnte sie nicht telefonisch erreichen

····➤ (prepare) machen (meal). **he got the breakfast** er machte das Frühstück

····➤ (cause) **get s.o. to do sth** jdn dazu bringen, etw zu tun. **get one's hair cut** sich (dat) die Haare schneiden lassen. **get one's hands dirty** sich (dat) die Hände schmutzig machen

····➤ **get the bus/train**. (travel by) den Bus/Zug nehmen; (be in time for, catch) den Bus/Zug erreichen

····➤ **have got** ([!]: have) haben. **I've got a cold** ich habe eine Erkältung

····➤ **have got to do sth** etw tun müssen. **I've got to hurry** ich muss mich beeilen

····➤ ([!]: understand) kapieren [!]. **I don't get it** ich kapiere nicht

• intransitive verb

····➤ (become) werden. **get older** älter werden. **the weather got worse** das Wetter wurde schlechter. **get to** kommen zu/ nach (town); (reach) erreichen. **get dressed** sich anziehen. **get married** heiraten.

• phrasal verbs

■ **get about** vi (move) sich bewegen; (travel) herumkommen; (spread) sich verbreiten. ■ **get at** vt (have access) herankommen an (+ acc); ([!]: criticize) anmachen [!]. (mean) **what are you getting at?** worauf willst du hinaus? ■ **get away** vi (leave) wegkommen; (escape) entkommen. ■ **get back** vi zurückkommen; vt (recover) zurückbekommen; **get one's own back** sich revanchieren. ■ **get by** vi vorbeikommen; (manage) sein Auskommen haben. ■ **get down** vi heruntersteigen; vt (depress) deprimieren; **get down to** sich [heran]machen an (+ acc). ■ **get in** vi (into bus) einsteigen; vt (fetch) hereinholen. ■ **get off** vi (dismount) absteigen; (from bus) aussteigen; (leave) wegkommen; (Jur) freigesprochen werden; vt (remove) abbekommen. ■ **get on** vi (mount) aufsteigen; (to bus) einsteigen; (be on good terms) gut auskommen (**with** mit + dat); (make progress) Fortschritte machen; **how are you getting on?** wie geht's? ■ **get out** vi herauskommen; (of car) aussteigen; **get out of** (avoid doing) sich drücken um; vt (take out) herausholen; herausbekommen (cork, stain). ■ **get over** vi hinübersteigen; vt (fig) hinwegkommen über (+ acc). ■ **get round** vi herumkommen; **I never get round to it** ich komme nie dazu; vt herumkriegen; (avoid) umgehen. ■ **get through** vi durchkommen. ■ **get up** vi aufstehen

get: ~away n Flucht f. **~-up** n Aufmachung f

ghastly /ˈgɑːstlɪ/ adj grässlich; (pale) blass

gherkin /ˈgɜːkɪn/ n Essiggurke f

ghost /gəʊst/ n Geist m, Gespenst nt. **~ly** adj geisterhaft

ghoulish /ˈguːlɪʃ/ adj makaber

giant /ˈdʒaɪənt/ n Riese m • adj riesig

gibberish /ˈdʒɪbərɪʃ/ n Kauderwelsch nt

giblets /ˈdʒɪblɪts/ npl Geflügelklein nt

giddiness /ˈgɪdɪnɪs/ n Schwindel m

giddy /ˈgɪdɪ/ adj schwindlig

gift /gɪft/ n Geschenk nt; (to charity) Gabe f; (talent) Begabung f. **~ed** adj begabt

gigantic /dʒaɪˈgæntɪk/ adj riesig, riesengroß

giggle /ˈgɪgl/ n Kichern nt • vi kichern

gild /gɪld/ vt vergolden

gilt /gɪlt/ adj vergoldet • n Vergoldung f. **~-edged** adj (Comm) mündelsicher

gimmick /ˈgɪmɪk/ n Trick m

gin /dʒɪn/ n Gin m

ginger /ˈdʒɪndʒə(r)/ adj rotblond; (cat) rot • n Ingwer m. **~bread** n Pfefferkuchen m

gingerly /ˈdʒɪndʒəlɪ/ adv vorsichtig

gipsy /ˈdʒɪpsɪ/ n = **gypsy**

giraffe /dʒɪˈrɑːf/ n Giraffe f

girder /ˈgɜːdə(r)/ n (Techn) Träger m

girl /gɜːl/ n Mädchen nt; (young woman) junge Frau f. **~ band** n Mädchenband f. **~friend** n Freundin f. **~ish** adj mädchenhaft

gist /dʒɪst/ n **the ~** das Wesentliche

give /gɪv/ n Elastizität f • v (pt **gave**, pp **given**) • vt geben/(as present) schenken (**to** dat); (donate) spenden; (lecture) halten; (one's name) angeben • vi geben; (yield)

g

nachgeben. ~ **away** vt verschenken; (betray) verraten; (distribute) verteilen. ~ **back** vt zurückgeben. ~ **in** vt einreichen •vi (yield) nachgeben. ~ **off** vt abgeben. ~ **up** vt/i aufgeben; ~ **oneself up** sich stellen. ~ **way** vi nachgeben; (Auto) die Vorfahrt beachten

glacier /ˈglæsɪə(r)/ n Gletscher m

glad /glæd/ adj froh (**of** über + acc)

gladly /ˈglædlɪ/ adv gern[e]

g

glamorous /ˈglæmərəs/ adj glanzvoll; (film star) glamourös

glamour /ˈglæmə(r)/ n [betörender] Glanz m

glance /glɑːns/ n [flüchtiger] Blick m •vi ~ **at** einen Blick werfen auf (+ acc). ~ **up** vi aufblicken

gland /glænd/ n Drüse f

glare /gleə(r)/ n grelles Licht nt; (look) ärgerlicher Blick m •vi ~ **at** böse ansehen

glaring /ˈgleərɪŋ/ adj grell; (mistake) krass

glass /glɑːs/ n Glas nt; (mirror) Spiegel m; ~**es** pl (spectacles) Brille f. ~**y** adj glasig

glaze /gleɪz/ n Glasur f

gleam /gliːm/ n Schein m •vi glänzen

glib /glɪb/ adj (pej) gewandt

glid|e /glaɪd/ vi gleiten; (through the air) schweben. ~**er** n Segelflugzeug nt. ~**ing** n Segelfliegen nt

glimmer /ˈglɪmə(r)/ n Glimmen nt •vi glimmen

glimpse /glɪmps/ vt flüchtig sehen

glint /glɪnt/ n Blitzen nt •vi blitzen

glisten /ˈglɪsn/ vi glitzern

glitter /ˈglɪtə(r)/ vi glitzern

global /ˈgləʊbl/ adj global

globaliz|e /ˈgləʊbəlaɪz/ vt globalisieren. ~**ation** n Globalisierung f

globe /gləʊb/ n Kugel f; (map) Globus m

gloom /gluːm/ n Düsterkeit f; (fig) Pessimismus m

gloomy /ˈgluːmɪ/ adj, **-ily** adv düster; (fig) pessimistisch

glorif|y /ˈglɔːrɪfaɪ/ vt (pt/pp **-ied**) verherrlichen

glorious /ˈglɔːrɪəs/ adj herrlich; (deed, hero) glorreich

glory /ˈglɔːrɪ/ n Ruhm m; (splendour) Pracht f •vi ~ **in** genießen

gloss /glɒs/ n Glanz m •adj Glanz- •vi ~ **over** beschönigen

glossary /ˈglɒsərɪ/ n Glossar nt

glossy /ˈglɒsɪ/ adj glänzend

glove /glʌv/ n Handschuh m

glow /gləʊ/ n Glut f; (of candle) Schein m •vi glühen; (candle:) scheinen. ~**ing** adj glühend; (account) begeistert

glucose /ˈgluːkəʊs/ n Traubenzucker m, Glukose f

glue /gluː/ n Klebstoff m •vt (pres p **gluing**) kleben (**to** an + acc)

glum /glʌm/ adj (**glummer, glummest**) niedergeschlagen

glut /glʌt/ n Überfluss m (**of** an + dat)

glutton /ˈglʌtən/ n Vielfraß m

GM abbr (**genetically modified**); ~ **crops/food** gentechnisch veränderte Feldfrüchte/ Nahrungsmittel

gnash /næʃ/ vt ~ **one's teeth** mit den Zähnen knirschen

gnat /næt/ n Mücke f

gnaw /nɔː/ vt/i nagen (**at** an + dat)

go /gəʊ/

3 sg pres tense **goes;** pt **went;** pp **gone**

• intransitive verb

····➤ gehen; (in vehicle) fahren. **go by air** fliegen. **where are you going?** wo gehst du hin? **I'm going to France** ich fahre nach Frankreich. **go to the doctor's/ dentist's** zum Arzt/Zahnarzt gehen. **go to the theatre/ cinema** ins Theater/Kino gehen. **I** must go to Paris/to the doctor's ich muss nach Paris/zum Arzt. **go shopping** einkaufen gehen. **go swimming** schwimmen gehen. **go to see s.o.** jdn besuchen [gehen]

....➤ (leave) weggehen; (on journey) abfahren. **I must go now** ich muss jetzt gehen. **we're going on Friday** wir fahren am Freitag

....➤ (work, function) (engine, clock) gehen

....➤ (become) werden. **go deaf** taub werden. **go mad** verrückt werden. **he went red** er wurde rot

....➤ (pass) (time) vergehen

....➤ (disappear) weggehen; (coat, hat, stain) verschwinden. **my headache/my coat/the stain has gone** mein Kopfweh/mein Mantel/der Fleck ist weg

....➤ (turn out, progress) gehen; verlaufen. **everything's going very well** alles geht od verläuft sehr gut. **how did the party go?** wie war die Party? **go smoothly/according to plan** reibungslos/planmäßig verlaufen

....➤ (match) zusammenpassen. **the two colours don't go [together]** die beiden Farben passen nicht zusammen

....➤ (cease to function) kaputtgehen; (fuse) durchbrennen. **his memory is going** sein Gedächtnis lässt nach

● auxiliary verb

....➤ **be going to** werden + inf. **it's going to rain** es wird regnen. **I'm not going to** ich werde es nicht tun

● noun

pl **goes**

....➤ (turn) **it's your go** du bist jetzt an der Reihe od dran

....➤ (attempt) Versuch. **have a go at doing sth** versuchen, etw zu tun. **have another go!** versuch's noch mal!

....➤ (energy, drive) Energie

....➤ (in phrases) **on the go** auf Trab. **make a go of sth** das Beste aus etw machen

● phrasal verbs

■ **go across** vi hinübergehen/-fahren; vt überqueren. ■ **go after** vt (pursue) jagen. ■ **go away** vi weggehen/-fahren; (on holiday or business) verreisen. ■ **go back** vi zurückgehen/-fahren. ■ **go back on** vt nicht [ein]halten (promise). ■ **go by** vi vorbeigehen/-fahren; (time) vergehen. ■ **go down** vi hinuntergehen/-fahren; (sun, ship) untergehen; (prices) fallen; (temperature, swelling) zurückgehen. ■ **go for** vt holen; (!: attack) losgehen auf (+ acc). ■ **go in** vi hineingehen/-fahren; ■ **go in for** teilnehmen an (+ dat) (competition); (take up) sich verlegen auf (+ acc). ■ **go off** vi weggehen/-fahren; (alarm clock) klingeln; (alarm, gun, bomb) losgehen; (light) ausgehen; (go bad) schlecht werden; vt: **go off sth** von etw abkommen. ■ **go off well** gut verlaufen. ■ **go on** vi weitergehen/-fahren; (light) angehen; (continue) weitermachen; (talking) fortfahren; (happen) vorgehen. ■ **go on at** ! herumnörgeln an (+ dat). ■ **go out** vi (from home) ausgehen; (leave) hinausgehen/-fahren; (fire, light) ausgehen; **go out to work/for a meal** arbeiten/essen gehen; **go out with s.o.** (!: date s.o.) mit jdm gehen !. ■ **go over** vi hinübergehen/-fahren; vt (rehearse) durchgehen. ■ **go round** vi herumgehen/-fahren; (visit) vorbeigehen; (turn) sich drehen; (be enough) reichen. ■ **go through** vi durchgehen/-fahren; vt (suffer) durchmachen; (rehearse) durchgehen; (bags) durchsuchen. ■ **go through with** vt zu Ende machen. ■ **go under** vi untergehen/-fahren; (fail) scheitern. ■ **go up** vi hinaufgehen/-fahren; (lift) hochfahren; (prices) steigen. ■ **go without** vt: **go without sth** auf etw (acc) verzichten; vi darauf verzichten

'**go-ahead** adj fortschrittlich; (enterprising) unternehmend ● n (fig) grünes Licht nt

goal /gəʊl/ n Ziel nt; (sport) Tor nt.

g

~keeper n Torwart m. **~-post** n Torpfosten m

goat /gəʊt/ n Ziege f

gobble /ˈgɒbl/ vt hinunterschlingen

God, god /gɒd/ n Gott m

god: ~child n Patenkind nt. **~-daughter** n Patentochter f. **~dess** n Göttin f. **~father** n Pate m. **~mother** n Patin f. **~parents** npl Paten pl. **~send** n Segen m. **~son** n Patensohn m

goggles /ˈgɒglz/ npl Schutzbrille f

going /ˈgəʊɪŋ/ adj (price, rate) gängig; (concern) gut gehend •n **it is hard ~** es ist schwierig

gold /gəʊld/ n Gold nt •adj golden

golden /ˈgəʊldn/ adj golden. **~ ˈwedding** n goldene Hochzeit f

gold: ~fish n inv Goldfisch m. **~-mine** n Goldgrube f. **~-plated** adj vergoldet. **~smith** n Goldschmied m

golf /gɒlf/ n Golf nt

golf: ~-club n Golfklub m; (implement) Golfschläger m. **~-course** n Golfplatz m. **~er** m Golfspieler(in) m(f)

gone /gɒn/ see **go**

good /gʊd/ adj (**better, best**) gut; (well-behaved) brav, artig; **~ at** gut in (+ dat); **a ~ deal** ziemlich viel; **~ morning/evening** guten Morgen/Abend •n **for ~** für immer; **do ~** Gutes tun; **do s.o. ~** jdm gut tun; **it's no ~** es ist nutzlos; (hopeless) da ist nichts zu machen

goodbye /gʊdˈbaɪ/ int auf Wiedersehen; (Teleph, Radio) auf Wiederhören

good: G~ ˈFriday n Karfreitag m. **~-ˈlooking** adj gut aussehend. **~-ˈnatured** adj gutmütig

goodness /ˈgʊdnɪs/ n Güte f; **thank ~!** Gott sei Dank!

goods /gʊdz/ npl Waren pl. **~ train** n Güterzug m

goodˈwill n Wohlwollen nt; (Comm) Goodwill m

gooey /ˈguːɪ/ adj [!] klebrig

google ® /ˈguːgl/ vt, vi googeln

goose /guːs/ n (pl **geese**) Gans f

gooseberry /ˈgʊzbərɪ/ n Stachelbeere f

goose: /guːs/ **~-flesh** n, **~-pimples** npl Gänsehaut f

gorge /gɔːdʒ/ n (Geog) Schlucht f •vt **~ oneself** sich vollessen

gorgeous /ˈgɔːdʒəs/ adj prachtvoll; [!] herrlich

gorilla /gəˈrɪlə/ n Gorilla m

gormless /ˈgɔːmlɪs/ adj [!] doof

gorse /gɔːs/ n inv Stechginster m

gory /ˈgɔːrɪ/ adj blutig; (story) blutrünstig

gosh /gɒʃ/ int [!] Mensch!

gospel /ˈgɒspl/ n Evangelium nt

gossip /ˈgɒsɪp/ n Klatsch m; (person) Klatschbase f •vi klatschen

got /gɒt/ see **get; have ~** haben; **have ~ to** müssen; **have ~ to do sth** etw tun müssen

Gothic /ˈgɒθɪk/ adj gotisch

gotten /ˈgɒtn/ see **get**

goulash /ˈguːlæʃ/ n Gulasch nt

gourmet /ˈgʊəmeɪ/ n Feinschmecker m

govern /ˈgʌvn/ vt/i regieren; (determine) bestimmen

government /ˈgʌvnmənt/ n Regierung f

governor /ˈgʌvənə(r)/ n Gouverneur m; (on board) Vorstandsmitglied nt; (of prison) Direktor m; ([!]: boss) Chef m

gown /gaʊn/ n [elegantes] Kleid nt; (Univ, Jur) Talar m

GP abbr **general practitioner**

GPS abbr (**Global Positioning System**) GPS nt

grab /græb/ vt (pt/pp **grabbed**) ergreifen; **~ [hold of]** packen

grace /greɪs/ n Anmut f; (before meal) Tischgebet nt; **three days' ~** drei Tage Frist. **~ful** adj anmutig

gracious /'greɪʃəs/ adj gnädig; (elegant) vornehm

grade /greɪd/ n Stufe f; (Comm) Güteklasse f; (Sch) Note f; (Amer, Sch: class) Klasse f; (Amer) = **gradient** •vt einstufen; (Comm) sortieren. ~ **crossing** n (Amer) Bahnübergang m

gradient /'greɪdɪənt/ n Steigung f; (downward) Gefälle nt

gradual /'grædʒʊəl/ adj allmählich

graduate /'grædʒʊət/ n Akademiker(in) m(f)

graffiti /grə'fi:ti/ npl Graffiti pl

graft /grɑ:ft/ n (Bot) Pfropfreis nt; (Med) Transplantat nt; (!: hard work) Plackerei f

grain /greɪn/ n (sand, salt, rice) Korn nt; (cereals) Getreide nt; (in wood) Maserung f

gram /græm/ n Gramm nt

grammar /'græmə(r)/ n Grammatik f. ~ **school** n ≈ Gymnasium nt

grammatical /grə'mætɪkl/ adj grammatisch

grand /grænd/ adj **(-er, -est)** großartig

grandad /'grændæd/ n ! Opa m

'**grandchild** n Enkelkind nt

'**granddaughter** n Enkelin f

grandeur /'grændʒə(r)/ n Pracht f

'**grandfather** n Großvater m. ~ **clock** n Standuhr f

grandiose /'grændɪəʊs/ adj grandios

grand: ~mother n Großmutter f. **~parents** npl Großeltern pl. ~ **pi'ano** n Flügel m. **~son** n Enkel m. **~stand** n Tribüne f

granite /'grænɪt/ n Granit m

granny /'grænɪ/ n ! Oma f

grant /grɑ:nt/ n Subvention f; (Univ) Studienbeihilfe f •vt gewähren; (admit) zugeben; **take sth for ~ed** etw als selbstverständlich hinnehmen

grape /greɪp/ n [Wein]traube f; **bunch of ~s** [ganze] Weintraube f

grapefruit /'greɪp-/ n invar Grapefruit f

graph /grɑ:f/ grafische Darstellung f

graphic /'græfɪk/ adj, **-ally** adv grafisch; (vivid) anschaulich

'**graph paper** n Millimeterpapier nt

grapple /'græpl/ vi ringen

grasp /grɑ:sp/ n Griff m •vt ergreifen; (understand) begreifen. **~ing** adj habgierig

grass /grɑ:s/ n Gras nt; (lawn) Rasen m. **~hopper** n Heuschrecke f

grassy /'grɑ:sɪ/ adj grasig

grate[1] /greɪt/ n Feuerrost m; (hearth) Kamin m

grate[2] vt (Culin) reiben

grateful /'greɪtfl/ adj dankbar (**to** dat)

grater /'greɪtə(r)/ n (Culin) Reibe f

gratify /'grætɪfaɪ/ vt (pt/pp **-ied**) befriedigen. **~ing** adj erfreulich

gratis /'grɑ:tɪs/ adv gratis

gratitude /'grætɪtju:d/ n Dankbarkeit f

gratuitous /grə'tju:ɪtəs/ adj (uncalled for) überflüssig

grave[1] /greɪv/ adj **(-r, -st)** ernst; **~ly ill** schwer krank

grave[2] n Grab nt. **~-digger** n Totengräber m

gravel /'grævl/ n Kies m

grave: ~stone n Grabstein m. **~yard** n Friedhof m

gravity /'grævətɪ/ n Ernst m; (force) Schwerkraft f

gravy /'greɪvɪ/ n [Braten]soße f

gray /greɪ/ adj (Amer) = **grey**

graze[1] /greɪz/ vi (animal:) weiden

graze[2] n Schürfwunde f •vt (car) streifen; (knee) aufschürfen

grease /gri:s/ n Fett nt; (lubricant) Schmierfett nt •vt einfetten; (lubricate) schmieren

greasy /'gri:sɪ/ adj fettig

g

great /greɪt/ adj (**-er, -est**) groß; ([!]: marvellous) großartig

great: ~-'aunt n Großtante f. **G~ 'Britain** n Großbritannien nt. **~-'grandchildren** npl Urenkel pl. **~-'grandfather** n Urgroßvater m. **~-'grandmother** n Urgroßmutter f

great|ly /'greɪtlɪ/ adv sehr. **~ness** n Größe f

great-'uncle n Großonkel m

Greece /gri:s/ n Griechenland nt

greed /gri:d/ n [Hab]gier f

greedy /'gri:dɪ/ adj, **-ily** adv gierig

Greek /gri:k/ adj griechisch •n Grieche m/Griechin f; (Lang) Griechisch nt

green /gri:n/ adj (**-er, -est**) grün; (fig) unerfahren •n Grün nt; (grass) Wiese f; **~s** pl Kohl m; **the G~s** pl (Pol) die Grünen pl

greenery /'gri:nərɪ/ n Grün nt

green: ~fly n Blattlaus f. **~grocer** n Obst- und Gemüsehändler m. **~house** n Gewächshaus nt

Greenland /'gri:nlənd/ n Grönland nt

greet /gri:t/ vt grüßen; (welcome) begrüßen. **~ing** n Gruß m; (welcome) Begrüßung f

grew /gru:/ see **grow**

grey /greɪ/ adj (**-er, -est**) grau •n Grau nt •vi grau werden. **~hound** n Windhund m

grid /grɪd/ n Gitter nt

grief /gri:f/ n Trauer f

grievance /'gri:vəns/ n Beschwerde f

grieve /gri:v/ vi trauern (**for** um)

grill /grɪl/ n Gitter nt; (Culin) Grill m; **mixed ~** Gemischtes nt vom Grill •vt/i grillen; (interrogate) [streng] verhören

grille /grɪl/ n Gitter nt

grim /grɪm/ adj (**grimmer, grimmest**) ernst; (determination) verbissen

grimace /grɪ'meɪs/ n Grimasse f •vi Grimassen schneiden

grime /graɪm/ n Schmutz m

grimy /'graɪmɪ/ adj schmutzig

grin /grɪn/ n Grinsen nt •vi (pt/pp **grinned**) grinsen

grind /graɪnd/ n ([!]: hard work) Plackerei f •vt (pt/pp **ground**) mahlen; (smooth, sharpen) schleifen; (Amer: mince) durchdrehen

grip /grɪp/ n Griff m; (bag) Reisetasche f •vt (pt/pp **gripped**) ergreifen; (hold) festhalten

gripping /'grɪpɪŋ/ adj fesselnd

grisly /'grɪzlɪ/ adj grausig

gristle /'grɪsl/ n Knorpel m

grit /grɪt/ n [grober] Sand m; (for roads) Streugut nt; (courage) Mut m •vt (pt/pp **gritted**) streuen (road)

groan /grəʊn/ n Stöhnen nt •vi stöhnen

grocer /'grəʊsə(r)/ n Lebensmittelhändler m; **~'s [shop]** Lebensmittelgeschäft nt. **~ies** npl Lebensmittel pl

groin /grɔɪn/ n (Anat) Leiste f

groom /gru:m/ n Bräutigam m; (for horse) Pferdepfleger(in) m(f) •vt striegeln (horse)

groove /gru:v/ n Rille f

grope /grəʊp/ vi tasten (**for** nach)

gross /grəʊs/ adj (**-er, -est**) fett; (coarse) derb; (glaring) grob; (Comm) brutto; (salary, weight) Brutto-. **~ly** adv (very) sehr

grotesque /grəʊ'tesk/ adj grotesk

ground[1] /graʊnd/ see **grind**

ground[2] n Boden m; (terrain) Gelände nt; (reason) Grund m; (Amer, Electr) Erde f; **~s** pl (park) Anlagen pl; (of coffee) Satz m

ground: ~ floor n Erdgeschoss nt. **~ing** n Grundlage f. **~less** adj grundlos. **~sheet** n Bodenplane f. **~work** n Vorarbeiten pl

group /gru:p/ n Gruppe f •vt gruppieren •vi sich gruppieren

grouse vi [!] meckern

grovel /'grɒvl/ vi (pt/pp **grovelled**) kriechen

grow /grəʊ/ v (pt **grew**, pp **grown**) •vi wachsen; (become) werden; (increase) zunehmen •vt anbauen. ~ **up** vi aufwachsen; (town:) entstehen

growl /graʊl/ n Knurren nt •vi knurren

grown /grəʊn/ see **grow**. ~**-up** adj erwachsen •n Erwachsene(r) m/f

growth /grəʊθ/ n Wachstum nt; (increase) Zunahme f; (Med) Gewächs nt

grub /grʌb/ n (larva) Made f; ([!]: food) Essen nt

grubby /'grʌbɪ/ adj schmuddelig

grudg|e /grʌdʒ/ n Groll m •vt ~**e s.o. sth** jdm etw missgönnen. ~**ing** adj widerwillig

gruelling /'gru:əlɪŋ/ adj strapaziös

gruesome /'gru:səm/ adj grausig

gruff /grʌf/ adj barsch

grumble /'grʌmbl/ vi schimpfen (**at** mit)

grumpy /'grʌmpɪ/ adj griesgrämig

grunt /grʌnt/ n Grunzen nt •vi grunzen

guarantee /gærən'ti:/ n Garantie f; (document) Garantieschein m •vt garantieren; garantieren für (quality, success)

guard /gɑ:d/ n Wache f; (security) Wächter m; (on train) ≈ Zugführer m; (Techn) Schutz m; **be on** ~ Wache stehen; **on one's** ~ auf der Hut •vt bewachen; (protect) schützen •vi ~ **against** sich hüten vor (+ dat). ~**-dog** n Wachhund m

guarded /'gɑ:dɪd/ adj vorsichtig

guardian /'gɑ:dɪən/ n Vormund m

guess /ges/ n Vermutung f •vt erraten •vi raten; (Amer: believe) glauben. ~**work** n Vermutung f

guest /gest/ n Gast m. ~**-house** n Pension f

guidance /'gaɪdəns/ n Führung f, Leitung f; (advice) Beratung f

guide /gaɪd/ n Führer(in) m(f); (book) Führer m; **[Girl] G~** Pfadfinderin f •vt führen, leiten. ~**book** n Führer m

guided /'gaɪdɪd/ adj ~ **tour** Führung f

guide: ~**-dog** n Blindenhund m. ~**lines** npl Richtlinien pl

guilt /gɪlt/ n Schuld f. ~**ily** adv schuldbewusst

guilty /'gɪltɪ/ adj adj schuldig (**of** gen); (look) schuldbewusst; (conscience) schlecht

guinea-pig /'gɪnɪ-/ n Meerschweinchen nt; (person) Versuchskaninchen nt

guitar /gɪ'tɑ:(r)/ n Gitarre f. ~**ist** n Gitarrist(in) m(f)

gulf /gʌlf/ n (Geog) Golf m; (fig) Kluft f

gull /gʌl/ n Möwe f

gullible /'gʌlɪbl/ adj leichtgläubig

gully /'gʌlɪ/ n Schlucht f; (drain) Rinne f

gulp /gʌlp/ n Schluck m •vi schlucken •vt ~ **down** hinunterschlucken

gum[1] /gʌm/ n (also pl **-s**) (Anat) Zahnfleisch nt

gum[2] n Gummi[harz] nt; (glue) Klebstoff m; (chewing gum) Kaugummi m

gummed /gʌmd/ •adj (label) gummiert

gun /gʌn/ n Schusswaffe f; (pistol) Pistole f; (rifle) Gewehr nt; (cannon) Geschütz nt

gun: ~**fire** n Geschützfeuer nt. ~**man** bewaffneter Bandit m

gunner /'gʌnə(r)/ n Artillerist m

gunpowder n Schießpulver nt

gurgle /'gɜ:gl/ vi gluckern; (of baby) glucksen

gush /gʌʃ/ vi strömen; (enthuse) schwärmen (**over** von)

gust /gʌst/ n (of wind) Windstoß m; (Naut) Bö f

gusto /'gʌstəʊ/ n **with** ~ mit Schwung

g

gusty /'gʌstɪ/ adj böig

gut /gʌt/ n Darm m; **~s** pl Eingeweide pl; ([!]: courage) Schneid m • vt (pt/pp **gutted**) (Culin) ausnehmen; **~ted by fire** ausgebrannt

gutter /'gʌtə(r)/ n Rinnstein m; (fig) Gosse f; (on roof) Dachrinne f

guy /gaɪ/ n [!] Kerl m

guzzle /'gʌzl/ vt/i schlingen; (drink) schlürfen

gym /dʒɪm/ n [!] Turnhalle f; (gymnastics) Turnen nt

gymnasium /dʒɪm'neɪzɪəm/ n Turnhalle f

gymnast /'dʒɪmnæst/ n Turner(in) m(f). **~ics** n Turnen nt

gym shoes pl Turnschuhe pl

gynaecolog|ist /gaɪnɪ'kɒlədʒɪst/ n Frauenarzt m /-ärztin f. **~y** n Gynäkologie f

gypsy /'dʒɪpsɪ/ n Zigeuner(in) m(f)

g h

Hh

habit /'hæbɪt/ n Gewohnheit f; (Relig: costume) Ordenstracht f; **be in the ~** die Angewohnheit haben **(of** zu)

habitat /'hæbɪtæt/ n Habitat nt

habitation /hæbɪ'teɪʃn/ n **unfit for human ~** für Wohnzwecke ungeeignet

habitual /hə'bɪtjʊəl/ adj gewohnt; (inveterate) gewohnheitsmäßig. **~ly** adv gewohnheitsmäßig; (constantly) ständig

hack¹ /hæk/ n (writer) Schreiberling m; (hired horse) Mietpferd nt

hack² vt hacken; **~ to pieces** zerhacken

hackneyed /'hæknɪd/ adj abgedroschen

'hacksaw n Metallsäge f

had /hæd/ see **have**

haddock /'hædək/ n inv Schellfisch m

haggard /'hægəd/ adj abgehärmt

haggle /'hægl/ vi feilschen **(over** um)

hail¹ /heɪl/ vt begrüßen; herbeirufen (taxi) • vi **~ from** kommen aus

hail² n Hagel m • vi hageln. **~stone** n Hagelkorn nt

hair /heə(r)/ n Haar nt; **wash one's ~** sich (dat) die Haare waschen

hair: ~brush n Haarbürste f. **~cut** n Haarschnitt m; **have a ~cut** sich (dat) die Haare schneiden lassen. **~-do** n [!] Frisur f. **~dresser** n Friseur m/ Friseuse f. **~-drier** n Haartrockner m; (hand-held) Föhn m. **~pin** n Haarnadel f. **~pin 'bend** n Haarnadelkurve f. **~-raising** adj haarsträubend. **~-style** n Frisur f

hairy /'heərɪ/ adj behaart; (excessively) haarig; ([!] frightening) brenzlig

hake /heɪk/ n inv Seehecht m

half /hɑːf/ n (pl **halves**) Hälfte f; **cut in ~** halbieren; **one and a ~** eineinhalb, anderthalb; **~ a dozen** ein halbes Dutzend; **~ an hour** eine halbe Stunde • adj & adv halb; **~ past two** halb drei; **[at] ~ price** zum halben Preis

half: ~-'hearted adj lustlos. **~-'term** n schulfreie Tage nach dem halben Trimester. **~-'timbered** adj Fachwerk-. **~-'time** n (Sport) Halbzeit f. **~-'way** adj **the ~-way mark/ stage** die Hälfte • adv auf halbem Weg

halibut /'hælɪbət/ n inv Heilbutt m

hall /hɔːl/ n Halle f; (room) Saal m;

(Sch) Aula f; (entrance) Flur m; (mansion) Gutshaus nt; **~ of residence** (Univ) Studentenheim nt

'hallmark n [Feingehalts]stempel m; (fig) Kennzeichen nt (**of** für)

hallo /hə'ləʊ/ int [guten] Tag! 🅸 hallo!

hallucination /həlu:sɪ'neɪʃn/ n Halluzination f

halo /'heɪləʊ/ n (pl **-es**) Heiligenschein m; (Astronomy) Hof m

halt /hɔ:lt/ n Halt m; **come to a ~** stehen bleiben; (traffic:) zum Stillstand kommen •vi Halt machen; **~!** halt! **~ing** adj, **-ly** adv zögernd

halve /hɑ:v/ vt halbieren; (reduce) um die Hälfte reduzieren

ham /hæm/ n Schinken m

hamburger /'hæmbɜ:gə(r)/ n Hamburger m

hammer /'hæmə(r)/ n Hammer m •vt/i hämmern (**at** an + acc)

hammock /'hæmək/ n Hängematte f

hamper vt behindern

hamster /'hæmstə(r)/ n Hamster m

hand /hænd/ n Hand f; (of clock) Zeiger m; (writing) Handscrift f; (worker) Arbeiter(in) m(f); (Cards) Blatt nt; **on the one/other ~** einer-/andererseits; **out of ~** außer Kontrolle; (summarily) kurzerhand; **in ~** unter Kontrolle; (available) verfügbar; **give s.o. a ~** jdm behilflich sein •vt reichen (**to** dat). **~ in** vt abgeben. **~ out** vt austeilen. **~ over** vt überreichen

hand: ~bag n Handtasche f. **~book** n Handbuch nt. **~brake** n Handbremse f. **~cuffs** npl Handschellen pl. **~ful** n Handvoll f; **be [quite] a ~ful** 🅸 nicht leicht zu haben sein

handicap /'hændɪkæp/ n Behinderung f; (Sport & fig) Handikap nt. **~ped** adj **mentally/physically ~ped** geistig/körperlich behindert

handkerchief /'hæŋkətʃɪf/ n (pl **~s** & **-chieves**) Taschentuch nt

handle /'hændl/ n Griff m; (of door) Klinke f; (of cup) Henkel m; (of broom) Stiel m •vt handhaben; (treat) umgehen mit; (touch) anfassen. **~bars** npl Lenkstange f

hand: ~made adj handgemacht. **~shake** n Händedruck m

handsome /'hænsəm/ adj gut aussehend; (generous) großzügig; (large) beträchtlich

hand: ~writing n Handschrift f. **~-'written** adj handgeschrieben

handy /'hændɪ/ adj handlich; (person) geschickt; **have/keep ~** griffbereit haben/halten

hang /hæŋ/ vt/i (pt/pp **hung**) hängen; **~ wallpaper** tapezieren •vt (pt/pp **hanged**) hängen (criminal) •n **get the ~ of it** 🅸 den Dreh herauskriegen. **~ about** vi sich herumdrücken. **~ on** vi sich festhalten (**to** an + dat); (🅸: wait) warten. **~ out** vi heraushängen; (🅸: live) wohnen •vt draußen aufhängen (washing). **~ up** vt/i aufhängen

hangar /'hæŋə(r)/ n Flugzeughalle f

hanger /'hæŋə(r)/ n [Kleider]bügel m

hang: ~-glider n Drachenflieger m. **~-gliding** n Drachenfliegen nt. **~man** n Henker m. **~over** n 🅸 Kater m 🅸. **~-up** n 🅸 Komplex m

hanker /'hæŋkə(r)/ vi **~ after sth** sich (dat) etw wünschen

hanky /'hæŋkɪ/ n 🅸 Taschentuch nt

haphazard /hæp'hæzəd/ adj planlos

happen /'hæpn/ vi geschehen, passieren; **I ~ed to be there** ich war zufällig da; **what has ~ed to him?** was ist mit ihm los? (become of) was ist aus ihm geworden? **~ing** n Ereignis nt

happi|ly /'hæpɪlɪ/ adv glücklich; (fortunately) glücklicherweise. **~ness** n Glück nt

happy /'hæpɪ/ adj glücklich. **~-go-'lucky** adj sorglos

h

harass /ˈhærəs/ vt schikanieren. **~ed** adj abgehetzt. **~ment** n Schikane f; (sexual) Belästigung f

harbour /ˈhɑ:bə(r)/ n Hafen m

hard /hɑ:d/ adj (**-er, -est**) hart; (difficult) schwer; **~ of hearing** schwerhörig •adv hart; (work) schwer; (pull) kräftig; (rain, snow) stark; **be ~ up** [!] knapp bei Kasse sein

hard: ~back n gebundene Ausgabe f. **~board** n Hartfaserplatte f. **~-boiled** adj hart gekocht **~disk** n Festplatte f

h

harden /ˈhɑ:dn/ vi hart werden

hard-ˈhearted adj hartherzig

hard|ly /ˈhɑ:dlɪ/ adv kaum; **~ly ever** kaum [jemals]. **~ness** n Härte f. **~ship** n Not f

hard: ~ ˈshoulder n (Auto) Randstreifen m. **~ware** n Haushaltswaren pl; (Computing) Hardware f. **~-ˈwearing** adj strapazierfähig. **~-ˈworking** adj fleißig

hardy /ˈhɑ:dɪ/ adj abgehärtet; (plant) winterhart

hare /heə(r)/ n Hase m

harm /hɑ:m/ n Schaden m; **it won't do any ~** es kann nichts schaden •vt **~ s.o.** jdm etwas antun. **~ful** adj schädlich. **~less** adj harmlos

harmonious /hɑ:ˈməʊnɪəs/ adj harmonisch

harmon|ize /ˈhɑ:mənaɪz/ vi (fig) harmonieren. **~y** n Harmonie f

harness /ˈhɑ:nɪs/ n Geschirr nt; (of parachute) Gurtwerk nt •vt anschirren (horse); (use) nutzbar machen

harp /hɑ:p/ n Harfe f. **~ist** n Harfenist(in) m(f)

harpsichord /ˈhɑ:psɪkɔ:d/ n Cembalo nt

harrowing /ˈhærəʊɪŋ/ adj grauenhaft

harsh /hɑ:ʃ/ adj (**-er, -est**) hart; (voice) rau; (light) grell. **~ness** n Härte f; Rauheit f

harvest /ˈhɑ:vɪst/ n Ernte f •vt ernten

has /hæz/ see **have**

hassle /ˈhæsl/ n [!] Ärger m •vt schikanieren

haste /heɪst/ n Eile f

hasten /ˈheɪsn/ vi sich beeilen (**to** zu); (go quickly) eilen •vt beschleunigen

hasty /ˈheɪstɪ/ adj, **-ily** adv hastig; (decision) voreilig

hat /hæt/ n Hut m; (knitted) Mütze f

hatch[1] /hætʃ/ n (for food) Durchreiche f; (Naut) Luke f

hatch[2] vi **~[out]** ausschlüpfen •vt ausbrüten

ˈhatchback n (Auto) Modell nt mit Hecktür

hate /heɪt/ n Hass m •vt hassen. **~ful** adj abscheulich

hatred /ˈheɪtrɪd/ n Hass m

haughty /ˈhɔ:tɪ/ adj, **-ily** adv hochmütig

haul /hɔ:l/ n (loot) Beute f •vt/i ziehen (**on** an + dat)

haunt /hɔ:nt/ n Lieblingsaufenthalt m •vt umgehen in (+ dat); **this house is ~ed** in diesem Haus spukt es

have /hæv/, unbetont /həv/, /əv/

3 sg pres tense **has**; pt and pp **had**

•transitive verb

····➤(possess) haben. **he has [got] a car** er hat ein Auto. **she has [got] a brother** sie hat einen Bruder. **we have [got] five minutes** wir haben fünf Minuten

····➤(eat) essen; (drink) trinken; (smoke) rauchen. **have a cup of tea** eine Tasse Tee trinken. **have a pizza** eine Pizza essen. **have a cigarette** eine Zigarette rauchen. **have breakfast/dinner/lunch** frühstücken/zu Abend essen/zu Mittag essen

····➤(take esp. in shop, restaurant)

nehmen. **I'll have the soup/the red dress** ich nehme die Suppe/ das rote Kleid. **have a cigarette!** nehmen Sie eine Zigarette!
····➤ (get, receive) bekommen. **I had a letter from her** ich bekam einen Brief von ihr. **have a baby** ein Baby bekommen
····➤ (suffer) haben (illness, pain, disappointment); erleiden (shock)
····➤ (organize) **have a party** eine Party veranstalten. **they had a meeting** sie hielten eine Versammlung ab
····➤ (take part in) **have a game of football** Fußball spielen. **have a swim** schwimmen
····➤ (as guest) **have s.o. to stay** jdn zu Besuch haben
····➤ **have had it** [!] (thing) ausgedient haben; (person) geliefert sein. **you've had it now** jetzt ist es aus
····➤ **have sth done** etw machen lassen. **we had the house painted** wir haben das Haus malen lassen. **have a dress made** sich (dat) ein Kleid machen lassen. **have a tooth out** sich (dat) einen Zahn ziehen lassen. **have one's hair cut** sich (dat) die Haare schneiden lassen
····➤ **have to do sth** etw tun müssen. **I have to go now** ich muss jetzt gehen
• auxiliary verb
····➤ (forming perfect and past perfect tenses) haben; (with verbs of motion and some others) sein. **I have seen him** ich habe ihn gesehen. **he has never been there** er ist nie da gewesen. **I had gone** ich war gegangen. **if I had known ...** wenn ich gewusst hätte ...
····➤ (in tag questions) nicht wahr. **you've met her, haven't you?** du kennst sie, nicht wahr?
····➤ (in short answers) **Have you seen the film? — Yes, I have** Hast du den Film gesehen? — Ja [, stimmt]
• **have on** vt (be wearing) anhaben; (dupe) anführen

havoc /'hævək/ n Verwüstung f

hawk /hɔ:k/ n Falke m

hawthorn /'hɔ:-/ n Hagedorn m

hay /heɪ/ n Heu nt. **~ fever** n Heuschnupfen m. **~stack** n Heuschober m

hazard /'hæzəd/ n Gefahr f; (risk) Risiko nt • vt riskieren. **~ous** adj gefährlich; (risky) riskant

haze /'heɪz/ n Dunst m

hazel /'heɪzl/ n Haselbusch m. **~-nut** n Haselnuss f

hazy /'heɪzɪ/ adj dunstig; (fig) unklar

he /hi:/ pron er

head /hed/ n Kopf m; (chief) Oberhaupt nt; (of firm) Chef(in) m(f); (of school) Schulleiter(in) m(f); (on beer) Schaumkrone f; (of bed) Kopfende nt; **~ first** kopfüber • vt anführen; (Sport) köpfen (ball) • vi **~ for** zusteuern auf (+ acc). **~ache** n Kopfschmerzen pl

head|er /'hedə(r)/ n Kopfball m; (dive) Kopfsprung m. **~ing** n Überschrift f

head: ~lamp, ~light n (Auto) Scheinwerfer m. **~line** n Schlagzeile f. **~long** adv kopfüber. **~'master** n Schulleiter m. **~'mistress** n Schulleiterin f. **~-on** adj & adv frontal. **~phones** npl Kopfhörer m. **~quarters** npl Hauptquartier nt; (Pol) Zentrale f. **~-rest** n Kopfstütze f. **~room** n lichte Höhe f. **~scarf** n Kopftuch nt. **~strong** adj eigenwillig. **~way** n **make ~way** Fortschritte machen. **~word** n Stichwort nt

heady /'hedɪ/ adj berauschend

heal /hi:l/ vt/i heilen

health /helθ/ n Gesundheit f

health: ~ farm n Schönheitsfarm f. **~ foods** npl Reformkost f. **~-food shop** n Reformhaus nt. **~ insurance** n Krankenversicherung f

healthy /'helθɪ/ adj, **-ily** adv gesund

heap /hi:p/ n Haufen m; **~s** [!] jede Menge • vt **~ [up]** häufen

hear /hɪə(r)/ vt/i (pt/pp **heard**) hören; **~,~!** hört, hört! **he would**

not ~ of it er ließ es nicht zu

hearing /ˈhɪərɪŋ/ n Gehör nt; (Jur) Verhandlung f. **~-aid** n Hörgerät nt

hearse /hɜːs/ n Leichenwagen m

heart /hɑːt/ n Herz nt; (courage) Mut m; **~s** pl (Cards) Herz nt; **by ~** auswendig

heart: ~ache n Kummer m. **~attack** n Herzanfall m. **~beat** n Herzschlag m. **~-breaking** adj herzzerreißend. **~-broken** adj untröstlich. **~burn** n Sodbrennen nt. **~en** vt ermutigen. **~felt** adj herzlich[st]

h

hearth /hɑːθ/ n Herd m; (fireplace) Kamin m

heart|ily /ˈhɑːtɪlɪ/ adv herzlich; (eat) viel. **~less** adj herzlos. **~y** adj herzlich; (meal) groß; (person) burschikos

heat /hiːt/ n Hitze f; (Sport) Vorlauf m • vt heiß machen; heizen (room). **~ed** adj geheizt; (swimming pool) beheizt; (discussion) hitzig. **~er** n Heizgerät nt; (Auto) Heizanlage f

heath /hiːθ/ n Heide f

heathen /ˈhiːðn/ adj heidnisch • n Heide m/Heidin f

heather /ˈheðə(r)/ n Heidekraut nt

heating /ˈhiːtɪŋ/ n Heizung f

heat wave n Hitzewelle f

heave /hiːv/ vt/i ziehen; (lift) heben; (!: throw) schmeißen

heaven /ˈhevn/ n Himmel m. **~ly** adj himmlisch

heavy /ˈhevɪ/ adj, **-ily** adv schwer; (traffic, rain) stark. **~weight** n Schwergewicht nt

heckle /ˈhekl/ vt [durch Zwischenrufe] unterbrechen. **~r** n Zwischenrufer m

hectic /ˈhektɪk/ adj hektisch

hedge /hedʒ/ n Hecke f. **~hog** n Igel m

heed /hiːd/ vt beachten

heel[1] /hiːl/ n Ferse f; (of shoe) Absatz m; **down at ~** heruntergekommen

heel[2] vi **~ over** (Naut) sich auf die Seite legen

hefty /ˈheftɪ/ adj kräftig; (heavy) schwer

height /haɪt/ n Höhe f; (of person) Größe f. **~en** vt (fig) steigern

heir /eə(r)/ n Erbe m. **~ess** n Erbin f. **~loom** n Erbstück nt

held /held/ see **hold**[2]

helicopter /ˈhelɪkɒptə(r)/ n Hubschrauber m

hell /hel/ n Hölle f; **go to ~!** ✖ geh zum Teufel! • int verdammt!

hello /həˈləʊ/ int [guten] Tag! ! hallo!

helm /helm/ n [Steuer]ruder nt

helmet /ˈhelmɪt/ n Helm m

help /help/ n Hilfe f; (employees) Hilfskräfte pl; **that's no ~** das nützt nichts • vt/i helfen (**s.o.** jdm); **~ oneself to sth** sich (dat) etw nehmen; **~ yourself** (at table) greif zu; **I could not ~ laughing** ich musste lachen; **it cannot be ~ed** es lässt sich nicht ändern; **I can't ~ it** ich kann nichts dafür

help|er /ˈhelpə(r)/ n Helfer(in) m(f). **~ful** adj, **-ly** adv hilfsbereit; (advice) nützlich. **~ing** n Portion f. **~less** adj hilflos

hem /hem/ n Saum m • vt (pt/pp **hemmed**) säumen; **~ in** umzingeln

hemisphere /ˈhemɪ-/ n Hemisphäre f

ˈhem-line n Rocklänge f

hen /hen/ n Henne f; (any female bird) Weibchen nt

hence /hens/ adv daher; **five years ~** in fünf Jahren. **~ˈforth** adv von nun an

ˈhenpecked adj **~ husband** Pantoffelheld m

her /hɜː(r)/ adj ihr • pron (acc) sie; (dat) ihr

herald /ˈherəld/ vt verkünden. **~ry** n Wappenkunde f

herb /hɜːb/ n Kraut nt

herbaceous /hɜːˈbeɪʃəs/ adj ~

border Staudenrabatte f

herd /hɜːd/ n Herde f. ~ **together** vt zusammentreiben

here /hɪə(r)/ adv hier; (to this place) hierher; **in** ~ hier drinnen; **come/ bring** ~ herkommen/herbringen

hereditary /həˈredɪtərɪ/ adj erblich

here|sy /ˈherəsɪ/ n Ketzerei f. ~**tic** n Ketzer(in) m(f)

here'with adv (Comm) beiliegend

heritage /ˈherɪtɪdʒ/ n Erbe nt. ~ **tourism** n Kulturtourismus m

hero /ˈhɪərəʊ/ n (pl **-es**) Held m

heroic /hɪˈrəʊɪk/ adj, **-ally** adv heldenhaft

heroin /ˈherəʊɪn/ n Heroin nt

hero|ine /ˈherəʊɪn/ n Heldin f. ~**ism** n Heldentum nt

heron /ˈhern/ n Reiher m

herring /ˈherɪŋ/ n Hering m

hers /hɜːz/ poss pron ihre(r), ihrs; **a friend of** ~ ein Freund von ihr; **that is** ~ das gehört ihr

her'self pron selbst; (reflexive) sich; **by** ~ allein

hesitant /ˈhezɪtənt/ adj zögernd

hesitat|e /ˈhezɪteɪt/ vi zögern. ~**ion** n Zögern nt; **without** ~**ion** ohne zu zögern

hexagonal /hekˈsægənl/ adj sechseckig

heyday /ˈheɪ-/ n Glanzzeit f

hi /haɪ/ int he! (hallo) Tag!

hiatus /haɪˈeɪtəs/ n (pl **-tuses**) Lücke f

hibernat|e /ˈhaɪbəneɪt/ vi Winterschlaf halten. ~**ion** n Winterschlaf m

hiccup /ˈhɪkʌp/ n Hick m; (**!**: hitch) Panne f; **have the** ~**s** den Schluckauf haben • vi hick machen

hid /hɪd/, **hidden** see **hide**[2]

hide v (pt **hid**, pp **hidden**) • vt verstecken; (keep secret) verheimlichen • vi sich verstecken

hideous /ˈhɪdɪəs/ adj hässlich; (horrible) grässlich

'hide-out n Versteck nt

hiding[1] /ˈhaɪdɪŋ/ n **!** **give s.o. a** ~ jdn verdreschen

hiding[2] n **go into** ~ untertauchen

hierarchy /ˈhaɪərɑːkɪ/ n Hierarchie f

high /haɪ/ adj (**-er, -est**) hoch; attrib hohe(r,s); (meat) angegangen; (wind) stark; (on drugs) high; **it's** ~ **time** es ist höchste Zeit • adv hoch; ~ **and low** überall • n Hoch nt; (temperature) Höchsttemperatur f

high: ~**brow** adj intellektuell. ~**chair** n Kinderhochstuhl m. ~**'-handed** adj selbstherrlich. ~**-'heeled** adj hochhackig. ~ **jump** n Hochsprung m

'highlight n (fig) Höhepunkt m; ~**s** pl (in hair) helle Strähnen pl • vt (emphasize) hervorheben

highly /ˈhaɪlɪ/ adv hoch; **speak** ~ **of** loben; **think** ~ **of** sehr schätzen. ~**-'strung** adj nervös

Highness /ˈhaɪnɪs/ n Hoheit f

high: ~ **season** n Hochsaison f. ~ **street** n Hauptstraße f. ~ **'tide** n Hochwasser nt. ~**way** n **public** ~**way** öffentliche Straße f

hijack /ˈhaɪdʒæk/ vt entführen. ~**er** n Entführer m

hike /haɪk/ n Wanderung f • vi wandern. ~**r** n Wanderer m

hilarious /hɪˈleərɪəs/ adj sehr komisch

hill /hɪl/ n Berg m; (mound) Hügel m; (slope) Hang m

hill: ~**side** n Hang m. ~**y** adj hügelig

him /hɪm/ pron (acc) ihn; (dat) ihm. ~**'self** pron selbst; (reflexive) sich; **by** ~**self** allein

hind /haɪnd/ adj Hinter-

hind|er /ˈhɪndə(r)/ vt hindern. ~**rance** n Hindernis nt

hindsight /ˈhaɪnd-/ n **with** ~ rückblickend

Hindu /ˈhɪnduː/ n Hindu m • adj Hindu-. ~**ism** n Hinduismus m

h

hinge /hɪndʒ/ n Scharnier nt; (on door) Angel f

hint /hɪnt/ n Wink m, Andeutung f; (advice) Hinweis m; (trace) Spur f •vi **~ at** anspielen auf (+ acc)

hip /hɪp/ n Hüfte f

hip 'pocket n Gesäßtasche f

hippopotamus /hɪpəˈpɒtəməs/ n (pl **-muses** or **-mi** /-maɪ/) Nilpferd nt

hire /ˈhaɪə(r)/ vt mieten (car); leihen (suit); einstellen (person); **~[out]** vermieten; verleihen

his /hɪz/ adj sein •poss pron seine(r), seins; **a friend of ~** ein Freund von ihm; **that is ~** das gehört ihm

hiss /hɪs/ n Zischen nt •vt/i zischen

historian /hɪˈstɔːrɪən/ n Historiker(in) m(f)

historic /hɪˈstɒrɪk/ adj historisch. **~al** adj geschichtlich, historisch

history /ˈhɪstərɪ/ n Geschichte f

hit /hɪt/ n (blow) Schlag m; (!: success) Erfolg m; **direct ~** Volltreffer m •vt/i (pt/pp **hit**, pres p **hitting**) schlagen; (knock against, collide with, affect) treffen; **~ the target** das Ziel treffen; **~ on** (fig) kommen auf (+ acc); **~ it off** gut auskommen (**with** mit); **~ one's head on sth** sich (dat) den Kopf an etw (dat) stoßen

hitch /hɪtʃ/ n Problem nt; **technical ~** Panne f •vt festmachen (**to** an + dat); **~ up** hochziehen. **~-hike** vi ! trampen. **~-hiker** n Anhalter(in) m(f)

hive /haɪv/ n Bienenstock m

hoard /hɔːd/ n Hort m •vt horten, hamstern

hoarding /ˈhɔːdɪŋ/ n Bauzaun m; (with advertisements) Reklamewand f

hoar-frost /ˈhɔː-/ n Raureif m

hoarse /hɔːs/ adj (**-r, -st**) heiser. **~ness** n Heiserkeit f

hoax /həʊks/ n übler Scherz m; (false alarm) blinder Alarm m

hobble /ˈhɒbl/ vi humpeln

hobby /ˈhɒbɪ/ n Hobby nt. **~-horse** n (fig) Lieblingsthema nt

hockey /ˈhɒkɪ/ n Hockey nt

hoe /həʊ/ n Hacke f •vt (pres p **hoeing**) hacken

hog /hɒg/ vt (pt/pp **hogged**) ! mit Beschlag belegen

hoist /hɔɪst/ n Lastenaufzug m •vt hochziehen; hissen (flag)

hold¹ /həʊld/ n (Naut) Laderaum m

hold² n Halt m; (Sport) Griff m; (fig: influence) Einfluss m; **get ~ of** fassen; (!: contact) erreichen •v (pt/pp **held**) •vt halten; (container:) fassen; (believe) meinen; (possess) haben; anhalten (breath) •vi (rope:) halten; (weather:) sich halten. **~ back** vt zurückhalten •vi zögern. **~ on** vi (wait) warten; (on telephone) am Apparat bleiben; **~ on to** (keep) behalten; (cling to) sich festhalten an (+ dat). **~ out** vt hinhalten •vi (resist) aushalten. **~ up** vt hochhalten; (delay) aufhalten; (rob) überfallen

'hold|all n Reisetasche f. **~er** n Inhaber(in) m(f); (container) Halter m. **~-up** n Verzögerung f; (attack) Überfall m

hole /həʊl/ n Loch nt

holiday /ˈhɒlədeɪ/ n Urlaub m; (Sch) Ferien pl; (public) Feiertag m; (day off) freier Tag m; **go on ~** in Urlaub fahren

holiness /ˈhəʊlɪnɪs/ n Heiligkeit f

Holland /ˈhɒlənd/ n Holland nt

hollow /ˈhɒləʊ/ adj hohl; (promise) leer •n Vertiefung f; (in ground) Mulde f. **~ out** vt aushöhlen

holly /ˈhɒlɪ/ n Stechpalme f

holster /ˈhəʊlstə(r)/ n Pistolentasche f

holy /ˈhəʊlɪ/ adj (**-ier, -est**) heilig. **H~ Ghost** or **Spirit** n Heiliger Geist m

homage /ˈhɒmɪdʒ/ n Huldigung f; **pay ~ to** huldigen (+ dat)

home /həʊm/ n Zuhause nt (house) Haus nt; (institution) Heim nt; (native land) Heimat f •adv **at ~** zu Hause; **come/go ~** nach Hause kommen/gehen

home: ~ ad'dress n Heimatanschrift f. **~ game** n Heimspiel nt. **~ help** n Haushaltshilfe f. **~land** n Heimatland nt. **~land security** innere Sicherheit f. **~less** adj obdachlos

homely /'həʊmlɪ/ adj adj gemütlich; (Amer: ugly) unscheinbar

home: ~-'made adj selbst gemacht. **H~ Office** n Innenministerium nt. **~ page** n Homepage f. **H~ 'Secretary** Innenminister m. **~sick** adj **be ~sick** Heimweh haben (**for** nach). **~sickness** n Heimweh nt. **~ 'town** n Heimatstadt f. **~work** n (Sch) Hausaufgaben pl

homo'sexual adj homosexuell •n Homosexuelle(r) m/f

honest /'ɒnɪst/ adj ehrlich. **~y** n Ehrlichkeit f

honey /'hʌnɪ/ n Honig m ([!]: darling) Schatz m

honey: ~comb n Honigwabe f. **~moon** n Flitterwochen pl; (journey) Hochzeitsreise f

honorary /'ɒnərərɪ/ adj ehrenamtlich; (member, doctorate) Ehren-

honour /'ɒnə(r)/ n Ehre f •vt ehren; honorieren (cheque). **~able** adj, **-bly** adv ehrenhaft

hood /hʊd/ n Kapuze f; (of car, pram) [Klapp]verdeck nt; (over cooker) Abzugshaube f; (Auto, Amer) Kühlerhaube f

hoof /hu:f/ n (pl **~s** or **hooves**) Huf m

hook /hʊk/ n Haken m •vt festhaken (**to** an + acc)

hook|ed /hʊkt/ adj **~ed nose** Hakennase f; **~ed on** [!] abhängig von; (keen on) besessen von. **~er** n (Amer, [x]) Nutte f

hookey /'hʊkɪ/ n **play ~** (Amer, [!]) schwänzen

hooligan /'hu:lɪgən/ n Rowdy m. **~ism** n Rowdytum nt

hooray /hʊ'reɪ/ int & n = **hurrah**

hoot /hu:t/ n Ruf m; **~s of laughter** schallendes Gelächter nt •vi (owl:) rufen; (car:) hupen; (jeer) johlen. **~er** n (of factory) Sirene f; (Auto) Hupe f

hoover /'hu:və(r)/ n **H~ ®** Staubsauger m •vt/i [staub]saugen

hop¹ /hɒp/ n, & **~s** pl Hopfen m

hop² vi (pt/pp **hopped**) hüpfen; **~ it!** [!] hau ab!

hope /həʊp/ n Hoffnung f; (prospect) Aussicht f (**of** auf + acc) •vt/i hoffen (**for** auf + acc); **I ~ so** hoffentlich

hope|ful /'həʊpfl/ adj hoffnungsvoll; **be ~ful that** hoffen, dass. **~fully** adv hoffnungsvoll; (it is hoped) hoffentlich. **~less** adj hoffnungslos; (useless) nutzlos; (incompetent) untauglich

horde /hɔ:d/ n Horde f

horizon /hə'raɪzn/ n Horizont m

horizontal /hɒrɪ'zɒntl/ adj horizontal. **~ 'bar** n Reck nt

horn /hɔ:n/ n Horn nt; (Auto) Hupe f

hornet /'hɔ:nɪt/ n Hornisse f

horoscope /'hɒrəskəʊp/ n Horoskop nt

horrible /'hɒrɪbl/ adj, **-bly** adv schrecklich

horrid /'hɒrɪd/ adj grässlich

horrific /hə'rɪfɪk/ adj entsetzlich

horrify /'hɒrɪfaɪ/ vt (pt/pp **-ied**) entsetzen

horror /'hɒrə(r)/ n Entsetzen nt

hors-d'œuvre /ɔ:'dɜ:vr/ n Vorspeise f

horse /hɔ:s/ n Pferd nt

horse: ~back n **on ~back** zu Pferde. **~man** n Reiter m. **~power** n Pferdestärke f. **~-racing** n Pferderennen nt. **~radish** n Meerrettich m. **~shoe** n Hufeisen nt

'horticulture n Gartenbau m

hose /həʊz/ n (pipe) Schlauch m •vt **~ down** abspritzen

hosiery /'həʊzɪərɪ/ n Strumpfwaren pl

h

hospitable /hɒ'spɪtəbl/ adj, **-bly** adv gastfreundlich

hospital /'hɒspɪtl/ n Krankenhaus nt

hospitality /hɒspɪ'tælətɪ/ n Gastfreundschaft f

host /həʊst/ n Gastgeber m

hostage /'hɒstɪdʒ/ n Geisel f

hostel /'hɒstl/ n [Wohn]heim nt

hostess /'həʊstɪs/ n Gastgeberin f

hostile /'hɒstaɪl/ adj feindlich; (unfriendly) feindselig

hostilit|y /hɒ'stɪlətɪ/ n Feindschaft f; **~ies** pl Feindseligkeiten pl

h

hot /hɒt/ adj (**hotter, hottest**) heiß; (meal) warm; (spicy) scharf; **I am** or **feel ~** mir ist heiß

hotel /həʊ'tel/ n Hotel nt

hot: ~head n Hitzkopf m. **~house** n Treibhaus nt. **~ly** adv (fig) heiß, heftig. **~plate** n Tellerwärmer m; (of cooker) Kochplatte f. **~ tap** n Warmwasserhahn m. **~-tempered** adj jähzornig. **~-'waterbottle** n Wärmflasche f

hound /haʊnd/ n Jagdhund m • vt (fig) verfolgen

hour /'aʊə(r)/ n Stunde f. **~ly** adj & adv stündlich

house[1] /haʊs/ n Haus nt; **at my ~** bei mir

house[2] /haʊz/ vt unterbringen

house: /haʊs/ **~breaking** n Einbruch m. **~hold** n Haushalt m. **~holder** n Hausinhaber(in) m(f). **~keeper** n Haushälterin f. **~keeping** n Hauswirtschaft f; (money) Haushaltsgeld nt. **~-plant** n Zimmerpflanze f. **~-trained** adj stubenrein. **~-warming** n **have a ~-warming party** Einstand feiern. **~wife** n Hausfrau f. **~work** n Hausarbeit f

housing /'haʊzɪŋ/ n Wohnungen pl; (Techn) Gehäuse nt

hovel /'hɒvl/ n elende Hütte f

hover /'hɒvə(r)/ vi schweben. **~craft** n Luftkissenfahrzeug nt

how /haʊ/ adv wie; **~ do you do?** guten Tag!; **and ~!** und ob!

how'ever adv (in question) wie; (nevertheless) jedoch, aber; **~ small** wie klein es auch sein mag

howl /haʊl/ n Heulen nt • vi heulen; (baby:) brüllen

hub /hʌb/ n Nabe f

huddle /'hʌdl/ vi **~ together** sich zusammendrängen

huff /hʌf/ n **in a ~** beleidigt

hug /hʌg/ n Umarmung f • vt (pt/pp **hugged**) umarmen

huge /hju:dʒ/ adj riesig

hull /hʌl/ n (Naut) Rumpf m

hullo /hə'ləʊ/ int = **hallo**

hum /hʌm/ n Summen nt; Brummen nt • vt/i (pt/pp **hummed**) summen; (motor:) brummen

human /'hju:mən/ adj menschlich • n Mensch m. **~ 'being** n Mensch m

humane /hju:'meɪn/ adj human

humanitarian /hju:mænɪ'teərɪən/ adj humanitär

humanity /hju:'mænətɪ/ n Menschheit f

humble /'hʌmbl/ adj (**-r, -st**), **-bly** adv demütig • vt demütigen

'humdrum adj eintönig

humid /'hju:mɪd/ adj feucht. **~ity** n Feuchtigkeit f

humiliat|e /hju:'mɪlɪeɪt/ vt demütigen. **~ion** n Demütigung f

humility /hju:'mɪlətɪ/ n Demut f

humorous /'hju:mərəs/ adj humorvoll; (story) humoristisch

humour /'hju:mə(r)/ n Humor m; (mood) Laune f; **have a sense of ~** Humor haben

hump /hʌmp/ n Buckel m; (of camel) Höcker m • vt schleppen

hunch /hʌntʃ/ n (idea) Ahnung f

'hunch|back n Bucklige(r) m/f

hundred /'hʌndrəd/ adj **one/a ~** [ein]hundert • n Hundert nt; (written figure) Hundert f. **~th** adj hundertste(r,s) • n Hundertstel nt.

~weight n ≈ Zentner m

hung /hʌŋ/ see **hang**

Hungarian /hʌŋ'geərɪən/ adj ungarisch • n Ungar(in) m(f)

Hungary /'hʌŋgərɪ/ n Ungarn nt

hunger /'hʌŋgə(r)/ n Hunger m. **~-strike** n Hungerstreik m

hungry /'hʌŋgrɪ/ adj , **-ily** adv hungrig; **be ~** Hunger haben

hunt /hʌnt/ n Jagd f; (for criminal) Fahndung f • vt/i jagen; fahnden nach (criminal); **~ for** suchen. **~er** n Jäger m; (horse) Jagdpferd nt. **~ing** n Jagd f

hurdle /'hɜːdl/ n (Sport & fig) Hürde f

hurl /hɜːl/ vt schleudern

hurrah /hʊ'rɑː/, **hurray** /hʊ'reɪ/ int hurra! • n Hurra nt

hurricane /'hʌrɪkən/ n Orkan m

hurried /'hʌrɪd/ adj eilig; (superficial) flüchtig

hurry /'hʌrɪ/ n Eile f; **be in a ~** es eilig haben • vi (pt/pp **-ied**) sich beeilen; (go quickly) eilen. **~ up** vi sich beeilen • vt antreiben

hurt /hɜːt/ n Schmerz m • vt/i (pt/pp **hurt**) weh tun (+ dat); (injure) verletzen; (offend) kränken

hurtle /'hɜːtl/ vi **~ along** rasen

husband /'hʌzbənd/ n [Ehe]mann m

hush /hʌʃ/ n Stille f • vt **~ up** vertuschen. **~ed** adj gedämpft

husky /'hʌskɪ/ adj heiser; (burly) stämmig

hustle /'hʌsl/ vt drängen • n Gedränge nt

hut /hʌt/ n Hütte f

hutch /hʌtʃ/ n [Kaninchen]stall m

hybrid /'haɪbrɪd/ adj hybrid • n Hybride f

hydraulic /haɪ'drɔːlɪk/ adj, **-ally** adv hydraulisch

hydroe'lectric /haɪdrəʊ-/ adj hydroelektrisch

hydrogen /'haɪdrədʒən/ n Wasserstoff m

hygien|e /'haɪdʒiːn/ n Hygiene f. **~ic** adj, **-ally** adv hygienisch

hymn /hɪm/ n Kirchenlied nt. **~-book** n Gesangbuch nt

hyphen /'haɪfn/ n Bindestrich m. **~ate** vt mit Bindestrich schreiben

hypno|sis /hɪp'nəʊsɪs/ n Hypnose f. **~tic** adj hypnotisch

hypno|tism /'hɪpnətɪzm/ n Hypnotik f. **~tist** n Hypnotiseur m. **~tize** vt hypnotisieren

hypochondriac /haɪpə'kɒndrɪæk/ n Hypochonder m

hypocrisy /hɪ'pɒkrəsɪ/ n Heuchelei f

hypocrit|e /'hɪpəkrɪt/ n Heuchler(in) m(f)

hypodermic /haɪpə'dɜːmɪk/ adj & n **~ [syringe]** Injektionsspritze f

hypothe|sis /haɪ'pɒθəsɪs/ n Hypothese f. **~tical** adj hypothetisch

hyster|ia /hɪ'stɪərɪə/ n Hysterie f. **~ical** adj hysterisch. **~ics** npl hysterischer Anfall m

Ii

I /aɪ/ pron ich

ice /aɪs/ n Eis nt • vt mit Zuckerguss überziehen (cake)

ice: ~berg /-bɜːg/ n Eisberg m. **~box** n (Amer) Kühlschrank m. **~-'cream** n [Speise]eis nt. **~-cube** n Eiswürfel m

Iceland /'aɪslənd/ n Island nt

ice: ~'lolly n Eis nt am Stiel. **~ rink** n Eisbahn f

icicle /'aɪsɪkl/ n Eiszapfen m

icing /'aɪsɪŋ/ n Zuckerguss m. ~ **sugar** n Puderzucker m

icon /'aɪkɒn/ n Ikone f

icy /'aɪsɪ/ adj, **-ily** adv eisig; (road) vereist

idea /aɪ'dɪə/ n Idee f; (conception) Vorstellung f; **I have no ~!** ich habe keine Ahnung!

ideal /aɪ'dɪəl/ adj ideal •n Ideal nt. **~ism** n Idealismus m. **~ist** n Idealist(in) m(f). **~istic** adj idealistisch. **~ize** vt idealisieren. **~ly** adv ideal; (in ideal circumstances) idealerweise

identical /aɪ'dentɪkl/ adj identisch; (twins) eineiig

identi|fication /aɪdentɪfɪ'keɪʃn/ n Identifizierung f; (proof of identity) Ausweispapiere pl. **~fy** vt (pt/pp **-ied**) identifizieren

identity /aɪ'dentətɪ/ n Identität f. ~ **card** n [Personal]ausweis m. ~ **theft** Identitätsdiebstahl m

idiom /'ɪdɪəm/ n [feste] Redewendung f. **~atic** adj, **-ally** adv idiomatisch

idiosyncrasy /ɪdɪə'sɪŋkrəsɪ/ n Eigenart f

idiot /'ɪdɪət/ n Idiot m. **~ic** adj idiotisch

idle /'aɪdl/ adj (**-r, -st**) untätig; (lazy) faul; (empty) leer; (machine) nicht in Betrieb •vi faulenzen; (engine:) leer laufen. **~ness** n Untätigkeit f; Faulheit f

idol /'aɪdl/ n Idol nt. **~ize** vt vergöttern

idyllic /ɪ'dɪlɪk/ adj idyllisch

i.e. abbr (**id est**) d.h.

if /ɪf/ conj wenn; (whether) ob; **as if** als ob

ignition /ɪg'nɪʃn/ n (Auto) Zündung f. ~ **key** n Zündschlüssel m

ignoramus /ɪgnə'reɪməs/ n Ignorant m

ignoran|ce /'ɪgnərəns/ n Unwissenheit f. **~t** adj unwissend

ignore /ɪg'nɔ:(r)/ vt ignorieren

ill /ɪl/ adj krank; (bad) schlecht; **feel ~ at ease** sich unbehaglich fühlen •adv schlecht

illegal /ɪ'li:gl/ adj illegal

illegible /ɪ'ledʒəbl/ adj, **-bly** adv unleserlich

illegitimate /ɪlɪ'dʒɪtɪmət/ adj unehelich; (claim) unberechtigt

illicit /ɪ'lɪsɪt/ adj illegal

illiterate /ɪ'lɪtərət/ adj **be ~** nicht lesen und schreiben können

illness /'ɪlnɪs/ n Krankheit f

illogical /ɪ'lɒdʒɪkl/ adj unlogisch

ill-treat /ɪl'tri:t/ vt misshandeln. **~ment** n Misshandlung f

illuminat|e /ɪ'lu:mɪneɪt/ vt beleuchten. **~ion** n Beleuchtung f

illusion /ɪ'lu:ʒn/ n Illusion f; **be under the ~ that** sich (dat) einbilden, dass

illustrat|e /'ɪləstreɪt/ vt illustrieren. **~ion** n Illustration f

illustrious /ɪ'lʌstrɪəs/ adj berühmt

image /'ɪmɪdʒ/ n Bild nt; (statue) Standbild nt; (exact likeness) Ebenbild nt; **[public] ~** Image nt

imagin|able /ɪ'mædʒɪnəbl/ adj vorstellbar. **~ary** adj eingebildet

imaginat|ion /ɪmædʒɪ'neɪʃn/ n Phantasie f; (fancy) Einbildung f. **~ive** adj phantasievoll; (full of ideas) einfallsreich

imagine /ɪ'mædʒɪn/ vt sich (dat) vorstellen; (wrongly) sich (dat) einbilden

im'balance n Unausgeglichenheit f

imbecile /'ɪmbəsi:l/ n Schwachsinnige(r) m/f; (pej) Idiot m

imitat|e /'ɪmɪteɪt/ vt nachahmen, imitieren. **~ion** n Nachahmung f, Imitation f

immaculate /ɪ'mækjʊlət/ adj tadellos; (Relig) unbefleckt

imma'ture adj unreif

immediate /ɪ'mi:dɪət/ adj sofortig; (nearest) nächste(r,s). **~ly** adv sofort; **~ly next to** unmittelbar neben •conj sobald

immemorial /ɪmə'mɔ:rɪəl/ adj **from time ~** seit Urzeiten

immense /ɪ'mens/ adj riesig; [!] enorm

immerse /ɪ'mɜ:s/ vt untertauchen

immigrant /'ɪmɪgrənt/ n Einwanderer m

immigration /ɪmɪ'greɪʃn/ n Einwanderung f

imminent /'ɪmɪnənt/ adj **be ~** unmittelbar bevorstehen

immobil|e /ɪ'məʊbaɪl/ adj unbeweglich. **~ize** vt (fig) lähmen; (Med) ruhig stellen. **~izer** n (Auto) Wegfahrsperre f

immodest /ɪ'mɒdɪst/ adj unbescheiden

immoral /ɪ'mɒrəl/ adj unmoralisch. **~ity** n Unmoral f

immortal /ɪ'mɔ:tl/ adj unsterblich. **~ity** n Unsterblichkeit f. **~ize** vt verewigen

immune /ɪ'mju:n/ adj immun (**to**/**from** gegen)

immunity /ɪ'mju:nətɪ/ n Immunität f

imp /ɪmp/ n Kobold m

impact /'ɪmpækt/ n Aufprall m; (collision) Zusammenprall m; (of bomb) Einschlag m; (fig) Auswirkung f

impair /ɪm'peə(r)/ vt beeinträchtigen

impart /ɪm'pɑ:t/ vt übermitteln (**to** dat); vermitteln (knowledge)

im'parti|al adj unparteiisch. **~'ality** n Unparteilichkeit f

im'passable adj unpassierbar

impassioned /ɪm'pæʃnd/ adj leidenschaftlich

im'passive adj unbeweglich

im'patien|ce n Ungeduld f. **~t** adj ungeduldig

impeccable /ɪm'pekəbl/ adj, **-bly** adv tadellos

impede /ɪm'pi:d/ vt behindern

impediment /ɪm'pedɪmənt/ n Hindernis nt; (in speech) Sprachfehler m

impel /ɪm'pel/ vt (pt/pp **impelled**) treiben

impending /ɪm'pendɪŋ/ adj bevorstehend

impenetrable /ɪm'penɪtrəbl/ adj undurchdringlich

imperative /ɪm'perətɪv/ adj **be ~** dringend notwendig sein •n (Gram) Imperativ m

imper'ceptible adj nicht wahrnehmbar

im'perfect adj unvollkommen; (faulty) fehlerhaft •n (Gram) Imperfekt nt. **~ion** n Unvollkommenheit f; (fault) Fehler m

imperial /ɪm'pɪərɪəl/ adj kaiserlich. **~ism** n Imperialismus m

im'personal adj unpersönlich

impersonat|e /ɪm'pɜ:səneɪt/ vt sich ausgeben als; (Theat) nachahmen, imitieren. **~or** n Imitator m

impertinen|ce /ɪm'pɜ:tɪnəns/ n Frechheit f. **~t** adj frech

imperturbable /ɪmpə'tɜ:bəbl/ adj unerschütterlich

impetuous /ɪm'petjʊəs/ adj ungestüm

impetus /'ɪmpɪtəs/ n Schwung m

implacable /ɪm'plækəbl/ adj unerbittlich

im'plant vt einpflanzen

implement¹ /'ɪmplɪmənt/ n Gerät nt

implement² /'ɪmplɪment/ vt ausführen. **~ation** n Ausführung f, Durchführung f

implication /ɪmplɪ'keɪʃn/ n Verwicklung f; **~s** pl Auswirkungen pl; **by ~** implizit

implicit /ɪm'plɪsɪt/ adj unausgesprochen; (absolute) unbedingt

implore /ɪm'plɔ:(r)/ vt anflehen

imply /ɪm'plaɪ/ vt (pt/pp **-ied**) andeuten; **what are you ~ing?**

was wollen Sie damit sagen?

impo'lite adj unhöflich

import[1] /'ɪmpɔːt/ n Import m, Einfuhr f

import[2] /ɪm'pɔːt/ vt importieren, einführen

importan|ce /ɪm'pɔːtns/ n Wichtigkeit f. **~t** adj wichtig

importer /ɪm'pɔːtə(r)/ n Importeur m

impos|e /ɪm'pəʊz/ vt auferlegen (**on** dat) •vi sich aufdrängen (**on** dat). **~ing** adj eindrucksvoll

impossi'bility n Unmöglichkeit f

im'possible adj, **-bly** adv unmöglich

impostor /ɪm'pɒstə(r)/ n Betrüger(in) m(f)

impoten|ce /'ɪmpətəns/ n Machtlosigkeit f; (Med) Impotenz f. **~t** adj machtlos; (Med) impotent

impoverished /ɪm'pɒvərɪʃt/ adj verarmt

im'practicable adj undurchführbar

im'practical adj unpraktisch

impre'cise adj ungenau

im'press vt beeindrucken; **~ sth [up]on s.o.** jdm etw einprägen

impression /ɪm'preʃn/ n Eindruck m; (imitation) Nachahmung f; (edition) Auflage f. **~ism** n Impressionismus m

impressive /ɪm'presɪv/ adj eindrucksvoll

im'prison vt gefangen halten; (put in prison) ins Gefängnis sperren

im'probable adj unwahrscheinlich

impromptu /ɪm'prɒmptjuː/ adj improvisiert •adv aus dem Stegreif

im'proper adj inkorrekt; (indecent) unanständig

impro'priety n Unkorrektheit f

improve /ɪm'pruːv/ vt verbessern; verschönern (appearance) •vi sich bessern; **~ [up]on** übertreffen. **~ment** n Verbesserung f; (in health) Besserung f

improvise /'ɪmprəvaɪz/ vt/i improvisieren

im'prudent adj unklug

impuden|ce /'ɪmpjʊdəns/ n Frechheit f. **~t** adj frech

impuls|e /'ɪmpʌls/ n Impuls m; **on [an] ~e** impulsiv. **~ive** adj impulsiv

im'pur|e adj unrein. **~ity** n Unreinheit f

in /ɪn/ prep in (+ dat/(into) + acc); **sit in the garden** im Garten sitzen; **go in the garden** in den Garten gehen; **in May** im Mai; **in 1992** [im Jahre] 1992; **in this heat** bei dieser Hitze; **in the evening** am Abend; **in the sky** am Himmel; **in the world** auf der Welt; **in the street** auf der Straße; **deaf in one ear** auf einem Ohr taub; **in the army** beim Militär; **in English/German** auf Englisch/Deutsch; **in ink/pencil** mit Tinte/Bleistift; **in a soft/loud voice** mit leiser/lauter Stimme; **in doing this, he ...** indem er das tut/tat, ... er •adv (at home) zu Hause; (indoors) drinnen; **he's not in yet** er ist noch nicht da; **all in** alles inbegriffen; (!: exhausted) kaputt; **day in, day out** tagaus, tagein; **have it in for s.o.** ! es auf jdn abgesehen haben; **send/go in** hineinschicken/-gehen; **come/bring in** hereinkommen/-bringen •adj (!: in fashion) in •n **the ins and outs** alle Einzelheiten pl

ina'bility n Unfähigkeit f

inac'cessible adj unzugänglich

in'accura|cy n Ungenauigkeit f. **~te** adj ungenau

in'ac|tive adj untätig. **~'tivity** n Untätigkeit f

in'adequate adj unzulänglich

inad'missable adj unzulässig

inadvertently /ɪnəd'vɜːtəntlɪ/ adv versehentlich

inad'visable adj nicht ratsam

inane /ɪ'neɪn/ adj albern

in'animate adj unbelebt

in'applicable adj nicht zutreffend

inap'propriate adj unangebracht

inar'ticulate adj undeutlich; **be ~** sich nicht gut ausdrücken können

inat'tentive adj unaufmerksam

in'audible adj, **-bly** adv unhörbar

inaugural /ɪ'nɔ:gjʊrl/ adj Antritts-

inau'spicious adj ungünstig

inborn /'ɪnbɔ:n/ adj angeboren

inbred /ɪn'bred/ adj angeboren

incalculable /ɪn'kælkjʊləbl/ adj nicht berechenbar; (fig) unabsehbar

in'capable adj unfähig; **be ~ of doing sth** nicht fähig sein, etw zu tun

incapacitate /ɪnkə'pæsɪteɪt/ vt unfähig machen

incarnation /ɪnkɑ:'neɪʃn/ n Inkarnation f

incendiary /ɪn'sendɪərɪ/ adj & n **~ [bomb]** Brandbombe f

incense[1] /'ɪnsens/ n Weihrauch m

incense[2] /ɪn'sens/ vt wütend machen

incentive /ɪn'sentɪv/ n Anreiz m

incessant /ɪn'sesnt/ adj unaufhörlich

incest /'ɪnsest/ n Inzest m, Blutschande f

inch /ɪntʃ/ n Zoll m • vi **~ forward** sich ganz langsam vorwärts schieben

incident /'ɪnsɪdənt/ n Zwischenfall m

incidental /ɪnsɪ'dentl/ adj nebensächlich; (remark) beiläufig; (expenses) Neben-. **~ly** adv übrigens

incinerat|e /ɪn'sɪnəreɪt/ vt verbrennen

incision /ɪn'sɪʒn/ n Einschnitt m

incisive /ɪn'saɪsɪv/ adj scharfsinnig

incite /ɪn'saɪt/ vt aufhetzen. **~ment** n Aufhetzung f

in'clement adj rau

inclination /ɪnklɪ'neɪʃn/ n Neigung f

incline /ɪn'klaɪn/ vt neigen; **be ~d to do sth** dazu neigen, etw zu tun • vi sich neigen

inclu|de /ɪn'klu:d/ vt einschließen; (contain) enthalten; (incorporate) aufnehmen (**in** in + acc). **~ding** prep einschließlich (+ gen). **~sion** n Aufnahme f

inclusive /ɪn'klu:sɪv/ adj Inklusiv-; **~ of** einschließlich (+ gen)

incognito /ɪnkɒg'ni:təʊ/ adv inkognito

inco'herent adj zusammenhanglos; (incomprehensible) unverständlich

income /'ɪnkəm/ n Einkommen nt. **~ tax** n Einkommensteuer f

'incoming adj ankommend; (mail, call) eingehend

in'comparable adj unvergleichlich

incom'patible adj unvereinbar; **be ~** (people:) nicht zueinander passen

in'competen|ce n Unfähigkeit f. **~t** adj unfähig

incom'plete adj unvollständig

incompre'hensible adj unverständlich

incon'ceivable adj undenkbar

incon'clusive adj nicht schlüssig

incongruous /ɪn'kɒŋgrʊəs/ adj unpassend

incon'siderate adj rücksichtslos

incon'sistent adj widersprüchlich; (illogical) inkonsequent; **be ~** nicht übereinstimmen

inconsolable /ɪnkən'səʊləbl/ adj untröstlich

incon'spicuous adj unauffällig

incontinen|ce /ɪn'kɒntɪnəns/ n Inkontinenz f. **~t** adj inkontinent

incon'venien|ce n Unannehmlichkeit f; (drawback) Nachteil m. **~t** adj ungünstig; **be ~t for s.o.** jdm nicht passen

incorporate /ɪn'kɔ:pəreɪt/ vt aufnehmen; (contain) enthalten

incor'rect adj inkorrekt

incorrigible /ɪn'kɒrɪdʒəbl/ adj unverbesserlich

incorruptible /ɪnkə'rʌptəbl/ adj unbestechlich

increase[1] /'ɪnkri:s/ n Zunahme f; (rise) Erhöhung f; **be on the ~** zunehmen

increas|e[2] /ɪn'kri:s/ vt vergrößern; (raise) erhöhen •vi zunehmen; (rise) sich erhöhen. **~ing** adj zunehmend

in'credi|ble adj, **-bly** adv unglaublich

incredulous /ɪn'kredjʊləs/ adj ungläubig

incriminate /ɪn'krɪmɪneɪt/ vt (Jur) belasten

incur /ɪn'kɜ:(r)/ vt (pt/pp **incurred**) sich (dat) zuziehen; machen (debts)

in'cura|ble adj, **-bly** adv unheilbar

indebted /ɪn'detɪd/ adj verpflichtet (**to** dat)

in'decent adj unanständig

inde'cision n Unentschlossenheit f

inde'cisive adj ergebnislos; (person) unentschlossen

indeed /ɪn'di:d/ adv in der Tat, tatsächlich; **very much ~** sehr

indefatigable /ɪndɪ'fætɪgəbl/ adj unermüdlich

in'definite adj unbestimmt. **~ly** adv unbegrenzt; (postpone) auf unbestimmte Zeit

indent /ɪn'dent/ vt (Printing) einrücken. **~ation** n Einrückung f; (notch) Kerbe f

inde'penden|ce n Unabhängigkeit f; (self-reliance) Selbstständigkeit f. **~t** adj unabhängig; selbstständig

indescriba|ble /ɪndɪ'skraɪbəbl/ adj, **-bly** adv unbeschreiblich

indestructible /ɪndɪ'strʌktəbl/ adj unzerstörbar

indeterminate /ɪndɪ'tɜ:mɪnət/ adj unbestimmt

index /'ɪndeks/ n Register nt

index: ~ card n Karteikarte f. **~ finger** n Zeigefinger m. **~-linked** adj (pension) dynamisch

India /'ɪndɪə/ n Indien nt. **~n** adj indisch; (American) indianisch •n Inder(in) m(f); (American) Indianer(in) m(f)

Indian 'summer n Nachsommer m

indicat|e /'ɪndɪkeɪt/ vt zeigen; (point at) zeigen auf (+ acc); (hint) andeuten; (register) anzeigen •vi (Auto) blinken. **~ion** n Anzeichen nt

indicative /ɪn'dɪkətɪv/ n (Gram) Indikativ m

indicator /'ɪndɪkeɪtə(r)/ n (Auto) Blinker m

in'differen|ce n Gleichgültigkeit f. **~t** adj gleichgültig; (not good) mittelmäßig

indi'gest|ible adj unverdaulich; (difficult to digest) schwer verdaulich. **~ion** n Magenverstimmung f

indigna|nt /ɪn'dɪgnənt/ adj entrüstet, empört. **~tion** n Entrüstung f, Empörung f

in'dignity n Demütigung f

indi'rect adj indirekt

indi'screet adj indiskret

indis'cretion n Indiskretion f

indi'spensable adj unentbehrlich

indisposed /ɪndɪ'spəʊzd/ adj indisponiert

indisputable /ɪndɪ'spju:təbl/ adj, **-bly** adv unbestreitbar

indi'stinct adj undeutlich

indistinguishable /ɪndɪ'stɪŋgwɪʃəbl/ adj **be ~** nicht zu unterscheiden sein

individual /ɪndɪ'vɪdjʊəl/ adj individuell; (single) einzeln •n Individuum nt. **~ity** n Individualität f

indi'visible adj unteilbar

indoctrinate /ɪn'dɒktrɪneɪt/ vt indoktrinieren

indolen|ce /'ɪndələns/ n Faulheit f. **~t** adj faul

indomitable /ɪn'dɒmɪtəbl/ adj unbeugsam

indoor /'ɪndɔ:(r)/ adj Innen-; (clothes) Haus-; (plant) Zimmer-; (Sport) Hallen-. **~s** adv im Haus, drinnen; **go ~s** ins Haus gehen

indulge /ɪn'dʌldʒ/ vt frönen (+ dat); verwöhnen (child) •vi **~ in** frönen (+ dat). **~nce** n Nachgiebigkeit f; (leniency) Nachsicht f. **~nt** adj [zu] nachgiebig; nachsichtig

industrial /ɪn'dʌstrɪəl/ adj Industrie-. **~ist** n Industrielle(r) m

industr|ious /ɪn'dʌstrɪəs/ adj fleißig. **~y** n Industrie f; (zeal) Fleiß m

inebriated /ɪ'ni:brɪeɪtɪd/ adj betrunken

in'edible adj nicht essbar

inef'fective adj unwirksam; (person) untauglich

inef'ficient adj unfähig; (organization) nicht leistungsfähig; (method) nicht rationell

in'eligible adj nicht berechtigt

inept /ɪ'nept/ adj ungeschickt

ine'quality n Ungleichheit f

inertia /ɪ'nɜ:ʃə/ n Trägheit f

inescapable /ɪnɪ'skeɪpəbl/ adj unvermeidlich

inestimable /ɪn'estɪməbl/ adj unschätzbar

inevitab|le /ɪn'evɪtəbl/ adj unvermeidlich. **~ly** adv zwangsläufig

ine'xact adj ungenau

inex'cusable adj unverzeihlich

inexhaustible /ɪnɪg'zɔ:stəbl/ adj unerschöpflich

inex'pensive adj preiswert

inex'perience n Unerfahrenheit f. **~d** adj unerfahren

inexplicable /ɪnɪk'splɪkəbl/ adj unerklärlich

in'fallible adj unfehlbar

infamous /'ɪnfəməs/ adj niederträchtig; (notorious) berüchtigt

infan|cy /'ɪnfənsɪ/ n frühe Kindheit f; (fig) Anfangsstadium nt. **~t** n Kleinkind nt. **~tile** adj kindisch

infantry /'ɪnfəntrɪ/ n Infanterie f

infatuated /ɪn'fætʃʊeɪtɪd/ adj vernarrt (**with** in + acc)

infect /ɪn'fekt/ vt anstecken, infizieren; **become ~ed** (wound:) sich infizieren. **~ion** n Infektion f. **~ious** adj ansteckend

inferior /ɪn'fɪərɪə(r)/ adj minderwertig; (in rank) untergeordnet •n Untergebene(r) m/f

inferiority /ɪnfɪərɪ'ɒrətɪ/ n Minderwertigkeit f. **~ complex** n Minderwertigkeitskomplex m

infern|al /ɪn'fɜ:nl/ adj höllisch. **~o** n flammendes Inferno nt

in'fertile adj unfruchtbar

infest /ɪn'fest/ vt **be ~ed with** befallen sein von; (place) verseucht sein mit

infi'delity n Untreue f

infighting /'ɪnfaɪtɪŋ/ n (fig) interne Machtkämpfe pl

infinite /'ɪnfɪnət/ adj unendlich

infinitive /ɪn'fɪnətɪv/ n (Gram) Infinitiv m

infinity /ɪn'fɪnətɪ/ n Unendlichkeit f

inflame /ɪn'fleɪm/ vt entzünden. **~d** adj entzündet

in'flammable adj feuergefährlich

inflammation /ɪnflə'meɪʃn/ n Entzündung f

inflammatory /ɪn'flæmətrɪ/ adj aufrührerisch

inflat|e /ɪn'fleɪt/ vt aufblasen; (with pump) aufpumpen. **~ion** n Inflation f. **~ionary** adj inflationär

in'flexible adj starr; (person) unbeugsam

inflict /ɪn'flɪkt/ vt zufügen (**on** dat); versetzen (blow) (**on** dat)

influen|ce /'ɪnflʊəns/ n Einfluss m •vt beeinflussen. **~tial** adj einflussreich

influenza /ɪnflʊ'enzə/ n Grippe f

inform /ɪn'fɔːm/ vt benachrichtigen; (officially) informieren; ~ **s.o. of sth** jdm etw mitteilen; **keep s.o. ~ed** jdn auf dem Laufenden halten • vi ~ **against** denunzieren

in'for|mal adj zwanglos; (unofficial) inoffiziell. **~'mality** n Zwanglosigkeit f

informant /ɪn'fɔːmənt/ n Gewährsmann m

informat|ion /ɪnfə'meɪʃn/ n Auskunft f; **a piece of ~ion** eine Auskunft. **~ive** adj aufschlussreich; (instructive) lehrreich

informer /ɪn'fɔːmə(r)/ n Spitzel m; (Pol) Denunziant m

infra-'red /ɪnfrə-/ adj infrarot

in'frequent adj selten

infringe /ɪn'frɪndʒ/ vt/i ~ **[on]** verstoßen gegen. **~ment** n Verstoß m

infuriat|e /ɪn'fjʊərɪeɪt/ vt wütend machen. **~ing** adj ärgerlich

ingenious /ɪn'dʒiːnɪəs/ adj erfinderisch; (thing) raffiniert

ingenuity /ɪndʒɪ'njuːətɪ/ n Geschicklichkeit f

ingrained /ɪn'greɪnd/ adj eingefleischt; **be** ~ (dirt:) tief sitzen

ingratiate /ɪn'greɪʃɪeɪt/ vt ~ **oneself** sich einschmeicheln (**with** bei)

in'gratitude n Undankbarkeit f

ingredient /ɪn'griːdɪənt/ n (Culin) Zutat f

ingrowing /'ɪngrəʊɪŋ/ adj (nail) eingewachsen

inhabit /ɪn'hæbɪt/ vt bewohnen. **~ant** n Einwohner(in) m(f)

inhale /ɪn'heɪl/ vt/i einatmen; (Med & when smoking) inhalieren

inherent /ɪn'hɪərənt/ adj natürlich

inherit /ɪn'herɪt/ vt erben. **~ance** n Erbschaft f, Erbe nt

inhibit|ed /ɪn'hɪbɪtɪd/ adj gehemmt. **~ion** n Hemmung f

inho'spitable adj ungastlich

in'human adj unmenschlich

inimitable /ɪ'nɪmɪtəbl/ adj unnachahmlich

initial /ɪ'nɪʃl/ adj anfänglich, Anfangs- • n Anfangsbuchstabe m; **my ~s** meine Initialen. **~ly** adv anfangs, am Anfang

initiat|e /ɪ'nɪʃɪeɪt/ vt einführen. **~ion** n Einführung f

initiative /ɪ'nɪʃətɪv/ n Initiative f

inject /ɪn'dʒekt/ vt einspritzen, injizieren. **~ion** n Spritze f, Injektion f

injur|e /'ɪndʒə(r)/ vt verletzen. **~y** n Verletzung f

in'justice n Ungerechtigkeit f; **do s.o. an** ~ jdm unrecht tun

ink /ɪŋk/ n Tinte f

inlaid /ɪn'leɪd/ adj eingelegt

inland /'ɪnlənd/ adj Binnen- • adv landeinwärts. **I~ Revenue** (UK) ≈ Finanzamt nt

in-laws /'ɪnlɔːz/ npl [!] Schwiegereltern pl

inlay /'ɪnleɪ/ n Einlegearbeit f

inlet /'ɪnlet/ n schmale Bucht f; (Techn) Zuleitung f

inmate /'ɪnmeɪt/ n Insasse m

inn /ɪn/ n Gasthaus nt

innate /ɪ'neɪt/ adj angeboren

inner /'ɪnə(r)/ adj innere(r,s). **~most** adj innerste(r,s)

innocen|ce /'ɪnəsəns/ n Unschuld f. **~t** adj unschuldig. **~tly** adv in aller Unschuld

innocuous /ɪ'nɒkjʊəs/ adj harmlos

innovat|ion /ɪnə'veɪʃn/ n Neuerung f. **~ive** adj innovativ. **~or** n Neuerer m

innumerable /ɪ'njuːmərəbl/ adj unzählig

inoculat|e /ɪ'nɒkjʊleɪt/ vt impfen. **~ion** n Impfung f

inof'fensive adj harmlos

in'operable adj nicht operierbar

in'opportune adj unpassend

inor'ganic adj anorganisch

'in-patient n [stationär behandelter] Krankenhauspatient m

input /'ɪnpʊt/ n Input m & nt

inquest /'ɪnkwest/ n gerichtliche Untersuchung f der Todesursache

inquir|e /ɪn'kwaɪə(r)/ vi sich erkundigen (**about** nach); **~e into** untersuchen • vt sich erkundigen nach. **~y** n Erkundigung f; (investigation) Untersuchung f

inquisitive /ɪn'kwɪzətɪv/ adj neugierig

in'sane adj geisteskrank; (fig) wahnsinnig

in'sanitary adj unhygienisch

in'sanity n Geisteskrankheit f

insatiable /ɪn'seɪʃəbl/ adj unersättlich

inscription /ɪn'skrɪpʃn/ n Inschrift f

inscrutable /ɪn'skru:təbl/ adj unergründlich; (expression) undurchdringlich

insect /'ɪnsekt/ n Insekt nt. **~icide** n Insektenvertilgungsmittel nt

inse'cur|e adj nicht sicher; (fig) unsicher. **~ity** n Unsicherheit f

in'sensitive adj gefühllos; **~ to** unempfindlich gegen

in'separable adj untrennbar; (people) unzertrennlich

insert[1] /'ɪnsɜ:t/ n Einsatz m

insert[2] /ɪn'sɜ:t/ vt einfügen, einsetzen; einstecken (key); einwerfen (coin). **~ion** n (insert) Einsatz m; (in text) Einfügung f

inside /ɪn'saɪd/ n Innenseite f; (of house) Innere(s) nt • attrib Innen- • adv innen; (indoors) drinnen; **go ~** hineingehen; **come ~** hereinkommen; **~ out** links [herum]; **know sth ~ out** etw in- und auswendig kennen • prep **~ [of]** in (+ dat/ (into) + acc)

insight /'ɪnsaɪt/ n Einblick m (**into** in + acc); (understanding) Einsicht f

insig'nificant adj unbedeutend

insin'cere adj unaufrichtig

insinuat|e /ɪn'sɪnjʊeɪt/ vt andeuten. **~ion** n Andeutung f

insipid /ɪn'sɪpɪd/ adj fade

insist /ɪn'sɪst/ vi darauf bestehen; **~ on** bestehen auf (+ dat) • vt **~ that** darauf bestehen, dass. **~ence** n Bestehen nt. **~ent** adj beharrlich; **be ~ent** darauf bestehen

'insole n Einlegesohle f

insolen|ce /'ɪnsələns/ n Unverschämtheit f. **~t** adj unverschämt

in'soluble adj unlöslich; (fig) unlösbar

in'solvent adj zahlungsunfähig

insomnia /ɪn'sɒmnɪə/ n Schlaflosigkeit f

inspect /ɪn'spekt/ vt inspizieren; (test) prüfen; kontrollieren (ticket). **~ion** n Inspektion f. **~or** n Inspektor m; (of tickets) Kontrolleur m

inspiration /ɪnspə'reɪʃn/ n Inspiration f

inspire /ɪn'spaɪə(r)/ vt inspirieren

insta'bility n Unbeständigkeit f; (of person) Labilität f

install /ɪn'stɔ:l/ vt installieren. **~ation** n Installation f

instalment /ɪn'stɔ:lmənt/ n (Comm) Rate f; (of serial) Fortsetzung f; (Radio, TV) Folge f

instance /'ɪnstəns/ n Fall m; (example) Beispiel nt; **in the first ~** zunächst; **for ~** zum Beispiel

instant /'ɪnstənt/ adj sofortig; (Culin) Instant- • n Augenblick m, Moment m. **~aneous** adj unverzüglich, unmittelbar

instant 'coffee n Pulverkaffee m

instantly /'ɪnstəntlɪ/ adv sofort

instead /ɪn'sted/ adv statt dessen; **~ of** statt (+ gen), anstelle von; **~ of me** an meiner Stelle; **~ of going** anstatt zu gehen

'instep n Spann m, Rist m

instigat|e /'ɪnstɪgeɪt/ vt anstiften; einleiten (proceedings). **~ion** n Anstiftung f; **at his ~ion** auf seine Veranlassung

instil /ɪn'stɪl/ vt (pt/pp **instilled**) einprägen (**into s.o.** jdm)

instinct /'ɪnstɪŋkt/ n Instinkt m. **~ive** adj instinktiv

institut|e /'ɪnstɪtju:t/ n Institut nt. **~ion** n Institution f; (home) Anstalt f

instruct /ɪn'strʌkt/ vt unterrichten; (order) anweisen. **~ion** n Unterricht m; Anweisung f; **~ions** pl **for use** Gebrauchsanweisung f. **~ive** adj lehrreich. **~or** n Lehrer(in) m(f); (Mil) Ausbilder m

i

instrument /'ɪnstrʊmənt/ n Instrument nt. **~al** adj Instrumental-

insu'bordi|nate adj ungehorsam. **~nation** n Ungehorsam m; (Mil) Insubordination f

insuf'ficient adj nicht genügend

insulat|e /'ɪnsjʊleɪt/ vt isolieren. **~ing tape** n Isolierband nt. **~ion** n Isolierung f

insult¹ /'ɪnsʌlt/ n Beleidigung f

insult² /ɪn'sʌlt/ vt beleidigen

insur|ance /ɪn'ʃʊərəns/ n Versicherung f. **~e** vt versichern

intact /ɪn'tækt/ adj unbeschädigt; (complete) vollständig

'intake n Aufnahme f

in'tangible adj nicht greifbar

integral /'ɪntɪgrl/ adj wesentlich

integrat|e /'ɪntɪgreɪt/ vt integrieren •vi sich integrieren. **~ion** n Integration f

integrity /ɪn'tegrətɪ/ n Integrität f

intellect /'ɪntəlekt/ n Intellekt m. **~ual** adj intellektuell

intelligen|ce /ɪn'telɪdʒəns/ n Intelligenz f; (Mil) Nachrichtendienst m; (information) Meldungen pl. **~t** adj intelligent

intelligible /ɪn'telɪdʒəbl/ adj verständlich

intend /ɪn'tend/ vt beabsichtigen; **be ~ed for** bestimmt sein für

intense /ɪn'tens/ adj intensiv; (pain) stark. **~ly** adv äußerst; (study) intensiv

intensify /ɪn'tensɪfaɪ/ v (pt/pp **-ied**) •vt intensivieren •vi zunehmen

intensity /ɪn'tensətɪ/ n Intensität f

intensive /ɪn'tensɪv/ adj intensiv; **be in ~ care** auf der Intensivstation sein

intent /ɪn'tent/ adj aufmerksam; **~ on** (absorbed in) vertieft in (+ acc) •n Absicht f

intention /ɪn'tenʃn/ n Absicht f. **~al** adj absichtlich

inter'acti|on n Wechselwirkung f. **~ve** adj interaktiv

intercede /ɪntə'si:d/ vi Fürsprache einlegen (**on behalf of** für)

intercept /ɪntə'sept/ vt abfangen

'interchange n Austausch m; (Auto) Autobahnkreuz nt

intercom /'ɪntəkɒm/ n [Gegen]sprechanlage f

'intercourse n (sexual) Geschlechtsverkehr m

interest /'ɪntrəst/ n Interesse nt; (Comm) Zinsen pl •vt interessieren; **be ~ed** sich interessieren (**in** für). **~ing** adj interessant. **~ rate** n Zinssatz m

interface /'ɪntəfeɪs/ n Schnittstelle f

interfere /ɪntə'fɪə(r)/ vi sich einmischen. **~nce** n Einmischung f; (Radio, TV) Störung f

interim /'ɪntərɪm/ adj Zwischen-; (temporary) vorläufig

interior /ɪn'tɪərɪə(r)/ adj innere(r,s), Innen- •n Innere(s) nt

interject /ɪntə'dʒekt/ vt einwerfen. **~ion** n Interjektion f; (remark) Einwurf m

interlude /'ɪntəlu:d/ n Pause f; (performance) Zwischenspiel nt

inter'marry vi untereinander heiraten; (different groups:) Mischehen schließen

intermediary /ɪntə'mi:dɪərɪ/ n

Vermittler(in) m(f)

intermediate /ɪntəˈmiːdɪət/ adj Zwischen-

interminable /ɪnˈtɜːmɪnəbl/ adj endlos [lang]

intermittent /ɪntəˈmɪtənt/ adj in Abständen auftretend

internal /ɪnˈtɜːnl/ adj innere(r,s); (matter, dispute) intern. **I~ Revenue** (USA) ≈ Finanzamt nt. **~ly** adv innerlich; (deal with) intern

interˈnational adj international • n Länderspiel nt; (player) Nationalspieler(in) m(f)

ˈInternet n Internet nt; **on the ~** im Internet

internment /ɪnˈtɜːnmənt/ n Internierung f

ˈinterplay n Wechselspiel nt

interpolate /ɪnˈtɜːpəleɪt/ vt einwerfen

interpret /ɪnˈtɜːprɪt/ vt interpretieren; auslegen (text); deuten (dream); (translate) dolmetschen • vi dolmetschen. **~ation** n Interpretation f. **~er** n Dolmetscher(in) m(f)

interrogat|e /ɪnˈterəgeɪt/ vt verhören. **~ion** n Verhör nt

interrogative /ɪntəˈrɒgətɪv/ adj & n **~ [pronoun]** Interrogativpronomen nt

interrupt /ɪntəˈrʌpt/ vt/i unterbrechen; **don't ~!** red nicht dazwischen! **~ion** n Unterbrechung f

intersect /ɪntəˈsekt/ vi sich kreuzen; (of lines) sich schneiden. **~ion** n Kreuzung f

interspersed /ɪntəˈspɜːst/ adj **~ with** durchsetzt mit

interˈtwine vi sich ineinanderschlingen

interval /ˈɪntəvl/ n Abstand m; (Theat) Pause f; (Mus) Intervall nt; **at hourly ~s** alle Stunde; **bright ~s** pl Aufheiterungen pl

interven|e /ɪntəˈviːn/ vi eingreifen; (occur) dazwischenkommen. **~tion** n Eingreifen nt; (Mil, Pol) Intervention f

interview /ˈɪntəvjuː/ n (in media) Interview nt; (for job) Vorstellungsgespräch nt • vt interviewen; ein Vorstellungsgespräch führen mit. **~er** n Interviewer(in) m(f)

intimacy /ˈɪntɪməsɪ/ n Vertrautheit f; (sexual) Intimität f

intimate /ˈɪntɪmət/ adj vertraut; (friend) eng; (sexually) intim

intimidat|e /ɪnˈtɪmɪdeɪt/ vt einschüchtern. **~ion** n Einschüchterung f

into /ˈɪntə/, vor einem Vokal /ˈɪntʊ/ prep in (+ acc); **be ~** [!] sich auskennen mit; **7 ~ 21** 21 [geteilt] durch 7

inˈtolerable adj unerträglich

inˈtoleran|ce n Intoleranz f. **~t** adj intolerant

intonation /ɪntəˈneɪʃn/ n Tonfall m

intoxicat|ed /ɪnˈtɒksɪkeɪtɪd/ adj betrunken; (fig) berauscht. **~ion** n Rausch m

intransigent /ɪnˈtrænsɪdʒənt/ adj unnachgiebig

inˈtransitive adj intransitiv

intrepid /ɪnˈtrepɪd/ adj kühn, unerschrocken

intricate /ˈɪntrɪkət/ adj kompliziert

intrigu|e /ɪnˈtriːg/ n Intrige f • vt faszinieren. **~ing** adj faszinierend

intrinsic /ɪnˈtrɪnsɪk/ adj **~ value** Eigenwert m

introduce /ɪntrəˈdjuːs/ vt vorstellen; (bring in, insert) einführen

introduct|ion /ɪntrəˈdʌkʃn/ n Einführung f; (to person) Vorstellung f; (to book) Einleitung f. **~ory** adj einleitend

introvert /ˈɪntrəvɜːt/ n introvertierter Mensch m

intru|de /ɪnˈtruːd/ vi stören. **~der** n Eindringling m. **~sion** n Störung f

i

intuit|ion /ɪntjuːˈɪʃn/ n Intuition f. **~ive** adj intuitiv

inundate /ˈɪnəndeɪt/ vt überschwemmen

invade /ɪnˈveɪd/ vt einfallen in (+ acc). **~r** n Angreifer m

invalid¹ /ˈɪnvəlɪd/ n Kranke(r) m/f

invalid² /ɪnˈvælɪd/ adj ungültig

inˈvaluable adj unschätzbar; (person) unersetzlich

inˈvariab|le adj unveränderlich. **~ly** adv immer

invasion /ɪnˈveɪʒn/ n Invasion f

invent /ɪnˈvent/ vt erfinden. **~ion** n Erfindung f. **~ive** adj erfinderisch. **~or** n Erfinder m

inventory /ˈɪnvəntrɪ/ n Bestandsliste f

invert /ɪnˈvɜːt/ vt umkehren. **~ed commas** npl Anführungszeichen pl

invest /ɪnˈvest/ vt investieren, anlegen; **~ in** (🄸: buy) sich (dat) zulegen

investigat|e /ɪnˈvestɪgeɪt/ vt untersuchen. **~ion** n Untersuchung f

invest|ment /ɪnˈvestmənt/ n Anlage f; **be a good ~ment** (fig) sich bezahlt machen. **~or** n Kapitalanleger m

invidious /ɪnˈvɪdɪəs/ adj unerfreulich; (unfair) ungerecht

invincible /ɪnˈvɪnsəbl/ adj unbesiegbar

inviolable /ɪnˈvaɪələbl/ adj unantastbar

inˈvisible adj unsichtbar

invitation /ɪnvɪˈteɪʃn/ n Einladung f

invit|e /ɪnˈvaɪt/ vt einladen. **~ing** adj einladend

invoice /ˈɪnvɔɪs/ n Rechnung f • vt **~ s.o.** jdm eine Rechnung schicken

inˈvoluntary adj, **-ily** adv unwillkürlich

involve /ɪnˈvɒlv/ vt beteiligen; (affect) betreffen; (implicate) verwickeln; (entail) mit sich bringen; (mean) bedeuten; **be ~d in** beteiligt sein an (+ dat); (implicated) verwickelt sein in (+ acc); **get ~d with s.o.** sich mit jdm einlassen. **~d** adj kompliziert. **~ment** n Verbindung f

inˈvulnerable adj unverwundbar; (position) unangreifbar

inward /ˈɪnwəd/ adj innere(r,s). **~s** adv nach innen

iodine /ˈaɪədiːn/ n Jod nt

IOU abbr Schuldschein m

Iran /ɪˈrɑːn/ n der Iran

Iraq /ɪˈrɑːk/ n der Irak

irascible /ɪˈræsəbl/ adj aufbrausend

irate /aɪˈreɪt/ adj wütend

Ireland /ˈaɪələnd/ n Irland nt

iris /ˈaɪərɪs/ n (Anat) Regenbogenhaut f, Iris f; (Bot) Schwertlilie f

Irish /ˈaɪərɪʃ/ adj irisch • n **the ~** pl die Iren. **~man** n Ire m. **~woman** n Irin f

iron /ˈaɪən/ adj Eisen-; (fig) eisern • n Eisen nt; (appliance) Bügeleisen nt • vt/i bügeln

ironic[al] /aɪˈrɒnɪk[l]/ adj ironisch

ironing /ˈaɪənɪŋ/ n Bügeln nt; (articles) Bügelwäsche f. **~-board** n Bügelbrett nt

ironmonger /ˈ-mʌŋgə(r)/ n **~'s [shop]** Haushaltswarengeschäft nt

irony /ˈaɪərənɪ/ n Ironie f

irrational /ɪˈræʃənl/ adj irrational

irreconcilable /ɪˈrekənsaɪləbl/ adj unversöhnlich

irrefutable /ɪrɪˈfjuːtəbl/ adj unwiderlegbar

irregular /ɪˈregjʊlə(r)/ adj unregelmäßig; (against rules) regelwidrig. **~ity** n Unregelmäßigkeit f; Regelwidrigkeit f

irrelevant /ɪ'reləvənt/ adj irrelevant

irreparable /ɪ'repərəbl/ adj nicht wieder gutzumachen

irreplaceable /ɪrɪ'pleɪsəbl/ adj unersetzlich

irrepressible /ɪrɪ'presəbl/ adj unverwüstlich; **be ~** (person:) nicht unterzukriegen sein

irresistible /ɪrɪ'zɪstəbl/ adj unwiderstehlich

irresolute /ɪ'rezəlu:t/ adj unentschlossen

irrespective /ɪrɪ'spektɪv/ adj **~ of** ungeachtet (+ gen)

irresponsible /ɪrɪ'spɒnsəbl/ adj, **-bly** adv unverantwortlich; (person) verantwortungslos

irreverent /ɪ'revərənt/ adj respektlos

irrevocable /ɪ'revəkəbl/ adj, **-bly** adv unwiderruflich

irrigat|e /'ɪrɪgeɪt/ vt bewässern. **~ion** n Bewässerung f

irritable /'ɪrɪtəbl/ adj reizbar

irritant /'ɪrɪtənt/ n Reizstoff m

irritat|e /'ɪrɪteɪt/ vt irritieren; (Med) reizen. **~ion** n Ärger m; (Med) Reizung f

is /ɪz/ see **be**

Islam /'ɪzlɑ:m/ n der Islam. **~ic** adj islamisch

island /'aɪlənd/ n Insel f. **~er** n Inselbewohner(in) m(f)

isolat|e /'aɪsəleɪt/ vt isolieren. **~ed** adj (remote) abgelegen; (single) einzeln. **~ion** n Isoliertheit f; (Med) Isolierung f

Israel /'ɪzreɪl/ n Israel nt. **~i** adj israelisch • n Israeli m/f

issue /'ɪʃu:/ n Frage f; (outcome) Ergebnis nt; (of magazine, stamps) Ausgabe f; (offspring) Nachkommen pl • vt ausgeben; ausstellen (passport); erteilen (order); herausgeben (book); **be ~d with sth** etw erhalten

it /ɪt/

• pronoun

····➤ (as subject) er (m), sie (f), es (nt); (in impersonal sentence) es. **where is the spoon? It's on the table** wo ist der Löffel? Er liegt auf dem Tisch. **it was very kind of you** es war sehr nett von Ihnen. **it's five o'clock** es ist fünf Uhr

····➤ (as direct object) ihn (m), sie (f), es (nt). **that's my pencil — give it to me** das ist mein Bleistift — gib ihn mir.

····➤ (as dative object) ihm (m), ihr (f), ihm (nt). **he found a track and followed it** er fand eine Spur und folgte ihr.

····➤ (after prepositions)

! Combinations such as with it, from it, to it are translated by the prepositions with the prefix **da-** (**damit**, **davon**, **dazu**). Prepositions beginning with a vowel insert an 'r' (**daran**, **darauf**, **darüber**). **I can't do anything with it** ich kann nichts damit anfangen. **don't lean on it!** lehn dich nicht daran!

····➤ (the person in question) es. **it's me** ich bin's. **is it you, Dad?** bist du es, Vater? **who is it?** wer ist da?

Italian /ɪ'tæljən/ adj italienisch • n Italiener(in) m(f); (Lang) Italienisch nt

italics /ɪ'tælɪks/ npl Kursivschrift f; **in ~s** kursiv

Italy /'ɪtəlɪ/ n Italien nt

itch /ɪtʃ/ n Juckreiz m; **I have an ~** es juckt mich • vi jucken; **I'm ~ing** [!] es juckt mich (**to** zu). **~y** adj **be ~y** jucken

item /'aɪtəm/ n Gegenstand m; (Comm) Artikel m; (on agenda) Punkt m; (on invoice) Posten m; (act) Nummer f

itinerary /aɪ'tɪnərərɪ/ n [Reise]route f

its /ɪts/ poss pron sein; (f) ihr

it's = it is, it has

itself /ɪt'self/ pron selbst; (reflexive) sich; **by ~** von selbst; (alone) allein

ivory /'aɪvərɪ/ n Elfenbein nt •attrib Elfenbein-

ivy /'aɪvɪ/ n Efeu m

Jj

jab /dʒæb/ n Stoß m; (!: injection) Spritze f •vt (pt/pp **jabbed**) stoßen

jabber /'dʒæbə(r)/ vi plappern

jack /dʒæk/ n (Auto) Wagenheber m; (Cards) Bube m •vt **~ up** (Auto) aufbocken

jacket /'dʒækɪt/ n Jacke f; (of book) Schutzumschlag m

'jackpot n **hit the ~** das große Los ziehen

jade /dʒeɪd/ n Jade m

jagged /'dʒægɪd/ adj zackig

jail /dʒeɪl/ = **gaol**

jam[1] /dʒæm/ n Marmelade f

jam[2] n Gedränge nt; (Auto) Stau m; (fam. difficulty) Klemme f •v (pt/pp **jammed**) •vt klemmen (**in** in + acc); stören (broadcast) •vi klemmen

Jamaica /dʒə'meɪkə/ n Jamaika nt

jangle /'dʒæŋgl/ vi klimpern •vt klimpern mit

January /'dʒænjʊərɪ/ n Januar m

Japan /dʒə'pæn/ n Japan nt. **~ese** adj japanisch •n Japaner(in) m(f); (Lang) Japanisch nt

jar /dʒɑ:(r)/ n Glas nt; (earthenware) Topf m

jargon /'dʒɑ:gən/ n Jargon m

jaunt /dʒɔ:nt/ n Ausflug m

jaunt|y /'dʒɔ:ntɪ/ adj, **-ily** adv keck

javelin /'dʒævlɪn/ n Speer m

jaw /dʒɔ:/ n Kiefer m

jazz /dʒæz/ n Jazz m. **~y** adj knallig

jealous /'dʒeləs/ adj eifersüchtig (**of** auf + acc). **~y** n Eifersucht f

jeans /dʒi:nz/ npl Jeans pl

jeer /dʒɪə(r)/ vi johlen; **~ at** verhöhnen

jelly /'dʒelɪ/ n Gelee nt; (dessert) Götterspeise f. **~fish** n Qualle f

jeopar|dize /'dʒepədaɪz/ vt gefährden. **~dy** n **in ~dy** gefährdet

jerk /dʒɜ:k/ n Ruck m •vt stoßen; (pull) reißen •vi rucken; (limb, muscle:) zucken. **~ily** adv ruckweise. **~y** adj ruckartig

jersey /'dʒɜ:zɪ/ n Pullover m; (Sport) Trikot nt; (fabric) Jersey m

jest /dʒest/ n **in ~** im Spaß

jet n (of water) [Wasser]strahl m; (nozzle) Düse f; (plane) Düsenflugzeug nt

jet: ~-'black adj pechschwarz. **~-pro'pelled** adj mit Düsenantrieb

jetty /'dʒetɪ/ n Landesteg m; (breakwater) Buhne f

Jew /dʒu:/ n Jude m /Jüdin f

jewel /'dʒu:əl/ n Edelstein m; (fig) Juwel nt. **~ler** n Juwelier m; **~ler's [shop]** Juweliergeschäft nt. **~lery** n Schmuck m

Jew|ess /'dʒu:ɪs/ n Jüdin f. **~ish** adj jüdisch

jib /dʒɪb/ vi (pt/pp **jibbed**) (fig) sich sträuben (**at** gegen)

jigsaw /'dʒɪgsɔ:/ n **~ [puzzle]** Puzzlespiel nt

jilt /dʒɪlt/ vt sitzen lassen

jingle /'dʒɪŋgl/ n (rhyme) Verschen nt •vi klimpern

jinx /dʒɪŋks/ n ! **it's got a ~ on it** es ist verhext

jittery /ˈdʒɪtərɪ/ adj [!] nervös

job /dʒɒb/ n Aufgabe f; (post) Stelle f, [!] Job m; **be a ~** [!] nicht leicht sein; **it's a good ~ that** es ist [nur] gut, dass. **~less** adj arbeitslos

jockey /ˈdʒɒkɪ/ n Jockei m

jocular /ˈdʒɒkjʊlə(r)/ adj spaßhaft

jog /ˈdʒɒg/ n Stoß m •v (pt/pp **jogged**) •vt anstoßen; **~ s.o.'s memory** jds Gedächtnis nachhelfen •vi (Sport) joggen. **~ging** n Jogging nt

john /dʒɒn/ n (Amer, [!]) Klo nt

join /dʒɔɪn/ n Nahtstelle f •vt verbinden (**to** mit); sich anschließen (+ dat) (person); (become member of) beitreten (+ dat); eintreten in (+ acc) (firm) •vi (roads:) sich treffen. **~ in** vi mitmachen. **~ up** vi (Mil) Soldat werden •vt zusammenfügen

joint /dʒɔɪnt/ adj gemeinsam •n Gelenk nt; (in wood, brickwork) Fuge f; (Culin) Braten m; ([!]: bar) Lokal nt

jok|e /dʒəʊk/ n Scherz m; (funny story) Witz m; (trick) Streich m •vi scherzen. **~er** n Witzbold m; (Cards) Joker m. **~ing** n **~ing apart** Spaß beiseite. **~ingly** adv im Spaß

jolly /ˈdʒɒlɪ/ adj lustig •adv [!] sehr

jolt /dʒəʊlt/ n Ruck m •vt einen Ruck versetzen (+ dat) •vi holpern

Jordan /ˈdʒɔːdn/ n Jordanien nt

jostle /ˈdʒɒsl/ vt anrempeln

jot /dʒɒt/ vt (pt/pp **jotted**) **~ [down]** sich (dat) notieren

journal /ˈdʒɜːnl/ n Zeitschrift f; (diary) Tagebuch nt. **~ese** n Zeitungsjargon m. **~ism** n Journalismus m. **~ist** n Journalist(in) m(f)

journey /ˈdʒɜːnɪ/ n Reise f

jovial /ˈdʒəʊvɪəl/ adj lustig

joy /dʒɔɪ/ n Freude f. **~ful** adj freudig, froh. **~ride** n [!] Spritztour f [im gestohlenen Auto]

jubil|ant /ˈdʒuːbɪlənt/ adj überglücklich. **~ation** n Jubel m

jubilee /ˈdʒuːbɪliː/ n Jubiläum nt

judder /ˈdʒʌdə(r)/ vi rucken

judge /dʒʌdʒ/ n Richter m; (of competition) Preisrichter m •vt beurteilen; (estimate) [ein]schätzen •vi urteilen (**by** nach). **~ment** n Beurteilung f; (Jur) Urteil nt; (fig) Urteilsvermögen nt

judic|ial /dʒuːˈdɪʃl/ adj gerichtlich. **~ious** adj klug

jug /dʒʌg/ n Kanne f; (small) Kännchen nt; (for water, wine) Krug m

juggle /ˈdʒʌgl/ vi jonglieren. **~r** n Jongleur m

juice /dʒuːs/ n Saft m

juicy /ˈdʒuːsɪ/ adj saftig; [!] (story) pikant

juke-box /ˈdʒuːk-/ n Musikbox f

July /dʒʊˈlaɪ/ n Juli m

jumble /ˈdʒʌmbl/ n Durcheinander nt •vt **~ [up]** durcheinander bringen. **~ sale** n [Wohltätigkeits]basar m

jump /dʒʌmp/ n Sprung m; (in prices) Anstieg m; (in horse racing) Hindernis nt •vi springen; (start) zusammenzucken; **make s.o. ~** jdn erschrecken; **~ at** (fig) sofort zugreifen bei (offer); **~ to conclusions** voreilige Schlüsse ziehen •vt überspringen. **~ up** vi aufspringen

jumper /ˈdʒʌmpə(r)/ n Pullover m, Pulli m

jumpy /ˈdʒʌmpɪ/ adj nervös

junction /ˈdʒʌŋkʃn/ n Kreuzung f; (Rail) Knotenpunkt m

June /dʒuːn/ n Juni m

jungle /ˈdʒʌŋgl/ n Dschungel m

junior /ˈdʒuːnɪə(r)/ adj jünger; (in rank) untergeordnet; (Sport) Junioren- •n Junior m

junk /dʒʌŋk/ n Gerümpel nt, Trödel m

junkie /ˈdʒʌŋkɪ/ n [✖] Fixer m

ˈjunk-shop n Trödelladen m

jurisdiction /dʒʊərɪsˈdɪkʃn/ n Gerichtsbarkeit f

jury /ˈdʒʊərɪ/ n **the ~** die

j

Geschworenen pl; (for competition) die Jury

just /dʒʌst/ adj gerecht • adv gerade; (only) nur; (simply) einfach; (exactly) genau; ~ **as tall** ebenso groß; **I'm** ~ **going** ich gehe schon

justice /ˈdʒʌstɪs/ n Gerechtigkeit f; **do** ~ **to** gerecht werden (+ dat)

justifiab|le /ˈdʒʌstɪfaɪəbl/ adj berechtigt. ~**ly** adv berechtigterweise

justi|fication /dʒʌstɪfɪˈkeɪʃn/ n Rechtfertigung f. ~**fy** vt (pt/pp **-ied**) rechtfertigen

justly /ˈdʒʌstlɪ/ adv zu Recht

jut /dʒʌt/ vi (pt/pp **jutted**) ~ **out** vorstehen

juvenile /ˈdʒu:vənaɪl/ adj jugendlich; (childish) kindisch • n Jugendliche(r) m/f. ~ **delinquency** n Jugendkriminalität f

Kk

kangaroo /kæŋgəˈru:/ n Känguru nt

kebab /kɪˈbæb/ n Spießchen nt

keel /ki:l/ n Kiel m • vi ~ **over** umkippen; (Naut) kentern

keen /ki:n/ adj (**-er, -est**) (sharp) scharf; (intense) groß; (eager) eifrig, begeistert; ~ **on** 🅧 erpicht auf (+ acc); ~ **on s.o.** von jdm sehr angetan; **be** ~ **to do sth** etw gerne machen wollen. ~**ly** adv tief. ~**ness** n Eifer m, Begeisterung f

keep /ki:p/ n (maintenance) Unterhalt m; (of castle) Bergfried m; **for** ~**s** für immer • v (pt/pp **kept**) • vt behalten; (store) aufbewahren; (not throw away) aufheben; (support) unterhalten; (detain) aufhalten; freihalten (seat); halten (promise, animals); führen, haben (shop); einhalten (law, rules); ~ **s.o. waiting** jdn warten lassen; ~ **sth to oneself** etw nicht weitersagen • vi (remain) bleiben; (food:) sich halten; ~ **left/right** sich links/ rechts halten; ~ **on doing sth** etw weitermachen; (repeatedly) etw dauernd machen; ~ **in with** sich gut stellen mit. ~ **up** vi Schritt halten • vt (continue) weitermachen

keep|er /ˈki:pə(r)/ n Wärter(in) m(f). ~**ing** n **be in** ~**ing with** passen zu

kennel /ˈkenl/ n Hundehütte f; ~**s** pl (boarding) Hundepension f; (breeding) Zwinger m

Kenya /ˈkenjə/ n Kenia nt

kept /kept/ see **keep**

kerb /kɜ:b/ n Bordstein m

kernel /ˈkɜ:nl/ n Kern m

ketchup /ˈketʃʌp/ n Ketschup m

kettle /ˈketl/ n [Wasser]kessel m; **put the** ~ **on** Wasser aufsetzen

key /ki:/ n Schlüssel m; (Mus) Tonart f; (of piano, typewriter) Taste f • vt ~ **in** eintasten

key: ~**board** n Tastatur f; (Mus) Klaviatur f. ~**hole** n Schlüsselloch nt. ~**-ring** n Schlüsselring m

khaki /ˈkɑ:kɪ/ adj khakifarben • n Khaki nt

kick /kɪk/ n [Fuß]tritt m; **for** ~**s** 🅧 zum Spaß • vt treten; ~ **the bucket** 🅧 abkratzen • vi (animal) ausschlagen

kid /kɪd/ n (🅧: child) Kind nt • vt (pt/ pp **kidded**) 🅧 ~ **s.o.** jdm etwas vormachen

kidnap /ˈkɪdnæp/ vt (pt/pp **-napped**) entführen. ~**per** n Entführer m. ~**ping** n Entführung f

kidney /ˈkɪdnɪ/ n Niere f

kill /kɪl/ vt töten; 🅧 totschlagen

(time): ~ **two birds with one stone** zwei Fliegen mit einer Klappe schlagen. ~**er** n Mörder(in) m(f). ~**ing** n Tötung f; (murder) Mord m

'**killjoy** n Spielverderber m

kilo /'ki:ləʊ/ n Kilo nt

kilo: /'kɪlə/: ~**gram** n Kilogramm nt. ~**metre** n Kilometer m. ~**watt** n Kilowatt nt

kilt /kɪlt/ n Schottenrock m

kind[1] /kaɪnd/ n Art f; (brand, type) Sorte f; **what ~ of car?** was für ein Auto? ~ **of** [!] irgendwie

kind[2] adj (**-er, -est**) nett; ~ **to animals** gut zu Tieren

kind|ly /'kaɪndlɪ/ adj nett •adv netterweise; (if you please) gefälligst. ~**ness** n Güte f; (favour) Gefallen m

king /kɪŋ/ n König m; (Draughts) Dame f. ~**dom** n Königreich nt; (fig & Relig) Reich nt

king: ~**fisher** n Eisvogel m. ~**-sized** adj extragroß

kink /kɪŋk/ n Knick m. ~**y** adj [!] pervers

kiosk /'ki:ɒsk/ n Kiosk m

kip /kɪp/ n **have a ~** [!] pennen •vi (pt/pp **kipped**) [!] pennen

kipper /'kɪpə(r)/ n Räucherhering m

kiss /kɪs/ n Kuss m •vt/i küssen

kit /kɪt/ n Ausrüstung f; (tools) Werkzeug nt; (construction ~) Bausatz m •vt (pt/pp **kitted**) ~**out** ausrüsten

kitchen /'kɪtʃɪn/ n Küche f •attrib Küchen-. ~**ette** n Kochnische f

kitchen: ~'**garden** n Gemüsegarten m. ~'**sink** n Spülbecken nt

kite /kaɪt/ n Drachen m

kitten /'kɪtn/ n Kätzchen nt

kitty /'kɪtɪ/ n (money) [gemeinsame] Kasse f

knack /næk/ n Trick m, Dreh m

knead /ni:d/ vt kneten

knee /ni:/ n Knie nt. ~**cap** n Kniescheibe f

kneel /ni:l/ vi (pt/pp **knelt**) knien; ~ **[down]** sich [nieder]knien

knelt /nelt/ see **kneel**

knew /nju:/ see **know**

knickers /'nɪkəz/ npl Schlüpfer m

knife /naɪf/ n (pl **knives**) Messer nt •vt einen Messerstich versetzen (+ dat)

knight /naɪt/ n Ritter m; (Chess) Springer m •vt adeln

knit /nɪt/ vt/i (pt/pp **knitted**) stricken; ~ **one's brow** die Stirn runzeln. ~**ting** n Stricken nt; (work) Strickzeug nt. ~**ting-needle** n Stricknadel f. ~**wear** n Strickwaren pl

knives /naɪvz/ npl see **knife**

knob /nɒb/ n Knopf m; (on door) Knauf m; (small lump) Beule f. ~**bly** adj knorrig; (bony) knochig

knock /nɒk/ n Klopfen nt; (blow) Schlag m; **there was a ~** es klopfte •vt anstoßen; ([!]: criticize) heruntermachen; ~ **a hole in sth** ein Loch in etw (acc) schlagen; ~ **one's head** sich (dat) den Kopf stoßen (**on** an + dat) •vi klopfen. ~ **about** vt schlagen •vi [!] herumkommen. ~ **down** vt herunterwerfen; (with fist) niederschlagen; (in car) anfahren; (demolish) abreißen; ([!]: reduce) herabsetzen. ~ **off** vt herunterwerfen; ([!]: steal) klauen; ([!]: complete quickly) hinhauen •vi ([!]: cease work) Feierabend machen. ~ **out** vt ausschlagen; (make unconscious) bewusstlos schlagen; (Boxing) k.o. schlagen. ~ **over** vt umwerfen; (in car) anfahren

knock: ~**-down** adj ~**-down prices** Schleuderpreise pl. ~**er** n Türklopfer m. ~**-out** n (Boxing) K.o. m

knot /nɒt/ n Knoten m •vt (pt/pp **knotted**) knoten

know /nəʊ/ vt/i (pt **knew**, pp **known**) wissen; kennen (person); können (language); **get to ~** kennen lernen •n **in the ~** [!] im Bild

know: ~**-all** n [!] Alleswisser m.

~-how n [!] [Sach]kenntnis f. **~ing** adj wissend. **~ingly** adv wissend; (intentionally) wissentlich

knowledge /ˈnɒlɪdʒ/ n Kenntnis f (**of** von/gen); (general) Wissen nt; (specialized) Kenntnisse pl. **~able** adj be **~able** viel wissen

knuckle /ˈnʌkl/ n [Finger]knöchel m; (Culin) Hachse f

kosher /ˈkəʊʃə(r)/ adj koscher

kudos /ˈkju:dɒs/ n [!] Prestige nt

Ll

lab /læb/ n [!] Labor nt

label /ˈleɪbl/ n Etikett nt •vt (pt/pp **labelled**) etikettieren

laboratory /ləˈbɒrətrɪ/ n Labor nt

laborious /ləˈbɔ:rɪəs/ adj mühsam

labour /ˈleɪbə(r)/ n Arbeit f; (workers) Arbeitskräfte pl; (Med) Wehen pl; **L~** (Pol) die Labourpartei •attrib Labour- •vi arbeiten •vt (fig) sich lange auslassen über (+ acc). **~er** n Arbeiter m

ˈ**labour-saving** adj arbeitssparend

lace /leɪs/ n Spitze f; (of shoe) Schnürsenkel m •vt schnüren

lack /læk/ n Mangel m (**of** an + dat) •vt **I ~ the time** mir fehlt die Zeit •vi **be ~ing** fehlen

laconic /ləˈkɒnɪk/ adj, **-ally** adv lakonisch

lacquer /ˈlækə(r)/ n Lack m; (for hair) [Haar]spray m

lad /læd/ n Junge m

ladder /ˈlædə(r)/ n Leiter f; (in fabric) Laufmasche f

ladle /ˈleɪdl/ n [Schöpf]kelle f •vt schöpfen

lady /ˈleɪdɪ/ n Dame f; (title) Lady f

lady: ~bird n, (Amer) **~bug** n Marienkäfer m. **~like** adj damenhaft

lag[1] /læg/ vi (pt/pp **lagged**) **~ behind** zurückbleiben; (fig) nachhinken

lag[2] vt (pt/pp **lagged**) umwickeln (pipes)

lager /ˈlɑ:gə(r)/ n Lagerbier nt

laid /leɪd/ see **lay**[3]

lain /leɪn/ see **lie**[2]

lake /leɪk/ n See m

lamb /læm/ n Lamm nt

lame /leɪm/ adj (**-r, -st**) lahm

lament /ləˈment/ n Klage f; (song) Klagelied nt •vt beklagen •vi klagen

laminated /ˈlæmɪneɪtɪd/ adj laminiert

lamp /læmp/ n Lampe f; (in street) Laterne f. **~post** n Laternenpfahl m. **~shade** n Lampenschirm m

lance /lɑ:ns/ vt (Med) aufschneiden

land /lænd/ n Land nt; **plot of ~** Grundstück nt •vt/i landen; **~ s.o. with sth** [!] jdm etw aufhalsen

landing /ˈlændɪŋ/ n Landung f; (top of stairs) Treppenflur m. **~-stage** n Landesteg m

land: ~lady n Wirtin f. **~lord** n Wirt m; (of land) Grundbesitzer m; (of building) Hausbesitzer m. **~mark** n Erkennungszeichen nt; (fig) Meilenstein m. **~owner** n Grundbesitzer m. **~scape** /-skeɪp/ n Landschaft f. **~slide** n Erdrutsch m

lane /leɪn/ n kleine Landstraße f; (Auto) Spur f; (Sport) Bahn f; **'get in ~'** (Auto) 'bitte einordnen'

language /ˈlæŋgwɪdʒ/ n Sprache f; (speech, style) Ausdrucksweise f

languid /ˈlæŋgwɪd/ adj träge

languish /ˈlæŋgwɪʃ/ vi schmachten

lanky /ˈlæŋkɪ/ adj schlaksig

lantern /ˈlæntən/ n Laterne f

lap¹ /læp/ n Schoß m

lap² n (Sport) Runde f; (of journey) Etappe f •vi (pt/pp **lapped**) plätschern (**against** gegen)

lap³ vt (pt/pp **lapped**) ~ **up** aufschlecken

lapel /ləˈpel/ n Revers nt

lapse /læps/ n Fehler m; (moral) Fehltritt m; (of time) Zeitspanne f •vi (expire) erlöschen; ~ **into** verfallen in (+ acc)

laptop /ˈlæptɒp/ n Laptop m

lard /lɑːd/ n [Schweine]schmalz nt

larder /ˈlɑːdə(r)/ n Speisekammer f

large /lɑːdʒ/ adj (**-r, -st**) & adv groß; **by and** ~ im Großen und Ganzen; **at** ~ auf freiem Fuß. ~**ly** adv großenteils

lark¹ /lɑːk/ n (bird) Lerche f

lark² n (joke) Jux m •vi ~ **about** herumalbern

laryngitis /lærɪnˈdʒaɪtɪs/ n Kehlkopfentzündung f

larynx /ˈlærɪŋks/ n Kehlkopf m

laser /ˈleɪzə(r)/ n Laser m

lash /læʃ/ n Peitschenhieb m; (eyelash) Wimper f •vt peitschen; (tie) festbinden (**to** an + acc). ~ **out** vi um sich schlagen; (spend) viel Geld ausgeben (**on** für)

lass /læs/ n Mädchen nt

lasso /ləˈsuː/ n Lasso nt

last /lɑːst/ adj & n letzte(r,s); ~ **night** heute od gestern Nacht; (evening) gestern Abend; **at** ~ endlich; **for the** ~ **time** zum letzten Mal; **the** ~ **but one** der/die/das vorletzte •adv zuletzt; (last time) das letzte Mal; **he/she went** ~ er/sie ging als Letzter/Letzte •vi dauern; (weather:) sich halten; (relationship:) halten. ~**ing** adj dauerhaft. ~**ly** adv schließlich, zum Schluss

latch /lætʃ/ n [einfache] Klinke f

late /leɪt/ adj & adv (**-r, -st**) spät; (delayed) verspätet; (deceased) verstorben; **the** ~**st news** die neuesten Nachrichten; **stay up** ~ bis spät aufbleiben; **arrive** ~ zu spät ankommen; **I am** ~ ich komme zu spät od habe mich verspätet; **the train is** ~ der Zug hat Verspätung. ~**comer** n Zuspätkommende(r) m/f. ~**ly** adv in letzter Zeit. ~**ness** n Zuspätkommen nt; (delay) Verspätung f

later /ˈleɪtə(r)/ adj & adv später; ~ **on** nachher

lateral /ˈlætərəl/ adj seitlich

lather /ˈlɑːðə(r)/ n [Seifen]schaum m

Latin /ˈlætɪn/ adj lateinisch •n Latein nt. ~ **Aˈmerica** n Lateinamerika nt

latitude /ˈlætɪtjuːd/ n (Geog) Breite f; (fig) Freiheit f

latter /ˈlætə(r)/ adj & n **the** ~ der/die/das Letztere

Latvia /ˈlætvɪə/ n Lettland nt

laudable /ˈlɔːdəbl/ adj lobenswert

laugh /lɑːf/ n Lachen nt; **with a** ~ lachend •vi lachen (**at/about** über + acc); ~ **at s.o.** (mock) jdn auslachen. ~**able** adj lachhaft, lächerlich

laughter /ˈlɑːftə(r)/ n Gelächter nt

launch¹ /lɔːntʃ/ n (boat) Barkasse f

launch² n Stapellauf m; (of rocket) Abschuss m; (of product) Lancierung f •vt vom Stapel lassen (ship); zu Wasser lassen (lifeboat); abschießen (rocket); starten (attack); (Comm) lancieren (product)

laund(e)rette /lɔːndret/ n Münzwäscherei f

laundry /ˈlɔːndrɪ/ n Wäscherei f; (clothes) Wäsche f

laurel /ˈlɒrl/ n Lorbeer m

lava /ˈlɑːvə/ n Lava f

lavatory /ˈlævətrɪ/ n Toilette f

lavender /ˈlævəndə(r)/ n Lavendel m

lavish /ˈlævɪʃ/ adj großzügig; (wasteful) verschwenderisch •vt ~

sth on s.o. jdn mit etw überschütten

law /lɔː/ n Gesetz nt; (system) Recht nt; **study ~** Jura studieren; **~ and order** Recht und Ordnung

law: ~-abiding adj gesetzestreu. **~court** n Gerichtshof m. **~ful** adj rechtmäßig. **~less** adj gesetzlos

lawn /lɔːn/ n Rasen m. **~-mower** n Rasenmäher m

lawyer /ˈlɔːjə(r)/ n Rechtsanwalt m /-anwältin f

lax /læks/ adj lax, locker

laxative /ˈlæksətɪv/ n Abführmittel nt

laxity /ˈlæksətɪ/ n Laxheit f

lay[1] /leɪ/ see **lie**[2]

lay[2] vt (pt/pp **laid**) legen; decken (table); **~ a trap** eine Falle stellen. **~ down** vt hinlegen; festlegen (rules, conditions). **~ off** vt entlassen (workers) •vi (🅸: stop) aufhören. **~ out** vt hinlegen; aufbahren (corpse); anlegen (garden); (Typography) gestalten

lay-by n Parkbucht f

layer /ˈleɪə(r)/ n Schicht f

lay: ~man n Laie m. **~out** n Anordnung f; (design) Gestaltung f; (Typography) Layout nt

laze /leɪz/ vi **~ [about]** faulenzen

laziness /ˈleɪzɪnɪs/ n Faulheit f

lazy /ˈleɪzɪ/ adj faul. **~-bones** n Faulenzer m

lead[1] /led/ n Blei nt; (of pencil) [Bleistift]mine f

lead[2] /liːd/ n Führung f; (leash) Leine f; (flex) Schnur f; (clue) Hinweis m, Spur f; (Theat) Hauptrolle f; (distance ahead) Vorsprung m; **be in the ~** in Führung liegen •vt/i (pt/pp **led**) führen; leiten (team); (induce) bringen; (at cards) ausspielen; **~ the way** vorangehen; **~ up to sth** (fig) etw (dat) vorangehen

leader /ˈliːdə(r)/ n Führer m; (of expedition, group) Leiter(in) m(f); (of orchestra) Konzertmeister m; (in newspaper) Leitartikel m. **~ship** n Führung f; Leitung f

leading /ˈliːdɪŋ/ adj führend; **~ lady** Hauptdarstellerin f

leaf /liːf/ n (pl **leaves**) Blatt nt •vi **~ through sth** etw durchblättern. **~let** n Merkblatt nt; (advertising) Reklameblatt nt; (political) Flugblatt nt

league /liːg/ n Liga f

leak /liːk/ n (hole) undichte Stelle f; (Naut) Leck nt; (of gas) Gasausfluss m •vi undicht sein; (ship:) leck sein, lecken; (liquid:) auslaufen; (gas:) ausströmen •vt auslaufen lassen; **~ sth to s.o.** (fig) jdm etw zuspielen. **~y** adj undicht; (Naut) leck

lean[1] /liːn/ adj (**-er, -est**) mager

lean[2] v (pt/pp **leaned** or **leant** /lent/) •vt lehnen (**against**/**on** an + acc) •vi (person) sich lehnen (**against**/**on** an + acc); (not be straight) sich neigen; **be ~ing against** lehnen an (+ dat). **~ back** vi sich zurücklehnen. **~ forward** vi sich vorbeugen. **~ out** vi sich hinauslehnen. **~ over** vi sich vorbeugen

leaning /ˈliːnɪŋ/ adj schief •n Neigung f

leap /liːp/ n Sprung m •vi (pt/pp **leapt** or **leaped**) springen; **he leapt at it** 🅸 er griff sofort zu. **~ year** n Schaltjahr nt

learn /lɜːn/ vt/i (pt/pp **learnt** or **learned**) lernen; (hear) erfahren; **~ to swim** schwimmen lernen

learn|ed /ˈlɜːnɪd/ adj gelehrt. **~er** n Anfänger m; **~er [driver]** Fahrschüler(in) m(f). **~ing** n Gelehrsamkeit f; **~ing curve** Lernkurve f

lease /liːs/ n Pacht f; (contract) Mietvertrag m •vt pachten

leash /liːʃ/ n Leine f

least /liːst/ adj geringste(r,s) •n **the ~** das wenigste; **at ~** wenigstens, mindestens; **not in the ~** nicht im Geringsten •adv am wenigsten

leather /ˈleðə(r)/ n Leder nt

leave /liːv/ n Erlaubnis f; (holiday)

Urlaub m; **on ~** auf Urlaub; **take one's ~** sich verabschieden • v (pt/pp **left**) • vt lassen; (go out of, abandon) verlassen; (forget) liegen lassen; (bequeath) vermachen (**to** dat); **~ it to me!** überlassen Sie es mir! **there is nothing left** es ist nichts mehr übrig • vi [weg]gehen/-fahren; (train, bus:) abfahren. **~ behind** vt zurücklassen; (forget) liegen lassen. **~ out** vt liegen lassen; (leave outside) draußen lassen; (omit) auslassen

leaves /li:vz/ see **leaf**

Lebanon /'lebənən/ n Libanon m

lecherous /'letʃərəs/ adj lüstern

lecture /'lektʃə(r)/ n Vortrag m; (Univ) Vorlesung f; (reproof) Strafpredigt f • vi einen Vortrag/eine Vorlesung halten (**on** über + acc) • vt **~ s.o.** jdm eine Strafpredigt halten. **~r** n Vortragende(r) m/f; (Univ) Dozent(in) m(f)

led /led/ see **lead**[2]

ledge /ledʒ/ n Leiste f; (shelf, of window) Sims m; (in rock) Vorsprung m

ledger /'ledʒə(r)/ n Hauptbuch nt

leech /li:tʃ/ n Blutegel m

leek /li:k/ n Stange f Porree; **~s** pl Porree m

left[1] /left/ see **leave**

left[2] adj linke(r,s) • adv links; (go) nach links • n linke Seite f; **on the ~** links; **from/to the ~** von/nach links; **the ~** (Pol) die Linke

left: ~-'handed adj linkshändig. **~-'luggage [office]** n Gepäckaufbewahrung f. **~overs** npl Reste pl. **~-'wing** adj (Pol) linke(r,s)

leg /leg/ n Bein nt; (Culin) Keule f; (of journey) Etappe f

legacy /'legəsɪ/ n Vermächtnis nt, Erbschaft f

legal /'li:gl/ adj gesetzlich; (matters) rechtlich; (department, position) Rechts-; **be ~** [gesetzlich] erlaubt sein

legality /lɪ'gæləti/ n Legalität f

legend /'ledʒənd/ n Legende f. **~ary** adj legendär

legi|ble /'ledʒəbl/ adj, **-bly** adv leserlich

legion /'li:dʒn/ n Legion f

legislat|e /'ledʒɪsleɪt/ vi Gesetze erlassen. **~ion** n Gesetzgebung f; (laws) Gesetze pl

legislative /'ledʒɪslətɪv/ adj gesetzgebend

legitimate /lɪ'dʒɪtɪmət/ adj rechtmäßig; (justifiable) berechtigt

leisure /'leʒə(r)/ n Freizeit f; **at your ~** wenn Sie Zeit haben. **~ly** adj gemächlich

lemon /'lemən/ n Zitrone f. **~ade** n Zitronenlimonade f

lend /lend/ vt (pt/pp **lent**) leihen (**s.o. sth** jdm etw)

length /leŋθ/ n Länge f; (piece) Stück nt; (of wallpaper) Bahn f; (of time) Dauer f

length|en /'leŋθən/ vt länger machen • vi länger werden. **~ways** adv der Länge nach

lengthy /'leŋθɪ/ adj langwierig

lenient /'li:nɪənt/ adj nachsichtig

lens /lenz/ n Linse f; (Phot) Objektiv nt; (of spectacles) Glas nt

lent /lent/ see **lend**

Lent n Fastenzeit f

lentil /'lentl/ n (Bot) Linse f

leopard /'lepəd/ n Leopard m

leotard /'li:ətɑ:d/ n Trikot nt

lesbian /'lezbɪən/ adj lesbisch • n Lesbierin f

less /les/ a, adv, n & prep weniger; **~ and ~** immer weniger

lessen /'lesn/ vt verringern • vi nachlassen; (value:) abnehmen

lesser /'lesə(r)/ adj geringere(r,s)

lesson /'lesn/ n Stunde f; (in textbook) Lektion f; (Relig) Lesung f; **teach s.o. a ~** (fig) jdm eine Lehre erteilen

lest /lest/ conj (literary) damit ... nicht

let /let/ vt (pt/pp **let**, pres p **letting**)

lassen; (rent) vermieten; ~ **alone** (not to mention) geschweige denn; ~ **us go** gehen wir; ~ **me know** sagen Sie mir Bescheid; ~ **oneself in for sth** [!] sich (dat) etw einbrocken. ~ **down** vt hinunter-/herunterlassen; (lengthen) länger machen; ~ **s.o. down** [!] jdn im Stich lassen; (disappoint) jdn enttäuschen. ~ **in** vt hereinlassen. ~ **off** vt abfeuern (gun); hochgehen lassen (firework, bomb); (emit) ausstoßen; (excuse from) befreien von; (not punish) frei ausgehen lassen. ~ **out** vt hinaus-/herauslassen; (make larger) auslassen. ~ **through** vt durchlassen. ~ **up** vi [!] nachlassen

'let-down n Enttäuschung f, [!] Reinfall m

lethal /'li:θl/ adj tödlich

letharg|ic /lɪ'θɑ:dʒɪk/ adj lethargisch. ~**y** n Lethargie f

letter /'letə(r)/ n Brief m; (of alphabet) Buchstabe m. ~**-box** n Briefkasten m. ~**-head** n Briefkopf m. ~**ing** n Beschriftung f

lettuce /'letɪs/ n [Kopf]salat m

'let-up n [!] Nachlassen nt

level /'levl/ adj eben; (horizontal) waagerecht; (in height) auf gleicher Höhe; (spoonful) gestrichen; **one's ~ best** sein Möglichstes •n Höhe f; (fig) Ebene f, Niveau nt; (stage) Stufe f; **on the ~** [!] ehrlich •vt (pt/pp **levelled**) einebnen

level 'crossing n Bahnübergang m

lever /'li:və(r)/ n Hebel m •vt ~ **up** mit einem Hebel anheben. ~**age** n Hebelkraft f

lewd /lju:d/ adj (**-er, -est**) anstößig

liabilit|y /laɪə'bɪlətɪ/ n Haftung f; ~**ies** pl Verbindlichkeiten pl

liable /'laɪəbl/ adj haftbar; **be ~ to do sth** etw leicht tun können

liaise /lɪ'eɪz/ vi [!] Verbindungsperson sein

liaison /lɪ'eɪzɒn/ n Verbindung f; (affair) Verhältnis nt

liar /'laɪə(r)/ n Lügner(in) m(f)

libel /'laɪbl/ n Verleumdung f •vt (pt/pp **libelled**) verleumden. ~**lous** adj verleumderisch

liberal /'lɪbərl/ adj tolerant; (generous) großzügig. **L~** adj (Pol) liberal •n Liberale(r) m/f

liberat|e /'lɪbəreɪt/ vt befreien. ~**ed** adj (woman) emanzipiert. ~**ion** n Befreiung f. ~**or** n Befreier m

liberty /'lɪbətɪ/ n Freiheit f; **take liberties** sich (dat) Freiheiten erlauben

librarian /laɪ'breərɪən/ n Bibliothekar(in) m(f)

library /'laɪbrərɪ/ n Bibliothek f

Libya /'lɪbɪə/ n Libyen nt

lice /laɪs/ see **louse**

licence /'laɪsns/ n Genehmigung f; (Comm) Lizenz f; (for TV) ≈ Fernsehgebühr f; (for driving) Führerschein m; (for alcohol) Schankkonzession f

license /'laɪsns/ vt eine Genehmigung/(Comm) Lizenz erteilen (+ dat); **be ~d** (car:) zugelassen sein; (restaurant:) Schankkonzession haben. ~**-plate** n (Amer) Nummernschild nt

lick /lɪk/ n Lecken nt; **a ~ of paint** ein bisschen Farbe •vt lecken; ([!]: defeat) schlagen

lid /lɪd/ n Deckel m; (of eye) Lid nt

lie[1] /laɪ/ n Lüge f; **tell a ~** lügen •vi (pt/pp **lied**, pres p **lying**) lügen; ~ **to** belügen

lie[2] vi (pt **lay**, pp **lain**, pres p **lying**) liegen; **here ~s ...** hier ruht ... ~ **down** vi sich hinlegen

'lie-in n **have a ~** [sich] ausschlafen

lieu /lju:/ n **in ~ of** statt (+ gen)

lieutenant /lef'tenənt/ n Oberleutnant m

life /laɪf/ n (pl **lives**) Leben nt; **lose one's ~** ums Leben kommen

life: ~-boat n Rettungsboot nt. ~ **coach** n Lebensberater(in) m(f).

~-guard n Lebensretter m. **~-jacket** n Schwimmweste f. **~less** adj leblos. **~like** adj naturgetreu. **~long** adj lebenslang. **~ preserver** n (Amer) Rettungsring m. **~-size(d)** adj ... in Lebensgröße. **~time** n Leben nt; **in s.o.'s ~time** zu jds Lebzeiten; **the chance of a ~time** eine einmalige Gelegenheit

lift /lɪft/ n Aufzug m, Lift m; **give s.o. a ~** jdn mitnehmen; **get a ~** mitgenommen werden •vt heben; aufheben (restrictions) •vi (fog:) sich lichten. **~ up** vt hochheben

light[1] /laɪt/ adj (**-er, -est**) (not dark) hell; **~ blue** hellblau •n Licht nt; (lamp) Lampe f; **have you [got] a ~?** haben Sie Feuer? •vt (pt/pp **lit** or **lighted**) anzünden (fire, cigarette); (illuminate) beleuchten. **~ up** vi (face:) sich erhellen

light[2] adj (**-er, -est**) (not heavy) leicht; **~ sentence** milde Strafe f •adv **travel ~** mit wenig Gepäck reisen

'**light-bulb** n Glühbirne f

lighten[1] /'laɪtn/ vt heller machen

lighten[2] vt leichter machen (load)

lighter /'laɪtə(r)/ n Feuerzeug nt

light: ~-'hearted adj unbekümmert. **~house** n Leuchtturm m. **~ing** n Beleuchtung f. **~ly** adv leicht; **get off ~ly** glimpflich davonkommen

lightning /'laɪtnɪŋ/ n Blitz m

'**lightweight** adj leicht •n (Boxing) Leichtgewicht nt

like[1] /laɪk/ adj ähnlich; (same) gleich •prep wie; (similar to) ähnlich (+ dat); **~ this** so; **what's he ~?** wie ist er denn? •conj (🅘: as) wie; (Amer: as if) als ob

like[2] vt mögen; **I should/would ~** ich möchte; **I ~ the car** das Auto gefällt mir; **~ dancing/singing** gern tanzen/singen •n **~s and dislikes** pl Vorlieben und Abneigungen pl

like|able /'laɪkəbl/ adj sympathisch. **~lihood** n Wahrscheinlichkeit f. **~ly** adj & adv wahrscheinlich; **not ~ly!** 🅘 auf gar keinen Fall!

'**like-minded** adj gleich gesinnt

liken /'laɪkən/ vt vergleichen (**to** mit)

like|ness /'laɪknɪs/ n Ähnlichkeit f. **~wise** adv ebenso

liking /'laɪkɪŋ/ n Vorliebe f; **is it to your ~?** gefällt es Ihnen?

lilac /'laɪlək/ n Flieder m

lily /'lɪlɪ/ n. Lilie f

limb /lɪm/ n Glied nt

lime /laɪm/ n (fruit) Limone f; (tree) Linde f. **~light** n **be in the ~light** im Rampenlicht stehen

limit /'lɪmɪt/ n Grenze f; (limitation) Beschränkung f; **that's the ~!** 🅘 das ist doch die Höhe! •vt beschränken (**to** auf + acc). **~ation** n Beschränkung f; **~ed** adj beschränkt. **~ed company** Gesellschaft f mit beschränkter Haftung

limousine /'lɪməzi:n/ n Limousine f

limp[1] /lɪmp/ n Hinken nt •vi hinken

limp[2] adj (**-er -est**) schlaff

limpid /'lɪmpɪd/ adj klar

line[1] /laɪn/ n Linie f; (length of rope, cord) Leine f; (Teleph) Leitung f; (of writing) Zeile f; (row) Reihe f; (wrinkle) Falte f; (of business) f; (Amer: queue) Schlange f; **in ~ with** gemäß (+ dat) •vt säumen (street)

line[2] vt füttern (garment); (Techn) auskleiden

lined[1] /laɪnd/ adj (wrinkled) faltig; (paper) liniert

lined[2] adj (garment) gefüttert

'**line dancing** n Linedance-Tanzen nt

linen /'lɪnɪn/ n Leinen nt; (articles) Wäsche f

liner /'laɪnə(r)/ n Passagierschiff nt

'**linesman** n (pl **men**) (Sport) Linienrichter m

linger /'lɪŋgə(r)/ vi [zurück]bleiben

lingerie /'læ̃ʒərɪ/ n Damenunterwäsche f

linguist /ˈlɪŋgwɪst/ n Sprachkundige(r) m/f

linguistic /lɪŋˈgwɪstɪk/ adj, **-ally** adv sprachlich

lining /ˈlaɪnɪŋ/ n (of garment) Futter nt; (Techn) Auskleidung f

link /lɪŋk/ n (of chain) Glied nt (fig) Verbindung f •vt verbinden; **~ arms** sich unterhaken

links /lɪŋks/ n or npl Golfplatz m

lint /lɪnt/ n Verbandstoff m

lion /ˈlaɪən/ n Löwe m; **~'s share** (fig) Löwenanteil m. **~ess** n Löwin f

lip /lɪp/ n Lippe f; (edge) Rand m; (of jug) Schnabel m

lip: ~-reading n Lippenlesen nt. **~-service** n **pay ~-service** ein Lippenbekenntnis ablegen (**to** zu). **~stick** n Lippenstift m

liqueur /lɪˈkjʊə(r)/ n Likör m

liquid /ˈlɪkwɪd/ n Flüssigkeit f •adj flüssig

liquidation /lɪkwɪˈdeɪʃn/ n Liquidation f

liquidize /ˈlɪkwɪdaɪz/ vt [im Mixer] pürieren. **~r** n Mixer m

liquor /ˈlɪkə(r)/ n Alkohol m. **~ store** n (Amer) Spirituosengeschäft nt

lisp /lɪsp/ n Lispeln nt •vt/i lispeln

list[1] /lɪst/ n Liste f •vt aufführen

list[2] vi (ship:) Schlagseite haben

listen /ˈlɪsn/ vi zuhören (**to** dat); **~ to the radio** Radio hören. **~er** n Zuhörer(in) m(f); (Radio) Hörer(in) m(f)

listless /ˈlɪstlɪs/ adj lustlos

lit /lɪt/ see **light**[1]

literacy /ˈlɪtərəsɪ/ n Lese- und Schreibfertigkeit f

literal /ˈlɪtərl/ adj wörtlich. **~ly** adv buchstäblich

literary /ˈlɪtərərɪ/ adj literarisch

literate /ˈlɪtərət/ adj **be ~** lesen und schreiben können

literature /ˈlɪtrətʃə(r)/ n Literatur f; [!] Informationsmaterial nt

lithe /laɪð/ adj geschmeidig

Lithuania /lɪθjʊˈeɪnɪə/ n Litauen nt

litre /ˈliːtə(r)/ n Liter m & nt

litter /ˈlɪtə(r)/ n Abfall m; (Zool) Wurf m. **~-bin** n Abfalleimer m

little /ˈlɪtl/ adj klein; (not much) wenig •adv & n wenig; **a ~** ein bisschen/wenig; **~ by ~** nach und nach

live[1] /laɪv/ adj lebendig; (ammunition) scharf; **~ broadcast** Live-Sendung f; **be ~** (Electr) unter Strom stehen

live[2] /lɪv/ vi leben; (reside) wohnen. **~ on** vt leben von; (eat) sich ernähren von •vi weiterleben

liveli|hood /ˈlaɪvlɪhʊd/ n Lebensunterhalt m. **~ness** n Lebendigkeit f

lively /ˈlaɪvlɪ/ adj lebhaft, lebendig

liver /ˈlɪvə(r)/ n Leber f

lives /laɪvz/ see **life**

livid /ˈlɪvɪd/ adj [!] wütend

living /ˈlɪvɪŋ/ adj lebend •n **earn one's ~** seinen Lebensunterhalt verdienen. **~-room** n Wohnzimmer nt

lizard /ˈlɪzəd/ n Eidechse f

load /ləʊd/ n Last f; (quantity) Ladung f; (Electr) Belastung f; **~s of** [!] jede Menge •vt laden (goods, gun); beladen (vehicle); **~ a camera** einen Film in eine Kamera einlegen. **~ed** adj beladen; ([!]: rich) steinreich

loaf /ləʊf/ n (pl **loaves**) Brot nt

loan /ləʊn/ n Leihgabe f; (money) Darlehen nt; **on ~** geliehen •vt leihen (to dat)

loath /ləʊθ/ adj **be ~ to do sth** etw ungern tun

loath|e /ləʊð/ vt verabscheuen. **~ing** n Abscheu m

loaves /ləʊvz/ see **loaf**[1]

lobby /ˈlɒbɪ/ n Foyer nt; (anteroom) Vorraum m; (Pol) Lobby f

lobster /ˈlɒbstə(r)/ n Hummer m

local /ˈləʊkl/ adj hiesig; (time, traffic)

Orts-; ~ **anaesthetic** örtliche Betäubung; **I'm not** ~ ich bin nicht von hier •n Hiesige(r) m/f; (!: public house) Stammkneipe f. ~ **call** n (Teleph) Ortsgespräch nt

locality /ləʊ'kælətɪ/ n Gegend f

localization /ləʊkəlaɪ'zeɪʃn/ n Lokalisierung f

locally /'ləʊkəlɪ/ adv am Ort

locat|e /ləʊ'keɪt/ vt ausfindig machen; **be** ~**ed** sich befinden. ~**ion** n Lage f; **filmed on** ~**ion** als Außenaufnahme gedreht

lock[1] /lɒk/ n (hair) Strähne f

lock[2] n (on door) Schloss nt; (on canal) Schleuse f •vt abschließen •vi sich abschließen lassen. ~ **in** vt einschließen. ~ **out** vt ausschließen. ~ **up** vt abschließen; einsperren (person)

locker /'lɒkə(r)/ n Schließfach nt; (Mil) Spind m

lock: ~**-out** n Aussperrung f. ~**smith** n Schlosser m

locomotive /ləʊkə'məʊtɪv/ n Lokomotive f

locum /'ləʊkəm/ n Vertreter(in) m(f)

locust /'ləʊkəst/ n Heuschrecke f

lodge /lɒdʒ/ n (porter's) Pförtnerhaus nt •vt (submit) einreichen; (deposit) deponieren •vi zur Untermiete wohnen (**with** bei); (become fixed) stecken bleiben. ~**r** n Untermieter(in) m(f)

lodging /'lɒdʒɪŋ/ n Unterkunft f; ~**s** npl möbliertes Zimmer nt

loft /lɒft/ n Dachboden m

lofty /'lɒftɪ/ adj hoch

log /lɒg/ n Baumstamm m; (for fire) [Holz]scheit nt; **sleep like a** ~ ! wie ein Murmeltier schlafen •vi ~ **off** sich abmelden; ~ **on** sich anmelden

loggerheads /'lɒgə-/ npl **be at** ~ ! sich in den Haaren liegen

logic /'lɒdʒɪk/ n Logik f. ~**al** adj logisch

logo /'ləʊgəʊ/ n Symbol nt, Logo nt

loiter /'lɔɪtə(r)/ vi herumlungern

loll /lɒl/ vi sich lümmeln

loll|ipop /'lɒlɪpɒp/ n Lutscher m. ~**y** n Lutscher m; (!: money) Moneten pl

London /'lʌndən/ n London nt •attrib Londoner. ~**er** n Londoner(in) m(f)

lone /ləʊn/ adj einzeln. ~**liness** n Einsamkeit f

lonely /'ləʊnlɪ/ adj einsam

lone|r /'ləʊnə(r)/ n Einzelgänger m. ~**some** adj einsam

long[1] /lɒŋ/ adj (**-er** /'lɒŋgə(r)/, **-est** /'lɒŋgɪst/) lang; (journey) weit; **a** ~ **time** lange; **a** ~ **way** weit; **in the** ~ **run** auf lange Sicht; (in the end) letzten Endes •adv lange; **all day** ~ den ganzen Tag; **not** ~ **ago** vor kurzem; **before** ~ bald; **no** ~**er** nicht mehr; **as** or **so** ~**as** solange; **so** ~**!** ! tschüs!

long[2] vi ~ **for** sich sehnen nach

long-'distance adj Fern-; (Sport) Langstrecken-

longing /'lɒŋɪŋ/ adj sehnsüchtig •n Sehnsucht f

longitude /'lɒŋgɪtju:d/ n (Geog) Länge f

long: ~ **jump** n Weitsprung m. ~**-lived** /-lɪvd/ adj langlebig. ~**-range** adj (Mil, Aviat) Langstrecken-; (forecast) langfristig. ~**-sighted** adj weitsichtig. ~**-sleeved** adj langärmelig. ~**-suffering** adj langmütig. ~**-term** adj langfristig. ~ **wave** n Langwelle. ~**-winded** /-'wɪndɪd/ adj langatmig

loo /lu:/ n ! Klo nt

look /lʊk/ n Blick m; (appearance) Aussehen nt; **[good]** ~**s** pl [gutes] Aussehen nt; **have a** ~ **at** sich (dat) ansehen; **go and have a** ~ sieh mal nach •vi sehen; (search) nachsehen; (seem) aussehen; **don't** ~ sieh nicht hin; ~ **here!** hören Sie mal! ~ **at** ansehen; ~ **for** suchen; ~ **forward to** sich freuen auf (+ acc); ~ **in on** vorbeischauen bei; ~ **into** (examine) nachgehen (+ dat); ~ **like** aussehen wie; ~ **on to** (room:) gehen auf (+ acc). ~ **after**

vt betreuen. ~ **down** vi hinuntersehen; ~ **down on s.o.** (fig) auf jdn herabsehen. ~ **out** vi hinaus-/heraussehen; (take care) aufpassen; ~ **out for** Ausschau halten nach; ~ **out!** Vorsicht! ~ **round** vi sich umsehen. ~ **up** vi aufblicken; ~ **up to s.o.** (fig) zu jdm aufsehen •vt nachschlagen (word)

'**look-out** n Wache f; (prospect) Aussicht f; **be on the ~ for** Ausschau halten nach

loom[1] /lu:m/ n Webstuhl m

loom[2] vi auftauchen

loony /'lu:nɪ/ adj [!] verrückt

loop /lu:p/ n Schlinge f; (in road) Schleife f. **~hole** n Hintertürchen nt; (in the law) Lücke f

loose /lu:s/ adj (**-r, -st**) lose; (not tight enough) locker; (inexact) frei; **be at a ~ end** nichts zu tun haben. ~ '**change** n Kleingeld nt

loosen /'lu:sn/ vt lockern

loot /lu:t/ n Beute f •vt/i plündern. **~er** n Plünderer m

lop /lɒp/ vt (pt/pp **lopped**) stutzen

lop'sided adj schief

lord /lɔ:d/ n Herr m; (title) Lord m; **House of L~ s** ≈ Oberhaus nt; **the L~'s Prayer** das Vaterunser

lorry /'lɒrɪ/ n Last[kraft]wagen m

lose /lu:z/ v (pt/pp **lost**) •vt verlieren; (miss) verpassen •vi verlieren; (clock:) nachgehen; **get lost** verloren gehen; (person) sich verlaufen. **~r** n Verlierer m

loss /lɒs/ n Verlust m; **be at a ~** nicht mehr weiter wissen

lost /lɒst/ see **lose**. ~ '**property office** n Fundbüro nt

lot[1] /lɒt/ Los nt; (at auction) Posten m; **draw ~s** losen (**for** um)

lot[2] n **the ~** alle; (everything) alles; **a ~ [of]** viel; (many) viele; **~s of** [!] eine Menge; **it has changed a ~** es hat sich sehr verändert

lotion /'ləʊʃn/ n Lotion f

lottery /'lɒtərɪ/ n Lotterie f. ~ **ticket** n Los nt

loud /laʊd/ adj (**-er, -est**) laut; (colours) grell •adv **[out]** ~ laut. ~ '**speaker** n Lautsprecher m

lounge /laʊndʒ/ n Wohnzimmer nt; (in hotel) Aufenthaltsraum m. •vi sich lümmeln

louse /laʊs/ n (pl **lice**) Laus f

lousy /'laʊzɪ/ adj [!] lausig

lout /laʊt/ n Flegel m, Lümmel m

lovable /'lʌvəbl/ adj liebenswert

love /lʌv/ n Liebe f; (Tennis) null; **in ~** verliebt •vt lieben; ~ **doing sth** etw sehr gerne machen. **~-affair** n Liebesverhältnis nt. ~ **letter** n Liebesbrief m

lovely /'lʌvlɪ/ adj schön

lover /'lʌvə(r)/ n Liebhaber m

love: ~ **song** n Liebeslied nt. ~ **story** n Liebesgeschichte f

loving /'lʌvɪŋ/ adj liebevoll

low /ləʊ/ adj (**-er, -est**) niedrig; (cloud, note) tief; (voice) leise; (depressed) niedergeschlagen •adv niedrig; (fly, sing) tief; (speak) leise •n (weather) Tief nt; (fig) Tiefstand m

low: **~brow** adj geistig anspruchslos. **~-cut** adj (dress) tief ausgeschnitten

lower /'ləʊə(r)/ adj & adv see **low** •vt niedriger machen; (let down) herunterlassen; (reduce) senken

low: ~-'**fat** adj fettarm. **~lands** /-ləndz/ npl Tiefland nt. ~ '**tide** n Ebbe f

loyal /'lɔɪəl/ adj treu. **~ty** n Treue f. **~ty card** n Treuekarte f

lozenge /'lɒzɪndʒ/ n Pastille f

Ltd abbr (**Limited**) GmbH

lubricant /'lu:brɪkənt/ n Schmiermittel nt

lubricat|e /'lu:brɪkeɪt/ vt schmieren. **~ion** n Schmierung f

lucid /'lu:sɪd/ adj klar. **~ity** n Klarheit f

luck /lʌk/ n Glück nt; **bad ~** Pech nt; **good ~!** viel Glück! **~ily** adv glücklicherweise, zum Glück

lucky /'lʌkɪ/ adj glücklich; (day,

number) Glücks-; **be** ~ Glück haben; (thing:) Glück bringen

lucrative /'lu:krətɪv/ adj einträglich

ludicrous /'lu:dɪkrəs/ adj lächerlich

lug /lʌg/ vt (pt/pp **lugged**) [!] schleppen

luggage /'lʌgɪdʒ/ n Gepäck nt

luggage: ~**-rack** in Gepäckablage f. ~**-van** n Gepäckwagen m

lukewarm /'lu:k-/ adj lauwarm

lull /lʌl/ n Pause f •vt ~ **to sleep** einschläfern

lullaby /'lʌləbaɪ/ n Wiegenlied nt

lumber /'lʌmbə(r)/ n Gerümpel nt; (Amer: timber) Bauholz nt •vt ~ **s.o. with sth** jdm etw aufhalsen. ~ **jack** n (Amer) Holzfäller m

luminous /'lu:mɪnəs/ adj leuchtend

lump /lʌmp/ n Klumpen m; (of sugar) Stück nt; (swelling) Beule f; (in breast) Knoten m; (tumour) Geschwulst f; **a** ~ **in one's throat** [!] ein Kloß im Hals

lump: ~ **sugar** n Würfelzucker m. ~ **'sum** n Pauschalsumme f

lumpy /'lʌmpɪ/ adj klumpig

lunacy /'lu:nəsɪ/ n Wahnsinn m

lunar /'lu:nə(r)/ adj Mond-

lunatic /'lu:nətɪk/ n Wahnsinnige(r) m/f

lunch /lʌntʃ/ n Mittagessen nt •vi zu Mittag essen

luncheon /'lʌntʃn/ n Mittagessen nt. ~ **voucher** n Essensbon m

lunch: ~**-hour** n Mittagspause f. ~**-time** n Mittagszeit f

lung /lʌŋ/ n Lungenflügel m; ~**s** pl Lunge f

lunge /lʌndʒ/ vi sich stürzen (**at** auf + acc)

lurch[1] /lɜ:tʃ/ n **leave in the** ~ [!] im Stich lassen

lurch[2] vi (person:) torkeln

lure /ljʊə(r)/ vt locken

lurid /'lʊərɪd/ adj grell; (sensational) reißerisch

lurk /lɜ:k/ vi lauern

luscious /'lʌʃəs/ adj lecker, köstlich

lush /lʌʃ/ adj üppig

lust /lʌst/ n Begierde f. ~**ful** adj lüstern

lustre /'lʌstə(r)/ n Glanz m

lusty /'lʌstɪ/ adj kräftig

luxuriant /lʌg'ʒʊərɪənt/ adj üppig

luxurious /lʌg'ʒʊərɪəs/ adj luxuriös

luxury /'lʌkʃərɪ/ n Luxus m •attrib Luxus-

lying /'laɪɪŋ/ see **lie**[1], **lie**[2]

lynch /lɪntʃ/ vt lynchen

lyric /'lɪrɪk/ adj lyrisch. ~**al** adj lyrisch; (enthusiastic) schwärmerisch. ~ **poetry** n Lyrik f. ~**s** npl [Lied]text m

Mm

mac /mæk/ n [!] Regenmantel m

macabre /mə'kɑ:br/ adj makaber

macaroni /mækə'rəʊnɪ/ n Makkaroni pl

machinations /mækɪ'neɪʃnz/ pl Machenschaften pl

machine /mə'ʃi:n/ n Maschine f •vt (sew) mit der Maschine nähen; (Techn) maschinell bearbeiten. ~**-gun** n Maschinengewehr nt

machinery /mə'ʃi:nərɪ/ n Maschinerie f

mackerel /'mækrl/ n inv Makrele f

mackintosh /'mækɪntoʃ/ n Regenmantel m

mad /mæd/ adj (**madder, maddest**)

verrückt; (dog) tollwütig; (!: angry) böse (**at** auf + acc)

madam /ˈmædəm/ n gnädige Frau f

mad ˈcow disease n ! Rinderwahnsinn m

madden /ˈmædn/ vt (make angry) wütend machen

made /meɪd/ see **make**; **~ to measure** maßgeschneidert

mad|ly /ˈmædlɪ/ adv ! wahnsinnig. **~man** n Irre(r) m. **~ness** n Wahnsinn m

madonna /məˈdɒnə/ n Madonna f

magazine /mægəˈziːn/ n Zeitschrift f; (Mil, Phot) Magazin nt

maggot /ˈmægət/ n Made f

magic /ˈmædʒɪk/ n Zauber m; (tricks) Zauberkunst f • adj magisch; (word, wand) Zauber-. **~al** adj zauberhaft

magician /məˈdʒɪʃn/ n Zauberer m; (entertainer) Zauberkünstler m

magistrate /ˈmædʒɪstreɪt/ n ≈ Friedensrichter m

m

magnet /ˈmægnɪt/ n Magnet m. **~ic** adj magnetisch. **~ism** n Magnetismus m

magnification /mægnɪfɪˈkeɪʃn/ n Vergrößerung f

magnificen|ce /mægˈnɪfɪsəns/ n Großartigkeit f. **~t** adj großartig

magnify /ˈmægnɪfaɪ/ vt (pt/pp **-ied**) vergrößern; (exaggerate) übertreiben. **~ing glass** n Vergrößerungsglas nt

magnitude /ˈmægnɪtjuːd/ n Größe f; (importance) Bedeutung f

magpie /ˈmægpaɪ/ n Elster f

mahogany /məˈhɒgənɪ/ n Mahagoni nt

maid /meɪd/ n Dienstmädchen nt; **old ~** (pej) alte Jungfer f

maiden /ˈmeɪdn/ adj (speech, voyage) Jungfern-. **~ name** n Mädchenname m

mail /meɪl/ n Post f • vt mit der Post schicken

mail: ~-bag n Postsack m. **~box** n (Amer) Briefkasten m. **~ing list** n Postversandliste f. **~man** n (Amer) Briefträger m. **~-order firm** n Versandhaus nt

maim /meɪm/ vt verstümmeln

main /meɪn/ adj Haupt- • n (water, gas, electricity) Hauptleitung f

main: ~land /-lənd/ n Festland nt. **~ly** adv hauptsächlich. **~stay** n (fig) Stütze f. **~ street** n Hauptstraße f

maintain /meɪnˈteɪn/ vt aufrechterhalten; (keep in repair) instand halten; (support) unterhalten; (claim) behaupten

maintenance /ˈmeɪntənəns/ n Aufrechterhaltung f; (care) Instandhaltung f; (allowance) Unterhalt m

maize /meɪz/ n Mais m

majestic /məˈdʒestɪk/ adj, **-ally** adv majestätisch

majesty /ˈmædʒəstɪ/ n Majestät f

major /ˈmeɪdʒə(r)/ adj größer • n (Mil) Major m; (Mus) Dur nt • vi **~ in** als Hauptfach studieren

majority /məˈdʒɒrətɪ/ n Mehrheit f; **in the ~** in der Mehrzahl

major road n Hauptverkehrsstraße f

make /meɪk/ n (brand) Marke f • v (pt/pp **made**) • vt machen; (force) zwingen; (earn) verdienen; halten (speech); treffen (decision); erreichen (destination) • vi **~ do** vi zurechtkommen (**with** mit). **~ for** vi zusteuern auf (+ acc). **~ off** vi sich davonmachen (**with** mit). **~ out** vt (distinguish) ausmachen; (write out) ausstellen; (assert) behaupten. **~ up** vt (constitute) bilden; (invent) erfinden; (apply cosmetics to) schminken; **~ up one's mind** sich entschließen • vi sich versöhnen; **~ up for sth** etw wieder gutmachen; **~ up for lost time** verlorene Zeit aufholen

ˈmake-believe n Phantasie f

maker /ˈmeɪkə(r)/ n Hersteller m

make: ~ shift adj behelfsmäßig • n Notbehelf m. **~-up** n Make-up nt

maladjusted /mælə'dʒʌstɪd/ adj verhaltensgestört

male /meɪl/ adj männlich •n Mann m; (animal) Männchen nt. ~ **nurse** n Krankenpfleger m. ~ **voice 'choir** n Männerchor m

malice /'mælɪs/ n Bosheit f

malicious /mə'lɪʃəs/ adj böswillig

malign /mə'laɪŋ/ vt verleumden

malignant /mə'lɪgnənt/ adj bösartig

mallet /'mælɪt/ n Holzhammer m

malnu'trition /mæl-/ n Unterernährung f

mal'practice n Berufsvergehen nt

malt /mɔ:lt/ n Malz nt

mal'treat /mæl-/ vt misshandeln. ~**ment** n Misshandlung f

mammal /'mæml/ n Säugetier nt

mammoth /'mæməθ/ adj riesig

man /mæn/ n (pl **men**) Mann m; (mankind) der Mensch; (chess) Figur f; (draughts) Stein m •vt (pt/pp **manned**) bemannen (ship); bedienen (pump); besetzen (counter)

manage /'mænɪdʒ/ vt leiten; verwalten (estate); (cope with) fertig werden mit; ~ **to do sth** es schaffen, etw zu tun •vi zurechtkommen; ~ **on** auskommen mit. ~**able** adj (tool) handlich; (person) fügsam. ~**ment** n Leitung f; **the ~ment** die Geschäftsleitung f

manager /'mænɪdʒə(r)/ n Geschäftsführer m; (of bank) Direktor m; (of estate) Verwalter m; (Sport) [Chef]trainer m. ~**ess** n Geschäftsführerin f. ~**ial** adj ~**ial staff** Führungskräfte pl

managing /'mænɪdʒɪŋ/ adj ~ **director** Generaldirektor m

mandat|e /'mændeɪt/ n Mandat nt. ~**ory** adj obligatorisch

mane /meɪn/ n Mähne f

manful /'mænfl/ adj mannhaft

man: ~**'handle** vt grob behandeln (person). ~**hole** n Kanalschacht m. ~**hood** n Mannesalter nt; (quality) Männlichkeit f. ~**-hour** n Arbeitsstunde f. ~**-hunt** n Fahndung f

man|ia /'meɪnɪə/ n Manie f. ~**iac** n Wahnsinnige(r) m/f

manicure /'mænɪkjʊə(r)/ n Maniküre f •vt maniküren

manifest /'mænɪfest/ adj offensichtlich

manifesto /mænɪ'festəʊ/ n Manifest nt

manifold /'mænɪfəʊld/ adj mannigfaltig

manipulat|e /mə'nɪpjʊleɪt/ vt handhaben; (pej) manipulieren. ~**ion** n Manipulation f

man'kind n die Menschheit

manly /'mænlɪ/ adj männlich

'man-made adj künstlich. ~ **fibre** n Kunstfaser f

manner /'mænə(r)/ n Weise f; (kind, behaviour) Art f; **[good/bad] ~s** [gute/schlechte] Manieren pl. ~**ism** n Angewohnheit f

manœuvrable /mə'nu:vrəbl/ adj manövrierfähig

manœuvre /mə'nu:və(r)/ n Manöver nt •vt/i manövrieren

manor /'mænə(r)/ n Gutshof m; (house) Gutshaus nt

'manpower n Arbeitskräfte pl

mansion /'mænʃn/ n Villa f

'manslaughter n Totschlag m

mantelpiece /'mæntl-/ n Kaminsims m & nt

manual /'mænjʊəl/ adj Hand- •n Handbuch nt

manufacture /mænjʊ'fæktʃə(r)/ vt herstellen •n Herstellung f. ~**r** n Hersteller m

manure /mə'njʊə(r)/ n Mist m

manuscript /'mænjʊskrɪpt/ n Manuskript nt

many /'menɪ/ adj viele •n **a good/ great** ~ sehr viele

map /mæp/ n Landkarte f; (of town) Stadtplan m

maple /'meɪpl/ n Ahorn m

mar /mɑː(r)/ vt (pt/pp **marred**) verderben

marathon /ˈmærəθən/ n Marathon m

marble /ˈmɑːbl/ n Marmor m; (for game) Murmel f

March /mɑːtʃ/ n März m

march n Marsch m •vi marschieren •vt marschieren lassen; ~ **s.o. off** jdn abführen

mare /ˈmeə(r)/ n Stute f

margarine /mɑːdʒəˈriːn/ n Margarine f

margin /ˈmɑːdʒɪn/ n Rand m; (leeway) Spielraum m; (Comm) Spanne f. **~al** adj geringfügig

marigold /ˈmærɪgəuld/ n Ringelblume f

marina /məˈriːnə/ n Jachthafen m

marine /məˈriːn/ adj Meeres- •n Marine f; (sailor) Marineinfanterist m

m

marital /ˈmærɪtl/ adj ehelich. ~ **status** n Familienstand m

maritime /ˈmærɪtaɪm/ adj See-

mark[1] /mɑːk/ n (former German currency) Mark f

mark[2] n Fleck m; (sign) Zeichen nt; (trace) Spur f; (target) Ziel nt; (Sch) Note f •vt markieren; (spoil) beschädigen; (characterize) kennzeichnen; (Sch) korrigieren; (Sport) decken; ~ **time** (Mil) auf der Stelle treten; (fig) abwarten. ~ **out** vt markieren

marked /mɑːkt/ adj, **~ly** adv deutlich; (pronounced) ausgeprägt

market /ˈmɑːkɪt/ n Markt m •vt vertreiben; (launch) auf den Markt bringen. **~ing** n Marketing nt. ~ **reˈsearch** n Marktforschung f

marking /ˈmɑːkɪŋ/ n Markierung f; (on animal) Zeichnung f

marksman /ˈmɑːksmən/ n Scharfschütze m

marmalade /ˈmɑːməleɪd/ n Orangenmarmelade f

maroon /məˈruːn/ adj dunkelrot

marooned /məˈruːnd/ adj (fig) von der Außenwelt abgeschnitten

marquee /mɑːˈkiː/ n Festzelt nt

marquetry /ˈmɑːkɪtrɪ/ n Einlegearbeit f

marriage /ˈmærɪdʒ/ n Ehe f; (wedding) Hochzeit f. **~able** adj heiratsfähig

married /ˈmærɪd/ see **marry** •adj verheiratet. ~ **life** n Eheleben nt

marrow /ˈmærəʊ/ n (Anat) Mark nt; (vegetable) Kürbis m

marr|y /ˈmærɪ/ vt/i (pt/pp **married**) heiraten; (unite) trauen; **get ~ied** heiraten

marsh /mɑːʃ/ n Sumpf m

marshal /ˈmɑːʃl/ n Marschall m; (steward) Ordner m

marshy /ˈmɑːʃɪ/ adj sumpfig

martial /ˈmɑːʃl/ adj kriegerisch. ~ **ˈlaw** n Kriegsrecht nt

martyr /ˈmɑːtə(r)/ n Märtyrer(in) m(f). **~dom** n Martyrium nt

marvel /ˈmɑːvl/ n Wunder nt •vi (pt/pp **marvelled**) staunen (**at** über + acc). **~lous** adj, **-ly** adv wunderbar

Marxis|m /ˈmɑːksɪzm/ n Marxismus m. **~t** adj marxistisch •n Marxist(in) m(f)

marzipan /ˈmɑːzɪpæn/ n Marzipan nt

mascot /ˈmæskət/ n Maskottchen nt

masculin|e /ˈmæskjʊlɪn/ adj männlich •n (Gram) Maskulinum nt. **~ity** n Männlichkeit f

mash /mæʃ/ n 🅸, **~ed potatoes** npl Kartoffelpüree nt

mask /mɑːsk/ n Maske f •vt maskieren

masochis|m /ˈmæsəkɪzm/ n Masochismus m. **~t** n Masochist m

mason /ˈmeɪsn/ n Steinmetz m. **~ry** n Mauerwerk nt

mass[1] /mæs/ n (Relig) Messe f

mass[2] n Masse f •vi sich sammeln; (Mil) sich massieren

massacre /ˈmæsəkə(r)/ n Massaker nt •vt niedermetzeln

massage /ˈmæsɑːʒ/ n Massage f •vt massieren

masseu|r /mæˈsɜː(r)/ n Masseur m. **~se** n Masseuse f

massive /ˈmæsɪv/ adj massiv; (huge) riesig

mass: ~ ˈmedia npl Massenmedien pl. **~-proˈduce** vt in Massenproduktion herstellen. **~proˈduction** n Massenproduktion f

mast /mɑːst/ n Mast m

master /ˈmɑːstə(r)/ n Herr m; (teacher) Lehrer m; (craftsman, artist) Meister m; (of ship) Kapitän m •vt meistern; beherrschen (language)

master: ~ly adj meisterhaft. **~-mind** n führender Kopf m •vt der führende Kopf sein von. **~piece** n Meisterwerk nt. **~y** n (of subject) Beherrschung f

mat /mæt/ n Matte f; (on table) Untersatz m

match[1] /mætʃ/ n Wettkampf m; (in ball games) Spiel nt; (Tennis) Match nt; (marriage) Heirat f; **be a good ~** (colours:) gut zusammenpassen; **be no ~ for s.o.** jdm nicht gewachsen sein •vt (equal) gleichkommen (+ dat); (be like) passen zu; (find sth similar) etwas Passendes finden zu •vi zusammenpassen

match[2] n Streichholz nt. **~box** n Streichholzschachtel f

mate[1] /meɪt/ n Kumpel m; (assistant) Gehilfe m; (Naut) Maat m; (Zool) Männchen nt; (female) Weibchen nt •vi sich paaren

mate[2] n (Chess) Matt nt

material /məˈtɪərɪəl/ n Material nt; (fabric) Stoff m; **raw ~s** Rohstoffe pl •adj materiell

material|ism /məˈtɪərɪəlɪzm/ n Materialismus m. **~istic** adj materialistisch. **~ize** vi sich verwirklichen

maternal /məˈtɜːnl/ adj mütterlich

maternity /məˈtɜːnətɪ/ n Mutterschaft f. **~ clothes** npl Umstandskleidung f. **~ ward** n Entbindungsstation f

mathematic|al /mæθəˈmætɪkl/ adj mathematisch. **~ian** n Mathematiker(in) m(f)

mathematics /mæθəˈmætɪks/ n Mathematik f

maths /mæθs/ n [!] Mathe f

matinée /ˈmætɪneɪ/ n (Theat) Nachmittagsvorstellung f

matrimony /ˈmætrɪmənɪ/ n Ehe f

matron /ˈmeɪtrən/ n (of hospital) Oberin f; (of school) Hausmutter f

matt /mæt/ adj matt

matted /ˈmætɪd/ adj verfilzt

matter /ˈmætə(r)/ n (affair) Sache f; (Phys: substance) Materie f; **money ~s** Geldangelegenheiten pl; **what is the ~?** was ist los? •vi wichtig sein; **~ to s.o.** jdm etwas ausmachen; **it doesn't ~** es macht nichts. **~-of-fact** adj sachlich

mattress /ˈmætrɪs/ n Matratze f

matur|e /məˈtjʊə(r)/ adj reif; (Comm) fällig •vi reifen; (person:) reifer werden; (Comm) fällig werden •vt reifen lassen. **~ity** n Reife f; (Comm) Fälligkeit f

mauve /məʊv/ adj lila

maximum /ˈmæksɪməm/ adj maximal •n (pl **-ima**) Maximum nt. **~ speed** n Höchstgeschwindigkeit f

may /meɪ/

pres **may**, pt **might**

• modal verb

····➤ (expressing possibility) können. **she may come** es kann sein, dass sie kommt; es ist möglich, dass sie kommt. **she might come** (more distant possibility) sie könnte kommen. **it may/might rain** es könnte regnen. **I may be wrong** vielleicht irre ich mich. **he may have missed his train** vielleicht hat er seinen Zug verpasst

····➤ (expressing permission) dürfen.

m

may I come in? darf ich reinkommen? **you may smoke** Sie dürfen rauchen
....➤ (expressing wish) **may the best man win!** auf dass der Beste gewinnt!
....➤ (expressing concession) **he may be slow but he's accurate** mag od kann sein, dass er langsam ist, aber dafür ist er auch genau
....➤ **may/might as well** ebenso gut können. **we may/might as well go** wir könnten eigentlich ebensogut [auch] gehen. **we might as well give up** da können wir gleich aufgeben

May n Mai m

maybe /ˈmeɪbiː/ adv vielleicht

ˈ**May Day** n der Erste Mai

mayonnaise /meɪəˈneɪz/ n Mayonnaise f

mayor /ˈmeə(r)/ n Bürgermeister m. **~ess** n Bürgermeisterin f; (wife of mayor) Frau Bürgermeister f

m

maze /meɪz/ n Irrgarten m; (fig) Labyrinth nt

me /miː/ pron (acc) mich; (dat) mir; **it's ~** [!] ich bin es

meadow /ˈmedəʊ/ n Wiese f

meagre /ˈmiːgə(r)/ adj dürftig

meal /miːl/ n Mahlzeit f; (food) Essen nt; (grain) Schrot m

mean[1] /miːn/ adj (**-er, -est**) (miserly) geizig; (unkind) gemein; (poor) schäbig

mean[2] adj mittlere(r,s) •n (average) Durchschnitt m

mean[3] vt (pt/pp **meant**) heißen; (signify) bedeuten; (intend) beabsichtigen; **I ~ it** das ist mein Ernst; **~ well** es gut meinen; **be meant for** (present:) bestimmt sein für; (remark:) gerichtet sein an (+ acc)

meaning /ˈmiːnɪŋ/ n Bedeutung f. **~ful** adj bedeutungsvoll. **~less** adj bedeutungslos

means /miːnz/ n Möglichkeit f, Mittel nt; **~ of transport** Verkehrsmittel nt; **by ~ of** durch; **by all ~!** aber natürlich! **by no ~** keineswegs •npl (resources) [Geld]mittel pl

meant /ment/ see **mean**[3]

ˈ**meantime** n **in the ~** in der Zwischenzeit •adv inzwischen

ˈ**meanwhile** adv inzwischen

measles /ˈmiːzlz/ n Masern pl

measure /ˈmeʒə(r)/ n Maß nt; (action) Maßnahme f •vt/i messen; **~ up to** (fig) herankommen an (+ acc). **~d** adj gemessen. **~ment** n Maß nt

meat /miːt/ n Fleisch nt

mechan|ic /mɪˈkænɪk/ n Mechaniker m. **~ical** adj mechanisch. **~ical engineering** Maschinenbau m

mechan|ism /ˈmekənɪzm/ n Mechanismus m. **~ize** vt mechanisieren

medal /ˈmedl/ n Orden m; (Sport) Medaille f

medallist /ˈmedəlɪst/ n Medaillengewinner(in) m(f)

meddle /ˈmedl/ vi sich einmischen (**in** in + acc); (tinker) herumhantieren (**with** an + acc)

media /ˈmiːdɪə/ see **medium** •n pl **the ~** die Medien pl

mediat|e /ˈmiːdɪeɪt/ vi vermitteln. **~or** n Vermittler(in) m(f)

medical /ˈmedɪkl/ adj medizinisch; (treatment) ärztlich •n ärztliche Untersuchung f. **~ insurance** n Krankenversicherung f. **~ student** n Medizinstudent m

medicat|ed /ˈmedɪkeɪtɪd/ adj medizinisch. **~ion** n (drugs) Medikamente pl

medicinal /mɪˈdɪsɪnl/ adj medizinisch; (plant) heilkräftig

medicine /ˈmedsən/ n Medizin f; (preparation) Medikament nt

medieval /medɪˈiːvl/ adj mittelalterlich

mediocr|e /miːdɪˈəʊkə(r)/ adj mittelmäßig. **~ity** n Mittelmäßigkeit f

meditat|e /'medɪteɪt/ vi nachdenken (**on** über + acc). **~ion** n Meditation f

Mediterranean /medɪtə'reɪnɪən/ n Mittelmeer nt • adj Mittelmeer-

medium /'mi:dɪəm/ adj mittlere(r,s); (steak) medium; **of ~ size** von mittlerer Größe • n (pl **media**) Medium nt: (means) Mittel nt

medium: ~-sized adj mittelgroß. **~ wave** n Mittelwelle f

medley /'medlɪ/ n Gemisch nt; (Mus) Potpourri nt

meek /mi:k/ adj (**-er, -est**) sanftmütig; (unprotesting, compliant) widerspruchslos

meet /mi:t/ v (pt/pp **met**) • vt treffen; (by chance) begegnen (+ dat); (at station) abholen; (make the acquaintance of) kennen lernen; stoßen auf (+ acc) (problem); bezahlen (bill); erfüllen (requirements) • vi sich treffen; (for the first time) sich kennen lernen

meeting /'mi:tɪŋ/ n Treffen nt; (by chance) Begegnung f; (discussion) Besprechung f; (of committee) Sitzung f; (large) Versammlung f

megalomania /megələ'meɪnɪə/ n Größenwahnsinn m

megaphone /'megəfəʊn/ n Megaphon nt

melancholy /'melənkəlɪ/ adj melancholisch • n Melancholie f

mellow /'meləʊ/ adj (**-er, -est**) (fruit) ausgereift; (sound, person) sanft • vi reifer werden

melodious /mɪ'ləʊdɪəs/ adj melodiös

melodramatic /melədrə'mætɪk/ adj, **-ally** adv melodramatisch

melody /'melədɪ/ n Melodie f

melon /'melən/ n Melone f

melt /melt/ vt/i schmelzen

member /'membə(r)/ n Mitglied nt; (of family) Angehörige(r) m/f; **M~ of Parliament** Abgeordnete(r) m/f. **~ship** n Mitgliedschaft f; (members) Mitgliederzahl f

memento /mɪ'mentəʊ/ n Andenken nt

memo /'meməʊ/ n Mitteilung f

memoirs /'memwɑ:z/ n pl Memoiren pl

memorable /'memərəbl/ adj denkwürdig

memorial /mɪ'mɔ:rɪəl/ n Denkmal nt. **~ service** n Gedenkfeier f

memorize /'meməraɪz/ vt sich (dat) einprägen

memory /'memərɪ/ n Gedächtnis nt; (thing remembered) Erinnerung f; (of computer) Speicher m; **from ~** auswendig; **in ~ of** zur Erinnerung an (+ acc)

men /men/ see **man**

menac|e /'menɪs/ n Drohung f; (nuisance) Plage f • vt bedrohen. **~ing** adj, **~ly** adv drohend

mend /mend/ vt reparieren; (patch) flicken; ausbessern (clothes)

'menfolk n pl Männer pl

menial /'mi:nɪəl/ adj niedrig

menopause /'menə-/ n Wechseljahre pl

mental /'mentl/ adj geistig; (!: mad) verrückt. **~ a'rithmetic** n Kopfrechnen nt. **~ 'illness** n Geisteskrankheit f

mentality /men'tælətɪ/ n Mentalität f

mention /'menʃn/ n Erwähnung f • vt erwähnen; **don't ~ it** keine Ursache; bitte

menu /'menju:/ n Speisekarte f

merchandise /'mɜ:tʃəndaɪz/ n Ware f

merchant /'mɜ:tʃənt/ n Kaufmann m; (dealer) Händler m. **~ 'navy** n Handelsmarine f

merci|ful /'mɜ:sɪfl/ adj barmherzig. **~fully** adv ! glücklicherweise. **~less** adj erbarmungslos

mercury /'mɜ:kjʊrɪ/ n Quecksilber nt

mercy /'mɜ:sɪ/ n Barmherzigkeit f, Gnade f; **be at s.o.'s ~** jdm ausgeliefert sein

mere /mɪə(r)/ adj bloß

merest /'mɪərɪst/ adj kleinste(r,s)

merge /mɜ:dʒ/ vi zusammenlaufen; (Comm) fusionieren

merger /'mɜ:dʒə(r)/ n Fusion f

meringue /mə'ræŋ/ n Baiser nt

merit /'merɪt/ n Verdienst nt; (advantage) Vorzug m; (worth) Wert m •vt verdienen

merry /'merɪ/ adj fröhlich

merry-go-round n Karussell nt

mesh /meʃ/ n Masche f

mesmerized /'mezməraɪzd/ adj (fig) [wie] gebannt

mess /mes/ n Durcheinander nt; (trouble) Schwierigkeiten pl; (something spilt) Bescherung f [!]; (Mil) Messe f; **make a ~ of** (botch) verpfuschen •vt **~ up** in Unordnung bringen; (botch) verpfuschen •vi **~ about** herumalbern; (tinker) herumspielen (**with** mit)

m

message /'mesɪdʒ/ n Nachricht f; **give s.o. a ~** jdm etwas ausrichten

messenger /'mesɪndʒə(r)/ n Bote m

Messrs /'mesəz/ n pl see **Mr**; (on letter) **~ Smith** Firma Smith

messy /'mesɪ/ adj schmutzig; (untidy) unordentlich

met /met/ see **meet**

metal /'metl/ n Metall nt •adj Metall-. **~lic** adj metallisch

metaphor /'metəfə(r)/ n Metapher f. **~ical** adj metaphorisch

meteor /'mi:tɪə(r)/ n Meteor m. **~ic** adj kometenhaft

meteorological /mi:tɪərə'lɒdʒɪkl/ adj Wetter-

meteorolog|ist /mi:tɪə'rɒlədʒɪst/ n Meteorologe m/ -gin f. **~y** n Meteorologie f

meter¹ /'mi:tə(r)/ n Zähler m

meter² n (Amer) = **metre**

method /'meθəd/ n Methode f; (Culin) Zubereitung f

methodical /mɪ'θɒdɪkl/ adj systematisch, methodisch

methylated /'meθɪleɪtɪd/ adj **~ spirit[s]** Brennspiritus m

meticulous /mɪ'tɪkjʊləs/ adj sehr genau

metre /'mi:tə(r)/ n Meter m & n; (rhythm) Versmaß nt

metric /'metrɪk/ adj metrisch

metropolis /mɪ'trɒpəlɪs/ n Metropole f

metropolitan /metrə'pɒlɪtən/ adj haupstädtisch; (international) weltstädtisch

mew /mju:/ n Miau nt •vi miauen

Mexican /'meksɪkən/ adj mexikanisch •n Mexikaner(in) m(f). **'Mexico** n Mexiko nt

miaow /mɪ'aʊ/ n Miau nt •vi miauen

mice /maɪs/ see **mouse**

micro: ~film n Mikrofilm m. **~light [aircraft]** n Ultraleichtflugzeug nt. **~phone** n Mikrofon nt. **~scope** /-skəʊp/ n Mikroskop nt. **~scopic** /-'skɒpɪk/ adj mikroskopisch. **~wave [oven]** n Mikrowellenherd m

mid /mɪd/ adj **~ May** Mitte Mai; **in ~ air** in der Luft

midday /mɪd'deɪ/ n Mittag m

middle /'mɪdl/ adj mittlere(r,s); **the M~ Ages** das Mittelalter; **the ~ class[es]** der Mittelstand; **the M~ East** der Nahe Osten •n Mitte f; **in the ~ of the night** mitten in der Nacht

middle: ~-aged adj mittleren Alters. **~-class** adj bürgerlich

midge /mɪdʒ/ n [kleine] Mücke f

midget /'mɪdʒɪt/ n Liliputaner(in) m(f)

Midlands /'mɪdləndz/ npl **the ~** Mittelengland n

'midnight n Mitternacht f

midriff /'mɪdrɪf/ n [!] Taille f

midst /mɪdst/ n **in the ~ of** mitten in (+ dat); **in our ~** unter uns

mid: ~summer n Hochsommer

m. ~**way** adv auf halbem Wege. ~**wife** n Hebamme f. ~'**winter** n Mitte f des Winters

might[1] /maɪt/ modal verb **I ~** vielleicht; **it ~ be true** es könnte wahr sein; **he asked if he ~ go** er fragte, ob er gehen dürfte; **you ~ have drowned** du hättest ertrinken können

might[2] n Macht f

mighty /'maɪtɪ/ adj mächtig

migraine /'mi:greɪn/ n Migräne f

migrat|e /maɪ'greɪt/ vi abwandern; (birds:) ziehen. ~**ion** n Wanderung f; (of birds) Zug m

mike /maɪk/ n ! Mikrofon nt

mild /maɪld/ adj (**-er, -est**) mild

mild|ly /'maɪldlɪ/ adv leicht; **to put it ~ly** gelinde gesagt. ~**ness** n Milde f

mile /maɪl/ n Meile f (= 1,6 km); ~**s too big** ! viel zu groß

mile|age /-ɪdʒ/ n Meilenzahl f; (of car) Meilenstand m

militant /'mɪlɪtənt/ adj militant

military /'mɪlɪtrɪ/ adj militärisch. ~ **service** n Wehrdienst m

milk /mɪlk/ n Milch f •vt melken

milk: ~**man** n Milchmann m. ~ **shake** n Milchmixgetränk nt. ~ **tooth** n Milchzahn m

milky /'mɪlkɪ/ adj milchig. **M~ Way** n (Astronomy) Milchstraße f

mill /mɪl/ n Mühle f; (factory) Fabrik f

millennium /mɪ'lenɪəm/ n Jahrtausend nt

milli|gram /'mɪlɪ-/ n Milligramm nt. ~**metre** n Millimeter m & nt

million /'mɪljən/ n Million f; **a ~ pounds** eine Million Pfund. ~**aire** n Millionär(in) m(f)

mime /maɪm/ n Pantomime f •vt pantomimisch darstellen

mimic /'mɪmɪk/ n Imitator m •vt (pt/pp **mimicked**) nachahmen

mince /mɪns/ n Hackfleisch nt •vt (Culin) durchdrehen; **not ~ words** kein Blatt vor den Mund nehmen

mince: ~**meat** n Masse f aus Korinthen, Zitronat usw; **make ~ meat of** (fig) vernichtend schlagen. ~'**pie** n mit 'mincemeat' gefülltes Pastetchen nt

mincer /'mɪnsə(r)/ n Fleischwolf m

mind /maɪnd/ n Geist m; (sanity) Verstand m; **give s.o. a piece of one's ~** jdm gehörig die Meinung sagen; **make up one's ~** sich entschließen; **be out of one's ~** nicht bei Verstand sein; **have sth in ~** etw im Sinn haben; **bear sth in ~** an etw (acc) denken; **have a good ~ to große** Lust haben, zu; **I have changed my ~** ich habe es mir anders überlegt •vt aufpassen auf (+ acc); **I don't ~ the noise** der Lärm stört mich nicht; **~ the step!** Achtung Stufe! •vi (care) sich kümmern (**about** um); **I don't ~** mir macht es nichts aus; **never ~!** macht nichts! **do you ~ if?** haben Sie etwas dagegen, wenn? **~ out** vi aufpassen

m

'**mindless** adj geistlos

mine[1] /maɪn/ poss pron meine(r), meins; **a friend of ~** ein Freund von mir; **that is ~** das gehört mir

mine[2] n Bergwerk nt; (explosive) Mine f •vt abbauen; (Mil) verminen

miner /'maɪnə(r)/ n Bergarbeiter m

mineral /'mɪnərl/ n Mineral nt. ~ **water** n Mineralwasser nt

minesweeper /'maɪn-/ n Minenräumboot nt

mingle /'mɪŋgl/ vi ~ **with** sich mischen unter (+ acc)

miniature /'mɪnɪtʃə(r)/ adj Klein- •n Miniatur f

mini|bus /'mɪnɪ-/ n Kleinbus m. ~**cab** n Kleintaxi nt

minim|al /'mɪnɪməl/ adj minimal. ~**um** n (pl **-ima**) Minimum nt •adj Mindest-

mining /'maɪnɪŋ/ n Bergbau m

miniskirt /'mɪnɪ-/ n Minirock m

minist|er /'mɪnɪstə(r)/ n Minister

m; (Relig) Pastor m. **~erial** adj ministeriell

ministry /'mɪnɪstrɪ/ n (Pol) Ministerium nt

mink /mɪŋk/ n Nerz m

minor /'maɪnə(r)/ adj kleiner; (less important) unbedeutend •n Minderjährige(r) m/f; (Mus) Moll nt

minority /maɪ'nɒrətɪ/ n Minderheit f

minor road n Nebenstraße f

mint[1] /mɪnt/ n Münzstätte f •adj (stamp) postfrisch; **in ~ condition** wie neu •vt prägen

mint[2] n (herb) Minze f; (sweet) Pfefferminzbonbon m & nt

minus /'maɪnəs/ prep minus, weniger; ([!]: without) ohne

minute[1] /'mɪnɪt/ n Minute f; **in a ~** (shortly) gleich; **~s** pl (of meeting) Protokoll nt

minute[2] /maɪ'nju:t/ adj winzig

mirac|le /'mɪrəkl/ n Wunder nt. **~ulous** adj wunderbar

mirror /'mɪrə(r)/ n Spiegel m •vt widerspiegeln

mirth /mɜ:θ/ n Heiterkeit f

misad'venture /mɪs-/ n Missgeschick nt

misappre'hension n Missverständnis nt; **be under a ~** sich irren

misbe'hav|e vi sich schlecht benehmen. **~iour** n schlechtes Benehmen nt

mis'calcu|late vt falsch berechnen •vi sich verrechnen. **~'lation** n Fehlkalkulation f

'miscarriage n Fehlgeburt f

miscellaneous /mɪsə'leɪnɪəs/ adj vermischt

mischief /'mɪstʃɪf/ n Unfug m

mischievous /'mɪstʃɪvəs/ adj schelmisch; (malicious) boshaft

miscon'ception n falsche Vorstellung f

mis'conduct n unkorrektes Verhalten nt; (adultery) Ehebruch m

miser /'maɪzə(r)/ n Geizhals m

miserable /'mɪzrəbl/ adj, **-bly** adv unglücklich; (wretched) elend

miserly /'maɪzəlɪ/ adv geizig

misery /'mɪzərɪ/ n Elend nt; ([!]: person) Miesepeter m

mis'fire vi fehlzünden; (go wrong) fehschlagen

'misfit n Außenseiter(in) m(f)

mis'fortune n Unglück nt

mis'givings npl Bedenken pl

mis'guided adj töricht

mishap /'mɪshæp/ n Missgeschick nt

misin'form vt falsch unterrichten

misin'terpret vt missdeuten

mis'judge vt falsch beurteilen

mis'lay vt (pt/pp **-laid**) verlegen

mis'lead vt (pt/pp **-led**) irreführen. **~ing** adj irreführend

mis'manage vt schlecht verwalten. **~ment** n Misswirtschaft f

misnomer /mɪs'nəʊmə(r)/ n Fehlbezeichnung f

'misprint n Druckfehler m

mis'quote vt falsch zitieren

misrepre'sent vt falsch darstellen

miss /mɪs/ n Fehltreffer m •vt verpassen; (fail to hit or find) verfehlen; (fail to attend) versäumen; (fail to notice) übersehen; (feel the loss of) vermissen •vi (fail to hit) nicht treffen. **~ out** vt auslassen

Miss n (pl **-es**) Fräulein nt

missile /'mɪsaɪl/ n [Wurf]geschoss nt; (Mil) Rakete f

missing /'mɪsɪŋ/ adj fehlend; (lost) verschwunden; (Mil) vermisst; **be ~** fehlen

mission /'mɪʃn/ n Auftrag m; (Mil) Einsatz m; (Relig) Mission f

missionary /'mɪʃənrɪ/ n Missionar(in) m(f)

mis'spell vt (pt/pp **-spelt** or

-spelled) falsch schreiben

mist /mɪst/ n Dunst m; (fog) Nebel m; (on window) Beschlag m •vi ~ **up** beschlagen

mistake /mɪ'steɪk/ n Fehler m; **by** ~ aus Versehen •vt (pt **mistook**, pp **mistaken**); ~ **for** verwechseln mit

mistaken /mɪ'steɪkən/ adj falsch; **be** ~ sich irren. ~**ly** adv irrtümlicherweise

mistletoe /'mɪsltəʊ/ n Mistel f

mistress /'mɪstrɪs/ n Herrin f; (teacher) Lehrerin f; (lover) Geliebte f

mis'trust n Misstrauen nt •vt misstrauen (+ dat)

misty /'mɪstɪ/ adj dunstig; (foggy) neblig; (fig) unklar

misunder'stand vt (pt/pp **-stood**) missverstehen. ~**ing** n Missverständnis nt

misuse[1] /mɪs'ju:z/ vt missbrauchen

misuse[2] /mɪs'ju:s/ n Missbrauch m

mitigating /'mɪtɪgeɪtɪŋ/ adj mildernd

mix /mɪks/ n Mischung f •vt mischen •vi sich mischen; ~ **with** (associate with) verkehren mit. ~ **up** vt mischen; (muddle) durcheinander bringen; (mistake for) verwechseln (**with** mit)

mixed /mɪkst/ adj gemischt; **be** ~ **up** durcheinander sein

mixer /'mɪksə(r)/ n Mischmaschine f; (Culin) Küchenmaschine f

mixture /'mɪkstʃə(r)/ n Mischung f; (medicine) Mixtur f; (Culin) Teig m

'mix-up n Durcheinander nt; (confusion) Verwirrung f; (mistake) Verwechslung f

moan /məʊn/ n Stöhnen nt •vi stöhnen; (complain) jammern

mob /mɒb/ n Horde f; (rabble) Pöbel m; (!: gang) Bande f •vt (pt/pp **mobbed**) herfallen über (+ acc); belagern (celebrity)

mobile /'məʊbaɪl/ adj beweglich •n Mobile nt; (telephone) Handy nt. ~ **'home** n Wohnwagen m. ~ **'phone** n Handy nt

mobility /mə'bɪlətɪ/ n Beweglichkeit f

mock /mɒk/ adj Schein- •vt verspotten. ~**ery** n Spott m

'mock-up n Modell nt

mode /məʊd/ n [Art und] Weise f; (fashion) Mode f

model /'mɒdl/ n Modell nt; (example) Vorbild nt; **[fashion]** ~ Mannequin nt •adj Modell-; (exemplary) Muster- •v (pt/pp **modelled**) •vt formen, modellieren; vorführen (clothes) •vi Mannequin sein; (for artist) Modell stehen

moderate[1] /'mɒdəreɪt/ vt mäßigen

moderate[2] /'mɒdərət/ adj mäßig; (opinion) gemäßigt. ~**ly** adv mäßig; (fairly) einigermaßen

moderation /mɒdə'reɪʃn/ n Mäßigung f; **in** ~ mit Maß[en]

modern /'mɒdn/ adj modern. ~**ize** vt modernisieren. ~ **'languages** npl neuere Sprachen pl

modest /'mɒdɪst/ adj bescheiden; (decorous) schamhaft. ~**y** n Bescheidenheit f

modif|ication /mɒdɪfɪ'keɪʃn/ n Abänderung f. ~**y** vt (pt/pp **-fied**) abändern

module /'mɒdju:l/ n Element nt; (of course) Kurseinheit f

moist /mɔɪst/ adj (**-er**, **-est**) feucht

moisten /'mɔɪsn/ vt befeuchten

moistur|e /'mɔɪstʃə(r)/ n Feuchtigkeit f. ~**izer** n Feuchtigkeitscreme f

molar /'məʊlə(r)/ n Backenzahn m

mole[1] /məʊl/ n Leberfleck m

mole[2] n (Zool) Maulwurf m

molecule /'mɒlɪkju:l/ n Molekül nt

molest /mə'lest/ vt belästigen

mollify /'mɒlɪfaɪ/ vt (pt/pp **-ied**) besänftigen

mollycoddle /'mɒlɪkɒdl/ vt verzärteln

molten /'məʊltən/ adj geschmolzen

mom /mɒm/ n (Amer fam) Mutti f

moment /'məʊmənt/ n Moment m, Augenblick m; **at the ~** im Augenblick, augenblicklich. **~ary** adj vorübergehend

momentous /mə'mentəs/ adj bedeutsam

momentum /mə'mentəm/ n Schwung m

monarch /'mɒnək/ n Monarch(in) m(f). **~y** n Monarchie f

monastery /'mɒnəstrɪ/ n Kloster nt

Monday /'mʌndeɪ/ n Montag m

money /'mʌnɪ/ n Geld nt

money: ~-box n Sparbüchse f. **~-lender** n Geldverleiher m. **~ order** n Zahlungsanweisung f

mongrel /'mʌŋgrəl/ n Promenadenmischung f

monitor /'mɒnɪtə(r)/ n (Techn) Monitor m •vt überwachen (progress); abhören (broadcast)

monk /mʌŋk/ n Mönch m

m

monkey /'mʌŋkɪ/ n Affe m

mono /'mɒnəʊ/ n Mono nt

monogram /'mɒnəgræm/ n Monogramm nt

monologue /'mɒnəlɒg/ n Monolog m

monopol|ize /mə'nɒpəlaɪz/ vt monopolisieren. **~y** n Monopol nt

monosyllable /'mɒnəsɪləbl/ n einsilbiges Wort nt

monotone /'mɒnətəʊn/ n **in a ~** mit monotoner Stimme

monoton|ous /mə'nɒtənəs/ adj eintönig, monoton; (tedious) langweillig. **~y** n Eintönigkeit f, Monotonie f

monster /'mɒnstə(r)/ n Ungeheuer nt; (cruel person) Unmensch m

monstrosity /mɒn'strɒsətɪ/ n Monstrosität f

monstrous /'mɒnstrəs/ adj ungeheuer; (outrageous) ungeheuerlich

month /mʌnθ/ n Monat m. **~ly** adj & adv monatlich •n (periodical) Monatszeitschrift f

monument /'mɒnjʊmənt/ n Denkmal nt. **~al** adj (fig) monumental

moo /mu:/ n Muh nt •vi (pt/pp **mooed**) muhen

mood /mu:d/ n Laune f; **be in a good/bad ~** gute/schlechte Laune haben

moody /'mu:dɪ/ adj launisch

moon /mu:n/ n Mond m; **over the ~** ! überglücklich

moon: ~light n Mondschein m. **~lighting** n ! ≈ Schwarzarbeit f. **~lit** adj mondhell

moor[1] /mʊə(r)/ n Moor nt

moor[2] vt (Naut) festmachen •vi anlegen

mop /mɒp/ n Mopp m; **~ of hair** Wuschelkopf m •vt (pt/pp **mopped**) wischen. **~ up** vt aufwischen

moped /'məʊped/ n Moped nt

moral /'mɒrl/ adj moralisch, sittlich; (virtuous) tugendhaft •n Moral f; **~s** pl Moral f

morale /mə'rɑ:l/ n Moral f

morality /mə'rælətɪ/ n Sittlichkeit f

morbid /'mɔ:bɪd/ adj krankhaft; (gloomy) trübe

more /mɔ:(r)/ a, adv & n mehr; (in addition) noch; **a few ~** noch ein paar; **any ~** noch etwas; **once ~** noch einmal; **~ or less** mehr oder weniger; **some ~ tea?** noch etwas Tee? **~ interesting** interessanter; **~ [and ~] quickly** [immer] schneller

moreover /mɔ:'rəʊvə(r)/ adv außerdem

morgue /mɔ:g/ n Leichenschauhaus nt

morning /'mɔ:nɪŋ/ n Morgen m; **in the ~** morgens, am Morgen; (tomorrow) morgen früh

Morocco /mə'rɒkəʊ/ n Marokko nt

moron /'mɔ:rɒn/ n ! Idiot m

morose /mə'rəʊs/ adj mürrisch

morsel /'mɔ:sl/ n Happen m

mortal /'mɔ:tl/ adj sterblich; (fatal)

tödlich •n Sterbliche(r) m/f. **~ity** n Sterblichkeit f. **~ly** adv tödlich

mortar /'mɔ:tə(r)/ n Mörtel m

mortgage /'mɔ:gɪdʒ/ n Hypothek f •vt hypothekarisch belasten

mortuary /'mɔ:tjʊərɪ/ n Leichenhalle f; (public) Leichenschauhaus nt; (Amer: undertaker's) Bestattungsinstitut nt

mosaic /məʊ'zeɪɪk/ n Mosaik nt

Moscow /'mɒskəʊ/ n Moskau nt

mosque /mɒsk/ n Moschee f

mosquito /mɒs'ki:təʊ/ n (pl **-es**) [Stech]mücke f, Schnake f; (tropical) Moskito m

moss /mɒs/ n Moos nt. **~y** adj moosig

most /məʊst/ adj der/die/das meiste; (majority) die meisten; **for the ~ part** zum größten Teil •adv am meisten; (very) höchst; **the ~ interesting day** der interessanteste Tag; **~ unlikely** höchst unwahrscheinlich •n das meiste; **~ of them** die meisten [von ihnen]; **at [the] ~** höchstens; **~ of the time** die meiste Zeit. **~ly** adv meist

MOT n ≈ TÜV m

motel /məʊ'tel/ n Motel nt

moth /mɒθ/ n Nachtfalter m; **[clothes-] ~** Motte f

'mothball n Mottenkugel f

mother /'mʌðə(r)/ n Mutter f

mother: ~hood n Mutterschaft f. **~-in-law** n (pl **~s-in-law**) Schwiegermutter f. **~land** n Mutterland nt. **~ly** adj mütterlich. **~-of-pearl** n Perlmutter f. **~-to-be** n werdende Mutter f

mothproof /'mɒθ-/ adj mottenfest

motif /məʊ'ti:f/ n Motiv nt

motion /'məʊʃn/ n Bewegung f; (proposal) Antrag m. **~less** adj bewegungslos

motivat|e /'məʊtɪveɪt/ vt motivieren. **~ion** n Motivation f

motive /'məʊtɪv/ n Motiv nt

motor /'məʊtə(r)/ n Motor m; (car) Auto nt •adj Motor-; (Anat) motorisch •vi [mit dem Auto] fahren

motor: ~ bike n [!] Motorrad nt. **~ boat** n Motorboot nt. **~ car** n Auto nt, Wagen m. **~ cycle** n Motorrad nt. **~-cyclist** n Motorradfahrer m. **~ing** n Autofahren nt. **~ist** n Autofahrer(in) m(f). **~ vehicle** n Kraftfahrzeug nt. **~way** n Autobahn f

mottled /'mɒtld/ adj gesprenkelt

motto /'mɒtəʊ/ n (pl **-es**) Motto nt

mould[1] /məʊld/ n (fungus) Schimmel m

mould[2] n Form f •vt formen (**into** zu). **~ing** n (decorative) Fries m

mouldy /'məʊldɪ/ adj schimmelig; ([!]: worthless) schäbig

mound /maʊnd/ n Hügel m; (of stones) Haufen m

mount n (animal) Reittier nt; (of jewel) Fassung f; (of photo, picture) Passepartout nt •vt (get on) steigen auf (+ acc); (on pedestal) montieren auf (+ acc); besteigen (horse); fassen (jewel); aufziehen (photo, picture) •vi aufsteigen; (tension:) steigen. **~ up** vi sich häufen; (add up) sich anhäufen

mountain /'maʊntɪn/ n Berg m

mountaineer /maʊntɪ'nɪə(r)/ n Bergsteiger(in) m(f). **~ing** n Bergsteigen nt

mountainous /'maʊntɪnəs/ adj bergig, gebirgig

mourn /mɔ:n/ vt betrauern •vi trauern (**for** um). **~er** n Trauernde(r) m/f. **~ful** adj trauervoll. **~ing** n Trauer f

mouse /maʊs/ n (pl **mice**) Maus f. **~trap** n Mausefalle f

moustache /mə'stɑ:ʃ/ n Schnurrbart m

mouth[1] /maʊð/ vt **~ sth** etw lautlos mit den Lippen sagen

mouth[2] /maʊθ/ n Mund m; (of animal) Maul nt; (of river) Mündung f

mouth: ~ful n Mundvoll m; (bite)

Bissen m. ~**-organ** n Mundharmonika f. ~**wash** n Mundwasser nt

movable /'mu:vəbl/ adj beweglich

move /mu:v/ n Bewegung f; (fig) Schritt m; (moving house) Umzug m; (in board game) Zug m; **on the ~** unterwegs; **get a ~ on** [!] sich beeilen •vt bewegen; (emotionally) rühren; (move along) rücken; (in board game) ziehen; (take away) wegnehmen; wegfahren (car); (rearrange) umstellen; (transfer) versetzen (person); verlegen (office); (propose) beantragen; **~ house** umziehen •vi sich bewegen; (move house) umziehen; **don't ~!** stillhalten! (stop) stillstehen! **~ along** vt/i weiterrücken. **~ away** vt/i wegrücken; (move house) wegziehen. **~ in** vi einziehen. **~ off** vi (vehicle:) losfahren. **~ out** vi ausziehen. **~ over** vt/i [zur Seite] rücken. **~ up** vi aufrücken

movement /'mu:vmənt/ n Bewegung f; (Mus) Satz m; (of clock) Uhrwerk nt

movie /'mu:vɪ/ n (Amer) Film m; **go to the ~s** ins Kino gehen

moving /'mu:vɪŋ/ adj beweglich; (touching) rührend

mow /məʊ/ vt (pt **mowed**, pp **mown** or **mowed**) mähen

mower /'məʊə(r)/ n Rasenmäher m

MP abbr **Member of Parliament**

Mr /'mɪstə(r)/ n (pl **Messrs**) Herr m

Mrs /'mɪsɪz/ n Frau f

Ms /mɪz/ n Frau f

much /mʌtʃ/ a, adv & n viel; **as ~ as** so viel wie; **~ loved** sehr geliebt

muck /mʌk/ n Mist m; ([!]: filth) Dreck m. **~ about** vi herumalbern; (tinker) herumspielen (**with** mit). **~ out** vt ausmisten. **~ up** vt [!] vermasseln; (make dirty) schmutzig machen

mucky /'mʌkɪ/ adj dreckig

mud /mʌd/ n Schlamm m

muddle /'mʌdl/ n Durcheinander nt; (confusion) Verwirrung f •vt **~ [up]** durcheinander bringen

muddy /'mʌdɪ/ adj schlammig; (shoes) schmutzig

'mudguard n Kotflügel m; (on bicycle) Schutzblech nt

muffle /'mʌfl/ vt dämpfen

muffler /'mʌflə(r)/ n Schal m; (Amer, Auto) Auspufftopf m

mug[1] /mʌg/ n Becher m; (for beer) Bierkrug m; ([!]: face) Visage f; ([!]: simpleton) Trottel m

mug[2] vt (pt/pp **mugged**) überfallen. **~ger** n Straßenräuber m. **~ging** n Straßenraub m

muggy /'mʌgɪ/ adj schwül

mule /mju:l/ n Maultier nt

mulled /mʌld/ adj **~ wine** Glühwein m

multi /'mʌltɪ/: **~coloured** adj vielfarbig, bunt. **~lingual** adj mehrsprachig. **~'national** adj multinational

multiple /'mʌltɪpl/ adj vielfach; (with pl) mehrere •n Vielfache(s) nt

multiplication /mʌltɪplɪ'keɪʃn/ n Multiplikation f

multiply /'mʌltɪplaɪ/ v (pt/pp **-ied**) •vt multiplizieren (**by** mit) •vi sich vermehren

multistorey adj **~ car park** Parkhaus nt

mum/mʌm/ n [!] Mutti f

mumble /'mʌmbl/ vt/i murmeln

mummy[1] /'mʌmɪ/ n [!] Mutti f

mummy[2] n (Archaeology) Mumie f

mumps /mʌmps/ n Mumps m

munch /mʌntʃ/ vt/i mampfen

municipal /mju:'nɪsɪpl/ adj städtisch

munitions /mju:'nɪʃnz/ npl Kriegsmaterial nt

mural /'mjʊərəl/ n Wandgemälde nt

murder /'mɜ:də(r)/ n Mord m •vt ermorden. **~er** n Mörder m. **~ess** n Mörderin f. **~ous** adj mörderisch

murky /'mɜ:kɪ/ adj düster

murmur /'mɜ:mə(r)/ n Murmeln nt •vt/i murmeln

muscle /ˈmʌsl/ n Muskel m

muscular /ˈmʌskjʊlə(r)/ adj Muskel-; (strong) muskulös

museum /mjuːˈzɪəm/ n Museum nt

mushroom /ˈmʌʃrʊm/ n [essbarer] Pilz m, esp Champignon m •vi (fig) wie Pilze aus dem Boden schießen

mushy /ˈmʌʃɪ/ adj breiig

music /ˈmjuːzɪk/ n Musik f; (written) Noten pl; **set to ~** vertonen

musical /ˈmjuːzɪkl/ adj musikalisch •n Musical nt. **~ box** n Spieldose f. **~ instrument** n Musikinstrument nt

musician /mjuːˈzɪʃn/ n Musiker(in) m(f)

ˈ**music-stand** n Notenständer m

Muslim /ˈmʊzlɪm/ adj muslimisch •n Muslim(in) m(f)

must /mʌst/ modal verb (nur Präsens) müssen; (with negative) dürfen •n **a ~** [!] ein Muss nt

mustard /ˈmʌstəd/ n Senf m

musty /ˈmʌstɪ/ adj muffig

mute /mjuːt/ adj stumm

mutilat|e /ˈmjuːtɪleɪt/ vt verstümmeln. **~ion** n Verstümmelung f

mutin|ous /ˈmjuːtɪnəs/ adj meuterisch. **~y** n Meuterei f •vi (pt/pp **-ied**) meutern

mutter /ˈmʌtə(r)/ n Murmeln nt •vt/i murmeln

mutton /ˈmʌtn/ n Hammelfleisch nt

mutual /ˈmjuːtjʊəl/ adj gegenseitig; ([!]: common) gemeinsam. **~ly** adv gegenseitig

muzzle /ˈmʌzl/ n (of animal) Schnauze f; (of firearm) Mündung f; (for dog) Maulkorb m

my /maɪ/ adj mein

myself /maɪˈself/ pron selbst; (reflexive) mich; **by ~** allein; **I thought to ~** ich habe mir gedacht

mysterious /mɪˈstɪərɪəs/ adj geheimnisvoll; (puzzling) mysteriös, rätselhaft

mystery /ˈmɪstərɪ/ n Geheimnis nt; (puzzle) Rätsel nt; **~ [story]** Krimi m

mysti|c[al] /ˈmɪstɪk[l]/ adj mystisch. **~cism** n Mystik f

mystified /ˈmɪstɪfaɪd/ adj **be ~** vor einem Rätsel stehen

mystique /mɪˈstiːk/ n geheimnisvoller Zauber m

myth /mɪθ/ n Mythos m; ([!]: untruth) Märchen nt. **~ical** adj mythisch; (fig) erfunden

mythology /mɪˈθɒlədʒɪ/ n Mythologie f

Nn

nab /næb/ vt (pt/pp **nabbed**) [!] erwischen

nag¹ /næg/ n (horse) Gaul m

nag² vt/i (pp/pp **nagged**) herumnörgeln (**s.o.** an jdm)

nail /neɪl/ n (Anat, Techn) Nagel m; **on the ~** [!] sofort •vt nageln (**to** an + acc)

nail: ~-brush n Nagelbürste f. **~-file** n Nagelfeile f. **~ scissors** npl Nagelschere f. **~ varnish** n Nagellack m

naïve /naɪˈiːv/ adj naiv. **~ty** n Naivität f

naked /ˈneɪkɪd/ adj nackt; (flame) offen; **with the ~ eye** mit bloßem Auge. **~ness** n Nacktheit f

name /neɪm/ n Name m; (reputation) Ruf m; **by ~** dem Namen nach; **by the ~ of** namens; **call s.o. ~s** [!]

jdn beschimpfen •vt nennen; (give a name to) einen Namen geben (+ dat); (announce publicly) den Namen bekannt geben von. **~less** adj namenlos. **~ly** adv nämlich

name: ~-plate n Namensschild nt. **~sake** n Namensvetter m/ Namensschwester f

nanny /ˈnænɪ/ n Kindermädchen nt

nap /næp/ n Nickerchen nt

napkin /ˈnæpkɪn/ n Serviette f

nappy /ˈnæpɪ/ n Windel f

narcotic /nɑːˈkɒtɪk/ n (drug) Rauschgift nt

narrat|e /nəˈreɪt/ vt erzählen. **~ion** n Erzählung f

narrative /ˈnærətɪv/ n Erzählung f

narrator /nəˈreɪtə(r)/ n Erzähler(in) m(f)

narrow /ˈnærəʊ/ adj (**-er, -est**) schmal; (restricted) eng; (margin, majority) knapp; **have a ~ escape** mit knapper Not davonkommen •vi sich verengen. **~-ˈminded** adj engstirnig

nasal /ˈneɪzl/ adj nasal; (Med & Anat) Nasen-

nasty /ˈnɑːstɪ/ adj übel; (unpleasant) unangenehm; (unkind) boshaft; (serious) schlimm

nation /ˈneɪʃn/ n Nation f; (people) Volk nt

national /ˈnæʃənl/ adj national; (newspaper) überregional; (campaign) landesweit •n Staatsbürger(in) m(f)

national: ~ ˈanthem n Nationalhymne f. **N~ ˈHealth Service** n staatlicher Gesundheitsdienst m. **N~ Inˈsurance** n Sozialversicherung f

nationalism /ˈnæʃənəlɪzm/ n Nationalismus m

nationality /næʃəˈnælətɪ/ n Staatsangehörigkeit f

national|ization /næʃənəlaɪˈzeɪʃn/ n Verstaatlichung f. **~ize** vt verstaatlichen

native /ˈneɪtɪv/ adj einheimisch; (innate) angeboren •n Eingeborene(r) m/f; (local inhabitant) Einheimische(r) m/f; **a ~ of Vienna** ein gebürtiger Wiener

native: ~ ˈland n Heimatland nt. **~ ˈlanguage** n Muttersprache f

natter /ˈnætə(r)/ vi [!] schwatzen

natural /ˈnætʃrəl/ adj natürlich; **~[-coloured]** naturfarben

natural: ~ ˈgas n Erdgas nt. **~ ˈhistory** n Naturkunde f

naturalist /ˈnætʃrəlɪst/ n Naturforscher m

natural|ization /nætʃrəlaɪˈzeɪʃn/ n Einbürgerung f. **~ize** vt einbürgern

nature /ˈneɪtʃə(r)/ n Natur f; (kind) Art f; **by ~** von Natur aus. **~ reserve** n Naturschutzgebiet nt

naughty /ˈnɔːtɪ/ adj, **-ily** adv unartig; (slightly indecent) gewagt

nausea /ˈnɔːzɪə/ n Übelkeit f

nautical /ˈnɔːtɪkl/ adj nautisch. **~ mile** n Seemeile f

naval /ˈneɪvl/ adj Marine-

nave /neɪv/ n Kirchenschiff nt

navel /ˈneɪvl/ n Nabel m

navigable /ˈnævɪgəbl/ adj schiffbar

navigat|e /ˈnævɪgeɪt/ vi navigieren •vt befahren (river). **~ion** n Navigation f

navy /ˈneɪvɪ/ n [Kriegs]marine f •adj **~ [blue]** marineblau

near /nɪə(r)/ adj (**-er, -est**) nah[e]; **the ~est bank** die nächste Bank •adv nahe; **draw ~** sich nähern •prep nahe an (+ dat/acc); in der Nähe von

near: ~by adj nahe gelegen, nahe liegend. **~ly** adv fast, beinahe; **not ~ly** bei weitem nicht. **~ness** n Nähe f. **~ side** n Beifahrerseite f. **~-sighted** adj (Amer) kurzsichtig

neat /niːt/ adj (**-er, -est**) adrett; (tidy) ordentlich; (clever) geschickt; (undiluted) pur. **~ness** n Ordentlichkeit f

necessarily /ˈnesəserəlɪ/ adv notwendigerweise; **not ~** nicht unbedingt

necessary /ˈnesəsərɪ/ adj nötig, notwendig

necessit|ate /nɪˈsesɪteɪt/ vt notwendig machen. **~y** n Notwendigkeit f; **work from ~y** arbeiten, weil man es nötig hat

neck /nek/ n Hals m; **~ and ~** Kopf an Kopf

necklace /ˈneklɪs/ n Halskette f

neckline n Halsausschnitt m

née /neɪ/ adj **~ X** geborene X

need /niːd/ n Bedürfnis nt; (misfortune) Not f; **be in ~ of** brauchen; **in case of ~** notfalls; **if ~ be** wenn nötig; **there is a ~ for** es besteht ein Bedarf an (+ dat); **there is no ~ for that** das ist nicht nötig •vt brauchen; **you ~ not go** du brauchst nicht zu gehen; **~ I come?** muss ich kommen? **I ~ to know** ich muss es wissen

needle /ˈniːdl/ n Nadel f

needless /ˈniːdlɪs/ adj unnötig; **~ to say** selbstverständlich, natürlich

ˈneedlework n Nadelarbeit f

needy /ˈniːdɪ/ adj bedürftig

negation /nɪˈgeɪʃn/ n Verneinung f

negative /ˈnegətɪv/ adj negativ •n Verneinung f; (photo) Negativ nt

neglect /nɪˈglekt/ n Vernachlässigung f •vt vernachlässigen; (omit) versäumen (**to** zu). **~ed** adj verwahrlost. **~ful** adj nachlässig

negligen|ce /ˈneglɪdʒəns/ n Nachlässigkeit f. **~t** adj nachlässig

negligible /ˈneglɪdʒəbl/ adj unbedeutend

negotiat|e /nɪˈgəʊʃɪeɪt/ vt aushandeln; (Auto) nehmen (bend) •vi verhandeln. **~ion** n Verhandlung f. **~or** n Unterhändler(in) m(f)

Negro /ˈniːgrəʊ/ adj Neger- •n (pl **-es**) Neger m

neigh /neɪ/ vi wiehern

neighbour /ˈneɪbə(r)/ n Nachbar(in) m(f). **~hood** n Nachbarschaft f. **~ing** adj Nachbar-. **~ly** adj [gut]nachbarlich

neither /ˈnaɪðə(r)/ adj & pron keine(r, s) [von beiden] •adv **~ ... nor** weder ... noch •conj auch nicht

neon /ˈniːɒn/ n Neon nt

nephew /ˈnevjuː/ n Neffe m

nepotism /ˈnepətɪzm/ n Vetternwirtschaft f

nerve /nɜːv/ n Nerv m; (!: courage) Mut m; (!: impudence) Frechheit f. **~-racking** adj nervenaufreibend

nervous /ˈnɜːvəs/ adj (afraid) ängstlich; (highly strung) nervös; (Anat, Med) Nerven-. **~ ˈbreakdown** n Nervenzusammenbruch m. **~ness** n Ängstlichkeit f

nervy /ˈnɜːvɪ/ adj nervös; (Amer: impudent) frech

nest /nest/ n Nest nt •vi nisten

nestle /ˈnesl/ vi sich schmiegen (**against** an + acc)

net[1] /net/ n Netz nt; (curtain) Store m

net[2] adj netto; (salary, weight) Netto-

ˈnetball n ≈ Korbball m

Netherlands /ˈneðələndz/ npl **the ~** die Niederlande pl

nettle /ˈnetl/ n Nessel f

ˈnetwork n Netz nt

neurolog|ist /njʊəˈrɒlədʒɪst/ n Neurologe m/ -gin f. **~y** n Neurologie f

neur|osis /njʊəˈrəʊsɪs/ n (pl **-oses** /-siːz/) Neurose f. **~otic** adj neurotisch

neuter /ˈnjuːtə(r)/ adj (Gram) sächlich •n (Gram) Neutrum nt •vt kastrieren; (spay) sterilisieren

neutral /ˈnjuːtrl/ adj neutral •n **in ~** (Auto) im Leerlauf. **~ity** n Neutralität f

never /ˈnevə(r)/ adv nie, niemals; (!: not) nicht; **~ mind** macht nichts; **well I ~!** ja so was! **~-ending** adj endlos

n

nevertheless /nevəðə'les/ adv dennoch, trotzdem

new /nju:/ adj (**-er, -est**) neu

new: ~comer n Neuankömmling m. **~fangled** /-'fæŋgld/ adj (pej) neumodisch. **~-laid** adj frisch gelegt

'**newly** adv frisch. **~-weds** npl Jungverheiratete pl

new: ~ 'moon n Neumond m. **~ness** n Neuheit f

news /nju:z/ n Nachricht f; (Radio, TV) Nachrichten pl; **piece of ~** Neuigkeit f

news: ~agent n Zeitungshändler m. **~ bulletin** n Nachrichtensendung f. **~letter** n Mitteilungsblatt nt. **~paper** n Zeitung f; (material) Zeitungspapier nt. **~reader** n Nachrichtensprecher(in) m(f)

New: ~ Year's 'Day n Neujahr nt. **~ Year's 'Eve** n Silvester nt. **~ Zealand** /'zi:lənd/ n Neuseeland nt

next /nekst/ adj & n nächste(r, s); **who's ~?** wer kommt als Nächster dran? **the ~ best** das nächstbeste; **~ door** nebenan; **my ~ of kin** mein nächster Verwandter; **~ to nothing** fast gar nichts; **the week after ~** übernächste Woche •adv als Nächstes; **~ to** neben

nib /nɪb/ n Feder f

nibble /'nɪbl/ vt/i knabbern (**at** an + dat)

nice /naɪs/ adj (**-r, -st**) nett; (day, weather) schön; (food) gut; (distinction) fein. **~ly** adv nett; (well) gut

niche /ni:ʃ/ n Nische f; (fig) Platz m

nick /nɪk/ n Kerbe f; (!: prison) Knast m; (!: police station) Revier nt; **in good ~** ! in gutem Zustand •vt einkerben; (steal) klauen; (!: arrest) schnappen

nickel /'nɪkl/ n Nickel nt; (Amer) Fünfcentstück nt

'**nickname** n Spitzname m

nicotine /'nɪkəti:n/ n Nikotin nt

niece /ni:s/ n Nichte f

Nigeria /naɪ'dʒɪərɪə/ n Nigeria nt. **~n** adj nigerianisch •n Nigerianer(in) m(f)

night /naɪt/ n Nacht f; (evening) Abend m; **at ~** nachts

night: ~-club n Nachtklub m. **~-dress** n Nachthemd nt. **~fall** n **at ~fall** bei Einbruch der Dunkelheit. **~-gown** n, ! **~ie** /'naɪtɪ/ n Nachthemd nt

nightingale /'naɪtɪŋgeɪl/ n Nachtigall f

night: ~-life n Nachtleben nt. **~ly** adj nächtlich •adv jede Nacht. **~mare** n Albtraum m. **~-time** n **at ~-time** bei Nacht

nil /nɪl/ n null

nimble /'nɪmbl/ adj (**-r, -st**), **-bly** adv flink

nine /naɪn/ adj neun •n Neun f. **~'teen** adj neunzehn. **~'teenth** adj neunzehnte(r, s)

ninetieth /'naɪntɪɪθ/ adj neunzigste(r, s)

ninety /'naɪntɪ/ adj neunzig

ninth /naɪnθ/ adj neunte(r, s)

nip /nɪp/ vt kneifen; (bite) beißen; **~ in the bud** (fig) im Keim ersticken •vi (!: run) laufen

nipple /'nɪpl/ n Brustwarze f; (Amer: on bottle) Sauger m

nitwit /'nɪtwɪt/ n ! Dummkopf m

no /nəʊ/ adv nein •n (pl **noes**) Nein nt •adj kein(e); (pl) keine; **in no time** [sehr] schnell; **no parking/smoking** Parken/Rauchen verboten; **no one** = **nobody**

nobility /nəʊ'bɪlətɪ/ n Adel m

noble /'nəʊbl/ adj (**-r, -st**) edel; (aristocratic) adlig. **~man** n Adlige(r) m

nobody /'nəʊbədɪ/ pron niemand, keiner •n **a ~** ein Niemand m

nocturnal /nɒk'tɜ:nl/ adj nächtlich; (animal, bird) Nacht-

nod /nɒd/ n Nicken nt •v (pt/pp **nodded**) •vi nicken •vt **~ one's head** mit dem Kopf nicken

noise /nɔɪz/ n Geräusch nt; (loud)

Lärm m. ~**less** adj geräuschlos

noisy /'nɔɪzɪ/ adj, **-ily** adv laut; (eater) geräuschvoll

nomad /'nəʊmæd/ n Nomade m. ~**ic** adj nomadisch; (life, tribe) Nomaden-

nominal /'nɒmɪnl/ adj nominell

nominat|e /'nɒmɪneɪt/ vt nominieren, aufstellen; (appoint) ernennen. ~**ion** n Nominierung f; Ernennung f

nominative /'nɒmɪnətɪv/ adj & n (Gram) ~ **[case]** Nominativ m

nonchalant /'nɒnʃələnt/ adj nonchalant; (gesture) lässig

nondescript /'nɒndɪskrɪpt/ adj unbestimmbar; (person) unscheinbar

none /nʌn/ pron keine(r)/keins; ~ **of it/this** nichts davon ●adv ~ **too** nicht gerade; ~ **too soon** [um] keine Minute zu früh; ~ **the less** dennoch

nonentity /nɒ'nentətɪ/ n Null f

non-ex'istent adj nicht vorhanden

non-'fiction n Sachliteratur f

nonplussed /nɒn'plʌst/ adj verblüfft

nonsens|e /'nɒnsəns/ n Unsinn m. ~**ical** adj unsinnig

non-'smoker n Nichtraucher m

non-'stop adv ununterbrochen; (fly) nonstop

non-'swimmer n Nichtschwimmer m

non-'violent adj gewaltlos

noodles /'nu:dlz/ npl Bandnudeln pl

noon /nu:n/ n Mittag m; **at** ~ um 12 Uhr mittags

noose /nu:s/ n Schlinge f

nor /nɔ:(r)/ adv noch ●conj auch nicht

Nordic /'nɔ:dɪk/ adj nordisch

norm /nɔ:m/ n Norm f

normal /'nɔ:ml/ adj normal. ~**ity** n Normalität f. ~**ly** adv normal; (usually) normalerweise

north /nɔ:θ/ n Norden m; **to the** ~ **of** nördlich von ●adj Nord-, nord- ●adv nach Norden

north: N~ America n Nordamerika nt. ~**-east** adj Nordost- ●n Nordosten m

norther|ly /'nɔ:ðəlɪ/ adj nördlich. ~**n** adj nördlich. **N~n Ireland** n Nordirland nt

north: N~ 'Pole n Nordpol m. **N~ 'Sea** n Nordsee f. ~**ward[s]** /-wəd[z]/ adv nach Norden. ~**-west** adj Nordwest- ●n Nordwesten m

Nor|way /'nɔ:weɪ/ n Norwegen nt. ~**wegian** adj norwegisch ●n Norweger(in) m(f)

nose /nəʊz/ n Nase

'nosebleed n Nasenbluten nt

nostalg|ia /nɒ'stældʒɪə/ n Nostalgie f. ~**ic** adj nostalgisch

nostril /'nɒstrəl/ n Nasenloch nt

nosy /'nəʊzɪ/ adj [!] neugierig

not /nɒt/

● adverb

····➤ nicht. **I don't know** ich weiß nicht. **isn't she pretty?** ist sie nicht hübsch?

····➤ **not a** kein. **he is not a doctor** er ist kein Arzt. **she didn't wear a hat** sie trug keinen Hut. **there was not a person to be seen** es gab keinen Menschen zu sehen. **not a thing** gar nichts. **not a bit** kein bisschen

····➤ (in elliptical phrases) **I hope not** ich hoffe nicht. **of course not** natürlich nicht. **not at all** überhaupt nicht; (in polite reply to thanks) keine Ursache; gern geschehen. **certainly not!** auf keinen Fall! **not I** ich nicht

····➤ **not ... but ...** nicht ... sondern .... **it was not a small town but a big one** es war keine kleine Stadt, sondern eine große

notab|le /'nəʊtəbl/ adj bedeutend; (remarkable) bemerkenswert. ~**ly** adv insbesondere

notation /nəʊ'teɪʃn/ n Notation f; (Mus) Notenschrift f

notch /nɒtʃ/ n Kerbe f

note /nəʊt/ n (written comment) Notiz f, Anmerkung f; (short letter) Briefchen nt, Zettel m; (bank ~) Banknote f, Schein m; (Mus) Note f; (sound) Ton m; (on piano) Taste f; **half/whole ~** (Amer) halbe/ganze Note f; **of ~** von Bedeutung; **make a ~ of** notieren •vt beachten; (notice) bemerken (**that** dass)

'**notebook** n Notizbuch nt

noted /'nəʊtɪd/ adj bekannt (**for** für)

note: ~paper n Briefpapier nt. **~worthy** adj beachtenswert

nothing /'nʌθɪŋ/ n, pron & adv nichts; **for ~** umsonst; **~ but** nichts als; **~ much** nicht viel; **~ interesting** nichts Interessantes

notice /'nəʊtɪs/ n (on board) Anschlag m, Bekanntmachung f; (announcement) Anzeige f; (review) Kritik f; (termination of lease, employment) Kündigung f; **give [in one's] ~** kündigen; **give s.o. ~** jdm kündigen; **take no ~!** ignoriere es! •vt bemerken. **~able** /-əbl/ adj, **-bly** adv merklich. **~-board** n Anschlagbrett nt

noti|fication /nəʊtɪfɪ'keɪʃn/ n Benachrichtigung f. **~fy** vt (pt/pp **-ied**) benachrichtigen

notion /'nəʊʃn/ n Idee f

notorious /nəʊ'tɔːrɪəs/ adj berüchtigt

notwith'standing prep trotz (+ gen) •adv trotzdem, dennoch

nought /nɔːt/ n Null f

noun /naʊn/ n Substantiv nt

nourish /'nʌrɪʃ/ vt nähren. **~ing** adj nahrhaft. **~ment** n Nahrung f

novel /'nɒvl/ adj neu[artig] •n Roman m. **~ist** n Romanschriftsteller(in) m(f). **~ty** n Neuheit f

November /nəʊ'vembə(r)/ n November m

novice /'nɒvɪs/ n Neuling m; (Relig) Novize m/Novizin f

now /naʊ/ adv & conj jetzt; **~ [that]** jetzt, wo; **just ~** gerade, eben; **right ~** sofort; **~ and again** hin und wieder; **now, now!** na, na!

'**nowadays** adv heutzutage

nowhere /'nəʊ-/ adv nirgendwo, nirgends

nozzle /'nɒzl/ n Düse f

nuance /'njuːɑ̃s/ n Nuance f

nuclear /'njuːklɪə(r)/ adj Kern-. **~ de'terrent** n nukleares Abschreckungsmittel nt

nucleus /'njuːklɪəs/ n (pl **-lei** /-lɪaɪ/) Kern m

nude /njuːd/ adj nackt •n (Art) Akt m; **in the ~** nackt

nudge /nʌdʒ/ vt stupsen

nud|ist /'njuːdɪst/ n Nudist m. **~ity** n Nacktheit f

nuisance /'njuːsns/ n Ärgernis nt; (pest) Plage f; **be a ~** ärgerlich sein

null /nʌl/ adj **~ and void** null und nichtig

numb /nʌm/ adj gefühllos, taub •vt betäuben

number /'nʌmbə(r)/ n Nummer f; (amount) Anzahl f; (Math) Zahl f •vt nummerieren; (include) zählen (**among** zu). **~-plate** n Nummernschild nt

numeral /'njuːmərl/ n Ziffer f

numerical /njuː'merɪkl/ adj numerisch; **in ~ order** zahlenmäßig geordnet

numerous /'njuːmərəs/ adj zahlreich

nun /nʌn/ n Nonne f

nurse /nɜːs/ n [Kranken]schwester f; (male) Krankenpfleger m; **children's ~** Kindermädchen nt •vt pflegen

nursery /'nɜːsərɪ/ n Kinderzimmer nt; (for plants) Gärtnerei f; **[day] ~** Kindertagesstätte f. **~ rhyme** n Kinderreim m. **~ school** n Kindergarten m

nursing /'nɜːsɪŋ/ n Krankenpflege f. **~ home** n Pflegeheim nt

nut /nʌt/ n Nuss f; (Techn)

[Schrauben]mutter f; (!: head) Birne f !; **be ~s** ! spinnen !. **~crackers** npl Nussknacker m. **~meg** n Muskat m

nutrient /'nju:trɪənt/ n Nährstoff m

nutrit|ion /nju:'trɪʃn/ n Ernährung f. **~ious** adj nahrhaft

'nutshell n Nussschale f; **in a ~** (fig) kurz gesagt

nylon /'naɪlɒn/ n Nylon nt

O /əʊ/ n (Teleph) null

oak /əʊk/ n Eiche f

OAP abbr (**old-age pensioner**) Rentner(in) m(f)

oar /ɔ:(r)/ n Ruder nt. **~sman** n Ruderer m

oasis /əʊ'eɪsɪs/ n (pl **oases** /-si:z/) Oase f

oath /əʊθ/ n Eid m; (swear-word) Fluch m

oatmeal /'əʊt-/ n Hafermehl nt

oats /əʊts/ npl Hafer m; (Culin) **[rolled] ~** Haferflocken pl

obedien|ce /ə'bi:dɪəns/ n Gehorsam m. **~t** adj gehorsam

obey /ə'beɪ/ vt/i gehorchen (+ dat); befolgen (instructions, rules)

obituary /ə'bɪtjʊərɪ/ n Nachruf m; (notice) Todesanzeige f

object[1] /'ɒbdʒɪkt/ n Gegenstand m; (aim) Zweck m; (intention) Absicht f; (Gram) Objekt nt; **money is no ~** Geld spielt keine Rolle

object[2] /əb'dʒekt/ vi Einspruch erheben (**to** gegen); (be against) etwas dagegen haben

objection /əb'dʒekʃn/ n Einwand m; **have no ~** nichts dagegen haben. **~able** adj anstößig; (person) unangenehm

objectiv|e /əb'dʒektɪv/ adj objektiv • n Ziel nt. **~ity** n Objektivität f

objector /əb'dʒektə(r)/ n Gegner m

obligation /ɒblɪ'geɪʃn/ n Pflicht f; **without ~** unverbindlich

obligatory /ə'blɪgətrɪ/ adj obligatorisch; **be ~** Vorschrift sein

oblig|e /ə'blaɪdʒ/ vt verpflichten; (compel) zwingen; (do a small service) einen Gefallen tun (+ dat). **~ing** adj entgegenkommend

oblique /ə'bli:k/ adj schräg; (angle) schief; (fig) indirekt

obliterate /ə'blɪtəreɪt/ vt auslöschen

oblivion /ə'blɪvɪən/ n Vergessenheit f

oblivious /ə'blɪvɪəs/ adj **be ~** sich (dat) nicht bewusst sein (**of** gen)

oblong /'ɒblɒŋ/ adj rechteckig • n Rechteck nt

obnoxious /əb'nɒkʃəs/ adj widerlich

oboe /'əʊbəʊ/ n Oboe f

obscen|e /əb'si:n/ adj obszön. **~ity** n Obszönität f

obscur|e /əb'skjʊə(r)/ adj dunkel; (unknown) unbekannt • vt verdecken; (confuse) verwischen. **~ity** n Dunkelheit f; Unbekanntheit f

observa|nce /əb'zɜ:vns/ n (of custom) Einhaltung f. **~nt** adj aufmerksam. **~tion** n Beobachtung f; (remark) Bemerkung f

observatory /əb'zɜ:vətrɪ/ n Sternwarte f

observe /əb'zɜ:v/ vt beobachten; (say, notice) bemerken; (keep, celebrate) feiern; (obey) einhalten. **~r** n Beobachter m

obsess /əb'ses/ vt **be ~ed by** besessen sein von. **~ion** n Besessenheit f; (persistent idea) fixe Idee f. **~ive** adj zwanghaft

obsolete /'ɒbsəli:t/ adj veraltet

obstacle /'ɒbstəkl/ n Hindernis nt

obstina|cy /'ɒbstɪnəsɪ/ n Starrsinn m. **~te** adj starrsinnig; (refusal) hartnäckig

obstruct /əb'strʌkt/ vt blockieren; (hinder) behindern. **~ion** n Blockierung f; Behinderung f; (obstacle) Hindernis nt. **~ive** adj **be ~ive** Schwierigkeiten bereiten

obtain /əb'teɪn/ vt erhalten. **~able** adj erhältlich

obtrusive /əb'tru:sɪv/ adj aufdringlich; (thing) auffällig

obtuse /əb'tju:s/ adj begriffsstutzig

obvious /'ɒbvɪəs/ adj offensichtlich, offenbar

occasion /ə'keɪʒn/ n Gelegenheit f; (time) Mal nt; (event) Ereignis nt; (cause) Anlass m, Grund m; **on the ~ of** anlässlich (+ gen)

occasional /ə'keɪʒənl/ adj gelegentlich. **~ly** adv gelegentlich, hin und wieder

O

occult /ɒ'kʌlt/ adj okkult

occupant /'ɒkjʊpənt/ n Bewohner(in) m(f); (of vehicle) Insasse m

occupation /ɒkjʊ'peɪʃn/ n Beschäftigung f; (job) Beruf m; (Mil) Besetzung f; (period) Besatzung f. **~al** adj Berufs-. **~al therapy** n Beschäftigungstherapie f

occupier /'ɒkjʊpaɪə(r)/ n Bewohner(in) m(f)

occupy /'ɒkjʊpaɪ/ vt (pt/pp **occupied**) besetzen (seat, (Mil) country); einnehmen (space); in Anspruch nehmen (time); (live in) bewohnen; (fig) bekleiden (office); (keep busy) beschäftigen

occur /ə'kɜ:(r)/ vi (pt/pp **occurred**) geschehen; (exist) vorkommen, auftreten; **it ~red to me that** es fiel mir ein, dass. **~rence** n Auftreten nt; (event) Ereignis nt

ocean /'əʊʃn/ n Ozean m

o'clock /ə'klɒk/ adv **[at] 7 ~** [um] 7 Uhr

octagonal /ɒk'tægənl/ adj achteckig

October /ɒk'təʊbə(r)/ n Oktober m

octopus /'ɒktəpəs/ n (pl **-puses**) Tintenfisch m

odd /ɒd/ adj (**-er, -est**) seltsam, merkwürdig; (number) ungerade; (not of set) einzeln; **forty ~** über vierzig; **~ jobs** Gelegenheitsarbeiten pl; **the ~ one out** die Ausnahme; **at ~ moments** zwischendurch

odd|ity /'ɒdɪtɪ/ n Kuriosität f. **~ly** adv merkwürdig; **~ly enough** merkwürdigerweise **~ment** n (of fabric) Rest m

odds /ɒdz/ npl (chances) Chancen pl; **at ~** uneinig; **~ and ends** Kleinkram m

ode /əʊd/ n Ode f

odious /'əʊdɪəs/ adj widerlich

odour /'əʊdə(r)/ n Geruch m. **~less** adj geruchlos

of /ɒv/, unbetont /əv/

• preposition

····▸ (indicating belonging, origin) von (+ dat); genitive. **the mother of twins** die Mutter von Zwillingen. **the mother of the twins** die Mutter der Zwillinge or von den Zwillingen. **the Queen of England** die Königin von England. **a friend of mine** ein Freund von mir. **a friend of the teacher's** ein Freund des Lehrers. **the brother of her father** der Bruder ihres Vaters. **the works of Shakespeare** Shakespeares Werke. **it was nice of him** es war nett von ihm

····▸ (made of) aus (+ dat). **a dress of cotton** ein Kleid aus Baumwolle

····▸ (following number) **five of us** fünf von uns. **the two of us** wir zwei. **there were four of us**

waiting wir waren vier, die warteten

····➤ (followed by number, description) von (+ dat). **a girl of ten** ein Mädchen von zehn Jahren. **a distance of 50 miles** eine Entfernung von 50 Meilen. **a man of character** ein Mann von Charakter. **a woman of exceptional beauty** eine Frau von außerordentlicher Schönheit. **a person of strong views** ein Mensch mit festen Ansichten

! **of** is not translated after measures and in some other cases: **a pound of apples** ein Pfund Äpfel; **a cup of tea** eine Tasse Tee; **a glass of wine** ein Glas Wein; **the city of Chicago** die Stadt Chicago; **the fourth of January** der vierte Januar

off /ɒf/ prep von (+ dat); **~ the coast** vor der Küste; **get ~ the ladder/bus** von der Leiter/aus dem Bus steigen • adv weg; (button, lid, handle) ab; (light) aus; (brake) los; (machine) abgeschaltet; (tap) zu; (on appliance) **'off'** 'aus'; **2 kilometres ~** 2 Kilometer entfernt; **a long way ~** weit weg; (time) noch lange hin; **~ and on** hin und wieder; **with his hat/coat ~** ohne Hut/Mantel; **20% ~** 20% Nachlass; **be ~** (leave) [weg]gehen; (Sport) starten; (food:) schlecht sein; **be well ~** gut dran sein; (financially) wohlhabend sein; **have a day ~** einen freien Tag haben

offal /'ɒfl/ n (Culin) Innereien pl

offence /ə'fens/ n (illegal act) Vergehen nt; **give/take ~** Anstoß erregen/nehmen (**at** an + dat)

offend /ə'fend/ vt beleidigen. **~er** n (Jur) Straftäter m

offensive /ə'fensɪv/ adj anstößig; (Mil, Sport) offensiv • n Offensive f

offer /'ɒfə(r)/ n Angebot nt; **on (special) ~** im Sonderangebot • vt anbieten (**to** dat); leisten (resistance); **~ to do sth** sich anbieten, etw zu tun. **~ing** n Gabe f

off'hand adj brüsk; (casual) lässig

office /'ɒfɪs/ n Büro nt; (post) Amt nt

officer /'ɒfɪsə(r)/ n Offizier m; (official) Beamte(r) m/ Beamtin f; (police) Polizeibeamte(r) m/ -beamtin f

official /ə'fɪʃl/ adj offiziell, amtlich • n Beamte(r) m/ Beamtin f; (Sport) Funktionär m. **~ly** adv offiziell

officious /ə'fɪʃəs/ adj übereifrig

'off-licence n Wein- und Spirituosenhandlung f

off-'load vt ausladen

'off-putting adj [!] abstoßend

off'set vt (pt/pp **-set**, pres p **-setting**) ausgleichen

'offshoot n Schössling m; (fig) Zweig m

'offshore adj (oil field) im Meer; (breeze) vom Land kommend • adv im/ins Ausland

off'side adj (Sport) abseits

off'stage adv hinter den Kulissen

off-'white adj fast weiß

often /'ɒfn/ adv oft; **every so ~** von Zeit zu Zeit

oh /əʊ/ int oh! ach! **oh dear**! o weh!

oil /ɔɪl/ n Öl nt; (petroleum) Erdöl nt • vt ölen

oil: ~field n Ölfeld nt. **~-painting** n Ölgemälde nt. **~ refinery** n [Erd]ölraffinerie f. **~-tanker** n Öltanker m. **~ well** n Ölquelle f

oily /'ɔɪlɪ/ adj ölig

ointment /'ɔɪntmənt/ n Salbe f

OK /əʊ'keɪ/ adj & int [!] in Ordnung; okay • adv (well) gut • vt (auch **okay**) (pt/pp **okayed**) genehmigen

old /əʊld/ adj (**-er, -est**) alt; (former) ehemalig

old: ~ 'age n Alter nt. **~-age 'pensioner** n Rentner(in) m(f). **~ boy** n ehemaliger Schüler. **~-'fashioned** adj altmodisch. **~ girl** ehemalige Schülerin f

olive /'ɒlɪv/ n Olive f; (colour) Oliv nt • adj olivgrün. **~ 'oil** n Olivenöl nt

O

Olympic /ə'lɪmpɪk/ adj olympisch •n **the ~s** pl die Olympischen Spiele pl

omelette /'ɒmlɪt/ n Omelett nt

ominous /'ɒmɪnəs/ adj bedrohlich

omission /ə'mɪʃn/ n Auslassung f; (failure to do) Unterlassung f

omit /ə'mɪt/ vt (pt/pp **omitted**) auslassen; **~ to do sth** es unterlassen, etw zu tun

omnipotent /ɒm'nɪpətənt/ adj allmächtig

on /ɒn/ prep auf (+ dat/(on to) + acc); (on vertical surface) an (+ dat/(on to) + acc); (about) über (+ acc); **on Monday** [am] Montag; **on Mondays** montags; **on the first of May** am ersten Mai; **on arriving** als ich ankam; **on one's finger** am Finger; **on the right/left** rechts/links; **on the Rhine** am Rhein; **on the radio/television** im Radio/Fernsehen; **on the bus/train** im Bus/Zug; **go on the bus/train** mit dem Bus/Zug fahren; **on me** (with me) bei mir; **it's on me** 🄵 das spendiere ich •adv (further on) weiter; (switched on) an; (brake) angezogen; (machine) angeschaltet; (on appliance) **'on'** 'ein'; **with/without his hat/coat on** mit/ohne Hut/Mantel; **be on** (film:) laufen; (event:) stattfinden; **be on at** 🄵 bedrängen (**zu** to); **it's not on** 🄵 das geht nicht; **on and on** immer weiter; **on and off** hin und wieder; **and so on** und so weiter

once /wʌns/ adv einmal; (formerly) früher; **at ~** sofort; (at the same time) gleichzeitig; **~ and for all** ein für alle Mal •conj wenn; (with past tense) als

'oncoming adj **~ traffic** Gegenverkehr m

one /wʌn/ adj ein(e); (only) einzig; **not ~** kein(e); **~ day/evening** eines Tages/Abends •n Eins f •pron eine(r)/eins; (impersonal) man; **which ~** welche(r,s); **~ another** einander; **~ by ~** einzeln; **~ never knows** man kann nie wissen

one: ~-parent 'family n Einelternfamilie f. **~'self** pron selbst; (reflexive) sich; **by ~self** allein. **~-sided** adj einseitig. **~-way** adj (street) Einbahn-; (ticket) einfach

onion /'ʌnjən/ n Zwiebel f

on-'line adv online

'onlooker n Zuschauer(in) m(f)

only /'əʊnlɪ/ adj einzige(r,s); **an ~ child** ein Einzelkind nt •adv & conj nur; **~ just** gerade erst; (barely) gerade noch

'onset n Beginn m; (of winter) Einsetzen nt

'on-shore adj (oil field) an Land; (breeze) vom Meer kommend

onward[s] /'ɒnwəd[z]/ adv vorwärts; **from then ~** von der Zeit an

ooze /u:z/ vi sickern

opaque /əʊ'peɪk/ adj undurchsichtig

open /'əʊpən/ adj offen; **be ~** (shop:) geöffnet sein; **in the ~ air** im Freien •n **in the ~** im Freien •vt öffnen, aufmachen; (start, set up) eröffnen •vi sich öffnen; (flower:) aufgehen; (shop:) öffnen, aufmachen; (be started) eröffnet werden. **~ up** vt öffnen, aufmachen

'open day n Tag m der offenen Tür

opener /'əʊpənə(r)/ n Öffner m

opening /'əʊpənɪŋ/ n Öffnung f; (beginning) Eröffnung f; (job) Einstiegsmöglichkeit f. **~ hours** npl Öffnungszeiten pl

open: ~-'minded adj aufgeschlossen. **~ 'sandwich** n belegtes Brot nt

opera /'ɒpərə/ n Oper f. **~ glasses** pl Opernglas n **~-house** n Opernhaus nt. **~-singer** n Opernsänger(in) m(f)

operate /'ɒpəreɪt/ vt bedienen (machine, lift); betätigen (lever, brake); (fig: run) betreiben •vi (Techn) funktionieren; (be in action) in Betrieb sein; (Mil & fig) operieren; **~ [on]** (Med) operieren

operatic /ɒpəˈrætɪk/ adj Opern-

operation /ɒpəˈreɪʃn/ n (see **operate**) Bedienung f; Betätigung f; Operation f; **in ~** (Techn) in Betrieb; **come into ~** (fig) in Kraft treten; **have an ~** (Med) operiert werden. **~al** adj einsatzbereit; **be ~al** in Betrieb sein; (law:) in Kraft sein

operative /ˈɒpərətɪv/ adj wirksam

operator /ˈɒpəreɪtə(r)/ n (user) Bedienungsperson f; (Teleph) Vermittlung f

operetta /ɒpəˈretə/ n Operette f

opinion /əˈpɪnjən/ n Meinung f; **in my ~** meiner Meinung nach. **~ated** adj rechthaberisch

opponent /əˈpəʊnənt/ n Gegner(in) m(f)

opportun|e /ˈɒpətjuːn/ adj günstig. **~ist** n Opportunist m

opportunity /ɒpəˈtjuːnətɪ/ n Gelegenheit f

oppos|e /əˈpəʊz/ vt Widerstand leisten (+ dat); (argue against) sprechen gegen; **be ~ed to sth** gegen etw sein; **as ~ed to** im Gegensatz zu. **~ing** adj gegnerisch

opposite /ˈɒpəzɪt/ adj entgegengesetzt; (house, side) gegenüberliegend; **~ number** (fig) Gegenstück nt; **the ~ sex** das andere Geschlecht •n Gegenteil nt •adv gegenüber •prep gegenüber (+ dat)

opposition /ɒpəˈzɪʃn/ n Widerstand m; (Pol) Opposition f

oppress /əˈpres/ vt unterdrücken. **~ion** n Unterdrücken f. **~ive** adj tyrannisch; (heat) drückend

opt /ɒpt/ vi **~ for** sich entscheiden für

optical /ˈɒptɪkl/ adj optisch

optician /ɒpˈtɪʃn/ n Optiker m

optimis|m /ˈɒptɪmɪzm/ n Optimismus m. **~t** n Optimist m. **~tic** adj, **-ally** adv optimistisch

optimum /ˈɒptɪməm/ adj optimal

option /ˈɒpʃn/ n Wahl f; (Comm) Option f. **~al** adj auf Wunsch erhältlich; (subject) wahlfrei

opu|lence /ˈɒpjʊləns/ n Prunk m. **~lent** adj prunkvoll

or /ɔː(r)/ conj oder; (after negative) noch; **or [else]** sonst; **in a year or two** in ein bis zwei Jahren

oral /ˈɔːrl/ adj mündlich; (Med) oral •n Mündliche(s) nt

orange /ˈɒrɪndʒ/ n Apfelsine f, Orange f; (colour) Orange nt •adj orangefarben

oratorio /ɒrəˈtɔːrɪəʊ/ n Oratorium nt

oratory /ˈɒrətərɪ/ n Redekunst f

orbit /ˈɔːbɪt/ n Umlaufbahn f •vt umkreisen

orchard /ˈɔːtʃəd/ n Obstgarten m

orches|tra /ˈɔːkɪstrə/ n Orchester nt. **~tral** adj Orchester-. **~trate** vt orchestrieren

ordeal /ɔːˈdiːl/ n (fig) Qual f

order /ˈɔːdə(r)/ n Ordnung f; (sequence) Reihenfolge f; (condition) Zustand m; (command) Befehl m; (in restaurant) Bestellung f; (Comm) Auftrag m; (Relig, medal) Orden m; **out of ~** (machine) außer Betrieb; **in ~ that** damit; **in ~ to help** um zu helfen •vt (put in ~) ordnen; (command) befehlen (+ dat); (Comm, in restaurant) bestellen; (prescribe) verordnen

orderly /ˈɔːdəlɪ/ adj ordentlich; (not unruly) friedlich •n (Mil, Med) Sanitäter m

ordinary /ˈɔːdɪnərɪ/ adj gewöhnlich, normal

ore /ɔː(r)/ n Erz nt

organ /ˈɔːgən/ n (Biology) Organ nt; (Mus) Orgel f

organic /ɔːˈgænɪk/ adj, **-ally** adv organisch; (without chemicals) biodynamisch; (crop) biologisch angebaut; (food) Bio-. **~ farming** n biologischer Anbau m

organism /ˈɔːgənɪzm/ n Organismus m

organist /ˈɔːgənɪst/ n Organist m

organization /ɔːgənaɪˈzeɪʃn/ n Organisation f

organize /'ɔːgənaɪz/ vt organisieren; veranstalten (event). **~r** n Organisator m; Veranstalter m

orgy /'ɔːdʒɪ/ n Orgie f

Orient /'ɔːrɪənt/ n Orient m. **o~al** adj orientalisch • n Orientale m/ Orientalin f

orientation /ɔːrɪən'teɪʃn/ n Orientierung f

origin /'ɒrɪdʒɪn/ n Ursprung m; (of person, goods) Herkunft f

original /ə'rɪdʒənl/ adj ursprünglich; (not copied) original; (new) originell • n Original nt. **~ity** n Originalität f. **~ly** adv ursprünglich

originate /ə'rɪdʒɪneɪt/ vi entstehen

ornament /'ɔːnəmənt/ n Ziergegenstand m; (decoration) Verzierung f. **~al** adj dekorativ

ornate /ɔː'neɪt/ adj reich verziert

ornithology /ɔːnɪ'θɒlədʒɪ/ n Vogelkunde f

orphan /'ɔːfn/ n Waisenkind nt, Waise f. **~age** n Waisenhaus nt

orthodox /'ɔːθədɒks/ adj orthodox

O

ostensible /ɒ'stensəbl/ adj, **-bly** adv angeblich

ostentat|ion /ɒsten'teɪʃn/ n Protzerei f [!]. **~ious** adj protzig [!]

osteopath /'ɒstɪəpæθ/ n Osteopath m

ostrich /'ɒstrɪtʃ/ n Strauß m

other /'ʌðə(r)/ adj, pron & n andere(r,s); **the ~ [one]** der/die/ das andere; **the ~ two** die zwei anderen; **no ~s** sonst keine; **any ~ questions?** sonst noch Fragen? **every ~ day** jeden zweiten Tag; **the ~ day** neulich; **the ~ evening** neulich abends; **someone/ something or ~** irgendjemand/ -etwas • adv anders; **~ than him** außer ihm; **somehow/somewhere or ~** irgendwie/irgendwo

'otherwise adv sonst; (differently) anders

ought /ɔːt/ modal verb **I/we ~ to stay** ich sollte/wir sollten eigentlich bleiben; **he ~ not to have done it** er hätte es nicht machen sollen

ounce /aʊns/ n Unze f (28,35 g)

our /'aʊə(r)/ adj unser

ours /'aʊəz/ poss pron unsere(r,s); **a friend of ~** ein Freund von uns; **that is ~** das gehört uns

ourselves /aʊə'selvz/ pron selbst; (reflexive) uns; **by ~** allein

out /aʊt/ adv (not at home) weg; (outside) draußen; (not alight) aus; (unconscious) bewusstlos; **be ~** (sun:) scheinen; (flower) blühen; (workers) streiken; (calculation:) nicht stimmen; (Sport) aus sein; (fig: not feasible) nicht infrage kommen; **~ and about** unterwegs; **have it ~ with s.o.** [!] jdn zur Rede stellen; **get ~!** [!] raus! **~ with it!** [!] heraus damit! • prep **~ of** aus (+ dat); **go ~ (of) the door** zur Tür hinausgehen; **be ~ of bed/ the room** nicht im Bett/im Zimmer sein; **~ of breath/danger** außer Atem/Gefahr; **~ of work** arbeitslos; **nine ~ of ten** neun von zehn; **be ~ of sugar** keinen Zucker mehr haben

'outboard adj **~ motor** Außenbordmotor m

'outbreak n Ausbruch m

'outbuilding n Nebengebäude nt

'outburst n Ausbruch m

'outcast n Ausgestoßene(r) m/f

'outcome n Ergebnis nt

'outcry n Aufschrei m [der Entrüstung]

out'dated adj überholt

out'do vt (pt **-did**, pp **-done**) übertreffen, übertrumpfen

'outdoor adj (life, sports) im Freien; **~ swimming pool** Freibad nt

out'doors adv draußen; **go ~** nach draußen gehen

'outer adj äußere(r,s)

'outfit n Ausstattung f; (clothes) Ensemble nt; ([!]: organization) Laden m

'outgoing adj ausscheidend; (mail)

ausgehend; (sociable) kontaktfreudig. **~s** npl Ausgaben pl

out'grow vi (pt **-grew**, pp **-grown**) herauswachsen aus

outing /'aʊtɪŋ/ n Ausflug m

'outlaw n Geächtete(r) m/f • vt ächten

'outlay n Auslagen pl

'outlet n Abzug m; (for water) Abfluss m; (fig) Ventil nt; (Comm) Absatzmöglichkeit f

'outline n Umriss m; (summary) kurze Darstellung f • vt umreißen

out'live vt überleben

'outlook n Aussicht f; (future prospect) Aussichten pl; (attitude) Einstellung f

out'moded adj überholt

out'number vt zahlenmäßig überlegen sein (+ dat)

'out-patient n ambulanter Patient m

'outpost n Vorposten m

'output n Leistung f; Produktion f

'outrage n Gräueltat f; (fig) Skandal m; (indignation) Empörung f. **~ous** adj empörend

'outright[1] adj völlig, total; (refusal) glatt

out'right[2] adv ganz; (at once) sofort; (frankly) offen

'outset n Anfang m

'outside[1] adj äußere(r,s); **~ wall** Außenwand f • n Außenseite f; **from the ~** von außen; **at the ~** höchstens

out'side[2] adv außen; (out of doors) draußen; **go ~** nach draußen gehen • prep außerhalb (+ gen); (in front of) vor (+ dat/acc)

out'sider n Außenseiter m

'outsize adj übergroß

'outskirts npl Rand m

out'spoken adj offen; **be ~** kein Blatt vor den Mund nehmen

out'standing adj hervorragend; (conspicuous) bemerkenswert; (Comm) ausstehend

'outstretched adj ausgestreckt

out'vote vt überstimmen

'outward /-wəd/ adj äußerlich; **~ journey** Hinreise f • adv nach außen. **~ly** adv nach außen hin, äußerlich. **~s** adv nach außen

out'wit vt (pt/pp **-witted**) überlisten

oval /'əʊvl/ adj oval • n Oval nt

ovation /əʊ'veɪʃn/ n Ovation f

oven /'ʌvn/ n Backofen m

over /'əʊvə(r)/ prep über (+ acc/dat); **~ dinner** beim Essen; **~ the phone** am Telefon; **~ the page** auf der nächsten Seite • adv (remaining) übrig; (ended) zu Ende; **~ again** noch einmal; **~ and ~** immer wieder; **~ here/there** hier/da drüben; **all ~** (everywhere) überall; **it's all ~** es ist vorbei; **I ache all ~** mir tut alles weh

overall[1] /'əʊvərɔ:l/ n Kittel m; **~s** pl Overall m

overall[2] /əʊvər'ɔ:l/ adj gesamt; (general) allgemein • adv insgesamt

over'balance vi das Gleichgewicht verlieren

over'bearing adj herrisch

'overboard adv (Naut) über Bord

'overcast adj bedeckt

over'charge vt **~ s.o.** jdm zu viel berechnen • vi zu viel verlangen

'overcoat n Mantel m

over'come vt (pt **-came**, pp **-come**) überwinden; **be ~ by** überwältigt werden von

over'crowded adj überfüllt

over'do vt (pt **-did**, pp **-done**) übertreiben; (cook too long) zu lange kochen; **~ it** (!: do too much) sich übernehmen

'overdose n Überdosis f

'overdraft n [Konto]überziehung f; **have an ~** sein Konto überzogen haben

over'due adj überfällig

over'estimate vt überschätzen

'overflow¹ n Überschuss m; (outlet) Überlauf m; ~ **car park** zusätzlicher Parkplatz m

over'flow² vi überlaufen

over'grown adj (garden) überwachsen

'overhang¹ n Überhang m

over'hang² vt/i (pt/pp **-hung**) überhängen (über + acc)

'overhaul¹ n Überholung f

over'haul² vt (Techn) überholen

over'head¹ adv oben

'overhead² adj Ober-; (ceiling) Decken-. **~s** npl allgemeine Unkosten pl

over'hear vt (pt/pp **-heard**) mit anhören (conversation)

over'heat vi zu heiß werden

over'joyed adj überglücklich

'overland adj & adv /--'-/ auf dem Landweg; ~ **route** Landroute f

over'lap vi (pt/pp **-lapped**) sich überschneiden

over'leaf adv umseitig

O

over'load vt überladen

over'look vt überblicken; (fail to see, ignore) übersehen

over'night¹ adv über Nacht; **stay** ~ übernachten

'overnight² adj Nacht-; ~ **stay** Übernachtung f

'overpass n Überführung f

over'pay vt (pt/pp **-paid**) überbezahlen

over'populated adj übervölkert

over'power vt überwältigen. **~ing** adj überwältigend

over'priced adj zu teuer

over'rated adj überbewertet

overre'act vi überreagieren. **~ion** n Überreaktion f

over'riding adj Haupt-

over'rule vt ablehnen; **we were ~d** wir wurden überstimmt

over'run vt (pt **-ran**, pp **-run**, pres p **-running**) überrennen; überschreiten (time); **be ~ with** überlaufen sein von

over'seas¹ adv in Übersee; **go ~** nach Übersee gehen

'overseas² adj Übersee-

over'see vt (pt **-saw**, pp **-seen**) beaufsichtigen

over'shadow vt überschatten

over'shoot vt (pt/pp **-shot**) hinausschießen über (+ acc)

'oversight n Versehen nt

over'sleep vi (pt/pp **-slept**) [sich] verschlafen

over'step vt (pt/pp **-stepped**) überschreiten

overt /əʊ'vɜːt/ adj offen

over'take vt/i (pt **-took**, pp **-taken**) überholen

over'throw vt (pt **-threw**, pp **-thrown**) (Pol) stürzen

'overtime n Überstunden pl •adv **work ~** Überstunden machen

over'tired adj übermüdet

overture /'əʊvətjʊə(r)/ n (Mus) Ouvertüre f; **~s** pl (fig) Annäherungsversuche pl

over'turn vt umstoßen •vi umkippen

over'weight adj übergewichtig; **be ~** Übergewicht haben

overwhelm /-'welm/ vt überwältigen. **~ing** adj überwältigend

over'work n Überarbeitung f •vt überfordern •vi sich überarbeiten

over'wrought adj überreizt

ow|e /əʊ/ vt schulden/ (fig) verdanken (**[to] s.o.** jdm); **~e s.o. sth** jdm etw schuldig sein. **'~ing to** prep wegen (+ gen)

owl /aʊl/ n Eule f

own¹ /əʊn/ adj & pron eigen; **it's my ~** es gehört mir; **a car of my ~** mein eigenes Auto; **on one's ~**

allein; **get one's ~ back** [!] sich revanchieren

own² vt besitzen; **I don't ~ it** es gehört mir nicht. **~ up** vi es zugeben

owner /'əʊnə(r)/ n Eigentümer(in) m(f), Besitzer(in) m(f); (of shop) Inhaber(in) m(f). **~ship** n Besitz m

oxygen /'ɒksɪdʒən/ n Sauerstoff m

oyster /'ɔɪstə(r)/ n Auster f

Pp

pace /peɪs/ n Schritt m; (speed) Tempo nt; **keep ~ with** Schritt halten mit •vi **~ up and down** auf und ab gehen. **~-maker** n (Sport & Med) Schrittmacher m

Pacific /pə'sɪfɪk/ adj & n **the ~ [Ocean]** der Pazifik

pacifist /'pæsɪfɪst/ n Pazifist m

pacify /'pæsɪfaɪ/ vt (pt/pp **-ied**) beruhigen

pack /pæk/ n Packung f; (Mil) Tornister m; (of cards) [Karten]spiel nt; (gang) Bande f; (of hounds) Meute f; (of wolves) Rudel nt; **a ~ of lies** ein Haufen Lügen •vt/i packen; einpacken (article); **be ~ed** (crowded) [gedrängt] voll sein. **~ up** vt einpacken •vi [!] (machine:) kaputtgehen

package /'pækɪdʒ/ n Paket nt. **~ holiday** n Pauschalreise f

packet /'pækɪt/ n Päckchen nt

packing /'pækɪŋ/ n Verpackung f

pact /pækt/ n Pakt m

pad /pæd/ n Polster nt; (for writing) [Schreib]block m •vt (pt/pp **padded**) polstern

padding /'pædɪŋ/ n Polsterung f; (in written work) Füllwerk nt

paddle¹ /'pædl/ n Paddel nt •vt (row) paddeln

paddle² vi waten

paddock /'pædək/ n Koppel f

padlock /'pædlɒk/ n Vorhängeschloss nt •vt mit einem Vorhängeschloss verschließen

paediatrician /pi:dɪə'trɪʃn/ n Kinderarzt m /-ärztin f

pagan /'peɪgən/ adj heidnisch •n Heide m/Heidin f

page¹ /peɪdʒ/ n Seite f

page² n (boy) Page m •vt ausrufen (person)

paid /'peɪd/ see **pay** •adj bezahlt; **put ~ to** [!] zunichte machen

pail /peɪl/ n Eimer m

pain /peɪn/ n Schmerz m; **be in ~** Schmerzen haben; **take ~s** sich (dat) Mühe geben; **~ in the neck** [!] Nervensäge f

pain: ~ful adj schmerzhaft; (fig) schmerzlich. **~-killer** n schmerzstillendes Mittel nt. **~less** adj schmerzlos

painstaking /'peɪnzteɪkɪŋ/ adj sorgfältig

paint /peɪnt/ n Farbe f •vt/i streichen; (artist:) malen. **~brush** n Pinsel m. **~er** n Maler m; (decorator) Anstreicher m. **~ing** n Malerei f; (picture) Gemälde nt

pair /peə(r)/ n Paar nt; **~ of trousers** Hose f •vi **~ off** Paare bilden

pajamas /pə'dʒɑ:məz/ n pl (Amer) Schlafanzug m

Pakistan /pɑ:kɪ'stɑ:n/ n Pakistan nt. **~i** adj pakistanisch •n Pakistaner(in) m(f)

pal /pæl/ n Freund(in) m(f)

palace /'pælɪs/ n Palast m

palatable /'pælətəbl/ adj schmackhaft

palate /'pælət/ n Gaumen m

palatial /pə'leɪʃl/ adj palastartig

pale adj (**-r, -st**) blass •vi blass werden. **~ness** n Blässe f

Palestin|e /'pælɪstaɪn/ n Palästina nt. **~ian** adj palästinensisch •n Palästinenser(in) m(f)

palette /'pælɪt/ n Palette f

palm /pɑ:m/ n Handfläche f; (tree, symbol) Palme f •vt **~ sth off on s.o.** jdm etw andrehen. **P~'Sunday** n Palmsonntag m

palpable /'pælpəbl/ adj tastbar; (perceptible) spürbar

palpitations /'pælpɪ'teɪʃnz/ npl Herzklopfen nt

paltry /'pɔ:ltrɪ/ adj armselig

pamper /'pæmpə(r)/ vt verwöhnen

pamphlet /'pæmflɪt/ n Broschüre f

pan /pæn/ n Pfanne f; (saucepan) Topf m; (of scales) Schale f

panacea /pænə'si:ə/ n Allheilmittel nt

'pancake n Pfannkuchen m

panda /'pændə/ n Panda m

pandemonium /pændɪ'məʊnɪəm/ n Höllenlärm m

P

pane /peɪn/ n [Glas]scheibe f

panel /'pænl/ n Tafel f, Platte f; **~ of experts** Expertenrunde f; **~ of judges** Jury f. **~ling** n Täfelung f

pang /pæŋ/ n **~s of hunger** Hungergefühl nt; **~s of conscience** Gewissensbisse pl

panic /'pænɪk/ n Panik f •vi (pt/pp **panicked**) in Panik geraten. **~-stricken** adj von Panik ergriffen

panoram|a /pænə'rɑ:mə/ n Panorama nt. **~ic** adj Panorama-

pansy /'pænzɪ/ n Stiefmütterchen nt

pant /pænt/ vi keuchen; (dog:) hecheln

panther /'pænθə(r)/ n Panther m

panties /'pæntɪz/ npl [Damen]slip m

pantomime /'pæntəmaɪm/ n [zu Weihnachten aufgeführte] Märchenvorstellung f

pantry /pæntrɪ/ n Speisekammer f

pants /pænts/ npl Unterhose f; (woman's) Schlüpfer m; (trousers) Hose f

'pantyhose n (Amer) Strumpfhose f

paper /'peɪpə(r)/ n Papier nt; (newspaper) Zeitung f; (exam~) Testbogen m; (exam) Klausur f; (treatise) Referat nt; **~s** pl (documents) Unterlagen pl; (for identification) [Ausweis]papiere pl •vt tapezieren

paper: ~back n Taschenbuch nt. **~-clip** n Büroklammer f. **~weight** n Briefbeschwerer m. **~work** n Schreibarbeit f

par /pɑ:(r)/ n (Golf) Par nt; **on a ~** gleichwertig (**with** dat)

parable /'pærəbl/ n Gleichnis nt

parachut|e /'pærəʃu:t/ n Fallschirm m •vi [mit dem Fallschirm] abspringen. **~ist** n Fallschirmspringer m

parade /pə'reɪd/ n Parade f; (procession) Festzug m •vt (show off) zur Schau stellen

paradise /'pærədaɪs/ n Paradies nt

paradox /'pærədɒks/ n Paradox nt. **~ical** paradox

paraffin /'pærəfɪn/ n Paraffin nt

paragraph /'pærəgrɑ:f/ n Absatz m

parallel /'pærəlel/ adj & adv parallel •n (Geog) Breitenkreis m; (fig) Parallele f

Paralympics /pærə'lɪmpɪks/ npl **the ~** die Paralympics pl

paralyse /'pærəlaɪz/ vt lähmen; (fig) lahmlegen

paralysis /pə'ræləsɪs/ n (pl **-ses** /-si:z/) Lähmung f

paramedic /pærə'medɪk/ n Rettungssanitäter(in) m(f)

parameter /pə'ræmɪtə(r)/ n Parameter m, Rahmen m

paranoid /'pærənɔɪd/ adj [krankhaft] misstrauisch

parapet /'pærəpɪt/ n Brüstung f

paraphernalia /pærəfə'neɪlɪə/ n Kram m

parasite /'pærəsaɪt/ n Parasit m, Schmarotzer m

paratrooper /'pærətruːpə(r)/ n Fallschirmjäger m

parcel /'pɑːsl/ n Paket nt

parch /pɑːtʃ/ vt austrocknen; **be ~ed** (person:) einen furchtbaren Durst haben

parchment /'pɑːtʃmənt/ n Pergament nt

pardon /'pɑːdn/ n Verzeihung f; (Jur) Begnadigung f; **~?** ! bitte? **I beg your ~** wie bitte? (sorry) Verzeihung! •vt verzeihen; (Jur) begnadigen

parent /'peərənt/ n Elternteil m; **~s** pl Eltern pl. **~al** adj elterlich

parenthesis /pə'renθəsɪs/ n (pl **-ses** /-siːz/) Klammer f

parish /'pærɪʃ/ n Gemeinde f. **~ioner** n Gemeindemitglied nt

park /pɑːk/ n Park m •vt/i parken. **~-and-ride** n Park-and-ride-Platz m

parking /'pɑːkɪŋ/ n Parken nt; **'no ~'** 'Parken verboten'. **~-lot** n (Amer) Parkplatz m. **~-meter** n Parkuhr f. **~ space** n Parkplatz m

parliament /'pɑːləmənt/ n Parlament nt. **~ary** adj parlamentarisch

parochial /pə'rəʊkɪəl/ adj Gemeinde-; (fig) beschränkt

parody /'pærədɪ/ n Parodie f •vt (pt/pp **-ied**) parodieren

parole /pə'rəʊl/ n **on ~** auf Bewährung

parquet /'pɑːkeɪ/ n **~ floor** Parkett nt

parrot /'pærət/ n Papagei m

parsley /'pɑːslɪ/ n Petersilie f

parsnip /'pɑːsnɪp/ n Pastinake f

parson /'pɑːsn/ n Pfarrer m

part /pɑːt/ n Teil m; (Techn) Teil nt; (area) Gegend f; (Theat) Rolle f; (Mus) Part m; **spare ~** Ersatzteil nt; **for my ~** meinerseits; **on the ~ of** vonseiten (+ gen); **take s.o.'s ~** für jdn Partei ergreifen; **take ~ in** teilnehmen an (+ dat) •adv teils •vt trennen; scheiteln (hair) •vi (people:) sich trennen; **~ with** sich trennen von

partial /'pɑːʃl/ adj Teil-; **be ~ to** mögen. **-ly** adv teilweise

particip|ant /pɑː'tɪsɪpənt/ n Teilnehmer(in) m(f). **~ate** vi teilnehmen (**in** an + dat). **~ation** n Teilnahme f

particle /'pɑːtɪkl/ n Körnchen nt; (Phys) Partikel nt; (Gram) Partikel f

particular /pə'tɪkjʊlə(r)/ adj besondere(r,s); (precise) genau; (fastidious) penibel; **in ~** besonders. **~ly** adv besonders. **~s** npl nähere Angaben pl

parting /'pɑːtɪŋ/ n Abschied m; (in hair) Scheitel m

partition /pɑː'tɪʃn/ n Trennwand f; (Pol) Teilung f •vt teilen

partly /'pɑːtlɪ/ adv teilweise

partner /'pɑːtnə(r)/ n Partner(in) m(f); (Comm) Teilhaber m. **~ship** n Partnerschaft f; (Comm) Teilhaberschaft f

partridge /'pɑːtrɪdʒ/ n Rebhuhn nt

part-'time adj & adv Teilzeit-; **be** or **work ~** Teilzeitarbeit machen

party /'pɑːtɪ/ n Party f, Fest nt; (group) Gruppe f; (Pol, Jur) Partei f

pass /pɑːs/ n Ausweis m; (Geog, Sport) Pass m; (Sch) ≈ ausreichend; **get a ~** bestehen •vt vorbeigehen/-fahren an (+ dat); (overtake) überholen; (hand) reichen; (Sport) abgeben, abspielen; (approve) annehmen; (exceed) übersteigen; bestehen (exam); machen (remark); fällen (judgement); (Jur) verhängen (sentence); **~ the time** sich (dat) die Zeit vertreiben; **~ one's hand over sth** mit der Hand über etw (acc) fahren •vi vorbeigehen/-fahren; (get by) vorbeikommen; (overtake) überholen; (time:) vergehen; (in exam) bestehen. **~ away** vi sterben. **~ down** vt herunterreichen; (fig) weitergeben. **~ out** vi ohnmächtig

P

werden. ~ **round** vt herumreichen. ~ **up** vt heraufreichen; (!: miss) vorübergehen lassen

passable /'pɑ:səbl/ adj (road) befahrbar; (satisfactory) passabel

passage /'pæsɪdʒ/ n Durchgang m; (corridor) Gang m; (voyage) Überfahrt f; (in book) Passage f

passenger /'pæsɪndʒə(r)/ n Fahrgast m; (Naut, Aviat) Passagier m; (in car) Mitfahrer m. ~ **seat** n Beifahrersitz m

passer-by /pɑ:sə'baɪ/ n (pl **-s-by**) Passant(in) m(f)

passion /'pæʃn/ n Leidenschaft f. ~**ate** adj leidenschaftlich

passive /'pæsɪv/ adj passiv •n Passiv nt

pass: ~**port** n [Reise]pass m. ~**word** n Kennwort nt; (Mil) Losung f

past /pɑ:st/ adj vergangene(r,s); (former) ehemalig; **that's all** ~ das ist jetzt vorbei •n Vergangenheit f •prep an (+ dat) ... vorbei; (after) nach; **at ten** ~ **two** um zehn nach zwei •adv vorbei; **go** ~ vorbeigehen

P

pasta /'pæstə/ n Nudeln pl

paste /peɪst/ n Brei m; (adhesive) Kleister m; (jewellery) Strass m •vt kleistern

pastel /'pæstl/ n Pastellfarbe f; (drawing) Pastell nt •attrib Pastell-

pastime /'pɑ:staɪm/ n Zeitvertreib m

pastr|y /'peɪstrɪ/ n Teig m; **cakes and** ~**ies** Kuchen und Gebäck

pasture /'pɑ:stʃə(r)/ n Weide f

pasty[1] /'pæstɪ/ n Pastete f

pat /pæt/ n Klaps m; (of butter) Stückchen nt •vt (pt/pp **patted**) tätscheln; ~ **s.o. on the back** jdm auf die Schulter klopfen

patch /pætʃ/ n Flicken m; (spot) Fleck m; **not a** ~ **on** ! gar nicht zu vergleichen mit •vt flicken. ~ **up** vt [zusammen]flicken; beilegen (quarrel)

patchy /'pætʃɪ/ adj ungleichmäßig

patent /'peɪtnt/ n Patent nt •vt patentieren. ~ **leather** n Lackleder nt

paternal /pə'tɜ:nl/ adj väterlich

path /pɑ:θ/ n (pl ~**s** /pɑ:ðz/) [Fuß]weg m, Pfad m; (orbit, track) Bahn f; (fig) Weg m

pathetic /pə'θetɪk/ adj mitleiderregend; (attempt) erbärmlich

patience /'peɪʃns/ n Geduld f; (game) Patience f

patient /'peɪʃnt/ adj geduldig •n Patient(in) m(f)

patio /'pætɪəʊ/ n Terrasse f

patriot /'pætrɪət/ n Patriot(in) m(f). ~**ic** adj patriotisch. ~**ism** n Patriotismus m

patrol /pə'trəʊl/ n Patrouille f •vt/i patrouillieren [in (+ dat)]; (police:) auf Streife gehen/fahren [in (+ dat)]. ~ **car** n Streifenwagen m

patron /'peɪtrən/ n Gönner m; (of charity) Schirmherr m; (of the arts) Mäzen m; (customer) Kunde m/Kundin f; (Theat) Besucher m. ~**age** n Schirmherrschaft f

patroniz|e /'pætrənaɪz/ vt (fig) herablassend behandeln. ~**ing** adj gönnerhaft

patter n (speech) Gerede nt

pattern /'pætn/ n Muster nt

paunch /pɔ:ntʃ/ n [Schmer]bauch m

pause /pɔ:z/ n Pause f •vi innehalten

pave /peɪv/ vt pflastern; ~ **the way** den Weg bereiten (**for** dat). ~**ment** n Bürgersteig m

paw /pɔ:/ n Pfote f; (of large animal) Pranke f, Tatze f

pawn[1] /pɔ:n/ n (Chess) Bauer m; (fig) Schachfigur f

pawn[2] vt verpfänden. ~ **broker** n Pfandleiher m

pay /peɪ/ n Lohn m; (salary) Gehalt nt; **be in the** ~ **of** bezahlt werden von •v (pt/pp **paid**) •vt bezahlen; zahlen (money); ~ **s.o. a visit** jdm einen Besuch abstatten; ~ **s.o. a compliment** jdm ein Kompliment machen •vi zahlen; (be profitable) sich bezahlt machen; (fig) sich lohnen; ~ **for sth** etw bezahlen. ~ **back** vt zurückzahlen. ~ **in** vt einzahlen. ~ **off** vt abzahlen (debt) •vi (fig) sich auszahlen

payable /'peɪəbl/ adj zahlbar; **make** ~ **to** ausstellen auf (+ acc)

payment /'peɪmənt/ n Bezahlung f; (amount) Zahlung f

pea /pi:/ n Erbse f

peace /pi:s/ n Frieden m; **for my** ~ **of mind** zu meiner eigenen Beruhigung

peace|ful adj friedlich. ~**maker** n Friedensstifter m

peach /pi:tʃ/ n Pfirsich m

peacock /'pi:kɒk/ n Pfau m

peak /pi:k/ n Gipfel m; (fig) Höhepunkt m. ~**ed 'cap** n Schirmmütze f. ~ **hours** npl Hauptbelastungszeit f; (for traffic) Hauptverkehrszeit f

peal /pi:l/ n (of bells) Glockengeläut nt; ~**s of laughter** schallendes Gelächter nt

'peanut n Erdnuss f

pear /peə(r)/ n Birne f

pearl /pɜ:l/ n Perle f

peasant /'peznt/ n Bauer m

peat /pi:t/ n Torf m

pebble /'pebl/ n Kieselstein m

peck /pek/ n Schnabelhieb m; (kiss) flüchtiger Kuss m •vt/i picken/(nip) hacken (**at** nach)

peculiar /pɪ'kju:lɪə(r)/ adj eigenartig, seltsam; ~ **to** eigentümlich (+ dat). ~**ity** n Eigenart f

pedal /'pedl/ n Pedal nt •vt fahren (bicycle) •vi treten

pedantic /pɪ'dæntɪk/ adj, **-ally** adv pedantisch

pedestal /'pedɪstl/ n Sockel m

pedestrian /pɪ'destrɪən/ n Fußgänger(in) m(f) •adj (fig) prosaisch. ~ **'crossing** n Fußgängerüberweg m. ~ **'precinct** n Fußgängerzone f

pedigree /'pedɪgri:/ n Stammbaum m •attrib (animal) Rasse-

pedlar /'pedlə(r)/ n Hausierer m

peek /pi:k/ vi [!] gucken

peel /pi:l/ n Schale f •vt schälen; •vi (skin:) sich schälen; (paint:) abblättern. ~ **ings** npl Schalen pl

peep /pi:p/ n kurzer Blick m •vi gucken. ~**-hole** n Guckloch nt

peer[1] /pɪə(r)/ vi ~ **at** forschend ansehen

peer[2] n Peer m; **his** ~**s** pl seinesgleichen

peg /peg/ n (hook) Haken m; (for tent) Pflock m, Hering m; (for clothes) [Wäsche]klammer f; **off the** ~ [!] von der Stange

pejorative /pɪ'dʒɒrətɪv/ adj abwertend

pelican /'pelɪkən/ n Pelikan m

pellet /'pelɪt/ n Kügelchen nt

pelt[1] /pelt/ n (skin) Pelz m, Fell nt

pelt[2] vt bewerfen •vi ~ **[down]** (rain:) [hernieder]prasseln

pelvis /'pelvɪs/ n (Anat) Becken nt

pen[1] /pen/ n (for animals) Hürde f

pen[2] n Federhalter m; (ballpoint) Kugelschreiber m

penal /'pi:nl/ adj Straf-. ~**ize** vt bestrafen; (fig) benachteiligen

penalty /'penltɪ/ n Strafe f; (fine) Geldstrafe f; (Sport) Strafstoß m; (Football) Elfmeter m

penance /'penəns/ n Buße f

pence /pens/ see **penny**

pencil /'pensɪl/ n Bleistift m •vt (pt/pp **pencilled**) mit Bleistift schreiben. ~**-sharpener** n Bleistiftspitzer m

pendulum /'pendjʊləm/ n Pendel nt

penetrat|e /'penɪtreɪt/ vt durchdringen; ~**e into** eindringen in (+ acc). ~**ing** adj durchdringend. ~**ion** n Durchdringen nt

'penfriend n Brieffreund(in) m(f)

P

penguin /'peŋgwɪn/ n Pinguin m

penicillin /penɪ'sɪlɪn/ n Penizillin nt

peninsula /pə'nɪnsʊlə/ n Halbinsel f

penis /'pi:nɪs/ n Penis m

penitentiary /penɪ'tenʃərɪ/ n (Amer) Gefängnis nt

pen: ~knife n Taschenmesser nt. **~-name** n Pseudonym nt

penniless /'penɪlɪs/ adj mittellos

penny /'penɪ/ n (pl **pence**; single coins **pennies**) Penny m; (Amer) Centstück nt; **the ~'s dropped** [!] der Groschen ist gefallen

pension /'penʃn/ n Rente f; (of civil servant) Pension f. **~er** n Rentner(in) m(f); Pensionär(in) m(f)

pensive /'pensɪv/ adj nachdenklich

pent-up /'pentʌp/ adj angestaut

penultimate /pe'nʌltɪmət/ adj vorletzte(r,s)

people /'pi:pl/ npl Leute pl, Menschen pl; (citizens) Bevölkerung f; **the ~** das Volk; **English ~** die Engländer; **~ say** man sagt; **for four ~** für vier Personen •vt bevölkern

P

pepper /'pepə(r)/ n Pfeffer m; (vegetable) Paprika m

pepper: ~mint n Pfefferminz nt; (Bot) Pfefferminze f. **~pot** n Pfefferstreuer m

per /pɜ:(r)/ prep pro; **~ cent** Prozent nt

percentage /pə'sentɪdʒ/ n Prozentsatz m; (part) Teil m

perceptible /pə'septəbl/ adj wahrnehmbar

percept|ion /pə'sepʃn/ n Wahrnehmung f. **~ive** adj feinsinnig

perch[1] /pɜ:tʃ/ n Stange f •vi (bird:) sich niederlassen

perch[2] n inv (fish) Barsch m

percussion /pə'kʌʃn/ n Schlagzeug nt. **~ instrument** n Schlaginstrument nt

perennial /pə'renɪəl/ adj (problem) immer wiederkehrend •n (Bot) mehrjährige Pflanze f

perfect[1] /'pɜ:fɪkt/ adj perfekt, vollkommen; ([!]: utter) völlig •n (Gram) Perfekt nt

perfect[2] /pə'fekt/ vt vervollkommnen. **~ion** n Vollkommenheit f; **to ~ion** perfekt

perfectly /'pɜ:fɪktlɪ/ adv perfekt; (completely) vollkommen, völlig

perforated /'pɜ:fəreɪtɪd/ adj perforiert

perform /pə'fɔ:m/ vt ausführen; erfüllen (duty); (Theat) aufführen (play); spielen (role) •vi (Theat) auftreten; (Techn) laufen. **~ance** n Aufführung f; (at theatre, cinema) Vorstellung f; (Techn) Leistung f. **~er** n Künstler(in) m(f)

perfume /'pɜ:fju:m/ n Parfüm nt; (smell) Duft m

perhaps /pə'hæps/ adv vielleicht

perilous /'perələs/ adj gefährlich

perimeter /pə'rɪmɪtə(r)/ n [äußere] Grenze f; (Geometry) Umfang m

period /'pɪərɪəd/ n Periode f; (Sch) Stunde f; (full stop) Punkt m •attrib (costume) zeitgenössisch; (furniture) antik. **~ic** adj, **-ally** adv periodisch. **~ical** n Zeitschrift f

peripher|al /pə'rɪfərl/ adj nebensächlich. **~y** n Peripherie f

perish /'perɪʃ/ vi (rubber:) verrotten; (food:) verderben; (to die) ums Leben kommen. **~able** adj leicht verderblich. **~ing** adj ([!]: cold) eiskalt

perjur|e /'pɜ:dʒə(r)/ vt **~e oneself** einen Meineid leisten. **~y** n Meineid m

perk[1] /pɜ:k/ n [!] [Sonder]vergünstigung f

perk[2] vi **~ up** munter werden

perm /pɜ:m/ n Dauerwelle f •vt **~ s.o.'s hair** jdm eine Dauerwelle machen

permanent /'pɜ:mənənt/ adj ständig; (job, address) fest. **~ly** adv ständig; (work, live) dauernd, permanent; (employed) fest

permissible /pə'mɪsəbl/ adj erlaubt

permission /pə'mɪʃn/ n Erlaubnis f

permit[1] /pə'mɪt/ vt (pt/pp **-mitted**) erlauben (**s.o.** jdm)

permit[2] /'pɜ:mɪt/ n Genehmigung f

perpendicular /pɜ:pən'dɪkjʊlə(r)/ adj senkrecht • n Senkrechte f

perpetual /pə'petjʊəl/ adj ständig, dauernd

perpetuate /pə'petjʊeɪt/ vt bewahren; verewigen (error)

perplex /pə'pleks/ vt verblüffen. **~ed** adj verblüfft

persecut|e /'pɜ:sɪkju:t/ vt verfolgen. **~ion** n Verfolgung f

perseverance /pɜ:sɪ'vɪərəns/ n Ausdauer f

persevere /pɜ:sɪ'vɪə(r)/ vi beharrlich weitermachen

Persia /'pɜ:ʃə/ n Persien nt

Persian /'pɜ:ʃn/ adj persisch; (cat, carpet) Perser-

persist /pə'sɪst/ vi beharrlich weitermachen; (continue) anhalten; (view:) weiter bestehen; **~ in doing sth** dabei bleiben, etw zu tun. **~ence** n Beharrlichkeit f. **~ent** adj beharrlich; (continuous) anhaltend

person /'pɜ:sn/ n Person f; **in ~** persönlich

personal /'pɜ:sənl/ adj persönlich. **~ 'hygiene** n Körperpflege f

personality /pɜ:sə'nælətɪ/ n Persönlichkeit f

personify /pə'sɒnɪfaɪ/ vt (pt/pp **-ied**) personifizieren, verkörpern

personnel /pɜ:sə'nel/ n Personal nt

perspective /pə'spektɪv/ n Perspektive f

persp|iration /pɜ:spɪ'reɪʃn/ n Schweiß m. **~ire** vi schwitzen

persua|de /pə'sweɪd/ vt überreden; (convince) überzeugen. **~sion** n Überredung f; (powers of ~sion) Überredungskunst f

persuasive /pə'sweɪsɪv/ adj beredsam; (convincing) überzeugend

pertinent /'pɜ:tɪnənt/ adj relevant (**to** für)

perturb /pə'tɜ:b/ vt beunruhigen

peruse /pə'ru:z/ vt lesen

pervers|e /pə'vɜ:s/ adj eigensinnig. **~ion** n Perversion f

pervert[1] /pə'vɜ:t/ vt verdrehen; verführen (person)

pervert[2] /'pɜ:vɜ:t/ n Perverse(r) m

pessimis|m /'pesɪmɪzm/ n Pessimismus m. **~t** n Pessimist m. **~tic** adj, **-ally** adv pessimistisch

pest /pest/ n Schädling m; ([!]: person) Nervensäge f

pester /'pestə(r)/ vt belästigen

pesticide /'pestɪsaɪd/ n Schädlingsbekämpfungsmittel nt

pet /pet/ n Haustier nt; (favourite) Liebling m • vt (pt/pp **petted**) liebkosen

petal /'petl/ n Blütenblatt nt

peter /'pi:tə(r)/ vi **~ out** allmählich aufhören

petition /pə'tɪʃn/ n Bittschrift f

pet 'name n Kosename m

petrified /'petrɪfaɪd/ adj vor Angst wie versteinert

petrol /'petrl/ n Benzin nt

petroleum /pɪ'trəʊlɪəm/ n Petroleum nt

petrol: ~-pump n Zapfsäule f. **~ station** n Tankstelle f. **~ tank** n Benzintank m

petticoat /'petɪkəʊt/ n Unterrock m

petty /'petɪ/ adj kleinlich. **~ 'cash** n Portokasse f

petulant /'petjʊlənt/ adj gekränkt

pew /pju:/ n [Kirchen]bank f

pharmaceutical /fɑ:mə'sju:tɪkl/ adj pharmazeutisch

pharmac|ist /'fɑ:məsɪst/ n Apotheker(in) m(f). **~y** n Pharmazie f; (shop) Apotheke f

phase /feɪz/ n Phase f • vt **~ in/out**

allmählich einführen/abbauen

Ph.D. (abbr **Doctor of Philosophy**) Dr. phil.

pheasant /'feznt/ n Fasan m

phenomen|al /fɪ'nɒmɪnl/ adj phänomenal. **~on** n (pl **-na**) Phänomen nt

philharmonic /fɪlɑ:'mɒnɪk/ n (orchestra) Philharmoniker pl

Philippines /'fɪlɪpi:nz/ npl Philippinen pl

philistine /'fɪlɪstaɪn/ n Banause m

philosoph|er /fɪ'lɒsəfə(r)/ n Philosoph m. **~ical** adj philosophisch. **~y** n Philosophie f

phlegmatic /fleg'mætɪk/ adj phlegmatisch

phobia /'fəʊbɪə/ n Phobie f

phone /fəʊn/ n Telefon nt; **be on the ~** Telefon haben; (be phoning) telefonieren •vt anrufen •vi telefonieren. **~ back** vt/i zurückrufen. **~ book** n Telefonbuch nt. **~ box** n Telefonzelle f. **~ card** n Telefonkarte f. **~-in** n (Radio) Hörersendung f. **~ number** n Telefonnummer f

phonetic /fə'netɪk/ adj phonetisch. **~s** n Phonetik f

P

phoney /'fəʊnɪ/ adj falsch; (forged) gefälscht

photo /'fəʊtəʊ/ n Foto nt, Aufnahme f. **~copier** n Fotokopiergerät nt. **~copy** n Fotokopie f •vt fotokopieren

photogenic /fəʊtəʊ'dʒenɪk/ adj fotogen

photograph /'fəʊtəgrɑ:f/ n Fotografie f, Aufnahme f •vt fotografieren

photograph|er /fə'tɒgrəfə(r)/ n Fotograf(in) m(f). **~ic** adj, **-ally** adv fotografisch. **~y** n Fotografie f

phrase /freɪz/ n Redensart f •vt formulieren. **~-book** n Sprachführer m

physical /'fɪzɪkl/ adj körperlich

physician /fɪ'zɪʃn/ n Arzt m/ Ärztin f

physic|ist /'fɪzɪsɪst/ n Physiker(in) m(f). **~s** n Physik f

physio'therap|ist /fɪzɪəʊ-/ n Physiotherapeut(in) m(f). **~y** n Physiotherapie f

physique /fɪ'zi:k/ n Körperbau m

pianist /'pɪənɪst/ n Klavierspieler(in) m(f); (professional) Pianist(in) m(f)

piano /pɪ'ænəʊ/ n Klavier nt

pick¹ /pɪk/ n Spitzhacke f

pick² n Auslese f; **take one's ~** sich (dat) aussuchen •vt/i (pluck) pflücken; (select) wählen, sich (dat) aussuchen; **~ and choose** wählerisch sein; **~ a quarrel** einen Streit anfangen; **~ holes in** [!] kritisieren; **~ at one's food** im Essen herumstochern. **~ on** vt wählen; ([!]: find fault with) herumhacken auf (+ dat). **~ up** vt in die Hand nehmen; (off the ground) aufheben; hochnehmen (baby); (learn) lernen; (acquire) erwerben; (buy) kaufen; (Teleph) abnehmen (receiver); auffangen (signal); (collect) abholen; aufnehmen (passengers); (police:) aufgreifen (criminal); sich holen (illness); [!] aufgabeln (girl); **~ oneself up** aufstehen •vi (improve) sich bessern

'**pickaxe** n Spitzhacke f

picket /'pɪkɪt/ n Streikposten m

pickle /'pɪkl/ n (Amer: gherkin) Essiggurke f; **~s** pl [Mixed] Pickles pl •vt einlegen

pick: ~pocket n Taschendieb m. **~-up** n (truck) Lieferwagen m

picnic /'pɪknɪk/ n Picknick nt •vi (pt/pp **-nicked**) picknicken

picture /'pɪktʃə(r)/ n Bild nt; (film) Film m; **as pretty as a ~** bildhübsch; **put s.o. in the ~** (fig) jdn ins Bild setzen •vt (imagine) sich (dat) vorstellen

picturesque /pɪktʃə'resk/ adj malerisch

pie /paɪ/ n Pastete f; (fruit) Kuchen m

piece /pi:s/ n Stück nt; (of set) Teil nt; (in game) Stein m; (writing) Artikel m; **a ~ of bread/paper** ein Stück Brot/Papier; **a ~ of news/advice** eine Nachricht/ein Rat; **take to ~s** auseinander nehmen •vt **~ together** zusammensetzen; (fig) zusammenstückeln. **~meal** adv stückweise

pier /pɪə(r)/ n Pier m; (pillar) Pfeiler m

pierc|e /pɪəs/ vt durchstechen. **~ing** adj durchdringend

pig /pɪg/ n Schwein nt

pigeon /ˈpɪdʒɪn/ n Taube f. **~-hole** n Fach nt

piggy|back /ˈpɪgɪbæk/ n **give s.o. a ~back** jdn huckepack tragen. **~bank** n Sparschwein nt

pigˈheaded adj [!] starrköpfig

pigment /ˈpɪgmənt/ n Pigment nt

pig: ~skin n Schweinsleder nt. **~sty** n Schweinestall m. **~tail** n [!] Zopf m

pilchard /ˈpɪltʃəd/ n Sardine f

pile¹ /paɪl/ n (of fabric) Flor m

pile² n Haufen m •vt **~ sth on to sth** etw auf etw (acc) häufen. **~ up** vt häufen •vi sich häufen

piles /paɪlz/ npl Hämorrhoiden pl

ˈpile-up n Massenkarambolage f

pilgrim /ˈpɪlgrɪm/ n Pilger(in) m(f). **~age** n Pilgerfahrt f, Wallfahrt f

pill /pɪl/ n Pille f

pillar /ˈpɪlə(r)/ n Säule f. **~-box** n Briefkasten m

pillow /ˈpɪləʊ/ n Kopfkissen nt. **~case** n Kopfkissenbezug m

pilot /ˈpaɪlət/ n Pilot m; (Naut) Lotse m •vt fliegen (plane); lotsen (ship). **~-light** n Zündflamme f

pimple /ˈpɪmpl/ n Pickel m

pin /pɪn/ n Stecknadel f; (Techn) Bolzen m, Stift m; (Med) Nagel m; **I have ~s and needles in my leg** [!] mein Bein ist eingeschlafen •vt (pt/pp **pinned**) anstecken (**to/on** an + acc); (sewing) stecken; (hold down) festhalten

pinafore /ˈpɪnəfɔ:(r)/ n Schürze f. **~ dress** n Kleiderrock m

pincers /ˈpɪnsəz/ npl Kneifzange f; (Zool) Scheren pl

pinch /pɪntʃ/ n Kniff m; (of salt) Prise f; **at a ~** [!] zur Not •vt kneifen, zwicken; (fam; steal) klauen; **~ one's finger** sich (dat) den Finger klemmen •vi (shoe:) drücken

pine¹ /paɪn/ n (tree) Kiefer f

pine² vi **~ for** sich sehnen nach

pineapple /ˈpaɪn-/ n Ananas f

ˈping-pong n Tischtennis nt

pink /pɪŋk/ adj rosa

pinnacle /ˈpɪnəkl/ n Gipfel m; (on roof) Turmspitze f

pin: ~point vt genau festlegen. **~stripe** n Nadelstreifen m

pint /paɪnt/ n Pint nt (0,57 l, Amer: 0,47 l)

pioneer /paɪəˈnɪə(r)/ n Pionier m •vt bahnbrechende Arbeit leisten für

pious /ˈpaɪəs/ adj fromm

pip¹ /pɪp/ n (seed) Kern m

pip² n (sound) Tonsignal nt

pipe /paɪp/ n Pfeife f; (for water, gas) Rohr nt •vt in Rohren leiten; (Culin) spritzen

pipe: ~-dream n Luftschloss nt. **~line** n Pipeline f; **in the ~line** [!] in Vorbereitung

piping /ˈpaɪpɪŋ/ adj **~ hot** kochend heiß

pirate /ˈpaɪərət/ n Pirat m

piss /pɪs/ vi [x] pissen

pistol /ˈpɪstl/ n Pistole f

piston /ˈpɪstən/ n (Techn) Kolben m

pit /pɪt/ n Grube f; (for orchestra) Orchestergraben m; (for audience) Parkett nt; (motor racing) Box f

pitch¹ /pɪtʃ/ n (steepness) Schräge f; (of voice) Stimmlage f; (of sound) [Ton]höhe f; (Sport) Feld nt; (of street-trader) Standplatz m; (fig: degree) Grad m •vt werfen; aufschlagen (tent) •vi fallen

pitch² n (tar) Pech nt. **~-ˈblack** adj pechschwarz. **~-ˈdark** adj stockdunkel

piteous /ˈpɪtɪəs/ adj erbärmlich

ˈpitfall n (fig) Falle f

pith /pɪθ/ n (Bot) Mark nt; (of orange) weiße Haut f

pithy /ˈpɪθɪ/ adj (fig) prägnant

piti|ful /ˈpɪtɪfl/ adj bedauernswert. **~less** adj mitleidslos

ˈpit stop n Boxenstopp m

pittance /ˈpɪtns/ n Hungerlohn m

pity /ˈpɪtɪ/ n Mitleid nt, Erbarmen nt; **[what a] ~!** [wie] schade! **take ~ on** sich erbarmen über (+ acc) •vt bemitleiden

pivot /ˈpɪvət/ n Drehzapfen m •vi sich drehen (**on** um)

pizza /ˈpi:tsə/ n Pizza f

placard /ˈplækɑ:d/ n Plakat nt

placate /pləˈkeɪt/ vt beschwichtigen

place /pleɪs/ n Platz m; (spot) Stelle f; (town, village) Ort m; (!: house) Haus nt; **out of ~** fehl am Platze; **take ~** stattfinden •vt setzen; (upright) stellen; (flat) legen; (remember) unterbringen !; **~ an order** eine Bestellung aufgeben; **be ~d** (in race) sich platzieren. **~-mat** n Set nt

P

placid /ˈplæsɪd/ adj gelassen

plague /pleɪg/ n Pest f •vt plagen

plaice /pleɪs/ n inv Scholle f

plain /pleɪn/ adj (**-er, -est**) klar; (simple) einfach; (not pretty) nicht hübsch; (not patterned) einfarbig; (chocolate) zartbitter; **in ~ clothes** in Zivil •adv (simply) einfach •n Ebene f. **~ly** adv klar, deutlich; (simply) einfach; (obviously) offensichtlich

plaintiff /ˈpleɪntɪf/ n Kläger(in) m(f)

plait /plæt/ n Zopf m •vt flechten

plan /plæn/ n Plan m •vt (pt/pp **planned**) planen; (intend) vorhaben

plane[1] /pleɪn/ n (tree) Platane f

plane[2] n Flugzeug nt; (Geometry & fig) Ebene f

plane[3] n (Techn) Hobel m •vt hobeln

planet /ˈplænɪt/ n Planet m

plank /plæŋk/ n Brett nt; (thick) Planke f

planning /ˈplænɪŋ/ n Planung f

plant /plɑ:nt/ n Pflanze f; (Techn) Anlage f; (factory) Werk nt •vt pflanzen; (place in position) setzen; **~ oneself** sich hinstellen. **~ation** n Plantage f

plaque /plɑ:k/ n [Gedenk]tafel f; (on teeth) Zahnbelag m

plaster /ˈplɑ:stə(r)/ n Verputz m; (sticking ~) Pflaster nt; **~ [of Paris]** Gips m •vt verputzen (wall); (cover) bedecken mit

plastic /ˈplæstɪk/ n Kunststoff m, Plastik nt •adj Kunststoff-, Plastik-; (malleable) formbar, plastisch

plastic ˈsurgery n plastische Chirurgie f

plate /pleɪt/ n Teller m; (flat sheet) Platte f; (with name, number) Schild nt; (gold and silverware) vergoldete/versilberte Ware f; (in book) Tafel f •vt (with gold) vergolden; (with silver) versilbern

platform /ˈplætfɔ:m/ n Plattform f; (stage) Podium nt; (Rail) Bahnsteig m; **~ 5** Gleis 5

platinum /ˈplætɪnəm/ n Platin nt

platitude /ˈplætɪtju:d/ n Plattitüde f

plausible /ˈplɔ:zəbl/ adj plausibel

play /pleɪ/ n Spiel nt; [Theater]stück nt; (Radio) Hörspiel nt; (TV) Fernsehspiel nt; **~ on words** Wortspiel nt •vt/i spielen; ausspielen (card); **~ safe** sichergehen. **~ down** vt herunterspielen. **~ up** vi ! Mätzchen machen

play: ~er n Spieler(in) m(f). **~ful** adj verspielt. **~ground** n Spielplatz m; (Sch) Schulhof m. **~group** n Kindergarten m

playing: ~-card n Spielkarte f. **~-field** n Sportplatz m

play: ~mate n Spielkamerad m. **~thing** n Spielzeug nt. **~wright** /-raɪt/ n Dramatiker m

plc abbr (**public limited company**) ≈ GmbH

plea /pli:/ n Bitte f; **make a ~ for** bitten um

plead /pli:d/ vi flehen (**for** um); **~ guilty** sich schuldig bekennen; **~ with s.o.** jdn anflehen

pleasant /'plezənt/ adj angenehm; (person) nett. **~ly** adv angenehm; (say, smile) freundlich

pleas|e /pli:z/ adv bitte •vt gefallen (+ dat); **~e s.o.** jdm eine Freude machen; **~e oneself** tun, was man will. **~ed** adj erfreut; **be ~ed with/about sth** sich über etw (acc) freuen. **~ing** adj erfreulich

pleasure /'pleʒə(r)/ n Vergnügen nt; (joy) Freude f; **with ~** gern[e]

pleat /pli:t/ n Falte f •vt fälteln

pledge /pledʒ/ n Versprechen nt •vt verpfänden; versprechen

plentiful /'plentɪfl/ adj reichlich

plenty /'plentɪ/ n eine Menge; (enough) reichlich; **~ of money/people** viel Geld/viele Leute

pliable /'plaɪəbl/ adj biegsam

pliers /'plaɪəz/ npl [Flach]zange f

plight /plaɪt/ n [Not]lage f

plinth /plɪnθ/ n Sockel m

plod /plɒd/ vi (pt/pp **plodded**) trotten; (work) sich abmühen

plonk /plɒŋk/ n [!] billiger Wein m

plot /plɒt/ n Komplott nt; (of novel) Handlung f; **~ of land** Stück nt Land •vt einzeichnen •vi ein Komplott schmieden

plough /plaʊ/ n Pflug m •vt/i pflügen

ploy /plɔɪ/ n [!] Trick m

pluck /plʌk/ n Mut m •vt zupfen; rupfen (bird); pflücken (flower); **~ up courage** Mut fassen

plucky /'plʌkɪ/ adj tapfer, mutig

plug /plʌg/ n Stöpsel m; (wood) Zapfen m; (cotton wool) Bausch m; (Electr) Stecker m; (Auto) Zündkerze f; ([!]: advertisement) Schleichwerbung f •vt zustopfen; ([!]: advertise) Schleichwerbung machen für. **~ in** vt (Electr) einstecken

plum /plʌm/ n Pflaume f

plumage /'plu:mɪdʒ/ n Gefieder nt

plumb|er /'plʌmə(r)/ n Klempner m. **~ing** n Wasserleitungen pl

plume /plu:m/ n Feder f

plump /plʌmp/ adj (**-er, -est**) mollig, rundlich •vt **~ for** wählen

plunge /plʌndʒ/ n Sprung m; **take the ~** [!] den Schritt wagen •vt/i tauchen

plural /'plʊərl/ adj pluralisch •n Mehrzahl f, Plural m

plus /plʌs/ prep plus (+ dat) •adj Plus- •n Pluszeichen nt; (advantage) Plus nt

plush[y] /'plʌʃ[ɪ]/ adj luxuriös

ply /plaɪ/ vt (pt/pp **plied**) ausüben (trade); **~ s.o. with drink** jdm ein Glas nach dem anderen eingießen. **~wood** n Sperrholz nt

p.m. adv (abbr **post meridiem**) nachmittags

pneumatic /nju:'mætɪk/ adj pneumatisch. **~ 'drill** n Presslufthammer m

pneumonia /nju:'məʊnɪə/ n Lungenentzündung f

poach /pəʊtʃ/ vt (Culin) pochieren; (steal) wildern. **~er** n Wilddieb m

pocket /'pɒkɪt/ n Tasche f; **be out of ~** [an einem Geschäft] verlieren •vt einstecken. **~-book** n Notizbuch nt; (wallet) Brieftasche f. **~-money** n Taschengeld nt

pod /pɒd/ n Hülse f

poem /'pəʊɪm/ n Gedicht nt

poet /'pəʊɪt/ n Dichter(in) m(f). **~ic** adj dichterisch

poetry /'pəʊɪtrɪ/ n Dichtung f

poignant /'pɔɪnjənt/ adj ergreifend

point /pɔɪnt/ n Punkt m; (sharp end) Spitze f; (meaning) Sinn m; (purpose) Zweck m; (Electr) Steckdose f; **~s** pl (Rail) Weiche f; **~ of view** Standpunkt m; **good/bad ~s** gute/schlechte Seiten; **what is the ~?** wozu? **the ~ is** es geht darum; **up to a ~** bis zu einem gewissen Grade; **be on the ~ of doing sth**

im Begriff sein, etw zu tun •vt richten (**at** auf + acc); ausfugen (brickwork) •vi deuten (**at/to** auf + acc); (with finger) mit dem Finger zeigen. ~ **out** vt zeigen auf (+ acc); ~ **sth out to s.o.** jdn auf etw (acc) hinweisen

point-'blank adj aus nächster Entfernung; (fig) rundweg

point|ed /'pɔɪntɪd/ adj spitz; (question) gezielt. ~**less** adj zwecklos, sinnlos

poise /pɔɪz/ n Haltung f

poison /'pɔɪzn/ n Gift nt •vt vergiften. ~**ous** adj giftig

poke /pəʊk/ n Stoß m •vt stoßen; schüren (fire); (put) stecken

poker[1] /'pəʊkə(r)/ n Schüreisen nt

poker[2] n (Cards) Poker nt

poky /'pəʊkɪ/ adj eng

Poland /'pəʊlənd/ n Polen nt

polar /'pəʊlə(r)/ adj Polar-. ~**'bear** n Eisbär m

Pole /pəʊl/ n Pole m/Polin f

pole[1] n Stange f

pole[2] n (Geog, Electr) Pol m

'pole-vault n Stabhochsprung m

police /pə'li:s/ npl Polizei f

police: ~**man** n Polizist m. ~ **station** n Polizeiwache f. ~**woman** n Polizistin f

policy[1] /'pɒlɪsɪ/ n Politik f

policy[2] n (insurance) Police f

Polish /'pəʊlɪʃ/ adj polnisch

polish /'pɒlɪʃ/ n (shine) Glanz m; (for shoes) [Schuh]creme f; (for floor) Bohnerwachs m; (for furniture) Politur f; (for silver) Putzmittel nt; (for nails) Lack m; (fig) Schliff m •vt polieren; bohnern (floor). ~ **off** vt [!] verputzen (food); erledigen (task)

polite /pə'laɪt/ adj höflich. ~**ness** n Höflichkeit f

politic|al /pə'lɪtɪkl/ adj politisch. ~**ian** n Politiker(in) m(f)

politics /'pɒlətɪks/ n Politik f

poll /pəʊl/ n Abstimmung f; (election) Wahl f; **[opinion]** ~ [Meinungs]umfrage f

pollen /'pɒlən/ n Blütenstaub m, Pollen m

polling /'pəʊlɪŋ/: ~**-booth** n Wahlkabine f. ~**-station** n Wahllokal nt

pollut|e /pə'lu:t/ vt verschmutzen. ~**ion** n Verschmutzung f

polo /'pəʊləʊ/ n Polo nt. ~**-neck** n Rollkragen m

polystyrene /pɒlɪ'staɪri:n/ n Polystyrol nt; (for packing) Styropor® nt

polythene /'pɒlɪθi:n/ n Polyäthylen nt. ~ **bag** n Plastiktüte f

pomp /pɒmp/ n Pomp m

pompous /'pɒmpəs/ adj großspurig

pond /pɒnd/ n Teich m

ponder /'pɒndə(r)/ vi nachdenken

ponderous /'pɒndərəs/ adj schwerfällig

pony /'pəʊnɪ/ n Pony nt. ~**-tail** n Pferdeschwanz m

poodle /'pu:dl/ n Pudel m

pool /pu:l/ n [Schwimm]becken nt; (pond) Teich m; (of blood) Lache f; (common fund) [gemeinsame] Kasse f; ~**s** pl [Fußball]toto nt •vt zusammenlegen

poor /pʊə(r)/ adj (**-er, -est**) arm; (not good) schlecht; **in** ~ **health** nicht gesund. ~**ly** adj **be** ~**ly** krank sein •adv ärmlich; (badly) schlecht

pop[1] /pɒp/ n Knall m •v (pt/pp **popped**) •vt ([!]: put) stecken (**in** in + acc) •vi knallen; (burst) platzen. ~ **in** vi [!] reinschauen. ~ **out** vi [!] kurz rausgehen

pop[2] n [!] Popmusik f, Pop m •attrib Pop-

'popcorn n Puffmais m

pope /pəʊp/ n Papst m

poplar /'pɒplə(r)/ n Pappel f

poppy /'pɒpɪ/ n Mohn m

popular /'pɒpjʊlə(r)/ adj beliebt, populär; (belief) volkstümlich. ~**ity**

n Beliebtheit f, Popularität f

populat|e /ˈpɒpjʊleɪt/ vt bevölkern. **~ion** n Bevölkerung f

pop-up /ˈpɒpʌp/ n Pop-up-Werbefenster nt

porcelain /ˈpɔːsəlɪn/ n Porzellan nt

porch /pɔːtʃ/ n Vorbau m; (Amer) Veranda f

porcupine /ˈpɔːkjʊpaɪn/ n Stachelschwein nt

pore /pɔː(r)/ n Pore f

pork /pɔːk/ n Schweinefleisch nt

porn /pɔːn/ n [!] Porno m

pornograph|ic /pɔːnəˈɡræfɪk/ adj pornographisch. **~y** n Pornographie f

porridge /ˈpɒrɪdʒ/ n Haferbrei m

port[1] /pɔːt/ n Hafen m; (town) Hafenstadt f

port[2] n (Naut) Backbord nt

port[3] n (wine) Portwein m

portable /ˈpɔːtəbl/ adj tragbar

porter /ˈpɔːtə(r)/ n Portier m; (for luggage) Gepäckträger m

ˈporthole n Bullauge nt

portion /ˈpɔːʃn/ n Portion f; (part, share) Teil nt

portrait /ˈpɔːtrɪt/ n Porträt nt

portray /pɔːˈtreɪ/ vt darstellen. **~al** n Darstellung f

Portug|al /ˈpɔːtjʊɡl/ n Portugal nt. **~uese** adj portugiesisch •n Portugiese m/-giesin f

pose /pəʊz/ n Pose f •vt aufwerfen (problem); stellen (question) •vi posieren; (for painter) Modell stehen

posh /pɒʃ/ adj [!] feudal

position /pəˈzɪʃn/ n Platz m; (posture) Haltung f; (job) Stelle f; (situation) Lage f, Situation f; (status) Stellung f •vt platzieren; **~ oneself** sich stellen

positive /ˈpɒzətɪv/ adj positiv; (definite) eindeutig; (real) ausgesprochen •n Positiv nt

possess /pəˈzes/ vt besitzen. **~ion** n Besitz m; **~ions** pl Sachen pl

possess|ive /pəˈzesɪv/ adj Possessiv-; **be ~ive about s.o.** zu sehr an jdm hängen

possibility /pɒsəˈbɪlətɪ/ n Möglichkeit f

possib|le /ˈpɒsəbl/ adj möglich. **~ly** adv möglicherweise; **not ~ly** unmöglich

post[1] /pəʊst/ n (pole) Pfosten m

post[2] n (place of duty) Posten m; (job) Stelle f

post[3] n (mail) Post f; **by ~** mit der Post •vt aufgeben (letter); (send by ~) mit der Post schicken; **keep s.o. ~ed** jdn auf dem Laufenden halten

postage /ˈpəʊstɪdʒ/ n Porto nt

postal /ˈpəʊstl/ adj Post-. **~ order** n ≈ Geldanweisung f

post: ~-box n Briefkasten m. **~card** n Postkarte f; (picture) Ansichtskarte f. **~code** n Postleitzahl f. **~-ˈdate** vt vordatieren

poster /ˈpəʊstə(r)/ n Plakat nt

posterity /pɒˈsterətɪ/ n Nachwelt f

posthumous /ˈpɒstjʊməs/ adj postum

post: ~man n Briefträger m. **~mark** n Poststempel m

post-mortem /-ˈmɔːtəm/ n Obduktion f

ˈpost office n Post f

postpone /pəʊstˈpəʊn/ vt aufschieben; **~ until** verschieben auf (+ acc). **~ment** n Verschiebung f

postscript /ˈpəʊstskrɪpt/ n Nachschrift f

posture /ˈpɒstʃə(r)/ n Haltung f

pot /pɒt/ n Topf m; (for tea, coffee) Kanne f; **~s of money** [!] eine Menge Geld

potato /pəˈteɪtəʊ/ n (pl **-es**) Kartoffel f

potent /ˈpəʊtənt/ adj stark

potential /pəˈtenʃl/ adj potenziell •n Potenzial nt

pot: ~-hole n Höhle f; (in road) Schlagloch nt. **~-shot** n **take a ~-shot at** schießen auf (+ acc)

potter /'pɒtə(r)/ n Töpfer(in) m(f). **~y** n Töpferei f; (articles) Töpferwaren pl

potty /'pɒtɪ/ adj [!] verrückt •n Töpfchen nt

pouch /paʊtʃ/ n Beutel m

poultry /'pəʊltrɪ/ n Geflügel nt

pounce /paʊns/ vi zuschlagen; **~ on** sich stürzen auf (+ acc)

pound[1] /paʊnd/ n (money & 0,454 kg) Pfund nt

pound[2] vi (heart:) hämmern; (run heavily) stampfen

pour /pɔ:(r)/ vt gießen; einschenken (drink) •vi strömen; (with rain) gießen. **~ out** vi ausströmen •vt ausschütten; einschenken (drink)

pout /paʊt/ vi einen Schmollmund machen

poverty /'pɒvətɪ/ n Armut f

powder /'paʊdə(r)/ n Pulver nt; (cosmetic) Puder m •vt pudern

power /'paʊə(r)/ n Macht f; (strength) Kraft f; (Electr) Strom m; (nuclear) Energie f; (Math) Potenz f. **~ cut** n Stromsperre f. **~ed** adj betrieben (**by** mit); **~ed by electricity** mit Elektroantrieb. **~ful** adj mächtig; (strong) stark. **~less** adj machtlos. **~-station** n Kraftwerk nt

practicable /'præktɪkəbl/ adj durchführbar, praktikabel

practical /'præktɪkl/ adj praktisch. **~ 'joke** n Streich m

practice /'præktɪs/ n Praxis f; (custom) Brauch m; (habit) Gewohnheit f; (exercise) Übung f; (Sport) Training nt; **in ~** (in reality) in der Praxis; **out of ~** außer Übung; **put into ~** ausführen

practise /'præktɪs/ vt üben; (carry out) praktizieren; ausüben (profession) •vi üben; (doctor:) praktizieren. **~d** adj geübt

praise /preɪz/ n Lob nt •vt loben. **~worthy** adj lobenswert

pram /præm/ n Kinderwagen m

prank /præŋk/ n Streich m

prawn /prɔ:n/ n Garnele f, Krabbe f

pray /preɪ/ vi beten. **~er** n Gebet nt

preach /pri:tʃ/ vt/i predigen. **~er** n Prediger m

pre-ar'range /pri:-/ vt im Voraus arrangieren

precarious /prɪ'keərɪəs/ adj unsicher

precaution /prɪ'kɔ:ʃn/ n Vorsichtsmaßnahme f

precede /prɪ'si:d/ vt vorangehen (+ dat)

preceden|ce /'presɪdəns/ n Vorrang m. **~t** n Präzedenzfall m

preceding /prɪ'si:dɪŋ/ adj vorhergehend

precinct /'pri:sɪŋkt/ n Bereich m; (traffic-free) Fußgängerzone f; (Amer: district) Bezirk m

precious /'preʃəs/ adj kostbar; (style) preziös •adv [!] **~ little** recht wenig

precipice /'presɪpɪs/ n Steilabfall m

precipitation /prɪsɪpɪ'teɪʃn/ n (rain) Niederschlag m

precis|e /prɪ'saɪs/ adj genau. **~ion** n Genauigkeit f

precocious /prɪ'kəʊʃəs/ adj frühreif

pre|con'ceived /pri:-/ adj vorgefasst. **~con'ception** n vorgefasste Meinung f

predator /'predətə(r)/ n Raubtier nt

predecessor /'pri:dɪsesə(r)/ n Vorgänger(in) m(f)

predicat|e /'predɪkət/ n (Gram) Prädikat nt. **~ive** adj prädikativ

predict /prɪ'dɪkt/ vt voraussagen. **~able** adj voraussehbar; (person) berechenbar. **~ion** n Voraussage f

pre'domin|ant /prɪ-/ adj vorherrschend. **~antly** adv hauptsächlich, überwiegend. **~ate** vi vorherrschen

preen /pri:n/ vt putzen

pre|fab /'pri:fæb/ n Ⓕ [einfaches] Fertighaus nt. **~'fabricated** adj vorgefertigt

preface /'prefɪs/ n Vorwort nt

prefect /'pri:fekt/ n Präfekt m

prefer /prɪ'fɜ:(r)/ vt (pt/pp **preferred**) vorziehen; **I ~ to walk** ich gehe lieber zu Fuß; **I ~ wine** ich trinke lieber Wein

prefera|ble /'prefərəbl/ adj **be ~ble** vorzuziehen sein (**to** dat). **~bly** adv vorzugsweise

preferen|ce /'prefərəns/ n Vorzug m. **~tial** adj bevorzugt

pregnan|cy /'pregnənsɪ/ n Schwangerschaft f. **~t** adj schwanger; (animal) trächtig

prehi'storic /pri:-/ adj prähistorisch

prejudice /'predʒʊdɪs/ n Vorurteil nt; (bias) Voreingenommenheit f •vt einnehmen (**against** gegen). **~d** adj voreingenommen

preliminary /prɪ'lɪmɪnərɪ/ adj Vor-

prelude /'prelju:d/ n Vorspiel nt

premature /'premətjʊə(r)/ adj vorzeitig; (birth) Früh-. **~ly** adv zu früh

pre'meditated /pri:-/ adj vorsätzlich

premier /'premɪə(r)/ adj führend •n (Pol) Premier[minister] m

première /'premɪeə(r)/ n Premiere f

premise /'premɪs/ n Prämisse f, Voraussetzung f

premises /'premɪsɪz/ npl Räumlichkeiten pl; **on the ~** im Haus

premium /'pri:mɪəm/ n Prämie f; **be at a ~** hoch im Kurs stehen

premonition /premə'nɪʃn/ n Vorahnung f

preoccupied /prɪ'ɒkjʊpaɪd/ adj [in Gedanken] beschäftigt

preparation /prepə'reɪʃn/ n Vorbereitung f; (substance) Präparat nt

preparatory /prɪ'pærətrɪ/ adj Vor-

prepare /prɪ'peə(r)/ vt vorbereiten; anrichten (meal) •vi sich vorbereiten (**for** auf + acc); **~d to** bereit zu

preposition /prepə'zɪʃn/ n Präposition f

preposterous /prɪ'pɒstərəs/ adj absurd

prerequisite /pri:'rekwɪzɪt/ n Voraussetzung f

Presbyterian /prezbɪ'tɪərɪən/ adj presbyterianisch •n Presbyterianer(in) m(f)

prescribe /prɪ'skraɪb/ vt vorschreiben; (Med) verschreiben

prescription /prɪ'skrɪpʃn/ n (Med) Rezept nt

presence /'prezns/ n Anwesenheit f, Gegenwart f; **~ of mind** Geistesgegenwart f

present[1] /'preznt/ adj gegenwärtig; **be ~** anwesend sein; (occur) vorkommen •n Gegenwart f; (Gram) Präsens nt; **at ~** zurzeit; **for the ~** vorläufig

present[2] n (gift) Geschenk nt

present[3] /prɪ'zent/ vt überreichen; (show) zeigen; vorlegen (cheque); (introduce) vorstellen; **~ s.o. with sth** jdm etw überreichen. **~able** adj **be ~able** sich zeigen lassen können

presentation /prezn'teɪʃn/ n Überreichung f

presently /'prezntlɪ/ adv nachher; (Amer: now) zurzeit

preservation /prezə'veɪʃn/ n Erhaltung f

preservative /prɪ'zɜ:vətɪv/ n Konservierungsmittel nt

preserve /prɪ'zɜ:v/ vt erhalten; (Culin) konservieren; (bottle) einmachen •n (Hunting & fig) Revier nt; (jam) Konfitüre f

preside /prɪ'zaɪd/ vi den Vorsitz haben (**over** bei)

presidency /'prezɪdənsɪ/ n Präsidentschaft f

president /'prezɪdənt/ n Präsident m; (Amer: chairman) Vorsitzende(r) m/

P

f. **~ial** adj Präsidenten-; (election) Präsidentschafts-

press /pres/ n Presse f •vt/i drücken; drücken auf (+ acc) (button); pressen (flower); (iron) bügeln; (urge) bedrängen; **~ for** drängen auf (+ acc); **be ~ed for time** in Zeitdruck sein. **~ on** vi weitergehen/-fahren; (fig) weitermachen

press: ~ cutting n Zeitungsausschnitt m. **~ing** adj dringend

pressure /'preʃə(r)/ n Druck m. **~-cooker** n Schnellkochtopf m

pressurize /'preʃəraɪz/ vt Druck ausüben auf (+ acc). **~d** adj Druck-

prestig|e /pre'sti:ʒ/ n Prestige nt. **~ious** adj Prestige-

presumably /prɪ'zju:məblɪ/ adv vermutlich

presume /prɪ'zju:m/ vt vermuten

presumpt|ion /prɪ'zʌmpʃn/ n Vermutung f; (boldness) Anmaßung f. **~uous** adj anmaßend

pretence /prɪ'tens/ n Verstellung f; (pretext) Vorwand m

pretend /prɪ'tend/ vt (claim) vorgeben; **~ that** so tun, als ob; **~ to be** sich ausgeben als

P

pretentious /prɪ'tenʃəs/ adj protzig

pretext /'pri:tekst/ n Vorwand m

prett|y /'prɪtɪ/ adj, **~ily** adv hübsch •adv (!: fairly) ziemlich

prevail /prɪ'veɪl/ vi siegen; (custom:) vorherrschen; **~ on s.o. to do sth** jdn dazu bringen, etw zu tun

prevalen|ce /'prevələns/ n Häufigkeit f. **~t** adj vorherrschend

prevent /prɪ'vent/ vt verhindern, verhüten; **~ s.o. [from] doing sth** jdn daran hindern, etw zu tun. **~ion** n Verhinderung f, Verhütung f. **~ive** adj vorbeugend

preview /'pri:vju:/ n Voraufführung f

previous /'pri:vɪəs/ adj vorhergehend; **~ to** vor (+ dat). **~ly** adv vorher, früher

prey /preɪ/ n Beute f; **bird of ~** Raubvogel m

price /praɪs/ n Preis m •vt (Comm) auszeichnen. **~less** adj unschätzbar; (fig) unbezahlbar

prick /prɪk/ n Stich m •vt/i stechen

prickl|e /'prɪkl/ n Stachel m; (thorn) Dorn m. **~y** adj stachelig; (sensation) stechend

pride /praɪd/ n Stolz m; (arrogance) Hochmut m •vt **~ oneself on** stolz sein auf (+ acc)

priest /pri:st/ n Priester m

prim /prɪm/ adj (**primmer, primmest**) prüde

primarily /'praɪmərɪlɪ/ adv hauptsächlich, in erster Linie

primary /'praɪmərɪ/ adj Haupt-. **~ school** n Grundschule f

prime[1] /praɪm/ adj Haupt-; (first-rate) erstklassig

prime[2] vt scharf machen (bomb); grundieren (surface)

Prime Minister /praɪ'mɪnɪstə(r)/ n Premierminister(in) m(f)

primitive /'prɪmɪtɪv/ adj primitiv

primrose /'prɪmrəʊz/ n gelbe Schlüsselblume f

prince /prɪns/ n Prinz m

princess /prɪn'ses/ n Prinzessin f

principal /'prɪnsəpl/ adj Haupt- •n (Sch) Rektor(in) m(f)

principally /'prɪnsəplɪ/ adv hauptsächlich

principle /'prɪnsəpl/ n Prinzip nt, Grundsatz m; **in/on ~** im/aus Prinzip

print /prɪnt/ n Druck m; (Phot) Abzug m; **in ~** gedruckt; (available) erhältlich; **out of ~** vergriffen •vt drucken; (write in capitals) in Druckschrift schreiben; (Computing) ausdrucken; (Phot) abziehen. **~ed matter** n Drucksache f

print|er /'prɪntə(r)/ n Drucker m. **~ing** n Druck m

'printout n (Computing) Ausdruck m

prior /'praɪə(r)/ adj frühere(r,s); **~ to** vor (+ dat)

priority /praɪ'ɒrətɪ/ n Priorität f, Vorrang m

prise /praɪz/ vt ~ **open/up** aufstemmen/hochstemmen

prison /'prɪzn/ n Gefängnis nt. **~er** n Gefangene(r) m/f

privacy /'prɪvəsɪ/ n Privatsphäre f; **have no ~** nie für sich sein

private /'praɪvət/ adj privat; (confidential) vertraulich; (car, secretary, school) Privat- •n (Mil) [einfacher] Soldat m; **in ~** privat; (confidentially) vertraulich

privation /praɪ'veɪʃn/ n Entbehrung f

privilege /'prɪvəlɪdʒ/ n Privileg nt. **~d** adj privilegiert

prize /praɪz/ n Preis m •vt schätzen

pro /prəʊ/ n ⓘ Profi m; **the ~s and cons** das Für und Wider

probability /prɒbə'bɪlətɪ/ n Wahrscheinlichkeit f

proba|ble /'prɒbəbl/ adj, **-bly** adv wahrscheinlich

probation /prə'beɪʃn/ n (Jur) Bewährung f

probe /prəʊb/ n Sonde f; (fig: investigation) Untersuchung f

problem /'prɒbləm/ n Problem nt; (Math) Textaufgabe f. **~atic** adj problematisch

procedure /prə'si:dʒə(r)/ n Verfahren nt

proceed /prə'si:d/ vi gehen; (in vehicle) fahren; (continue) weitergehen/-fahren; (speaking) fortfahren; (act) verfahren

proceedings /prə'si:dɪŋz/ npl Verfahren nt; (Jur) Prozess m

proceeds /'prəʊsi:dz/ npl Erlös m

process /'prəʊses/ n Prozess m; (procedure) Verfahren nt; **in the ~** dabei •vt verarbeiten; (Admin) bearbeiten; (Phot) entwickeln

procession /prə'seʃn/ n Umzug m, Prozession f

processor /'prəʊsesə(r)/ n Prozessor m

proclaim /prə'kleɪm/ vt ausrufen

proclamation /prɒklə'meɪʃn/ n Proklamation f

procure /prə'kjʊə(r)/ vt beschaffen

prod /prɒd/ n Stoß m •vt stoßen

prodigy /'prɒdɪdʒɪ/ n **[infant] ~** Wunderkind nt

produce[1] /'prɒdju:s/ n landwirtschaftliche Erzeugnisse pl

produce[2] /prə'dju:s/ vt erzeugen, produzieren; (manufacture) herstellen; (bring out) hervorholen; (cause) hervorrufen; inszenieren. (play); (Radio, TV) redigieren. **~r** n Erzeuger m, Produzent m; Hersteller m; (Theat) Regisseur m; (Radio, TV) Redakteur(in) m(f)

product /'prɒdʌkt/ n Erzeugnis nt, Produkt nt. **~ion** n Produktion f; (Theat) Inszenierung f

productiv|e /prə'dʌktɪv/ adj produktiv; (land, talks) fruchtbar. **~ity** n Produktivität f

profession /prə'feʃn/ n Beruf m. **~al** adj beruflich; (not amateur) Berufs-; (expert) fachmännisch; (Sport) professionell •n Fachmann m; (Sport) Profi m

professor /prə'fesə(r)/ n Professor m

proficien|cy /prə'fɪʃnsɪ/ n Können nt. **~t** adj **be ~t in** beherrschen

profile /'prəʊfaɪl/ n Profil nt; (character study) Porträt nt

profit /'prɒfɪt/ n Gewinn m, Profit m •vi **~ from** profitieren von. **~able** adj, **-bly** adv gewinnbringend; (fig) nutzbringend

profound /prə'faʊnd/ adj tief

program /'prəʊgræm/ n Programm nt; •vt (pt/pp **programmed**) programmieren

programme /'prəʊgræm/ n Programm nt; (Radio, TV) Sendung f. **~r** n (Computing) Programmierer(in) m(f)

progress[1] /'prəʊgres/ n Vorankommen nt; (fig) Fortschritt m; **in ~** im Gange; **make ~** (fig) Fortschritte machen

progress[2] /prə'gres/ vi

P

vorankommen; (fig) fortschreiten. **~ion** n Folge f; (development) Entwicklung f

progressive /prəˈgresɪv/ adj fortschrittlich. **~ly** adv zunehmend

prohibit /prəˈhɪbɪt/ vt verbieten (**s.o.** jdm). **~ive** adj unerschwinglich

project[1] /ˈprɒdʒekt/ n Projekt nt; (Sch) Arbeit f

project[2] /prəˈdʒekt/ vt projizieren (film); (plan) planen • vi (jut out) vorstehen

projector /prəˈdʒektə(r)/ n Projektor m

prolific /prəˈlɪfɪk/ adj fruchtbar; (fig) produktiv

prologue /ˈprəʊlɒg/ n Prolog m

prolong /prəˈlɒŋ/ vt verlängern

promenade /prɒməˈnɑːd/ n Promenade f • vi spazieren gehen

prominent /ˈprɒmɪnənt/ adj vorstehend; (important) prominent; (conspicuous) auffällig

promiscuous /prəˈmɪskjʊəs/ adj **be ~ous** häufig den Partner wechseln

P

promis|e /ˈprɒmɪs/ n Versprechen nt • vt/i versprechen (**s.o.** jdm). **~ing** adj viel versprechend

promot|e /prəˈməʊt/ vt befördern; (advance) fördern; (publicize) Reklame machen für; **be ~ed** (Sport) aufsteigen. **~ion** n Beförderung f; (Sport) Aufstieg m; (Comm) Reklame f

prompt /prɒmpt/ adj prompt, unverzüglich; (punctual) pünktlich • adv pünktlich • vt/i veranlassen (**to** zu); (Theat) soufflieren (+ dat). **~er** n Souffleur m/Souffleuse f. **~ly** adv prompt

prone /prəʊn/ adj **be** or **lie ~** auf dem Bauch liegen; **be ~ to** neigen zu

pronoun /ˈprəʊnaʊn/ n Fürwort nt, Pronomen nt

pronounce /prəˈnaʊns/ vt aussprechen; (declare) erklären. **~d** adj ausgeprägt; (noticeable) deutlich. **~ment** n Erklärung f

pronunciation /prənʌnsɪˈeɪʃn/ n Aussprache f

proof /pruːf/ n Beweis m; (Typography) Korrekturbogen m. **~-reader** n Korrektor m

prop[1] /prɒp/ n Stütze f • vt (pt/pp **propped**) **~ against** lehnen an (+ acc). **~ up** vt stützen

prop[2] n (Theat, [!]) Requisit nt

propaganda /prɒpəˈgændə/ n Propaganda f

propel /prəˈpel/ vt (pt/pp **propelled**) [an]treiben. **~ler** n Propeller m

proper /ˈprɒpə(r)/ adj richtig; (decent) anständig

property /ˈprɒpətɪ/ n Eigentum nt; (quality) Eigenschaft f; (Theat) Requisit nt; (land) [Grund]besitz m; (house) Haus nt

prophecy /ˈprɒfəsɪ/ n Prophezeiung f

prophesy /ˈprɒfɪsaɪ/ vt (pt/pp **-ied**) prophezeien

prophet /ˈprɒfɪt/ n Prophet m. **~ic** adj prophetisch

proportion /prəˈpɔːʃn/ n Verhältnis nt; (share) Teil m; **~s** pl Proportionen; (dimensions) Maße. **~al** adj proportional

proposal /prəˈpəʊzl/ n Vorschlag m; (of marriage) [Heirats]antrag m

propose /prəˈpəʊz/ vt vorschlagen; (intend) vorhaben; einbringen (motion) • vi einen Heiratsantrag machen

proposition /prɒpəˈzɪʃn/ n Vorschlag m

proprietor /prəˈpraɪətə(r)/ n Inhaber(in) m(f)

propriety /prəˈpraɪətɪ/ n Korrektheit f; (decorum) Anstand m

prose /prəʊz/ n Prosa f

prosecut|e /ˈprɒsɪkjuːt/ vt strafrechtlich verfolgen. **~ion** n strafrechtliche Verfolgung f; **the ~ion** die Anklage. **~or** n **[Public] P~or** Staatsanwalt m

prospect /'prɒspekt/ n Aussicht f

prospect|ive /prə'spektɪv/ adj (future) zukünftig. **~or** n Prospektor m

prospectus /prə'spektəs/ n Prospekt m

prosper /'prɒspə(r)/ vi gedeihen, florieren; (person) Erfolg haben. **~ity** n Wohlstand m

prosperous /'prɒspərəs/ adj wohlhabend

prostitut|e /'prɒstɪtju:t/ n Prostituierte f. **~ion** n Prostitution f

prostrate /'prɒstreɪt/ adj ausgestreckt

protagonist /prəʊ'tægənɪst/ n Kämpfer m; (fig) Protagonist m

protect /prə'tekt/ vt schützen (**from** vor + dat); beschützen (person). **~ion** n Schutz m. **~ive** adj Schutz-; (fig) beschützend. **~or** n Beschützer m

protein /'prəʊti:n/ n Eiweiß nt

protest[1] /'prəʊtest/ n Protest m

protest[2] /prə'test/ vi protestieren

Protestant /'prɒtɪstənt/ adj protestantisch • n Protestant(in) m(f)

protester /prə'testə(r)/ n Protestierende(r) m/f

prototype /'prəʊtə-/ n Prototyp m

protrude /prə'tru:d/ vi [her]vorstehen

proud /praʊd/ adj stolz (**of** auf + acc)

prove /pru:v/ vt beweisen • vi **~to be** sich erweisen als

proverb /'prɒvɜ:b/ n Sprichwort nt

provide /prə'vaɪd/ vt zur Verfügung stellen; spenden (shade); **~ s.o. with sth** jdn mit etw versorgen od versehen • vi **~ for** sorgen für

provided /prə'vaɪdɪd/ conj **~ [that]** vorausgesetzt [dass]

providen|ce /'prɒvɪdəns/ n Vorsehung f. **~tial** adj **be ~tial** ein Glück sein

provinc|e /'prɒvɪns/ n Provinz f; (fig) Bereich m. **~ial** adj provinziell

provision /prə'vɪʒn/ n Versorgung f (of mit); **~s** pl Lebensmittel pl. **~al** adj vorläufig

provocat|ion /prɒvə'keɪʃn/ n Provokation f. **~ive** adj provozierend; (sexually) aufreizend

provoke /prə'vəʊk/ vt provozieren; (cause) hervorrufen

prow /praʊ/ n Bug m

prowl /praʊl/ vi herumschleichen

proximity /prɒk'sɪmətɪ/ n Nähe f

pruden|ce /'pru:dns/ n Umsicht f. **~t** adj umsichtig; (wise) klug

prudish /'pru:dɪʃ/ adj prüde

prune[1] /pru:n/ n Backpflaume f

prune[2] vt beschneiden

pry /praɪ/ vi (pt/pp **pried**) neugierig sein

psalm /sɑ:m/ n Psalm m

psychiatric /saɪkɪ'ætrɪk/ adj psychiatrisch

psychiatr|ist /saɪ'kaɪətrɪst/ n Psychiater(in) m(f). **~y** n Psychiatrie f

psychic /'saɪkɪk/ adj übersinnlich

psycho|a'nalysis /saɪkəʊ-/ n Psychoanalyse f. **~'analyst** n Psychoanalytiker(in) m(f)

psychological /saɪkə'lɒdʒɪkl/ adj psychologisch; (illness) psychisch

psycholog|ist /saɪ'kɒlədʒɪst/ n Psychologe m/ -login f. **~y** n Psychologie f

P.T.O. abbr (**please turn over**) b.w.

pub /pʌb/ n 🅱 Kneipe f

puberty /'pju:bətɪ/ n Pubertät f

public /'pʌblɪk/ adj öffentlich; **make ~** publik machen • n **the ~** die Öffentlichkeit

publican /'pʌblɪkən/ n [Gast]wirt m

publication /pʌblɪ'keɪʃn/ n Veröffentlichung f

public: ~ 'holiday n gesetzlicher Feiertag m. **~ 'house** n [Gast]wirtschaft f

P

publicity /pʌb'lɪsətɪ/ n Publicity f; (advertising) Reklame f

publicize /'pʌblɪsaɪz/ vt Reklame machen für

public: ~ **'school** n Privatschule f; (Amer) staatliche Schule f. **~-'spirited** adj **be ~-spirited** Gemeinsinn haben

publish /'pʌblɪʃ/ vt veröffentlichen. **~er** n Verleger(in) m(f); (firm) Verlag m. **~ing** n Verlagswesen nt

pudding /'pʊdɪŋ/ n Pudding m; (course) Nachtisch m

puddle /'pʌdl/ n Pfütze f

puff /pʌf/ n (of wind) Hauch m; (of smoke) Wölkchen nt •vt blasen, pusten; ~ **out** ausstoßen. •vi keuchen; ~ **at** paffen an (+ dat) (pipe). **~ed** adj (out of breath) aus der Puste. ~ **pastry** n Blätterteig m

pull /pʊl/ n Zug m; (jerk) Ruck m; ([!]: influence) Einfluss m •vt ziehen; ziehen an (+ dat) (rope); ~ **a muscle** sich (dat) einen Muskel zerren; ~ **oneself together** sich zusammennehmen; ~ **one's weight** tüchtig mitarbeiten; ~ **s.o.'s leg** [!] jdn auf den Arm nehmen. ~ **down** vt herunterziehen; (demolish) abreißen. ~ **in** vt hereinziehen •vi (Auto) einscheren. ~ **off** vt abziehen; [!] schaffen. ~ **out** vt herausziehen •vi (Auto) ausscheren. ~ **through** vt durchziehen •vi (recover) durchkommen. ~ **up** vt heraufziehen; ausziehen (plant) •vi (Auto) anhalten

pullover /'pʊləʊvə(r)/ n Pullover m

pulp /pʌlp/ n Brei m; (of fruit) [Frucht]fleisch nt

pulpit /'pʊlpɪt/ n Kanzel f

pulse /pʌls/ n Puls m

pulses /'pʌlsɪz/ npl Hülsenfrüchte pl

pummel /'pʌml/ vt (pt/pp **pummelled**) mit den Fäusten bearbeiten

pump /pʌmp/ n Pumpe f •vt pumpen; [!] aushorchen. ~ **up** vt (inflate) aufpumpen

pumpkin /'pʌmpkɪn/ n Kürbis m

pun /pʌn/ n Wortspiel nt

punch¹ /pʌntʃ/ n Faustschlag m; (device) Locher m •vt boxen; lochen (ticket); stanzen (hole)

punch² n (drink) Bowle f

punctual /'pʌŋktjʊəl/ adj pünktlich. **~ity** n Pünktlichkeit f

punctuat|e /'pʌŋktjʊeɪt/ vt mit Satzzeichen versehen. **~ion** n Interpunktion f

puncture /'pʌŋktʃə(r)/ n Loch nt; (tyre) Reifenpanne f •vt durchstechen

punish /'pʌnɪʃ/ vt bestrafen. **~able** adj strafbar. **~ment** n Strafe f

punt /pʌnt/ n (boat) Stechkahn m

puny /'pju:nɪ/ adj mickerig

pup /pʌp/ n = **puppy**

pupil /'pju:pl/ n Schüler(in) m(f); (of eye) Pupille f

puppet /'pʌpɪt/ n Puppe f; (fig) Marionette f

puppy /'pʌpɪ/ n junger Hund m

purchase /'pɜ:tʃəs/ n Kauf m; (leverage) Hebelkraft f •vt kaufen. **~r** n Käufer m

pure /pjʊə(r)/ adj (**-r, -st**), **-ly** adv rein

purge /pɜ:dʒ/ n (Pol) Säuberungsaktion f •vt reinigen

puri|fication /pjʊərɪfɪ'keɪʃn/ n Reinigung f. **~fy** vt (pt/pp **-ied**) reinigen

puritanical /pjʊərɪ'tænɪkl/ adj puritanisch

purity /'pjʊərɪtɪ/ n Reinheit f

purple /'pɜ:pl/ adj [dunkel]lila

purpose /'pɜ:pəs/ n Zweck m; (intention) Absicht f; (determination) Entschlossenheit f; **on** ~ absichtlich. **~ful** adj entschlossen. **~ly** adv absichtlich

purr /pɜ:(r)/ vi schnurren

purse /pɜ:s/ n Portemonnaie nt; (Amer: handbag) Handtasche f

pursue /pə'sju:/ vt verfolgen; (fig)

nachgehen (+ dat). **~r** n Verfolger(in) m(f)

pursuit /pə'sju:t/ n Verfolgung f; Jagd f; (pastime) Beschäftigung f

pus /pʌs/ n Eiter m

push /pʊʃ/ n Stoß m; **get the ~** ⓘ hinausfliegen •vt/i schieben; (press) drücken; (roughly) stoßen. **~ off** vt hinunterstoßen •vi (ⓘ: leave) abhauen. **~ on** vi (continue) weitergehen/-fahren; (with activity) weitermachen. **~ up** vt hochschieben; hochtreiben (price)

push: ~-button n Druckknopf m. **~-chair** n [Kinder]sportwagen m

pushy /'pʊʃɪ/ adj ⓘ aufdringlich

puss /pʊs/ n, **pussy** n Mieze f

put /pʊt/ vt (pt/pp **put**, pres p **putting**) tun; (place) setzen; (upright) stellen; (flat) legen; (express) ausdrücken; (say) sagen; (estimate) schätzen (**at** auf + acc); **~ aside** or **by** beiseite legen •vi **~ to sea** auslaufen •adj **stay ~** dableiben. **~ away** vt wegräumen. **~ back** vt wieder hinsetzen/-stellen/-legen; zurückstellen (clock). **~ down** vt hinsetzen/-stellen/-legen; (suppress) niederschlagen; (kill) töten; (write) niederschreiben; (attribute) zuschreiben (**to** dat). **~ forward** vt vorbringen; vorstellen (clock). **~ in** vt hineinsetzen/-stellen/-legen; (insert) einstecken; (submit) einreichen •vi **~ in for** beantragen. **~ off** vt ausmachen (light); (postpone) verschieben; **~ s.o. off** jdn abbestellen; (disconcert) jdn aus der Fassung bringen. **~ on** vt anziehen (clothes, brake); sich (dat) aufsetzen (hat); (Culin) aufsetzen; anmachen (light); aufführen (play); annehmen (accent); **~ on weight** zunehmen. **~ out** vt hinaussetzen/-stellen/-legen; ausmachen (fire, light); ausstrecken (hand); (disconcert) aus der Fassung bringen; **~ s.o./oneself out** jdm/sich Umstände machen. **~ through** vt durchstecken; (Teleph) verbinden (**to** mit). **~ up** vt errichten (building); aufschlagen (tent); aufspannen (umbrella); anschlagen (notice); erhöhen (price); unterbringen (guest) •vi (at hotel) absteigen in (+ dat); **~ up with sth** sich (dat) etw bieten lassen

putrid /'pju:trɪd/ faulig

putt /pʌt/ n Putt m

putty /'pʌtɪ/ n Kitt m

puzzl|e /'pʌzl/ n Rätsel nt; (jigsaw) Puzzlespiel nt •vt **it ~es me** es ist mir rätselhaft. **~ing** adj rätselhaft

pyjamas /pə'dʒɑ:məz/ npl Schlafanzug m

pylon /'paɪlən/ n Mast m

pyramid /'pɪrəmɪd/ n Pyramide f

python /'paɪθn/ n Pythonschlange f

Qq

quack /kwæk/ n Quaken nt; (doctor) Quacksalber m •vi quaken

quadrangle /'kwɒdræŋgl/ n Viereck nt; (court) Hof m

quadruped /'kwɒdrʊped/ n Vierfüßer m

quadruple /'kwɒdrʊpl/ adj vierfach •vt vervierfachen •vi sich vervierfachen

quaint /kweɪnt/ adj (**-er, -est**) malerisch; (odd) putzig

quake /kweɪk/ n ⓘ Erdbeben nt •vi beben; (with fear) zittern

qualif|ication /kwɒlɪfɪ'keɪʃn/ n Qualifikation f; (reservation) Einschränkung f. **~ied** adj qualifiziert; (trained) ausgebildet; (limited) bedingt

qualify /ˈkwɒlɪfaɪ/ v (pt/pp **-ied**) •vt qualifizieren; (entitle) berechtigen; (limit) einschränken •vi sich qualifizieren

quality /ˈkwɒlətɪ/ n Qualität f; (characteristic) Eigenschaft f

qualm /kwɑːm/ n Bedenken pl

quantity /ˈkwɒntətɪ/ n Quantität f, Menge f; **in ~** in großen Mengen

quarantine /ˈkwɒrəntiːn/ n Quarantäne f

quarrel /ˈkwɒrl/ n Streit m •vi (pt/pp **quarrelled**) sich streiten. **~some** adj streitsüchtig

quarry¹ /ˈkwɒrɪ/ n (prey) Beute f

quarry² n Steinbruch m

quart /kwɔːt/ n Quart nt

quarter /ˈkwɔːtə(r)/ n Viertel nt; (of year) Vierteljahr nt; (Amer) 25-Cent-Stück nt; **~s** pl Quartier nt; **at [a] ~ to six** um Viertel vor sechs •vt vierteln; (Mil) einquartieren (**on** bei). **~-ˈfinal** n Viertelfinale nt

quarterly /ˈkwɔːtəlɪ/ adj & adv vierteljährlich

quartet /kwɔːˈtet/ n Quartett nt

quartz /kwɔːts/ n Quarz m

quay /kiː/ n Kai m

queasy /ˈkwiːzɪ/ adj **I feel ~** mir ist übel

queen /kwiːn/ n Königin f; (Cards, Chess) Dame f

queer /kwɪə(r)/ adj (**-er, -est**) eigenartig; (dubious) zweifelhaft; (ill) unwohl

quell /kwel/ vt unterdrücken

quench /kwentʃ/ vt löschen

query /ˈkwɪərɪ/ n Frage f; (question mark) Fragezeichen nt •vt (pt/pp **-ied**) infrage stellen; reklamieren (bill)

quest /kwest/ n Suche f (**for** nach)

question /ˈkwestʃn/ n Frage f; (for discussion) Thema nt; **out of the ~** ausgeschlossen; **the person in ~** die fragliche Person •vt infrage stellen; **~ s.o.** jdn ausfragen; (police:) jdn verhören. **~able** adj zweifelhaft. **~ mark** n Fragezeichen nt

questionnaire /kwestʃəˈneə(r)/ n Fragebogen m

queue /kjuː/ n Schlange f •vi **~ [up]** Schlange stehen, sich anstellen (**for** nach)

quibble /ˈkwɪbl/ vi Haarspalterei treiben

quick /kwɪk/ adj (**-er, -est**) schnell; **be ~!** mach schnell! •adv schnell. **~en** vt beschleunigen •vi sich beschleunigen

quick: ~sand n Treibsand m. **~-tempered** adj aufbrausend

quid /kwɪd/ n inv [!] Pfund nt

quiet /ˈkwaɪət/ adj (**-er, -est**) still; (calm) ruhig; (soft) leise; **keep ~ about** [!] nichts sagen von •n Stille f; Ruhe f

quiet|en /ˈkwaɪətn/ vt beruhigen •vi **~en down** ruhig werden. **~ness** n Stille f; Ruhe f

quilt /kwɪlt/ n Steppdecke f. **~ed** adj Stepp-

quintet /kwɪnˈtet/ n Quintett nt

quirk /kwɜːk/ n Eigenart f

quit /kwɪt/ v (pt/pp **quitted** or **quit**) •vt verlassen; (give up) aufgeben; **~ doing sth** aufhören, etw zu tun •vi gehen

quite /kwaɪt/ adv ganz; (really) wirklich; **~ [so]!** genau! **~ a few** ziemlich viele

quits /kwɪts/ adj quitt

quiver /ˈkwɪvə(r)/ vi zittern

quiz /kwɪz/ n Quiz nt •vt (pt/pp **quizzed**) ausfragen. **~zical** adj fragend

quota /ˈkwəʊtə/ n Anteil m; (Comm) Kontingent nt

quotation /kwəʊˈteɪʃn/ n Zitat nt; (price) Kostenvoranschlag m; (of shares) Notierung f. **~ marks** npl Anführungszeichen pl

quote /kwəʊt/ n [!] = **quotation; in ~s** in Anführungszeichen •vt/i zitieren

Rr

rabbi /'ræbaɪ/ n Rabbiner m; (title) Rabbi m

rabbit /'ræbɪt/ n Kaninchen nt

rabid /'ræbɪd/ adj fanatisch; (animal) tollwütig

rabies /'reɪbi:z/ n Tollwut f

race[1] /reɪs/ n Rasse f

race[2] n Rennen nt; (fig) Wettlauf m •vi [am Rennen] teilnehmen; (athlete, horse:) laufen; ([!]: rush) rasen •vt um die Wette laufen mit; an einem Rennen teilnehmen lassen (horse)

race: ~course n Rennbahn f. **~horse** n Rennpferd nt. **~track** n Rennbahn f

racial /'reɪʃl/ adj rassisch; (discrimination) Rassen-

racing /'reɪsɪŋ/ n Rennsport m; (horse-) Pferderennen nt. **~ car** n Rennwagen m. **~ driver** n Rennfahrer m

racis|m /'reɪsɪzm/ n Rassismus m. **~t** adj rassistisch •n Rassist m

rack[1] /ræk/ n Ständer m; (for plates) Gestell nt •vt **~ one's brains** sich (dat) den Kopf zerbrechen

rack[2] n **go to ~ and ruin** verfallen; (fig) herunterkommen

racket /'rækɪt/ n (Sport) Schläger m; (din) Krach m; (swindle) Schwindelgeschäft nt

racy /'reɪsɪ/ adj schwungvoll; (risqué) gewagt

radar /'reɪdɑ:(r)/ n Radar m

radian|ce /'reɪdɪəns/ n Strahlen nt. **~t** adj strahlend

radiat|e /'reɪdɪeɪt/ vt ausstrahlen •vi (heat:) ausgestrahlt werden; (roads:) strahlenförmig ausgehen. **~ion** n Strahlung f

radiator /'reɪdɪeɪtə(r)/ n Heizkörper m; (Auto) Kühler m

radical /'rædɪkl/ adj radikal •n Radikale(r) m/f

radio /'reɪdɪəʊ/ n Radio nt; **by ~** über Funk •vt funken (message)

radio|'active adj radioaktiv. **~ac'tivity** n Radioaktivität f

radish /'rædɪʃ/ n Radieschen nt

radius /'reɪdɪəs/ n (pl **-dii** /-dɪaɪ/) Radius m, Halbmesser m

raffle /'ræfl/ n Tombola f

raft /rɑ:ft/ n Floß nt

rafter /'rɑ:ftə(r)/ n Dachsparren m

rag /ræg/ n Lumpen m; (pej: newspaper) Käseblatt nt

rage /reɪdʒ/ n Wut f; **all the ~** [!] der letzte Schrei •vi rasen

ragged /'rægɪd/ adj zerlumpt; (edge) ausgefranst

raid /reɪd/ n Überfall m; (Mil) Angriff m; (police) Razzia f •vt überfallen; (Mil) angreifen; (police) eine Razzia durchführen in (+ dat); (break in) eindringen in (+ acc). **~er** n Eindringling m; (of bank) Bankräuber m

rail /reɪl/ n Schiene f; (pole) Stange f; (hand~) Handlauf m; (Naut) Reling f; **by ~** mit der Bahn

railings /'reɪlɪŋz/ npl Geländer nt

'railroad n (Amer) = **railway**

'railway n [Eisen]bahn f. **~ station** n Bahnhof m

rain /reɪn/ n Regen m •vi regnen

rain: ~bow n Regenbogen m. **~coat** n Regenmantel m. **~fall** n Niederschlag m

rainy /'reɪnɪ/ adj regnerisch

raise /reɪz/ n (Amer) Lohnerhöhung f •vt erheben; (upright) aufrichten; (make higher) erhöhen; (lift)

r

[hoch]heben; aufziehen (child, animal); aufwerfen (question); aufbringen (money)

raisin /'reɪzn/ n Rosine f

rake /reɪk/ n Harke f, Rechen m •vt harken, rechen

rally /'rælɪ/ n Versammlung f; (Auto) Rallye f; (Tennis) Ballwechsel m •vt sammeln

ram /ræm/ n Schafbock m •vt (pt/pp **rammed**) rammen

rambl|e /'ræmbl/ n Wanderung f •vi wandern; (in speech) irrereden. **~er** n Wanderer m; (rose) Kletterrose f. **~ing** adj weitschweifig; (club) Wander-

ramp /ræmp/ n Rampe f; (Aviat) Gangway f

rampage[1] /'ræmpeɪdʒ/ n **be/go on the ~** randalieren

rampage[2] /ræm'peɪdʒ/ vi randalieren

ramshackle /'ræmʃækl/ adj baufällig

ran /ræn/ see **run**

ranch /rɑːntʃ/ n Ranch f

random /'rændəm/ adj willkürlich; **a ~ sample** eine Stichprobe •n **at ~** aufs Geratewohl; (choose) willkürlich

rang /ræŋ/ see **ring**[2]

range /reɪndʒ/ n Serie f, Reihe f; (Comm) Auswahl f, Angebot nt (**of** an + dat); (of mountains) Kette f; (Mus) Umfang m; (distance) Reichweite f; (for shooting) Schießplatz m; (stove) Kohlenherd m •vi reichen; **~ from ... to** gehen von ... bis. **~r** n Aufseher m

rank /ræŋk/ n (row) Reihe f; (Mil) Rang m; (social position) Stand m; **the ~ and file** die breite Masse •vt/i einstufen; **~ among** zählen zu

ransack /'rænsæk/ vt durchwühlen; (pillage) plündern

ransom /'rænsəm/ n Lösegeld nt; **hold s.o. to ~** Lösegeld für jdn fordern

rape /reɪp/ n Vergewaltigung f •vt vergewaltigen

rapid /'ræpɪd/ adj schnell. **~ity** n Schnelligkeit f

rapist /'reɪpɪst/ n Vergewaltiger m

raptur|e /'ræptʃə(r)/ n Entzücken nt. **~ous** adj begeistert

rare[1] /reə(r)/ adj (**-r, -st**) selten

rare[2] adj (Culin) englisch gebraten

rarefied /'reərɪfaɪd/ adj dünn

rarity /'reərətɪ/ n Seltenheit f

rascal /'rɑːskl/ n Schlingel m

rash[1] /ræʃ/ n (Med) Ausschlag m

rash[2] adj (**-er, -est**) voreilig

rasher /'ræʃə(r)/ n Speckscheibe f

raspberry /'rɑːzbərɪ/ n Himbeere f

rat /ræt/ n Ratte f; ([!]: person) Schuft m; **smell a ~** [!] Lunte riechen

rate /reɪt/ n Rate f; (speed) Tempo nt; (of payment) Satz m; (of exchange) Kurs m; **~s** pl (taxes) ≈ Grundsteuer f; **at any ~** auf jeden Fall; **at this ~** auf diese Weise •vt einschätzen; **~ among** zählen zu •vi **~ as** gelten als

rather /'rɑːðə(r)/ adv lieber; (fairly) ziemlich; **~!** und ob!

rating /'reɪtɪŋ/ n Einschätzung f; (class) Klasse f; (sailor) [einfacher] Matrose m; **~s** pl (Radio, TV) ≈ Einschaltquote f

ratio /'reɪʃɪəʊ/ n Verhältnis nt

ration /'ræʃn/ n Ration f •vt rationieren

rational /'ræʃənl/ adj rational. **~ize** vt/i rationalisieren

rattle /'rætl/ n Rasseln nt; (of windows) Klappern nt; (toy) Klapper f •vi rasseln; klappern •vt rasseln mit

raucous /'rɔːkəs/ adj rau

rave /reɪv/ vi toben; **~ about** schwärmen von

raven /'reɪvn/ n Rabe m

ravenous /'rævənəs/ adj heißhungrig

ravine /rə'viːn/ n Schlucht f

raving /'reɪvɪŋ/ adj **~ mad** [!] total verrückt

ravishing /ˈrævɪʃɪŋ/ adj hinreißend

raw /rɔː/ adj (**-er, -est**) roh; (not processed) Roh-; (skin) wund; (weather) nasskalt; (inexperienced) unerfahren; **get a ~ deal** [!] schlecht wegkommen. **~ maˈterials** npl Rohstoffe pl

ray /reɪ/ n Strahl m

razor /ˈreɪzə(r)/ n Rasierapparat m. **~ blade** n Rasierklinge f

re /riː/ prep betreffs (+ gen)

reach /riːtʃ/ n Reichweite f; (of river) Strecke f; **within/out of ~** in/außer Reichweite •vt erreichen; (arrive at) ankommen in (+ dat); (~ as far as) reichen bis zu; kommen zu (decision, conclusion); (pass) reichen •vi reichen (**to** bis zu); **~ for** greifen nach

reˈact /riːˈækt/ vi reagieren (**to** auf + acc)

reˈaction /rɪ-/ n Reaktion f. **~ary** adj reaktionär

reactor /rɪˈæktə(r)/ n Reaktor m

read /riːd/ vt/i (pt/pp **read** /red/) lesen; (aloud) vorlesen (**to** dat); (Univ) studieren; ablesen (meter). **~ out** vt vorlesen

readable /ˈriːdəbl/ adj lesbar

reader /ˈriːdə(r)/ n Leser(in) m(f); (book) Lesebuch nt

readily /ˈredɪlɪ/ adv bereitwillig; (easily) leicht

reading /ˈriːdɪŋ/ n Lesen nt; (Pol, Relig) Lesung f

reaˈdjust /riː-/ vt neu einstellen •vi sich umstellen (**to** auf + acc)

ready /ˈredɪ/ adj fertig; (willing) bereit; (quick) schnell; **get ~** sich fertig machen; (prepare to) sich bereitmachen

ready: ~-ˈmade adj fertig. **~-to-ˈwear** adj Konfektions-

real /rɪəl/ adj wirklich; (genuine) echt; (actual) eigentlich •adv (Amer, [!]) echt. **~ estate** n Immobilien pl

realis|m /ˈrɪəlɪzm/ n Realismus m. **~t** n Realist m. **~tic** adj, **-ally** adv realistisch

reality /rɪˈælətɪ/ n Wirklichkeit f

realization /rɪəlaɪˈzeɪʃn/ n Erkenntnis f

realize /ˈrɪəlaɪz/ vt einsehen; (become aware) gewahr werden; verwirklichen (hopes, plans); einbringen (price)

really /ˈrɪəlɪ/ adv wirklich; (actually) eigentlich

realm /relm/ n Reich nt

realtor /ˈriːəltə(r)/ n (Amer) Immobilienmakler m

reap /riːp/ vt ernten

reapˈpear /riː-/ vi wiederkommen

rear[1] /rɪə(r)/ adj Hinter-; (Auto) Heck- •n **the ~** der hintere Teil; **from the ~** von hinten

rear[2] vt aufziehen •vi **~ [up]** (horse:) sich aufbäumen

rearˈrange /riː-/ vt umstellen

reason /ˈriːzn/ n Grund m; (good sense) Vernunft f; (ability to think) Verstand m; **within ~** in vernünftigen Grenzen •vi argumentieren; **~ with** vernünftig reden mit. **~able** adj vernünftig; (not expensive) preiswert. **~ably** adv (fairly) ziemlich

reasˈsur|ance /riː-/ n Beruhigung f; Versicherung f. **~e** vt beruhigen; **~e s.o. of sth** jdm etw (gen) versichern

rebel[1] /ˈrebl/ n Rebell m

rebel[2] /rɪˈbel/ vi (pt/pp **rebelled**) rebellieren. **~lion** n Rebellion f. **~lious** adj rebellisch

reˈbound[1] /rɪ-/ vi abprallen

ˈrebound[2] /riː-/ n Rückprall m

reˈbuild /riː-/ vt (pt/pp **-built**) wieder aufbauen

rebuke /rɪˈbjuːk/ n Tadel m •vt tadeln

reˈcall /rɪ-/ n Erinnerung f •vt zurückrufen; abberufen (diplomat); (remember) sich erinnern an (+ acc)

recant /rɪˈkænt/ vi widerrufen

recap /ˈriːkæp/ vt/i [!] = **recapitulate**

recapitulate /riːkəˈpɪtjʊleɪt/ vt/i

r

zusammenfassen; rekapitulieren

re'capture /ri:-/ vt wieder gefangen nehmen (person); wieder einfangen (animal)

reced|e /rɪ'si:d/ vi zurückgehen. **~ing** adj (forehead, chin) fliehend

receipt /rɪ'si:t/ n Quittung f; (receiving) Empfang m; **~s** pl (Comm) Einnahmen pl

receive /rɪ'si:v/ vt erhalten, bekommen; empfangen (guests). **~r** n (Teleph) Hörer m; (of stolen goods) Hehler m

recent /'ri:sənt/ adj kürzlich erfolgte(r,s). **~ly** adv vor kurzem

receptacle /rɪ'septəkl/ n Behälter m

reception /rɪ'sepʃn/ n Empfang m; **~ [desk]** (in hotel) Rezeption f: **~ist** n Empfangsdame f

receptive /rɪ'septɪv/ adj aufnahmefähig; **~ to** empfänglich für

recess /rɪ'ses/ n Nische f; (holiday) Ferien pl

recession /rɪ'seʃn/ n Rezession f

re'charge /ri:-/ vt [wieder] aufladen

recipe /'resəpɪ/ n Rezept nt

recipient /rɪ'sɪpɪənt/ n Empfänger m

recital /rɪ'saɪtl/ n (of poetry, songs) Vortrag m; (on piano) Konzert nt

recite /rɪ'saɪt/ vt aufsagen; (before audience) vortragen

reckless /'reklɪs/ adj leichtsinnig; (careless) rücksichtslos. **~ness** n Leichtsinn m; Rücksichtslosigkeit f

reckon /'rekən/ vt rechnen; (consider) glauben • vi **~ on/with** rechnen mit

re'claim /rɪ-/ vt zurückfordern; zurückgewinnen (land)

reclin|e /rɪ'klaɪn/ vi liegen. **~ing seat** n Liegesitz m

recluse /rɪ'klu:s/ n Einsiedler(in) m(f)

recognition /rekəg'nɪʃn/ n Erkennen nt; (acknowledgement) Anerkennung f; **in ~** als Anerkennung (**of** gen)

recognize /'rekəgnaɪz/ vt erkennen; (know again) wieder erkennen; (acknowledge) anerkennen

re'coil /rɪ-/ vi zurückschnellen; (in fear) zurückschrecken

recollect /rekə'lekt/ vt sich erinnern an (+ acc). **~ion** n Erinnerung f

recommend /rekə'mend/ vt empfehlen. **~ation** n Empfehlung f

recon|cile /'rekənsaɪl/ vt versöhnen; **~cile oneself to** sich abfinden mit. **~ciliation** n Versöhnung f

reconnaissance /rɪ'kɒnɪsns/ n (Mil) Aufklärung f

reconnoitre /rekə'nɔɪtə(r)/ vi (pres p **-tring**) auf Erkundung ausgehen

recon'sider /ri:-/ vt sich (dat) noch einmal überlegen

recon'struct /ri:-/ vt wieder aufbauen; rekonstruieren (crime)

record[1] /rɪ'kɔ:d/ vt aufzeichnen; (register) registrieren; (on tape) aufnehmen

record[2] /'rekɔ:d/ n Aufzeichnung f; (Jur) Protokoll nt; (Mus) [Schall]platte f; (Sport) Rekord m; **~s** pl Unterlagen pl; **off the ~** inoffiziell; **have a [criminal] ~** vorbestraft sein

recorder /rɪ'kɔ:də(r)/ n (Mus) Blockflöte f

recording /rɪ'kɔ:dɪŋ/ n Aufnahme f

re-'count[1] /ri:-/ vt nachzählen

're-count[2] /ri:-/ n (Pol) Nachzählung f

recover /rɪ'kʌvə(r)/ vt zurückbekommen • vi sich erholen. **~y** n Wiedererlangung f; (of health) Erholung f

recreation /rekrɪ'eɪʃn/ n Erholung f; (hobby) Hobby nt. **~al** adj Freizeit-; **be ~al** erholsam sein

recruit /rɪ'kru:t/ n (Mil) Rekrut m; **new ~** (member) neues Mitglied nt;

(worker) neuer Mitarbeiter m •vt rekrutieren; anwerben (staff). **~ment** n Rekrutierung f; Anwerbung f

rectang|le /'rektæŋgl/ n Rechteck nt. **~ular** adj rechteckig

rectify /'rektɪfaɪ/ vt (pt/pp **-ied**) berichtigen

rector /'rektə(r)/ n Pfarrer m; (Univ) Rektor m. **~y** n Pfarrhaus nt

recur /rɪ'kɜː(r)/ vi (pt/pp **recurred**) sich wiederholen; (illness:) wiederkehren

recurren|ce /rɪ'kʌrəns/ n Wiederkehr f. **~t** adj wiederkehrend

recycle /riː'saɪkl/ vt wieder verwerten

red /red/ adj (**redder, reddest**) rot •n Rot nt

redd|en /'redn/ vt röten •vi rot werden. **~ish** adj rötlich

re'decorate /riː-/ vt renovieren; (paint) neu streichen; (wallpaper) neu tapezieren

redeem /rɪ'diːm/ vt einlösen; (Relig) erlösen

redemption /rɪ'dempʃn/ n Erlösung f

red: ~-haired adj rothaarig. **~-'handed** adj **catch s.o. ~-handed** jdn auf frischer Tat ertappen. **~ 'herring** n falsche Spur f. **~-hot** adj glühend heiß. **~ 'light** n (Auto) rote Ampel f. **~ness** n Röte f

re'do /riː-/ vt (pt **-did**, pp **-done**) noch einmal machen

re'double /riː-/ vt verdoppeln

red 'tape n [!] Bürokratie f

reduc|e /rɪ'djuːs/ vt verringern, vermindern; (in size) verkleinern; ermäßigen (costs); herabsetzen (price, goods); (Culin) einkochen lassen. **~tion** n Verringerung f; (in price) Ermäßigung f; (in size) Verkleinerung f

redundan|cy /rɪ'dʌndənsɪ/ n Beschäftigungslosigkeit f. **~t** adj überflüssig; **make ~t** entlassen; **be made ~t** beschäftigungslos werden

reed /riːd/ n [Schilf]rohr nt; **~s** pl Schilf nt

reef /riːf/ n Riff nt

reek /riːk/ vi riechen (**of** nach)

reel /riːl/ n Rolle f, Spule f •vi (stagger) taumeln •vt **~ off** (fig) herunterrasseln

refectory /rɪ'fektərɪ/ n Refektorium nt; (Univ) Mensa f

refer /rɪ'fɜː(r)/ v (pt/pp **referred**) •vt verweisen (**to** an + acc); übergeben, weiterleiten (matter) (**to** an + acc) •vi **~ to** sich beziehen auf (+ acc); (mention) erwähnen; (concern) betreffen; (consult) sich wenden an (+ acc); nachschlagen in (+ dat) (book); **are you ~ring to me**? meinen Sie mich?

referee /refə'riː/ n Schiedsrichter m; (Boxing) Ringrichter m; (for job) Referenz f •vt/i (pt/pp **refereed**) Schiedsrichter/Ringrichter sein (bei)

reference /'refərəns/ n Erwähnung f; (in book) Verweis m; (for job) Referenz f; **with ~ to** in Bezug auf (+ acc); **make [a] ~ to** erwähnen. **~ book** n Nachschlagewerk nt

referendum /refə'rendəm/ n Volksabstimmung f

re'fill[1] /riː-/ vt nachfüllen

'refill[2] /riː-/ n (for pen) Ersatzmine f

refine /rɪ'faɪn/ vt raffinieren. **~d** adj fein, vornehm. **~ment** n Vornehmheit f; (Techn) Verfeinerung f. **~ry** n Raffinerie f

reflect /rɪ'flekt/ vt reflektieren; (mirror:) [wider]spiegeln; **be ~ed in** sich spiegeln in (+ dat) •vi nachdenken (**on** über + acc). **~ion** n Reflexion f; (image) Spiegelbild nt; **on ~ion** nach nochmaliger Überlegung. **~or** n Rückstrahler m

reflex /'riːfleks/ n Reflex m

reflexive /rɪ'fleksɪv/ adj reflexiv

reform /rɪ'fɔːm/ n Reform f •vt

r

reformieren •vi sich bessern

refrain[1] /rɪ'freɪn/ n Refrain m

refrain[2] vi ~ **from doing sth** etw nicht tun

refresh /rɪ'freʃ/ vt erfrischen. **~ing** adj erfrischend. **~ments** npl Erfrischungen pl

refrigerat|e /rɪ'frɪdʒəreɪt/ vt kühlen. **~or** n Kühlschrank m

re'fuel /riː-/ vt/i (pt/pp **-fuelled**) auftanken

refuge /'refjuːdʒ/ n Zuflucht f; **take ~** Zuflucht nehmen

refugee /refjʊ'dʒiː/ n Flüchtling m

'refund[1] /riː-/ **get a ~** sein Geld zurückbekommen

re'fund[2] /rɪ-/ vt zurückerstatten

refusal /rɪ'fjuːzl/ n (see **refuse**[1]) Ablehnung f; Weigerung f

refuse[1] /rɪ'fjuːz/ vt ablehnen; (not grant) verweigern; ~ **to do sth** sich weigern, etw zu tun •vi ablehnen; sich weigern

refuse[2] /'refjuːs/ n Müll m

refute /rɪ'fjuːt/ vt widerlegen

re'gain /rɪ-/ vt wiedergewinnen

regal /'riːgl/ adj königlich

regard /rɪ'gaːd/ n (heed) Rücksicht f; (respect) Achtung f; **~s** pl Grüße pl; **with ~ to** in Bezug auf (+ acc) •vt ansehen, betrachten (**as** als). **~ing** prep bezüglich (+ gen). **~less** adv ohne Rücksicht (**of** auf + acc)

regatta /rɪ'gætə/ n Regatta f

regime /reɪ'ʒiːm/ n Regime nt

regiment /'redʒɪmənt/ n Regiment nt. **~al** adj Regiments-

region /'riːdʒən/ n Region f; **in the ~ of** (fig) ungefähr. **~al** adj regional

register /'redʒɪstə(r)/ n Register nt; (Sch) Anwesenheitsliste f •vt registrieren; (report) anmelden; einschreiben (letter); aufgeben (luggage) •vi (report) sich anmelden

registrar /redʒɪ'straː(r)/ n Standesbeamte(r) m

registration /redʒɪ'streɪʃn/ n Registrierung f; Anmeldung f. **~ number** n Autonummer f

registry office /'redʒɪstrɪ-/ n Standesamt nt

regret /rɪ'gret/ n Bedauern nt •vt (pt/pp **regretted**) bedauern. **~fully** adv mit Bedauern

regrettab|le /rɪ'gretəbl/ adj bedauerlich. **~ly** adv bedauerlicherweise

regular /'regjʊlə(r)/ adj regelmäßig; (usual) üblich •n (in pub) Stammgast m; (in shop) Stammkunde m. **~ity** n Regelmäßigkeit f

regulat|e /'regjʊleɪt/ vt regulieren. **~ion** n (rule) Vorschrift f

rehears|al /rɪ'hɜːsl/ n (Theat) Probe f. **~e** vt proben

reign /reɪn/ n Herrschaft f •vi herrschen, regieren

rein /reɪn/ n Zügel m

reindeer /'reɪndɪə(r)/ n inv Rentier nt

reinforce /riːɪn'fɔːs/ vt verstärken. **~ment** n Verstärkung f; **send ~ments** Verstärkung schicken

reiterate /riː'ɪtəreɪt/ vt wiederholen

reject /rɪ'dʒekt/ vt ablehnen. **~ion** n Ablehnung f

rejects /'riːdʒekts/ npl (Comm) Ausschussware f

rejoic|e /rɪ'dʒɔɪs/ vi (literary) sich freuen. **~ing** n Freude f

re'join /rɪ-/ vt sich wieder anschließen (+ dat); wieder beitreten (+ dat) (club, party)

rejuvenate /rɪ'dʒuːvəneɪt/ vt verjüngen

relapse /rɪ'læps/ n Rückfall m •vi einen Rückfall erleiden

relate /rɪ'leɪt/ vt (tell) erzählen; (connect) verbinden

relation /rɪ'leɪʃn/ n Beziehung f; (person) Verwandte(r) m/f. **~ship** n Beziehung f; (link) Verbindung f; (blood tie) Verwandtschaft f; (affair) Verhältnis nt

relative /'relətɪv/ n Verwandte(r) m/f •adj relativ; (Gram) Relativ-. **~ly** adv relativ, verhältnismäßig

relax /rɪ'læks/ vt lockern, entspannen •vi sich lockern, sich entspannen. **~ation** n Entspannung f. **~ing** adj entspannend

relay[1] /ri:'leɪ/ vt (pt/pp **-layed**) weitergeben; (Radio, TV) übertragen

relay[2] /'ri:leɪ/ n **~ [race]** n Staffel f

release /rɪ'li:s/ n Freilassung f, Entlassung f; (Techn) Auslöser m •vt freilassen; (let go of) loslassen; (Techn) auslösen; veröffentlichen (information)

relent /rɪ'lent/ vi nachgeben. **~less** adj erbarmungslos; (unceasing) unaufhörlich

relevan|ce /'reləvəns/ n Relevanz f. **~t** adj relevant (**to** für)

reliab|ility /rɪlaɪə'bɪlətɪ/ n Zuverlässigkeit f. **~le** adj zuverlässig

relian|ce /rɪ'laɪəns/ n Abhängigkeit f (**on** von). **~t** adj angewiesen (**on** auf + acc)

relic /'relɪk/ n Überbleibsel nt; (Relig) Reliquie f

relief /rɪ'li:f/ n Erleichterung f; (assistance) Hilfe f; (replacement) Ablösung f; (Art) Relief nt

relieve /rɪ'li:v/ vt erleichtern; (take over from) ablösen; **~ of** entlasten von

religion /rɪ'lɪdʒən/ n Religion f

religious /rɪ'lɪdʒəs/ adj religiös

relinquish /rɪ'lɪŋkwɪʃ/ vt loslassen; (give up) aufgeben

relish /'relɪʃ/ n Genuss m; (Culin) Würze f •vt genießen

reluctan|ce /rɪ'lʌktəns/ n Widerstreben nt. **~t** adj widerstrebend; **be ~t** zögern (**to** zu). **~tly** adv ungern, widerstrebend

rely /rɪ'laɪ/ vi (pt/pp **-ied**) **~ on** sich verlassen auf (+ acc); (be dependent on) angewiesen sein auf (+ acc)

remain /rɪ'meɪn/ vi bleiben; (be left) übrig bleiben. **~der** n Rest m. **~ing** adj restlich. **~s** npl Reste pl; **[mortal] ~s** [sterbliche] Überreste pl

remand /rɪ'mɑ:nd/ n **on ~** in Untersuchungshaft •vt **~ in custody** in Untersuchungshaft schicken

remark /rɪ'mɑ:k/ n Bemerkung f •vt bemerken. **~able** adj, **-bly** adv bemerkenswert

re|marry /ri:-/ vi wieder heiraten

remedy /'remədɪ/ n [Heil]mittel nt (**for** gegen); (fig) Abhilfe f •vt (pt/pp **-ied**) abhelfen (+ dat); beheben (fault)

rememb|er /rɪ'membə(r)/ vt sich erinnern an (+ acc); **~er to do sth** daran denken, etw zu tun •vi sich erinnern

remind /rɪ'maɪnd/ vt erinnern (**of** an + acc). **~er** n Andenken nt; (letter, warning) Mahnung f

reminisce /remɪ'nɪs/ vi sich seinen Erinnerungen hingeben. **~nces** npl Erinnerungen pl. **~nt** adj **be ~nt of** erinnern an (+ acc)

remnant /'remnənt/ n Rest m

remorse /rɪ'mɔ:s/ n Reue f. **~ful** adj reumütig. **~less** adj unerbittlich

remote /rɪ'məʊt/ adj fern; (isolated) abgelegen; (slight) gering. **~ con'trol** n Fernsteuerung f; (for TV) Fernbedienung f

remotely /rɪ'məʊtlɪ/ adv entfernt; **not ~** nicht im Entferntesten

re'movable /rɪ-/ adj abnehmbar

removal /rɪ'mu:vl/ n Entfernung f; (from house) Umzug m. **~ van** n Möbelwagen m

remove /rɪ'mu:v/ vt entfernen; (take off) abnehmen; (take out) herausnehmen

render /'rendə(r)/ vt machen; erweisen (service); (translate) wiedergeben; (Mus) vortragen

renegade /'renɪgeɪd/ n Abtrünnige(r) m/f

renew /rɪ'nju:/ vt erneuern;

verlängern (contract). **~al** n Erneuerung f; Verlängerung f

renounce /rɪ'naʊns/ vt verzichten auf (+ acc)

renovat|e /'renəveɪt/ vt renovieren. **~ion** n Renovierung f

renown /rɪ'naʊn/ n Ruf m. **~ed** adj berühmt

rent /rent/ n Miete f •vt mieten; (hire) leihen; **~ [out]** vermieten; verleihen. **~al** n Mietgebühr f; Leihgebühr f

renunciation /rɪnʌnsɪ'eɪʃn/ n Verzicht m

re'open /ri:-/ vt/i wieder aufmachen

re'organize /ri:-/ vt reorganisieren

rep /rep/ n [!] Vertreter m

repair /rɪ'peə(r)/ n Reparatur f; **in good/bad ~** in gutem/schlechtem Zustand •vt reparieren

repatriat|e /ri:'pætrɪeɪt/ vt repatriieren

re'pay /ri:-/ vt (pt/pp **-paid**) zurückzahlen; **~ s.o. for sth** jdm etw zurückzahlen. **~ment** n Rückzahlung f

repeal /rɪ'pi:l/ n Aufhebung f •vt aufheben

repeat /rɪ'pi:t/ n Wiederholung f •vt/i wiederholen; **~ after me** sprechen Sie mir nach. **~ed** adj wiederholt

r

repel /rɪ'pel/ vt (pt/pp **repelled**) abwehren; (fig) abstoßen. **~lent** adj abstoßend

repent /rɪ'pent/ vi Reue zeigen. **~ance** n Reue f. **~ant** adj reuig

repercussions /ri:pə'kʌʃnz/ npl Auswirkungen pl

repertoire /'repətwɑ:(r)/, **repertory** n Repertoire nt

repetit|ion /reprɪ'tɪʃn/ n Wiederholung f. **~ive** adj eintönig

re'place /rɪ-/ vt zurücktun; (take the place of) ersetzen; (exchange) austauschen. **~ment** n Ersatz m

'replay /ri:-/ n (Sport) Wiederholungsspiel nt; **[action] ~** Wiederholung f

replenish /rɪ'plenɪʃ/ vt auffüllen (stocks); (refill) nachfüllen

replica /'replɪkə/ n Nachbildung f

reply /rɪ'plaɪ/ n Antwort f (**to** auf + acc) •vt/i (pt/pp **replied**) antworten

report /rɪ'pɔ:t/ n Bericht m; (Sch) Zeugnis nt; (rumour) Gerücht nt; (of gun) Knall m •vt berichten; (notify) melden; **~ s.o. to the police** jdn anzeigen •vi berichten (**on** über + acc); (present oneself) sich melden (**to** bei). **~er** n Reporter(in) m(f)

reprehensible /reprɪ'hensəbl/ adj tadelnswert

represent /reprɪ'zent/ vt darstellen; (act for) vertreten, repräsentieren. **~ation** n Darstellung f

representative /reprɪ'zentətɪv/ adj repräsentativ (**of** für) •n Bevollmächtigte(r) m/(f); (Comm) Vertreter(in) m(f); (Amer, Politics) Abgeordnete(r) m/f

repress /rɪ'pres/ vt unterdrücken. **~ion** n Unterdrückung f. **~ive** adj repressiv

reprieve /rɪ'pri:v/ n Begnadigung f; (fig) Gnadenfrist f •vt begnadigen

reprimand /'reprɪmɑ:nd/ n Tadel m •vt tadeln

'reprint¹ /ri:-/ n Nachdruck m

re'print² /ri:-/ vt neu auflegen

reprisal /rɪ'praɪzl/ n Vergeltungsmaßnahme f

reproach /rɪ'prəʊtʃ/ n Vorwurf m •vt Vorwürfe pl machen (+ dat). **~ful** adj vorwurfsvoll

repro'duc|e /ri:-/ vt wiedergeben, reproduzieren •vi sich fortpflanzen. **~tion** n Reproduktion f; (Biology) Fortpflanzung f

reptile /'reptaɪl/ n Reptil nt

republic /rɪ'pʌblɪk/ n Republik f. **~an** adj republikanisch •n Republikaner(in) m(f)

repugnan|ce /rɪ'pʌgnəns/ n Widerwille m. **~t** adj widerlich

repuls|ion /rɪ'pʌlʃn/ n Widerwille m. **~ive** adj abstoßend, widerlich

reputable /'repjʊtəbl/ adj (firm) von gutem Ruf; (respectable) anständig

reputation /repjʊ'teɪʃn/ n Ruf m

request /rɪ'kwest/ n Bitte f •vt bitten

require /rɪ'kwaɪə(r)/ vt (need) brauchen; (demand) erfordern; **be ~d to do sth** etw tun müssen. **~ment** n Bedürfnis nt; (condition) Erfordernis nt

re'sale /ri:-/ n Weiterverkauf m

rescue /'reskju:/ n Rettung f •vt retten. **~r** n Retter m

research /rɪ'sɜ:tʃ/ n Forschung f •vt erforschen; (in media) recherchieren. **~er** n Forscher m; (for media) Rechercheur m

resem|blance /rɪ'zembləns/ n Ähnlichkeit f. **~ble** vt ähneln (+ dat)

resent /rɪ'zent/ vt übel nehmen; einen Groll hegen gegen (person). **~ful** adj verbittert. **~ment** n Groll m

reservation /rezə'veɪʃn/ n Reservierung f; (doubt) Vorbehalt m; (enclosure) Reservat nt

reserve /rɪ'zɜ:v/ n Reserve f; (for animals) Reservat nt; (Sport) Reservespieler(in) m(f) •vt reservieren; (client:) reservieren lassen; (keep) aufheben; sich (dat) vorbehalten (right). **~d** adj reserviert

reservoir /'rezəvwɑ:(r)/ n Reservoir nt

re'shuffle /ri:-/ n (Pol) Umbildung f •vt (Pol) umbilden

residence /'rezɪdəns/ n Wohnsitz m; (official) Residenz f; (stay) Aufenthalt m

resident /'rezɪdənt/ adj ansässig (**in** in + dat); (housekeeper, nurse) im Haus wohnend •n Bewohner(in) m(f); (of street) Anwohner m. **~ial** adj Wohn-

residue /'rezɪdju:/ n Rest m; (Chemistry) Rückstand m

resign /rɪ'zaɪn/ vt **~ oneself to** sich abfinden mit •vi kündigen; (from public office) zurücktreten. **~ation** n Resignation f; (from job) Kündigung f; Rücktritt m. **~ed** adj resigniert

resilient /rɪ'zɪlɪənt/ adj federnd; (fig) widerstandsfähig

resin /'rezɪn/ n Harz nt

resist /rɪ'zɪst/ vt/i sich widersetzen (+ dat), (fig) widerstehen (+ dat). **~ance** n Widerstand m. **~ant** adj widerstandsfähig

resolut|e /'rezəlu:t/ adj entschlossen. **~ion** n Entschlossenheit f; (intention) Vorsatz m; (Pol) Resolution f

resolve /rɪ'zɒlv/ n Entschlossenheit f; (decision) Beschluss m •vt beschließen; (solve) lösen

resort /rɪ'zɔ:t/ n (place) Urlaubsort m; **as a last ~** wenn alles andere fehlschlägt •vi **~ to** (fig) greifen zu

resound /rɪ'zaʊnd/ vi widerhallen

resource /rɪ'sɔ:s/ n **~s** pl Ressourcen pl. **~ful** adj findig

respect /rɪ'spekt/ n Respekt m, Achtung f (**for** vor + dat); (aspect) Hinsicht f; **with ~ to** in Bezug auf (+ acc) •vt respektieren, achten

respect|able /rɪ'spektəbl/ adj, **-bly** adv ehrbar; (decent) anständig; (considerable) ansehnlich. **~ful** adj respektvoll

respective /rɪ'spektɪv/ adj jeweilig. **~ly** adv beziehungsweise

respiration /respə'reɪʃn/ n Atmung f

respite /'respaɪt/ n [Ruhe]pause f; (delay) Aufschub m

respond /rɪ'spɒnd/ vi antworten; (react) reagieren (**to** auf + acc)

response /rɪ'spɒns/ n Antwort f; Reaktion f

responsibility /rɪspɒnsɪ'bɪlətɪ/ n Verantwortung f; (duty) Verpflichtung f

responsib|le /rɪ'spɒnsəbl/ adj verantwortlich; (trustworthy) verantwortungsvoll. **~ly** adv verantwortungsbewusst

rest[1] /rest/ n Ruhe f; (holiday)

Erholung f; (interval & Mus) Pause f; **have a ~** eine Pause machen; (rest) sich ausruhen •vt ausruhen; (lean) lehnen (**on** an/auf + acc) •vi ruhen; (have a rest) sich ausruhen

rest[2] n **the ~** der Rest; (people) die Übrigen pl •vi **it ~s with you** es ist an Ihnen (**to** zu)

restaurant /'rest(ə)rɒnt/ n Restaurant nt, Gaststätte f

restful /'restfl/ adj erholsam

restive /'restɪv/ adj unruhig

restless /'restlɪs/ adj unruhig

restoration /restə'reɪʃn/ n (of building) Restaurierung f

restore /rɪ'stɔ:(r)/ vt wiederherstellen; restaurieren (building)

restrain /rɪ'streɪn/ vt zurückhalten; **~ oneself** sich beherrschen. **~ed** adj zurückhaltend. **~t** n Zurückhaltung f

restrict /rɪ'strɪkt/ vt einschränken; **~ to** beschränken auf (+ acc). **~ion** n Einschränkung f; Beschränkung f. **~ive** adj einschränkend

'rest room n (Amer) Toilette f

result /rɪ'zʌlt/ n Ergebnis nt, Resultat nt; (consequence) Folge f; **as a ~** als Folge (**of** gen) •vi sich ergeben (**from** aus); **~ in** enden in (+ dat); (lead to) führen zu

r

resume /rɪ'zju:m/ vt wieder aufnehmen •vi wieder beginnen

résumé /'rezʊmeɪ/ n Zusammenfassung f

resumption /rɪ'zʌmpʃn/ n Wiederaufnahme f

resurrect /rezə'rekt/ vt (fig) wieder beleben. **~ion** n **the R~ion** (Relig) die Auferstehung

resuscitat|e /rɪ'sʌsɪteɪt/ vt wieder beleben. **~ion** n Wiederbelebung f

retail /'ri:teɪl/ n Einzelhandel m •adj Einzelhandels- •adv im Einzelhandel •vt im Einzelhandel verkaufen •vi **~ at** im Einzelhandel kosten. **~er** n Einzelhändler m

retain /rɪ'teɪn/ vt behalten

retaliat|e /rɪ'tælɪeɪt/ vi zurückschlagen. **~ion** n Vergeltung f; **in ~ion** als Vergeltung

retarded /rɪ'tɑ:dɪd/ adj zurückgeblieben

reticen|ce /'retɪsns/ n Zurückhaltung f. **~t** adj zurückhaltend

retina /'retɪnə/ n Netzhaut f

retinue /'retɪnju:/ n Gefolge nt

retire /rɪ'taɪə(r)/ vi in den Ruhestand treten; (withdraw) sich zurückziehen. **~d** adj im Ruhestand. **~ment** n Ruhestand m

retiring /rɪ'taɪərɪŋ/ adj zurückhaltend

retort /rɪ'tɔ:t/ n scharfe Erwiderung f; (Chemistry) Retorte f •vt scharf erwidern

re'trace /rɪ-/ vt **~ one's steps** denselben Weg zurückgehen

re'train /ri:-/ vt umschulen •vi umgeschult werden

retreat /rɪ'tri:t/ n Rückzug m; (place) Zufluchtsort m •vi sich zurückziehen

re'trial /ri:-/ n Wiederaufnahmeverfahren nt

retrieve /rɪ'tri:v/ vt zurückholen; (from wreckage) bergen; (Computing) wieder auffinden

retrograde /'retrəgreɪd/ adj rückschrittlich

retrospect /'retrəspekt/ n **in ~** rückblickend. **~ive** adj rückwirkend; (looking back) rückblickend

return /rɪ'tɜ:n/ n Rückkehr f; (giving back) Rückgabe f; (Comm) Ertrag m; (ticket) Rückfahrkarte f; (Aviat) Rückflugschein m; **by ~ [of post]** postwendend; **in ~** dafür; **in ~ for** für; **many happy ~s!** herzlichen Glückwunsch zum Geburtstag! •vt zurückgehen/-fahren; (come back) zurückkommen •vt zurückgeben; (put back) zurückstellen/-legen;

(send back) zurückschicken

return ticket n Rückfahrkarte f; (Aviat) Rückflugschein m

reunion /ri:'ju:nɪən/ n Wiedervereinigung f; (social gathering) Treffen nt

reunite /ri:ju:'naɪt/ vt wieder vereinigen

re'use vt wieder verwenden

rev /rev/ n (Auto, [!]) Umdrehung f •vt/i ~ **[up]** den Motor auf Touren bringen

reveal /rɪ'vi:l/ vt zum Vorschein bringen; (fig) enthüllen. **~ing** adj (fig) aufschlussreich

revel /'revl/ vi (pt/pp **revelled**) **~ in sth** etw genießen

revelation /revə'leɪʃn/ n Offenbarung f, Enthüllung f

revenge /rɪ'vendʒ/ n Rache f; (fig & Sport) Revanche f •vt rächen

revenue /'revənju:/ n [Staats]einnahmen pl

revere /rɪ'vɪə(r)/ vt verehren. **~nce** n Ehrfurcht f

Reverend /'revərənd/ adj **the ~ X** Pfarrer X; (Catholic) Hochwürden X

reverent /'revərənt/ adj ehrfürchtig

reversal /rɪ'vɜ:sl/ n Umkehrung f

reverse /rɪ'vɜ:s/ adj umgekehrt •n Gegenteil nt; (back) Rückseite f; (Auto) Rückwärtsgang m •vt umkehren; (Auto) zurücksetzen •vi zurücksetzen

revert /rɪ'vɜ:t/ vi **~ to** zurückfallen an (+ acc)

review /rɪ'vju:/ n Rückblick m (**of** auf + acc); (re-examination) Überprüfung f; (Mil) Truppenschau f; (of book, play) Kritik f, Rezension f •vt zurückblicken auf (+ acc); überprüfen (situation); rezensieren (book, play). **~er** n Kritiker m, Rezensent m

revis|e /rɪ'vaɪz/ vt revidieren; (for exam) wiederholen. **~ion** n Revision f; Wiederholung f

revival /rɪ'vaɪvl/ n Wiederbelebung f

revive /rɪ'vaɪv/ vt wieder beleben; (fig) wieder aufleben lassen •vi wieder aufleben

revolt /rɪ'vəʊlt/ n Aufstand m •vi rebellieren •vt anwidern. **~ing** adj widerlich, eklig

revolution /revə'lu:ʃn/ n Revolution f; (Auto) Umdrehung f. **~ary** adj revolutionär. **~ize** vt revolutionieren

revolve /rɪ'vɒlv/ vi sich drehen; **~ around** kreisen um

revolv|er /rɪ'vɒlvə(r)/ n Revolver m. **~ing** adj Dreh-

revue /rɪ'vju:/ n Revue f; (satirical) Kabarett nt

revulsion /rɪ'vʌlʃn/ n Abscheu m

reward /rɪ'wɔ:d/ n Belohnung f •vt belohnen. **~ing** adj lohnend

re'write /ri:-/ vt (pt **rewrote**, pp **rewritten**) noch einmal [neu] schreiben; (alter) umschreiben

rhetoric /'retərɪk/ n Rhetorik f. **~al** adj rhetorisch

rheumatism /'ru:mətɪzm/ n Rheumatismus m, Rheuma nt

Rhine /raɪn/ n Rhein m

rhinoceros /raɪ'nɒsərəs/ n Nashorn nt, Rhinozeros nt

rhubarb /'ru:bɑ:b/ n Rhabarber m

rhyme /raɪm/ n Reim m •vt reimen •vi sich reimen

rhythm /'riðm/ n Rhythmus m. **~ic[al]** adj, **-ally** adv rhythmisch

rib /rɪb/ n Rippe f

ribbon /'rɪbən/ n Band nt; (for typewriter) Farbband nt

rice /raɪs/ n Reis m

rich /rɪtʃ/ adj (**-er, -est**) reich; (food) gehaltvoll; (heavy) schwer •n **the ~** pl die Reichen; **~es** pl Reichtum m

ricochet /'rɪkəʃeɪ/ vi abprallen

rid /rɪd/ vt (pt/pp **rid**, pres p **ridding**) befreien (**of** von); **get ~ of** loswerden

riddance /'rɪdns/ n **good ~!** auf

Nimmerwiedersehen!

ridden /'rɪdn/ see **ride**

riddle /'rɪdl/ n Rätsel nt

riddled /'rɪdld/ adj ~ **with** durchlöchert mit

ride /raɪd/ n Ritt m; (in vehicle) Fahrt f; **take s.o. for a ~** ⊡ jdn reinlegen • v (pt **rode**, pp **ridden**) • vt reiten (horse); fahren mit (bicycle) • vi reiten; (in vehicle) fahren. **~r** n Reiter(in) m(f); (on bicycle) Fahrer(in) m(f)

ridge /rɪdʒ/ n Erhebung f; (on roof) First m; (of mountain) Grat m, Kamm m

ridicule /'rɪdɪkju:l/ n Spott m • vt verspotten, spotten über (+ acc)

ridiculous /rɪ'dɪkjʊləs/ adj lächerlich

riding /'raɪdɪŋ/ n Reiten nt • attrib Reit-

riff-raff /'rɪfræf/ n Gesindel nt

rifle /'raɪfl/ n Gewehr nt • vt plündern; ~ **through** durchwühlen

rift /rɪft/ n Spalt m; (fig) Riss m

rig /rɪg/ n Ölbohrturm m; (at sea) Bohrinsel f • vt (pt/pp **rigged**) ~ **out** ausrüsten; ~ **up** aufbauen

right /raɪt/ adj richtig; (not left) rechte(r,s); **be ~** (person:) Recht haben; (clock:) richtig gehen; **put ~** wieder in Ordnung bringen; (fig) richtig stellen; **that's ~!** das stimmt! • adv richtig; (directly) direkt; (completely) ganz; (not left) rechts; (go) nach rechts; ~ **away** sofort • n Recht nt; (not left) rechte Seite f; **on the ~** rechts; **from/to the ~** von/nach rechts; **be in the ~** Recht haben; **by ~s** eigentlich; **the R~** (Pol) die Rechte. ~ **angle** n rechter Winkel m

rightful /'raɪtfl/ adj rechtmäßig

right-'handed adj rechtshändig

rightly /'raɪtlɪ/ adv mit Recht

right-'wing adj (Pol) rechte(r,s)

rigid /'rɪdʒɪd/ adj starr; (strict) streng. **~ity** n Starrheit f; Strenge f

rigorous /'rɪgərəs/ adj streng

rigour /'rɪgə(r)/ n Strenge f

rim /rɪm/ n Rand m; (of wheel) Felge f

rind /raɪnd/ n (on fruit) Schale f; (on cheese) Rinde f; (on bacon) Schwarte f

ring[1] /rɪŋ/ n Ring m; (for circus) Manege f; **stand in a ~** im Kreis stehen • vt umringen

ring[2] n Klingeln nt; **give s.o. a ~** (Teleph) jdn anrufen • v (pt **rang**, pp **rung**) • vt läuten; ~ **[up]** (Teleph) anrufen • vi (bells:) läuten; (telephone:) klingeln. ~ **back** vt/i (Teleph) zurückrufen

ring: ~leader n Rädelsführer m. ~ **road** n Umgehungsstraße f

rink /rɪŋk/ n Eisbahn f

rinse /rɪns/ n Spülung f; (hair colour) Tönung f • vt spülen

riot /'raɪət/ n Aufruhr m; **~s** pl Unruhen pl; **run ~** randalieren • vi randalieren. **~er** n Randalierer m. **~ous** adj aufrührerisch; (boisterous) wild

rip /rɪp/ n Riss m • vt/i (pt/pp **ripped**) zerreißen; ~ **open** aufreißen. ~ **off** vt ⊡ neppen

ripe /raɪp/ adj (**-r, -st**) reif

ripen /'raɪpn/ vi reifen • vt reifen lassen

ripeness /'raɪpnɪs/ n Reife f

'rip-off n ⊡ Nepp m

ripple /'rɪpl/ n kleine Welle f

rise /raɪz/ n Anstieg m; (fig) Aufstieg m; (increase) Zunahme f; (in wages) Lohnerhöhung f; (in salary) Gehaltserhöhung f; **give ~ to** Anlass geben zu • vi (pt **rose**, pp **risen**) steigen; (ground:) ansteigen; (sun, dough:) aufgehen; (river:) entspringen; (get up) aufstehen; (fig) aufsteigen (**to** zu). **~r** n **early ~r** Frühaufsteher m

rising /'raɪzɪŋ/ adj steigend; (sun) aufgehend • n (revolt) Aufstand m

risk /rɪsk/ n Risiko nt; **at one's own ~** auf eigene Gefahr • vt riskieren

risky /'rɪskɪ/ adj riskant

rite /raɪt/ n Ritus m

ritual /ˈrɪtjʊəl/ adj rituell •n Ritual nt

rival /ˈraɪvl/ adj rivalisierend •n Rivale m/Rivalin f. **~ry** n Rivalität f; (Comm) Konkurrenzkampf m

river /ˈrɪvə(r)/ n Fluss m

rivet /ˈrɪvɪt/ n Niete f •vt [ver]nieten; **~ed by** (fig) gefesselt von

road /rəʊd/ n Straße f; (fig) Weg m

road: ~-map n Straßenkarte f. **~ safety** n Verkehrssicherheit f. **~side** n Straßenrand m. **~way** n Fahrbahn f. **~-works** npl Straßenarbeiten pl. **~worthy** adj verkehrssicher

roam /rəʊm/ vi wandern

roar /rɔː(r)/ n Gebrüll nt; **~s of laughter** schallendes Gelächter nt •vi brüllen; (with laughter) schallend lachen. **~ing** adj (fire) prasselnd; **do a ~ing trade** [!] ein Bombengeschäft machen

roast /rəʊst/ adj gebraten, Brat-; **~ beef/pork** Rinder-/Schweinebraten m •n Braten m •vt/i braten; rösten (coffee, chestnuts)

rob /rɒb/ vt (pt/pp **robbed**) berauben (**of** gen); ausrauben (bank). **~ber** n Räuber m. **~bery** n Raub m

robe /rəʊb/ n Robe f; (Amer: bathrobe) Bademantel m

robin /ˈrɒbɪn/ n Rotkehlchen nt

robot /ˈrəʊbɒt/ n Roboter m

robust /rəʊˈbʌst/ adj robust

rock¹ /rɒk/ n Fels m; **on the ~s** (ship) aufgelaufen; (marriage) kaputt; (drink) mit Eis

rock² vt/i schaukeln

rock³ n (Mus) Rock m

rockery /ˈrɒkərɪ/ n Steingarten m

rocket /ˈrɒkɪt/ n Rakete f

rocking: ~-chair n Schaukelstuhl m. **~-horse** n Schaukelpferd nt

rocky /ˈrɒkɪ/ adj felsig; (unsteady) wackelig

rod /rɒd/ n Stab m; (stick) Rute f; (for fishing) Angel[rute] f

rode /rəʊd/ see **ride**

rodent /ˈrəʊdnt/ n Nagetier nt

rogue /rəʊg/ n Gauner m

role /rəʊl/ n Rolle f

roll /rəʊl/ n Rolle f; (bread) Brötchen nt; (list) Liste f; (of drum) Wirbel m •vi rollen; **be ~ing in money** [!] Geld wie Heu haben •vt rollen; walzen (lawn); ausrollen (pastry). **~ over** vi sich auf die andere Seite rollen. **~ up** vt aufrollen; hochkrempeln (sleeves) •vi [!] auftauchen

roller /ˈrəʊlə(r)/ n Rolle f; (lawn, road) Walze f; (hair) Lockenwickler m. **~ blind** n Rollo nt. **R~blades®** npl Rollerblades® mpl. **~-coaster** n Berg-und-Talbahn f. **~-skate** n Rollschuh m

ˈrolling-pin n Teigrolle f

Roman /ˈrəʊmən/ adj römisch •n Römer(in) m(f)

romance /rəˈmæns/ n Romantik f; (love-affair) Romanze f; (book) Liebesgeschichte f

Romania /rəʊˈmeɪnɪə/ n Rumänien nt. **~n** adj rumänisch •n Rumäne m/-nin f

romantic /rəʊˈmæntɪk/ adj, **-ally** adv romantisch. **~ism** n Romantik f

Rome /rəʊm/ n Rom nt

romp /rɒmp/ vi [herum]tollen

roof /ruːf/ n Dach nt; (of mouth) Gaumen m •vt **~ [over]** überdachen. **~-top** n Dach nt

rook /rʊk/ n Saatkrähe f; (Chess) Turm m

room /ruːm/ n Zimmer nt; (for functions) Saal m; (space) Platz m. **~y** adj geräumig

roost /ruːst/ n Hühnerstange f

root¹ /ruːt/ n Wurzel f; **take ~** anwachsen •vi Wurzeln schlagen. **~ out** vt (fig) ausrotten

root² vi **~ about** wühlen; **~ for s.o.** [!] für jdn sein

rope /rəʊp/ n Seil nt; **know the ~s**

r

[!] sich auskennen. ~ **in** vt [!] einspannen

rose¹ /rəʊz/ n Rose f; (of watering-can) Brause f

rose² see **rise**

rostrum /ˈrɒstrəm/ n Podium nt

rosy /ˈrəʊzɪ/ adj rosig

rot /rɒt/ n Fäulnis f; ([!]: nonsense) Quatsch m •vi (pt/pp **rotted**) [ver]faulen

rota /ˈrəʊtə/ n Dienstplan m

rotary /ˈrəʊtərɪ/ adj Dreh-; (Techn) Rotations-

rotat|e /rəʊˈteɪt/ vt drehen •vi sich drehen; (Techn) rotieren. **~ion** n Drehung f; **in ~ion** im Wechsel

rote /rəʊt/ n **by ~** auswendig

rotten /ˈrɒtn/ adj faul; [!] mies; (person) fies

rough /rʌf/ adj (**-er, -est**) rau; (uneven) uneben; (coarse, not gentle) grob; (brutal) roh; (turbulent) stürmisch; (approximate) ungefähr •adv **sleep ~** im Freien übernachten •vt **~ it** primitiv leben. **~ out** vt im Groben entwerfen

roughage /ˈrʌfɪdʒ/ n Ballaststoffe pl

rough ˈdraft n grober Entwurf m

rough|ly /ˈrʌflɪ/ adv (see **rough**) rau; grob; roh; ungefähr. **~ness** n Rauheit f

ˈrough paper n Konzeptpapier nt

round /raʊnd/ adj (**-er, -est**) rund •n Runde f; (slice) Scheibe f; **do one's ~s** seine Runde machen •prep um (+ acc); **~ the clock** rund um die Uhr •adv **all ~** ringsherum; **ask s.o. ~** jdn einladen •vt biegen um (corner). **~ off** vt abrunden. **~ up** vt aufrunden; zusammentreiben (animals); festnehmen (criminals)

roundabout /ˈraʊndəbaʊt/ adj **~ route** Umweg m •n Karussell nt; (for traffic) Kreisverkehr m

round ˈtrip n Rundreise f

rous|e /raʊz/ vt wecken; (fig) erregen. **~ing** adj mitreißend

route /ruːt/ n Route f; (of bus) Linie f

routine /ruːˈtiːn/ adj routinemäßig •n Routine f; (Theat) Nummer f

row¹ /rəʊ/ n (line) Reihe f

row² vt/i rudern

row³ /raʊ/ n [!] Krach m •vi [!] sich streiten

rowdy /ˈraʊdɪ/ adj laut

rowing boat /ˈrəʊɪŋ-/ n Ruderboot nt

royal /rɔɪəl/ adj königlich

royalt|y /ˈrɔɪəltɪ/ n Königtum nt; (persons) Mitglieder pl der königlichen Familie; **-ies** pl (payments) Tantiemen pl

RSI abbr (**repetitive strain injury**) chronisches Überlastungssyndrom nt

rub /rʌb/ vt (pt/pp **rubbed**) reiben; (polish) polieren; **don't ~ it in** [!] reib es mir nicht unter die Nase. **~ off** vt abreiben •vi abgehen. **~ out** vt ausradieren

rubber /ˈrʌbə(r)/ n Gummi m; (eraser) Radiergummi m. **~ band** n Gummiband nt

rubbish /ˈrʌbɪʃ/ n Abfall m, Müll m; ([!]: nonsense) Quatsch m; ([!]: junk) Plunder m. **~ bin** n Abfalleimer m. **~ dump** n Abfallhaufen m; (official) Müllhalde f

rubble /ˈrʌbl/ n Trümmer pl

ruby /ˈruːbɪ/ n Rubin m

rudder /ˈrʌdə(r)/ n [Steuer]ruder nt

rude /ruːd/ adj (**-r, -st**) unhöflich; (improper) unanständig. **~ness** n Unhöflichkeit f

rudimentary /ruːdɪˈmentərɪ/ adj elementar; (Biology) rudimentär

ruffian /ˈrʌfɪən/ n Rüpel m

ruffle /ˈrʌfl/ vt zerzausen

rug /rʌg/ n Vorleger m, [kleiner] Teppich m; (blanket) Decke f

rugged /ˈrʌgɪd/ adj (coastline) zerklüftet

ruin /ˈruːɪn/ n Ruine f; (fig) Ruin m •vt ruinieren

rule /ru:l/ n Regel f; (control) Herrschaft f; (government) Regierung f; (for measuring) Lineal nt; **as a ~** in der Regel •vt regieren, herrschen über (+ acc); (fig) beherrschen; (decide) entscheiden; ziehen (line) •vi regieren, herrschen. **~ out** vt ausschließen

ruled /ru:ld/ adj (paper) liniert

ruler /'ru:lə(r)/ n Herrscher(in) m(f); (measure) Lineal nt

ruling /'ru:lɪŋ/ adj herrschend; (factor) entscheidend; (Pol) regierend •n Entscheidung f

rum /rʌm/ n Rum m

rumble /'rʌmbl/ n Grollen nt •vi grollen; (stomach:) knurren

rummage /'rʌmɪdʒ/ vi wühlen; **~ through** durchwühlen

rumour /'ru:mə(r)/ n Gerücht nt •vt **it is ~ed that** es geht das Gerücht, dass

rump /rʌmp/ n Hinterteil nt. **~ steak** n Rumpsteak nt

run /rʌn/ n Lauf m; (journey) Fahrt f; (series) Serie f, Reihe f; (Theat) Laufzeit f; (Skiing) Abfahrt f; (enclosure) Auslauf m; (Amer: ladder) Laufmasche f; **~ of bad luck** Pechsträhne f; **be on the ~** flüchtig sein; **in the long ~** auf lange Sicht •v (pt **ran**, pp **run**, pres p **running**) •vi laufen; (flow) fließen; (eyes:) tränen; (bus:) verkehren; (butter, ink:) zerfließen; (colours:) [ab]färben; (in election) kandidieren •vt laufen lassen; einlaufen lassen (bath); (manage) führen, leiten; (drive) fahren; eingehen (risk); (Journalism) bringen (story); **~ one's hand over sth** mit der Hand über etw (acc) fahren. **~ away** vi weglaufen. **~ down** vi hinunter-/herunterlaufen; (clockwork:) ablaufen; (stocks:) sich verringern •vt (run over) überfahren; (reduce) verringern; ([!]: criticize) heruntermachen. **~ in** vi hinein-/hereinlaufen. **~ off** vi weglaufen •vt abziehen (copies). **~ out** vi hinaus-/herauslaufen; (supplies, money:) ausgehen; **I've ~ out of sugar** ich habe keinen Zucker mehr. **~ over** vt überfahren. **~ up** vi hinauf-/herauflaufen; (towards) hinlaufen •vt machen (debts); auflaufen lassen (bill); (sew) schnell nähen

'runaway n Ausreißer m

run-'down adj (area) verkommen

rung¹ /rʌŋ/ n (of ladder) Sprosse f

rung² see **ring²**

runner /'rʌnə(r)/ n Läufer m; (Bot) Ausläufer m; (on sledge) Kufe f. **~ bean** n Stangenbohne f. **~-up** n Zweite(r) m/f

running /'rʌnɪŋ/ adj laufend; (water) fließend; **four times ~** viermal nacheinander •n Laufen nt; (management) Führung f, Leitung f; **be/not be in the ~** eine/keine Chance haben

runny /'rʌnɪ/ adj flüssig

run: ~-up n (Sport) Anlauf m; (to election) Zeit f vor der Wahl. **~way** n Start- und Landebahn f

rupture /'rʌptʃə(r)/ n Bruch m •vt/i brechen

rural /'rʊərəl/ adj ländlich

ruse /ru:z/ n List f

rush¹ /rʌʃ/ n (Bot) Binse f

rush² n Hetze f; **in a ~** in Eile •vi sich hetzen; (run) rasen; (water:) rauschen •vt hetzen, drängen. **~-hour** n Hauptverkehrszeit f, Stoßzeit f

Russia /'rʌʃə/ n Russland nt. **~n** adj russisch •n Russe m/Russin f; (Lang) Russisch nt

rust /rʌst/ n Rost m •vi rosten

rustle /'rʌsl/ vi rascheln •vt rascheln mit; (Amer) stehlen (cattle). **~ up** vt [!] improvisieren

'rustproof adj rostfrei

rusty /'rʌstɪ/ adj rostig

rut /rʌt/ n Furche f

ruthless /'ru:θlɪs/ adj rücksichtslos. **~ness** n Rücksichtslosigkeit f

rye /raɪ/ n Roggen m

Ss

sabbath /'sæbəθ/ n Sabbat m

sabot|age /'sæbətɑ:ʒ/ n Sabotage f • vt sabotieren

sachet /'sæʃeɪ/ n Beutel m; (scented) Kissen nt

sack n Sack m; **get the ~** [!] rausgeschmissen werden • vt [!] rausschmeißen

sacred /'seɪkrɪd/ adj heilig

sacrifice /'sækrɪfaɪs/ n Opfer nt • vt opfern

sacrilege /'sækrɪlɪdʒ/ n Sakrileg nt

sad /sæd/ adj (**sadder, saddest**) traurig: (loss, death) schmerzlich. **~den** vt traurig machen

saddle /'sædl/ n Sattel m • vt satteln; **~ s.o. with sth** [!] jdm etw aufhalsen

sadist /'seɪdɪst/ n Sadist m. **~ic** adj, **-ally** adv sadistisch

sad|ly /'sædlɪ/ adv traurig; (unfortunately) leider. **~ness** n Traurigkeit f

safe /seɪf/ adj (**-r, -st**) sicher; (journey) gut; (not dangerous) ungefährlich; **~ and sound** gesund und wohlbehalten • n Safe m. **~guard** n Schutz m • vt schützen. **~ly** adv sicher; (arrive) gut

safety /'seɪftɪ/ n Sicherheit f. **~-belt** n Sicherheitsgurt m. **~-pin** n Sicherheitsnadel f. **~-valve** n [Sicherheits]ventil nt

sag /sæg/ vi (pt/pp **sagged**) durchhängen

saga /'sɑ:gə/ n Saga f; (fig) Geschichte f

said /sed/ see **say**

sail /seɪl/ n Segel nt; (trip) Segelfahrt f • vi segeln; (on liner) fahren; (leave) abfahren (**for** nach) • vt segeln mit

sailing /'seɪlɪŋ/ n Segelsport m. **~-boat** n Segelboot nt. **~-ship** n Segelschiff nt

sailor /'seɪlə(r)/ n Seemann m; (in navy) Matrose m

saint /seɪnt/ n Heilige(r) m/f. **~ly** adj heilig

sake /seɪk/ n **for the ~ of ...** um ... (gen) willen; **for my/your ~** um meinet-/deinetwillen

salad /'sæləd/ n Salat m. **~-dressing** n Salatsoße f

salary /'sælərɪ/ n Gehalt nt

sale /seɪl/ n Verkauf m; (event) Basar m; (at reduced prices) Schlussverkauf m; **for ~** zu verkaufen

sales|man n Verkäufer m. **~woman** n Verkäuferin f

saliva /sə'laɪvə/ n Speichel m

salmon /'sæmən/ n Lachs m

saloon /sə'lu:n/ n Salon m; (Auto) Limousine f; (Amer: bar) Wirtschaft f

salt /sɔ:lt/ n Salz nt • adj salzig; (water, meat) Salz- • vt salzen; (cure) pökeln; streuen (road). **~-cellar** n Salzfass nt. **~ 'water** n Salzwasser nt. **~y** adj salzig

salute /sə'lu:t/ n (Mil) Gruß m • vt/i (Mil) grüßen

salvage /'sælvɪdʒ/ n (Naut) Bergung f • vt bergen

salvation /sæl'veɪʃn/ n Rettung f; (Relig) Heil nt

same /seɪm/ adj & pron **the ~** der/die/das gleiche; (pl) die gleichen; (identical) der-/die-/dasselbe; (pl) dieselben • adv **the ~** gleich; **all the ~** trotzdem

sample /'sɑ:mpl/ n Probe f; (Comm) Muster nt • vt probieren; kosten (food)

sanatorium /sænə'tɔ:rɪəm/ n Sanatorium nt

S

sanction /'sæŋkʃn/ n Sanktion f •vt sanktionieren

sanctuary /'sæŋktjʊərɪ/ n (Relig) Heiligtum nt; (refuge) Zuflucht f; (for wildlife) Tierschutzgebiet nt

sand /sænd/ n Sand m •vt ~ **[down]** [ab]schmirgeln

sandal /'sændl/ n Sandale f

sand: ~bank n Sandbank f. **~paper** n Sandpapier nt. **~-pit** n Sandkasten m

sandwich /'sænwɪdʒ/ n; Sandwich m •vt **~ed between** eingeklemmt zwischen

sandy /'sændɪ/ adj sandig; (beach, soil) Sand-; (hair) rotblond

sane /seɪn/ adj (**-r, -st**) geistig normal; (sensible) vernünftig

sang /sæŋ/ see **sing**

sanitary /'sænɪtərɪ/ adj hygienisch; (system) sanitär. ~ **napkin** n (Amer), ~ **towel** n [Damen]binde f

sanitation /sænɪ'teɪʃn/ n Kanalisation und Abfallbeseitigung pl

sanity /'sænətɪ/ n [gesunder] Verstand m

sank /sæŋk/ see **sink**

sap /sæp/ n (Bot) Saft m •vt (pt/pp **sapped**) schwächen

sarcas|m /'sɑ:kæzm/ n Sarkasmus m. **~tic** adj, **-ally** adv sarkastisch

sardine /sɑ:'di:n/ n Sardine f

sash /sæʃ/ n Schärpe f

sat /sæt/ see **sit**

satchel /'sætʃl/ n Ranzen m

satellite /'sætəlaɪt/ n Satellit m. **~television** n Satellitenfernsehen nt

satin /'sætɪn/ n Satin m

satire /'sætaɪə(r)/ n Satire f

satirical /sə'tɪrɪkl/ adj satirisch

satirist /'sætərɪst/ n Satiriker(in) m(f)

satisfaction /sætɪs'fækʃn/ n Befriedigung f; to **my** ~ zu meiner Zufriedenheit

satisfactory /sætɪs'fæktərɪ/ adj, **-ily** adv zufrieden stellend

satisf|y /'sætɪsfaɪ/ vt (pp/pp **-fied**) befriedigen; zufrieden stellen (customer); (convince) überzeugen; **be ~ied** zufrieden sein. **~ying** adj befriedigend; (meal) sättigend

satphone /'sætfəʊn/ n Satellitentelefon nt

saturate /'sætʃəreɪt/ vt durchtränken; (Chemistry & fig) sättigen

Saturday /'sætədeɪ/ n Samstag m

sauce /sɔ:s/ n Soße f; (cheek) Frechheit f. **~pan** n Kochtopf m

saucer /'sɔ:sə(r)/ n Untertasse f

saucy /'sɔ:ʃɪ/ adj frech

Saudi Arabia /saʊdɪə'reɪbɪə/ n Saudi-Arabien n

sauna /'sɔ:nə/ n Sauna f

saunter /'sɔ:ntə(r)/ vi schlendern

sausage /'sɒsɪdʒ/ n Wurst f

savage /'sævɪdʒ/ adj wild; (fierce) scharf; (brutal) brutal •n Wilde(r) m/f. **~ry** n Brutalität f

save /seɪv/ n (Sport) Abwehr f •vt retten (**from** vor + dat); (keep) aufheben; (not waste) sparen; (collect) sammeln; (avoid) ersparen; (Sport) verhindern (goal) •vi ~ **[up]** sparen

saver /'seɪvə(r)/ n Sparer m

saving /'seɪvɪŋ/ n (see **save**) Rettung f; Sparen nt; Ersparnis f; **~s** pl (money) Ersparnisse pl

S

savour /'seɪvə(r)/ n Geschmack m •vt auskosten. **~y** adj würzig

saw[1] /sɔ:/ see **see**[1]

saw[2] n Säge f •vt/i (pt **sawed**, pp **sawn** or **sawed**) sägen

saxophone /'sæksəfəʊn/ n Saxophon nt

say /seɪ/ n Mitspracherecht nt; **have one's** ~ seine Meinung sagen •vt/i (pt/pp **said**) sagen; sprechen (prayer); **that is to** ~ das heißt; **that goes without ~ing** das versteht sich von selbst. **~ing** n Redensart f

scab /skæb/ n Schorf m; (pej) Streikbrecher m

scaffolding /ˈskæfəldɪŋ/ n Gerüst nt

scald /skɔːld/ vt verbrühen

scale[1] /skeɪl/ n (of fish) Schuppe f

scale[2] n Skala f; (Mus) Tonleiter f; (ratio) Maßstab m •vt (climb) erklettern. **~ down** vt verkleinern

scales /skeɪlz/ npl (for weighing) Waage f

scalp /skælp/ n Kopfhaut f

scamper /ˈskæmpə(r)/ vi huschen

scan /skæn/ n (Med) Szintigramm nt •v (pt/pp **scanned**) •vt absuchen; (quickly) flüchtig ansehen; (Med) szintigraphisch untersuchen

scandal /ˈskændl/ n Skandal m; (gossip) Skandalgeschichten pl. **~ize** vt schockieren. **~ous** adj skandalös

Scandinavia /skændɪˈneɪvɪə/ n Skandinavien nt. **~n** adj skandinavisch •n Skandinavier(in) m(f)

scanner /ˈskænə(r)/ n Scanner m

scanty /ˈskæntɪ/ adj, **-ily** adv spärlich; (clothing) knapp

scapegoat /ˈskeɪp-/ n Sündenbock m

scar /skɑː(r)/ n Narbe f

scarc|e /skeəs/ adj (**-r, -st**) knapp; **make oneself ~e** [!] sich aus dem Staub machen. **~ely** adv kaum. **~ity** n Knappheit f

scare /skeə(r)/ n Schreck m; (panic) [allgemeine] Panik f •vt Angst machen (+ dat); **be ~d** Angst haben (**of** vor + dat)

scarf /skɑːf/ n (pl **scarves**) Schal m; (square) Tuch nt

scarlet /ˈskɑːlət/ adj scharlachrot

scary /ˈskeərɪ/ adj unheimlich

scathing /ˈskeɪðɪŋ/ adj bissig

scatter /ˈskætə(r)/ vt verstreuen; (disperse) zerstreuen •vi sich zerstreuen. **~ed** adj verstreut; (showers) vereinzelt

scatty /ˈskætɪ/ adj [!] verrückt

scene /siːn/ n Szene f; (sight) Anblick m; (place of event) Schauplatz m; **behind the ~s** hinter den Kulissen

scenery /ˈsiːnərɪ/ n Landschaft f; (Theat) Szenerie f

scenic /ˈsiːnɪk/ adj landschaftlich schön

scent /sent/ n Duft m; (trail) Fährte f; (perfume) Parfüm nt. **~ed** adj parfümiert

sceptic|al /ˈskeptɪkl/ adj skeptisch. **~ism** n Skepsis f

schedule /ˈʃedjuːl/ n Programm nt; (of work) Zeitplan m; (timetable) Fahrplan m; **behind ~** im Rückstand; **according to ~** planmäßig •vt planen

scheme /skiːm/ n Programm nt; (plan) Plan m; (plot) Komplott nt •vi Ränke schmieden

schizophrenic /skɪtsəˈfrenɪk/ adj schizophren

scholar /ˈskɒlə(r)/ n Gelehrte(r) m/f. **~ly** adj gelehrt. **~ship** n Gelehrtheit f; (grant) Stipendium nt

school /skuːl/ n Schule f; (Univ) Fakultät f •vt schulen

school: ~boy n Schüler m. **~girl** n Schülerin f. **~ing** n Schulbildung f. **~master** n Lehrer m. **~mistress** n Lehrerin f. **~-teacher** n Lehrer(in) m(f)

scien|ce /ˈsaɪəns/ n Wissenschaft f. **~tific** adj wissenschaftlich. **~tist** n Wissenschaftler(in) m(f)

scissors /ˈsɪzəz/ npl Schere f; **a pair of ~** eine Schere

scoff[1] /skɒf/ vi **~ at** spotten über (+ acc)

scoff[2] vt [!] verschlingen

scold /skəʊld/ vt ausschimpfen

scoop /skuːp/ n Schaufel f; (Culin) Portionierer m; (story) Exklusivmeldung f •vt **~ out** aushöhlen; (remove) auslöffeln

scooter /ˈskuːtə(r)/ n Roller m

scope /skəʊp/ n Bereich m; (opportunity) Möglichkeiten pl

scorch /skɔ:tʃ/ vt versengen. **~ing** adj glühend heiß

score /skɔ:(r)/ n [Spiel]stand m; (individual) Punktzahl f; (Mus) Partitur f; (Cinema) Filmmusik f; **on that ~** was das betrifft •vt erzielen; schießen (goal); (cut) einritzen •vi Punkte erzielen; (Sport) ein Tor schießen; (keep score) Punkte zählen. **~r** n Punktezähler m; (of goals) Torschütze m

scorn /skɔ:n/ n Verachtung f •vt verachten. **~ful** adj verächtlich

Scot /skɒt/ n Schotte m/Schottin f

Scotch /skɒtʃ/ adj schottisch •n (whisky) Scotch m

Scot|land /'skɒtlənd/ n Schottland nt. **~s, ~tish** adj schottisch

scoundrel /'skaʊndrl/ n Schurke m

scour /'skaʊə(r)/ vt (search) absuchen; (clean) scheuern

scout /skaʊt/ n (Mil) Kundschafter m; **[Boy] S~** Pfadfinder m

scowl /skaʊl/ n böser Gesichtsausdruck m •vi ein böses Gesicht machen

scram /skræm/ vi [!] abhauen

scramble /'skræmbl/ n Gerangel nt •vi klettern; **~ for** sich drängen nach. **~d 'egg[s]** n[pl] Rührei nt

scrap[1] /skræp/ n ([!]: fight) Rauferei f •vi sich raufen

scrap[2] n Stückchen nt; (metal) Schrott m; **~s** pl Reste; **not a ~** kein bisschen •vt (pt/pp **scrapped**) aufgeben

'scrapbook n Sammelalbum nt

scrape /skreɪp/ vt schaben; (clean) abkratzen; (damage) [ver]schrammen. **~ through** vi gerade noch durchkommen. **~ together** vt zusammenkriegen

scrappy /'skræpɪ/ adj lückenhaft

'scrapyard n Schrottplatz m

scratch /skrætʃ/ n Kratzer m; **start from ~** von vorne anfangen; **not be up to ~** zu wünschen übrig lassen •vt/i kratzen; (damage) zerkratzen

scrawl /skrɔ:l/ n Gekrakel nt •vt/i krakeln

scream /skri:m/ n Schrei m •vt/i schreien

screech /skri:tʃ/ n Kreischen nt •vt/i kreischen

screen /skri:n/ n Schirm m; (Cinema) Leinwand f; (TV) Bildschirm m •vt schützen; (conceal) verdecken; vorführen (film); (examine) überprüfen; (Med) untersuchen

screw /skru:/ n Schraube f •vt schrauben. **~ up** vt festschrauben; (crumple) zusammenknüllen; zusammenkneifen (eyes); (sl: bungle) vermasseln

'screwdriver n Schraubenzieher m

scribble /'skrɪbl/ n Gekritzel nt •vt/i kritzeln

script /skrɪpt/ n Schrift f; (of speech, play) Text m; (Radio, TV) Skript nt; (of film) Drehbuch nt

scroll /skrəʊl/ n Rolle f • vt **~ up/down** nach oben/unten rollen. **~ bar** n Rollbalken m

scrounge /skraʊndʒ/ vt/i schnorren. **~r** n Schnorrer m

scrub[1] /skrʌb/ n (land) Buschland nt, Gestrüpp nt

scrub[2] vt/i (pt/pp **scrubbed**) schrubben

scruff /skrʌf/ n **by the ~ of the neck** beim Genick

scruffy /'skrʌfɪ/ adj vergammelt

scrum /skrʌm/ n Gedränge nt

scruple /'skru:pl/ n Skrupel m

scrupulous /'skru:pjʊləs/ adj gewissenhaft

scuffle /'skʌfl/ n Handgemenge nt

sculpt|or /'skʌlptə(r)/ n Bildhauer(in) m(f). **~ure** n Bildhauerei f; (piece of work) Skulptur f, Plastik f

scum /skʌm/ n Schmutzschicht f; (people) Abschaum m

scurry /'skʌrɪ/ vi (pt/pp **-ied**) huschen

scuttle[1] /'skʌtl/ vt versenken (ship)

scuttle[2] vi schnell krabbeln

sea /si:/ n Meer nt, See f; **at ~** auf See; **by ~** mit dem Schiff. **~food** n Meeresfrüchte pl. **~gull** n Möwe f

seal[1] /si:l/ n (Zool) Seehund m

seal[2] n Siegel nt •vt versiegeln; (fig) besiegeln. **~ off** vt abriegeln

'sea-level n Meeresspiegel m

seam /si:m/ n Naht f; (of coal) Flöz nt

'seaman n Seemann m; (sailor) Matrose m

seance /'seɪɑ:ns/ n spiritistische Sitzung f

search /sɜ:tʃ/ n Suche f; (official) Durchsuchung f •vt durchsuchen; absuchen (area) •vi suchen (**for** nach). **~ engine** n Suchmaschine f. **~ing** adj prüfend, forschend. **~light** n [Such]scheinwerfer m. **~-party** n Suchmannschaft f

sea: ~sick adj seekrank. **~side** n **at/to the ~side** am/ans Meer

season /'si:zn/ n Jahreszeit f; (social, tourist, sporting) Saison f •vt (flavour) würzen. **~al** adj Saison-. **~ing** n Gewürze pl

'season ticket n Dauerkarte f

seat /si:t/ n Sitz m; (place) Sitzplatz m; (bottom) Hintern m; **take a ~** Platz nehmen •vt setzen; (have seats for) Sitzplätze bieten (+ dat); **remain ~ed** sitzen bleiben. **~-belt** n Sicherheitsgurt m; **fasten one's ~-belt** sich anschnallen

sea: ~weed n [See]tang m. **~worthy** adj seetüchtig

seclu|ded /sɪ'klu:dɪd/ adj abgelegen. **~sion** n Zurückgezogenheit f

second /'sekənd/ adj zweite(r,s); **on ~ thoughts** nach weiterer Überlegung •n Sekunde f; (Sport) Sekundant m; **~s** pl (goods) Waren zweiter Wahl •adv (in race) an zweiter Stelle •vt unterstützen (proposal)

secondary /'sekəndrɪ/ adj zweitrangig; (Phys) Sekundär-. **~ school** n höhere Schule f

second: ~-best adj zweitbeste(r,s). **~ 'class** adv (travel, send) zweiter Klasse. **~-class** adj zweitklassig

'second hand n (on clock) Sekundenzeiger m

second-'hand adj gebraucht •adv aus zweiter Hand

secondly /'sekəndlɪ/ adv zweitens

second-'rate adj zweitklassig

secrecy /'si:krəsɪ/ n Heimlichkeit f

secret /'si:krɪt/ adj geheim; (agent, police) Geheim-; (drinker, lover) heimlich •n Geheimnis nt

secretarial /sekrə'teərɪəl/ adj Sekretärinnen-; (work, staff) Sekretariats-

secretary /'sekrətərɪ/ n Sekretär(in) m(f)

secretive /'si:krətɪv/ adj geheimtuerisch

secretly /'si:krɪtlɪ/ adv heimlich

sect /sekt/ n Sekte f

section /'sekʃn/ n Teil m; (of text) Abschnitt m; (of firm) Abteilung f; (of organization) Sektion f

sector /'sektə(r)/ n Sektor m

secular /'sekjʊlə(r)/ adj weltlich

secure /sɪ'kjʊə(r)/ adj sicher; (firm) fest; (emotionally) geborgen •vt sichern; (fasten) festmachen; (obtain) sich (dat) sichern

securit|y /sɪ'kjʊərətɪ/ n Sicherheit f; (emotional) Geborgenheit f; **~ies** pl Wertpapiere pl

sedan /sɪ'dæn/ n (Amer) Limousine f

sedate /sɪ'deɪt/ adj gesetzt

sedative /'sedətɪv/ adj beruhigend •n Beruhigungsmittel nt

sediment /'sedɪmənt/ n [Boden]satz m

seduce /sɪ'dju:s/ vt verführen

seduct|ion /sɪ'dʌkʃn/ n Verführung f. **~ive** adj verführerisch

see /si:/ v (pt **saw**, pp **seen**) •vt sehen; (understand) einsehen; (imagine) sich (dat) vorstellen; (escort) begleiten; **go and ~**

nachsehen; (visit) besuchen; ~ **you later!** bis nachher! ~**ing that** da •vi sehen; (check) nachsehen; ~ **about** sich kümmern um. ~ **off** vt verabschieden; (chase away) vertreiben. ~ **through** vt (fig) durchschauen (person)

seed /si:d/ n Samen m; (of grape) Kern m; (fig) Saat f; (Tennis) gesetzter Spieler m; **go to** ~ Samen bilden; (fig) herunterkommen. ~**ed** adj (Tennis) gesetzt

seedy /'si:dɪ/ adj schäbig; (area) heruntergekommen

seek /si:k/ vt (pt/pp **sought**) suchen

seem /si:m/ vi scheinen

seen /si:n/ see **see**[1]

seep /si:p/ vi sickern

seethe /si:ð/ vi ~ **with anger** vor Wut schäumen

'**see-through** adj durchsichtig

segment /'segmənt/ n Teil m; (of worm) Segment nt; (of orange) Spalte f

segregat|e /'segrɪgeɪt/ vt trennen. ~**ion** n Trennung f

seize /si:z/ vt ergreifen; (Jur) beschlagnahmen; ~ **s.o. by the arm** jdn am Arm packen. ~ **up** vi (Techn) sich festfressen

seldom /'seldəm/ adv selten

select /sɪ'lekt/ adj ausgewählt; (exclusive) exklusiv •vt auswählen; aufstellen (team). ~**ion** n Auswahl f

self /self/ n (pl **selves**) Ich nt

self: ~**-as'surance** n Selbstsicherheit f. ~**-as'sured** adj selbstsicher. ~**-'catering** n Selbstversorgung f. ~**-'centred** adj egozentrisch. ~**-'confidence** n Selbstbewusstsein nt, Selbstvertrauen nt. ~**-'confident** adj selbstbewusst. ~**-'conscious** adj befangen. ~**-con'tained** adj (flat) abgeschlossen. ~**-con'trol** n Selbstbeherrschung f. ~**-de'fence** n Selbstverteidigung f; (Jur) Notwehr f. ~**-em'ployed** selbstständig. ~**-e'steem** n Selbstachtung f. ~**-'evident** adj offensichtlich. ~**-in'dulgent** adj maßlos. ~**-'interest** n Eigennutz m

self|ish /'selfɪʃ/ adj egoistisch, selbstsüchtig. ~**less** adj selbstlos

self: ~**-'pity** n Selbstmitleid nt. ~**-'portrait** n Selbstporträt nt. ~**-re'spect** n Selbstachtung f. ~**-'righteous** adj selbstgerecht. ~**-'sacrifice** n Selbstaufopferung f. ~**-'satisfied** adj selbstgefällig. ~**-'service** n Selbstbedienung f •attrib Selbstbedienungs-. ~**-suf'ficient** adj selbstständig

sell /sel/ v (pt/pp **sold**) •vt verkaufen; **be sold out** ausverkauft sein •vi sich verkaufen. ~ **off** vt verkaufen

seller /'selə(r)/ n Verkäufer m

Sellotape® /'seləʊ-/, n ≈ Tesafilm® m

'**sell-out** n **be a** ~ ausverkauft sein; ([!]: betrayal) Verrat sein

selves /selvz/ see **self**

semester /sɪ'mestə(r)/ n Semester nt

semi|breve /'semɪbri:v/ n (Mus) ganze Note f. ~**circle** n Halbkreis m. ~**'circular** adj halbkreisförmig. ~**'colon** n Semikolon nt. ~**-de'tached** adj & n ~**-detached [house]** Doppelhaushälfte f. ~**-'final** n Halbfinale nt

seminar /'semɪnɑ:(r)/ n Seminar nt

senat|e /'senət/ n Senat m. ~**or** n Senator m

send /send/ vt/i (pt/pp **sent**) schicken; ~ **for** kommen lassen (person); sich (dat) schicken lassen (thing). ~**er** n Absender m. ~**-off** n Verabschiedung f

senil|e /'si:naɪl/ adj senil

senior /'si:nɪə(r)/ adj älter; (in rank) höher •n Ältere(r) m/f; (in rank) Vorgesetzte(r) m/f. ~ '**citizen** n Senior(in) m(f)

seniority /si:nɪ'ɒrətɪ/ n höheres Alter nt; (in rank) höherer Rang m

sensation /sen'seɪʃn/ n Sensation

f; (feeling) Gefühl nt. **~al** adj sensationell

sense /sens/ n Sinn m; (feeling) Gefühl nt; (common ~) Verstand m; **make ~** Sinn ergeben •vt spüren. **~less** adj sinnlos; (unconscious) bewusstlos

sensible /'sensəbl/ adj, **-bly** adv vernünftig; (suitable) zweckmäßig

sensitiv|e /'sensətɪv/ adj empfindlich; (understanding) einfühlsam. **~ity** n Empfindlichkeit f

sensual /'sensjʊəl/ adj sinnlich. **-ity** n Sinnlichkeit f

sensuous /'sensjʊəs/ adj sinnlich

sent /sent/ see **send**

sentence /'sentəns/ n Satz m; (Jur) Urteil nt; (punishment) Strafe f •vt verurteilen

sentiment /'sentɪmənt/ n Gefühl nt; (opinion) Meinung f; (sentimentality) Sentimentalität f **~al** adj sentimental. **~ality** n Sentimentalität f

sentry /'sentrɪ/ n Wache f

separable /'sepərəbl/ adj trennbar

separate[1] /'sepərət/ adj getrennt, separat

separat|e[2] /'sepəreɪt/ vt trennen •vi sich trennen. **~ion** n Trennung f

September /sep'tembə(r)/ n September m

septic /'septɪk/ adj vereitert

sequel /'si:kwl/ n Folge f; (fig) Nachspiel nt

sequence /'si:kwəns/ n Reihenfolge f

serenade /serə'neɪd/ n Ständchen nt •vt **~ s.o.** jdm ein Ständchen bringen

seren|e /sɪ'ri:n/ adj gelassen. **~ity** n Gelassenheit f

sergeant /'sɑ:dʒənt/ n (Mil) Feldwebel m; (in police) Polizeimeister m

serial /'sɪərɪəl/ n Fortsetzungsgeschichte f; (Radio, TV) Serie f. **~ize** vt in Fortsetzungen veröffentlichen/ (Radio, TV) senden

series /'sɪəri:z/ n inv Serie f

serious /'sɪərɪəs/ adj ernst; (illness, error) schwer. **~ness** n Ernst m

sermon /'sɜ:mən/ n Predigt f

servant /'sɜ:vənt/ n Diener(in) m(f)

serve /sɜ:v/ n (Tennis) Aufschlag m •vt dienen (+ dat); bedienen (customer, guest); servieren (food); verbüßen (sentence); **it ~s you right!** das geschieht dir recht! •vi dienen; (Tennis) aufschlagen. **~r** n (Computing) Server m

service /'sɜ:vɪs/ n Dienst m; (Relig) Gottesdienst m; (in shop, restaurant) Bedienung f; (transport) Verbindung f; (maintenance) Wartung f; (set of crockery) Service nt; (Tennis) Aufschlag m; **~s** pl Dienstleistungen pl; (on motorway) Tankstelle und Raststätte f; **in the ~s** beim Militär; **out of/in ~** (machine:) außer/ in Betrieb •vt (Techn) warten

service: ~ area n Tankstelle und Raststätte f. **~ charge** n Bedienungszuschlag m. **~man** n Soldat m. **~ station** n Tankstelle f

serviette /sɜ:vɪ'et/ n Serviette f

servile /'sɜ:vaɪl/ adj unterwürfig

session /'seʃn/ n Sitzung f

set /set/ n Satz m; (of crockery) Service nt; (of cutlery) Garnitur f; (TV, Radio) Apparat m; (Math) Menge f; (Theat) Bühnenbild nt; (Cinema) Szenenaufbau m; (of people) Kreis m •adj (ready) fertig, bereit; (rigid) fest; (book) vorgeschrieben; **be ~ on doing sth** entschlossen sein, etw zu tun •v (pt/pp **set**, pres p **setting**) •vt setzen; (adjust) einstellen; stellen (task, alarm clock); festsetzen, festlegen (date, limit); aufgeben (homework); zusammenstellen (questions); [ein]fassen (gem); einrichten (bone); legen (hair); decken (table) •vi (sun:) untergehen; (become hard) fest werden. **~ back** vt zurücksetzen; (hold up) aufhalten; (!: cost) kosten. ~ **off** vi losgehen; (in vehicle) losfahren •vt auslösen (alarm); explodieren lassen (bomb). ~ **out** vi losgehen; (in vehicle) losfahren •vt auslegen; (state) darlegen. ~ **up** vt aufbauen; (fig) gründen

settee /se'ti:/ n Sofa nt, Couch f

setting /'setɪŋ/ n Rahmen m; (surroundings) Umgebung f

settle /'setl/ vt (decide) entscheiden; (agree) regeln; (fix) festsetzen; (calm) beruhigen; (pay) bezahlen •vi sich niederlassen; (snow, dust:) liegen bleiben; (subside) sich senken; (sediment:) sich absetzen. ~ **down** vi sich beruhigen; (permanently) sesshaft werden. ~ **up** vi abrechnen

settlement /'setlmənt/ n (see **settle**) Entscheidung f; Regelung f; Bezahlung f; (Jur) Vergleich m; (colony) Siedlung f

settler /'setlə(r)/ n Siedler m

'set-up n System nt

seven /'sevn/ adj sieben. ~**'teen** adj siebzehn. ~**'teenth** adj siebzehnte(r,s)

seventh /'sevnθ/ adj siebte(r,s)

seventieth /'sevntɪɪθ/ adj siebzigste(r,s)

seventy /'sevntɪ/ adj siebzig

several /'sevrl/ adj & pron mehrere, einige

sever|e /sɪ'vɪə(r)/ adj (**-r, -st**), **-ly** adv streng; (pain) stark; (illness) schwer. ~**ity** n Strenge f; Schwere f

sew /səʊ/ vt/i (pt **sewed**, pp **sewn** or **sewed**) nähen

sewage /'su:ɪdʒ/ n Abwasser nt

sewer /'su:ə(r)/ n Abwasserkanal m

sewing /'səʊɪŋ/ n Nähen nt; (work) Näharbeit f. ~ **machine** n Nähmaschine f

sewn /səʊn/ see **sew**

sex /seks/ n Geschlecht nt; (sexuality, intercourse) Sex m. ~**ist** adj sexistisch

sexual /'seksjʊəl/ adj sexuell. ~ **'intercourse** n Geschlechtsverkehr m

sexuality /seksjʊ'ælətɪ/ n Sexualität f

sexy /'seksɪ/ adj sexy

shabby /'ʃæbɪ/ adj, **-ily** adv schäbig

shack /ʃæk/ n Hütte f

shade /ʃeɪd/ n Schatten m; (of colour) [Farb]ton m; (for lamp) [Lampen]schirm m; (Amer: window-blind) Jalousie f •vt beschatten

shadow /'ʃædəʊ/ n Schatten m •vt (follow) beschatten

shady /'ʃeɪdɪ/ adj schattig; (!: disreputable) zwielichtig

shaft /ʃɑ:ft/ n Schaft m; (Techn) Welle f; (of light) Strahl m; (of lift) Schacht m

shaggy /'ʃægɪ/ adj zottig

shake /ʃeɪk/ n Schütteln nt •v (pt **shook**, pp **shaken**) •vt schütteln; (shock) erschüttern; ~ **hands with s.o.** jdm die Hand geben •vi wackeln; (tremble) zittern. ~ **off** vt abschütteln

shaky /'ʃeɪkɪ/ adj wackelig; (hand, voice) zittrig

shall /ʃæl/ v aux **we ~ see** wir werden sehen; **what ~ I do?** was soll ich machen?

shallow /'ʃæləʊ/ adj (**-er, -est**) seicht; (dish) flach; (fig) oberflächlich

sham /ʃæm/ adj unecht •n Heuchelei f •vt (pt/pp **shammed**) vortäuschen

shambles /'ʃæmblz/ n Durcheinander nt

shame /ʃeɪm/ n Scham f; (disgrace) Schande f; **be a ~** schade sein; **what a ~!** wie schade!

shame|ful /'ʃeɪmfl/ adj schändlich. ~**less** adj schamlos

shampoo /ʃæm'pu:/ n Shampoo nt •vt schamponieren

shan't /ʃɑ:nt/ = **shall not**

shape /ʃeɪp/ n Form f; (figure) Gestalt f •vt formen (**into** zu). ~**less** adj formlos; (clothing) unförmig

S

share /ʃeə(r)/ n [An]teil m; (Comm) Aktie f •vt/i teilen. ~**holder** n Aktionär(in) m(f)

shark /ʃɑːk/ n Hai[fisch] m

sharp /ʃɑːp/ adj (**-er, -est**) scharf; (pointed) spitz; (severe) heftig; (sudden) steil; (alert) clever; (unscrupulous) gerissen •adv scharf; (Mus) zu hoch; **at six o'clock** ~ Punkt sechs Uhr •n (Mus) Kreuz nt. ~**en** vt schärfen; [an]spitzen (pencil)

shatter /'ʃætə(r)/ vt zertrümmern; (fig) zerstören; ~**ed** (person:) erschüttert; (!: exhausted) kaputt •vi zersplittern

shave /ʃeɪv/ n Rasur f; **have a** ~ sich rasieren •vt rasieren •vi sich rasieren. ~**r** n Rasierapparat m

shawl /ʃɔːl/ n Schultertuch nt

she /ʃiː/ pron sie

shears /ʃɪəz/ npl [große] Schere f

shed[1] /ʃed/ n Schuppen m

shed[2] vt (pt/pp **shed**, pres p **shedding**) verlieren; vergießen (blood, tears); ~ **light on** Licht bringen in (+ acc)

sheep /ʃiːp/ n inv Schaf nt. ~**-dog** n Hütehund m

sheepish /'ʃiːpɪʃ/ adj verlegen

sheer /ʃɪə(r)/ adj rein; (steep) steil; (transparent) hauchdünn

sheet /ʃiːt/ n Laken nt, Betttuch nt; (of paper) Blatt nt; (of glass, metal) Platte f

S

shelf /ʃelf/ n (pl **shelves**) Brett nt, Bord nt; (set of shelves) Regal nt

shell /ʃel/ n Schale f; (of snail) Haus nt; (of tortoise) Panzer m; (on beach) Muschel f; (Mil) Granate f •vt pellen; enthülsen (peas); (Mil) [mit Granaten] beschießen. ~ **out** vi ! blechen

'shellfish n inv Schalentiere pl; (Culin) Meeresfrüchte pl

shelter /'ʃeltə(r)/ n Schutz m; (air-raid ~) Luftschutzraum m •vt schützen (**from** vor + dat) •vi sich unterstellen. ~**ed** adj geschützt; (life) behütet

shelve /ʃelv/ vt auf Eis legen; (abandon) aufgeben

shelving /'ʃelvɪŋ/ n (shelves) Regale pl

shepherd /'ʃepəd/ n Schäfer m •vt führen

sherry /'ʃerɪ/ n Sherry m

shield /ʃiːld/ n Schild m; (for eyes) Schirm m; (Techn & fig) Schutz m •vt schützen (**from** vor + dat)

shift /ʃɪft/ n Verschiebung f; (at work) Schicht f •vt rücken; (take away) wegnehmen; (rearrange) umstellen; schieben (blame) (**on to** auf + acc) •vi sich verschieben; (!: rush) rasen

shifty /'ʃɪftɪ/ adj (pej) verschlagen

shimmer /'ʃɪmə(r)/ n Schimmer m •vi schimmern

shin /ʃɪn/ n Schienbein nt

shine /ʃaɪn/ n Glanz m •v (pt/pp **shone**) •vi leuchten; (reflect light) glänzen; (sun:) scheinen •vt ~ **a light on** beleuchten

shingle /'ʃɪŋgl/ n (pebbles) Kiesel pl

shiny /'ʃaɪnɪ/ adj glänzend

ship /ʃɪp/ n Schiff nt •vt (pt/pp **shipped**) verschiffen

ship: ~**building** n Schiffbau m. ~**ment** n Sendung f. ~**per** n Spediteur m. ~**ping** n Versand m; (traffic) Schifffahrt f. ~**shape** adj & adv in Ordnung. ~**wreck** n Schiffbruch m. ~**wrecked** adj schiffbrüchig. ~**yard** n Werft f

shirt /ʃɜːt/ n [Ober]hemd nt; (for woman) Hemdbluse f

shit /ʃɪt/ n (vulgar) Scheiße f •vi (pt/pp **shit**) (vulgar) scheißen

shiver /'ʃɪvə(r)/ n Schauder m •vi zittern

shoal /ʃəʊl/ n (fish) Schwarm m

shock /ʃɒk/ n Schock m; (Electr) Schlag m; (impact) Erschütterung f •vt einen Schock versetzen (+ dat); (scandalize) schockieren. ~**ing** adj schockierend; (!: bad) fürchterlich

shoddy /'ʃɒdɪ/ adj minderwertig

shoe /ʃu:/ n Schuh m; (of horse) Hufeisen nt •vt (pt/pp **shod**, pres p **shoeing**) beschlagen (horse)

shoe: ~horn n Schuhanzieher m. **~-lace** n Schnürsenkel m. **~-string** n **on a ~-string** [!] mit ganz wenig Geld

shone /ʃɒn/ see **shine**

shoo /ʃu:/ vt scheuchen •int sch!

shook /ʃʊk/ see **shake**

shoot /ʃu:t/ n (Bot) Trieb m; (hunt) Jagd f •v (pt/pp **shot**) •vt schießen; (kill) erschießen; drehen (film) •vi schießen. **~ down** vt abschießen. **~ out** vi (rush) herausschießen. **~ up** vi (grow) in die Höhe schießen/ (prices:) schnellen

shop /ʃɒp/ n Laden m, Geschäft nt; (workshop) Werkstatt f; **talk ~** [!] fachsimpeln •vi (pt/pp **shopped**, pres p **shopping**) einkaufen; **go ~ping** einkaufen gehen

shop: ~ assistant n Verkäufer(in) m(f). **~keeper** n Ladenbesitzer(in) m(f). **~-lifter** n Ladendieb m. **~-lifting** n Ladendiebstahl m

shopping /ˈʃɒpɪŋ/ n Einkaufen nt; (articles) Einkäufe pl; **do the ~** einkaufen. **~ bag** n Einkaufstasche f. **~ centre** n Einkaufszentrum nt. **~ trolley** n Einkaufswagen m

shop-ˈwindow n Schaufenster nt

shore /ʃɔ:(r)/ n Strand m; (of lake) Ufer nt

short /ʃɔ:t/ (**er, -est**) kurz; (person) klein; (curt) schroff; **a ~ time ago** vor kurzem; **be ~ of ...** zu wenig ... haben; **be in ~ supply** knapp sein •adv kurz; (abruptly) plötzlich; (curtly) kurz angebunden; **in ~** kurzum; **~ of** (except) außer; **go ~** Mangel leiden

shortage /ˈʃɔ:tɪdʒ/ n Mangel m (**of** an + dat); (scarcity) Knappheit f

short: ~bread n ≈ Mürbekekse pl. **~ ˈcircuit** n Kurzschluss m. **~coming** n Fehler m. **~ ˈcut** n Abkürzung f

shorten /ˈʃɔ:tn/ vt [ab]kürzen; kürzer machen (garment)

short: ~hand n Kurzschrift f, Stenographie f. **~ list** n engere Auswahl f

short|ly /ˈʃɔ:tlɪ/ adv in Kürze; **~ly before/after** kurz vorher/danach. **~ness** n Kürze f; (of person) Kleinheit f

shorts /ʃɔ:ts/ npl Shorts pl

short: ~-ˈsighted adj kurzsichtig. **~-sleeved** adj kurzärmelig. **~ ˈstory** n Kurzgeschichte f. **~-ˈtempered** adj aufbrausend. **~-term** adj kurzfristig. **~ wave** n Kurzwelle f

shot /ʃɒt/ see **shoot** •n Schuss m; (pellets) Schrot m; (person) Schütze m; (Phot) Aufnahme f; (injection) Spritze f; ([!]: attempt) Versuch m; **like a ~** [!] sofort. **~gun** n Schrotflinte f. **~-put** n (Sport) Kugelstoßen nt

should /ʃʊd/ modal verb **you ~ go** du solltest gehen; **I ~ have seen him** ich hätte ihn sehen sollen; **I ~ like** ich möchte; **this ~ be enough** das müsste eigentlich reichen; **if he ~ be there** falls er da sein sollte

shoulder /ˈʃəʊldə(r)/ n Schulter f •vt schultern; (fig) auf sich (acc) nehmen. **~-blade** n Schulterblatt nt

shout /ʃaʊt/ n Schrei m •vt/i schreien. **~ down** vt niederschreien

shouting /ˈʃaʊtɪŋ/ n Geschrei nt

shove /ʃʌv/ n Stoß m •vt stoßen; ([!]: put) tun •vi drängeln. **~ off** vi [!] abhauen

shovel /ˈʃʌvl/ n Schaufel f •vt (pt/pp **shovelled**) schaufeln

show /ʃəʊ/ n (display) Pracht f; (exhibition) Ausstellung f, Schau f; (performance) Vorstellung f; (Theat, TV) Show f; **on ~** ausgestellt •v (pt **showed**, pp **shown**) •vt zeigen; (put on display) ausstellen; vorführen (film) •vi sichtbar sein; (film:) gezeigt werden. **~ in** vt hereinführen. **~ off** vi [!] angeben •vt vorführen; (flaunt) angeben mit. **~ up** vi [deutlich] zu sehen sein; ([!]: arrive) auftauchen •vt deutlich zeigen; ([!]: embarrass) blamieren

shower /'ʃaʊə(r)/ n Dusche f; (of rain) Schauer m; **have a ~** duschen •vt **~ with** überschütten mit •vi duschen

'show-jumping n Springreiten nt

shown /ʃəʊn/ see **show**

show: ~-off n Angeber(in) m(f). **~room** n Ausstellungsraum m

showy /'ʃəʊɪ/ adj protzig

shrank /ʃræŋk/ see **shrink**

shred /ʃred/ n Fetzen m; (fig) Spur f •vt (pt/pp **shredded**) zerkleinern; (Culin) schnitzeln. **~der** n Reißwolf m; (Culin) Schnitzelwerk nt

shrewd /ʃru:d/ adj (**-er, -est**) klug. **~ness** n Klugheit f

shriek /ʃri:k/ n Schrei m •vt/i schreien

shrill /ʃrɪl/ adj, **-y** adv schrill

shrimp /ʃrɪmp/ n Garnele f, Krabbe f

shrink /ʃrɪŋk/ vi (pt **shrank**, pp **shrunk**) schrumpfen; (garment:) einlaufen; (draw back) zurückschrecken (**from** vor + dat)

shrivel /'ʃrɪvl/ vi (pt/pp **shrivelled**) verschrumpeln

Shrove /ʃrəʊv/ n **~'Tuesday** Fastnachtsdienstag m

shrub /ʃrʌb/ n Strauch m

shrug /ʃrʌg/ n Achselzucken nt •vt/i (pt/pp **shrugged**) **~ [one's shoulders]** die Achseln zucken

shrunk /ʃrʌŋk/ see **shrink**

shudder /'ʃʌdə(r)/ n Schauder m •vi schaudern; (tremble) zittern

shuffle /'ʃʌfl/ vi schlurfen •vt mischen (cards)

shun /ʃʌn/ vt (pt/pp **shunned**) meiden

shunt /ʃʌnt/ vt rangieren

shut /ʃʌt/ v (pt/pp **shut**, pres p **shutting**) •vt zumachen, schließen •vi sich schließen; (shop:) schließen, zumachen. **~ down** vt schließen; stilllegen (factory) •vi schließen. **~ up** vt abschließen; (lock in) einsperren •vi [!] den Mund halten

shutter /'ʃʌtə(r)/ n [Fenster]laden m; (Phot) Verschluss m

shuttle /'ʃʌtl/ n (textiles) Schiffchen nt

shuttle service n Pendelverkehr m

shy /ʃaɪ/ adj (**-er, -est**) schüchtern; (timid) scheu. **~ness** n Schüchternheit f

siblings /'sɪblɪŋz/ npl Geschwister pl

Sicily /'sɪsɪlɪ/ n Sizilien nt

sick /sɪk/ adj krank; (humour) makaber; **be ~** (vomit) sich übergeben; **be ~ of sth** [!] etw satt haben; **I feel ~** mir ist schlecht

sick|ly /'sɪklɪ/ adj kränklich. **~ness** n Krankheit f; (vomiting) Erbrechen nt

side /saɪd/ n Seite f; **on the ~** (as sideline) nebenbei; **~ by ~** nebeneinander; (fig) Seite an Seite; **take ~s** Partei ergreifen (**with** für) •attrib Seiten- •vi **~ with** Partei ergreifen für

side: ~board n Anrichte f. **~-effect** n Nebenwirkung f. **~lights** npl Standlicht nt. **~line** n Nebenbeschäftigung f. **~-show** n Nebenattraktion f. **~-step** vt ausweichen (+ dat). **~walk** n (Amer) Bürgersteig m. **~ways** adv seitwärts

siding /'saɪdɪŋ/ n Abstellgleis nt

siege /si:dʒ/ n Belagerung f; (by police) Umstellung f

sieve /sɪv/ n Sieb nt •vt sieben

sift /sɪft/ vt sieben; (fig) durchsehen

sigh /saɪ/ n Seufzer m •vi seufzen

sight /saɪt/ n Sicht f; (faculty) Sehvermögen nt; (spectacle) Anblick m; (on gun) Visier nt; **~s** pl Sehenswürdigkeiten pl; **at first ~** auf den ersten Blick; **lose ~ of** aus dem Auge verlieren; **know by ~** vom Sehen kennen •vt sichten

'sightseeing n **go ~** die Sehenswürdigkeiten besichtigen

sign /saɪn/ n Zeichen nt; (notice) Schild nt •vt/i unterschreiben; (author, artist:) signieren. **~ on** vi (as unemployed) sich arbeitslos melden; (Mil) sich verpflichten

signal /'sɪgnl/ n Signal nt •vt/i (pt/pp **signalled**) signalisieren; **~ to s.o.** jdm ein Signal geben

signature /'sɪgnətʃə(r)/ n Unterschrift f; (of artist) Signatur f

significan|ce /sɪg'nɪfɪkəns/ n Bedeutung f. **~t** adj (important) bedeutend

signify /'sɪgnɪfaɪ/ vt (pt/pp **-ied**) bedeuten

signpost /'saɪn-/ n Wegweiser m

silence /'saɪləns/ n Stille f; (of person) Schweigen nt •vt zum Schweigen bringen. **~r** n (on gun) Schalldämpfer m; (Auto) Auspufftopf m

silent /'saɪlənt/ adj still; (without speaking) schweigend; **remain ~** schweigen

silhouette /sɪlu:'et/ n Silhouette f; (picture) Schattenriss m •vt **be ~d** sich als Silhouette abheben

silicon /'sɪlɪkən/ n Silizium nt

silk /sɪlk/ n Seide f •attrib Seiden-

silky /'sɪlkɪ/ adj seidig

sill /ʃɪl/ n Sims m & nt

silly /'ʃɪlɪ/ adj dumm, albern

silver /'sɪlvə(r)/ adj silbern; (coin, paper) Silber- •n Silber nt

silver: ~-plated adj versilbert. **~ware** n Silber nt

similar /'sɪmɪlə(r)/ adj ähnlich. **~ity** n Ähnlichkeit f

simmer /'sɪmə(r)/ vi leise kochen, ziehen •vt ziehen lassen

simple /'sɪmpl/ adj (**-r, -st**) einfach; (person) einfältig. **~-'minded** adj einfältig

simplicity /sɪm'plɪsətɪ/ n Einfachheit f

simpli|fication /sɪmplɪfɪ'keɪʃn/ n Vereinfachung f. **~fy** vt (pt/pp **-ied**) vereinfachen

simply /'sɪmplɪ/ adv einfach

simulat|e /'sɪmjʊleɪt/ vt vortäuschen; (Techn) simulieren

simultaneous /sɪml'teɪnɪəs/ adj gleichzeitig

sin /sɪn/ n Sünde f •vi (pt/pp **sinned**) sündigen

since /sɪns/

• preposition

····> seit (+ dat). **he's been living here since 1991** er wohnt* seit 1991 hier. **I had been waiting since 8 o'clock** ich wartete* [schon] seit 8 Uhr. **since seeing you** seit ich dich gesehen habe. **how long is it since your interview?** wie lange ist es seit deinem Vorstellungsgespräch?

• adverb

····> seitdem. **I haven't spoken to her since** seitdem habe ich mit ihr nicht gesprochen. **the house has been empty ever since** das Haus steht seitdem leer. **he has since remarried** er hat danach wieder geheiratet. **long since** vor langer Zeit

• conjunction

····> seit. **since she has been living in Germany** seit sie in Deutschland wohnt*. **since they had been in London** seit sie in London waren*. **how long is it since he left?** wie lange ist es her, dass er weggezogen ist? **it's a year since he left** es ist ein Jahr her, dass er weggezogen ist

····> (because) da. **since she was ill, I had to do it** da sie krank war, musste ich es tun

! *Note the different tenses in German

sincere /sɪn'sɪə(r)/ adj aufrichtig; (heartfelt) herzlich. **~ly** adv aufrichtig; **Yours ~ly** Mit freundlichen Grüßen

sincerity /sɪn'serətɪ/ n Aufrichtigkeit f

sinful /'sɪnfl/ adj sündhaft

sing /sɪŋ/ vt/i (pt **sang**, pp **sung**) singen

singe /sɪndʒ/ vt (pres p **singeing**) versengen

singer /ˈsɪŋə(r)/ n Sänger(in) m(f)

single /ˈsɪŋgl/ adj einzeln; (one only) einzig; (unmarried) ledig; (ticket) einfach; (room, bed) Einzel- •n (ticket) einfache Fahrkarte f; (record) Single f; **~s** pl (Tennis) Einzel nt •vt **~ out** auswählen

single: ~-handed adj & adv allein. **~ ˈparent** n Alleinerziehende(r) m/f

singly /ˈsɪŋglɪ/ adv einzeln

singular /ˈsɪŋgjʊlə(r)/ adj eigenartig; (Gram) im Singular •n Singular m

sinister /ˈsɪnɪstə(r)/ adj finster

sink /sɪŋk/ n Spülbecken nt •v (pt **sank**, pp **sunk**) •vi sinken •vt versenken (ship); senken (shaft). **~ in** vi einsinken; (🅘: be understood) kapiert werden

sinner /ˈsɪnə(r)/ n Sünder(in) m(f)

sip /sɪp/ n Schlückchen nt •vt (pt/pp **sipped**) in kleinen Schlucken trinken

siphon /ˈsaɪfn/ n (bottle) Siphon m. **~ off** vt mit einem Saugheber ablassen

sir /sɜː(r)/ n mein Herr; **S~** (title) Sir; **Dear S~s** Sehr geehrte Herren

siren /ˈsaɪrən/ n Sirene f

sister /ˈsɪstə(r)/ n Schwester f; (nurse) Oberschwester f. **~-in-law** n Schwägerin f

sit /sɪt/ v (pt/pp **sat**, pres p **sitting**) •vi sitzen; (sit down) sich setzen; (committee:) tagen •vt setzen; machen (exam). **~ back** vi sich zurücklehnen. **~ down** vi sich setzen. **~ up** vi [aufrecht] sitzen; (rise) sich aufsetzen; (not slouch) gerade sitzen

site /saɪt/ n Gelände nt; (for camping) Platz m; (Archaeology) Stätte f

sitting /ˈsɪtɪŋ/ n Sitzung f; (for meals) Schub m

situat|e /ˈsɪtjʊeɪt/ vt legen; **be ~ed** liegen. **~ion** n Lage f; (circumstances) Situation f; (job) Stelle f

six /sɪks/ adj sechs. **~teen** adj sechzehn. **~teenth** adj sechzehnte(r,s)

sixth /sɪksθ/ adj sechste(r,s)

sixtieth /ˈsɪkstɪɪθ/ adj sechzigste(r,s)

sixty /ˈsɪkstɪ/ adj sechzig

size /saɪz/ n Größe f

sizzle /ˈsɪzl/ vi brutzeln

skate /skeɪt/ n Schlittschuh m •vi Schlittschuh laufen. **~board** n Skateboard nt •vi Skateboard fahren. **~boarding** n Skateboardfahren nt. **~r** n Eisläufer(in) m(f)

skating /ˈskeɪtɪŋ/ n Eislaufen nt. **~-rink** n Eisbahn f

skeleton /ˈskelɪtn/ n Skelett nt. **~ ˈkey** n Dietrich m

sketch /sketʃ/ n Skizze f; (Theat) Sketch m •vt skizzieren

sketchy /ˈsketʃɪ/ adj, **-ily** adv skizzenhaft

ski /skiː/ n Ski m •vi (pt/pp **skied**, pres p **skiing**) Ski fahren or laufen

skid /skɪd/ n Schleudern nt •vi (pt/pp **skidded**) schleudern

skier /ˈskiːə(r)/ n Skiläufer(in) m(f)

skiing /ˈskiːɪŋ/ n Skilaufen nt

skilful /ˈskɪlfl/ adj geschickt

skill /skɪl/ n Geschick nt. **~ed** adj geschickt; (trained) ausgebildet

skim /skɪm/ vt (pt/pp **skimmed**) entrahmen (milk)

skimp /skɪmp/ vt sparen an (+ dat)

skimpy /ˈskɪmpɪ/ adj knapp

skin /skɪn/ n Haut f; (on fruit) Schale f •vt (pt/pp **skinned**) häuten; schälen (fruit)

skin: ~-deep adj oberflächlich. **~-diving** n Sporttauchen nt

skinny /ˈskɪnɪ/ adj dünn

skip[1] /skɪp/ n Container m

skip[2] n Hüpfer m •v (pt/pp **skipped**)

vi hüpfen; (with rope) seilspringen •vt überspringen

skipper /'skɪpə(r)/ n Kapitän m

'skipping-rope n Sprungseil nt

skirmish /'skɜ:mɪʃ/ n Gefecht nt

skirt /skɜ:t/ n Rock m •vt herumgehen um

skittle /'skɪtl/ n Kegel m

skive /skaɪv/ vi [!] blaumachen

skull /skʌl/ n Schädel m

sky /skaɪ/ n Himmel m. **~light** n Dachluke f. **~ marshal** n bewaffneter Flugbegleiter m. **~scraper** n Wolkenkratzer m

slab /slæb/ n Platte f; (slice) Scheibe f; (of chocolate) Tafel f

slack /slæk/ adj (**-er, -est**) schlaff, locker; (person) nachlässig; (Comm) flau •vi bummeln

slacken /'slækn/ vi sich lockern; (diminish) nachlassen •vt lockern; (diminish) verringern

slain /sleɪn/ see **slay**

slam /slæm/ v (pt/pp **slammed**) •vt zuschlagen; (put) knallen [!]; ([!]: criticize) verreißen •vi zuschlagen

slander /'slɑ:ndə(r)/ n Verleumdung f •vt verleumden

slang /slæŋ/ n Slang m. **~y** adj salopp

slant /slɑ:nt/ Schräge f; **on the ~** schräg •vt abschrägen; (fig) färben (report) •vi sich neigen

slap /slæp/ n Schlag m •vt (pt/pp **slapped**) schlagen; (put) knallen [!] •adv direkt

slapdash adj [!] schludrig

slash /slæʃ/ n Schlitz m •vt aufschlitzen; [drastisch] reduzieren (prices)

slat /slæt/ n Latte f

slate /sleɪt/ n Schiefer m •vt [!] heruntermachen; verreißen (performance)

slaughter /'slɔ:tə(r)/ n Schlachten nt; (massacre) Gemetzel nt •vt schlachten; abschlachten (men)

Slav /slɑ:v/ adj slawisch •n Slawe m/ Slawin f

slave /sleɪv/ n Sklave m/ Sklavin f •vi **~ [away]** schuften

slavery /'sleɪvərɪ/ n Sklaverei f

slay /sleɪ/ vt (pt **slew**, pp **slain**) ermorden

sledge /sledʒ/ n Schlitten m

sleek /sli:k/ adj (**-er, -est**) seidig; (well-fed) wohlgenährt

sleep /sli:p/ n Schlaf m; **go to ~** einschlafen; **put to ~** einschläfern •v (pt/pp **slept**) •vi schlafen •vt (accommodate) Unterkunft bieten für. **~er** n Schläfer(in) m(f); (Rail) Schlafwagen m; (on track) Schwelle f

sleeping: ~-bag n Schlafsack m. **~-pill** n Schlaftablette f

sleep: ~less adj schlaflos. **~-walking** n Schlafwandeln nt

sleepy /'sli:pɪ/ adj, **-ily** adv schläfrig

sleet /sli:t/ n Schneeregen m

sleeve /sli:v/ n Ärmel m; (for record) Hülle f. **~less** adj ärmellos

sleigh /sleɪ/ n [Pferde]schlitten m

slender /'slendə(r)/ adj schlank; (fig) gering

slept /slept/ see **sleep**

slew see **slay**

slice /slaɪs/ n Scheibe f •vt in Scheiben schneiden

slick /slɪk/ adj clever

slid|e /slaɪd/ n Rutschbahn f; (for hair) Spange f; (Phot) Dia nt •v (pt/pp **slid**) •vi rutschen •vt schieben. **~ing** adj gleitend; (door, seat) Schiebe-

slight /slaɪt/ adj (**-er, -est**) leicht; (importance) gering; (acquaintance) flüchtig; (slender) schlank; **not in the ~est** nicht im Geringsten; **~ly better** ein bisschen besser •vt kränken, beleidigen •n Beleidigung f

slim /slɪm/ adj (**slimmer, slimmest**) schlank; (volume) schmal; (fig) gering •vi eine Schlankheitskur machen

slim|e /slaɪm/ n Schleim m. **~y** adj schleimig

S

sling /slɪŋ/ n (Med) Schlinge f •vt (pt/pp **slung**) [!] schmeißen

slip /slɪp/ n (mistake) Fehler m, [!] Patzer m; (petticoat) Unterrock m; (paper) Zettel m; **give s.o. the ~** [!] jdm entwischen; **~ of the tongue** Versprecher m •v (pt/pp **slipped**) •vi rutschen; (fall) ausrutschen; (go quickly) schlüpfen •vt schieben; **~ s.o.'s mind** jdm entfallen. **~ away** vi sich fortschleichen. **~ up** vi [!] einen Schnitzer machen

slipper /'slɪpə(r)/ n Hausschuh m

slippery /'slɪpərɪ/ adj glitschig; (surface) glatt

slipshod /'slɪpʃɒd/ adj schludrig

'**slip-up** n [!] Schnitzer m

slit /slɪt/ n Schlitz m •vt (pt/pp **slit**) aufschlitzen

slither /'slɪðə(r)/ vi rutschen

slog /slɒg/ n **[hard] ~** Schinderei f •vi (pt/pp **slogged**) schuften

slogan /'sləʊgən/ n Schlagwort nt; (advertising) Werbespruch m

slop|e /sləʊp/ n Hang m; (inclination) Neigung f •vi sich neigen. **~ing** adj schräg

sloppy /'slɒpɪ/ adj schludrig; (sentimental) sentimental

slosh /slɒʃ/ vi [!] schwappen

slot /slɒt/ n Schlitz m; (TV) Sendezeit f •v (pt/pp **slotted**) •vt einfügen •vi sich einfügen (**in** in + acc)

'**slot-machine** n Münzautomat m; (for gambling) Spielautomat m

slouch /slaʊtʃ/ vi sich schlecht halten

slovenly /'slʌvnlɪ/ adj schlampig

slow /sləʊ/ adj (**-er, -est**) langsam; **be ~** (clock:) nachgehen; **in ~ motion** in Zeitlupe •adv langsam •vt verlangsamen •vi **~ down, ~ up** langsamer werden. **~ness** n Langsamkeit f

sludge /slʌdʒ/ n Schlamm m

slug /slʌg/ n Nacktschnecke f

sluggish /'slʌgɪʃ/ adj träge

sluice /slu:s/ n Schleuse f

slum /slʌm/ n Elendsviertel nt

slumber /'slʌmbə(r)/ n Schlummer m •vi schlummern

slump /slʌmp/ n Sturz m •vi fallen; (crumple) zusammensacken; (prices:) stürzen; (sales:) zurückgehen

slung /slʌŋ/ see **sling**

slur /slɜ:(r)/ vt (pt/pp **slurred**) undeutlich sprechen

slurp /slɜ:p/ vt/i schlürfen

slush /slʌʃ/ n [Schnee]matsch m; (fig) Kitsch m

slut /slʌt/ n Schlampe f [!]

sly /slaɪ/ adj (**-er, -est**) verschlagen •n **on the ~** heimlich

smack /smæk/ n Schlag m, Klaps m •vt schlagen •adv [!] direkt

small /smɔ:l/ adj (**-er, -est**) klein •adv **chop up ~** klein hacken •n **~ of the back** Kreuz nt

small: ~ ads npl Kleinanzeigen pl. **~ 'change** n Kleingeld nt. **~pox** n Pocken pl. **~ talk** n leichte Konversation f

smart /smɑ:t/ adj (**-er, -est**) schick; (clever) schlau, clever; (brisk) flott; (Amer, fam: cheeky) frech •vi brennen

smarten /'smɑ:tn/ vt **~ oneself up** mehr auf sein Äußeres achten

smash /smæʃ/ n Krach m; (collision) Zusammenstoß m; (Tennis) Schmetterball m •vt zerschlagen; (strike) schlagen; (Tennis) schmettern •vi zerschmettern; (crash) krachen (**into** gegen). **~ing** adj [!] toll

smear /smɪə(r)/ n verschmierter Fleck m; (Med) Abstrich m; (fig) Verleumdung f •vt schmieren; (coat) beschmieren (**with** mit); (fig) verleumden •vi schmieren

smell /smel/ n Geruch m; (sense) Geruchssinn m •v (pt/pp **smelt** or **smelled**) •vt riechen; (sniff) riechen an (+ dat) •vi riechen (**of** nach)

smelly /'smelɪ/ adj übel riechend

smelt /smelt/ see **smell**

smile /smaɪl/ n Lächeln nt •vi lächeln; **~ at** anlächeln

smirk /smɜ:k/ vi feixen

smith /smɪθ/ n Schmied m

smock /smɒk/ n Kittel m

smog /smɒg/ n Smog m

smoke /sməʊk/ n Rauch m •vt/i rauchen; (Culin) räuchern. **~less** adj rauchfrei; (fuel) rauchlos

smoker /'sməʊkə(r)/ n Raucher m; (Rail) Raucherabteil nt

smoking /'sməʊkɪŋ/ n Rauchen nt; **'no ~'** 'Rauchen verboten'

smoky /'sməʊkɪ/ adj verraucht; (taste) rauchig

smooth /smu:ð/ adj (**-er, -est**) glatt •vt glätten. **~ out** vt glatt streichen

smother /'smʌðə(r)/ vt ersticken; (cover) bedecken; (suppress) unterdrücken

smoulder /'sməʊldə(r)/ vi schwelen

smudge /smʌdʒ/ n Fleck m •vt verwischen •vi schmieren

smug /smʌg/ adj (**smugger, smuggest**) selbstgefällig

smuggl|e /'smʌgl/ vt schmuggeln. **~er** n Schmuggler m. **~ing** n Schmuggel m

snack /snæk/ n Imbiss m. **~-bar** n Imbissstube f

snag /snæg/ n Schwierigkeit f, [!] Haken m

snail /sneɪl/ n Schnecke f; **at a ~'s pace** im Schneckentempo

snake /sneɪk/ n Schlange f

snap /snæp/ n Knacken nt; (photo) Schnappschuss m •attrib (decision) plötzlich •v (pt/pp **snapped**) •vi [entzwei]brechen; **~ at** (bite) schnappen nach; (speak sharply) [scharf] anfahren •vt zerbrechen; (say) fauchen; (Phot) knipsen. **~ up** vt wegschnappen

snappy /'snæpɪ/ adj (smart) flott; **make it ~!** ein bisschen schnell!

'snapshot n Schnappschuss m

snare /sneə(r)/ n Schlinge f

snarl /snɑ:l/ vi [mit gefletschten Zähnen] knurren

snatch /snætʃ/ n (fragment) Fetzen pl •vt schnappen; (steal) klauen; entführen (child); **~ sth from s.o.** jdm etw entreißen

sneak /sni:k/ n [!] Petze f •vi schleichen; ([!]: tell tales) petzen •vt (take) mitgehen lassen •vi **~ in/ out** sich hinein-/hinausschleichen

sneakers /'sni:kəz/ npl (Amer) Turnschuhe pl

sneer /snɪə(r)/ vi höhnisch lächeln; (mock) spotten

sneeze /sni:z/ n Niesen nt •vi niesen

snide /snaɪd/ adj [!] abfällig

sniff /snɪf/ vi schnüffeln •vt schnüffeln an (+ dat)

snigger /'snɪgə(r)/ vi [boshaft] kichern

snip /snɪp/ n Schnitt m •vt/i **~ [at]** schnippeln an (+ dat)

snippet /'snɪpɪt/ n Schnipsel m; (of information) Bruchstück nt

snivel /'snɪvl/ vi (pt/pp **snivelled**) flennen

snob /snɒb/ n Snob m. **~bery** n Snobismus m. **~bish** adj snobistisch

snoop /snu:p/ vi [!] schnüffeln

snooty /'snu:tɪ/ adj [!] hochnäsig

snooze /snu:z/ n Nickerchen nt •vi dösen

snore /snɔ:(r)/ vi schnarchen

snorkel /'snɔ:kl/ n Schnorchel m

snort /snɔ:t/ vi schnauben

snout /snaʊt/ n Schnauze f

snow /snəʊ/ n Schnee m •vi schneien; **~ed under with** (fig) überhäuft mit

snow: ~ball n Schneeball m. **~board** n Snowboard nt. **~-drift** n Schneewehe f. **~drop** n Schneeglöckchen nt. **~fall** n Schneefall m. **~flake** n Schneeflocke f. **~man** n Schneemann m. **~plough** n Schneepflug m

snub /snʌb/ n Abfuhr f •vt (pt/pp **snubbed**) brüskieren

'snub-nosed adj stupsnasig

snuffle /'snʌfl/ vi schnüffeln

snug /snʌg/ adj (**snugger, snuggest**) behaglich, gemütlich

snuggle /'snʌgl/ vi sich kuscheln (**up to** an + acc)

so /səʊ/ adv so; **so am I** ich auch; **so I see** das sehe ich; **that is so** das stimmt; **so much the better** umso besser; **if so** wenn ja; **so as to** um zu; **so long!** [!] tschüs! •pron **I hope so** hoffentlich; **I think so** ich glaube schon; **I'm afraid so** leider ja; **so saying/doing, he/she ...** indem er/sie das sagte/tat, ... •conj (therefore) also; **so that** damit; **so what!** na und! **so you see** wie du siehst

soak /səʊk/ vt nass machen; (steep) einweichen; ([!]: fleece) schröpfen •vi weichen; (liquid:) sickern. **~ up** vt aufsaugen

soaking /'səʊkɪŋ/ adj & adv **~ [wet]** patschnass [!]

soap /səʊp/ n Seife f. **~ opera** n Seifenoper f. **~ powder** n Seifenpulver nt

soapy /'səʊpɪ/ adj seifig

soar /sɔː(r)/ vi aufsteigen; (prices:) in die Höhe schnellen

sob /sɒb/ n Schluchzer m •vi (pt/pp **sobbed**) schluchzen

sober /'səʊbə(r)/ adj nüchtern; (serious) ernst; (colour) gedeckt. **~ up** vi nüchtern werden

S

'so-called adj sogenannt

soccer /'sɒkə(r)/ n [!] Fußball m

sociable /'səʊʃəbl/ adj gesellig

social /'səʊʃl/ adj gesellschaftlich; (Admin, Pol, Zool) sozial

socialis|m /'səʊʃəlɪzm/ n Sozialismus m. **~t** adj sozialistisch •n Sozialist m

socialize /'səʊʃəlaɪz/ vi [gesellschaftlich] verkehren

socially /'səʊʃəlɪ/ adv gesellschaftlich; **know ~** privat kennen

social: ~ se'curity n Sozialhilfe f. **~ worker** n Sozialarbeiter(in) m(f)

society /sə'saɪətɪ/ n Gesellschaft f; (club) Verein m

sociolog|ist /səʊsɪ'ɒlədʒɪst/ n Soziologe m. **~y** n Soziologie f

sock /sɒk/ n Socke f; (kneelength) Kniestrumpf m

socket /'sɒkɪt/ n (of eye) Augenhöhle f; (of joint) Gelenkpfanne f; (wall plug) Steckdose f

soda /'səʊdə/ n Soda nt; (Amer) Limonade f. **~ water** n Sodawasser nt

sodden /'sɒdn/ adj durchnässt

sofa /'səʊfə/ n Sofa nt. **~ bed** n Schlafcouch f

soft /sɒft/ adj (**-er, -est**) weich; (quiet) leise; (gentle) sanft; ([!]: silly) dumm. **~ drink** n alkoholfreies Getränk nt

soften /'sɒfn/ vt weich machen; (fig) mildern •vi weich werden

soft: ~ toy n Stofftier nt. **~ware** n Software f

soggy /'sɒgɪ/ adj aufgeweicht

soil[1] /sɔɪl/ n Erde f, Boden m

soil[2] vt verschmutzen

solar /'səʊlə(r)/ adj Sonnen-

sold /səʊld/ see **sell**

soldier /'səʊldʒə(r)/ n Soldat m •vi **~ on** [unbeirrbar] weitermachen

sole[1] /səʊl/ n Sohle f

sole[2] n (fish) Seezunge f

sole[3] adj einzig. **~ly** adv einzig und allein

solemn /'sɒləm/ adj feierlich; (serious) ernst

solicitor /sə'lɪsɪtə(r)/ n Rechtsanwalt m/-anwältin f

solid /'sɒlɪd/ adj fest; (sturdy) stabil; (not hollow, of same substance) massiv; (unanimous) einstimmig; (complete) ganz

solidarity /sɒlɪ'dærətɪ/ n Solidarität f

solidify /səˈlɪdɪfaɪ/ vi (pt/pp **-ied**) fest werden

solitary /ˈsɒlɪtərɪ/ adj einsam; (sole) einzig

solitude /ˈsɒlɪtju:d/ n Einsamkeit f

solo /ˈsəʊləʊ/ n Solo nt •adj Solo-; (flight) Allein- •adv solo. **~ist** n Solist(in) m(f)

solstice /ˈsɒlstɪs/ n Sonnenwende f

soluble /ˈsɒljʊbl/ adj löslich

solution /səˈlu:ʃn/ n Lösung f

solvable /ˈsɒlvəbl/ adj lösbar

solve /sɒlv/ vt lösen

solvent /ˈsɒlvənt/ n Lösungsmittel nt

sombre /ˈsɒmbə(r)/ adj dunkel; (mood) düster

some /sʌm/ adj & pron etwas; (a little) ein bisschen; (with pl noun) einige; (a few) ein paar; (certain) manche(r,s); (one or the other) [irgend]ein; **~ day** eines Tages; **I want ~** ich möchte etwas/ (pl) welche; **will you have ~ wine?** möchten Sie Wein? **do ~ shopping** einkaufen

some: ~body /-bədɪ/ pron & n jemand; (emphatic) irgendjemand. **~how** adv irgendwie. **~one** pron & n = **somebody**

somersault /ˈsʌməsɔ:lt/ n Purzelbaum m [!]; (Sport) Salto m; **turn a ~** einen Purzelbaum schlagen/einen Salto springen

ˈsomething pron & adv etwas; (emphatic) irgendetwas; **~ different** etwas anderes; **~ like this** so etwas [wie das]

some: ~time adv irgendwann •adj ehemalig. **~times** adv manchmal. **~what** adv ziemlich. **~where** adv irgendwo; (go) irgendwohin

son /sʌn/ n Sohn m

song /sɒŋ/ n Lied nt. **~bird** n Singvogel m

ˈson-in-law n (pl **~s-in-law**) Schwiegersohn m

soon /su:n/ adv (**-er, -est**) bald; (quickly) schnell; **too ~** zu früh; **as ~ as possible** so bald wie möglich; **~er or later** früher oder später; **no ~er had I arrived than** ... kaum war ich angekommen, da ...; **I would ~er stay** ich würde lieber bleiben

soot /sʊt/ n Ruß m

sooth|e /su:ð/ vt beruhigen; lindern (pain). **~ing** adj beruhigend; lindernd

sophisticated /səˈfɪstɪkeɪtɪd/ adj weltgewandt; (complex) hoch entwickelt

sopping /ˈsɒpɪŋ/ adj & adv **~ [wet]** durchnässt

soppy /ˈsɒpɪ/ adj [!] rührselig

soprano /səˈprɑ:nəʊ/ n Sopran m; (woman) Sopranistin f

sordid /ˈsɔ:dɪd/ adj schmutzig

sore /sɔ:(r)/ adj (**-r, -st**) wund; (painful) schmerzhaft; **have a ~ throat** Halsschmerzen haben •n wunde Stelle f. **~ly** adv sehr

sorrow /ˈsɒrəʊ/ n Kummer m

sorry /ˈsɒrɪ/ adj (sad) traurig; (wretched) erbärmlich; **I am ~** es tut mir Leid; **she is** or **feels ~ for him** er tut ihr Leid; **I am ~ to say** leider; **~!** Entschuldigung!

sort /sɔ:t/ n Art f; (brand) Sorte f; **he's a good ~** [!] er ist in Ordnung •vt sortieren. **~ out** vt sortieren; (fig) klären

sought /sɔ:t/ see **seek**

soul /səʊl/ n Seele f

sound¹ /saʊnd/ adj (**-er, -est**) gesund; (sensible) vernünftig; (secure) solide; (thorough) gehörig •adv **be ~ asleep** fest schlafen

sound² n (strait) Meerenge f

sound³ n Laut m; (noise) Geräusch nt; (Phys) Schall m; (Radio, TV) Ton m; (of bells, music) Klang m; **I don't like the ~ of it** [!] das hört sich nicht gut an •vi [er]tönen; (seem) sich anhören •vt (pronounce) aussprechen; schlagen (alarm); (Med) abhorchen (chest)

soundly /ˈsaʊndlɪ/ adv solide; (sleep) fest; (defeat) vernichtend

'**soundproof** adj schalldicht

soup /suːp/ n Suppe f

sour /'saʊə(r)/ adj (**-er, -est**) sauer; (bad-tempered) griesgrämig, verdrießlich

source /sɔːs/ n Quelle f

south /saʊθ/ n Süden m; **to the ~ of** südlich von •adj Süd-, süd- •adv nach Süden

south: S~ 'Africa n Südafrika nt. **S~ A'merica** n Südamerika nt. **~-'east** n Südosten m

southerly /'sʌðəlɪ/ adj südlich

southern /'sʌðən/ adj südlich

'**southward[s]** /-wəd[z]/ adv nach Süden

souvenir /suːvə'nɪə(r)/ n Andenken nt, Souvenir nt

Soviet /'səʊvɪət/ adj (History) sowjetisch; **~ Union** Sowjetunion f

sow[1] /saʊ/ n Sau f

sow[2] /səʊ/ vt (pt **sowed**, pp **sown** or **sowed**) säen

soya /'sɔɪə/ n **~ bean** Sojabohne f

spa /spɑː/ n Heilbad nt

space /speɪs/ n Raum m; (gap) Platz m; (Astronomy) Weltraum m •vt **~ [out]** [in Abständen] verteilen

space: ~craft n Raumfahrzeug nt. **~ship** n Raumschiff nt

spacious /'speɪʃəs/ adj geräumig

spade /speɪd/ n Spaten m; (for child) Schaufel f; **~s** pl (Cards) Pik nt

Spain /speɪn/ n Spanien nt

span[1] /spæn/ n Spanne f; (of arch) Spannweite f •vt (pt/pp **spanned**) überspannen; umspannen (time)

span[2] see **spick**

Span|iard /'spænjəd/ n Spanier(in) m(f). **~ish** adj spanisch •n (Lang) Spanisch nt; **the ~ish** pl die Spanier

spank /spæŋk/ vt verhauen

spanner /'spænə(r)/ n Schraubenschlüssel m

spare /speə(r)/ adj (surplus) übrig; (additional) zusätzlich; (seat, time) frei; (room) Gäste-; (bed, cup) Extra- •n (part) Ersatzteil nt •vt ersparen; (not hurt) verschonen; (do without) entbehren; (afford to give) erübrigen. **~ 'wheel** n Reserverad nt

sparing /'speərɪŋ/ adj sparsam

spark /spɑːk/ n Funke nt. **~[ing]-plug** n (Auto) Zündkerze f

sparkl|e /'spɑːkl/ n Funkeln nt •vi funkeln. **~ing** adj funkelnd; (wine) Schaum-

sparrow /'spærəʊ/ n Spatz m

sparse /spɑːs/ adj spärlich. **~ly** adv spärlich; (populated) dünn

spasm /'spæzm/ n Anfall m; (cramp) Krampf m. **~odic** adj, **-ally** adv sporadisch

spastic /'spæstɪk/ adj spastisch [gelähmt] •n Spastiker(in) m(f)

spat /spæt/ see spit[2]

spatter /'spætə(r)/ vt spritzen; **~ with** bespritzen mit

spawn /spɔːn/ n Laich m •vt (fig) hervorbringen

speak /spiːk/ v (pt **spoke**, pp **spoken**) •vi sprechen (**to** mit) **~ing!** (Teleph) am Apparat! •vt sprechen; sagen (truth). **~ up** vi lauter sprechen; **~ up for oneself** seine Meinung äußern

speaker /spiːkə(r)/ n Sprecher(in) m(f); (in public) Redner(in) m(f); (loudspeaker) Lautsprecher m

spear /spɪə(r)/ n Speer m •vt aufspießen

spec /spek/ n **on ~** [!] auf gut Glück

special /'speʃl/ adj besondere(r,s), speziell. **~ist** n Spezialist m; (Med) Facharzt m/-ärztin f. **~ity** n Spezialität f

special|ize /'speʃəlaɪz/ vi sich spezialisieren (**in** auf + acc). **~ly** adv speziell; (particularly) besonders

species /'spiːʃiːz/ n Art f

specific /spə'sɪfɪk/ adj bestimmt; (precise) genau; (Phys) spezifisch. **~ally** adv ausdrücklich

specification /spesɪfɪ'keɪʃn/ n (also ~**s**) pl genaue Angaben pl

specify /'spesɪfaɪ/ vt (pt/pp **-ied**) [genau] angeben

specimen /spesɪmən/ n Exemplar nt; (sample) Probe f; (of urine) Urinprobe f

speck /spek/ n Fleck m

speckled /'spekld/ adj gesprenkelt

spectacle /'spektəkl/ n (show) Schauspiel nt; (sight) Anblick m. ~**s** npl Brille f

spectacular /spek'tækjʊlə(r)/ adj spektakulär

spectator /spek'teɪtə(r)/ n Zuschauer(in) m(f)

speculat|e /'spekjʊleɪt/ vi spekulieren. ~**ion** n Spekulation f. ~**or** n Spekulant m

sped /sped/ see **speed**

speech /spi:tʃ/ n Sprache f; (address) Rede f. ~**less** adj sprachlos

speed /spi:d/ n Geschwindigkeit f; (rapidity) Schnelligkeit f •vi (pt/pp **sped**) schnell fahren •(pt/pp **speeded**) (go too fast) zu schnell fahren. ~ **up** (pt/pp **speeded up**) •vt/i beschleunigen

speed: ~**boat** n Rennboot nt. ~ **camera** n Geschwindigkeitsüberwachungskamera f. ~ **dating** n Speeddating nt. ~**ing** n Geschwindigkeitsüberschreitung f. ~ **limit** n Geschwindigkeitsbeschränkung f

speedometer /spi:'dɒmɪtə(r)/ n Tachometer m

speedy /'spi:dɪ/ adj, **-ily** adv schnell

spell[1] /spel/ n Weile f; (of weather) Periode f

spell[2] v (pt/pp **spelled** or **spelt**) •vt schreiben; (aloud) buchstabieren; (fig: mean) bedeuten •vi richtig schreiben; (aloud) buchstabieren. ~ **out** vt buchstabieren; (fig) genau erklären

spell[3] n Zauber m; (words) Zauberspruch m. ~**bound** adj wie verzaubert

'spell checker n Rechtschreibprogramm nt

spelling /'spelɪŋ/ n (of a word) Schreibweise f; (orthography) Rechtschreibung f

spelt /spelt/ see **spell**[2]

spend /spend/ vt/i (pt/pp **spent**) ausgeben; verbringen (time)

spent /spent/ see **spend**

sperm /spɜ:m/ n Samen m

sphere /sfɪə(r)/ n Kugel f; (fig) Sphäre f

spice /spaɪs/ n Gewürz nt; (fig) Würze f

spicy /'spaɪsɪ/ adj würzig, pikant

spider /'spaɪdə(r)/ n Spinne f

spik|e /spaɪk/ n Spitze f; (Bot, Zool) Stachel m; (on shoe) Spike m. ~**y** adj stachelig

spill /spɪl/ v (pt/pp **spilt** or **spilled**) •vt verschütten •vi überlaufen

spin /spɪn/ v (pt/pp **spun**, pres p **spinning**) •vt drehen; spinnen (wool); schleudern (washing) •vi sich drehen

spinach /'spɪnɪdz/ n Spinat m

spindl|e /'spɪndl/ n Spindel f. ~**y** adj spindeldürr

spin-'drier n Wäscheschleuder f

spine /spaɪn/ n Rückgrat nt; (of book) [Buch]rücken m; (Bot, Zool) Stachel m. ~**less** adj (fig) rückgratlos

'spin-off n Nebenprodukt nt

spinster /'spɪnstə(r)/ n ledige Frau f

spiral /'spaɪrl/ adj spiralig •n Spirale f •vi (pt/pp **spiralled**) sich hochwinden. ~ **'staircase** n Wendeltreppe f

spire /'spaɪə(r)/ n Turmspitze f

spirit /'spɪrɪt/ n Geist m; (courage) Mut m; ~**s** pl (alcohol) Spirituosen pl; **in low** ~**s** niedergedrückt. ~ **away** vt verschwinden lassen

spirited /'spɪrɪtɪd/ adj lebhaft; (courageous) beherzt

spiritual /'spɪrɪtjʊəl/ adj geistig; (Relig) geistlich

spit¹ /spɪt/ n (for roasting) [Brat]spieß m

spit² n Spucke f •vt/i (pt/pp **spat**, pres p **spitting**) spucken; (cat:) fauchen; (fat:) spritzen; **it's ~ting with rain** es tröpfelt

spite /spaɪt/ n Boshaftigkeit f; **in ~ of** trotz (+ gen) •vt ärgern. **~ful** adj gehässig

splash /splæʃ/ n Platschen nt; (🅸: drop) Schuss m; **~ of colour** Farbfleck m •vt spritzen; **~ s.o. with sth** jdn mit etw bespritzen •vi spritzen. **~ about** vi planschen

splendid /ˈsplendɪd/ adj herrlich, großartig

splendour /ˈsplendə(r)/ n Pracht f

splint /splɪnt/ n (Med) Schiene f

splinter /ˈsplɪntə(r)/ n Splitter m •vi zersplittern

split /splɪt/ n Spaltung f; (Pol) Bruch m; (tear) Riss m •v (pt/pp **split**, pres p **splitting**) •vt spalten; (share) teilen; (tear) zerreißen •vi sich spalten; (tear) zerreißen; **~ on s.o.** 🅸 jdn verpfeifen. **~ up** vt aufteilen •vi (couple:) sich trennen

splutter /ˈsplʌtə(r)/ vi prusten

spoil /spɔɪl/ n **~s** pl Beute f •v (pt/pp **spoilt** or **spoiled**) •vt verderben; verwöhnen (person) •vi verderben. **~sport** n Spielverderber m

spoke¹ /spəʊk/ n Speiche f

spoke², **spoken** see **speak**

ˈspokesman n Sprecher m

sponge /spʌndʒ/ n Schwamm m •vt abwaschen •vi **~ on** schmarotzen bei. **~-bag** n Waschbeutel m. **~-cake** n Biskuitkuchen m

sponsor /ˈspɒnsə(r)/ n Sponsor m; (godparent) Pate m/Patin f •vt sponsern

spontaneous /spɒnˈteɪnɪəs/ adj spontan

spoof /spuːf/ n 🅸 Parodie f

spooky /ˈspuːkɪ/ adj 🅸 gespenstisch

spool /spuːl/ n Spule f

spoon /spuːn/ n Löffel m •vt löffeln. **~ful** n Löffel m

sporadic /spəˈrædɪk/ adj, **-ally** adv sporadisch

sport /spɔːt/ n Sport m •vt [stolz] tragen. **~ing** adj sportlich

sports: ~car n Sportwagen m. **~ coat** n, **~ jacket** n Sakko m. **~man** n Sportler m. **~woman** n Sportlerin f

sporty /ˈspɔːtɪ/ adj sportlich

spot /spɒt/ n Fleck m; (place) Stelle f (dot) Punkt m; (drop) Tropfen m; (pimple) Pickel m; **~s** pl (rash) Ausschlag m; **on the ~** auf der Stelle •vt (pt/pp **spotted**) entdecken

spot: ~ ˈcheck n Stichprobe f. **~less** adj makellos; (🅸: very clean) blitzsauber. **~light** n Scheinwerfer m; (fig) Rampenlicht nt

spotted /ˈspɒtɪd/ adj gepunktet

spouse /spaʊz/ n Gatte m/Gattin f

spout /spaʊt/ n Schnabel m, Tülle f •vi schießen (**from** aus)

sprain /spreɪn/ n Verstauchung f •vt verstauchen

sprang /spræŋ/ see **spring²**

sprawl /sprɔːl/ vi sich ausstrecken

spray¹ /spreɪ/ n (of flowers) Strauß m

spray² n Sprühnebel m; (from sea) Gischt m; (device) Spritze f; (container) Sprühdose f; (preparation) Spray nt •vt spritzen; (with aerosol) sprühen

spread /spred/ n Verbreitung f; (paste) Aufstrich m; (🅸: feast) Festessen nt •v (pt/pp **spread**) •vt ausbreiten; streichen (butter, jam); bestreichen (bread, surface); streuen (sand, manure); verbreiten (news, disease); verteilen (payments) •vi sich ausbreiten. **~ out** vt ausbreiten; (space out) verteilen •vi sich verteilen

spree /spriː/ n 🅸 **go on a shopping ~** groß einkaufen gehen

sprightly /ˈspraɪtlɪ/ adj rüstig

spring¹ /sprɪŋ/ n Frühling m •attrib Frühlings-

spring² n (jump) Sprung m; (water)

Quelle f; (device) Feder f; (elasticity) Elastizität f •v (pt **sprang**, pp **sprung**) •vi springen; (arise) entspringen (**from** dat) •vt **~ sth on s.o.** jdn mit etw überfallen

spring: ~-'cleaning n Frühjahrsputz m. **~time** n Frühling m

sprinkl|e /'sprɪŋkl/ vt sprengen; (scatter) streuen; bestreuen (surface). **~ing** n dünne Schicht f

sprint /sprɪnt/ n Sprint m •vi rennen; (Sport) sprinten. **~er** n Kurzstreckenläufer(in) m(f)

sprout /spraʊt/ n Trieb m; **[Brussels] ~s** pl Rosenkohl m •vi sprießen

sprung /sprʌŋ/ see **spring**[2]

spud /spʌd/ n [!] Kartoffel f

spun /spʌn/ see **spin**

spur /spɜ:(r)/ n Sporn m; (stimulus) Ansporn m; **on the ~ of the moment** ganz spontan •vt (pt/pp **spurred**) **~ [on]** (fig) anspornen

spurn /spɜ:n/ vt verschmähen

spurt /spɜ:t/ n (Sport) Spurt m; **put on a ~** spurten •vi spritzen

spy /spaɪ/ n Spion(in) m(f) •vi spionieren; **~ on s.o.** jdm nachspionieren. •vt ([!]: see) sehen

spying /'spaɪɪŋ/ n Spionage f

squabble /'skwɒbl/ n Zank m •vi sich zanken

squad /skwɒd/ n Gruppe f; (Sport) Mannschaft f

squadron /'skwɒdrən/ n (Mil) Geschwader nt

squalid /'skwɒlɪd/ adj schmutzig

squall /skwɔ:l/ n Bö f •vi brüllen

squalor /'skwɒlə(r)/ n Schmutz m

squander /'skwɒndə(r)/ vt vergeuden

square /skweə(r)/ adj quadratisch; (metre, mile) Quadrat-; (meal) anständig; **all ~** [!] quitt •n Quadrat nt; (area) Platz m; (on chessboard) Feld nt •vt (settle) klären; (Math) quadrieren

squash /skwɒʃ/ n Gedränge nt; (drink) Fruchtsaftgetränk nt; (Sport) Squash nt •vt zerquetschen; (suppress) niederschlagen. **~y** adj weich

squat /skwɒt/ adj gedrungen •vi (pt/pp **squatted**) hocken; **~ in a house** ein Haus besetzen. **~ter** n Hausbesetzer m

squawk /skwɔ:k/ vi krächzen

squeak /skwi:k/ n Quieken nt; (of hinge, brakes) Quietschen nt •vi quieken; quietschen

squeal /skwi:l/ n Kreischen nt •vi kreischen

squeamish /'skwi:mɪʃ/ adj empfindlich

squeeze /skwi:z/ n Druck m; (crush) Gedränge nt •vt drücken; (to get juice) ausdrücken; (force) zwängen

squiggle /'skwɪgl/ n Schnörkel m

squint /skwɪnt/ n Schielen nt •vi schielen

squirm /skwɜ:m/ vi sich winden

squirrel /'skwɪrl/ n Eichhörnchen nt

squirt /skwɜ:t/ n Spritzer m •vt/i spritzen

St abbr (**Saint**) St.; (**Street**) Str.

stab /stæb/ n Stich m; ([!]: attempt) Versuch m •vt (pt/pp **stabbed**) stechen; (to death) erstechen

stability /stə'bɪlətɪ/ n Stabilität f

stable[1] /'steɪbl/ adj (**-r, -st**) stabil

stable[2] n Stall m; (establishment) Reitstall m

stack /stæk/ n Stapel m; (of chimney) Schornstein m •vt stapeln

stadium /'steɪdɪəm/ n Stadion nt

staff /stɑ:f/ n (stick & Mil) Stab m •(& pl) (employees) Personal nt; (Sch) Lehrkräfte pl •vt mit Personal besetzen. **~-room** n (Sch) Lehrerzimmer nt

stag /stæg/ n Hirsch m

stage /steɪdʒ/ n Bühne f; (in journey) Etappe f; (in process) Stadium nt; **by** or **in ~s** in Etappen •vt aufführen; (arrange) veranstalten

stagger /'stægə(r)/ vi taumeln •vt

staffeln (holidays); versetzt anordnen (seats); **I was ~ed** es hat mir die Sprache verschlagen. **~ing** adj unglaublich

stagnant /'stægnənt/ adj stehend; (fig) stagnierend

stagnate /stæg'neɪt/ vi (fig) stagnieren

stain /steɪn/ n Fleck m; (for wood) Beize f •vt färben; beizen (wood); **~ed glass** farbiges Glas nt. **~less** adj (steel) rostfrei

stair /steə(r)/ n Stufe f; **~s** pl Treppe f. **~case** n Treppe f

stake /steɪk/ n Pfahl m; (wager) Einsatz m; (Comm) Anteil m; **be at ~** auf dem Spiel stehen •vt **~ a claim to sth** Anspruch auf etw (acc) erheben

stale /steɪl/ adj (**-r, -st**) alt; (air) verbraucht. **~mate** n Patt nt

stalk /stɔ:k/ n Stiel m, Stängel m

stall /stɔ:l/ n Stand m; **~s** pl (Theat) Parkett nt •vi (engine:) stehen bleiben; (fig) ausweichen •vt abwürgen (engine)

stalwart /'stɔ:lwət/ adj treu •n treuer Anhänger m

stamina /'stæmɪnə/ n Ausdauer f

stammer /'stæmə(r)/ n Stottern nt •vt/i stottern

stamp /stæmp/ n Stempel m; (postage ~) [Brief]marke f •vt stempeln; (impress) prägen; (put postage on) frankieren •vi stampfen. **~ out** vt [aus]stanzen; (fig) ausmerzen

stampede /stæm'pi:d/ n wilde Flucht f •vi in Panik fliehen

stance /stɑ:ns/ n Haltung f

stand /stænd/ n Stand m; (rack) Ständer m; (pedestal) Sockel m; (Sport) Tribüne f; (fig) Einstellung f •v (pt/pp **stood**) •vi stehen; (rise) aufstehen; (be candidate) kandidieren; (stay valid) gültig bleiben; **~ still** stillstehen; **~ firm** (fig) festbleiben; **~ to reason** logisch sein; **~ in for** vertreten; **~ for** (mean) bedeuten •vt stellen; (withstand) standhalten (+ dat); (endure) ertragen; vertragen (climate); (put up with) aushalten; haben (chance); **~ s.o. a beer** jdm ein Bier spendieren; **I can't ~ her** [!] ich kann sie nicht ausstehen. **~ by** vi daneben stehen; (be ready) sich bereithalten •vt **~ by s.o.** (fig) zu jdm stehen. **~ down** vi (retire) zurücktreten. **~ out** vi hervorstehen; (fig) herausragen. **~ up** vi aufstehen; **~ up for** eintreten für; **~ up to** sich wehren gegen

standard /'stændəd/ adj Normal- •n Maßstab m; (Techn) Norm f; (level) Niveau nt; (flag) Standarte f; **~s** pl (morals) Prinzipien pl. **~ize** vt standardisieren; (Techn) normen

'stand-in n Ersatz m

standing /'stændɪŋ/ adj (erect) stehend; (permanent) ständig •n Rang m; (duration) Dauer f. **~-room** n Stehplätze pl

stand: ~-offish /stænd'ɒfɪʃ/ adj distanziert. **~point** n Standpunkt m. **~still** n Stillstand m; **come to a ~still** zum Stillstand kommen

stank /stæŋk/ see **stink**

staple[1] /'steɪpl/ adj Grund-

staple[2] n Heftklammer f •vt heften. **~r** n Heftmaschine f

star /stɑ:(r)/ n Stern m; (asterisk) Sternchen nt; (Theat, Sport) Star m •vi (pt/pp **starred**) die Hauptrolle spielen

starboard /'stɑ:bəd/ n Steuerbord nt

starch /stɑ:tʃ/ n Stärke f •vt stärken. **~y** adj stärkehaltig; (fig) steif

stare /steə(r)/ n Starren nt •vt starren; **~ at** anstarren

stark /stɑ:k/ adj (**-er, -est**) scharf; (contrast) krass

starling /'stɑ:lɪŋ/ n Star m

start /stɑ:t/ n Anfang m, Beginn m; (departure) Aufbruch m; (Sport) Start m; **from the ~** von Anfang an; **for a ~** erstens •vi anfangen, beginnen; (set out) aufbrechen; (engine:) anspringen; (Auto, Sport) starten; (jump) aufschrecken; **to ~**

with zuerst •vt anfangen, beginnen; (cause) verursachen; (found) gründen; starten (car, race); in Umlauf setzen (rumour). **~er** n (Culin) Vorspeise f; (Auto, Sport) Starter m. **~ing-point** n Ausgangspunkt m

startle /'stɑ:tl/ vt erschrecken

starvation /stɑ:'veɪʃn/ n Verhungern nt

starve /stɑ:v/ vi hungern; (to death) verhungern •vt verhungern lassen

state /steɪt/ n Zustand m; (Pol) Staat m; **~ of play** Spielstand m; **be in a ~** (person:) aufgeregt sein •attrib Staats-, staatlich •vt erklären; (specify) angeben

stately /'steɪtlɪ/ adj stattlich. **~ 'home** n Schloss nt

statement /'steɪtmənt/ n Erklärung f; (Jur) Aussage f; (Banking) Auszug m

'statesman n Staatsmann m

static /'stætɪk/ adj statisch; **remain ~** unverändert bleiben

station /'steɪʃn/ n Bahnhof m; (police) Wache f; (radio) Sender m; (space, weather) Station f; (Mil) Posten m; (status) Rang m •vt stationieren; (post) postieren. **~ary** adj stehend; **be ~ary** stehen

stationery /'steɪʃənrɪ/ n Briefpapier nt; (writing materials) Schreibwaren pl

'station-wagon n (Amer) Kombi[wagen] n

statistic /stə'tɪstɪk/ n statistische Tatsache f. **~al** adj statistisch. **~s** n & pl Statistik f

statue /'stætju:/ n Statue f

stature /'stætʃə(r)/ n Statur f; (fig) Format nt

status /'steɪtəs/ n Status m, Rang m

statut|e /'stætju:t/ n Statut nt. **~ory** adj gesetzlich

staunch /stɔ:ntʃ/ adj (**-er, -est**) treu

stave /steɪv/ vt **~ off** abwenden

stay /steɪ/ n Aufenthalt m •vi bleiben; (reside) wohnen; **~ the night** übernachten. **~ behind** vi zurückbleiben. **~ in** vi zu Hause bleiben; (Sch) nachsitzen. **~ up** vi (person:) aufbleiben

steadily /'stedɪlɪ/ adv fest; (continually) stetig

steady /'stedɪ/ adj fest; (not wobbly) stabil; (hand) ruhig; (regular) regelmäßig; (dependable) zuverlässig

steak /steɪk/ n Steak nt

steal /sti:l/ vt/i (pt **stole**, pp **stolen**) stehlen (**from** dat). **~ in/out** vi sich hinein-/hinausstehlen

stealthy /stelθɪ/ adj heimlich

steam /sti:m/ n Dampf m •vt (Culin) dämpfen, dünsten •vi dampfen. **~ up** vi beschlagen

'steam engine n Dampfmaschine f; (Rail) Dampflokomotive f

steamer /'sti:mə(r)/ n Dampfer m

steamy /'sti:mɪ/ adj dampfig

steel /sti:l/ n Stahl m

steep /sti:p/ adj steil; ([!]: exorbitant) gesalzen

steeple /'sti:pl/ n Kirchturm m

steer /stɪə(r)/ vt/i (Auto) lenken; (Naut) steuern; **~ clear of s.o./sth** jdm/ etw aus dem Weg gehen. **~ing** n (Auto) Lenkung f. **~ing-wheel** n Lenkrad nt

stem[1] /stem/ n Stiel m; (of word) Stamm m

stem[2] vt (pt/pp **stemmed**) eindämmen; stillen (bleeding)

stench /stentʃ/ n Gestank m

stencil /'stensl/ n Schablone f

step /step/ n Schritt m; (stair) Stufe f; **~s** pl (ladder) Trittleiter f; **in ~** im Schritt; **~ by ~** Schritt für Schritt; **take ~s** (fig) Schritte unternehmen •vi (pt/pp **stepped**) treten; **~ in** (fig) eingreifen. **~ up** vt (increase) erhöhen, steigen; verstärken (efforts)

step: ~brother n Stiefbruder m. **~child** n Stiefkind nt. **~daughter** n Stieftochter f. **~father** n Stiefvater m.

~**-ladder** n Trittleiter f. ~**mother** n Stiefmutter f. ~**sister** n Stiefschwester f. ~**son** n Stiefsohn m

stereo /ˈsterɪəʊ/ n Stereo nt; (equipment) Stereoanlage f. ~**phonic** adj stereophon

stereotype /ˈsterɪətaɪp/ n stereotype Figur f

steril|e /ˈsteraɪl/ adj steril. ~**ize** vt sterilisieren

sterling /ˈstɜːlɪŋ/ adj Sterling-; (fig) gediegen •n Sterling m

stern[1] /stɜːn/ adj (**-er, -est**) streng

stern[2] n (of boat) Heck nt

stew /stjuː/ n Eintopf m; **in a** ~ [!] aufgeregt •vt/i schmoren; ~**ed fruit** Kompott nt

steward /ˈstjuːəd/ n Ordner m; (on ship, aircraft) Steward m. ~**ess** n Stewardess f

stick[1] /stɪk/ n Stock m; (of chalk) Stück nt; (of rhubarb) Stange f; (Sport) Schläger m

stick[2] v (pt/pp **stuck**) •vt stecken; (stab) stechen; (glue) kleben; ([!]: put) tun; ([!]: endure) aushalten •vi stecken; (adhere) kleben, haften (**to** an + dat); (jam) klemmen; ~ **at it** [!] dranbleiben; ~ **up** for [!] eintreten für; **be stuck** nicht weiterkönnen; (vehicle:) festsitzen, festgefahren sein; (drawer:) klemmen; **be stuck with sth** [!] etw am Hals haben. ~ **out** vi abstehen; (project) vorstehen •vt hinausstrecken; herausstrecken (tongue)

sticker /ˈstɪkə(r)/ n Aufkleber m

ˈ**sticking plaster** n Heftpflaster nt

sticky /ˈstɪkɪ/ adj klebrig; (adhesive) Klebe-

stiff /stɪf/ adj (**-er, -est**) steif; (brush) hart; (dough) fest; (difficult) schwierig; (penalty) schwer; **be bored** ~ [!] sich zu Tode langweilen. ~**en** vt steif machen •vi steif werden. ~**ness** n Steifheit f

stifl|e /ˈstaɪfl/ vt ersticken; (fig) unterdrücken. ~**ing** adj **be** ~**ing** zum Ersticken sein

still /stɪl/ adj still; (drink) ohne Kohlensäure; **keep** ~ stillhalten; **stand** ~ stillstehen •adv noch; (emphatic) immer noch; (nevertheless) trotzdem; ~ **not** immer noch nicht

ˈ**stillborn** adj tot geboren

still ˈ**life** n Stillleben nt

stilted /ˈstɪltɪd/ adj gestelzt, geschraubt

stimulant /ˈstɪmjʊlənt/ n Anregungsmittel nt

stimulat|e /ˈstɪmjʊleɪt/ vt anregen. ~**ion** n Anregung f

stimulus /ˈstɪmjʊləs/ n (pl **-li** /-laɪ/) Reiz m

sting /stɪŋ/ n Stich m; (from nettle, jellyfish) Brennen nt; (organ) Stachel m •v (pt/pp **stung**) •vt stechen •vi brennen; (insect:) stechen

stingy /ˈstɪndʒɪ/ adj geizig, [!] knauserig

stink /stɪŋk/ n Gestank m •vi (pt **stank**, pp **stunk**) stinken (**of** nach)

stipulat|e /ˈstɪpjʊleɪt/ vt vorschreiben. ~**ion** n Bedingung f

stir /stɜː(r)/ n (commotion) Aufregung f •v (pt/pp **stirred**) vt rühren •vi sich rühren

stirrup /ˈstɪrəp/ n Steigbügel m

stitch /stɪtʃ/ n Stich m; (Knitting) Masche f; (pain) Seitenstechen nt; **be in** ~**es** [!] sich kaputtlachen •vt nähen

stock /stɒk/ n Vorrat m (**of** an + dat); (in shop) [Waren]bestand m; (livestock) Vieh nt; (lineage) Abstammung f; (Finance) Wertpapiere pl; (Culin) Brühe f; (plant) Levkoje f; **in/out of** ~ vorrätig/nicht vorrätig; **take** ~ (fig) Bilanz ziehen •adj Standard- •vt (shop:) führen; auffüllen (shelves). ~ **up** vi sich eindecken (**with** mit)

stock: ~**broker** n Börsenmakler m. **S**~ **Exchange** n Börse f

stocking /ˈstɒkɪŋ/ n Strumpf m

stock: ~**market** n Börse f.

~-taking n (Comm) Inventur f

stocky /ˈstɒkɪ/ adj untersetzt

stodgy /ˈstɒdʒɪ/ adj pappig [und schwer verdaulich]

stoke /stəʊk/ vt heizen

stole /stəʊl/, **stolen** see **steal**

stomach /ˈstʌmək/ n Magen m. **~-ache** n Magenschmerzen pl

stone /stəʊn/ n Stein m; (weight) 6,35kg • adj steinern; (wall, Age) Stein- • vt mit Steinen bewerfen; entsteinen (fruit). **~-cold** adj eiskalt. **~-ˈdeaf** n [!] stocktaub

stony /ˈstəʊnɪ/ adj steinig

stood /stʊd/ see stand

stool /stuːl/ n Hocker m

stoop /stuːp/ n **walk with a ~** gebeugt gehen • vi sich bücken

stop /stɒp/ n Halt m; (break) Pause f; (for bus) Haltestelle f; (for train) Station f; (Gram) Punkt m; (on organ) Register nt; **come to a ~** stehen bleiben; **put a ~ to sth** etw unterbinden • v (pt/pp **stopped**) • vt anhalten, stoppen; (switch off) abstellen; (plug, block) zustopfen; (prevent) verhindern; **~ s.o. doing sth** jdn daran hindern, etw zu tun; **~ doing sth** aufhören, etw zu tun; **~ that!** hör auf damit! • vi anhalten; (cease) aufhören; (clock:) stehen bleiben • int halt!

stop: ~gap n Notlösung f. **~over** n (Aviat) Zwischenlandung f

stoppage /ˈstɒpɪdʒ/ n Unterbrechung f; (strike) Streik m

stopper /ˈstɒpə(r)/ n Stöpsel m

stop-watch n Stoppuhr f

storage /ˈstɔːrɪdʒ/ n Aufbewahrung f; (in warehouse) Lagerung f; (Computing) Speicherung f

store /stɔː(r)/ n (stock) Vorrat m; (shop) Laden m; (department ~) Kaufhaus nt; (depot) Lager nt; **in ~** auf Lager; **be in ~ for s.o.** (fig) jdm bevorstehen • vt aufbewahren; (in warehouse) lagern; (Computing) speichern. **~-room** n Lagerraum m

storey /ˈstɔːrɪ/ n Stockwerk nt

stork /stɔːk/ n Storch m

storm /stɔːm/ n Sturm m; (with thunder) Gewitter nt • vt/i stürmen. **~y** adj stürmisch

story /ˈstɔːrɪ/ n Geschichte f; (in newspaper) Artikel m; ([!]: lie) Märchen nt

stout /staʊt/ adj (**-er, -est**) beleibt; (strong) fest

stove /stəʊv/ n Ofen m; (for cooking) Herd m

stow /stəʊ/ vt verstauen. **~away** n blinder Passagier m

straggl|e /ˈstrægl/ vi hinterherhinken. **~er** n Nachzügler m. **~y** adj strähnig

straight /streɪt/ adj (**-er, -est**) gerade; (direct) direkt; (clear) klar; (hair) glatt; (drink); pur; **be ~** (tidy) in Ordnung sein • adv gerade; (directly) direkt, geradewegs; (clearly) klar; **~ away** sofort; **~ on** or **ahead** geradeaus; **~ out** (fig) geradeheraus; **sit**/**stand up ~** gerade sitzen/stehen

straighten /ˈstreɪtn/ vt gerade machen; (put straight) gerade richten • vi gerade werden; **~ [up]** (person:) sich aufrichten. **~ out** vt gerade biegen

straightˈforward adj offen; (simple) einfach

strain /ˈstreɪn/ n Belastung f; **~s** pl (of music) Klänge pl • vt belasten; (overexert) überanstrengen; (injure) zerren (muscle); (Culin) durchseihen; abgießen (vegetables). **~ed** adj (relations) gespannt. **~er** n Sieb nt

strait /streɪt/ n Meerenge f; **in dire ~s** in großen Nöten

strand[1] /strænd/ n (of thread) Faden m; (of hair) Strähne f

strand[2] vt **be ~ed** festsitzen

strange /streɪndʒ/ adj (**-r, -st**) fremd; (odd) seltsam, merkwürdig. **~ly** adv seltsam, merkwürdig; **~ enough** seltsamerweise. **~r** n Fremde(r) m/f

strangle /ˈstræŋgl/ vt erwürgen; (fig) unterdrücken

strap /stræp/ n Riemen m; (for safety)

S

Gurt m; (to grasp in vehicle) Halteriemen m; (of watch) Armband nt; (shoulder~) Träger m •vt (pt/pp **strapped**) schnallen

strapping /'stræpɪŋ/ adj stramm

strategic /strə'ti:dʒɪk/ adj, **-ally** adv strategisch

strategy /'strætədʒɪ/ n Strategie f

straw /strɔ:/ n Stroh nt; (single piece, drinking) Strohhalm m; **that's the last ~** jetzt reicht's aber

strawberry /'strɔ:bərɪ/ n Erdbeere f

stray /streɪ/ adj streunend •n streunendes Tier nt •vi sich verirren; (deviate) abweichen

streak /stri:k/ n Streifen m; (in hair) Strähne f; (fig: trait) Zug m

stream /stri:m/ n Bach m; (flow) Strom m; (current) Strömung f; (Sch) Parallelzug m •vi strömen

'**streamline** vt (fig) rationalisieren. **~d** adj stromlinienförmig

street /stri:t/ n Straße f. **~car** n (Amer) Straßenbahn f. **~lamp** n Straßenlaterne f

strength /streŋθ/ n Stärke f; (power) Kraft f; **on the ~ of** auf Grund (+ gen). **~en** vt stärken; (reinforce) verstärken

strenuous /'strenjʊəs/ adj anstrengend

stress /stres/ n (emphasis) Betonung f; (strain) Belastung f; (mental) Stress m •vt betonen; (put a strain on) belasten. **~ful** adj stressig [!]

stretch /stretʃ/ n (of road) Strecke f; (elasticity) Elastizität f; **at a ~** ohne Unterbrechung; **have a ~** sich strecken •vt strecken; (widen) dehnen; (spread) ausbreiten; fordern (person); **~ one's legs** sich (dat) die Beine vertreten •vt sich erstrecken; (become wider) sich dehnen; (person:) sich strecken. **~er** n Tragbahre f

strict /strɪkt/ adj (**-er, -est**) streng; **~ly speaking** streng genommen

stride /straɪd/ n [großer] Schritt m; **take sth in one's ~** mit etw gut fertig werden •vi (pt **strode**, pp **stridden**) [mit großen Schritten] gehen

strident /straɪdnt/ adj schrill; (colour) grell

strife /straɪf/ n Streit m

strike /straɪk/ n Streik m; (Mil) Angriff m; **be on ~** streiken •v (pt/pp **struck**) •vt schlagen; (knock against, collide with) treffen; anzünden (match); stoßen auf (+ acc) (oil, gold); abbrechen (camp); (impress) beeindrucken; (occur to) einfallen (+ dat); **~ s.o. a blow** jdm einen Schlag versetzen •vi treffen; (lightning:) einschlagen; (clock:) schlagen; (attack) zuschlagen; (workers:) streiken

striker /'straɪkə(r)/ n Streikende(r) m/f

striking /'straɪkɪŋ/ adj auffallend

string /strɪŋ/ n Schnur f; (thin) Bindfaden m; (of musical instrument, racket) Saite f; (of bow) Sehne f; (of pearls) Kette f; **the ~s** (Mus) die Streicher pl; **pull ~s** [!] seine Beziehungen spielen lassen •vt (pt/pp **strung**) (thread) aufziehen (beads)

stringent /'strɪndʒnt/ adj streng

strip /strɪp/ n Streifen m •v (pt/pp **stripped**) •vt ablösen; ausziehen (person, clothes); abziehen (bed); abbeizen (wood, furniture); auseinander nehmen (machine); (deprive) berauben (of gen); **~ sth off sth** etw von etw entfernen •vi (undress) sich ausziehen

stripe /straɪp/ n Streifen m. **~d** adj gestreift

stripper /'strɪpə(r)/ n Stripperin f; (male) Stripper m

strive /straɪv/ vi (pt **strove**, pp **striven**) sich bemühen (**to** zu); **~ for** streben nach

strode /strəʊd/ see **stride**

stroke[1] /strəʊk/ n Schlag m; (of pen)

Strich m; (Swimming) Zug m; (style) Stil m; (Med) Schlaganfall m; **~ of luck** Glücksfall m

stroke² •vt streicheln

stroll /strəʊl/ n Bummel m [!] •vi bummeln [!]. **~er** n (Amer: pushchair) [Kinder]sportwagen m

strong /strɒŋ/ adj (**-er** /-gə(r)/, **-est** /-gɪst/) stark; (powerful, healthy) kräftig; (severe) streng; (sturdy) stabil; (convincing) gut

strong: ~hold n Festung f; (fig) Hochburg f. **~-room** n Tresorraum m

strove /strəʊv/ see **strive**

struck /strʌk/ see **strike**

structural /'strʌktʃərl/ adj baulich

structure /'strʌktʃə(r)/ n Struktur f; (building) Bau m

struggle /'strʌgl/ n Kampf m; **with a ~** mit Mühe •vt kämpfen; **~ to do sth** sich abmühen, etw zutun

strum /strʌm/ v (pt/pp **strummed**) •vt klimpern auf (+ dat) •vi klimpern

strung /strʌŋ/ see **string**

strut¹ /strʌt/ n Strebe f

strut² vi (pt/pp **strutted**) stolzieren

stub /stʌb/ n Stummel m; (counterfoil) Abschnitt m. **~ out** vt (pt/pp **stubbed**) ausdrücken (cigarette)

stubble /'stʌbl/ n Stoppeln pl

stubborn /'stʌbən/ adj starrsinnig; (refusal) hartnäckig

stubby /'stʌbɪ/ adj (**-ier, -iest**) kurz und dick

stuck /stʌk/ see **stick²**. **~-'up** adj [!] hochnäsig

stud /stʌd/ n Nagel m; (on clothes) Niete f; (for collar) Kragenknopf m; (for ear) Ohrstecker m

student /'stju:dnt/ n Student(in) m(f); (Sch) Schüler(in) m(f)

studio /'stju:dɪəʊ/ n Studio nt; (for artist) Atelier nt

studious /'stju:dɪəs/ adj lerneifrig; (earnest) ernsthaft

stud|y /'stʌdɪ/ n Studie f; (room) Arbeitszimmer nt; (investigation) Untersuchung f; **~ies** pl Studium nt •v (pt/pp **studied**) •vt studieren; (examine) untersuchen •vi lernen; (at university) studieren

stuff /stʌf/ n Stoff m; ([!]: things) Zeug nt •vt vollstopfen; (with padding, Culin) füllen; ausstopfen (animal); (cram) [hinein]stopfen. **~ing** n Füllung f

stuffy /'stʌfɪ/ adj stickig; (old-fashioned) spießig

stumbl|e /'stʌmbl/ vi stolpern; **~e across** zufällig stoßen auf (+ acc). **~ing-block** n Hindernis nt

stump /stʌmp/ n Stumpf m •**~ up** vt/i [!] blechen. **~ed** adj [!] überfragt

stun /stʌn/ vt (pt/pp **stunned**) betäuben

stung /stʌŋ/ see **sting**

stunk /stʌŋk/ see **stink**

stunning /'stʌnɪŋ/ adj [!] toll

stunt /stʌnt/ n [!] Kunststück nt

stupendous /stju:'pendəs/ adj enorm

stupid /'stju:pɪd/ adj dumm. **~ity** n Dummheit f. **~ly** adv dumm; **~ly [enough]** dummerweise

sturdy /'stɜ:dɪ/ adj stämmig; (furniture) stabil; (shoes) fest

stutter /'stʌtə(r)/ n Stottern nt •vt/i stottern

sty /staɪ/ n (pl **sties**) Schweinestall m

style /staɪl/ n Stil m; (fashion) Mode f; (sort) Art f; (hair~) Frisur f; **in ~** in großem Stil

stylish /'staɪlɪʃ/ adj, **-ly** adv stilvoll

stylist /'staɪlɪst/ n Friseur m/ Friseuse f. **~ic** adj, **-ally** adv stilistisch

suave /swɑ:v/ adj (pej) gewandt

sub'conscious /sʌb-/ adj

unterbewusst •n Unterbewusstsein nt

'subdivi|de vt unterteilen. **~sion** n Unterteilung f

subdue /səb'dju:/ vt unterwerfen. **~d** adj gedämpft; (person) still

subject¹ /'sʌbdʒɪkt/ adj **be ~ to sth** etw (dat) unterworfen sein •n Staatsbürger(in) m(f); (of ruler) Untertan m; (theme) Thema nt; (of investigation) Gegenstand m; (Sch) Fach nt; (Gram) Subjekt nt

subject² /səb'dʒekt/ vt unterwerfen (**to** dat); (expose) aussetzen (**to** dat)

subjective /səb'dʒektɪv/ adj subjektiv

subjunctive /səb'dʒʌŋktɪv/ n Konjunktiv m

sublime /sə'blaɪm/ adj erhaben

subma'rine n Unterseeboot nt

submerge /səb'mɜ:dʒ/ vt untertauchen; **be ~d** unter Wasser stehen •vi tauchen

submission /səb'mɪʃn/ n Unterwerfung f

submit /səb'mɪt/ v (pt/pp **-mitted**, pres p **-mitting**) •vt vorlegen (**to** dat); (hand in) einreichen •vi sich unterwerfen (**to** dat)

subordinate¹ /sə'bɔ:dɪnət/ adj untergeordnet •n Untergebene(r) m/f

subordinate² /sə'bɔ:dɪneɪt/ vt unterordnen (**to** dat)

subscribe /səb'skraɪb/ vi spenden; **~ to** (fig); abonnieren (newspaper). **~r** n Spender m; Abonnent m

subscription /səb'skrɪpʃn/ n (to club) [Mitglieds]beitrag m; (to newspaper) Abonnement nt; **by ~** mit Spenden; (buy) im Abonnement

subsequent /'sʌbsɪkwənt/ adj folgend; (later) später

subside /səb'saɪd/ vi sinken; (ground:) sich senken; (storm:) nachlassen

subsidiary /səb'sɪdɪərɪ/ adj untergeordnet •n Tochtergesellschaft f

subsid|ize /'sʌbsɪdaɪz/ vt subventionieren. **~y** n Subvention f

substance /'sʌbstəns/ n Substanz f

sub'standard adj unzulänglich; (goods) minderwertig

substantial /səb'stænʃl/ adj solide; (meal) reichhaltig; (considerable) beträchtlich. **~ly** adv solide; (essentially) im Wesentlichen

substitut|e /'sʌbstɪtju:t/ n Ersatz m; (Sport) Ersatzspieler(in) m(f) •vt **~e A for B** B durch A ersetzen •vi **~e for s.o.** jdn vertreten. **~ion** n Ersetzung f

subterranean /sʌbtə'reɪnɪən/ adj unterirdisch

'subtitle n Untertitel m

subtle /'sʌtl/ adj (**-r, -st**), **-tly** adv fein; (fig) subtil

subtract /səb'trækt/ vt abziehen, subtrahieren. **~ion** n Subtraktion f

suburb /'sʌbɜ:b/ n Vorort m. **~an** adj Vorort-. **~ia** n die Vororte pl

'subway n Unterführung f; (Amer: railway) U-Bahn f

succeed /sək'si:d/ vi Erfolg haben; (plan:) gelingen; (follow) nachfolgen (+ dat); **I ~ed** es ist mir gelungen; **he ~ed in escaping** es gelang ihm zu entkommen •vt folgen (+ dat)

success /sək'ses/ n Erfolg m. **~ful** adj, **-ly** adv erfolgreich

succession /sək'seʃn/ n Folge f; (series) Serie f; (to title, office) Nachfolge f; (to throne) Thronfolge f; **in ~** hintereinander

successive /sək'sesɪv/ adj aufeinander folgend

successor /sək'sesə(r)/ n Nachfolger(in) m(f)

succumb /sə'kʌm/ vi erliegen (**to** dat)

such /sʌtʃ/
• adjective
····➤ (of that kind) solch. **such a book** ein solches Buch; so ein Buch [!]. **such a person** ein solcher Mensch; so ein Mensch [!]. **such people** solche Leute. **such a thing** so etwas. **no such example** kein solches Beispiel. **there is no such thing** so etwas gibt es nicht; das gibt es gar nicht. **there is no such person** eine solche Person gibt es nicht. **such writers as Goethe and Schiller** Schriftsteller wie Goethe und Schiller
····➤ (so great) solch; derartig. **I've got such a headache!** ich habe solche Kopfschmerzen! **it was such fun!** das machte solchen Spaß! **I got such a fright that ...** ich bekam einen derartigen od [!] so einen Schrecken, dass ...
····➤ (with adjective) so. **such a big house** ein so großes Haus. **he has such lovely blue eyes** er hat so schöne blaue Augen. **such a long time** so lange
• pronoun
····➤ **as such** als solcher/solche/solches. **the thing as such** die Sache als solche. (strictly speaking) **this is not a promotion as such** dies ist im Grunde genommen keine Beförderung
····➤ **such is**: **such is life** so ist das Leben. **such is not the case** das ist nicht der Fall
····➤ **such as** wie [zum Beispiel]

suchlike /ˈsʌtʃlaɪk/ pron [!] dergleichen

suck /ʃʌk/ vt/i saugen; lutschen (sweet). ~ **up** vt aufsaugen • vi ~ **up to s.o.** [!] sich bei jdm einschmeicheln

suction /ˈsʌkʃn/ n Saugwirkung f

sudden /ˈsʌdn/ adj plötzlich; (abrupt) jäh • n **all of a** ~ auf einmal

sue /suː/ vt (pres p **suing**) verklagen (**for** auf + acc) • vi klagen

suede /sweɪd/ n Wildleder nt

suet /ˈsuːɪt/ n [Nieren]talg m

suffer /ˈsʌfə(r)/ vi leiden (**from** an + dat) • vt erleiden; (tolerate) dulden

suffice /səˈfaɪs/ vi genügen

sufficient /səˈfɪʃnt/ adj genug, genügend; **be** ~ genügen

suffocat|e /ˈsʌfəkeɪt/ vt/i ersticken. ~**ion** n Ersticken nt

sugar /ˈʃʊgə(r)/ n Zucker m • vt zuckern; (fig) versüßen. ~ **basin,** ~**-bowl** n Zuckerschale f. ~**y** adj süß; (fig) süßlich

suggest /səˈdʒest/ vt vorschlagen; (indicate, insinuate) andeuten. ~**ion** n Vorschlag m; Andeutung f; (trace) Spur f. ~**ive** adj anzüglich

suicidal /suːɪˈsaɪdl/ adj selbstmörderisch

suicide /ˈsuːɪsaɪd/ n Selbstmord m

suit /suːt/ n Anzug m; (woman's) Kostüm nt; (Cards) Farbe f; (Jur) Prozess m • vt (adapt) anpassen (**to** dat); (be convenient for) passen (+ dat); (go with) passen zu; (clothing:) stehen (**s.o.** jdm); **be** ~**ed for** geeignet sein für; ~ **yourself!** wie du willst!

suit|able /ˈsuːtəbl/ adj geeignet; (convenient) passend; (appropriate) angemessen; (for weather, activity) zweckmäßig. ~**ably** adv angemessen; zweckmäßig

ˈsuitcase n Koffer m

suite /swiːt/ n Suite f; (of furniture) Garnitur f

sulk /sʌlk/ vi schmollen. ~**y** adj schmollend

sullen /ˈsʌlən/ adj mürrisch

sultry /ˈsʌltrɪ/ adj (**-ier, -iest**) (weather) schwül

sum /sʌm/ n Summe f; (Sch) Rechenaufgabe f • vt/i (pt/pp **summed**) ~ **up** zusammenfassen; (assess) einschätzen

summar|ize /ˈsʌməraɪz/ vt zusammenfassen. ~**y** n Zusammenfassung f • adj, **-ily** adv summarisch; (dismissal) fristlos

summer /ˈsʌmə(r)/ n Sommer m. ~**time** n Sommer m

summery /'sʌmərɪ/ adj sommerlich

summit /'sʌmɪt/ n Gipfel m. **~ conference** n Gipfelkonferenz f

summon /'sʌmən/ vt rufen; holen (help); (Jur) vorladen

summons /'sʌmənz/ n (Jur) Vorladung f •vt vorladen

sumptuous /'sʌmptjʊəs/ adj prunkvoll; (meal) üppig

sun /sʌn/ n Sonne f •vt (pt/pp **sunned**) **~ oneself** sich sonnen

sun: ~bathe vi sich sonnen. **~-bed** n Sonnenbank f. **~burn** n Sonnenbrand m

Sunday /'sʌndeɪ/ n Sonntag m

'sunflower n Sonnenblume f

sung /sʌŋ/ see **sing**

'sunglasses npl Sonnenbrille f

sunk /sʌŋk/ see **sink**

sunny /'sʌnɪ/ adj (**-ier, -iest**) sonnig

sun: ~rise n Sonnenaufgang m. **~-roof** n (Auto) Schiebedach nt. **~set** n Sonnenuntergang m. **~shade** n Sonnenschirm m. **~shine** n Sonnenschein m. **~stroke** n Sonnenstich m. **~-tan** n [Sonnen]bräune f. **~-tanned** adj braun [gebrannt]. **~-tan oil** n Sonnenöl nt

super /'su:pə(r)/ adj [!] prima, toll

superb /sʊ'pɜ:b/ adj erstklassig

superficial /su:pə'fɪʃl/ a oberflächlich

superfluous /sʊ'pɜ:flʊəs/ adj überflüssig

superintendent /su:pərɪn'tendənt/ n (of police) Kommissar m

superior /su:'pɪərɪə(r)/ a überlegen; (in rank) höher •n Vorgesetzte(r) m/f. **~ity** n Überlegenheit f

superlative /su:'pɜ:lətɪv/ a unübertrefflich •n Superlativ m

'supermarket n Supermarkt m

super'natural adj übernatürlich

supersede /su:pə'si:d/ vt ersetzen

superstiti|on /su:pə'stɪʃn/ n Aberglaube m. **~ous** adj abergläubisch

supervis|e /'su:pəvaɪz/ vt beaufsichtigen; überwachen (work). **~ion** n Aufsicht f; Überwachung f. **~or** n Aufseher(in) m(f)

supper /'sʌpə(r)/ n Abendessen nt

supple /'sʌpl/ adj geschmeidig

supplement /'sʌplɪmənt/ n Ergänzung f; (addition) Zusatz m; (to fare) Zuschlag m; (book) Ergänzungsband m; (to newspaper) Beilage f •vt ergänzen. **~ary** adj zusätzlich

supplier /sə'plaɪə(r)/ n Lieferant m

supply /sə'plaɪ/ n Vorrat m; **supplies** pl (Mil) Nachschub m •vt (pt/pp **-ied**) liefern; **~ s.o. with sth** jdn mit etw versorgen

support /sə'pɔ:t/ n Stütze f; (fig) Unterstützung f •vt stützen; (bear weight of) tragen; (keep) ernähren; (give money to) unterstützen; (speak in favour of) befürworten; (Sport) Fan sein von. **~er** n Anhänger(in) m(f); (Sport) Fan m

suppose /sə'pəʊz/ vt annehmen; (presume) vermuten; (imagine) sich (dat) vorstellen; **be ~d to do sth** etw tun sollen; **not be ~d to** [!] nicht dürfen; **I ~ so** vermutlich. **~dly** adv angeblich

supposition /sʌpə'zɪʃn/ n Vermutung f

suppress /sə'pres/ vt unterdrücken. **~ion** n Unterdrückung f

supremacy /su:'preməsɪ/ n Vorherrschaft f

supreme /su:'pri:m/ adj höchste(r,s); (court) oberste(r,s)

sure /ʃʊə(r)/ adj (**-r, -st**) sicher; **make ~** sich vergewissern (**of** gen); (check) nachprüfen •adv (Amer, [!]) klar; **~ enough** tatsächlich. **~ly** adv sicher; (for emphasis) doch; (Amer: gladly) gern

surf /'sɜ:f/ n Brandung f •vi surfen

surface /'sɜ:fɪs/ n Oberfläche f •vi (emerge) auftauchen

'surfboard n Surfbrett nt

surfing /'sɜ:fɪŋ/ n Surfen nt

surge /sɜ:dʒ/ n (of sea) Branden nt; (fig) Welle f •vi branden; **~ forward** nach vorn drängen

surgeon /'sɜ:dʒən/ n Chirurg(in) m(f)

surgery /'sɜ:dʒərɪ/ n Chirurgie f; (place) Praxis f; (room) Sprechzimmer nt; (hours) Sprechstunde f; **have ~** operiert werden

surgical /'sɜ:dʒɪkl/ adj chirurgisch

surly /'sɜ:lɪ/ adj mürrisch

surname /'sɜ:neɪm/ n Nachname m

surpass /sə'pɑ:s/ vt übertreffen

surplus /'sɜ:pləs/ adj überschüssig •n Überschuss m (**of** an + dat)

surpris|e /sə'praɪz/ n Überraschung f •vt überraschen; **be ~ed** sich wundern (**at** über + acc). **~ing** adj überraschend

surrender /sə'rendə(r)/ n Kapitulation f •vi sich ergeben; (Mil) kapitulieren •vt aufgeben

surround /sə'raʊnd/ vt umgeben; (encircle) umzingeln; **~ed by** umgeben von. **~ing** adj umliegend. **~ings** npl Umgebung f

surveillance /sə'veɪləns/ n Überwachung f; **be under ~** überwacht werden

survey¹ /'sɜ:veɪ/ n Überblick m; (poll) Umfrage f; (investigation) Untersuchung f; (of land) Vermessung f; (of house) Gutachten nt

survey² /sə'veɪ/ vt betrachten; vermessen (land); begutachten (building). **~or** n Landvermesser m; Gutachter m

survival /sə'vaɪvl/ n Überleben nt; (of tradition) Fortbestand m

surviv|e /sə'vaɪv/ vt überleben •vi überleben; (tradition:) erhalten bleiben. **~or** n Überlebende(r) m/f; **be a ~or** nicht unterzukriegen sein

susceptible /sə'septəbl/ adj empfänglich/ (Med) anfällig (**to** für)

suspect¹ /sə'spekt/ vt verdächtigen; (assume) vermuten; **he ~s nothing** er ahnt nichts

suspect² /'sʌspekt/ adj verdächtig •n Verdächtige(r) m/f

suspend /sə'spend/ vt aufhängen; (stop) [vorläufig] einstellen; (from duty) vorläufig beurlauben. **~ders** npl (Amer: braces) Hosenträger pl

suspense /sə'spens/ n Spannung f

suspension /sə'spenʃn/ n (Auto) Federung f. **~ bridge** n Hängebrücke f

suspici|on /sə'spɪʃn/ n Verdacht m; (mistrust) Misstrauen nt; (trace) Spur f. **~ous** adj misstrauisch; (arousing suspicion) verdächtig

sustain /sə'steɪn/ vt tragen; (fig) aufrechterhalten; erhalten (life); erleiden (injury)

sustenance /'sʌstɪnəns/ n Nahrung f

swagger /'swægə(r)/ vi stolzieren

swallow¹ /'swɒləʊ/ vt/i schlucken. **~ up** vt verschlucken; verschlingen (resources)

swallow² n (bird) Schwalbe f

swam /swæm/ see **swim**

swamp /swɒmp/ n Sumpf m •vt überschwemmen

swan /swɒn/ n Schwan m

swank /swæŋk/ vi [!] angeben

swap /swɒp/ n [!] Tausch m •vt/i (pt/pp **swapped**) [!] tauschen (**for** gegen)

swarm /swɔ:m/ n Schwarm m •vi schwärmen; **be ~ing with** wimmeln von

swat /swɒt/ vt (pt/pp **swatted**) totschlagen

sway /sweɪ/ vi schwanken; (gently) sich wiegen •vt (influence) beeinflussen

swear /sweə(r)/ v (pt **swore**, pp **sworn**) •vt schwören •vi schwören (**by** auf + acc); (curse) fluchen. **~-word** n Kraftausdruck m

S

sweat /swet/ n Schweiß m • vi schwitzen

sweater /'swetə(r)/ n Pullover m

Swed|e n Schwede m/Schwedin f. **~en** n Schweden nt. **~ish** adj schwedisch

sweep /swi:p/ n Schornsteinfeger m; (curve) Bogen m; (movement) ausholende Bewegung f • v (pt/pp **swept**) • vt fegen, kehren • vi (go swiftly) rauschen; (wind:) fegen

sweeping /'swi:pɪŋ/ adj ausholend; (statement) pauschal; (changes) weit reichend

sweet /swi:t/ adj (**-er, -est**) süß; **have a ~ tooth** gern Süßes mögen • n Bonbon m & nt; (dessert) Nachtisch m

sweeten /'swi:tn/ vt süßen

sweet: ~heart n Schatz m. **~ness** n Süße f. **~ 'pea** n Wicke f. **~-shop** n Süßwarenladen m

swell /swel/ n Dünung f • v (pt **swelled**, pp **swollen** or **swelled**) • vi [an]schwellen; (wood:) aufquellen • vt anschwellen lassen; (increase) vergrößern. **~ing** n Schwellung f

swelter /'sweltə(r)/ vi schwitzen

swept /swept/ see **sweep**

swerve /swɜ:v/ vi einen Bogen machen

swift /swɪft/ adj (**-er, -est**) schnell

swig /swɪg/ n ! Schluck m

swim /swɪm/ n **have a ~** schwimmen • vi (**pt swam**, pp **swum**) schwimmen; **my head is ~ming** mir dreht sich der Kopf. **~mer** n Schwimmer(in) m(f)

swimming /'swɪmɪŋ/ n Schwimmen nt. **~-baths** npl Schwimmbad nt. **~-pool** n Schwimmbecken nt; (private) Swimmingpool m

'swimsuit n Badeanzug m

swindle /'swɪndl/ n Schwindel m, Betrug m • vt betrügen. **~r** n Schwindler m

swine /swaɪn/ n (pej) Schwein nt

swing /swɪŋ/ n Schwung m; (shift) Schwenk m; (seat) Schaukel f; **in full ~** in vollem Gange • (pt/pp **swung**) • vi schwingen; (on swing) schaukeln; (dangle) baumeln; (turn) schwenken • vt schwingen; (influence) beeinflussen

swipe /swaɪp/ n ! Schlag m • vt ! knallen; (steal) klauen

swirl /swɜ:l/ n Wirbel m • vt/i wirbeln

Swiss /swɪs/ adj Schweizer-, schweizerisch • n Schweizer(in) m(f); **the ~** pl die Schweizer. **~ 'roll** n Biskuitrolle f

switch /swɪtʃ/ n Schalter m; (change) Wechsel m; (Amer, Rail) Weiche f • vt wechseln; (exchange) tauschen • vi wechseln; **~ to** umstellen auf (+ acc). **~ off** vt ausschalten; abschalten (engine). **~ on** vt einschalten

switchboard n [Telefon]zentrale f

Switzerland /'swɪtsələnd/ n die Schweiz

swivel /'swɪvl/ v (pt/pp **swivelled**) • vt drehen • vi sich drehen

swollen /'swəʊlən/ see **swell**

swoop /swu:p/ n (by police) Razzia f • vi **~ down** herabstoßen

sword /sɔ:d/ n Schwert nt

swore /swɔ:(r)/ see **swear**

sworn /swɔ:n/ see **swear**

swot /swɒt/ n ! Streber m • vt (pt/pp **swotted**) ! büffeln

swum /swʌm/ see **swim**

swung /swʌŋ/ see **swing**

syllable /'sɪləbl/ n Silbe f

syllabus /'sɪləbəs/ n Lehrplan m; (for exam) Studienplan m

symbol /'sɪmbəl/ n Symbol nt (**of** für). **~ic** adj, **-ally** adv symbolisch **~ism** n Symbolik f. **~ize** vt symbolisieren

symmetr|ical /sɪ'metrɪkl/ adj symmetrisch. **~y** n Symmetrie f

sympathetic /sɪmpə'θetɪk/ adj, **-ally** adv mitfühlend; (likeable) sympathisch

sympathize /'sɪmpəθaɪz/ vi mitfühlen

S

sympathy /ˈsɪmpəθɪ/ n Mitgefühl nt; (condolences) Beileid nt

symphony /ˈsɪmfənɪ/ n Sinfonie f

symptom /ˈsɪmptəm/ n Symptom nt

synagogue /ˈsɪnəgɒg/ n Synagoge f

synchronize /ˈsɪŋkrənaɪz/ vt synchronisieren

synonym /ˈsɪnənɪm/ n Synonym nt. **~ous** adj synonym

synthesis /ˈsɪnθəsɪs/ n (pl **-ses** /-siːz/) Synthese f

synthetic /sɪnˈθetɪk/ adj synthetisch

Syria /ˈsɪrɪə/ n Syrien nt

syringe /sɪˈrɪndʒ/ n Spritze f

syrup /ˈsɪrəp/ n Sirup m

system /ˈsɪstəm/ n System nt. **~atic** adj, **-ally** adv systematisch

Tt

tab /tæb/ n (projecting) Zunge f; (with name) Namensschild nt; (loop) Aufhänger m; **pick up the ~** [!] bezahlen

table /ˈteɪbl/ n Tisch m; (list) Tabelle f; **at [the] ~** bei Tisch. **~-cloth** n Tischdecke f. **~spoon** n Servierlöffel m

tablet /ˈtæblɪt/ n Tablette f; (of soap) Stück nt

ˈ**table tennis** n Tischtennis nt

tabloid /ˈtæblɔɪd/ n kleinformatige Zeitung f; (pej) Boulevardzeitung f

taciturn /ˈtæsɪtɜːn/ adj wortkarg

tack /tæk/ n (nail) Stift m; (stitch) Heftstich m; (Naut & fig) Kurs m • vt festnageln; (sew) heften • vi (Naut) kreuzen

tackle /ˈtækl/ n Ausrüstung f • vt angehen (problem); (Sport) angreifen

tact /tækt/ n Takt m, Taktgefühl nt. **~ful** adj taktvoll

tactic|al /ˈtæktɪkl/ adj taktisch. **~s** npl Taktik f

tactless /ˈtæktlɪs/ adj taktlos. **~ness** n Taktlosigkeit f

tag /tæg/ n (label) Schild nt • vi (pt/pp **tagged**) **~ along** mitkommen

tail /teɪl/ n Schwanz m; **~s** pl (tailcoat) Frack m; **heads or ~s?** Kopf oder Zahl? • vt ([!]: follow) beschatten • vi **~ off** zurückgehen

tail: ~back n Rückstau m. **~ light** n Rücklicht nt

tailor /ˈteɪlə(r)/ n Schneider m. **~-made** adj maßgeschneidert

taint /teɪnt/ vt verderben

take /teɪk/ v (pt **took**, pp **taken**) • vt nehmen: (with one) mitnehmen; (take to a place) bringen; (steal) stehlen; (win) gewinnen; (capture) einnehmen; (require) brauchen; (last) dauern; (teach) geben; machen (exam, subject, holiday, photograph); messen (pulse, temperature); **~ sth to the cleaner's** etw in die Reinigung bringen; **be ~n ill** krank werden; **~ sth calmly** etw gelassen aufnehmen • vi (plant:) angehen; **~ after s.o.** jdm nachschlagen; (in looks) jdm ähnlich sehen; **~ to** (like) mögen; (as a habit) sich (dat) angewöhnen. **~ away** vt wegbringen; (remove) wegnehmen; (subtract) abziehen; **'to ~ away'** 'zum Mitnehmen'. **~ back** vt zurücknehmen; (return) zurückbringen. **~ down** vt herunternehmen; (remove) abnehmen; (write down) aufschreiben. **~ in** vt hineinbringen; (bring indoors) hereinholen; (to one's home) aufnehmen; (understand) begreifen; (deceive) hereinlegen; (make smaller) enger machen. ~ **off** vt abnehmen; ablegen (coat); sich (dat) ausziehen (clothes); (deduct) abziehen; (mimic) nachmachen •vi (Aviat) starten. ~ **on** vt annehmen; (undertake) übernehmen; (engage) einstellen; (as opponent) antreten gegen. ~ **out** vt hinausbringen; (for pleasure) ausgehen mit; ausführen (dog); (remove) herausnehmen; (withdraw) abheben (money); (from library) ausleihen; ~ **it out on s.o.** [!] seinen Ärger an jdm auslassen. ~ **over** vt hinüberbringen; übernehmen (firm, control) •vi ~ **over from s.o.** jdn ablösen. ~ **up** vt hinaufbringen; annehmen (offer); ergreifen (profession); sich (dat) zulegen (hobby); in Anspruch nehmen (time); einnehmen (space); aufreißen (floorboards); ~ **sth up with s.o.** mit jdm über etw (acc) sprechen

take: ~**-away** n Essen nt zum Mitnehmen; (restaurant) Restaurant nt mit Straßenverkauf. ~**-off** n (Aviat) Start m, Abflug m. ~**-over** n Übernahme f

takings /'teɪkɪŋz/ npl Einnahmen pl

talcum /'tælkəm/ n ~ **[powder]** Körperpuder m

tale /teɪl/ n Geschichte f

talent /'tælənt/ n Talent nt

talk /tɔ:k/ n Gespräch nt; (lecture) Vortrag m •vi reden, sprechen (**to/with** mit) •vt reden; ~ **s.o. into sth** jdn zu etw überreden. ~ **over** vt besprechen

talkative /'tɔ:kətɪv/ adj gesprächig

tall /tɔ:l/ adj (**-er, -est**) groß; (building, tree) hoch. ~ **'story** n übertriebene Geschichte f

tally /'tælɪ/ vi übereinstimmen

tame /teɪm/ adj (**-r, -st**) zahm; (dull) lahm [!] •vt zähmen. ~**r** n Dompteur m

tamper /'tæmpə(r)/ vi ~ **with** sich (dat) zu schaffen machen an (+ dat)

tampon /'tæmpɒn/ n Tampon m

tan /tæn/ adj gelbbraun •n Gelbbraun nt; (from sun) Bräune f •v (pt/pp **tanned**) •vt gerben (hide) •vi braun werden

tang /tæŋ/ n herber Geschmack m; (smell) herber Geruch m

tangible /'tændʒɪbl/ adj greifbar

tangle /'tæŋgl/ n Gewirr nt; (in hair) Verfilzung f •vt ~ **[up]** verheddern •vi sich verheddern

tank /tæŋk/ n Tank m; (Mil) Panzer m

tanker /'tæŋkə(r)/ n Tanker m; (lorry) Tank[last]wagen m

tantrum /'tæntrəm/ n Wutanfall m

tap /tæp/ n Hahn m; (knock) Klopfen nt; **on** ~ zur Verfügung •v (pt/pp **tapped**) •vt klopfen an (+ acc); anzapfen (barrel, tree); erschließen (resources); abhören (telephone) •vi klopfen. ~**-dance** n Stepp[tanz] m •vi Stepp tanzen, steppen

tape /teɪp/ n Band nt; (adhesive) Klebstreifen m; (for recording) Tonband nt •vt mit Klebstreifen zukleben; (record) auf Band aufnehmen

'tape-measure n Bandmaß nt

taper /'teɪpə(r)/ vi sich verjüngen

'tape recorder n Tonbandgerät nt

tar /tɑ:(r)/ n Teer m •vt (pt/pp **tarred**) teeren

target /'tɑ:gɪt/ n Ziel nt; (board) [Ziel]scheibe f

tarnish /'tɑ:nɪʃ/ vi anlaufen

tarpaulin /tɑ:'pɔ:lɪn/ n Plane f

tart[1] /tɑ:t/ adj (**-er, -est**) sauer

tart[2] n ≈ Obstkuchen m; (individual) Törtchen nt; (sl: prostitute) Nutte f •vt ~ **oneself up** [!] sich auftakeln

tartan /'tɑ:tn/ n Schottenmuster nt; (cloth) Schottenstoff m

task /tɑ:sk/ n Aufgabe f; **take s.o. to** ~ jdm Vorhaltungen machen. ~ **force** n Sonderkommando nt

tassel /'tæsl/ n Quaste f

taste /teɪst/ n Geschmack m; (sample) Kostprobe f •vt kosten, probieren; schmecken (flavour) •vi schmecken (**of** nach). ~**ful** adj (fig)

t

geschmackvoll. **~less** adj geschmacklos

tasty /'teɪstɪ/ adj lecker

tat /tæt/ see **tit**[2]

tatters /'tætəz/ npl **in ~s** in Fetzen

tattoo /tə'tu:/ n Tätowierung f •vt tätowieren

tatty /'tætɪ/ adj schäbig; (book) zerfleddert

taught /tɔ:t/ see **teach**

taunt /tɔ:nt/ n höhnische Bemerkung f •vt verhöhnen

taut /tɔ:t/ adj straff

tawdry /'tɔ:drɪ/ adj billig und geschmacklos

tax /tæks/ n Steuer f •vt besteuern; (fig) strapazieren. **~able** adj steuerpflichtig. **~ation** n Besteuerung f

taxi /'tæksɪ/ n Taxi nt •vi (pt/pp **taxied**, pres p **taxiing**) (aircraft:) rollen. **~ driver** n Taxifahrer m. **~ rank** n Taxistand m

'taxpayer n Steuerzahler m

tea /ti:/ n Tee m. **~-bag** n Teebeutel m. **~-break** n Teepause f

teach /ti:tʃ/ vt/i (pt/pp **taught**) unterrichten; **~ s.o. sth** jdm etw beibringen. **~er** n Lehrer(in) m(f). **~ing** n Unterrichten nt

tea: ~-cloth n (for drying) Geschirrtuch nt. **~cup** n Teetasse f

teak /ti:k/ n Teakholz nt

team /ti:m/ n Mannschaft f; (fig) Team nt; (of animals) Gespann nt

'teapot n Teekanne f

tear[1] /teə(r)/ n Riss m •v (pt **tore**, pp **torn**) •vt reißen; (damage) zerreißen; **~ oneself away** sich losreißen •vi [zer]reißen; (run) rasen. **~ up** vt zerreißen

tear[2] /tɪə(r)/ n Träne f. **~ful** adj weinend. **~fully** adv unter Tränen. **~gas** n Tränengas nt

tease /ti:z/ vt necken

tea: ~-set n Teeservice nt. **~ shop** n Café nt. **~spoon** n Teelöffel m

teat /ti:t/ n Zitze f; (on bottle) Sauger m

'tea-towel n Geschirrtuch nt

technical /'teknɪkl/ adj technisch; (specialized) fachlich. **~ity** n technisches Detail nt; (Jur) Formfehler m. **~ly** adv technisch; (strictly) streng genommen. **~ term** n Fachausdruck m

technician /tek'nɪʃn/ n Techniker m

technique /tek'ni:k/ n Technik f

technological /teknə'lɒdʒɪkl/ adj technologisch

technology /tek'nɒlədʒɪ/ n Technik f

teddy /'tedɪ/ n **~ [bear]** Teddybär m

tedious /'ti:dɪəs/ adj langweilig

tedium /'ti:dɪəm/ n Langeweile f

teenage /'ti:neɪdʒ/ adj Teenager-; **~ boy/girl** Junge m/Mädchen nt im Teenageralter. **~r** n Teenager m

teens /ti:nz/ npl **the ~** die Teenagerjahre pl

teeter /'ti:tə(r)/ vi schwanken

teeth /ti:θ/ see **tooth**

teeth|e /ti:ð/ vi zahnen. **~ing troubles** npl (fig) Anfangsschwierigkeiten pl

teetotal /ti:'təʊtl/ adj abstinent. **~ler** n Abstinenzler m

telebanking /'telɪbæŋkɪŋ/ n Telebanking nt

telecommunications /telɪkəmju:nɪ'keɪʃnz/ npl Fernmeldewesen nt

telegram /'telɪgræm/ n Telegramm nt

telegraph /'telɪgrɑ:f/ **~ pole** n Telegrafenmast m

telephone /'telɪfəʊn/ n Telefon nt; **be on the ~** Telefon haben; (be telephoning) telefonieren •vt anrufen •vi telefonieren

telephone: ~ booth n, **~ box** n Telefonzelle f. **~ directory** n Telefonbuch nt. **~ number** n Telefonnummer f

tele'photo /telɪ-/ adj ~ **lens** Teleobjektiv nt

telescop|e /'telɪskəʊp/ n Teleskop nt, Fernrohr nt. **~ic** adj (collapsible) ausziehbar

televise /'telɪvaɪz/ vt im Fernsehen übertragen

television /'telɪvɪʒn/ n Fernsehen nt; **watch ~** fernsehen; **~ [set]** Fernseher m [!]

teleworking /'telɪwɜ:kɪŋ/ n Telearbeit f

tell /tel/ vt/i (pt/pp **told**) sagen (**s.o.** jdm); (relate) erzählen; (know) wissen; (distinguish) erkennen; **~ the time** die Uhr lesen; **time will ~** das wird man erst sehen; **his age is beginning to ~** sein Alter macht sich bemerkbar. **~ off** vt ausschimpfen

telly /'telɪ/ n [!] = **television**

temp /temp/ n [!] Aushilfssekretärin f

temper /'tempə(r)/ n (disposition) Naturell nt; (mood) Laune f; (anger) Wut f; **lose one's ~** wütend werden •vt (fig) mäßigen

temperament /'temprəmənt/ n Temperament nt. **~al** adj temperamentvoll; (moody) launisch

temperate /'tempərət/ adj gemäßigt

temperature /'temprətʃə(r)/ n Temperatur f; **have** or **run a ~** Fieber haben

temple[1] /'templ/ n Tempel m

temple[2] n (Anat) Schläfe f

t

tempo /'tempəʊ/ n Tempo nt

temporary /'tempərərɪ/ adj, **-ily** adv vorübergehend; (measure, building) provisorisch

tempt /tempt/ vt verleiten; (Relig) versuchen; herausfordern (fate); (entice) [ver]locken; **be ~ed** versucht sein (**to** zu). **~ation** n Versuchung f. **~ing** adj verlockend

ten /ten/ adj zehn

tenaci|ous /tɪ'neɪʃəs/ adj, **-ly** adv hartnäckig. **~ty** n Hartnäckigkeit f

tenant /'tenənt/ n Mieter(in) m(f); (Comm) Pächter(in) m(f)

tend /tend/ vi **~ to do sth** dazu neigen, etw zu tun

tendency /'tendənsɪ/ n Tendenz f; (inclination) Neigung f

tender /'tendə(r)/ adj zart; (loving) zärtlich; (painful) empfindlich. **~ly** adv zärtlich. **~ness** n Zartheit f; Zärtlichkeit f

tendon /'tendən/ n Sehne f

tenner /'tenə(r)/ n [!] Zehnpfundschein m

tennis /'tenɪs/ n Tennis nt. **~-court** n Tennisplatz m

tenor /'tenə(r)/ n Tenor m

tense /tens/ adj (**-r, -st**) gespannt •vt anspannen (muscle)

tension /'tenʃn/ n Spannung f

tent /tent/ n Zelt nt

tentative /'tentətɪv/ adj, **-ly** adv vorläufig; (hesitant) zaghaft

tenterhooks /'tentəhʊks/ npl **be on ~** wie auf glühenden Kohlen sitzen

tenth /tenθ/ adj zehnte(r,s) •n Zehntel nt

tenuous /'tenjʊəs/ adj schwach

tepid /'tepɪd/ adj lauwarm

term /tɜ:m/ n Zeitraum m; (Sch) ≈ Halbjahr nt; (Univ) ≈ Semester nt; (expression) Ausdruck m; **~s** pl (conditions) Bedingungen pl; **in the short/long ~** kurz-/langfristig; **be on good/bad ~s** gut/nicht gut miteinander auskommen

terminal /'tɜ:mɪnl/ adj End-; (Med) unheilbar •n (Aviat) Terminal m; (of bus) Endstation f; (on battery) Pol m; (Computing) Terminal nt

terminat|e /'tɜ:mɪneɪt/ vt beenden; lösen (contract); unterbrechen (pregnancy) •vi enden

terminology /tɜ:mɪ'nɒlədʒɪ/ n Terminologie f

terminus /'tɜ:mɪnəs/ n (pl **-ni** /-naɪ/) Endstation f

terrace /'terəs/ n Terrasse f; (houses) Häuserreihe f. **~d house** n Reihenhaus nt

terrain /teˈreɪn/ n Gelände nt

terrible /ˈterəbl/ adj, **-bly** adv schrecklich

terrific /təˈrɪfɪk/ adj [!] (excellent) sagenhaft; (huge) riesig

terri|fy /ˈterɪfaɪ/ vt (pt/pp **-ied**) Angst machen (+ dat); **be ~fied** Angst haben. **~fying** adj Furcht erregend

territorial /terɪˈtɔːrɪəl/ adj Territorial-

territory /ˈterɪtərɪ/ n Gebiet nt

terror /ˈterə(r)/ n [panische] Angst f; (Pol) Terror m. **~ism** n Terrorismus m. **~ist** n Terrorist(in) m(f). **~ize** vt terrorisieren

terse /tɜːs/ adj kurz, knapp

test /test/ n Test m; (Sch) Klassenarbeit f; **put to the ~** auf die Probe stellen •vt prüfen; (examine) untersuchen (**for** auf + acc)

testament /ˈtestəmənt/ n Testament nt

testify /ˈtestɪfaɪ/ v (pt/pp **-ied**) •vt beweisen; **~ that** bezeugen, dass •vi aussagen

testimonial /testɪˈməʊnɪəl/ n Zeugnis nt

testimony /ˈtestɪmənɪ/ n Aussage f

ˈtest-tube n Reagenzglas nt

tether /ˈteðə(r)/ n **be at the end of one's ~** am Ende seiner Kraft sein •vt anbinden

text /tekst/ n Text m •vt/i texten. **~book** n Lehrbuch nt

textile /ˈtekstaɪl/ adj Textil- •n **~s** pl Textilien pl

ˈtext message n SMS-Nachricht f

texture /ˈtekstʃə(r)/ n Beschaffenheit f; (of cloth) Struktur f

Thai /taɪ/ adj thailändisch. **~land** n Thailand nt

Thames /temz/ n Themse f

than /ðən/, betont /ðæn/ conj als

thank /θæŋk/ vt danken (+ dat); **~ you [very much]** danke [schön]. **~ful** adj dankbar. **~less** adj undankbar

thanks /θæŋks/ npl Dank m; **~!** [!] danke! **~ to** dank (+ dat or gen)

that /ðæt/

pl **those**

• adjective

····➤ der (m), die (f), das (nt), die (pl); (just seen or experienced) dieser (m), diese (f), dieses (nt), diese (pl). **I'll never forget that day** den Tag werde ich nie vergessen. **I liked that house** dieses Haus hat mir gut gefallen

• pronoun

····➤ der (m), die (f), das (nt), die (pl). **that is not true** das ist nicht wahr. **who is that in the garden?** wer ist das [da] im Garten? **I'll take that** ich nehme den/die/das. **I don't like those** die mag ich nicht. **is that you?** bist du es? **that is why** deshalb

····➤ **like that** so. **don't be like that!** sei doch nicht so! **a man like that** ein solcher Mann; so ein Mann [!]

····➤ (after prepositions) da .... **after that** danach. **with that** damit. **apart from that** außerdem

····➤ (relative pronoun) der (m), die (f), das (nt), die (pl). **the book that I'm reading** das Buch, das ich lese. **the people that you got it from** die Leute, von denen du es bekommen hast. **everyone that I know** jeder, den ich kenne. **that is all that I have** das ist alles, was ich habe

• adverb

····➤ so. **he's not 'that stupid** so blöd ist er [auch wieder] nicht. **it wasn't 'that bad** so schlecht war es auch nicht. **a nail about 'that long** ein etwa so langer Nagel

····➤ (relative adverb) der (m), die (f), das (nt), die (pl). **the day that I first met her** der Tag, an dem ich sie zum ersten Mal sah. **at the speed that he was going** bei der Geschwindigkeit, die er hatte

t

• conjunction
····➤ dass. **I don't think that he'll come** ich denke nicht, dass er kommt. **we know that you're right** wir wissen, dass du Recht hast. **I'm so tired that I can hardly walk** ich bin so müde, dass ich kaum gehen kann
····➤ **so that** (purpose) damit; (result) sodass. **he came earlier so that they would have more time** er kam früher, damit sie mehr Zeit hatten. **it was late, so that I had to catch the bus** es war spät, sodass ich den Bus nehmen musste

thatch /θætʃ/ n Strohdach nt. **~ed** adj strohgedeckt

thaw /θɔː/ n Tauwetter nt •vt/i auftauen; **it's ~ing** es taut

the /ðə/, vor einem Vokal /ðɪː/ def art der/die/das; (pl) die; **play ~ piano/violin** Klavier/Geige spielen •adv **~ more ~ better** je mehr, desto besser; **all ~ better** umso besser

theatre /'θɪətə(r)/ n Theater nt; (Med) Operationssaal m

theatrical /θɪ'ætrɪkl/ adj Theater-; (showy) theatralisch

theft /θeft/ n Diebstahl m

their /ðeə(r)/ adj ihr

theirs /ðeəz/ poss pron ihre(r), ihrs; **a friend of ~** ein Freund von ihnen; **those are ~** die gehören ihnen

them /ðem/ pron (acc) sie; (dat) ihnen

theme /θiːm/ n Thema nt. **~ park** n Themenpark m

them'selves pron selbst; (reflexive) sich; **by ~** allein

then /ðen/ adv dann; (at that time in past) damals; **by ~** bis dahin; **since ~** seitdem; **before ~** vorher; **from ~ on** von da an; **now and ~** dann und wann; **there and ~** auf der Stelle •adj damalig

theology /θɪ'ɒlədʒɪ/ n Theologie f

theoretical /θɪə'retɪkl/ adj theoretisch

theory /'θɪərɪ/ n Theorie f; **in ~** theoretisch

therap|ist /'θerəpɪst/ n Therapeut(in) m(f). **~y** n Therapie f

there /ðeə(r)/ adv da; (with movement) dahin, dorthin; **down/up ~ da** unten/oben; **~ is/are** da ist/sind; (in existence) es gibt •int **~, ~!** nun, nun!

there: ~abouts adv da [in der Nähe]; **or ~abouts** (roughly) ungefähr. **~fore** /-fɔː(r)/ adv deshalb, also

thermometer /θə'mɒmɪtə(r)/ n Thermometer nt

Thermos® /'θɜːməs/ n **~ [flask]** Thermosflasche ® f

thermostat /'θɜːməstæt/ n Thermostat m

these /ðiːz/ see **this**

thesis /'θiːsɪs/ n (pl **-ses** /-siːz/) Dissertation f; (proposition) These f

they /ðeɪ/ pron sie; **~ say** (generalizing) man sagt

thick /θɪk/ adj (**-er, -est**) dick; (dense) dicht; (liquid) dickflüssig; (!: stupid) dumm •adv dick •n **in the ~ of** mitten in (+ dat). **~en** vt dicker machen; eindicken (sauce) •vi dicker werden; (fog:) dichter werden; (plot:) kompliziert werden. **~ness** n Dicke f; Dichte f; Dickflüssigkeit f

thief /θiːf/ n (pl **thieves**) Dieb(in) m(f)

thigh /θaɪ/ n Oberschenkel m

thimble /'θɪmbl/ n Fingerhut m

thin /θɪn/ adj (**thinner, thinnest**) dünn •adv dünn •v (pt/pp **thinned**) •vt verdünnen (liquid) •vi sich lichten

thing /θɪŋ/ n Ding nt; (subject, affair) Sache f; **~s** pl (belongings) Sachen pl; **for one ~** erstens; **just the ~!** genau das Richtige! **how are ~s?** wie geht's? **the latest ~** ! der letzte Schrei

think /θɪŋk/ vt/i (pt/pp **thought**) denken (**about/of** an + acc); (believe) meinen; (consider) nachdenken; (regard as) halten für; **I ~ so** ich glaube schon; **what do you ~ of it?** was halten Sie davon? **~ over** vt sich (dat) überlegen. **~ up** vt sich (dat) ausdenken

third /θɜːd/ adj dritte(r,s) •n Drittel nt. **~ly** adv drittens. **~-rate** adj drittrangig

thirst /θɜːst/ n Durst m. **~y** adj, **-ily** adv durstig; **be ~y** Durst haben

thirteen /θɜːˈtiːn/ adj dreizehn. **~th** adj dreizehnte(r,s)

thirtieth /ˈθɜːtɪɪθ/ adj dreißigste(r,s)

thirty /ˈθɜːtɪ/ adj dreißig

this /ðɪs/ adj (pl **these**) diese(r,s); (pl) diese; **~ one** diese(r,s) da; **I'll take ~** ich nehme diesen/diese/dieses; **~ evening/morning** heute Abend/Morgen; **these days** heutzutage •pron (pl **these**) das, dies[es]; (pl) die, diese; **~ and that** dies und das; **~ or that** dieses oder das da; **like ~** so; **~ is Peter** das ist Peter; (Teleph) hier [spricht] Peter; **who is ~?** wer ist das? (Teleph, Amer) wer ist am Apparat?

thistle /ˈθɪsl/ n Distel f

thorn /θɔːn/ n Dorn m

thorough /ˈθʌrə/ adj gründlich

thoroughbred n reinrassiges Tier nt; (horse) Rassepferd nt

thorough|ly /ˈθʌrəlɪ/ adv gründlich; (completely) völlig; (extremely) äußerst. **~ness** n Gründlichkeit f

those /ðəʊz/ see **that**

though /ðəʊ/ conj obgleich, obwohl; **as ~** als ob •adv [!] doch

thought /θɔːt/ see **think** •n Gedanke m; (thinking) Denken nt. **~ful** adj nachdenklich; (considerate) rücksichtsvoll. **~less** adj gedankenlos

thousand /ˈθaʊznd/ adj **one/a ~** [ein]tausend •n Tausend nt. **~th** adj tausendste(r,s) •n Tausendstel nt

thrash /θræʃ/ vt verprügeln; (defeat) [vernichtend] schlagen

thread /θred/ n Faden m; (of screw) Gewinde nt •vt einfädeln; auffädeln (beads). **~bare** adj fadenscheinig

threat /θret/ n Drohung f; (danger) Bedrohung f

threaten /ˈθretn/ vt drohen (+ dat); (with weapon) bedrohen; **~ s.o. with sth** jdm etw androhen •vi drohen. **~ing** adj drohend; (ominous) bedrohlich

three /θriː/ adj drei. **~fold** adj & adv dreifach

thresh /θreʃ/ vt dreschen

threshold /ˈθreʃəʊld/ n Schwelle f

threw /θruː/ see **throw**

thrift /θrɪft/ n Sparsamkeit f. **~y** adj sparsam

thrill /θrɪl/ n Erregung f; [!] Nervenkitzel m •vt (excite) erregen; **be ~ed with** sich sehr freuen über (+ acc). **~er** n Thriller m. **~ing** adj erregend

thrive /θraɪv/ vi (pt **thrived** or **throve**, pp **thrived** or **thriven** /ˈθrɪvn/) gedeihen (**on** bei); (business:) florieren

throat /θrəʊt/ n Hals m; **cut s.o.'s ~** jdm die Kehle durchschneiden

throb /θrɒb/ n Pochen nt •vi (pt/pp **throbbed**) pochen; (vibrate) vibrieren

throes /θrəʊz/ npl **in the ~ of** (fig) mitten in (+ dat)

throne /θrəʊn/ n Thron m

throttle /ˈθrɒtl/ vt erdrosseln

through /θruː/ prep durch (+ acc); (during) während (+ gen); (Amer: up to & including) bis einschließlich •adv durch; **wet ~** durch und durch nass; **read sth ~** etw durchlesen •adj (train) durchgehend; **be ~** (finished) fertig sein; (Teleph) durch sein

throughout /θruːˈaʊt/ prep **~ the country** im ganzen Land; **~ the night** die Nacht durch •adv ganz; (time) die ganze Zeit

throve /θrəʊv/ see **thrive**

throw /θrəʊ/ n Wurf m •vt (pt

threw, pp **thrown**) werfen; schütten (liquid); betätigen (switch); abwerfen (rider); (!: disconcert) aus der Fassung bringen; ! geben (party); ~ **sth to s.o.** jdm etw zuwerfen. ~ **away** vt wegwerfen. ~ **out** vt hinauswerfen; (~ away) wegwerfen; verwerfen (plan). ~ **up** vt hochwerfen •vi sich übergeben

'throw-away adj Wegwerf-

thrush /θrʌʃ/ n Drossel f

thrust /θrʌst/ n Stoß m; (Phys) Schub m •vt (pt/pp **thrust**) stoßen; (insert) stecken

thud /θʌd/ n dumpfer Schlag m

thug /θʌg/ n Schläger m

thumb /θʌm/ n Daumen m •vt ~ **a lift** ! per Anhalter fahren. ~**tack** n (Amer) Reißzwecke f

thump /θʌmp/ n Schlag m; (noise) dumpfer Schlag m •vt schlagen •vi hämmern; (heart:) pochen

thunder /'θʌndə(r)/ n Donner m •vi donnern. ~**clap** n Donnerschlag m. ~**storm** n Gewitter nt. ~**y** adj gewittrig

Thursday /'θɜːzdeɪ/ n Donnerstag m

thus /ðʌs/ adv so

thwart /θwɔːt/ vt vereiteln; ~ **s.o.** jdm einen Strich durch die Rechnung machen

tick[1] /tɪk/ n **on** ~ ! auf Pump

tick[2] n (sound) Ticken nt; (mark) Häkchen nt; (!: instant) Sekunde f •vi ticken •vt abhaken. ~ **off** vt abhaken; ! rüffeln

t

ticket /'tɪkɪt/ n Karte f; (for bus, train) Fahrschein m; (Aviat) Flugschein m; (for lottery) Los nt; (for article deposited) Schein m; (label) Schild nt; (for library) Lesekarte f; (fine) Strafzettel m. ~ **collector** n Fahrkartenkontrolleur m. ~ **office** n Fahrkartenschalter m; (for entry) Kasse f

tick|le /'tɪkl/ n Kitzeln nt •vt/i kitzeln. ~**lish** adj kitzlig

tidal /'taɪdl/ adj ~ **wave** Flutwelle f

tide /taɪd/ n Gezeiten pl; (of events) Strom m; **the ~ is in/out** es ist Flut/Ebbe •vt ~ **s.o. over** jdm über die Runden helfen

tidiness /'taɪdɪnɪs/ n Ordentlichkeit f

tidy /'taɪdɪ/ adj, **-ily** adv ordentlich •vt ~ **[up]** aufräumen

tie /taɪ/ n Krawatte f; Schlips m; (cord) Schnur f; (fig: bond) Band nt; (restriction) Bindung f; (Sport) Unentschieden nt; (in competition) Punktgleichheit f •v (pres p **tying**) •vt binden; machen (knot) •vi (Sport) unentschieden spielen; (have equal scores, votes) punktgleich sein. ~ **up** vt festbinden; verschnüren (parcel); fesseln (person); **be ~d up** (busy) beschäftigt sein

tier /tɪə(r)/ n Stufe f; (of cake) Etage f; (in stadium) Rang m

tiger /'taɪgə(r)/ n Tiger m

tight /taɪt/ adj (**-er, -est**) fest; (taut) straff; (clothes) eng; (control) streng; (!: drunk) blau •adv fest

tighten /'taɪtn/ vt fester ziehen; straffen (rope); anziehen (screw); verschärfen (control) •vi sich spannen

tightrope n Hochseil nt

tights /taɪts/ npl Strumpfhose f

tile /taɪl/ n Fliese f; (on wall) Kachel f; (on roof) [Dach]ziegel m •vt mit Fliesen auslegen; kacheln (wall); decken (roof)

till[1] /tɪl/ prep & conj = **until**

till[2] n Kasse f

tilt /tɪlt/ n Neigung f •vt kippen; [zur Seite] neigen (head) •vi sich neigen

timber /'tɪmbə(r)/ n [Nutz]holz nt

time /taɪm/ n Zeit f; (occasion) Mal nt; (rhythm) Takt m; ~**s** (Math) mal; **at ~s** manchmal; **~ and again** immer wieder; **two at a ~** zwei auf einmal; **on ~** pünktlich; **in ~** rechtzeitig; (eventually) mit der Zeit; **in no ~** im Handumdrehen; **in a year's ~** in einem Jahr; **behind ~** verspätet; **behind the ~s** rückständig; **for the ~ being** vorläufig; **what is the ~?** wie spät ist es? wie viel Uhr ist es? **did you**

have a nice ~? hat es dir gut gefallen? •vt stoppen (race); **be well ~d** gut abgepasst sein

time: ~ bomb n Zeitbombe f. **~less** adj zeitlos. **~ly** adj rechtzeitig. **~-switch** n Zeitschalter m. **~-table** n Fahrplan m; (Sch) Stundenplan m

timid /'tɪmɪd/ adj scheu; (hesitant) zaghaft

timing /'taɪmɪŋ/ n (Sport, Techn) Timing nt

tin /tɪn/ n Zinn nt; (container) Dose f •vt (pt/pp **tinned**) in Dosen konservieren. **~ foil** n Stanniol nt; (Culin) Alufolie f

tinge /tɪndʒ/ n Hauch m

tingle /'tɪŋgl/ vi kribbeln

tinker /'tɪŋkə(r)/ vi herumbasteln (**with** an + dat)

tinkle /'tɪŋkl/ n Klingeln nt •vi klingeln

tinned /tɪnd/ adj Dosen-

'tin opener n Dosenöffner m

tinsel /'tɪnsl/ n Lametta nt

tint /tɪnt/ n Farbton m •vt tönen

tiny /'taɪnɪ/ adj winzig

tip[1] /tɪp/ n Spitze f

tip[2] n (money) Trinkgeld nt; (advice) Rat m, [!] Tipp m; (for rubbish) Müllhalde f •v (pt/pp **tipped**) •vt (tilt) kippen; (reward) Trinkgeld geben (**s.o.** jdm) •vi kippen. **~ out** vt auskippen. **~ over** vt/i umkippen

tipped /tɪpt/ adj Filter-

tipsy /'tɪpsɪ/ adj [!] beschwipst

tiptoe /'tɪptəʊ/ n **on ~** auf Zehenspitzen

tiptop /tɪp'tɒp/ adj [!] erstklassig

tire /'taɪə(r)/ vt/i ermüden. **~d** adj müde; **be ~d of sth** etw satt haben; **~d out** [völlig] erschöpft. **~less** adj unermüdlich. **~some** adj lästig

tiring /'taɪrɪŋ/ adj ermüdend

tissue /tɪʃu:/ n Gewebe nt; (handkerchief) Papiertaschentuch nt

tit /tɪt/ n (bird) Meise f

'titbit n Leckerbissen m

title /'taɪtl/ n Titel m

to /tu:/, unbetont /tə/

• preposition

····➤ (destinations: most cases) zu (+ dat). **go to work/the station** zur Arbeit/zum Bahnhof gehen. **from house to house** von Haus zu Haus. **go/come to s.o.** zu jdm gehen/kommen

····➤ (with name of place or points of compass) nach. **to Paris/Germany** nach Paris/Deutschland. **to Switzerland** in die Schweiz. **from East to West** von Osten nach Westen. **I've never been to Berlin** ich war noch nie in Berlin

····➤ (to cinema, theatre, bed) in (+ acc). **to bed with you!** ins Bett mit dir!

····➤ (to wedding, party, university, the toilet) auf (+ acc).

····➤ (up to) bis zu (+ dat). **to the end** bis zum Schluss. **to this day** bis heute. **5 to 6 pounds** 5 bis 6 Pfund

····➤ (give, say, write) + dat. **give/say sth to s.o.** jdm etw geben/sagen. **she wrote to him/the firm** sie hat ihm/an die Firma geschrieben

····➤ (address, send, fasten) an (+ acc). **she sent it to her brother** sie schickte es an ihren Bruder

····➤ (in telling the time) vor. **five to eight** fünf vor acht. **a quarter to ten** Viertel vor zehn

• before infinitive

····➤ (after modal verb) (not translated). **I want to go** ich will gehen. **he is learning to swim** er lernt schwimmen. **you have to** du musst [es tun]

····➤ (after adjective) zu. **it is easy to forget** es ist leicht zu vergessen

····➤ (expressing purpose, result) um ... zu. **he did it to annoy me** er tat es, um mich zu ärgern. **she was too tired to go** sie war zu müde um zu gehen

• adverb

····➤ **be to** (door, window) angelehnt sein. **pull a door to** eine Tür anlehnen

····➤ **to and fro** hin und her

toad /təʊd/ n Kröte f

toast /təʊst/ n Toast m •vt toasten (bread); (drink a ~ to) trinken auf (+ acc). **~er** n Toaster m

tobacco /tə'bækəʊ/ n Tabak m. **~nist's [shop]** n Tabakladen m

toboggan /tə'bɒgən/ n Schlitten m •vi Schlitten fahren

today /tə'deɪ/ n & adv heute; **~ week** heute in einer Woche

toddler /'tɒdlə(r)/ n Kleinkind nt

toe /təʊ/ n Zeh m; (of footwear) Spitze f •vt **~ the line** spuren. **~nail** n Zehennagel m

toffee /'tɒfɪ/ n Karamell m & nt

together /tə'geðə(r)/ adv zusammen; (at the same time) gleichzeitig

toilet /'tɔɪlɪt/ n Toilette f. **~ bag** n Kulturbeutel m. **~ paper** n Toilettenpapier nt

toiletries /'tɔɪlɪtrɪz/ npl Toilettenartikel pl

token /'təʊkən/ n Zeichen nt; (counter) Marke f; (voucher) Gutschein m •attrib symbolisch

told /təʊld/ see **tell** •adj **all ~** insgesamt

tolerable /'tɒlərəbl/ adj, **-bly** adv erträglich; (not bad) leidlich

toleran|ce /'tɒlərəns/ n Toleranz f. **~t** adj tolerant

tolerate /'tɒləreɪt/ vt dulden, tolerieren; (bear) ertragen

toll /təʊl/ n Gebühr f; (for road) Maut f (Aust); **death ~** Zahl f der Todesopfer

tomato /tə'mɑːtəʊ/ n (pl **-es**) Tomate f

tomb /tuːm/ n Grabmal nt

'tombstone n Grabstein m

'tom-cat n Kater m

tomorrow /tə'mɒrəʊ/ n & adv morgen; **~ morning** morgen früh; **the day after ~** übermorgen; **see you ~!** bis morgen!

ton /tʌn/ n Tonne f; **~s of** [!] jede Menge

tone /təʊn/ n Ton m; (colour) Farbton m •vt **~ down** dämpfen; (fig) mäßigen. **~ up** vt kräftigen; straffen (muscles)

tongs /tɒŋz/ npl Zange f

tongue /tʌŋ/ n Zunge f; **~ in cheek** [!] nicht ernst

tonic /'tɒnɪk/ n Tonikum nt; (for hair) Haarwasser nt; (fig) Wohltat f; **~ [water]** Tonic nt

tonight /tə'naɪt/ n & adv heute Nacht; (evening) heute Abend

tonne /tʌn/ n Tonne f

tonsil /'tɒnsl/ n (Anat) Mandel f. **~litis** n Mandelentzündung f

too /tuː/ adv zu; (also) auch; **~ much/little** zu viel/zu wenig

took /tʊk/ see **take**

tool /tuːl/ n Werkzeug nt; (for gardening) Gerät nt. **~bar** n Werkzeugleiste f

tooth /tuːθ/ n (pl **teeth**) Zahn m

tooth: ~ache n Zahnschmerzen pl. **~brush** n Zahnbürste f. **~less** adj zahnlos. **~paste** n Zahnpasta f. **~pick** n Zahnstocher m

top¹ /tɒp/ n (toy) Kreisel m

top² n oberer Teil m; (apex) Spitze f; (summit) Gipfel m; (Sch) Erste(r) m/f; (top part or half) Oberteil nt; (head) Kopfende nt; (of road) oberes Ende nt; (upper surface) Oberfläche f; (lid) Deckel m; (of bottle) Verschluss m; (garment) Top nt; **at the/on ~** oben; **on ~ of** oben auf (+ dat/acc); **on ~ of that** (besides) obendrein; **from ~ to bottom** von oben bis unten •adj oberste(r,s); (highest) höchste(r,s); (best) beste(r,s) •vt (pt/pp **topped**) an erster Stelle stehen auf (+ dat) (list); (exceed) übersteigen; (remove the ~ of) die Spitze abschneiden von. **~ up** vt nachfüllen, auffüllen

top: ~ 'hat n Zylinder[hut] m. **~-heavy** adj kopflastig

topic /'tɒpɪk/ n Thema nt. **~al** adj aktuell

topple /'tɒpl/ vt/i umstürzen

torch /tɔːtʃ/ n Taschenlampe f; (flaming) Fackel f

t

tore /tɔ:(r)/ see **tear**[1]

torment[1] /ˈtɔ:ment/ n Qual f

torment[2] /tɔ:ˈment/ vt quälen

torn /tɔ:n/ see **tear**[1] •adj zerrissen

torpedo /tɔ:ˈpi:dəʊ/ n (pl **-es**) Torpedo m •vt torpedieren

torrent /ˈtɒrənt/ n reißender Strom m. **~ial** adj (rain) wolkenbruchartig

tortoise /ˈtɔ:təs/ n Schildkröte f. **~shell** n Schildpatt nt

tortuous /ˈtɔ:tjʊəs/ adj verschlungen; (fig) umständlich

torture /ˈtɔ:tʃə(r)/ n Folter f; (fig) Qual f •vt foltern; (fig) quälen

toss /tɒs/ vt werfen; (into the air) hochwerfen; (shake) schütteln; (unseat) abwerfen; mischen (salad); wenden (pancake); **~ a coin** mit einer Münze losen •vi **~ and turn** (in bed) sich [schlaflos] im Bett wälzen

tot[1] /tɒt/ n kleines Kind nt; ([!]: of liquor) Gläschen nt

tot[2] vt (pt/pp **totted**) **~ up** [!] zusammenzählen

total /ˈtəʊtl/ adj gesamt; (complete) völlig, total •n Gesamtzahl f; (sum) Gesamtsumme f •vt (pt/pp **totalled**); (amount to) sich belaufen auf (+ acc)

totalitarian /təʊtælɪˈteərɪən/ adj totalitär

totally /ˈtəʊtəlɪ/ adv völlig, total

totter /ˈtɒtə(r)/ vi taumeln

touch /tʌtʃ/ n Berührung f; (sense) Tastsinn m; (Mus) Anschlag m; (contact) Kontakt m; (trace) Spur f; (fig) Anflug m; **get/be in ~** sich in Verbindung setzen/in Verbindung stehen (**with** mit) •vt berühren; (get hold of) anfassen; (lightly) tippen auf/an (+ acc); (brush against) streifen [gegen]; (fig: move) rühren; anrühren (food, subject); **don't ~ that!** fass das nicht an! •vi sich berühren; **~ on** (fig) berühren. **~ down** vi (Aviat) landen. **~ up** vt ausbessern

touch|ing /ˈtʌtʃɪŋ/ adj rührend. **~y** adj empfindlich

tough /tʌf/ adj (**-er, -est**) zäh; (severe, harsh) hart; (difficult) schwierig; (durable) strapazierfähig

toughen /ˈtʌfn/ vt härten; **~ up** abhärten

tour /tʊə(r)/ n Reise f, Tour f; (of building, town) Besichtigung f; (Theat, Sport) Tournee f; (of duty) Dienstzeit f •vt fahren durch •vi herumreisen

touris|m /ˈtʊərɪzm/ n Tourismus m, Fremdenverkehr m. **~t** n Tourist(in) m(f) •attrib Touristen-. **~t office** n Fremdenverkehrsbüro nt

tournament /ˈtʊənəmənt/ n Turnier nt

ˈtour operator n Reiseveranstalter m

tousle /ˈtaʊzl/ vt zerzausen

tow /təʊ/ n **give s.o./a car a ~** jdn/ein Auto abschleppen •vt schleppen; ziehen (trailer)

toward[s] /təˈwɔ:dz/ prep zu (+ dat); (with time) gegen (+ acc); (with respect to) gegenüber (+ dat)

towel /ˈtaʊəl/ n Handtuch nt. **~ling** n (cloth) Frottee nt

tower /ˈtaʊə(r)/ n Turm m •vi **~ above** überragen. **~ block** n Hochhaus nt. **~ing** adj hoch aufragend

town /taʊn/ n Stadt f. **~ ˈhall** n Rathaus nt

tow-rope n Abschleppseil nt

toxic /ˈtɒksɪk/ adj giftig

toy /tɔɪ/ n Spielzeug nt •vi **~ with** spielen mit; stochern in (+ dat) (food). **~shop** n Spielwarengeschäft nt

trac|e /treɪs/ n Spur f •vt folgen (+ dat); (find) finden; (draw) zeichnen; (with tracing-paper) durchpausen

track /træk/ n Spur f; (path) [unbefestigter] Weg m; (Sport) Bahn f; (Rail) Gleis nt; **keep ~ of** im Auge behalten •vt verfolgen. **~ down** vt aufspüren; (find) finden

ˈtracksuit n Trainingsanzug m

tractor /ˈtræktə(r)/ n Traktor m

t

trade /treɪd/ n Handel m; (line of business) Gewerbe nt; (business) Geschäft nt; (craft) Handwerk nt; **by ~** von Beruf •vt tauschen; **~ in** (give in part exchange) in Zahlung geben •vi handeln (**in** mit)

'trade mark n Warenzeichen nt

trader /'treɪdə(r)/ n Händler m

trade: ~ 'union n Gewerkschaft f. **~ 'unionist** n Gewerkschaftler(in) m(f)

trading /'treɪdɪŋ/ n Handel m

tradition /trə'dɪʃn/ n Tradition f. **~al** adj traditionell

traffic /'træfɪk/ n Verkehr m; (trading) Handel m

traffic: ~ circle n (Amer) Kreisverkehr m. **~ jam** n [Verkehrs]stau m. **~ lights** npl [Verkehrs]ampel f. **~ warden** n ≈ Hilfspolizist m; (woman) Politesse f

tragedy /'trædʒədɪ/ n Tragödie f

tragic /'trædʒɪk/ adj, **-ally** adv tragisch

trail /treɪl/ n Spur f; (path) Weg m, Pfad m •vi schleifen; (plant:) sich ranken •vt verfolgen, folgen (+ dat); (drag) schleifen

trailer /'treɪlə(r)/ n (Auto) Anhänger m; (Amer: caravan) Wohnwagen m; (film) Vorschau f

train /treɪn/ n Zug m; (of dress) Schleppe f •vt ausbilden; (Sport) trainieren; (aim) richten auf (+ acc); erziehen (child); abrichten/(to do tricks) dressieren (animal); ziehen (plant) •vi eine Ausbildung machen; (Sport) trainieren. **~ed** adj ausgebildet

trainee /treɪ'ni:/ n Auszubildende(r) m/f; (Techn) Praktikant(in) m(f)

train|er /'treɪnə(r)/ n (Sport) Trainer m; (in circus) Dompteur m; **~ers** pl Trainingsschuhe pl. **~ing** n Ausbildung f; (Sport) Training nt; (of animals) Dressur f

trait /treɪt/ n Eigenschaft f

traitor /'treɪtə(r)/ n Verräter m

tram /træm/ n Straßenbahn f

tramp /træmp/ n Landstreicher m •vi stapfen; (walk) marschieren

trample /'træmpl/ vt/i trampeln

trance /trɑ:ns/ n Trance f

tranquil /'træŋkwɪl/ adj ruhig. **~lity** n Ruhe f

tranquillizer /'træŋkwɪlaɪzə(r)/ n Beruhigungsmittel nt

transaction /træn'zækʃn/ n Transaktion f

transcend /træn'send/ vt übersteigen

transfer¹ /'trænsfɜ:(r)/ n (see **transfer²**) Übertragung f; Verlegung f; Versetzung f; Überweisung f; (Sport) Transfer m; (design) Abziehbild nt

transfer² /træns'fɜ:(r)/ v (pt/pp **transferred**) •vt übertragen; verlegen (firm, prisoners); versetzen (employee); überweisen (money); (Sport) transferieren •vi [über]wechseln; (when travelling) umsteigen

transform /træns'fɔ:m/ vt verwandeln. **~ation** n Verwandlung f. **~er** n Transformator m

transfusion /træns'fju:ʒn/ n Transfusion f

transistor /træn'zɪstə(r)/ n Transistor m

transit /'trænsɪt/ n Transit m; (of goods) Transport m; **in ~** (goods) auf dem Transport

transition /træn'sɪʒn/ n Übergang m. **~al** adj Übergangs-

translat|e /træns'leɪt/ vt übersetzen. **~ion** n Übersetzung f. **~or** n Übersetzer(in) m(f)

transmission /trænz'mɪʃn/ n Übertragung f

transmit /trænz'mɪt/ vt (pt/pp **transmitted**) übertragen. **~ter** n Sender m

transparen|cy /træns'pærənsɪ/ n (Phot) Dia nt. **~t** adj durchsichtig

transplant¹ /'trænsplɑ:nt/ n Verpflanzung f, Transplantation f

transplant² /træns'plɑ:nt/ vt

umpflanzen; (Med) verpflanzen

transport[1] /ˈtrænspɔːt/ n Transport m

transport[2] /trænˈspɔːt/ vt transportieren. **~ation** n Transport m

transpose /trænsˈpəʊz/ vt umstellen

trap /træp/ n Falle f; ([!]: mouth) Klappe f; **pony and ~** Einspänner m • vt (pt/pp **trapped**) [mit einer Falle] fangen; (jam) einklemmen; **be ~ped** festsitzen; (shut in) eingeschlossen sein. **~'door** n Falltür f

trash /træʃ/ n Schund m; (rubbish) Abfall m; (nonsense) Quatsch m. **~can** n (Amer) Mülleimer m. **~y** adj Schund-

trauma /ˈtrɔːmə/ n Trauma nt. **~tic** adj traumatisch

travel /ˈtrævl/ n Reisen nt • v (pt/pp **travelled**) • vi reisen; (go in vehicle) fahren; (light, sound:) sich fortpflanzen; (Techn) sich bewegen • vt bereisen; fahren (distance). **~ agency** n Reisebüro nt. **~ agent** n Reisebürokaufmann m

traveller /ˈtrævələ(r)/ n Reisende(r) m/f; (Comm) Vertreter m; **~s** pl (gypsies) Zigeuner pl. **~'s cheque** n Reisescheck m

trawler /ˈtrɔːlə(r)/ n Fischdampfer m

tray /treɪ/ n Tablett nt; (for baking) [Back]blech nt; (for documents) Ablagekorb m

treacher|ous /ˈtretʃərəs/ adj treulos; (dangerous, deceptive) tückisch. **~y** n Verrat m

tread /tred/ n Schritt m; (step) Stufe f; (of tyre) Profil nt • v (pt **trod**, pp **trodden**) • vi (walk) gehen; **~ on/in** treten auf/ in (+ acc) • vt treten

treason /ˈtriːzn/ n Verrat m

treasure /ˈtreʒə(r)/ n Schatz m • vt in Ehren halten. **~r** n Kassenwart m

treasury /ˈtreʒərɪ/ n Schatzkammer f; **the T~** das Finanzministerium

treat /triːt/ n [besonderes] Vergnügen nt • vt behandeln; **~ s.o. to sth** jdm etw spendieren

treatment /ˈtriːtmənt/ n Behandlung f

treaty /ˈtriːtɪ/ n Vertrag m

treble /ˈtrebl/ adj dreifach; **~ the amount** dreimal so viel • n (Mus) Diskant m; (voice) Sopran m • vt verdreifachen • vi sich verdreifachen

tree /triː/ n Baum m

trek /trek/ n Marsch m • vi (pt/pp **trekked**) latschen

trellis /ˈtrelɪs/ n Gitter nt

tremble /ˈtrembl/ vi zittern

tremendous /trɪˈmendəs/ adj gewaltig; ([!]: excellent) großartig

tremor /ˈtremə(r)/ n Zittern nt; **[earth] ~** Beben nt

trench /trentʃ/ n Graben m; (Mil) Schützengraben m

trend /trend/ n Tendenz f; (fashion) Trend m. **~y** adj [!] modisch

trepidation /trepɪˈdeɪʃn/ n Beklommenheit f

trespass /ˈtrespəs/ vi **~ on** unerlaubt betreten

trial /ˈtraɪəl/ n (Jur) [Gerichts]verfahren nt, Prozess m; (test) Probe f; (ordeal) Prüfung f; **be on ~** auf Probe sein; (Jur) angeklagt sein (**for** wegen); **by ~ and error** durch Probieren

triang|le /ˈtraɪæŋgl/ n Dreieck nt; (Mus) Triangel m. **~ular** adj dreieckig

tribe /traɪb/ n Stamm m

tribunal /traɪˈbjuːnl/ n Schiedsgericht nt

tributary /ˈtrɪbjʊtərɪ/ n Nebenfluss m

tribute /ˈtrɪbjuːt/ n Tribut m; **pay ~** Tribut zollen (**to** dat)

trick /trɪk/ n Trick m; (joke) Streich m; (Cards) Stich m; (feat of skill) Kunststück nt • vt täuschen, [!] hereinlegen

trickle /ˈtrɪkl/ vi rinnen

trick|ster /ˈtrɪkstə(r)/ n Schwindler

m. **~y** adj adj schwierig

tricycle /'traɪsɪkl/ n Dreirad nt

tried /traɪd/ see **try**

trifl|e /'traɪfl/ n Kleinigkeit f; (Culin) Trifle nt. **~ing** adj unbedeutend

trigger /'trɪgə(r)/ n Abzug m; (fig) Auslöser m •vt ~ **[off]** auslösen

trim /trɪm/ adj (**trimmer, trimmest**) gepflegt •n (cut) Nachschneiden nt; (decoration) Verzierung f; (condition) Zustand m •vt schneiden; (decorate) besetzen. **~ming** n Besatz m; **~mings** pl (accessories) Zubehör nt; (decorations) Verzierungen pl

trio /'tri:əʊ/ n Trio nt

trip /trɪp/ n Reise f; (excursion) Ausflug m •v (pt/pp **tripped**) •vt ~ **s.o. up** jdm ein Bein stellen •vi stolpern (**on/over** über + acc)

tripe /traɪp/ n Kaldaunen pl; (nonsense) Quatsch m

triple /'trɪpl/ adj dreifach •vt verdreifachen •vi sich verdreifachen

triplets /'trɪplɪts/ npl Drillinge pl

triplicate /'trɪplɪkət/ n **in ~** in dreifacher Ausfertigung

tripod /'traɪpɒd/ n Stativ nt

tripper /'trɪpə(r)/ n Ausflügler m

trite /traɪt/ adj banal

triumph /'traɪʌmf/ n Triumph m •vi triumphieren (**over** über + acc). **~ant** adj triumphierend

trivial /'trɪvɪəl/ adj belanglos. **~ity** n Belanglosigkeit f

t

trod, **trodden** see **tread**

trolley /'trɒlɪ/ n (for food) Servierwagen m; (for shopping) Einkaufswagen m; (for luggage) Kofferkuli m; (Amer: tram) Straßenbahn f

trombone /trɒm'bəʊn/ n Posaune f

troop /tru:p/ n Schar f; **~s** pl Truppen pl

trophy /'trəʊfɪ/ n Trophäe f; (in competition) ≈ Pokal m

tropics /'trɒpɪks/ npl Tropen pl. **~al** adj tropisch; (fruit) Süd-

trot /trɒt/ n Trab m •vi (pt/pp **trotted**) traben

trouble /'trʌbl/ n Ärger m; (difficulties) Schwierigkeiten pl; (inconvenience) Mühe f; (conflict) Unruhe f; (Med) Beschwerden pl; (Techn) Probleme pl; **get into ~** Ärger bekommen; **take ~** sich (dat) Mühe geben •vt (disturb) stören; (worry) beunruhigen •vi sich bemühen. **~-maker** n Unruhestifter m. **~some** adj schwierig; (flies, cough) lästig

trough /trɒf/ n Trog m

troupe /tru:p/ n Truppe f

trousers /'traʊzəz/ npl Hose f

trousseau /'tru:səʊ/ n Aussteuer f

trout /traʊt/ n inv Forelle f

trowel /'traʊəl/ n Kelle f

truant /'tru:ənt/ n **play ~** die Schule schwänzen

truce /tru:s/ n Waffenstillstand m

truck /trʌk/ n Last[kraft]wagen m; (Rail) Güterwagen m

trudge /trʌdʒ/ vi latschen

true /tru:/ adj (**-r, -st**) wahr; (loyal) treu; (genuine) echt; **come ~** in Erfüllung gehen; **is that ~?** stimmt das?

truly /'tru:lɪ/ adv wirklich; (faithfully) treu; **Yours ~** mit freundlichen Grüßen

trump /trʌmp/ n (Cards) Trumpf m •vt übertrumpfen

trumpet /'trʌmpɪt/ n Trompete f. **~er** n Trompeter m

truncheon /'trʌntʃn/ n Schlagstock m

trunk /trʌŋk/ n [Baum]stamm m; (body) Rumpf m; (of elephant) Rüssel m; (for travelling) [Übersee]koffer m; (Amer: of car) Kofferraum m; **~s** pl Badehose f

trust /trʌst/ n Vertrauen nt; (group of companies) Trust m; (organization) Treuhandgesellschaft f; (charitable) Stiftung f •vt trauen (+ dat), vertrauen (+ dat); (hope) hoffen •vi vertrauen (**in/to** auf + acc)

trustee /trʌs'ti:/ n Treuhänder m

'trust|ful /ˈtrʌstfl/ adj, **-ly** adv, **~ing** adj vertrauensvoll. **~worthy** adj vertrauenswürdig

truth /tru:θ/ n (pl **-s** /tru:ðz/) Wahrheit f. **~ful** adj ehrlich

try /traɪ/ n Versuch m •v (pt/pp **tried**) •vt versuchen; (sample, taste) probieren; (be a strain on) anstrengen; (Jur) vor Gericht stellen; verhandeln (case) •vi versuchen; (make an effort) sich bemühen. **~ on** vt anprobieren; aufprobieren (hat). **~ out** vt ausprobieren

trying /ˈtraɪɪŋ/ adj schwierig

T-shirt /ˈti:-/ n T-Shirt nt

tub /tʌb/ n Kübel m; (carton) Becher m; (bath) Wanne f

tuba /ˈtju:bə/ n (Mus) Tuba f

tubby /ˈtʌbɪ/ adj rundlich

tube /tju:b/ n Röhre f; (pipe) Rohr nt; (flexible) Schlauch m; (of toothpaste) Tube f; (Rail, [!]) U-Bahn f

tuberculosis /tju:bɜ:kjʊˈləʊsɪs/ n Tuberkulose f

tubular /ˈtju:bjʊlə(r)/ adj röhrenförmig

tuck /tʌk/ n Saum m; (decorative) Biese f •vt (put) stecken. **~ in** vt hineinstecken; **~ s.o. in** or **up** jdn zudecken •vi ([!]: eat) zulangen

Tuesday /ˈtju:zdeɪ/ n Dienstag m

tuft /tʌft/ n Büschel nt

tug /tʌg/ n Ruck m; (Naut) Schleppdampfer m •v (pt/pp **tugged**) •vt ziehen •vi zerren (**at** an + dat)

tuition /tju:ˈɪʃn/ n Unterricht m

tulip /ˈtju:lɪp/ n Tulpe f

tumble /ˈtʌmbl/ n Sturz m •vi fallen. **~down** adj verfallen. **~-drier** n Wäschetrockner m

tumbler /ˈtʌmblə(r)/ n Glas nt

tummy /ˈtʌmɪ/ n [!] Bauch m

tumour /ˈtju:mə(r)/ n Tumor m

tumult /ˈtju:mʌlt/ n Tumult m

tuna /ˈtju:nə/ n Thunfisch m

tune /tju:n/ n Melodie f; **out of ~** (instrument) verstimmt •vt stimmen; (Techn) einstellen. **~ in** vt einstellen •vi **~ in to a station** einen Sender einstellen. **~ up** vi (Mus) stimmen

tuneful /ˈtju:nfl/ adj melodisch

Tunisia /tju:ˈnɪzɪə/ n Tunesien nt

tunnel /ˈtʌnl/ n Tunnel m •vi (pt/pp **tunnelled**) einen Tunnel graben

turban /ˈtɜ:bən/ n Turban m

turbine /ˈtɜ:baɪn/ n Turbine f

turbulen|ce /ˈtɜ:bjʊləns/ n Turbulenz f. **~t** adj stürmisch

turf /tɜ:f/ n Rasen m; (segment) Rasenstück nt

Turk /tɜ:k/ n Türke m/Türkin f

turkey /ˈtɜ:kɪ/ n Truthahn m

Turk|ey n die Türkei. **~ish** adj türkisch

turmoil /ˈtɜ:mɔɪl/ n Aufruhr m; (confusion) Durcheinander nt

turn /tɜ:n/ n (rotation) Drehung f; (bend) Kurve f; (change of direction) Wende f; (Theat) Nummer f; ([!]: attack) Anfall m; **do s.o. a good ~** jdm einen guten Dienst erweisen; **take ~s** sich abwechseln; **in ~** der Reihe nach; **out of ~** außer der Reihe; **it's your ~** du bist an der Reihe •vt drehen; (~ over) wenden; (reverse) umdrehen; (Techn) drechseln (wood); **~ the page** umblättern; **~ the corner** um die Ecke biegen •vi sich drehen; (~ round) sich umdrehen; (car:) wenden; (leaves:) sich färben: (weather:) umschlagen; (become) werden; **~ right/left** nach rechts/links abbiegen; **~ to s.o.** sich an jdn wenden. **~ away** vt abweisen •vi sich abwenden. **~ down** vt herunterschlagen (collar); herunterdrehen (heat, gas); leiser stellen (sound); (reject) ablehnen; abweisen (person). **~ in** vt einschlagen (edges) •vi (car:) einbiegen; ([!]: go to bed) ins Bett gehen. **~ off** vt zudrehen (tap);

t

ausschalten (light, radio); abstellen (water, gas, engine, machine) • vi abbiegen. ~ **on** vt aufdrehen (tap); einschalten (light, radio); anstellen (water, gas, engine, machine). ~ **out** vt (expel) vertreiben, [!] hinauswerfen; ausschalten (light); abdrehen (gas); (produce) produzieren; (empty) ausleeren; [gründlich] aufräumen (room, cupboard) • vi (go out) hinausgehen; (transpire) sich herausstellen. ~ **over** vt umdrehen. ~ **up** vt hochschlagen (collar); aufdrehen (heat, gas); lauter stellen (sound, radio) • vi auftauchen

turning /'tɜ:nɪŋ/ n Abzweigung f. **~-point** n Wendepunkt m

turnip /'tɜ:nɪp/ n weiße Rübe f

turn: ~-out n (of people) Beteiligung f. **~over** n (Comm) Umsatz m; (of staff) Personalwechsel m. **~pike** n (Amer) gebührenpflichtige Autobahn f. **~table** n Drehscheibe f; (on record player) Plattenteller m. **~-up** n [Hosen]aufschlag m

turquoise /'tɜ:kwɔɪz/ adj türkis[farben] • n (gem) Türkis m

turret /'tʌrɪt/ n Türmchen nt

turtle /'tɜ:tl/ n Seeschildkröte f

tusk /tʌsk/ n Stoßzahn m

tutor /'tju:tə(r)/ n [Privat]lehrer m

tuxedo /tʌk'si:dəʊ/ n (Amer) Smoking m

TV /ti:'vi:/ abbr **television**

tweed /twi:d/ n Tweed m

tweezers /'twi:zəz/ npl Pinzette f

twelfth /twelfθ/ adj zwölfter(r,s)

twelve /twelv/ adj zwölf

twentieth /'twentɪɪθ/ adj zwanzigste(r,s)

twenty /'twentɪ/ adj zwanzig

twice /twaɪs/ adv zweimal

twig /twɪg/ n Zweig m

twilight /'twaɪ-/ n Dämmerlicht nt

twin /twɪn/ n Zwilling m • attrib Zwillings-

twine /twaɪn/ n Bindfaden m

twinge /twɪndʒ/ n Stechen nt; ~ **of conscience** Gewissensbisse pl

twinkle /'twɪŋkl/ n Funkeln nt • vi funkeln

twin 'town n Partnerstadt f

twirl /twɜ:l/ vt/i herumwirbeln

twist /twɪst/ n Drehung f; (curve) Kurve f; (unexpected occurrence) überraschende Wendung f • vt drehen; (distort) verdrehen; ([!]: swindle) beschummeln; ~ **one's ankle** sich (dat) den Knöchel verrenken • vi sich drehen; (road:) sich winden. **~er** n [!] Schwindler m

twit /twɪt/ n [!] Trottel m

twitch /twɪtʃ/ n Zucken nt • vi zucken

twitter /'twɪtə(r)/ n Zwitschern nt • vi zwitschern

two /tu:/ adj zwei

two: ~-faced adj falsch. **~-piece** adj zweiteilig. **~-way** adj **~-way traffic** Gegenverkehr m

tycoon /taɪ'ku:n/ n Magnat m

tying /'taɪɪŋ/ see **tie**

type /taɪp/ n Art f, Sorte f; (person) Typ m; (printing) Type f • vt mit der Maschine schreiben, [!] tippen • vi Maschine schreiben, [!] tippen. **~writer** n Schreibmaschine f. **~written** adj maschinegeschrieben

typical /'tɪpɪkl/ adj typisch (**of** für)

typify /'tɪpɪfaɪ/ vt (pt/pp **-ied**) typisch sein für

typing /'taɪpɪŋ/ n Maschineschreiben nt

typist /'taɪpɪst/ n Schreibkraft f

tyrannical /tɪ'rænɪkl/ adj tyrannisch

tyranny /'tɪrənɪ/ n Tyrannei f

tyrant /'taɪrənt/ n Tyrann m

tyre /'taɪə(r)/ n Reifen m

Uu

ugl|iness /'ʌglɪnɪs/ n Hässlichkeit f. **~y** adj hässlich; (nasty) übel

UK abbr **United Kingdom**

ulcer /'ʌlsə(r)/ n Geschwür nt

ultimate /'ʌltɪmət/ adj letzte(r,s); (final) endgültig; (fundamental) grundlegend, eigentlich. **~ly** adv schließlich

ultimatum /ʌltɪ'meɪtəm/ n Ultimatum nt

ultra'violet adj ultraviolett

umbrella /ʌm'brelə/ n [Regen]schirm m

umpire /'ʌmpaɪə(r)/ n Schiedsrichter m •vt/i Schiedsrichter sein (bei)

umpteen /ʌmp'ti:n/ adj [!] zig. **~th** adj [!] zigste(r,s)

un'able /ʌn-/ adj **be ~ to do sth** etw nicht tun können

una'bridged adj ungekürzt

unac'companied adj ohne Begleitung; (luggage) unbegleitet

unac'countable adj unerklärlich

unac'customed adj ungewohnt; **be ~ to sth** etw (acc) nicht gewohnt sein

un'aided adj ohne fremde Hilfe

unanimous /ju:'nænɪməs/ adj einmütig; (vote, decision) einstimmig

un'armed adj unbewaffnet

unas'suming adj bescheiden

unat'tended adj unbeaufsichtigt

un'authorized adj unbefugt

una'voidable adj unvermeidlich

una'ware adj **be ~ of sth** sich (dat) etw (gen) nicht bewusst sein. **~s** adv **catch s.o. ~s** jdn überraschen

un'bearable adj, **-bly** adv unerträglich

unbeat|able /ʌn'bi:təbl/ adj unschlagbar. **~en** adj ungeschlagen; (record) ungebrochen

unbe'lievable adj unglaublich

un'biased adj unvoreingenommen

un'block vt frei machen

un'bolt vt aufriegeln

un'breakable adj unzerbrechlich

un'button vt aufknöpfen

uncalled-for /ʌn'kɔ:ldfɔ:(r)/ adj unangebracht

un'canny adj unheimlich

un'ceasing adj unaufhörlich

un'certain adj (doubtful) ungewiss; (origins) unbestimmt; **be ~** nicht sicher sein. **~ty** n Ungewissheit f

un'changed adj unverändert

un'charitable adj lieblos

uncle /'ʌŋkl/ n Onkel m

un'comforta|ble adj, **-bly** adv unbequem; **feel ~** (fig) sich nicht wohl fühlen

un'common adj ungewöhnlich

un'compromising adj kompromisslos

uncon'ditional adj, **~ly** adv bedingungslos

un'conscious adj bewusstlos; (unintended) unbewusst; **be ~ of sth** sich (dat) etw (gen) nicht bewusst sein. **~ly** adv unbewusst

uncon'ventional adj unkonventionell

unco'operative adj nicht hilfsbereit

un'cork vt entkorken

uncouth /ʌn'ku:θ/ adj ungehobelt

un'cover vt aufdecken

unde'cided adj unentschlossen; (not settled) nicht entschieden

undeniable /ʌndɪ'naɪəbl/ adj, **-bly** adv unbestreitbar

under /'ʌndə(r)/ prep unter (+ dat/acc); ~ **it** darunter; ~ **there** da drunter; ~ **repair** in Reparatur; ~ **construction** im Bau; ~ **age** minderjährig •adv darunter

'undercarriage n (Aviat) Fahrwerk nt, Fahrgestell nt

'underclothes npl Unterwäsche f

under'cover adj geheim

'undercurrent n Unterströmung f; (fig) Unterton m

'underdog n Unterlegene(r) m

under'done adj nicht gar; (rare) nicht durchgebraten

under'estimate vt unterschätzen

under'fed adj unterernährt

under'foot adv am Boden

under'go vt (pt **-went**, pp **-gone**) durchmachen; sich unterziehen (+ dat) (operation, treatment)

under'graduate n Student(in) m(f)

under'ground[1] adv unter der Erde; (mining) unter Tage

'underground[2] adj unterirdisch; (secret) Untergrund- •n (railway) U-Bahn f. ~ **car park** n Tiefgarage f

'undergrowth n Unterholz nt

'underhand adj hinterhältig

under'lie vt (pt **-lay**, pp **-lain**, pres p **-lying**) zugrunde liegen (+ dat)

under'line vt unterstreichen

under'lying adj eigentlich

under'mine vt (fig) unterminieren, untergraben

underneath /ʌndə'ni:θ/ prep unter (+ dat/acc) •adv darunter

'underpants npl Unterhose f

'underpass n Unterführung f

under'privileged adj unterprivilegiert

under'rate vt unterschätzen

'undershirt n (Amer) Unterhemd nt

under'stand vt/i (pt/pp **-stood**) verstehen; **I ~ that ...** (have heard) ich habe gehört, dass ... **~able** adj verständlich. **~ably** adv verständlicherweise

under'standing adj verständnisvoll •n Verständnis nt; (agreement) Vereinbarung f; **reach an ~** sich verständigen

'understatement n Untertreibung f

under'take vt (pt **-took**, pp **-taken**) unternehmen; ~ **to do sth** sich verpflichten, etw zu tun

'undertaker n Leichenbestatter m; **[firm of] ~s** Bestattungsinstitut n

under'taking n Unternehmen nt; (promise) Versprechen nt

'undertone n (fig) Unterton m; **in an ~** mit gedämpfter Stimme

under'value vt unterbewerten

'underwater[1] adj Unterwasser-

under'water[2] adv unter Wasser

'underwear n Unterwäsche f

under'weight adj untergewichtig; **be ~** Untergewicht haben

'underworld n Unterwelt f

unde'sirable adj unerwünscht

un'dignified adj würdelos

un'do vt (pt **-did**, pp **-done**) aufmachen; (fig) ungeschehen machen

un'done adj offen; (not accomplished) unerledigt

un'doubted adj unzweifelhaft. **~ly** adv zweifellos

un'dress vt ausziehen; **get ~ed** sich ausziehen •vi sich ausziehen

un'due adj übermäßig

und'uly adv übermäßig

un'earth vt ausgraben; (fig) zutage bringen. **~ly** adj unheimlich; **at an ~ly hour** [!] in aller Herrgottsfrühe

un'easy adj unbehaglich

uneco'nomic adj, **-ally** adv unwirtschaftlich

u

unem'ployed adj arbeitslos •npl **the ~** die Arbeitslosen

unem'ployment n Arbeitslosigkeit f

un'ending adj endlos

un'equal adj unterschiedlich; (struggle) ungleich. **~ly** adv ungleichmäßig

unequivocal /ʌnɪ'kwɪvəkl/ adj eindeutig

un'ethical adj unmoralisch; **be ~** gegen das Berufsethos verstoßen

un'even adj uneben; (unequal) ungleich; (not regular) ungleichmäßig; (number) ungerade

unex'pected adj unerwartet

un'fair adj ungerecht, unfair. **~ness** n Ungerechtigkeit f

un'faithful adj untreu

unfa'miliar adj ungewohnt; (unknown) unbekannt

un'fasten vt aufmachen; (detach) losmachen

un'favourable adj ungünstig

un'feeling adj gefühllos

un'fit adj ungeeignet; (incompetent) unfähig; (Sport) nicht fit; **~ for work** arbeitsunfähig

un'fold vt auseinander falten, entfalten; (spread out) ausbreiten •vi sich entfalten

unfore'seen adj unvorhergesehen

unforgettable /ʌnfə'getəbl/ adj unvergesslich

unforgivable /ʌnfə'gɪvəbl/ adj unverzeihlich

un'fortunate adj unglücklich; (unfavourable) ungünstig; (regrettable) bedauerlich; **be ~** (person:) Pech haben. **~ly** adv leider

un'founded adj unbegründet

unfurl /ʌn'fɜ:l/ vt entrollen

un'furnished adj unmöbliert

ungainly /ʌn'geɪnlɪ/ adj unbeholfen

un'grateful adj undankbar

un'happiness n Kummer m

un'happy adj unglücklich; (not content) unzufrieden

un'harmed adj unverletzt

un'healthy adj ungesund

un'hurt adj unverletzt

unification /ju:nɪfɪ'keɪʃn/ n Einigung f

uniform /'ju:nɪfɔ:m/ adj einheitlich •n Uniform f

unify /'ju:nɪfaɪ/ vt (pt/pp **-ied**) einigen

uni'lateral /ju:nɪ-/ adj einseitig

uni'maginable adj unvorstellbar

unim'portant adj unwichtig

unin'habited adj unbewohnt

unin'tentional adj unabsichtlich

union /'ju:nɪən/ n Vereinigung f; (Pol) Union f; (trade ~) Gewerkschaft f

unique /ju:'ni:k/ adj einzigartig. **~ly** adv einmalig

unison /'ju:nɪsn/ n **in ~** einstimmig

unit /'ju:nɪt/ n Einheit f; (Math) Einer m; (of furniture) Teil nt, Element nt

unite /ju:'naɪt/ vt vereinigen •vi sich vereinigen

united /ju:'naɪtɪd/ adj einig. **U~ 'Kingdom** n Vereinigtes Königreich nt. **U~ 'Nations** n Vereinte Nationen pl. **U~ States [of America]** n Vereinigte Staaten pl [von Amerika]

unity /'ju:nətɪ/ n Einheit f; (harmony) Einigkeit f

universal /ju:nɪ'vɜ:sl/ adj allgemein

universe /'ju:nɪvɜ:s/ n [Welt]all nt, Universum nt

university /ju:nɪ'vɜ:sətɪ/ n Universität f •attrib Universitäts-

un'just adj ungerecht

un'kind adj unfreundlich; (harsh) hässlich

un'known adj unbekannt

un'lawful adj gesetzwidrig

unleaded /ʌn'ledɪd/ adj bleifrei

un'leash vt (fig) entfesseln

unless /ən'les/ conj wenn ... nicht; **~ I am mistaken** wenn ich mich nicht irre

un'like prep im Gegensatz zu (+ dat)

un'likely adj unwahrscheinlich

un'limited adj unbegrenzt

un'load vt entladen; ausladen (luggage)

un'lock vt aufschließen

un'lucky adj unglücklich; (day, number) Unglücks-; **be ~** Pech haben; (thing:) Unglück bringen

un'married adj unverheiratet. **~ 'mother** n ledige Mutter f

un'mask vt (fig) entlarven

unmistakable /ʌnmɪ'steɪkəbl/ adj, **-bly** adv unverkennbar

un'natural adj unnatürlich; (not normal) nicht normal

un'necessary adj, **-ily** adv unnötig

un'noticed adj unbemerkt

unob'tainable adj nicht erhältlich

unob'trusive adj unaufdringlich; (thing) unauffällig

unof'ficial adj inoffiziell

un'pack vt/i auspacken

un'paid adj unbezahlt

un'pleasant adj unangenehm

un'plug vt (pt/pp **-plugged**) den Stecker herausziehen von

un'popular adj unbeliebt

un'precedented adj beispiellos

unpre'dictable adj unberechenbar

unpre'pared adj nicht vorbereitet

unpre'tentious adj bescheiden

un'profitable adj unrentabel

un'qualified adj unqualifiziert; (fig: absolute) uneingeschränkt

un'questionable adj unbezweifelbar; (right) unbestreitbar

unravel /ʌn'rævl/ vt (pt/pp **-ravelled**) entwirren; (Knitting) aufziehen

un'real adj unwirklich

un'reasonable adj unvernünftig

unre'lated adj unzusammenhängend; **be ~** nicht verwandt sein; (events:) nicht miteinander zusammenhängen

unre'liable adj unzuverlässig

un'rest n Unruhen pl

un'rivalled adj unübertroffen

un'roll vt aufrollen •vi sich aufrollen

unruly /ʌn'ru:lɪ/ adj ungebärdig

un'safe adj nicht sicher

unsatis'factory adj unbefriedigend

un'savoury adj unangenehm; (fig) unerfreulich

unscathed /ʌn'skeɪðd/ adj unversehrt

un'screw vt abschrauben

un'scrupulous adj skrupellos

un'seemly adj unschicklich

un'selfish adj selbstlos

un'settled adj ungeklärt; (weather) unbeständig; (bill) unbezahlt

unshakeable /ʌn'ʃeɪkəbl/ adj unerschütterlich

unshaven /ʌn'ʃeɪvn/ adj unrasiert

unsightly /ʌn'saɪtlɪ/ adj unansehnlich

un'skilled adj ungelernt; (work) unqualifiziert

un'sociable adj ungesellig

unso'phisticated adj einfach

un'sound adj krank, nicht gesund; (building) nicht sicher; (advice) unzuverlässig; (reasoning) nicht stichhaltig

un'stable adj nicht stabil; (mentally) labil

un'steady adj, **-ily** adv unsicher; (wobbly) wackelig

un'stuck adj **come ~** sich lösen; (!: fail) scheitern

unsuc'cessful adj erfolglos; **be ~** keinen Erfolg haben

un'suitable adj ungeeignet; (inappropriate) unpassend; (for weather, activity) unzweckmäßig

unthinkable /ʌn'θɪŋkəbl/ adj unvorstellbar

un'tidiness n Unordentlichkeit f

un'tidy adj, **-ily** adv unordentlich

un'tie vt aufbinden; losbinden (person, boat, horse)

until /ən'tɪl/ prep bis (+ acc); **not ~** erst; **~ the evening** bis zum Abend •conj bis; **not ~** erst wenn; (in past) erst als

un'told adj unermesslich

un'true adj unwahr; **that's ~** das ist nicht wahr

unused[1] /ʌn'ju:zd/ adj unbenutzt; (not utilized) ungenutzt

unused[2] /ʌn'ju:st/ adj **be ~ to sth** etw nicht gewohnt sein

un'usual adj ungewöhnlich

un'veil vt enthüllen

un'wanted adj unerwünscht

un'welcome adj unwillkommen

un'well adj **be** or **feel ~** sich nicht wohl fühlen

unwieldy /ʌn'wi:ldɪ/ adj sperrig

un'willing adj widerwillig; **be ~ to do sth** etw nicht tun wollen

un'wind v (pt/pp **unwound**) •vt abwickeln •vi sich abwickeln; (!: relax) sich entspannen

un'wise adj unklug

un'worthy adj unwürdig

un'wrap vt (pt/pp **-wrapped**) auswickeln; auspacken (present)

un'written adj ungeschrieben

up /ʌp/ adv oben; (with movement) nach oben; (not in bed) auf; (road) aufgerissen; (price) gestiegen; **be up for sale** zu verkaufen sein; **up there** da oben; **up to** (as far as) bis; **time's up** die Zeit ist um; **what's up?** ! was ist los? **what's he up to?** ! was hat er vor? **I don't feel up to it** ich fühle mich dem nicht gewachsen; **go up** hinaufgehen; **come up** heraufkommen •prep **be up on sth** [oben] auf etw (dat) sein; **up the mountain** oben am Berg; (movement) den Berg hinauf; **be up the tree** oben im Baum sein; **up the road** die Straße entlang; **up the river** stromaufwärts; **go up the stairs** die Treppe hinaufgehen

'upbringing n Erziehung f

up'date vt auf den neuesten Stand bringen

up'grade vt aufstufen

upheaval /ʌp'hi:vl/ n Unruhe f; (Pol) Umbruch m

up'hill adj (fig) mühsam •adv bergauf

up'hold vt (pt/pp **upheld**) unterstützen; bestätigen (verdict)

upholster /ʌp'həʊlstə(r)/ vt polstern. **~y** n Polsterung f

'upkeep n Unterhalt m

up'market adj anspruchsvoll

upon /ə'pɒn/ prep auf (+ dat/acc)

upper /'ʌpə(r)/ adj obere(r,s); (deck, jaw, lip) Ober-; **have the ~ hand** die Oberhand haben •n (of shoe) Obermaterial nt

upper class n Oberschicht f

'upright adj aufrecht

'uprising n Aufstand m

'uproar n Aufruhr m

up'set[1] vt (pt/pp **upset**, pres p **upsetting**) umstoßen; (spill) verschütten; durcheinander bringen (plan); (distress) erschüttern; (food:) nicht bekommen (+ dat); **get ~ about sth** sich über etw (acc) aufregen

'upset[2] n Aufregung f; **have a stomach ~** einen verdorbenen Magen haben

'upshot n Ergebnis nt

upside 'down adv verkehrt herum; **turn ~** umdrehen

up'stairs[1] adv oben; (go) nach oben

'upstairs[2] adj im Obergeschoss

'upstart n Emporkömmling m

up'stream adv stromaufwärts

'uptake n **slow on the ~** schwer von Begriff; **be quick on the ~** schnell begreifen

'upturn n Aufschwung m

upward /'ʌpwəd/ adj nach oben; (movement) Aufwärts-; **~ slope** Steigung f •adv **~[s]** aufwärts, nach oben

uranium /jʊ'reɪnɪəm/ n Uran nt

urban /'ɜ:bən/ adj städtisch

urge /ɜ:dʒ/ n Trieb m, Drang m •vt drängen; **~ on** antreiben

urgen|cy /'ɜ:dʒənsɪ/ n Dringlichkeit f. **~t** adj dringend

urine /'jʊərɪn/ n Urin m, Harn m

us /ʌs/ pron uns; **it's us** wir sind es

US[A] abbr USA pl

usable /'ju:zəbl/ adj brauchbar

usage /'ju:sɪdʒ/ n Brauch m; (of word) [Sprach]gebrauch m

use¹ /ju:s/ n (see **use²**) Benutzung f; Verwendung f; Gebrauch m; **be (of) no ~** nichts nützen; **it is no ~** es hat keinen Zweck; **what's the ~?** wozu?

use² /ju:z/ vt benutzen (implement, room, lift); verwenden (ingredient, method, book, money); gebrauchen (words, force, brains); **~ [up]** aufbrauchen

used¹ /ju:zd/ adj gebraucht; (towel) benutzt; (car) Gebraucht-

used² /ju:st/ pt **be ~ to sth** an etw (acc) gewöhnt sein; **get ~ to** sich gewöhnen an (+ acc); **he ~ to say** er hat immer gesagt; **he ~ to live here** er hat früher hier gewohnt

useful /'ju:sfl/ adj nützlich. **~ness** n Nützlichkeit f

useless /'ju:slɪs/ adj nutzlos; (not usable) unbrauchbar; (pointless) zwecklos

user /'ju:zə(r)/ n Benutzer(in) m(f)

usher /'ʌʃə(r)/ n Platzanweiser m; (in court) Gerichtsdiener m

usherette /ʌʃə'ret/ n Platzanweiserin f

USSR abbr (History) UdSSR f

usual /'ju:ʒʊəl/ adj üblich. **~ly** adv gewöhnlich

utensil /ju:'tensl/ n Gerät nt

utility /ju:'tɪlətɪ/ adj Gebrauchs-

utilize /'ju:tɪlaɪz/ vt nutzen

utmost /'ʌtməʊst/ adj äußerste(r,s), größte(r,s) •n **do one's ~** sein Möglichstes tun

utter¹ /'ʌtə(r)/ adj völlig

utter² vt von sich geben (sigh, sound); sagen (word)

U-turn /'ju:-/ n (fig) Kehrtwendung f; **'no ~s'** (Auto) 'Wenden verboten'

Vv

vacan|cy /'veɪkənsɪ/ n (job) freie Stelle f; (room) freies Zimmer nt; **'no ~cies'** 'belegt'. **~t** adj frei; (look) [gedanken]leer

vacate /və'keɪt/ vt räumen

vacation /və'keɪʃn/ n (Univ & Amer) Ferien pl

vaccinat|e /'væksɪneɪt/ vt impfen. **~ion** n Impfung f

vaccine /'væksi:n/ n Impfstoff m

vacuum /'vækjʊəm/ n Vakuum nt, luftleerer Raum m •vt saugen. **~ cleaner** n Staubsauger m

vagina /və'dʒaɪnə/ n (Anat) Scheide f

vague /veɪg/ adj **(-r,-st)** vage; (outline) verschwommen

vain /veɪn/ adj **(-er,-est)** eitel; (hope,

attempt) vergeblich; **in ~** vergeblich. **~ly** adv vergeblich

valiant /'vælɪənt/ adj tapfer

valid /'vælɪd/ adj gültig; (claim) berechtigt; (argument) stichhaltig; (reason) triftig. **~ity** n Gültigkeit f

valley /'vælɪ/ n Tal nt

valour /'vælə(r)/ n Tapferkeit f

valuable /'væljʊəbl/ adj wertvoll. **~s** npl Wertsachen pl

valuation /væljʊ'eɪʃn/ n Schätzung f

value /'vælju:/ n Wert m; (usefulness) Nutzen m •vt schätzen. **~ 'added tax** n Mehrwertsteuer f

valve /vælv/ n Ventil nt; (Anat) Klappe f; (Electr) Röhre f

van /væn/ n Lieferwagen m

vandal /'vændl/ n Rowdy m. **~ism** n mutwillige Zerstörung f. **~ize** vt demolieren

vanilla /və'nɪlə/ n Vanille f

vanish /'vænɪʃ/ vi verschwinden

vanity /'vænətɪ/ n Eitelkeit f

vapour /'veɪpə(r)/ n Dampf m

variable /'veərɪəbl/ adj unbeständig; (Math) variabel; (adjustable) regulierbar

variant /'veərɪənt/ n Variante f

variation /veərɪ'eɪʃn/ n Variation f; (difference) Unterschied m

varied /'veərɪd/ adj vielseitig; (diet:) abwechslungsreich

variety /və'raɪətɪ/ n Abwechslung f; (quantity) Vielfalt f; (Comm) Auswahl f; (type) Art f; (Bot) Abart f; (Theat) Varieté nt

various /'veərɪəs/ adj verschieden. **~ly** adv unterschiedlich

varnish /'vɑ:nɪʃ/ n Lack m •vt lackieren

vary /'veərɪ/ v (pt/pp **-ied**) •vi sich ändern; (be different) verschieden sein •vt [ver]ändern; (add variety to) abwechslungsreicher gestalten

vase /vɑ:z/ n Vase f

vast /vɑ:st/ adj riesig; (expanse) weit. **~ly** adv gewaltig

vat /væt/ n Bottich m

VAT /vi:eɪ'ti:, væt/ abbr (**value added tax**) Mehrwertsteuer f, MwSt.

vault¹ /vɔ:lt/ n (roof) Gewölbe nt; (in bank) Tresor m; (tomb) Gruft f

vault² n Sprung m •vt/i **~ [over]** springen über (+ acc)

VDU abbr (**visual display unit**) Bildschirmgerät nt

veal /vi:l/ n Kalbfleisch nt •attrib Kalbs-

veer /vɪə(r)/ vi sich drehen; (Auto) ausscheren

vegetable /'vedʒtəbl/ n Gemüse nt; **~s** pl Gemüse nt •attrib Gemüse-; (oil, fat) Pflanzen-

vegetarian /vedʒɪ'teərɪən/ adj vegetarisch •n Vegetarier(in) m(f)

vegetation /vedʒɪ'teɪʃn/ n Vegetation f

vehement /'vi:əmənt/ adj heftig

vehicle /'vi:ɪkl/ n Fahrzeug nt

veil /veɪl/ n Schleier m •vt verschleiern

vein /veɪn/ n Ader f; (mood) Stimmung f; (manner) Art f

velocity /vɪ'lɒsətɪ/ n Geschwindigkeit f

velvet /'velvɪt/ n Samt m

vending-machine /'vendɪŋ-/ n [Verkaufs]automat m

vendor /'vendə(r)/ n Verkäufer(in) m(f)

veneer /və'nɪə(r)/ n Furnier nt; (fig) Tünche f. **~ed** adj furniert

venerable /'venərəbl/ adj ehrwürdig

Venetian /və'ni:ʃn/ adj venezianisch. **v~ blind** n Jalousie f

vengeance /'vendʒəns/ n Rache f; **with a ~** gewaltig

Venice /'venɪs/ n Venedig nt

venison /'venɪsn/ n (Culin) Reh[fleisch] nt

venom /'venəm/ n Gift nt; (fig) Hass m. **~ous** adj giftig

vent /vent/ n Öffnung f

ventilat|e /'ventɪleɪt/ vt belüften. **~ion** n Belüftung f; (installation) Lüftung f. **~or** n Lüftungsvorrichtung f; (Med) Beatmungsgerät nt

ventriloquist /ven'trɪləkwɪst/ n Bauchredner m

venture /'ventʃə(r)/ n Unternehmung f •vt wagen •vi sich wagen

venue /'venju:/ n (for event) Veranstaltungsort m

veranda /və'rændə/ n Veranda f

verb /vɜ:b/ n Verb nt. **~al** adj mündlich; (Gram) verbal

verbose /vɜ:'bəʊs/ adj weitschweifig

verdict /'vɜ:dɪkt/ n Urteil nt

verge /vɜ:dʒ/ n Rand m •vi **~ on** (fig) grenzen an (+ acc)

verify /'verɪfaɪ/ vt (pt/pp **-ied**) überprüfen; (confirm) bestätigen

vermin /'vɜ:mɪn/ n Ungeziefer nt

vermouth /'vɜ:məθ/ n Wermut m

versatil|e /'vɜ:sətaɪl/ adj vielseitig. **~ity** n Vielseitigkeit f

verse /vɜ:s/ n Strophe f; (of Bible) Vers m; (poetry) Lyrik f

version /'vɜ:ʃn/ n Version f; (translation) Übersetzung f; (model) Modell nt

versus /'vɜ:səs/ prep gegen (+ acc)

vertical /'vɜ:tɪkl/ adj senkrecht •n Senkrechte f

vertigo /'vɜ:tɪgəʊ/ n (Med) Schwindel m

verve /vɜ:v/ n Schwung m

very /'verɪ/ adv sehr; **~ much** sehr; (quantity) sehr viel; **~ probably** höchstwahrscheinlich; **at the ~ most** allerhöchstens •adj (mere) bloß; **the ~ first** der/die/das allererste; **the ~ thing** genau das Richtige; **at the ~ end/beginning** ganz am Ende/Anfang; **only a ~ little** nur ein ganz kleines bisschen

vessel /'vesl/ n Schiff nt; (receptacle & Anat) Gefäß nt

vest /vest/ n [Unter]hemd nt; (Amer: waistcoat) Weste f

vestige /'vestɪdʒ/ n Spur f

vestry /'vestrɪ/ n Sakristei f

vet /vet/ n Tierarzt m /-ärztin f •vt (pt/pp **vetted**) überprüfen

veteran /'vetərən/ n Veteran m

veterinary /'vetərɪnərɪ/ adj tierärztlich. **~ surgeon** n Tierarzt m /-ärztin f

veto /'vi:təʊ/ n (pl **-es**) Veto nt

VHF abbr (**very high frequency**) UKW

via /'vaɪə/ prep über (+ acc)

viable /'vaɪəbl/ adj lebensfähig; (fig) realisierbar; (firm) rentabel

viaduct /'vaɪədʌkt/ n Viadukt nt

vibrat|e /vaɪ'breɪt/ vi vibrieren. **~ion** n Vibrieren nt

vicar /'vɪkə(r)/ n Pfarrer m. **~age** n Pfarrhaus nt

vice[1] /vaɪs/ n Laster nt

vice[2] n (Techn) Schraubstock m

vice[3] adj Vize-; **~ 'chairman** stellvertretender Vorsitzender m

vice versa /vaɪsɪ'vɜ:sə/ adv umgekehrt

vicinity /vɪ'sɪnətɪ/ n Umgebung f; **in the ~ of** in der Nähe von

vicious /'vɪʃəs/ adj boshaft; (animal) bösartig

victim /'vɪktɪm/ n Opfer nt. **~ize** vt schikanieren

victor /'vɪktə(r)/ n Sieger m

victor|ious /vɪk'tɔ:rɪəs/ adj siegreich. **~y** n Sieg m

video /'vɪdɪəʊ/ n Video nt; (recorder) Videorecorder m •attrib Video-

video: ~ cas'sette n Videokassette f. **~ game** n Videospiel nt. **~ recorder** n Videorecorder m

Vienn|a /vɪ'enə/ n Wien nt. **~ese** adj Wiener

view /vju:/ n Sicht f; (scene)

Aussicht f, Blick m; (picture, opinion) Ansicht f; **in my ~** meiner Ansicht nach; **in ~ of** angesichts (+ gen); **be on ~** besichtigt werden können •vt sich (dat) ansehen; besichtigen (house); (consider) betrachten •vi (TV) fernsehen. **~er** n (TV) Zuschauer(in) m(f)

view: ~finder n (Phot) Sucher m. **~point** n Standpunkt m

vigilan|ce /ˈvɪdʒɪləns/ n Wachsamkeit f. **~t** adj wachsam

vigorous /ˈvɪgərəs/ adj kräftig; (fig) heftig

vigour /ˈvɪgə(r)/ n Kraft f; (fig) Heftigkeit f

vile /vaɪl/ adj abscheulich

villa /ˈvɪlə/ n (for holidays) Ferienhaus nt

village /ˈvɪlɪdʒ/ n Dorf nt. **~r** n Dorfbewohner(in) m(f)

villain /ˈvɪlən/ n Schurke m; (in story) Bösewicht m

vindicat|e /ˈvɪndɪkeɪt/ vt rechtfertigen. **~ion** n Rechtfertigung f

vindictive /vɪnˈdɪktɪv/ adj nachtragend

vine /vaɪn/ n Weinrebe f

vinegar /ˈvɪnɪgə(r)/ n Essig m

vineyard /ˈvɪnjɑːd/ n Weinberg m

vintage /ˈvɪntɪdʒ/ adj erlesen •n (year) Jahrgang m. **~ ˈcar** n Oldtimer m

viola /vɪˈəʊlə/ n (Mus) Bratsche f

violat|e /ˈvaɪəleɪt/ vt verletzen; (break) brechen; (disturb) stören; (defile) schänden. **~ion** n Verletzung f; Schändung f

violen|ce /ˈvaɪələns/ n Gewalt f; (fig) Heftigkeit f. **~t** adj gewalttätig; (fig) heftig. **~tly** adv brutal; (fig) heftig

violet /ˈvaɪələt/ adj violett •n (flower) Veilchen nt

violin /vaɪəˈlɪn/ n Geige f, Violine f. **~ist** n Geiger(in) m(f)

VIP abbr (**very important person**) Prominente(r) m/f

viper /ˈvaɪpə(r)/ n Kreuzotter f

virgin /ˈvɜːdʒɪn/ adj unberührt •n Jungfrau f. **~ity** n Unschuld f

viril|e /ˈvɪraɪl/ adj männlich. **~ity** n Männlichkeit f

virtual /ˈvɜːtjʊəl/ adj **a ~ ...** praktisch ein ... **~ly** adv praktisch

virtu|e /ˈvɜːtjuː/ n Tugend f; (advantage) Vorteil m; **by** or **in ~e of** auf Grund (+ gen)

virtuoso /vɜːtjʊˈəʊzəʊ/ n (pl **-si** /-ziː/) Virtuose m

virtuous /ˈvɜːtjʊəs/ adj tugendhaft

virus /ˈvaɪərəs/ n Virus nt

visa /ˈviːzə/ n Visum nt

visibility /vɪzəˈbɪlətɪ/ n Sichtbarkeit f; (range) Sichtweite f

visi|ble /ˈvɪzəbl/ adj, **-bly** adv sichtbar

vision /ˈvɪʒn/ n Vision f; (sight) Sehkraft f; (foresight) Weitblick m

visit /ˈvɪzɪt/ n Besuch m •vt besuchen; besichtigen (town, building). **~or** n Besucher(in) m(f); (in hotel) Gast m; **have ~ors** Besuch haben

visor /ˈvaɪzə(r)/ n Schirm m; (Auto) [Sonnen]blende f

vista /ˈvɪstə/ n Aussicht f

visual /ˈvɪzjʊəl/ adj visuell. **~ disˈplay unit** n Bildschirmgerät nt

visualize /ˈvɪzjʊəlaɪz/ vt sich (dat) vorstellen

vital /ˈvaɪtl/ adj unbedingt notwendig; (essential to life) lebenswichtig. **~ity** n Vitalität f. **~ly** adv äußerst

vitamin /ˈvɪtəmɪn/ n Vitamin nt

vivaci|ous /vɪˈveɪʃəs/ adj lebhaft. **~ty** n Lebhaftigkeit f

vivid /ˈvɪvɪd/ adj lebhaft; (description) lebendig

vocabulary /vəˈkæbjʊlərɪ/ n Wortschatz m; (list) Vokabelverzeichnis nt; **learn ~** Vokabeln lernen

vocal /ˈvəʊkl/ adj stimmlich; (vociferous) lautstark

vocalist /ˈvəʊkəlɪst/ n Sänger(in) m(f)

vocation /vəˈkeɪʃn/ n Berufung f. **~al** adj Berufs-

vociferous /vəˈsɪfərəs/ adj lautstark

vodka /ˈvɒdkə/ n Wodka m

vogue /vəʊg/ n Mode f

voice /vɔɪs/ n Stimme f •vt zum Ausdruck bringen. **~ mail** n Voicemail f

void /vɔɪd/ adj leer; (not valid) ungültig; **~ of** ohne •n Leere f

volatile /ˈvɒlətaɪl/ adj flüchtig; (person) sprunghaft

volcanic /vɒlˈkænɪk/ adj vulkanisch

volcano /vɒlˈkeɪnəʊ/ n Vulkan m

volley /ˈvɒlɪ/ n (of gunfire) Salve f; (Tennis) Volley m

volt /vəult/ n Volt nt. **~age** n (Electr) Spannung f

voluble /ˈvɒljʊbl/ adj, **-bly** adv redselig; (protest) wortreich

volume /ˈvɒlju:m/ n (book) Band m; (Geometry) Rauminhalt m; (amount) Ausmaß nt; (Radio, TV) Lautstärke f

voluntary /ˈvɒləntərɪ/ adj, **-ily** adv freiwillig

volunteer /vɒlənˈtɪə(r)/ n Freiwillige(r) m/f •vt anbieten; geben (information) •vi sich freiwillig melden

vomit /ˈvɒmɪt/ n Erbrochene(s) nt •vt erbrechen •vi sich übergeben

voracious /vəˈreɪʃəs/ adj gefräßig; (appetite) unbändig

vot|e /vəʊt/ n Stimme f; (ballot) Abstimmung f; (right) Wahlrecht nt •vi abstimmen; (in election) wählen. **~er** n Wähler(in) m(f)

vouch /vaʊtʃ/ vi **~ for** sich verbürgen für. **~er** n Gutschein m

vowel /ˈvaʊəl/ n Vokal m

voyage /ˈvɔɪɪdz/ n Seereise f; (in space) Reise f, Flug m

vulgar /ˈvʌlgə(r)/ adj vulgär, ordinär. **~ity** n Vulgarität f

vulnerable /ˈvʌlnərəbl/ adj verwundbar

vulture /ˈvʌltʃə(r)/ n Geier m

Ww

wad /wɒd/ n Bausch m; (bundle) Bündel nt. **~ding** n Wattierung f

waddle /ˈwɒdl/ vi watscheln

wade /weɪd/ vi waten

wafer /ˈweɪfə(r)/ n Waffel f

waffle[1] /ˈwɒfl/ vi [!] schwafeln

waffle[2] n (Culin) Waffel f

waft /wɒft/ vt/i wehen

wag /wæg/ v (pt/pp **wagged**) •vt wedeln mit •vi wedeln

wage /weɪdʒ/ n (also **~s**) pl Lohn m

wager /ˈweɪdʒə(r)/ n Wette f

wagon /ˈwægən/ n Wagen m; (Rail) Waggon m

wail /weɪl/ n [klagender] Schrei m •vi heulen; (lament) klagen

waist /weɪst/ n Taille f. **~coat** n Weste f. **~line** n Taille f

wait /weɪt/ n Wartezeit f; **lie in ~ for** auflauern (+ dat) •vi warten (**for** auf + acc); (at table) servieren; **~ on** bedienen •vt **~ one's turn** warten, bis man an der Reihe ist

waiter /ˈweɪtə(r)/ n Kellner m; **~!** Herr Ober!

waiting: ~-list n Warteliste f. **~-room** n Warteraum m; (doctor's) Wartezimmer nt

waitress /ˈweɪtrɪs/ n Kellnerin f

waive /weɪv/ vt verzichten auf (+ acc)

wake¹ /weɪk/ n Totenwache f •v (pt **woke**, pp **woken**) ~ **up** •vt [auf]wecken •vi aufwachen

wake² n (Naut) Kielwasser nt; **in the ~ of** im Gefolge (+ gen)

Wales /weɪlz/ n Wales nt

walk /wɔ:k/ n Spaziergang m; (gait) Gang m; (path) Weg m; **go for a ~** spazieren gehen •vi gehen; (not ride) laufen, zu Fuß gehen; (ramble) wandern; **learn to ~** laufen lernen •vt ausführen (dog). ~ **out** vi hinausgehen (; workers:) in den Streik treten; ~ **out on s.o.** jdn verlassen

walker /'wɔ:kə(r)/ n Spaziergänger(in) m(f); (rambler) Wanderer m/Wanderin f

walking /'wɔ:kɪŋ/ n Gehen nt; (rambling) Wandern nt. ~**-stick** n Spazierstock m

wall /wɔ:l/ n Wand f; (external) Mauer f; **drive s.o. up the ~** [!] jdn auf die Palme bringen •vt ~ **up** zumauern

wallet /'wɒlɪt/ n Brieftasche f

'**wallflower** n Goldlack m

wallop /'wɒləp/ vt (pt/pp **walloped**) [!] schlagen

wallow /'wɒləʊ/ vi sich wälzen; (fig) schwelgen

'**wallpaper** n Tapete f •vt tapezieren

walnut /'wɔ:lnʌt/ n Walnuss f

waltz /wɔ:lts/ n Walzer m •vi Walzer tanzen

wander /'wɒndə(r)/ vi umherwandern, [!] bummeln; (fig: digress) abschweifen. ~ **about** vi umherwandern

wangle /'wæŋgl/ vt [!] organisieren

want /wɒnt/ n Mangel m (**of** an + dat); (hardship) Not f; (desire) Bedürfnis nt •vt wollen; (need) brauchen; ~ **[to have] sth** etw haben wollen; ~ **to do sth** etw tun wollen; **I ~ you to go** ich will, dass du gehst; **it ~s painting** es müsste gestrichen werden •vi **he doesn't ~ for anything** ihm fehlt es an nichts. ~**ed** adj (criminal) gesucht

war /wɔ:(r)/ n Krieg m; **be at ~** sich im Krieg befinden

ward /wɔ:d/ n [Kranken]saal m; (unit) Station f; (of town) Wahlbezirk m; (child) Mündel nt •vt ~ **off** abwehren

warden /'wɔ:dn/ n (of hostel) Heimleiter(in) m(f); (of youth hostel) Herbergsvater m; (supervisor) Aufseher(in) m(f)

warder /'wɔ:də(r)/ n Wärter(in) m(f)

wardrobe /'wɔ:drəʊb/ n Kleiderschrank m; (clothes) Garderobe f

warehouse /'weəhaʊs/ n Lager nt; (building) Lagerhaus nt

wares /weəz/ npl Waren pl

war: ~**fare** n Krieg m. ~**like** adj kriegerisch

warm /wɔ:m/ adj (**-er, -est**) warm; (welcome) herzlich; **I am ~** mir ist warm •vt wärmen. ~ **up** vt aufwärmen •vi warm werden; (Sport) sich aufwärmen. ~**-hearted** adj warmherzig

warmth /wɔ:mθ/ n Wärme f

warn /wɔ:n/ vt warnen (**of** vor + dat). ~**ing** n Warnung f; (advance notice) Vorwarnung f; (caution) Verwarnung f

warp /wɔ:p/ vt verbiegen •vi sich verziehen

warrant /'wɒrənt/ n (for arrest) Haftbefehl m; (for search) Durchsuchungsbefehl m •vt (justify) rechtfertigen; (guarantee) garantieren

warranty /'wɒrəntɪ/ n Garantie f

warrior /'wɒrɪə(r)/ n Krieger m

'**warship** n Kriegsschiff nt

wart /wɔ:t/ n Warze f

'**wartime** n Kriegszeit f

war|y /'weərɪ/ adj, **-ily** adv vorsichtig; (suspicious) misstrauisch

was /wɒz/ see **be**

wash /wɒʃ/ n Wäsche f; (Naut) Wellen pl; **have a ~** sich waschen • vt waschen; spülen (dishes); aufwischen (floor); **~ one's hands** sich (dat) die Hände waschen • vi sich waschen. **~ out** vt auswaschen; ausspülen (mouth). **~ up** vt/i abwaschen, spülen • vi (Amer) sich waschen

washable /'wɒʃəbl/ adj waschbar

wash-basin n Waschbecken nt

washer /'wɒʃə(r)/ n (Techn) Dichtungsring m; (machine) Waschmaschine f

washing /'wɒʃɪŋ/ n Wäsche f. **~-machine** n Waschmaschine f. **~-powder** n Waschpulver nt. **~-'up** n Abwasch m; **do the ~-up** abwaschen, spülen. **~-'up liquid** n Spülmittel nt

wasp /wɒsp/ n Wespe f

waste /weɪst/ n Verschwendung f; (rubbish) Abfall m; **~s** pl Öde f • adj (product) Abfall- • vt verschwenden • vi **~ away** immer mehr abmagern

waste: ~ful adj verschwenderisch. **~ land** n Ödland nt. **~ 'paper** n Altpapier nt. **~-'paper basket** n Papierkorb m

watch /wɒtʃ/ n Wache f; (timepiece) [Armband]uhr f • vt beobachten; sich (dat) ansehen (film, match); (keep an eye on) achten auf (+ acc); **~ television** fernsehen • vi zusehen. **~ out** vi Ausschau halten (**for** nach); (be careful) aufpassen

watch: ~-dog n Wachhund m. **~ful** adj wachsam. **~man** n Wachmann m

water /'wɔːtə(r)/ n Wasser nt; **~s** pl Gewässer nt • vt gießen (garden, plant); (dilute) verdünnen • vi (eyes:) tränen; **my mouth was ~ing** mir lief das Wasser im Munde zusammen. **~ down** vt verwässern

water: ~-colour n Wasserfarbe f; (painting) Aquarell nt. **~cress** n Brunnenkresse f. **~fall** n Wasserfall m

'watering-can n Gießkanne f

water: ~-lily n Seerose f. **~logged** adj **be ~logged** (ground:) unter Wasser stehen. **~ polo** n Wasserball m. **~proof** adj wasserdicht. **~-skiing** n Wasserskilaufen nt. **~tight** adj wasserdicht. **~way** n Wasserstraße f

watery /'wɔːtərɪ/ adj wässrig

watt /wɒt/ n Watt nt

wave /weɪv/ n Welle f; (gesture) Handbewegung f; (as greeting) Winken nt • vt winken mit; (brandish) schwingen; wellen (hair); **~ one's hand** winken • vi winken (**to** dat); (flag:) wehen. **~length** n Wellenlänge f

waver /'weɪvə(r)/ vi schwanken

wavy /'weɪvɪ/ adj wellig

wax /wæks/ n Wachs nt; (in ear) Schmalz nt • vt wachsen. **~works** n Wachsfigurenkabinett nt

way /weɪ/ n Weg m; (direction) Richtung f; (respect) Hinsicht f; (manner) Art f; (method) Art und Weise f; **~s** pl Gewohnheiten pl; **on the ~** auf dem Weg (**to** nach/zu); (under way) unterwegs; **a little/long ~** ein kleines/ganzes Stück; **a long ~ off** weit weg; **this ~** hierher; (like this) so; **which ~** in welche Richtung; (how) wie; **by the ~** übrigens; **in some ~s** in gewisser Hinsicht; **either ~** so oder so; **in this ~** auf diese Weise; **in a ~** in gewisser Weise; **lead the ~** vorausgehen; **make ~** Platz machen (**for** dat); **'give ~'** (Auto) 'Vorfahrt beachten'; **go out of one's ~** (fig) sich (dat) besondere Mühe geben (**to** zu); **get one's [own] ~** seinen Willen durchsetzen • adv weit; **~ behind** weit zurück. **~ 'in** n Eingang m

way 'out n Ausgang m; (fig) Ausweg m

WC abbr WC nt

we /wiː/ pron wir

weak /wiːk/ adj (**-er, -est**) schwach; (liquid) dünn. **~en** vt schwächen • vi schwächer werden. **~ling** n

W

Schwächling m. **~ness** n Schwäche f

wealth /welθ/ n Reichtum m; (fig) Fülle f (**of** an + dat). **~y** adj reich

weapon /'wepən/ n Waffe f; **~s of mass destruction** Massenvernichtungswaffen pl

wear /weə(r)/ n (clothing) Kleidung f; **~ and tear** Abnutzung f, Verschleiß m •v (pt **wore**, pp **worn**) •vt tragen; (damage) abnutzen; **what shall I ~?** was soll ich anziehen? •vi sich abnutzen; (last) halten. **~ off** vi abgehen; (effect:) nachlassen. **~ out** vt abnutzen; (exhaust) erschöpfen •vi sich abnutzen

weary /'wɪərɪ/ adj, **-ily** adv müde

weather /'weðə(r)/ n Wetter nt; **in this ~** bei diesem Wetter; **under the ~** [!] nicht ganz auf dem Posten •vt abwettern (storm); (fig) überstehen

weather: ~-beaten adj verwittert; wettergegerbt (face). **~ forecast** n Wettervorhersage f

weave[1] /wi:v/ vi (pt/pp **weaved**) sich schlängeln (**through** durch)

weave[2] n (of cloth) Bindung f •vt (pt **wove**, pp **woven**) weben. **~r** n Weber m

web /web/ n Netz nt; **the W~** das Web. **~master** n Webmaster m. **~ page** n Webseite f. **~site** n Website f

wed /wed/ vt/i (pt/pp **wedded**) heiraten. **~ding** n Hochzeit f

wedding: ~ day n Hochzeitstag m. **~ dress** n Hochzeitskleid nt. **~-ring** n Ehering m, Trauring m

wedge /wedʒ/ n Keil m •vt festklemmen

Wednesday /'wenzdeɪ/ n Mittwoch m

wee /wi:/ adj [!] klein •vi Pipi machen

weed /wi:d/ n Unkraut nt •vt/i jäten. **~ out** vt (fig) aussieben

'weedkiller n Unkrautvertilgungsmittel nt

weedy /'wi:dɪ/ adj [!] spillerig

week /wi:k/ n Woche f. **~day** n Wochentag m. **~end** n Wochenende nt

weekly /'wi:klɪ/ adj & adv wöchentlich •n Wochenzeitschrift f

weep /wi:p/ vi (pt/pp **wept**) weinen

weigh /weɪ/ vt/i wiegen. **~ down** vt (fig) niederdrücken. **~ up** vt (fig) abwägen

weight /weɪt/ n Gewicht nt; **put on/lose ~** zunehmen/abnehmen

weight-lifting n Gewichtheben nt

weighty /'weɪtɪ/ adj schwer; (important) gewichtig

weir /wɪə(r)/ n Wehr nt.

weird /wɪəd/ adj (**-er, -est**) unheimlich; (bizarre) bizarr

welcome /'welkəm/ adj willkommen; **you're ~!** nichts zu danken! **you're ~ to (have) it** das können Sie gerne haben •n Willkommen nt •vt begrüßen

weld /weld/ vt schweißen. **~er** n Schweißer m

welfare /'welfeə(r)/ n Wohl nt; (Admin) Fürsorge f. **W~ State** n Wohlfahrtsstaat m

well[1] /wel/ n Brunnen m; (oil **~**) Quelle f

well[2] adv (**better, best**) gut; **as ~** auch; **as ~ as** (in addition) sowohl ... als auch; **~ done!** gut gemacht! •adj gesund; **he is not ~** es geht ihm nicht gut; **get ~ soon!** gute Besserung! •int nun, na

well: ~-behaved adj artig. **~-being** n Wohl nt

wellingtons /'welɪŋtənz/ npl Gummistiefel pl

well: ~-known adj bekannt. **~-off** adj wohlhabend; **be ~-off** gut dransein. **~-to-do** adj wohlhabend

Welsh /welʃ/ adj walisisch •n (Lang) Walisisch nt; **the ~** pl die Waliser. **~man** n Waliser m

went /went/ see **go**

wept /wept/ see **weep**

were /wɜː(r)/ see **be**

west /west/ n Westen m; **to the ~ of** westlich von •adj West-, west- •adv nach Westen. **~erly** adj westlich. **~ern** adj westlich •n Western m

West: ~ 'Germany n Westdeutschland nt. **~ 'Indian** adj westindisch •n Westinder(in) m(f). **~ 'Indies** /-'ɪndɪz/ npl Westindische Inseln pl

'westward[s] /-wəd[z]/ adv nach Westen

wet /wet/ adj (**wetter, wettest**) nass; (fam: person) weichlich, lasch; **'~ paint'** 'frisch gestrichen' •vt (pt/pp **wet** or **wetted**) nass machen

whack /wæk/ vt [!] schlagen. **~ed** adj [!] kaputt

whale /weɪl/ n Wal m

wharf /wɔːf/ n Kai m

what /wɒt/

•pronoun

····➤(in questions) was. **what is it?** was ist das? **what do you want?** was wollen Sie? **what is your name?** wie heißen Sie? **what?** ([!]: say that again) wie?; was? **what is the time?** wie spät ist es? (indirect) **I didn't know what to do** ich wusste nicht, was ich machen sollte

! The equivalent of a preposition with **what** in English is a special word in German beginning with wo- (wor- before a vowel): **for what? what for?** = wofür? wozu? **from what?** wovon? **on what?** worauf? worüber? **under what?** worunter? **with what?** womit? etc. **what do you want the money for?** wozu willst du das Geld? **what is he talking about?** wovon redet er?

····➤(relative pronoun) was. **do what I tell you** tu, was ich dir sage. **give me what you can** gib mir, so viel du kannst. **what little I know** das bisschen, das ich weiß. **I don't agree with what you are saying** ich stimme dem nicht zu, was Sie sagen

····➤(in phrases) **what about me?** was ist mit mir? **what about a cup of coffee?** wie wäre es mit einer Tasse Kaffee? **what if she doesn't come?** was ist, wenn sie nicht kommt? **what of it?** was ist dabei?

•adjective

····➤(asking for selection) welcher (m), welche (f), welches (nt), welche (pl). **what book do you want?** welches Buch willst du haben? **what colour are the walls?** welche Farbe haben die Wände? **I asked him what train to take** ich habe ihn gefragt, welchen Zug ich nehmen soll

····➤(asking how much/many) **what money does he have?** wie viel Geld hat er? **what time is it?** wie spät ist es? **what time does it start?** um wie viel Uhr fängt es an?

····➤**what kind of ...?** was für [ein(e)]? **what kind of man is he?** was für ein Mensch ist er?

····➤(in exclamations) was für (+ nom). **what a fool you are!** was für ein Dummkopf du doch bist! **what cheek/luck!** was für eine Frechheit/ein Glück! **what a huge house!** was für ein riesiges Haus! **what a lot of people!** was für viele Leute!

what'ever adj [egal] welche(r,s) •pron was ... auch; **~ is it?** was ist das bloß?; **~ he does** was er auch tut; **nothing ~** überhaupt nichts

whatso'ever pron & adj ≈ **whatever**

wheat /wiːt/ n Weizen m

wheel /wiːl/ n Rad nt; (pottery) Töpferscheibe f; (steering **~**) Lenkrad nt; **at the ~** am Steuer •vt (push) schieben •vi kehrtmachen; (circle) kreisen

wheel: ~barrow n Schubkarre f. **~chair** n Rollstuhl m. **~-clamp** n Parkkralle f

when /wen/ adv wann; **the day ~** der Tag, an dem •conj wenn; (in the past) als; (although) wo ... doch; **~ swimming/reading** beim

Schwimmen/Lesen

when'ever conj & adv [immer] wenn; (at whatever time) wann immer; ~ **did it happen?** wann ist das bloß passiert?

where /weə(r)/ adv & conj wo; ~ **[to]** wohin; ~ **[from]** woher

whereabouts[1] /weərə'baʊts/ adv wo

'**whereabouts**[2] n Verbleib m; (of person) Aufenthaltsort m

where'as conj während; (in contrast) wohingegen

whereu'pon adv worauf[hin]

wher'ever conj & adv wo immer; (to whatever place) wohin immer; (from whatever place) woher immer; (everywhere) überall wo; ~ **possible** wenn irgend möglich

whether /'weðə(r)/ conj ob

which /wɪtʃ/

•adjective

····➤(in questions) welcher (m), welche (f), welches (nt), welche (pl). **which book do you need?** welches Buch brauchst du? **which one?** welcher/welche/welches? **which ones?** welche? **which one of you did it?** wer von euch hat es getan? **which way?** (which direction) welche Richtung?; (where) wohin?; (how) wie?

····➤(relative) **he always comes at one at which time I'm having lunch/by which time I've finished** er kommt immer um ein Uhr; dann esse ich gerade zu Mittag/bis dahin bin ich schon fertig

•pronoun

····➤(in questions) welcher (m), welche (f), welches (nt), welche (pl). **which is which?** welcher/welche/welches ist welcher/welche/welches? **which of you?** wer von euch?

····➤(relative) der (m), die (f), das (nt), die (pl); (genitive) dessen (m, nt), deren (f, pl); (dative) dem (m, nt), der (f), denen (pl); (referring to a clause) was. **the book which I gave you** das Buch, das ich dir gab. **the trial, the result of which we are expecting** der Prozess, dessen Ergebnis wir erwarten. **the house of which I was speaking** das Haus, von dem od wovon ich redete. **after which** wonach; nach dem. **on which** worauf; auf dem. **the shop opposite which we parked** der Laden, gegenüber dem wir parkten. **everything which I tell you** alles, was ich dir sage

which'ever adj & pron [egal] welche(r,s); ~ **it is** was es auch ist

while /waɪl/ n Weile f; **a long** ~ lange; **be worth** ~ sich lohnen; **it's worth my** ~ es lohnt sich für mich •conj während; (as long as) solange; (although) obgleich •vt ~ **away** sich (dat) vertreiben

whilst /waɪlst/ conj während

whim /wɪm/ n Laune f

whimper /'wɪmpə(r)/ vi wimmern; (dog:) winseln

whine /waɪn/ vi winseln

whip /wɪp/ n Peitsche f; (Pol) Einpeitscher m •vt (pt/pp **whipped**) peitschen; (Culin) schlagen. **~ped 'cream** n Schlagsahne f

whirl /wɜːl/ vt/i wirbeln. **~pool** n Strudel m. **~-wind** n Wirbelwind m

whirr /wɜː(r)/ vi surren

whisk /wɪsk/ n (Culin) Schneebesen m •vt (Culin) schlagen

whisker /'wɪskə(r)/ n Schnurrhaar nt

whisky /'wɪskɪ/ n Whisky m

whisper /'wɪspə(r)/ n Flüstern nt •vt/i flüstern

whistle /'wɪsl/ n Pfiff m; (instrument) Pfeife f •vt/i pfeifen

white /waɪt/ adj (**-r, -st**) weiß •n Weiß nt; (of egg) Eiweiß nt; (person) Weiße(r) m/f

white: ~ **'coffee** n Kaffee m mit Milch. **~-'collar worker** n Angestellte(r) m. ~ **'lie** n Notlüge f

whiten /'waɪtn/ vt weiß machen •vi weiß werden

whiteness /ˈwaɪtnɪs/ n Weiß nt

Whitsun /ˈwɪtsn/ n Pfingsten nt

whiz[z] /wɪz/ vi (pt/pp **whizzed**) zischen. **~-kid** n [!] Senkrechtstarter m

who /huː/ pron wer; (acc) wen; (dat) wem • rel pron der/die/das, (pl) die

who'ever pron wer [immer]; **~ he is** wer er auch ist; **~ is it?** wer ist das bloß?

whole /həʊl/ adj ganz; (truth) voll • n Ganze(s) nt; **as a ~** als Ganzes; **on the ~** im Großen und Ganzen; **the ~ of Germany** ganz Deutschland

whole: ~food n Vollwertkost f. **~-'hearted** adj rückhaltlos. **~meal** adj Vollkorn-

'**wholesale** adj Großhandels- • adv en gros; (fig) in Bausch und Bogen. **~r** n Großhändler m

wholly /ˈhəʊlɪ/ adv völlig

whom /huːm/ pron wen; **to ~** wem • rel pron den/die/das, (pl) die; (dat) dem/der/dem, (pl) denen

whopping /ˈwɒpɪŋ/ adj [!] Riesen-

whore /hɔː(r)/ n Hure f

whose /huːz/ pron wessen; **~ is that?** wem gehört das? • rel pron dessen/deren/dessen, (pl) deren

why /waɪ/ adv warum; (for what purpose) wozu; **that's ~** darum

wick /wɪk/ n Docht m

wicked /ˈwɪkɪd/ adj böse; (mischievous) frech, boshaft

wicker /ˈwɪkə(r)/ n Korbgeflecht nt • attrib Korb-

wide /waɪd/ adj (**-r,-st**) weit; (broad) breit; (fig) groß • adv weit; (off target) daneben; **~ awake** hellwach; **far and ~** weit und breit. **~ly** adv weit; (known, accepted) weithin; (differ) stark

widen /ˈwaɪdn/ vt verbreitern; (fig) erweitern • vi sich verbreitern

'**widespread** adj weit verbreitet

widow /ˈwɪdəʊ/ n Witwe f. **~ed** adj verwitwet. **~er** n Witwer m

width /wɪdθ/ n Weite f; (breadth) Breite f

wield /wiːld/ vt schwingen; ausüben (power)

wife /waɪf/ n (pl **wives**) [Ehe]frau f

wig /wɪg/ n Perücke f

wiggle /ˈwɪgl/ vi wackeln • vt wackeln mit

wild /waɪld/ adj (**-er, -est**) wild; (animal) wild lebend; (flower) wild wachsend; (furious) wütend • adv wild; **run ~** frei herumlaufen • n **in the ~** wild; **the ~s** pl die Wildnis f

wilderness /ˈwɪldənɪs/ n Wildnis f; (desert) Wüste f

wildlife n Tierwelt f

will[1] /wɪl/

• modal verb

past **would**

····> (expressing the future) werden. **she will arrive tomorrow** sie wird morgen ankommen. **he will be there by now** er wird jetzt schon da sein

····> (expressing intention) (present tense) **will you go?** gehst du? **I promise I won't do it again** ich verspreche, ich machs nicht noch mal

····> (in requests) **will/would you please tidy up?** würdest du bitte aufräumen? **will you be quiet!** willst du ruhig sein!

····> (in invitations) **will you have/ would you like some wine?** wollen Sie/möchten Sie Wein?

····> (negative: refuse to) nicht wollen. **they won't help me** sie wollen mir nicht helfen. **the car won't start** das Auto will nicht anspringen

····> (in tag questions) nicht wahr. **you'll be back soon, won't you?** du kommst bald wieder, nicht wahr? **you will help her, won't you?** du hilfst ihr doch, nicht wahr?

····> (in short answers) **Will you be there? — Yes I will** Wirst du da sein? — Ja

will[2] n Wille m; (document) Testament nt

willing /ˈwɪlɪŋ/ adj willig; (eager) bereitwillig; **be ~** bereit sein. **~ly** adv bereitwillig; (gladly) gern. **~ness** n Bereitwilligkeit f

willow /ˈwɪləʊ/ n Weide f

ˈ**will-power** n Willenskraft f

wilt /wɪlt/ vi welk werden, welken

wily /ˈwaɪlɪ/ adj listig

win /wɪn/ n Sieg m •v (pt/pp **won**; pres p **winning**) •vt gewinnen; bekommen (scholarship) •vi gewinnen; (in battle) siegen. **~ over** vt auf seine Seite bringen

wince /wɪns/ vi zusammenzucken

winch /wɪntʃ/ n Winde f •vt **~ up** hochwinden

wind[1] /wɪnd/ n Wind m; ([!]: flatulence) Blähungen pl •vt **~ s.o.** jdm den Atem nehmen

wind[2] /waɪnd/ v (pt/pp **wound**) •vt (wrap) wickeln; (move by turning) kurbeln; aufziehen (clock) vi (road:) sich winden. **~ up** vt aufziehen (clock); schließen (proceedings)

wind: ~ farm n Windpark m. **~ instrument** n Blasinstrument nt. **~mill** n Windmühle f

window /ˈwɪndəʊ/ n Fenster nt; (of shop) Schaufenster nt

window: ~-box n Blumenkasten m. **~-cleaner** n Fensterputzer m. **~-pane** n Fensterscheibe f. **~-shopping** n Schaufensterbummel m. **~-sill** n Fensterbrett nt

ˈ**windpipe** n Luftröhre f

ˈ**windscreen** n, (Amer) ˈ**windshield** n Windschutzscheibe f. **~-wiper** n Scheibenwischer m

wind surfing n Windsurfen nt

windy /ˈwɪndɪ/ adj windig

wine /waɪn/ n Wein m

wine: ~-bar n Weinstube f. **~glass** n Weinglas nt. **~-list** n Weinkarte f

winery /ˈwaɪnərɪ/ n (Amer) Weingut nt

ˈ**wine-tasting** n Weinprobe f

wing /wɪŋ/ n Flügel m; (Auto) Kotflügel m; **~s** pl (Theat) Kulissen pl

wink /wɪŋk/ n Zwinkern nt; **not sleep a ~** kein Auge zutun •vi zwinkern; (light:) blinken

winner /ˈwɪnə(r)/ n Gewinner(in) m(f); (Sport) Sieger(in) m(f)

winning /ˈwɪnɪŋ/ adj siegreich; (smile) gewinnend. **~-post** n Zielpfosten m. **~s** npl Gewinn m

wint|er /ˈwɪntə(r)/ n Winter m. **~ry** adj winterlich

wipe /waɪp/ n **give sth a ~** etw abwischen •vt abwischen; aufwischen (floor); (dry) abtrocknen. **~ out** vt (cancel) löschen; (destroy) ausrotten. **~ up** vt aufwischen

wire /ˈwaɪə(r)/ n Draht m

wiring /ˈwaɪərɪŋ/ n [elektrische] Leitungen pl

wisdom /ˈwɪzdəm/ n Weisheit f; (prudence) Klugheit f. **~ tooth** n Weisheitszahn m

wise /waɪz/ adj (**-r, -st**) weise; (prudent) klug

wish /wɪʃ/ n Wunsch m •vt wünschen; **~ s.o. well** jdm alles Gute wünschen; **I ~ you could stay** ich wünschte, du könntest hier bleiben •vi sich (dat) etwas wünschen. **~ful** adj **~ful thinking** Wunschdenken nt

wistful /ˈwɪstfl/ adj wehmütig

wit /wɪt/ n Geist m, Witz m; (intelligence) Verstand m; (person) geistreicher Mensch m; **be at one's ~s' end** sich (dat) keinen Rat mehr wissen

witch /wɪtʃ/ n Hexe f. **~craft** n Hexerei f

with /wɪð/ prep mit (+ dat); **~ fear/cold** vor Angst/Kälte; **~ it** damit; **I'm going ~ you** ich gehe mit; **take it ~ you** nimm es mit; **I haven't got it ~ me** ich habe es nicht bei mir

withˈ**draw** v (pt **-drew**, pp **-drawn**) •vt zurückziehen; abheben (money)

•vi sich zurückziehen. **~al** n Zurückziehen nt; (of money) Abhebung f; (from drugs) Entzug m

wither /'wɪðə(r)/ vi [ver]welken

with'hold vt (pt/pp **-held**) vorenthalten (**from s.o.** jdm)

with'in prep innerhalb (+ gen) •adv innen

with'out prep ohne (+ acc); **~ my noticing it** ohne dass ich es merkte

with'stand vt (pt/pp **-stood**) standhalten (+ dat)

witness /'wɪtnɪs/ n Zeuge m/ Zeugin f •vt Zeuge/Zeugin sein (+ gen); bestätigen (signature)

witticism /'wɪtɪsɪzm/ n geistreicher Ausspruch m

witty /'wɪtɪ/ adj witzig, geistreich

wives /waɪvz/ see **wife**

wizard /'wɪzəd/ n Zauberer m

wizened /'wɪznd/ adj verhutzelt

wobb|le /'wɒbl/ vi wackeln. **~ly** adj wackelig

woke, woken /wəʊk, 'wəʊkn/ see **wake**[1]

wolf /wʊlf/ n (pl **wolves** /wʊlvz/) Wolf m

woman /'wʊmən/ n (pl **women**) Frau f. **~izer** n Schürzenjäger m

womb /wu:m/ n Gebärmutter f

women /'wɪmɪn/ npl see **woman**

won /wʌn/ see **win**

wonder /'wʌndə(r)/ n Wunder nt; (surprise) Staunen nt •vt/i sich fragen; (be surprised) sich wundern; **I ~** da frage ich mich; **I ~ whether she is ill** ob sie wohl krank ist? **~ful** adj wunderbar

won't /wəʊnt/ = **will not**

wood /wʊd/ n Holz nt; (forest) Wald m; **touch ~!** unberufen!

wood: ~ed /-ɪd/ adj bewaldet. **~en** adj Holz-; (fig) hölzern. **~pecker** n Specht m. **~wind** n Holzbläser pl. **~work** n (wooden parts) Holzteile pl; (craft) Tischlerei f. **~worm** n Holzwurm m

wool /wʊl/ n Wolle f •attrib Woll-. **~len** adj wollen

woolly /'wʊlɪ/ adj wollig; (fig) unklar

word /wɜ:d/ n Wort nt; (news) Nachricht f; **by ~ of mouth** mündlich; **have a ~ with** sprechen mit; **have ~s** einen Wortwechsel haben. **~ing** n Wortlaut m. **~ processor** n Textverarbeitungssystem nt

wore /wɔ:(r)/ see **wear**

work /wɜ:k/ n Arbeit f; (Art, Literature) Werk nt; **~s** pl (factory, mechanism) Werk nt; **at ~** bei der Arbeit; **out of ~** arbeitslos •vi arbeiten; (machine, system:) funktionieren; (have effect) wirken; (study) lernen; **it won't ~** (fig) es klappt nicht •vt arbeiten lassen; bedienen (machine); betätigen (lever). **~ off** vt abarbeiten. **~ out** vt ausrechnen; (solve) lösen •vi gut gehen, [!] klappen. **~ up** vt aufbauen; sich (dat) holen (appetite); **get ~ed up** sich aufregen

workable /'wɜ:kəbl/ adj (feasible) durchführbar

worker /'wɜ:kə(r)/ n Arbeiter(in) m(f)

working /'wɜ:kɪŋ/ adj berufstätig; (day, clothes) Arbeits-; **be in ~ order** funktionieren. **~ class** n Arbeiterklasse f

work: ~man n Arbeiter m; (craftsman) Handwerker m. **~manship** n Arbeit f. **~shop** n Werkstatt f

world /wɜ:ld/ n Welt f; **in the ~** auf der Welt; **think the ~ of s.o.** große Stücke auf jdn halten. **~ly** adj weltlich; (person) weltlich gesinnt. **~-wide** adj & adv /-'-/ weltweit

worm /wɜ:m/ n Wurm m

worn /wɔ:n/ see **wear** •adj abgetragen. **~-out** adj abgetragen; (carpet) abgenutzt; (person) erschöpft

worried /'wʌrɪd/ adj besorgt

worry /'wʌrɪ/ n Sorge f •v (pt/pp

worried) • vt beunruhigen; (bother) stören • vi sich beunruhigen, sich (dat) Sorgen machen. **~ing** adj beunruhigend

worse /wɜːs/ adj & adv schlechter; (more serious) schlimmer • n Schlechtere(s) nt; Schlimmere(s) nt

worsen /ˈwɜːsn/ vt verschlechtern • vi sich verschlechtern

worship /ˈwɜːʃɪp/ n Anbetung f; (service) Gottesdienst m • vt (pt/pp **-shipped**) anbeten

worst /wɜːst/ adj schlechteste(r,s); (most serious) schlimmste(r,s) • adv am schlechtesten; am schlimmsten • n **the ~** das Schlimmste

worth /wɜːθ/ n Wert m; **£10's ~ of petrol** Benzin für £10 • adj **be ~ £5** £5 wert sein; **be ~ it** (fig) sich lohnen. **~less** adj wertlos. **~while** adj lohnend

worthy /ˈwɜːðɪ/ adj würdig

would /wʊd/ modal verb **I ~ do it** ich würde es tun, ich täte es; **~ you go?** würdest du gehen? **he said he ~n't** er sagte, er würde es nicht tun; **what ~ you like?** was möchten Sie?

wound¹ /wuːnd/ n Wunde f • vt verwunden

wound² /waʊnd/ see **wind²**

wove, woven see **weave²**

wrangle /ˈræŋgl/ n Streit m

wrap /ræp/ n Umhang m • vt (pt/pp **wrapped**) **~ [up]** wickeln; einpacken (present) • vi **~ up warmly** sich warm einpacken. **~per** n Hülle f. **~ping** n Verpackung f

wrath /rɒθ/ n Zorn m

wreath /riːθ/ n (pl **~s** /-ðz/) Kranz m

wreck /rek/ n Wrack nt • vt zerstören; zunichte machen (plans); zerrütten (marriage). **~age** n Wrackteile pl; (fig) Trümmer pl

wren /ren/ n Zaunkönig m

wrench /rentʃ/ n Ruck m; (tool) Schraubenschlüssel m; **be a ~** (fig) weh tun • vt reißen; **~ sth from s.o.** jdm etw entreißen

wrestl|e /ˈresl/ vi ringen. **~er** n Ringer m. **~ing** n Ringen nt

wretch /retʃ/ n Kreatur f. **~ed** adj elend; (very bad) erbärmlich

wriggle /ˈrɪgl/ n Zappeln nt • vi zappeln; (move forward) sich schlängeln; **~ out of sth** [!] sich vor etw (dat) drücken

wring /rɪŋ/ vt (pt/pp **wrung**) wringen; (**~** out) auswringen; umdrehen (neck); ringen (hands)

wrinkle /ˈrɪŋkl/ n Falte f; (on skin) Runzel f • vt kräuseln • vi sich kräuseln, sich falten. **~d** adj runzlig

wrist /rɪst/ n Handgelenk nt. **~-watch** n Armbanduhr f

write /raɪt/ vt/i (pt **wrote**, pp **written**, pres p **writing**) schreiben. **~ down** vt aufschreiben. **~ off** ˈ vt abschreiben; zu Schrott fahren (car)

ˈwrite-off n ≈ Totalschaden m

writer /ˈraɪtə(r)/ n Schreiber(in) m(f); (author) Schriftsteller(in) m(f)

writhe /raɪð/ vi sich winden

writing /ˈraɪtɪŋ/ n Schreiben nt; (handwriting) Schrift f; **in ~** schriftlich. **~-paper** n Schreibpapier nt

written /ˈrɪtn/ see **write**

wrong /rɒŋ/ adj falsch; (morally) unrecht; (not just) ungerecht; **be ~** nicht stimmen; (person:) Unrecht haben; **what's ~?** was ist los? • adv falsch; **go ~** (person:) etwas falsch machen; (machine:) kaputtgehen; (plan:) schief gehen • n Unrecht nt • vt Unrecht tun (+ dat). **~ful** adj ungerechtfertigt. **~fully** adv (accuse) zu Unrecht

wrote /rəʊt/ see **write**

wrung /rʌŋ/ see **wring**

wry /raɪ/ adj (**-er, -est**) ironisch; (humour) trocken

Xx

Xmas /'krɪsməs, 'eksməs/ n [!] Weihnachten nt

X-ray /'eks-/ n (picture) Röntgenaufnahme f; **~s** pl Röntgenstrahlen pl •vt röntgen; durchleuchten (luggage)

Yy

yacht /jɒt/ n Jacht f; (for racing) Segeljacht f. **~ing** n Segeln nt

yank /jæŋk/ vt [!] reißen

Yank n [!] Ami m [!]

yap /jæp/ vi (pt/pp **yapped**) (dog:) kläffen

yard[1] /jɑːd/ n Hof m; (for storage) Lager nt

yard[2] n Yard nt (= 0,91 m)

yarn /jɑːn/ n Garn nt; ([!]: tale) Geschichte f

yawn /jɔːn/ n Gähnen nt •vi gähnen

year /jɪə(r)/ n Jahr nt; (of wine) Jahrgang m; **for ~s** jahrelang. **~ly** adj & adv jährlich

yearn /jɜːn/ vi sich sehnen (**for** nach). **~ing** n Sehnsucht f

yeast /jiːst/ n Hefe f

yell /jel/ n Schrei m •vi schreien

yellow /'jeləʊ/ adj gelb •n Gelb nt

yelp /jelp/ vi jaulen

yes /jes/ adv ja; (contradicting) doch •n Ja nt

yesterday /'jestədeɪ/ n & adv gestern; **~'s paper** die gestrige Zeitung; **the day before ~** vorgestern

yet /jet/ adv noch; (in question) schon; (nevertheless) doch; **as ~** bisher; **not ~** noch nicht; **the best ~** das bisher beste •conj doch

Yiddish /'jɪdɪʃ/ n Jiddisch nt

yield /jiːld/ n Ertrag m • vt bringen; abwerfen (profit) • vi nachgeben; (Amer, Auto) die Vorfahrt beachten

yoga /'jəʊgə/ n Yoga m

yoghurt /'jɒgət/ n Joghurt m

yoke /jəʊk/ n Joch nt; (of garment) Passe f

yolk /jəʊk/ n Dotter m, Eigelb nt

you /juː/ pron du; (acc) dich; (dat) dir; (pl) ihr; (acc, dat) euch; (formal) (nom & acc, sg & pl) Sie; (dat, sg & pl) Ihnen; (one) man; (acc) einen; (dat) einem; **all of ~** ihr/Sie alle; **I know ~** ich kenne dich/euch/Sie; **I'll give ~ the money** ich gebe dir/euch/Ihnen das Geld; **it does ~ good** es tut einem gut; **it's bad for ~** es ist ungesund

young /jʌŋ/ adj (**-er** /-gə(r)/, **-est** /-gɪst/) jung •npl (animals) Junge pl; **the ~** die Jugend f. **~ster** n Jugendliche(r) m/f; (child) Kleine(r) m/f

your /jɔː(r)/ adj dein; (pl) euer; (formal) Ihr

yours /jɔːz/ poss pron deine(r), deins; (pl) eure(r), euers; (formal, sg & pl) Ihre(r), Ihr[e]s; **a friend of ~**

ein Freund von dir/Ihnen/euch; **that is** ~ das gehört dir/Ihnen/euch

your'self pron (pl **-selves**) selbst; (reflexive) dich; (dat) dir; (pl) euch; (formal) sich; **by** ~ allein

youth /ju:θ/ n (pl **youths** /-ð:z/) Jugend f; (boy) Jugendliche(r) m. **~ful** adj jugendlich. ~ **hostel** n Jugendherberge f

Yugoslavia /ju:gə'slɑ:vɪə/ n Jugoslawien nt

Zz

zeal /zi:l/ n Eifer m

zealous /'zeləs/ adj eifrig

zebra /'zebrə/ n Zebra nt. ~ **'crossing** n Zebrastreifen m

zero /'zɪərəʊ/ n Null f

zest /zest/ n Begeisterung f

zigzag /'zɪgzæg/ n Zickzack m •vi (pt/pp **-zagged**) im Zickzack laufen/ (in vehicle) fahren

zinc /zɪŋk/ n Zink nt

zip /zɪp/ n ~ **[fastener]** Reißverschluss m •vt ~ **[up]** den Reißverschluss zuziehen an (+ dat)

'zip code n (Amer) Postleitzahl f

zipper /'zɪpə(r)/ n Reißverschluss m

zodiac /'zəʊdɪæk/ n Tierkreis m

zone /zəʊn/ n Zone f

zoo /zu:/ n Zoo m

zoological /zu:ə'lɒdʒɪkl/ adj zoologisch

zoolog|ist /zu:'ɒlədʒɪst/ n Zoologe m/-gin f. **~y** n Zoologie f

zoom /zu:m/ vi sausen. ~ **lens** n Zoomobjektiv nt

Grammar and Verbs

Summary of German grammar

Regular verbs

Most German verbs are regular and add the same endings to their stem. You find the stem by taking away the **-en** (or sometimes just **-n**) from the end of the infinitive. The infinitive of the verb, for example **machen**, is the form you look up in the dictionary. The stem of **machen** is **mach-**. There are six endings for each tense, to go with the different pronouns:

ich = *I*	**du** = *you*	**er/sie/es** = *he/she/it*
wir = *we*	**ihr** = *you*	**sie/Sie** = *they/you* (*polite form*).

Present tense

For example, *I make*, *I am making*, or *I do make*:

infinitive	ich	du	er/sie/es	wir	ihr	sie/Sie
machen	**mache**	**machst**	**macht**	**machen**	**macht**	**machen**

Imperfect tense

For example, *I made*, *I was making*, or *I used to make*:

infinitive	ich	du	er/sie/es	wir	ihr	sie/Sie
machen	**machte**	**machtest**	**machte**	**machten**	**machtet**	**machten**

Future tense

For example, *I will make* or *I shall make*. This is formed by using the present tense of **werden**, which is the equivalent of *will* or *shall*, with the infinitive verb: **ich werde machen**.

infinitive	ich	du	er/sie/es	wir	ihr	sie/Sie
werden	**werde**	**wirst**	**wird**	**werden**	**werdet**	**werden**

Perfect tense

For example, *I made* or *I have made*. For most German verbs the perfect is formed by using the present tense of **haben**, which is the equivalent of *have*, with the past participle: **ich habe gemacht.** Some verbs take **sein** instead of **haben**, and these are all marked (***sein***) in the dictionary. They are mainly verbs expressing motion and involving a change of place:

he drove to Berlin today = **er ist heute nach Berlin gefahren**

Or they express a change of state, and this includes verbs meaning to happen (**geschehen**, **passieren**, **vorkommen**):

he woke up = **er ist aufgewacht**

infinitive	ich	du	er/sie/es	wir	ihr	sie/Sie
haben	**habe**	**hast**	**hat**	**haben**	**habt**	**haben**
sein	**bin**	**bist**	**ist**	**sind**	**seid**	**sind**

Irregular verbs and other forms

Some German verbs are irregular and change their stem or add different endings. All the irregular verbs that appear in the dictionary are given in the section *German irregular verbs* on pp.615–620.

The subjunctive

This is a form of the verb that is used to express speculation, doubt, or unlikelihood. It is rarely used in English (*if I were you* instead of *if I was you* is an exceptional example), but is still used in both written and spoken German.

Present tense

infinitive	ich	du	er/sie/es	wir	ihr	sie/Sie
machen	**mache**	**machest**	**mache**	**machen**	**machet**	**machen**
sein	**sei**	**sei(e)st**	**sei**	**seien**	**seid**	**seien**

Imperfect tense

For regular verbs this is the same as the normal imperfect forms, but irregular verbs vary.

infinitive	ich	du	er/sie/es	wir	ihr	sie/Sie
machen	**machte**	**machtest**	**machte**	**machten**	**machtet**	**machten**
werden	**würde**	**würdest**	**würde**	**würden**	**würdet**	**würden**

sein	wäre	wär(e)st	wäre	wären	wär(e)t	wären

The imperfect subjunctive of werden is used with an infinitive to form the conditional tense. This tense expresses what would happen if something else occurred.

he would go = **er würde gehen**
I wouldn't do that = **das würde ich nicht machen**

Reflexive verbs

The object of a reflexive verb is the same as its subject. In German, the object is a reflexive pronoun. This is usually in the accusative (I wash = **ich wasche mich**). The reflexive pronouns of some verbs are in the dative (I imagine = **ich stelle mir vor**), and these are marked in the English–German part of the dictionary with (*dat*).

infinitive	ich	du	er/sie/es	wir	ihr	sie/Sie
sich waschen	**wasche mich**	**wäschst dich**	**wäscht sich**	**waschen uns**	**wascht euch**	**waschen sich**
sich vorstellen	**stelle mir vor**	**stellst dir vor**	**stellt sich vor**	**stellen uns vor**	**stellt euch vor**	**stellen sich vor**

The passive

In the passive form, the subject of the verb experiences the action rather than performs it: he was asked = **er wurde gefragt**. In German, the passive is formed using parts of **werden** with the past participle:

PRESENT PASSIVE	*it is done*	**es wird gemacht**
IMPERFECT PASSIVE	*it was done*	**es wurde gemacht**
FUTURE PASSIVE	*it will be done*	**es wird gemacht werden**
PERFECT PASSIVE	*it has been done*	**es ist gemacht worden**

When forming the perfect passive, note that the past participle of **werden** becomes **worden** rather than **geworden**.

Separable verbs

Separable verbs are marked in the German–English part of the dictionary with the label *sep*. In the perfect tense, the **ge-** of the past participle comes between the prefix and the verb, for example **er/sie/es hat an**ge**fangen**.

Articles

There are two articles in English, the definite article *the* and the indefinite article *a/an*. The way these are translated into German depends on the gender, number, and case of the noun with which the article goes.

There are three genders of nouns in German: masculine (**der Mann** = the man), feminine (**die Frau** = the woman), and neuter (**das Buch** = the book). There are two forms of number: singular (**der Baum** = the tree) and plural (**die Bäume** = the trees). And there are four cases, which show the part a noun plays in a sentence: nominative, accusative, genitive, and dative.

Definite article

the = **der/die/das**, (plural) = **die**

	SINGULAR			PLURAL
	masculine	feminine	neuter	all genders
NOMINATIVE	**der** Mann	**die** Frau	**das** Buch	**die** Bäume
ACCUSATIVE	**den** Mann	**die** Frau	**das** Buch	**die** Bäume
GENITIVE	**des** Mannes	**der** Frau	**des** Buches	**der** Bäume
DATIVE	**dem** Mann	**der** Frau	**dem** Buch	**den** Bäumen

Indefinite article

a/an = ein/eine/ein. This article can only be singular.

	masculine	feminine	neuter
NOMINATIVE	**ein** Mann	**eine** Frau	**ein** Buch
ACCUSATIVE	**einen** Mann	**eine** Frau	**ein** Buch
GENITIVE	**eines** Mannes	**einer** Frau	**eines** Buches
DATIVE	**einem** Mann	**einer** Frau	**einem** Buch

Nouns

In German, all nouns start with a capital letter: **das Buch** = the book.

Gender

There are three genders of nouns in German: masculine (**der Mann** = the man), feminine (**die Frau** = the woman), and neuter (**das Buch** = the book). These three examples are logical, with masculine for a male person, feminine for a female person, and neuter for an object. But it is not always like this with German nouns. Gender is sometimes determined by a noun's ending. For example, **das Mädchen** (= the girl) is neuter rather than feminine, simply because the ending **-chen** is always neuter.

The gender of German nouns is given in the dictionary. There are some general rules regarding the gender of groups of nouns, but individual genders must be checked by looking them up.

Masculine nouns

- male persons and animals: **der Arbeiter** = worker; **der Bär** = bear
- 'doers' and 'doing' instruments ending in **-er** in German: **der Gärtner** = gardener; **der Computer** = computer
- days, months, and seasons: (**der**) **Montag** = Monday
- words ending in **-ich**, **-ig**, and **-ling**: **der Honig** = honey; **der Lehrling** = apprentice
- words ending in **-ismus**, **-ist**, and **-ant**.

Feminine nouns

- female persons and animals: **die Schauspielerin** = actress; **die Henne** = hen; the feminine form of professions and animals is made by adding **-in** to the masculine (**der Schauspieler/die Schauspielerin** = actor/actress)
- nouns ending in **-ei**, **-ie**, **-ik**, **-in**, **-ion**, **-heit**, **-keit**, **-schaft**, **-tät**, **-ung**, **-ur**: **die Gärtnerei** = gardening; **die Energie** = energy
- most nouns ending in **-e**: **die Blume** = flower; note that there are many exceptions, including **der Name** = name, **der Käse** = cheese, **das Ende** = end.

Neuter nouns

- names of continents, most countries, and towns: (**das**) **Deutschland** = Germany; (**das**) **Köln** = Cologne

- nouns ending in **-chen** and **-lein** (indicating *small*): **das Mädchen**, **das Fräulein** = girl.
- most (but not all!) nouns beginning with **Ge-** or ending in **-nis**, **-tel**, or **-um**: **das Geheimnis** = secret; **das Zentrum** = centre
- infinitives of verbs used as nouns: **das Lachen** = laughter; das Essen = food.

Compound nouns

When two nouns are put together to make one compound noun, it takes the gender of the second noun:

der Brief + die Marke = die Briefmarke.

Plural

There are no absolutely definitive rules for the plural forms of German nouns. Plurals generally add an ending (**der Freund**, **die Freunde**), and change a vowel to an umlaut (**der Gast**, **die Gäste**; **das Haus**, **die Häuser**). Feminine words ending in **-heit**, **-keit**, and **-ung** add **-en** to make the plural (**die Abbildung**, **die Abbildungen**).

The plurals of all nouns are given in the German–English part of the dictionary.

Case

There are four cases, which show the part a noun plays in a sentence: nominative, accusative, genitive, and dative. The noun's article changes according to the case, and the ending of the noun changes in some cases:

	SINGULAR masculine	feminine	neuter
NOMINATIVE	der Mann	die Frau	das Buch
ACCUSATIVE	den Mann	die Frau	das Buch
GENITIVE	des **Mannes**	der Frau	des **Buches**
DATIVE	dem Mann	der Frau	dem Buch

	PLURAL masculine	feminine	neuter
NOMINATIVE	die Männer	die Frauen	die Bücher
ACCUSATIVE	die Männer	die Frauen	die Bücher
GENITIVE	der Männer	der Frauen	der Bücher
DATIVE	den **Männern**	den Frauen	den **Büchern**

The nominative is used for the subject of a sentence; in sentences with **sein** (to be) and **werden** (to become), the noun after the verb is in the nominative.

the dog barked = **der Hund bellte**
that is my car = **das ist mein Wagen**

The accusative is used for the direct object and after some prepositions (listed on p.612):

she has a son = **sie hat einen Sohn**

The genitive shows possession, and is also used after some prepositions (listed on p.612):

my husband's dog = **der Hund meines Mannes**

The dative is used for the indirect object. Some German verbs, such as **helfen**, take only the dative. The dative is also used after some prepositions (listed on p.612):

she gave the books to the children = **sie gab den Kindern die Bücher**

The following sentence combines all four cases:

der Mann gibt der Frau den Bleistift des Mädchens = *the man gives the woman the girl's pencil*
der Mann is the subject (in the nominative)
gibt is the verb
der Frau is the indirect object (in the dative)
den Bleistift is the direct object (in the accusative)
des Mädchens is in the genitive (showing possession).

Adjectives

An adjective is a word qualifying a noun. In German, an adjective in front of a noun adds endings that vary with the noun's gender, number, and case. Adjectives that come after a noun do not add endings.

With the definite article

Adjectives following **der/die/das** take these endings:

	SINGULAR masculine	feminine	neuter	PLURAL all genders
NOMINATIVE	der rot**e** Hut	die rot**e** Lampe	das rot**e** Buch	die rot**en** Autos
ACCUSATIVE	den rot**en** Hut	die rot**e** Lampe	das rot**e** Buch	die rot**en** Autos
GENITIVE	des rot**en** Hutes	der rot**en** Lampe	des rot**en** Buches	der rot**en** Autos
DATIVE	dem rot**en** Hut	der rot**en** Lampe	dem rot**en** Buch	den rot**en** Autos

Some German adjectives follow the pattern of the definite article, and adjectives after them change their endings in the same way as after **der/die/das**. For example, **dieser/diese/dieses** (= this):

	SINGULAR masculine	feminine	neuter	PLURAL all genders
NOMINATIVE	dieser	diese	dieses	diese
ACCUSATIVE	diesen	diese	dieses	diese
GENITIVE	dieses	dieser	dieses	dieser
DATIVE	diesem	dieser	diesem	diesen

Other common examples are:

jeder/jede/jedes = *every, each*
solcher/solche/solches = such
jener/jene/jenes = *that*
welcher/welche/welches = which
mancher/manche/manches = *many a, some*

With the indefinite article

Adjectives following **ein/eine/ein** take these endings:

	SINGULAR masculine	feminine	neuter
NOMINATIVE	ein rot**er** Hut	eine rot**e** Lampe	ein rot**es** Buch
ACCUSATIVE	einen rot**en** Hut	eine rot**e** Lampe	ein rot**es** Buch
GENITIVE	eines rot**en** Hutes	einer rot**en** Lampe	eines rot**en** Buches
DATIVE	einem rot**en** Hut	einer rot**en** Lampe	einem rot**en** Buch

Some German adjectives follow the pattern of the indefinite article, and adjectives after them change their endings in the same way as after **ein/eine/ein**. They are:

dein	= *your*	**kein**	= *no*
euer	= *your*	**mein**	= *my*
Ihr	= *your*	**sein**	= *his/its*
ihr	= *her/their*	**unser**	= *our*

These adjectives can also go with plural nouns: no cars = **keine Autos**. All genders take the same endings in the plural:

	PLURAL all genders
NOMINATIVE	kein**e** roten Autos
ACCUSATIVE	kein**e** roten Autos
GENITIVE	kein**er** roten Autos
DATIVE	kein**en** roten Autos

Without an article

Adjectives in front of a noun on their own, without an article, take the following endings:

	SINGULAR masculine	feminine	neuter	PLURAL all genders
NOMINATIVE	gut**er** Wein	frisch**e** Milch	kalt**es** Bier	alt**e** Leute
ACCUSATIVE	gut**en** Wein	frisch**e** Milch	kalt**es** Bier	alt**e** Leute
GENITIVE	gut**en** Weins	frisch**er** Milch	kalt**en** Biers	alt**er** Leute
DATIVE	gut**em** Wein	frisch**er** Milch	kalt**em** Bier	alt**en** Leuten

Adjectives as nouns

In German, adjectives can be used as nouns, spelt with a capital letter: **alt** = old, **ein Alter** = an old man, **eine Alte** = an old woman.

With the definite article (**der/die/das**), these nouns take the following endings:

	SINGULAR masculine	feminine	PLURAL both genders
NOMINATIVE	der Fremde	die Fremde	die Fremden
ACCUSATIVE	den Fremden	die Fremde	die Fremden
GENITIVE	des Fremden	der Fremden	der Fremden
DATIVE	dem Fremden	der Fremden	den Fremden

The feminine noun refers to a female stranger or foreigner.

With the indefinite article (**ein/eine/ein**), these nouns take the following endings:

	SINGULAR masculine	feminine	PLURAL both genders without an article
NOMINATIVE	ein Fremder	eine Fremde	Fremde
ACCUSATIVE	einen Fremden	eine Fremde	Fremde
GENITIVE	eines Fremden	einer Fremden	Fremder
DATIVE	einem Fremden	einer Fremden	Fremden

Comparative and superlative

In English, the comparative of the adjective *small* is *smaller*, and of *difficult* is *more difficult*. The superlatives are *smallest* and *most difficult*. In German, there is just one way to form the comparative and superlative: by adding the endings **-er** and -(**e**)**ste**:

small, smaller, smallest = **klein**, **kleiner**, **der/die/das kleinste**

Many adjectives change their vowel to an umlaut in the comparative and superlative:

cold, colder, coldest = **kalt**, **kälter**, **der/die/das kälteste**

Some important adjectives are irregular:

big, bigger, biggest = **groß**, **größer**, **der/die/das größte**
good, better, best = **gut**, **besser**, **der/die/das beste**
high, higher, highest = **hoch**, **höher**, **der/die/das höchste**
much, more, most = **viel**, **mehr**, **der/die/das meiste**
near, nearer, nearest = **nah**, **näher**, **der/die/das nächste**

Comparative and superlative adjectives take the same endings as basic adjectives:

a smaller child = **ein kleineres Kind**
the coldest month = **der kälteste Monat**

Adverbs

In German almost all adjectives can also be used as adverbs, describing a verb, an adjective, or another adverb.

she sings beautifully = **sie singt schön**

Some words, such as **auch** (= also), **fast** (= almost), **immer** (= always), and **leider** (= unfortunately) are used only as adverbs:

she is very clever = **sie ist sehr klug**

Comparative and superlative

The comparative is formed by adding **-er** to the basic adverb, and the superlative by putting **am** in front of the basic adverb and adding the ending -(**e**)**sten**:

clearly, more clearly, most clearly = **klar**, **klarer**, **am klarsten**

Some important adverbs are irregular:

soon, earlier, at the earliest = **bald**, **früher**, **am frühesten**
well, better, best = **gut**, **besser**, **am besten**
willingly, more willingly, most willingly = **gern**, **lieber**, **am liebsten**

Pronouns

Pronouns are words—such as *he*, *which*, and *mine* in English—that stand instead of a noun.

Personal pronouns

These pronouns, such as he/she/it = **er/sie/es**, refer to people or things.

	I	you	he/it	she/it	it	we	you	they	you
NOMINATIVE	ich	du	er	sie	es	wir	ihr	sie	Sie
ACCUSATIVE	mich	dich	ihn	sie	es	uns	euch	sie	Sie
DATIVE	mir	dir	ihm	ihr	ihm	uns	euch	ihnen	Ihnen
	me	*you*	*him/it*	*her/it*	*it*	*us*	*you*	*them*	*you*

The genitive form is not given, because it is so rarely used.

In German there are two forms for you, **du** and **Sie**. **Du** is less formal and is used when speaking to someone you know well, a child, or a family member. When speaking to a person or a group of people you do not know very well, use the polite form, **Sie**.

German pronouns agree in gender with the noun they refer to. In the nominative case, it might be translated by **er** or **sie**, as well as **es**:

it (the pencil) is red = **er (der Bleistift) ist rot**
it (the rose) is beautiful = **sie (die Rose) ist schön**
it (the car) is expensive = **es (das Auto) ist teuer**

Possessive pronouns

The possessive pronouns are:

mine = **meiner/meine/mein(e)s**
yours (informal singular) = **deiner/deine/dein(e)s**
his = **seiner/seine/sein(e)s**
hers = **ihrer/ihre/ihr(e)s**
its = **seiner/seine/sein(e)s**
ours = **unserer/unsere/unser(e)s**
yours (informal plural) = **eurer/eure/eures**
theirs = **ihrer/ihre/ihr(e)s**
yours (polite) = **Ihrer**, **Ihre**, **Ihr(e)s**

They all take endings like **meiner/meine/mein(e)s**, as follows:

	SINGULAR			PLURAL
	masculine	feminine	neuter	all genders
NOMINATIVE	meiner	meine	mein(e)s	meine
ACCUSATIVE	meinen	meine	mein(e)s	meine
GENITIVE	meines	meiner	meines	meiner
DATIVE	meinem	meiner	meinem	meinen

As can be seen in the table, in the neuter form an -e- can be added (making **meines**). This applies to all the possessive pronouns, but the extra **-e-** is rare.

Relative pronouns

These pronouns are used to introduce and link a new clause. In English they are *who*, *which*, *that*, and *what*. In German they are **der**, **die**, or **das**, depending on the noun referred to:

	SINGULAR			PLURAL
	masculine	feminine	neuter	all genders
NOMINATIVE	der	die	das	die
ACCUSATIVE	den	die	das	die
GENITIVE	dessen	deren	dessen	deren
DATIVE	dem	der	dem	denen

Relative pronouns can be left out in English, but never in German:

the book (*that*) *I'm reading* = **das Buch, das ich lese**

They agree in gender and number with the noun they refer back to:

the man who visited us = **der Mann, der uns besucht hat** (**der** is masculine singular)

But the case of the pronoun depends on its function in the clause it introduces:

the pencil I bought yesterday = **der Bleistift, den ich gestern gekauft habe**

(**den** is masculine singular, but accusative because it is the object of the clause it introduces)

Interrogative pronouns

These pronouns are used to ask questions:

who? = **wer?**
what? = **was?**
which? = **welcher/welche/welches?**

Wer changes as follows:

NOMINATIVE	wer?
ACCUSATIVE	wen?
GENITIVE	wessen?
DATIVE	wem?

Reflexive pronouns

The object of a reflexive verb is the same as its subject. In German, the object is a reflexive pronoun. This is usually in the accusative (I wash = **ich wasche** *mich*). The reflexive pronouns of some verbs are in the dative (I imagine = **ich stelle** *mir* **vor**).

Indefinite pronouns

These pronouns do not refer to identifiable people or objects. In German, many indefinite pronouns, such as **etwas** (= something) and **nichts** (= nothing), never change. But some do take endings:

	someone	no one
NOMINATIVE	jemand	niemand
ACCUSATIVE	jemanden	niemanden
DATIVE	jemandem	niemandem

The genitive case is rarely used.

Prepositions

Prepositions are small words like *in*, that stand in front of a noun or pronoun. In German, the noun following a preposition always has to be in one of three cases—dative, accusative, or genitive.

Prepositions can be prefixes and form separable verbs:

to walk along the street = **die Straße entlanggehen**
he is walking along the street = **er geht die Straße entlang**

In the dictionary, the case governed by a preposition is given:

mit (+ dat) means **mit** always takes the dative case.

The most common case used after prepositions is the dative. The following prepositions always take the dative:

aus	mit	von
außer	nach	zu
bei	seit	

Some prepositions always take the accusative:

bis	entlang	gegen	um
durch	für	ohne	

Some prepositions always take the genitive:

anstatt	während
trotz	wegen

There is a group of prepositions that can take the dative or the accusative, depending on the sentence. They are:

an	in	unter
auf	neben	vor
hinter	über	zwischen

If the phrase containing one of these prepositions describes position—where something is happening—the dative case is used:

she sat in the kitchen = **sie saß in der Küche**

But if the phrase containing the preposition describes movement—motion towards something—the accusative follows:

she went into the kitchen = **sie ging in die Küche**

Some forms of the definite article are usually shortened when used with prepositions:

am (an dem); **ans** (an das); **aufs** (auf das); **beim** (bei dem);
durchs (durch das); **fürs** (für das); **im** (in dem); **ins** (in das); **ums** (um das); **vom** (von dem); **zum** (zu dem); **zur** (zu der).

Conjunctions

Conjunctions are small words, such as *and* = **und**, which join clauses together in a sentence.

These common conjunctions link clauses together:

aber = *but*
denn = *for*
oder = *or*
sondern = *but* (on the contrary)
und = *and*

These conjunctions do not change normal word order in the two clauses:

ich gehe, und er kommt auch = *I am going, and he is coming too*

But there are many other conjunctions that send the verb to the end of the subordinate clause:

als = *when*, = *as*	**daß** = *that*	**weil** = *because*
bevor = *before*	**ob** = *whether*	
bis = *until*	**während** = *while*	
da = *since*	**wenn** = *when*, = *if*	

er konnte nicht in die Schule gehen, weil er krank war =
he couldn't go to school, because he was ill

Word order

The basic rule for German word order is that the verb comes second in a sentence. The subject of the sentence usually comes before the verb:

meine Mutter fährt am Freitag nach Köln =
my mother is going to Cologne on Friday

When the verb is made up of two parts, such as in the perfect and the future tenses, the auxiliary verb comes second in the sentence, while the past participle (in the perfect) or infinitive (in the future tense) goes to the end:

wir haben sehr lang gewartet = *we waited a very long time*
sie wird sicher bald kommen = *she is sure to turn up soon*

Past participles and infinitives go to the end in other sentences too:

ich kann dieses Lied nicht leiden = *I can't stand this song*
du musst hier bleiben = *you must stay here*

When a sentence starts with a subordinate clause, the verb stays in second place:

da ich kein Geld hatte, blieb ich zu Hause =
since I had no money, I stayed at home

In the clause itself, the verb goes to the end:

er konnte nicht in die Schule gehen, weil er krank war

The relative pronouns **der**, **die**, and **das**, as well as a number of conjunctions, send the verb to the end of the clause:

der Junge, der hier wohnt = *the boy who lives here*

When separable verbs separate, the prefix goes to the end:

der Film fängt um acht Uhr an = *the film starts at 8 o'clock*

In questions and commands, the verb is usually first in the sentence:

kommst du heute Abend? = *are you coming this evening?*
komm schnell rein! = *come in quickly!*

When there are a number of phrases in a sentence, the usual order for the different elements is 1 time, 2 manner, 3 place:

wir fahren heute mit dem Auto nach München =
we are driving to Munich today
(*time* = **heute**; *manner* = **mit dem Auto**; *place* = **nach München**)

German irregular verbs

Infinitive	Past tense	Past participle
abwägen	wog (wöge) ab	abgewogen
ausbedingen	bedang (bedänge) aus	ausbedungen
backen (du bäckst, er bäckt)	buk (büke)	gebacken
befehlen (du befiehlst, er befiehlt)	befahl (beföhle, befähle)	befohlen
beginnen	begann (begänne)	begonnen
beißen (du/er beißt)	biss (bisse)	gebissen
bergen (du birgst, er birgt)	barg (bärge)	geborgen
bewegen[2]	bewog (bewöge)	bewogen
biegen	bog (böge)	gebogen
bieten	bot (böte)	geboten
binden	band (bände)	gebunden
bitten	bat (bäte)	gebeten
blasen (du/er bläst)	blies	geblasen
bleiben	blieb	geblieben
bleichen*	blich	geblichen
braten (du brätst, er brät)	briet	gebraten
brechen (du brichst, er bricht)	brach (bräche)	gebrochen
brennen	brannte (brennte)	gebrannt
bringen	brachte (brächte)	gebracht
denken	dachte (dächte)	gedacht
dreschen (du drischst, er drischt)	drosch (drösche)	gedroschen
dringen	drang (dränge)	gedrungen
dürfen (ich/er darf, du	durfte (dürfte)	gedurft

Infinitive	Past tense	Past participle
darfst)		
empfehlen (du empfiehlst, er empfiehlt)	empfahl (empföhle)	empfohlen
erlöschen (du erlischst, er erlischt)	erlosch (erlösche)	erloschen
erschrecken (du erschrickst, er erschrickt)	erschrak (erschäke)	erschrocken
erwägen	erwog (erwöge)	erwogen
essen (du/er isst)	aß (äße)	gegessen
fahren (du fährst, er fährt)	fuhr (führe)	gefahren
fallen (du fällst, er fällt)	fiel	gefallen
fangen (du fängst, er fängt)	fing	gefangen
fechten (du fichtst, er ficht)	focht (föchte)	gefochten
finden	fand (fände)	gefunden
flechten (du flichtst, er flicht)	flocht (flöchte)	geflochten
fliegen	flog (flöge)	geflogen
fliehen	floh (flöhe)	geflohen
fließen (du/er fließt)	floss (flösse)	geflossen
fressen (du/er frisst)	fraß (fräße)	gefressen
frieren	fror (fröre)	gefroren
gären*	gor (göre)	gegoren
gebären (du gebierst, sie gebiert)	gebar (gebäre)	geboren
geben (du gibst, er gibt)	gab (gäbe)	gegeben
gedeihen	gedieh	gediehen
gehen	ging	gegangen
gelingen	gelang (gelänge)	gelungen
gelten (du giltst, er gilt)	galt (gölte, gälte)	gegolten
genesen (du/er genest)	genas (genäse)	genesen
genießen (du/er genießt)	genoss (genösse)	genossen
geschehen (es geschieht)	geschah (geschähe)	geschehen
gewinnen	gewann (gewönne, gewänne)	gewonnen
gießen (du/er gießt)	goss (gösse)	gegossen
gleichen	glich	geglichen
gleiten	glitt	geglitten
glimmen	glomm (glömme)	geglommen
graben (du gräbst, er gräbt)	grub (grübe)	gegraben

Infinitive	Past tense	Past participle
greifen	griff	gegriffen
haben (du hast, er hat)	hatte (hätte)	gehabt
halten (du hältst, er hält)	hielt	gehalten
hängen[2]	hing	gehangen
hauen	haute	gehauen
heben	hob (höbe)	gehoben
heißen (du/er hießt)	hieß	geheißen
helfen (du hilfst, er hilft)	half (hülfe)	geholfen
kennen	kannte (kennte)	gekannt
klingen	klang (klänge)	geklungen
kneifen	kniff	gekniffen
kommen	kam (käme)	gekommen
können (ich/er kann, du kannst)	konnte (könnte)	gekonnt
kriechen	kroch (kröche)	gekrochen
laden (du lädst, er lädt)	lud (lüde)	geladen
lassen (du/er lässt)	ließ	gelassen
laufen (du läufst, er läuft)	lief	gelaufen
leiden	litt	gelitten
leihen	lieh	geliehen
lesen (du/er liest)	las (läse)	gelesen
liegen	lag (läge)	gelegen
lügen	log (löge)	gelogen
mahlen	mahlte	gemahlen
meiden	mied	gemieden
melken	molk (mölke)	gemolken
messen (du/er misst)	maß (mäße)	gemessen
misslingen	misslang (misslänge)	misslungen
mögen (ich/er mag, du magst)	mochte (möchte)	gemocht
müssen (ich/er muss, du musst	musste (müsste)	gemusst
nehmen (du nimmst, er nimmt)	nahm (nähme)	genommen
nennen	nannte (nennte)	genannt
pfeifen	pfiff	gepfiffen
preisen (du/er preist)	pries	gepriesen
raten (du rätst, er rät)	riet	geraten
reiben	rieb	gerieben
reißen (du/er reißt)	riss	gerissen
reiten	ritt	geritten
rennen	rannte (rennte)	gerannt

Infinitive	Past tense	Past participle
riechen	roch (röche)	gerochen
ringen	rang (ränge)	gerungen
rinnen	rann (ränne)	geronnen
rufen	rief	gerufen
salzen* (du/er salzt)	salzte	gesalzen
saufen (du säufst, er säuft)	soff (söffe)	gesoffen
saugen*	sog (söge)	gesogen
schaffen[1]	schuf (schüfe)	geschaffen
scheiden	schied	geschieden
scheinen	schien	geschienen
scheißen (du/er scheißt)	schiss	geschissen
schelten (du schiltst, er schilt)	schalt (schölte)	gescholten
scheren[1]	schor (schöre)	geschoren
schieben	schob (schöbe)	geschoben
schießen (du/er schießt)	schoss (schösse)	geschossen
schlafen (du schläfst, er schläft)	schlief	geschlafen
schlagen (du schlägst, er schlägt)	schlug (schlüge)	geschlagen
schleichen	schlich	geschlichen
schleifen[2]	schliff	geschliffen
schließen (du/er schießt)	schloss (schlösse)	geschlossen
schlingen	schlang (schlänge)	geschlungen
schmeißen (du/er schmeißt)	schmiss (schmisse)	geschmissen
schmelzen (du/er schmilzt)	schmolz (schmölze)	geschmolzen
schneiden	schnitt	geschnitten
schrecken* (du schrickst, er schrickt)	schrak (schräke)	geschreckt
schreiben	schrieb	geschrieben
schreien	schrie	geschrie[e]n
schreiten	schritt	geschritten
schweigen	schwieg	geschwiegen
schwellen (du schwillst, er schwillt)	schwoll (schwölle)	geschwollen
schwimmen	schwamm (schwömme)	geschwommen
schwinden	schwand (schwände)	geschwunden
schwingen	schwang (schwänge)	geschwungen
schwören	schwor (schwüre)	geschworen

Infinitive	Past tense	Past participle
sehen (du siehst, er sieht)	sah (sähe)	gesehen
sein (ich bin, du bist, er ist,wir sind, ihr seid, sie sind)	war (wäre)	gewesen
senden[1]	sandte (sendete)	gesandt
sieden	sott (sötte)	gesotten
singen	sang (sänge)	gesungen
sinken	sank (sänke)	gesunken
sitzen (du/er sitzt)	saß (säße)	gesessen
sollen (ich/er soll, du sollst)	sollte	gesollt
spalten*	spaltete	gespalten
spinnen	spann (spönne, spänne)	gesponnen
sprechen (du sprichst, er spricht)	sprach (spräche)	gesprochen
sprießen (du/er sprießt)	spross (sprösse)	gesprossen
springen	sprang (spränge)	gesprungen
stechen (du stichst, er sticht)	stach (stäche)	gestochen
stehen	stand (stünde, stände)	gestanden
stehlen (du stiehlst, er stiehlt)	stahl (stähle)	gestohlen
steigen	stieg	gestiegen
sterben (du stirbst, er stirbt)	starb (stürbe)	gestorben
stinken	stank (stänke)	gestunken
stoßen (du/er stößt)	stieß	gestoßen
streichen	strich	gestrichen
streiten	stritt	gestritten
tragen (du trägst, er trägt)	trug (trüge)	getragen
treffen (du triffst, er trifft)	traf (träfe)	getroffen
treiben	trieb	getrieben
treten (du trittst, er tritt)	trat (träte)	getreten
triefen*	troff (tröffe)	getroffen
trinken	trank (tränke)	getrunken
trügen	trog (tröge)	getrogen
tun (du tust, er tut)	tat (täte)	getan
verderben (du verdirbst, er verdirbt)	verdarb (verdürbe)	verdorben
vergessen (du/er vergisst)	vergaß (vergäße)	vergessen
verlieren	verlor (verlöre)	verloren

Infinitive	Past tense	Past participle
verzeihen	verzieh	verziehen
wachsen[1] (du/er wächst)	wuchs (wüchse)	gewachsen
waschen (du wäschst, er wäscht)	wusch (wüsche)	gewaschen
wenden[2] *	wandte (wendete)	gewandt
werben (du wirbst, er wirbt)	warb (würbe)	geworben
werden (du wirst, er wird)	wurde (würde)	geworden
werfen (du wirfst, er wirft)	warf (würfe)	geworfen
wiegen[1]	wog (wöge)	gewogen
winden	wand (wände)	gewunden
wissen (ich/er weiß, du weißt)	wusste (wüsste)	gewusst
wollen (ich/er will, du willst)	wollte	gewollt
wringen	wrang (wränge)	gewrungen
ziehen	zog (zöge)	gezogen
zwingen	zwang (zwänge)	gezwungen